Register for Free Membership to

T0228959

solutions@syngress.com

Over the last few years, Syngress has published many best-selling and critically acclaimed books, including Tom Shinder's *Configuring ISA Server 2000*, Brian Caswell and Jay Beale's *Snort 2.0 Intrusion Detection*, and Angela Orebaugh and Gilbert Ramirez's *Ethereal Packet Sniffing*. One of the reasons for the success of these books has been our unique **solutions@syngress.com** program. Through this site, we've been able to provide readers a real time extension to the printed book.

As a registered owner of this book, you will qualify for free access to our members-only solutions@syngress.com program. Once you have registered, you will enjoy several benefits, including:

- Four downloadable e-booklets on topics related to the book. Each booklet is approximately 20-30 pages in Adobe PDF format. They have been selected by our editors from other best-selling Syngress books as providing topic coverage that is directly related to the coverage in this book.

- A comprehensive FAQ page that consolidates all of the key points of this book into an easy to search web page, providing you with the concise, easy to access data you need to perform your job.

- A "From the Author" Forum that allows the authors of this book to post timely updates links to related sites, or additional topic coverage that may have been requested by readers.

Just visit us at **www.syngress.com/solutions** and follow the simple registration process. You will need to have this book with you when you register.

Thank you for giving us the opportunity to serve your needs. And be sure to let us know if there is anything else we can do to make your job easier.

SYNGRESS®

Dedications

This book is dedicated to:
As always, our families: the kids (Kris and Kniki), the brothers (Rich and D),
and our parents, including the ones who are no longer with us.

Our friends, many of whom are also our business colleagues.

Our cats, who walked on the keyboards, slept on our desks and helped us to
keep it all in perspective through the long process of writing this book.

As with all the others, we also dedicate this book to each other. Not many
people are lucky enough to be able to work with their spouses, to spend
twenty-four hours a day, most days, in each other's company, and to enjoy it this
much. We are truly blessed.

Dr. Tom Shinder's
Configuring
ISA Server
2004

Dr. Thomas W. Shinder
Debra Littlejohn Shinder

KEY	SERIAL NUMBER
001	HJIRTCV764
002	PO9873D5FG
003	829KM8NJH2
004	JKGGGBSR29
005	CVPLQ6WQ23
006	VBP965T5T5
007	HJJJ863WD3E
008	2987GVTWMK
009	629MP5SDJT
010	IMWQ295T6T

PUBLISHED BY
Syngress Publishing, Inc.
800 Hingham Street
Rockland, MA 02370

Dr. Tom Shinder's Configuring ISA Server 2004

Printed in the United States of America
Transferred to Digital Printing, 2011
ISBN: 1-931836-19-1

Publisher: Andrew Williams   Page Layout and Art: Patricia Lupien
Acquisitions Editor: Jaime Quigley   Copy Editor: Edwina Lewis
Technical Editor: Martin Grasdal   Indexer: Richard Carlson
Cover Designer: Michael Kavish

Distributed by O'Reilly Media, Inc. in the United States and Canada.
For information on rights and translations, contact Matt Pedersen, Director of Sales and Rights, at Syngress Publishing; email matt@syngress.com or fax to 781-681-3585.

Acknowledgments

Syngress would like to acknowledge the following people for their kindness and support in making this book possible.

Syngress books are now distributed in the United States and Canada by O'Reilly Media, Inc. The enthusiasm and work ethic at O'Reilly is incredible and we would like to thank everyone there for their time and efforts to bring Syngress books to market: Tim O'Reilly, Laura Baldwin, Mark Brokering, Mike Leonard, Donna Selenko, Bonnie Sheehan, Cindy Davis, Grant Kikkert, Opol Matsutaro, Steve Hazelwood, Mark Wilson, Rick Brown, Leslie Becker, Jill Lothrop, Tim Hinton, Kyle Hart, Sara Winge, C. J. Rayhill, Peter Pardo, Leslie Crandell, Valerie Dow, Regina Aggio, Pascal Honscher, Preston Paull, Susan Thompson, Bruce Stewart, Laura Schmier, Sue Willing, Mark Jacobsen, Betsy Waliszewski, Dawn Mann, Kathryn Barrett, John Chodacki, and Rob Bullington. And a hearty welcome to Aileen Berg—glad to be working with you.

The incredibly hard working team at Elsevier Science, including Jonathan Bunkell, Ian Seager, Duncan Enright, David Burton, Rosanna Ramacciotti, Robert Fairbrother, Miguel Sanchez, Klaus Beran, Emma Wyatt, Rosie Moss, Chris Hossack, Mark Hunt, and Krista Leppiko, for making certain that our vision remains worldwide in scope.

David Buckland, Marie Chieng, Lucy Chong, Leslie Lim, Audrey Gan, Pang Ai Hua, and Joseph Chan of STP Distributors for the enthusiasm with which they receive our books.

Kwon Sung June at Acorn Publishing for his support.

David Scott, Tricia Wilden, Marilla Burgess, Annette Scott, Andrew Swaffer, Stephen O'Donoghue, Bec Lowe, and Mark Langley of Woodslane for distributing our books throughout Australia, New Zealand, Papua New Guinea, Fiji Tonga, Solomon Islands, and the Cook Islands.

Winston Lim of Global Publishing for his help and support with distribution of Syngress books in the Philippines.

About the Authors

Thomas W. Shinder, MD is an MCSE and has been awarded the Microsoft Most Valuable Professional (MVP) award for his work with ISA Server and is recognized in the firewall community as one of the foremost experts on ISA Server. Tom has consulted with major companies and organizations such as Microsoft Corp., Xerox, Lucent Technologies, FINA Oil, Hewlett-Packard, and the U.S. Department of Energy.

Tom practiced medicine in Oregon, Texas, and Arkansas before turning his growing fascination with computer technology into a new career shortly after marrying his wife, Debra Littlejohn Shinder, in the mid 90s. They co-own TACteam (Trainers, Authors, and Consultants), through which they teach technology topics and develop courseware, write books, articles, whitepapers and corporate product documentation and marketing materials, and assist small and large businesses in deploying technology solutions.

Tom co-authored, with Deb, the best selling *Configuring ISA Server 2000* (Syngress Publishing, ISBN: 1-928994-29-6), *Dr. Tom Shinder's ISA Server and Beyond* (Syngress, ISBN: 1-931836-66-3), and *Troubleshooting Windows 2000 TCP/IP* (Syngress, ISBN: 1-928994-11-3). He has contributed to several other books on subjects such as the Windows 2000 and Windows 2003 MCSE exams and has written hundreds of articles on Windows server products for a variety of electronic and print publications.

Tom is the "primary perpetrator" on ISAserver.org (www.isaserver.org), where he answers hundreds of questions per week on the discussion boards and is the leading content contributor.

Debra Littlejohn Shinder is an MCSE and has been awarded Microsoft's Most Valuable Professional (MVP) award in the area of Server Security. She is a former police officer and college level criminal justice instructor, which led her to her interest in computer security and computer crime. She has authored a number of books on computer operating systems, networking, and security. These include *Scene of the Cybercrime: Computer Forensics Handbook* (Syngress, ISBN: 1-931836-65-5), and *Computer Networking Essentials*, published by Cisco Press. She is co-author, with her husband, Dr. Thomas Shinder, of the best selling *Configuring ISA Server 2000* (Syngress Publishing, ISBN: 1-928994-29-6), *Dr. Tom Shinder's ISA Server and Beyond* (Syngress, ISBN: 1-931836-66-3), and *Troubleshooting Windows 2000 TCP/IP* (Syngress, ISBN: 1-928994-11-3).

Deb is also a technical editor, developmental editor, and contributor to over 15 additional books on subjects such as the Windows 2000 and Windows 2003 MCSE exams, CompTIA Security+ exam and TruSecure's ICSA certification. She formerly edited the Brainbuzz A+ Hardware News and currently edits Sunbelt Software's *WinXP News* (www.winxpnews.com). Her articles are regularly published on TechRepublic's TechProGuild site and Windowsecurity.com, and have appeared in print magazines such as Windows IT Pro Magazine (formerly Windows & .NET) and she has authored training material, corporate whitepapers, marketing material, and product documentation for Microsoft Corporation, DigitalThink, Sunbelt Software, CNET and other technology companies. Deb currently specializes in security issues and Microsoft products.

Deb and Tom live and work in the Dallas-Ft Worth area and occasionally teach computer networking and security classes at Eastfield College.

Technical Editor

Martin Grasdal (MCSE+I, MCT, CNE, CNI, CTT, A+) An independent consultant with over 10 years experience in the computer industry, Martin has a wide range of networking and IT managerial experience. He has been an MCT since 1995 and an MCSE since 1996. His training and networking experience covers a number of products, including NetWare, Lotus Notes, Windows NT, Windows 2000, Windows 2003, Exchange Server, IIS, and ISA Server, among others. Martin currently works actively as a consultant, author and editor. His recent consulting experience includes contract work for Microsoft as a Technical Contributor to the MCP Program on projects related to server technologies. Martin lives in Edmonton, Alberta, Canada with his wife Cathy and their two sons.

A Note From the Publisher

We started Syngress in 1997 with the mission of creating great individual books instead of manufacturing them from an assembly line. We have been blessed since then to have attracted some magnificent people who shared our mission, and first among them are Debra Littlejohn Shinder and Thomas Shinder, M.D.

They have worked with us as editors, authors, "on-air" talent, consultants, and at times, critics; always in the spirit of publishing the best book possible. In the process, they have opened doors for us we didn't even know existed.

They are both firmly rooted in a work ethic befitting a cop and a physician. (Deb's the Cop, Tom's the Doc). They demand quality because, at the end of the day, it's their names on the book and their reputations on the line.

Most importantly, they combine technical brilliance with a passion for teaching. It's a combination that's hard to find, and because of it, they have made over 250,000 IT professionals' life a little bit easier.

A heartfelt thank you.

Chris Williams
President and Co-Founder

Amorette Pedersen
Vice President of Marketing, Co-Founder

Andrew Williams
Publisher

Syngress Publishing
December 2004

From Deb and Tom Shinder, Authors

ISA Server has been a big part of our lives for the last four years. This is our third book about Microsoft's rapidly evolving firewall and caching solution, and we're more excited than ever about its new incarnation, ISA Server 2004.

We've been in on this one from the very beginning, and we've had a chance to experience the changes, additions and improvements through the alpha and beta stages of the software.

This book was a joint effort between the two of us, but it was also a team effort. There are dozens of people who contributed to the cause, without whom this book could not have been written:

We are deeply indebted to those on the ISA Server teams at Microsoft for involving us in the development, documentation and marketing of ISA. We especially want to thank those in Redmond, Dallas and Charlotte: Mike Nash, Steve Brown, Tony Bailey, Joseph Landes, Josue Fontanez, Marcus Schmidt, Risa Coleman, Mark Mortimer, Red Johnston, Dave Gardner, Joel Sloss, Julia Polk, Steve Riley, Zach Gutt, Mike Chan, Suzanne Kalberer, Kelly Mondloch, Alan Wood, Clint Denham, Ellen Prater, Scott Jiles, Sibylle Haupert, Amy Logan, Ari Fruchter, Ronen Boazi, Barclay Neira, Ben Guterson, Colin Lyth, Eric Rosencrantz, Jan Shanahan, Jim Edwards, and Walter Boyd, and we also want to thank Joern Wettern and Ronald Beekelaar for all their help and support.

We also want to thank the ISA team in Israel: Avi Nathan, Adina Hagege, Keren Master, Ron Mondri, Itai Greenberg, Yossi Siles, Sigalit Bar, Nathan Bigman, Linda Lior, Neta Amit, Amit Finkelstein, Meir Shmouely, Nir Ben Zvi, Opher Dubrovsky, Oren Trutner, Yigal Edery, Ziv Mador, Raz Goren, Mooly Beeri, Nir Caliv, Ziv Caspi, Gergory Bershansky, Ariel Katz, Dan Bar-Lev, Max Uritsky, Ronen Barenboim, Nir Michalowitz and Uri Barash.

Thank you to the hardware vendors who gave us the opportunity to work with their ISA Server-based appliances: John Curtis, John Amaral, Mike Druar, Kevin Murphy, Erika Batten, Bonnie Anderson, and Mark Roden, of Network Engines, Abdul Azhan of RimApp, Marc Semadeni of Hewlett Packard, and Yong Thye Lin and Yong Ping Lin of Celestix.

We want to thank our technical editor, Martin Grasdal, for his painstaking efforts to ensure that every procedure we outlined worked, that our descriptions and instructions were accurate and complete, and that our text was understandable – even the parts that we wrote at the end of an 18 hour day when we were hanging onto consciousness and our sanity by virtue of sheer willpower and numerous cups of coffee. We also thank Edwina Lewis, our copy editor, who wrestled with the terminology, whose eagle eye spotted our typos, and who stayed sweet and cheerful even when we got a little grumpy.

We also want to thank Stephen Chetcuti and Sean Buttgieg of Isaserver.org (www.isaserver.org) and Windowsecurity.com (www.windowsecurity.com), who provided us with forums in which we were able to promote both ISA Server itself and this book, and through which we got to know other ISA Server fans all over the world.

Thank you, too, to John Sheesley at Tech Republic/TechProGuild (www.techproguild.com), which hosted our series of articles on ISA Server 2004, and Amy Eisenberg and Patricia Colby, at Windows IT Pro Magazine (formerly Windows & .NET), which featured a number of our ISA Server 2004 articles.

We want to recognize all the other ISA Server MVPs whose ideas and help were invaluable in writing this book: Chris Gregory, Kai Wilke, Stefaan Pouseele, Jason Ballard, Bud Ratliff, Christian Groebner, Dieter Rauscher, Frédéric Esnouf, Jesper Hanno, Philippe Mathon, Phil Windell, Slav Pidgorny, Abraham Martínez Fernández .

In addition, special thanks to those who've supported and maintained the MVP program: Jerry Bryant, Emily Freet, Janni Clark, and John Eddy.

In addition, we want to thank the participants in the ISA Server newsgroups, mailing lists and message boards whose questions inspired many of the scenarios in this book, and others who contributed in various ways. In particular, we extend our gratitude to John Tolmachoff, Jeffrey Martin, Amy Babinchak, Steve Moffat, Greg Mulholland, Shawn Quillman, Joseph Kravitz, Tiago de Aviz, David Farinic, Aman Bedi, Bill Stewart, AWJ (Al), Susan Bradley, and many, many others. Thanks guys!

We also want to give special recognition to Jim Harrison. Jim Harrison works for Microsoft on the ISA Server QA team and maintains the exceptional Web site: www.isatools.org. Many of us would be lost without Jim's tools and his constant prodding to be better networkers and firewall admins than we are today.

All of the above were instrumental in the development and production of this book, but any errors or omissions lie solely on our heads. We tried to make the manuscript as accurate and mistake-free as possible, but perfection is a goal rather than an achievement. If we've left anyone out, please accept our sincerest apologies (these last days of finishing up the manuscript have been hectic, to say the least) and let us know so we can correct the mistake in the next edition of the book.

Lastly, we want to say a special thank you to the folks at Syngress Publishing who pushed us to do this book, who showed extraordinary patience and understanding as deadlines slipped, and who believed in us from the beginning: Andrew Williams, our publisher, and Jaime Quigley, our editor. Hey, guys, believe it or not, it's finally finished!

Contents

Appendix A: Network Security Basics is available at www.syngress.com/solutions

Download the bonus chapter "Configuring Entperprise Networks, Caching Arrays, and Network Load Balancing," from www.syngress.com/solutions after the release of ISA Server 2004 Enterprise Edition.

Evolution of a Firewall: From Proxy 1.0 to ISA 2004

Topics in this Chapter:

- The Book: What It Covers and Who It's For
- Security: The New Star of the Show
- Firewalls: The Guardians at the Gateway
- ISA: From Proxy Server to Full-Featured Firewall

The Book: What it Covers and Who It's For

Our first ISA Server book, *Configuring ISA Server 2000: Building Firewalls for Windows 2000* (Syngress Publishing), addressed Microsoft's first attempt at producing an enterprise-level network firewall product. As with most first attempts, ISA 2000 was in many ways a learning experience—both for Microsoft and for those of us who used and managed it.

With ISA 2000, Microsoft provided full-fledged, multilayered firewall functionality that went far beyond the traditional packet filtering firewall, with "extras" such as intrusion detection and prevention (IDS/IDP) and Web caching – features that many other firewall vendors either don't include at all or offer as add-on modules or separate products at extra cost.

Inevitably, ISA was compared with other popular firewall products such as CheckPoint's Firewall-1/VPN-1 and Cisco's PIX, along with the plethora of low-cost security "appliances" from vendors such as NetScreen, Watchguard, SonicWall, Symantec, and many others that have flooded the market over the last few years. Although it proved to be a strong competitor, ISA administrators quickly started compiling "wish lists" of features and functionalities that could make ISA even better.

NOTE

Some might argue that customer "wish lists" have even, in some cases, resulted in the inclusion of features that are unnecessary or worse, as well as the elimination of desirable features. According to the product team, features such as the H.323 gateway – included in ISA 2000 – were dropped from ISA 2004 due to lack of customer interest. On the other hand, ISA 2004 added the ability to forward all traffic to an internal server ("all-port forwarding") because of pressure from users of low-cost firewall appliances that included this feature.

As with any software product, there were quirks to be ironed out. And as the security landscape became even more complex and brand new threats appeared, new technologies were needed and old ones needed to be improved. Microsoft set about creating a new incarnation of ISA Server, one that would incorporate many of the features users asked for and that would improve ease of use as well as security.

Some of the changes in ISA 2004 are profound – so profound that Microsoft seriously considered changing the product name completely before deciding to stick with "Internet Security and Acceleration Server" to better build on the existing user base and avoid market confusion. As we worked with ISA 2004 from the alpha stage through private and public betas, we saw it evolve into a hard-core comprehensive security product that can serve many purposes in a variety of network scenarios.

It's in the Book: What We Cover

Writing the ISA 2000 book, like working with the software itself, was yet another learning experience. As we continued to work with ISA after it was finished, we discovered new questions (and new answers) that we wished we'd included. Readers provided us with valuable feedback about what they wanted to see addressed. We took all of that into consideration as we laid out the game plan for this book on ISA Server 2004.

Two Parts for Two Purposes

In working with ISA 2000 users locally and around the world through www.isaserver.org, www.windowsecurity.com, and other Internet forums, we found that many network administrators' questions about ISA began even before their organizations committed to deploying it. They wanted hard information on ISA's features, how those features work "under the hood," and how ISA compares to other popular firewall solutions in the same price categories. Some users, new to the security aspects of networking, expressed a wish for more background information – how firewalls and VPNs work, and even some basic TCP/IP concepts that are essential to understanding firewall functionality.

Thus, we've divided this book into two distinct sections:

- **Part One: ISA Server 2004 Concepts.** This section (consisting of chapters 1 through 3) is meant to be an "appetizer." It provides a background understanding of computer security in general, firewalls in particular, and ISA Server specifically. We follow the development of ISA from its humble origins in MS Proxy Server. We answer the often-asked question "Why should I trust Microsoft when it comes to security?" We explain the different firewall models and architectures and describe the ISA 2004 feature set (including "under the hood" information about how the features work). We even include an entire chapter on comparing ISA 2004 with other popular firewall solutions in the same price category.

- **Part Two: ISA Server 2004 How-Tos.** This longer section (consisting of chapters 4 through 11) provides the "main course"—step-by-step instructions in how to install and manage ISA Server 2004 in common networking scenarios, taking into account different network configurations, business models, and ISA Server roles. Here you'll find all the details about how to create and use firewall access policies, how to publish network services to the Internet, how to use ISA Server to protect remote access and VPN connections, how ISA Server works in conjunction with Exchange Server, how to make best use of ISA Server's Web caching, and other "bonus" functionalities that distinguish ISA Server from its competitors.

You'll also find, at the end of the book, an appendix covering some TCP/IP and network security basics. This additional material is for those who need a refresher in TCP/IP security vulnerabilities. Some of this material is taken from *Configuring ISA Server 2000* and is most useful for readers who are not familiar with that book. Like dessert, it's optional.

We believe this structure will make the book easier to use and will also make it more valuable to a wider audience.

TIP _____

Although some readers have asked us for more conceptual information and broader background information, more experienced readers or those with specific questions and problems might want to skip the first chapters and go right to the "how to" sections.

If you're looking for specific scenarios that address your own situation or answers to troubleshooting problems that occur in your ISA deployment, we have tried to make it easy for you to find and flip to the section of this book that you need. We have put in numerous tips and tricks for dealing with ISA in the real world and provided references to give you more information about related topics that you could come across as you work with ISA. Following the adage that a picture can be worth a thousand words, we've also provided many diagrams and screenshots to illustrate exactly what we're talking about in the text.

Chapter-by-Chapter Game Card

We've laid out the book in such a way that it can be used as a reference, with individual "how to" sections that are not dependent upon one another. We've also provided a logical order for those who are working through the book progressively, so that you can learn the terminology and concepts first and then proceed to the walk-throughs.

Chapter One: Evolution of a Firewall: Proxy Server to ISA 2004

This first chapter begins with a section entitled *Security: The New Star of the Show*, an overview of the new, high-profile role of security in the new millennium. In *Security: What's Microsoft Got to Do with It?* we discuss Microsoft's new commitment to security as a number one priority with their Trustworthy Computing Initiative. We address the ever-changing nature of the security landscape in *Security: A Moving Target*. Then we look at the best practices for securing your valuables, whether physical or electronic, in *Security: A Multilayered Approach*, where we examine the popular "defense-in-depth" concept.

In the next section of the chapter, we get more specific as we examine the role of the firewall in *Firewalls: The Guardians at the Gateway*. We examine the history and philosophy behind today's firewalls and discuss the differences between different firewall models (host vs. network-based, hardware vs. software-based). Next, we look at the features and functionality offered by modern firewall products and how firewalls have evolved from simple packet filtering proxies to comprehensive "security solutions."

The last part of the chapter, *ISA Server: From Proxy Server to Full-Featured Firewall*, zooms in on the focus of the rest of the book: ISA Server. We follow Microsoft's venture into the security market from the time when ISA Server was just a glint in MS Proxy Server's eye to the release of ISA Server 2004. We discuss what it can do for you and your company, how it gives you two products for the price of one, and how caching fits in. We also speculate on what the future holds for ISA Server and Microsoft's increasing integration of security features into their software.

Chapter Two: Examining the ISA Server 2004 Feature Set

This chapter provides an in-depth look at each of ISA 2004's main features: the old (those that were ported over from ISA 2000), the new (and improved), and the missing in action (features included in ISA 2000 that were dropped in the new version).

In the first section, *Old Features Get New Functionality*, we focus closely on ISA 2000 features that have been enhanced or expanded, such as VPN administration, user authentication, firewall rules, user- and group-based access policies, Outlook Web Access (OWA) publishing and secure Web publishing, FTP support, caching rules, the SMTP message screener, improvements to logging and reporting, and the updated graphical interface.

We also examine, in detail, the many new features built into ISA 2004, including its multinetworking capabilities, VPN quarantine and other new VPN features, firewall user groups, customizable protocol definitions and support for complex protocols, delegation of basic authentication, SecurID authentication support for Web proxy clients, firewall-generated forms for forms-base authentication, PPTP server publishing, SSL VPN for accessing terminal services, forced encryption for secure Exchange RPC connections, new HTTP filtering features, link translation, and new management features.

In the next section, we go *Under the Hood* to discuss how some of ISA 2004's most important features work, covering the underlying technologies of Application Layer Filtering (ALF), VPN quarantine, and SSL Bridging.

Finally, for those who still aren't satisfied with everything that ISA 2004 can do out of the box, we discuss *Adding Features and Functionality with Third Party Products.*

Chapter Three: Stalking the Competition: How ISA 2004 Stacks Up

In response to many reader inquiries, we devote an entire chapter to a discussion of the 2004 firewall market and how ISA Server 2004 stacks up against the competition. In this chapter, we discuss the current firewall and caching server market(s) and look at the various points of comparison, including:

- Licensing structures, initial costs, and Total Cost of Operations (administrative overhead, support contracts, add-ons, and upgrades).
- Specifications
- Firewall and IDS/IDP features
- VPN features
- Web caching features
- Certification

We look at how various firewall products implement application-layer filtering, platform support and system requirements, VPN features, capacity and client licensing issues, interoperability and integration with other network components, such as Exchange, SharePoint, Active Directory, and non-Microsoft operating systems and the interface and ease of use.

Specifically, we look at how ISA Server 2004 stacks up against the following popular firewall and/or caching products:

- CheckPoint NG software and Nokia appliances (which run CheckPoint)
- Cisco PIX firewall/VPN appliances
- NetScreen/Juniper Networks firewall/VPN appliances
- SonicWall firewall/VPN appliances
- Symantec firewall/VPN software and appliances
- Watchguard firewall/VPN appliances
- Linux-based open source firewall software
- BlueCoat firewall/VPN/caching appliances
- Novell Volera caching products
- Squid open source caching software

We look at the strengths and weaknesses of each competing product in comparison to ISA Server 2004, and we also discuss how ISA 2004 can be effectively used in conjunction with third-party firewall products to provide multilayered security for both inner and outer network perimeters.

Chapter Four: Preparing the Network Infrastructure for ISA 2004

One of the most common problems we've encountered in troubleshooting ISA Server 2000 installations was the lack of an appropriate supporting infrastructure. We anticipate similar problems for ISA Server 2004 installations that do not have the appropriate supporting network infrastructures *before* installing the ISA Server 2004 firewall.

There are a number of key network infrastructure issues that we discuss in this chapter:

- Understanding the ISA Server 2004 networking model
- Configuring the routing table on the ISA Server 2004 firewall
- DHCP support for the ISA Server 2004 firewall and ISA Server 2004 clients
- WINS support for the ISA Server 2004 firewall and ISA Server 2004 clients
- DNS support for the ISA Server 2004 firewall and the ISA Server 2004 clients
- RADIUS (Internet Authentication Server IAS) support for the ISA Server 2004 firewall and ISA Server 2004 clients
- Certificate Services support for the ISA Server 2004 firewall and ISA Server 2004 clients

In Chapter Four, we go over each of the critical network services that must be in place to support your ISA Server 2004 firewall and hosts that connect through the ISA Server 2004 firewall. In addition, we discuss the ISA Server 2004 concepts of Networks, Network Sets, Network Relationships, and access control across networks. We also include a discussion of the "network within a network configuration" and how to solve the problem it poses using ISA Server 2004 and the internal network router configuration.

Chapter Five: Configuring ISA 2004 Clients and Automating Client Provisioning

This chapter looks at the three ISA 2004 network client types:

- The SecureNAT client
- The Firewall client
- The Web proxy client

Each of these client types works differently to allow the client computer access to the Internet or other outside network through the ISA server. We give detailed explanations of how each client type works "under the hood." Each has advantages and disadvantages, and the "best" client choice depends on a number of factors, including the client operating system, which protocols the client machine needs to access, and whether you want to (or policy or circumstances permit you to) install extra software on the client machines. We provide you with the info you need to make the right decisions concerning which client type(s) should be deployed in a given situation.

After gaining an understanding of the client options, we provide step-by-step instructions that illustrate how to configure each client type, with special considerations to keep in mind for each. We deal with common problems posed by different client types, such as name resolution issues and how to solve the problem of "loopback" through the ISA server by deploying a split DNS infrastructure.

Because manually installing or configuring a large number of clients in an enterprise environment can be a daunting task, we also provide instructions on how to automate the client provisioning process to reduce administrative overhead. In this section, we cover various ways to automate the configurations of the Web proxy and firewall clients, including:

- Configuring DHCP servers to support Web proxy and firewall client autodiscovery

- Configuring DNS servers to support Web proxy and firewall client autodiscovery

- Automating Web proxy client configuration with group policy

- Automating Web proxy client configuration with Internet Explorer Administration Kit (IEAK)

You'll learn how to automate the installation process for the firewall client software, either by using group policy-based software installation and management or by creating and using a silent installation script. We also discuss the use of System Management Server (SMS) to deploy the firewall client software.

Chapter Six: Installing and Configuring the ISA Server 2004 Software

This chapter begins with separate step-by-step instructions on how to install ISA Server in each of two possible configurations:

- **Installing ISA 2004 on a multihomed server**. If the ISA Server is to act as a firewall, either dedicated solely to firewall functions or as a combination firewall and caching server, it must be installed on a machine that has multiple network interfaces.

- **Installing ISA 2004 on a single-NIC server.** Unlike ISA 2000, ISA 2004 no longer has a caching-only installation mode, but by installing the software on a server that has only a single network interface, you accomplish the same thing since the single-adapter server cannot be used as a firewall.

ISA Server 2004 can run on either a Windows 2000 Server or a Windows Server 2003 machine. We discuss some of the differences in functionality based on which operating system you use and point out some of the things you need to watch for during installation, to avoid problems later.

The old Local Address Table (LAT) from ISA Server 2000 is gone, so you can install multiple network interfaces to create multiple internal networks (taking advantage of one of ISA 2004's great new features: multinetworking), in addition to multiple public or private address DMZs. We discuss how to do that in this chapter.

ISA Server 2004 includes a number of network templates that are positioned to help the new ISA Server 2004 firewall administrators get up and running as quickly as possible. We examine the front-end firewall, edge firewall, back-end firewall, trihomed DMZ, and unihomed firewall templates, and see how they can be used to assist the ISA Server 2004 firewall administrator get up and running with simple and complex networking setups. We also explore the new graphical user interface and how to navigate through it to perform the common administrative tasks.

We explore upgrade issues: specifically, we show you how to upgrade an ISA Server 2000 computer to ISA Server 2004, as well as the upgrade procedure for a Microsoft Proxy Server 2.0 machine, which requires first upgrading to ISA Server 2000 and then to ISA Server 2004.

Finally, The chapter includes a "Quick Start" section that provides the basics on how to get ISA 2004 up and running as quickly as possible, and instructions on how to create a temporary "all open" outbound access policy to allow you to verify that your ISA server is working after you install it.

TIP

Deployment of ISA Server 2004 on a production network will proceed much more smoothly if you first test the product in a prototype environment; this allows you to determine how ISA Server 2004 will interact with your existing network services and applications. Using virtualization software such as Microsoft's Virtual PC or VMWare is the most cost-effective method to simulate an enterprise-level network with full functionality without investing in additional hardware.

Chapter Seven: Creating and Using ISA 2004 Firewall Access Rules

ISA Server 2004 Access Rules set the new ISA Server 2004 firewall apart from its predecessor, ISA Server 2000. Unlike ISA Server 2000, the ISA Server 2004 firewall uses a unified rule base wherein Access Rules and Publishing Rules are processed from the top down. You no longer need to try to figure out which rule will be active at what time as you did with ISA Server 2000. Now you know that the first rule on the list that matches the connection request parameters will handle the request.

ISA Server 2004 Access Rules control traffic based on a number of parameters, with the core parameters being the following: source, destination, protocol, and user. However, you can fine-tune each rule so that it is applied at a certain time of day, to a specific user set, and/or to a specific server. You can use Access Rules to block sites, files, pop-ups and peer-to-peer applications. ISA Server 2004 Access Rules give you total control over what connections are allowed (and not allowed) through the ISA firewall.

One of the major improvements in ISA Server 2004 is the ability to create virtually any rule element within the Access Rule wizard. The inability to create policy elements "on the fly" with ISA Server 2000 was a major point of contention. It was a common occurrence that the ISA Server 2000 firewall administrator would begin to create a Protocol Rule and forget that the required Protocol Definition had not yet been created. ISA Server 2004 allows you to create each policy element from within the wizard.

In this chapter, we discuss how ISA Server 2004 Access Rules work and how to configure them to control access through the firewall. In addition, we discuss the procedures required to create your policy elements in advance, and we show you how to use the Access Rule toolset to simplify creation of Access Rules. Specific examples are provided, showing how to allow and deny Instant Messaging (IM) and Peer-to-Peer (P2P) applications, how to allow access to remote Exchange Servers, and much more.

Chapter Eight: Publishing Network Services to the Internet with ISA 2004

Publishing network services allows you to make servers and services on your corporate network accessible to users across the Internet and from other untrusted remote locations. Publishing services on the corporate network is fraught with danger because it exposes valuable network resources to the Internet. The challenge is to provide remote access to your network servers and services without compromising security. This is where the ISA Server 2004 firewall shines. As a sophisticated and stateful application-layer filtering firewall, the ISA Server 2004 firewall can make short work out of attackers who try to compromise your servers.

In this chapter, we discuss Web and Server Publishing rules. Web Publishing Rules allow you to securely publish Web sites and services to the Internet so that Internet users can access these servers. Web Publishing Rules provide the highest level of security available to published Web services because of their unique ability to perform SSL-to-SSL bridging and delegation of basic authentication. In addition, the HTTP Security filter allows you to control virtually any aspect of the HTTP communications moving through the firewall; the filter drops suspicious and dangerous connections before they ever reach the published Web site.

Server Publishing Rules can be used to publish virtually any service. You can use Server Publishing Rules to allow inbound access to HTTP (if you don't want to use a Web Publishing Rule, you can use a Server Publishing Rule), HTTPS, FTP, NNTP, SMTP, POP3, IMAP4. VNC, pcAnywhere, Terminal Services, and more. In addition, you can publish PPTP and L2TP/IPSec VPN servers behind an ISA Server 2004 firewall. You can publish virtually any TCP/UDP based protocol.

In this chapter, we go over the concepts and the step-by-step procedures required to publish virtually any network service using Web and Server Publishing Rules. We provide specific instructions showing you how to publish all the popular Internet protocols, as well as how to publish some more obscure services using customized configurations and using the firewall client on the published server.

Chapter Nine: Creating Remote Access and Site-to-Site VPNs with ISA Firewalls

Probably the most exciting and powerful new feature included with the ISA Server 2004 firewall is its significantly improved VPN server and gateway functionality. ISA Server 2000 could be configured to allow the ISA Server 2000 firewall to be a VPN server and VPN gateway, but the ISA Server 2000 firewall did not expose the VPN connections to firewall policy. In contrast, with ISA Server 2004, VPN remote access and gateway-to-gateway connections are all exposed to firewall policy in the same way as any other connection made through the ISA Server 2004 firewall.

The ISA Server 2004 firewall's VPN features allow you to control what resources VPN clients can connect to on a user/group basis. For example, if you want a group of users to only be able to connect to the Exchange Server using the secure Exchange RPC protocol via the Outlook 2002 client when connected over a VPN, you can create a firewall policy that limits this group to the Exchange Server only, and only when using the protocols required to connect using the full Outlook MAPI client.

The ISA Server 2004 firewall can now create gateway-to-gateway VPN connections using IPSec tunnel mode. This allows you to connect the ISA Server 2004 firewall to other VPN gateways made by third-party vendors using IPSec tunnel mode. Now you can bring the ISA Server 2004 firewall into a branch office and easily connect it to the non-Microsoft VPN server or concentrator at the main office. However, if you choose to use ISA Server 2004 firewalls as VPN gateways at both the main and branch offices, you can benefit from the higher security derived from using L2TP/IPSec as your site-to-site VPN protocol.

In this chapter, we cover the concepts and step-by-step procedures required to make the ISA Server 2004 firewall both a VPN Remote Access Server (RAS) and a VPN gateway (used for site-to-site VPN connections). This includes connecting to third-party VPN gateways and also addresses the special cases of publishing PPTP and L2TP/IPSec VPN servers behind the ISA Server 2004 firewall. Another issue that is addressed is providing outbound access for VPN clients that use PPTP, L2TP/IPSec NAT-T and third-party IPSec NAT-T solutions.

Chapter Ten: Stateful Inspection and Application Layer Filtering

One of the most compelling features of ISA 2004 is its "deep" application layer filtering (ALF) capabilities. With ALF, you can protect against application layer attacks, prevent users from visiting dangerous or offensive Web sites, and even provide first-line defense against spam at the firewall level. With ALF, you can perform protocol-specific tasks and control access to and from your network based on application (FTP, H.323, SOCKS4, etc.).

In this chapter, we discuss the benefits of ALF and how it fits into your network security plan, and provide step-by-step instructions in how to configure the application filters and Web filters that come with ISA 2004, as well as how to use add-in filters to further expand ISA 2004's application layer filtering functionality. Here you will learn how to use the DNS filter, the POP intrusion detection filter, the RPC, PPTP and SMTP filters, the Web Proxy filter, and many more. We'll also discuss filters that enable

OWA forms-based authentication, SecurID authentication, and RADIUS authentication, and you'll learn all about link translation and enforcing configurable HTTP policy with the appropriate filters.

Chapter Eleven: Accelerating Web Performance with ISA 2004 Caching Capabilities

One of ISA Server 2004's biggest competitive advantages is that it is not only a firewall and VPN server and gateway; it is also a Web-caching server. The Web-caching component allows you to speed up Web access for your corporate network users and potentially reduce overall bandwidth usage on all your Internet links.

In this chapter, we go over the concepts and step-by-step procedures required to configure the ISA Server 2004 firewall as a Web-caching server. You'll learn about the settings required to optimize Web-caching performance and how to configure Web proxy chaining to improve Web performance for your branch office users and reduce overall bandwidth usage on branch office links to the Main office.

Chapter Twelve: Using ISA 2004: Monitoring, Reports and Logging

The Monitoring node in the ISA Server 2004 management console is a huge improvement over the same feature in ISA Server 2000, providing a handy "Dashboard" view that lets you see the "big picture" of what's happening in various monitoring areas, along with performance information.

An intuitive tabbed interface makes it easy to quickly delve into more details about specific monitoring areas, and we will provide step-by-step instructions on how to configure alerts, how to use session and services information, how to configure logging and generate reports, and how to use the connectivity verification feature.

Appendix: Network Security Basics

In order to understand what a firewall does and how various firewall features work, it is essential that you have an understanding of the TCP/IP protocol stack and how common intrusions and attacks exploit characteristics of the protocols at different layers of the Open Systems Interconnect (OSI) and Department of Defense (DOD) networking models to do their dirty work.

Readers who do not have previous networking experience or who need a quick review of basic TCP/IP concepts and exploits should check out Appendix A before proceeding through the rest of the book.

This Book's For You: Our Target Audience

This book is for anyone who wants to know what ISA Server 2004 is all about, how it differs from ISA 2000 and from third party firewall and caching products, and how to get the most out of it to protect your network and improve Web content performance for your internal and external users.

This book is *not* designed as an exam prep or study guide. Although it contains useful conceptual information and step-by-step exercises that will provide readers with a better understanding of ISA Server 2004, and can serve as a background supplement to training kits and courses designed to prepare candidates for the MCSA/MCSE exam, the purpose of this book is to address real-world installation, configuration, management, and troubleshooting issues encountered on the job. Its structure and content are not based on exam objectives, and exam candidates should not consider it a primary source of preparation.

Tools and Traps…

Microsoft Certification Exam 70-350

At the time of the writing of this book, Microsoft Certification Exam 70-350, Installing, Configuring and Administering Microsoft Internet Security and Acceleration (ISA) Server 2004, has not been written and objectives are not yet available. Check the Microsoft Learning Web site at www.microsoft.com/learning/mcpexams/default.asp for information about the exam.

For those who want to get a head start on studying for the ISA Server 2004 exam, a good starting place is the exam preparation guide for Exam 70-227, *Installing, Configuring and Administering Microsoft Internet Security and Acceleration (ISA) Server 2000, Enterprise Edition.* At the time of this writing, Exam 70-227 not only counts as an elective for the Microsoft Certified Systems Administrator (MCSA) and Microsoft Certified Systems Engineer (MCSE) certification paths, but is also a core security exam for the MCSA and MCSE security specialty certification paths. It is expected that Exam 70-350 will similarly count toward the security specialist certifications.

As with all current Microsoft certification exams, the most important preparation will be hands-on work with the product in a variety of networking situations. Deploying ISA Server 2004, either on a home network, on a business network, or in a virtual network environment, and working with it on a daily basis is the best way to gain the intimate familiarity with the interface, concepts, and administrative tasks that are necessary to understand to successfully answer the exam questions.

This book is based in large part on our own trials and tribulations (as well as the occasional "Eureka!" moment) that we've experienced working with ISA Server 2004. In this book, we are talking to people much like ourselves – experienced Windows network administrators who want to secure their networks and speed up Web access for their users without having to make a full-time vocation of it, learn programming, recompile kernels, or struggle with a brand new command syntax. We're talking to people who want a security solution that is built to interoperate with their Windows domain controllers and Microsoft servers such as Exchange and SharePoint. We're talking to experienced ISA 2000 administrators, those who are brand new to the world of firewalls, and those who are migrating from third-party firewall products.

A book is, by its very nature, a one-way conversation that flows from author to reader. However, we have built each of our books on questions and comments from our readers, and we don't consider the subject closed when the book is finally printed and on the shelves. Rather, that's just the beginning of a dialog, and the input we get from you will help us in writing the next book, article or courseware project. You can reach us through the www.syngress.com Web site and you can find a wealth of additional and updated information about ISA Server 2004 at www.isaserver.org and on our Web site at www.msfirewall.org.

Security: The New Star of the Show

The new millennium ushered in a new era. In computing, as in most other aspects of everyday life, the focus shifted heavily toward a newly urgent concern: security. World events created a sudden realization that we live in much more perilous times than we previously imagined. It's no coincidence that Microsoft's first serious venture into the firewall market came in the year 2000, with the release of their first full-fledged firewall product, Internet Acceleration and Security Server (ISA).

Since then, the world's largest software company has continued to strengthen its commitment to creating products that not only offer features and functionality, but also provide protection from the hackers, crackers and network attackers who seem to lurk around every virtual corner.

As we discussed in our first ISA Server book, a comprehensive security solution must be able to address different types of security threats. A number of different factors are involved in protecting your network from security threats. Your overall security plan should be designed to protect some or all of the following:

- Confidentiality of sensitive data
- Integrity of both sensitive and non-sensitive data
- Availability of sensitive and non-sensitive data
- Verification of the source or origin of data
- Network operability (protection from malicious destruction of system files via viruses or direct intrusion)

Security threats come in many "flavors," but they can be broadly divided into two categories: external and internal. A denial-of-service (DOS) attack perpetuated by a hacker at a remote location is an external security threat. Accidental deletion of important files by a company employee onsite is an internal threat. Although a firewall's first function is to protect from external threats—those that attempt to penetrate your LAN from the Internet, ISA Server also allows you to restrict outgoing network traffic, and in that way it offers protection from some (although certainly not all) internal security threats as well.

In this chapter, we will discuss how ISA Server has evolved as the nature of computing itself has evolved. To fully understand what ISA Server is and where it came from, we have to go way back to before it was even a glint in Bill Gates' eye, and look at how Microsoft has viewed the issue of security (and how that view has changed) from the beginnings of Windows up to today.

Security: What's Microsoft Got to Do with It?

Proponents of alternative operating systems (OS) are quick to proclaim that all Microsoft products are inherently insecure. As with many myths, this one is based on facts, but they are outdated facts. Windows, unlike UNIX, was originally designed to run on single-user PCs rather than as a network operating system. In that scenario, security features are less important, and user-friendliness took precedence.

A Brief History of the Rise of Windows

The focus on user-friendliness led to the popularity of Windows, first on the desktop and then in the server space. Other desktop operating systems such as Apple's Mac OS and current UNIX-based OS X and various distributions of Linux appeal to niche audiences, and even older operating systems such as MS-DOS and OS/2 are still in use in some business settings. However, Windows has, by far, the largest installed base, especially in the consumer and business client computing markets. Most new PCs come with the latest version of Windows pre-installed by the hardware manufacturer. This means most computer users are familiar with the Windows interface. The fact that this is the interface users want is supported by the fact that the most popular graphical desktop environments for UNIX/Linux (for example, KDE) make those operating systems "look like" Windows.

At the beginning of the 1990s, Novell's NetWare was the "server of choice" for most businesses, while universities and ISPs commonly ran UNIX networks. By the end of the 1990s, Windows NT had all but crowded NetWare out of its own market.

Something else happened in the 90s: the commercialization of the Internet and its subsequent availability to consumers and businesses at low prices changed the nature of computing. No longer are personal computers used primarily as standalone machines for creating word processing documents, crunching numbers or playing single-user games. Now most home and office computers are connected to the global network, either directly or through a local area network (LAN). The popularity of the Internet for conducting research, corresponding with others via e-mail and live chat, "Web surfing," and playing multiuser games also led to an increase in the number of home LANs, many of which are set up specifically for the purpose of sharing an Internet connection.

A New Emphasis on Security

As computing changed from a solitary activity to an interactive one, Windows had to change, too. Networking is all about accessibility, but the nature of networking also demands limits on that accessibility. Microsoft might be fairly thought of as a "late-comer" to the security front, just as they were a bit slow to get on board with the idea of Internet connectivity. However, as the threat level rose and the importance of security became obvious, each successive Windows OS included more features designed to protect it and its data from unauthorized access and attack.

This change in focus from features and functionality to security didn't arise spontaneously. Microsoft—along with other software companies—learned the hard way how important security is to them and to their customers. The Code Red and Nimda worms hit Windows servers hard in 2001, and this served as a "wakeup call." Soon after, the company introduced the concept of Trustworthy Computing.

The advantages of using Microsoft over its competition—which were a major factor in its success over that competition—also became a significant factor in its security vulnerabilities. For example, Microsoft, through its published APIs, made it easy to write applications that could interact with the OS. (It was not easy to write an NetWare Loadable Module (NLM) for a NetWare operating system.) As MS grew more successful, enmity toward the company increased, and those APIs and other hooks to the OS were leveraged by motivated hackers.

The Trustworthy Computing Initiative

With security, as with Internet connectivity, once Microsoft decides to embrace a concept, the company's leaders and employees pour their considerable resources into getting it right. With their Trustworthy Computing initiative, Microsoft made their commitment to security a number one priority. Today's Windows operating systems include a multiplicity of built-in security features. Services that present special security risks, such as Internet Information Server (IIS), are turned off and locked down by default. The company has also turned its attention and talents to creating and improving software devoted exclusively to providing various aspects of security, including Microsoft Identity and Integration Server (MIIS), Microsoft Baseline Security Analyzer (MBSA), Software Update Services (SUS), and of course, ISA Server.

NOTE

Software Update Services (SUS) is being renamed to Windows Update Services (WUS); the new product is still in beta testing at this writing.

The Trustworthy Computing Initiative includes the "SD³ Security Framework," the components of which are explained in Table 1.1.

Table 1.1 The SD³ Security Framework

SD3 Component	How It Is Implemented
Secure by Design	Programmers receive training in security. Code is reviewed for security issues. The software design process includes threat modeling, and security protections are built into the code.
Secure by Default	The software is configured to be more secure "out of the box," with services and features that pose a security risk locked down or turned off by default.
Secure in Deployment	Security tools are provided free of charge to help administrators monitor and address security issues. Automated updates ensure easier and more widespread installation of security fixes and enhancements.

NOTE

A fourth component was added to the framework after its inception: Communications. This refers to a two-way communication process that includes listening to (and indeed, soliciting) customers' security concerns and disseminating information about security to customers and the public.

Microsoft is also emphasizing security in their relationships with third-party developers, partner companies, and customers. The Microsoft Web site reported that Microsoft expected to provide security training for more than half a million customers between February and June 2004, via a series of security "events" to be held at various locations. They have created a marketing campaign to make users of their products – both at the consumer and the corporate levels – more security-aware. A good example is the rollout of Service Pack 2 for Windows XP. The Service Pack addresses many security issues, and the company expects to spend millions of dollars on distribution of a CD through various outlets.

In addition to correcting security flaws in the code, service packs also include changes to the interface and explanations to help end users more clearly understand the security consequences of taking particular actions. For example, the Authenticode warning and functionality have been changed to eliminate software "nagging" to install ActiveX code. This addresses the problem of software that repeatedly asks users to install it, resulting in many users eventually giving in and saying "Yes" out of frustration.

The MCSE/MCSA certification paths now include a Security Specialist option, and Exam 70-298, *Designing Security for a Microsoft Windows Server 2003 Network,* is a core Design exam in the Server 2003 MCSE track.

The Role of ISA Server 2004 in Microsoft's Security Initiative

An update to ISA Server 2000 – building a better firewall – is a logical progression in the company's security initiative. An illustration of the new emphasis on security is the fact that Bill Gates highlighted a demonstration of the ISA Server 2004 beta in his keynote address at COMDEX in November 2003.

With ISA 2004, Microsoft hopes to go head-to-head against the "big players" in the enterprise firewall market, CheckPoint and Cisco, and also compete with a plethora of low-cost turnkey firewall/VPN appliances marketed by NetScreen, WatchGuard, SonicWall and several other vendors.

ISA Server Firewall Fallacies

In working with network administrators through isaserver.org, Microsoft events, and other forums, we constantly hear myths, half-truths and even outright fallacies about ISA Server. This section will address some of the most common, including:

- Software firewalls are inherently weak. Only hardware firewalls can be trusted to secure a network.

- You can't trust any service running on the Windows operating system to be secure. You could never secure a firewall running on a Windows OS.

- ISA machines make for good proxy servers, but I need a real firewall to protect my network.

- ISA firewalls run on an Intel hardware platform, and only firewalls that have all "solid state" components can be firewall. A firewall should have no moving parts.

- I have a firewall and an 'ISA Server.'

- A real firewall should be a nightmare to configure, and ideally, should use a command-line interface (CLI) to make it accessible only to highly trained individuals.

Fallacy #1: Software Firewalls are Inherently Weak

As an ISA firewall administrator, you'll probably run into people who:

- Don't know what an ISA firewall is,

- Think it's some sort of caching server, akin to the old CacheFlow product (purchased by Bluecoat) or Squid, or

- Believe only hardware firewalls are inviolate, and so-called "software" firewalls are as penetrable as warm custard and aren't meant to be perimeter data center or enterprise firewalls.

Teaching the ones who never heard of an ISA firewall can be a profoundly rewarding experience. You get to tell them about how an ISA firewall provides strong inbound and outbound access controls in ways that no other firewall can provide; how it blocks file-sharing programs; how it prevents malicious users from violating network security policies, such as downloading copyrighted material; how the ISA firewall provides superior protection for Microsoft Exchange services, including OWA and MAPI/RPC, and how it is so easy to configure that it blows away all other firewalls on the market (if you don't believe it, look at Checkpoint NG's management interface).

The other two types test our patience.

First, there's the "ISA is a Web Proxy or caching server thingie, I think" person. This one probably read some industry rag or attended a conference where a security or firewall "guru" who's never seen an ISA firewall, proudly and oracularly stated: "ISA Server is just an update to Proxy Server 2.0".

If this were true, Microsoft probably would have called it Proxy Server 3.0. There was a reason they chose to go with a whole new name: ISA firewalls are honest-to-goodness, enterprise-class firewalls that provide the strong inbound and outbound access control and application-layer filtering you need to protect *today's* networks, not the networks of yesteryear at which traditional packet filter-based firewalls were aimed.

The "hardware firewalls descended from heaven" people are the most difficult. They've been told over the years that IBM's application specific integrated circuit (ASIC-based) firewalls are the "acme" of all possible firewalls, and any firewall not based on ASIC is a lowly software firewall and doesn't even deserve the name of "firewall". One wonders how they reconcile their dogma with the fact that the number one selling firewall product is CheckPoint, a (gasp!) software-based firewall.

The hardware firewall fantasy is actually based on a historical reality. In the past, firewalls could provide a reasonable level of security and performance using simple packet filtering mechanisms that look at source and destination addresses and ports and protocols, and make quick decisions. Since the logic is "burned in" to the ASIC, it's not easy to hack the basic system. However, attackers have learned that you don't need to hack the core instruction set in order to get around the relatively poor security hardware-based systems provide.

You can find an excellent article debunking the myth of ASIC superiority at www.issadvisor.com/viewtopic.php?t=368. The author makes a very good case showing that hardware firewalls will never be able to keep pace with modern threat evolution and that one-box software-based firewalls are the future of network firewalls and perimeter security. Therein lies the big advantage conferred by the ISA firewall: it can be quickly upgraded and enhanced to meet not only today's threats, but also the exploits against which you'll need a defense in the future.

The ISA firewall, be it ISA Server 2000 or ISA Server 2004, is the ideal mainline enterprise firewall ("mainline" in this context meaning that it protects mission critical systems). However, you'll see the "ASIC is the only firewall" fallacy over and over. For example, the article at http://infosecuritymag.techtarget.com/ss/0,295796,sid6_iss346 _art676,00.html perpetuates the misconception that ISA firewalls aren't suited to be enterprise perimeter firewalls. Comments such as, "ISA 2004 isn't going to replace mainline, perimeter firewalls, nor is it intended as a sole layer of protection for Microsoft apps, but it's a pretty good addition to the layers of the security onion," imply that there is only a single network or security perimeter.

In fact, enterprise networks contain many security perimeters, as we discussed earlier in this chapter. No, we wouldn't want the ISA firewall as the Internet edge or at edges of very high traffic backbone segments, because only a very simple (and thus fast) packet filtering firewall can meet the packet-passing *performance* requirements there. However, it is important to realize that high-speed packet passing with simple packet filters and "fix-ups" does *not* equal acceptable security. These hardware-based packet-passing firewalls are useful for very high traffic perimeters, but are of little or no use at the perimeters bordering the server and client systems because of their lack of deep application-layer intelligence.

Fallacy #2: You Can't Trust Any Service Running on the Windows Operating System to be Secure.

This is a common fallacy based on factors we discussed earlier in this chapter. We are often asked about how we can run ISA Server 2004 firewalls on a machine running the Windows operating system, given the number of security holes and bug fixes the base operating system requires. It's a valid question. Here are some facts to consider about Windows and running the ISA firewall on top of it:

- **Not all hotfixes apply to the ISA Server 2004 firewall**. Many of these hotfixes are service based. Since you don't run client or server services on the ISA Server 2004 firewall machine, most of the hotfixes are irrelevant.

- **Some of the hotfixes do address issues with the core operating system components, such as Remote Procedure Call (RPC) (which was exploited by the Blaster worm).** Since the ISA Server 2004 firewall applies security policy to *all* interfaces, you would have to create a firewall policy that allows the attack access to the firewall. In the specific case of RPC, the secure RPC filter blocks Blaster and related attacks. IIS problems are a non-issue, because you do not run IIS services (with the exception of maybe the IIS SMTP service) on the firewall. Other services are only accessible if you open up the ports to the firewall to allow the attack in. A properly configured ISA Server 2004 firewall, therefore, is much more secure than the based operating system because network access to the firewall is severely truncated.

- **Other hotfixes apply to stability issues.** You will need to apply these hotfixes and service packs. However, all firewall vendors issue regular fixes (if they don't, they're not paying attention, and their software is vulnerable – even if they don't know it, and even if they haven't acknowledged the vulnerabilities to the public).

- **Some hotfixes require restarting.** You can also schedule the restart for a convenient time. Note that you will not need to install all hotfixes because not all of them (or even a significant number of them) will apply to your ISA Server 2004 firewall. The number of restarts required should be negligible.

- **The underlying OS on the ISA Server 2004 firewall can be hardened.** In fact, there is a profile in the Windows Server 2003 SP1 Security Configuration Wizard (SCW) that allows you to easily harden the underlying OS, automatically, using the SCW.

- **You can harden the underlying OS manually, if you don't want to use the SCW or don't have access to it.** There will be an OS hardening guide that will be released concurrently with ISA Server 2004. It will walk you through the process of hardening the underlying OS, while leaving the ISA Server 2004 firewall services unaffected. This was a significant issue with ISA Server 2000 because many of us attempted to harden the OS, and it had side effects of which we weren't aware or that we didn't intend.

While the issue of the underlying operating system is a factor in the security of any application, the underlying Windows Server 2003 OS is not a significant vulnerability when properly configured. As for Windows 2000, securing the underlying OS may be bit more of an issue, but you can still harden the OS to an extent that rivals any hardware firewall.

If you can't trust any services running on a Windows operating system, then how can you trust the underlying OS for your Exchange, SQL, SharePoint and other Microsoft server installations?

Fallacy #3: ISA Firewalls Make Good Proxy Servers, But I Need a Real Firewall to Protect My Network

It's true that ISA Server 2004 machines make good proxy servers. In fact, ISA Server 2004 is a *proxy firewall*, which is the most sophisticated and most secure type of firewall you can use because it can filter at the highest (application) layer. In addition to being a proxy firewall, ISA Server 2004 is also a packet-filtering and circuit-layer firewall.

As we discuss later in the chapter, in the section dealing with firewall architecture, the conventional packet-filtering firewall uses a very simple mechanism to control inbound and outbound access: source and destination port, source and destination IP address, and for ICMP, source and destination IP address together with ICMP type and code. Packet filters must be explicitly created for each inbound and outbound connection. More sophisticated packet filters can dynamically open response ports. ISA Server 2004 firewalls are able to dynamically open ports via their *dynamic packet-filtering* feature.

The "circuit-layer" firewall is akin to what most commentators refer to as the "stateful firewall." It should be noted that the term "stateful" can mean whatever you want it to mean. It was introduced as a marketing term, and like most marketing terms, was designed to sell products, not to quantify and specify any specific feature or behavior. However, most industry experts think of *stateful filtering* (in contrast to *stateful inspection*) as a mechanism where the stateful filter tracks the connection state at the transport (layer 4) level. TCP includes a number of fields that define connection states, while the User Datagram Protocol (UDP) does not. Because of this, UDP communications must have a *pseudostate* enforced by the stateful-filtering device. Stateful filtering is helpful in protecting against a number of sub-application layer attacks, such as session hijacking.

Most consumer grade (and many very expensive commercial grade hardware firewalls) stop there. They can perform simple packet filtering, dynamic packet filtering, and stateful packet filtering (stateful filtering). These firewalls also often provide advanced routing features, which places them more in the class of a network router than that of a true modern firewall. In contrast, the routing features of ISA Server 2004 firewalls are less impressive than you see in traditional packet filter-based firewalls.

As we've discussed earlier, the packet-filtering firewall is useful at the Internet edge because of its processing speed. The primary problem with these firewalls is that they really do not provide the level of protection required to stop exploits from reaching the inner perimeters, where advanced application-layer inspection must be performed.

This is where proxy firewalls enter the equation. A proxy firewall is able to inspect the entire contents of an application-layer communication by deconstructing and reconstructing the entire application-layer message. For example, the proxy firewall deconstructs the entire HTTP message, examines the commands and data within the message, statefully inspects the contents and compares those with the application-layer rules, and then passes or blocks the communication based on the application layer rules configured for the HTTP protocol.

One of the more common HTTP exploits is the directory traversal attack. Many popular worms take advantage of directory traversal to access executables on the Web server that allow the attacker to take control of the Web server. For example, consider the following URL:

```
www.iusepixfirewalls.com/scripts/..%5c../winnt/system32/cmd.exe?/c+dir+c:\
```

The code contained in this URL executes the cmd.exe file and runs the "`dir c:\`" command, which lists all files in the C:\ directory. Note the "`%5c`" string. This is a Web server escape code. Escape codes represent normal characters in the form of %nn, where nn stands for a two-character entry. The escape code "`%5c`" represents the character "\". The IIS root directory enforcer might not check for escape codes and allow the request to be executed. The Web server's operating system understands escape codes and executes the command.

Escape codes are also very useful for bypassing poorly written filters enforced on input received from users. If the filter looks for "../", then the attacker could easily change the input to "`%2e%2e/`". This has the same meaning as "../", but is not detected by the filter. The escape code %2e represents the character "." (dot). The ISA Server 2004 firewall, being a sophisticated stateful inspection (application-layer aware) firewall, easily blocks these exploits (as did ISA 2000). Although modern Web server software has been updated to prevent directory traversal attacks, this still serves as an example of how the ISA Server firewall can protect older Web servers.

Proxy firewalls have the potential to block exploits for any application-layer protocol. Other application-layer protocols include SMTP, NNTP, Instant Messaging protocols, POP3, IMAP4, and others. Blended firewalls such as ISA Server 2004, which are combined stateful-filtering and stateful- (application-layer) inspection firewalls, can easily be upgraded with software to block the most recent application-layer attacks. In contrast, packet filter-based firewalls are totally unaware of application-layer attacks, and even hardware firewalls with rudimentary application-layer inspection cannot be quickly upgraded to meet the latest application-layer exploits because of the limits of ASIC (hardware) processing and development.

Fallacy #4: ISA Firewalls Run on an Intel Hardware Platform and Firewalls Should Have "No Moving Parts"

We've heard this one a number of times and it always leaves us scratching our heads. Why should a firewall have no moving parts, yet our Exchange server, SQL server, Web server, FTP server, and any other mission-critical service work fine with moving parts? Here are some advantages to using the Intel PC-based platform for firewalls:

- When the memory, processor, or network card goes bad on the device, you can replace it at commodity hardware prices. You do not need to go back to the solid state hardware vendor and pay premium prices for their proprietary versions of hardware components.

- When you want to upgrade memory, processor, storage, NIC, or any other component, you can use commodity hardware and add that to your machine. You do not need to go to the source hardware vendor to obtain overpriced upgrades to your box.

- Because the ISA Server 2004 software is hard disk based, you do not have the memory and storage restrictions that solid state devices have. You can install on-box application-layer filters, increase the cache size, tweak performance and security settings, and perform fine-tuned customizations required by your environment.

- The "no moving parts" aspect pertains primarily to hard disks. Hard disk Mean Time Before Failure (MTBF) values are now in years. Even lowly IDE drives last 3+ years with normal use. And when the disk fails, the ISA Server 2004 firewall configuration is easy to restore because the entire configuration is stored in a simple .xml file. You can have it back up and running within 15 minutes with the right disaster recovery plan. Compare that to fried memory in a hardware device, requiring that the entire device be returned to the manufacturer.

NOTE

Even with ASIC-based firewalls, log files and reports have to be stored somewhere, so hard disk storage space – either on the device itself or on the network – is still necessary.

The disaster recovery aspect is perhaps the most compelling reason for using a "software" firewall. A single ISA Server 2004 firewall or an entire array of ten ISA Server 2004 firewalls can be rebuilt in a matter of minutes without having to replace the entire box or requiring you to obtain hardware pieces from the vendor. And if you're using removable drives, it's easily possible to be up and running for the entire array in less than 30 minutes.

Fallacy #5: "I Have a Firewall and an 'ISA Server'"

We've heard this one countless times: "I have a firewall and I want to place an ISA Server behind it. How do I do that"? These comments come from ISA fans, so we know there's no intent to denigrate the ISA firewall. Instead, this is an indication that even ISA firewall administrators themselves don't realize that ISA firewalls are *the* firewalls for their networks, and the packet filters they put in front of the ISA firewalls are typically performing basic packet filtering, which helps with processor off-loading.

This fallacy is easily corrected by changing the wording to: "I have a packet-filtering firewall in front of my ISA firewall; how do I get them to work together?" or "I have a Sonicwall firewall in front of my ISA firewall; how do I get them to work together?"

To be fair, we have to admit that not everyone uses the ISA Server 2004 firewall as a firewall. You do have the option to install the ISA Server 2004 firewall in single network interface card (NIC) mode, which is comparable to the "cache only" mode that ISA Server 2000 included. In single NIC mode, however, you are wasting half of the capability of the ISA Server 2004 firewall. Most of the firewall functionality is removed, and the machine provides limited functionality as a Web proxy server only.

This is not to imply that the ISA Server 2004 firewall in single NIC mode is not secure. Enough of the firewall functionality is left in place to allow the ISA Server 2004 firewall to protect itself, and to secure the Web-proxied connections made through the single NIC ISA Server 2004 firewall. The ISA Server 2004 single NIC firewall only allows connections to itself that you explicitly allow via the firewall's system policy. The only connections it allows to corporate network hosts are those that you explicitly allow via Web Publishing Rules, and the only outbound connections that can be made through the single NIC ISA Server 2004 firewall are those you allow via a truncated HTTP/HTTPS-only list of Access Rules.

While we would prefer to see all organizations use the ISA Server 2004 firewall for its intended use—that is, as a full featured, blended stateful packet-filtering and application-layer firewall—we do realize that larger organizations have spent literally millions of dollars on other firewall solutions and aren't inclined to just throw them away in favor of ISA Server. However, these organizations do want to benefit from the reverse proxy components offered by ISA for superior OWA, OMA, ActiveSync and IIS protection. For this reason, it's important to point out that the ISA Server 2004 firewall, even in its "crippled" single NIC mode, provides a high level of protection for forward and reverse proxy connections.

Security: A Policy-Based Approach

A police department couldn't do a community much good without laws to enforce. Likewise, a firewall and other security mechanisms aren't very useful to your network unless you have policies in place, defining the rules and guidelines that they will enforce.

An enormous amount of a company's most crucial information, including financial data, personnel records, customer information, and trade secrets, is concentrated in one virtual "place": the organization's network. This renders it vulnerable to unauthorized access and accidental or intentional destruction, both from within and (assuming the local network is connected to the Internet, as most today are) from outside intruders. Implementation of security measures, to be effective, must be based on an organized plan that takes into account all aspects of the organization's security needs. There must be rules and guidelines governing how the plan is put into action. These are disseminated throughout the organization, as *policies.* The firewall is the enforcement mechanism for these policies.

What is a Security Policy?

A security policy, as the term is generally understood, refers to a written document that defines an organization's approach to security or a specific security area (in this case, computer and network security) and lays down a set of rules to be followed in implementing the organization's security philosophy.

NOTE

Guidelines usually function as recommended procedures, rather than hard-and-fast rules. Guidelines can supplement policies, but do not replace them.

Organizations may establish both written and unwritten rules pertaining to security matters, and may issue a number of different types of documents dealing with these issues.

Security Standards and Specifications

Standards and *specifications* are generally requirements to be met in implementing system-specific security procedures, and may be used to measure or rate the overall reliability, compatibility, or other characteristics of the system. For example, the U.S. government has developed criteria defined in the *Department of Defense Trusted Computer System Evaluation Criteria* handbook (also called the "orange book") and the *Trusted Network Interpretation of the TCSEC* (the "red book") for rating security implementations. Other countries have similar rating systems. The International Organization for Standardization (ISO) has developed ISO 17799 as an internationally recognized set of "best practices" regarding IT security. Your security policy may specify adherence to particular standards or specifications.

Evaluating Security Needs

If we accept the definition of security policy provided above, it becomes obvious that there is not, and cannot be, a one-size-fits-all IT security policy that will work equally well for all organizations. Security needs differ, based on:

- Risk factors
- The perceived and actual threat level
- Organizational vulnerabilities
- The organization's philosophy (open vs closed system)
- Legal factors
- Available funds

It is important to analyze all of these factors carefully in developing a policy that offers both adequate protection and a desirable level of access.

Security features are now built into the operating system software; Windows NT, 2000, XP, and Windows Server 2003 include numerous security features. IT security products, both hardware and software, abound. Security training and numerous security certifications are available, and IT professionals are seeking them out.

These are all important components of an organization's overall security plan, but they are not enough. Effective coordination and interaction of all these parts requires one more thing: a comprehensive security policy.

Defining Areas of Responsibility

To assess security needs accurately, someone should review the company's infrastructure, processes, and procedures, and involve personnel at all levels of the organization and from as many different departments as possible. Ideally, the tasks will be performed by a carefully selected team that includes, at a minimum, members of management, IT personnel, and a company legal representative. Each team member should be assigned specific areas of responsibility, and deadlines for completion should be assigned. Steps involved in developing policy include:

- Analyzing risk factors
- Assessing threats and threat levels
- Analyzing organizational and network vulnerabilities
- Analyzing organizational philosophy
- Analyzing legal factors
- Analyzing cost factors
- Assessing security solutions

Analyzing Risk Factors

Before the policy development team can set policies, they need to determine both the nature and the level of the security risks to the organization. Traditionally, risk analysis involves:

- Determining to what types of security breaches the organization is vulnerable
- For each type, determining the probability of such a breach occurring
- For each type, determining the extent of the loss that would be suffered if the breach did occur

This is known as *quantitative risk analysis*.

Tools and Traps...

Quantitative Risk Analysis Formula

The industry-standard formula for quantitative risk analysis is:

(ALE = SLE x ARO). That is, Annualized Loss Expectancy (ALE) = Single Loss Exposure (SLE) x Annualized Rate of Occurrence (ARO).

SLE is calculated as asset value x exposure factor. So, for example, let's assume that there is an 80 percent risk factor that a major virus outbreak would occur at least once a year, and that 60 percent of computers on the network would be infected before the virus was contained. Consider further that the cost of removing the virus from the workstations is something like $60/workstation (based on an hourly rate and amount of time) and that you had 500 workstations. The SLE would be 500 x $60 x 0.6 = $18,000. The ALE would be $18,000 x 0.8 (ARO) = $14,400.

Note that this example does not assign a cost to the loss of data and worker productivity, so the actual costs would be greater.

Another type of risk analysis, *qualitative risk analysis,* disregards the probability element and focuses on potential threats and the characteristics of the system/network that make it vulnerable to these threats. Then, methods are developed for preventing or reducing the likelihood of breaches, detecting when breaches do occur, and decreasing and repairing the damage done if a breach does occur.

Risk analysis tools are available to help identify threats and vulnerabilities, rate the threat level, estimate the impact on the organization, and recommend solutions. An example is the COBRA Risk Consultant from C&A Systems Security Ltd. COBRA methodology is used by major corporations and governmental entities.

Why is a risk analysis necessary? There are several reasons, including the following:

- From the IT professional's point of view, a detailed risk analysis is the first, and perhaps most important step, in justifying to management the cost to implement needed security measures.

- From the business manager's point of view, the risk analysis document provides a solid, objective basis for making budgetary and personnel-impacting decisions.

- Data collected during the risk analysis process forces both IT and management to face and acknowledge threats and vulnerabilities of which they may not have been aware or which they may have been able to previously ignore.

- Risk analysis allows the organization to focus resources on the existing threats and vulnerabilities, and avoid wasting time and funds on unnecessary measures.

Because the risk analysis process involves personnel throughout the organization, it can raise security awareness and help to make appropriate security practices the responsibility of everyone who uses the computers and network. This is a basic tenet of crime prevention.

Assessing Threats and Threat Levels

The dictionary defines a *threat* as "somebody or something likely to cause harm." The threat assessment portion of the risk analysis should include:

- Sources of potential threats
- Nature of potential threats
- Likelihood of occurrence of each potential threat type
- Estimated impact of each potential threat type

Sources of potential threats can be divided into internal and external. Although many security policies focus on the threat of a security breach from outside the network/organization (across the Internet), in actuality, many organizations will find that their biggest potential losses come from inside – the deliberate or unintentional actions of employees, contractors and others who have legitimate access to the network. It is important to address both categories when performing a threat assessment.

Further defining threat sources requires that the assessment team determine both *who* and *what* may pose a threat to the network. For example, persons who may pose a threat include most of the cybercriminal types discussed in Chapter 3; for example:

- Random hackers, motivated by fun, the personal challenge of breaking into the network, or competition with other hackers.
- Data thieves who target the organization and information specifically; this includes corporate espionage.
- Emotionally-motivated persons, such as ex-employees out for revenge, business competitors who want to damage the company's ability to do business, or persons with a grudge against the company, its personnel, or the industry to which it belongs.
- Persons who accidentally or inadvertently cause damage or data loss (most often an internal threat, such as the employee who is "experimenting" and unintentionally deletes important files from the server).

The nature of possible threats is the "*what*" in this equation. Any of the above persons could initiate threats of one or more of the following natures:

- Unauthorized access to data
- Unauthorized disclosure of information
- Destruction of data
- Modification or corruption of data
- Introduction of viruses, worms or Trojans
- Denial or interruption of service or network congestion/slowdown

---

NOTE

A thorough threat-assessment program will not overlook the threats posed by events such as fire, flood, and power loss, as well as those caused by human agents.

The next step in threat analysis consists of assigning a likelihood or probability to each type of threat event. A high probability indicates that the threat event is more likely than not to occur, as when there is a history of its occurrence in the past. A medium probability indicates that the threat event may or may not occur. A low probability indicates that the threat event is not likely to occur, although it is possible. Finally, the assessment team must evaluate the probable impact on the organization for each potential threat event. For example:

- If the company's customer database were destroyed, how would this affect such activities as sales and billing?

- If the company network was down for one day, what is the potential cost to the company in tangibles and intangibles such as lost sales or lost employee productivity, for example?

- If the company's client records were made public, what is the potential loss in terms of lawsuits, withdrawal of client business, and other profit-affecting considerations?

Once all of these questions have been asked and answered, it is a relatively simple matter to construct a threat assessment matrix that will put this information into perspective and help the policy development team focus the company's security policies on the threat areas of highest likelihood and most significant impact.

Analyzing Organizational and Network Vulnerabilities

A network's *technical vulnerabilities* are those characteristics or configurations that can be exploited by an attacker to gain unauthorized access or misuse your network and its resources. Network vulnerabilities are often referred to as *security holes*. Security holes should be identified as part of the policy development process. These vulnerabilities can be caused by a programming characteristic or (mis)configuration of the operating system, a protocol or service, or an application. Examples might include:

- Operating system code that allows hackers to crash a computer by accessing a file whose path contains certain reserved words

- Unnecessary open TCP/UDP ports that hackers can use to get into or obtain information about the system

- A web browser's handling of JavaScript that allows malicious code to execute unwanted commands

The network's connection(s) to the Internet and other networks obviously affect vulnerability. Data on a network that is connected 24/7 via a high-speed link is more vulnerable than on a network that is only intermittently connected to the outside. A network that allows multiple outside connections (such as modems and phone lines on a number of different computers) increases vulnerability to outside attack. Dial-up modem connections merit special consideration. While a dial-up connection is less open to intrusion than a fulltime dedicated connection – both because it is connected to the outside for a shorter time period, reducing the window of opportunity for intrusion, and because it will usually have a dynamic IP address, making it harder for an intruder to locate it on multiple occasions – allowing workstations on the network to have modems and phone lines can create a huge security risk.

If improperly configured, a computer with a dial-up connection to the Internet that is also cabled to the internal network can act as a router, allowing outside intruders to access not just the workstation connected to the modem, but other computers on the LAN. One reason for allowing modems at individual workstations is to allow users to dial up connections to other private networks. A more secure way to do this is to remove the modems and have the users establish a virtual private networking (VPN) connection with the other private network through the LAN's Internet connection. The best security policy is to have as few connections from the internal network to the outside as possible, and control access at those entry points (the *network perimeter*).

> **NOTE**
>
> Third party software tools known as *vulnerability scanners* are designed to discover the vulnerabilities on a network, using a database of known commonly exploited weaknesses and probing for those weaknesses on your network.

Organizational vulnerabilities are those areas and data that are open to danger or harm if exposed to an attack. In order to determine these vulnerabilities, the policy team should first identify the assets that could be exposed to the types of threats previously identified. For example:

- The company's financial records
- Trade secrets
- Personnel information
- Customer/client information
- Private correspondence
- Intellectual property
- Marketing and business strategy documents
- Network integrity
- System and program files

There are a number of factors that should be considered when assessing vulnerabilities, including the nature of the data that goes through the organization's network. The vulnerability of data that is highly confidential (such as trade secrets) or irreplaceable (such as original artwork or writing) should be of highest priority. Vulnerability is also affected by the size of the organization and network. A larger number of persons who have access to the network indicates a greater chance of exposure to someone who will want to do harm.

Analyzing Organizational Factors

The next step in evaluating security needs is to determine the philosophy of the organization's management regarding security vs. accessibility. It is important to remember that the two are conflicting characteristics—the more of one that a system has, the less of the other it will have. The organizational philosophy will determine where on the security-access continuum this particular network will fall (and thus will determine its policies).

Some companies institute a highly structured, formal management style. Employees are expected to respect a strict chain of command, and information is generally disseminated on a "need to know" basis. Governmental agencies, especially those that are law-enforcement-related such as police departments and investigative agencies, often follow this philosophy. This is sometimes referred to as the *paramilitary model*.

Other companies, particularly those in "creative" industries and other fields that are subject to little state regulation, are built on the opposite premise: that all employees should have as much information and input as possible, that managers should function as "team leaders" rather than authoritarian supervisors, and that restrictions on employee actions should be imposed only when necessary for the efficiency and productivity of the organization. This is sometimes called the *"one big happy family"* model. Creativity is valued more than "going by the book," and job satisfaction is considered an important aspect of enhancing employee performance and productivity.

In business management circles, these two diametrically opposed models are called *Theory X* (traditional paramilitary style) and *Theory Y* (modern, team-oriented approach). Although there are numerous other management models that have been popularized in recent years, such as Management by Objective (MBO) and Total Quality Management (TQM), each company's management style will fall somewhere on the continuum between Theory X and Theory Y. The management model is based on the personal philosophies of the company's top decision-makers regarding the relationship between management and employees.

The management model can have a profound influence on what is or is not acceptable in planning security for the network. A "deny all access" based security policy that is viewed as appropriate in a Theory X organization may meet with so much resentment and employee dissatisfaction in a Theory Y company that it disrupts business operations. Policy makers must always consider the company "atmosphere" as part of security planning. If there are good reasons to implement strict security in a Theory Y atmosphere, the restrictions will probably have to be justified to management and "sold" to employees, whereas those same restrictions might be accepted without question in a more traditional organization.

Analyzing Legal Factors

Security needs are dependent not only on the wishes of company managers, but may also be dictated or at least guided by the criminal and civil law in a particular jurisdiction. If the company's industry is subject to government regulations, or the information on its network falls under privacy protection acts, or company contracts prohibit disclosure of information on the company network, these are legal factors that must be considered in establishing security policies.

Damage and Defense...

When Security is Mandatory

In the United States, as in many other countries, there are laws governing privacy protection in specific industries that will affect an organization's security plan and policies. For example, the Health Insurance Portability and Accountability Act (HIPAA) governs electronic storage and transmission of patient information and requires that physicians and other healthcare providers implement certain security standards, provide notification to patients of the privacy measures in place, and document every disclosure of patient information to outside entities (with some exceptions). All medical practices were required to comply with HIPAA by April 2003. Violation of the HIPAA regulations can result in fines ranging from $100 (per violation) to $250,000 and up to ten years in prison in cases of deliberate disclosure of patient information with the intent to sell, transfer, or use it for personal gain or commercial or malicious purposes.

HIPAA is federal law; some states also have laws that impose even more stringent privacy protections on the healthcare industry.

Other industries are governed by similar laws. For example, the Gramm-Leach-Bliley (GLB) Act imposes restrictions on financial institutions regarding disclosure of clients' personal information, with similar penalties for violation.

It is important to protect your company from liability that might be incurred if employees or others using the network violate laws. Thus it is essential that the security policy development team include one or more attorneys who are well versed in applicable laws (for example, the Data Protection Act in the United Kingdom, the Digital Millennium Copyright Act in the United States), and who are familiar with the terms of the company's contracts with partners, vendors, clients, and others.

Analyzing Cost Factors

Finally, the needs evaluation must take into account the monetary cost of implementing heightened security. Determining the funds available for security upgrades will affect security policies by forcing the development team to differentiate the organization's security *needs* from security "wants." This is where a quantitative risk analysis can be helpful, since it relies on verifiable data to measure the cost/benefit.

Cost factors may also force the team to prioritize security needs so that those threats that are most likely or most imminent can be addressed, those assets that are most important can be protected, and those vulnerabilities that are most egregious can be closed first.

Assessing Security Solutions

Once the company has identified and documented its security needs and established a working budget for addressing those needs, it is possible to assess solutions and determine which one(s) meet those needs within that budget. Network security solutions can be generally divided into three broad categories: policy-only solutions, hardware solutions, and software solutions.

Policy-only Solutions

While most hardware and software security measures will have accompanying policies that prescribe when and how they are to be deployed and used, many security measures consist of policy only. For example:

- Policies that prohibit users from disclosing their passwords to anyone else
- Policies that require users to lock their workstations when they leave their desks
- Policies that require users to get permission before installing any software on their machines
- Policies that prohibit users from allowing anyone else to use the computer after they've logged in

Of course, in many cases, policies will be enforced via software or hardware. For example, a policy that prohibits users from shutting down the computer can be enforced by a Group Policy setting in the Local Security policy object. A policy that requires users to change their passwords every 30 days can be enforced by setting passwords to expire after that time period.

Hardware Solutions

Hardware-based security solutions involve adding some physical device such as a dedicated firewall to protect the network, or a smart card reader for logon authentication. Removal of floppy and CD drives from desktop computers to prevent unauthorized copying of files to removable media or introduction of viruses is also a hardware-based solution. Other security hardware devices include:

- Keystroke capture devices for monitoring computer use
- Hardware tokens for storing security keys

- Cryptographic hardware devices for offloading the processing of crypto operations

- Biometric authentication devices such as fingerprint or retina scanners

Hardware solutions may be more costly than software-only solutions, but offer several advantages. Hardware security is usually more secure because there is less exposure of security information such as private keys, and it is more difficult to tamper with hardware than software. Hardware solutions also often offer faster performance.

Software Solutions

Software solutions include intrusion detection systems, packet/circuit/application-filtering software, and security-auditing software, as well as software firewall packages such as Microsoft's Internet Security and Acceleration (ISA) Server, which combine these functions. Other software security solutions are: antivirus programs such as those made by Symantec and McAfee, "spyware" used to monitor how computers are being used (including packet-sniffer software that can capture and analyze network traffic) and network-management packages that incorporate security features. Operating system and application "fixes" that patch security holes can also be placed in this category.

As you can see, the firewall is only one of many mechanisms designed to enforce your security policies. This leads us to the concept of *multilayered security.*

Security: A Multilayered Approach

A generic definition of *security* (from the American Heritage Dictionary) is, "freedom from risk or danger; safety." This definition is perhaps a little misleading when it comes to computer and networking security, as it implies a degree of protection that is inherently impossible in the modern connectivity-oriented computing environment.

This is why the same dictionary provides another definition, specific to computer science: "The *level to which* a program or device is safe from unauthorized use [emphasis added]." Implicit in this definition is the caveat that the objectives of *security* and *accessibility* – the two top priorities on the minds of many network administrators – are, by their very natures, diametrically opposed. The more accessible the data is, the less secure it is. Likewise, the more tightly you secure it, the more you impede accessibility. Any security plan is an attempt to strike the proper balance between the two.

The first step is to determine *what* needs to be protected, and to what degree. Because not every asset is equally valuable, some assets will need stronger protection than others. This leads to the concept of instituting multiple layers of security. Multilayered security is a broad concept that applies not just to information security, but physical security as well. The term "defense-in-depth" has been embraced by the IT community to describe this concept in relation to protecting computers and networks, although the term was originally used by the military. In the following sections, we discuss the importance of multilayered security and defense-in-depth solutions.

The Importance of Multilayered Security

An effective security plan does not rely on one technology or solution, but instead takes a multilayered approach. Compare this to a business's physical security measures; most companies don't depend on just the locks on the buildings' doors to keep intruders and thieves out. Instead, they may also have perimeter security (a fence), perhaps additional external security such as a guard or guard dog, external and internal alarm systems, and to protect special valuables, further internal safeguards such as a vault. IT security should be similarly layered. For example:

- Firewalls at network entry points (and possibly a DMZ or screened subnet between the LAN and the network interface connected to the Internet) that function as perimeter protection

- Password protection at local computers, requiring user authentication to log on, to keep unauthorized persons out

- Access permissions set on individual network resources to restrict access of those who are "in" (logged onto the network)

- Encryption of data sent across the network or stored on disk to protect what is especially valuable, sensitive or confidential

- Servers, routers and hubs located in locked rooms to prevent those with physical access from hijacking data

With a multilayered approach, it is not just IT security that should be layered, but the whole approach to security by the organization. That is, security needs to focus on technology, operations, and people. For example, having good security policies and practices, having good hiring practices, and providing training and user education are all part of multilayered security.

Multiple Walls of Fire

Because large networks have more than one "entry" point, firewalls themselves can be most effectively deployed at multiple levels of the enterprise network. Going back to the analogy with physical security, in protecting your home or business from intruders, you establish more than one perimeter. You might delineate an outer perimeter with a fence that goes around the property. Within that fence, the walls of your home or office building create an inner perimeter.

Likewise, a large network will place firewalls on the "edge" (where the company network connects to the Internet). Individual departments or subnets may also use firewalls to create inner perimeters and protect the servers and client computers inside from those in other departments or subnets within the company network.

Multiple firewalls can also be deployed to perform different functions. In our analogy, you have a fence designed to keep people out of your yard. You might also have a large dog, which serves as protection at the same level (protecting the outer perimeter) but who is more discerning than a fence. The dog is able to recognize your friends and family members who frequently enter the property and let them pass through, while barking and growling if a stranger comes through the fence.

Packet-filtering firewalls act like the fence. They have little "intelligence." They screen based on simple criteria contained in the packet headers. An application-layer filtering firewall placed within the "fence" (behind the packet-filtering firewall) is more discerning. Just as the dog can examine the characteristics of the person attempting to enter your property to determine whether he or she is a friend or stranger, the application filters can examine the inside of the data packets to determine whether they contain dangerous signatures.

Layering firewalls or using different types of firewalls together to serve different purposes greatly enhances the effectiveness of your security plan. We discuss the different types of firewalls (packet-filtering, circuit-filtering and application-filtering) in more detail in the next section, under the subsection titled *Firewalls: Features and Functionality.*

Firewalls: The Guardians at the Gateway

The CERT Coordination Center Web site documents the fact that the number of reported security breaches is increasing at a rate of 50 to 100 percent every year. More sophisticated attack tools are being created by hackers to automate the attack process, and thus, reduce the level of technical expertise needed to launch network attacks. "Script kiddies" don't have to have programming knowledge to attack your servers and networks, but wide access to these tools makes "script kiddies" a growing and significant threat. We can only expect this to get worse in the future. Because of the growing threat, every network or individual computer that is connected to the Internet should have protection from hack attacks, viruses and unwanted e-mail (spam).

At the same time the attacker base is increasing, businesses and individuals are relying more and more on fast, secure communications. They need the ability to conduct research on the Web, to send messages to co-workers, customers and partners over the Internet, and to access their company networks from home or when they're on the road via dial-in remote access or virtual private networking (VPN). All this must be done securely, without sacrificing performance.

A firewall provides the protection that today's businesses must have by filtering incoming and outgoing packets and blocking the ones that are not authorized so they cannot enter the network. Many firewall vendors extend the functionality of their firewall products by including other features, such as VPN gateways and Web-caching proxies. These combination products, often referred to as *comprehensive security solutions*, and often incorporated in a turn-key hardware appliance, protect from attacks while at the same time providing secure remote VPN access and speeding up Web access.

A firewall creates a point through which all data must pass in order to move from one network or computer to another. The firewall software can examine, log, and block particular packets based on criteria set by administrators, such as packet size, source address, and even file type or data content.

Firewalls: History and Philosophy

The term "firewall" was around long before the advent of computer networks. It was used to describe a fireproof barrier that prevents a fire in one part of a building or a vehicle from crossing over to another part. To network professionals, a firewall is a software program (which may be installed on a regular computer or on a dedicated hardware appliance) that is able to block undesirable network packets (for example, those that contain attacks, viruses or unwanted commercial email). The firewall serves as a barrier that prevents these packets from crossing over from the Internet or another network to the local network. In the case of "personal" firewalls (also called "host-based" firewalls), the protection is provided to the local computer, especially when it is directly connected to the Internet via a modem or broadband connection.

In the beginning of computer networking, networks were closed systems, with only the computers within a building or small geographic area connected to each other. However, soon networks grew and became more complex, and computers in widely separated geographic locations were able to communicate with one another over wide area networking links. The first attempt at a wide-spread network was the ARPANET, which was made up of a small, elite community of government and university computer users. Eventually, it expanded and became the Internet. In the 1990s, Internet access became easier and more affordable. Commercial Internet Service Providers (ISPs) sprang up everywhere, enabling computer owners to access the Internet from home at a reasonable cost. Soon commercial and individual users all over the world who were not known to one another were able to communicate and transact business. E-commerce became a viable way to purchase products and services, and online banking and other financial services heightened the need for protective mechanisms.

One of the first Internet viruses, the Morris Worm, hit a number of major educational institutions in 1988. This made companies and individual Internet users more aware of the dangers posed by information entering the network from outside. Necessity soon mothered the invention of the firewall.

The first firewalls were routers. A router connects two networks and is the logical place to set up a "checkpoint" where packets could be evaluated and blocked or allowed through. These first router-based firewalls were designed more for the purpose of keeping data in than for keeping it out. Routers separated networks into segments called subnets (for example, different departments in a company or university). There are several advantages in doing this, one of which is so that problems in one segment won't affect computers in the other segments. IP routers with filtering capabilities designed to keep intruders or unauthorized users out soon followed. These were very rudimentary firewalls by today's standards. They could only block or allow packets based on IP address or TCP/UDP port numbers. They had no way to examine the content of the data because they worked at the network layer of the OSI networking model.

A "bastion host" is a gateway designed specifically for the purpose of defending an internal network from external attacks. One of the first commercial firewalls of this type, which used filters and application gateways (application proxies), was made by DEC in the early 1990s. In 1993, an open source firewall from Trusted Information System (TIS) called the Firewall Toolkit (FWTK) was released, and TIS also produced a commercial firewall based on the same code, which it called Gauntlet. CheckPoint came out with the Firewall-1 (FW-1) software in 1994. It was the first popular firewall to use a friendly graphical interface, and was later used as the basic for firewall appliances made by Nokia.

Over the years, network attackers have grown more sophisticated and network protocols have grown more numerous and complex. This has caused firewalls to evolve from simple packet-filtering routers into dedicated multilevel security devices.

Firewalls: Understanding the Architecture

Firewalls can be classified in several different ways: by vendor/brand, by features, or by architectural model. In the following subsections, we look at a couple of important architectural elements:

- Hardware vs. software models
- Host-based vs. network models

Hardware vs. Software Model

The first architectural consideration we discuss is the physical architecture: firewalls can be either software- or hardware-based. Although this is standard terminology, it's not completely accurate. All firewalls consist of both software and hardware. The real distinction lies in how the product is marketed. "Software firewalls" are sold as software applications that can be installed on a standard operating system and hardware platform. "Hardware firewalls" are sold only as a "package deal," with the firewall software preinstalled on specific hardware, often running on a proprietary operating system designed for no purpose other than to run the firewall application.

Understanding the Hardware Firewall Model

You buy a hardware-based firewall as one unit: hardware (often called an "appliance") with the firewall software preinstalled. Most hardware firewalls run on proprietary operating systems designed specifically to run the firewall software, although some appliances run the firewall on Linux or BSD. Proprietary operating systems don't include many of the networking services that would be found on a general purpose OS. This is considered a security advantage in that the operating system is already automatically "hardened" and not vulnerable to some of the exploits that can be used against a general purpose OS.

An appliance is a self-contained box designed for a specific purpose. Some appliances actually serve more than one purpose, and these are often referred to as "security appliances" instead of "firewall appliances" by their vendors. Many appliances include VPN gateway functionality along with the firewall, and some also include other functionalities such as Web caching. Some vendors sell different hardware components (called security *blades*) that plug into the firewall chassis. For instance, NetScreen's IDP blade plugs into their firewall box.

Some firewall appliances are basically PCs, with the same types of hard disks, memory, and other components as a standard PC. Others are called "solid state" because they have virtually no moving parts. They use flash memory and no hard disks. Since high-speed solid-state circuits are used instead of mechanical disks, which are constrained by the need to physically rotate, solid-state storage is faster.

An Application Specific Integrated Circuit (ASIC) is a chip that is created to control the functions of a particular application. ASIC-based firewalls use a chip designed for the firewall application.

Hardware-based firewalls have both advantages and disadvantages. Solid state technology and the use of optimized operating systems with no unnecessary services allows for faster performance. Solid state technology also makes for greater reliability because there is no mechanical point of failure as with hard disk-based firewalls.

However, hardware-based firewalls are less adaptable and more difficult to upgrade. Because ASIC chips are mass-produced, and because of the cost of hardware redesigns, it takes longer for these products to be changed to adapt to new threats. It's difficult for appliance vendors to keep up with the increases in computer processing power. A standard PC to run firewall software almost always costs less than an appliance with the same processing power and memory. In addition, software-based firewalls can more easily be integrated with other network devices, which use the same technologies as the firewall. The proprietary operating systems used by ASIC-based firewalls make it harder to port add-on programs.

Another advantage of ASIC technology, encryption algorithms for VPN and SSL burned into the chip, is being countered by the fact that Intel has started building encryption algorithms into their regular chips that can be utilized by software-based firewalls.

Finally, the dynamic nature and complexity of algorithms used for deep application-layer filtering makes it less suitable for ASIC technology. Some performance comparisons have shown that software-based products had both performance and reliability advantages over ASIC-based firewalls.

Understanding the Software Firewall Model

A so-called "software firewall" is a firewall product that is marketed as a software program that can be installed on one or more different operating systems and one or more different hardware platforms. ISA Server 2004 is a software firewall that can be installed on a PC running either Windows 2000 Server or Windows Server 2003.

Some firewall products are marketed both as software programs and preinstalled on appliances. CheckPoint NG is a software firewall that can be installed on PCs running Windows NT or 2000 or Linux, on Sun's Solaris or IBM's AIX variety of UNIX. It is also the basis of Nokia firewall appliances.

NOTE

ISA Server 2004 is expected to be available preinstalled on a turnkey appliance product, in addition to being sold as a software firewall. At the time of this writing, several hardware vendors had already built ISA-based appliances or were discussing licensing ISA 2004 from Microsoft to do so. The authors have had the opportunity to beta test some of these appliances, and in fact, are running two of them on our production network.

The key point is that you buy these firewalls as a software package and install them on a supported operating system, which can serve other functions besides running the firewall software.

Like its hardware counterpart, the software firewall model has both advantages and disadvantages. Because the software firewall usually runs on a standard general purpose network operating system such as Windows, UNIX/Linux or Solaris, you may already have a system on which you can install it, saving the cost of hardware.

Configuration and management is usually easy, since the software runs on an OS familiar to the administrator. Another major advantage is the ability to upgrade the hardware easily. You can add a new processor or more memory relatively inexpensively. You can also replace the box completely and install the software on a new system (licensing agreement permitting).

Yet another advantage is that, in many cases, you can download an evaluation version of the software firewall to try out before you buy (just try getting a hardware vendor to loan you an appliance to try out for a while, unless you're a high priority customer).

Software firewalls also have disadvantages. They are generally slower than hardware-based firewalls, and because they run on standard operating systems, the underlying OS may be more vulnerable to exploits than a proprietary OS, if it has not been properly hardened.

Host-based vs. Network-based Model

Another way to categorize firewalls depends on whether the firewall product is designed to run on a single host computer that it protects, or is designed to sit in front of a group of computers and protect the entire network or subnet. This distinction determines whether the firewall is built on a host-based or network-based model.

Understanding the Host-based Firewall Model

The more common marketing term for the low-cost host-based firewall is "personal firewall." A personal firewall is installed on a workstation or portable computer to protect it from common network attacks. Personal firewalls generally sell for under $100, and there are many freeware personal firewalls, as well. Windows XP and Windows Server 2003 include a built-in personal firewall, the Internet Connection Firewall (ICF).

A simple host-based firewall blocks incoming packets based on source or destination IP address and port number, using preconfigured rules that take into account the normal behavior of installed applications and operating system components. More sophisticated versions can also filter packets based on content (see the section titled *Multilayered Filtering* later in this chapter).

Any computer that connects directly to the Internet without a network-based firewall should have a host-based firewall installed. This would include almost all computers that connect to the Internet over an analog modem connection, as well as those that have direct broadband connections (unless the broadband "modem" or "router" has built-in firewall software that is enabled).

Many company policies require that any computer connecting to their networks via dial-in remote access or virtual private networking (VPN) have a personal firewall installed and enabled. This is to prevent Internet-based attacks from being spread from the remote clients to the corporate network. The corporate network-based firewall is usually the entity that enforces these policies.

Understanding the Network-based Firewall Model

Network-based firewalls, as the name implies, protect entire networks or subnets rather than individual computers. A network-based firewall is usually a dedicated computer or appliance that runs no software other than the firewall software, and perhaps related programs or "modules" such as caching, intrusion detection/prevention, and network anti-virus software. There are two approaches to adding these extra features:

- **"On box."** The extra features are either integrated into the firewall application or are installed on the same machine via add-on programs.

- **"Off box."** The extra features are implemented on separate computers that work in conjunction with the firewall computer or appliance.

Virtual private networking and some level of intrusion detection are integrated into most network firewall applications. Caching, anti-virus, and other "extras" can be integrated in the firewall software (as with ISA Server), can be installed as add-ons on the same machine (as with CheckPoint), or can be implemented as separate computers or appliances (as with Cisco PIX).

Network-based firewalls are much more expensive than personal firewalls, due to their increased complexity and functionality. Network-based firewalls are constructed to handle much more traffic than a personal firewall and support more protocols and simultaneous connections. Most are designed to use sophisticated management tools that allow for remote administration, centralized administration of multiple firewalls, and detailed, configurable monitoring, reporting and logging functions. Network-based firewalls range from relatively simple "edge" firewalls designed to operate as the network's only firewall to enterprise-level firewalls that can be chained together in an hierarchical structure to provide multiple layers of protection from the packet level to the application level, or that can provide load-balancing across a cluster of firewalls at the same level of the network.

Firewalls: Features and Functionality

The firewall's primary function is simple: protecting the network. Modern firewalls use multiple sophisticated methods to accomplish that mission.

- **First line of defense against network attacks**. In addition to blocking packets that originate from particular source IP addresses or particular domains or specific e-mail addresses, an effective firewall can recognize the "signatures" or specific characteristics of packets that comprise common types of network attacks, such as Denial of Service (DOS) attacks or IP spoofing (forgery of the source address in an IP packet). This is a function of the firewall's intrusion detection system/intrusion prevention system (IDS/IPS).

- **First line of defense against viruses and spam.** An effective firewall must also be able to recognize viruses, worms, Trojan horses, and other malicious code designed to do damage to computer programs or data on your network, send data back to an unauthorized party without your knowledge or consent, and/or use the systems on your network as intermediaries (zombies) to launch attacks against other remote computers.

- **"After the fact" forensic tool.** The firewall's primary role is to prevent attackers, malicious code, and unauthorized users from entering the network, but it also fills an important secondary role as a forensic tool after an attack or attempted attack. Modern firewalls record events in logs that can be used to generate reports used in incident response and as evidence in prosecuting security breach cases. A good logging/reporting system is essential to provide a usable audit trail and fill any existing security holes.

NOTE

A good firewall is an effective means of preventing many types of security breaches, but no firewall will guarantee 100 percent security for your network. Hackers have ways to breach network security, such as social engineering, that circumvent the protections provided by firewalls. Thus, it is important that a true multilayered approach to security also focus on training, user education, human resource policies and practices, and so forth.

Some important features included in modern firewalls include:

- Multilayered filtering
- VPN gateways
- Intrusion detection and prevention
- Anti-virus
- Web caching
- Advanced management tools

In the following sections, we'll discuss each in more detail.

Multilayered Filtering

There are three basic firewall types, based on the level at which the firewall performs filtering actions. Early firewalls filtered only at one level, usually the packet level. Most modern firewalls use multilayered filtering to provide for better security. A multilayered firewall is sometimes called a *hybrid* firewall. A multilayered firewall performs two or more of the following levels of filtering:

- Packet filtering
- Circuit filtering
- Application-layer filtering

These three layers of filtering and their relationships to the Open Systems Interconnection (OSI) networking model are illustrated in Figure 1.1 and discussed in more detail in the following subsections.

NOTE

The OSI model was developed by the International Organization for Standardization (ISO) to provide a multilayered model that vendors of networking software and hardware products could use to ensure better compatibility between their products. For more information, see www.cisco.com/univercd/cc/td/doc/cisintwk/ito_doc/introint.htm.

Figure 1.1 Three Layers of Filtering with OSI Networking

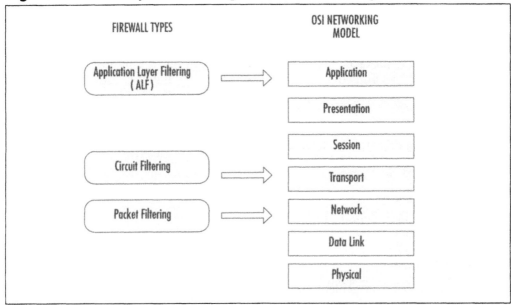

Packet Filtering

The first firewalls were packet-filtering firewalls that work at the Network layer of the OSI networking model. They examine the packet headers that contain IP addresses and packet options and block or allow traffic through the firewall based on that information. A packet filtering firewall can use one of three technologies:

- *Static-packet filtering*: rules are set manually and particular ports stay open or closed until changed manually

- *Dynamic-packet filtering*: more intelligent filtering in which rules can be changed dynamically based on events or conditions, and thus ports are opened only when needed and then closed

- *Stateful-packet filtering*: uses a table to maintain connection states of sessions so that packets must pass through in sequence as authorized by the filter policies.

NOTE

Stateful inspection is a technology by which a deeper analysis of the information contained in the packets (up to the application layer) is performed, and subsequent filtering decisions are based on what the firewall "learned" from packets that it examined previously.

Circuit Filtering

A circuit-filtering firewall (also called a circuit-level gateway) works at the transport and session layers of the OSI model. It can examine the TCP handshake information that is sent between computers to verify that a session request is legitimate.

Circuit filters operate at a higher layer of the OSI model, the Transport layer (Host-to-Host layer in the DOD model). Circuit filters restrict access on the basis of host machines (not users) by processing the information found in the TCP and UDP packet headers. This allows administrators to create filters that would, for example, prohibit anyone using Computer A from using FTP to access Computer B.

When circuit filters are used, access control is based on TCP data streams or UDP datagrams. Circuit filters can act based on TCP and UDP status flags and sequencing information, in addition to source and destination addresses and port numbers. Circuit-level filtering allows administrators to inspect sessions, rather than packets. A session is sometimes thought of as a connection, but actually a session can be made up of more than one connection. Sessions are established only in response to a user request, which adds to security.

Circuit filters don't restrict access based on user information; they also cannot interpret the meanings of the packets. That is, they cannot distinguish between a **GET** command and a **PUT** command sent by an application program. To do this, application filtering must be used.

Application-Layer Filtering

Application-layer filtering (ALF) is performed by application gateways, also called application proxies. ALF firewalls operate at the application layer of the OSI model and can actually examine the *content* of the data (for example, a URL contained in an HTTP communication or a command contained in an FTP communication).

There are times when the best tactic is to filter packets based on the information contained in the data itself. Packet filters and circuit filters don't use the contents of the data stream in making filtering decisions, but this *can* be done with application filtering. An application filter operates at the top layer of the networking model, the (appropriately named) Application layer. Application filters can use the packet header information, but are also able to allow or reject packets on the basis of the data contents and the user information.

Administrators can use application filtering to control access based on the identity of the user, and/or based on the particular task the user is attempting to perform. With application filters, criteria can be set based on commands issued by the application. This means, for example, the administrator could restrict a particular user from downloading files to a specified computer, using FTP. At the same time, he/she could allow that user to upload files via FTP to that same computer. This is possible because different commands are issued depending on whether the user is retrieving files from the server or depositing them there.

Application gateways are considered by many firewall experts to be the most secure of the filtering technologies. This is because the criteria they use for filtering covers a broader span than the other methods. Sometimes hackers write malicious programs that use the port address of an authorized application, such as port 53, which is the DNS address. A packet or circuit filter would not be able to recognize that the packet is not a valid DNS request or response, and would allow it to pass through. An application filter, however, is able to examine the contents of the packet and determine that it should *not* be allowed.

There are drawbacks to this filtering type. The biggest problem is that there must be a separate application gateway for every Internet service that the firewall needs to support. This makes for more configuration work; however, this weakness is also a strength that adds to the security of the firewall. Since a gateway for each service must be explicitly enabled, an administrator won't accidentally allow services that pose a threat to the network. Application filtering is the most sophisticated level of filtering performed by the firewall service and is especially useful in protecting the network against specific types of attacks such as malicious SMTP commands or attempts to penetrate the local DNS servers.

Another drawback to application filtering is performance—or the lack thereof. Application filtering is a slow process because the data inside the packets must be examined. Consequently, you probably would not want to place an ALF firewall on the network edge when you have a very fast incoming connection (such as an OC-3 line). Instead, simple (and fast) packet-filtering firewalls should be placed there, and application filtering can be done further downstream, closer to the application itself.

VPN Gateway

Most modern firewalls include integrated VPN gateways. VPN gateways allow remote users to connect to a VPN server or the entire internal network via a virtual private networking "tunnel" that goes through the public Internet, or alternatively, allows two local area networks in different locations to connect to one another securely over the Internet. These two types of VPNs are referred to as client-to-server VPNs and site-to-site VPNs.

Client-to-Server VPN

The client-to-server VPN is used when individual remote computers (such as those of employees working from home or executives who are on the road with their laptop computers) connect to the company LAN by first establishing a connection to the Internet and then using VPN client software, VPN tunneling protocols (such as PPTP or L2TP) to establish a connection to the company LAN that is also connected to the Internet. Because the data sent through this "tunnel" is encrypted (using protocols such as MPPE or IPSec), the connection is also private.

Site-to-Site VPN

A site-to-site VPN is used to connect entire networks to each other. As in the case of client-to-server VPNs, both sides of the "virtual network" must be connected to the Internet. The same tunneling and encryption protocols are used. The difference is that with the site-to-site VPN, there is a gateway at both ends of the connection (instead of an individual client computer at one end). Some firewalls support only site-to-site VPNs.

ISA Server VPN Support

ISA Server 2004 supports the following VPN protocols:

- Point-to-Point Tunneling Protocol (PPTP)
- Layer 2 Tunneling Protocol/IPSec (L2TP/IPSec)
- IPSec Tunnel Mode

PPTP and L2TP/IPSec VPN protocols can be used in both remote access and site-to-site VPN connections. IPSec Tunnel Mode can be used *only* in site-to-site VPN connections.

IPSec Tunnel Mode is used *only* for compatibility with third-party VPN servers. It should not be used when site-to-site connections are created between an ISA Server 2004 firewall and another Microsoft VPN product (Windows 2000/Windows Server 2003 RRAS or ISA Server 2000).

The ISA Server 2004 VPN feature supports both types of VPN connections: client-to-server (also called Remote Access VPN) and site-to-site.

The Remote Access VPN allows individual computers configured as VPN clients to connect to the ISA Server 2004 firewall and access resources on the corporate network.

Remote Access VPN clients can use either the PPTP or L2TP/IPSec VPN protocol. Advanced authentication mechanisms, such as SecurID, RADIUS, EAP/TLS certificates, biometric, and others are supported by the ISA Server 2004 VPN Remote Access Server.

Site-to-Site VPNs allow the ISA Server 2004 firewall to connect to another VPN server and join entire networks to each other over the Internet. Site-to-site VPNs allow organizations to remove expensive dedicated leased lines, which leads to significant cost reductions.

A major competitive advantage for ISA Server 2004 is that firewall access policies are applied to VPN remote access and site-to-site connections. In contrast to competitors' products that allow VPN clients full access to the corporate network, the ISA Server 2004 VPN connections are exposed to the firewall's access policies. The enables the ISA Server 2004 firewall administrator to set restrictive access controls on VPN connections on a per-user basis. When the user establishes a VPN connection with the ISA Server 2004 firewall, that user can only access resources he needs to get the job done. No other network resources will be available.

All Windows operating systems include the Windows VPN client software. Advantages of using the Windows VPN client include:

- No need to install third party software
- No need to troubleshoot compatibility issues between the third-party VPN client software and the Windows operating system
- Simplified configuration and deployment of the VPN client using the Connection Manager Administration Kit (CMAK)
- Support for IETF RFC Internet standard IPSec NAT Traversal

ISA Server 2004 also includes VPN security features such as VPN quarantine, which we discuss in Chapter 2, *The ISA Server 2004 Feature Set*.

Intrusion Detection and Prevention

Many firewalls (including ISA Server) incorporate an intrusion detection system (IDS) that can recognize that an attack of a specific type is being attempted and can perform a predefined action when such an intrusion is identified.

Intrusion detection systems can recognize many different common forms of network intrusion, such as port scans, LAND attacks, Ping of Death, UDP bombs, out of band attacks, and others. Special detection filters may also be built in, such as a POP (Post Office Protocol) intrusion detection filter that analyzes POP mail traffic to guard against POP buffer overflows, or a DNS intrusion detection filter that can be configured to look for DNS hostname overflow or length overflow attacks.

ISA Server 2004 includes a collection of intrusion detection filters that are licensed from Internet Security Systems (ISS). These intrusion detection filters are focused on detecting and blocking network layer attacks. In addition, ISA Server 2004 includes intrusion detection filters that detect and block application layer attacks.

ISA Server 2004 can detect the follow intrusions or attacks:

- Windows out-of-band (WinNuke)
- Land
- Ping of Death
- IP half scan
- UDP bomb
- Port scan
- DNS host name overflow
- DNS length overflow
- DNS zone transfer
- POP3 buffer overflow
- SMTP buffer overflow

When the ISA Server 2004 firewall detects one of these attacks, the following actions can be carried out:

- An alert is sent to the ISA Server 2004 Event Log
- ISA Server 2004 services can be stopped or restarted
- An administrative script or program can be run
- An e-mail message can be sent to an administrator's mailbox or pager

One disadvantage is that the intrusion detection system included with ISA Server 2004 is not configurable, and you cannot create your own intrusion signatures. However, third-party applications, such as Internet Security System's **Real Secure** IDS, can be used to extend the intrusion detection features at an additional cost to the customer.

Web Caching

Web caching is another important feature that can be built into the firewall software. ISA Server is one of only a few popular firewalls that include Web caching functionality at no extra charge. Many firewall vendors require that you either purchase an add-on module (CheckPoint), purchase a separate hardware appliance (Cisco), or use a third-party caching solution in conjunction with their firewalls. ISA Server is one of the only major firewall products (with BlueCoat being the other) that combines firewall and Web caching.

The amount of Web traffic has been growing consistently within most Internet-connected organizations. In many cases, users visit the same Web sites on a regular basis, or multiple users within the organization visit the same sites and view the same pages. At the same time, overall network and Internet traffic is steadily increasing, often to the point of near saturation of available Internet bandwidth.

Web caching provides a way to reduce network traffic for both outbound Web requests from your internal users to Web servers on the Internet and inbound Web requests from external users to the Web servers you host on your internal network.

In the following subsections, we discuss these caching methods:

- Forward caching
- Reverse caching
- Distributed caching
- Hierarchical caching

Forward Caching

Some ISPs charge T-1 and T-3 users on a usage basis. One way to reduce Internet bandwidth consumption is to store frequently-accessed Web objects on the local network, where they can be retrieved by internal users without going out to a server on the Internet. This is forward Web caching, and it has the added advantage of making access for internal users faster because they are retrieving the Web objects (pages, graphics, sound files, and others) over a fast LAN connection, typically 100Mbps or more, instead of a slower Internet connection at perhaps 1.5Mbps.

Reverse Caching

Another type of Web caching, called reverse caching, reduces traffic on the internal network and speeds access for external users when the company hosts its own Web sites. In this case, frequently requested objects on the internal Web servers are cached at the network edge, on a proxy server, so that the load on the Web servers is reduced.

Distributed Caching

Multiple Web-caching servers can be used together to provide for more efficient caching. As the name implies, distributed caching distributes the cached Web objects across two or more caching servers. These servers are all on the same level on the network. Figure 1.2 illustrates how distributed caching works.

Figure 1.2 Distributed Caching Uses Multiple Servers at the Same Level of the Network.

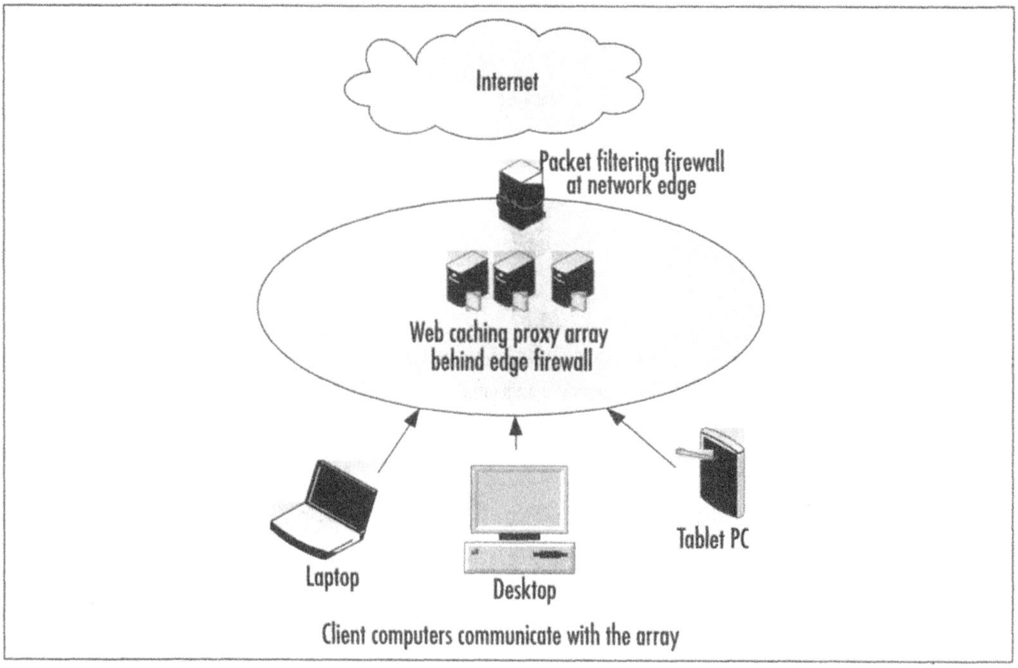

Hierarchical Caching

Hierarchical caching is another way of using multiple Web-caching servers. Caching servers are placed at different levels on the network. Upstream caching servers communicate with downstream proxies. For example, a caching server is placed at each branch office. These servers communicate with the caching array at the main office. This is illustrated in Figure 1.3.

Figure 1.3 Hierarchical Caching Uses Multiple Web Proxy Servers at Different Levels

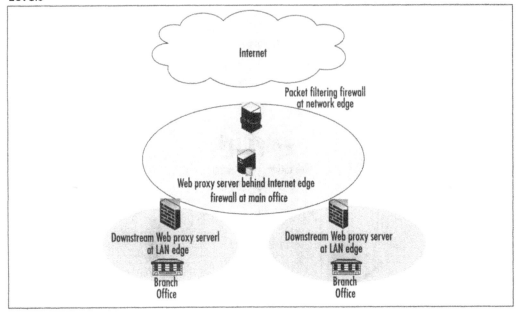

Hierarchical caching uses bandwidth more efficiently than distributed caching. However, distributed caching has lower disk space requirements. The best of both worlds, hybrid-caching schemes combine distributed and hierarchical caching. This improves performance and efficiency. Figure 1.4 illustrates a hybrid-caching scheme.

Figure 1.4 Hybrid Caching Combines Distributed and Hierarchical Caching Methods

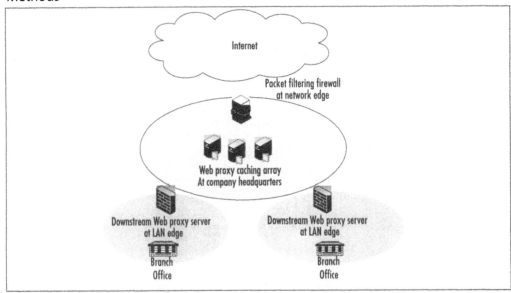

Firewalls: Role and Placement on the Network

Firewalls can be simple or sophisticated. There are a number of different roles that firewalls can play on the network, depending on where they're placed within the network infrastructure and what they're expected to do there.

A small organization might have only a single firewall that protects the internal network from attacks coming from the external network. Large organizations usually deploy multiple firewalls in different locations and roles. This provides more complete coverage, as well as allowing you to take advantage of the strengths of different firewall types and achieve better performance. Firewalls can be placed in a number of different roles, including the following:

- **Front-end firewalls** The front-end firewall is also called an "edge" firewall because it sits at the edge of the internal network, between the LAN and the Internet. The front-end firewall has a network interface on the corporate network and another network interface that connects directly to the Internet. All data that comes into and goes out of the corporate network will be exposed to the firewall and must be examined by its filters before being blocked or allowed to pass in or out.

- **Back-end firewalls** A back-end firewall also sits at the edge of the internal network, but not at the edge of the Internet. Instead, it is placed behind one or more front-end firewalls. A typical scenario has the front-end firewall(s) performing packet filtering, and after packets have been allowed through, they then must go through the back-end firewall that performs deeper application-layer filtering. This spreads the processing load and allows both the front and back-end firewalls to perform their respective duties at higher speed.

- **Perimeter networks** Servers that need to be available to the Internet (such as Web servers) can be placed between a front-end and a back-end firewall so that the internal network is not directly exposed to them. The area in between the firewalls is called a perimeter network, screened network, or demilitarized zone (DMZ).

- **Application-filtering gateway within the perimeter network** An application-layer filtering (ALF) capable firewall can be placed within the perimeter network between the front-end and back-end firewalls to reduce the attack surface and provide a very high level of security. Because it takes the burden of content filtering off the edge firewalls, their performance is enhanced. The edge firewalls can be simple, fast packet-filtering firewalls.

- **Departmental firewalls** Firewalls can be deployed within the internal network to protect individual subnets. This protects particular departments or other divisions of the network, not only from the Internet, but from other departments or divisions. In this scenario, a firewall sits between a departmental subnet and the rest of the internal network.

- **Branch office firewalls** Branch offices that are connected to the larger internal network, for example via a site-to-site VPN connection, should be protected by a firewall at their own Internet edge.

- **Telecommuter firewalls** Remote users such as telecommuters or traveling executives who connect back to the corporate network via remote access VPN should have firewall protection for their remote machines. This can be accomplished via personal firewall software or simple low-cost firewall appliances designed for this purpose.

- **Multiple firewall configurations** Firewalls from different vendors may have to work together in multiple firewall configurations. For effective protection, firewalls must be designed to interoperate with one another and with network operating systems and application servers deployed on the network.

Firewall placement and roles will be discussed in more detail in Chapter 4, *Preparing the Network Infrastructure to Support ISA Server 2004 Firewalls.*

ISA: From Proxy Server to Full-Featured Firewall

ISA Server did not spring, full-formed, from Microsoft's development teams. Instead, it is a product that evolved slowly, becoming more of a full-fledged firewall, and then a comprehensive security solution with each incarnation. ISA Server had its roots in MS Proxy Server. In less than a decade, it has grown into something quite different.

ISA: A Glint in MS Proxy Server's Eye

Proxy servers have been around for quite a while. Despite its new name, ISA Server *is* a proxy server, but it is also much more. The original meaning of *proxy* was "one who is authorized to act for another." Perhaps the most famous—or infamous—use of the word came about in relation to the practice of marriage by proxy, in which a substitute "stood in" for one of the parties, allowing a wedding ceremony to be performed even though the groom (or less commonly, the bride) was not physically present. Proxy weddings at one time were a popular way for a couple to get "hitched" while the groom was serving in the military.

Proxy servers are so named because they, like the hapless stand-in who says, "I do," when it's really someone else who does, act as go-betweens to allow something to take place (in this case, network communications) between systems that must remain separate.

Proxy servers "stand in" between the computers on a LAN and those on the public network outside. Another good analogy is the gatekeeper who is stationed at the entrance to an estate to check all incoming visitors to ensure that they are on the list of invited guests. The proxy can actually hide the computers on the LAN from outsiders. Only the IP address of the proxy server is "visible" to others on the Internet; internal computers use private IP addresses (nonroutable over the Internet) that cannot be seen from the other side of the proxy.

In fact, a proxy can go further and function more like a prison guard, who not only makes certain that only authorized persons get in, but also sees that only those who have permission go out. Just as the guard checks his list before letting anyone in or out, the proxy *filters* outgoing and incoming data according to predefined criteria. At this point, the proxy is behaving as a *firewall*.

In the Beginning: MS Proxy Server

Microsoft released its first version of a proxy server in November 1996. It included some unique features such as Winsock proxy capability, which allowed for the use of applications that traditional proxy servers didn't support.

Unfortunately, though, version 1.0 suffered from some significant limitations that prevented it from becoming popular as a caching and security solution for large enterprise networks. One big drawback was the lack of redundancy. While its rivals, such as Netscape's proxy server, used distributed caching across multiple servers to provide fault tolerance, the first version of the Microsoft proxy did not include such a feature. The Microsoft proxy seemed better suited to smaller networks and perhaps to those in which its caching and security features were less mission critical.

The redundancy issue was addressed in Proxy Server, version 2. In fact, Microsoft surpassed Netscape's implementation by introducing the concept of proxy server *arrays*. An array is a group of two or more proxy servers that run as mirrors of one another and function as one entity under a common name. With version 2, multiple proxies could be chained together for better load balancing, and Microsoft even developed a new protocol, called Cache Array Routing Protocol (CARP), for sharing data between proxy servers.

NOTE

CARP is a proprietary (Microsoft-only) protocol. It is used for management of multiple user Web requests across an array of proxy servers. The Internet Cache Protocol (ICP) is a similar protocol used by vendors of other proxy solutions (for example, Novell's Border Manager). Although the functionality of CARP and ICP are similar, they use different hashing algorithms. CARP offers some advantages over ICP, especially in terms of performance, because CARP does not exchange query messages between servers, as does ICP. In addition, CARP eliminates the problem of unnecessary redundancy of content on the servers in an array.

Automatic synchronization was added to propagate configuration changes to all the servers in an array. Caching capabilities were expanded to include support for both File Transfer Protocol (FTP) and HyperText Transfer Protocol (HTTP) caching. All these services were easily configured.

Also new to version 2 was the *reverse proxy* feature, which allowed for publishing Web content from protected Web servers. Multiple Web sites could be published on a single proxy server, using multihoming support. In addition, version 2 included *reverse hosting* (in which the proxy server listens for and responds to incoming Web requests on behalf of multiple servers sitting behind it) and the ability to publish other services through *server binding*.

From the beginning, Microsoft's Proxy Server got high marks for ease of setup and configuration, compared with competing products. The second version also included the snap-in administration module for the Internet Information Server (IIS) 4.0 Microsoft Management Console (MMC), which gave administrators a convenient and powerful way to manage individual or multiple proxy servers.

Microsoft's First Real Firewall: ISA Server 2000

The third implementation of Microsoft's Proxy Server got a whole new name because it included a number of enhancements that go beyond the definition of a proxy server. Released with the beginning of the new millennium, Internet Security and Acceleration (ISA) Server 2000 was, at least, a full-fledged firewall solution in addition to its caching and acceleration abilities.

NOTE

What is or is not a firewall is a matter of contention within the network security community. All agree that firewalls are programs (or groups of programs) located at the gateway to a network and that they protect the resources of that internal network from the outside. The National Institute of Standards and Technology (NIST), in SP-800-10, defines a firewall as an *approach* to security that helps implement a larger security policy by creating a perimeter defense through which all incoming and outgoing traffic must pass, thus controlling access to or from a protected network or site.

Some industry players use a broad definition of firewall that includes proxy servers. Under this premise, Microsoft marketed Proxy Server 2.0 as a firewall, but some security experts argued that it was not and that in order to meet the standard of "firewall," there must be more than just a router, bastion host, or other device(s) providing security to the network. These purists demand that to be considered a firewall, implementation must be policy-based.

In addition to its multilayer firewall functionality (packet filtering, circuit filtering, and application filtering), ISA Server 2000 offered such new or improved features as:

- **Integrated virtual private networking (VPN)** ISA Server can be used to set up either a remote access VPN between a client and gateway or a multiple member VPN tunnel from server to server.

- **Integration with Active Directory** ISA access policies and server configuration information are integrated with the Windows 2000 Active Directory for easier and more secure administration.

- **Intrusion detection** This exciting new feature can be set up to send you an alert if or when a particular type of attack is attempted against your network (for example, if an outsider attempts to scan your ports).

- **Support for Secure Network Address Translation (SecureNAT)** The extensible NAT architecture that is implemented by ISA provides a secure connection for clients that don't have the firewall client software installed, including Macintosh and UNIX clients and other non-Microsoft operating systems that are running Transmission Control Protocol/Internet Protocol (TCP/IP).

- **Bandwidth allocation** The amount of bandwidth allocated to a specific user, communication, client, or destination can be controlled by quality-of-service rules that an administrator creates to optimize network traffic usage.

- **Secure server publishing** Internal servers can be made accessible to specific clients while the servers are protected from unauthorized access.

- **Enterprise management** ISA, like Windows 2000, was designed for greater scalability and more focus on the enterprise market than previous Microsoft products. ISA allows you to set enterprise-level policies as well as array-level policies, and management of ISA arrays is easily centralized.

- **Monitoring and report generation** ISA server allows you to monitor its performance and create detailed security and access logs and graphical reports. Report generation can be scheduled, and remote administration lets administrators keep tabs on the use and performance of the ISA server from an off-site location.

- **E-mail content screening** ISA Server provides for screening of e-mail content by keyword to allow administrators to implement and enforce strict security policies.

- **H.323 Gatekeeper functionality** This feature allows for use of videoconferencing software, such as Microsoft NetMeeting, through the proxy, and NetMeeting directory functionality (replacing some of the functionality of ILS).

- **Enhanced software** This software can be used for streaming media, including live stream splitting, and caching of Windows Media content (when using Windows Media Server).

New and Improved: ISA Server 2004

ISA Server 2000 has slowly but surely increased its market share against competitors since its introduction. According to IDC, Microsoft's growth in sales and market share was one of the fastest in the firewall industry in 2002/2003. However, many ISA users compiled "wish lists" of features and improvements they wanted to see in the next version. Microsoft responded with an intensive effort by the ISA team to provide a friendlier and more intuitive graphical interface, building in better support for key features such as VPN, more flexible and comprehensive policies, support for multiple networks, and easier customization.

ISA Server 2004 added many new features and improved others, along with completely revamping the interface, to greatly increase the functionality, especially at the enterprise level. Table 1.2 shows some of the features that are new in ISA 2004. These are discussed in more detail in Chapter 2.

Table 1.2 What's New in ISA Server 2004

New Feature	What it does
Multiple Network support	Allows you to configure more than one network, each with distinct relationships to other networks. You can define access policies relative to the networks. Unlike ISA Server 2000, where all network traffic was inspected relative to a local address table (LAT) that only included addresses on the local network, with ISA Server 2004 you can apply the firewall and security features to traffic between any networks or network objects.
Per-network policies	The new multinetworking features of ISA Server 2004 enable you to protect your network against internal and external security threats, by limiting communication between clients even within your own organization. Multinetworking functionality supports sophisticated perimeter network (also known as a DMZ, demilitarized zone, or screened subnet) scenarios, allowing you to configure how clients in different networks access the perimeter network. Access policy between networks can then be based on the unique security zone represented by each network.
Routed and NAT network relationships	You can use ISA Server 2004 to define routing relationship between networks, depending on the type of access and communication required between the networks. In some cases, you may want more secure, less transparent communication between the networks; for these scenarios you can define a network address translation (NAT) relationship. In other scenarios, you want to simply route traffic through ISA Server; in this case, you can define a routed relationship. In contrast to ISA Server 2000, packets moving between routed networks are fully exposed to ISA Server 2004 stateful filtering and inspection mechanisms.

Continued

Table 1.2 What's New in ISA Server 2004

New Feature	What it does
Stateful filtering and inspection for VPN	Virtual private network (VPN) clients are configured as a separate network zone. Therefore, you can create distinct policies for VPN clients. The firewall rule engine discriminately checks requests from VPN clients, statefully filtering and inspecting these requests and dynamically opening connections, based on the access policy.
Stateful filtering and inspection for traffic moving through site-to-site VPN tunnel	Networks joined by an ISA Server 2000 site-to-site link where considered trusted network and firewall policy was not applied to communication moving through the link. ISA Server 2004 introduces stateful filtering and inspection for all communications moving through a site-to-site VPN connection. This allows you to control resources specific hosts or networks can access on the opposite side of the link. User/group-based access policies can be used to gain granular control over resource utilization via the link.
Secure NAT client support for VPN clients connected to ISA Server 2004 VPN server	With ISA Server 2000, only VPN clients configured as firewall clients could access the Internet via their connected ISA Server 2000 VPN server. ISA Server 2004 expands VPN client support by allowing SecureNAT clients to access the Internet without the firewall client installed on the client system. You can also enhance corporate network security by forcing user/group-based firewall policy on VPN SecureNAT clients.
VPN Quarantine	ISA Server 2004 leverages the Windows Server 2003 VPN Quarantine feature. VPN Quarantine allows you to quarantine VPN clients on a separate network until they meet a predefined set of security requirements. VPN clients passing security tests are allowed network access based on VPN client firewall policies. VPN clients who fail security testing may be provided limited access to servers that will help them meet network security requirements.
Ability to publish PPTP VPN servers	You could only publish L2TP/IPSec NAT-T VPN servers using ISA Server 2000. ISA Server 2004 Server Publishing Rules allow you to publish IP protocols and allow you to publish PPTP servers. The ISA Server 2004 smart PPTP application filter performs the complex connection management. In addition, you can easily publish the Windows Server 2003 NAT-T L2TP/IPSec VPN server using ISA Server 2004 Server Publishing.

Continued

Table 1.2 What's New in ISA Server 2004

New Feature	What it does
IPSec tunnel mode support for site to site VPN links	ISA Server 2000 could use the PPTP and L2TP/IPSec VPN protocols to join networks over the Internet using a VPN site to site link. ISA Server 2004 improves site-to-site link support by allowing you to use IPSec tunnel mode as the VPN protocol.
Extended protocol support	ISA Server 2004 extends ISA Server 2000 functionality, by allowing you to control access and usage of any protocol, including IP-level protocols. This enables users to use applications such as ping and tracert and to create VPN connections PPTP. In addition, IPSec traffic can be enabled through ISA Server.
Support for complex protocols requiring multiple primary connections	Many streaming media and voice/video applications require that the firewall manage complex protocols. ISA Server 2000 was able to manage complex protocols, but required that the firewall administrator create complex scripts to create protocol definitions requiring multiple primary outbound connections. ISA Server 2004 greatly improves this situation by allowing you to create protocol definitions within an easy-to-use New Protocol Wizard.
Customizable protocol definitions	ISA Server 2004 allows you to control the source and destination port number for any protocol for which you create a Firewall Rule. This allows the ISA Server 2004 firewall administrator a very high level of control over what packets are allowed inbound and outbound through the firewall.
Firewall user groups	ISA Server 2000 utilized users and groups created in the Active Directory or on the local firewall computer for user/group-based access control. ISA Server 2004 also uses these sources, but allows you to create custom firewall groups that consist of preexisting groups in the local accounts database or Active Directory domain. This increases your flexibility to control access based on user or group membership because the firewall administrator can create custom security groups from these existing groups. This removes the requirement that the firewall administrator be a domain administrator in order to credit custom security groups for inbound or outbound access control.

Continued

Table 1.2 What's New in ISA Server 2004

New Feature	What it does
Forwarding of firewall client credentials to Web Proxy service	The HTTP Redirector had to forward requests to the Web Proxy service in order for firewall clients to benefit from the Web cache in ISA Server 2000. User credentials were removed during this process and the request failed if user credentials were required. ISA Server 2004 removes the problem by allowing firewall clients to access the Web cache via the HTTP filter.
RADIUS support for Web Proxy client authentication	In order for ISA Server 2000 to authenticate Web proxy clients, the machine must have been a member of the Active Directory domain, or the user account must exist on the firewall computer's local user database. ISA Server 2004 allows you to authenticate users in the Active Directory and other authentication databases by using RADIUS to query the Active Directory. Web publishing rules can also use RADIUS to authenticate remote connections.
Delegation of basic authentication	Published Web sites are protected from unauthenticated access by requiring the ISA Server 2004 firewall to authenticate the user before the connection is forwarded to the published Web site. This prevents exploits from unauthenticated users ever reaching the published Web server.
Preservation of source IP address in Web publishing rules	ISA Server 2000 Web Publishing Rules replaced the source IP address of the remote client with the IP address of the internal interface of the firewall before forwarding the request to the published Web server. ISA Server 2004 corrects this problem by allowing you to choose on a per-rule basis whether the firewall should replace the original IP address with its own, or forward the original IP address of the remote client to the Web server.
SecurID authentication for Web proxy clients	ISA Server 2004 can authenticate remote connections using SecurID two-factor authentication. This provides a very high level of authentication security because a user must "know" something and "have" something to gain access to the published Web server.
Form-based authentication	ISA Server 2004 can generate the forms used by Outlook Web Access sites for forms-based authentication. This enhances security for remote access to OWA sites by preventing unauthenticated users from contacting the OWA server.

Continued

Table 1.2 What's New in ISA Server 2004

New Feature	What it does
Remote access to terminal services using SSL VPN	Windows Server 2003 Service Pack 1 machines support RDP over SSL to allow secure SSL VPN connection to Windows Server 2003 Terminal Services. ISA Server 2004 allows you to securely publish your terminal server using secure SSL VPN technology.
Secure Web Publishing Wizard	The new Secure Web Server Publishing Wizard allows you to create secure SSL VPN tunnels to Web sites on your internal network. The SSL Bridging option allows ISA Server 2004 to decrypt encrypted traffic and expose the traffic to the HTTP policy's stateful inspection mechanism. The SSL Tunneling option relays unmodified encrypted traffic to the published Web server.
Forced encryption for secure Exchange RPC connections	RPC policy can be set on the ISA Server 2004 firewall to prevent non-encrypted communications from remote Outlook MAPI clients connecting over the Internet. This enhances network and Exchange security by preventing user credentials and data from being exchanged in a non-encrypted format.
HTTP filtering on a per-rule basis	ISA Server 2004 HTTP policy allows the firewall to perform deep HTTP stateful inspection (application-layer filtering). The extent of the inspection is configured on a per-rule basis. This allows you to configure custom constraints for HTTP inbound and outbound access.
Ability to block access to all executable content	You can configure ISA Server 2004 HTTP policy to block all connection attempts to Windows executable content, regardless of the file extension used on the resource.
Ability to control HTTP file downloads by file extension	ISA Server 2004 HTTP policy allows you allow all files extensions, allow all except a specified group of extensions, or block all extensions except for a specified group.
Application of HTTP filtering to all ISA Server 2004 client connections	ISA Server 2000 could block content for Web Proxy client-based HTTP and FTP connections via MIME type (for HTTP) or file extension (for FTP). ISA Server 2004 HTTP policy allows you to control HTTP access for all ISA Server 2004 client connections.

Continued

Table 1.2 What's New in ISA Server 2004

New Feature	What it does
Ability to block HTTP content based on keywords or strings (signatures)	ISA Server 2004 deep HTTP inspection allows you to create "HTTP Signatures" that can be compared against the Request URL, Request headers, Request body, Response headers, and Response body. This allows you precise control over what content internal and external users can access through the ISA Server 2004 firewall.
Ability to control which HTTP methods are allowed	You can control which HTTP methods (also known as "HTTP verbs") are allowed through the firewall by setting access controls on user access to various methods. For example, you can limit the HTTP POST method to prevent users from sending data to Web sites using the HTTP POST method.
Ability to block unencrypted Exchange RPC connections from full Outlook MAPI clients	ISA Server 2004 Secure Exchange Server Publishing Rules allow remote users to connect to Exchange using the fully-functional Outlook MAPI client over the Internet. However, the Outlook client must be configured to use secure RPC, so that the connection is encrypted. ISA Server 2004 RPC policy allows you to block all non-encrypted Outlook MAPI client connections.
FTP policy	ISA Server 2004 FTP policy can be configured to allow users to upload and download via FTP, or you can limit user FTP access to download only.
Link Translator	Some published Web sites may include references to internal names of computers. Because only the ISA Server 2004 firewall and external namespace, and not the internal network namespace, is available to external clients, these references will appear as broken links. ISA Server 2004 includes a link translation feature that allows you to create a dictionary of definitions for internal computer names that map to publicly-known names.
Real-time monitoring of log entries	ISA Server 2004 allows you to see Firewall, Web Proxy and SMTP Message Screener logs in real time. The monitoring console displays the log entries as they are recorded in the firewall's log file.

Continued

Table 1.2 What's New in ISA Server 2004

New Feature	What it does
Built-in log query facility	You can query the log files using the built-in log query facility. Logs can be queried for information contained in any field recorded in the logs. You can limit the scope of the query to a specific time frame. The results appear in the ISA Server 2004 console and can be copied to the clipboard and pasted into another application for more detailed analysis.
Connection verifiers	You can verify connectivity by regularly monitoring connections to a specific computer or URL from the ISA Server 2004 computer using Connection Verifiers. You can configure which method to use to determine connectivity: ping, TCP connect to a port, or HTTP GET. You can select which connection to monitor, by specifying an IP address, computer name, or URL.
Report publishing	ISA Server 2004 report jobs can be configured to automatically save a copy of a report to a local folder or network file share. The folder or file share the reports are saved in can be mapped to Web site virtual directory so that other users can view the report. You can also manually publish reports that have not been configured to automatically publish after report creation.
E-mail notification of report creation	You can configure a report job to send you an e-mail message after a report job is completed.
Ability to customize time for log summary creation	ISA Server 2000 was hard-coded to create log summaries at 12:30 AM. Reports are based on information contained in log summaries. ISA Server 2004 allows you to easily customize the time when log summaries are created. This gives you increased flexibility in determining the time of day reports are created.
Ability to log to an MSDE database	Logs can now be stored in MSDE format. Logging to a local database enhances query speed and flexibility.
Ability to import and export configuration data	ISA Server introduces the ability to export and import configuration information. You can use this feature to save configuration parameters to an XML file, and then import the information from the file to another server.

Continued

Table 1.2 What's New in ISA Server 2004

New Feature	What it does
Delegated Permissions Wizard for firewall administrator roles	The Administration Delegation Wizard helps you assign administrative roles to users and to groups of users. These predefined roles delegate the level of administrative control users are allowed over specified ISA Server 2004 services.

In addition to these new features, there are many enhancements and improvements to features that were already included in ISA Server 2000. In Chapter 2, we delve into those, as well.

NOTE

Some of the features mentioned in the table could be added to ISA Server 2000 by means of Feature Pack 1, but were not included "out of the box" as they are with ISA Server 2004.

ISA: A Personal Philosophy

As we've worked with the product from alpha stage on, we've been reading a lot of things about the upcoming release of ISA Server 2004. While much of what we read is good, factual information, some just feeds the fallacies we discussed earlier in this chapter. Just check out some of these not-so-quotable quotes:

- "It is a good clean up update, but I won't say it is major. It doesn't all of a sudden make them a competitor to CheckPoint." (www.infoworld.com/article/04/05/03/HNisaserver_1.html)

- "They insist ISA Server is a firewall, but it is a server. It is Gartner's strong belief that firewalls are gateway packet and stream processing devices and not servers. The market supports that; most new installations are appliances." (www.infoworld.com/article/04/05/03/HNisaserver_1.html)

- "I've worked with large enterprises where we've used Cisco [Systems] on the front end with ISA behind it," said Chris Darrow, a consultant at TCP-IP Inc., a Sacramento, Calif .-based consulting firm. "It's a good addition to a Checkpoint or Cisco firewall, but I still would not use it alone." (http://searchwin2000.techtarget.com/originalContent/0,289142,sid1_gci967964,00.html)

- "Franco, under the subject "Strange Setup" wondered why a Microsoft ISA server is dual-homed to bypass a firewall. Follow-up posters explained that the ISA Server requires such a setup and that it is a good HTTP proxy/cache/authenticator for a Windows network. (Read: Better than the firewall is.) All

other traffic should still go through the firewall."
(http://sandbox.rulemaker.net/ngps/infosec/fwiz/fwiz-2004-02-28)

- Common themes that run through these types of comments and discussions include:

- Belief in the myth of "hardware" firewall. We dispelled that myth in the ISAServer.org newsletter last March.
(www.isaserver.org/pages/newsletters/march2004.asp)

- The assumption that Cisco and Checkpoint (and other traditional firewall) solutions are inherently more secure, without any understanding of the ISA Server 2004 firewall and without stating what precisely it is that controls their belief that these other firewall products provide better protection.

- The presumption that software running on a Microsoft Windows operating system can't be trusted (presumably the proponents of this belief don't use Microsoft Exchange or Microsoft SQL servers, since they also run on Microsoft operating systems).

- The assumption that you should put your weakest link directly in front of the most valued corporate assets (sort of like putting a security guard with a machine gun in the front of the Bank, and a poodle at the open entrance to the safe)

It's clear that a number of commentators and industry analysts don't understand the nature of firewall security in the 21st century and still cling to the marketing material they received in 1997 from the leaders in the firewall space. The problem with this is that the glorified "stateful packet filter" of yesteryear just can't stack up to a serious application-layer-aware firewall like ISA Server 2004.

In the following subsections, we discuss our personal firewall philosophy, based on the "defense in depth" approach to network security, and where we believe ISA Server 2004 should fit into your network security plan.

Defense in Depth

As mentioned previously, "defense-in-depth" has been adopted in the IT community to describe the multilayered approach to security. In its broadest scope, defense-in-depth focuses not only on technology, but also on operations and people. An example is the design of a castle: the moats, high walls, multiple walls, narrow windows, and lack of straight corridors leading from the perimeter to the center, provide a kind of defense in depth that focuses on technology. However, if the castle administrators did not plan for long sieges (operations) and did not guarantee the loyalty of their soldiers (people), the castle would be vulnerable.

Just about every firewall administrator has heard the old joke: the IT guy's boss asks, "is our network secure?" and the response is: "of course, we have a firewall!" Unfortunately, this is the attitude of many real-life network and firewall administrators. They consider the firewall at the edge of the network as the primary mode of defense against all network security issues. From a defense-in-depth point of view, the firewall administrator is not qualified or competent to answer this question. The firewall administrator has no control over the hiring and training practices of the company, which can create just as much risk (or more) than an improperly configured firewall.

Even from a purely technological point of view, the sad fact is that while the Internet edge firewall is a key component of your network security scheme, it is only one part, and that single part does not provide *defense in depth* – an absolute necessity in today's high risk environment. Technological defense in depth refers to the security philosophy that there are multiple partitions or security zones that must be protected, with the interface between each zone representing a specific *edge* that requires a customized approach to security and access control.

The number of security zones that require protection varies with the organization and how the organization has its network laid out. Smaller organizations might have just a single network segment sitting behind an Internet edge firewall. Larger organizations often have very complex networks with multiple security zones and security zones within security zones. Regardless of the complexity of your network, the principle of least privilege should be your guiding principle in determining firewall placement and configuration.

Rings of Fire(walls)

To help demonstrate how security zones dictate access control and firewall configuration and placement, we'll go over a typical enterprise-level network and how it segregates its security zones. We will call these zones "rings." You can think of each ring as being comparable to a layer in an onion, with the center of the onion representing your core network assets that need to be protected at all costs. These rings are:

- Ring 1: The Internet Edge
- Ring 2: The Backbone Edge
- Ring 3: The Asset Network Edge
- Ring 4: Local Host Security

Ring 1: The Internet Edge

Figure 1.5 shows the outermost ring, which is the Internet edge.

Figure 1.5 Ring 1 represents the Internet edge

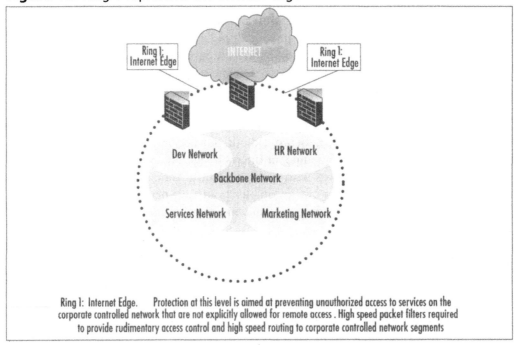

Ring 1: Internet Edge.   Protection at this level is aimed at preventing unauthorized access to services on the corporate controlled network that are not explicitly allowed for remote access . High speed packet filters required to provide rudimentary access control and high speed routing to corporate controlled network segments

The Internet edge is the first point of attack for external hosts. Because of this, most network and firewall administrators believe they should put their most intelligent and powerful firewalls at this location. If you don't think about this too much, it makes sense. But if you consider how this approach flies in the face of how you secure anything else in this world, you'll realize that the Internet edge firewall should *not* be your most secure or sophisticated firewall, it should be your *fastest* firewall.

Think about how a bank secures the money assets it has inside. First, there are the Federal agencies that hover unseen around all of our lives. This "outermost" level of bank security doesn't stop too many bank robberies in progress, but it helps deter law-abiding citizens from deciding to rob a bank when they have nothing else to do that day. The next layer of defense, moving inward toward the core band assets, is the local police department. They drive around all day, and maybe they'll be in front of the bank when the bank robber is about to begin the hold-up. This is a little closer to home than the federal agents, but the local police can't be in front of the bank all of the time, and when they do respond, its after the fact when the perpetrator is long gone.

The next ring closer to the core bank assets might be represented by the front door or parking lot cameras. The bank security people monitoring those cameras might be able to stop a robbery from taking place if they are vigilant and identify the criminal right before he begins the robbery attempt. The problem with this approach is they can't really do anything until the robber does something that suggests that the robbery attempt is in progress. However, this method is more sophisticated and more likely to stop a robbery attempt in progress than the Federal security ring or the local policy security ring.

The next ring is between the outside of the bank and the area around the tellers. There is typically an armed guard of some sort located in this area. The armed guard provides a better level of protection because he can stop a robbery as it begins, *if* he identifies it and captures or shoots the robber before the robber shoots him. The armed guard in the lobby provides a much higher level of security than the cameras watching outside the building, the local police cruising the streets and the Feds miles away at a regional office.

The next ring of security lies at the interface between the bank vault where the money is kept and the lobby and teller area. If the robber flies past the Feds, arrives when there's no police car in sight, looks like a typical customer and isn't flagged by the security cameras, and shoots the armed guard before the armed guard shoots him, the final hurdle is the bank vault door. Unless the guy is a munitions expert or a safe cracker, the bank vault door will stop him every time.

The bank vault door provides the highest level of security, and it's the most "hardened" and "impenetrable" of the bank defenses. That's why it's put right in front of the bank's core assets — to protect these assets in the event that an intruder gets past all the other rings of security designed to protect the bank's assets.

However, no ring, no matter how well protected, is impenetrable. Let's assume the robber isn't a munitions expert or a safe cracker. Instead, he'll be likely to use what we in computer security call *social engineering*. In this case, the social engineering method might consist of threatening the lives of the customers and tellers if the bank vault door is not opened by the bank manager. Since you can always find more money, but human life tickets only have one punch in them, the bank manager opens the vault door. Of course, if the robber has inside help from a disloyal employee, we have another type of security issue. This "human factor" can render most of the technological defenses useless.

At this point, you might think that the game is over and the robber won. He's penetrated the last defense ring and the money is his (let's overlook the fact that in order to really win the robbery game, you also have to successfully leave the bank with the cash). However, there is the last layer of defense, and that is the defense the money itself can provide. The bags of money might have exploding ink bags in them that will activate if they are moved or removed at the wrong time or the incorrect way, or maybe the money is marked and is easily identified if it is spent in public. This equates to your firewall's auditing and logging mechanisms that can provide a trail by which you might be able to identify and prove the case against the hacker who hacks into your network.

The point of this story is that the bank, and most other entities that secure their core assets, put their most hardened, most sophisticated, and most impenetrable barriers right in front of those assets. The enemy is always at his best at the outermost ring, and by the time he's made it to the innermost ring, he's either completely exhausted his resources or ready to give up. In either case, meeting stronger defensive mechanisms as he continues to get weaker only helps accelerate his ultimate defeat.

Now, with these facts in mind, how do you explain the attitude of network and firewall administrators who claim, "while I think an ISA firewall is great, I wouldn't feel comfortable if I didn't have a PIX in front of it"? The real irony is that these network and firewall administrators are doing the right thing – but for the wrong reason. They've been beaten over the head for years by "firewall experts" and "hardware firewall" marketeers with the idea that only an ASIC ("hardware") firewall can be secure; so-called "software firewalls" are inherently insecure because of reasons X, Y, and Z. Reason "X" always has to do with something about the underlying operating system, and after repeating with great enthusiasm, "Windows is not secure," for several minutes, they never seem to get around to reasons "Y" and "Z".

The truth is that the hardware firewall *does belong at the Internet edge* of the network, but not for the reasons the "firewall experts" proclaim. The actual reason is that while traditional firewalls cannot provide a high level of security for modern Internet connected networks, they *can* pass packets very quickly and do *stateful* packet filtering. This speed is very important for organizations that have multigigabit connections to the Internet. High security, application application-layer aware firewalls cannot handle this volume of traffic and provide the deep application-layer stateful inspection required of a modern network firewall.

NOTE

Placing a different type of firewall at the Internet edge can also be thought of as an example of "security through diversity," as it does confer a security advantage. At the same time, it also introduces complexity that can have disadvantages. For example, administrators will have to be trained on the different products.

Because of all this, the hardware firewalls should in fact be placed on the Internet edge. They can handle the high volume of traffic, perform basic packet filters and allow inbound traffic only to services that you intend to provide to remote users (outbound access control isn't very effective for high speed packet filtering firewalls at the Internet edge). For example, if you intend to provide only HTTP, HTTPS and IMAP4 access to resources on the corporate network, the high speed stateful packet filtering firewall will only allow new inbound connection requests for TCP ports 80, 143 and 443. The high speed packet filtering firewall can quickly determine the destination port and validity of the layer 4 and below information, and accept or reject the traffic. While this approach provides a small measure of security, it is far from what is required to protect modern networks.

Ring 2: The Backbone Edge

Ring 2 is the *Backbone Edge* that marks a line between the internal interfaces of the Internet Edge firewalls and the external interfaces of the backbone segment firewalls.

Figure 1.6 shows the placement of the four Backbone Edge firewalls surrounding the edges of the corporate backbone network.

Figure 1.6 The Backbone Edge

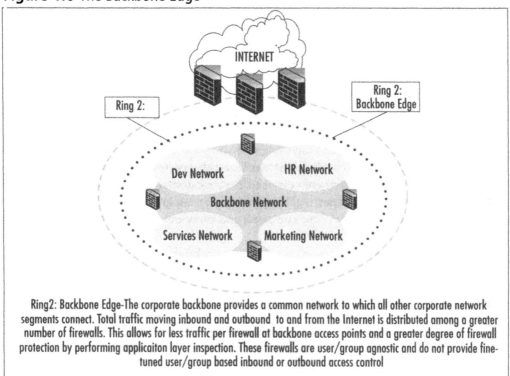

Ring2: Backbone Edge-The corporate backbone provides a common network to which all other corporate network segments connect. Total traffic moving inbound and outbound to and from the Internet is distributed among a greater number of firewalls. This allows for less traffic per firewall at backbone access points and a greater degree of firewall protection by performing applicaiton layer inspection. These firewalls are user/group agnostic and do not provide fine-tuned user/group based inbound or outbound access control

The corporate backbone network provides a common network to which all other corporate network segments connect. The total traffic moving inbound and outbound through the backbone firewalls is lower on a per-firewall basis than the Internet Edge firewalls because there are more of them. For example, you might have two high speed packet filtering firewalls on the Internet Edge, with each handling 5 gigabits/second for a total of 10 gigabits/second between them. There are four Backbone Edge firewalls, and assuming that the load is shared equally among these, each of the Backbone Edge firewalls handles 2.5 gigabits/second.

The Backbone Edge firewalls can start to perform the real work of a network firewall: stateful application layer inspection of both inbound and outbound traffic. Because modern exploits are aimed at the application layer (that's where the "money" is), the backbone application layer firewalls do the job of checking the validity of the communications moving through them. For example, if you allow inbound HTTP, the stateful inspection application layer aware firewalls on the Backbone Edge can start to apply real network security by checking the details of the HTTP communication and blocking suspicious connections through the firewall.

This is a good location for the ISA Server 2004 firewall. Because the ISA Server 2004 firewall is the model of a stateful inspection application layer aware firewall, it can perform the heavy lifting required to protect the corporate-backbone network and the network inside of it, as well as making sure that inappropriate traffic (such as worm-generated traffic) does not cross the Backbone Edge ring. The volume of traffic in this example is not a problem for ISA Server 2004 firewalls, as they have been tested and confirmed to be multigigabit firewalls, based on their hardware configuration and firewall rule base.

Ring 3: The Asset Network Edge

Ring 3 is at the border of the backbone network and the networks that contain the corporate assets. Corporate assets can represent user workstations, servers, departmental LANs, management networks, and anything else you want to protect from unauthorized access. The line between the backbone network and the assets networks is the *Asset Network Edge*. This is the ring where you need the strongest, most sophisticated level of protection, because if the intruder is able to violate the integrity of this ring, he is in the position to directly access your corporate assets and carry out what might turn out to be a successful attack.

Figure 1.7 shows the location of the Asset Network Edges in ring 3.

Figure 1.7 The Asset Network Edge

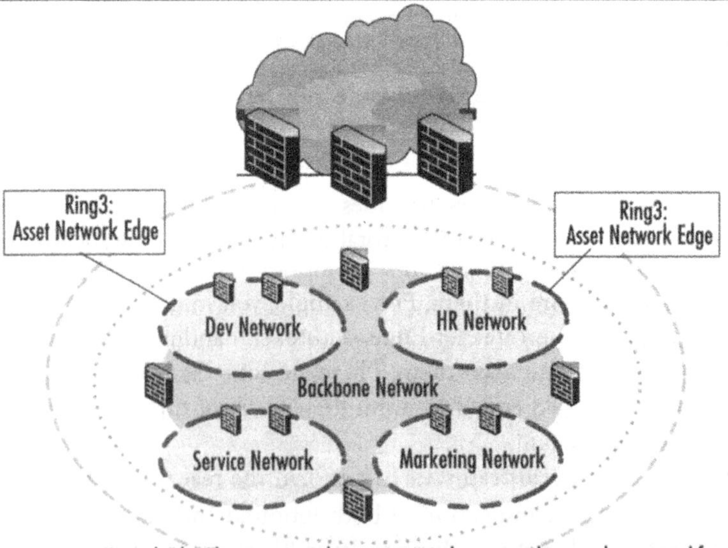

Ring: Asset Network Edge-The asset networks contain criitical resources that must be protected from attacks originating from outside the asset network and must stop outgoing attacks originating from the asset networks. Traffic inbound and outboud through the asset network firewalls are less on a per firewall basis than deeper application layer inspection and strong user/group based access control for inbound and outbound access through the asset network firewalls. Asset networks might represent departmental LANs, user LANs, network services segments/networks, management networks, and others.The most secure and powerful firewalls must be placed at this level because it's the last line of network defense.

It is at this level that an ISA Server 2004 firewall becomes critical. In contrast to a packet filter hardware device, you need *real* firewall protection when you get this close to the "money." Simple packet filtering is inadequate when it comes to protecting resources in the network asset ring. Not only must we ensure that all incoming connections are subjected to deep application layer inspection, we must also control what leaves the asset networks by using strong user/group-based access control.

Strong outbound user/group-based access control is an absolute requirement. In contrast to the typical hardware packet-filtering firewall that lets everything out, the firewalls at the Asset Network Edge must be able to control outbound connections based on user/group membership. Reasons for this include:

- You must be able to log the user names of all outbound connections so that you can hold users accountable for their Internet activity.

- You must be able to log the application the user used to access Internet content; this allows you to determine if applications not allowed by network-use policy are being used and enables you to take effective countermeasures.

- Your organization can be held legally responsible for material leaving your network (pornography, viruses, attacks); therefore, you must be able to block inappropriate material.

- Sensitive corporate information can be transferred outside the network from Asset Network locations. You must be able to block this and record user names and applications the users are using to transfer proprietary information to a location outside your network.

The ISA Server 2004 firewall is the ideal firewall for the Asset Network Edge because it meets all of these requirements. When the systems behind the firewall are properly configured as Firewall and Web Proxy clients, you are able to:

- Record the user names for all TCP and UDP connections made to the Internet (or any other network to which the user might connect by going through the ISA Server 2004 firewall).

- Record the applications the user uses to make these TCP and UDP connections through the ISA Server 2004 firewall.

- Block connections to any domain name or IP address based on user name or group membership.

- Block access to any content outside the network based on user name or group membership.

- Block transfer of information from the Asset Network to any other network based on user name or group membership.

All this deep application-layer stateful inspection and access control requires processing power. You should size your servers appropriately to meet the requirements of powerful stateful application-layer processing. Fortunately, even with complex rule sets, the ISA Server 2004 firewall is able to handle well over 1.5 gigabits/second per server, and even higher traffic volumes with the appropriate hardware configuration.

Ring 4: Local Host Security

The last ring is Ring 4, the *Host-based security* ring. This represents the junction between the host systems and the network to which they are directly attached. Figure 1.8 shows the position of ring 4.

Figure 1.8 Host-based Security Ring

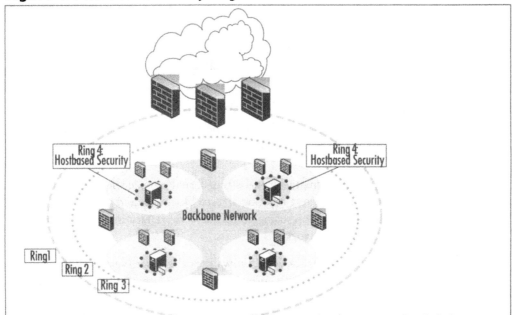

Ring 4: Host-based Security. This is the most important and the most neglected security ring. When the barbarians are at the gate, you better have your best and most powerful defensive weapons available because this is your last chance to protect your vital assets. Host based security includes host-based firewalls, disabling unused services that increase the "attack surface" using IPSec filters if available to allow only the required traffic, and insuring that the operating system software, applications, and services on the host are configured to allow only legitimate traffic and drop exploits automatically. This also requires that the software on the host systems are written with security in mind and are not susceptible to known attacks such as buffer overflows

Approaches to host-based security are somewhat different from what you see with network firewall protection, but the principles are the same. Host-based security requires that you control what is allowed inbound and outbound to the host machine and that the applications on the hosts are designed with security in mind. Some of the things you should consider when dealing with the Host-based Security ring include:

■ Using a Host-based firewall to control which incoming and outgoing connections are allowed and which applications can send and receive data. This is the typical "personal firewall" approach, but can be expanded to support server applications in addition to providing personal firewall support for user workstations.

- IPSec policy (on systems that support it) can be used to control what is allowed inbound and outbound from and to specific hosts. If a particular workstation or server does not need to connect to all possible computers, you can lock it down using IPSec policies to limit connections to a predefined collection of machines.

- Applications and services running on the hosts must be designed with security in mind. That means these applications and services are not vulnerable to common attacks such as buffer overflow and social attacks (such as HTML e-mail exploits and opening attachments).

- Anti-virus software must be used to block viruses that come from other network locations or are introduced by compromised hotfixes and software.

- Anti-scumware software must be installed to protect the machines and prevent adware and other malicious software from being installed on the machine.

- Anti-spam software must be installed on the machine if an e-mail client is installed. Anti-spam software should also be installed on SMTP relays that handle inbound and outbound mail, not only to block spam that carries a potentially dangerous payload, but also to reduce losses in employee productivity related to spam.

The Host-based Security ring is the last defense. The ISA Server 2004 and the Asset Network can help with this to a certain extent, but no firewall can completely make up for weaknesses found at the host layer. Network firewall security is helpful for controlling access from corporate network to corporate network and attacks coming from non-local networks that must traverse the ISA Server 2004 firewall, but only host-based security can handle attacks coming from the local network where the connection does not traverse a network firewall.

Note that for smaller networks that might have a single ring, which is the Internet Edge ring, the entire discussion is moot. The only reason to put a packet-filtering traditional firewall in front of the ISA firewall on a one-perimeter network is to waste money. You'd be better off buying two ISA firewalls, or buying another sophisticated application-layer firewall, with the ISA firewall behind the other application-layer firewall, so that the ISA firewall can implement the strong user/group-based security that is required for an in-depth defense of your network.

Summary

The importance of security began to "hit home" with network administrators years ago, but the events of the new millennium – including both an increased level of cyber-attacks and the physical attacks on the United States and its allies here and abroad – have heightened our awareness that today's world is a dangerous place and that danger extends to the computer networks that hold data on which many aspects of our lives depend. Protecting digital assets has become a top priority for businesses and individuals, and a key element in protecting any computer that connects to a network (and that includes most of them these days) is the firewall.

ISA Server 2004 has its origins in Microsoft Proxy Server, and later, ISA Server 2000, but Microsoft sees it as an entirely new product. The user interface has been completely changed, key features have been added (and some features have been removed), and ISA has grown into a full-fledged firewall that is designed to compete with the "big guys" in the firewall industry, both enterprise-level software firewalls and appliance-type hardware firewall devices.

Microsoft's reputation when it comes to security has suffered because of an early emphasis on features and functionality at the expense of security. However, the company has done a complete turnaround in priorities and today spends millions of dollars on security each year. The Trustworthy Computing initiative, with its SD^3 – Secure by Design, Secure by Default, Secure in Deployment – three-pronged goal puts an emphasis on security that has been incorporated into the design of ISA Server 2004 at every level.

ISA Server 2004 takes a policy-based approach to security and makes it easy for administrators to enforce the security policies decided upon by management. Developing appropriate policies is a key step in planning your firewall deployment, and that includes evaluating security needs, analyzing risk factors, assessing threats and threat levels, analyzing organizational and network vulnerabilities, analyzing organizational factors that affect security, analyzing legal factors, and finally, analyzing cost factors.

In order to be effective, a good security plan must take a multilayered approach. This means recognizing that most networks contain more than one perimeter and implementing multiple security measures (which may include multiple firewalls) to best protect the important assets (mission-critical applications and data) at the core of the network.

Firewalls act as the guardians at the gateway (the entrance to the network or subnet). The first firewalls were simple packet-filtering devices, but today's sophisticated multilayered firewalls can filter at the network, transport, and application layers of the OSI networking model to provide security coverage on a much broader scale. ISA Server 2004 is a packet-filtering, circuit-filtering and application-layer-filtering network-based software firewall that also includes VPN gateway functionality, intrusion detection and prevention, and Web caching to accelerate performance for both internal and external users.

ISA Server 2004 includes many new features, and improvements and enhancements have been made to many of the features that it shares with ISA 2000. As you go through this book, you will first learn the concepts behind the latest incarnation of ISA, then you'll learn how to install, configure, manage, use, and troubleshoot it in a detailed, step-by-step fashion.

Let's begin!

Chapter 2

Examining the ISA Server 2004 Feature Set

Topics in this Chapter:

- The New GUI: More Than Just a Pretty Interface

- Teaching Old Features New Tricks

- New Features on the Block

- Missing in Action: Gone, but Not Forgotten

ISA 2004 retains many of the same features that administrators know and love from ISA 2000, and, in many cases, has improved on them to make them even more functional and easy to use. For example, enhancements and improvements have been made to Virtual Private Networks (VPN) administration, authentication, firewall rules, Outlook Web Access (OWA) publishing, FTP support, secure Web publishing, cache rules, the SMTP message screener, customization of reports, and more.

ISA 2004 also adds an abundance of new features, such as support for multiple networks, stateful filtering and inspection for VPN traffic, VPN quarantine, firewall user groups, firewall generation of forms used by OWA for forms-based authentication, link translation, and much more.

The graphical user interface (GUI) has been completely reworked for a more intuitive and user-friendly experience.

In this chapter, we provide an overview of ISA 2004's new GUI and discuss old features that have been improved as well as new additions that will make the ISA Server administrator's job easier. We also look at some features present in ISA 2000 that have been removed in ISA 2004, making the product leaner and meaner, and reflecting Microsoft's focus on marketing ISA 2004 first and foremost as a firewall/security product that can compete with top competitors in that market, and then, as a caching/acceleration server, adding value and saving money for organizations that need both functions, but don't want to have to buy two separate products or expensive add-ons for their firewalls.

The New GUI: More Than Just a Pretty Interface

First, we'll look at the first thing the ISA user sees the graphical interface. There's no question that ISA 2004's interface is more intuitive than the ISA 2000 interface. Improving the user experience by making the interface friendlier was a major goal of the development team, and they've done a good job. It's easy for someone who isn't familiar with ISA 2000 to sit down at the ISA 2004 interface and click his or her way to performing many of the common firewall administrative tasks without consulting the Help file.

Examining the Graphical Interface

Figure 2.1 shows the ISA Server 2000 management GUI, and Figure 2.2 shows the new ISA Server 2004 GUI. As you can see, the former looks pretty much like any other Microsoft Management Console (MMC), with its simple left-pane tree and right details pane.

Figure 2.1 The ISA 2000 Interface — A Simple MMC

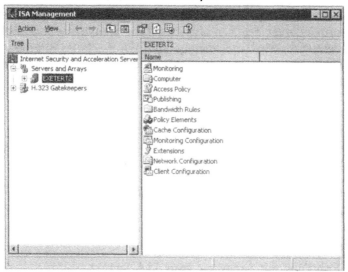

The ISA Server 2004 console is much richer, with a three-pane window that still includes the familiar tree structure in the left pane, but gives you tabbed pages in the middle and right panes that make it easy to select the type of tasks you want to perform and get precise help in performing them. No longer do you have to click through dozens of dialog boxes within dialog boxes in order to find the configuration setting you want. Instead, common management tasks are, literally, at your fingertips. This point-and-click interface can easily be learned by any IT administrator, without extensive training.

Figure 2.2 The ISA Server 2004 Management GUI — A Handy Three-part Tabbed Interface

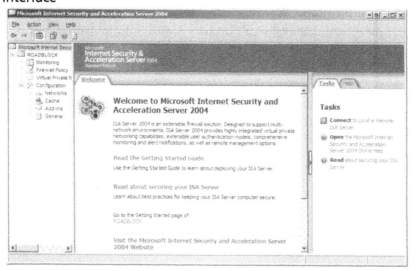

NOTE

You can use the management console to connect to remote ISA servers as well as the local ISA Server. You can also install the management console on a workstation or non-ISA server and manage your ISA machines remotely. You select the ISA computer you want to manage by clicking **Connect to Local or Remote ISA Server** in the right console pane, on the **Tasks** tab.

Clicking the top node in the management console's left pane (labeled **Microsoft Internet Security and Acceleration Server 2004**) displays the Welcome page in the middle pane. This interface provides quick links to the following options:

- **The Getting Started Guide**, an HTML document (Figure 2.3), provides detailed guidance for installing and configuring ISA Server 2004 and includes a "Feature Walk-Through" that shows you scenarios for performing specific common tasks.

- **Best Practices for Securing your ISA Server** takes you to the Security and Administration section of the ISA Server 2004 Help file. There is also a link to the Guides and Articles page on the ISA Server Website, http://www.microsoft.com/isaserver/techinfo/howto/, where you can find the most current version of the Security Best Practices document.

- **The Getting Started Page** (not to be confused with the Getting Start Guide) provides a logically-organized task-driven list of steps that allow you to quickly and easily set up your ISA Server (discussed in the next section).

- **The Microsoft ISA 2004 Web site** at www.microsoft.com/isaserver has product updates, customer support information, and the latest news about ISA Server.

- **Partner Products Web site** offers an extensive list of third-party add-ons to enhance the functionality of ISA Server, with links to partner sites, case studies, and partner news and reviews.

Figure 2.3 The ISA Server 2003 Getting Started Guide — Installation Instructions and a Features Walk-through

Examining The Management Nodes

Depending on your selection in the left pane, the middle pane displays different click-able configuration items. The left pane nodes include:

- ISA Server (Name) Top Node
- Monitoring Node
- Firewall Policy Node
- Virtual Private Networks (VPN) Node
- Configuration Node

The Configuration Node contains four subnodes:

- Networks
- Cache
- Add-ins
- General

In the following subsections, we'll take a look at each of the nodes and their inter-faces and what you can do with each.

ISA Server (Name) Top Node

If you select the node representing your ISA Server firewall (in the figures, the firewall's name is ROADBLOCK), the middle pane will display the **Getting Started with ISA Server 2004** page, shown in Figure 2.4. Again, don't confuse this with the Getting Started Guide.

Figure 2.4 Selecting the ISA Server Name — Left Pane Displays Getting Started Page

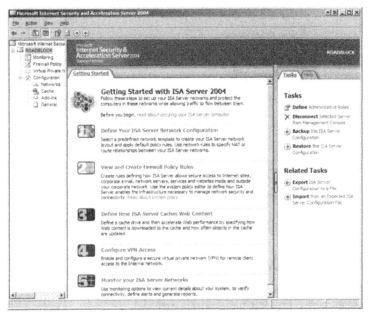

The Getting Started page makes it easy to set up the ISA Server firewall and/or caching server. You will see options here for performing the following tasks:

- **Defining Your ISA Server Network Configuration** allows you to select a predefined network template that you can use to create the layout for your ISA Server network and apply default policy rules. You can specify the NAT or routed relationship between multiple ISA server networks.

- **View and Create Firewall Policy Rules** lets you configure rules that will determine how your ISA Server allows secure access to internal and external Web sites, other Internet sites, servers, e-mail, and other services.

- **Define How ISA Server Caches Web** configures caching, first by defining a cache drive and then by creating caching rules to control how the Web content will be downloaded to the cache and the frequency of cache updates.

- **Configure VPN Access** allows you to create a VPN gateway to allow remote users to connect to your Internal network via virtual private networking.

- **Monitor your ISA Server Network** supplies options to view system details and verify connectivity (including monitoring in real time, which users are connected to which Web sites, and application usage). You can also create alerts to notify administrators of specified events via e-mail and set up generation of one-time or scheduled reports.

NOTE

Each of the options on the **Getting Started** page actually takes you to one of the nodes shown in the left pane. Thus, clicking "**Define Your ISA Server Network Configuration**" takes you to the same interface as clicking the **Networks** node under "**Configuration**" in the left pane; clicking "**View and Create Firewall Policy Rules**" takes you to the same interface as clicking **Firewall Policy** in the left pane, and so forth. After you become familiar with the ISA 2004 management console, you'll probably find it easier to just click the appropriate node in the left pane, but the **Getting Started** page brings together in an ordered list all of the configuration options you need when you first set up your ISA Server computer.

When the top ISA Server node is selected, in the **Tasks** tab of the right pane you'll see clickable icons for performing several tasks that relate to the ISA server as a whole. These include:

- **Define Administrative Roles** invokes the Administration Delegation Wizard, which you can use to assign administrative roles to individual users or groups. The roles define what permissions those users will have to administer the ISA Server.

- **Disconnect Selected Server from Management Console** will disconnect you from the local or remote ISA Server.

- **Backup this ISA Server Configuration** allows you to save the ISA configuration as an .XML file.

- **Restore this ISA Server Configuration** allows you to use the .XML file created by the Backup option to restore a configuration.

Related Tasks include exporting and importing ISA server configuration files (in .XML format).

ISA Server Secrets

How Does Backup/Restore Differ from Export/Import?

A popular question we get is: "How do the Backup and Restore functions differ from the Export and Import functions?" It's a good question, because at first glance, they look the same. In both cases, you're saving the ISA Server configuration to an .XML file and then bringing it back and applying it to the ISA server. The only difference you'll see between the two dialog boxes for saving the file is that the Export dialog box includes two checkboxes that you won't see when saving the file using the Backup feature:

- Export user permission settings
- Export confidential information (encryption will be used)

Both of these function sets allow you to save configuration information, but the export/import feature gives you more granular control over *what* information you save and how you save it.

With Backup/Restore, the server's general configuration information is saved. This consists of firewall policy rules, rule elements, alert configurations, cache configuration, and VPN configuration. You have no option to save only some of this information; it's an "all-or-nothing" deal.

With the Export/Import, you can save the entire configuration, or just specific parts of it. For example, you can save just the networks, or just one network; just the Web chaining rules, or even just one specific chaining rule; just selected firewall policies; just the cache configuration, and so forth. If you select to export the entire configuration, the following will be saved:

- Access rules
- Publishing rules
- Rule elements
- Alert configuration
- Cache configuration
- ISA Server properties and all general configuration information

You can choose whether to export confidential information such as user passwords, pre-shared keys for IPSec, and RADIUS shared secrets. You can also choose whether to export user permission settings. With the Backup function, you have no choice: the confidential information and user permission settings are automatically saved. Either way, when you save confidential information, it is encrypted for protection. You specify a password during the export operation, and you'll have to enter it when you import the configuration.

Continued

Why export an entire configuration rather than using Backup? This is often used to clone a server, creating a second ISA Server with the identical configuration. If you need to have several ISA Server firewalls configured as duplicates (for example, for several branch offices), this is the fastest way to do it.

An important fact to note is that when you export an entire configuration, the certificate settings are included. If you import the configuration to another ISA Server that doesn't have the same certificates installed, the firewall service won't start.

We will revisit the Getting Started tasks in more detail in Chapter Six, *Installing and Configuring the ISA Server 2004 Software.*

Monitoring Node

The *monitoring node* in ISA Server 2004 is a big improvement over the ISA Server 2000 monitoring and logging interface. This is a busy node, with seven tabbed pages displayed in the middle pane:

- The Dashboard
- Alerts
- Sessions
- Services
- Reports
- Connectivity
- Logging

The *Dashboard* is just what its name implies: a "big picture" view that summarizes each of the areas represented by a tab (except Logging). Like the dashboard of a car, you're able to keep an eye on what's going on with all the different areas from one interface. The Dashboard is shown in Figure 2.5.

Figure 2.5 The Dashboard — A "Big Picture" View of All Monitoring Areas at One Glance

The Dashboard also provides you with system performance information; you are able to see in graph format, the number of packets allowed per second (x10) and the number of packets dropped per second.

Each of the Dashboard sections contains an icon that indicates the status of that area:

- **Checkmark inside a green circle**: indicates that all is okay

- **Exclamation point inside a yellow triangle**: indicates a warning

- **X inside a red circle:** indicates a problem or potential problem

You can get more detailed information about each monitoring area by clicking on the appropriate tab.

We will go into more detail about how to use the Dashboard in Chapter 12, *Using ISA Server 2004 Monitoring, Logging and Reporting Tools.*

The *Alerts* tab provides information about significant events that have occurred (for example, when services start or shut down, an intrusion is detected, the connection limit is exceeded, and so on). You can configure what actions will trigger alerts. The Alerts tab is shown in Figure 2.6.

Figure 2.6 The Alerts Tab Notifies You of Significant Events That Occur on the ISA Server

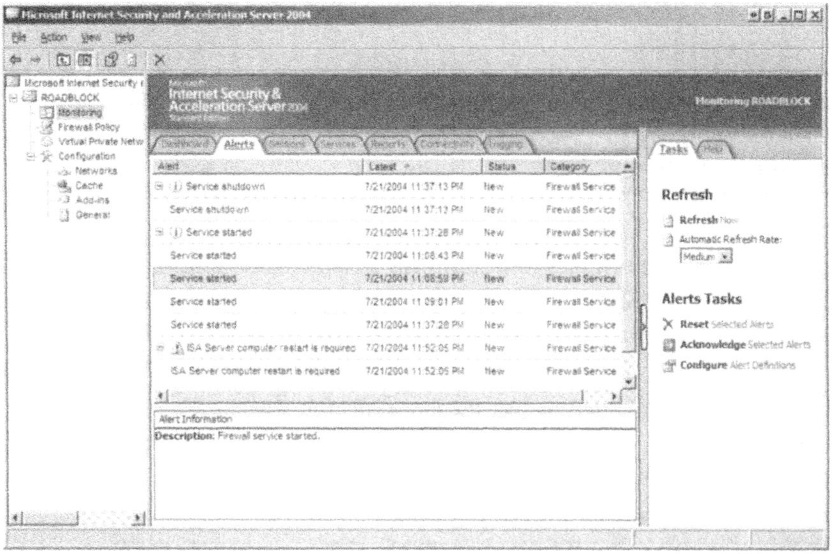

As you can see in Figure 2.6, if you click on an alert, more information about it will be displayed in the bottom middle pane. Alerts are marked by icons to indicate the relative importance of each. The icons will be familiar to Windows administrators, as they are the same ones used in the Event Viewer's system and application logs:

- **A lowercase "i" in a white circle:** indicates an informational alert. No action is necessary.

- **An exclamation point in a yellow triangle:** indicates a warning. Action may be required.

- **An "X" inside a red circle** indicates an error, a problem or potential problem that demands immediate attention.

The right task pane allows you to refresh the Alerts window manually, or you can set an automatic refresh rate (none, low, medium, or high). Under **Alerts Tasks,** you can reset selected alerts by clicking the alert(s) you want to reset (you can highlight multiple alerts by holding down CTRL while you select them) and then clicking **Reset.** You will be asked if you're sure you want to reset the alert. Click **Yes** to do so.

You can also choose **Acknowledge** to indicate that you are handling the alert. This will not remove it from the Alerts window; however, the alert will be removed from the Dashboard view.

Finally, you can configure alerts by choosing from a list of predefined alert events, and you can specify the number of times an event must occur, or the number of events per second, in order to trigger an alert. You can also specify what should happen when an alert is triggered (send e-mail to an administrator, run a specified program, log to the Windows event log, or start or stop a specified service or services).

We will discuss how to configure alerts step-by-step in Chapter 12, *Using ISA Server 2004 Monitoring, Logging and Reporting Tools.*

TIP

If you reset a group of alerts, all of the alerts in the group will disappear from the Alerts window. You won't see them there again unless/until the actions occur again to trigger them.

The *Sessions* tab makes it easy for administrators to view who is and has been connected through the ISA Server firewall and what applications they use. This information can be filtered for easier perusal. The Sessions window is shown in Figure 2.7.

We will discuss how to use the Sessions information in more detail in Chapter 12, *Using ISA Server 2004 Monitoring, Logging and Reporting Tools.*

Figure 2.7 Using the Sessions Tab —View Information About Who Has Connected Through the ISA Server Firewall

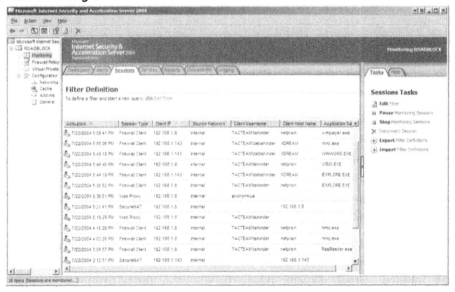

The *Services* tab shows you the status and uptime of the ISA Server and ISA-related services that are running on the Windows 2000 or Server 2003 computer. You can stop and start the services from this window, either from the **Services Tasks** section of the right pane or by right-clicking the service you want to start or stop. The Services tab is shown in Figure 2.8. We will discuss the Services tab more in Chapter 12, *Using ISA Server 2004 Monitoring, Logging and Reporting Tools.*

Figure 2.8 The Services Tab — Stop and Start ISA-related Services

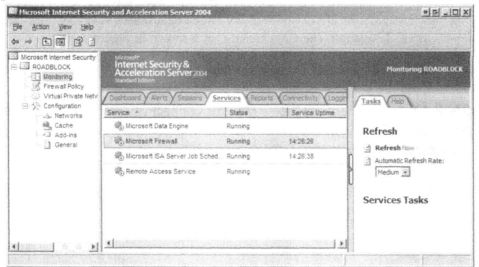

You can use the *Reports* tab, shown in Figure 2.9, to generate a one-time report or configure scheduled report jobs. A New Report Wizard walks you through the steps of creating a one-time report. Report jobs can schedule reports daily, weekly, or monthly. You can specify what information to include in the reports. We will discuss step-by-step procedures for generating reports in Chapter 12, *Using ISA Server 2004 Monitoring, Logging and Reporting Tools.*

Figure 2.9 The Reports Tab — Generate Reports from the Logs

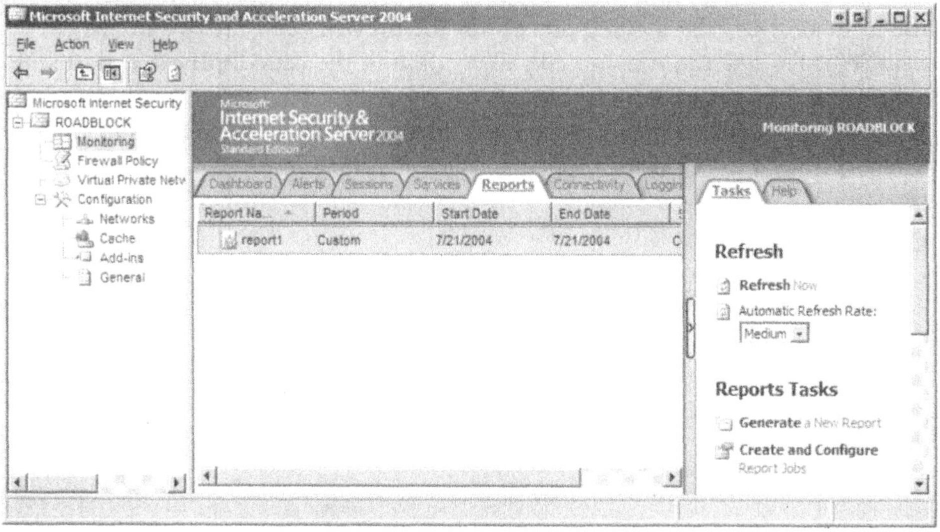

The *Connectivity* tab allows you to create, export, and import connectivity verifiers. These are objects that monitor the connectivity status between the ISA Server computer and a specific computer or URL. Connectivity can be determined via PING messages, TCP port, or HTTP request. The Connectivity tab is shown in Figure 2.10.

We will show you how to configure and use connectivity verifiers in Chapter 12, *Using ISA Server 2004 Monitoring, Logging and Reporting Tools.*

Figure 2.10 The Connectivity Tab — Monitor Connectivity Status Between the ISA Server and a Specific Computer or URL

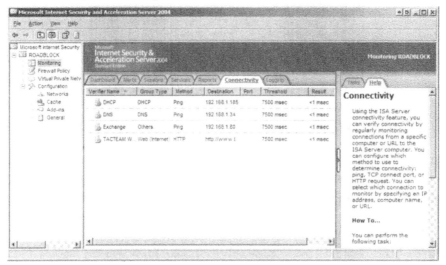

The last tab in the Monitoring window is the *Logging* tab, shown in Figure 2.11. You can use it to configure the logging process for the firewall, Web Proxy, and SMTP Message Screener logs. You can also edit filters to limit the data displayed, export and import filter definitions, and query the logs.

We will discuss how to how to configure, filter, and query the log files in Chapter 12, *Using ISA Server 2004 Monitoring, Logging and Reporting Tools.*

Figure 2.11 The Logging Tab — Filter and Query Data in the ISA Log Files

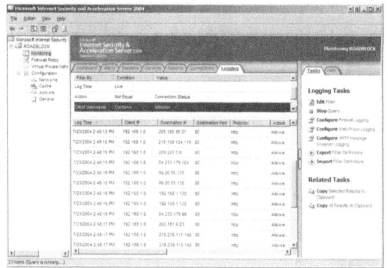

Firewall Policy Node

If you select Firewall Policy, the middle pane displays a list of firewall policy rules, and the right pane contains tabs labeled Toolbox, Tasks, and Help, as shown in Figure 2.12.

Figure 2.12 Firewall Policy — Configure Rules

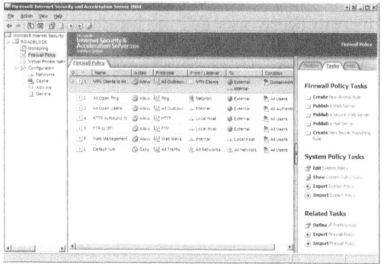

The *firewall policy node* is the "heart" of the ISA Server interface. This is where you create access rules, Web publishing rules, mail server publishing rules, and other server publishing rules to control access to and from your network. In addition, you can edit system policy, define IP preferences, and export and import both system policies and firewall policies. New access rules are created easily using the New Access Rule wizard, shown in Figure 2.13.

Figure 2.13 New Access Wizard — Create New Access and Publishing Rules

You will learn all the step-by-step details for creating and using access policies and publishing rules in Chapter 7, *Creating and Using ISA Server 2004 Firewall Access Policy,* and Chapter 8, *Publishing Network Services to the Internet with ISA Server 2004.*

Virtual Private Networks (VPN) Node

It's easy to set up your ISA Server firewall to act as a VPN gateway for remote access users or site-to-site VPN. The *Virtual Private Networks node*, shown in Figure 2.14, provides a friendly interface for performing common VPN configuration tasks and controlling client access.

Figure 2.14 Virtual Private Networks Node to Configure VPNs

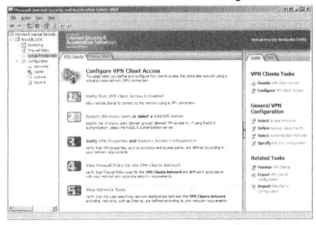

The middle pane displays a list of configuration tasks, including:

- Verifying that VPN client access is enabled
- Specifying the Windows users who are allowed VPN access or selecting a RADIUS server for authentication
- Verifying VPN properties and remote access configuration
- Viewing firewall policy rules for the VPN clients network
- Viewing rules that specify network relationships between the VPN clients network and other networks

From the right Tasks pane, you can configure client access (specifying number of simultaneous VPN connections, selecting groups for which VPN access is allowed, specifying allowed VPN protocols, and mapping users from non-Windows namespaces). You can even disable all VPN access with a single click.

We take you through the processes involved in creating and managing VPNs in Chapter 9, *Protecting Remote Access and VPN Communications with ISA Server 2004.*

Configuration Node: Networks Subnode

The *Configuration node* has four subnodes. If you select the *Networks subnode*, the middle pane displays a tabbed set of pages that includes *networks*, *network sets*, *network rules*, and *Web chaining*, as shown in Figure 12.15.

Figure 2.15 The Networks Tab — Configure Networks, Network Sets, Network Rules and Web Chaining

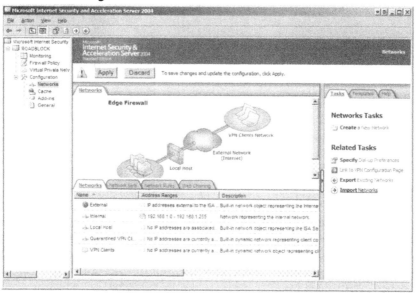

The right pane will contain tabs labeled **Tasks, Templates,** and **Help.**

The *Networks* tab is used to create and configure networks in a multiple network environment. The *Network Sets* tab lets you group networks and apply rules to a group, or set, of networks. The *Network Rules* tab is used to create, export, and import rules that define whether and what type of connectivity is allowed between different networks using translated (NAT) or routed connections. The *Web Chaining* tab is used to create Web chaining rules that allow you to route requests from clients to an upstream ISA Server or an alternate location.

We will discuss multiple network configurations in a bonus chapter *Configuring Enterprise Networks, Caching Arrays and Network Load Balancing,* to be made available free to purchasers of this book from www.syngress.com/solutions after the release of ISA Server 2004 Enterprise Edition.

Configuration Node: Cache Subnode

The *Cache subnode,* shown in Figure 2.16, is used to configure caching on your ISA Server.

Figure 2.16 The Cache Subnode — Configure or Disable Caching on your ISA Server

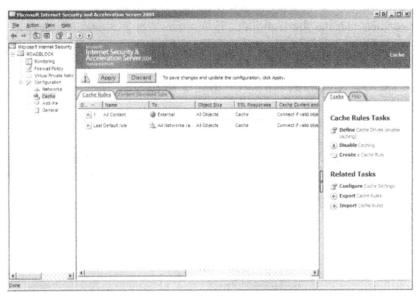

You can define cache drives where cached content will be stored and create cache rules via the New Cache Rule wizard. The rules apply to specific networks and determine how objects stored in the cache are to be retrieved when requested, as well as when content is to be cached, and limits on the size of cached objects. You can configure general cache settings here and export and import cache rules. You can also disable caching altogether, making the ISA Server function solely as a firewall.

We show you the step-by-step procedures for configuring and using ISA Server as a caching server in Chapter 11, *Accelerating Web Performance with ISA Server 2004 Caching Capabilities.*

Configuration Node: Add-ins Subnode

The *Add-ins subnode* is used to configure ISA Server's application layer filtering (ALF). This is where you enable, view, modify, and disable application filters and Web filters. Some filters are installed and enabled by default when you install ISA Server. The Add-ins subnode is shown in Figure 2.17.

Figure 2.17 The Add-ins Node — Configure Application and Web Filters

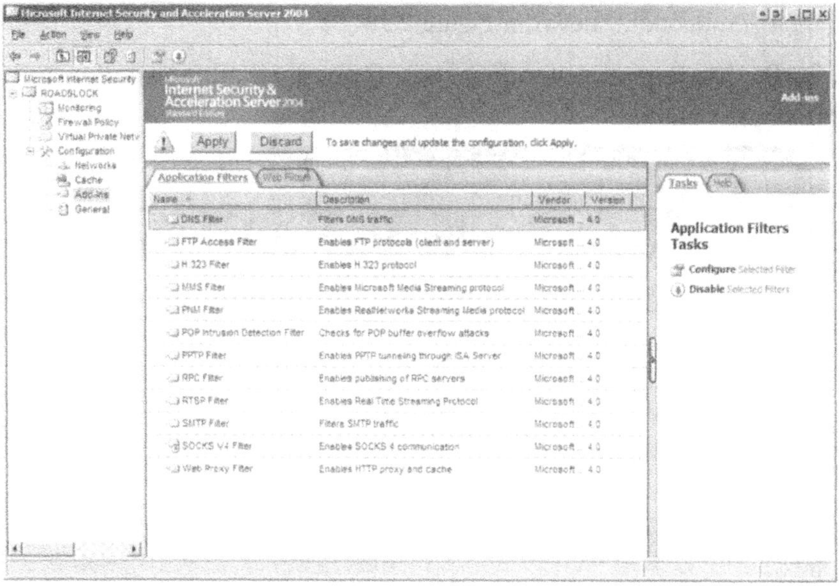

Configuration Node: General Subnode

Finally, the *General subnode* includes general administrative tasks, including:

- **Delegation of administration** to grant permissions for users and groups to perform specific administrative tasks;

- **Configuration of firewall chaining** to specify how requests from Firewall clients and SecureNAT clients are to be forwarded to upstream servers

- **Specification of Dial-up preferences** if you use a dial-up account

- **Specification of certificate revocation** so the ISA Server can verify that incoming certificates are not in the Certificate Revocation List (CRL)

- **Definition of Firewall client settings**, including application settings

- **Viewing of ISA Server computer details,** such as ISA version, name, product ID, creation date and installation directory

- **Configuration of link translation** to select content types that define the pages to which link translation will be applied

This subnode also allows you to perform advanced security tasks, such as the following:

- Define RADIUS servers
- Enable intrusion detection and DNS attack detection
- Define IP preferences
- Define connection limits

The *General* subnode is shown in Figure 2.18.

Figure 2.18 The General subnode is used for general administrative and advanced security tasks

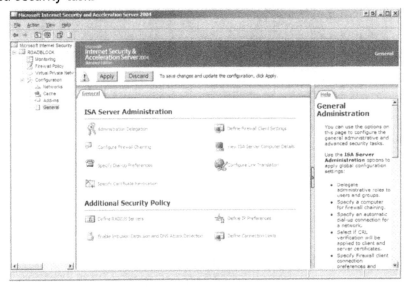

Teaching Old Features New Tricks

The GUI isn't the only feature that has been enhanced and improved in ISA 2004. In fact, many of the familiar tasks that firewall administrators performed with ISA 2000 have been made easier in ISA 2004. In the following sections, we will discuss some of the most significant of these improvements, grouped into the following categories:

- Remote Management
- Firewall Features
- Virtual Private Networking and Remote Access
- Web Cache and Web Proxy
- Monitoring and Reporting

Enhanced and Improved Remote Management

Administrators need the ability to manage ISA Server firewalls from remote locations: from their own desktop machines, from their portable computers when on the road or at another site, and sometimes even from computers over which they don't have control, such as public access computers. If your company has multiple ISA Server installations in different locations, you don't want to have to physically visit every ISA Server machine to perform management tasks on each.

NOTE

If you wish, you can copy the ISA Server 2004 Help file to your workstation or non-ISA server, so that you can have it at hand even if you are not connected to the ISA Server computer via the ISA management console or terminal services/remote desktop. To do so, navigate to the Microsoft ISA Server folder on the ISA Server (usually installed in the Program Files folder) and find the **isa.chm** file. Copy this file to your workstation or non-ISA server's hard disk, and you will be able to access the ISA Help files without connecting to the ISA Server.

With ISA 2004, there are several different ways to remotely manage your firewalls. In the following subsection, we will discuss three methods of remote management:

- The ISA 2004 Management Console
- Windows 2000 Terminal Services or Server 2003 Remote Desktop
- Third-party Web interface

Remote Management via the ISA Server 2004 Management Console

You can connect to a remote ISA Server or to multiple ISA Server firewalls with the management console. Each ISA Server will have its own top node in the left pane, as shown in Figure 2.19

Figure 2.19 You can connect to multiple ISA Server firewalls simultaneously with the management console

To connect to a second or subsequent ISA Server, click **Connect to Local or Remote ISA Server** in the right pane, and enter the name or IP address of the remote server and credentials to access it, as shown in Figure 2.20.

TIP

If you are unable to connect, see the instructions below to add your computer to the Remote Management Computers list in the ISA Firewall Policy node.

Figure 2.20 Use "Connect To" Dialog Box to Add Remote ISA Server to Management Console

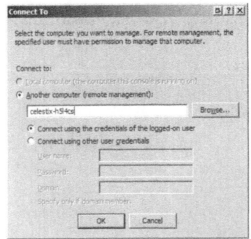

NOTE

You can only connect to ISA Server 2004 firewalls remotely with the management console. If you try to connect to an ISA Server 2000 firewall, you will receive the message, "A failure occurred. The task was not activated."

In order to manage an ISA Server remotely, the system policy must be configured to allow remote management. To configure the system policy:

1. On the ISA Server computer, click the **Firewall Policy** node in the left pane of the management console.

2. Click the **System Policy** rule labeled, "Allow remote management from selected computers using MMC," to view the rule.

3. To add a computer to it, in the right pane, click **Edit System Policy** under **System Policy Tasks.** This opens the **System Policy Editor**.

4. In the right pane of the **Editor**, under **Configuration Groups**, navigate to **Remote Management** and click **Microsoft Management Console (MMC)**.

5. Click the **From** tab, and by default you'll see **Remote Management Computers** in the box labeled **This rule applies to traffic from these sources,** as shown in Figure 2.21.

Figure 2.21 Use System Policy Editor to Configure Remote Management Computers

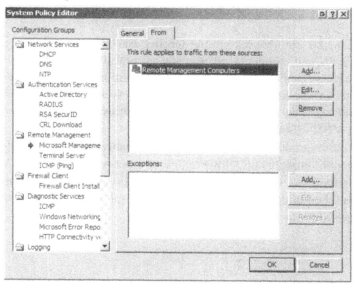

6. Double-click **Remote Management Computers**.

7. In the properties box, as shown in Figure 2.22, click **Add** and select
    Computer, Address Range, or Subnet.

Figure 2.22 Add A Computer, Address Range or Subnet to List of
Remote Management Computers

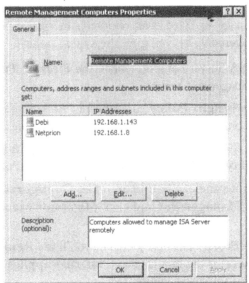

You can add the IP address of a single computer from which you want to remotely
manage the ISA Server, a range of addresses, or an entire subnet. The computers to
which this rule applies will be the only ones from which you can manage the ISA
Server.

You can also add network entities (entire networks, network sets, computers, address
ranges, subnets, and computer sets) directly to the rule instead of adding them to the
Remote Management Computers list. This is useful if, for example, you want to allow
VPN clients to remotely management the ISA Server. In that case, click **Add** on the
From tab page, then in the **Add Network Entities** dialog box, expand **Networks**,
and select **VPN clients.**

Best (most secure) practice is to add individual computers to the Remote
Management Computers list. However, if you need to manage the ISA Server from different workstations around the organization and do not know in advance which computers you'll be using, you may prefer to allow a subnet, address range, or even the entire
Internal network (*not* recommended).

ISA Server Secrets

Installing the Management Console

Before you can manage your ISA Server from a computer that doesn't have ISA Server installed, you will need to install the management console. You can install the console on Windows Server 2003, Windows XP, and Windows 2000 computers.

To do so, insert the ISA Server CD or navigate to the ISA Server installation files on a file server. Double click the **isaautorun.exe** file to start the ISA Server 2004 setup program. Click **Install ISA Server 2004** on the Setup front page.

If you are installing the console on a computer that is not running Windows 2000 Server or Windows Server 2003, you will get a message that ISA Server 2004 cannot be installed on this machine. Click **Continue** anyway, and you will be shown a list of the components that can be installed, including the management console. Proceed through the installation wizard to install the management console on your computer. It will appear in your Programs list as "Microsoft ISA Server."

After you have connected to the remote ISA Server computer via the management console, you can perform any administrative tasks you would be able to perform sitting at the local ISA Server. This is a big improvement over the ISA Server 2000 remote management console. For example, with ISA Server 2000, you could not configure or manage VPNs. With ISA 2004, you can manage all elements of the ISA Server remotely.

Remote Management via Terminal Services/Remote Desktop

Another way to manage your ISA Server from a remote computer is via terminal services (if you are running ISA Server 2004 on a Windows 2000 server) or Remote Desktop (if you are running ISA Server 2004 on a Windows Server 2003 machine). The advantage of this method is that you don't have to install the ISA Server management console software on the remote computer.

If you are using a Windows XP or Server 2003 computer to remotely manage ISA, you don't have to install any software at all because the Remote Desktop Connection (RDC) client software is already installed (you'll find it under **Programs | Accessories | Communications**).

If you want to use a Windows 2000 or 9x computer to manage your ISA server, you'll need to install the terminal services client or RDC client software first.

NOTE

If ISA is running on Windows 2000 Server, the server will need to have terminal services installed and running in either remote admin or application server mode. If ISA is running on a Windows Server 2003 computer, you will need to ensure that **Allow users to connect remotely to this computer** is checked on the **Remote** tab in the **System** properties applet of Control Panel. In addition, your user account must have permission to connect to the server via terminal services or Remote Desktop.

When all of the above hurdles have been crossed, it's easy to manage the ISA Server via terminal services/remote desktop. Connect to the server as you would to any terminal server/Remote Desktop server, and the server's desktop will appear in a window on your desktop, allowing you to perform any administrative tasks you could perform sitting at the server locally, as shown in Figure 2.23.

Figure 2.23 With Terminal Services or the RDC Client, the ISA Server's Desktop Appears in the Desktop Window

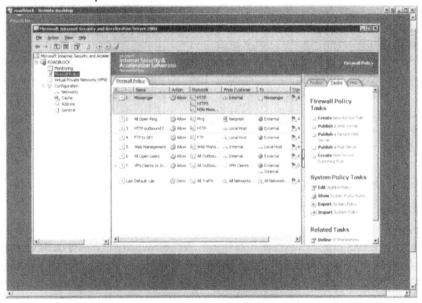

As with remote management using the management console, you might need to modify the ISA Server's system policy to allow management via terminal services before you'll be able to use this remote management method. The procedure is the same, except after you click **Edit System Policy** in the right pane of the ISA management console (with **Firewall Policy** selected in the left pane), you click **Terminal Server** under **Remote Management.** Then, on the **From** tab, click the **Add** button to add networks, network sets, computers, computer sets, IP ranges, or subnets. These are the computers that will be allowed to manage the ISA Server via terminal services/Remote Desktop.

Third-Party Remote Management Web GUI

Third-party vendors provide Web interfaces that can be used to manage ISA Server machines from any computer. No software has to be installed on the client machine, and no special configuration is necessary on the ISA Server. However, you might need to use the Internet Explorer browser, and/or the browser's security settings may have to be configured to use the Web GUI (for example, ActiveX controls might have to be enabled). You also might have to add the ISA Server's Web site to your Trusted Sites or Local Intranet security zone.

Two examples of Web interfaces for ISA-based firewall appliances are shown in Figure 2.24. The first shows the RoadBLOCK appliance marketed by RimApp (www.rimapp.com). The second shows the NS6000 appliance marketed by Network Engines (www.networkengines.com). You can see that Web interfaces can differ dramatically. Appliance vendors can add many enhancements that make the ISA-based firewall more functional, providing unique features based on their customers' priorities. Other vendors that have partnered with Microsoft to make ISA-based appliances include Hewlett-Packard, Celestix Networks and Advantis.

Figure 2.24 Third-Party Vendors Provide Web Interfaces for ISA-based Firewall Appliances

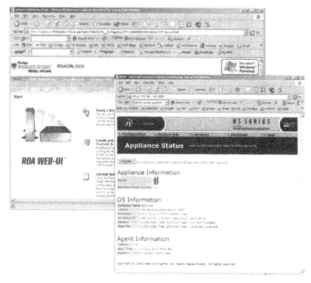

Enhanced and Improved Firewall Features

The firewall functionality is Microsoft's biggest focus in ISA Server 2004, perhaps more so than in ISA 2000. While it is still known as "Internet Security *and* Acceleration Server," the emphasis in both development and marketing has been more on the security function and less on the acceleration. ISA 2004 is designed to compete with popular firewall products that do not include caching functionality out of the box. Thus, it's only natural that many improvements have been made to ISA's security and firewall features. including better protocol support, improved authentication, easier access for popular services (OWA and FTP), expanded ability to define network objects, improvements to firewall rules functionality, improvements to server publishing and Web publishing.

Better Protocol Support

ISA Server 2004 allows you to control access and usage of any protocol, including IP-level (Layer 3) protocols such as the Internet Control Message Protocol (ICMP). This makes it possible for users to use applications such as ping and tracert, and also allows them to create VPN connections using the Point-to-Point Tunneling Protocol (PPTP). Internet Protocol security (IPSec) traffic can also be enabled through ISA Server, whereas you could not control IPSec with ISA 2000.

At the Transport layer (Layer 4), ISA Server 2004 also adds new support for port redirection and better FTP support. With ISA Server 2004, a connection that is received on one port can be redirected to a different port number, and FTP servers can be published on alternate port numbers without the requirement for any special configuration on the client by simply creating an FTP server publishing rule.

Streaming media and voice/video applications frequently require the firewall to manage *complex protocols*. A complex protocol is one that needs to make multiple connections. ISA Server 2000 can manage complex protocols, but this requires you to be able to create complex scripts in order to create protocol definitions for protocols that require multiple primary outbound connections. With ISA Server 2004, you can create protocol definitions easily with the New Protocol Wizard. These protocol definitions can be created "on the fly" when creating an access rule, or you can create a new protocol in the **Firewall Policy** node by selecting **Protocols** from the **Toolbox** tab in the right pane, and clicking **New,** as shown in Figure 2.25.

Figure 2.25 ISA Server 2004 Makes it Easy to Create New Protocol Definitions

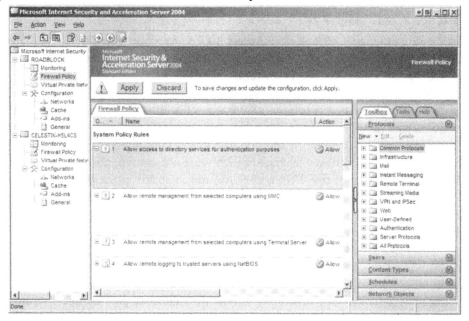

In addition, with ISA Server 2004, you can control the source and destination port numbers for any protocol for which you create a Firewall Rule. This gives the ISA Server 2004 firewall administrator a very high level of control over exactly which packets are allowed through the firewall.

Improved Authentication

Improvements have been made to the authentication process in ISA Server 2004. Users can be authenticated via the built-in Windows authentication or Remote Authentication Dial-In User Service (RADIUS) or other namespaces. You can apply rules to users or user groups in any namespace. Using the software development kit, third-party vendors can extend these built-in authentication types to provide for additional authentication mechanisms.

A common authentication problem with ISA Server 2000 has been solved: in ISA 2000, the HTTP redirector had to forward requests to the Web Proxy service so that firewall clients could benefit from the Web cache. During this process, user credentials were removed, and then the request failed if user credentials were required. ISA Server 2004 fixes this problem by allowing Firewall clients to access the Web cache via the HTTP filter, without requiring separate authentication with the Web Proxy service.

With ISA Server 2000, there were also some authentication issues with the Hotmail Web site. This required the site to be configured for direct access. The improved HTTP filter in ISA Server 2004 fixes this problem, too. Now all users can access Hotmail via an easily-configured firewall rule without any need for special configuration on either the client or the firewall.

Easier Access for Popular Services such as OWA and FTP

It is now easier to set up Outlook Web Access (OWA) to work with ISA 2004, thanks to the OWA Publishing wizard. SSL VPNs provide clientless remote access via secure connections using the Secure Sockets Layer (SSL) protocol.

The ISA Server 2004 OWA Publishing Wizard walks you through the process of setting up a firewall rule that creates an OWA SSL VPN to your Exchange Server. All network elements can be created "on the fly," and you never need to leave the wizard in order to create a policy element. In addition, the OWA Publishing Wizard now supports Outlook Mobile Access and ActiveSynch, which were not configurable via the wizard in ISA 2000. Configuration of the Web listener was not included in the Wizard in ISA 2000, whereas it is with ISA 2004. The Web listener is also much more configurable; in ISA 2000, you had to set properties globally for the Web listener. That is, if you enabled the HTTP listener, it was enabled for all Web listeners. With ISA 2004, you can set properties individually for each Web listener.

It was difficult to configure outbound access to FTP servers listening on non-standard ports in ISA Server 2000, and it required the Firewall Client. ISA Server 2004 allows you to access Internet FTP servers listening on alternate port numbers without requiring any special configuration on the client or on the ISA Server 2004 firewall. Also, FTP server publishing on alternate port numbers was a problem in ISA Server 2000, but it's easy in ISA Server 2004, requiring nothing more than creating an FTP Server Publishing Rule. You will learn how to do this in Chapter 8, *Publishing Network Services to the Internet with ISA 2004*.

Tools and Traps...

How Secure Sockets Works

Netscape originally developed Secure Sockets Layer (SSL) as a security protocol to be used in transmitting information via a Web browser. Netscape licensed the public key cryptography from RSA. SSL uses public key (asymmetric) encryption to provide authentication and protect the confidentiality and integrity of messages exchanged between two computers. Here is a simplified version of how it works:

1. A client computer sends a request for a secure connection to the server.

2. The server sends its authentication certificate and its public key to the client.

Continued

3. The client checks to determine if the certificate is valid, and if so, the client sends the server a randomly-generated encryption key that has been encrypted with the server's public key.

4. The server decrypts the encryption key, using its private key that matches the public key with which the client encrypted it.

5. The client and server can now exchange data securely using session-based symmetric key encryption.

Expanded Ability to Define Network Objects

With ISA Server 2000, you defined network objects based on IP addresses (client address sets) or fully-qualified domain names (destination sets). With ISA Server 2004, you have much more flexibility in defining network objects. You can specify them according to the following categories:

- **Networks:** In this context, a network is defined as a range of IP addresses.
- **Network sets:** This is a group of networks.
- **Computers:** A computer is defined here as representing a single IP address. To apply a rule to a computer with multiple NICs or with multiple IP addresses assigned to a single NIC, you would use a computer set, an address range, or even a subnet.
- **Address ranges:** This is just what it sounds like: a range of IP addresses.
- **Subnets:** A subnet is also defined as a range of IP addresses, in this case, the addresses make up a sub network.
- **Computer sets:** As a network set is a group of networks, a computer set is a group of computers (or more specifically, a group of non–sequential IP addresses).
- **URL set:** This is a group of Uniform Resource Locators (Web addresses).
- **Domain name set:** This is a group of domain names.
- **Web listener:** This is a software construct that determines which IP addresses and ports will be used to "listen" for Web requests.

These network objects define the source and destination for Firewall Rules. Whenever you create a rule, you specify source and destination objects to which the rule is to be applied. The full list of categories with their subcategories is shown in Figure 2.26.

Figure 2.26 ISA Server 2004 — Providing Great Flexibility in Defining Network Objects

You will learn about working with network objects in Chapter 4, *Preparing the Network Infrastructure for ISA 2004.*

Improvements to Firewall Rules Functionality

The core component of controlling access through the ISA firewall is the firewall policy, which consists of system policy rules, publishing rules and access rules (together, these are called firewall policy rules). ISA Server 2004 includes a new set of rule Wizards that make it easier than ever to create access policies. With ISA 2000, outbound access policies required IP Packet Filters, Site and Content Rules, and Protocol Rules. ISA Server 2004 access policies can be created by using the sophisticated Firewall Rule Wizard that allows you to configure any required policy element "on the fly." You do not need to leave the rule wizard to create a network object as you did with ISA 2000; any network object or relationship that is needed for the rule can be created within the new Wizard.

ISA Server 2000 access control was based on Allow and Deny rules. Generally, Deny rules were processed first, and then Allow rules were processed. ISA Server 2004 rules processing has been completely revamped. System policy rules are processed first, then user-defined rules. The firewall rules now represent an ordered list, in which connection parameters are first compared to the top listed rule. ISA Server 2004 moves down the list of rules until it finds a rule that matches the connection parameters, and then it enforces the matching rule's policy. This approach to firewall policy makes it much easier to troubleshoot problems and determine why a specific connection was Allowed or Denied.

To change the order of rules in the list, right-click the rule you want to move and select **Move Down** or **Move Up** as shown in Figure 2.27.

Figure 2.27 Changing the Order in which Access and Publishing Rules are Processed

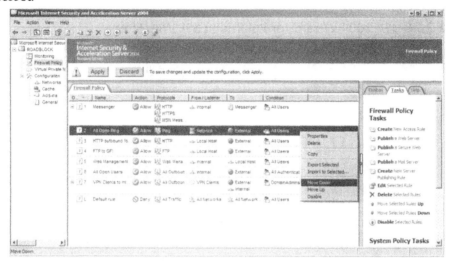

> **NOTE**
>
> You can change the order of the user-defined (publishing and access) rules, but you cannot change the order of the System Policy Rules.

ISA Server 2000 allowed you to specify which sites and protocols users could access, but you could not allow a user to access a particular site with a selected protocol or use a particular protocol to access a specific site. ISA Server 2004's enhanced firewall rules allow you to define the source and destination for each individual protocol that a user or group is allowed to access. This increases the flexibility with which you can control both inbound and outbound access through the ISA firewall.

System Policy Rules are discussed in detail in Chapter 6, *Installing and Configuring the ISA Server 2004 Software.* You will learn all the details of creating and working with user-defined firewall rules in Chapter 7, *Creating and Using ISA 2004 Firewall Access Policy,* and Chapter 8, *Publishing Network Services to the Internet with ISA 2004.*

Improvements to Server Publishing and Web Publishing

Several improvements have been made to server publishing and Web publishing in ISA 2004. In ISA Server 2000, the Server Publishing Rules forwarded incoming connections to a published server on the same port where the original request was received. ISA Server 2004 allows you to receive a connection on a particular port number and then redirect the request to a different port number on the published server.

With ISA Server 2004, you can place servers behind the firewall, either on the corporate network or on a perimeter network, and securely publish their services. Unlike ISA 2000, ISA 2004 has two separate Web Publishing Wizards. The first is for publishing a secure Web server that will allow remote users to access the Web server via SSL (shown in Figure 2.28).

Figure 2.28 ISA 2004 Wizard for Publishing SSL Web Sites

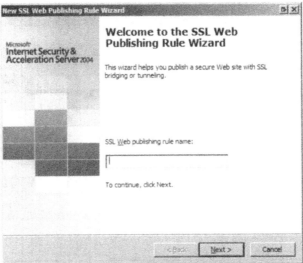

There is also a new Mail Server Publishing Wizard that will allow you to publish any IMAP, POP3, SMTP or RPC-based mail server or NNTP news server, or you can publish Outlook Web Access, Outlook Mobile Access, or Exchange ActiveSynch. ISA 2000 included the Mail Server Security Wizard and a separate OWA Publishing Wizard that was categorized under Web publishing. The ISA 2000 Wizard did not include support for OMA or ActiveSynch.

The improved Web Publishing Wizards allow you to publish Web sites easily and quickly. For example, configuration of the Web listener was not included in the wizard in ISA 2000, whereas it is with ISA 2004. The Web listener is also much more configurable; in ISA 2000, you had to set properties globally for the Web listener. That is, if you enabled the HTTP listener, it was enabled for all Web listeners. With ISA 2004, you can set properties individually for each Web listener.

In ISA 2000, prior to creating a server publishing rule or a Web publishing rule, you had to create a number of new policy elements that would be required by the rule. With ISA 2004, policy elements can be created "on the fly" within the Rule Wizard.

Enhanced and Improved Virtual Private Networking and Remote Access

Virtual private networking (VPN) is becoming increasingly important to companies, because of the proliferation of employees who telecommute, executives, and sales personnel who need network access either while traveling or after-hours from home, as well as partners and others outside the organization who need to access the corporate network. ISA Server 2004 includes many improvements and enhancements to VPN and remote access functionality, including:

- More flexibility for site-to-site VPN links
- Better control over VPN clients
- PPTP server publishing
- Forced Encryption for Secure Exchange RPC Connections

In the following subsections, we look at what's been improved in each of these categories.

More Flexibility for Site-to-Site VPN Links

ISA Server 2004 has improved VPN capabilities that allow it to create site-to-site links to other VPN servers, using IPSec in tunnel mode. This increases the level of interoperability of VPN networking over that offered by ISA Server 2000. This means that ISA Server 2004 can be placed at a branch office and a tunnel mode IPSec site-to-site link can connect the branch office network to the main office network, even if the main office is using a third-party edge firewall such as a Cisco PIX, Check Point, or any other firewall that supports IPSec VPNs. ISA Server 2000 could use only the PPTP and L2TP/IPSec VPN protocols to join networks over the Internet using a VPN site-to-site link.

With ISA Server 2000, networks joined by a site-to-site link were considered trusted networks; thus, firewall policy was not applied to communications that moved through the link. ISA Server 2004 introduces stateful filtering and inspection for all communications moving through a site-to-site VPN connection. This means you can control which resources specific hosts or networks can access on the opposite side of the link. User/group-based access policies can be used to granularly control resource utilization via the link.

Better Control Over VPN Clients

Unlike with ISA 2000, the ISA Server 2004 firewall policy is applied to *all* network interfaces. This includes VPN interfaces. For better security and control, you can limit the VPN clients to a selected set of servers and protocols on the internal network. For example, you might want to allow VPN clients to have full Outlook MAPI client access to the Exchange Server on the internal network, but you might not want these users to have access to any other servers or protocols on the network. In this case, you can configure the ISA Server 2004 Firewall Rules to limit VPN users' access to only the Exchange Server's MAPI client services and nothing else.

VPN clients are configured as a separate network zone. This means that you can create distinct policies for VPN clients. The firewall rule engine discriminately checks requests from VPN clients, statefully filtering and inspecting these requests and dynamically opening connections, based on the access policy.

In ISA Server 2000, only VPN clients that were configured as Firewall clients could access the Internet via their connected ISA Server 2000 VPN server. ISA Server 2004 improves VPN client support by allowing SecureNAT clients to access the Internet without requiring that the Firewall client be installed on the client computer. You can also enhance the corporate network's security by forcing user/group-based firewall policy on SecureNAT clients that are connecting via VPN.

PPTP Server Publishing

Publishing of VPN servers has also been improved. You could only publish L2TP/IPSec NAT-T VPN servers using ISA Server 2000. ISA Server 2004 allows you to publish PPTP VPN servers located behind the ISA Server 2004 firewall. The ISA Server 2004 smart PPTP application filter performs the complex connection management. In addition, you can easily publish the Windows Server 2003 NAT-T L2TP/IPSec VPN server using ISA Server 2004 Server Publishing. ISA Server 2004 also supports NAT-T-compliant IPSec-based VPN servers located behind the firewall.

Forced Encryption for Secure Exchange RPC Connections

RPC policy can be set on the ISA Server 2004 firewall to prevent non-encrypted communications from remote Outlook MAPI clients connecting over the Internet. This enhances network and Exchange security by preventing user credentials and data from being exchanged in a non-encrypted format.

Enhanced and Improved Web Cache and Web Proxy

It's important to remember that despite Microsoft's emphasis on the security side, ISA Server 2004 is more than a firewall; it's also a functional caching server. Several improvements have been made to the Web Cache and Web Proxy features in ISA Server. These include:

- Improvements to the Cache Rule Wizard
- More Flexibility in Caching of SSL Content
- Path Mapping for Web Publishing Rules
- Enhancements to Scheduled Content Download

In the following subsections, we discuss each of these improvements and enhancements in more detail.

Improvements to the Cache Rule Wizard

As with ISA Server 2000, cache rules can be created via a handy wizard interface. However, the Cache Rules Wizard has been improved in ISA Server 2004. For one thing, you can find it. In the ISA Server 2000 interface, cache rules were set up via the "New Routing Rule" Wizard, as shown in Figure 2.29, located rather non-intuitively in the Network Configuration node of the left console pane (*not* the Cache Configuration node where one might expect it to be).

Figure 2.29 Cache Rules in ISA 2000

With ISA Server 2004, cache rules are created from the **Configuration | Cache** node—right where most folks would naturally look—either by right-clicking the Cache node and selecting **New** and then **Cache Rule,** as shown in Figure 2.30, or by simply clicking **Create a Cache Rule** in the right **Tasks** pane, also shown in Figure 2.30.

Figure 2.30 Creating A Cache Rule in ISA Server 2004

In addition, you have more flexibility and clarity in selecting the network entities to which your rule will apply. In ISA Server 2000, your choices were: all destinations, all internal destinations, all external destinations, a specified destination set, or all destinations except a selected set.

With ISA Server 2004, you can apply the cache rule to any of the list of network entities discussed earlier: entire networks, network sets, individual computers, address ranges, subnets, computer sets, domain name sets, or URL sets.

You can also configure the circumstances when retrieved content is stored in the cache much more granularly in the in ISA Server 2004 wizard. In addition to selecting to store content in the cache if the source and request headers indicate to cache, you can also select to cache dynamic content, to cache content for offline browsing, and to cache content requiring user authentication on a per-rule basis.

We discuss the Cache Rule Wizard in more detail in Chapter 11, *Accelerating Web Performance with ISA Server 2004 Caching Capabilities.*

More Flexibility in Caching of SSL Content

With ISA Server 2000, there was no way to select *not* to cache SSL content. This was a problem because, since SSL is secure content, you might not want it to be stored in the cache because of security concerns.

With ISA Server 2004, this problem is solved. When you create a cache rule, SSL content is cached by default, but you can select not to cache it by unchecking a checkbox on the Cache Advanced Configuration page. Alternatively, after the rule has been created, you can configure it not to cache SSL content by right-clicking the rule, selecting **Properties** and selecting the **Advanced** tab, then unchecking the checkbox as shown in Figure 2.31.

Figure 2.31 ISA Server 2004 — You can Select *Not* to Cache SSL Content

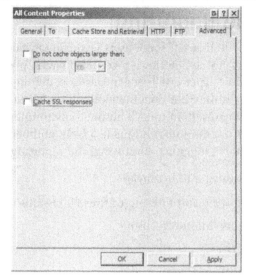

The ability to control whether or not SSL responses will be cached is a welcome addition to ISA Server 2004.

Path Mapping for Web Publishing Rules

ISA Server 2000 Web Publishing Rules required that the path the user included in the original request be the same path as on the published Web server. ISA Server 2004 significantly improves the flexibility of Web Publishing by allowing you to redirect the path sent to the firewall by the user to any path of choice on the published Web server.

When you configure path mapping in ISA Server 2004, ISA replaces the path that is contained in the request with the path that you have mapped.

Path mapping is configured by editing the Web publishing rule after it is created. In the publishing rule's **Properties** dialog box, select the **Paths** tab, and add the path to which you want requests mapped in the format **/path/***.

You will learn more about path mapping when we discuss creating publishing rules in Chapter 8, *Publishing Network Services to the Internet with ISA 2004.*

Enhancements to Scheduled Content Download

The scheduled content download feature has also been improved in ISA Server 2004. With ISA Server 2000, you could not schedule content for download from sites that required user authentication. This limited your ability to automate the content download process.

With ISA Server 2004, you can now specify an account to be used for authentication, thus allowing you to schedule content download jobs from sites that require authentication.

Enhanced and Improved Monitoring and Reporting

One part of ISA Server 2000 that left some users less than satisfied was the monitoring and reporting functionality (to be fair, this is a complaint with many other vendors' firewalls, as well). Certainly, the "paper trail"—or in this case, the digital trail—is not nearly as exciting as some other features, but documentation is an essential element of protecting your network, and yourself, in today's business environment.

Microsoft has listened to customers and made a large number of improvements and additions to ISA Server 2004's logging, monitoring, and reporting functions, including:

- Real-time monitoring of log entries
- Real-time monitoring and filtering of firewall sessions
- A built-in log-querying mechanism
- Connection verifiers
- Ability to customize reports
- Ability to publish reports
- E-mail notification for report jobs
- Ability to configure time of log summary
- Better SQL logging
- Ability to log to an MSDE database

We take a brief look at each of these in the following subsections.

Real-time Monitoring of Log Entries

With ISA Server 2004, you are able to see Firewall, Web Proxy, and SMTP Message Screener logs in real time. The monitoring console displays the log entries as they are recorded in the firewall's log file (Figure 2.32). This is in contrast to ISA Server 2000, where you had to consult the actual log file (by default, created daily) or generate a report in order to see the logged information.

Figure 2.32 Monitor Logs in Real Time with ISA Server 2004

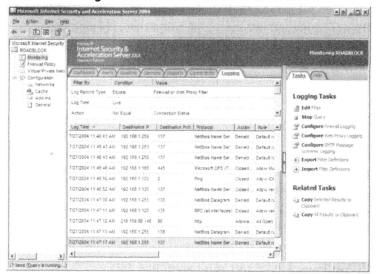

Real-time Monitoring and Filtering of Firewall Sessions

ISA Server 2004 allows you to view all active connections to the firewall. Using the **Sessions** tab in the **Monitoring** console, as shown in Figure 2.33, you can sort or disconnect individual or groups of sessions. You can also filter the entries in the Sessions interface to focus on specific sessions in which you're interested, using the built-in sessions filtering feature.

Figure 2.33 The Sessions Feature — View All Active Connections Through the Firewall

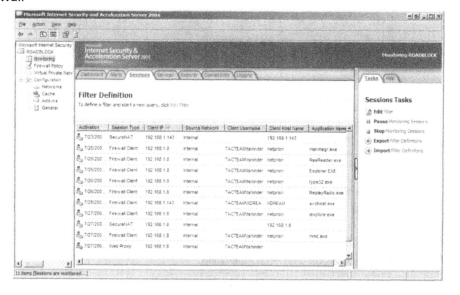

As shown, you can see the session type (whether the client is connecting via the firewall client, SecureNAT or as a Web Proxy client), the user's IP address, the user name and client computer name, and even the application that is being used.

This is useful for troubleshooting purposes and for determining if users are using unauthorized or problematic applications.

A Built-in Log-Querying Mechanism

With ISA Server 2004, you can query the log files using the built-in log-query mechanism. You can query the logs for information contained in any field recorded in the log files. The results appear in the ISA Server 2004 console's log viewer and can be copied to the clipboard and pasted into another application for more detailed analysis.

You can configure filters to limit the results of the query. For example, you can limit the scope of the query to a specific time frame, or specify that the query use live (real-time) data. Configuration is simple, as shown in Figure 2.34.

Figure 2.34 Configure Filters to Limit Query Results

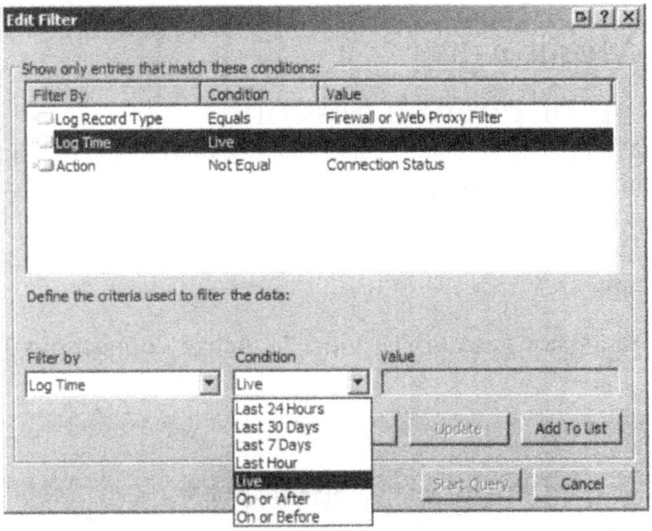

NOTE

The log viewer can be used to view information about the Firewall and Web Proxy logs, but not the SMTP Message Screener log.

You can filter by many different criteria in addition to the log time, including (but not limited to) client or destination IP address, user name, protocol, server name, service, or URL.

We discuss how to filter queries in much more detail in Chapter 12, *Using ISA Server 2004's Monitoring, Logging and Reporting Tools.*

Connection Verifiers

ISA Server 2004 provides the ability to verify connectivity by regularly monitoring connections to a specific computer or URL from the ISA Server 2004 computer, using Connection Verifiers through the **Connectivity** tab on the **Monitoring** console. You can configure which method to use to determine connectivity: ping, TCP connect to a port, or HTTP GET. You can select which connection to monitor, by specifying an IP address, computer name, or URL.

A Connectivity Verifier Wizard walks you through the process of creating new connection verifiers.

Better Customization of Reports

ISA Server 2000 allowed some limited customization of the reports generated by the firewall. However, ISA Server 2004 includes an enhanced report customization feature that allows you to include more information in the firewall reports.

The New Report Wizard helps you customize one-time reports, and the New Report Job Wizard helps you customize scheduled report jobs. In either case, you can select the content to be included, time period covered, and whether/where to publish the report.

Ability to Publish Reports

With ISA Server 2004, individual reports or report jobs can be configured to automatically save a copy of a report to a local folder or network file share. The published reports are saved in HTML format, and the folder or file share in which the reports are saved can be mapped to a Web site virtual directory so that other users can view the report. You can also manually publish reports that have not been configured to automatically publish after report creation.

E-mail Notification for Report Jobs

In both the New Report Wizard and the New Report Job Wizard in ISA 2004, you can configure a report or report job to send you or another administrator an e-mail message after a report or job is completed. You can customize the message to be sent, and if you have configured the report to be published, you can automatically include a link to the report within the e-mail message.

Ability to Configure Time of Log Summary

ISA Server 2000 was hard-coded to create log summaries at 12:30 A.M. each day. Reports are based on information contained in log summaries, so this limited the time of day when an accurate report could be generated. ISA Server 2004 allows you to easily customize the time for creating log summaries. This, in turn, gives you increased flexibility in determining the time of day your reports are to be created.

The default time is still 12:30 A.M., but changing it is as easy as clicking the **Up** and **Down** arrows in a box, as shown in Figure 2.35.

Figure 2.35 With ISA Server 2004, You Can Change the Time when the Log Summaries are Generated

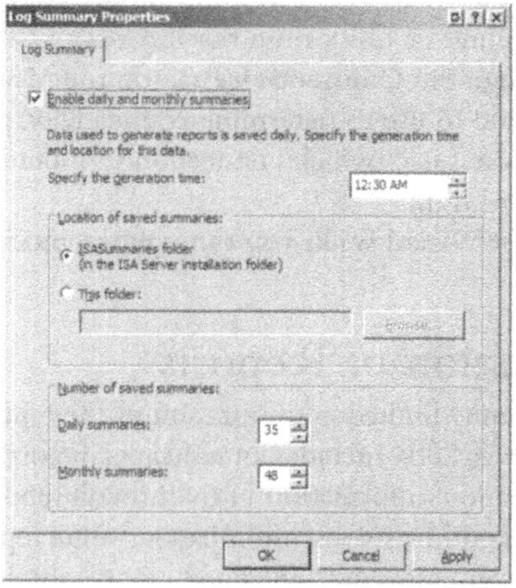

Better SQL Logging

With ISA Server 2004, you can log to a SQL database that is located on another machine on the Internal network. ISA Server 2004 SQL logging has also been optimized to provide much higher performance in comparison to SQL logging in ISA Server 2000.

We discuss how to set up logging to a remote SQL server in Chapter 12, *Using ISA Server 2004's Monitoring, Logging and Reporting Tools.*

Ability to Log to an MSDE Database

With ISA Server 2004, logs can now be stored in Microsoft Data Engine (MSDE) format. Logging to a local database enhances query speed and flexibility. Data that you save in an MSDE database can be viewed in the log viewer and saved in a text file.

TIP

If you have a SQL Server 2000 license, you can use your SQL tools (such as Enterprise Manager, query tools, and so on.) to view the database and conduct queries.

We discuss how to set up logging to an MSDE database in Chapter 12, *Using ISA Server 2004's Monitoring, Logging and Reporting Tools.*

New Features on the Block

In addition to all the improved features discussed in the previous section, Microsoft has added a number of completely new features to ISA Server 2004. In the following sections, we look at three of the most significant new features:

- Multi-networking support
- New Application Layer Filtering (ALF) features
- VPN Quarantine Control

Multi-Networking Support

A big limitation of ISA 2000 was the fact that it did not support multiple networks. Today's complex networks demand that you be able to work with multiple networks and define the relationships between them. With ISA Server 2004, Microsoft has introduced a multi-networking model that is appropriate for the interconnected networks used by many corporations. Now you can create network rules and control how different networks communicate with one another.

ISA Server 2004 includes several built-in network definitions, including:

- The Internal network (includes the addresses on the primary protected network)
- The External network (includes addresses that don't belong to any other network)
- The VPN clients network (includes the addresses assigned to VPN clients)
- The Local host network (includes the IP addresses on the ISA Server)

You can configure one or more networks, each with distinct relationships to each other network. In ISA Server 2000, all traffic was inspected relative to a local address table (LAT), which included only address ranges on the Internal network, but ISA Server 2004 extends the firewall and security features to apply to traffic between any networks or network objects.

Per-network Policies

ISA Server 2004's new multi-networking features make it easy for you to protect your network against internal and external security threats, by limiting communication between clients, even within your own organization. Multi-networking functionality supports sophisticated perimeter network (also known as a DMZ, demilitarized zone, or screened subnet) scenarios, allowing you to configure how clients in different networks access the perimeter network. Access policy between networks can be based on the unique security zone that is represented by each network.

Network Relationships

You can also use ISA Server 2004 to define the routing relationship between networks, depending on the type of access and communication required between the networks. For example, in some cases you would want more secure, less transparent communication between the networks. You can define a network address translation (NAT) relationship for these networks. In other scenarios, you might want to just route traffic through the ISA Server; in this case, you would define a routed relationship. Unlike with ISA Server 2000, the packets that move between the routed networks are all fully exposed to ISA Server 2004's stateful filtering and inspection mechanisms.

Network Templates

ISA Server 2004 provides network templates that you can use to easily configure firewall policy governing the traffic between multiple networks. These are designed to address common scenarios, including:

- ISA Server as edge firewall
- Perimeter network (DMZ)
- ISA as front-end firewall with a third-party back end firewall
- ISA Server deployed between a perimeter network and the Internal network
- Caching/Web Proxy server with a single NIC

You will learn more about how to configure multi-networking, create networking rules and apply network templates in Chapter 4, *Preparing the Network Infrastructure for ISA Server 2004.*

New Application Layer Filtering (ALF) Features

Application Layer Filtering is one of ISA Server 2004's strong points; unlike a traditional packet filtering firewall, ISA can delve deep into application layer communications to protect your network from the many modern exploits that occur at this layer. ISA Server 2000's ALF functionality has been enhanced by the addition of the following new features:

- Per-rule HTTP filtering
- Ability to block access to all executables
- Ability to control HTTP downloads by file extension
- Application of HTTP filtering to all client connections
- Control of HTTP access based on signatures
- Control over allowed HTTP methods
- Ability to force secure Exchange RPC connections
- Policy-based control over FTP
- Link Translation

In the following subsections, we'll have a look at each of these.

Per-rule HTTP Filtering

ISA Server 2004's HTTP policy allows the firewall to perform deep HTTP stateful inspection (application layer filtering). You can configure the extent of the inspection on a per-rule basis. This means that you can configure custom constraints for HTTP inbound and outbound access. With ISA Server 2000, HTTP filtering had to be performed globally, using a version of URLscan installed with Feature Pack 1 for ISA Server 2000.

Ability to Block Access to All Executables

You can configure ISA Server 2004's HTTP policy to block all connection attempts to Windows executable content, regardless of the file extension used on the resource. This blocks all responses in which the first word of the downloaded binary is MZ. You can also block by file extension (see the next subsection).

WARNING
_____

Blocking all *Windows* executables does not necessarily block all file types that can be dangerous. For example, .pif and .com files are not blocked by this filter because the first two bytes of the binaries are not MZ. You can block these other potentially dangerous file types by configuring filters to block by file extension.

_____

NOTE
_____

The first two bytes of the file contain its file signature. The MZ file signature, originally used for MS-DOS executable files, stands for the name of Microsoft programmer Mark Zbikowski.

_____

Ability to Control HTTP Downloads by File Extension

ISA Server 2004's HTTP policy makes it easy for you to allow all files extensions, allow all except a specified group of extensions, or block all extensions except for a specified group. This gives you a lot of flexibility in controlling what types of files can be downloaded by users, especially since this is done on a per-rule basis. This means you can apply the blocking of certain extensions to specific users or groups.

Application of HTTP Filtering to All Client Connections

ISA Server 2000 was able to block content for Web Proxy clients based on HTTP and FTP connections by MIME type (for HTTP) or file extension (for FTP). With ISA Server 2004's HTTP policy, you can control HTTP access for all ISA Server 2004 client connections, regardless of client type. There was no deep inspection of outbound connections, out of the box, with ISA Server 2000.

Control of HTTP Access Based on Signatures

ISA Server 2004's deep HTTP inspection also allows you to create "HTTP Signatures" that can be compared to the Request URL, Request headers, Request body, Response headers, and Response body. This allows you to exercise extremely precise control over the content that internal and external users can access through the ISA Server 2004 firewall.

A signature is a character string for which ISA Server will search the request body, request header, response body, and/or response header. If the string is found, the data will be blocked. You can search for either a text or binary string. Blocking based on text signatures can only be done if the HTTP requests and responses are UTF-8 encoded.

Control Over Allowed HTTP Methods

You can control which HTTP methods are to be allowed through the firewall by setting access controls on user access to various methods. For example, you can limit the HTTP POST method to prevent users from sending data to Web sites using the HTTP POST method. You can select to allow all methods, allowed selected methods, or block specified methods and allow all others.

> **NOTE**
>
> HTTP methods are commands that tell the server what action to perform on a given request. They are also sometimes referred to as "HTTP verbs" because they consist of action words: GET (retrieve the data identified by theURI), PUT (store the data under the URL), POST (create an object linked to the specified object), and so on.

Ability to Force Secure Exchange RPC Connections

ISA Server 2004's Secure Exchange Server Publishing Rules allow remote users to connect to the Exchange server by using the fully functional Outlook MAPI client over the Internet. However, the Outlook client must be configured to use secure RPC so that the connection will be encrypted. ISA Server 2004's RPC policy allows you to block all non-encrypted Outlook MAPI client connections.

With traditional firewalls, you have to open a number of ports to enable remote access to Exchange RPC services with the Outlook MAPI client, creating a security risk. With ISA Server 2004, the RPC filter solves this problem.

Policy-based Control Over FTP

You can configure ISA Server 2004's FTP policy to allow users to upload and download via FTP, or you can limit user FTP access to download only. This gives you more control over FTP activity and more granular security. By selecting **Read Only** on the **Protocols** tab when you configure FTP filtering, you block FTP uploads.

The FTP access filter is more functional than a user-defined FTP protocol because it dynamically opens specified ports for the secondary connection and can perform the address translation that is required by the secondary connection. The filter is also able to differentiate between read and write permissions, so you can granularly control access.

Link Translation

Some of your published Web sites might include references to the NetBIOS names of computers. Only the ISA Server 2004 firewall and external namespace, and not the internal network namespace, is available to external clients. That means when external clients try to access the sites via these links, these references will appear to be broken links.

ISA Server 2004 includes a link translation feature, which allows you to create a dictionary of definitions for internal computer names that map to publicly-known names. This is especially useful, for example, when publishing SharePoint Web sites. The link translation directory can also translate requests that are made to ports other than the standard ports, and the link translator will include the port number when it sends the URL back to the client.

NOTE

Although link translation was not available as a feature of ISA Server 2000 out of the box, it can be added to ISA 2000 by installing Feature Pack 1.

TIP

By default, link translation only works with HTML documents, but you can add other content groups if you wish.

> **WARNING**
>
> If your document contains internal links that have not been mapped to their appropriate external links in the link translation dictionary, the internal NetBIOS names will be exposed to external users. This can pose a security risk because it allows outsiders to know what the internal computer names are.

VPN Quarantine Control

This is another feature that was not available in ISA Server 2000. ISA Server 2004 leverages the Network Access Quarantine Control feature built into Windows Server 2003 to provide VPN quarantine, which allows you to quarantine VPN clients on a separate network until they meet a predefined set of security requirements. Even if ISA Server 2004 is installed on Windows 2000, you can still use quarantine control, with some limitations. In either case, you are able to specify conditions that VPN clients must meet in order to be allowed on the Internal network, such as the following:

- Security updates and service packs must be installed
- Anti-virus software must be installed and enabled
- Personal firewall software must be installed and enabled

VPN clients that pass the pre-defined security tests are allowed network access based on the VPN client firewall policies. VPN clients who fail security testing may be provided limited access to servers that will help them meet network security requirements (for example, servers where they can download the patches and updates they need).

Benefits of ISA Server 2004 VPN Quarantine Control

VPN quarantine control is an exciting feature that helps to protect your network from remote users who establish VPN connections from client computers that don't have their security patches and service packs up to date, don't have anti-virus software installed and enabled, and/or don't have personal firewalls to prevent Internet attacks. A number of other firewall vendors offer similar functionality, although usually with a different name—but in most cases, you must use their proprietary VPN client software (at extra cost) to take advantage of this feature. With ISA Server 2004, no special client software is required; clients use the PPTP or L2TP clients built into all modern Windows operating systems.

Options for Using VPN Quarantine Control

To use VPN quarantine control through Routing and Remote Access, ISA Server 2004 needs to be installed on a Windows Server 2003 computer. You are then able to quarantine VPN clients based on RADIUS server policies. If ISA Server 2004 is installed on a Windows 2000 server, you can still enable quarantine mode via the ISA Server and set a firewall policy for the Quarantined VPN clients network.

Quarantine control is great for enforcing compliance with your organization's security policy when users access the network from an outside location using a VPN, but setting it up is not a no-brainer. You must create Connection Manager profiles and connectoids for your VPN clients using the Connection Manager Administration Kit (CMAK) that comes with Windows 2000 server and Windows Server 2004.

You can then enable quarantine on the server, either using RADIUS policy or using ISA Server policy. Microsoft recommends that you use RADIUS policy if you are running ISA on a Windows Server 2003 computer and you have a RADIUS server on the network. Otherwise, you'll have to use ISA Server policy.

You can set the amount of time that a client will stay in quarantine when trying to connect through the VPN. If the client doesn't comply with the security policy requirements within this specified time period, allowing it to move from the Quarantined VPN clients network to the VPN clients network, it will be disconnected. If you have certain clients that should not be quarantined even if they don't pass the security test (the big boss's computer, for example), you can create an exemption list so that quarantine won't be applied to them.

Requirements for Enabling VPN Quarantine Control

To use quarantine control, you have to install a listener component on the ISA Server firewall. This is a software construct that listens for messages from the VPN clients that tell the ISA server that the quarantine control script has been run successfully. The listener listens for messages from the notifier component. The ISA Server 2004 Resource Kit contains a listener, the Remote Access Quarantine Agent service (Rqs.exe), and a notifier component (Rqc.exe) that you can use, or you can create your own listener. When the client computer is in compliance with the security policies, the notifier sends a notification message to the listener, and the client is removed from quarantine.

Here's the tricky part: you have to be adept at scripting to create the quarantine script that will be run on the client computer by the Connection Manager profile.

WARNING

The notification message isn't encrypted nor is it authenticated. This means it is possible for a hacker to spoof the message.

What about clients that don't comply with the policy? You can set up a Web server that allows anonymous access for those clients to download instructions and/or software that's needed to come into compliance. The quarantined clients can access this server, but cannot access other resources on the network.

We discuss how to configure ISA Server 2004 quarantine control policies in Chapter 9, *Creating Remote Access and Site-to-Site VPNs with ISA Firewalls.*

Missing in Action: Gone but Not Forgotten

ISA Server 2004 offers some great new features and many improvements and enhancements to features that were present, but less functional or less friendly, in ISA Server 2000. However, we would be remiss if we didn't mention that there are a few features you might have used in ISA Server 2000 that are "missing in action" when it comes to ISA Server 2004.

Most ISA Server firewall administrators won't miss these features, as they were ones that either were not used much or didn't work well in ISA 2000. However, take note, and if you have a specific need for these features, you might consider not upgrading to ISA 2004, or adding a third-party product that can handle these functions. The most significant "gone but not forgotten features" are:

■ Live media stream splitting

■ The H.323 gateway

■ Bandwidth control

■ Active caching

Let's briefly address what each of these features does and why Microsoft chose not to include them in ISA Server 2004.

Live Media Stream Splitting

ISA Server 2000 was able to split live media streams using Windows Media Technologies (WMT) to reduce the amount of bandwidth used for streaming audio or video, depending on the number of internal clients that were viewing the same streaming media. If a large number of people within your organization often viewed or listened to the same streaming media source, this could be beneficial. The feature could be applied to streams that used a WMT server located on the internal network, or you could install the WMT server on the ISA Server itself.

According to customer feedback, most companies implementing ISA Server did not use the streaming media splitting feature, so Microsoft did not include it in ISA Server 2004.

H.323 Gateway

The H.323 gateway is used for call handling and routing of Voice over IP (VoIP) calls. VoIP allows you to make voice calls over the Internet instead of using telephone company lines. This can result in a big savings in long distance charges for organizations that must make many long distance calls.

Problems were reported with memory leaks in the ISA Server gatekeeper service when malformed packets were directed at the service. These attacks had no effect if the H.323 gateway was not configured on the ISA Server. Although the problem was corrected with ISA Server 2000 Service Pack 1, many users stopped using the H.323 gateway service or did not use it because of these problems and because configuration of the H.323 gateway was difficult for many ISA Server users to figure out. Further, many newer VoIP products use the Session Initiation Protocol (SIP) instead of H.323. SIP is less complex and was designed as an alternative to H.323. Cisco and other vendors market IP phones that are based on SIP (Cisco also has its own proprietary VoIP protocol called Skinny). In order for H.323 to be effective, both sides of the connection have to have an H.323 gateway.

Microsoft dropped support for the H.323 gateway in ISA Server 2004 because of low usage due to these causes.

Bandwidth Control

ISA Server 2000 included a bandwidth control feature. You could right-click on the Bandwidth Rules node and check a box to enable bandwidth control, then set an effective bandwidth in Kbps. Effective bandwidth refers to either the actual bandwidth used by a device such as a modem, or overall network bandwidth. You could use bandwidth rules to specify which connections would have priority over others.

Although it seemed like a good idea, users complained that bandwidth controls in ISA Server 2000 didn't work, or didn't work as expected. Users expected bandwidth controls to limit the amount of bandwidth that could be used by each connection. This was not how it worked. Instead, the bandwidth rules were used by the quality of service (QoS) packet scheduling service to determine how connections should be prioritized. More disconcertingly, even when you understood what the bandwidth rules did and didn't do and configured them correctly, there were widespread problems with the rules ceasing to work over time. The only solution seemed to be to reformat and reinstall the operating system and ISA Server—not something that the average firewall administrator wants to do on a regular basis.

For these reasons, support for the bandwidth control feature was dropped in ISA Server 2004.

Active Caching

ISA Server 2000 supported not only forward/reverse and distributed/hierarchical caching types, but also supported active caching. This feature would automatically initiate requests to update objects that were stored in cache without any intervention from the user. These updates could be triggered based on the amount of time the object had been cached or when it had last been retrieved from the source server. When active caching was enabled, ISA Server would automatically refresh the cache content before objects expired. The ISA server kept track of which objects in the cache were most popular, and re-cached them even if no one had requested them.

You were able to configure the active caching policy to determine how frequently objects should be updated to balance the need for up-to-date cached objects with network performance concerns.

Although active caching can ensure that frequently-requested objects are kept up to date, it also can use a lot of network bandwidth and impact overall network performance. Active caching was not enabled by default in ISA Server 2000, and input from customers indicated that it was not a feature that was important to most Microsoft ISA Server users. In keeping with Microsoft's emphasis on firewall functionality in ISA Server 2004, the active caching feature was left out.

Summary

ISA Server 2004 is loaded with features. This chapter discussed the completely revamped graphical user interface, which is one of the most obvious changes that has been made to the ISA Server software. With ISA Server 2004, Microsoft has taken another big step away from Proxy Server and into the arena of serious firewall products. Although it is built on the shoulders of ISA Server 2000, ISA Server 2004 is, in many ways, a completely new product rather than a version upgrade. The emphasis is, more than ever, on security.

ISA Server 2004 still retains many of the same features that were available in ISA Server 2000, but most of them have been improved or enhanced. From more functional wizards to greater configuration flexibility to entirely new ways to perform old familiar firewall administration tasks, ISA Server has seen a lot of changes.

Microsoft has also added some brand new features to ISA Server 2004. The most extensive and perhaps the most welcome new feature is multi-networking support, which extends ISA Server 2004's ability to function as the firewall of choice in large, complex networking environments. New Application Layer Filtering (ALF) features give ISA Server 2004 even more of an edge when it comes to such functions as front-line defense against spam, and VPN quarantine control gives administrators a powerful way to ensure that remote VPN clients must meet the same standards in regard to security configurations as do the clients on the Internal network.

In this chapter, we did not attempt to cover every single feature that has been improved or added to ISA Server. We did attempt to give you a good idea of some of the differences between ISA Server 2004 and its predecessor. This chapter didn't go into details on how to use all of these new and improved features, but we introduced you to many of them and will provide step-by-step instructions for their use in later chapters of the book.

We also took a moment to mourn a few dearly departed friends: features we had grown to love (or in some cases, not love) in ISA Server 2000 that didn't make it into ISA Server 2004. Overall, we think ISA Server 2004's feature set is a solid one, and we find it much easier to set up and administer. The extent of our faith in ISA Server 2004 can be illustrated by the fact that we currently have multiple ISA Server 2004 machines protecting our own network. Feature-for-feature, we believe ISA Server is one of the best firewall/caching solutions available for the money. In the next chapter, we'll compare it to some of its competitors and show you why we think it stacks up.

Solutions Fast Track

New GUI: More Than Just a Pretty Face

☑ Improving the user experience by making the interface friendlier was a major goal of the ISA Server 2004 development team, and they've done a good job.

☑ The ISA Server 2004 console is much richer than that of ISA 2000, with a three-pane window that still includes the familiar tree structure in the left pane, but gives you tabbed pages in the middle and right panes that make it easy to select the type of tasks you want to perform and get precise help in performing them.

☑ The left pane nodes include: ISA Server (Name) Top Node, Monitoring Node, Firewall Policy Node, Virtual Private Networks (VPN) Node, and Configuration Node.

☑ The Configuration Node contains four subnodes: Networks, Cache, Add-ins, and General.

☑ The Getting Started page makes it easy to set up the ISA Server firewall and/or caching server.

☑ The *Dashboard* is just what its name implies — a "big picture" view that summarizes each of the Monitoring areas represented by a tab (except Logging).

☑ The firewall policy node is the "heart" of the ISA Server interface. This is where you create access rules, Web publishing rules, mail server publishing rules, and other server publishing rules to control access to and from your network.

☑ The *Virtual Private Networks* node provides a friendly interface for performing common VPN configuration tasks and controlling client access.

☑ The *Networks* tab (Configuration node) is used to create and configure networks in a multiple network environment.

☑ The *Cache* subnode is used to define cache drives, create cache rules, configure general cache settings or disable caching altogether, making the ISA server function solely as a firewall.

☑ The *Add-ins* subnode is used to configure ISA Server's application layer filtering (ALF). This is where you enable, view, modify, and disable application filters and Web filters.

☑ The *General* subnode includes general administrative tasks.

Teaching Old Features New Tricks

☑ If your company has multiple ISA Server installations in different locations, you don't want to have to physically visit every ISA Server machine to perform management tasks on each.

☑ Three ways to remotely manage your ISA Server firewalls are: the ISA Server management console, Windows 2000 terminal services or Server 2003 remote desktop, and through a third-party Web interface.

☑ ISA Server 2004 allows you to control access and usage of any protocol, including IP-level protocols.

☑ Improvements have been made to the authentication process in ISA Server 2004. Users can be authenticated via the built-in Windows authentication or Remote Authentication Dial-In User Service (RADIUS) or other namespaces.

☑ It is now easier to set up Outlook Web Access (OWA) to work with ISA 2004, thanks to the OWA Publishing wizard.

☑ With ISA Server 2004, you have more flexibility in defining network objects because you can specify them according to the following categories: Networks, Network sets, Computers, Computer sets, Address ranges, Subnets, URL sets, Domain name sets, and Web listeners.

☑ ISA Server 2004 includes a new set of rule wizards that make it easier than ever to create access policies.

☑ In ISA Server 2000, the Server Publishing Rules forwarded incoming connections to a published server on the same port where the original request was received. ISA Server 2004 allows you to receive a connection on a particular port number and then redirect the request to a different port number on the published server.

☑ ISA Server 2004 includes many improvements and enhancements to VPN and remote access functionality, including more flexibility for site-to-site VPN links, better control over VPN clients, PPTP server publishing, and forced Encryption for Secure Exchange RPC Connections.

☑ Several improvements have been made to the Web Cache and Web Proxy features in ISA Server, including improvements to the Cache Rule Wizard, more flexibility in caching of SSL content, path mapping for Web Publishing Rules, and enhancements to scheduled content download.

☑ Microsoft has listened to customers and made a number of improvements and additions to ISA Server 2004's logging, monitoring, and reporting functions. These include real-time monitoring of log entries, real-time monitoring and filtering of firewall sessions, a built-in log querying mechanism, connection verifiers, ability to customize reports, ability to publish reports, e-mail notification for report jobs, ability to configure time of log summary, better SQL logging, and the ability to log to an MSDE database.

New Features on the Block

☑ With ISA Server 2004, Microsoft has introduced a multi-networking model that is appropriate for interconnected networks used by many corporations.

☑ Now you can create network rules and control how different networks communicate with one another.

☑ ISA Server 2004 includes several built-in network definitions, including: the Internal network (includes the addresses on the primary protected network), the External network (includes addresses that don't belong to any other network), the VPN clients network (includes the addresses assigned to VPN clients), and the Local host network (includes the IP addresses on the ISA Server).

☑ ISA Server 2004's new multi-networking features make it easy for you to protect your network against internal and external security threats by limiting communication between clients, even within your own organization.

☑ You can use ISA Server 2004 to define the routing relationship between networks, depending on the type of access and communication required between the networks.

☑ ISA Server 2004 provides network templates that you can use to easily configure firewall policy governing the traffic between multiple networks.

☑ ISA Server 2004's HTTP policy allows the firewall to perform deep HTTP stateful inspection (application layer filtering). You can configure the extent of the inspection on a per-rule basis.

☑ You can configure ISA Server 2004's HTTP policy to block all connection attempts to Windows executable content, regardless of the file extension used on the resource.

☑ ISA Server 2004's HTTP policy makes it easy for you to allow all file extensions, allow all except a specified group of extensions, or block all extensions except for a specified group.

☑ With ISA Server 2004's HTTP policy, you can control HTTP access for all ISA Server 2004 client connections, regardless of client type.

☑ ISA Server 2004's deep HTTP inspection also allows you to create "HTTP Signatures" that can be compared to the Request URL, Request headers, Request body, Response headers, and Response body.

☑ You can control which HTTP methods are allowed through the firewall by setting access controls on user access to various methods.

☑ ISA Server 2004's Secure Exchange Server Publishing Rules allow remote users to connect to the Exchange server by using the fully-functional Outlook MAPI client over the Internet.

☑ You can configure ISA Server 2004's FTP policy to allow users to upload and download via FTP, or you can limit user FTP access to download only.

☑ ISA Server 2004 includes a link translation feature, which allows you to create a dictionary of definitions for internal computer names that map to publicly-known names.

☑ ISA Server 2004 leverages the Network Access Quarantine Control feature built into Windows Server 2003 to provide VPN quarantine, which allows you to quarantine VPN clients on a separate network until they meet a predefined set of security requirements.

☑ ISA Server 2004 adds support for port redirection and the ability to publish FTP servers on alternate ports.

Missing in Action: Gone But Not Forgotten

☑ ISA Server 2000 was able to split live media streams using Windows Media Technologies (WMT) to reduce the amount of bandwidth used for streaming audio or video, depending on the number of internal clients that were viewing the same streaming media. According to customer feedback, most companies implementing ISA Server did not use the streaming media splitting feature, so Microsoft did not include it in ISA Server 2004.

☑ The H.323 gateway is used for call handling and routing of Voice over IP (VoIP) calls. Microsoft dropped support for the H.323 gateway in ISA Server 2004 because of low usage.

☑ ISA Server 2000 included a bandwidth control feature, but users complained that bandwidth controls in ISA Server 2000 didn't work, or didn't work as expected. Support for the bandwidth control feature was dropped in ISA Server 2004.

☑ ISA Server 2000 supported not only forward/reverse and distributed/hierarchical caching types, but also supported active caching. This feature would automatically initiate requests to update objects that were stored in cache without any intervention from the user. In keeping with Microsoft's emphasis on firewall functionality in ISA Server 2004, the active caching feature was left out.

Frequently Asked Questions

The following Frequently Asked Questions, answered by the authors of this book, are designed to both measure your understanding of the concepts presented in this chapter and to assist you with real-life implementation of these concepts. To have your questions about this chapter answered by the author, browse to **www.syngress.com/solutions** and click on the **"Ask the Author"** form. You will also gain access to thousands of other FAQs at ITFAQnet.com.

Q: Is ISA Server 2004 a firewall or a cache server?

A: ISA Server 2000 can be configured as an integrated firewall and caching solution, or it can be deployed as a locked-down firewall only. The caching feature is disabled by default and is enabled only after a firewall administrator acts to enable it. Organizations require a robust firewall solution. The ISA Server 2004 firewall secures their networks with ISA Server 2004 dynamic packet filtering (stateful filtering), intrusion detection, system hardening, and deep application layer inspection. Microsoft's emphasis in developing and marketing ISA Server 2004 is on its firewall functionality.

Q: Does implementing the cache functionality compromise the security of ISA Server as a firewall?

A: No. The cache is a sophisticated memory and disk-based storage engine that allows improved network access performance by storing frequently retrieved objects. The Web cache is integrated into the firewall service engine that provides Hypertext Transfer Protocol (HTTP) connectivity, filtering capabilities, and security-related tasks such as content screening and Uniform Resource Locator (URL) blocking.

Q: Can I deploy only the firewall functionality?

A: The ISA Server 2004 firewall architecture is quite different than the ISA Server 2000 architecture. Because of this, the ISA Server 2004 firewall does not distinguish between firewall and caching services – all services are mediated by the hardened firewall service. You can completely disable Web caching if your organization does not require it.

Q: Do I have to run Active Directory to use an ISA Server 2004 firewall?

A: No. Active Directory is not required. While the ISA Server 2004 firewall can leverage the users and groups contained in the Active Directory to provide granular inbound and outbound access control that no other firewall on the market can provide, you do not need an Active Directory or NT domain to benefit from an ISA Server 2004 firewall.

Q: How does ISA Server handle streaming media?

A: ISA Server 2004 includes application filters that manage complex media streaming connections. It specifically supports Microsoft Windows Media–based streaming, RealAudio and Apple QuickTime. ISA Server 2004 has dropped support for media stream splitting.

Q: How do ISA Server 2004 access policies differ from ISA Server 2000

A: ISA Server 2000 access policy was based on Protocol Rules, Site and Content Rules, IP Packet Filters, Server Publishing Rules and Web Publishing Rules where deny rules were processed before allow rules. In contrast, ISA Server 2004 access policy is a single, unified ordered list of Firewall Rules that are applied from top to bottom. The rule highest on the list that matches the characteristics of the connection is applied.

Q: How does ISA Server 2004 support Exchange Server?

A: ISA Server 2004 provides a unique level of protection for Microsoft Exchange Servers. Remote access to Microsoft Exchange can be done in a highly secure fashion using ISA Server 2004 secure RPC publishing, secure Outlook Web Access Publishing, and secure POP3/IMAP4/SMTP publishing. The firewall performs SSL-to-SSL bridging, which provides a level of inspection of SSL stream content that no other firewall in ISA Server 2004's class can provide. In addition, the ISA Server 2004 firewall can perform form-based authentication on behalf of the OWA site on the internal network by generating the log on the form itself. This prevents non-authenticated connections to the OWA site.

Q: Can I put a VPN Server behind the ISA Server 2004 firewall?

A: Yes. Unlike ISA Server 2000, you can publish non-TCP/UDP protocols (GRE) using ISA Server 2004. You can publish a PPTP or NAT-T compliant L2TP/IPSec VPN server located behind the ISA Server 2004 firewall. In fact, you can make the ISA Server 2004 firewall a VPN server itself and publish a VPN server located behind the ISA Server 2004 firewall.

Q: What is ISA Server 2004 Multi-networking?

A: ISA Server 2004 multi-networking greatly increases the flexibility you have in deploying the firewall and expands on the LAT-based network view used by ISA Server 2000 firewalls. ISA Server 2004 firewalls apply firewall policy to all network interfaces and the firewall administrator can set the routing relationship between these interfaces. Each Firewall Rule includes a reference to the source and destination network. Unlike with other firewalls, you do not need to create rules for each interface because the ISA Server 2004 firewall automatically creates the required stateful filters to allow or deny the connection based on interfaces used for the source and destination networks.

Q: What is the Firewall System Policy?

A: Firewall System Policy is a default set of Firewall Rules that allows the ISA Server 2004 firewall to communicate with vital network infrastructure services on the internal network. The Firewall System Policy takes effect immediately after the ISA Server 2004 software is installed. The firewall administrator can adjust Firewall System Policy after the firewall is started the first time.

Q: What VPN Protocols does ISA Server 2004 support?

A: ISA Server 2004 supports PPTP and L2TP/IPSec for client/server VPN connections. When ISA Server 2004 is installed on Windows Server 2003, the VPN client can take advantage of IPSec NAT traversal (NAT-T). This allows the VPN client, VPN server, or both to be located behind NAT devices and use a secure L2TP/IPSec connection. ISA Server 2004 firewalls support PPTP, L2TP/IPSec, and IPSec tunneling more for site-to-site VPN links.

Q: What is Application Layer Filtering?

A: Application layer filtering allows the ISA Server 2004 firewall to determine the validity of communications moving through it by examining application layer protocol commands and data. The ISA Server 2004 firewall is configured to recognize legitimate commands and data for the application layer protocol, then pass valid connections and reject invalid ones. Traditional firewalls are not able to assess the validity of a connection attempt or message because they are only aware of source and destination IP addresses and port numbers. Traditional firewalls pass exploit code because they do not understand application layer protocols. ISA Server 2004 firewalls have a deep understanding of the most popular application layer protocols used on the Internet today. This understanding allows

ISA Server 2004 firewalls to protect your network from known and unknown exploits now and in the future.

Q: Does ISA Server 2004 Application Layer Filtering have an effect on performance?

A: Deep inspection of application layer protocol commands and data does incur some memory, disk, and processing overhead. The level of overhead is determined by the number of rules and communications per second the firewall evaluates. Larger Firewall rule sets generate greater overhead than smaller ones. ISA Server 2004 includes a built-in Performance console you can use to evaluate effects of different rule set configurations. Because ISA Server 2004 runs on PC architecture hardware, it's simple to upgrade the hardware component that performance analysis indicates is causing a bottleneck. Traditional hardware firewalls require that you purchase a new license, or worse, purchase a new device when hardware upgrades are required.

Q: Can I customize the presentation of the information displayed in ISA Server 2004 reports?

A: The ISA Server 2004 reporting engine allows you to customize many components of the built-in ISA Server 2004 reports. For example, you can increase the number of user names that appear in the Web usage report, the number of sites that appear in the Web usage report, and the sort order of applications that appear in the application usage report. This is just a small sample of the customizations you can make to the ISA Server 2004 reports.

Chapter 3

Stalking the Competition: How ISA 2004 Stacks Up

Topics in this Chapter:

- Firewall Comparative Issues

- Comparing ISA 2004 to Other Firewall Products

Firewall Comparative Issues

It hasn't been easy, trying to do our part to introduce ISA Server to the IT security community. Once we get past the basic question mentioned in Chapter 1 ("Is ISA Server really a firewall?"), the next thing potential users want to know is inevitably, "How does ISA Server compare to other firewalls?"

Often, the question comes as a challenge from CheckPoint or PIX aficionados. Other times it comes from new or experienced network administrators who have been tasked with the responsibility of selecting or recommending a firewall solution for their companies and who are confused and overwhelmed by the plethora of marketing material, claims of firewall vendors, and kudos or complaints they hear from other firewall users.

In order to intelligently answer the question, we've had to become acquainted not only with ISA Server 2004 itself, but with the features and pricing/licensing structures of competing products. This chapter is designed to serve three main purposes:

- Provide answers to some common questions for readers who are responsible for selecting a firewall and/or caching product for their networks.

- Provide a rational basis for selecting ISA Server 2004 that is predicated on evidence and fact, rather than bias.

- Provide "ammunition" for readers who already know they want to implement ISA Server 2004 on their networks and need to convince their companies' management.

If you take a look at the product lines of most of the major firewall appliance vendors, you'll find several different models, not to mention a variety of different licensing schemes, as well as plenty of add-ons that enhance functionality and come at extra cost.

Constructing an intelligent comparison of the products of different vendors can be a daunting task, and often there is no clear-cut "winner" in such a comparison. Instead, you find that making the right choice depends very much on your existing network infrastructure, the role you want the firewall to play, and a tradeoff of some features for others.

We often hear network administrators lament, "I can buy a SonicWall firewall for under $500. ISA Server costs three times that and doesn't even include the hardware." That's true — as far as it goes. Here is the rest of the story:

- The under-$500 SonicWall (or NetScreen, or WatchGuard) is not intended for use on a large or even medium-sized business network. These low-cost firewall appliances are the SOHO (Small Office/Home Office) and "telecommuter" models.

- SOHO firewalls are limited to a small number of users (usually 10-25), and telecommuter firewalls are designed to protect the single computer of someone working from home and connecting to the company network remotely (more like a personal firewall).

- SOHO and telecommuter firewalls may not support remote access VPN, or may come with only a single VPN license; additional VPN clients will cost extra. They may support a limited number of VPN tunnels (5-10), even with extra licenses.

- Low-end firewalls run on low-powered hardware. For example, the SonicWall SOHO 3 uses a 133MHz processor and 16MB of RAM, whereas you can select the hardware on which to install ISA Server and other software-based firewalls (as long as it meets the minimum requirements needed to run the OS and firewall).

- Performance/throughput for low-cost firewalls is often very low (for example, 75Mbps firewall throughput, in comparison to ISA Server's tested throughput of up to 1.5Gbps).

As you dig deeper into the comparative features, you begin to realize that a simple cost comparison is meaningless. A comparative analysis must also take into account the administrative overhead, licensing structure, and feature sets of the products being compared. To say, "I can buy a firewall for under $500" is like saying, "I can buy a watch for $5," or "I can buy a new car for $10,000." All of those statements are true, but many consumers still choose to spend $50 or $500 or even $5000 for a watch and $20,000, $30,000, or much more for a new car. Why? Most would tell you that issues of reliability, features, and longevity are important factors. Of course, status may also play a part in their decisions, especially at the extreme high end of the price scale.

Of course, if the under-$500 firewalls were all anyone needed to protect their networks, the same vendors wouldn't also offer firewalls that cost three, five, ten, or sometimes twenty times as much as their low-end products.

This chapter does not attempt to make the case that ISA Server is "the best" firewall product for every network in every situation. It does provide facts supporting our contention that ISA Server is a serious contender in the business firewall market and can hold its own in a competition with the "big boys" (Cisco and Check Point) and the many low-cost firewall/VPN appliances currently in use.

NOTE

In an enterprise environment, it is often neither necessary nor desirable to choose a single firewall solution for all applications. A good "defense-in-depth" strategy will often "mix and match" products from multiple vendors for the most effective protection against modern threats. For example, a company might decide to deploy one or more fast packet filtering firewalls, such as PIX, at the Internet edge and put a deep application layer filtering firewall, such as ISA Server, within the DMZ or in front of each departmental subnet.

In the following sections, we examine some factors that you should take into consideration when comparing different firewall products. These are separated into three broad categories:

- **Cost and licensing.** This includes not only the initial capital investment in the software, hardware, or appliance, but also special licensing considerations (such as the requirement for separate licenses for VPN clients), add-on modules and enhancements that are required to provide full competitive functionality, support contracts, the comparative cost of upgrading, and other factors that impact Total Cost of Ownership (TCO), such as administrative overhead, training requirements, and so on.

- **Specifications and features.** This refers to architecture and operating system, throughput and concurrent sessions supported, filtering features, and intrusion detection and prevention features, VPN features (protocol support, client support, number of tunnels supported, VPN quarantine/security), Web caching functionality (if any), and integration and interoperability with Windows and other servers.

- **Certification.** Certification by independent entities such as ICSA Labs in the U.S. and Checkmark in the U.K. can ensure that firewalls meet minimum criteria based on standardized testing.

The comparative analysis in this chapter is based on information gathered from vendor documentation, vendor queries, questionnaires targeting administrators who use the various products, and hands-on evaluation of (some of) the products.

WARNING

The information in this chapter is current as of the time of the research and writing, but the security software market is constantly changing. New products are introduced and existing products are upgraded on a daily basis. Changes in business structure or ownership are common (for example, one of the major companies addressed in this analysis, NetScreen, was bought by Juniper Networks a short time before the writing of this document) and might or might not result in changes to the products themselves.

The following analysis will compare ISA Server 2004's cost, features, and functionality with some of its primary competitors in the firewall market. The competitors we address in this chapter are:

- CheckPoint (including Nokia appliances)
- Cisco's PIX security appliances
- NetScreen security appliances (now owned by Juniper Networks)
- SonicWall security appliances

- Watchguard security appliances

- Symantec's Enterprise Firewall software (including Symantec appliances)

- Blue Coat Systems ProxySG appliances

- Open source firewalls (IPchains, Juniper FWTK, IPCop)

This by no means includes all available firewall products on the market today; however, it does include those with the largest market shares.

The Cost of Firewall Operations

To the network/security administrator, the cost of a firewall may not be first on the list of priorities in selecting the best product for your situation. You want the one that will get the job done most effectively and efficiently, and that will be easiest for you and your staff to deploy, manage, and update. However, to those who may have the ultimate decision-making authority (the Chief Financial Officer, purchasing agent, or small business owner), cost is a *very* important consideration.

It's important to remember, however, that cost involves a lot more than just the initial purchase price of an appliance or software/hardware package. Budget-minded decision-makers are concerned with the "bottom line," or the entire financial impact of the decision spread over the lifetime of the product. In comparing different products, you need to address each of the following:

- Capital investment

- Add-on modules and enhancements

- Licensing structures

- Support

- Upgrade

- Total Cost of Ownership

We address each of these in the following subsections.

Capital Investment

By "capital investment," we refer to both the initial cost of the software license and/or the hardware device, plus any additional add-on modules, client licenses, or other components that are required to deploy the firewall or caching solution with full functionality on your network. Many vendors advertise a "base price" that doesn't necessarily include everything that's required for what you want to do (for example, if you want to use the firewall as a VPN gateway, you may have to purchase licenses that are not included in the price of the firewall for each VPN client).

Add-on Modules and Enhancements

Many firewall products provide some of their functionality through add-on modules or additional "off-box" devices or software. For example, most firewall vendors don't provide Web caching as a standard feature of the firewall, but some allow you to add it through a software module (for example, CheckPoint) or offer an additional hardware device that performs the function (such as Cisco). ISA Server 2004, along with BlueCoat, builds Web caching into the firewall so that you save hundreds or even thousands of dollars because you don't have to buy additional software and/or devices to get that functionality.

To accurately compare the cost of ISA Server with these devices, you must also factor in the cost of add-ons required to give the same level of functionality ISA Server has "out of the box."

Some features and functionalities provided by vendors through add-ons include:

- Web caching
- IDS/IDP
- Virus scanning and detection
- Centralized management of multiple firewalls
- Report generation
- High availability/load balancing
- PKI/Smart card authentication

ISA Server 2004 includes many of these features right out of the box, so they don't add any extra cost.

In addition, it's important to note that because they don't include a hard disk to which log files can be written, ASIC devices often require separate computer hardware for logging. For example, you may need to set up a server to collect the PIX logs. This is often forgotten in cost considerations. People often complain that ISA requires the purchase of computer hardware and an OS license, but recording ASIC-generated log files frequently requires this expenditure, too.

Licensing Structures

Software licensing structures can be confusing, at best. However, it's important to understand each product's licensing structure in order to make a valid comparison. The licensing structure can greatly affect the total cost of the firewall/security device. Some vendors grant licenses on a subscription basis, requiring that you pay for the software license again each year. Others charge an initial licensing fee, with no additional fee required unless/until you upgrade to a new version of the product (and you may get a discounted licensing fee when you upgrade versus someone who is buying the product for the first time).

Licenses may also vary in price depending on how you intend to use the firewall. For example, the license for a second firewall in a failover/fault tolerance cluster may be lower than for the first license for the active firewall. Vendors may use different terminology to distinguish between licensing levels. For example, Cisco makes its PIX licenses available as either Restricted (R) or Unrestricted (U) licenses, in addition to Failover mode (FO) licenses. The licensing mode is defined by your activation key. A Restricted (R) license puts a limit on the number of interfaces that are supported, as well as the amount of RAM that will be available to the software. An Unrestricted (UR) license allows you to use all of the RAM that the hardware supports and the maximum number of interfaces supported by the hardware. A Restricted license does not support Failover configuration, while an Unrestricted license does. You can also buy a special "R to UR" license to upgrade from a Restricted license to an Unrestricted one or an "FO to R" or "FO to UR" license to upgrade from a Failover license to a Restricted or Unrestricted license.

Some firewalls are licensed according to number of "users." The firewall may enforce this by sending a ping and counting the replies from responding hosts (in which case, network printers and other devices that are assigned IP addresses might be counted as "users") or by keeping track of the number of internal nodes that are accessing the Internet on the external interface. For example, Check Point FireWall-1 (FW-1) listens for IP traffic on all internal interfaces and keeps count of the different IP addresses. When the number of IP addresses exceeds the license limit, e-mail notifications will be sent to administrators and the event will be logged.

Many vendors also have volume licensing plans or corporate licensing plans that offer lower rates to large customers or those who buy a large number of firewalls. Software firewall vendors may also offer evaluation licenses that expire after a specified number of days.

NOTE

One notable advantage of software firewalls such as ISA Server 2004, Check Point and Symantec Enterprise firewall is the ability to easily "try before you buy" by installing an evaluation version of the product.

You'll also want to consider whether additional licenses, other than for the firewall software itself, are needed for full functionality. Some vendors charge extra for VPN licenses for each VPN connection. Even when the cost is relatively low ($15-35 per license is typical), this can add up fast if you have hundreds of VPN users. You might also have to obtain an extra license to use certain features, such as 3DES encryption. Finally, you may need additional licenses to run add-on modules. For example, running the Motif GUI to connect to a Check Point FW-1 management console in FW-1 4.1 and above requires that you pay extra for a Motif license. LDAP (Lightweight Directory Access Protocol) functionality also requires an extra license if you want to use it with FW-1.

Support Costs

Another "hidden" cost factor that you should consider in comparing the cost of various solutions is the cost of support, which can vary widely depending on the vendor. Support contracts can cost from less than a hundred to several thousand dollars per year.

Some vendors include free support for a set period of time. For example, Cisco provides free tech support for 90 days, while Check Point FW-1 requires that you purchase a support/upgrade contract to access their tech support, with such contracts costing as much as 50 percent of the original software price, per year.

Some vendors have different levels of support contracts. For example, Symantec offers Gold, Platinum, and Premium Platinum Maintenance and Support contracts on their firewall products. Gold support provides telephone support during regular business hours, Monday through Friday, while Platinum support provides after-hours support. With Premium Platinum support, you get a Technical Account Manager and three additional technical contacts (Gold and regular Platinum provide for two technical contacts).

If you plan to purchase a support contract, the cost should be factored into your comparison.

> **NOTE**
>
> Some vendors require that you maintain the support agreement on a yearly basis. This means that if you let a support agreement lapse for a year, the vendor may require that you buy a support agreement for the current year *and* the lapsed year.

Upgrade Costs

The cost to upgrade the firewall is another important cost factor you must consider when doing a cost comparison. Software firewalls that are installed on standard hardware can easily take advantage of the addition of a faster or additional processor, faster network cards, more RAM, or installation on a new, more powerful machine. Hardware appliances, on the other hand, may have to be replaced completely, or may be more costly to upgrade. For example, the Cisco PIX Firewall Classic, 10000, and 510 models have been discontinued and cannot run PIX firewall software version 6.0 or later. This means if you want the features of the new software, you'll have to purchase a new PIX appliance.

> **NOTE**
>
> Another important consideration is if/when you need to upgrade to more powerful hardware for your software-based firewall, you can "repurpose" the original hardware to act as a file server, workstation, or in another role on the network. A hardware-based security appliance running a proprietary operating system has less potential for reuse.

Whether you have a "hardware firewall" or a "software firewall," the cost of upgrading the software at periodic intervals is also important. You'll want to consider the following:

- Are updates and fixes available free, or do you have to pay for them?

- Are there discounts for upgrade versions of the software, or must you buy the full version?

Another consideration might be the administrative overhead required to perform the upgrade. For example, upgrading a PIX running version 5.0 or earlier doesn't provide a way to use Trivial File Transfer Protocol (TFTP) to transfer the software image directly to the device's flash memory, so you have to enter boothelper or monitor mode. Newer versions of the PIX software support a command that allows you to copy the software image directly from the TFTP server to the device. Either way, you'll have to use a command line interface to enter the appropriate commands to upgrade the software.

Total Cost of Ownership

When all of the cost factors are taken into consideration, you can come up with a Total Cost of Ownership (TCO) for each product in order to make a more accurate price comparison. In calculating the TCO for each of the competing products, you must consider not only each of the direct costs we discussed in the preceding paragraphs, but also indirect costs such as:

- **Learning curve**: cost of materials, training courses, and such, required for administrators to learn to configure and manage the firewall.

- **Administrative overhead**: relative amount of administrative time required to configure and manage the firewall; level of administrative expertise required (which can increase personnel costs).

- **Productivity costs**: affect on productivity of network users.

- **Downtime costs**: both productivity losses and loss of revenues, for example from potential e-commerce sales, related to the deployment and reliability of the firewall.

Most TCO models divide all cost factors into two broad categories: acquisition costs and on-going or operational costs. The first category includes the purchase price of the hardware, the initial licensing fees for the software, and one-time installation costs, including the cost of administrative time, hiring of consultants if applicable, initial training, and so on. The second category includes vendor support contracts, internal IT administrative costs, hiring of independent consultants for troubleshooting and maintenance, hardware maintenance and upgrades, software updates and upgrades, on-going training, and other support costs. Of course, some of these costs will vary from one customer to another, depending on the way the firewall will be deployed and the experience and skill sets of current personnel.

NOTE

There is more price flexibility and you have more control over TCO with software firewalls because you can take advantage of competitive pricing among different hardware vendors, whereas with hardware-based firewalls, you may be limited to a small selection of different hardware configurations with less of a price variance between different resellers.

Specifications and Features

Once cost issues are out of the way and a budget is determined, the second broad category for comparison deals with features and functionalities for each product. We can divide this category into the following subcategories:

- General specifications (both hardware and software specs)
- Firewall features (including related features such as intrusion detection)
- VPN gateway functionality
- Web-caching features (if included)
- Firewall certification

Let's look at each of these separately.

General Specifications

General specifications relate to the included hardware (for appliances) or the minimum hardware requirements (for software firewalls), as well as how scalable, extensible, and reliable the product has proven to be in deployment, and whether and how it supports high availability/fault tolerance features such as clustering/failover and load balancing. Other important points of comparison include compatibility and interoperability with other software and devices on the network, and ease of use (which directly affects administrative overhead). The list below provides a starting point for comparing these specifications:

- **Hardware specifications.** This includes hardware architecture (software firewall, hard disk-based appliance, ASIC appliance). For software firewalls, you'll want to know the minimum system requirements as well as the maximum hardware resources that the firewall can utilize. This subcategory also includes processor speed, amount of memory, number of ports (and port type: 10/100 Ethernet, gigabit Ethernet, and so on), disk size (for hard disk-based devices), and other physical factors. This is an especially important point of comparison for hardware-based firewalls, since you may not be able to easily upgrade the hardware.

- **Scalability.** This refers to the ability of the software firewall or device to scale up as the organization and network grow. You'll want to consider such factors as how many connections the firewall can handle and how many simultaneous VPN tunnels are supported, as well as other factors, depending on your particular network setup. You'll also want the ability to configure multiple devices to work together and to provide for centralized management.

- **Extensibility.** This refers to the ease with which in-house developers or third parties can create add-ons to enhance the functionality of the firewall.

- **Reliability.** This refers to minimizing downtime and is a product of several factors, including hardware and software factors. For example, a reliability advantage of ASIC-based devices is the lack of moving parts, which eliminates the possibility of mechanical failure. Software reliability depends on programming accuracy and complexity of both the firewall application and the underlying operating system, as well as interoperability with any other applications (add-on modules, third-party enhancements, or other applications) running on the box. One element of reliability is *fault tolerance,* which refers to the ability of a system to continue to operate after a failure of one or more components.

- **High availability.** This is closely related to reliability and refers to redundancies (such as redundant power supplies or clustering of multiple firewalls with automatic failover) to ensure that functionality continues in case of hardware or software failure.

- **Load balancing.** This refers to the ability to spread the processing load across multiple firewall devices to enhance performance and accommodate increases in traffic.

- **Compatibility/interoperability.** This refers to the firewall's ability to interoperate with other devices, servers and clients on the network; for example, can the firewall integrate with your mail server to provide protection for RPC communications? In particular, if you are operating in a Windows network environment, you'll want to know how well the firewall integrates with Active Directory (can it use AD user and group accounts for authentication?), Exchange, SharePoint, and other Microsoft server products you have deployed on the network.

- **Ease of use.** This refers to simplicity of installation and configuration (applicable to software-based firewalls), user-friendliness of the management interface (GUI, Web-based, or CLI), and how easy it is to remotely manage the firewall and to centrally manage multiple firewalls.

TIP

Some factors, such as ease of use, are not quantifiable, but are rather the result of subjective assessment. An interface that seems friendly to one user might be confusing to another. Unlike hardware specifications or software features, such as number of VPN tunnels supported, you can't depend on vendor documentation to determine how easy an interface is to use. We recommend that when evaluating this factor, you talk with firewall administrators who have been using the product, or ideally, try the product yourself in a test lab environment. This is especially easy in the case of software firewalls that offer trial versions, and it is a step that shouldn't be skipped, as you'll be dealing with the interface every day.

Firewall and Related Features

There are several firewall-specific features that you should look for when comparing different vendors' products. Product data sheets from vendor Web sites can provide a starting point, but as you narrow your choices, you'll want to dig deeper and read independent product reviews and/or talk to IT professionals who have personally worked with the particular products you're considering.

Keep in mind that a vendors' claim that it supports a particular feature might not tell the full story; you must also evaluate *how* that feature is implemented. For example, Application Layer Filtering (ALF) might mean only that there are filters to detect a few application layer attacks, such as DNS or POP3 buffer overflows. The firewall might not support *deep* ALF (examination of the contents of data packets for particular administrator-defined text strings, for example).

TIP

Advertising material will always be slanted to show the product in the best light. Also note that different vendors often use different terminology to describe the same features, which makes it more difficult to compare products based only on vendor documentation. For example, the feature that Microsoft calls "SSL bridging" is referred to as "SSL termination and initiation" by some other vendors.

Some important firewall features to compare include the following:

■ **Application Layer Filtering**: Most modern firewall products now incorporate some form of ALF, but the level of ALF support can vary widely from one product to another. The most common implementation provides filters that check for application level attacks, such as those that exploit DNS and POP3. Another type of ALF is URL scanning, which allows you to screen Web requests and reject those that don't comply with administrator-defined rules based on content, character set, length, HTTP methods (verbs), headers, extensions, and so on. SMTP filters and screeners can inspect e-mail traffic and can be used as an anti-spam mechanism to block messages from particular domains, source addresses, or containing particular content.

- **Protocol support**: In comparing protocol support, you should not only determine which protocols are supported by a particular product, but *how* each is supported. For example, can access policies be applied to a particular application, service or protocol? What about VPN policy? Quality of Service (QoS), if applicable? Determine exactly which application filters are included with the product; find out which add-on filters are available for it, and look into how easy (or difficult) it is to create your own filters. Depending on your organization's needs, you might want to look for support for the following categories of applications, services and protocols: Authentication/security services (HTTPS, IPSEC, ISAKMP/IKE, LDAP, RADIUS, SecurID, TACACS/TACACS+, CVP), Mail services (POP3, SMTP, IMAP), Internet services (IM, file sharing, NNTP, PCAnywhere), Enterprise services (DCOM, Citrix ICA, Sun NFS, Lotus Notes, SQL), routing protocols (EGP, IGRP, GRP, OSPF, RIP), TCP/UDP services (Bootp, Finger, Echo, FTP, NetBEUI, NetBIOS over IP, SMB, RAS, PPTP), RPC services, ICMP services, and multi-media streaming services.

- **Intrusion Detection**: Most modern firewalls include some level of built-in intrusion detection and prevention (IDS/IDP). Some products provide IDS as a separate module or offer an "off-box" IDS solution. Other firewalls include rudimentary IDS but offer a more sophisticated version of IDS/IDP at extra cost. Compare the common attacks that the firewall's IDS is configured to detect (for example, WinNuke, Ping of Death, Teardrop, and buffer overflow attacks are common, but the first three are older attacks from which most modern systems with updated patches are already protected). You also might want to consider how IDS alerts are sent (for example, e-mail, pager), and you might also want to check availability of IDS add-on products (both from the firewall vendor and from third parties) to increase IDS effectiveness.

NOTE

An important element in evaluating IDS effectiveness is the number of "false positives" that the IDS returns.

- **Firewall throughput/Number of connections**: The size of your organization will determine your needs when it comes to how many simultaneous firewall sessions are supported. This number can vary widely from vendor to vendor and from one product to another within a single vendor's line. You'll also want to consider firewall throughput in megabits per second or gigabits per second (Mbps or Gbps). Note that this will generally be a different (and higher) number than VPN throughput because of VPN overhead, especially when strong encryption such as 3DES or AES is used for VPN connections. Throughput and connection specs are often the primary differentiating factors between different appliance models made by the same vendor, but when you buy a software firewall, these numbers may also depend on the hardware on which you install it.

■ **Logging/Reporting**: Most modern firewalls include some level of logging, but the sophistication and scope of the logs varies. Consider the logging format and how easy it is to import the logs into spreadsheets or other programs, as well as your organization's logging needs. Will text logs do, or do you need to be able to log data to a SQL database? Some firewalls come with reporting functions that analyze and aggregate the information that's contained in the logs into configurable reports. Others offer this feature as an add-on module. Also, consider the availability of third-party log file analysis and reporting software.

VPN Features

Most modern firewalls, other than those intended only as personal firewalls or "telecommuter" models, include integrated VPN gateways. Virtual private networking is an essential element of remote access communications for many organizations. Employees depend on VPN to work from home or when on the road. There are several factors to consider when comparing VPN support of different security devices.

■ **VPN Protocol Support**: What VPN protocol(s) are supported: IPSec, PPTP, L2TP, SSL VPN? Is NAT Traversal (NAT-T) supported? What authentication protocols are supported for VPN connections? Is two-factor authentication (ActivCard, Authenex, SecurID) supported? What encryption methods are supported (DES, 3DES, AES)? Some vendors require an extra license at extra cost to use strong encryption.

■ **Remote access/site-to-site VPN**: Organizational needs determine whether you need support for site-to-site VPN (connecting two networks), remote access VPN connections, also called client-server VPN (which allows an individual computer to connect to the network), or both. Some low cost firewalls support only site-to-site VPN.

■ **VPN client**: Remote access VPN connections require VPN client software on the client computer (SSL VPNs are made through the Web browser). All modern versions of Windows include Microsoft's PPTP and L2TP clients built into the OS. Many firewall/VPN devices require proprietary client software, which may have to be licensed at extra cost. In some cases, you can use the Microsoft clients with third-party firewalls for basic VPN operation, but you will need the vendor's proprietary software for advanced functionality.

■ **VPN connections/throughput**: Organizational needs will determine the number of simultaneous VPN connections needed. In firewall documentation, this is often expressed as number of VPN tunnels supported. If multiple VPN protocols are supported, check the number of allowed connections per protocol (for example, the number of PPTP connections supported may be different from the number of L2TP connections). VPN throughput is generally expressed in Mbps. Throughput will differ depending on the encryption method used. For example, AES throughput will be slower than 3DES.

■ **VPN quarantine:** This is the ability to block or allow VPN connections based on administrator-defined conditions (such as whether the client is running an anti-virus program or firewall, or whether security updates have been installed). Users whose machines don't meet the criteria can be forwarded to a Web site where they can download the needed updates. Some vendors refer to this as remote policy enforcement, client configuration verification, or by other terms, and offer it through a third-party software package or extra-cost VPN client software.

NOTE

NAT Traversal, or NAT-T, is a technology that makes it possible to use IPSec with Network Address Translation, something that formerly did not work. Microsoft defines NAT-T as "a set of capabilities that allows network-aware applications to discover they are behind a NAT device, learn the external IP address, and configure port mappings to forward packets from the external port of the NAT to the internal port used by the application—all in an automated fashion so the user does not have to manually configure port mappings or other such mechanisms."

Web-Caching Features

There are a number of features to consider in comparing Web-caching solutions. Which features you need will be dependent on such factors as the size and structure of your organization, how and how much external Web access is used by those on your network, and whether your organization hosts its own Web servers.

■ **Forward caching:** All Web caching servers support forward caching. This is used to accelerate response to outbound requests when users on the internal network request a Web object from a server on the Internet. Frequently-requested objects are stored on the caching server, and thus, can be retrieved via the faster local network connection. Studies of ISA Server show that in the typical business network environment, 35 to 50 percent of requests can be retrieved from the forward cache.

■ **Reverse caching:** Reverse caching is used when the organization has internal Web sites that are available to external Internet users. The caching server stores objects that are frequently requested from the internal Web servers and serves them to Internet users. This speeds access for the external users and lightens the load on the internal Web servers, thus reducing traffic on the Internal network.

- **Distributed caching**: This is a means of spreading the load over multiple caching servers that operate on a peer basis.

- **Hierarchical caching**: This is a means of placing multiple caching servers on the network in an hierarchical arrangement so that requests are serviced first from the local cache, then from a centralized cache before going out to the Internet server for the request. Distributed and hierarchical caching can be used in combination.

- **Caching Rules**: Caching servers can use administrator-defined rules to determine how to process requests from internal and external Web clients. Rules can control access to specific protocols, control bandwidth, or control content. Rules may be applied based on user accounts or group memberships.

Firewall Certification

Another factor that may or may not be important to your organization is whether the firewall product you're considering has been "certified." Certification means that some organization has determined that the firewall meets specific minimal standards. To be meaningful, certification should be done by an independent entity (not a vendor) based on a standardized course of hands-on testing in a lab (not just a "paper" comparison of features).

ICSA Labs (a division of TruSecure Corporation) is the most well recognized organization providing testing and certification of firewalls and other network security products. ICSA testing is currently done against the Modular Firewall Product Certification Criteria version 4, as described at http://www.icsalabs.com/html/communities/firewalls/certification/criteria/criteria_4.0.shtml.

ICSA testing is based on hands-on evaluation of the firewall products using a "black box" approach based on functionality.

In the United Kingdom, NSS Network Testing Laboratories provides Checkmark certification for computer security products. See http://www.nss.co.uk/Certification/Certification.htm. Other testing/certification programs that have been developed to evaluate computer security products include the Information Technology Security Evaluation Criteria (ITSEC), recognized by France, Germany, the Netherlands and the UnitedKingdom, and the United States Department of Defense Trusted Computer System Evaluation Criteria (TCSEC). These government evaluation programs have given way to the Common Criteria Security Evaluation process, which was ratified as a standard through the International Organization for Standardization (ISO).

NOTE

ISA Server 2000 was certified under MFPCC version 3a, running on Windows 2000 Server. ICSA lab report (updated November 2001) is at http://www. icsalabs.com/html/communities/firewalls/certification/rxvendors/microsoft-isas2000/labreport_cid303.shtml. At the time of publication, ISA Server 2004 had not yet undergone ICSA certification testing.

Comparing ISA 2004 to Other Firewall Products

In this section, we will compare ISA Server 2004's specifications, features and functionality to selected competitive products. Because many vendors market multiple models of firewalls, we have attempted to choose each vendor's product that is most similar in usage, target market, and price point to ISA Server 2004. Comparing ISA Server, which is designed for the medium-to-large business network, to personal and SOHO firewalls would be meaningless. Likewise, we have not attempted to compare ISA Server to high-end enterprise level firewalls that cost ten times as much.

Specifically, we will look at how ISA Server 2004 stacks up against selected models of the following vendors' firewall products:

- CheckPoint
- Cisco PIX
- NetScreen
- SonicWall
- WatchGuard
- Symantec Enterprise Firewall
- BlueCoat SG

ISA Server 2004 Comparative Points

Microsoft defines ISA Server 2004 as "an advanced application layer firewall, VPN, and Web cache solution that enables customers to easily maximize existing IT investments by improving network security and performance. ISA Server 2004 is a member of the Microsoft Windows Server System™, a comprehensive and integrated server infrastructure designed to meet the needs of developers and IT professionals." Let's quickly review some of its key features and specifications in the context of our comparative analysis model.

Key Features and General Specifications

ISA Server 2004 offers the following key features for advanced protection against hackers, crackers, and network attackers:

- **Multi-layer inspection** helps protect IT assets and corporate intellectual property such as IIS, Exchange Server, Sharepoint, and other network infrastructure from hackers, viruses, and unauthorized use with comprehensive and flexible policies, customizable protocol filters, and network-routing relationships.

- **Advanced Application Layer Filtering** (ALF) enables complex application traffic to access the Internet while ensuring high levels of security, performance, and protection against the latest types of attacks.

- **Secure inbound traffic and protection from "inside attacks" via VPN client connections** are achieved through unified firewall and VPN policy management, deep content inspection, and VPN Quarantine integration.

- **Integrated multi-networking capabilities, network templates, and stateful routing and inspection** make it easy to deploy ISA Server into existing IT environments as an edge, departmental, or branch office firewall without changing the network architecture.

ISA Server 2004 provides enhanced ease-of-use features that include:

- **Simple, easy to learn and use management tools** that shorten ramp-up time for new security administrators while making it easier to avoid security breaches due to firewall misconfiguration.

- **Prevention of network access downtime** by allowing administrators to securely and remotely manage firewall and Web cache services.

- **Savings on bandwidth costs** by reducing outbound Internet traffic and serving content locally, and the ability to distribute the content of Web servers and e-commerce applications closer to customers efficiently and cost-effectively.

- **Integration with Windows Active Directory, third-party VPN solutions, and other existing infrastructure** that simplifies the task of securing corporate applications, users, and data in a pure Windows environment or in a mixed environment.

- **ISA Server's thriving community of partners, users, and Web resources** that, along with Microsoft's formal support programs, provides multiple avenues for support and information.

High performance is a high priority in today's business environment, and ISA Server 2004 offers the features most wanted by performance-conscious organizations:

- **Ability to provide fast, secure anywhere/anytime access** to corporate applications and data, such as Microsoft Exchange Server.

- **A safe, reliable, and high-performance infrastructure** for enabling both inbound and outbound Internet data access and single sign-on through multiple Internet-standard authentication mechanisms.

- **An integrated single-server solution** that puts only the necessary services at the edge of the network, including firewall security, VPN, and Web cache.

- **A way to scale out the security infrastructure** as networking needs grow with a flexible multi-network architecture.

- **Enhanced network performance and reduced bandwidth costs** with Web caching in corporate data centers and branch offices.

Next, we'll look at some of the general specifications we discussed as points of comparison and how ISA Server 2004 fits into those specifications.

Hardware Platform Support and System Requirements

ISA Server 2004 is a software firewall, which can be installed on Windows 2000 Server (service pack 4 or above) or Windows Server 2003. Internet Explorer 6 or later must be installed. Minimum hardware requirements are as follows:

- 300 MHz processor
- 256MB RAM
- NTFS formatted disk with 150MB free space
- One NIC for each network connected to the ISA server

NOTE

The minimum supported hardware requirements listed by Microsoft should be considered an absolute minimum for installing ISA Server 2004; these are not optimum hardware specifications. ISA Server 2004 performance will increase dramatically with upgraded hardware. We recommend, as a realistic base hardware specification, at least an 800MHz processor and 1GB of RAM. Also, note that if you are using ISA Server as a Web-caching server, you'll need more disk space for the cache.

Reliability

System reliability is a very important consideration for a mission-critical device such as a network firewall. Some factors supporting ISA Server 2004's reliability include the following:

- Windows Update can be used to automatically update the ISA Server 2004 underlying operating system.

- There are plans to add functionality to the Windows Update site that will enable the ISA Server 2004 firewall software to update itself. When this feature will be available is not known at the time of this writing.

- Underlying hardware quality is a major factor in system reliability. Redundant hardware components, such as power supplies, network interfaces, and software or hardware RAID can significantly improve overall reliability of the firewall.

- Firewall configuration backup tools are included in the ISA Server 2004 firewall's user interface. These are easy to use and allow the firewall administrator to back up the entire firewall configuration and restore it to the same machine or to another machine.

Scalability

Scalability can be divided into at least two common categories:

- **Outward scalability** refers to the ability to adapt to expansion of the network as it grows beyond the original location and adds remote offices, telecommuters, and more.

- **Upward scalability** refers to the ability to adapt to the growing number of users and increase in traffic as the network grows larger.

ISA Server 2004 can scale outwards and upward by using the built-in Network Load Balancing Service that is included in the underlying Windows Server 2003 operating system. ISA Server 2004 can also scale upwards by adding memory (RAM), disk space, a more powerful processor and more processors. The number of processors supported in the final version of the product has not yet been announced.

Extensibility

Extensibility refers to the product's ability to add features and functionality through vendor-provided, third-party or in-house software add-ons, scripts, and other components. Because ISA Server 2004 is a "software" firewall, it supports almost unlimited extension of its application layer filtering and other access control and networking components. Many of its competitors in the hardware firewall market require the customer to upgrade to an entirely new hardware device, or require a separate off-box hardware/software solution, to add new features and functions.

The ISA Server 2004 firewall can be extended by the customer at no added cost by using the free ISA Server 2004 Software Development Kit (SDK).

The ISA Server 2004 firewall can likewise be extended by third-party vendors, and the customer can purchase third-party solutions from these vendors. Add-ons can provide such extra or enhanced features as virus detection and blocking, high availability and load balancing, access controls, content security, advanced intrusion detection, authentication (for example, ability to use RSA SecurID tokens), caching enhancement, and more sophisticated monitoring, logging and reporting.

NOTE

For a discussion of some of the add-on products available for ISA Server, see our article in the May 2004 issue of Windows & .NET magazine, *Improving on ISA Server* by Deb and Tom Shinder, or check out the Software Add-ons section at www.isaserver.org.

High Availability

High availability refers to the product's ability to recover from a failure with minimal or no downtime for the network and its users. The Windows Server 2003 Network Load Balancing (NLB) service supports high availability NLB arrays. If one member of the ISA Server 2004 NLB array becomes unavailable, another machine in the NLB array can service requests for inbound and outbound connections. This provides fault tolerance in case of hardware or software problems that put one of the servers out of commission.

Third-party vendors can augment the Windows NLB service with their own custom software solutions. There are also a number of hardware vendors that provide high-speed application layer-aware high-availability solutions for ISA Server 2004 firewalls.

Compatibility/Interoperability

Compatibility and interoperability issues for comparison include (but are not limited to) the following:

- Active Directory integration
- Exchange integration
- Operation in a mixed network environment

We take a closer look at each of these in the following subsections.

Active Directory Integration

ISA Server 2004 firewalls machines can join the Active Directory domain on the internal network and use the user database contained in that domain, or other trusted domains, to authenticate users for inbound and outbound access.

The ISA Server 2004 Firewall client application enables the ISA Server 2004 firewall to authenticate all Active Directory domain and trusted domain users. This authentication is transparent to the user and enables the firewall to obtain user and application information for all TCP and UDP connections. This information is stored in the ISA Server 2004 firewall logs and can be implemented to audit user Internet activity and to track applications with which the user has accessed the Internet.

ISA Server 2004 firewalls support RADIUS authentication. The Windows 2000 Server and Windows Server 2003 operating systems include the Internet Authentication Server (IAS) service, which is Microsoft's implementation of RADIUS. An IAS server can forward inbound and outbound authentication requests to an Active Directory domain controller for authentication. When IAS or another RADIUS server is implemented to authenticate users, the ISA Server 2004 firewall does not need to join the Active Directory domain to perform authentication.

NOTE

RADIUS authentication is supported for inbound and outbound Web proxy communications and inbound VPN connections only. Note that the Firewall Client cannot use RADIUS to authenticate to an Active Directory domain.

Exchange Integration

Exchange Integration is one of the major selling points for ISA Server 2004 and provides a major competitive advantage over competing firewalls. Here are some of the key factors that play into ISA Server 2004's superior ability to integrate with Exchange servers:

- **ISA Server 2004 SSL-to-SSL bridging** allows remote access to an Outlook Web Access (OWA) site located behind the ISA Server 2004 firewall. Most competing firewalls are not able to filter HTTP communications hidden inside an SSL tunnel and pass those through the firewall. In contrast, the ISA Server 2004 SSL-to-SSL bridging feature enables the ISA Server 2004 firewall to "unwrap" the encrypted SSL communication, expose the HTTP content to ISA Server 2004's sophisticated application layer filters, and then wrap the HTTP communication back into an SSL tunnel and forward the SSL-secured information to the OWA site. Unlike competing firewalls, ISA Server 2004 will not let hackers hide their exploits in an SSL-encrypted tunnel. The ISA Server 2004 SSL-to-SSL bridging feature can be extended to support the Outlook 2003/Exchange Server 2003 RPC over HTTP protocol. We anticipate that in the future, hackers will come up with a method to attack

Microsoft Exchange Servers using communications hidden inside an RPC over HTTPS (SSL) communication. Competing firewalls that don't support SSL bridging will not be able to protect against these attacks because they are not able to ascertain the contents of the RPC over HTTPS (SSL) communication. In contrast, the ISA Server 2004 firewall will be able to use its SSL-to-SSL Bridging feature to inspect the RPC over HTTPS (SSL) communication and block these exploits.

■ **The ISA Server 2004 Secure Exchange RPC filter** enables Exchange Server organizations to provide remote access to the company Exchange Server using the native Outlook 2000/2002/2003 client. No matter where the user is located, whether on the intranet or at a remote site a continent away, the user can open his laptop, open Outlook and "Outlook Just Works." Significant enhancements in user satisfaction and productivity are realized when using ISA Server 2004 firewalls to publish Microsoft Exchange using Secure Exchange RPC Publishing. The only competitor at the time of this writing that provides this feature is Checkpoint's Firewall-1, which recently licensed this RPC filter from Microsoft.

■ **ISA Server 2004 firewalls support forms-based authentication** is supported for all versions of Microsoft Exchange Server. Forms-based authentication uses a logon form that is normally generated by the Exchange Server machine. Many competing firewalls allow the initial connection to reach the Exchange Server so that the Exchange Sever can generate the logon form to return to the user who wants to log onto the OWA Web site. In contrast, ISA Server 2004 firewalls generate the logon form at the firewall and send the firewall-generated logon form to the user on the Internet. The user fills in the form and sends the credentials to the firewall, where the firewall authenticates the user. Only after the user authenticates with the firewall via the firewall-generated logon form is the user allowed access to the Exchange OWA Web site. In addition, ISA Server 2004 is a significant "value-add" for owners of Microsoft Exchange 2000 and Exchange 5.5 because these versions of Exchange do not support forms-based authentication; in this case, the ISA Server 2004 firewall can generate the logon form for these previous versions of Exchange. In addition, you can use forms-based authentication to prevent users from accessing attachments from OWA sessions and prevent cookies and cached information from remaining on the client machine from which the remote user accesses the OWA site.

■ **The ISA Server 2004 SMTP Message Screener** enables organizations to carry out a spam and virus attachment "e-mail defense in-depth" program beginning at the network perimeter. While most organizations will require more comprehensive spam and virus checking applications on the back end, such as on the Exchange Server machine or on an internal SMTP relay, the customer will be able to use the ISA Server 2004 SMTP Message Screener as a "front line" spam/virus screener to block e-mail based on keywords contained in the subject or body of a message and block attachments with defined sizes, file extensions, and file names. Both of these features can be used to reduce the load on the organization's primary spam and virus filtering devices. At the time of this writing, no other firewall in ISA Server 2004's price class offers this functionality at no additional cost.

- **The ISA Server 2004 HTTP filter** exposes all HTTP communications to the restrictions set for the file on a per-rule basis. This filter can be paired up with the ISA Server 2004 SSL-to-SSL Bridging feature to provide protection for secure Exchange OWA Web Publishing to allow the firewall administrator total control over the HTTP traffic that moves into and out of the OWA Web site. None of the competitors in ISA Server 2004's class provide this level of deep HTTP inspection for SSL-secured OWA connections.

Operation in a Mixed Network Environment

There are two primary factors involved in placing ISA Server 2004 in a mixed environment:

- Mixed client operating systems
- Mixed network infrastructure that is already in place

ISA Server 2004 works well with a mix of client operating systems. The Web Proxy and SecureNAT client configurations are supported by all operating systems. The Web Proxy client is a machine with its Web browser configured to use the ISA Server 2004 firewall as its Web Proxy server. All modern browsers support Web Proxy client configuration. The network administrator does not need to touch the client operating systems to make computers Web proxy clients. There are multiple methods available to automatically configure client browsers, such as DNS/DHCP wpad entries, Windows Group Policy, IEAK, and logon scripts.

On machines using the SecureNAT configuration, the client operating system has a default gateway configured that forwards Internet-bound requests to the ISA Server 2004 firewall machine. Again, the network administrator does not need to manually configure these systems, as the default gateway setting on client operating systems can easily be set using DHCP.

Ease of Use

An important element in ease of use for any software product is the user interface. ISA Server 2004 provides administrators with a friendly graphical interface that not only has many advantages over most of its competitors, but also is a big improvement over the ISA Server 2000 interface. The high points of the ISA Server 2004 graphical interface include the following:

- **Intuitive Interface** The ISA Server 2004 firewall has major advantages over other firewalls in its class in this area. The ISA Server 2004 interface was designed to provide the administrator an easy to use and intuitive configuration and management system. This is a major advantage for ISA Server 2004, as the core firewall configuration interface is easily discoverable, and a secure firewall configuration can be set up in a matter of a few hours without requiring comprehensive experience and training courses. The ISA Server 2004 interface is also a big improvement over the ISA Server 2000 interface.

■ **Management Scripts** ISA Server 2004 allows the administrator to use scripts to manage the server. Virtually any feature that can be configured using the UI can also be set using an administrative script. The ISA Server 2004 CD-ROM includes the complete ISA Server 2004 SDK, free of charge. Organizations that have programmers on staff can create complex scripts and custom add-ons for their ISA Server 2004 firewall. This is a competitive advantage for those organizations that sport such expertise, since most other commercial firewalls do not provide such comprehensive development tools at no extra cost.

■ **Easy to Use Management and Configuration Wizards** Firewall configuration is an inherently difficult process. A single misconfiguration can lead to potentially disastrous results. In order to reduce the risk of misconfiguration, ISA Server 2004 includes dozens of configuration wizards that walk firewall administrators through what would otherwise be complex tasks. Each wizard provides the appropriate options for the task at hand, and almost every step includes a link to the comprehensive Help system included with the ISA Server 2004 firewall. This is a big advantage for the ISA Server 2004 firewall.

■ **Comprehensive Help System** Perhaps one of the most frustrating experiences in firewall administration is the experience of trying out a new procedure and needing to find out how the procedure is performed and the meaning of the terms used by the firewall management interface. The ISA Server 2004 firewall provides a comprehensive Help system that provides detailed discussions of the concepts used when configuring the firewall and also provides step-by-step procedures. The help file also contains links to the online knowledge base where more comprehensive material on custom configurations can be found.

■ **Easy to Troubleshoot Rule Base** ISA Server 2000 firewall administrators had a difficult time determining which rule applied to a particular connection. This complicated troubleshooting of the firewall rule base when connections were either allowed or denied and the reason for such wasn't clear. In contrast, the ISA Server 2004 firewall rule base is an ordered list. All connections moving through the firewall are compared to rules in the firewall rule base, and the rule base is evaluated from the top down. This makes it easy for the ISA Server 2004 administrator to determine what rule allowed or denied a connection.

- **Easy Extensibility** In-house programmers and third-party companies can easily develop add-on packages using the freely available SDK, and administrators can add ISAPI filters to expand ISA's functionality.

Remote Management

Remote management is important because so many organizations are spread out over a large geographic area. Administrators must be able to manage the firewall(s) without traveling physically to their locations. Some remote management solutions for ISA Server 2004 firewalls include the following:

- **ISA Server 2004 Remote Console** ISA Server 2004 firewall administrators can install the same ISA Server 2004 management console that's used on the firewall machine itself on a management station anywhere on the network. The remote management console can also be used to manage multiple ISA Server 2004 firewalls. This greatly simplifies management of multiple firewalls. The firewall administrator can connect to multiple firewalls, and each firewall's name will appear in the left pane of the console, which is easy to navigate. In contrast, Web-based management interfaces provided by other vendors often require that the firewall administrator have many browser windows open and then try to manage the firewalls through each of these windows.

- **Remote Desktop Protocol Management** Another effective method for managing one or multiple ISA Server 2004 firewalls is with the Remote Desktop Protocol (RDP). You can use RDP to manage the ISA server via the terminal services client installed on Windows 2000 and previous operating systems or via the Remote Desktop Connection client built into Windows XP and Server 2003. This allows the ISA Server 2004 firewall administrator to connect to the local console of one or more firewalls over the network. While the Remote Desktop client requires that you open multiple windows in order to connect to multiple ISA Server 2004 firewalls, you can use the Windows Server 2003 Remote Desktops utility to manage multiple firewalls in a single RDP interface and move between machines by clicking on the name of the firewall in the left pane of the console.

Logging/Reporting

One of the major ease-of-use improvements seen in ISA Server 2004, as compared to ISA Server 2000, is the logging and reporting facility. The following features represent major improvements over what was available in ISA Server 2000 and over what is provided by many of the competitors:

- **Dashboard** The ISA Server 2004 Dashboard provides a single interface from which the firewall administrator can get information about Connectivity, Service status, Report status, Alerts, active Sessions, and overall System

Performance. The Dashboard provides a large amount of information in a single location and is presented in an attractive and easy-to-interpret fashion.

- **Alerts** The Alerts feature is enhanced by providing all the Alert information relating to firewall activity in a single location within the ISA Server 2004 management console. Firewall administrators do not need to go into the Event Viewer to see details of a Firewall Alert. In addition, an Alert can either be reset (which removes the Alert from the Interface), or it can be Acknowledged (the Alert stays in the interface, but is marked as Acknowledged). The ISA Server 2004 firewall allows you to use a number of pre-configured Alerts and also allows the firewall administrator to create his own Alerts with custom Alert actions.

- **Sessions** The Sessions panel enables Firewall administrators to view active connections through the firewall. Sessions can be filtered so that the Firewall administrator can focus on connections of special interest. In addition, connections to the firewall can be terminated using the Sessions console.

- **Connectivity Monitors** ISA Server 2004 Connectivity Monitors enable the Firewall administrator to keep tabs on a number of network services that are vital to network and Internet connectivity. Connectivity Monitors are grouped into several classes: Active Directory, DHCP, DNS, Published Servers, Web (Internet) and Others. Each of these groups represents services that are critical to network functionality. An Alert can be triggered when a Connectivity Monitor indicates a failure in a network service.

- **Reporting** The built-in reporting feature allows the administrator to create reports on firewall activity. Reports can be created to run once or can be scheduled on a recurring basis. A report configuration Wizard makes it easy to create a report. Information included in the report is focused on protocol usage, most popular sites, cache performance and most active users.

- **Logging** ISA Server 2004 logging allows the firewall administrator to view connection information in real time. Real-time logging can be used to quickly troubleshoot firewall configuration problems and to respond to attacks in real time. In addition, the firewall administrator can use database queries against the firewall logs and drill down on specific information of interest. ISA Server 2004's logging is database driven, allowing for greater flexibility. ISA Server allows log storage using the Microsoft Data Engine (MSDE) database, SQL, or file storage. MSDE ships with ISA Server and if you already have a SQL license, you can perform custom queries against it.

Most of ISA's competitors have similar logging and reporting features. However, a competitive advantage here is that these features are included with the product and do not require expensive add-ons, as some competitive products do. One disadvantage of ISA Server's logging and reporting is that the built-in reporting feature is not customizable to the extent that some customers require. They will need to purchase third-party products to obtain information about per-user usage statistics and per-site usage.

Firewall and Related Features

Now let's take a look at some of ISA Server 2004's firewall and related features in depth.

Application Layer Filtering Capabilities

One of the major strengths of ISA Server 2004 is its ability to perform application layer filtering (ALF). The application layer filtering feature allows the ISA Server 2004 firewall to protect against attacks that are based on weaknesses or holes in a specific application layer protocol or service.

ISA Server 2004's most impressive application layer filtering feature is its advanced HTTP security filter. The ISA Server 2004 HTTP security filter can be configured to examine and block HTTP communications based on virtually any aspect of the HTTP communication. Examples of how the advanced HTTP security filter can be used include:

- Blocking Java scripts
- Blocking ActiveX controls
- Blocking file-sharing applications
- Blocking downloads based on file extension or MIME type
- Blocking uploads via HTTP
- Blocking malformed HTTP connections
- Blocking URLs based on any component of the URL
- Blocking Web pages containing keywords or phrases

In addition to the HTTP security filter, ISA Server 2004 firewalls provide application filters for the following protocols:

- DNS
- FTP
- H.323
- MMS (Microsoft Media Streaming)
- PNM (RealNetworks Streaming)
- POP intrusion detection
- PPTP
- RPC
- Exchange RPC
- RTSP (Real Time Streaming Protocol)
- SMTP
- SOCKS V4

- Web Proxy (responsible for Web Proxy functionality)
- SecurID
- RADIUS
- Link Translation
- OWA Forms-based Authentication

Most of the competitors have similar application layer filtering features. However, there are some application layer filtering and inspection features that set ISA Server 2004 firewalls apart from the competition:

- **Secure Exchange RPC Filter** With the exception of Checkpoint NG, ISA Server 2004 and ISA Server 2000 firewalls are the only ones that can provide secure inbound and outbound access to Microsoft Exchange using the full Outlook MAPI client. The ISA Server 2004 firewall's Secure Exchange RPC Filter allows external users access to the full range of Exchange Server services via the full Outlook 2000, Outlook 2002 and Outlook 2003 MAPI client. In addition, the network can be configured so that regardless of the users' locations, whether inside or outside the corporate network, "Outlook just works" without requiring reconfiguration of any of the Outlook client settings.

- **Link Translation Filter** Based on research, ISA Server 2004 is one of the only firewalls that allows rewriting of URLs in reverse proxy scenarios. This is a tremendous boon to organizations that require remote access to Web applications that were not written with remote access connections from the Internet in mind. The Link Translation Filter removes the requirement of rewriting LAN-based Web applications for use on the Internet. This feature alone can save an organization tens of thousands of dollars per application.

- **OWA Forms-based Filter** This unique feature of ISA Server 2004 allows the firewall to generate the logon form that users see when they log on to an Outlook Web Access (OWA) Web site. This increases the security of the OWA site because users must authenticate first before a connection is allowed to the OWA site. In addition, user credentials are not cached on the computer connected to the OWA site. This feature is useful in circumstances when users log on to the OWA site from untrusted computers, such as airport Web kiosks. Another security feature provided by forms-based authentication is an authentication time-out, so that if users are idle for a period of time, reauthentication is required. Finally, the forms-based application feature extends these features to all versions of Exchange Outlook Web Access, including Exchange 5.5, Exchange 2000 and Exchange 2003. Without ISA Server 2004, only Exchange 2003 supports the advantages of forms-based authentication.

Protocol Support

Protocol support is a critically important issue for users located behind the firewall. A firewall must be able to support all protocols required by users on the network. If a firewall cannot support a protocol that users require, that firewall will be quickly replaced with one that does provide the required protocol support. In addition, organizations require granular control over protocol access; not all users should have access to the same protocols. Some users require limited protocol access, while others require access to a broad range of protocols.

Key features of ISA Server 2004 protocol support include:

- **Application Layer Filters** There are a number of application layer filters included with ISA Server 2004 that provide protocol support. Examples of these protocol support application layer filters include the FTP filter, the H.323 filter, the MMS filter, and the PNM filter. These filters manage the connections for these "complex" protocols. Users would not be able to use these protocols if there were no application layer filters for them. In addition, application layer filters are required to support SecureNAT client access to "complex" protocols.

- **Firewall client** The Firewall client software provides a unique level of accessibility to machines that have the software installed. The Firewall client software allows the machine to use virtually any protocol to connect to the Internet, including all "complex" protocols. The most compelling feature of the Firewall client software is that application filters do not need to be written to support complex protocols. The Firewall client software works together with the Firewall service on the ISA Server 2004 firewall to manage the connections. No other firewall currently on the market can make the same claim. The Firewall client can be easily installed without requiring the network administrator to touch the machines. The software can be installed via SMS, Active Directory Group Policy Software Distribution, or logon and management scripts.

- **ISA Server 2004 Software Development Kit** Organizations can create their own application filters using the information and tools included with the ISA Server 2004 Software Development Kit (SDK). Application filters can be created to perform tasks such as blocking downloads for SecureNAT and Firewall clients. Any organization with C++ programmers on staff can use the ISA Server 2004 SDK at no extra charge.

- **VPN Protocol Support** Unlike many other firewalls in ISA Server 2004's class, the ISA Server 2004 firewall can apply stateful filtering and stateful inspection to connections made via a VPN link. This allows the ISA Server 2004 firewall to provide full protocol support to VPN clients when these clients connect to the corporate network through the VPN, or when they connect to the Internet via the VPN connection. This means corporate firewall policy can be applied to VPN clients without losing vital protocol support.

Intrusion Detection

ISA Server 2004 includes a collection of intrusion-detection filters that are licensed from Internet Security Systems (ISS). These intrusion-detection filters are focused on detecting and blocking network layer attacks. In addition, ISA Server 2004 includes intrusion-detection filters that detect and block application layer attacks.

ISA Server 2004 can detect the follow intrusions or attacks:

- Windows out-of-band (WinNuke)
- Land
- Ping of Death
- IP half scan
- UDP bomb
- Port scan
- DNS host name overflow
- DNS length overflow
- DNS zone transfer
- POP3 buffer overflow
- SMTP buffer overflow

When the ISA Server 2004 firewall detects one of these attacks, the following actions can be carried out:

- An alert sent to the ISA Server 2004 Event Log
- ISA Server 2004 services stopped or restarted
- An administrative script or program run
- An e-mail message sent to an administrator's mailbox or pager

One competitive disadvantage of ISA Server is that the intrusion-detection system included with ISA Server 2004 is not configurable, and you cannot create your own intrusion signatures. However, third-party applications, such as Internet Security System's **Real Secure** IDS, can be used to extend the intrusion-detection features at an additional cost.

VPN Functionality

ISA Server 2004 supports the following VPN protocols:

- Point-to-Point Tunneling Protocol (PPTP)
- Layer 2 Tunneling Protocol/IPSec (L2TP/IPSec)
- IPSec Tunnel Mode

PPTP and L2TP/IPSec VPN protocols can be used in both remote access and site-to-site VPN connections. Site-to-site IPSec Tunnel Mode can be used *only* in site-to-site VPN connections.

IPSec Tunnel Mode is used *only* for compatibility with third-party VPN servers. It should not be used when site–to-site connections are created between an ISA Server 2004 firewall and another Microsoft VPN product (Windows 2000/Windows Server 2003 RRAS or ISA Server 2000).

Remote Access/Site-to-Site VPN

The ISA Server 2004 VPN feature supports two types of VPN connections:

- Remote Access VPN
- Site-to-Site VPN

The Remote Access VPN allows individual computers configured as VPN clients to connect to the ISA Server 2004 firewall and access resources on the corporate network. Remote Access VPN clients can use either the PPTP or L2TP/IPSec VPN protocol. Advanced authentication mechanisms, such as SecurID, RADIUS, EAP/TLS certificates, biometric, and others are supported by the ISA Server 2004 VPN remote access server.

Site-to-site VPNs allow the ISA Server 2004 firewall to connect to another VPN server and join entire networks to each other over the Internet. Site-to-site VPNs allow organizations to remove expensive dedicated leased lines, which leads to significant cost reductions.

A major advantage of ISA Server 2004 is that firewall access policies are applied to VPN remote access and site-to-site connections. In contrast to many competitors' products that allow VPN clients full access to the corporate network, the ISA Server 2004 VPN connections are exposed to the firewall's access policies. The enables the ISA Server 2004 firewall administrator to set restrictive access controls on VPN connections on a per-user basis. When the user establishes a VPN connection with the ISA Server 2004 firewall, that user can only access resources he needs to get the job done. No other network resources will be available.

NOTE

A common problem with some third-party VPN services is that additional configuration may be required to support single sign-on. That is, unless the third-party VPN service has a way of integrating with Active Directory, users are forced to log on twice. Even when integration with AD is supported, additional configuration is often required. This is a big advantage of ISA Server's Active Directory integration when compared to many third-party firewall/VPN devices.

VPN Client Support

All Windows operating systems include the Windows VPN client software. Advantages of using the Windows VPN client include:

- **No Third-Party Software Required** This is a significant competitive advantage. Users do not need to install any extra software and can configure their VPN connections using an intuitive and easy-to-use VPN client connection Wizard. The VPN client software requires minimal configuration, and most users can connect to the ISA Server 2004 firewall in minutes.

- **No Compatibility Issues** The Windows VPN client was designed from the ground up to work with the client operating system on which it runs. In contrast, third-party VPN client software may or may not work correctly on the client Windows operating system and may have known or unknown conflicts with other networking components of the Windows operating system. In addition, troubleshooting issues are minimized because the customer can call Microsoft and get VPN client problems addressed. In contrast, when the customer uses a third-party VPN client, he is often bounced between the operating system vendor and the third-party vendor before the final solution to the problem is discovered.

- **Simplified VPN Configuration and Deployment** The Microsoft Connection Manager Administration Kit (CMAK) included with Windows 2000 and Windows Server 2003 makes it easy to create a VPN client that is preconfigured with the correct VPN client settings. The CMAK configures the VPN client software and packages it in an executable file. The file can be e-mailed, sent on disk, or downloaded from a server by corporate VPN users. The user only needs to double-click on the file, and it is automatically installed without requiring the user to make decisions. In contrast to the products of many competitors, this VPN client automation feature is provided at no additional cost to the customer. CMAK is also used to create client connection profiles to work with the VPN quarantine feature (discussed in the next section).

- **Support for IETF RFC IPSec NAT Traversal** NAT traversal (NAT-T) is a mechanism used to allow IPSec VPN connections across firewalls and network devices that use network address translation (NAT). This is a very common configuration and almost all organizations use NAT in one form or another because it reduces the number of public IP addresses needed. ISA's competitors have developed a number of different NAT traversal mechanisms, many of which are incompatible with one another and increase the complexity of firewall configurations. In contrast, the Microsoft VPN client uses industry standard NAT Traversal, which is firewall friendly.

VPN Quarantine

The ISA Server 2004 VPN quarantine feature increases the security of VPN client connections by "pre-qualifying" VPN clients before they are allowed to connect to the corporate network. The VPN clients must meet a set of requirements before the connection to the corporate network is enabled. They remain in a special "quarantine network" until they meet the corporate security standards. Quarantine policy can require that VPN clients have the latest security updates installed, the latest services packs, up-to-date virus definition files, and more. VPN quarantine policies are managed centrally and there is no need to distribute quarantine files to individual VPN clients.

The VPN quarantine feature is a significant competitive advantage for ISA Server 2004. No additional software needs to be purchased and there are no limited license fees required. There is no limit on the number of VPN clients that can connect through the VPN quarantine security feature.

ISA's competitors provide managed VPN client solutions similar to the VPN quarantine feature, but at potentially larger costs to the organization. You frequently need to install the competitors' proprietary VPN client software to obtain these advantages. In contrast, the ISA Server 2004 VPN quarantine feature works right out of the box with any Windows VPN client. You can create the managed clients using the Connection Manager Administration Kit, then the managed client software is quickly and easily deployed to users in the field.

VPN Throughput/Connections

VPN throughput is dependent on the hardware platform on which Windows and ISA Server 2004 are installed. Adding processors and encryption off-load cards will significantly increase throughput and VPN performance.

Web-Caching Features

In addition to ISA Server 2004's firewall and VPN features, the ISA Server 2004 firewall can also act as a Web proxy server. The ISA Server 2004 machine can be deployed as a combined firewall and Web-caching server, or as a dedicated Web-caching server.

NOTE

If the ISA Server 2004 firewall is configured as a Web-caching-only server, it loses the majority of its firewall network protection features.

Forward Caching

Forward caching takes place when a user on a network protected by the ISA Server 2004 firewall makes a request for static Web content. The requested content is placed in the Web cache after the first user makes a request. The next (and subsequent) user who requests the same content from the Internet has the content delivered from the Web cache on the ISA Server 2004 machine instead of from the Internet Web server. This reduces the amount of traffic on the Internet connection and reduces overall network costs. In addition, the content is delivered to the user much more quickly from cache than it is from the actual Web server. This increases user satisfaction and productivity.

The primary benefit of ISA Server 2004's forward caching is cost savings realized by reduced bandwidth usage on the Internet connection.

Reverse Caching

Reverse caching takes place when a user on the Internet makes a request for Web content that is located on a Web server published by a ISA Server 2004 Web Publishing Rule. The ISA Server 2004 firewall retrieves the content from the Web server on the Internal network or another network protected by the firewall and returns that information to the Internet user who requested the content. The ISA Server 2004 machine caches the content it retrieves from the Web server on the Internal network. When subsequent users request the same information, the content is served from the ISA Server 2004 cache instead of being retrieved from the originating Web site.

There are two principle advantages to the reverse caching scenario:

- **Reverse Caching Reduces Network Bandwidth Usage** Reverse caching reduces the bandwidth usage on the Internal network because cached content is served directly from the ISA Server 2004 machine. No bandwidth is required on the internal network, which makes this bandwidth available to users on the internal network to get their work done. Corporate networks that are already "bandwidth challenged" will benefit from this configuration.

- **Reverse Caching Keeps Web Content Available** An even more compelling advantage to reverse caching is its ability to make Web site content available when the Web server is offline. Web servers can go offline when routine maintenance needs to be performed or after the server experiences a hardware or software crash. Regardless of the reason for the server being offline, the time offline can create a negative experience for Internet users when they try to access content on the site. The ISA Server 2004 reverse caching feature enables you to take the Web server offline and still have Web site content available to Internet users because the content is served from the ISA Server 2004 cache.

Comparing ISA 2004 to Check Point

According to its Web site and marketing material, at the time of this writing Check Point has 97 of 100 Fortune 100 businesses as customers, and (along with Cisco PIX) is the major ISA Server competitor in the large- and medium-business markets. According to information from International Data Corp. as reported December 17, 2003 by TechTarget (http://searchsecurity.techtarget.com/originalContent/0,289142,sid14 _gci941717,00.html), CheckPoint remains the leader in overall firewall/VPN technologies with a market share of 48 percent.

NOTE

When considering market share figures, it is important to keep in mind that many large companies practice "defense in depth" by deploying multiple firewalls made by different vendors. Thus, the fact that 97 percent of Fortune 500 companies use Check Point does not mean that they don't also use other firewall products along with Check Point.

Among security appliances, Nokia (which runs the Check Point FW-1/VPN-1 software on its proprietary IPSO operating system) was ranked third, after Cisco and NetScreen.

In this section, we will provide an overview of Check Point firewall software and Nokia appliances. We will look at Check Point's general specifications, platform support and system requirements, application layer filtering capabilities, VPN support, and Web-caching abilities, and examine how ISA Server 2004 stacks up against them.

Check Point: General Specifications

Check Point NG is the current ("next generation") version of the Firewall-1 and VPN-1 security products. Check Point provides an NG security suite, which includes FW-1 Pro, VPN-1 Pro, SmartCenter/SmartCenter Pro, Check Point Express, SmartView Monitor/Reporter, SmartUpdate, ClusterXL, and the SecuRemote and SecureClient VPN clients. A time-limited evaluation version of the suite can be downloaded at: https://www.checkpoint.com/GetSecure/MediaEngine?action=MP_OrderStart.

FW-1/VPN-1 can be purchased as a software firewall/VPN product that can be installed on any of several operating systems (see "Platform Requirements") or on a Nokia appliance, running on Nokia's proprietary IPSO operating system. You can buy the Nokia appliance with Check Point software installed, or you can download the software from Check Point (by providing your logon ID) and do the installation yourself. You can also download an updated image of the IPSO operating system to install before installing the NG software.

Check Point FireWall-1 and Check Point VPN-1 are licensed for a specified number of IP addresses (25, 50, 100, 250, Unlimited). Proprietary VPN-1 client software (VPN-1 SecureClient) is purchased as an option, at extra cost.

Pricing varies per reseller and there are many different products offered by Check Point (as well as appliances offered by other vendors, such as Nokia, that run the Check Point FW-1/VPN-1 software). Below are some typical software costs from popular resellers (based on information from Hardware Central) at the time of this writing:

FW-1 gateway with SmartCenter for a single security enforcement point that protects 100 IP addresses costs from $5150 to$5516.

According to Check Point's website, pricing starts at:

■ $24,100 for enterprise solutions (500+ users)

■ $4,995 for medium businesses (100 – 500 users)

■ $399 for branch office solutions★

★VPN-1 Edge for branch offices includes VPN functionality and stateful inspection firewall only (does not support application layer filtering/security servers).

FW-1 and VPN-1 have yearly subscription licenses that require you to pay every year for use of FW-1. VPN-1 SecuRemote client software is free. However, the more advanced VPN-1 SecureClient for Windows and Macintosh (which includes personal firewall and security configuration control for individual desktops) is priced from $2300 for 25 IP addresses to $40,000 for 1000 IP addresses.

Adding a content-filtering server (UFP or CVP) adds extra cost, with the amount depending on the hardware and software deployed.

NOTE

URL Filtering Protocol (UFP) servers hold lists of URLs designated as permitted or denied. Content Vectoring Protocol (CVP) servers analyze the data stream and allow or deny connections based on policy rules.

Check Point: Platform Support and System Requirements

The Check Point FireWall-1 software firewall runs on the following operating systems:

■ Windows NT/2000

■ Sun Solaris

■ Linux (RedHat)

■ Check Point SecurePlatform

■ Nokia IPSO (UNIX-based proprietary OS)

■ IBM AIX

When installing on a Windows machine, Check Point FW-1 NG requires 40MB of free disk space, a 300MHz or better processor and at least 128MB of RAM. This is for the primary management and enforcement module. For the GUI clients, you need an additional 40MB of disk space and 32MB of RAM.

Check Point FW-1/VPN-1 products are marketed both as software solutions and pre-installed on hardware appliances.

Except for appliances, the underlying operating system must be properly configured before FW-1 will run correctly. OS patches and upgrades can cause problems. Support for Solaris 2.7 didn't occur for two years after the OS release, and FW-1 still did not support Windows Server 2003 nine months after its release.

How does ISA Server 2004 compare? Like Check Point, ISA Server 2004 is a software firewall and can be installed on a variety of hardware configurations. Unlike Check Point, ISA Server 2004 cannot be installed on UNIX. Minimum system requirements are similar for the two.

ISA Server 2004 is designed specifically to integrate with Windows and take advantage of its features, including:

- Network Load Balancing (NLB)
- VPN quarantine
- Active Directory
- Windows DHCP, DNS, and WINS services
- RADIUS Internet Authentication

All these Windows services are included "on the box" with the underlying Windows 2000 Server or Server 2003 operating system at no extra cost.

Check Point: Application Layer Filtering Capabilities

Check Point provides application filtering with its newest "NG with Application Intelligence" products. Check Point calls its application proxies "security servers" and uses the term "Application Intelligence" to refer to application layer attack prevention technologies integrated in FireWall-1 and SmartDefense. Check Point is relatively new to application layer filtering (this feature was not included with its versions prior to 4.0).

Content filtering can be done via a URL Filtering Protocol (UFP) Server for FW-1 (SurfControl) plug-in. The plug-in provides a category list of classified Web sites and can be installed on the FW-1 machine or a separate server. Content filtering can also be done via a Content Vectoring Protocol (CVP) server. Content filtering appliances and services such as Websense can interoperate with FW-1.

How does ISA Server 2004 compare? ISA Server 2004 performs intelligent stateful inspection using "smart" application filters. Not only can you determine the validity of data moving through the firewall in request and response headers, you can also filter by "signature" (text string) for keyword filtering or filter for particular file types. Like FW-1, ISA 2004 works with Websense, SurfControl, and other third-party filtering products.

ISA Server 2004 inspects all aspects of HTTP communications. The SMTP filter protects from invalid SMTP commands that cause buffer overflows, and the SMTP message screener blocks spam and mail containing dangerous attachments. ISA Server's RPC filtering protects from exploits and malicious code directed to the RPC services and ensures that only valid connections get through to the Exchange server. DNS filtering prevents application layer attacks aimed at published DNS servers, and the POP3 filters protect published POP3 mail servers from attack. ISA Server's SDK allows easy development of web and application filters.

Check Point: VPN Support

Check Point provides a number of different VPN solutions:

- VPN-1 Edge: for remote sites/branch offices
- VPN-1 Express: mid-sized businesses with multiple sites and up to 500 users
- VPN-1 Pro: complex enterprise-level networks (includes FW-1)
- VSX: VLAN environments, datacenters, large segmented networks

All support stateful inspection, URL filtering, site-to-site VPN, remote access VPN, and X.509 certificates. SmartDefense intrusion detection, content filtering and application proxy (Security Server), stateful failover, and load balancing are supported only by VPN-1 Express, VPN-1 Pro and VSX. Other VPN features include:

- One-click VPNs (ability to create a VPN with a one-step operation).
- IPSec encryption and authentication
- SecuRemote uses 128-256 bit AES and 56-168 bit 3DES for data encryption
- VPN QoS support via optional module (FloodGate-1)
- Support for SSL-based VPNs via Web browser
- Support for Microsoft L2TP VPN clients

Check Point's SecureClient (extra cost VPN client software) provides functionality similar to ISA's VPN Quarantine (Check Point calls it "client configuration verification") and also provides a personal firewall for the client machine.

How does ISA Server 2004 compare? ISA Server 2004 supports user- and group-based access control, and site-to-site and remote VPN, with both stateful inspection and stateful filtering to allow you to control what moves through the VPN. VPN connections are exposed to firewall policies like any other connection; this provides granular control of protocols that can be used, servers to which they can connect, time of day/duration of connection, and IP address from which connection is allowed. In addition:

- ISA Server supports X.509 certificates for IPSec encryption, and pre-shared keys for organizations that don't want to implement a PKI.
- ISA Server VPN wizards make it easy to set up VPNs. ISA Server supports use of CMAK to create a VPN connectoid that allows users to connect to VPN with one click, and supports an automatically downloadable phone book. CMAK also allows you to customize routes for VPN clients. CMAK wizards make it easy for the administrator as well as the user.

- ISA Server uses IETF RFC Internet standard L2TP IPSec Nat Traversal (NAT-T) protocol to connect to Server 2003 VPNs.

- ISA Server 2004 supports 3DES encryption.

- ISA Server 2004 does not support VPN QoS; however, QoS has limited functionality outside the corporate network because every intervening router must also support it, and the likelihood of this is low.

- ISA Server supports SSL tunneling.

- ISA Server 2004 supports both Microsoft PPTP and L2TP clients.

- ISA Server supports VPN quarantine through Windows Server 2003's quarantine feature using the standard Windows PPTP and L2TP clients at no extra cost.

Check Point: Web Caching

Web-caching functionality is not included in the basic Check Point software; it can be added through the purchase of an extra module or via an "off-box" solution.

How does ISA Server 2004 compare? ISA Server 2004 includes Web-caching functionality at no extra charge. Forward caching allows the ISA Server 2004 firewall to cache objects retrieved by internal users from external Web servers. Reverse caching allows the ISA Server 2004 firewall to cache objects retrieved by remote users from servers that have been published by the ISA Server 2004 firewall. Web objects requested by remote users are cached on the ISA Server 2004 firewall, and subsequent requests for the same objects are served from the firewall's Web cache instead of forwarding the request to the published Web server located behind the ISA Server 2004 firewall.

Fast RAM caching allows the ISA Server 2004 firewall to keep most frequently-accessed items in memory. This optimizes response time by retrieving items from memory rather than from disk. ISA Server 2004 gives you an optimized disk cache store that minimizes disk access for both read and write operations. ISA Server 2004 also supports Web proxy chaining, which allows the ISA Server 2004 firewall to forward Web requests to an upstream Web proxy server.

Comparing ISA 2004 to Cisco PIX

Cisco offers PIX "security appliances" in a number of different models and configurations. These range from small, relatively inexpensive models that are aimed at small offices and telecommuters (such as the PIX 501) to high performance, high-dollar models marketed to enterprise customers and service network providers (such as the PIX 535), with a number of "in-between" models targeted at businesses of various sizes.

Check Point is acknowledged by most sources as the overall market share leader (taking into account that its product is sold both as a software firewall and installed on Nokia appliances). However, when it comes to firewall appliances, Cisco topped the appliance market in 2003 with 34.3 percent of the market, according to International

Data Corp information reported by CNET News at http://news.com.com/2100-7355-5079045.html.

PIX firewalls are typically deployed as edge firewalls, and to create perimeter networks (DMZs). Their hardware is optimized for fast performance (as with all hardware-based firewalls), and the simplicity of their packet-filtering functionality makes them especially appropriate at the Internet edge.

In this section, we provide an overview of PIX appliances. We look at Cisco PIX's general specifications, platform support and system requirements, application layer filtering capabilities, VPN support and Web-caching abilities, and examine how ISA Server 2004 stacks up against them.

Cisco PIX: General Specifications

PIX firewalls are generally licensed for an unlimited number of users. Cisco VPN client software (which is not required, but adds functionality) is typically priced at $30 to $50 per client. Customers with support contracts and encryption entitlement can download the client at no charge. PIX firewalls have Common Criteria EAL4 certification.

PIX series 500 firewalls cover a broad range. At the time of this writing, available PIX models included:

- **PIX 501**: designed for use in small offices and by telecommuters. Provides up to 10Mbps firewall throughput, 3Mbps VPN throughput (using 3DES encryption). Includes one 10baseT interface and a four-port 10/100 integrated switch.

- **PIX 506E**: designed for use in branch/remote offices. Provides up to 20Mbps firewall throughput, 16 Mbps VPN throughput (using 3DES encryption). Provides two autosense 10BaseT interfaces.

- **PIX 515E**: designed for use by small-to-medium businesses and within the enterprise environment. Provides up to 188Mbps firewall throughput, integrated support for 2000 IPSec tunnels. Supports up to six 10/100 interfaces.

- **PIX 525**: designed for enterprise and service provider environments. Provides over 360Mbps firewall throughput, up to 70Mbps VPN throughput (using 3DES encryption), support for 2000 IPSec tunnels. Can handle 280,000 simultaneous firewall sessions. Supports up to eight 10/100 interfaces or three gigabit Ethernet interfaces.

- **PIX 535**: designed for large enterprise and service provider environments. Provides over 1Gbps firewall throughput, 95Mbps VPN throughput (using 3DES encryption), support for 2000 IPSec tunnels. Can handle 500,000 simultaneous firewall sessions. Supports up to ten 10/100 interfaces or nine gigabit Ethernet interfaces.

Cost ranges from under $500 for the PIX 501 with 10 user licenses ($795 for unlimited users) to over $20,000 for the PIX 535. Specifically, at the time of this writing, typical pricing for each of the PIX models was as shown below:

- PIX 501: $495 to $795
- PIX 506E: $959
- PIX 515E: $2495 to $2695
- PIX 525: $10,920 to $14,759
- PIX 535: $20,000 to $24,000

The PIX software is the same on all appliance models. The difference is in the hardware, specifically in processor speed, amount of RAM, throughput, number of connections allowed, maximum number of interfaces, and whether failover is supported. Table 3.1 illustrates the different hardware configurations for the different models.

Table 3.1: PIX Model-by-Model Feature Comparison

Model	501	506E	515E	525	535
Processor	133MHz	300MHz	433MHz	600MHz	1GHz
RAM	16MB	32MB	32MB, 64MB	256MB	1GB
Flash memory	8MB	8MB	16MB	16MB	16MB
Throughput	10Mbps	20Mbps	188Mbps	360Mbps	1Gbps
Connections	7,500	25,000	130,000	280,000	500,000
Max. number of interfaces	1, + 1 four-port switch	2	6	8	10
Failover	No	No	Yes	Yes	Yes

How does ISA Server compare? ISA Server 2004 is a software firewall, and thus, is not tied to a particular vendor's hardware. This gives you more flexibility and allows throughput based on the hardware configuration on which you install it. ISA Server has been tested at firewall throughput up to 1.59 Gbps. There is no software limit on the number of interfaces; ISA Server supports as many interfaces as the hardware allows.

Cisco PIX: Platform Support and System Requirements

Cisco's appliances run on the proprietary PIX OS embedded operating system. The OS is built specifically for security services, and thus, is a "hardened" OS. It is based on the Cisco IOS operating system used by Cisco routers, with fewer commands and a few that are extra or differently named. Administrators not familiar with the OS must learn a new operating system.

Hardware configurations vary by PIX model, as shown in Table 3.1

How does ISA Server 2004 compare? ISA Server 2004 runs on standard Intel PCs that are easily upgraded and can be installed on Windows 2000 Server or Windows Server 2003, providing a standardized, familiar management interface and the flexibility to use hardware of your choice. This makes ISA Server more scalable than appliances that are tied to the hardware.

The Windows Server 2003 OS can be "hardened" by applying a series of special profiles included in Server 2003 SP2 for the Security Configuration wizard. Microsoft also provides a system hardening guide that includes specific configuration recommendations and deployment strategies for ISA Server 2004. The document can be downloaded at http://www.microsoft.com/technet/prodtechnol/isa/2004/plan/securityhardening-guide.mspx.

Cisco PIX: Application Layer Filtering Capabilities

PIX firewalls provide "stateful application inspection" via the Adaptive Security Algorithm (ASA), to discern IP addressing information embedded in the user data packet or open secondary channels on dynamically assigned ports (for example, FTP, H.323). This allows NAT to translate the embedded addresses. PIX firewalls include support for a type of URL filtering that is designed to work with third-party content-filtering services WebSense and N2H2. With this feature, you can allow or deny access to Web sites based on administrator-created lists of acceptable and unacceptable sites. This requires a subscription and access to NetPartner's WebSense server or N2H2 server over the Internet. The PIX captures the URL requests and queries the database on the WebSense or N2H2 server, and then denies or allows the request based on the acceptable use policy set by the administrator. Content filtering blocks ActiveX or Java applets.

Cisco calls their application proxies "fixup protocols." They are handled via the "fixup" command. These proxies include: FTP, HTTP, H.323, ils, rsh, rtsp, SMTP, SIP, Skinny, and SQL. Application layer protocols supported by the intrusion-detection feature in the native PIX services don't have to be configured.

How does ISA Server 2004 compare? ISA Server 2004 performs intelligent stateful inspection using "smart" application filters. Not only can you determine the validity of data moving through the firewall in request and response headers, you can also filter by "signature" (text string) for keyword filtering or filter for particular file types. ISA 2004 can also work with Websense and other third-party filtering products.

ISA Server 2004 inspects all aspects of HTTP communications. ISA's SMTP filter protects from invalid SMTP commands that cause buffer overflows, and the SMTP message screener blocks spam and mail containing dangerous attachments.

ISA Server's RPC filtering protects from exploits and malicious code directed to the RPC services and ensures that only valid connections get through to the Exchange server.

DNS filtering prevents application layer attacks aimed at published DNS servers, and the POP3 filters protect published POP3 mail servers from attack.

ISA Server's SDK allows for easy development of web and application filters.

Cisco PIX: VPN Support

Cisco PIX firewalls all include VPN support. They support Cisco software VPN clients (for Windows, Linux, Solaris, and Mac OS X), Cisco hardware VPN clients (PIX 501 and 506E, Cisco 800 and 1700 series routers), and Microsoft PPTP and L2TP clients. Data is encrypted using 56-bit DES, 168-bit 3DES, or 256-bit AES.

> **NOTE**
>
> PIX users can download a 3DES/AES or 56-bit DES encryption license free from Cisco's Web site.

VPN policy configuration enforcement (which is similar to ISA Server 2004's VPN quarantine feature) is provided with the Cisco Secure VPN client v.3.x. or above. VPN access policies and configuration requirements are downloaded from a central gateway and "pushed" to the client upon establishing the VPN connection. Customers who have purchased support contracts and encryption entitlement can download the client software at no extra cost.

How does ISA Server 2004 compare? ISA Server 2004 can apply firewall policy to the VPN interfaces. Perhaps more significantly, ISA Server does not require any software to be added to VPN clients. ISA Server supports the PPTP and L2TP/IPSec VPN clients that are built into Windows 9x/ME, Windows XP, Windows NT, 2000, and Server 2003 operating systems. ISA Server's VPN quarantine allows administrators to enforce specific conditions VPN clients must meet before being allowed to connect (for example, latest service pack/updates must be installed) and direct clients to a server to download and install the required updates.

ISA Server's VPN wizards make it easy for administrators to set up VPNs, and the CMAK can be used to provide easy one-click connections for clients.

Cisco PIX: Web Caching

As with Check Point, Web-caching functionality is not included with the Cisco firewall/VPN; it is available at extra cost through purchase of the Cisco Content Engine.

Cisco Application and Content Networking Software (ACNS) is deployed on Cisco Content Engine caching modules/devices, which range in price from $2500 to over $18,000, to provide integrated caching and content delivery. Content Engines are caching appliances that run on the Cisco IOS. Cisco cache software runs on the Content Engine to provide streaming media splitting and caching, proxy-style caching (HTTP, FTP, SSL tunneling), and transparent caching.

For transparent caching, the cache software and ACNS support the Web Cache Communication Protocol (WCCP), a protocol developed by Cisco to redirect specified traffic to the Web cache. WCCP has also been used by CacheFlow (now BlueCoat), NetApp, and Squid.

How does ISA Server 2004 compare? ISA Server 2004 includes Web-caching functionality at no extra charge. Forward caching allows the ISA Server 2004 firewall to cache objects retrieved by internal users from external Web servers. Reverse caching allows the ISA Server 2004 firewall to cache objects retrieved by remote users from servers that have been published by the ISA Server 2004 firewall. Web objects requested by remote users are cached on the ISA Server 2004 firewall, and subsequent requests for the same objects are served from the firewall's Web cache instead of forwarding the request to the published Web server located behind the ISA Server 2004 firewall.

Fast RAM caching allows the ISA Server 2004 firewall to keep most frequently accessed items in memory. This optimizes response time by retrieving items from memory rather than from disk. ISA Server 2004 gives you an optimized disk cache store that minimizes disk access for both read and write operations. ISA Server 2004 also supports Web proxy chaining, which allows the ISA Server 2004 firewall to forward Web requests to an upstream Web proxy server.

Comparing ISA 2004 to NetScreen

NetScreen ranked second among security appliance vendors in 2003, with a 16 percent market share, according to the information provided by to International Data Corp. (IDC) and published by CNET News at http://news.com.com/2100-7355-5079045.html.

Juniper Networks signed an agreement to acquire NetScreen Technologies in February, 2004. Juniper Networks markets carrier-class and service provider/large enterprise routers and switches.

In this section, we provide an overview of NetScreen firewall appliances. We look at NetScreen's general specifications, platform support and system requirements, application layer filtering capabilities, VPN support and Web caching abilities, and examine how ISA Server 2004 stacks up against them.

NOTE

Juniper Networks is not related to the Juniper Firewall Tool Kit (FWTK), an open source firewall utility for Linux/UNIX, which we discuss later in this chapter under the section titled *Comparing ISA 2004 to Open Source Firewalls.*

NetScreen: General Specifications

NetScreen appliances include firewall and IPSec VPN capabilities. They also incorporate antivirus functionality based on Trend Micro AV technology. The firewall component uses stateful inspection and limited application layer inspection.

NetScreen appliances are built on Application Specific Integrated Circuit (ASIC) architecture, which embeds RISC processors and accelerates processing. Appliances run the proprietary real time ScreenOS firmware in flash memory, rather than on a hard disk. This gives the appliance some advantages over traditional disk-based machines, in that there is less chance for mechanical failure.

NetScreen makes a number of different appliances, ranging from the low-end 5 series (5XP, 5XP Elite, 5GT, 5GT Plus, 5XT, 5XT Elite) to the high-end 200, 500, and 5000 series. Mid-range models include the NetScreen 25 and 50. Prices range from under $500 to almost $100,000. At the time of this writing, typical pricing for each of the NetScreen models is as shown below:

- NetScreen 5XP (10 user): $495
- NetScreen 5GT: $495
- NetScreen 5XT: $695
- NetScreen 5XP Elite (unlimited): $995
- NetScreen 5GT Plus: $995
- NetScreen 5XT Elite: $1195
- NetScreen 25: $3495
- NetScreen 50: $5695
- NetScreen 204: $9995
- NetScreen 208: $14,245
- NetScreen 500: $22,500
- NetScreen 5200: $99,000

The cost of add-ons for more functionality can significantly increase the capital investment required. For example, at the time of this writing, NetScreen IDP (intrusion detection and prevention) appliances range from $7995 for the IDP 10 to $34,995 for the IDP 500. NetScreen remote VPN client licenses (v.8) cost $95 for 10 users, $195 for 100 users, and $995 for 1000 users. NetScreen remote security VPN client (which also provides personal firewalls for remote users) cost $345 for 10 users, $2495 for 100 users, and $19,995 for 1000 users.

Table 3.2 compares features available on popular models that are most competitive with ISA Server 2004.

Table 3.2 NetScreen Model-by-Model Feature Comparison

Feature	NetScreen 200 Series	NetScreen 50	NetScreen 25	NetScreen 5XP
Concurrent sessions	128,000	8,000	4,000	2,000
Firewall throughput	400 to 550Mbps	170Mbps	100Mbps	10Mbps
VPN throughput with 3DES	200Mbps	50Mbps	20Mbps	10Mbps
Policies	4,000	1,000	500	100

Continued

Table 3.2 NetScreen Model-by-Model Feature Comparison

Feature	NetScreen 200 Series	NetScreen 50	NetScreen 25	NetScreen 5XP
Transparent mode (all interfaces)	Yes	Yes	Yes	Yes
Route mode (all interfaces)	Yes	Yes	Yes	Yes
NAT	Yes	Yes	Yes	Yes
PAT	Yes	Yes	Yes	Yes
Virtual IP	4	2	2	1
Mapped IP	4,000	1,000	1,000	32
Static IP routes	256	60	60	16
Dedicated VPN tunnels	1000	100	25	10
High availability	Yes	Future ScreenOS	No	No

All models of the NetScreen appliance support the following features:

- Manual key, IKE, PKI (X.509) authentication, PKCS 7 and 10 certificate requests
- DES, 3DES and AES encryption
- Automated certificate enrollment (SCEP)
- Certification authorities: VeriSign, Microsoft, Entrust, RSA Keon, iPlanet (Netscape), Baltimore, DOD PKI
- RADIUS, RSA SecureID, LDAP external databases

How does ISA Server compare? ISA Server 2004 is a software firewall, and thus, is not tied to a particular vendor's hardware. This gives you more flexibility and allows throughput based on the hardware configuration on which you install it. ISA Server has been tested at firewall throughput up to 1.59 Gbps. There is no software limit on the number of interfaces; ISA Server supports as many interfaces as the hardware allows.

The Windows Server 2003 OS can be "hardened" by applying a series of special profiles included in Server 2003 SP2 for the Security Configuration wizard. Microsoft also provides a system hardening guide that includes specific configuration recommendations and deployment strategies for ISA Server 2004. The document can be downloaded at www.microsoft.com/technet/prodtechnol/isa/2004/plan/securityhardeningguide.mspx.

NetScreen: Platform Support and System Requirements

NetScreen appliances run on the proprietary ScreenOS operating system, which in turn runs on proprietary ASIC-based hardware. The NetScreen firewall software cannot be installed on general purpose PC operating systems. ScreenOS is hardened and optimized for the specific purpose of running the firewall software.

Hardware configurations vary by NetScreen model, as shown in Table 3.2

How does ISA Server 2004 compare? ISA Server 2004 runs on standard Intel PCs that are easily upgraded and can be installed on Windows 2000 Server or Windows Server 2003, providing a standardized, familiar management interface and the flexibility to use hardware of your choice. This makes ISA Server more scalable than appliances that are tied to the hardware.

NetScreen: Application Layer Filtering Capabilities

Netscreen firewalls provide "deep inspection" technology for application layer protection to integrate intrusion detection and prevention for common Internet-originating attacks that exploit the following protocols:

- HTTP
- POP3
- IMAP
- SMTP
- FTP
- DNS

Intrusion-detection technology was acquired when NetScreen bought OneSecure. For more sophisticated intrusion detection, NetScreen markets a separate product, NetScreen-IDP, that can be deployed behind the firewall and in front of mission critical servers.

All models of NetScreen appliances support Websense (external URL filtering service).

How does ISA Server 2004 compare? ISA Server 2004 performs intelligent stateful inspection using "smart" application filters. Not only can you determine the validity of data moving through the firewall in request and response headers, you can also filter by "signature" (text string) for keyword filtering or filter for particular file types. ISA 2004 supports Websense and other third-party filtering products and services.

ISA Server 2004 inspects all aspects of HTTP communications. The SMTP filter protects from invalid SMTP commands that cause buffer overflows, and the SMTP message screener blocks spam and mail containing dangerous attachments. ISA Server's RPC filtering protects from exploits and malicious code directed to the RPC services and ensures that only valid connections get through to the Exchange server. DNS filtering prevents application layer attacks aimed at published DNS servers, and the POP3 filters protect published POP3 mail servers from attack. ISA Server's SDK allows easy development of web and application filters.

NetScreen: VPN Support

NetScreen firewall appliances all include VPN support. They support NetScreen proprietary VPN client software, available both as remote client and remote security client (the latter includes personal firewall protection for remote users). VPN client software licenses cost extra.

Data is encrypted using 56-bit DES, 168-bit 3DES or 256-bit AES. NetScreen supports authentication via X.509 certificates in a PKI environment. Certificates must be obtained from a certification authority (a separate system running CA software, either within the Internal network or a public CA such as Verisign).

- NetScreen supports IPSec and SSL VPNs.
- NetScreen supports remote access and site-to-site VPNs.
- VPN throughput is dependent on the appliance model (hardware).

Enforcement of firewall protection on client machines is accomplished by using NetScreen Remote Security Client (at extra cost) which installs personal firewall software on the client machine and enforces updates over the Web. This provides some of the functionality of VPN quarantine. VPN policies are tied to user accounts rather than machines. Policies will not be retrieved unless the firewall software is installed and operational.

How does ISA Server 2004 compare? ISA Server 2004 supports user- and group-based access control, site-to-site and remote VPN with both stateful inspection and stateful filtering to allow you to control what moves through the VPN. VPN connections are exposed to firewall policies like any other connection; this provides granular control of protocols that can be used, servers to which they can connect, time of day/duration of connection, and IP address from which connection is allowed. In addition:

- ISA Server supports X.509 certificates for IPSec encryption, and pre-shared keys for organizations that don't want to implement a PKI.
- ISA Server VPN wizards make it easy to set up VPNs. ISA Server supports use of CMAK to create a VPN connectoid that allows users to connect to VPN with one click, and an automatically downloadable phone book. CMAK also allows you to customize routes for VPN clients. CMAK wizards make it easy for the administrator as well as the user.
- ISA Server uses IETF RFC Internet standard L2TP IPSec Nat Traversal (NAT-T) protocol to connect to Server 2003 VPNs.
- ISA Server 2004 supports 3DES encryption.
- ISA Server 2004 does not support VPN QoS; however, QoS has limited functionality outside the corporate network because every intervening router must also support it, and the likelihood of this is low.

- ISA Server supports SSL tunneling.

- ISA Server 2004 supports both Microsoft PPTP and L2TP clients.

- ISA Server supports VPN quarantine through Windows Server 2003's quarantine feature using the standard Windows PPTP and L2TP clients at no extra cost.

NetScreen: Web Caching

NetScreen firewall/VPN appliances do not provide Web-caching functionality. Web caching/acceleration can be added to a network using NetScreen products by implementing a caching solution such as ISA Server on the network.

How does ISA Server 2004 compare? ISA Server 2004 includes Web-caching functionality at no extra charge. Forward caching allows the ISA Server 2004 firewall to cache objects retrieved by internal users from external Web servers. Reverse caching allows the ISA Server 2004 firewall to cache objects retrieved by remote users from servers that have been published by the ISA Server 2004 firewall. Web objects requested by remote users are cached on the ISA Server 2004 firewall, and subsequent requests for the same objects are served from the firewall's Web cache instead of forwarding the request to the published Web server located behind the ISA Server 2004 firewall.

Fast RAM caching allows the ISA Server 2004 firewall to keep most frequently accessed items in memory. This optimizes response time by retrieving items from memory, rather than from disk. ISA Server 2004 gives you an optimized disk cache store that minimizes disk access for both read and write operations. ISA Server 2004 also supports Web proxy chaining, which allows the ISA Server 2004 firewall to forward Web requests to an upstream Web proxy server.

Comparing ISA 2004 to SonicWall

SonicWall was ranked fourth (after Cisco, Netscreen and Nokia) among security appliance vendors in 2003, with a 5.4 percent market share, according to International Data Corp. information published by CNET News at http://news.com.com/2100-7355-5079045.html.

In this section, we provide an overview of SonicWall appliances. We look at SonicWall's general specifications, platform support and system requirements, application layer filtering capabilities, VPN support and Web caching abilities, and examine how ISA Server 2004 stacks up against them.

SonicWall: General Specifications

SonicWall's line of firewall/VPN appliances use ASIC architecture and are based on stateful inspection technology that is ICSA certified. The following SonicWall appliances are available at the time of this writing:

- SOHO3: for small businesses or branch offices

- SOHO TZW: has built in wireless gateway

- TELE3: for telecommuters

- TELE TZ: for telecommuters; includes "WorkPort" architecture that physically separates corporate and home network

- TELE TZX: as above; includes integrated four-port MDIX switch for connecting multiple network devices

- TELE3 SP/TELE3 SPi: for Point of Sale (POS) businesses with failover from broadband to analog modem connection; supports bandwidth on demand and usage management of ISDN connection

- PRO 100: for small-to-large businesses; unlimited network nodes; integrated DMZ (perimeter network)

- TZ 170: for small businesses and IT administrators with limited resources; includes integrated five-port MDIX switch and security processor (system on a chip); policy-based NAT; optional upgrade adds ISP failover and load balancing

- PRO 230: rack-mount; supports multiple protected zones; user-level authentication, bandwidth management, DHCP relay through VPN tunnels, automatic security updates

- PRO 330: for business critical networks; includes high availability, guaranteed automatic failover when configured with mirror appliance, redundant power

- PRO 3060: for complex networks; uses next-gen SonicOS 2.0; optional upgrade provides hardware failover, ISP failover, and automated secondary VPN gateway; supports hardware AES, processor includes dedicated cryptographic accelerator; multiple interfaces per security zone, policy-based NAT

- PRO 4060: enterprise class firewall with same features as 3060; includes one year 8-hour day/5-day week support and on-going software updates.

Table 3.3 shows a comparison of the specifications and features among the different SonicWall models.

Table 3.3 SonicWall Model-by-Model Feature Comparison

Model	Processor	RAM	Interfaces	Concur. Connections	FW users	FW through-put	3DES Through-put	VPN tunnels/policies
SOHO3	133MHz	16MB	2 10/100 baseT	6000	10/25/50/ Unlim	75Mbps (bi-dir)	20Mbps	10
SOHO TZW	133MHz	16MB	2 10/100 baseT	6000	10/25	75Mbps (bi-dir)	20Mbps	10
TELE3	133MHz	16MB	2 10/100 baseT	6000	5	75Mbps (bi-dir)	20Mbps	5
TELE TZ	133MHz	16MB	3 10/100 baseT	6000	5	75Mbps (bi-dir)	20Mbps	5
TELE TZX	133MHz	16MB	3 10/100 baseT, 4 port switch	6000	5	75Mbps (bi-dir)	20Mbps	5
TELE3 SP/SPi	133MHz	16MB	2 10/100 baseT, 1 v.90, 1 ISDN	6000	10	75Mbps (bi-dir)	20Mbps	10
PRO 100	133MHz	16MB	3 10/100 baseT	6000	Unlim	75Mbps (bi-dir)	20Mbps	50
TZ 170	SonicWall Security Processor	64MB	7 10/100 baseT	6000	10/25/ unlim	90Mbps (bi-dir)	30+Mbps	5-50/ 2-10 site-to-site pol-icies
PRO 230	233MHz	64MB	3 10/100 baseT	30,000	Unlim	190Mbps (bi-dir)	25Mbps	500

Continued

Table 3.3 SonicWall Model-by-Model Feature Comparison

Model	Processor	RAM	Interfaces	Concur. Connections	FW users	FW through-put	3DES Through-put	VPN tunnels/policies
PRO 330	233MHz Strongarm RISC	64MB	3 10/100 baseT	128,000	Unlim	190Mbps (bi-dir)	45Mbps	1000
PRO 3060	2GHz Intel	256MB	6 10/100 baseT	128,000	Unlim	300+Mbps (bi-dir)	75Mbps (same for AES)	500-1000
PRO 4060	2GHz Intel	256MB	6 10/100 baseT	500,000	Unlim	300+Mbps (bi-dir)	190Mbps (same for AES)	1000/3000

SonicWall appliances cover a wide range of price points, depending on the model and reseller. Typical prices at the time of this writing are:

- SonicWall SOHO3: $445 (10 users) $645 (25) $795 (50)
- SonicWall TZW: $449 (10 users) $599 (25)
- SonicWall TZ170: $410 (10 users) $576 (25) $825 (unlim.)
- SonicWall Tele3 TZX: $493
- SonicWall Tele3 SP: $534
- SonicWall Pro 230: $1655 (unlim.)
- SonicWall Pro 3060: $2319 (unlim.)
- SonicWall Pro 4060: $4995 (unlim.)

Add-ons, upgrades and services for SonicWall products are priced as follows at the time of this writing:

- VPN for SonicWall SOHO: $410
- SonicWall VPN for PRO 100: $576
- SonicWall VPN client: $451 (10 user) $659 (50) $825 (100)
- Content filtering add-on: $75   (5 node) $495 (50) $695 (unlim)
- VPN upgrade for SOHO: $495

(Source: http://www.tribecaexpress.com/sonicwall_firewalls_price.htm)

SonicWall Content Filtering Service (CFS) requires a one-year subscription fee and is priced according to number of nodes. For unlimited node products, at the time of this writing, list price is $695 per year for the standard service, $995/year for the PRO 3060 and PRO 4060 SonicWall devices. (Source: http://www.sonicguard.com/ContentFilteringService.asp).

Other add-ons include:

- Anti-virus subscription: varies from $136/year for 5 users to $19,195/year for 1000 users
- Global Management System: $1655 for software plus 10 node licenses; $12,446 for 100 incremental node licenses
- Support contracts: vary from $95 (SOHO 10 node) to $20,749 (GMS unlimited)

(Source: www.tribecaexpress.com/sonicwall_firewalls_price.htm)

SonicWall: Platform Support and System Requirements

SonicWall appliances run on dedicated ASIC-based hardware devices with specifications as shown in the table above. The appliances run the single-purpose SonicOS operating system. There are two current versions of the operating system:

- SonicOS v.2.0s, which runs on lower-end products and is a simpler version of the OS that uses wizards to guide users through configuration options.

- SonicOS v.2.0e, which runs on the higher end products (PRO 3060 and 4060) and allows you to define security zones for which you can set separate security policies and define user groups to which policies can be applied.

How does ISA Server 2004 compare? ISA Server 2004 runs on standard Intel PCs that are easily upgraded and can be installed on Windows 2000 Server or Windows Server 2003, providing a standardized, familiar management interface and the flexibility to use hardware of your choice. This makes ISA Server more scalable than ASIC appliances that are tied to the hardware.

The Windows Server 2003 OS can be "hardened" by applying a series of special profiles included in Server 2003 SP2 for the Security Configuration wizard. Microsoft also provides a system hardening guide that includes specific configuration recommendations and deployment strategies for ISA Server 2004. The document can be downloaded at http://www.microsoft.com/technet/prodtechnol/isa/2004/plan/securityhardening-guide.mspx.

SonicWall: Application Layer Filtering Capabilities

Content filtering can be accomplished via SonicWall's subscription-based Content Filtering Service (CFS). This requires that you pay a subscription fee for deep filtering of Web content. URL ratings of Web sites and those sites that are rated as acceptable (according to administrator-defined policies) are cached on the local appliance as part of the service.

The service comes in both standard and premium editions. The standard edition only filters the sites that are in its database. The premium edition also analyzes pages that aren't in the database and adds them. There are also special editions of the service available for governmental and educational institutions.

CFS standard edition filters Web content according to 14 pre-defined categories:

- Violence
- Hate/racism
- Intimate apparel
- Nudism
- Pornography
- Weapons
- Adult/mature content
- Cult/occult
- Illegal drugs
- Drugs
- Criminal skills

- Sex education
- Gambling
- Alcohol/tobacco

The premium edition adds more categories, such as Abortion, Arts/Entertainment, Auctions, Brokerage/Trading, Humor/Jokes, News/Media, Personals/Dating, Religion, Streaming Media/MP3, Software Downloads, and many more (for a total of 52 categories).

The premium edition runs only on fourth-generation SonicWall products and requires the enhanced SonicOS. CFS does not run on older first-generation SonicWall products, but its predecessor, SonicWall Content Filter List (CFL) can be used on older models.

How does ISA Server 2004 compare? ISA Server includes deep application layer filtering at no extra cost. However, ISA 2004 can also use Websense or other third-party products and services if desired.

NOTE

There are performance and administrative overhead costs involved in configuring filters for a wide range of content and Web sites. In cases in which a subscription service is an attractive option, ISA Server 2004 can also provide content filtering through subscription services such as Websense.

ISA Server 2004 performs intelligent stateful inspection using "smart" application filters. Not only can you determine the validity of data moving through the firewall in request and response headers, you can also filter by "signature" (text string) for keyword filtering or filter for particular file types.

ISA Server 2004 inspects all aspects of HTTP communications. The SMTP filter protects against invalid SMTP commands that cause buffer overflows, and the SMTP message screener blocks spam and mail containing dangerous attachments.

ISA Server's RPC filtering protects against exploits and malicious code directed to the RPC services and ensures that only valid connections get through to the Exchange server.

DNS filtering prevents application layer attacks aimed at published DNS servers, and the POP3 filters protect published POP3 mail servers from attack.

ISA Server does not require an extra cost subscription service to perform application layer filtering.

SonicWall: VPN Support

SonicWall appliances include VPN support. PRO models support from 500 to 3000 simultaneous VPN tunnels. SonicWall appliances support IPSec and PPTP VPNs.

SonicWall uses proprietary VPN Client 8.0 (extra license cost), which is needed to use automatic certificate support, L2TP and to access VPN gateway using DNS, WINS, and LMHOST resolution instead of IP addresses.

SonicWall Client Policy Provisioning allows clients to automatically download VPN configuration data from the VPN gateway with the proprietary Global VPN client.

At the time of this writing, the appliances come with a limited number of VPN client licenses included, depending on the model, as shown in the list below.

- SOHO TZW: 1
- TZ 170:   1
- PRO 2040:   10
- PRO 306:   25
- PRO 406:   1000

If the number of VPN users exceeds this number, additional client licenses must be purchased.

Some models do not include any VPN client licenses. These include the following:

- TELE3
- TELE3 TZ
- TELE3 TZX
- TELE3 SP
- SOHO3 10-node
- SOHO3 25-node
- SOHO3 50-node
- TZ 170 10-node

How does ISA Server 2004 compare? In ISA Server 2004, the number of simultaneous VPN connections depend on the operating system, from 1000 (Standard edition), depending on the operating system on which it is installed. In addition, ISA Server supports IPSec VPNs for site-to-site connections, and both PPTP and the more secure L2TP for remote access connections. ISA Server can apply firewall policy to the VPN interfaces.

ISA Server does not require any software to be added to VPN clients. ISA Server supports the PPTP and L2TP/IPSec VPN clients that are built into Windows 9x/ME, Windows XP, Windows NT, 2000, and Server 2003 operating systems. There is no extra cost for the VPN clients.

ISA Server's VPN quarantine allows administrators to enforce specific conditions VPN clients must meet before being allowed to connect (for example, latest service pack/updates must be installed) and direct clients to server to download and install the required updates. ISA Server's VPN quarantine is a function of Windows Server 2003 and allows you to block VPN access if the client does not meet pre-defined configuration criteria, including installation of current service packs and hotfixes, operational antivirus and firewall. No proprietary client software is required to use VPN-Q, and there is no extra cost to apply it to any number of clients up to the limits of the operating system.

SonicWall: Web Caching

SonicWall products do not include Web caching on the basic box; however, if you subscribe to the Content Filtering Service (CFS), acceptable Web sites—as defined by your policies and checked against the CFS database—are cached on the local appliance for faster returns.

How does ISA Server 2004 compare? ISA Server 2004 includes Web caching functionality at no extra charge. Forward caching allows the ISA Server 2004 firewall to cache objects retrieved by internal users from external Web servers. Reverse caching allows the ISA Server 2004 firewall to cache objects retrieved by remote users from servers that have been published by the ISA Server 2004 firewall. Web objects requested by remote users are cached on the ISA Server 2004 firewall, and subsequent requests for the same objects are served from the firewall's Web cache instead of forwarding the request to the published Web server located behind the ISA Server 2004 firewall.

Fast RAM caching allows the ISA Server 2004 firewall to keep most frequently accessed items in memory. This optimizes response time by retrieving items from memory rather than from disk. ISA Server 2004 gives you an optimized disk cache store that minimizes disk access for both read and write operations. ISA Server 2004 also supports Web proxy chaining, which allows the ISA Server 2004 firewall to forward Web requests to an upstream Web proxy server.

Comparing ISA 2004 to WatchGuard

According to information provided by International Data Corp. and published by CNET News at http://news.com.com/2100-7355-5079045.html, Watchguard was ranked fifth (after Cisco, NetScreen, Nokia, and SonicWall) among security appliance vendors in 2003, with a 4 percent market share.

In this section, we provide an overview of WatchGuard appliances. We look at WatchGuard's general specifications, platform support and system requirements, application layer filtering capabilities, VPN support and Web caching abilities, and examine how ISA Server 2004 stacks up against them.

Watchguard: General Specifications

Watchguard is offering the following appliance models at the time of this writing:

- SOHO 6: designed for small businesses and remote offices; provides stateful packet filtering and VPN capability

- Firebox X: designed for small to mid-sized enterprises; scalable to grow with the business

- Firebox Vclass: designed for medium-sized enterprises; supports high-speed networking and advanced networking features

A comparison of the features among the various WatchGuard appliance models is shown in Table 3.4.

Table 3.4 WatchGuard Model-by-Model Feature Comparison

Feature	Firebox X	SOHO 6	Firebox Vclass
Firewall throughput	Up to 275 Mbps	Up to 75 Mbps	Up to 2 Gbps
VPN throughput	Up to 100Mbps	Up to 20Mbps	Up to 1.1 Gbps
Concurrent sessions	500,000	7000	500,000
Interfaces	6 10/100 (3 active)	6 10/100	V200, V100: 2 1000BaseSX Fiber Gigabit Ethernet 2 Dedicated HA V80, V60, V60L: 4 10/100 2 Dedicated HA V10:2 10/100
VPN tunnels	Up to 1000	Up to 10	Up to 40,000
ALF	HTTP, SMTP, FTP, DNS, H.323, DCE-RPC, RTSP	HTTP	SMTP, HTTP
Spam filtering	Optional addition	No	No
URL filtering	Optional	Optional	No
High availabililty	Active/passive	No	Active Passive Active/active (optional)
QoS	No	No	Yes
VLAN tagging	No	No	Yes

Continued

Table 3.4 WatchGuard Model-by-Model Feature Comparison

Feature	Firebox X	SOHO 6	Firebox Vclass
Mobile user VPN licenses	Up to 1000	Up to 10 (optional)	Up to 20
Network diagnostic tools	No	No	Yes
Command line interface	No	No	Yes
Real time monitoring	Yes	No	Yes
Historical reporting	Yes	No	No
Upgradability	To be available March 2004	Upgrade from 10 to 25 or 50 users	V60L upgrade to V60

At the time of this writing, typical pricing for various WatchGuard Firebox models is shown in the following list:

- SOHO 6 / 10 users: $549
- SOHO 6 / 50 users: $899
- Firebox III 700/ 250 users: $2490
- Firebox III 2500/ 5000 users: $5790
- Firebox V10 / unlimited (20/75Mbps): $799
- Firebox V60 / unlimited (100/200Mbps): $599
- Firebox V80 /unlimited (150/200Mbps): $8490
- Firebox V100 / unlimited (300/600Mbps): $14,490

Additional user licenses may be required for SOHO and Firebox V10 (10 users supported out of box). VPN Manager software is required for more than one VPN site with SOHO models:

- Four Fireboxes: $796
- 20 Fireboxes: $2796
- Unlimited Fireboxes: $6396

VPN client software cost:

- 5 user: $220
- 50 user: $1800

Vclass MU VPN client software cost:

- 100 user: $780

- 1000 user: $1440

Centralized Policy Manager (CPM) is used for multiple Vclass appliances. The cost of the CPM for Windows NT/2000 is as follows:

- 10 appliances: $2840
- 100 appliances: $12,680

(Watchguard pricing information was gathered from http://www.securehq.com/group.wml&storeid=1&deptid=76&groupid=222&sessionid=200437249417233)

WatchGuard: Platform Support and System Requirements

The Watchguard appliances run a proprietary operating system and firewall software (Security Management System) that can be configured in three ways:

- InternetGuard: protects corporate networks and bastion hosts and defines corporate-level security.

- GroupGuard: protects departmental systems, restricts flow of information and packets, and defines Internet privileges at the group level.

- HostGuard: protects specific servers.

How does ISA Server 2004 compare? ISA Server 2004 runs on standard Intel PCs that are easily upgraded and can be installed on Windows 2000 Server or Windows Server 2003, providing a standardized, familiar management interface and the flexibility to use hardware of your choice. This makes ISA Server more scalable than ASIC appliances that are tied to the hardware and more user-friendly than appliance-based firewalls.

The Windows Server 2003 OS can be "hardened" by applying a series of special profiles included in Server 2003 SP2 for the Security Configuration wizard. Microsoft also provides a system hardening guide that includes specific configuration recommendations and deployment strategies for ISA Server 2004. The document can be downloaded at http://www.microsoft.com/technet/prodtechnol/isa/2004/plan/securityhardening-guide.mspx.

WatchGuard: Application Layer Filtering Capabilities

Watchguard Fireboxes (except the lower cost models – SOHO and V10) support application proxies to block common application-layer attacks. You can set protocol rules for HTTP, FTP and SMTP. Firebox III models 500, 700, 1000, 2500, and 4500, and Firebox Vclass models V60L, V60, V80, V100, and V200 support the following proxies:

- SMTP: inspects content of ingoing and outgoing e-mail; denies executable attachments, filters by address, filters malformed headers, spoofed domain names and message IDs, specifies maximum number of message recipients and maximum message size, allows specific characters in e-mail addresses.

- HTTP: blocks Web traffic on ports other than 80, filters MIME content, Java, ActiveX, removes unknown headers, removes cookies, filters content to comply with use policies.

- FTP: Filters FTP server commands, uses read-only rules to control file changes, sets time limits for idle connections.

- DNS: Checks for malformed headers and packets, filters header content for class, type, and length abnormalities.

- H.323: Limits open ports.

The Vclass firewalls provide built-in intrusion detection, with configurable logs and alarms for the following attacks:

- Java script blocking

- IP source route

- Denial of service (DoS)

- Distributed denial of service (DDoS)

- Ping of Death

- ICMP flood

- TCP SYN flood

- UDP flood

Automatic logs are embedded in the ASIC to detect the following attacks:

- LAND

- Teardrop

- NewTear

- OpenTear

- Overdrop

- Jolt2

- SSPING

- Bonk/Boink

- Smurf

- Twinge

How does ISA Server 2004 compare? ISA Server 2004's intrusion detection mechanism can detect the following types of attacks:

- Windows out-of-band (WinNuke)

- Land

- Ping of Death

- IP half scan
- UDP bomb
- Port scan
- DNS host name overflow
- DNS length overflow
- DNS zone transfer
- POP3 buffer overflow
- SMTP buffer overflow

ISA Server includes deep application layer filtering at no extra cost. ISA Server 2004 performs intelligent stateful inspection using "smart" application filters. Not only can you determine the validity of data moving through the firewall in request and response headers, you can also filter by "signature" (text string) for keyword filtering or filter for particular file types. ISA 2004 supports Websense and other third-party filtering products and services.

ISA Server 2004 inspects all aspects of HTTP communications. The SMTP filter protects against invalid SMTP commands that cause buffer overflows, and the SMTP message screener blocks spam and mail containing dangerous attachments.

ISA Server's RPC filtering protects against exploits and malicious code directed to the RPC services and ensures that only valid connections get through to the Exchange server.

ISA Server's DNS filtering prevents application layer attacks aimed at published DNS servers, and the POP3 filters protect published POP3 mail servers from attack.

WatchGuard: VPN Support

The number of VPN tunnels and VPN throughput for WatchGuard Fireboxes varies widely depending on the model. The lower cost appliances (SOHO, Firebox III 700, Firebox V10) support a low number or no VPN clients. VPN support for various models is shown in Table 3.5.

Table 3.5 WatchGuard Model-by-Model VPN Support Comparison

Model	VPN throughput	Max VPN clients	Free VPN Clients included	VPN sites
SOHO 6	20 Mbps	5	0	1/5
Firebox III 700	5 Mbps	150	0	1000
Firebox III 2500	75 Mbps	1000	50	1000
Firebox V10	20 Mbps	0	0	10
Firebox V60	100 Mbps	400*	20	400*

Continued

Table 3.5 WatchGuard Model-by-Model VPN Support Comparison

Model	VPN throughput	Max VPN clients	Free VPN Clients included	VPN sites
Firebox V80	150 Mbsp	8000*	20	8000*
Firebox V100	300 Mbps	20,000*	20	20,000*

Total client plus site connections

Firebox V80, WatchGuard's enterprise level firewall, supports the following VPN protocols:

- IPSec with IKE
- L2TP over IPSec for external L2TP servers
- PPTP over IPSec for external PPTP servers
- IPSec Security Services
- Tunnel and Transport Mode
- ESP (Encapsulated Security Payload)
- AH (Authentication Header)
- AH + ESP
- IPSec Encryption and Authentication
- DES and 3DES
- MD5 and SHA-1
- RSA
- Digital Signature Standard (DSS)
- Certificate Management
- Automatic Certificate Revocation List (CRL) through LDAP Server
- Digital Certificates X.509 v2 and v3, PKCS #10, and PKCS #7

Watchguard Fireboxes require a proprietary Mobile User VPN client, which must be distributed, along with security configuration policy, to each client machine. The VPN client includes personal firewall software for the client computer.

How does ISA Server 2004 compare? ISA Server 2004's VPN wizards make it easy to set up VPNs. ISA Server supports the use of the Connection Manager Administration Kit (CMAK) to create VPN connectoids that allow users to connect to the VPN server with one click, and supports an automatically downloadable phone book. CMAK also allows you to customize routes for VPN clients. CMAK wizards make it easier for the administrator as well as the user.

ISA Server uses IETF RFC Internet standard L2TP IPSec Nat Traversal (NAT-T) protocol to connect to Server 2003 VPNs. ISA Server 2004 supports DES, 3DES and AES encryption.

ISA Server 2004 supports both remote access and site-to-site VPNs. ISA Server can apply firewall policy to the VPN interfaces.

ISA Server 2004 supports both Microsoft PPTP and L2TP clients. ISA Server does not require any software to be added to VPN clients. ISA Server supports the PPTP and L2TP/IPSec VPN clients that are built into Windows 9x/ME, Windows XP, Windows NT, 2000, and Server 2003 operating systems.

ISA Server's VPN quarantine allows administrators to enforce specific conditions VPN clients must meet before being allowed to connect (for example, latest service pack/updates must be installed, antivirus and personal software must be installed and operational) and direct clients to server to download and install the required updates. This goes further than Watchguard's Mobile User VPN client, which enforces use and update of firewall software.

WatchGuard: Web Caching

Watchguard appliances do not include Web caching functionality. Web caching/acceleration can be added to a network using Watchguard products by implementing a caching solution such as ISA Server on the network.

How does ISA Server 2004 compare? ISA Server 2004 includes Web caching functionality at no extra charge. Forward caching allows the ISA Server 2004 firewall to cache objects retrieved by internal users from external Web servers. Reverse caching allows the ISA Server 2004 firewall to cache objects retrieved by remote users from servers that have been published by the ISA Server 2004 firewall. Web objects requested by remote users are cached on the ISA Server 2004 firewall, and subsequent requests for the same objects are served from the firewall's Web cache instead of forwarding the request to the published Web server located behind the ISA Server 2004 firewall.

Fast RAM caching allows the ISA Server 2004 firewall to keep most frequently accessed items in memory. This optimizes response time by retrieving items from memory rather than from disk. ISA Server 2004 gives you an optimized disk cache store that minimizes disk access for both read and write operations. ISA Server 2004 also supports Web proxy chaining, which allows the ISA Server 2004 firewall to forward Web requests to an upstream Web proxy server.

Comparing ISA 2004 to Symantec Enterprise Firewall

Symantec is well known for the popular Norton anti-virus software and its comprehensive virus database available on the Web. The company posted a 31 percent increase in revenues for fiscal third quarter ending 01/02/2004. Enterprise security, administration, and services represented 51 percent of total revenues (Source: http://www.symantec.com/press/2004/n040121.html).

Symantec markets low-cost basic firewall/VPN appliances for SOHO, small businesses and remote locations, as well as enterprise-level gateway security appliances that provide application layer filtering, centralized management, and high availability. Symantec also offers a software firewall product that runs on the Windows and Solaris operating systems.

In this section, we will provide an overview of Symantec Enterprise firewall software and appliances. We will look at Symantec's general specifications, platform support and system requirements, application layer filtering capabilities, VPN support and Web caching abilities, and examine how ISA Server 2004 stacks up against them.

Symantec: General Specifications

Symantec's firewall/VPN products that are available at the time of this writing can be broken into three major categories, as shown in Table 3.6.

Table 3.6 Symantec Firewall/VPN Product Categories

Firewall/VPN appliances (small/remote office)	Gateway security appliances (enterprise)	Firewall/VPN software (enterprise)
Symantec Firewall/VPN 100	SGS 5420	Symantec Enterprise Firewall
Symantec Firewall/VPN 200	SGS 5440	
Symantec Firewall/VPN 200R	SGS 5460	

Table 3.7 shows key features of Symantec's small/remote office firewall/VPN appliances at the time of this writing:

Table 3.7 Symantec Small/Remote Office Firewall/VPN Model-by-Model Comparison

Feature	Firewall/VPN 100	Firewall/VPN 200	Firewall/VPN 200R
Stateful inspection firewall functionality	Yes	Yes	Yes
Intrusion detection	Yes	Yes	Yes
Remote access VPN	No	No	Yes
Gateway-to-Gateway VPN	Yes	Yes	Yes
VPN client included	No	No	Yes
IPSec/VPN pass-through	Yes	Yes	Yes
DSL/cable interface	Yes	Yes	Yes
T-1/ISDN interface	Yes	Yes	Yes

Continued

Table 3.7 Symantec Small/Remote Office Firewall/VPN Model-by-Model Comparison

Feature	Firewall/VPN 100	Firewall/VPN 200	Firewall/VPN 200R
PPPoE support	Yes	Yes	Yes
10/100 LAN ports	4	8	8
WAN ports	1	2	2
Load balancing	No	Yes	Yes
Number of users (recommended)	15-25	30-40	30-40
Failover	Analog dialup with external modem	Analog dialup with external modem	Analog dialup with external modem
Configuration	Web interface	Web interface	Web interface
Processor	ARM7	ARM7	ARM7
WAN throughput (bi-directional)	8Mbps	8Mbps	8Mbp
Web caching	No	No	No
Application layer content filtering	No	No	No
Built-in DHCP server	Yes	Yes	Yes
NAT	Yes	Yes	Yes

Symantec's current enterprise gateway security appliances, at the time of this writing, comprise the 5400 series (SGS 5430, SGS 5440 and SGS 5460). Table 3.8 compares features of the three enterprise gateway security appliances.

Table 3.8 Symantec Enterprise Gateway Appliance Model-by-Model Comparison

Feature	SGS 5420	SGS 5440	SGS 5460
Stateful inspection firewall functionality	Yes	Yes	Yes
WAN Ports	6	6	8
10/100 ports	6	0	0
Gigabit ports	0	6	8
Maximum nodes (recommended)	500	2500	4500
Concurrent connections	64,000	190,000	200,000
Stateful throughput	200Mbps	1.4Gbps	1.8Gbps
Full inspection	95Mbps	680Mbps	730Mbps
VPN w/3DES	90Mbps	400Mbps	600Mbps

Continued

Table 3.8 Symantec Enterprise Gateway Appliance Model-by-Model Comparison

Feature w/AES	SGS 5420 30Mbps	SGS 5440 80Mbps	SGS 5460VPN 90Mbps
Memory	512MB	1GB	2GB
Hard disk	40GB	80GB	80GB
Signature-based intrusion detection	Yes	Yes	Yes
IPSec compliant VPN	Yes	Yes	Yes
Application layer inspection	Yes	Yes	Yes
HTTP content filtering	Yes	Yes	Yes
Web caching	No	No	No
Anti-spam protection	Yes	Yes	Yes

Symantec markets two software packages that are designed to run on Windows NT/2000 or Solaris; these are the Symantec Enterprise Firewall and Symantec Enterprise VPN. The current version is 7.0 at the time of this writing. The Symantec Enterprise Firewall is ICSA certified.

This software is also the basis for the enterprise security gateway appliances. Symantec Enterprise Firewall 7.0 includes:

- Hybrid architecture firewall
- Deep packet inspection
- Application proxy
- Automated system hardening
- Wide range of user authentication methods (RADIUS, LDAP, digital certificates, S/Key, Defender, SecureID, Windows domain authentication)
- Integrated Web content filtering
- Integrated load balancing
- EAL-4 certification
- AES support
- NAT: both inbound and outbound for VPN and non-VPN traffic
- WebNOT URL filtering

Symantec Enterprise VPN includes:

- Support for IPSec VPNs; interoperates with other IPSec-compliant VPN clients and servers

- Operates independently of firewall and integrates into networks with non-Symantec firewalls
- One-step configuration and one-step connect
- Remote centralized management for large scale deployments.

The cost of the Symantec firewall/VPN appliances for small or remote offices, at the time of this writing, is as follows:

- Symantec Firewall/VPN 100: $499
- Symantec Firewall/VPN 200: $899
- Symantec Firewall/VPN 200R: $1199

The cost of the Symantec enterprise gateway security appliances, at the time of this writing, is shown in the following list. These prices are for a base license (50-node firewall, one client-to-gateway VPN session).

- Symantec SGS 5420: $2999.99
- Symantec SGS 5440: $6899.98
- Symantec SGS 5460: $11,534.98

A base license is for a 50-node firewall, unlimited gateway-to-gateway VPN, and one client-to-gateway VPN session. The base license also includes one year of Gold Maintenance support service and content updates of virus definitions, attack signatures, and URL filtering via LiveUpdate.

The appliance itself contains all supported security features, but several of the security functions have to be licensed separately, including the following:

- Optional Event Manager plug-in for centralized logging, alerting and reporting
- Optional Advanced Manager plug-in (included Event Manager) for centralized management of rule sets and security policies
- Optional high availability and load balancing
- Optional enhanced anti-virus engine
- Optional hybrid anomaly intrusion prevention and detection engine (real-time monitoring, detection and prevention using protocol anomaly detection and attack signatures)
- Additional concurrent VPN sessions

Symantec: Platform Support and System Requirements

SGS is based on the Raptor firewall plus the Recourse Intrusion Detection System (IDS) plus Symantec's Antivirus. The software version of the Symantec Enterprise Firewall will run on Windows NT/2000 or Solaris. Windows machines require a 400 MHz PIII processor, 256MB of RAM, and 8 GB of disk space. Solaris machines require

Solaris 7 or 8, Sun UltraSPARC I or II sbus or PCI bus, 256MB of RAM and 8 GB of disk space.

How does ISA Server 2004 compare? ISA Server 2004 runs on standard Intel PCs that are easily upgraded and can be installed on Windows 2000 Server or Windows Server 2003, providing a standardized, familiar management interface and the flexibility to use hardware of your choice.

The Windows Server 2003 OS can be "hardened" by applying a series of special profiles included in Server 2003 SP2 for the Security Configuration wizard. Microsoft also provides a system hardening guide that includes specific configuration recommendations and deployment strategies for ISA Server 2004. The document can be downloaded at http://www.microsoft.com/technet/prodtechnol/isa/2004/plan/securityhardening-guide.mspx.

Symantec: Application Layer Filtering Capabilities

Symantec provides application layer filtering for intrusion detection, HTTP and SMTP/POP3 protection, and FTP filtering (virus and attack protection). The firewall uses ManHunt (which Symantec purchased from Recourse Technologies) for IDS. ManHunt monitors as passive IDS or actively blocks specified attacks. Symantec uses WebNot content filtering for URL screening. Anti-spam filtering is also sold as a separate optional function.

How does ISA Server 2004 compare? ISA Server 2004's built-in intrusion detection examines the HTTP, POP3, IMAP, SMTP, FTP, and DNS protocols. ISA Server 2004 performs intelligent stateful inspection using "smart" application filters. Not only can you determine the validity of data moving through the firewall in request and response headers, you can also filter by "signature" (text string) for keyword filtering or filter for particular file types.

ISA Server 2004 inspects all aspects of HTTP communications. The SMTP filter protects against invalid SMTP commands that cause buffer overflows, and the SMTP message screener blocks spam and mail containing dangerous attachments. ISA Server's RPC filtering protects against exploits and malicious code directed to the RPC services and ensures that only valid connections get through to the Exchange server. DNS filtering prevents application layer attacks aimed at published DNS servers, and the POP3 filters protect published POP3 mail servers from attack.

ISA Server was built from the beginning to perform ALF, and ISA Server's SDK allows easy development of new web and application filters.

Symantec: VPN Support

The Symantec Enterprise VPN 7.0 runs on Windows NT/2000 and Solaris 7/8 and is included in the Enterprise Gateway appliances. The Symantec Enterprise VPN client runs on Windows 9x, ME, 2000, NT 4.0 and XP. Enterprise VPN software is integrated with the Enterprise Firewall software on Symantec's security appliances.

Symantec Enterprise VPN includes:

- Support for IPSec VPNs; interoperates with other IPSec-compliant VPN clients and servers
- Operation independent of firewall and integrates into networks with non-Symantec firewalls
- One-step configuration for administrators and one-step connect for clients
- Remote centralized management for large-scale deployments.

The Enterprise VPN client includes personal firewall software; remote policies create a bootstrap file for clients, and the VPN server performs ProxySecured scanning of VPN connections.

How does ISA Server 2004 compare? In ISA Server 2004, the number of simultaneous VPN connections depend on the operating system, from 1000 (Standard edition), and up. ISA Server supports IPSec VPNs for site-to-site connections and both PPTP and the more secure L2TP for remote access connections. ISA Server can apply firewall policy to the VPN interfaces.

ISA Server does not require any software to be added to VPN clients. ISA Server supports the PPTP and L2TP/IPSec VPN clients that are built into Windows 9x/ME, Windows XP, Windows NT, 2000, and Server 2003 operating systems.

ISA Server's VPN quarantine allows administrators to enforce specific conditions VPN clients must meet before being allowed to connect (for example, latest service pack/updates must be installed) and direct clients to server to download and install the required updates.

ISA Server's VPN quarantine is a function of Windows Server 2003 and allows you to block VPN access if the client does not meet pre-defined configuration criteria, including installation of current service packs and hotfixes, operational anti-virus and firewall. No proprietary client software is required to use VPN-Q, and there is no extra cost to apply it to any number of clients up to the limits of the operating system.

Symantec: Web Caching

Symantec firewalls do not perform Web caching. A separate appliance or third-party Web caching solution must be implemented to provide this functionality on the network.

How does ISA Server 2004 compare? ISA Server 2004 includes Web caching functionality at no extra charge. Forward caching allows the ISA Server 2004 firewall to cache objects retrieved by internal users from external Web servers. Reverse caching allows the ISA Server 2004 firewall to cache objects retrieved by remote users from servers that have been published by the ISA Server 2004 firewall. Web objects requested by remote users are cached on the ISA Server 2004 firewall, and subsequent requests for the same objects are served from the firewall's Web cache instead of forwarding the request to the published Web server located behind the ISA Server 2004 firewall.

Fast RAM caching allows the ISA Server 2004 firewall to keep most frequently accessed items in memory. This optimizes response time by retrieving items from memory rather than from disk. ISA Server 2004 gives you an optimized disk cache store that minimizes disk access for both read and write operations. ISA Server 2004 also supports Web proxy chaining, which allows the ISA Server 2004 firewall to forward Web requests to an upstream Web proxy server.

Comparing ISA 2004 to Blue Coat SG

Blue Coat Systems is one of ISA Server's few competitors that markets an integrated firewall and Web caching solution. It was originally known as CacheFlow, then in 2002 the company changed its name and shifted its focus to the security market. The company's Web site claims more than 3,000 customers and over 14,000 appliances shipped worldwide, with over 70 percent of the Dow-Jones Industrial companies as customers. According to IDC, Blue Coat has a 33 percent share of the content management market, making it number one in that area. Blue Coat appliances are ICSA certified.

In this section, we provide an overview of Blue Coat SG appliances. We look at Blue Coat's general specifications, platform support and system requirements, application layer filtering capabilities, VPN support and Web caching abilities, and examine how ISA Server 2004 stacks up against them.

Blue Coat: General Specifications

Blue Coat offers three series of security and caching appliances:

- SG 400: designed for small to medium sized businesses with up to 250 users

- SG 800: designed for enterprise networks with up to 2000 users

- SG 8000: designed for enterprise networks with 1000 to 10,000+ users, providing an expandable modular platform that allows customization of disk size, memory and interfaces.

Configurations of the different models are shown in Table 3.9.

Table 3.9 Blue Coat SG Model-by-Model Comparison

Model	Disk	Memory	Interfaces
SG400-0	One 40GB IDE	256MB	Two 10/100
SG400-1	Two 40GB IDE	512MB	Two 10/100
SG800-0	One 18GB or one 36GB Ultra SCSI	512MB	Two 10/100
SG800-0B	Two 18GB or two 36GB Ultra SCSI	768MB	Two 10/100

Continued

Table 3.9 Blue Coat SG Model-by-Model Comparison

Model	Disk	Memory	Interfaces
SG800-1	One 73GB Ultra SCSI	1GB	Two 10/100; one expansion slot for 10/100, 10/10/1000 or SX
SG800-2	Two 73GB Ultra SCSI	1.5GB	Two 10/100; one expansion slot for 10/100, 10/10/1000 or SX
SG800-3	Four 73GB Ultra SCSI	2GB	Two 10/100; one expansion slot for 10/100, 10/10/1000 or SX
SG8000-1*	Two 15,000 RPM 73GB	1GB	Four 10/100/1000
SG8000-2*	Four 15,000 RPM 73GB	2GB	Four 10/100/1000
SG8000-3*	Six 15,000 RPM 73GB	3GB	Four 10/100/1000
SG8000-4*	Eight 15,000 RPM 73GB	4GB	Four 10/100/1000

* *SG8000 series are all dual processor with two 3.2GHz Xeon processors*

Cost of the Blue Coat SG appliances, at the time of this writing, is as follows:

- SG400 starts at $3495
- SG800 starts at $5995
- SG8000 starts at $40,000

Content filtering license costs extra; for 500 users, a two-year site license costs $9140 at the time of this writing.

Blue Coat: Platform Support and System Requirements

Blue Coat appliances run on a proprietary hardened SGOS operating system. The SGOS and integrated firewall and caching software are installed on proprietary disk-based appliance hardware (not ASIC).

How does ISA Server 2004 compare? ISA Server 2004 runs on standard Intel PCs that are easily upgraded and can be installed on Windows 2000 Server or Windows Server 2003, providing a standardized, familiar management interface and the flexibility to use hardware of your choice. This makes ISA Server more scalable than appliances that are tied to the hardware and more user-friendly than Blue Coat.

The Windows Server 2003 OS can be "hardened" by applying a series of special profiles included in Server 2003 SP2 for the Security Configuration wizard. Microsoft also provides a system hardening guide that includes specific configuration recommendations and deployment strategies for ISA Server 2004. The document can be downloaded at http://www.microsoft.com/technet/prodtechnol/isa/2004/plan/securityhardening-guide.mspx.

Blue Coat: Application Layer Filtering Capabilities

Blue Coat appliances provide packet-filtering rules that are defined using Content Policy Language (CPL) and Access Control Lists (ACLs). The SG appliances support NTLM, LDAP, and RADIUS authentication.

The Blue Coat SG appliances support content filtering via the major filtering vendors (WebSense, SurfControl, SmartFilter). Policies can be defined to provide MIME-type filtering. Filtering of content headers is supported. Third party anti-virus software is required to filter for malicious code downloaded from the Web. The SG appliances integrate with Symantec and TrendMicro via ICAP for real-time AV scanning of Web content.

Active content can be blocked, Web content can be stripped and replaced, and the information in content headers can be limited, stripped, or replaced. You can block or log Peer-to-Peer and IM traffic, and control clients' actions (for example, prevent them from downloading files). Pop-up ad blocking is also included.

Blue Coat uses a "policy-processing engine" that utilizes security triggers that can be based on a variety of factors, including users/groups, protocols, time of day, location, or content type.

Blue Coat appliances support bandwidth management.

How does ISA Server compare? ISA Server provides packet filtering, circuit filtering and application layer filtering, along with stateful inspection/stateful filtering. ISA Server includes deep application layer filtering at no extra cost.

ISA Server 2004 performs intelligent stateful inspection using "smart" application filters. Not only can you determine the validity of data moving through the firewall in request and response headers, you can also filter by "signature" (text string) for keyword filtering or filter for particular file types.

ISA Server 2004 inspects all aspects of HTTP communications. The SMTP filter protects from invalid SMTP commands that cause buffer overflows, and the SMTP message screener blocks spam and mail containing dangerous attachments.

ISA Server's RPC filtering protects from exploits and malicious code directed to the RPC services and ensures that only valid connections get through to the Exchange server.

DNS filtering prevents application layer attacks aimed at published DNS servers and the POP3 filters protect published POP3 mail servers from attack.

Blue Coat: VPN Support

VPN support is not included in the basic Blue Coat Firewall and Web caching appliances.

How does ISA Server 2004 compare? ISA Server 2004 supports the following VPN protocols:

- Point-to-Point Tunneling Protocol (PPTP)
- Layer 2 Tunneling Protocol/IPSec (L2TP/IPSec)
- IPSec Tunnel Mode
- The ISA Server 2004 VPN feature supports two types of VPN connections:
- Remote Access VPN
- Site-to-site VPN

Firewall access policies are applied to VPN remote access and site-to-site connections. ISA Server uses the PPTP and L2TP VPN clients included free with all Windows operating systems.

Blue Coat: Web Caching

The SG appliances support the following:

- Forward caching
- Reverse caching
- Active caching
- Distributed caching
- Hierarchical caching
- Streaming media caching

Client browsers can be automatically configured via a Proxy Autoconfiguration (PAC) file.

Reverse caching is accomplished by using a layer 4/7 switch or a router that supports WCCP. This redirects Web requests so that they are sent to the cache instead of the originating server.

Statistics (size, usage and changes) for all Web objects served are kept by the OS, then used to create "refresh patterns" for each object. These are used by the Active caching function. You cannot schedule the refreshing for particular times.

How does ISA Server 2004 compare? ISA Server 2004 includes Web caching functionality at no extra charge. Forward caching allows the ISA Server 2004 firewall to cache objects retrieved by internal users from external Web servers. Reverse caching allows the ISA Server 2004 firewall to cache objects retrieved by remote users from servers that have been published by the ISA Server 2004 firewall. Web objects requested by remote users are cached on the ISA Server 2004 firewall, and subsequent requests for the same objects are served from the firewall's Web cache instead of forwarding the request to the published Web server, located behind the ISA Server 2004 firewall.

Fast RAM caching allows the ISA Server 2004 firewall to keep most frequently accessed items in memory. This optimizes response time by retrieving items from memory rather than from disk. ISA Server 2004 gives you an optimized disk cache store that minimizes disk access for both read and write operations. ISA Server 2004 also supports Web proxy chaining, which allows the ISA Server 2004 firewall to forward Web requests to an upstream Web proxy server.

Comparing ISA 2004 to Open Source Firewalls

Open source firewalls are developed and distributed under the GNU General Public License (GPL) and other open source licenses; as with other open source programs, the source code is available free to anyone who wants it. This results in peer review that theoretically makes it easier for flaws in the software to be discovered and fixed.

Open source firewalls are popular with highly technical individuals (such as hackers, both of the black and white hat varieties) and those who advocate and are familiar with open source operating systems. The obvious advantage (cost) is often offset by the following disadvantages:

- **Difficult to use**: a high level of technical expertise is often required to configure open source software. Many (although not all) rely on command-line interfaces (CLI) and obscure commands that must be learned; this can take time, especially if administrators are not already familiar with the underlying OS.

- **Lack of documentation**: Because the software is developed for free, programmers may not have the time nor the inclination to prepare commercial-grade documentation and Help files for the products. Combined with the inherently less intuitive interfaces, this makes the learning curve for new users even steeper and more frustrating, and thus, adds hidden cost in terms of administrative time to get up to speed.

- **Weak or missing logging and alerting; no real time monitoring**: these are "extra" features that are often left out of open source firewall products. They may be less important in a home use or a lab environment but are essential to a corporate business environment where administrators must be able to track events, provide forensics information for investigation of security incidents, and justify decisions with well documented information.

Despite these drawbacks, a number of open source firewall products have gained popularity in some business circles. Some of the most well established include IPchains, the Juniper Firewall Tool Kit (FWTK), and IPCop.

IPChains/IP Tables

IPchains is a part of the Linux core operating system that provides packet filtering and Network Address Translation (often referred to as IP Masquerade in the Linux community). Administrators can create "chains" or tables of rules that can be applied to each incoming or outgoing packet. The rules are applied in the order in which you create them. The rules can be bundled into "chains" for specified types of traffic.

IPchains perform firewall functionality in the traditional sense of the word: packet filtering at the network layer of the OSI model. It can redirect higher level streambased protocols such as SMTP, POP, NNTP, and DNS, but can't examine the contents to ensure that the data inside the packets are valid for the protocol.

IPTables is similar to IPchains but performs stateful inspection, whereas IPchains is stateless. Both support port redirection and are often used in conjunction with other products such as Squid or FWTK for application proxies.

VPN functionality can be added with free open source software that can be downloaded from the Internet.

How does ISA Server 2004 compare? ISA Server 2004 is a full-featured multi-layered firewall and Web-caching product that offers easy management through a graphical interface and enterprise-level performance and centralized management.

ISA Server provides sophisticated application layer filtering capability and built-in IDS functionality. ISA Server includes full VPN gateway functionality supporting PPTP, L2TP and IPSec VPNs.

FWTK/ipfirewall

The Juniper Firewall ToolKit was developed by Obtuse Systems to run on Linux and BSD/FreeBSD. It was based on ipfirewall and offered as a toolkit for building proxy firewalls.

Ipfirewall is a kernel packet filter that comes with FreeBSD. It allows you to set up a machine as a packet-filtering router or you can use it on machines that aren't configured as routers as a personal firewall to filter incoming and outgoing packets.

Using ipfirewall is anything but user friendly. You must add options to the operating system's kernel configuration file and recompile the kernel. The default when you install ipfirewall is, "deny ip from any to any." This means everything is effectively blocked so that you may not be able to reboot back into the server after you install the firewall.

Configuration is done through the ipfw utility. This is a command line utility that can be used to enable and disable the firewall, add and delete rules, move them to different sets, and so on. You can have up to 65,535 rules. The firewall compares each packet to each rule and performs whatever action you have set on the matching rule(s). A default rule (allow or deny) determines whether all packets are blocked by default or allowed by default.

Dynamic rules with limited lifetimes can be created to open the firewall "on demand" to legitimate traffic.

How does ISA Server 2004 compare? ISA Server 2004 is a full-featured multi-layered firewall and Web caching product that offers easy management through a graphical interface and enterprise-level performance and centralized management.

ISA Server provides sophisticated application layer filtering capability and built-in IDS functionality. ISA Server includes full VPN gateway functionality supporting PPTP, L2TP and IPSec VPNs.

IPCop

IPCop is a user-friendly firewall that runs on Linux and is managed from a Web UI, thus it can be managed remotely. It includes NAT functionality to protect a small LAN.

It is based on the Smoothwall code and licensed under the GNU GPL. The firewall is based on ipchains, but the graphical interface makes it much easier to manage.

IPCop is more full-featured than command line open source firewalls. It includes VPN (IPSec only) and Snort IDS. It is implemented as an operating system/firewall combination that is installed as one package. The OS is a "cut down" distro of Linux with extra services removed.

IPCop supports up to three network interfaces, allowing you to set up a DMZ. The interfaces are color coded green, red and orange (for internal, external and DMZ) for ease of setup. Access from the DMZ network to the internal network can be provided via "DMZ pinholes").

A Web proxy service (Squid) is included but disabled by default.

How does ISA Server 2004 compare? ISA Server 2004 is a full-featured multi-layered firewall and Web-caching product that offers easy management through a graphical interface and enterprise-level performance and centralized management.

ISA Server provides sophisticated application layer filtering capability and built-in IDS functionality. ISA Server includes full VPN gateway functionality supporting PPTP, L2TP and IPSec VPNs.

Summary

Table 3.10 summarizes the comparison between ISA Server 2004 and its top competing commercial firewall products at the time of this writing:

Table 3.10 ISA 2004 vs. Competing Firewall Products

Feature	ISA Server	Check-Point NG/Nokia 350	Cisco PIX 515E	Netscreen 50	SonicWall Pro 230	Watch-Guard V80	Symantec 5420
Architecture	Software	Appliance Software	Appliance	Appliance (ASIC)	Appliance	Appliance	Appliance[1]
Operating system	Windows 2000, Windows Server 2003	IPSO; also runs on Windows NT/2000, Solaris, Linux, AIX	PIX OS (based on IOS)	ScreenOS	SonicOS (2 versions, simple & enhanced)	Proprietary	Proprietary[1]
Firewall throughput	Tested up to 1.59Gbps)	350Mbps	188Mbps	170Mbps	190Mbps	200Mbps	200Mbps
Interfaces	No software limit	4 10/100	6	4 10/100	3 10/100	4 10/100 2 HA ports	6
VPN tunnels	1000 (Standard) 16,000+ PPTP,	12,500	2000	100	500	8000	*
VPN support	PPTP, L2TP, IPSec, SSL	IPSec, SSL, L2TP	IKE/IPSec, L2TP, PPTP	IPSEC, SSL	IPSec, PPTP	IPSec, L2TP (other models support PPTP)	IPSec
VPN client	Free w/all Windows OS	Proprietary or MS L2TP client[3]	Proprietary, MS L2TP, PPTP[3]	Proprietary, costs extra	Proprietary, bundled (10)	Proprietary, costs extra	Proprietary, per-tunnel lic.

Continued

Table 3.10 ISA 2004 vs. Competing Firewall Products

Feature	ISA Server	Check-Point NG/Nokia 350	Cisco PIX 515E	Netscreen 50	SonicWall Pro 230	Watch-Guard V80	Symantec 5420
VPN Quarantine	Included as part of Windows Server 2003; allows enforcement of client configuration: SP installation, anti-virus, firewall; works with free VPN client included with Windows OS	Referred to as "client configuration verification." Requires Secure Client VPN client (extra cost)	Configurations downloaded and "pushed" to clients from central gateway; requires Cisco Secure VPN client v3.x	Limited; enforcement of personal firewall and updates. Requires Net Screen Remote Security Client (extra cost)	VPN configuration data is downloaded from VPN gateway by clients using proprietary Global VPN client software	Limited; enforcement of personal firewall Requires proprietary Mobile User VPN client	Enterprise VPN client includes personal firewall software; remote policies create bootstrap file for client; server performs ProxySecured scanning of VPN connections
IDS	Based on technology licensed from ISS	ISS Real Secure IDS; inline/passive inspection of TCP stream	Protects against 55 attacks; separate IDS appliance avail.	DS included lbased on OneSecure; IDP available extra	DoS attack detection and prevention	IDS, IDP included, protocol anomaly detection	Hybrid anomaly IDS/IDP (Recourse)
ALF	Deep application layer including character string filtering; HTTP, SMTP, DNS, FTP, POP3, IMAP	NG App Layer Intelligence; includes application proxies, content filtering via UFP	Fixups; ASA; URL filtering w/Websense or N2H2; CF blocks Java/ActiveX	HTTP, POP3, IMAP, SMTP, FTP, DNS, Supports WebSense	CFS subscription svc.	SMTP, HTTP proxies	Attack signatures; HTTP, FTP & SMTP sent to virus scan, content filtering

Continued

Table 3.10 ISA 2004 vs. Competing Firewall Products

Feature	ISA Server	Check-Point NG/Nokia 350	Cisco PIX 515E	Netscreen 50	SonicWall Pro 230	Watch-Guard V80	Symantec 5420
Management UI	Familiar Windows MMC for local and remote management, CLI, Terminal Svc/remote desktop	CLI, SNMP, FTP, Telnet, SSH, Web: Voyager (local) Horizon Mgr (remote)	PIX Device Mgr (PDM); CLI, Telnet, SSH, console port	Web (HTTP, HTTPS), CLI, Telnet, SSH, Global Pro (option)	Web UI, CLI, SNMP, Global Mgmt System (centralized)	Java-based GUI; CLI; Multi-box mgmt (CPM) optional	Web-based (SSL) UI, Symantec Mgmt console
Web Caching	Included at no extra cost; Forward/reverse product	Not included; add-on product	Not included; Cisco Content Engine costs extra	Not included	With CFS subscription	Not included	Not included
High availability	Uses load balancing, failover included in W2000/2003 at no extra cost.	Clustering not supported on this model	Failover with purchase of second appliance	Supports active/ passive mode only (A/A on other series)	Hardware failover is a "value added service"	Supports active/ passive (A/A optional at extra cost)	A/A, A/P, LB (max cluster size 8)
Add-ons (extra cost options)	Wide variety 3rd party add-ons for extensibility	Management, IDS, Cluster, Content filtering, reports, caching	Content engine (caching), IDS, anti-virus, content filtering	IDP, spam filtering (SurfControl), AV	AV, Content filtering add-on; GSM for multi mgmt	A/A HA, virus scan, live security update svc.	AV, content filtering, addi-tional VPN clients, HA/LB
Licensing	Based on Edition (SE or EE), no extra cost for VPN client licenses	Yearly subscrip. License, Secure-Client VPN client extra	Based on functionality; R, UR, F, VPN client extra	Baseline, advanced lic., VPN client extra	Unlim firewall user; VPN client license extra	Unlim user licenses; VPN client license extra	Base lic. 50 node FW, 1 client VPN session
Price	$1499 (Standard)	$3695	$4989 (UR)	$5695	$1699	$12,995	$2999

[1] Symantec Enterprise Firewall software that runs on 5400 series appliances can also be purchased as a software firewall that will run on Windows or Solaris.
[2] Windows Server 2003 Standard edition supports 1000 PPTP and 1000 L2TP connections. Windows Server 2003 Enterprise and DataCenter editions theoretically support unlimited VPN connections, but the Registry restricts PPTP to 16,384 and L2TP to 30,000 on these editions.

Comparing Architecture

All of ISA Server 2004's competitors except CheckPoint, Symantec, and the open source products (IPchains, FWTK, and IPCop) are marketed as appliances with the hardware and software sold together. Most run on proprietary operating systems. Many use ASIC solid state architectures.

Although the appliance form factor offers some advantages—turnkey installation without having to install an OS or software, OS optimized for the software, high performance for ASIC hardware—it also offers disadvantages: more difficulty in upgrading, less flexibility in hardware configuration, inability of the hardware to "keep up" with increases in processing power. In some respects, comparing an appliance to a software-based firewall or caching solution is comparing apples and oranges, especially in terms of price comparison. For example, important considerations in choosing an appliance include processor, memory, and number of network interfaces. With a software solution, you control these features by the hardware on which you choose to install the software, rather than being locked into one of the choices offered by the vendor.

As a software-based solution, ISA Server offers more flexibility in terms of hardware scalability than do the appliance-based solutions. ISA Server 2004 is also expected to be offered on security appliances by several vendors, allowing it to compete more directly with other appliance products.

Comparing Functionality

All of ISA Server's competitors except one (Blue Coat) compete in only one of ISA's dual functions: firewall/VPN or Web caching. Thus, although a PIX or NetScreen appliance might seem to offer equal firewall/VPN functionality at the same or a lower price than ISA Server, it provides no caching functionality. Adding that caching function raises the price of the alternate solution substantially, sometimes more than doubling it. When the cost of adding a caching solution to the competing firewall product is factored in, ISA Server generally offers a more attractive price point.

Blue Coat, which does provide both firewall and caching functionality, suffers from one drawback, but it's a big one: no VPN support.

Comparing Cost

When compared objectively (using comparable hardware, and factoring in the need for both firewall and caching functionality), ISA compares favorably in price to every competitor—except, of course, the open source products. You can't compete with "free," at least not on the basis of price.

However, the open source products fall short in other areas:

- IPchains/FWTK and similar products based on aspects of the Linux or UNIX kernel provide only rudimentary firewall functionality. They are adequate packet-filtering firewalls but do not provide the sophisticated application layer filtering or built-in VPN gateway support taken for granted with all the commercial products.

- IPchains/FWTK and similar products use command-line interfaces and text files for configuration and management. Considerable expertise and knowledge of the underlying *NIX operating system are required to use them. Because they are freeware, support from the developers is sparse or non-existent. Documentation is spotty, and you may have to rely on voluntary community support (mailing lists, Web boards) or pay big bucks for third-party support if you have problems.

- Some freeware products, such as IPCop, are more user friendly and offer easy installation and graphical interface management. IPCop even includes a Web proxy/caching solution: Squid. It also includes the Snort intrusion-detection system. However, it is designed for home and SOHO users, not for large enterprise deployment. It does not provide deep application layer filtering, and it suffers the same lack of formal support as other open source products.

Every firewall product has advantages and disadvantages, and selecting the right one for your network is not always easy. If we seem to be excited about ISA Server 2004, that's because we are. We've been working with it and comparing it to other popular products for months, and we believe ISA Server 2004 stacks up well against all of its top competitors, based on cost factors, features and functionality, and ease of use issues. That's why we wrote this book.

This chapter provides you with a basis of comparison in selecting a firewall solution for your organization. If you select ISA Server 2004, the rest of the book will show you how to prepare for, deploy, configure, and manage it in a variety of real-world networking scenarios. We hope you'll come along for the ride.

Solutions Fast Track

Firewall Comparative Issues

- ☑ If you take a look at the product lines of most of the major firewall "appliance" vendors, you'll find from three to ten or more different models, not to mention a variety of different licensing schemes and plenty of "add-ons" that enhance functionality and come at extra cost.

☑ Constructing an intelligent comparison of the products of different vendors can be a daunting task, and often there is no clear-cut "winner" in such a comparison. Instead, you find that making the right choice depends very much on your existing network infrastructure, the role you want the firewall to play, and a tradeoff of some features for others.

☑ As you dig deeper into the comparative features, you begin to realize that a simple cost comparison is meaningless. A comparative analysis must also take into account the administrative overhead, licensing structure, and feature sets of the products being compared.

☑ To those who may have the ultimate decision-making authority (the Chief Financial Officer, purchasing agent, or small business owner), cost is a *very* important consideration. It's important to remember, however, that cost involves a lot more than just the initial purchase price of an appliance or software/hardware package.

☑ In comparing different products, you need to address each of the following: Capital investment, Add-on modules and enhancements, Licensing structures, Support, Upgrade, and Total Cost of Ownership (TCO)

☑ In calculating the TCO for each of the competing products, you must consider not only each of the direct costs we discuss in the preceding paragraphs, but also indirect costs such as learning curve, administrative overhead, productivity and downtime costs.

☑ Once we get cost issues out of the way and determine a budget within which we must work, the second broad category for comparison deals with the features and functionalities of each product.

☑ General specifications relate to the included hardware (for appliances) or the minimum hardware requirements (for software firewalls), as well as how scalable, extensible and reliable the product has proven to be in deployment, and whether and how it supports high availability/fault tolerance features such as clustering/failover and load balancing.

☑ Product data sheets from vendor Web sites can provide a starting point, but as you narrow down your choices, you'll want to dig deeper and read independent product reviews and/or talk to IT professionals who have personally worked with the particular products you're considering.

☑ Some important firewall features to compare include Application Layer Filtering (ALF), protocol support, intrusion detection, firewall throughput and number of simultaneous connections supported, logging and reporting capabilities.

☑ Most modern firewalls, other than those intended only as personal firewalls or "telecommuter" models, include integrated VPN gateways. There are several factors to consider when comparing VPN support of different security devices.

☑ Some factors to consider when comparing VPN functionality include VPN protocol support, types of VPN supported (remote access and/or site-to-site), VPN client costs and functionality, number of simultaneous VPN connections allowed, VPN throughput, VPN quarantine capabilities.

☑ There are a number of features to consider in comparing Web-caching solutions. Which features you need will be dependent on factors such as the size and structure of your organization, how and how much external Web access is used by those on your network, and whether your organization hosts its own Web servers.

☑ Some factors to consider when comparing Web-caching capability include forward-caching capability, reverse-caching capability, support for distributed and hierarchical caching, and use of caching rules.

☑ Another factor that may or may not be important to your organization is whether the firewall product you're considering has been "certified." To be meaningful, certification should be done by an independent entity (not a vendor) based on a standardized course of hands-on testing in a lab (not just a "paper" comparison of features).

☑ ICSA Labs is the most well recognized organization providing testing and certification of firewalls and other network security products.

Comparing ISA 2004 to Other Firewall Products

☑ Microsoft defines ISA Server 2004 as "an advanced application layer firewall, VPN, and Web cache solution that enables customers to easily maximize existing IT investments by improving network security and performance."

☑ ISA Server 2004 includes the following key features: multi-layer inspection, advanced application layer filtering, secure inbound traffic and protection from "inside attacks" via VPN client connections, integrated multi-networking capabilities, network templates, and stateful routing and inspection.

☑ ISA Server 2004's ease of use features include: simple, easy to learn and use management tools; prevention of network access downtime; savings on bandwidth costs; integration with Windows Active Directory, third party VPN solutions and other existing infrastructure; a thriving community of partners, users and Web resources.

☑ ISA Server 2004's high-performance features include: ability to provide fast, secure anywhere/anytime access; a safe, reliable and high-performance infrastructure; an integrated single-server solution; a way to scale out the security infrastructure; enhanced network performance, and reduced bandwidth costs.

☑ ISA Server 2004 is a software firewall, which can be installed on Windows 2000 Server (with Service Pack 4 or above) or Windows Server 2003. Internet Explorer 6, or later, must be installed.

☑ ISA Server is reliable, scalable, and extensible, and supports high availability through the Windows Server 2003 Network Load Balancing (NLB) service.

☑ ISA Server offers compatibility and interoperability with Active Directory, with Exchange server and other Microsoft Server System products, and in a mixed network environment.

☑ ISA Server 2004 provides administrators with a friendly graphical interface that not only has many advantages over most of its competitors, but also is a big improvement over the ISA Server 2000 interface.

☑ ISA Server 2004 provides remote management capability through the ISA Server management console and the Remote Desktop Protocol (RDP).

☑ ISA Server 2004 provides improved logging and reporting through the dashboard, alerts, the sessions panel, connectivity monitors, the report configuration wizard, and the ability to view connection information in real time.

☑ One of the major strengths of ISA Server 2004 is its ability to perform application layer filtering (ALF). The application layer filtering feature allows the ISA Server 2004 firewall to protect against attacks that are based on weaknesses or holes in a specific application layer protocol or service.

☑ ISA Server 2004 includes the following features that set it apart from the competition: secure Exchange RPC filter, link translation filter, and the OWA forms-based filter.

☑ ISA Server 2004 includes a collection of intrusion detection filters that are licensed from Internet Security Systems (ISS). These intrusion detection filters are focused on detecting and blocking network layer attacks. In addition, ISA Server 2004 includes intrusion detection filters that detect and block application layer attacks.

☑ ISA Server 2004 supports the following VPN protocols: Point-to-Point Tunneling Protocol (PPTP), Layer 2 Tunneling Protocol/IPSec (L2TP/IPSec), and IPSec Tunnel Mode.

☑ The ISA Server 2004 VPN feature supports two types of VPN connections: Remote Access VPN and Site-to-site VPN.

☑ The ISA Server 2004 VPN quarantine feature increases the security of VPN client connections by "pre-qualifying" VPN clients before they are allowed to connect to the corporate network.

☑ In addition to ISA Server 2004's firewall and VPN features, the ISA Server 2004 firewall can also act as a Web proxy server. The ISA Server 2004 machine can be deployed as a combined firewall and Web-caching server, or as a dedicated Web-caching server.

☑ ISA Server 2004 supports forward and reverse caching, and multiple ISA servers can be configured to use distributed and hierarchical caching.

☑ Check Point's add-on modules have to be purchased at extra cost, in many cases for functionality that is included at no extra charge with ISA Server.

☑ Check Point includes no Web-caching functionality; this must be added as an off-box solution or via add-on modules.

☑ Check Point's SecureClient software costs extra, and is needed to add VPN client configuration verification, similar to ISA Server's VPN quarantine feature that is included at no extra cost.

☑ Cisco PIX requires add-on third party products to provide functionalities such as deep content inspection that are included with ISA Server at no cost.

☑ Cisco PIX includes no Web caching functionality; this must be added by purchasing a Cisco Content Engine or a third-party caching solution.

☑ Enforcement of VPN configuration policy for PIX requires the proprietary Cisco Secure VPN client v3.x or above.

☑ NetScreen requires that additional appliances or third party products be purchased to provide functionalities included with ISA Server (more sophisticated intrusion detection/deep content inspection, caching).

☑ NetScreen uses a proprietary VPN client or security client (which includes personal firewall) that must be purchased at extra cost.

☑ VPN configuration enforcement with NetScreen only enforces client firewall policy.

☑ SonicWall requires that additional appliances or third-party products be purchased to provide functionalities included with ISA Server (more sophisticated intrusion detection/deep content inspection, caching).

☑ NetScreen uses a proprietary VPN client that must be purchased at extra cost.

☑ Downloading of client configuration data from VPN gateway requires security client.

☑ WatchGuard does not include application proxies on its low cost models. ALF includes only HTTP, FTP, DNS.

☑ WatchGuard provides no Web-caching functionality. Cost of adding a caching solution must be factored in when comparing cost with ISA server.

☑ WatchGuard uses proprietary remote VPN client software that must be purchased at extra cost.

☑ Symantec requires that additional appliances or third party products be purchased to provide functionalities included with ISA Server (more sophisticated intrusion detection/deep content inspection, caching).

☑ Symantec provides no Web-caching functionality. Cost of adding a caching solution must be factored in when comparing cost with ISA server.

☑ Symantec uses proprietary remote VPN client software that must be purchased at extra cost.

☑ Blue Coat is the only one of ISA Server 2004's major competitors that includes Web-caching functionality.

☑ Blue Coat does not include site-to-site VPN gateway or remote access VPN functionality.

☑ Blue Coat requires that content filtering be done through a third-party service.

☑ Open source firewalls are more popular with highly technical individuals (such as hackers) and those who advocate and are familiar with open source operating systems.

☑ The cost advantage of open source firewalls is often offset by difficulty of use, lack of documentation, lack of technical support, and weak or missing logging and alerting features.

☑ IPChains provides rudimentary firewall functionality and does not include services usually taken for granted in commercial firewall products such as ALF, VPN gateway, IDS, and others.

☑ The Juniper Firewall ToolKit was developed by Obtuse Systems to run on Linux and BSD/FreeBSD. It was based on ipfirewall and offered as a toolkit for building proxy firewalls.

☑ Ipfirewall is a kernel packet filter that comes with FreeBSD. It performs network-layer packet filtering only; application-layer filtering must be done by another program/service.

☑ IPCop is a user-friendly firewall that runs on Linux and is managed from a Web UI, thus it can be managed remotely. It includes NAT functionality to protect a small LAN. It is based on the Smoothwall code and licensed under the GNU GPL. The firewall is based on ipchains.

☑ IPCop was designed for home and SOHO users rather than enterprise-level networks.

Frequently Asked Questions

The following Frequently Asked Questions, answered by the authors of this book, are designed to both measure your understanding of the concepts presented in this chapter and to assist you with real-life implementation of these concepts. To have your questions about this chapter answered by the author, browse to **www.syngress.com/solutions** and click on the **"Ask the Author"** form. You will also gain access to thousands of other FAQs at ITFAQnet.com.

Q. Why doesn't Microsoft offer ISA Server as a turn-key security appliance?

A. Microsoft is working with partners to provide security appliances running ISA Server, which can compete more directly with other hardware-based firewall and caching products for those who prefer the advantages of the appliance form factor over the flexibility and easy upgradeability of a software-based solution. Companies offering ISA Server 2004-based appliances include Hewlett-Packard, Network Engines, RimApp, and other hardware vendors. These ISA 2004 appliances will run on a hardened version of the Windows server OS and will provide the turn-key convenience of an appliance with all the deep integration into Windows networks that only ISA Server 2004 can offer.

Q. Is ISA Server's underlying operating system (Windows 2000 Server or Windows Server 2003) inherently insecure, and does this make the firewall insecure as well?

A. No, and no. Microsoft's security initiative began in earnest with the release of Windows 2000 server, which included a level of security orders of magnitude above its older operating systems. Windows 2000 introduced numerous new security features such as Kerberos authentication, file encryption, Active Directory, the Security Configuration Manager, Transport Layer Security (TLS), IPSec, PKI support, smart card authentication, L2TP VPN, and more. That trend has continued and intensified with the release of Windows Server 2003, which is built on a "secure by design" and "secure by default" philosophy, wherein services such as IIS are disabled out of the box.

ISA Server 2004 uses the Windows Server 2003 Security Configuration Wizard (included in SP2), which includes a special ISA Server profile to harden the OS specifically for running the ISA firewall.

Q. How can ISA Server compete with low-cost NetScreen and SonicWall devices that are priced under $500?

A. If you examine the specifications for the low-end devices, you'll find that they are intended for SOHO or telecommuter use. They cost less, but they also give you less functionality. For example, they provide far fewer simultaneous VPN tunnels, fewer concurrent firewall sessions, and/or much slower throughput. ISA Server was not designed for SOHO/telecommuter use (although it can perform well in those situations). It is designed for medium-to-large networks, and its specifications reflect that. Additionally, the low-cost firewalls mentioned don't provide any Web-caching functionality at all. Adding another caching solution on the network will bring the true total price up considerably.

Q. Most popular firewalls, such as PIX, SonicWall, and NetScreen, seem to come in several different models. Why does ISA Server only come in two editions? How can ISA Server scale to meet the needs of small to very large organizations with only two editions?

A. That's the difference between appliances and software-based firewalls. If you read the fine print, you'll see that the firewall software itself is the same for all those different models (although some of its functions may be disabled on some models unless you buy extra licenses). The differences between the models are generally hardware differences: processor(s), amount of memory, number and type of network interfaces, and so on. With ISA Server, you can install the software on any machine that meets the minimum requirements. Thus, you have complete control over the hardware specs, rather than being forced to choose between a set number of models.

Q. Why does ISA Server support only CARP for communications between caching servers, when other caching proxies support a number of different protocols, such as ICP, HTCP, Cache Digests, and WCCP?

A. The Cache Array Routing Protocol (CARP) was selected as the protocol of choice for communications between distributed ISA Server caches because it is the most optimum for this purpose. CARP supports both server-side and client-side routing requests. Server-side routing is similar to that supported by WCCP and ICP. Client-side routing is more efficient because the client is able to predetermine which array member is responsible for the URL, and can send its request directly to that array member. CARP uses a more efficient method for caching content across multiple servers in that CARP, unlike ICP, ensures that cached Web content is not duplicated on servers and that the CARP algorithm provides a deterministic method for locating the server that holds the cached content.

Q. How does ISA Server's VPN quarantine feature compare to similar features provided by other firewall/VPN vendors?

A. VPN quarantine is provided through the Network Access Quarantine feature of Windows Server 2003. It allows you to block connections from VPN clients that don't meet a number of administrator-defined criteria; for example, service packs and hot fixes must be current; antivirus software must be installed and operational, and personal firewall software must be installed and operational. Other vendors that provide similar functionality usually do so through the use of their proprietary VPN client software. This software may be different and cost more than their standard proprietary VPN client. If the standard client supports this functionality, the firewall may come with only a limited number of VPN client licenses and you must purchase extra ones for more VPN users. Some vendors' client configuration enforcement extends only to requiring personal firewall software be installed and does not enforce service pack and hotfix requirements. ISA Server's VPN quarantine feature works with the Windows VPN client software that is built into all modern Windows operating systems, and there is no extra cost for any of this functionality.

Q. Why would I pay for ISA Server when I can use free open source firewall and caching programs such as IPChains and Squid, which run on Linux, an open source operating system?

A. As Robert A. Heinlein, famous science fiction author, once said: TANSTAAFL ("There ain't no such thing as a free lunch"). The price you pay for "free" software comes in many forms:

- Frustration and administrative time spent learning obscure commands, or misconfigurations resulting from a single typo in a text-based configuration file
- The cost of third-party books or support contracts when you find that documentation for the open source code is sparse and difficult to understand, and support from the developers is non-existent

■ The need to implement a commercial product later instead of, or in addition to, the open source "solution" because the free product does not provide all the features you need, or is so user-unfriendly that you can't figure out how to implement them.

Specifically, IPchains/iptables and FWTK are very rudimentary firewalls that don't include the application layer filtering, VPN gateway, and other features you expect from a commercial product. IPCop is more user-friendly, but is designed for SOHO and home users, not for the enterprise. None of the open source products are designed to integrate into Microsoft networks and provide seamless support for Exchange mail servers, SharePoint collaboration servers, and other Microsoft products as ISA Server does.

Chapter 4

ISA 2004 Network Concepts and Preparing the Network Infrastructure

Topics in this Chapter:

- Our Approach to ISA Firewall Network Design and Defense Tactics

- Tom and Deb Shinder's Configuring ISA 2004 Network Layout

- How ISA Firewalls Define Networks and Network Relationships

- Web Proxy Chaining as a Form of Network Routing

- Firewall Chaining as a Form of Network Routing

- Configuring the ISA Firewall as a DHCP Server

In this chapter, we will discuss a disparate group of issues that relate to the ISA firewall's Networking capabilities. We'll start with a detailed discussion of how we see the ISA firewall and its proper place on corporate networks. Then, we'll cover the network layout we use for all the scenarios discussed in this book. Included in this discussion will be a detailed description on how you can configure VMware to replicate the configurations in this book.

Next, we'll dig into the deep details on how the ISA firewall "sees" Networks, and how you configure the firewall to communicate on local and non-local networks. We'll also discuss some topics that don't fit neatly into any category, but seem to fit best into this "Network Concepts" chapter. We'll finish up with a discussion of the supporting Network Services that you will need to consider when setting up an ISA firewall. This is a critical discussion because the ISA firewall benefits from the services and support of a wide variety of network services.

In some of the discussions in this chapter, we'll cover concepts and procedures that will be discussed in much more detail in other chapters of this book. We understand if you find yourself frustrated with some terms or concepts in this chapter that haven't yet been defined. Be patient and look up those terms or concepts in other chapters in this book. You're also welcome to post a question on the www.isaserver.org message boards. Just write **BOOK** at the beginning of the title in your post and reference that page number of the book that you're having problems with, then send me an e-mail message at tshinder@isaserver.org with the link to your post.

Our Approach to ISA Firewall Network Design and Defense Tactics

Every book has its own unique approach to a subject, and that's certainly true for this book's approach to ISA firewalls. You'll notice throughout this book that we refer to the ISA 2004 product as the "ISA firewall" or "ISA firewall" or even "ISA firewall." We've made it a point to bring together the name "ISA" with the term "firewall". We do this because it's important to get the point across that the ISA firewall is indeed an enterprise-ready firewall that, at this point of time, is capable of providing a higher level of firewall protection than virtually any other firewall on the market.

It is from this vantage point that we approach all of the discussion of the ISA firewall in this book. The ISA firewall can be placed anywhere on your network: as a front-end Internet edge perimeter firewall, as a back-end departmental or asset-segment firewall, and even as a firewall that is dedicated to protecting a collection of vital network services. The level of flexibility in placing the ISA firewall in relation to other networking services and firewalls is a testament to the ISA firewall's power in protecting your network resources, no matter where those resources are located.

If you've made it this far in the book, then we can assume that you already have an ISA firewall in place, or you are considering placing an ISA firewall somewhere on your network. In both situations, it's likely that you're going to have to deal with network infrastructure people, or even DMZ or router administrators, who have bought into the hardware firewall vendors' marketing schemes that have convinced them that "hardware firewalls" are the only way to get true firewall security.

To make your life easier when discussing firewall issues with these "hardware firewall experts," we will discuss our approach and philosophy regarding the ISA firewall and how it compares with the marketing approaches of the hardware firewall vendors. We will discuss the following subjects that will help clarify the situation and help you put any ISA firewall detractors against the wall and on the defensive:

- Defense in Depth
- ISA Firewall Fallacies
- Why ISA Belongs in Front of Critical Assets
- A Better Network and Firewall Topology

By the time you're done with this section, you'll have the fact ammo you need to get an ISA firewall solution in place to protect your network.

NOTE

The goal of this section is to show that the ISA firewall represents a true enterprise-grade network firewall. The goal is *not* to demonstrate that it's the firewall that will meet everyone's needs in all possible scenarios. Other firewalls include features an organization may require that the ISA firewall does not support. In the same way, the ISA firewall includes critical security features that other firewalls do not.

Defense in Depth

Just about every firewall administrator has heard the old joke where the guy's boss asks him, "Is our network secure?" and the response is, "Of course; we have a firewall!" Unfortunately, this is the attitude of many real-life network and firewall administrators. They consider the network edge firewall as their primary defense against all network attacks and attackers.

The sad fact is that the network edge firewall is only a small single piece of your overall security plan. While the Internet edge firewall is a key component of your network security scheme, its only *one part*, and that single part does very little to provide *defense in depth*.

Defense in depth refers to the security philosophy that there are multiple partitions or security zones within an organization and each of these must be protected. The interface between security zones represents a specific *edge*, with each edge requiring a customized approach to security and access control.

The number of security zones varies with the organization and how the organization's network is laid out. Smaller organizations may have just a single network segment sitting behind an Internet edge firewall. Larger organizations may have very complex networks with multiple security zones, and these organizations may also have security zones within security zones. Each security zone requires its own level of inbound and outbound access control, and firewall policy should be customized by meeting each security zone's unique access control requirements.

Regardless of the complexity of your network, the *principle of least privilege* leads you to the correct path to firewall placement and configuration. The principle of least privilege states that access is allowed only for those users who require the resource, and access is allowed only to those resources that users are allowed to access. For example, if you have a collection of users who require access to the Microsoft Web site and no other sites, and the only protocol they need to use is HTTP, and they should only have access to the Microsoft Web site using the HTTP protocol between the hours of 9:00 A.M. and 5:00 P.M., then the firewall should enforce this access policy. Allowing users access to resources that they do not require in order to complete their work only increases the overall attack surface (exposure) of your network.

To help demonstrate how security zones dictate access control, firewall configuration and firewall placement, we'll go over a typical enterprise-level network and how it might segregate its security zones. We will call these zones "Rings," and each ring is comparable to a layer in an onion, with the center of the onion containing your core network assets that require the highest level of network level security and access control.

These rings are:

- Ring 1: The Internet Edge
- Ring 2: The Backbone Edge
- Ring 3: The Asset Network Edge
- Ring 4: Local Host Security

Figure 4.1 shows the outermost ring, which is the Internet edge.

Figure 4.1 Ring 1: Internet Edge

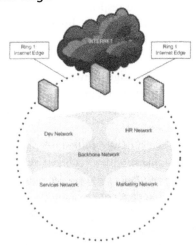

Ring 1: Internet Edge. Protection at this level is aimed at preventing unauthorized access to services on the corporate controlled network that are not explicitly allowed for remote access. High speed packet filters required to provide rudimentary access control and high speed routing to corporate controlled network segments.

The *Internet edge* is the first point of attack for externally-situated hosts. Because most of us have a greater fear of the unknown than of the known, network and firewall administrators believe they should put their most intelligent and powerful firewalls at this location. If you don't think about this too much, this makes sense.

The problem is that the great majority of network attacks occur from *inside* the network, and that you should put your most powerful defenses *closest* to the most valuable assets. If you consider how the approach of putting the strongest defenses at the edge flies in the face of how you secure anything else in this world, you'll realize that the Internet edge firewall should *not* be your most secure or sophisticated firewall, it should be your *fastest* firewall.

We first cover the logic behind putting the strongest defenses closest to the most valued assets, and then we'll discuss the rationale behind making the outermost firewall the fastest firewall.

Think about how a bank secures its cash assets. First, there are Federal agencies that hover unseen around all of our lives. This "outermost" level of bank security doesn't stop many bank robberies in progress, though it helps in preventing law-abiding citizens from deciding to rob a bank when they have nothing else to do that day.

The next layer of defense, moving inward toward the bank's core assets, is the local police department. The police drive around town and maybe they'll be in front of the bank when the bank robber is about to begin the hold-up. While this can provide a small measure of security, the police can't be in front of the bank *all the time*, and when they do respond, it's *after* the fact. The police typically arrive when the perpetrator is long gone

The next ring, closer to the core bank assets, can be represented by the front door cameras (more likely parking lot cameras). The bank security personnel may be able to stop a robbery from taking place *if* they are vigilant and identify the criminal right before the robbery attempt begins. The problem with this approach is they can't stop the guy until he does something suggesting a robbery attempt is in progress. You can't stop somebody these days just because he's wearing a sock over his head and carrying an empty pillow case. If he has a gun, but has a concealed carry permit, you still can't do anything to him unless he's displaying is illegally, or perhaps taking it into the bank (depending on your local or federal laws). However, the security cameras are more sophisticated and more likely to stop a robbery attempt in progress than the Federal security ring or the local policy security ring.

The next ring is the one at the border of the outside of the bank and the area between the tellers. There is typically an armed guard in this area. The armed guard provides a better level of protection because he can stop a robbery as it begins, *if* he identifies a robbery taking place, and *if* he shoots the robber before the robber shoots him. The armed guard in the lobby definitely provides a much higher level of security than the cameras watching outside the building, the local police cruising the streets, and the Feds.

The next ring of security lies at the interface between the inside of the bank vault and the lobby and teller area, which is the door of the bank vault. If the robber flies past the Fed, arrives when there's no police car in sight, looks like a typical customer and isn't flagged by the security cameras, and shoots the armed guard before the armed guard shoots him (I'm assuming that the robber isn't in a country or state that allows its citizens to carry weapons legally; if the bank were in this one of these areas, the robber would also have to survive armed citizens), the final hurdle is the bank vault door. Unless the robber is a munitions expert or some kind of safe cracker, the bank vault door will stop him every time.

The bank vault door provides the highest level of security, and it's the most "hardened" and "impenetrable" of the bank defenses. That's why it's put directly in front of the bank's core assets, to protect these assets in the event that an intruder gets past all other security rings.

However, no security ring, no matter how well protected is impenetrable. (Remind the "hardware firewall experts" of this fact the next time they tell you about the inviolate nature of "hardware" firewalls.)

Let's assume the robber isn't a munitions expert or a safe cracker. Instead, he'll use the coward's way out and take advantage of *social engineering* (coward computer hackers use similar methods). In this case, the bank robber social engineers this situation by threatening the lives of customers and tellers if the bank vault door is not opened by the bank manager.

Since you can always find more money, but human life tickets are only good for one punch, the bank manager opens the vault door.

At this point, you might think the game is over and the robber has won. He's penetrated the last defense ring, and the money is his (overlook the fact that in order to win the robbery game, the robber also has to successfully leave the bank with the cash).

However, there is another layer of defense, and that is the defense the money itself can provide. The bags of money may have exploding ink in them, which explodes and covers the robber with a bright shade of pink if the cash is moved or removed at the wrong time or the incorrect way. Or, maybe if the money is moved inappropriately, anesthetic gas is pumped into the vault, or maybe the money is marked and is easily identified if it is spent in public. If the bank hopes to recoup its money, it must make sure that methods of protection are applied to the money itself, as that is the last ring of defense the bank has in protecting its assets.

The point of this story is that the bank, and any other entity that secures its core assets, puts its most hardened, most sophisticated and most impenetrable barriers closest to those assets. The enemy is always at his best at the outermost ring. By the time he's made it to the innermost ring, he's either completely exhausted his resources or ready to give up. In either case, the enemy should meet stronger defensive mechanisms as he continues to get weaker. This helps accelerate his ultimate defeat. Table 4.1 reveals several defense rings protecting bank assets.

Table 4.1 Defense Rings Protecting Bank Assets

Bank Defense Layer	Implementation
Federal Agencies	Outermost layer of protection. Helps keep honest people honest
Local Police Department	Provides protection in the rare event that they happen to be in front of the bank during a robbery in progress; responds only after the fact
Perimeter Cameras	Allows vigilant security personnel to proactively stop a robbery if they can identify the robbery is about to begin
Bank Guard	Bank guard can shoot the robber if the robber doesn't shoot him first. Able to respond to robbery in progress and provide much more security than the levels above
Bank Vault Door	Strongest level of protection placed directly in front of critical bank resources.
Exploding Ink, Anesthetic Gas, and other devices	Represents "host-based" protection and increases the recoverability of assets if they are stolen

With this bank vault scenario protection scheme in mind, how do you explain the attitude of many network and firewall administrators who claim, "While I think an ISA firewall is great, I wouldn't feel comfortable if I didn't have a hardware firewall in front of the ISA firewall."

This kind of statement implies that the ISA firewall might not be as "strong" as the traditional hardware packet-filtering firewall. Does it make sense that you should put your "weakest link" (in terms of network firewall protection) directly in front of your core network assets?

The irony is that these network and firewall administrators are doing the right thing. It's just that they're doing it for the wrong reason. They've been beaten over the head for years by "firewall experts" and "hardware firewall" marketeers with the idea that only the ASIC ("hardware") firewalls can be secure; so-called "software firewalls" are inherently insecure because of reasons "X, Y and Z".

Reason "X" always has something to do with the underlying operating system. After repeating with excellent elocution and perfect tempo, "Windows is not secure," for several minutes, they never get around to reasons "Y" and "Z". Table 4.2 provides information on reasons Y and Z.

Table 4.2 Hardware Firewall Vendors Reasons for Why Software Firewalls are Insecure

Hardware Firewall Vendor's Reason	Explanation
X	The Windows operating system can't be secured
Y	Hardware firewall vendors sell hardware firewalls with big margins
Z	Hardware firewall vendors sell replacement parts and add-ons with even *bigger* margins

The truth is hardware firewalls *do belong at the Internet edge* of the network. But not for the reasons the "firewall experts" proclaim. The actual reason is that while traditional hardware stateful-filtering firewalls cannot provide the high level of security required by modern Internet-connected networks, they *can* pass packets very quickly and do *stateful*-packet filtering. The speed is very important for organizations that have multi-gigabit connections to the Internet. Because of the amount of processing they must do, high-security, application-layer aware firewalls cannot handle this volume of traffic and provide the deep application-layer stateful inspection required of a modern network firewall.

Stateful-*filtering* hardware firewalls can handle the high volume of traffic, perform basic packet filtering, and allow inbound traffic only to services that you intend to provide to remote users (outbound access control isn't very effective for high-speed packet-filtering firewalls at the Internet edge).

For example, if you intend to provide only HTTP, HTTPS and IMAP4 access to resources on the corporate network, the high-speed stateful packet-filtering firewall will only accept new inbound connection requests for TCP ports 80, 143 and 443. The high-speed packet-filtering firewall can quickly determine the destination port and validity of information at layer 4 and below and accept or reject the traffic, based on this rudimentary analysis. While this approach provides a marginal level measure of security, it is far from what is required to protect modern networks with Internet-facing hosts.

So the next time you hear someone say, "I wouldn't be comfortable without having a hardware firewall in front of the ISA firewall," you'll know that he's right, but his discomfort is based on the wrong reasons because he doesn't understand that you increase security as you move inward, not reduce it.

Ring 2 is the *Backbone Edge* that marks a line between the internal interfaces of the Internet Edge firewalls and the external interfaces of the backbone segment firewalls. Figure 4.2 shows the placement of the four Backbone Edge firewalls surrounding the edges of the corporate backbone network.

Figure 4.2 Ring 2: The Backbone Edge

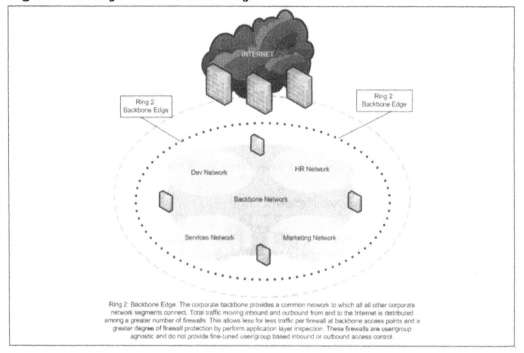

The corporate backbone network provides a common network to which all other corporate network segments connect. The total traffic moving inbound and outbound through backbone firewalls is lower on a *per-firewall* basis than the Internet Edge firewalls because there are more of them.

For example, you might have two high-speed packet-filtering firewalls on the Internet Edge handling 5 gigabits/second each for a total of 10 gigabits/second between them. There are four Backbone Edge firewalls, and assuming that the load is shared equally among these, each of the Backbone Edge firewalls handles 2.5 gigabits/second.

The Backbone Edge firewalls can begin the real firewall work required to protect the corporate assets by performing *stateful application-layer inspection* of both inbound and outbound traffic. Since modern exploits are aimed at the application layer (because that's where the "money" is), the backbone application-layer firewalls can do the job of checking the application layer validity of the communications moving through them.

For example, if you allow inbound HTTP, the stateful inspection application layer-aware firewalls on the Backbone Edge start to apply real network security by checking the details of the HTTP communication and block suspicious connections through the firewall.

This is a good location for the ISA firewall. Since the ISA firewall is considered the model of a stateful application-layer inspection firewall, it can perform the heavy lifting required to protect the corporate backbone network and the network inside of it, as well as ensure that inappropriate traffic (such as worm-generated traffic) does not cross the Backbone Edge ring. Traffic volume in this example isn't a problem for ISA firewalls, as they have been tested and confirmed as multi-gigabit firewalls, based on their hardware configuration and firewall rule base.

The next security perimeter is at Ring 3. Ring 3 is at the border of the backbone network and the networks containing the corporate assets. Corporate assets can represent user workstations, servers, departmental LANs, management networks, and anything else you don't want unauthorized access to. The line demarcating the backbone network and the asset networks is the *Asset Network Edge*. This is the ring where you need the strongest, most sophisticated level of protection. If an intruder is able to violate the integrity of this ring, they are in the position to directly access your corporate assets and carry out a successful attack.

Figure 4.3 shows the location of the Asset Network Edges in Ring 3.

Figure 4.3 Ring 3 at the Asset Network Edge

Ring 3: Asset Network Edge. The asset networks contain your critical resources that must be protected from attacks originating from outside the asset network and must stop outgoing attacks originating from the asset networks. Traffic inbound and outbound through the asset network firewalls are less on a per firewall basis than that seen on the backbone network firewalls because it is distributed across more firewalls. This allows even deeper application layer inspection and strong user/group based access control for inbound and outbound access through the asset network firewalls. Asset networks might represent departmental LANs, user LANs, network services segments/networks, management networks, and others. The most secure and most powerful firewalls must be placed at this level because it's the last line of network defense

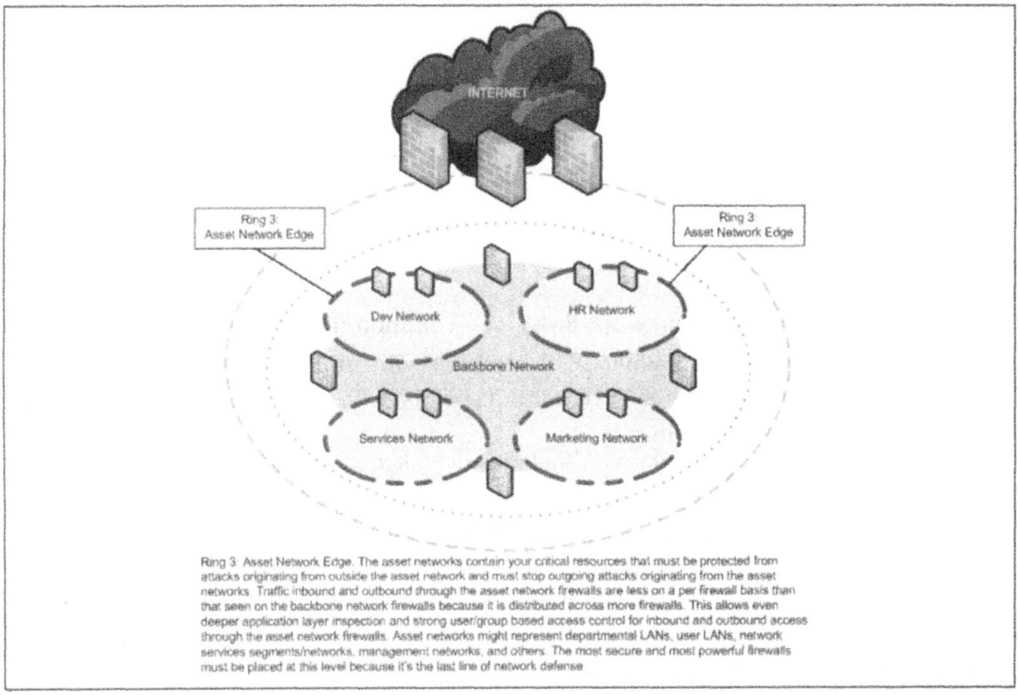

It is at Ring 3 that the ISA firewall becomes critical. In contrast to a packet-filtering hardware device, you need *real* firewall protection. Simple packet filtering is inadequate when it comes to protecting resources in the network asset ring. Not only must you ensure that all incoming connections are subjected to deep, stateful application-layer inspection, you must also ensure that outbound connections from the asset networks are subjected to strong user/group-based access control.

Strong outbound user/group-based access control is an absolute requirement. In contrast to typical hardware packet-filtering devices that let everything out, firewalls at the Asset Network Edge must be able to control outbound connections based on user/group-based membership. Reasons for this are listed below.

- You must be able to log the user name of all outbound connections so that you can make users accountable for their Internet activity.

- You must be able to log the application the user used to access Internet content; this allows you to determine if applications not allowed by network use policy are being used and enables you to take effective countermeasures.

- Your organization may be held responsible for material leaving your network; therefore, you must be able to block inappropriate material from leaving your network.

- Sensitive corporate information may be transferred outside the network from Asset Network locations. You must be able to block outbound transfer of proprietary information *and* record user names and the names of the software applications used to transfer proprietary information to external locations.

The ISA firewall is the ideal firewall for the Asset Network edges because it meets all of these requirements. When systems are properly configured as Firewall and Web Proxy clients, you are able to:

- Record the user name for all TCP and UDP connections made to the Internet (or any other network the user might connect to by going through the ISA firewall).

- Record the software application used to make these TCP and UDP connections through the ISA firewall.

- Block connections to any domain name or IP address based on user name or group membership.

- Block access to any content outside the Asset Network based on user name or group membership.

- Block transfer of information from the Asset Network to any other network based on user name or group membership.

Deep stateful application-layer inspection and access control requires processing power. Servers should be sized appropriately to meet the requirements of powerful stateful application-layer processing. Fortunately, even with complex rule sets, the ISA firewall is able to handle well over 1.5 gigabits/second per server, and even higher traffic volumes with the appropriate hardware configuration.

Ring 4 represents the deepest security perimeter in this model. Ring 4 is the *Host-based security* ring. The Host-based security ring represents the junction between host systems and the network to which they are directly attached. The following figure shows the position of Ring 4.

Figure 4.4 Ring 4: Host-based Security

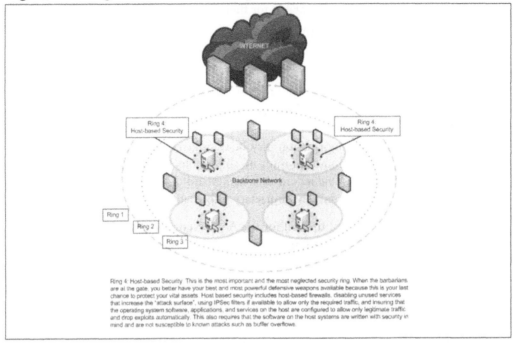

Ring 4: Host-based Security. This is the most important and the most neglected security ring. When the barbarians are at the gate, you better have your best and most powerful defensive weapons available because this is your last chance to protect your vital assets. Host based security includes host-based firewalls, disabling unused services that increase the 'attack surface', using IPSec filters, if available to allow only the required traffic, and insuring that the operating system software, applications, and services on the host are configured to allow only legitimate traffic and drop exploits automatically. This also requires that the software on the host systems are written with security in mind and are not susceptible to known attacks such as buffer overflows.

Approaches to Host-based security are somewhat different than what you see with network firewall protection, but the principles are the same. Host-based security requires that you control what is allowed inbound and outbound to the host machine and that the applications on the hosts are designed with security in mind. Some of the things you should consider when dealing with the Host-based Security ring are listed below.

- A Host-based firewall can be used to control what incoming and outgoing connections are allowed and what applications can send and receive data. This is the typical "personal firewall" approach, but it can be expanded to support Server applications, in addition to providing personal firewall support for user workstations.

- IPSec policy (on systems that support it) can be used to control what is allowed inbound and outbound from and to specific hosts. If a particular workstation or server does not need to connect to all possible computers, you can lock them down using IPSec policies to limit connections to a predefined collection of machines.

- Applications and services running on the hosts must be designed with security in mind. That means these applications and services are not vulnerable to common attacks such as buffer overflow and social attacks (such as HTML e-mail exploits and opening attachments).

- Antivirus software must be used to block viruses that come from other network locations or are introduced by compromised hotfixes and software.

- Anti-scumware software must be installed to protect the machines, to prevent Adware and other malicious software from being installed on the machine.

- Anti-spam software must be installed on the machine if an e-mail client is installed. Anti-spam software should also be installed on SMTP relays that handle inbound and outbound mail to block spam that carries not only potentially dangerous payload, but also to reduce losses in employee productivity related to spam.

- Users and installed services should run with least privilege to limit the impact malicious software can have should it be executed. For example, a lot of adware, scumware, spyware, viruses, and rootkits will fail to install if the compromised user account does not have admin or power user rights.

The Host-based security is the last defense. No firewall can completely make up for weaknesses found at the host layer. Network firewall security is helpful for control access from corporate network to corporate network and attacks coming from non-local networks that must traverse the ISA firewall, but only Host-based security can handle attacks coming from the local network where the connection does not traverse a network firewall.

Now that you have a good grounding in the varieties of security perimeters, you realize that comments like, "I wouldn't feel comfortable putting an ISA firewall in without putting a hardware packet filter in front of it," are akin to saying, "I wouldn't feel comfortable putting a ICBM missile silo in unless I can put a poodle in front of it."

Note that for smaller networks that might have a single ring, which is the Internet Edge ring, the entire discussion is moot. The only reason to put a packet-filtering traditional firewall in front of the ISA firewall is to waste money. You'd be better off buying two ISA firewalls, or buying two sophisticated application-layer firewalls with the ISA firewall behind the other application-layer firewall. This ensures that the ISA firewall can implement the strong user/group-based security you require.

ISA Firewall Fallacies

There are a collection of misconceptions and fallacies that are commonly associated with the ISA firewall. As an ISA firewall administrator, you'll need to be able to address these fallacies and educate colleagues and managers. Some common ISA firewall fallacies include:

- Software firewalls are inherently weak. Only hardware firewalls can be trusted to secure a network.

- You can't trust any service running on the Windows operating system to be secure. You could never secure a firewall running on a Windows OS.

- ISA machines make for good proxy servers, but I need a real firewall to protect my network.

- ISA firewalls run on an Intel hardware platform, and only firewalls that have all "solid state" components can be firewall. A firewall should have no moving parts if you want to consider it to be a firewall.

- "I have a firewall and an ISA Server."

- A real firewall should be a nightmare to configure, and ideally, should use a command line interface to make it accessible only to individuals who have attended expensive vendor training classes.

Let's take each of these ISA firewall fallacies one at a time.

Software Firewalls are Inherently Weak

As an ISA firewall admin, you've probably run into people who:

- Don't know what an ISA firewall is

- Think it's some sort of caching server, akin to the old CacheFlow product (purchased by Bluecoat) or Squid

- Believe only hardware firewalls are "secure" and so-called "software" firewalls aren't suitable at the datacenter perimeter

Teaching people who have never heard of an ISA firewall can be a lot of fun. You get to tell them about how an ISA firewall provides strong inbound *and* outbound access controls in ways no other firewall currently on the market can provide, how the ISA firewall blocks file sharing programs, how it prevents malicious users from violating network security policies (such as downloading copyrighted material), how the ISA firewall provides superior protection for Microsoft Exchange services including OWA and MAPI/RPC, and how it is so easy to configure that it blows away all other enterprise-grade firewalls on the market.

You will encounter a number of network and firewall administrators who have heard of the ISA firewall, but have the misconception that "ISA is a Web Proxy or caching server thingie," (to quote a firewall expert I once encountered at a security conference).

ISA firewalls are honest-to-goodness, enterprise-class firewalls that provide the strong inbound and outbound access control and application-layer filtering you need to protect *today's* networks, not the networks of the 1990s where traditional packet filter-based firewalls were good enough.

The "only hardware firewalls can be made secure" believers are the most recalcitrant. They've been told over the years that hardware (ASIC-based) firewalls are the *acme* of firewalls, and any firewall not based on ASIC is an inadequate software firewall and should more properly be referred to as a proxy. I have to wonder how they reconcile this dogma with the fact that the number-one selling firewall product is CheckPoint, a software-based firewall.

The hardware firewall fantasy is based on a historical reality. In the 1990s, hardware firewalls could provide a reasonable level of security and performance using simple packet-filtering mechanisms that look at source and destination addresses, ports, and protocols, and make quick decisions. Since firewall-filtering logic is "burnt-in" to the ASIC (Application Specific Integrated Circuit), it's not easy to hack the basic system. However, twenty-first century attackers have learned you don't need to hack the packet-filtering firewall's core instruction set to get around the relatively poor network security that stateful filtering hardware-based systems provide.

You can find an excellent article debunking the myth of ASIC superiority at http://www.issadvisor.com/viewtopic.php?t=368. The author makes a very good case for avoiding hardware firewalls because they will never be able to keep pace with modern threat evolution and that one-box software-based firewalls are the future of network firewalls and perimeter security. Herein lies the massive advantage conferred by your ISA firewall: it can be quickly upgraded and enhanced to meet not only today's threats, but also the exploits against which you're sure to need defense in the future.

You Can't Trust Any Service Running on the Windows Operating System to be Secure

This is a common point of contention among the "hardware firewall" enthusiasts. I'm often asked about how we can feel secure running ISA firewalls on Windows operating systems, given the number of security holes and bug fixes the base operating system requires. This is a good and valid question. Here the highlights you should consider regarding the issue of the underlying Windows operating system and running the ISA firewall on top of it.

- Not all hotfixes apply to the ISA firewall in its role as network firewall. Many of these hotfixes are services based. Since you don't run client or server services on the ISA firewall machine, most of the hotfixes are irrelevant.

- Some of the hotfixes address issues with core operating system components, such as RPC (which the Blaster worm took advantage of). Since the ISA firewall applies security policy to *all* interfaces, you would have to create a Access Rule allowing the attack access to the firewall. In the specific case of RPC, the secure RPC filter blocks Blaster and related attacks. IIS problems are a non-issue because you do not run IIS services (with the exception of maybe the IIS SMTP service) on the firewall. Other services are only accessible if you open up the ports to the firewall to allow the attack in. A properly configured ISA firewall, therefore, is much more secure than the based operating system because network access to the firewall is severely truncated.

- Other hotfixes apply to stability issues. You need to apply these hotfixes and service packs. However, all firewall vendors issue regular fixes (if they don't, then they're not paying attention and their software *is* vulnerable, even if they don't know it, and even if they haven't acknowledged the vulnerabilities to you).

- Some hotfixes require restarting. You can schedule the restart for a convenient time. Note that you will not need to install all hotfixes because not all of them, or even a significant number of them, apply to the ISA firewall. The number of restarts required should be negligible.

- If you can't trust services running on a Windows operating system, then how can you trust the underlying OS for your Exchange, SQL, SharePoint and other Microsoft server installations?

- The underlying OS on the ISA firewall can be hardened. In fact, there is a profile in the Windows Server 2003 SP1 Security Configuration Wizard (SCW) allowing you to harden the underlying OS automatically using the SCW.

- You can harden the underlying OS manually if you don't want to use the SCW or don't have access to it. There will be a OS hardening guide that releases concurrently with ISA 2004 that will walk you through the process of hardening the underlying OS while leaving the ISA firewall services unaffected. This was a significant issue with ISA Server 2000 because many of us attempted to harden the OS and it had side effects that we weren't aware of.

While the issue of the underlying operating system is a factor, you can see that the underlying Windows Server 2003 OS is definitely not a significant factor. As for Windows 2000, securing the underlying OS may be bit more of an issue, but you can still harden the OS to an extent that it rivals any hardware firewall.

ISA Firewalls Make Good Proxy Servers, but I Need a "Real Firewall" to Protect My Network

It's true that ISA firewalls make great proxy servers. In fact, the ISA firewall is both a stateful filtering *and* proxy firewall. Blended firewalls of this type are the most sophisticated and most secure firewalls available today.

The conventional packet-filtering firewall uses a very simple mechanism to control inbound and outbound access: source and destination port, source and destination IP address, and for ICMP, source and destination IP address together with ICMP type and code. Packet filters must be explicitly created for each inbound and outbound connection. More sophisticated packet filters can dynamically open response ports. ISA firewalls are able to dynamically open ports via their *dynamic packet-filtering* feature.

The "circuit layer" firewall is akin to what most commentators refer to as the "stateful filtering firewall" It should be noted that the term "stateful" can mean whatever you want it to mean. It was introduced as a marketing term, and like most marketing terms, was designed to sell product, not to quantify and specify any specific feature or behavior.

However, most people think of *stateful filtering* (in contrast to *stateful inspection*) as a mechanism where the stateful filter tracks the connection state at the transport (layer 4) level. The TCP protocol can define session state, while UDP does not. Because of this, UDP communications must have a *pseudo-state* enforced by the stateful-filtering device. Stateful filtering is helpful in protecting against a number of sub-application layer attacks, such as session hijacking.

Most hardware firewalls stop there. They can perform simple packet filtering, dynamic packet filtering, and stateful packet filtering (stateful filtering). These firewalls also often provide advanced routing features, which places them more in the class of a network router than a true modern firewall. In contrast, the routing features of ISA firewalls are less impressive than you see in traditional packet filter-based firewalls.

As we've discussed earlier, the packet-filter firewall is useful on Ring 1, at the Internet Edge, because of their processing speed. The primary problem with these firewalls is that they really do not provide the level of protection you require to stop exploits from reaching Rings 2 and 3, where advanced application-layer inspection must be performed.

This is where the proxy firewalls enter the mix. A proxy firewall is able to *inspect* the entire contents of an application-layer communication by deconstructing and reconstructing the entire application layer message. For example, the proxy firewall reconstructs the entire HTTP message, examines the commands and data within the message, statefully inspects the contents and compares those with the application layer rules. The proxy firewall then allows or denies the communication based on the application layer rules configured for the HTTP protocol.

For example, one of the more common HTTP exploits is the directory traversal attack. Many popular worms take advantage of directory traversal to access executables on a Web server. For example, the following URL:

```
http://www.iusepixfirewalls.com/scripts/..%5c../winnt/system32/
cmd.exe?/c+dir+c:\
```

executes the cmd.exe file and runs the "dir c:\" command which lists all files in the C:\ directory. Note the "%5c" string. This is a Web server escape code. Escape codes represent normal characters in the form of %nn, where nn stands for a two-character entry. The escape code "%5c" represents the character "\". The IIS root directory enforcer might not check for escape codes and allow the request to be executed. The Web server's operating system understands escape codes and executes the command.

Escape codes are also very useful for bypassing poorly written filters enforced on input received from users. If the filter looks for "../" (dot dot slash), then the attacker could easily change the input to "%2e%2e/". This has the same meaning as "../", but is not detected by the filter. The escape code %2e represents the character "." (dot). The ISA firewall, being a sophisticated stateful application-layer inspection firewall, easily blocks these exploits.

Proxy firewalls have the potential to block exploits for any application layer protocol. Other application layer protocols include SMTP, NNTP, Instant Messaging protocols, POP3, IMAP4 and all others. Blended firewalls like ISA 2004, which combine stateful filtering and stateful application-layer inspection, can easily be upgraded with software to block the most recent application layer-attack. In contrast, stateful filtering firewalls are totally unaware of application-layer attacks, and even hardware firewalls with rudimentary application-layer inspection cannot be quickly upgraded to meet the latest application-layer exploit because of the limits of ASIC (hardware) processing and development.

ISA Firewalls Run on an Intel Hardware Platform, and Firewalls Should Have "No Moving Parts"

Why does a firewall require no moving parts, while my Exchange, SQL, Web, FTP and any other mission critical run fine with "moving parts"? Usually, the term "moving parts" has something to do with Intel platforms and hard disks. Here are some advantages to using the Intel PC-based platform for firewalls.

- When memory, processor, or network card goes bad on the device, you can replace it at commodity hardware prices. You do not need to go back to the solid state hardware vendor and pay premium prices for their versions of hardware components.

- When you want to upgrade memory, processor, storage, NIC, or any other component, you can use commodity hardware and add that to your machine. You do not need to go to the source hardware vendor to obtain overpriced upgrades.

- Because the ISA firewall software is hard-disk based, you do not have the memory and storage restrictions of straightjacket solid state devices. You can install on-box application-layer filters, increase the cache size, tweak performance and security settings, and perform fine-tuned customizations required by your environment.

- The "no moving parts" aspect pertains primarily to hard disks. Hard disk MTBF values are in years. Even low-end IDE drives last 3+ years with normal use. When the disk fails, the ISA firewall configuration is easy to restore because the entire configuration is stored in a simple .xml file. You can be back up and running within 15 minutes with the right disaster-recovery plan. Compare that to fried memory in a hardware device where the entire device must be returned to the manufacturer.

The disaster recovery aspect is perhaps the most compelling reason for using a "software" firewall. A single ISA firewall, or an entire array of 10 ISA firewalls, can be rebuilt in a matter of minutes without requiring you to replace the entire box or requiring you to obtain hardware pieces from the vendor. And if you're using removable drives, it's a literal no-brainer to be up in running for the entire array in less than 30 minutes!

"I Have a Firewall and an ISA Server"

"I've got a firewall, and I want to place an ISA Server behind it; how do I do that?" These comments often come from ISA fans, so I know there's no intent to denigrate the ISA firewall. Instead, this indicates that the ISA firewalls admins don't realize that ISA firewalls are *the* firewalls for their network and the stateful packet-filtering devices they put in front of the ISA firewalls are performing basic packet filtering which helps with processor off-loading.

To be fair, not everyone uses the ISA firewall as a firewall. You do have the option to install the ISA firewall in single NIC mode, which is comparable to the "cache only" mode that ISA Server 2000 included. In single NIC mode, the ISA firewall functionality is truncated. Most of the firewall functionality is removed, and the machine provides limited functionality as a Web Proxy server only.

This is not to imply that the ISA firewall in single NIC mode is not secure. Enough of the firewall functionality is left in place to allow the ISA firewall to protect itself and to secure the Web-proxied connections made through the single NIC ISA firewall. The ISA firewall in single NIC configuration only allows connections to *itself* that you explicitly allow via the firewall's system policy. The only connections it allows to corporate network hosts are those you explicitly allow via Web Publishing Rules, and the only outbound connections that can be made through the single NIC ISA firewall are those you allow via an HTTP/HTTPS-only list of Access Rules.

While I would prefer to see all organizations use the 2004 firewall for its intended use, which is as a full-featured, blended stateful packet-filtering and stateful application-layer inspection firewall, I do realize that larger organizations may have already spent, literally, millions of dollars on other firewall solutions. These organizations do want to benefit from the reverse proxy components the ISA firewall provides to obtain superior OWA, OMA, ActiveSync and IIS protection. For this reason, it's important to point out that the ISA firewall, even in the "crippled" single NIC mode, provides a high level of protection for forward and reverse proxy connections.

Why ISA Belongs in Front of Critical Assets

We've covered a lot of ground, so let's sum up the reasons why the ISA firewall belongs in front of your critical network assets.

- ISA firewalls run on commodity hardware, which keeps costs in check while allowing you the luxury of upgrading the hardware with commodity components when you need to "scale up" the hardware.

- Being a "software" firewall, the firewall configuration can be quickly upgraded with application-aware enhancing software from Microsoft and from third-party vendors.

- Being a "software" firewall, you can quickly replace broken components without returning the entire firewall to the vendor or requiring that you have several hot or cold standbys waiting in the wings.

- The ISA firewall provides sophisticated and comprehensive stateful application-layer inspection, in addition to stateful packet filtering, to protect against common network-layer attacks and modern application-layer attacks.

- The ISA firewall should be placed behind high-speed packet-filtering firewalls. This is important on networks that have multi-gigabit connections to the Internet. The packet-filtering firewalls reduce the total amount of traffic that each back end ISA firewall needs to process. This reduces the total amount of processing overhead required on the ISA firewalls and allows the ISA firewalls to provide the true, deep stateful application-layer inspection required to protect your network assets.

- While the ISA firewall can't match the pure packet-passing capabilities of traditional hardware ASIC firewalls, the ISA firewall provides a much higher level of firewall functionality via its stateful packet filtering and stateful application-layer inspection features.

- The ISA firewall is able to authenticate all communications moving through the firewall. This argues for placing the firewall directly in front of the Asset Networks. Ideally, another non-authenticating ISA firewall is placed in front of the authenticating ISA firewall so that sophisticated stateful application-layer inspection and stateful packet filtering is done before those connections reach the ISA firewalls performing authentication.

A Better Network and Firewall Topology

At this point we've put to rest the belief that hardware firewalls are more secure than an ISA firewall. With that understanding in mind, where exactly should we place the ISA firewall?

The answer depends on the size of your network and the number of rings or security zones you need to protect. If you have a large network, then the four-ring approach we discussed will work best, with the Backbone Network and the Asset Network protected by ISA firewalls. The Backbone Network ISA firewall is configured for full stateful filtering and stateful application-layer inspection without outbound access controls, while the Asset Network ISA firewalls provide stateful filtering and stateful application-layer inspection, as well as inbound *and* outbound user/group-based access controls.

Figure 4.5 recaps the Backbone and Asset Network configuration.

Figure 4.5 Backbone and Asset Network

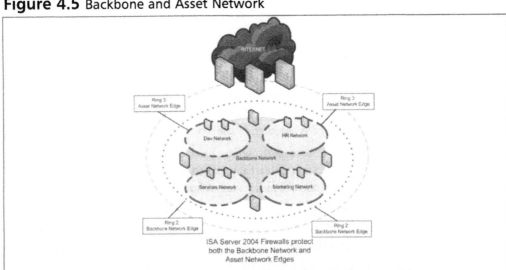

Simpler network configurations may not have multiple rings or have multi-gigabit network connections. For these networks, there is no reason to place a fast packet-filtering firewall at the Internet Edge ring.

However, you do want to host publicly-accessible services on a DMZ segment between the Internet Edge and the Asset Edge. This represents your DMZ segment. You can safely and confidently place the ISA firewall at the Internet Edge and be confident that you have a higher level of security and access control than you would have with a conventional-packet filtering firewall. In addition, you can configure the Internal (back-end) ISA firewall for strong inbound and outbound user/group-based access control.

The firewall in Figure 4.6 depicts of the DMZ Firewall Segment configuration.

Figure 4.6 DMZ Firewall Segment

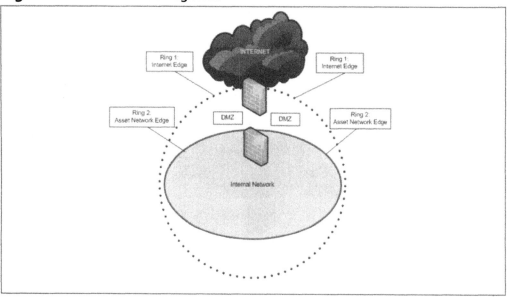

The most simple configuration requires only a single firewall situated at the Internet edge. In that case, you can place a single ISA firewall at the Internet Edge and benefit from its full firewall functionality knowing that it provides your network a far higher level of security and protection then what you would derive from a simple high-speed packet filter-based firewall.

Tom and Deb Shinder's Configuring ISA 2004 Network Layout

Throughout this book, we will give examples of how to configure the ISA firewall. Each of the exercises and configuration options will be within the context of the sample network we configured for this book. You can replicate this configuration on a lab network. Your lab network can consist of computers, or you can use operating system virtualization software to simulate the lab network configuration we use in this book. Microsoft Virtual PC and VMware Workstation are the two most popular operating system virtualization applications. We prefer, and have used, VMware extensively in our ISA firewall testing and modeling environment because of its advanced networking features. However, Microsoft Virtual PC or Virtual Server is adequate for most ISA firewall testing scenarios.

Figure 4.7 depicts the machines and some of the details of the machines in the lab network that forms that basis of the discussions in this book.

Figure 4.7 Lab Network Details

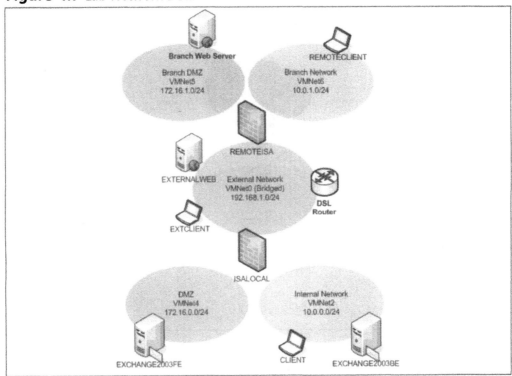

Tables 4.3 and 4.4 provide most of the salient details of the machines participating in the lab network setup.

Table 4.3 Lab Network Details

Setting	EXCHANGE 2003BE	CLIENT	EXCHANGE 2003FE	ISALOCAL	EXTCLIENT
IP Address	10.0.0.2	10.0.0.3	172.16.0.2	Int: 10.0.0.1 Ext: 192.168.1.70 Dmz: 172.16.0.1	192.168.1.90
Default Gateway	10.0.0.1 A	10.0.0.1	172.16.0.1	192.168.1.60	N/
DNS	10.0.0.2	10.0.0.2	10.0.0.2	Int: 10.0.0.2 Ext: N/A Dmz: N/A	N/A
WINS	10.0.1.2	10.0.0.2	10.0.0.2	Int: 10.0.0.2 Ext: N/A Dmz: N/A	N/A
Operating System	Windows Server 2003	Windows XP	Windows Server 2003	Windows Server 2003	Windows XP
Services	DC (msfirewall.org)[5] DNS WINS DHCP RADIUS Enterprise CA	None	Exchange 2003	ISA 2004	None
RAM[1] Allocation	128MB	128MB	128MB	128MB	64MB
VMNet[2]	2	2	4	Int: 2 Ext: 0 Dmz: 4	N/A

Table 4.4 Lab Network Details

Setting	DSL ROUTER	REMOTEISA	BRANCHWEB SERVER	REMOTE CLIENT	EXTERNAL WEB
IP Address	Int: 192.168.1.60 Ext: Public	Int: 10.0.1.1 Ext: 192.168.1.71	172.16.1.2	10.0.1.2	192.168.1.24[3]
Default Gateway	Public Gateway	192.168.1.60	172.16.1.1	10.0.1.1	N/A
DNS	Public	Public[4]	N/A	N/A	N/A
WINS	N/A	N/A	N/A	N/A	N/A
Operating System	N/A	Windows Server 2003	Windows Server 2003	Windows XP	Windows 2000
Services	N/A	ISA 2004	SMTP WWW NNTP FTP	N/A	SMTP WWW NNTP FTP
RAM Allocation	N/A	128MB	64MB	128MB	64MB
VMNet	N/A	Int: 6 Ext: 0 Dmz: 5	5	6	N/A

[1] The RAM allocation is the amount of Host system memory dedicated to the virtual machine. If you are not using virtual machines, you may want to use the amount of memory suggested for each operating system.

[2] The VMNet is the VMware virtual Ethernet segment that the virtual machine's interface is connected to. If a virtual machine has more than one interface, the VMNet for each interface is listed.

[3] The EXTERNALWEB server is a live Web server on the lab network.

[4] The REMOTEISA ISA firewall uses a public DNS server so that the ISA firewall can resolve public host names.

[5] The Active Directory domain name used on the internal network is *msfirewall.org*. We will simulate a split DNS configuration so that internal and external network hosts are able to connect to hosted resources using the same Active Directory domain name.

This lab network configuration forms the basis of all the exercises and examples provided in this book. If you plan to mirror this network on all physical machines, then you can ignore the memory allocations noted in the tables. Those memory allocations were used in our VMware network test lab so that we could run up to seven virtual machines simultaneously on the host operating system. Although the virtual machine performance was a bit sluggish when running more than four VMs on a Pentium 4 1.5GHz machine with 1 GB of memory, performance was good enough to allow for viable scenario testing

We place the lab hosts on different VMnets so that the networks are completely segmented. Each VMnet represents its own Ethernet broadcast domain. This allows us to simulate actual network communications as they would take place on any other wired network and simplifies log file and Network Monitor analysis. We highly recommend that you place each network ID on a different VMnet when testing your own ISA firewall configuration scenarios.

Note that not all machines are required for all scenarios. For any given scenario discussed in this book, only a subset of the machines described in the figure and table above are required. You also do not need to create a virtual machine for each host listed in the tables. For example, the Windows XP machine can act as the CLIENT, EXTERNALCLIENT and REMOTECLIENT. The only thing you need to do is change the machine name, the IP addressing information, and the VMnet on the virtual machine.

One major advantage of using virtual machines over physical devices is that you can create snapshots of the baseline configuration for each host in your virtual ISA firewall lab. You can save a snapshot of each virtual machine right after you have created its baseline configuration. You can then return to this snapshot when you're done testing a particular scenario.

Detailed instructions on how to configure the individual machines on the lab network are beyond the scope of this book. However, we will go over the detailed procedure on how to create the virtual machine for the ISALOCAL computer using VMware Workstation 4.0. After going through this example, you will have a good enough understanding on how to use VMware to create the rest of the virtual machines for our sample ISA firewall virtual network.

NOTE

Our decision to use VMware is based on our extensive experience with the product since it was first released to the general public. We do not want to give the impression that we believe that VMware is a superior to Virtual PC as an operating system virtualization option. Microsoft uses Virtual PC extensively in their own testing and training environments. We have tested ISA firewalls on the Virtual PC platform and found virtual machine performance actually appeared slightly better. However, VMware has better support for the networking scenarios we typically try to reproduce in our labs, and so for testing firewall scenarios, it provides a slightly better option. You can get more information on Virtual PC at www.microsoft.com/windows/virtualpc/default.mspx. Also, we want to recommend that you do not install VMware on a domain controller, as it has the potential of interfering with the browser service and the DCs role as master browser or domain master browser.

We used VMware 4.5.1 build-7568 when writing this book.

Creating the ISALOCAL Virtual Machine

The first step is to obtain the VMware Workstation software. You can download a trial version and test VMware before purchasing it. Go to http://www.vmware.com/download/ to find the download link. Make sure to review the system requirements before installing the VMware software. You can find these at http://www.vmware.com/support/ws45/doc/

Run the VMware Workstation executable after downloading the file. You will need to restart the host operating system after installation is complete.

The ISALOCAL virtual machine runs the ISA firewall software on Windows Server 2003. You can install the Windows Server 2003 operating system from a CD-ROM drive connected to your host operating system, or you can use a CD image file (".iso image"). These .iso images are used extensively on the MSDN download site. If you only have a CD-ROM copy of Windows Server 2003, you should consider creating an .iso file from the CD. This will make creating virtual machines using VMware Workstation much easier, as you can mount the .iso file as a CD-ROM drive and boot to the .iso CD-ROM drive to install Windows Server 2003.

You can also create your own .iso files. This can be of great help when working with Virtual machines, as you can mount the .iso files as virtual CD-ROM drives. For example, you might want to create an .iso file for your ISA 2004 CD. There are a number of software applications that allow you to do this. One that we've had success with is WinISO, which you can find at www.winiso.com/

TIP

You can download an evaluation version of the Windows Server 2003 Enterprise Edition software at https://microsoft.order-5.com/windowsserver2003evaldl/

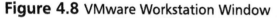

This trial software is provided as an .iso file that you can mount as a virtual CD-ROM Drive.

In this example, we'll use an .iso file. After placing the .iso file on the local hard disk of your host operating system, perform the following steps to create the ISALOCAL virtual machine:

1. Open the VMware application. In the **VMware Workstation** window (Figure 4.8), click the **New Virtual Machine** icon.

Figure 4.8 VMware Workstation Window

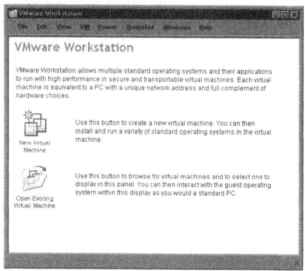

2. Click **Next** on the **Welcome to the New Virtual Machine Wizard** page.

3. On the **Select the Appropriate Configuration** page, select the **Custom** option. Click **Next**.

4. On the **Select a Guest Operating System** page (as shown in Figure 4.9), select the **Microsoft Windows** option. Select **Windows Server 2003 Enterprise Edition** from the **Version** list. Click **Next**.

Figure 4.9 Guest Operating System Page

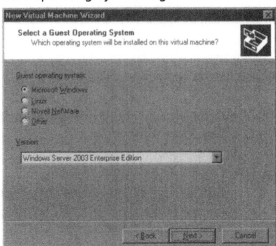

5. On the **Name the Virtual Machine** page (Figure 4.10), enter a **Virtual machine name** in the text box. In this example, name the machine **ISA-LOCAL**. Enter a path for the virtual machine in the **Location** text box. Click **Next**.

Figure 4.10 Name the Virtual Machine Page

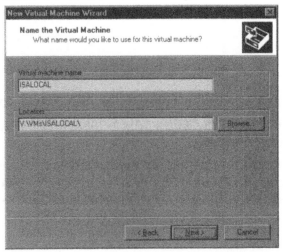

6. On the **Memory for the Virtual Machine** page (Figure 4.11), assign the amount of host system memory you want to allocate to this virtual machine. In our ISA firewall virtual firewall network, the ISALOCAL machine has 128MB of memory allocated to it. Enter **128** in the memory text box. Click **Next**.

Figure 4.11 Memory for the Virtual Machine Page

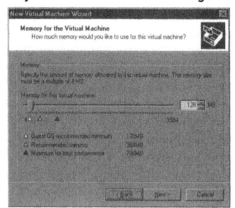

7. On the **Network Type** page (Figure 4.12), select the **Use bridged networking** option. This option allows the first network interface card in the virtual machine to connect to the live network to which the host operating system is connected. You can assign a valid IP address on this interface in the virtual machine and communicate with all machines on the live network and connect to the Internet via the live network's gateway. This is the interface that will act as the external interface of the ISALOCAL ISA firewall virtual machine. The ISALOCAL VM will use this interface to connect to the live network's Internet gateway (which is a DSL router on our network). We will later add two more network interface cards to this virtual machine that will be used to connect the ISALOCAL virtual machine to VMnet2 (the Internal network) and VMNet4 (the DMZ network). Click **Next**.

Figure 4.12 Network Type Page

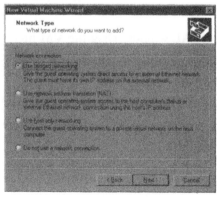

8. On the **Select I/O Adapter Types** page, use the default settings, and click **Next**.

9. On the **Select a Disk** page, select the **Create a New Virtual Disk** option. This will create a virtual hard disk file on the host operating system's drive. This virtual machine will see this file as a hard disk. Click **Next**.

10. On the **Select a Disk Type** page, select the **IDE (Recommended)** option, and click **Next**.

11. On the **Specify Disk Capacity** page (Figure 4.13), use the default value, **4.0** for the **Disk size (GB)** entry. Although the Windows Server 2003 and ISA firewall software will not require this amount of disk space, you do not need to worry about the virtual disk file using up this amount of space on your host system's physical disk. The value you enter on this page represents the maximum size the virtual machines disk will grow. While the virtual machine will always see its hard disk size as the size you enter on this page, the actual virtual disk file on the host operating system grows dynamically to accommodate the amount of space required by the data placed on the virtual machine's hard disk. Click **Next**.

Figure 4.13 Specify Disk Capacity Page

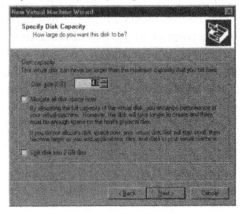

12. Accept the default name for the disk file on the **Specify Disk File** page, and click **Finish**.

13. In the **ISALOCAL** window, click the **VM** menu, and then click **Settings**.

14. In the **Virtual Machine Control Panel** dialog box, click the **Hardware** tab. On the **Hardware** tab, click **Add**.

15. Click **Next** on the **Welcome to the Add Hardware Wizard** page.

16. On the **Hardware Type** page (Figure 4.14), select the **Ethernet Adapter** option and click **Next**.

Figure 4.14 Hardware Type Page

17. On the **Network Type** page, select the **Custom** option. Select **VMNet2** from the drop-down list. This network interface will be the interface connected to the Internal network. Click **Finish**.

18. The second network interface card shows up as **NIC 2** in the **Device** list.

19. In the **Virtual Machine Control Panel** dialog box, click the **Hardware** tab. On the **Hardware** tab, click **Add**.

20. Click **Next** on the **Welcome to the Add Hardware Wizard** page.

21. On the **Hardware Type** page (Figure 4.15), select the **Ethernet Adapter** option, and click **Next**.

Figure 4.15 The Hardware Type page

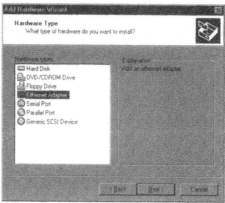

22. On the **Network Type** page, select the **Custom** option. Select **VMNet4** from the drop-down list. This network interface will be the interface connected to the DMZ network. Click **Finish**.

23. The second network interface card shows up as **NIC 3** in the **Device** list.

24. Click on the **CD-ROM 1 (IDE 1:0)** entry in the **Device** list.

25. On the right side of the dialog box (Figure 4.16), select the **Use ISO image** option and use the **Browse** button to locate the Windows Server 2003 .iso file.

Figure 4.16 Selecting an .iso image

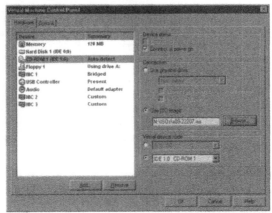

26. Click on the **USB Controller** entry in the **Device** list. Click **Remove**.

27. Click **OK** in the **Virtual Machine Control Panel** dialog box.

Now that the virtual machine hardware settings are configured, we can begin installing Windows Server 2003. Perform the following steps to complete the Windows Server 2003 operating system installation:

1. Click the **Start this virtual machine** link on the left side of the **ISA-LOCAL – VMware Workstation** window (Figure 4.17). The machine will boot the CD-ROM disk represented by the .iso file.

Figure 4.17 Starting the Virtual Machine

2. Press **ENTER** when you see the **Setup Notification** page.

3. Press **ENTER** on the **Welcome to Setup** page.

4. Press **F8** on the **Windows Licensing Agreement** page.

5. Press **ENTER** on the Partition Setup page.

6. Accept the default selection **Format the partition using the NTFS file system** option on the formatting page and press **ENTER.** The partition is quickly formatted.

7. The file copy phase proceeds to copy the Windows Server 2003 files from the .iso image to the virtual disk. The virtual machine will automatically reboot after the files are copied.

8. The installation routine enters graphical interface mode after the reboot.

9. Click **Next** on the **Regional and Language Options** settings page.

10. Enter your **Name** and **Organization** on the **Personalize Your Software** page. Click **Next.**

11. Enter your product key in the **Your Product Key** dialog box. Click **Next.**

12. On the **Licensing Modes** page, enter the value **500** in the **Per server. Number of concurrent connections** text box. Click **Next.**

13. On the **Computer Name** and **Administrator Password** page, enter **ISA-LOCAL** in the **Computer name** text box. Enter **password** in the **Administrator password** and **confirm password** text boxes. Click **Next.**

14. Click **Yes** in the **Windows Setup** dialog box indicating that the password you entered is not secure.

15. Enter the correct date, time, and time zone settings in the **Date and Time Settings** dialog box. Click **Next.**

16. On the **Networking Settings** page, select **Typical settings,** and click **Next.**

17. Accept the default option on the **Workgroup or Computer Domain** page. After you have installed the EXCHANGE2003BE machine on the Internal network (VMNet2), you should join the ISALOCAL machine to the msfire-wall.org domain. Click **Next.**

18. The installation continues, and then the virtual machine restarts.

19. Log on to the ISALOCAL machine using the Administrator account and the password you created.

Now that the Windows Server 2003 software is installed, we can configure the network interface cards in the virtual machine with the proper IP addressing information. Perform the following steps to configure the ISALOCAL virtual machine's network interface cards and configure other operating system options:

1. After logging on to the ISALOCAL virtual machine, click the **VM** menu, and click the **Install VMware Tools** command.

2. Click **Install** in the **ISALOCAL** dialog box.

3. Click **Next** on the **Welcome to the installation wizard for VMware Tools** page.

4. On the **Setup Type** page, select **Complete,** and click **Next**.

5. Click **Install** on the **Ready to Install the Program** page.

6. For each of the **Hardware Installation** dialog boxes, click the **Continue Anyway** button.

7. Click **Yes** on the **VMware Tools Installation** dialog box, informing you that hardware acceleration is not enabled on the virtual machine.

8. If the installation page for Windows Server 2003 appears, close it.

9. Minimize the notepad window that has the **HWAccel.txt** file opened.

10. On the **Settings** tab of the **Display Properties** dialog box, click **Advanced**.

11. In the **Default Monitor and Standard VGA Graphics Adapter Properties** dialog box, click the **Troubleshoot** tab.

12. On the **Troubleshoot** tab, drag the slider bar all the way over to the **Full** setting. Click **Apply,** and then click **OK**.

13. Click **OK** in the **Display Properties** dialog box.

14. Click **Finish** on the **Installation Wizard Completed** page.

15. Click **Yes** on the **VMware Tools** dialog box. This will restart the Windows Server 2003 ISALOCAL virtual machine.

16. Log on as Administrator.

The next step is to configure the network interface cards in the virtual machine. Perform the following steps to configure the network interface cards:

1. Right-click on an empty area on the desktop, and click **Properties**.

2. In the **Display Properties** dialog box, click the **Desktop** tab.

3. On the **Desktop** tab, click **Customize Desktop**.

4. In the **Desktop Items** dialog box, click the **General** tab. On the **General** tab, put checkmarks in the **My Documents, My Computer, My Network Places,** and **Internet Explorer** checkboxes. Click **OK**.

5. Click **Apply,** and then click **OK** in the **Display Properties** dialog box.

6. Right-click the **My Network Places** icon on the desktop, and click **Properties**.

7. Right-click the **Local Area Connection** icon in the **Network Connections** window, and click **Rename**. Name the connection **WAN**.

8. Right-click on **Local Area Connection 2**, and click **Rename**. Name this connection **LAN**.

9. Right-click on **Local Area Connection 3**, and click **Rename**. Name this connection **DMZ**.

Now we can assign IP addressing information to each of the interfaces. We'll begin with the external interface of the ISA firewall virtual machine.

1. Right-click on the **WAN** interface, and click **Properties**.

2. In the **WAN Properties** dialog box, click the **Internet Protocol (TCP/IP)** entry, and click **Properties**.

3. On the **General** tab of the **Internet Protocol (TCP/IP) Properties** dialog box (Figure 4.18), enter the IP addressing information as seen in the following figure.

Figure 4.18 Entering IP Addressing Information

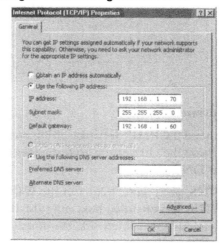

4. Click the **Advanced** button.

5. In the **Advanced TCP/IP Settings** dialog box, click the **DNS** tab. On the **DNS** tab, remove the checkmark from the **Register this connection's addresses in DNS** checkbox. Click **OK**.

6. Click **OK** in the **Internet Protocol (TCP/IP) Properties** dialog box.

7. Click **Close** in the **WAN Properties** dialog box.

Perform the following steps to configure the **LAN** interface's IP addressing information:

1. Right click on the **LAN** interface, and click **Properties**.

2. In the **LAN Properties** dialog box, click the **Internet Protocol (TCP/IP)** entry, and click **Properties**.

3. On the **General** tab of the **Internet Protocol (TCP/IP) Properties** dialog box (Figure 4.19), enter the IP addressing information as seen in the following figure.

Figure 4.19 Entering IP Addressing Information

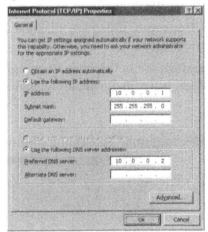

4. Click the **Advanced** button.

5. In the **Advanced TCP/IP Settings** dialog box, click the **DNS** tab. On the **DNS** tab, remove the checkmark from the **Register this connection's addresses in DNS** checkbox.

6. Click the **WINS** tab (Figure 4.20). On the **WINS** tab, click **Add**. In the **TCP/IP WINS Server** dialog box, enter the IP address of the WINS server. On our ISA firewall virtual network, the domain controller will also act as a WINS server. Enter **10.0.0.2** into this dialog box. Click **Add**.

Figure 4.20 Entering a WINS Server Address

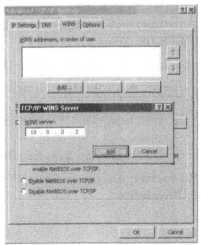

7. Click **OK** in the **Advanced TCP/IP Settings** dialog box.

8. Click **OK** in the **Internet Protocol (TCP/IP) Properties** dialog box.

9. Click **OK** in the **LAN Properties** dialog box.

We'll finish up by configuring the IP addressing information for the DMZ interface on the ISA firewall machine. Perform the following steps to configure the DMZ interface:

1. Right-click on the **DMZ** interface, and click **Properties**.

2. In the **DMZ Properties** dialog box, click **Internet Protocol (TCP/IP)**, and click **Properties**.

3. On the **General** tab of the **Internet Protocol (TCP/IP) Properties** dialog box (Figure 4.21), enter the IP addressing information as seen in the following figure.

Figure 4.21 Entering IP Addressing Information

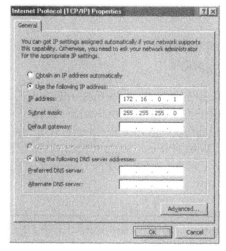

4. Click the **Advanced** button.

5. In the **Advanced TCP/IP Settings** dialog box, click the **DNS** tab. On the **DNS** tab, remove the checkmark from the **Register this connection's addresses in DNS** checkbox. Click **OK**.

6. Click **OK** in the **Internet Protocol (TCP/IP) Properties** dialog box.

7. Click **Close** in the **DMZ Properties** dialog box.

The Windows Server 2003 operating system is now ready for the ISA firewall software. At this point, you should save a snapshot of the configuration. Click the **Snapshot** menu in the **ISALOCAL – VMware Workstation** window, and click **Save Snapshot**. This allows you to get back to the base operating system configuration in the event that you want to start from a clean environment again. When we get to installing the ISA firewall software in Chapter 6, we'll describe how to save another snapshot of the configuration *after* installing the ISA firewall software.

The procedures used to install and configure the ISALOCAL virtual machine can be used to install the other virtual machines in the ISA firewall virtual network. Pay close attention to the IP addressing information for each virtual machine and make sure that you assign each virtual machine to the correct VMnet. You can test whether machines are connected to the correct VMnet by having the ISALOCAL or REMOTEISA machines ping hosts on their respective networks. For example, after creating the EXCHANGE2003BE machine, ping **10.0.0.2** from the ISALOCAL machine. If you do not get a ping reply back, the most likely reason for the failure is that you either misconfigured the IP addressing information on one of the machines, or the machines are not on the same VMnet.

If you are interested in the most simple setup that will allow you to test the majority of scenarios in this book, you can use the following virtual machines:

- ISALOCAL
- ISAREMOTE
- CLIENT
- EXCHANGE2003BE
- REMOTECLIENT

Note that you do not need to go through the entire configuration again for the REMOTECLIENT machine. You can copy the directory for the CLIENT machine to another location, and then reconfigure the name, IP addressing information, and VMnet in the copy. That will allow you to have a REMOTECLIENT that you can communicate with when we do the site-to-site VPN exercises in Chapter 9.

TIP

VMware Workstation 4.0 only supports three virtual NICs out of the box. However, with the kind help of Alessandro Perilli (http://www.virtualization.info/) you can add a fourth NIC to a single VMware virtual machine. Here's what you do:

Open a related .vmx file and add these lines to the bottom:
Ethernet3.present = "TRUE"
ethernet3.addressType = "generated"
ethernet3.generatedAddress = "00:0c:29:cb:7d:8f"
ethernet3.generatedAddressOffset = "30"
ethernet3.connectionType = "custom"
ethernet3.vnet = "VMnet3"
You cannot change the Ethernet number and the AddressOffset.
You can change the address.Type, the generatedAddress, the connectionType and the vnet.

How ISA Firewall's Define Networks and Network Relationships

One of the primary limitations of the ISA Server 2000 firewall was its simplistic view of the network. The ISA Server 2000 firewall recognized only two types of networks: trusted and untrusted. Trusted networks were included in the ISA Server 2000 firewall's Local Address Table (LAT). Any network that wasn't in the LAT was considered untrusted. ISA firewall policy was applied to all communications between LAT and non-LAT hosts. Communications between LAT hosts were routed through the ISA Server 2000 firewall without being subjected to the ISA Server 2000 firewall's stateful filtering and application-layer inspection mechanisms.

This was problematic for ISA Server 2000 firewall administrators who wanted to create DMZ segments that were directly connected to the ISA Server 2000 firewall. For example, an ISA Server 2000 firewall might be configured with three network interfaces. This configuration could include an internal interface connecting to the internal network, a DMZ interface connected to a public access DMZ segment, and an external interface, which connects the firewall to the Internet.

In ISA Server 2000, this trihomed DMZ configuration highlights most of the limitations of the ISA Server 2000 networking model.

- All communications between LAT and non-NAT hosts had to be NATed. This meant that all connections between the internal network and the Internet, and the internal network and the DMZ segment, were NATed.

- The ISA Server 2000 firewall did not apply stateful application-layer inspection to connections between Internet hosts and machines on the DMZ segment. These connections were routed by the ISA Server 2000 firewall from the Internet to the DMZ segment and only stateful filtering was done on the connections, similar to what you see with a typical hardware firewall.

- Communications between DMZ hosts and hosts on the internal network had to be accomplished via Server and Web Publishing Rules because the Internal network saw the DMZ segment as just another untrusted network.

- Outbound connections from the internal network to the DMZ segment were subject to the same Access Policy as those between the internal network and the Internet. For example, if you allowed outbound FTP access from the Internal network, FTP access was allowed to *all* non-LAT networks. If you allowed outbound access to a particular protocol, internal network users had access to that protocol at *all* sites.

- With the ISA Server 2000 firewall, it was possible to substitute private addresses for public address in the DMZ segment. However, the ISA Server 2000 firewall did not recognize this segment as a DMZ, and the DMZ segment had to be placed on the LAT. Because the ISA Server 2000 firewall only applied firewall policy on communications between LAT and non-LAT hosts, no firewall filtering was done between the internal network and the private address DMZ segment. While you could use RRAS packet filters to create a "poor man's" DMZ segment, the RRAS packet filters provided even less flexibility and security than a hardware firewall's stateful packet-filtering mechanisms.

Microsoft recognized these limitations in the ISA Server 2000 firewall and corrected them. The ISA firewall no longer uses the LAT. The LAT is no longer required because the ISA firewall does not implicitly trust any network. In ISA Server 2000, the LAT determined which networks were trusted and which were not. Because the networking model of the new ISA firewall does not trust any networks by default, the LAT is not part of the ISA firewalls configuration. All communications moving through the ISA firewall are subject to the ISA firewall's stateful filtering and stateful application-layer inspection mechanisms.

Another major improvement to the ISA firewall's networking model is that you now have control over the routing relationship between the any two networks. For example, if you wanted to replicate the trihomed DMZ setup where you have an external interface, internal interface and DMZ interface, you can use public or private addresses on the DMZ segment and create a route or NAT relationship between the internal network and the DMZ segment. You can even choose between a route or NAT relationship between the internal network and the Internet. This is especially helpful if you have public addresses on your internal network and you want to continue using them without NATing outbound connections to the Internet.

Table 4.5 shows what's new and improved in the ISA firewall's networking model versus the ISA Server 2000.

Table 4.5 New and Improved Features in the ISA Firewall's Networking Model

Feature	Description
All Access Rules include a source and destination network element	Access Rules control what communications move through the firewall. Two of the key components of an Access Rule are the source of the connection request and the destination requested. That allows you fined-tuned control over protocol access through the firewall. You can allow users IRC access, but only when the request comes from a specific internal network and the destination is another network on the corporate LAN. IRC requests to any other network, including the Internet, are denied.
All communications moving through the ISA firewall are subjected to stateful filtering and stateful application-layer inspection	All connections made through the ISA firewall are subjected to the ISA firewall's Access Policies. There are no trusted networks in the ISA 2004 networking scheme. While you can choose to route all communications from one network to another via an Access Rule, there is never a requirement to do so.

Continued

Table 4.5 New and Improved Features in the ISA Firewall's Networking Model

Feature	Description
Communications between any two networks can be routed or NATed	You can choose to route or to NAT connections between any two networks. You can choose a NAT relationship if you need to hide addresses on one network from another network, or you can route packets from one network to another network if you need to use protocols that do not function across NATed connections. The ability to choose the routing relationship between any two networks provides a great deal more flexibility than the ISA Server 2000 method of always NATing between LAT and non-NAT networking and always routing between LAT networks.
Firewall client and Web Proxy client configurations can be created on a per network basis	You can create multiple Internal networks and control access between these internal networks using Access Rules. Each network can have its own customized Web Proxy and Firewall client configuration and support. You may want one network to have Web Proxy client access but not Firewall client access, while at the same time, you want another internal network to have Firewall client access but not Web Proxy client access. You couldn't do this with the ISA Server 2000 firewall.
The ISA firewall is defined as a unique network	One of the most important jobs for a firewall is the ability to protect itself. One major limitation to the ISA Server 2000 firewall is that the packet-filtering mechanism only applied to non-LAT interfaces. This left LAT interfaces completely open to connections from any LAT host. The ISA firewall defines all its own interfaces as part of a *Local Host* network, and explicit Access Rules must be created to allow connections to *any* interface on the ISA firewall.
VPN clients belong to a separate network	The ISA Server 2000 firewall treated VPN clients as LAT hosts and did not apply firewall policy to VPN client connections. The ISA firewall applies both stateful filtering and stateful application-layer inspection to all connections from VPN clients to any other network. VPN clients can be locked down to access on the protocols and locations you want them to access.

Continued

Table 4.5 New and Improved Features in the ISA Firewall's Networking Model

Feature	Description
Quarantined VPN clients represent a separate network	The ISA firewall supports VPN Quarantine. You can configure the ISA firewall to require VPN clients to pass a security check before being moved to the VPN clients network. This allows you to create custom Access Rules that apply to quarantined VPN clients, which allows them to update their systems to meet network security requirements.
Networks can be grouped to simplify policy Access Rule configuration	You can group networks to simplify access control. For example, you may wish to grant users access from Internal networks A and B to access resources on a DMZ network. You can create Networks A and B and then create a network group that includes both of them and then allow access to the Network Group. The Network Group then simplifies creating Access Rules on subsequent occasions when you want to create Access Rules for these two networks.
Granular control over Network Objects	You have control access based on more than just a source and destination network. You can set computer objects, address ranges, subnets, computer sets, URL sets and domain name sets. Each of these Network Objects can be used to control access by using them for source and destination in Access Rules.
SecureNAT client support for VPN clients	The ISA Server 2000 firewall's VPN server required that VPN clients be configured as either Web Proxy or Firewall clients to access the Internet through the ISA firewall they were connected to. The ISA firewall allows VPN clients to act as enhanced SecureNAT clients and allows them to access the Internet through the same ISA firewall to which they created the VPN link. The VPN client SecureNAT client configuration is enhanced because the VPN client's log-on credentials can be used to allow for user/group-based access control between the VPN client and any other network.

We will cover all of these issues in more detail throughout this book.

ISA 2004 Multinetworking

The ISA 2004 marketing team has assigned the term "multinetworking" to the ISA firewall's new and improved networking feature set. Like most marketing terms, it's hard to pin down exactly what multinetworking actually means. It could mean the ISA firewall's ability to control access between any two networks using stateful filtering and stateful application-layer inspection. It could mean the ISA firewall's ability to create multiple types of Network Objects and use those network objects in Access Rules. Or, it could mean the ability to create multiple internal networks, multiple DMZ networks, and multiple external networks. Or, it could mean all of the above. Like the term "stateful," it has no specific meaning and can be used in just about any way you like.

WARNING

One thing that multinetworking does *not* mean is the ability to support multiple default gateways on the ISA firewall. This means you can't have one external interface connected to a DSL line, a second external interface connected to a cable line and a third external interface connected to a T1 line, and expect to use all three interfaces to connect to the Internet. While you can use all of these interface to connect to Internet-based computers, only one of these interfaces can be used to connect to the Internet at large, because the other two interfaces will require explicit routing table entries to connect to specific Internet hosts or networks. If you wish to use multiple Internet connections to connect to the Internet at large, check out Rainfinity's RainConnect. RainConnect allows you to connect multiple interface interfaces on the ISA firewall, and also provides for bandwidth aggregation and prioritization. It also allows you to publish resources on a protected network behind the ISA firewall and have those published resources available through all Internet connections and load balance them across the connections.

To get a better idea of how the ISA 2004 multinetworking model works, let's look at a network diagram. Figure 4.22 shows a typical ISA firewall multinetworking configuration.

Figure 4.22 ISA Firewall Multinetworking

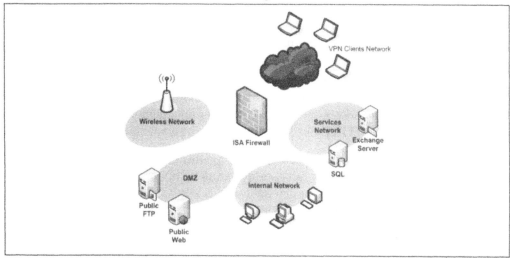

There are four *protected* networks directly connected to the ISA firewall in this example. A protected includes all networks defined on the ISA firewall except for the default External network. The default External network represents the Internet. The four protected networks in the diagram are the **Wireless Network**, **DMZ**, **Internal Network** and **Services Network**.

Using the ISA firewall's new network model, you could create the following access rules:

- Wireless clients can access the Internet but are not allowed access to any of the other protected networks. Users on the Wireless segment can VPN to the ISA firewall and gain access to the Internal network segment if access is required.

- Servers on the DMZ segment are allowed access to servers on the Services Network segment. For example, the Public Web server could be granted access to the Exchange Server, but not the SQL server. In this way, the Public Web server can act as an RPC over HTTP proxy for Outlook 2003 users. Hosts on the DMZ segment would not be allowed access to the Internet and they would not be allowed access to any other protected network segments.

- Users and machines on the Internal network can be granted access to resources on the Internet and the Services network. This allows them to use selected resources that you allow on the Internet and also have access to the Exchange Server. Users on the Internal network would not have access to resources on the Wireless network or the DMZ segment.

- Machines on the Services Network can be granted access to selected sites on the Internet (such as the Windows Update site). They could also be allowed restricted access to the Internal network. For example, the Exchange Server may be a member of the Internet network domain and need to communicate with domain controllers on the Internal network.

- VPN clients can be allowed access to resources on the DMZ, Internet, Internal Network and Services Network. You can control which VPN clients can access resources on which network via user/group based access control. For example, you may have a user group named *ExchangeUsers* and you want them to use the Outlook MAPI client to connect to the Exchange Server, but no other resources. You can create an access rule to allow members of the group access to the Exchange Server, but only using the secure Exchange RPC calls to get to the Exchange Server. If members of this group attempted to use any other protocol, such as HTTP or CIFS, their connection attempts would be denied.

The multinetworking features allows you very granular access control over what destination a host on any network can access. Even the VPN clients, which traditionally had access to everything on the corporate network once they connected, can now be locked down tight after establishing the VPN link.

The ISA Firewall's Default Networks

In order to get a better understanding of the ISA firewall's multinetworking feature and how the ISA firewall views networks and how they are used, let's take a look at the default networks on the ISA firewall. You will see these default networks created on the ISA firewall immediately after installation is complete.

- Local Host Network
- Internal Network
- External Network (default)
- VPN Clients Network
- Quarantined VPN Clients Network

ISA 2004 Networks must meet the following criteria:

- The ISA firewall must have one or more adapters. If the ISA firewall has a single adapter, then all addresses are considered part of the Internal Network.
- A Network Interface Card can have one or more IP addresses. The IP address on a particular interface must belong to the Local Host Network and to the Network to which that Interface is directly connected.
- With the exception of the Local Host, VPN Clients, and VPN Quarantine Networks, an IP address can only belong to *one* Network.
- All addresses belonging to a single NIC must belong to the *same Network*

In the following sections we will looks at each of the default networks in more detail.

Local Host Network

The *Local Host Network* is a built-in Network Object that defines all the IP addresses on all the interfaces on the ISA firewall. For example, if the ISA firewall has three network interfaces, and there are ten IP addresses bound to the external interface, two IP addresses bound to the DMZ interface and one IP address bound to the internal interface, then all 13 addresses would comprise the Local Host Network. You never have to explicitly define any of the addresses on the Local Host Network; addresses are automatically added to the Local Host Network when you add addresses to the interfaces.

You can find the **Properties** of the Local Host Network in the **ServerName\Configuration\Networks** node. Click on the **Networks** tab in the **Details** pane and right-click on **Local Host**, and click **Properties**. The Local Host Network's **Properties** dialog box appears in Figure 4.23.

Figure 4.23 Configuring a Web Proxy Listener on the Local Host Network

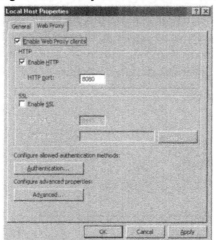

There are two tabs on the **Local Host Network Properties** dialog box. The **General** tab provides an explanation of the Local Host Network. The **Web Proxy** tab enables a Web Proxy listener for the Local Host Network. The Web Proxy listener is disabled by default. Put a checkmark in the **Enable Web Proxy clients** checkbox if you want applications running on the ISA firewall to act as Web Proxy clients.

WARNING

Do *not* enable the Local Host Network web listener to allow protected network hosts access to the Internet. The Local Host Network web listener is only used by the ISA firewall machine itself. No other machine on protected or non-protected Networks uses the Local Host web listener.

For example, if you want to use the Web browser on the ISA firewall itself, you would enable the Web Proxy listener and then configure the browser to use an IP address on one of the interfaces on the ISA firewall as its Web Proxy server. If the IP address on the Internal interface of the ISA firewall is **192.168.1.1**, you would use that IP address when configuring the browser as a Web Proxy client. You must also enable the Web Proxy listener on the Local Host Network if you want to use Scheduled Content Download jobs.

An important issue regarding the Local Host Network is that, like the VPN clients and VPN Quarantine Networks, the addresses assigned to it are not mutually exclusive of addresses assigned to other networks. In all other situations, addresses assigned to other Networks cannot be assigned to any other network.

For example, if the Internal interface of the ISA firewall is assigned the address **192.168.1.1**, then that address *must be included* in the Internal network's list of addresses. If the ISA firewall has the address **172.16.0.1** assigned to the DMZ interface, then that address *must be included* in the list of addresses defining the DMZ network. It's a common error where the ISA firewall administrator will leave out the addresses assigned to the Local Host Network because they think they cannot include these addresses because of the general principle that addresses cannot be assigned to two different Networks.

TIP

You can use addresses on the Local Host Network to publish services running on the ISA firewall. For example, you can configure an SMTP relay on the ISA firewall and bind the SMTP virtual server to the internal interface of the ISA firewall. You then publish that IP address when creating an SMTP Server Publishing Rule. You can also publish the Remote Desktop Server running on the ISA firewall by binding the Remote Desktop Server to one of the interfaces of the ISA firewall and then publishing that interface address using a Server Publishing Rule.

Internal Network

The ISA 2004 Internal Network is quite different from the ISA Server 2000 Internal network. In ISA Server 2000, any network contained in the LAT was considered an Internal network. All communications between LAT (Internal Network) hosts were *not* filtered and firewalled by ISA Server 2000 firewall. The reason for this is that only communications between LAT and non-LAT clients were firewalled by the ISA Server 2000 firewall.

In contrast to the ISA Server 2000 firewall's approach to Internal and external networks, the ISA firewall's concept of Internal network is related to the System Policy Rules that are automatically configured on the ISA firewall.

In order to understand the Internal Network's role, you have to have a basic understanding of the ISA 2004 System Policy. The ISA 2004 System Policy is a collection of 30 Access Rules that control inbound and outbound access to and from the ISA firewall. These rules are created by default and you can customize them, or even disable them, if you like. Examples of ISA 2004 System Policy rules include:

- Allow access to directory services for authentication purposes
- Allow Kerberos authentication from ISA Server to trusted servers
- Allow Microsoft CIFS from ISA Server to trusted servers
- Allow NetBIOS from ISA Server to trusted servers

For each of the System Policy Access Rules, communications are by default assigned from the Local Host network to the Internal Network. The ISA firewall's concept of the Internal network is the network where your main infrastructure servers are located. That way, the default System Policy rules allow communications with the organization's Active Directory servers, DNS servers, DHCP servers, WINS servers, and file servers. However, this concept of the Internal network applies to make setup of the ISA firewall simple, as the Internal network is defined during setup of the ISA firewall software. You are in no way limited to that definition of the Internal network.

One thing that's important to note that is you can create multiple *internal* networks. Notice that I've used a lower case "i" in this case. An internal network can be any network that is protected by the ISA firewall. In fact, you can create DMZ networks and call them internal networks. Only the default Internal network (with an upper case "I") has special meaning to the ISA firewall, and that special meaning is related to System Policy.

TIP

We recommend that you take advantage of the default Internal Network and place all of your infrastructure servers behind the same NIC. This makes installation and configuration of the ISA firewall much easier because you can leverage the default System Policy rules.

You can view the Properties of the default Internal Network by going to the **ServerName\Configuration\Networks** node. The configuration options for the default Internal network are the same as any other network you create on the ISA firewall. We can use the Internal network configuration options as a model on which you can create and configure other internal or perimeter Networks on the ISA firewall.

Click on the **Networks** tab in the **Details** pane, and then double-click on the **Internal** network. Click on the **Addresses** tab, and you'll see something like Figure 4.24.

Figure 4.24 Defining the Internal Network Addresses

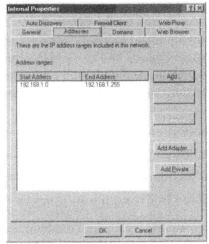

On the **Addresses** tab, you enter the addresses on *all* networks located behind the Internal Network adapter. In the example shown in Figure 4.25, the internal network includes all addresses in the 192.168.1.0/24 range. These addresses were defined when the ISA firewall software was installed.

You can also easily add addresses in the private address range. Click the **Add Private** button to add addresses in any of the private network ID address ranges. Figure 4.25 shows the fly out menu from the **Add Private** button.

Figure 4.25 Adding Private Network Addresses

Do not use private address ranges that are not in use on the Internal network, and do not address an entire private address range to the Internal network if the entire private address range is not in use on the Internal network. This can cause conflicts if you have other networks that use subnets of the private network address range. For example, you may have the Internal Network using IP addresses **192.168.1.0-192.168.1.255** and another internal network using IP addresses **192.168.2.0-192.168.2.255**. If you assign the Internal network the address range **192.168.0.0-192.168.255.255**, you will create a conflict that prevents you from using the **192.168.2.0/24** network addresses for the second internal network. We recommend that you *never* use the **Add Private** button when configuring addresses for networks.

A better way to add addresses to the Internet network (and other networks you create) is to use the **Add Adapter** button. Figure 4.26 illustrates the effect of clicking the **Add Adapter** button.

Figure 4.26 Adding Addresses via the Routing Table

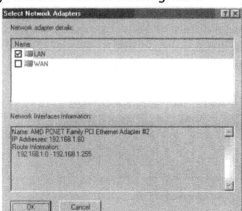

In the **Select Network Adapters** dialog box you can select the NIC connected to the Internal network and use the addresses in the Windows Routing Table to define the network. This is a much more reliable method of defining a particular network, since the Windows Routing Table should always have knowledge of all networks reachable from the ISA firewall. This knowledge of all reachable networks can be done either via manual configuration of the Windows Routing Table or by using a dynamic routing protocol such as RIP or OSPF.

The last method available for adding addresses to the Network is to use the **Add** button. Figure 4.27 illustrates the effect of clicking the **Add** button.

Figure 4.27 Entering an Address Range

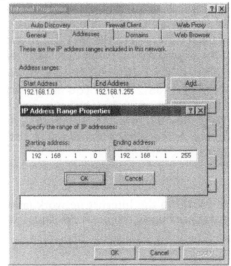

Click the **Domains** tab (Figure 4.28). Here you enter a list of internal network domains. When the firewall client connects to a host located in one of these domains, the connection request bypasses the Firewall client application. The primary rationale for this is that if all the machines located in the same domain are located behind the same NIC, then the Firewall client machine can communicate directly without looping back through the ISA firewall. This reduces the overall load on the ISA firewall and improves client performance because the connection doesn't incur any Firewall processing overhead. Further, the Domains tab can be used to control the behavior of Web Proxy clients when accessing external sites. We will discuss the relationship between the Domains tab and Web Proxy clients later in this chapter. See Figure 4.28 to see how to enter local domains.

Figure 4.28 Entering Local Domains

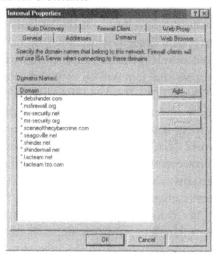

You have to be careful with the entries you make on the **Domains** tab if your internal network domain extends across multiple NICs. Figure 4.29 shows an example of one scenario where the domain extends across multiple network interfaces.

Figure 4.29 Domain Extending Across Internal Networks

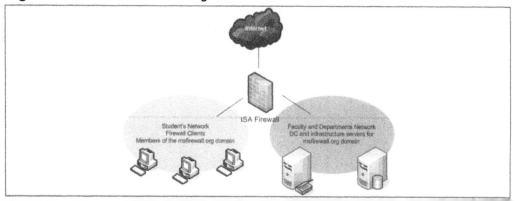

This is an example of a simple campus network configuration. There are three network interfaces on the ISA firewall. One interface connects the ISA firewall to the Internet. The second interface connects the ISA firewall with the Internet network, and a third interface connects the ISA firewall to a second internal network. The Internal network (with a capital "I," which is the Faculty and Departments network) contains the Active Directory servers and other infrastructure servers. The other internal network (the Student's Network) contains student machines which have been made members of the campus Active Directory domain, and these machines also have the Firewall client installed.

The Internal network domain name is *msfirewall.org*. You would include this domain name on the Domains tab. When any host on the Internal network contacts any other host in the msfirewall.org domain, the Firewall client machines on the Internet network will bypass the ISA firewall and connect directly to the hosts in the msfirewall.org domain located behind the Internal network adapter. Since there are no hosts on the Internal network that need to initiate connections to hosts on the Student's network, all is well. That's because all msfirewall.org servers are located behind the Internal network adapter.

Now suppose we place enter msfirewall.org into the **Domains** tab on the DMZ network, and we create an access rule (we will go over the details of Access Rules in Chapter 7) that allows HTTP, HTTPS, FTP, SMTP and POP3 to authenticate clients on the Student's Network into the Internal network. What would happen when machines configured as *only* Firewall clients on the Student's network try to connect to a POP3 server on the Internal network? That's right – the connection request fails. That's because the Student's Network Interface on the ISA firewall was configured with the msfirewall.org domain on its **Domains** tab. Since the machine configured as a Firewall client will bypass the Firewall client configuration when connecting to resources on domains listed on the **Domains** tab, the connect never even makes it to the ISA firewall.

What if the Firewall client machine on the Student's Network were configured as SecureNAT client as well as a Firewall client? In this case, the connection attempt from the host on the student's network to a member server on the Internal network in the msfirewall.org domain would be sent to the Student Network interface on the ISA firewall. The connection request in this case would be denied because the SecureNAT client cannot send credentials to the ISA firewall.

TIP

You can also enter external network domains on to the **Domains** tab. This will allow hosts that are also configured as Web Proxy and/or SecureNAT clients to bypass their Firewall client configuration to access Internet resources in those domains. This is useful in those rare circumstances where the Firewall client may not be compatible with a particular piece of software on the Firewall client computer.

In the **Internal Properties** dialog box, click on the **Web Browser** tab. Figure 4.30 shows what you will see in the dialog box.

Figure 4.30 Configuring Domains for Web Proxy Direct Access

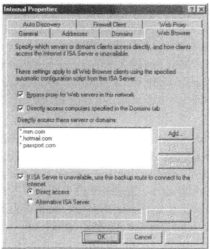

The settings on this tab control Web browsers on the Internal network that are configured to use the autoconfiguration script (we will discuss the autoconfiguration script in detail in Chapter 5).You have the options:

- **Bypass proxy for Web servers in this network.** This is an interesting setting. The Help file states: *"**Bypass proxy for web servers in this network.** Select this option if the Web browser on the Firewall client computer should bypass the ISA Server computer when accessing local Web servers."* The question is, *what is a local Web server?* Local to what? The answer is that *local* means to any Web server located at an address included in this Network's Address range. So, in the case of the Internal network, when a Web Proxy client configured with the autoconfiguration script attempts to connect to a Web server whose address is also on the Internal network, then the Web Proxy client will *bypass* the Web Proxy on the ISA firewall and connect directly to the Web server on the Internal network. This is a good thing.This prevents hosts located behind the same network adapter from looping back through the ISA firewall to access resources behind the same network interface.

- **Directly access computers specified on the Domains tab.**This allows the Web Proxy client configured with the autoconfiguration script to use the domains listed on the **Domains** tab for *Direct Access*. Direct Access for Web Proxy clients allows the Web Proxy client computer to bypass the Web Proxy on the ISA firewall and connect directly to the destination, either via the machines SecureNAT client configuration or via the machines Firewall client configuration.This is useful if you want to leverage the domains already entered on the domains tab and use them for Direct Access. However, beware of issues like those mentioned earlier with the Student's Network and Internal Network in the trihomed DMZ configuration.

■ **Directly access these servers or domains.** You can add a list of domains or IP addresses that you want Web Proxy clients configured with for the Autoconfiguration script to bypass the Web Proxy on the ISA firewall. In the example provided in the figure, we have entered a list of domains that should be bypassed when you want to use Outlook Express to access a Hotmail account. When the Web Proxy client computer connects to these domains, the Web Proxy client configuration is ignored, and the client uses alternate client configuration to access these sites, such as SecureNAT or Firewall client configurations.

■ **If ISA Server is unavailable, use this backup route to connect to the Internet: Direct access or Alternative ISA Server.** This option is a bit misleading because it implies that the entire ISA firewall must be unavailable before one of the options is triggered. In fact, the ISA firewall can be just fine, but if there is a problem with the ISA firewall's Web Proxy, then one of the alternatives is used. The **Direct Access** option allows a machine configured as a Web Proxy client to use an alternate client configuration to access the Internet or other destination network. This can be either its SecureNAT client configuration or via its Firewall client configuration. The **Alternative ISA Server** option allows you to enter the FQDN or IP address of an alternate ISA firewall to which the Web Proxy client can connect to reach the Internet. Do not use the **Browse** button to find an alternate server. If you use a FQDN in the **Alternative ISA Server** text box, then make surethe ISA firewall can resolve that FQDN to the correct IP address so that the ISA firewall can locate the alternate Web Proxy.

TIP

It is a little known fact that one of the most powerful methods you can use to control access for Web Proxy clients is the autoconfiguration script. You should *always* configure the Web Proxy clients to use *only* the autoconfiguration script if at all possible. The only exception to this is when you use WPAD and autodiscovery to assign configuration information to the Web Proxy clients. When you use autodiscovery, the autoconfiguration script information is automatically copied to the Web Proxy client. The autoconfiguration scripts make it possible to easily create a bypass list for Web Proxy clients so that they can use alternate client configuration to access problematic sites that do not work with CERN-compliant Web Proxy servers (like ISA 2004).

Click on the **Web Proxy** tab. The Web Proxy tab defines the outbound *Web Listener* for the Network. Web Proxy clients on this network use this Web listener to connect to the Web Proxy on the ISA firewall. The outbound Web Proxy listener for the Network is enabled by placing a checkmark in the **Enable Web Proxy clients** checkbox. A checkmark must also be in the **Enable HTTP** checkbox for Web browsers configured as Web Proxy clients to connect to the Web Proxy on this Network. See these steps illustrated in Figure 4.31.

Figure 4.31 The Web Proxy tab

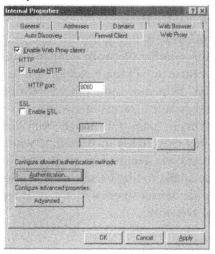

Many people have wondered for years about the **Enable SSL** checkbox on the **Web Proxy** page. This option was also available in ISA Server 2000. This setting posed a curious problem because if you enabled this option and then tried to configure the Web browser to connect to the default SSL port on the outbound Web Proxy SSL listener, the connection attempt would fail. The reason for this is that the Web browser that is configured as a Web Proxy client *cannot establish an SSL connection with the Web Proxy listener*. The initial connection between the Web Proxy client and the outbound Web Proxy listener must always be over HTTP.

If the connection between the Web Proxy client and the outbound Web Proxy listener must always be HTTP, then why did they make the **Enable SSL** option available on the **Web Proxy** tab? The reason is that in a *Web Proxy Chaining* scenario, you can configure a downstream Web Proxy server to forward Web requests to an upstream Web Proxy server using an SSL connection. This setup allows for *outbound HTTP- to-SSL bridging* between the downstream Web Proxy and the upstream Web Proxy.

TIP

It's always been a mystery to us why the Web browser wasn't designed to support SSL connections to the Web Proxy on the ISA firewall. This would allow an SSL-secured connection between the client and the Web Proxy, even though the URL might be for HTTP content on the Internet. While you might think that such a feature wouldn't be of much value, the fact is that it's more likely that someone has a sniffer on your network than there is on any interposed networks between yours and the destination host. There is also a greater chance that the person running the sniffer on your network is looking for specific data, such as user names and passwords. Perhaps future versions of the Internet Explorer Web client will support this type of configuration.

External Network (default)

The default External network created during ISA firewall setup includes all addresses that are not already defined by another Network on the ISA firewall. The default External Network doesn't contain any dialog boxes for you to perform customer configurations. Any address that isn't defined by some other Network on the ISA firewall is automatically included in the default External Network.

This is especially interesting in light of the Single NIC ISA firewall configuration. When you install the ISA firewall software on a machine with a single NIC, or when you apply the Single NIC Network Template to an existing configuration, all addresses in the IPv4 address range are added to the default Internal Network. Because all possible IP addresses are included in the default Internal Network, there are no addresses available for the default External Network.

TIP

In a single NIC ISA firewall configuration, all addresses are considered Internal. Because there are no addresses considered External, you cannot use the External Network in your Access Rules in a single NIC ISA firewall configuration. We will discuss this issue in more detail when we cover the Single NIC Network Template.

VPN Clients Network

The VPN Clients Network is one of the "virtual" or "just in time" Networks. When a VPN client or VPN gateway connects to the ISA firewall, that address is dynamically added to the VPN Clients Network. Access Rules can then be created to control traffic to and from the VPN Clients Network.

For example, suppose you use DHCP to assign addresses to VPN clients and gateways. When a VPN client connects to the ISA firewall, the address assigned to the VPN client is moved to the list of addresses included in the VPN Clients Network. Access Rules using the VPN Clients Network for Source or Destination address are then applied to the address assigned to the VPN client or gateway. When the VPN client or gateway disconnects from the ISA firewall, that address is dynamically removed from the VPN Clients Network.

TIP

You have the option to assign IP addresses to VPN clients and gateways using either DHCP or a static address pool. We recommend that you use DHCP as it simplifies things quite a bit. If you use a static address pool, you'll need to remove those addresses from the definition of the Internal Network if you choose to use subnet addresses for the VPN client's static address pool. We'll discuss this issue in more detail in Chapter 9 on configuring the ISA firewall as a VPN server and gateway.

Quarantined VPN Clients Network

The Quarantined VPN Clients Network is a "virtual" or "just in time" Network where addresses are dynamically assigned to this Network when quarantined VPN clients connect to the ISA firewall. The Quarantined VPN Client Network is only used when VPN Quarantine is enabled on the ISA firewall.

At the present time, VPN Quarantine represents more of a development platform than something that the average ISA firewall administrator can actually put into practice. The good news is that Frederic Esnouf, an MVP for ISA firewalls, has put together a very nice VPN Quarantine package that is easy to install and configure. Check out Frederic's excellent VPN Quarantine solution at **http://fesnouf.online.fr/programs/QSS/qssinaction/QssInAction.htm**

TIP

If you haven't completed the complex development requirements for VPN Quarantine, and then enabled VPN Quarantine on the ISA firewall, then all VPN clients and gateways will be quarantined and they will never leave the VPN Quarantine Network. For this reason, we recommend that you do not enable VPN Quarantine on the ISA firewall unless you have developer-level knowledge and a deep understanding of the development platform that underlies VPN Quarantine.

Creating New Networks

You will need to create new Networks whenever a new Network is introduced into your environment. A common reason to add a new Network is when you install additional NICs into the ISA firewall. Since all addresses located behind any particular NIC are considered a Network by the ISA firewall, you need to create a new Network when additional NICs are added to the firewall.

An interesting application of the Network concept relates to how you can use them for Networks located *in front of* the external interface of the ISA firewall. The external interface of the ISA firewall doesn't always need to be directly connected to the

Internet. Many organizations will use the ISA firewall as the back-end ISA firewall because they need the strongest level of firewall protection available closest to their corporate assets. The external interface of the back-end ISA firewall will be connected to a network under corporate control, and therefore, one that you can identify and configure as a Network Object in the ISA firewall configuration interface.

For example, suppose the back-end ISA firewall is has two NICs: one NIC is connected to a DMZ segment and one NIC is connected to a corporate asset network. Since you know the addresses used in the DMZ Network, you can create a Network Object that defines the address range used in the DMZ, and then use that Network Object to control traffic to and from the DMZ as it moves through the back-end ISA firewall.

In the following exercise, we'll add a new Network Object to an ISA firewall where we've installed an additional NIC to support a DMZ segment. This ISA firewall already had an external interface on network ID 192.168.1.0/24 and an internal interface on network ID 10.0.0.0/24. The new NIC is assigned the IP address 172.16.0.1/16 and we'll create a new Network for this DMZ interface.

Perform the following steps to create the New Network.

1. In the **Microsoft Internet Security and Acceleration Server 2004** management console, expand the server name and then expand the **Configuration** node. Click the **Networks** node.

2. Click the **Tasks** tab in the Task Pane. Click the **Create a New Network** link.

3. On the **Welcome to the New Network Wizard** page, enter a name for the new Network in the **Network name** text box. In this example we'll name it **DMZ**. Click **Next**.

4. On the **Network Type** page, select the **Perimeter Network** option (Figure 4.32). Notice in this dialog box that you have four options.

■   **Internal Network** Use the **Internal Network** option to create new internal Networks. Internal networks are generally considered to be networks on the "inside" of the ISA firewall. This isn't a hard and fast distinction because the ISA firewall doesn't really see the world in terms of internal versus external, as the ISA firewall applies stateful filtering and stateful application-layer inspection on *all* communications moving through the firewall. The notation as "internal" is more of an accounting consideration here. When you choose this option, you will have the chance to configure this Network using the **Properties** dialog box, to set options similar to those you can set with the default Internal Network.

■   **Perimeter Network** Use the **Perimeter Network** option when creating new DMZ segments. There are no practical differences between the settings created by the Wizard when you create a Perimeter versus an Internal Network. You have the same options in the **Properties** dialog box after you create a Perimeter Network as you have when you create an Internal

Network. The main value is that you can easily identify in the user interface which Networks are internal and which are DMZs.

- **VPN Site-to-Site Network** Use the **VPN Site-to-Site Network** option when you need to create a site-to-site VPN connection with another office. This Wizard walks you through the creation of the address ranges and VPN configuration of a site-to-site VPN.

- **External Network** Use the **External Network** option when you create a network that lies on the "outside" of the ISA firewall. Although the ISA firewall doesn't really see the network world as inside or outside, you can use as a rule of thumb that any network directly reachable from the interface on the ISA firewall that has the default gateway assigned to it is considered an external network. Note that you have the same configuration options in the **Properties** dialog box when you create a new External Network as you have when you create new Internal or Perimeter Networks.

5. Click **Next**.

See Figure 4.32 for defining the Network type and using a Perimeter Network.

Figure 4.32 Defining the Network Type

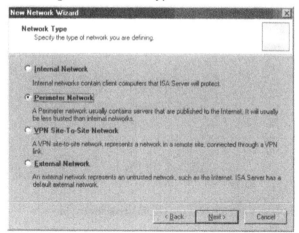

6. On the **Network Addresses** page (Figure 4.33), you define the address range(s) for the new Network. You have three choices.

- **Add** When you select the **Add** button, you can manually add the address range. This is useful if you don't want to define an entire network ID, or you want to add several non-contiguous ranges of IP addresses to the Network.

- **Add Adapter** When you select the **Add Adapter** button, a dialog box appears that allows you to select an adapter to define the new Network. The addresses added are based on the Windows routing table entries that apply to that adapter. If you have configured the Windows routing table correctly prior to creating the new Network, all the correct addresses will be added. This is the easiest way to define a new Network if the routing table contains the correct information.

■ **Add Private** When you select the **Add Private** button, a fly-out menu appears showing you're the three private network IDs. We highly recommend that you do not use this option because most organizations will use subnets of private network IDs throughout the organization.

In this example we'll select the **Add Adapter** option. This brings up the **Select Network Adapters** dialog box. Put a checkmark in the **DMZ** checkbox (in this example we renamed the adapters with meaningful names in the **Network and Dial-up Connections** Window). You'll see the addresses that will be assigned to the Network based on the Route Information listed in the **Network Interfaces Information** section. Click **OK**. See Figure 4.33 for how to select a Network adapter.

Figure 4.33 Selecting a Network Adapter

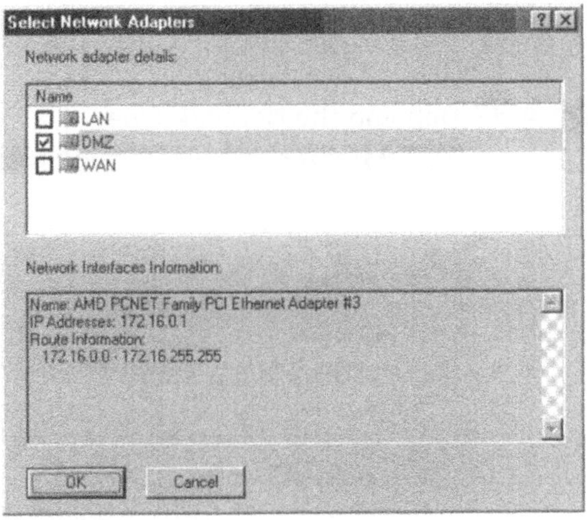

7   Click **Next** on the **Network Addresses** page.

8   Click **Finish** on the **Completing the New Network Wizard** page.

9.   Click **Apply** to save the changes and update the firewall policy.

10.   Click **OK** in the **Apply New Configuration** dialog box.

11.   The new Network appears in the list in the **Networks** tab (See Figure 4.34).

Figure 4.34 The New Network Appears in the List of Networks

Name ▲	Address Ranges	Description
DMZ	172.16.0.0 - 172.16.255.255	
External	IP addresses external to the ISA ...	Built-in network object representing the Internet.
Internal	10.0.0.0 - 10.0.0.255 10.255.255.255	Network representing the internal network.
Local Host	No IP addresses are associated ...	Built-in network object representing the ISA Server co
Quarantined VPN Cli...	No IP addresses are currently as...	Built-in dynamic network representing client computers
VPN Clients	No IP addresses are currently as...	Built-in dynamic network object representing client cor

Controlling Routing Behavior with Network Rules

Even though you've created a new Network, you can't use it for anything until you define the route relationship between that Network and other Networks it communicates with. You control this route relationship using *Network Rules*.

There are three route relationships available when you create a Network Rule.

- **Route** The ISA firewall documentation defines a route relationship as a "reciprocal" relationship. In practice, you use a route relationship when the Source and Destination Network defined by the Network Rule support routing between them. For example, if the source Network and the Destination Network both use public addresses, then you can define a Route relationship. If both the source and destination Network use private addresses, then you can use a route relationship. If the source network uses private addresses and the destination uses public addresses, then you can't use a route relationship (in most cases, there are exceptions when the ISA firewall is configured with a routing table entry that allows routing from private to public networks). Another key feature of the route relationship is that the source IP address is always preserved (with the exception of Publishing Rules, where you can control whether or not the source IP address is preserved, and the Server IP address is always replaced by the listener address). Use a Route relationship when the source and destination Networks support a route relationship, and you need to support protocols that are not NAT friendly.

- **NAT** The ISA firewall documentation defines a NAT relationship as directional. The directional nature of the NAT relationship means that you have to be mindful of the Source and Destination Network when configuring the Network Rule. When you use a NAT relationship, the source IP address is replaced with the address on the interface that connection is *exiting*. For example, suppose you create a NAT relationship between the default Internal Network and the DMZ Network. The source Network is the Internal Network and the destination Network is the DMZ Network. When communications leave the Internal Network to the DMZ Network, the source IP address is changed to the address on the network interface the communication is exiting, which in this case is the DMZ interface. If you created a Network Rule where the DMZ Network is the Source Network and the Internal Network is the Destination Network, then communications leaving the DMZ Network would have the source IP address replaced with the interface that the communication is exiting, which in this case is the Internal Network interface. Also note that when you define a NAT relationship, communications are *one-way* for both Web Publishing and Access Rules.

You must create a Network Rule for any communication between a specific Source and Destination Network. We've seen a number of situations where everything was set up right on the ISA firewall, but a particular Access Policy did not work because either there was no Network Rule controlling the route relationship between the Source and Destination, or the wrong route relationship was configured. We'll talk more about these route relationships later in this chapter in the discussions on the various ISA firewall Network Templates.

In the following exercise, you'll create a Network Rule that controls the route relationship between the Internal Network and the DMZ Network. Because both Networks are using private addresses we'll configure a Route relationship between the Networks. We prefer to use a Route relationship in this scenario because it allows us greater flexibility in the protocols we can pass between the Internal Network and the DMZ. However, if you want to hide the IP addresses of the hosts on the Internal Network when they're connecting to hosts on the DMZ Network, then you should use a NAT relationship, while keeping in mind that you'll not have support for protocols that do not work with NAT.

Perform the following steps to create the Network Rule:

1. In the **Microsoft Internet Security and Acceleration Server 2004** management console, expand the server name, and then expand the **Configuration** node. Click on the **Networks** node.

2. On the **Networks** node, click the **Network Rules** tab in the **Details** pane of the console.

3. On the **Task** pane, click the **Tasks** tab. Click the **Create a New Network Rule** link.

4. On the **Welcome to the New Network Rule Wizard** page, enter a name for the rule in the **Network rule name** text box. In this example we'll name the rule **Internal ▪ ⑧DMZ**. Click **Next**.

5. On the **Network Traffic Sources** page, click **Add**.

6. In the **Add Network Entities** dialog box, click the **Networks** folder. Double-click the **Internal** network. Click **Close**.

7. Click **Next** on the **Network Traffic Sources** page.

8. On the **Network Traffic Destinations** page, click **Add**.

9. In the **Add Network Entities** dialog box, click the **Networks** folder. Double-click the **DMZ** network. Click **Close**.

10. Click **Next** on the **Network Traffic Destinations** page.

11. On the **Network Relationship** page, select the **Route** option (see Figure 4.35). Click **Next**.

Figure 4.35 Defining a Route Relationship

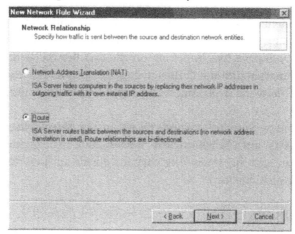

12. lick **Finish** on the **Completing the New Network Rule Wizard** page.

13. Click **Apply** to save the changes and update the firewall policy.

14. Click **OK** in the **Apply New Configuration** dialog box.

15. You will see the new Network Rule on the **Network Rules** tab in the **Details** pane of the **Microsoft Internet Security and Acceleration Server 2004** management console.

The ISA 2004 Network Objects

You always need to configure a source and a destination when creating Access Policies on the ISA firewall. The ISA firewall uses *Network Objects* to identify sources and destinations. The ISA firewall's Network Objects give you a lot of flexibility when creating Access Policy because you can get very granular control over what hosts can communicate with other hosts.

The ISA firewall's Network Objects include:

- Networks
- Network Sets
- Computers
- Address Ranges

- Subnets
- Computer Sets
- URL Sets
- Domain Name Sets
- Web Listeners

Networks

We've already spent a lot of time discussing the Network *Network Object*. Networks are collections of addresses that are reachable from a particular interface on the ISA firewall. For example, if you have two Interfaces on the ISA firewall with one interface connected to the Internet and one connected to the corporate network, then the definition of the Internal Network is all addresses located behind the internal interface of the ISA firewall.

You create new Network *Network Objects* in the **Networks** node of the **Microsoft Internet Security and Acceleration Server 2004** management console. See our earlier discussion on creating a new Network for details on how to create and configure Network Network Objects.

Network Sets

Network Sets represent collections of Networks. There are two default Network Sets:

- All Networks (and local host)
- All Protected Networks

The **All Networks (and local host)** Network Sets Network Object includes all possible addresses. You should rarely, if ever, need to use this Network Object. You might want to use this Network Object when performing testing, or if you want to use the ISA firewall as more of a stateful filtering router rather than a firewall.

The **All Protected Networks** Network Object includes all Networks defined on the ISA firewall *except* for the default External Network. You might use the **All Protected Networks** Network Object when you want to apply an Access Rule that controls outbound access for all networks behind the ISA firewall.

You can view the properties of the default **Network Sets** Network Objects by performing the following steps:

1. In the **Microsoft Internet Security and Acceleration Server 2004** management console, expand the server name, and then click the **Firewall Policy** node.

2. In the Task pane, click the **Toolbox** tab. Click the **Network Objects** link. The link expands and shows you a list of folders representing the ISA firewalls Network Objects.

3. Click on the **Network Sets** folder. There you will see the two default Network Sets.

4. Double-click the Network Sets to see the **Properties** of the Network Set (see Figure 4.36)

Figure 4.36 Defining Network Sets

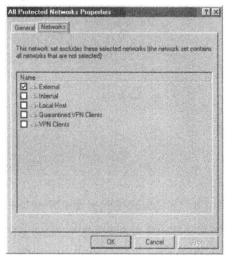

You can also create new Network Sets if you want to create Access Policy that applies to a specific collection of Networks. Suppose you want to create a Network Set that includes the VPN Clients Network and the Internal Network. You might use this set if you want to create an Access Rule that controls communications from both of these sources. Perform the following steps to create such as Network Set.

1. In the **Microsoft Internet Security and Acceleration Server 2004** management console, expand the server name and then click the **Firewall Policy** node.

2. In the Task pane, click the **Toolbox** tab. Click the **Network Objects** link. The link expands and shows you a list of folders representing the ISA firewalls Network Objects.

3. Click on the **Network Sets** folder. Click the **New** menu and then click **Network Set**.

4. On the **Welcome to the New Network Set Wizard** page, enter a name for the set in the **Network set name** text box. In this example, we'll name the set **VPN and Internal**. Click **Next**.

5. On the **Network Selection** page, select the **Includes all select networks** option. Notice that you also have the **Includes all networks except the selected network** option. Use this option if you want to create a large Network Set and only want to exclude a small number of Networks. In the **Name** list, put a checkmark in the **VPN Clients** and **Internal** checkboxes. Click **Next**. These steps are illustrated in Figure 4.37.

Figure 4.37 Creating a New Network Set

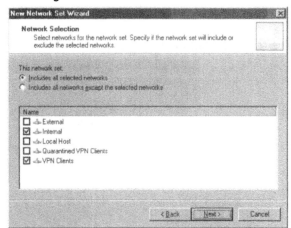

6. Click **Finish** on the **Completing the New Network Set Wizard** page.

7. Click **Apply** to save the changes and update the firewall policy

8. Click **OK** in the **Apply New Configuration** dialog box.

9. The new Network Set appears in the **Network Sets** list.

Computers

You can create Computer Objects to get very fined tuned control over the source and destination hosts that are allowed to communicate with one another. For example, suppose you have a DNS server on the corporate Network that is configured to use a DNS forwarder at your ISP. You don't want to allow users to use an external DNS server, and you don't want the DNS server on the corporate network to perform recursion. You can limit the DNS server to using the DNS protocol only when it communicates with the DNS forwarder at the ISP. The ISA firewall will drop all connections the DNS server on the corporate Network tries to make to other DNS servers.

There are no default Computer Objects. You perform the following steps to create a new computer object.

1. In the **Microsoft Internet Security and Acceleration Server 2004** management console, expand the server name and then click the **Firewall Policy** node.

2. In the Task pane, click the **Toolbox** tab. Click the **Network Objects** link.

3. Click the **New** menu, and click **Computer**.

4. In the **New Computer Rule Element** dialog box, enter the name of the computer. In this example we'll name the computer **DNS Server**. If you know the IP address of the computer, you can enter the address in the **Computer IP Address** text box. If you don't know the address, you can use the **Browse** button and locate the computer and the ISA firewall will attempt

to resolve the name of that machine for you. Enter an optional description for this Computer Object in the **Description (optional)** text box. Click **OK**. These steps for creating a new computer object are shown in Figure 4.38.

Figure 4.38 Creating a New Computer Object

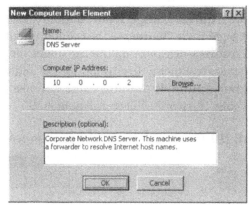

5. The new computer object appears in the list of Computer Objects.

6. Click **Apply** to save the changes and update the firewall policy.

7. Click **OK** in the **Apply New Configuration** dialog box.

Address Ranges

The **Address Ranges** Network Object allows you to create collections of contiguous IP addresses. For example, you might have a group of Web servers on an ISA firewall protected- network services segment, and you want to apply the same Access Rule to all the machines on this segment. Or perhaps you're working in a "network within a Network" environment and you want to control what users on one Network can access on another network. You can create address ranges representing each network within the Network and control access by using the Address Ranges Network Objects representing each network.

NOTE

In the phrase "network within a Network" the lower case "n" refers to a network ID while the upper case "N" refers to a Network defined on the ISA firewall.

There are no default Address Ranges. You can add new address ranges by performing the following steps.

1. In the **Microsoft Internet Security and Acceleration Server 2004** management console, expand the server name, and then click the **Firewall Policy** node.

2. In the Task pane, click the **Toolbox** tab. Click the **Network Objects** link.

3. Click the **New** menu, and click **Address Range**.

4. In the **New Address Range Rule Element** dialog box, enter a name for the Address Range in the **Name** text box. Enter the first address for the range in the **Start Address** text box and the last address in the range in the **End Address** text box. Enter a description for the address range in the **Description (optional)** text box. Click **OK**. See the steps for creating a new Address Range Network Object in Figure 4.39.

Figure 4.39 Creating a New Address Range Network Object

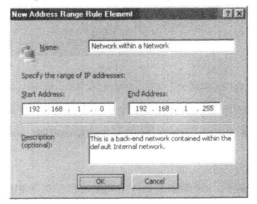

5. The new Address Range appears in the list of **Address Ranges**.

6. Click **Apply** to save the changes and update the firewall policy.

7. Click **OK** in the **Apply New Configuration** dialog box.

Subnets

The **Subnets** Network Object allows you to define groups of hosts located on the same subnet. In the previous example we created an Address Set that included an entire subnet. A better way to do it when an entire subnet is involved is to create a Subnet Network Object. There are no default Subnet Network Objects. You can create a new Subnet Network Object by performing the following steps.

1. In the **Microsoft Internet Security and Acceleration Server 2004** management console, expand the server name, and then click the **Firewall Policy** node.

2. In the Task pane, click the **Toolbox** tab. Click the **Network Objects** link.

3. Click the **New** menu, and click **Subnet**.

4. In the **New Subnet Rule Element** dialog box, enter a name for the subnet in the **Name** text box. Enter the network ID for the subnet in the **Network address** text box, and then enter the number of bits used in the subnet mask in the text box after the forward slash. The **Network mask** will be filled in automatically for you. Enter a description for this subnet in the **Description (optional)** text box. Click **OK**. See Creating a new Subnet Network Object in Figure 4.40.

Figure 4.40 Creating a new Subnet Network Object

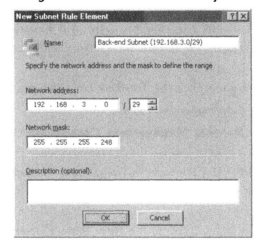

5. The new **Subnet** will appear in the list of subnets.
6. Click **Apply** to save the changes and update the firewall policy.
7. Click **OK** in the **Apply New Configuration** dialog box.

Computer Sets

The Computer Set Network Object is a collection of IP addresses for computers that have a common function or purpose. For example, you might create a computer set for all the servers on your network that never have logged-on users, or you might create a computer set for all non-Windows machines that do not support the Firewall client and you still need some measure of access control.

There are three default Computer Sets:

- Anywhere
- IPSec Remote Gateways
- Remote Management Computers

The **Anywhere Computer Set** includes all addresses in the IPv4 address range. You can use this Computer Set when you need to allow communications for broadcast-based protocols. For example, when you want to make the external interface of the ISA firewall a DHCP client, you can use the Anywhere Computer Set to allow the client to broadcast a DHCP Request message.

The **IPSec Remote Gateways** Computer Set is automatically populated when you create a site-to-site VPN connection using IPSec tunnel mode. You should not need to manually add entries into this Computer Set because the Remote Site VPN Wizards do the work for you.

The **Remote Management Computers** Computer Set is used by the ISA firewall's System Policy to allow connections from machines running the ISA remote MMC console. You can manually add your remote management computers by doing the following:

1. In the **Microsoft Internet Security and Acceleration Server 2004** management console, expand the server name, and then click the **Firewall Policy** node.

2. In the Task pane, click the **Toolbox** tab. Click the **Network Objects** link.

3. Click the **Computer Sets** folder.

4. Click the **Remote Management Computers** icon, and click the **Edit** menu.

5. Click **Add** in the **Remote Management Computers Properties** dialog box. Click the **Computer**, **Address Range** or **Subnet** entry from the fly-out menu.

6. Fill out the information in the **New Rule Element** dialog box, and click **OK**.

7. Click **Apply** to save the changes and update the firewall policy.

8. Click **OK** in the **Apply New Configuration** dialog box.

You can also create your own computer sets. We typically create Computer Sets for servers that do not have logged-on users. For example, your organization is operating a high-security environment and you require authentication for all inbound and outbound access. To meet your high-security requirements, you install the Firewall client on all your client operating systems.

The problem is that some of your servers do not have logged-on users, such as your outbound SMTP relay or Exchange Server. In order for these machines to access the Internet while at the same time exerting some level of access control, you can use a Computer Set and add the machines that do not have logged-on users to the Computer Set.

You can create a new Computer Set by performing the following steps:

1. In the **Microsoft Internet Security and Acceleration Server 2004** management console, expand the server name, and then click the **Firewall Policy** node.

2. In the Task Pane, click the **Toolbox** tab. Click the **Network Objects** link.

3. Click the **Computer Sets** folder.

4. Click the **New Menu**.

5. In the **New Computer Set Rule Element** dialog box, enter a name for the set in the **Name** text box. In this example we'll name it **Mail Relays**.

6. Click **Add**. Select **Computer, Address Range**, or **Subnet**. In this example we'll select **Computer**.

7. In the **New Computer Rule Element** dialog box, enter a name for the Computer Set in the **Name** text box. In this example, we'll name it **BORAX**. In the **Computer IP Address** text box, enter the IP address of a server belonging to this group. You can use the **Browse** button if you don't remember the IP address, but the address must be resolvable via DNS. Enter a description for the Computer in the **Description (optional)** text box. Click **OK**. You can see an example for Creating a New Network Set Network Object in Figure 4.41.

Figure 4.41 Creating a New Network Set Network Object

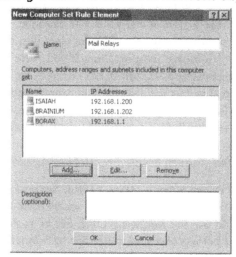

8. Click **Apply** to save the changes and update the firewall policy.

9. Click **OK** in the **Apply New Configuration** dialog box.

URL Sets

A URL Set Network Object is a collection of one or more URLs. You can use URL Sets to get fine-tuned control over what Web sites users can access through the ISA firewall. URL Sets are used only when an HTTP or FTP request is made through the ISA firewall. If you try to use a URL Set in a rule that applies to a non-HTTP or FTP protocol, the URL Set will not be applied, even if you create such a rule.

For example, suppose you create a URL Set containing the URL *mail.isaserverorg.com*. You want to allow users to access their mail by connecting to the mail server using the

SMTP protocol at mail.isaserverorg.com so you create an Access Rule allowing all users access to the URL Set containing the mail.isaserverorg.com domain. When users try to connect, the connection attempt will fail because URL Sets are not applied to non-HTTP/FTP protocols.

There are no default URL sets. However, there are several key facts about URL Sets you should keep in mind when creating Access Rules using a URL Set:

- You can specify both the protocol and port in a URL included in the URL set. However, only the FQDN and the path will be considered – the protocol and port will be ignored. The protocol and port are controlled by other aspects of an Access Rule.

- You can use wildcards when creating an entry in a URL set. For example, http://*.isaserver.org, http://www.isaserver.org/* or even http://*.isaserver.org/*. However, you must put the wildcards at the beginning or the end of the entry. You cannot put them anywhere else. For example, http://*.isaserver.org/*/articles would not be a legal.

- When creating URL Set entries for sites that require SSL, make sure that you do **not** include a path of any kind. For example, when you log on to a Hotmail account through the Web browser you must be able to access the URL https://loginnet.passport.com. If you were to create a URL Set entry for https://loginnet.passport.com/* the connection attempt would be denied. The reason for this is that the ISA firewall cannot perform stateful application-layer inspection for outgoing SSL connections. Because of this, the ISA firewall cannot access any paths once the SSL link is established. Since the ISA firewall has a URL Set entry that includes a path, but it cannot determine the path inside the SSL tunnel, it will drop the connection as a more secure option.

In the following example we'll create a URL Set you can use to allow Outlook Express and Microsoft Outlook 2003 users to access their Hotmail accounts through the ISA firewall. You could use the following URL Set in an Access Rule that applies to all users, or to users that belong to a Computer Set or Subnet or some other Network Object as the source location.

Perform the following steps to create a URL Set:

1. In the **Microsoft Internet Security and Acceleration Server 2004** management console, expand the server name, and then click the **Firewall Policy** node.

2. In the Task pane, click the **Toolbox** tab. Click the **Network Objects** link.

3. Click the **URL Sets** folder.

4. Click the **New Menu**, and then click **URL Set**.

5. In the **New URL Set Rule Element** dialog box, enter a name for the URL Set in the **Name** text box. In this example we'll name it **Hotmail Access**. Click **New**. In the text box above the **New** button, enter the first URL. In this example enter **http://*.passport.com**, and press ENTER. Repeat the

procedure and add the following URLs: **http://*.passport.net**, **http://*.msn.com**, **http://*.hotmail.com**. Click **OK**. Figure 4.42 shows how to create a new URL Set Network Object.

Figure 4.42 Creating a new URL Set Network Object

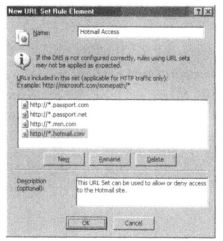

6. Click **Apply** to save the changes and update the firewall policy
7. Click **OK** in the **Apply New Configuration** dialog box

Domain Name Sets

Domain Name Set Network Objects are very similar to URL Sets except that they can be applied to all protocols, and they do not include path statements, only FQDNs. URL Sets support wildcards at the beginning of the FQDN, such as *.isaserver.org. They do not support wildcards at the end of the FQDN because that would include a path in a URL, and only URL Sets support path statements.

There are two default Domain Name Sets:

- **Microsoft Error Reporting Sites**
- **System Policy Allowed Sites**

The **Microsoft Error Reporting Sites** Domain Name Set includes the domains ***.watson.microsoft.com** and **watson.microsoft.com**. This Domain Name Set is used in a System Policy Rule that allows the ISA firewall to send error information to Microsoft for analysis.

The **System Policy Allow Sites** Domain Name Set includes the ***.microsoft.com**, ***.windows.com** and ***.windowsupdate.com** domains. There are System Policy Rules that use this Domain Name Set to allow the ISA firewall to contact Windows Update and obtain other information from Microsoft Web site properties.

Domain Name Sets have a very similar functionality to that provided by the URL Sets, and if you don't need path statements in your Access Rule, then you can use either one if you're controlling HTTP/HTTPS or Web Proxy tunnel FTP access. However, if you want to control any other protocol, then you need to use Domain Name Sets, since URL Sets are used just for HTTP/HTTPS/FTP.

You can create your own Domain Name Sets by performing the following steps:

1. In the **Microsoft Internet Security and Acceleration Server 2004** management console, expand the server name, and then click the **Firewall Policy** node.

2. In the Task pane, click the **Toolbox** tab. Click the **Network Objects** link.

3. Click the **Domain Name Sets** folder.

4. Click the **New Menu**, and then click **Domain Name Set**.

5. In the **New Domain Name Set Policy Element** dialog box, enter a name for the Domain Name Set in the **Name** text box. Click **New**. Enter a domain name or fully-qualified domain name in the text box, and press ENTER. Enter a description of the Domain Name Set in the **Description (optional)** text box. Click **OK**. See Creating a New Domain Name Set Network Object in Figure 4.43 .

Figure 4.43 Creating a New Domain Name Set Network Object

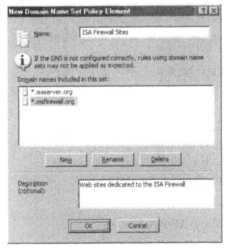

6. The new Domain Name Set appears in the list of **Domain Name Sets** (Figure 4.44).

Figure 4.44 Viewing the New Domain Name Set

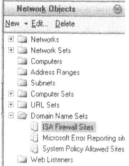

7. Click **Apply** to save the changes and update the firewall policy.

8. Click **OK** in the **Apply New Configuration** dialog box.

TIP

URL Sets and Domain Name Sets are powerful tools for blocking dangerous and offensive Web sites. However, you might find it a bit tedious manually entering 10,000 URLs or domains into a URL Set or Domain Name Set. The solution to this problem is to use a script to import thousands of entries into a Domain Name Set or URL set from a text file. First, visit http://www.mvps.org/win-help2002/hosts.htm to obtain the text file with the offensive URLs or domains. Next, check out my article "Strong Outbound Access Control using the ISA Firewall (2004): Using Scripts to Populate URL Sets and Domain Name Sets" at http://isaserver.org/articles/2004domainseturlset.html. With the HOSTS file and the script in hand, you'll be able to quickly create URL or Domain Name Sets to block thousands of offensive sites.

Web Listeners

Web Listeners represent a significant departure from the rest of the Network Object we've discussed in this section. A Web listener doesn't really fit into a Network location as it can't be used as a source or destination in any Access Rule or Publishing Rule. However, I suppose the ISA firewall development team needed to put them somewhere, and the Network Objects group was a good as any.

A Web Listener is used to accept incoming connections to Web sites, and they are an integral part of Web Publishing Rules. Each Web Publishing Rule requires a Web listener to accept the incoming connection to the Published Web site. Separate Web listeners can be created for HTTP and SSL connections, and you can create Web listeners for IP addresses on each interface on the ISA firewall.

We will discuss Web Listeners in detail in Chapter 8, where we dig deeply into Web Publishing and Web Publishing Rules.

ISA Firewall Network Templates

There are a number of approaches you can take when installing and configuring the ISA firewall. The approach we usually take is to install the ISA firewall software on a hardened version of Windows Server 2003 and then manually configure all the networks connected to the ISA firewall. We create the Networks, set the route relationships between the Networks using Network Rules, and then create the fine-tuned inbound and outbound access policies. Once you understand how the ISA firewall works, you can configure an ISA firewall with 10 network interface cards with a powerful inbound and outbound and intranet access policy in less than an hour. Compare that to a similarly configured PIX and you'll truly appreciate the security and ease of use of an ISA firewall.

If you want to get up and running quickly and you don't want to spend a lot of time learning about how the ISA firewall works, you have the option of using an ISA firewall Network Template. There are Network Templates that configure the ISA firewall in the following roles:

- Edge Firewall
- Front Firewall
- Back Firewall
- Trihomed DMZ Firewall (3-Leg Firewall)
- Unihomed Web Caching-only Firewall (Single NIC template)

In this section we'll go over the details of each Network Template, what they do and how they work.

Edge Firewall Template

The Edge Firewall Template is applied when the ISA firewall is on the Internet edge of the corporate network. The Internet edge is where the ISA firewall has a network interface directly connected to the Internet, and at least one other network interface connected to a network under your administrative control. The Edge Firewall Template assumes that you have at least one External interface and at least one Internal interface.

You will find the following key changes made to the ISA firewall configuration after running the Edge Firewall Template:

- A Network Rule is created that sets the route relationship between the Internal and VPN Clients Networks as Route.
- The default Internal Network remains; the Template does not remove the default Internal Network that you created during installation of the ISA firewall.

The Edge Firewall Template is the one that most closely preserves your default networking settings.

The policies in Table 4.6 are available to you when you run the Edge Firewall Template. Be very sure that you understand each of these policies *before* running the template. Then after running the template, review your firewall policies and make sure that you completely understand what you have done. We highly recommend that you begin with the **Block all** policy. This provides the most secure configuration and insures that you do not inadvertently create a security hole in your firewall. Later, you can create Access Rules and Publishing Rules on the ISA firewall to control outbound and inbound access. Table 4.6 describes the Firewall Policies Available with the Edge Firewall Template.

Table 4.6 Firewall Policies available with the Edge Firewall Template

Policy name	Description	Rules created
Block all	This policy blocks all network access through ISA Server. This option does not create any access rules other than the default rule which blocks all access. Use this option when you want to define firewall policy on your own.	None.
Block Internet access, allow access to ISP network services	This policy blocks all network access through ISA Server, except for access to External network services, such as DNS. This option is useful when services are provided by your ISP. Use this option when you want to define firewall policy on your own.	Allow DNS from Internal network and VPN Clients network to External network (Internet).
Allow limited Web access	This policy allows limited Web access using HTTP, HTTPS, and FTP only. All other network access is blocked.	Allow HTTP, HTTPS, and FTP from Internal network to External network. Allow all protocols from VPN Clients network to Internal network.
Allow limited Web access, allow access to ISP network services	This policy allows limited Web access using HTTP, HTTPS, and FTP, and allows access to ISP network services. All other network access is blocked.	Allow HTTP, HTTPS, and FTP from Internal network and VPN Clients network to External network (Internet). Allow DNS from Internal Network and VPN Clients Network to External Network (Internet).

Continued

Table 4.6 Firewall Policies available with the Edge Firewall Template

Policy name	Description	Rules created
		Allow all protocols from VPN Clients Network to Internal Network.
Allow access for all protocols	This policy allows unrestricted access to the Internet through ISA Server. ISA Server will prevent access from the Internet to protected networks.	Allow all protocols from Internal network and VPN Clients network to External network (Internet). Allow VPN Clients network to Internal network.

Perform the following steps to apply the Edge Firewall Template:

1. In the **Microsoft Internet Security and Acceleration Server 2004** management console, expand the server name and then expand the **Configuration** node. Click on the **Networks** node.

2. In the **Networks** node, click the **Templates** tab in the Task pane. The top-listed Network Template is the **Edge Firewall Template**. Click the **Edge Firewall Template**.

3. Click **Next** on the **Welcome to the Network Template Wizard** page.

4. On the **Export the ISA Server Configuration** page you have the option of backing up your current ISA firewall's configuration. This is a valuable feature because the Network Template will overwrite the current Network configuration and Firewall Policy. If you back up the current configuration, you can restore it very easily in the event that you don't like what the Network Template Wizard does to your firewall. Click **Export**.

5. In the **Export Configuration** dialog box, enter a name for the current ISA firewall configuration in the **File name** text box. In this example, we'll name the configuration file **Pre-Edge Firewall Template**. Notice that the configuration is saved in .xml format. You do not need to **Export user permission settings** or **Export confidential information (encryption will be used)** because you are not chaining user permissions with this template, and you are probably not going to use this backup file to move this ISA firewall's configuration to another machine. You just want to back up the current Network and firewall policy. Click **Export**.

6. The **Exporting** dialog box appears. Click **OK** when the wizard informs you that it **Successfully exported the configuration**.

7. Click **Next** on the **Export the ISA Server Configuration** page.

8. On the **Internal Network IP Addresses** page, set the addresses that represent the Internal Network. The Network Template Wizard will pull the same addresses you used for your Internal Network when you installed the ISA firewall. You do have the option to add more addresses to the default Internal Network by using the **Add**, **Add Adapter**, and **Add Private** buttons. The **Add** button allows you to manually enter a range or ranges of addresses. The **Add Adapter** button allows you to leverage the Windows routing table to automatically add addresses to the Internal Network, and the **Add Private** button automatically adds entire network IDs to the addresses included in the default Internal Network. In this example, and in most situations, you will not change the addresses on this page. Click **Next**. See the Internal Network IP Addresses page in Figure 4.45.

Figure 4.45 Defining the IP addresses

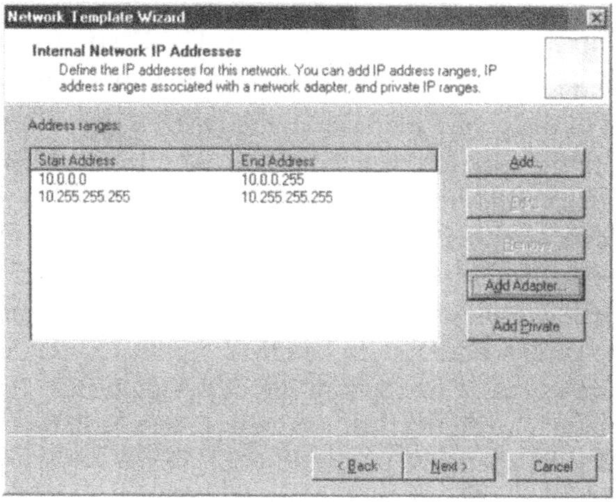

9. On the **Select a Firewall Policy** page, select the appropriate firewall policy for your organization. Refer to Table X above for details on each Firewall Policy. We highly recommend that you select the **Block All** firewall policy, and then later manually configure firewall policy after you understand how the ISA firewall's policies work. This will minimize the chance of you creating a configuration that is not as secure as you want. In this example, we'll select the **Block all** Firewall Policy, and click **Next.**

10. Click **Finish** on the **Completing the Network Template Wizard** page.

11. Click **Apply** to save the changes and update the firewall policy.

12. Click **OK** in the **Apply New Configuration** dialog box.

At this point, no traffic is allowed inbound or outbound through the ISA firewall because we selected the most secure firewall policy in the Network Template. You can now customize the ISA firewall's Firewall Policies to meet your organization's needs.

Trihomed (3-Leg) or DMZ Template

The trihomed DMZ Template allows you to configure the ISA firewall with three or more network adapters to use the additional network adapters are Perimeter network or DMZ segments. The trihomed DMZ Network Template is interesting because it sets some interesting Network Rules, which might be counterintuitive to the majority of ISA firewall administrators.

After running the trihomed DMZ Network Template, you'll find that:

- A new Network Object, the **Perimeter** Network Object, is created.

- A Network Rule named **Perimeter Access** sets a Route relationship from the Perimeter Network to the Internet

- A Network Rule name **Perimeter Configuration** sets a NAT relationship between the **Internal and VPN Clients** network and the **Perimeter** Network.

The Network Rules are a bit problematic. The **Perimeter Access** Network Rule sets a route relationship between the Perimeter Network and the Internet. This means that you'll need to use public addresses in the DMZ segment. You're going to find that things don't work the way you planned if you use private addresses in the DMZ segment. If you use this trihomed DMZ Network Template you'll need to change the **Perimeter Access** Network Rule to NAT if you use private addresses in the DMZ segment. Even more problematic is that the Template sets the route relationship between the DMZ segment and the Internal network to NAT. While this is a reasonable configuration if you use public addresses on the DMZ segment, it isn't our preferred configuration when private addresses are used on the DMZ segment.

The **Perimeter Configuration** Network Rule sets the route relationship between the Internal and VPN clients Networks to NAT. While NAT will work, it doesn't work with all protocols, and you can run into issues that you wouldn't have problems with if you chose a Route relationship between the Internal and VPN Clients Networks and the DMZ segment. If you use public addresses on the DMZ segment, then you need to leave the route relationship as NAT. But if you are using private addresses on the trihomed DMZ segment, then change the route relationship to Route.

You can choose from one of the policies listed in Table 4.7 when running the trihomed DMZ Network Template. Again, we highly recommend that you select the **Block all** firewall policy, and then configure the ISA firewall with the specific Access Rules and Publishing Rules required for your organization. Firewall policies are shown in Table 4.7 .

Table 4.7 Firewall Policies Available for the Trihomed (3-Leg) Network Template

Policy name	Description	Rules created
Block all	This policy blocks all network access through ISA Server. This option does not create any access rules other than the default rule which blocks all access. Use this option when you want to define firewall policy on your own.	None.
Block Internet access, allow access to network services on the perimeter network	This policy blocks all network access through ISA Server, except for access to network services (DNS) on the perimeter network. Use this option when you want to define the firewall policy on your own.	Allow DNS traffic from Internal network and VPN Clients network to perimeter network.
Block Internet access, allow access to ISP network services	This policy blocks all network access through ISA Server, except for access to external network services, such as DNS. This option is useful when network services are provided by your ISP. Use this option when you want to define firewall policy on your own.	Allow DNS traffic from Internal network, VPN Clients network, and perimeter network to External network (Internet).
Allow limited Web access	This policy allows limited Web access using only HTTP, HTTPS, and FTP and blocks all other network access.	Allow HTTP, HTTPS, and FTP from Internal network and VPN Clients network to perimeter network and External network (Internet). Allow all protocols from VPN Clients network to Internal network.
Allow limited Web access, allow access to network services on perimeter network	This policy allows limited Web access using only HTTP, HTTPS, and FTP, and allows access to network services on the perimeter network. All other network access is blocked. This option is useful when network infrastructure services are available in the perimeter network.	Allow HTTP, HTTPS, and FTP from Internal network and VPN Clients network to perimeter network and External network (Internet). Allow DNS traffic from Internal network and VPN Clients network to perimeter network.

Continued

Table 4.7 Firewall Policies Available for the Trihomed (3-Leg) Network Template

Policy name	Description	Rules created
		Allow all protocols from VPN Clients network to Internal network.
Allow limited Web access, allow ISP network services	This policy allows limited Internet access and allows access to network services, such as DNS, provided by your ISP. All other network access is blocked.	Allow HTTP, HTTPS, FTP from Internal network and VPN Clients network to the External network (Internet). Allow DNS from Internal network, VPN Clients network, and perimeter network to External network (Internet). Allow all protocols from VPN Clients network to Internal network.
Allow all protocols	This policy allows unrestricted access to the Internet through ISA Server. ISA Server will prevent access from the Internet to protected networks. You can modify the access rules later to block specific types of network access.	Allow all protocols from Internal network and VPN Clients network to perimeter network and External network (Internet). Allow all protocols from VPN Clients network to Internal network.

Perform the following steps to apply the Edge Firewall Template:

1. In the **Microsoft Internet Security and Acceleration Server 2004** management console, expand the server name, and then expand the **Configuration** node. Click on the **Networks** node.

2. In the **Networks** node, click the **Templates** tab in the Task Pane. Select the **3-Leg Perimeter** Network Template by double-clicking it..

3. Click **Next** on the **Welcome to the Network Template Wizard** page.

4. On the **Export the ISA Server Configuration** page, you have the option of backing up your current ISA firewall's configuration. This is a valuable feature because the Network Template will overwrite the current Network configuration and Firewall Policy. If you back up the current configuration, you can

restore it very easily in the event that you don't like what the Network Template Wizard does to your firewall. Click **Export**.

5. In the **Export Configuration** dialog box, enter a name for the current ISA firewall configuration in the **File name** text box. In this example, we'll name the configuration file **Pre-3-Leg Perimeter Template**. Notice that the configuration is saved in .xml format. You do not need to **Export user permission settings** or **Export confidential information (encryption will be used)** because you are not chaining user permissions with this template, and you are probably not going to use this backup file to move this ISA firewall's configuration to another machine. You just want to back up the current Network and firewall policy. Click **Export**.

6. The **Exporting** dialog box appears. Click **OK** when the wizard informs you that it **Successfully exported the configuration**.

7. Click **Next** on the **Export the ISA Server Configuration** page.

8. On the **Internal Network IP Addresses** page, configure a list of addresses that define the Internal Network. The addresses that appear by default are those addresses that you already defined as part of the Internal Network during the installation of the ISA firewall software. You have the option to add more addresses by clicking the **Add**, **Add Adapter** or **Add Private** button. We recommend that you use the **Add Adapter** button and avoid the use of the **Add Private** button. Click **Next**.

9. Configure the addresses that are part of the new DMZ segment on the **Perimeter Network IP Addresses** page. Again, you have the option of using the **Add**, **Add Adapter** or the **Add Private** buttons. In this example, we'll use the **Add Adapter** button. Click **Add Adapter**.

10. Select the Adapter representing the DMZ interface, and the put a checkmark in the checkbox network to that adapter. It's important that you select the adapter first. If you don't, you will not see the correct information in the **Network Interfaces Information** box (Figure 4.46). This box shows the list of addresses that will be used to define the DMZ Network. Click **OK**.

Figure 4.46 Selecting the Network Adapter

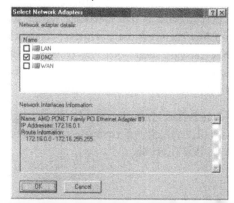

11. Click **Next** on the **Perimeter Network IP Addresses** page.

12. On the **Select a Firewall Policy** page, select the firewall policy that applies to your organization's requirements. We highly recommend that you select the **Block all** policy, and configure a policy based on your requirements later. Select the **Block all** policy, and click **Next**.

13. Click **Finish** on the **Completing the Network Template Wizard** page.

14. Click **Apply** to save the changes and update the firewall policy.

15. Click **OK** in the **Apply New Configuration** dialog box.

Front Firewall Template

The Front Firewall Network Template is used when the ISA firewall is in front of another firewall. This makes the ISA firewall a front-end firewall and the firewall located behind the front-end ISA firewall is the back-end firewall. The back-end firewall can be an ISA firewall, or a third-party firewall; it will make no different to the front-end ISA firewall.

The Front Firewall Template makes some interesting assumptions about your network infrastructure and the characteristics of the network located behind the front-end ISA firewall. These include:

- The Front Firewall Template assumes that the network behind the ISA firewall is a perimeter network. After running the Front Firewall Template, the front-end ISA firewall will not have an "Internal" network defined. The new Perimeter Network defined by the Template will replace the role of the former default Internal Network.

- A new Network Rule named **Perimeter Access** is created. This Network Rule sets a route relationship between the **Perimeter** and **VPN Clients Network** and the **External** network. The assumption is that you'll be using public addresses on the network behind the front-end ISA firewall. If you're not using public addresses on the network behind the front-end ISA firewall, this default Network Rule is going to cause problems. If you're using private addresses on the network behind the front-end ISA firewall, change the route relationship in the **Perimeter Access** Network Rule to NAT.

- An issue that you'll have to deal with in certain circumstances when you have a front-end ISA firewall is the "network within a Network" issue. If you have a route relationship between the perimeter network and the network behind the back-end ISA firewall, then you'll need to include all the addresses in the network behind the back-end ISA firewall in the definition of the **Perimeter** Network on the front-end ISA firewall.

The last issue deserves more attention, as the issue might not be immediately evident. Figure 4.47 shows an example of a front-end/back-end ISA firewall configuration where both firewalls are ISA firewalls.

Figure 4.47 Route Relationships in a Network behind a Network

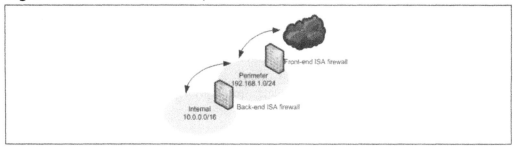

In this example the back-end ISA firewall defines its Internal Network as 10.0.0.0/24, and the perimeter network is part of its default External network. Note that you don't have to define the perimeter network as part of the default External network on the back-end ISA firewall. You could actually create a new Network Object called Perimeter Network and assign the network ID of the perimeter network to that Network Object. However, in this example, we'll just assume that the perimeter network is part of the back-end ISA firewall's default external network. There is also a Network Rule on the back-end ISA firewall that sets a Route relationship between the back-end ISA firewall's Internal Network and its External Network.

The front-end ISA firewall has had the Front Firewall Template applied to it, so it doesn't have an Internal network. Instead, the Internal Network has been replaced by the Perimeter Network, as we discussed earlier. The addresses included in the front-end ISA firewall's Perimeter Network include all those in the Network ID of the perimeter network, which in this case is 192.168.1.0/24. On the front-end ISA firewall there is a NAT relationship between the perimeter network and the Internet.

Now imagine that a host on the Internal network behind the back-end ISA firewall tries to connect to resources on the Internet. What will happen? Since there is a Route relationship between the back-end ISA firewall's Internal Network and the perimeter network, the source IP address of the host on the Internal network will be retained. When the front-end ISA firewall receives the connection request, it will see the Internal Network host's original IP address and assume that the connection is using a spoofed address and deny the connection attempt.

Why? Because ISA firewalls always detect a spoof when it receives a packet on an interface from an IP address that is not reachable from that interface. Since the front-end ISA firewall does not have a definition for network ID 10.0.0.0/16, it makes it part of its default External Network. Since External Network hosts cannot connect directly with the Internal interface of the ISA firewall, the front-end ISA firewall drops the connection because it thinks it's a spoof. This is a good thing, as the ISA firewall's spoof detection is a key component of its IDS/IPS system.

You can correct this problem by adding the back-end ISA firewall's Internal Network addresses to the front-end ISA firewall's list of addresses for the perimeter Network and add a route for the back-end ISA firewall's internal network into the front-end ISA firewall's routing table. Now the front-end ISA firewall knows that the back-end ISA firewall's Internal Network is reachable from the front-end ISA firewall's Perimeter Network interface, and it will not drop the connection as a spoofed packet.

It's important to note that this is still a secure configuration. The ISA firewall is still able to detect truly spoofed packets on all interfaces, including the External interface.

Table 4.8 shows the Firewall Policy options you have with the Front Firewall Network Template. Again, we strongly encourage you to use the **Block all** template, and then create your own custom firewall policies so that they precisely match your organization's requirements.

Table 4.8 Firewall Policies Available for the Trihomed (3-Leg) Network Template

Policy name	Description	Rules created
Block all	This policy blocks all network access through ISA Server. This option does not create any access rules other than the default rule which blocks all access. Use this option when you want to define firewall policy on your own.	None.
Block Internet access, allow access to ISP network services	This policy blocks all network access through ISA Server, except for access to External network services, such as DNS. This option is useful when network services are provided by your ISP. Use this option when you want to define firewall policy on your own.	Allow DNS from VPN Clients network and perimeter network to External network (Internet).
Block Internet access (network services are on the perimeter network)	This policy blocks all network access through ISA Server, except for access to network services, such as DNS, on the perimeter network. Use this option when you want to to define the firewall policy on your own.	Allow DNS from Internal network and VPN Clients network to perimeter network.
Allow limited Web access (network services are on the perimeter network)	This policy allows limited Web access. All other network access is blocked.	Allow HTTP, HTTPS, and FTP from VPN Clients network and perimeter network to External network (Internet). Allow all protocols from VPN Clients network to perimeter network.

Continued

Table 4.8 Firewall Policies Available for the Trihomed (3-Leg) Network Template

Policy name	Description	Rules created
Allow limited Web access, allow ISP network services	This policy allows limited Web access, and allows access to network services, such as DNS, provided by your ISP. All other network access is blocked.	Allow HTTP, HTTPS, and FTP from perimeter network and VPN Clients network to the External network (Internet). Allow DNS from Internal network, VPN Clients network, and perimeter network to External network (Internet). Allow all protocols from VPN Clients network to perimeter network.
Allow unrestricted access	This policy allows unrestricted access to the Internet through ISA Server. ISA Server will prevent access from the Internet to protected networks. You can modify the access rules later to block specific types of network access.	Allow all protocols from perimeter network and VPN Clients network to External network (Internet). Allow all protocols from VPN Clients network to perimeter network

Perform the following steps to apply the Edge Firewall Template:

1. In the **Microsoft Internet Security and Acceleration Server 2004** management console, expand the server name and then expand the **Configuration** node. Click on the **Networks** node.

2. In the **Networks** node, click the **Templates** tab in the Task pane. Select the **Front Firewall** Network Template by double-clicking it.

3. Click **Next** on the **Welcome to the Network Template Wizard** page.

4. On the **Export the ISA Server Configuration** page, you have the option of backing up your current ISA firewall's configuration. This is a valuable feature because the Network Template will overwrite the current Network configuration and Firewall Policy. If you back up the current configuration, you can restore it very easily in the event that you don't like what the Network Template Wizard does to your firewall. Click **Export**.

5. In the **Export Configuration** dialog box, enter a name for the current ISA firewall configuration in the **File name** text box. In this example we'll name

the configuration file **Pre-Front Firewall Template**. Notice that the config-uration is saved in .xml format. You do not need to **Export user permission settings** or **Export confidential information (encryption will be used)** because you are not chaining user permissions with this template, and you are probably not going to use this backup file to move this ISA firewall's configu-ration to another machine. You just want to back up the current Network and firewall policy. Click **Export**.

6.   The **Exporting** dialog box appears. Click **OK** when the wizard informs you that it **Successfully exported the configuration**.

7.   Click **Next** on the **Export the ISA Server Configuration** page.

8.   On the **Perimeter Network IP Addresses** page, configure a list of addresses that define the Internal Network. The addresses that appear by default are those addresses that you defined as part of the Internal Network during the installation of the ISA firewall software. You have the option to add more addresses by clicking **Add, Add Adapter** or **Add Private**. We recommend that you use the **Add Adapter** button, and avoid the use of the **Add Private** button. Click **Next**.

9.   On the **Select a Firewall Policy** page, select the firewall policy that applies to your organization's requirements. We highly recommend that you select the **Block all** policy, and configure a policy based on your requirements later. Select the **Block all** policy, and click **Next**.

10.   Click **Finish** on the **Completing the Network Template Wizard** page.

11.   Click **Apply** to save the changes and update the firewall policy.

12.   Click **OK** in the **Apply New Configuration** dialog box.

Back Firewall Template

The Back Firewall Template is very similar to the Edge Firewall Template. The main dif-ference between the Edge Firewall Template and the Back Firewall Template is that the network diagram in the **Microsoft Internet Security and Acceleration Server 2004** management console is different, depending on which template you select. Figure 4.48 shows the network diagram for the Back Firewall Template and the Figure 4.49 shows the network diagram for the Edge Firewall Template.

Figure 4.48 Network Diagram for Back Firewall Template

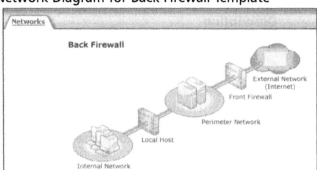

Figure 4.49 Network Diagram for Edge Firewall Template

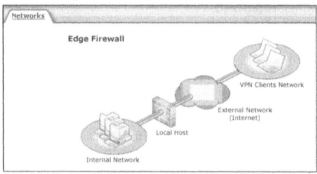

Firewall Polices you can choose from when using the Back Firewall Template are listed in Table 4.9. We recommend that you choose the **Block all** template, and then create custom policies based on your organization's security requirements.

Table 4.9 Firewall Policies Available for the Back Firewall Template

Policy name	Description	Rules created
No access: Block all	This policy blocks all network access through ISA Server. This option does not create any access rules other than the default rule that blocks all access. Use this option when you want to define firewall policy on your own.	None.
No access: Block Internet access (network services are in the perimeter network)	This policy blocks all network access through ISA Server, except for access to network services (DNS) on the perimeter network.	Use this option when you want to define firewall policy on your own. Allow DNS from Internal network and VPN Clients network to perimeter network.

Continued

Table 4.9 Firewall Policies Available for the Back Firewall Template

Policy name	Description	Rules created
No access: Block Internet access, allow access to ISP network services	This policy blocks all network access through ISA Server, except for access to External network services, such as DNS. This option is useful when network services are provided by your ISP. Use this option when you want to define the firewall policy access rules on your own.	Allow DNS from Internal network and VPN Clients network to External network (Internet), excluding perimeter address ranges.
Restricted access: Allow limited Web access	This policy allows limited Web access. All other network access is blocked.	Allow HTTP, HTTPS, and FTP from Internal network and VPN Clients network to External network (Internet). Allow all protocols from VPN Clients network to Internal network.
Restricted access: Allow limited Web access (network services are on perimeter network)	This policy allows limited Web access, and allows access to network services on the perimeter network. All other network access is blocked.	Allow HTTP, HTTPS, and FTP from Internal network and VPN Clients network to perimeter network and External network (Internet). Allow DNS from Internal network and VPN Clients network to perimeter network. Allow all protocols from VPN Clients network to Internal network.
Restricted access: Allow limited Web access, allow ISP network services	This policy allows limited Web access, and allows access to network services, such as DNS, provided by your ISP. All other network access is blocked.	Allow HTTP, HTTPS, and FTP from Internal network and VPN Clients network to External network (Internet).

Continued

Table 4.9 Firewall Policies Available for the Back Firewall Template

Policy name	Description	Rules created
		Allow DNS from Internal network and VPN Clients network to External network (Internet), except for perimeter address range. Allow all protocols from VPN Clients network to Internal network.
Unrestricted Internet access: Allow all protocols	This policy allows unrestricted access to the Internet through ISA Server. ISA Server will prevent access from the Internet to protected networks. You can modify the access rules later to block specific types of network access.	Allow all protocols from Internal network and VPN Clients network to External network (Internet) and perimeter address range. Allow all protocols from VPN Clients network to Internal network.

Perform the following steps to apply the Back Firewall Template:

1. In the **Microsoft Internet Security and Acceleration Server 2004** management console, expand the server name, and then expand the **Configuration** node. Click on the **Networks** node.

2. In the **Networks** node, click the **Templates** tab in the Task pane. Double-click the **Back Firewall Template**.

3. Click **Next** on the **Welcome to the Network Template Wizard** page.

4. On the **Export the ISA Server Configuration** page, you have the option of backing up your current ISA firewall's configuration. This is a valuable feature because the Network Template will overwrite the current Network configuration and Firewall Policy. If you back up the current configuration, you can restore it very easily in the event that you don't like what the Network Template Wizard does to your firewall. Click **Export**.

5. In the **Export Configuration** dialog box, enter a name for the current ISA firewall configuration in the **File name** text box. In this example we'll name the configuration file **Pre-Edge Firewall Template**. Notice that the configuration is saved in .xml format. You do not need to **Export user permission settings** or **Export confidential information (encryption will be used)**

because you are not chaining user permissions with this template, and you are probably not going to use this backup file to move this ISA firewall's configuration to another machine. You just want to back up the current Network and firewall policy. Click **Export**.

6. The **Exporting** dialog box appears. Click **OK** when the wizard informs you that it **Successfully exported the configuration**.

7. Click **Next** on the **Export the ISA Server Configuration** page.

8. On the **Internal Network IP Addresses** page, set the addresses that represent the Internal Network. The Network Template Wizard will pull the same addresses you used for your Internal Network when you installed the ISA firewall. You have the option to add more addresses to the default Internal Network by using **Add**, **Add Adapter** and **Add Private**. The **Add** button allows you to manually enter a range or ranges of addresses. The **Add Adapter** button allows you to leverage the Windows routing table to automatically add addresses to the Internal Network, and the **Add Private** button automatically adds entire network IDs to the addresses included in the default Internal Network. In this example, and in most situations, you will not change the addresses on this page. Click **Next**.

9. On the **Select a Firewall Policy** page, select the appropriate firewall policy for your organization. Refer to Table 4.9 for details on each Firewall Policy. We highly recommend that you select the **Block All** firewall policy, and then later manually configure a firewall policy after you understand how the ISA firewall's policies work. This will minimize the chance of creating a configuration that is not as secure as you want. In this example, we'll select the **Block all** Firewall Policy, and click **Next**. Figure 4.50 depicts Selecting a Firewall Policy.

Figure 4.50 Selecting a Firewall Policy

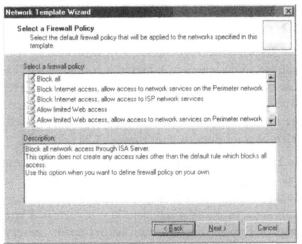

10. Click **Finish** on the **Completing the Network Template Wizard** page.

11. Click **Apply** to save the changes and update the firewall policy.

12. Click **OK** in the **Apply New Configuration** dialog box.

Single Network Adapter or Unihomed Network Template

The Single Network Adapter Network Template is used when you want to run the ISA firewall with a single NIC. You do not need to run the Single Network Adapter Template if you installed the ISA firewall on a single NIC machine. You will need to create your on Access Policy, which is our preferred method of configuring the ISA firewall. The Single Adapter Network Template does not create an Access Policy.

TIP

If you do use the single NIC configuration on a multiple NIC machine, you can connect multiple network segments to the ISA firewall machine. However, the ISA firewall will only be able to forward connections using HTTP, HTTPS, and Web Proxy tunneled FTP.

The Single Network Adapter Template can be run on machines that have multiple Network Interface cards. If the machine has multiple NICs, you will need to disable all NICs except for one. However, if you use multiple network interfaces, keep in mind that all interfaces are considered Internal and that there are no addresses that are considered external to the machine with a single NIC template applied to it.

Some important considerations regarding the Single Network Adapter Template are:

- After the Template is applied to the ISA firewall, all addresses will be considered Internal. The Single NIC ISA firewall has no conception of Internal or External, since there is only a single interface. All Access Rules will have the source and destination networks as Internal.

- Only the HTTP, HTTPS, and Web Proxy tunneled FTP protocols are supported on a single NIC ISA firewall.

- You cannot use the Firewall client when the ISA firewall has a single NIC. This means you lose the significant protection, access control, and enhanced logging capabilities provided when the Firewall client is installed on client workstations.

- The machine is used only for forward and reverse Web Proxy and caching. You cannot create additional protocols and you cannot create Access Rules supporting non-"Web" protocols.

- The ISA firewall's strong firewall capabilities are retained to the extent that the firewall is able to protect itself. No connections can be made to the ISA firewall until you create Access Rules that compromise the security of the ISA firewall itself.

■ You cannot make the ISA firewall a VPN server.

■ You cannot create Server Publishing Rules, only Web Publishing Rules.

We recommend that you use the unihomed (single NIC) ISA firewall configuration only when you have another ISA firewall in production on the network. The other ISA firewall provides the strong stateful filtering and strong stateful application-layer inspection, and the single NIC ISA firewall takes over the processing overhead for SSL-to-SSL bridging (we'll discuss this in more detail in Chapter 8 on Publishing Servers to the Internet).

Perform the following steps to apply the Single Network Adapter Template:

1. In the **Microsoft Internet Security and Acceleration Server 2004** management console, expand the server name, and then expand the **Configuration** node. Click on the **Networks** node.

2. In the **Networks** node, click the **Templates** tab in the Task pane. Double-click the **Single Network Adapter** Template.

3. Click **Next** on the **Welcome to the Network Template Wizard** page.

4. On the **Export the ISA Server Configuration** page, you have the option of backing up your current ISA firewall's configuration. This is a valuable feature because the Network Template will overwrite the current Network configuration and Firewall Policy. If you back up the current configuration, you can restore it very easily in the event that you don't like what the Network Template Wizard does to your firewall. Click **Export**.

5. In the **Export Configuration** dialog box, enter a name for the current ISA firewall configuration in the **File name** text box. In this example, we'll name the configuration file **Pre-Single NIC Template**. Notice that the configuration is saved in .xml format. You do not need to **Export user permission settings** or **Export confidential information (encryption will be used)** because you are not chaining user permissions with this template, and you are probably not going to use this backup file to move this ISA firewall's configuration to another machine. You just want to back up the current Network and firewall policy. Click **Export**.

6. The **Exporting** dialog box appears. Click **OK** when the wizard informs you that it **Successfully exported the configuration**.

7. Click **Next** on the **Export the ISA Server Configuration** page.

8. On the **Internal Network IP Addresses** page (Figure 4.51), you see a list of all addresses in the IPv4 range with the exception of the addresses in the loopback network. Click **Next**.

Figure 4.51 Defining the IP addresses

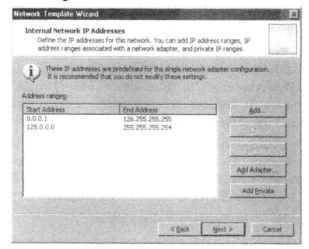

9. On the **Select a Firewall Policy** page, you have the choice of a single Default NIC policy. Select that policy and click **Next**.

10. Click **Finish** on the **Completing the Network Template Wizard** page.

Dynamic Address Assignment on the ISA Firewall's External Interface

Many smaller organizations do not have static IP addresses that they can assign to the external interface of the ISA firewall. The ISA firewall does support dynamic address assignment on any of its interfaces. We strongly recommend that you never use dynamic address assignment on any interface except the external interface of the ISA firewall.

You will need to change the System Policy on the ISA firewall in order to obtain a dynamic address on the external interface. Perform the following steps to make the required changes to System Policy:

1. Open the **Microsoft Internet Security and Acceleration Server 2004** management console, expand the server name, and click the **Firewall Policy** node.

2. On the **Firewall Policy Node**, click the **Tasks** tab in the Task pane. In the **System Policy Tasks** group, click the **Show System Policy Rules** link.

3. The **System Policy Rules** appear before the **Firewall Policy** rules that you create. Right-click Policy Rule #8 **Allow DHCP replies from DHCP server to ISA Server** and click **Edit System Policy**.

4. The System Policy Editor opens and the focus is on the **DHCP** entry in the **Network Services** group in the **Configuration Groups** section. Click the **From** tab.

5. On the **From** tab, click **Add**.

6. In the **Add Network Entities** dialog box, click the **New** menu. Click **Computer**.

7. In the **New Computer Rule Element** dialog box, enter a name for your public DHCP server in the **Name** text box. In this example we'll name it **ISP DHCP Server**. Enter the IP address of your ISP's DHCP server in the **Computer IP Address** text box. Enter a description for this Computer Object in the **Description (optional)** text box. Click **OK**.

8. In the **Add Network Entities** dialog box, click the **Computers** folder, and then double-click your **ISP DHCP server** entry. If you don't yet know the IP address of your ISP's DHCP server, you can click the **Networks** folder and double-click the **External** network. Click **Close**.

9. Click **OK** in the **System Policy Editor**.

10. Click **Apply** to save the changes and update the firewall policy.

11. Click **OK** in the **Apply New Configuration** dialog box.

12. Now set your external interface to use dynamic address assignment. If you run Network Monitor on the external interface of the ISA firewall, you'll see something like the following (Figure 4.52):

Figure 4.52 Network Monitor Trace of DHCP Conversation

```
DHCP    Discover    (xid=114D6560)    0.0.0.0          255.255.255.255
DHCP    Offer       (xid=114D6560)    192.168.1.185    255.255.255.255
DHCP    Request     (xid=114D6560)    0.0.0.0          255.255.255.255
DHCP    ACK         (xid=114D6560)    192.168.1.185    255.255.255.255
```

If you do not know the IP address of your DHCP server, you can find that out by using the **ipconfig /all** command. The resulting printout will display the IP address of your ISP's DHCP server.

Dial-up Connection Support for ISA firewalls, Including VPN Connections to the ISP

Some organizations are in locations where ISP support is very limited. These companies must use a dial-up modem connection or a VPN connection in order to connect to their local ISP. The ISA firewall supports dial-up connections to the Internet. The dial-up connection can be an analog modem connection or a VPN connection. Both type of connections are configured in the ISA firewall's **Network Connections** window. The connection you create is known as a *connectoid*, and the connectoid appears in the **Network Connections** window as an icon.

You then configure the ISA firewall to use the connectoid. One of the most common issues we see with new ISA firewall administrators is that they only create the connectoid and expect the ISA firewall to use it, or they configure the dial-up connection in the **Microsoft Internet Security and Acceleration Server 2004** management console but do not set it up in the **Network Connections** window.

There are two steps you need to perform to use a dial-up connection with the ISA firewall:

- Create a dial-up connectoid
- Configure the ISA firewall to use the connectoid
- Create an Access Rule allowing the ISA firewall to use the VPN protocol (this is only required if you are using a VPN connection for the dial-up link)

We'll go through an example of how to create a VPN connectoid and use that VPN connectoid in the ISA firewall's dial-up configuration. This is a common scenario for DSL users in Europe. We'll also discuss all the options available, so that dial-up modem users can also benefit from these instructions.

WARNING

We have identified issues with the ISA firewall and automatic dialing when using VPN dial-up connections. In a number of installations we find that the dial-up connection will not automatically dial. In this circumstance, you will need to enable the VPN connection manually and configure it so that it automatically redials when the connection is dropped. Analog modem connections do not seem to have this problem.

The first step is to create the VPN connectoid. Perform the following steps to create the VPN connectoid on a Windows Server 2003 machine. The procedures are very similar on Windows 2000 as well.

1. Right-click **My Network Places** on the desktop, and click **Properties**.

2. In the **Network Connections** window, click the **New Connection Wizard** link.

3. Click **Next** on the **Welcome to the New Connection Wizard** page.

4. On the **Network Connection Type** page, select the **Connection to the network at my workplace**, and click **Next**.

5. On the **Network Connection** page, select the **Virtual Private Network connection** option, and click **Next**.

6. On the **Connection Name** page, enter a name for the VPN connectoid in the **Company Name** text box. In this example, we'll name the connectoid **VPN to ISP**, and click **Next**.

7. On the **VPN Server Selection** page, enter the IP address of your ISP's VPN server in the **Host name or IP address** text box. Click **Next**.

8. On the **Connection Availability** page, select the **Anyone's use** option, and click **Next**.

9. On the **Completing the New Connection Wizard** page, click **Finish**.

10. In the **Connect VPN to ISP dialog** box, click **Properties**.

11. In the **Connect VPN to ISP** dialog box, click the **Options** tab. In the **Redialing** options frame, put a checkmark in the **Redial if line is dropped** option. In the **Redial attempts** text box, enter **99**. In the **Time between redial attempts** drop-down list, select **5 seconds**. In the **Idle time before hanging up** drop-down list, select **Never**.

12. In the **Connect VPN to ISP** dialog box, enter the user name and password your ISP assigned to you when you purchased your account. Put a checkmark in the **Save this user name and password for the following users** checkbox. Select the **Anyone who uses this computer** option.

13. Click **Connect** to test the connectoid to confirm that you can connect to your ISP using this connectoid.

The next step is to configure the ISA firewall to use this connectoid:

1. In the **Microsoft Internet Security and Acceleration Server 2004** management console, expand the server name, and then expand the **Configuration** node. Click the **General** node.

2. On the **General** node, click the **Specify Dial-Up Preferences** link.

3. In the **Dialing Configuration** dialog box, you have the following options:

■ **I will dial the connection myself** Use this option when you want to dial the dial-up connection first *before* users on protected Networks can access the Internet through the connection. This requires operator intervention to initiate the connection, but after the connection is established, the connection can be configured to automatically redial if it is dropped. Use this option for VPN connections and for any connection where the automatic dialing doesn't work for you properly.

■ **Allow automatic dialing to this network** This option allows the ISA firewall to automatically dial the connection in response to Web Proxy, Firewall, and SecureNAT clients on a protected Network behind the ISA firewall. Be careful with this option if you're using a VPN connection. If you enable this option, and the connection doesn't dial up correctly, then disable it and use the **I will dial the connection myself** option instead.

■ **Configure this dial-up connection as the default gateway** This option allows the ISA firewall to replace its current default gateway settings and use the VPN server it connects to as the new default gateway. This is the option you will use in the majority of cases if you are connecting to the ISP using a dial-up connection.

- **Use the following dial-up connection** This option allows you to select the dial-up connectoid you created.

- **Use this account** Enter the user account name that you used when you created the dial up connectoid. Do *not* enter local domain credentials. You must enter the actual credentials that your ISP assigned to you for your Internet account.

4. Click **Apply**, and then click **OK**.

If you use a VPN connection for your dial-up link, then you will need to create an Access Rule on the ISA firewall that allows the local host network to use the PPTP or L2TP/IPSec VPN protocol. If your ISP is using another VPN protocol (such as a proprietary IPSec NAT-T protocol), then you will need to create an access rule that allows the use of that protocol. Most ISPs should be using either PPTP or L2TP/IPSec for ease of use or for enhanced security.

Perform the following steps to create the Access Rule allowing the VPN connection:

1. In the **Microsoft Internet Security and Acceleration Server 2004** management console, expand the server name, and then click the **Firewall Policy** node.

2. In the **Firewall Policy** node, click the **Tasks** tab on the Task pane. Click the **Create a New Access Rule** link.

3. On the **Welcome to the New Access Rule Wizard** page, enter a name for the rule in the **Access Rule name** text box. In this example, we'll name the rule **PPTP to ISP**. Click **Next**.

4. Select **Allow** on the **Rule Action** page. Click **Next**.

5. On the **Protocols** page, choose **Selected protocols** from the **This rule applies to** drop-down list. Click **Add**.

6. In the **Add Protocols** dialog box (Figure 4.53), click the **VPN and IPSec** folder, and double-click **PPTP**. Click **Close** (if you are using a protocol other than PPTP, then select the appropriate VPN protocol).

Figure 4.53 Selecting the VPN protocol

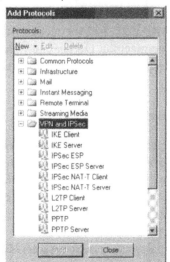

7. Click **Next** on the **Protocols** page.

8. On the **Access Rule Sources** page, click **Add**.

9. In the **Add Network Entities** dialog box, click the **Networks** folder, and then double-click **Local Host**. Click **Close**.

10. Click **Next** on the **Access Rule Sources** page.

11. On the **Access Rule Destinations** page, click **Add**.

12. In the **Add Network Entities** dialog box, click the **New** menu, and click **Computer**.

13. In the **New Computer Rule Element** dialog box, enter a name for your ISP's VPN server in the **Name** text box. In this example, we'll name the VPN server **ISP VPN Server**. Enter the IP address of the ISP's VPN server in the **Computer IP address** text box. Click **OK**.

14. Click the **Computers** folder in the **Add Network Entities** dialog box, and double-click the **ISP VPN Server** entry. Click **Close**.

15. Click **Next** on the **Access Rule Destinations** page.

16. Click **Next** on the **User Sets** page.

17. Click **Finish** on the **Completing the New Access Rule Wizard** page.

18. Click **Apply** to save the changes and update the firewall policy.

19. Click **OK** in the **Apply New Configuration** dialog box.

This configuration allows the ISA firewall to connect to the VPN server at the ISP. However, you still need to create Access Rules that allow inbound and outbound access to and from the ISA firewall's protected Networks. We will discuss in depth how to create Access Policy in Chapter 7.

"Network Behind a Network" Scenarios (Advanced ISA Firewall Configuration)

In order to fully appreciate the issues with the "network within a Network" scenario, we need to cover some ground that we covered earlier in the chapter. Once we refresh ourselves on these key topics of the ISA firewall's networking model, we can then examine in detail the issues involved with the "network within a Network" scenario. This is a common point of confusion among new ISA firewall administrators, so pay close attention to the following discussions.

The new ISA firewall's multinetworking feature represents a major departure from the ISA Server 2000 firewall's approach to networking. In ISA Server 2000, networks are seen as either trusted or untrusted. In ISA Server 2000, there is a necessary relationship between trusted networks and the *Local Address Table (LAT)*. It is not possible to have one without the other. Trusted networks are defined by the networks listed in the LAT. Networks not included in the LAT are untrusted. Communications moving between LAT hosts (hosts with IP addresses contained in the LAT) are not exposed to the ISA Server 2000 firewall's stateful filtering and stateful application-layer inspection mechanisms.

The LAT is gone in the ISA firewall. The ISA firewall's concept of multinetworking includes as its basic tenet that no network is trusted by default, and all communications moving through the ISA firewall are exposed to the firewall's stateful filtering and stateful application-layer inspection mechanisms. This provides for a much higher level of security and access control than you could ever obtain with the ISA Server 2000 firewall. By severing the relationship between the LAT and trusted networks, the new ISA firewall gives administrators a much more refined granular level of control over communications that move between networks.

The *Network Object* is one of the key concepts you must understand in order to get the most out of your ISA firewall. Key issues regarding the ISA firewall's Network concept include:

- An interface can belong to only one network.
- An interface cannot belong to two or more networks.
- You can place as many network interface cards in the ISA firewall as your hardware supports.
- All IP addresses located behind a network interface are part of the same Network.
- All IP addresses defined on the ISA firewall are considered *Protected Networks*.
- Any IP address that isn't defined on the ISA firewall is considered part of the default External network.

- The VPN Clients Network and the Quarantined VPN Clients Network are *virtual* or *dynamically-created* Networks in that addresses are added to and removed from these networks when VPN clients connect and disconnect.

- The network directly connected to a particular interface might be considered the *root* of a particular network. For example, if you were using network ID **10.0.0.0/16** on the ISA firewall's on setup network, then other networks behind it might be **10.1.0.0/16**, **10.2.0.0/16**, and so on. You could then summarize the entire Network associated with that adapter as **10.0.0.0/8** and that would include all the networks located behind that interface.

You could also include networks behind the same interface that do not summarize. For example, you might have the ISA firewall on subnet network ID be **10.0.0.0/16** and another network located behind that network be **172.16.0.0/16**. The ISA firewall doesn't have a problem with this configuration. You just include all the addresses in both Network IDs when defining the Network that network interface represents.

When you have multiple networks defined by a single network interface, the networks that aren't part of the on subnet network are considered *networks within a Network*. Figure 4.54 hows an example of a network within a Network. The ISA firewall must be configured with a routing table entry that provides the gateway address to the networks behind the on subnet network. In Figure 4.54, the routing table entry on the ISA firewall would send all connections to network ID **10.10.10.0/24** to **10.0.0.100**.

Figure 4.54 shows the basic setup in the lab network I'll be using to demonstrate some of the issues you'll run into while working with networks within a Network configurations. The on subnet network is network ID **10.0.0.0/24**, and the network located behind the Checkpoint server is network ID **10.10.10.0/24**. I used a Checkpoint Server in this example because it's what I had available, but it could be any firewall device or packet-filtering router. You could replace the Checkpoint server with a hardware router, layer-3 switch, or even a VPN gateway that connects another network to one of the ISA firewall's Protected Networks. See Figure 4.54 for the Back-end "network within a Network."

Figure 4.54 Back-end "Network within a Network"

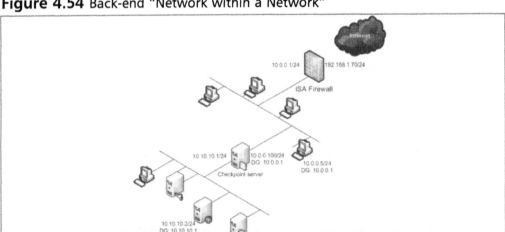

As a quick overview, the SecureNAT client is any machine configured with a default gateway address that routes connections to the Internet through the ISA firewall. If the SecureNAT client is located on a network directly attached to the ISA firewall, then the default gateway of the SecureNAT client is the IP address on the ISA firewall's interface that the SecureNAT client is connected to. If the SecureNAT client is located on a network ID different from the ISA firewall's interface, then the SecureNAT client is configured with a default gateway address of a router that will forward Internet-bound requests to the ISA firewall's interface.

In Figure 4.54, the host with IP address **10.0.0.5/24** uses the default gateway **10.0.0.1** because it's on the same network ID as the ISA firewall's local interface. The host with IP address **10.10.10.224** has a default gateway **10.10.10.1**, which routes Internet-bound requests to the local interface of the Checkpoint server. The Checkpoint server is configured with a default gateway address **10.0.0.1**, which is the interface on the ISA firewall on the same Network as the Checkpoint Server. The Checkpoint server forwards the Internet-bound connections to the ISA firewall, and the ISA firewall sends them to the Internet host.

Firewall clients work quite a bit differently. The Firewall client is configured with the name or IP address of the ISA firewall. The Firewall client software intercepts all TCP and UDP connections made by Winsock applications the Firewall client computer and *remotes* them (sends them directly to) the IP address of the Firewall client listener on the ISA firewall's interface that is on the same Network as the Firewall client machine.

For example in Figure 4.54, the client with IP address **10.0.0.5/24** is configured as a Firewall client, and the Firewall client software is configured to use address **10.0.0.1** as its default gateway. A firewall client on the back-end network with address **10.10.10.2/24** also has its Firewall client application configured to use IP address **10.0.0.1**. The Firewall client machine sends communications mediated by the Firewall client software *directly to the ISA firewall*. This means that the Firewall client is independent of the organization's current routing infrastructure. The only requirement is that the organization's routing infrastructure know the route to the networks where the ISA firewall's interface is located.

While these differences might seem straightforward when dealing with Internet-bound connections, there are some special considerations you're going to have to take into account when dealing with network within a Network scenarios. If you don't understand these differences, you'll end up frustrated and confused with your network within a Network configurations.

Figure 4.55 shows the request and response paths between a SecureNAT client on the *on subnet* network and a server on the back-end network (the network within a Network). When the SecureNAT client on the *on subnet* network sends a connection request to the host on the back-end network, the SecureNAT client sends the request to the ISA firewall's interface on the same Network as the SecureNAT client. The ISA firewall forwards the request to the interface on the Checkpoint server that can route to the back-end network, and then the Checkpoint server forwards the connection to the destination host. The response path is through the Checkpoint server and then directly to the SecureNAT client, because the Checkpoint server can forward response directly to the client and does not need to use its gateway address to do so. Figure 4.55 shows a SecureNAT Client connecting to a network within a Network.

Figure 4.55 A SecureNAT Client Connecting to a Network within a Network

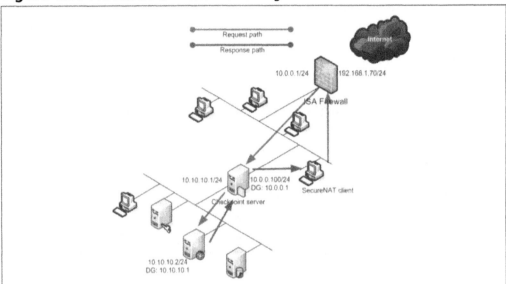

Now let's take a look at how the Firewall client works. Figure 4.56 shows two scenarios: the first scenario is the Firewall client connecting to a non-local network. A non-local Network is any network that isn't on the same Network where the Firewall client computer is located. The non-local Network could be a somewhere on the Internet, or a network located behind another interface connected to the ISA firewall. The second scenario shows a Firewall client connection to a local network, which is a network defined as being on the same Network as the Firewall client making the request.

The first scenario is illustrated by the Firewall client located on the right. This Firewall client machine attempts to connect to a Terminal Server at address 131.107.1.1. The Access Rule on the ISA firewall requires authentication before the connection request to the RDP server on the Internet is allowed. The Firewall client automatically forwards the user's credentials to the ISA firewall, and if the Access Rule allowing the outbound RDP connection applies to that user, the connection is forwarded to the remote RDP server on the Internet.

The second scenario also depicts a Firewall client machine on the same subnet as the ISA firewall's local interface, but this time the RDP connection is to a host on the back-end network within a Network.

This is where problems creep in. The Firewall client software automatically downloads a list of all IP addresses defined for the Network that the Firewall client belongs to. In this example, the Firewall client's Network includes all the addresses in the 10.0.0.0/24 and 10.10.10.0/24 ranges. The Firewall client software compares the destination address of the connection request to the addresses defined for the Network to which the Firewall client belongs. If the destination is on a non-local Network, then the connection is *remoted* to the ISA firewall's local interface, and the ISA firewall proxies the connection to the non-local network. However, if the destination address is for a host on the same Network as the Firewall client, then the Firewall client software will ignore the connection.

When the Firewall client ignores the connection, the destination host must be located on the same network ID as the Firewall client machine making the request, or the Firewall client machine must also be configured as a SecureNAT client, with a default gateway address that is able to route the connection to the destination network ID. In this second scenario, the Firewall client is also configured as a SecureNAT client.

When the Firewall client in this second scenario attempts to establish an RDP connection to a host on the back-end network, the Firewall client software will ignore the connection because the back-end network is part of the same Network as the *on subnet* network. Since the SecureNAT client is unable to send credentials to the ISA firewall, the connection request will fail if the Access Rule allowing RDP connections requires authentication. This is what takes place in this second scenario.

Note that if the Access Rule did not require authentication, then the second scenario would work because the Firewall client would be able to fail over to the SecureNAT client configuration and connect to the back-end network host. Of course, the entire point of using the Firewall client is to allow strong user/group-based authentication. Figure 4.56 illustrates Firewall Client Paths through Local and non-Local Networks.

Figure 4.56 Firewall Client Paths through Local and non-Local Networks

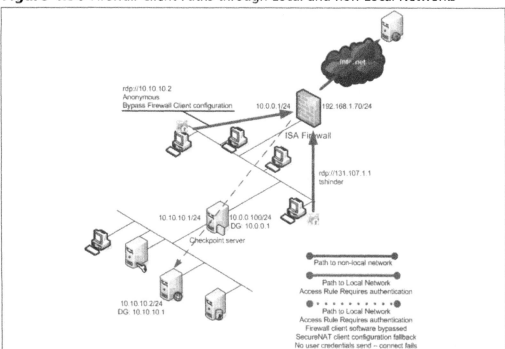

Log file entries in show the connections to the remote RDP server and the RDP server on the same network. The second and third lines in the log show RDP connections to a host on another Network. The Firewall client detects that the connection is destined to a host on another network and intercepts the connection and remotes it, along with the user credentials, to the ISA firewall. You can see the user information in the **Client Username** column, which confirms that the connection was handled by the Firewall client.

On the fifth, eighth and ninth lines of the log file, you see RDP connection attempts to a machine on the back-end network that is part of the same Network as the Firewall client computer. Because the destination is on the same network as the Firewall client computer, the Firewall client ignores the request and the SecureNAT client configuration takes over. You can see that the rule allowing connections to the back-end network with the Network denies the connection. The connection is denied because the rule is configured to require users to authenticate before connecting. The SecureNAT client can never send credentials to the ISA firewall, so the connection fails. See the log file entries showing these connections in Figure 4.57 .

Figure 4.57 Log Files Showing Firewall Client and SecureNAT Client

Client IP	Destination IP	Destinati...	Action	Rule	Client Username
172.16.0.1	172.16.255.255	138	Denied Connection	Default rule	
10.0.0.5	192.168.1.185	3389	Initiated Connection	All Open Internal to Back End	ISALOCAL\tshinder
10.0.0.5	192.168.1.185	3389	Closed Connection	All Open Internal to Back End	ISALOCAL\tshinder
192.168.1.101	192.168.1.255	138	Denied Connection	Default rule	
10.0.0.5	10.10.10.2	3389	Denied Connection	All Open Internal to Back End	
10.0.0.1	10.0.0.100	137	Closed Connection	Allow NetBIOS from ISA Server...	
192.168.1.101	192.168.1.255	137	Denied Connection	Default rule	
10.0.0.5	10.10.10.2	3389	Denied Connection	All Open Internal to Back End	
10.0.0.5	10.10.10.2	3389	Denied Connection	All Open Internal to Back End	

What is the solution to this problem? The best solution is to configure the machines as Firewall clients so they can access resources on the other Networks, and for *on subnet* hosts, configure the machines as SecureNAT clients, but use a gateway address that is *not the IP address of the ISA firewall on the same Network*.

The machines on the *on subnet* network should be configured as Firewall clients. When connections are made to other Networks, the Firewall client will handle the connection. When connections are made to hosts on the same Network, the SecureNAT client will take over and the default gateway address is set as the back-end router's interface to the back-end network with a Network. Since the back-end router has a default gateway set to the ISA firewall's interface on the same Network, any SecureNAT client request that needs to be routed to the Internet can be done by the back-end router. This would be required if the host on the *on subnet* network needs to use a non-Winsock protocol (non-TCP or UDP) such as ICMP (for ping and tracert).

With this configuration you don't need to make any changes on the back-end network within a Network. The Firewall clients on this network still remote their Winsock requests destined to other Networks to the ISA firewall's interface on the same Network. The SecureNAT client configuration is still set to the back-end router and that router already knows the route to all internal subnets, so the ISA firewall never even has a chance to deny the request, since it never sees it. The back-end client's SecureNAT client configuration allows a direct connection to other hosts on the same Network. Figure 4.58 shows the recommended configuration.

Figure 4.58 Using an Alternate Default Gateway Address for On Subnet Hosts

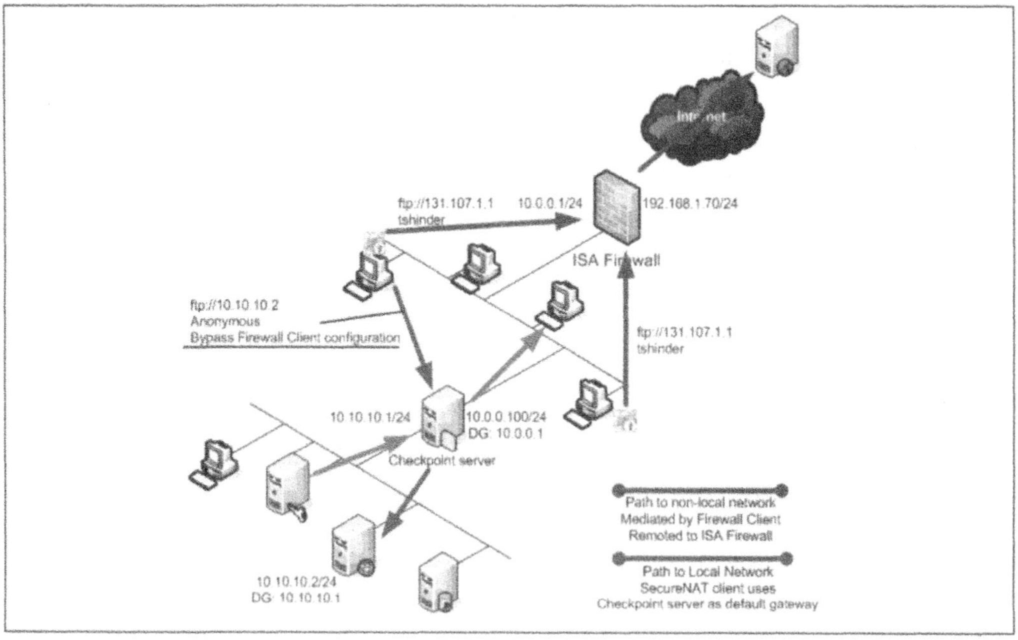

The network-within-a-Network scenario is a completely workable scenario, and all it requires is that you include all addresses behind a specific interface to be included in that Network. The primary limitation in this scenario is that you can't use the Firewall client to perform user/group-based access controls to control traffic moving between network IDs located on the same ISA firewall-defined Network.

While this might, at first, seem like a disappointing limitation, the fact is that the ISA firewall controls traffic *traversing* the firewall. While we can do some tricks with access rules to control traffic from one IP address group to another, the truth is that in order for the ISA firewall, or any firewall, to do the real work of a firewall, the connections must traverse the firewall, but just be routed from one network to another behind the same interface.

An example of one such trick is to use the Subnet or Address Range objects to control access to other machines located on the same Network. In fact, you can get even more granular and use Computer objects. Note that this is useful only for the machines located on the on subnet network. You would have to create router ACLs on any back-end subnets to obtain a similar level of control.

Web Proxy Chaining as a Form of Network Routing

Web Proxy Chaining is a method you can use to forward Web Proxy connections from one ISA firewall to another ISA firewall. Web Proxy chains consist of upstream and downstream ISA firewalls. The upstream ISA firewalls are those closer to the Internet connection, and the downstream ISA firewalls are those further away from the Internet connection. Downstream ISA firewalls forward Web Proxy requests to upstream ISA firewalls. The first ISA firewall in the Web Proxy chain is the one closest to the Internet and the one responsible for obtaining the Internet content.

Web Proxy Chaining is useful in a number of scenarios.

- Branch office ISA firewalls can be chained to upstream ISA firewalls at the corporate office.

- Departmental ISA firewalls, which protect department-specific networks within the organization can be chained to upstream ISA firewalls located on a network services segment or upstream ISA firewalls that are directly connected to the Internet.

- ISPs or large corporate customers can chain downstream ISA firewall Web caching arrays with upstream ISA firewall or ISA firewall Web caching array.

The advantage of using Web Proxy chaining is that you can reduce the overall bandwidth utilization on both the Internet link and all links between the downstream and upstream ISA firewalls in the Web Proxy chain. Figure 4.59 shows an example of a Web Proxy chain and the flow of information through the chain.

Figure 4.59 WebProxyChaining.vsd

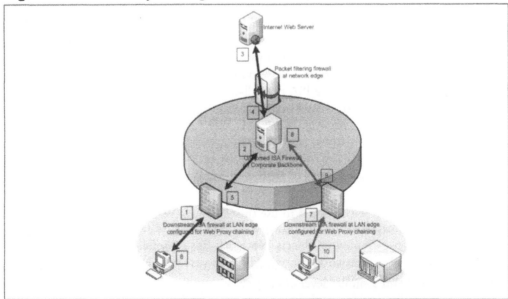

1. A client on a protected Network behind an ISA firewall makes a request for a Web page located on an Internet Web server. The connection request is sent through the ISA firewall protecting the departmental LAN.

2. The ISA firewall forwards the connection request to a unihomed ISA firewall located on the corporate backbone. The departmental ISA firewall is configured to use Web Proxy chaining to connect to the unihomed ISA firewall. Since the unihomed ISA firewall is able to protect itself from attack, there is little concern regarding attacks originating from hosts on the backbone network, or hosts located in the simple hardware packet filter firewall in front of the unihomed ISA firewall.

3. The unihomed Web caching-only ISA firewall forwards the connection request through the simple hardware packet filter-based router.

4. The Internet Web server returns the response to the unihomed ISA firewall through the simple hardware packet filter-based firewall.

5. The unihomed ISA firewall forwards the response to the departmental ISA firewall. However, before forwarding the response to the departmental ISA firewall, the unihomed ISA firewall places the Web content in its cache. The Web content in the response is returned to the departmental ISA firewall from the unihomed ISA firewall's Web cache.

6. The departmental ISA firewall returns the response to the client that issued the request. However, before the departmental ISA firewall returns the content, it places the content in its Web cache. It is from this Web cache that the departmental ISA firewall obtains the content to return to the protected host that issued the request.

7. A host on another network makes a request for the same Web page. This host is also protected by an ISA firewall. The host makes a request for the Web page by going through its ISA firewall.

8. The ISA firewall is Web chained to the unihomed ISA firewall on the corporate backbone. It forwards the connection request to the unihomed ISA firewall. The unihomed ISA firewall checks to see if the content is contained in its Web cache before forwarding the request to the Internet Web server.

9. The unihomed ISA firewall has the requested content in its Web cache and returns the content to the departmental ISA firewall that forwarded the request. The unihomed ISA firewall did not need to send the request to the Internet Web server because that information was already contained in its Web cache.

10. The departmental ISA firewall forwards the Web content to the host that initiated the request.

You can see in this example that not only is bandwidth saved on the Internet link, but bandwidth can also be saved on the backbone link. You would see this bandwidth savings when another host on either of the ISA firewall protected networks makes a request for the same Web content. In this case, the departmental ISA firewalls will have the information already in their local Web caches, and they will not need to forward the request to the unihomed ISA firewall on the corporate backbone. This reduces overall bandwidth utilization on the corporate backbone.

Another powerful application of Web chaining is when you configure the downstream ISA firewalls to connect to a Web-caching array.. Figure 4.60 shows how a Web-caching array could be set up for an organization.

Figure 4.60 A Web-cached Array Configured for an Organization

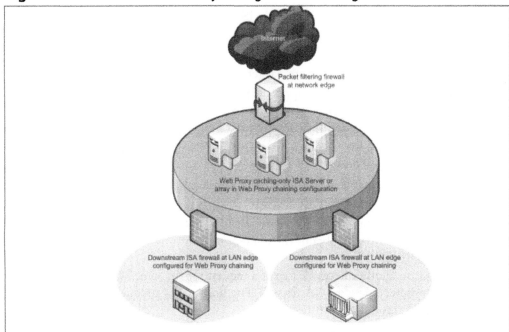

In this example, the downstream ISA firewalls are configured in a Web-chaining configuration with the array. The Web-caching array provides configuration information to the downstream ISA firewalls, including the names of the machines participating in the array. If one of the array members goes offline for some reason, the downstream ISA firewalls will try another array member that is online. In addition, when an array member goes offline, the array is aware that the array member is unavailable and removes the offline machine from the array. The remaining array members inform the downstream departmental ISA firewalls of the machines in the array that are online. This prevents the downstream ISA firewalls from attempting connections with an offline array member.

Configuration of Web Proxy chaining is done on the **Web Chaining** tab in the **Network** node. Perform the following steps to configure Web Proxy chaining:

1. In the **Microsoft Internet Security and Acceleration Server 2004** management console, expand the server name, and then expand the **Configuration** node. Click the **Networks** node.

2. In the **Networks** node, click the **Web Chaining** tab in the **Details** pane.

3. Click the **Tasks** tab in the Task pane, and click **Create New Web Chaining Rule**.

4. On the **Welcome to the New Web Chaining Rule Wizard** page, enter a name for the rule in the **Web chaining rule name** text box. In this example, we'll name the rule **Chain to ISA-1**. Click **Next**.

5. On the **Web Chaining Rule Destination** page you tell the ISA firewall what requests should be chained to the upstream firewall. You can choose to chain all requests to the upstream firewall, or you can chain requests for specific URLs to the upstream ISA firewall. In this example, we'll chain all requests to the upstream firewall. Click the **Add** button to add the sites.

6. In the **Add Network Entities** dialog box, click the **Networks** folder, and then double-click the **External** network. Click **Close**.

7. Click **Next** on the **Web Chaining Rule Destination** page.

8. On the **Request Action** page (Figure 4.61), inform the ISA firewall how requests for the destination you configured on the last page should be routed. You have the following options:

■ **Retrieve requests directly from the specified location** This option configures the ISA firewall to send requests for the destination specified on the last page directly to the specified server and not send them to an upstream ISA firewall. What this means is, if the ISA firewall is configured to connect to the Internet in some way other than via a Web Proxy chain, the ISA firewall will forward the connection via that link. If the ISA firewall does not have access to the Internet other than from a Web Proxy chain, then the connection will fail. This configuration option actually represents the default behavior of the ISA firewall, which is to not use Web Proxy chaining, but instead to send the connection to the Internet site being requested.

■ **Redirect requests to a specified upstream server** This option forwards the request to an upstream Web Proxy server. This is the option that creates the Web Proxy chain between this server and the upstream ISA firewall. The **Allow delegation of basic authentication credentials** option is a bit of a mystery. What credentials? For what destinations? Who are we authenticating against? Are we authenticating with a Web site? An upstream Web Proxy? All of the above? None of the above? At this time we cannot definitively state what this option is for. It's possible that this option is used when Web Proxy chaining is implemented while accessing internal Web sites, but we can't commit to that answer. We'll keep you updated when we find out what this option means.

- **Redirect requests to**   This option allows you to redirect requests for the site specified on the previous page to another Web site. For example, suppose you want to redirect requests for a list of forbidden Web sites to a specific site on your corporate network. You would select this option, and then enter the IP address or FQDN for your internal site. You an also specify the HTTP **Port** and the **SSL Port**.

- **Use automatic dialup**   The **Use automatic dial-up** option allows you to use a dial-up connection for this rule. If your external interface is a dial-up connection, then select this option if you want to use the dial-up connection to reach the destination you specified on the previous page. You can also use this option if you have a NIC and a dial-up connection on the same ISA firewall. The NIC can be used for regular Internet connection, and the dial-up connection can be used for chained connections.

Figure 4.61 shows Configuring the Request Action.

Figure 4.61 Configuring the Request Action

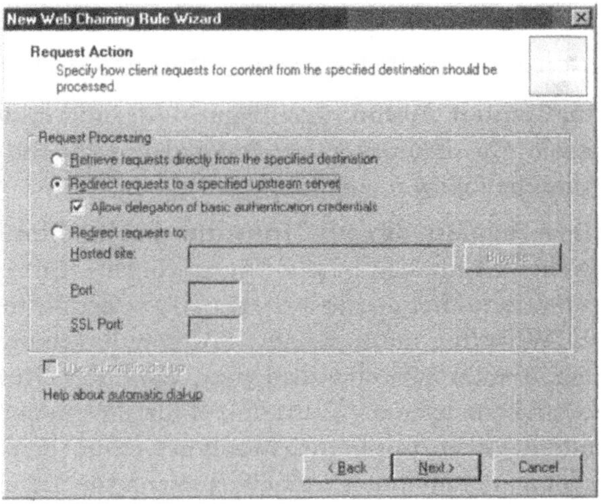

9.   In this example, we'll use **Redirect requests to a specified upstream server** and **disable the Allow delegation of basic authentication credentials**. Click **Next**.

10.   On the **Primary Routing** page, enter the IP address or FQDN of the upstream ISA firewall. If you enter the FQDN, make sure that the downstream ISA firewall can resolve that name to the correct IP address on the upstream. The **Port** and **SSL** Port text boxes contain defaults that work with all other ISA firewalls. Note that the **SSL port** is not used for SSL connections from clients behind the downstream ISA firewall in the Web Proxy chain. SSL connections from clients behind the downstream ISA firewall are tunneled in the Web Proxy connection to the upstream ISA firewall's TCP port 8080. The SSL Port is used when you want to secure the Web Proxy chain link between the upstream and

downstream ISA firewall using SSL. We don't have space in this book to include the details of this type of configuration, but we'll include it in an upcoming article on www.isaserver.org, so be on the lookout for it.

Figure 4.62 shows how to route to the upstream Web Proxy.

Figure 4.62 Routing to the Upstream Web Proxy

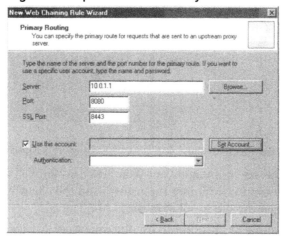

I highly recommend that you require authentication on the upstream Web Proxy. When authentication is forced on the upstream Web Proxy, the downstream Web Proxy must be able to send credentials to the upstream to access the Internet. You can configure credentials for the downstream Web Proxy in the Web Proxy chain by putting a checkmark in the **Use this account** checkbox. Click the **Set Account** button. In the **Set Account** dialog box (Figure 4.63), enter the user name in the **User** text box in the **COMPUTERNAME\Username** format. The user account is configured in the local user database of the upstream ISA firewall. If the upstream ISA firewall is a member of a domain, then you can use the DOMAINNAME\Username format. Enter the password, and confirm the password in the **Password** and **Confirm password** text boxes. Click **OK** in the **Set Account** dialog box. In the **Authentication** drop-down list, select the **Integrated Windows** option. If you are configuring Web Proxy chaining to a non-ISA firewall Web Proxy server, then you will have to use basic authentication. If you use basic authentication, make sure that the Web Proxy chain link is configured to use SSL, because the basic credentials are sent in clear text. Click **Next** on the **Primary Routing** page. Figure 4.63 shows setting the credentials.

Figure 4.63 Setting Credentials

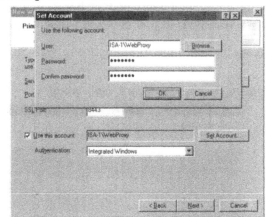

11. On the **Backup Action** page, you have the following options:

- **Ignore requests** If the upstream Web Proxy in the Web Proxy chain is not available, this option will drop the request, and the client will receive an error indicating that the site is not available.

- **Retrieve requests directly from the specified location** This option allows the downstream ISA firewall in the Web Proxy chain to use another method, outside the Web Proxy chain configuration, to connect to the Web site. This would be the case if the external interface of the ISA firewall was able to reach the destination site without going through the Web Proxy chain.

- **Route requests to an upstream server** This option allows the downstream ISA firewall in the Web Proxy chain to use another ISA firewall in a second Web Proxy chain. This option allows you to set a *second* Web Proxy chain configuration on the downstream ISA firewall, which is used only when the first upstream ISA firewall becomes unavailable.

- **Use automatic dial-up** This option should be enabled if a dial-up connection is used to connect the downstream ISA firewall to the Internet, or if you want requests for the destinations configured for this rule to use a dial-up connection instead of the ISA firewalls primary connection (which would be a dedicated NIC)

12. Select the **Ignore requests** option, and click **Next** on the **Backup Action** page.

13. Click **Finish** on the **Completing the New Web Chaining Rule Wizard** page.

The downstream ISA firewall is now configured in a Web Proxy chaining relationship with the upstream. Remember to configure an Access Rule on the upstream ISA firewall that allows the account you configured in the Web Chaining Rule access to the Internet using the HTTP, HTTPS, and FTP protocols.

> **Tip**
>
> When you configure Web Proxy chaining, the downstream ISA firewall can be configured with a user account it can use if the credentials the client used to authenticate with the downstream ISA firewall are not recognized by the upstream firewall. This is what we did in the scenario we configured above.
>
> In this scenario, the logged-on user name on the upstream ISA firewall will be the name you used to authenticate in the Web Proxy Chaining Rule.
>
> **However**, if the upstream ISA firewall can authenticate the user that issued the initial connection, because the upstream firewall belongs to the same domain as the client and downstream ISA firewall, or **if** the upstream ISA firewall has that user name located in its local SAM, then the user that issued the request will appear in both the downstream and upstream ISA firewall logs.

Firewall Chaining as a Form of Network Routing

Firewall chaining is similar to Web Proxy chaining. In a Firewall chaining arrangement, the downstream ISA firewall is configured to be a Firewall client of the upstream ISA firewall. The advantages of the Firewall chaining configuration over the Web Proxy configuration is that Firewall chaining supports all TCP and UDP Winsock protocols, not just Web protocols (HTTP/HTTPS/FTP). In addition, Web Proxy chaining supports complex protocols that require secondary connections.

We have not been able to get Firewall chaining to work with the ISA firewall, so we will not cover the details of the configuration in this book. If this feature is repaired in a future service pack or feature pack, we will post this information as a detailed tutorial on www.isaserver.org.

Configuring the ISA Firewall as a DHCP Server

Some organizations may want the ISA firewall to act more like a traditional SOHO router, where the ISA firewall acts as a DHCP Server for the corporate network. You can install the DHCP service on the ISA firewall and create Access Rules that allow the ISA firewall to provide IP addressing information to hosts on the corporate network.

We will assume that you have already installed the DHCP server. The next step is to configure the ISA firewall to allow the DHCP Request and DHCP replies with messages required to assign corporate network clients IP addressing information.

Perform the following steps to create the DHCP Request Access Rule:

1. In the **Microsoft Internet Security and Acceleration Server 2004** management console, expand the server name, and then click the **Firewall Policy** node. In the Task pane, click the **Tasks** tab. Click the **Create a New Access Rule** link.

2. On the Welcome to the New Access Rule Wizard page, enter a name for the rule in the Access Rule name text box. In this example, we'll name the rule DHCP Request. Click Next.

3. Select the **Allow** option on the **Rule Action** page. Click **Next**.

4. On the **Protocols** page, select the **Selected protocols** option from the **This rule applies to** list. Click **Add**.

5. In the **Add Network Entities** dialog box, click the **Infrastructure** folder, and then double-click the **DHCP Request** entry. Click **Close**.

6. Click **Next** on the **Protocols** page.

7. On the **Access Rule Sources** page, click **Add**.

8. In the **Add Network Entities** dialog box, click the **Networks** folder, and double-click the **Internal** entry. Click **Close**.

9. Click **Next** on the **Access Rule Sources** page.

10. On the **Access Rule Destinations** page, click **Add**.

11. In the **Add Network Entities** dialog box, click the **Networks** folder and double click the **Local Host** entry. Click **Close**.

12. Click **Next** on the **Access Rule Destinations** page.

13. Click **Next** on the **User Sets** page.

14. Click **Finish** on the **Completing the New Access Rule Wizard** page.

15. Click **Apply** to save the changes and update the firewall policy.

16. Click **OK** in the **Apply New Configuration** dialog box.

The next step is to create the DHCP Reply Access Rule:

17. Right-click the **DHCP Request** rule, and click **Copy**.

18. Right-click the **DHCP Request** rule, and click **Paste**.

19. Double-click on the **DHCP Request (1)** rule, and click **Properties**.

20. On the **General** tab of the **DHCP Request (1)** rule, change the name of the rule to **DHCP Reply** in the **Name** text box.

21. Click the **Protocols** tab. Click the **DHCP (request)** entry, and click **Remove**. Click **Add**. In the **Protocols** dialog box, click the **Infrastructure** folder, and double-click the **DHCP (reply)** entry. Click **Close**.

22. Click the **From** tab. Click the **Internal** entry, and click the **Remove** button. Click the **Add** button. In the **Add Network Entities** dialog box, click the **Networks** folder, and double-click the **Local Host** entry. Click **Close**.

23. Click the **To** tab. Click the **Local Host** entry, and click **Remove**. Click **Add**. In the **Add Network Entities** dialog box, click the **Networks** folder, and double-click the **Internal** entry. Click **Close**.

24. Click **Apply**, and then click **OK**.

25. Click **Apply** to save the changes and update the firewall policy.

26. Click **OK** in the **Apply New Configuration** dialog box.

This configuration allows the DHCP server on the ISA firewall to provide IP addressing information to hosts on the Internal Network.

WARNING

The DHCP server will also be able to provide IP addresses to VPN clients. However, you cannot install the DHCP Relay Agent on the ISA firewall and allow VPN clients to obtain DHCP options

Summary

In this chapter we focused on the ISA firewall's networking capabilities. As a prelude to the discussion, we went over our concept of how the ISA firewall fits within an existing corporate firewall infrastructure. We then discussed the details of the sample lab network we used when developing the scenarios discussed in this book. Included in that discussion were detailed instructions in how to configure VMware virtual machines to support the ISA firewalls and other machines in our sample network.

We then drilled down on the ISA firewall's view of the network. The new ISA firewall breaks away from the ISA Server 2000 approach of internal and external networks, where internal networks were trusted and external networks as untrusted. The new ISA firewall does not trust any network, and the default Internal network is quite different from the concept of "internal" network that previous versions of this product supported. We also went over all the ISA firewall Network Objects and the Network Templates that can be used to simplify configuration of the ISA firewall's network settings.

We finished up with a discussion of various topics related to the ISA firewall's networking feature sets, including Web Proxy chaining, Firewall chaining, and using the ISA firewall as a DHCP server.

Solutions Fast Track

Our Approach to the ISA Firewall Network Design and Defense Tactics

☑ Traditional Firewalls are simple stateful filtering devices, sometimes referred to as "stateful packet inspection." All modern firewalls perform stateful filtering.

☑ Attacks on networks now take place at the application layer and only stateful application-layer inspection firewalls like the ISA firewall can meet the challenge of protecting against these modern "Layer 7" attacks.

☑ Simple stateful packet-filtering firewalls should be placed on the Internet edge of the network if the effective Internet bandwidth exceeds the rate at which the stateful application-layer filtering ISA firewall can effectively process traffic (about 400Mbps). If the Internet "pipe" exceeds the ISA firewall's bandwidth limits, place stateful packet-filtering firewalls in front of the ISA stateful application-layer inspection firewall to offload some processing.

☑ There are multiple security perimeters on any network. Stateful filtering and stateful application-layer inspection should ideally be done at each perimeter.

☑ The Windows operating system can be hardened to the extent that it is no more or less penetrable than any other firewall, including hardware firewalls.

☑ Because ISA firewalls provide a significantly higher level of protection than stateful filtering "hardware" firewalls, the ISA firewalls should be placed closest to the core network assets.

Tom and Deb Shinder's Configuring ISA 2004 Network Layout

☑ The sample network layout in this chapter provides the information you need to replicate the network topology we use in the discussions and exercises through out book.

☑ We used VMware Workstation 4.51 as our test bed environment. Each network ID was placed on a separate VMNet virtual switch, which allowed us to segregate the Ethernet broadcast domain for each network in the same way a network router would do.

☑ Out of the box VMware 4.51 supports only three network adapters per virtual machine. Thanks to Alessandro Perilli for the great tip he provided us on how to install a four NIC on a VMware virtual machine.

How ISA Firewalls Define Networks and Network Relationships

☑ The ISA firewall does not use the old LAT-based concept where "internal" networks were trusted and external networks are untrusted. The new ISA firewall performs stateful filtering and stateful application-layer inspection on all interfaces, including its VPN interfaces.

☑ The term "multinetworking" refers to the ISA firewall's approach to networks. Networks are defined based on the location behind a particular NIC installed on the ISA firewall, and route relationships are defined between those networks

☑ Communications between any two hosts on a Network should never be looped back through the ISA firewall. Hosts located on the same network should always communicate directly with one another.

☑ The ISA firewall contains five default networks: Local Host, Internal, External, VPN Clients, and Quarantined VPN Clients.

☑ The Local Host Network includes addresses bound to the ISA firewall.

☑ The Internal Network includes all addresses located behind the NIC you designate as the default Internal network during installation of the ISA firewall software.

☑ The default External Network includes all addresses that are not defined as part of a Network on the ISA firewall.

☑ The VPN Clients Network includes all addresses in use by VPN clients and gateways at any point in time.

☑ The Quarantined VPN Clients Network includes all addresses of VPN clients and gateways that are currently in quarantine.

☑ You can create your own Internal, Perimeter, VPN site-to-site, and External Networks.

☑ All communications between Networks must have a Network Rule that defines the route relationship between the source and destination Network. You can have either a Route or a NAT relationship between any two Networks.

☑ A Route relationship is bidirectional, and the source IP address of the communicating hosts is always preserved.

☑ A NAT relationship is unidirectional, and the source IP address of a host behind the NATed Network is always replaced by the primary IP address on the interface that the connections leave on the NATed host Network.

☑ The ISA firewall supports nine Network Object types: Networks, Network Sets, Computers, Address Ranges, Subnets, Computer Sets, URL Sets, Domain Name Sets, and Web Listeners. Each of these Network Objects can be used to control the source and destination of any communication moving through the ISA firewall.

☑ The ISA firewall includes five Network Templates out of the box: Edge Firewall, Front Firewall, Back Firewall, Trihomed DMZ (3-Leg Firewall), and Unihomed Web Caching-only Firewall (Singe NIC Template).

☑ The Unihomed Web Caching-only Firewall Template is unusual because all addresses are included as part of its default Internal Network. This means there are no external addresses, and all source and destination addresses in Access Rules must be from Internal to Internal.

☑ The ISA firewall supports dial-up connections to the Internet. Automatic dialing may not work properly for dial-up VPN connections used to establish the Internet link.

☑ The ISA firewall supports dynamic address assignment on its external interface. However, you must configure the ISA firewall's System Policy to support dynamic address assignment.

☑ The "network within a Network" scenario is one where there are multiple network IDs located behind the same ISA firewall network interface card. All addresses located behind a particular ISA firewall NIC are part of the same

Network, and the ISA firewall must be configured with routing table entries that indicate the correct gateway for each network ID located behind that interface.

Web Proxy Chaining as a Form of Network Routing

- ☑ Web Proxy chaining allows you to connect ISA firewall Web Proxy servers to one another to route requests to the Internet.

- ☑ Upstream Web Proxy servers are closer to the Internet link, and downstream Web Proxy servers are further away from the Internet link.

- ☑ Web Proxy Chaining is sometime referred to as "Web Routing" because you can configure Web Proxy Chaining of some requests and not others.

- ☑ Web Proxy Chaining saves bandwidth on both the Internet link and any links between the upstream and downstream Web proxies in the Web Proxy chain.

Firewall Chaining as a Form of Network Routing

- ☑ Firewall Chaining allows you to connect ISA firewalls in a manner that allows the downstream ISA firewall to be a Web Proxy client of the upstream. Unfortunately, it does not appear to work at this time.

Configuring the ISA Firewall as a DHCP Server

- ☑ The ISA firewall can be configured as a DHCP server for the corporate network.

- ☑ The DHCP server on the ISA firewall can provide DHCP options to DHCP clients on the corporate network.

- ☑ The DHCP server on the ISA firewall can supply IP addresses to VPN clients and gateways, but it cannot supply DHCP options to the VPN clients and gateways. However, if you place a DHCP server on the corporate network, and configure a DHCP Relay Agent on the ISA firewall, then you can assign DHCP options to VPN clients.

Frequently Asked Questions

The following Frequently Asked Questions, answered by the authors of this book, are designed to both measure your understanding of the concepts presented in this chapter and to assist you with real-life implementation of these concepts. To have your questions about this chapter answered by the author, browse to **www.syngress.com/solutions** and click on the **"Ask the Author"** form. You will also gain access to thousands of other FAQs at ITFAQnet.com.

Q: My clients on the corporate Network are able to connect to all Web sites except the Web sites we manage on our Internal network. What's up with that?

A: The most likely reason for this problem is that your corporate network clients are attempting to access the Web sites by looping back through the ISA firewall. You can correct this problem by configuring the Web Proxy and Firewall clients to use direct access for internal IP addresses and domains, and to configuring a split DNS so that internal network hosts resolve names for internal resources to their internal IP addresses.

Q: I have two interfaces on my ISA firewall: one interface connected to the Internet and one interface connected to the corporate network. There are five network IDs managed by a router on the corporate network. I created four internal Networks for the network IDs that weren't covered by the default Internal network. Now I'm seeing errors on my ISA firewall indicating that my other Internal Networks are not "reachable" from the Internal Network interface. What gives?

A: All IP addresses behind a single NIC on the ISA firewall are considered part of the same Network. The ISA firewall's view of Networks is that communications between different Networks must traverse the ISA firewall. Any communications that take place directly between two hosts take place on the same Network. So, even though you have multiple Network IDs located behind the same Network interface on the ISA firewall, the ISA firewall considers them all a single Network because the ISA firewall doesn't handle communications between any two hosts located behind the same ISA firewall NIC. This discourages the poor practice of looping back through the ISA firewall to reach hosts on the same Network.

Q: I have a single NIC ISA firewall and have run the Single NIC Network Template on it. I've created Access Rules that allow communications from Internal to External, but the Access Rules do not work. What's the problem here?

A: The problem is that when you run the Single NIC Network Template on the ISA firewall, the Internal network changes so that all addresses in the IPv4 range are included in the definition of the Internal Network (with the exception of the loopback network ID). All Access Rules created on a unihomed ISA firewall on which the Single NIC Network Template is run should include the source and destination networks as Internal, or you can use other Network Objects to represent the source and destinations.

Q: I've installed a DHCP server on my ISA firewall, and I've also installed a DHCP Relay Agent on the firewall. I want to use the DHCP Relay Agent to provide DHCP options to my VPN clients, but its not working. Why?

A: When the DHCP server is installed on the ISA firewall, you will not be able to assign DHCP options to the VPN clients even after installing the DHCP Relay Agent. However, if you install a DHCP server on the corporate network and configure a DHCP Relay Agent on the ISA firewall, you will then be able to assign your VPN clients DHCP options.

Q: I used a DHCP-assigned address on the external interface of my ISA firewall. I was able to get an address before installing the ISA firewall software. Now it doesn't work. What do I need to do to get a DHCP-assigned address again?

A: You need to change the System Policy on the ISA firewall so that it accepts DHCP replies from either the default External Network, or better, from the specific IP address of your ISP's DHCP server.

ISA 2004 Client Types and Automating Client Provisioning

Topics in this Chapter:

- Understanding ISA 2004 Client Types
- Automating ISA 2004 Client Provisioning
- Automating Installation of the Firewall Client

☑ Summary

☑ Solutions Fast Track

☑ Frequently Asked Questions

One of the most misunderstood, but most critical, issues relating to the installation and management of ISA 2004 firewalls is that of ISA 2004 client types. Some of these client types have a classic client/server relationship with the ISA firewall. That is, the client makes a request for data from the server; the server subsequently performs the work of retrieving the data, and returning the data to the client. The client/server relationship is dependent on client software installed on the client computer that makes it possible to communicate with the particular services running on the server.

In the case of ISA, the client might request data in the form of a Web page on the Internet; the ISA firewall would perform the work of retrieving the Web page and delivering it to the client. However, not all ISA 2004 clients have a classic client/server relationship with the firewall, and each client type accesses networks outside its own in a different fashion. In addition, some applications work with one ISA 2004 client type but not with another. It is critical to determine the ISA 2004 client type before you install and configure ISA 2004 firewall. Failure to implement the correct client type can lead to the misconception that the firewall is not working correctly.

All machines connecting to resources by going through the ISA 2004 firewall are considered clients of the ISA firewall. This does not imply that all machines need to have client software installed or need their applications configured to connect directly with the ISA firewall computer. In the context of ISA 2004, the "client" does not always participate in the classic "client/server" relationship with the ISA 2004 firewall.

Understanding ISA 2004 Client Types

Computers that go through the ISA firewall to access resources outside their networks fall into one or more ISA 2004 client type categories. These are:

- The SecureNAT client
- The Firewall client
- The Web Proxy client

A single machine can be configured to act as multiple ISA 2004 client-types. For example, a Windows XP computer can be configured as a SecureNAT, Firewall and Web Proxy client. Another Windows XP computer can be configured as only a Firewall and Web Proxy client. A Linux machine can be configured as a SecureNAT client and Web Proxy client.

Table 5.1 provides an overview of the ISA 2004 client types, how each is installed or configured, which operating systems each supports, protocols supported by each, type of user-level authentication each supports, and special deployment considerations for each type.

Table 5.1 Overview of ISA 2004 Client Types

Feature	SecureNAT client	Firewall client	Web Proxy client
Installation of client software required?	No. SecureNAT clients require only a default gateway address that can route Internet-bound requests through the ISA 2004 firewall. The default gateway is set in the TCP/IP properties for the computer's network adapter.	Yes. The Firewall client software must be installed from an installation share on the network. The Firewall client installation share can be on the ISA 2004 firewall itself, or (preferably) on a File Server located somewhere on the network.	No. However, Web browsers on client computers must be configured to use the ISA 2004 firewall as their Web Proxy. The proxy is set in the Web browser's connection settings.
Operating system support	SecureNAT clients support all operating systems. The SecureNAT client type can be used with Windows, MacOS, Unix, Linux, and any other operating system that supports TCP/IP networking.	The Firewall client supports all post-Windows 95 platforms, from Windows 98 to Windows Server 2003.	The Web ProxyProxy client supports all platforms, but does so by way of a Web application. All Web browsers that can be configured to use a proxy server can function as Web ProxyProxy clients.
Protocol support	All simple protocols are supported by SecureNAT. Complex protocols (those requiring multiple connections) require an application filter be installed on the ISA Server 2004 firewall.	The Firewall client supports all Winsock applications that use the TCP and UDP protocols; the Firewall client does not mediate non-TCP/UDP connections.	The Web ProxyProxy client supports HTTP, HTTPS (SSL), and HTTP tunneled FTP (Web proxied FTP)

Continued

Table 5.1 Overview of ISA 2004 Client Types

Feature	SecureNAT client	Firewall client	Web Proxy client
User-level authentication supported?	No. SecureNAT clients cannot authenticate with the ISA 2004 firewall unless the client applications support SOCKS 5 and a SOCKS 5 application filter is installed on the firewall.	Yes. The Firewall client enables strong user/group-based access control by transparently forwarding client credentials to the ISA 2004 firewall.	Yes. Web Proxy clients will authenticate with the ISA 2004 firewall if the firewall requests credentials. No credentials are sent if an anonymous access rule enabling the connection is available to the Web Proxy client.
Deployment Considerations	All non-Windows operating systems can be configured as SecureNAT clients if they require protocol access outside of HTTP/HTTPS and FTP. All post-Windows 95 Windows operating systems should be configured as Firewall clients if at all possible. All servers published via Server Publishing Rules should be configured as SecureNAT clients. Use SecureNAT on Windows clients (except for published servers) only when outbound ICMP or PPTP is required.	All Windows operating systems supporting Firewall client installation (post-Windows 95) should have the Firewall client installed unless there are technical or management barriers that prevent this. The Firewall client increases the overall level of security and accessibility for all machines with the Firewall client software installed.	All browsers should be configured as Web Proxy clients when authentication is required for Web (HTTP/HTTPS/FTP) access. If user authentication is not required, Web Proxy configuration is not required because the ISA 2004 firewall will provide transparent Web ProxyProxy functionality for Firewall and SecureNAT clients.

Understanding the ISA 2004 SecureNAT Client

A SecureNAT client is any device configured with a default gateway address that can route Internet-bound connections through the ISA 2004 firewall. That is, the ISA firewall's role is closely related to the role of a router for outbound access. The SecureNAT client does not have a traditional client/server relationship with the ISA Server. There are three network scenarios in which the SecureNAT client is most commonly found:

- Simple
- Complex
- VPN client

A "simple network scenario" is one that has only a single subnet located behind the ISA 2004 firewall computer. For example, you have an ISA 2004 firewall sitting at the edge of the network with an interface directly connected to the Internet and a second interface connected to the Internal network. All the machines behind the ISA 2004 firewall are on a single subnet (for example, 10.0.0.0/8). There are no routers on the Internal network. Figure 5.1 depicts a typical simple network scenario.

Figure 5.1 SecureNAT Simple Network Scenario

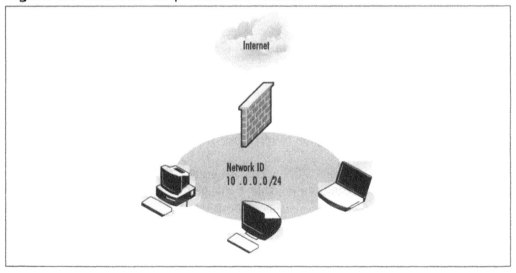

In the simple network scenario, the default gateway of the SecureNAT client is configured as the IP address of the Internal interface of the ISA 2004 firewall. You can manually configure the default gateway address, or you can use DHCP to automatically assign addresses to the SecureNAT clients. The DHCP server can be on the ISA 2004 firewall itself, or it can be located on a separate machine on the Internal network.

In the "complex network scenario," the Internal network consists of multiple network IDs that are managed by a router or series of routers or layer 3 switch(s). In the case of the complex network, the default gateway address assigned to each SecureNAT client depends on the location of the SecureNAT client computer. The gateway address for the SecureNAT client will be a router that allows the SecureNAT client access to other networks within the organization, as well as the Internet. The routing infrastructure must be configured to support the SecureNAT client so that Internet-bound requests are forwarded to the Internal interface of the ISA 2004 firewall. Figure 5.2 depicts the SecureNAT complex network scenario.

Figure 5.2 SecureNAT Complex Network Scenario

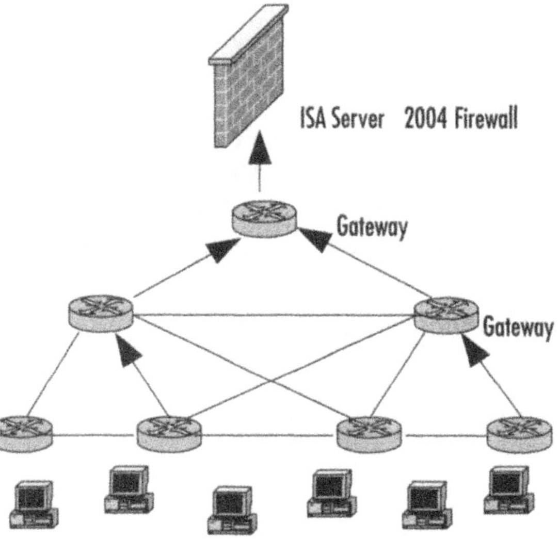

The "VPN client scenario" applies to machines that have created a VPN connection with the ISA 2004 firewall.

With ISA Server 2000, when a VPN client computer establishes a connection with the VPN server, the VPN client's routing table is changed so that the default gateway is an address on the VPN server. Unless changes are made to the default client configuration, the client will not be able to connect to resources on the Internet while connected to the ISA Server 2000 VPN server.

It was possible to configure the ISA Server 2000 VPN client as a Firewall or Web Proxy client and allow the VPN client access to the Internet through the ISA Server 2000 firewall. Alternatively, the ISA Server 2000 VPN client could be configured to allow split tunneling.

In contrast to ISA Server 2000, the ISA 2004 VPN server does not require you to configure the VPN clients to be Firewall or Web Proxy clients in order to access the Internet through the same ISA 2004 VPN server to which they connect. Because the VPN clients are not configured as Web Proxy or Firewall clients, they are de facto

SecureNAT clients. This allows VPN users to access the corporate network via the VPN connection, while at the same time allowing them to access the Internet via their connection to the ISA firewall, and removes the risks inherent in split tunneling.

Note that you do not need to have a deep understanding of VPN client routing table configuration or how different versions of the Windows VPN client handle default route assignments. Just remember that when a VPN client creates a VPN connection with the ISA 2004 firewall/VPN server, that client will be able to connect to the Internet via the ISA 2004 firewall based on access rules that you configure.

WARNING!

Split tunneling represents a significant security risk and should never be enabled on your VPN clients. ISA 2004 supports VPN client SecureNAT connections to the Internet through the same ISA 2004 firewall to which they connect, and thus, obviates the need for split tunneling. In addition, the ISA 2004 firewall enhances the SecureNAT client support for VPN clients by enabling user/group-based access controls for VPN clients. We will discuss the issue of split tunneling and the risks it imposes, in addition to the enhanced SecureNAT client support for VPN clients, in detail in **Chapter 8 Remote Access and Site-to-Site Virtual Private Networking.**

SecureNAT Client Limitations

While SecureNAT clients are the simplest ISA 2004 client types to configure, they are also the least capable and the least secure of the three ISA 2004 client types. Limitations of the SecureNAT client include:

- Inability to authenticate with the firewall for strong user/group-based access control

- Inability to take advantage of complex protocols without the aid of an application filter

- Dependency on the routing infrastructure to access the Internet

- Requirement for a Protocol Definition to be configured on the ISA 2004 firewall to support connections made through the ISA 2004 firewall

SecureNAT clients do not send credentials to the ISA 2004 firewall because, in order for credentials to be sent to the firewall, there must be a client software component configured to send them. The basic TCP/IP protocol stack does not provide for user authentication and requires an application component to send user credentials.

The Firewall and Web Proxy clients can send user credentials, but the SecureNAT client cannot. The Firewall client uses the Firewall client software to send user credentials, and Web browsers configured to use the ISA 2004 firewall as a Web Proxy have the built-in capability to send user credentials. You cannot use strong user/group-based outbound access controls for machines configured *only* as SecureNAT clients.

SecureNAT clients cannot connect to the Internet (or any other location through the ISA 2004 firewall) using complex protocols without the aid of an application filter installed on the ISA firewall. A complex protocol is one that requires multiple primary or secondary connections. A classic case of a complex protocol would be FTP standard (Port) mode connections.

When the standard or port mode FTP client establishes a connection to the FTP server, the initial connection (the "control channel") is established on TCP port 21. The FTP client and server then negotiate a port number on which the FTP client can receive the data (the file to download), and the FTP server returns the data from its own TCP port 20 to the negotiated port. This inbound connection is a *new* primary connection request and not represent a response to the primary outbound connection made by the FTP client when it established the control channel session.

The firewall must be aware of the communications going on between the FTP standard mode client and the FTP server so that the correct ports are available for the new inbound connection request to the ISA 2004 firewall. This is accomplished on ISA 2004 via its intelligent FTP Access Application Filter. Figure 5.3 depicts the FTP standard mode client and server communications.

Figure 5.3 FTP Standard Mode Client/Server Communications

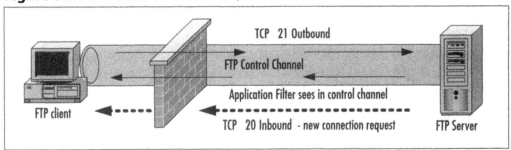

This SecureNAT limitation regarding complex protocols is especially problematic when it comes to Internet games and voice/video applications. These applications typically require multiple inbound and outbound primary connections. The SecureNAT client will not be able to use these applications unless there are specific application filters on the firewall to support them. In contrast, the Firewall client is easily able to handle applications requiring multiple inbound and outbound primary connections without installing anything extra on the firewall.

Of course, there's an exception to every rule, and here's the exception to the statement above: Complex protocol support for SecureNAT clients is possible *if* the application installed on the SecureNAT client is designed to work with a SOCKS proxy. In this case, the application is explicitly configured to communicate with the ISA 2004 firewall's SOCKS 4 application filter. The SOCKS 4 application filter can manage the connections on behalf of the SecureNAT client machine's application.

Warning!

Although SecureNAT clients running SOCKS 4 applications might be able to support complex protocols for the application configured to use the SOCKS proxy, the SOCKS proxy will *not* enable the client to benefit from user/group authentication. The SOCKS 4 proxy application filter on the ISA 2004 firewall does not accept user credentials that would enable user/group-based access control. However, if you require user authentication for SOCKS clients, you might want to consider COrnerpost Software's Surrogate Socket 5.0 application (http://www.cornerpostsw.com/surrogatesocket50/surrogatesocket50.asp).

The SecureNAT client is dependent on the organization's routing infrastructure. Unlike the Firewall and Web Proxy clients, which send their Internet connection requests directly to the ISA 2004 firewall (and thus, only need to know the route to the Internal interface of the ISA 2004 firewall machine), the SecureNAT client depends on the routing infrastructure to forward Internet-bound requests to the Internal interface of the ISA 2004 firewall. If the connection encounters a router in the path that does not route Internet-bound connections through the ISA 2004 firewall, the connection attempt will fail.

Tip

There must be a protocol definition created on the ISA 2004 firewall for each protocol you want the SecureNAT client to access. This is true even when you configure an Access Rule that allows the SecureNAT client access to all protocols. For the SecureNAT client, "all protocols" means all protocols for which there is a Protocol Definition. This is in contrast to the Firewall client, where an Access Rule specifying all protocols means all TCP and UDP protocols, regardless of whether or not there is a Protocol Definition for a particular protocol.

Because of the limitations of SecureNAT, a computer should only be configured as a SecureNAT client when at least one of the following conditions exists:

- The machine does not support Firewall client software (non-Windows clients) and requires protocol support outside of what the Web Proxy client can provide (protocols other than HTTP/HTTPS and FTP upload).

- The machine requires outbound access to the ICMP and PPTP.

- For administrative or political reasons, you cannot install the Firewall client on machines requiring protocol access outside of that provided by the Web Proxy client configuration.

Disadvantages of the SecureNAT configuration are summarized in Table 5.2.

Table 5.2 Disadvantages of the SecureNAT Client Configuration

Disadvantage	Implication
Inability to authenticate with the ISA 2004 firewall	The SecureNAT client is unable to send user credentials (user name and password) to the ISA 2004 firewall. This prevents the use of strong user/group-based outbound access control over Internet access. The only outbound access control available for SecureNAT clients is based on a client source IP address.
Inability to use complex protocols	Complex protocols require multiple primary and/or secondary connections. Internet games, voice/video applications, and instant messaging applications often require complex protocol support. The SecureNAT client cannot access Internet applications using complex protocols without the assistance of an application filter installed on the ISA 2004 firewall machine. The only exception to this is when the application installed on the SecureNAT client is configured to support SOCKS proxies. The ISA 2004 firewall includes a built-in SOCKS 4 filter.
Dependency on the existing network routing infrastructure	The SecureNAT client does not forward connections directly to the ISA 2004 firewall. Instead, it depends on the organization's routing infrastructure. Each router along the path from the SecureNAT client to the ISA 2004 firewall must be aware that the path to the Internet is through the ISA 2004 firewall. This may require reconfiguring network routers with new gateways of last resort (default gateways).
User information is not included in the Firewall and Web Proxy logs	The user name is only included in Firewall and Web Proxy logs when a client sends that information to the ISA firewall. A client piece is *always* required to send user information to the firewall since there are no provisions in the layer 1 through 6 headers to provide this information. Only the Firewall client and Web Proxy client configurations can send user information to the ISA firewall and have this information included in the log files. SecureNAT client connections allow for logging of the source IP address, but user information is never recorded for machines configured as *only* SecureNAT clients.

SecureNAT Client Advantages

Despite the limitations discussed in the foregoing section, you should not conclude that the SecureNAT client is all bad. In fact, some of the SecureNAT client's weaknesses also represent the SecureNAT client's strengths. Advantages of the SecureNAT client configuration include:

- Support for non-Windows client operating systems
- Support for non-TCP/UDP protocols (for example PPTP[GRE] and ICMP)
- No requirement for client software installation or configuration

The primary purpose of the SecureNAT client configuration is to enable non-Microsoft operating systems access to a broader range of protocols than is supported by the Web Proxy client configuration. The Firewall client works only with Windows operating systems. Without the SecureNAT client configuration, the only protocols that would be available to non-Microsoft operating systems are those provided by the Web Proxy client configuration (HTTP/HTTPS and FTP download).

The SecureNAT client has an important use for Microsoft operating systems, as well. The Firewall client software intercepts outbound TCP and UDP connections established by Winsock applications and forwards them to the ISA 2004 firewall. However, the Firewall client software does not intercept non-TCP/UDP communications. Networking protocols such as ICMP and GRE (used in the PPTP VPN protocol) do not use UDP or TCP as a transport protocol, and thus, are not evaluated by the Firewall client. You must configure client computers as SecureNAT clients to support outbound access through the ISA 2004 firewall using these protocols.

One significant downside of this situation is that you cannot use user/group-based access controls over which hosts can create outbound connections using non-TCP/UDP protocols. For example, you might want to allow outbound PPTP VPN connections for a specific group of users. This is not possible because PPTP requires GRE; this bypasses the Firewall client software, and therefore, no user information is passed to the ISA 2004 firewall. If you create an outbound PPTP Access Rule that requires user authentication, the connection attempt will fail. The only method available to control an outbound PPTP connection is by source IP address. We will cover this subject in more detail in Chapter 8.

NOTE

ICMP is most commonly used by the ping utility, although other utilities such as tracert also use ICMP. GRE is required if you wish to allow clients outbound access to external VPN servers using the PPTP VPN protocols. In contrast, outbound VPN clients that use the L2TP/IPSec NAT Traversal (NAT-T) protocol do not have to be configured as SecureNAT clients. L2TP/IPSec NAT-T uses only UDP ports 500 and 4500 for outbound access to L2TP/IPSec NAT-T VPN servers. Because of this, you can use the Firewall client configuration to force strong user/group-based access controls over L2TP/IPSec VPN connections.

Probably the most common reason for implementing the SecureNAT client configuration is to avoid installing or configuring client software. Firewall and network administrators are loath to install software on client computers that imposes itself on the network stack. In addition, there is a perception that significant administrative overhead is involved with installing the ISA 2004 Firewall client and configuring the Web Proxy client, although in reality, there is not.

In fact, there is an extremely low likelihood that the Firewall client software will interfere with networking components of any client software, and the administrative overhead is very small when you automate the Firewall client and Web Proxy client installation and configuration.

We will discuss how to automate client installation and configuration later in this chapter. Table 5.3 details the advantages of the SecureNAT client configuration.

Table 5.3 Advantages of the SecureNAT Client Configuration

Advantage	Implication
Provides additional protocol support for non-Windows operating systems	Non-Windows operating systems do not support the Firewall client software. If you wish to provide support for protocols other than those allowed via the Web Proxy client configuration (that is, HTTP/HTTPS/FTP download), the SecureNAT configuration is your only option for non-Windows operating system clients such as Linux, UNIX, and Macintosh.
Support for non-TCP/UDP Protocols	The SecureNAT client is the only ISA 2004 client configuration that supports non-TCP/UDP protocols. Ping, tracert, and PPTP are some of the non-TCP/UDP protocols that require the SecureNAT client configuration. Note that you cannot exert strong user/group-based access controls for non-TCP/UDP protocols because the SecureNAT client configuration does not support user authentication.
Does not require client software installation or configuration	The SecureNAT client does not require any specific software be installed or configured on the client computers. The only requirement is that the default gateway address on the client machine be configured so that Internet-bound requests are forwarded through the ISA 2004 firewall.

Continued

Table 5.3 Advantages of the SecureNAT Client Configuration

Advantage	Implication
Best configuration - for published servers	When publishing a server to the Internet, the server often needs to not only accept connections *from* Internet-based hosts, but also needs to initiate new connections. The best example is an SMTP relay configured for both inbound and outbound relay. The SMTP relay does not need to be configured as a SecureNAT client to receive inbound connections from remote SMTP servers (because you have the option to replace the original source IP address of the Internet host with the IP address of the ISA 2004 firewall). However, the SMTP relay *does* need to be configured as a SecureNAT client to send outbound mail to Internet SMTP servers. We will cover this issue in more detail in Chapter 10.

Name Resolution for SecureNAT Clients

As we discussed earlier in the context of network services support, name resolution is a critical issue not only when installing the ISA 2004 firewall software on the server, but for all types of ISA 2004 clients. Each ISA 2004 client resolves names in its own way. The SecureNAT client resolves names for hosts on the Internal and External networks using the DNS server address configured on the SecureNAT client's own network interfaces.

The fact that the SecureNAT client must be able to resolve names based on its own TCP/IP configuration can pose challenges for Internet-connected organizations that require access to resources both while connected to the corporate network and when those same hosts must leave the Internal network and connect to corporate resources from remote locations. In addition, there are significant challenges when SecureNAT clients attempt to "loop back" through the ISA 2004 firewall to access resources on the Internal or other protected networks.

SecureNAT clients must be configured to use a DNS server that can resolve both Internal network names and Internet host names. Most organizations host their own DNS servers within the confines of the corporate network. In this case, the SecureNAT client should be configured to use the Internal DNS server that can resolve Internal and Internet host names.

Name Resolution and "Looping Back" Through the ISA 2004 Firewall

Consider the example of an organization that uses the domain name *internal.net* for resources located on the Internal network behind the ISA 2004 firewall. The organization uses the same domain name to host resources for remote users and publishes those resources on the Internal network. For example, the company hosts its own Web server on the Internal network, and the IP address of that Web server on the Internal network is **192.168.1.10**.

The organization also hosts its own public DNS servers and has entered the IP address **222.222.222.1** into the DNS database for the host name www.internal.net. External users use this name, www.internal.net, to access the company's Web server. The Web server is published using ISA 2004 Web Publishing Rules and external users have no problem accessing the published Web server.

Problems arise when SecureNAT clients on the Internal network try to reach the same Web server; the connection attempts always fail. The reason for this is that the SecureNAT clients are configured to use the same DNS server that is used by the external clients to resolve the name www.internal.net. This name resolves to the public address on the external interface of the ISA 2004 firewall that is used in the Web Publishing Rule. The SecureNAT client resolves the name www.internal.net to this address and forwards the connection to the external interface of the ISA 2004 firewall. The ISA 2004 firewall then forwards the request to the Web server on the Internal network.

The Web server then responds *directly to the SecureNAT client computer.* The reason for this is that the source IP address in the request forwarded by the ISA 2004 firewall to the Web Server on the Internal network is the IP address of the SecureNAT client. This causes the Web server on the Internal network to recognize the IP address as one on its local network and respond directly to the SecureNAT client. The SecureNAT client computer drops the response from the Web server because it sent the request to the public IP address of the ISA 2004 firewall, not to the IP address of the Web server on the Internal network. The response is dropped because the SecureNAT client sees this as a response to a connection it did not request. Figure 5.4 depicts the SecureNAT client looping back through the ISA 2004 firewall.

Figure 5.4 SecureNAT "Loop Back"

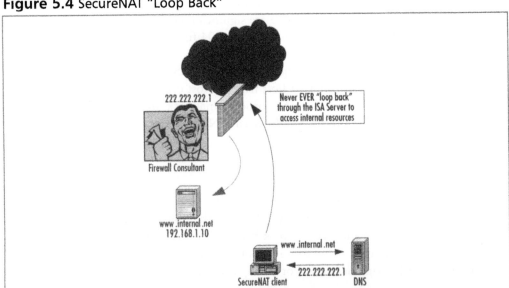

The solution to this problem is the split DNS infrastructure. In almost all cases in which the organization requires remote access to resources located on the Internal network, the split DNS infrastructure provides the solution to name resolution problems for SecureNAT and roaming clients (hosts that move between the Internal network and locations outside the corporate network).

In a split DNS infrastructure, the SecureNAT client is configured to use an Internal DNS server that resolves names for resources based on the resource's Internal network address. Remote hosts can resolve the same names, but the external hosts resolve the same names to the IP address on the external interface of the ISA 2004 firewall that publishes the resource. This prevents the SecureNAT client from looping back through the ISA 2004 firewall, and connection attempts to published servers succeed for the SecureNAT clients. Figure 5.5 demonstrates how the split DNS infrastructure solves the "looping back" issue for SecureNAT clients. Table 5.4 summarizes important DNS considerations for SecureNAT clients.

NOTE

For this reason, Web developers should never "hard code" IP addresses or names in links returned to Web users. For example, a Web developer might code a link that points to **http://192.168.1.1/info** into a Web page response to a user. Internal network clients can access this link because the IP address is that of the Web server on the Internal network, but remote access users will not be able to connect to this resource because the address is not accessible from the Internet. Many Java applications suffer from this type of poor coding, and even some Microsoft applications, such as SharePoint Portal Server (although some of these problems can be solved using the ISA 2004 firewall's Link Translator feature).

Figure 5.5 A Split DNS Solves the SecureNAT Paradox

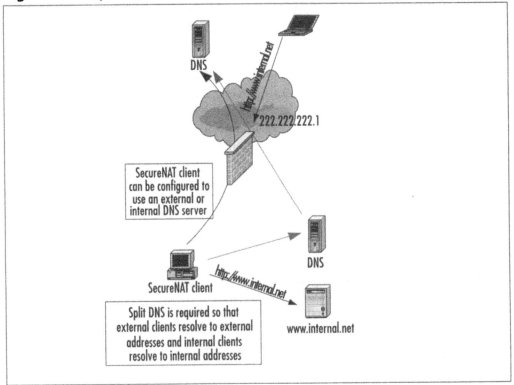

Table 5.4 DNS Considerations for SecureNAT Clients

SecureNAT DNS Consideration	Implications
Internal and external host name resolution	The SecureNAT client must be able to resolve all host names via its locally-configured DNS server address. The DNS server must be able to resolve Internal network names, as well as external Internet host names. If the DNS server the SecureNAT client is configured to use is not able to resolve local names or Internet names, the name resolution request may fail and the connection attempt will be aborted.

Continued

Table 5.4 DNS Considerations for SecureNAT Clients

SecureNAT DNS Consideration	Implications
Looping back through the ISA 2004 firewall	SecureNAT clients must not loop back through the ISA 2004 firewall to access Internal network resources. The most common situation where this occurs is when a server on the Internal network has been published to the Internet. The SecureNAT client is configured with a DNS server that resolves the name of the server to the IP address on the external interface of the ISA 2004 firewall. The SecureNAT client sends a connection request to that IP address and the connection request fails. The solution is to design and configure a split DNS infrastructure.
Organizations with Internal DNS servers	Organizations with Internal DNS servers should configure those servers to resolve both internal and external host names. The Internal DNS servers are authoritative for the Internal network names. The DNS servers should be configured to either perform recursion against Internet DNS servers or use a forwarder to resolve Internet host names. Note that an organization may elect to use different servers for local and external name resolution, but the SecureNAT clients DNS point of contact must have a mechanism in place to resolve both internal and external names.
Organizations without Internal DNS servers	Smaller organizations may not have a DNS server on the Internal network. In this case, alternate methods are used for local name resolution, such as WINS, NetBIOS broadcast name resolution, or local HOSTS files. The SecureNAT clients should be configured to use a DNS server located on the Internet (such as their ISP's DNS server) or configure a caching-only DNS server on the ISA 2004 firewall computer.

Continued

Table 5.4 DNS Considerations for SecureNAT Clients

SecureNAT DNS Consideration	Implications
SecureNAT client cannot connect to the Internet	The most common reason for SecureNAT clients failing to connect to Internet resources is a name resolution failure. Check that the SecureNAT client is configured to use a DNS server that can resolve Internet host names. You can use the **nslookup** utility to test name resolution on the SecureNAT client computer.
SecureNAT client cannot connect to servers on the Internal network	The most common reason for SecureNAT clients failing to connect to local resources using DNS host names is name resolution failure. Check that the DNS server configured on the SecureNAT client is able to resolve names on the Internal network. Note that if the SecureNAT client is configured to use an Internet-based DNS server (such as your ISP's DNS server), the SecureNAT client will not be able to resolve local DNS host names. This can be solved by configuring the SecureNAT client to use an Internal DNS server that can resolve local and Internet host names, or by using an alternate method of Internal network host name resolution, such as a local HOSTS file.
SecureNAT clients should be configured to use an Internal network DNS Server	Although small organizations may not have a DNS server responsible for name resolution on the Internal network, you should avoid using public DNS servers for your SecureNAT clients. Instead, configure the ISA 2004 firewall as a caching-only DNS server, and configure the SecureNAT clients to use the caching-only DNS server on the ISA 2004 firewall. Configure the caching-only DNS server on the ISA 2004 firewall to use a trusted DNS server, such as your ISP's DNS server, as a forwarder. This reduces the risks inherent from allowing SecureNAT clients to communicate directly with Internet DNS servers. The caching-only DNS server on the ISA 2004 firewall can be configured to prevent common DNS exploits, such as cache poisoning.

Understanding the ISA 2004 Firewall Client

The Firewall client software is an optional client piece that can be installed on any supported Windows operating system to provide enhanced security and accessibility. The Firewall client software provides the following enhancements to Windows clients:

- Allows strong user/group-based authentication for all Winsock applications using the TCP and UDP protocols

- Allows user and application information to be recorded in the ISA 2004 firewall's log files

- Provides enhanced support for network applications, including complex protocols that require secondary connections

- Provides "proxy" DNS support for Firewall client machines

- Allows you to publish servers requiring complex protocols without the aid of an application filter

- The network routing infrastructure is transparent to the Firewall client

Allows Strong User/Group-Based Authentication for All Winsock Applications Using TCP and UDP Protocols

The Firewall client software transparently sends user information to the ISA 2004 firewall. This allows you to create Access Rules that apply to users and groups and allow or deny access to any protocol, site, or content, based on a user account or group membership. This strong user/group-based outbound access control is extremely important. Not all users require the same level of access, and users should only be allowed access to protocols, sites, and content they require to do their jobs.

NOTE

The concept of allowing users access to only the protocols, sites, and content they require is based on the principle of *least privilege*. The principle of least privilege applies to both inbound and outbound access. For inbound access scenarios, Server and Web Publishing rules allow traffic from external hosts to Internal network resources in a highly controlled and monitored fashion. The same should be true for outbound access. In traditional network environments, inbound access is highly limited while users are allowed outbound access to virtually any resource they desire. This weak approach to outbound access control can put not only the corporate network at risk, but other networks as well, as Internet worms can easily traverse firewalls that do not restrict outbound access.

The Firewall client automatically sends user credentials (user name and password) to the ISA 2004 firewall. The user must be logged on with a user account that is either in the Windows Active Directory or NT domain, or the user account must be mirrored on the ISA 2004 firewall. For example, if you have an Active Directory domain, users should log on to the domain, and the ISA 2004 firewall must be a member of the domain. The ISA 2004 firewall is able to authenticate the user and allows or denies access based on the user's domain credentials.

If you do not have a Windows domain, you can still use the Firewall client software to control outbound access based on user/group. In this case, you must mirror the accounts that users log on to on their workstations to user accounts stored in the local Security Account Manager (SAM) on the ISA 2004 firewall computer.

For example, a small business does not use the Active Directory, but they do want strong outbound access control based on user/group membership. Users log on to their machine with local user accounts. You can enter the same user names and passwords on the ISA 2004 firewall, and the ISA 2004 firewall will be able to authenticate the users based on the same account information used when logging on to their local machines.

Windows 9x clients can be configured to forward domain credentials if they have the Active Directory client software installed. You can obtain the client software and installation instructions at http://support.microsoft.com/default.aspx?kbid=288358

Allows User and Application Information to be Recorded in the ISA 2004 Firewall's Log Files

A major benefit of using the Firewall client is that when the user name is sent to the ISA 2004 firewall, that user name is included in the ISA 2004 firewall's log files. This allows you to easily query the log files for usernames and obtain precise information on that user's Internet activity.

In this context, the Firewall client provides not only a high level of security by allowing you to control outbound access based on user/group accounts, but also provides a high level of accountability. Users will be less enthusiastic about sharing their account information with other users when they know that their Internet activity is being tracked based on their account name, and they are held responsible for that activity.

Provides Enhanced Support for Network Applications, Including Complex Protocols Requiring Secondary Connections

Unlike the SecureNAT client, which requires an application filter to support complex protocols requiring secondary connections, the Firewall client can support virtually any Winsock application using TCP or UDP protocols, regardless of the number of primary or secondary connections, without requiring an application filter.

The ISA 2004 firewall makes it easy for you to configure Protocol Definitions reflecting multiple primary or secondary connections and then create Access Rules based on these Protocol Definitions. This provides a significant advantage in terms of Total Cost of Ownership (TCO) because you do not need to purchase applications that are SOCKS proxy aware, and you do not need to incur the time and cost overhead involved with creating customer application filters to support "off-label" Internet applications.

Provides "Proxy" DNS Support for Firewall Client Machines

In contrast to the SecureNAT client, the Firewall client does not need to be configured with a DNS server that can resolve Internet host names. The ISA 2004 firewall can perform a "proxy" DNS function for Firewall clients.

For example, when a Firewall client sends a connection request for ftp://ftp.microsoft .com, the request is sent directly to the ISA 2004 firewall. The ISA 2004 firewall resolves the name for the Firewall client based on the DNS settings on the ISA 2004 firewall's network interface cards. The ISA 2004 firewall returns the IP address to the Firewall client machine, and the Firewall client machine sends the FTP request to the IP address for the ftp.microsoft.com FTP site. The ISA 2004 firewall also caches the results of the DNS queries it makes for Firewall clients. Unlike ISA Server 2000, which cached this information for a default period of 6 hours, the ISA 2004 firewall caches the entries for a period determined by the TTL on the DNS record. This speeds up name resolution for subsequent Firewall client connections to the same sites. Figure 5.6 shows the name resolution sequence for the Firewall client.

Figure 5.6 Firewall Name Resolution Sequence

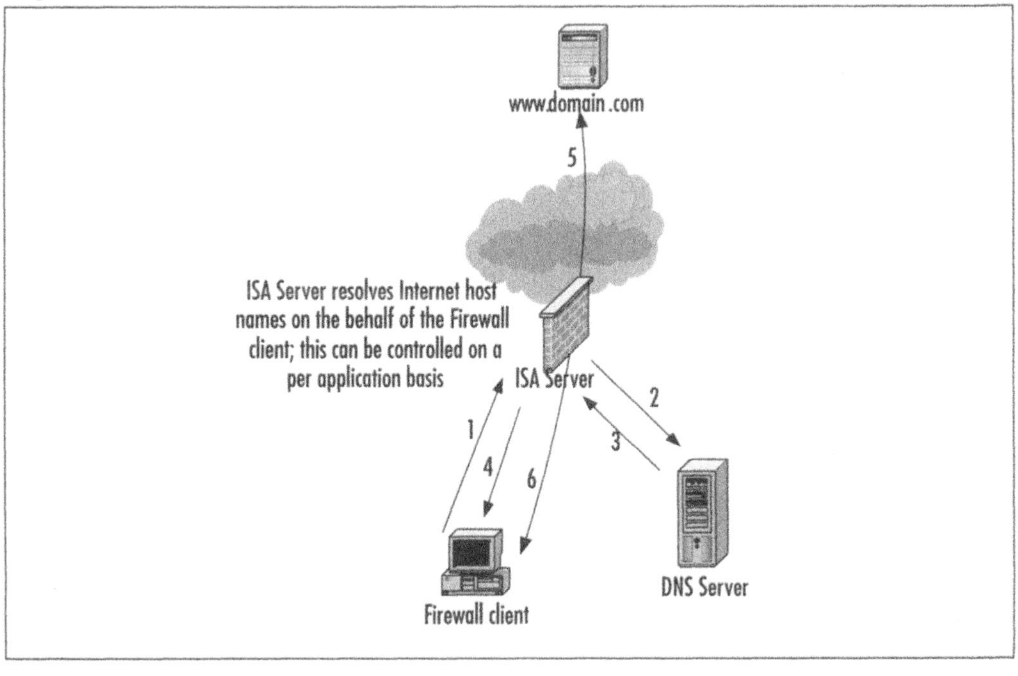

1. The Firewall client sends a request for ftp.microsoft.com.

2. The ISA 2004 firewall sends a DNS query to an Internal DNS server.

3. The DNS server resolves the name ftp.microsoft.com to its IP address and returns the result to the ISA 2004 firewall.

4. The ISA 2004 firewall returns the IP address of ftp.microsoft.com to the Firewall client that made the request.

5. The Firewall client sends a request to the IP address for ftp.microsoft.com and the connection is complete.

6. The Internet server returns requested information to the Firewall client via the Firewall client connection made to the ISA 2004 firewall.

The Network Routing Infrastructure Is Transparent to the Firewall Client

The final major benefit conferred by the Firewall client is that the routing infrastructure is virtually transparent to the Firewall client machine. In contrast to the SecureNAT client, which depends on its default gateway and the default gateway settings on routers throughout the corporate network, the Firewall client machine only needs to know the route to the IP address on the Internal interface of the ISA 2004 firewall.

The Firewall client machine "remotes" or sends requests directly to the IP address of the ISA 2004 firewall. Since corporate routers are typically aware of all routes on the corporate network, there is no need to make changes to the routing infrastructure to support Firewall client connections to the Internet. Figure 5.7 depicts the "remoting" of these connections directly to the ISA 2004 firewall computer. Table 5.5 summarizes the advantages of the Firewall client application.

Figure 5.7 Firewall Client Connections to the ISA 2004 Firewall are Independent of the Default Gateway Configurations on Interposed Routers

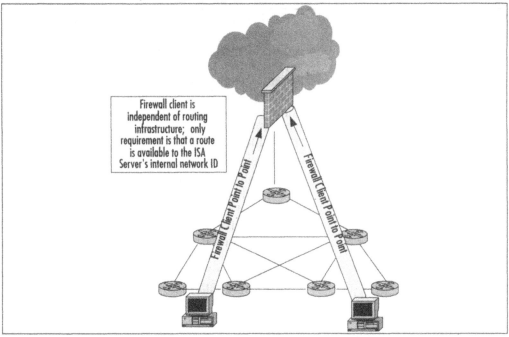

Table 5.5 Advantages of the Firewall Client Configuration

Firewall Client Advantage	Implication
Strong user/group based authentication for Winsock TCP and UDP protocols	Strong user/group based authentication for Winsock applications using TCP and UDP allows you fine-tuned granular control over outbound access and makes it possible for you to implement the principle of least privilege, which protects not only your own network, but other corporations' networks as well.
User name and application information is saved in the ISA 2004 firewall's logs	While strong user/group-based access controls increase the security the firewall provides for your network, user name and application name information saved in the ISA 2004 firewall's logs increases accountability and enables you to easily research what sites, protocols, and applications any user running the Firewall client software has accessed.

Continued

Table 5.5 Advantages of the Firewall Client Configuration

Firewall Client Advantage	Implication
Enhanced support for network applications and protocols	The Firewall client can access virtually any TCP or UDP-based protocol, even those used by complex protocols that require multiple primary and/or secondary connections. In contrast, the SecureNAT client requires an application filter on the ISA 2004 firewall to support complex protocols. The overall effect is that the Firewall client reduces the TCO of the ISA 2004 firewall solution.
Proxy DNS support for Firewall clients	The ISA 2004 firewall can resolve names on behalf of Firewall clients. This offloads the Internet host name resolution responsibility from the Firewall client computer and allows the ISA 2004 firewall to keep a DNS cache of recent name resolution requests. This DNS proxy feature also enhances the security configuration for Firewall clients because it eliminates the requirement that the Firewall client be configured to use a public DNS server to resolve Internet host names.
Enables publishing servers that require a complex networking protocol	Web and Server Publishing Rules support simple protocols, with the exception of those that have an application installed on the ISA 2004 firewall, such as the FTP Access application filter. You can install Firewall client software on a published server to support complex protocols, such as those that might be required if you wished to run a game server on your network. It is important to note the Microsoft no longer officially supports this configuration and they recommend that you have a C++ programmer code an application filter to support your application.
The network routing infrastructure is virtually transparent to the firewall client	Unlike the SecureNAT client, which relies on the organization's routing infrastructure to use the ISA 2004 firewall as its Internet access firewall, the Firewall client only needs to know the route to the IP address on the Internal interface of the ISA 2004 firewall. This significantly reduces the administrative overhead required to support the Firewall client versus the SecureNAT client.

How the Firewall Client Works

The details of how the Firewall client software actually works are not fully documented in the Microsoft literature. In fact, if you do a network trace of Firewall client communications using the Microsoft Network Monitor, you'll see that the Network Monitoring is unable to decode the Firewall client communications. However, Ethereal does have a rudimentary Firewall client filter you can use (www.ethereal.com).

What we do know is that the ISA 2004 Firewall client, unlike previous versions, uses only TCP 1745 for the Firewall client *Control Channel*. Over this control channel, the Firewall client communicates directly with the ISA 2004 firewall service to perform name resolution and network application-specific commands (such as those used by FTP and Telnet). The firewall service uses the information gained through the control channel and sets up a connection between the Firewall client and the destination server on the Internet. The ISA firewall *proxies* the connection between the Firewall client and the destination server.

> **NOTE**
>
> The Firewall client only establishes a control channel connection when connecting to resources not located on the Internal network.

In ISA Server 2000, the Internal network was defined by the Local Address Table (LAT). The ISA 2004 firewall does not use a LAT because of its enhanced multinetworking capabilities. Nevertheless, the Firewall client must have some mechanism in place to determine which communications should be sent to the firewall service on the ISA 2004 firewall and which should be sent directly to the destination host with which the Firewall client wants to communicate.

The Firewall client solves this problem using addresses defined by the **Internal Network**. The internal network for any specific Firewall client consists of all the addresses reachable from the network interface that is connected to the Firewall client's own network. This situation gets interesting on a multihomed ISA 2004 firewall that has multiple internal networks associated with different network adapters. In general, all hosts located behind the same network adapter (regardless of network ID) are considered part of the same internal network and all communications between hosts on the same internal network should bypass the Firewall client.

Addresses for the Internal network are defined during installation of the ISA 2004 firewall software, but you can create other "Internal" networks as required.

> **ISA 2004 SECURITY ALERT**
>
> You may have multiple interfaces on the same ISA 2004 firewall computer. However, only a single network may have the name **Internal**. The Internal network consists of a group of machines that have an implicit trust in each other (at least enough trust to not require a network firewall to control communica-

tions between them). You can have multiple internal networks, but additional internal networks cannot be included in the Internal address range of another Internal network.

This means you cannot use the centrally-configured network address range configured for the Internal network and additional Internal networks to bypass the Firewall client when communicating between Internal networks connected to the ISA 2004 firewall via different network interfaces. However, the centralized configuration of the Firewall client can be done per network, so you can control the Firewall client settings on a per network basis. This allows you a measure of control over how the Firewall client configuration settings are managed on each network. However, this solution does not help in the *network within a network scenario*, where there are multiple network IDs located behind the same network interface card.

In the network within the network scenario, you can use a Local LAT (locallat.txt) file to override the centralized Internal network settings. For more information on the ISA 2004 firewall's concept of the Internal network, please see Chapter 4.

The most significant improvement the ISA 2004 Firewall client has over previous versions of the Firewall client (Winsock Proxy Client 2.0 and ISA Server 2000) is that you now have the option to use an encrypted channel between the Firewall client and the ISA 2004 firewall.

Remember, the Firewall client sends user credentials transparently to the ISA 2004 firewall. The ISA 2004 Firewall client encrypts the channel so that user credentials will not be intercepted by someone who may be "sniffing" the network with a network analyzer (such as Microsoft Network Monitor or Ethereal). Note that you do have the option of configuring the ISA 2004 firewall to allow both secure encrypted and non-encrypted control channel communications.

For a very thorough empirical study on how the Firewall client application works with the firewall service in ISA Server 2000, check out Stefaan Pouseele's article **Understanding the Firewall Client Control Channel** at: www.isaserver.org/articles/Understanding_the_Firewall_Client_Control_Channel .html.

NOTE

If Internet Protocol security (IPSec) transport mode is enabled for a network so that the Firewall client machine uses IPSec transport mode to connect to the ISA 2004 firewall, you may experience unusual and unpredictable connectivity issues. If Firewall clients in the network do not behave as expected, disable **IP routing** at the ISA 2004 firewall console. In the **Microsoft Internet Security and Acceleration Server 2004** management console, expand the server, and then expand the **Configuration** node; click the **General** node. In the details pane, click **Define IP Preferences**. On the **IP Routing** tab, verify that the **Enable IP Routing** check box is *not* selected. Note that disabling **IP Routing** can significantly degrade the performance of your SecureNAT clients

Installing the Firewall Client Share

The Firewall client share contains the installation files for the Firewall client. Regardless of the method you use to distribute the Firewall client, you must install the Firewall client share on either the ISA 2004 firewall or a file server on the Internal network. We recommend that you do not install the Firewall client installation share on the ISA 2004 firewall.

When the Firewall client share is installed on the ISA 2004 firewall, a Firewall System Policy Rule (a type of Access Rule that is processed before using defined Access Rules) is created that allows a number of potentially risky protocols access to the firewall machine. These protocols include:

- Microsoft Common Internet File System (CIFS) (TCP)
- Microsoft CIFS (UDP)
- NetBIOS Datagram
- NetBIOS Name Service
- NetBIOS Session

In addition, File and Printer Sharing must be enabled on the Internal interface. These Microsoft File and Printer sharing services and protocols, as well as the Client for Microsoft Networks service, can pose a significant risk to the ISA 2004 firewall and should be disabled, if at all possible, on all ISA 2004 network interfaces. You can disable these services and still make the Firewall client share available to network users by installing the Firewall client share on another machine on the corporate network.

Do the following to install the Firewall client share on a file server on the Internal network:

1. Place the ISA 2004 CD into the CD tray on the file server, and let the **Autorun** menu appear. Click **Install ISA Server 2004**.

2. Click **Next** on the Welcome to the Installation Wizard for Microsoft ISA 2004 page.

3. Select **I accept the terms in the license agreement** and click **Next**.

4. Enter your **User Name**, **Organization** and **Product Serial Number** in the text boxes provided. Click **Next**.

5. On the Setup Type page, select **Custom** and click **Next**.

6. Click the **Firewall Services** icon, and click **This feature will not be available**. Click the **ISA Server Management** icon, and click **This feature will not be available**. Click the **Firewall Client Installation Share** icon, and click **This feature, and all subfeatures, will be installed on local hard drive** (see Figure 5.8). Click **Next**.

Figure 5.8 Installing the Firewall Client Installation Files

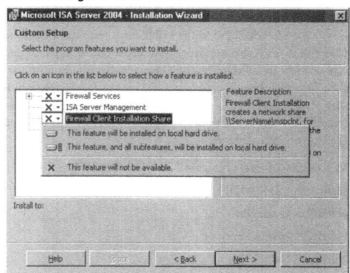

7. Click **Install** on the **Ready to Install the Program** page.

8. Click **Finish** on the **Installation Wizard Completed** page.

9. Close the **Autorun** page.

The Firewall client installation share is installed in the default local path **<Program Files>\ \Microsoft ISA Server\clients** with a share name of **mspclnt**. The default **Share Permissions** on the folder is **Everyone Read**. The default NTFS permissions on the share are:

- **Administrators** Full Control
- **Authenticated Users** Read & Execute, List Folder Contents and Read
- **System** Full Control

Installing the Firewall Client

There are a number of methods you can use to install the Firewall client software. These include:

- Using an SMB/CIFS connection to a share on a file server
- Active Directory Group Policy Software Management
- Silent Installation Script
- Systems Management Server (SMS)

In this section, we will cover the manual installation of the Firewall client. Users who choose this method of installing the Firewall client software must be local administrators on the machine on which they install the software.

For example, if the machine is a laptop computer that is also a member of the corporate domain, make sure the user has a local account on the laptop that is a member of the Administrators group. Have the user log off the domain and log on to the local computer. The user can then connect to the Firewall client share on the network file server if the local user account has the same name and password as a domain account (assuming that the file server belongs to the domain). The user may need to enter network credentials when connecting to the File server if the laptop's local account the user is currently logged into is not mirrored on the file server or in the Active Directory (if the file server and the user are members of the same Active Directory domain).

All users of the computer have access to the Firewall client software after it is installed. That means the user can log off from the local account and log back in with domain credentials and still use the Firewall client software. Note that the Web Proxy settings are not applied to all user accounts, so subsequent users will need to use the Firewall client applications to automatically configure their browsers. We will cover that procedure later in this chapter.

If you do not allow your users to be members of the Administrators group on their local machines, you must use one of the automated approaches to install the Firewall client software *before* the user logs on. You can use Active Directory Group Policy Software Assignment or Systems Management Server (SMS) to accomplish this task.

Some things to take note of regarding installation of the Firewall client software:

- Do **not** install the Firewall client software on the ISA 2004 firewall machine.

- Do **not** install the Firewall client software on a domain controller or other network servers. The only exception to this rule is when you must publish a server that requires complex protocol support. For example, many game servers require multiple primary and secondary connections. In this case, the Firewall client must be installed on the published server

- The Firewall client software begins working immediately after installation is complete. You do not need to restart the computer.

- You can install the Firewall client on any version of Windows (except Windows 95) as long as Internet Explorer 5.0 is installed.

Perform the following steps to install the Firewall client software from a file share on the Internal network:

1. Click **Start** and then click **Run**.

2. In the **Run** dialog box, enter **\\FILESERVER\mspclnt\setup** (where FILE-SERVER is the name of the ISA 2004 firewall) and click **OK**.

3. Click **Next** on the **Welcome to the Install Wizard for Microsoft Firewall Client** page.

4. Click **Next** on the **Destination Folder** page.

5. On the **ISA Server Computer Selection** page, select **Connect to this ISA Server computer**, and enter **isafirewall.msfirewall.org** (where

isafirewall.msfirewall.org is the name of the 2004 firewall) in the text box below
it. Click **Next**.

6. Click **Install** on the **Ready to Install the Program** page.

7. Click **Finish** on the **Install the Wizard Completed** page.

8. You will see the Firewall client icon in the system tray (see Figure 5.9). If there
    is an active TCP or UDP connection to a network that is not the Internal net-
    work, the icon will have a GREEN up-pointing arrow.

Figure 5.9 Firewall Client Icon

10:47 AM

TIP

VPN clients can install the Firewall client software while connected to the network using a VPN client connection.

ISA 2004 SECURITY ALERT

Settings you specify during setup of the Firewall client apply to all user accounts
on the client computer. Changes made in the Firewall Client dialog box on the
Firewall client machine after installation are only applied to the logged-on user
account. Changes are not applied to other users or to applications running under
system accounts. In order to make a change in Firewall Client settings for all
accounts after installation is complete, modify settings in the *Common.ini* and
Management.ini files. These files are located in the **Documents and Settings\All
Users\Local Settings\Application Data\Microsoft\Firewall Client 2004** folder.
You must restart the Firewall Client (FwcAgent) service on computers running
Windows Server 2003, Windows XP, Windows 2000, and Windows NT after modifying Common.ini. You must restart the computer on computers running
Windows 9x. Changes to Management.ini do not require a service or computer
restart. We will discuss the Management.ini and Common.ini configuration files in
more detail later in this section.

Firewall Client Configuration

There are two places where you can configure the Firewall client software: at the
Microsoft Internet Security and Acceleration Server 2004 management console and
at the Firewall client computer itself. Configuration changes made in the **Microsoft**

Internet Security and Acceleration Server 2004 management console apply to all Firewall client computers, and those made at the client apply only to that individual client.

Centralized Configuration Options at the ISA 2004 Firewall Computer

Centralized Firewall client configuration options are carried out in the **Microsoft Internet Security and Acceleration Server 2004** management console. Firewall client configuration is done for each network configured to support Firewall client connections. Firewall client connections can be made from:

- Perimeter Networks
- Internal Networks

All other network types do not support Firewall client connections. When Firewall client connections are enabled for a network, incoming connections to the ISA 2004 firewall to TCP and UDP ports 1745 are enabled to the interface connected to that network.

You can reach the Firewall client configuration interface by opening the **Microsoft Internet Security and Acceleration Server 2004** management console, expanding the server name and then expanding the **Configuration** node. In the **Configuration** node, click the **Networks** node, and then click the **Networks** tab in the **Details** pane. Right click on the **Internal** network and click **Properties**.

On the **Firewall Client** tab, put a checkmark in the **Enable Firewall client support for this network** check box, as shown in Figure 5.10. In the **Firewall client configuration** frame, enter the name of the ISA 2004 firewall computer in the **ISA Server name or IP address** text box.

Figure 5.10 The Internal Network Properties Dialog Box

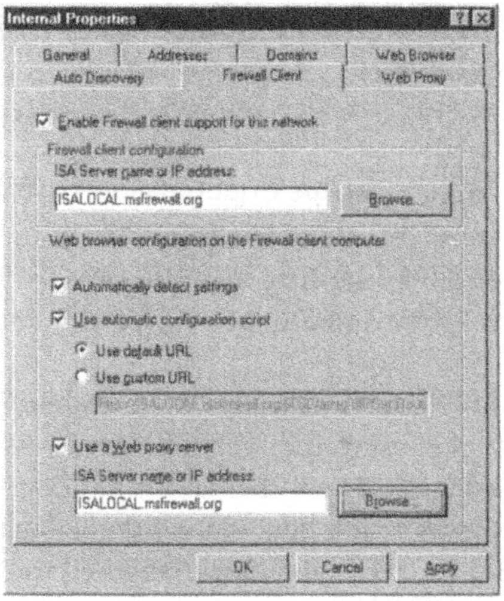

The default setting is to use the computer (also known as the "NetBIOS" name). However, you should replace the NetBIOS name with the fully-qualified domain name (FQDN) of the ISA 2004 firewall. When you replace the computer name with the FQDN, the Firewall client machines can use the DNS queries to correctly resolve the name of the ISA 2004 firewall. This will avoid one of the most common troubleshooting issues with Firewall client connectivity.

Make sure there is an entry for this name in your Internal network's DNS server. By default, all the interfaces on the ISA 2004 firewall will automatically register their names in the DNS, but if your DNS server does not support dynamic updates, you'll need to manually enter a Host (A) record for the ISA 2004 firewall.

We recommend that you disable automatic DNS registration for all interfaces on the ISA 2004 firewall. There reason for this is that you may want to enable Firewall client support for multiple internal or perimeter network interfaces on the ISA 2004 firewall. In this example, you would create a manual entry for each interface in the DNS. For example, the Internal network interface could be reached using the name *isainternal.msfirewall.org* and the perimeter network interface could be reached using the name *isaperimeter.msfirewall.org*. All you need to do is manually create Host (A) entries in your DNS to support this configuration.

NOTE

The most common problem ISA 2004 administrators encounter with the Firewall client is name resolution of the ISA 2004 firewall. If you do not have a DNS server on your network, use the IP address of the ISA 2004 firewall in the **ISA Server name or IP address** text box. Never use the default name that the software automatically enters into the text box; using the default name is a very common reason for Firewall client failures.

The Web Proxy client configuration settings are available in the **Web browser configuration on the Firewall client computer** frame. These settings will be automatically applied to the Web browser *when the Firewall client is installed*. Note that you can change the settings later and the Web browsers will automatically update themselves with the new settings.

The **Automatically detect settings** option allows the Web browser to automatically detect the Web Proxy service and configure itself based on the settings you configure on the **Web Browser** tab of the **Internal Properties** dialog box. Note that autodetection relies on Web Proxy AutoDiscovery (WPAD) entries being placed in DNS and/or DHCP.

The **Use automatic configuration script** option allows you to assign a proxy autoconfiguration file (PAC) address to the Web browser. The Web browser will then connect to the location you specify or use the default location; the default location is on the ISA 2004 firewall itself. Note that when you use the default location, you obtain the same information you would receive if you had configured the Web browser to use the **Automatically detect settings** option.

The **Use default URL** option automatically configures the browser to connect to the ISA 2004 firewall for autoconfiguration information. You can use the **Use custom URL** option if you want to create your own PAC file that overrides the settings on the automatically-generated file at the ISA 2004 firewall. You can find more information on PAC files and proxy client autoconfiguration files in **Using Automatic Configuration and Automatic Proxy** at www.microsoft.com/ resources/documentation/ie/5/all/reskit/en-us/part5/ch21auto.mspx

The **Use a Web Proxy server** option allows you to configure the Web browser to use the ISA 2004 as its Web Proxy, but without the benefits of the autoconfiguration script. This setting provides higher Web browsing performance than the SecureNAT client configuration, but you do not benefit from the settings contained in the autoconfiguration script. The most important configuration settings in the autoconfiguration script include site names and addresses that should be used for *Direct Access*. For this reason, we recommend that you avoid this option unless you do not wish to use Direct Access to bypass the Web Proxy to access selected Web sites.

NOTE

Web Proxy client Direct Access configuration allows you to bypass the Web Proxy for selected Web sites. Some Web sites do not conform to Internet standards (Java sites are the most common offenders), and therefore, do not work properly through Web Proxy servers. You can configure these sites for Direct Access and the client machine will bypass the Web Proxy and use an alternate method (such as through the machine's SecureNAT or Firewall client configuration) to connect to the destination Web site. In order for the client to use an alternate method to connect, the client machine must be configured as a Firewall and/or SecureNAT client.

Click the **Domains** tab, as shown in Figure 5.11.

Figure 5.11 The Domains Tab

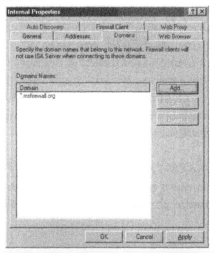

The **Domains** tab contains domains for which the Firewall client computer will not use the Firewall client software to establish a connection. The entries on the **Domains** tab have the same effect as adding machines in these domains to the Internal network (or whatever the network is named for which you are configuring Firewall client Properties). When a Firewall client makes a connection to a host that is located in one of the domains contained in the **Domains** tab, the Firewall client software is not used and the Firewall client machine attempts to connect directly to the destination host.

You can add domains by clicking the **Add** button, and enter the domain in the the **Domain Properties** dialog box, as shown in Figure 5.12.

Figure 5.12 The Domain Properties Dialog Box

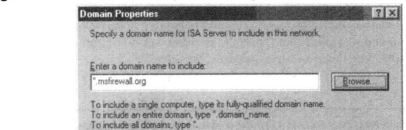

Note that you can use wildcards when specifying a domain. If you want to specify a single computer, just enter the fully-qualified domain name (FQDN) of that host. If you want to include all hosts in a single domain, then use an asterisk (★) just to the left of the leftmost period in the FQDN. If you want to avoid using the Firewall client for all domains, then just enter an asterisk. If you choose this option, the Firewall client will never be used, and the client will depend on its Web Proxy or SecureNAT client settings to connect to hosts through the ISA 2004 firewall. Click **OK** after making your entry.

You should always include all Internal network domains in the **Domains** tab, as you usually want to allow direct connections to hosts located in the same domain. This prevents clients from "looping back" throught the ISA 2004 firewall to access hosts located on the same network as the client making the request.

For example, if domain members are located on multiple subnets behind a single network interface representing a single network on the ISA 2004 firewall, you do *not* want hosts on the network to go through the ISA 2004 firewall to connect to hosts on the same network. This puts unneeded stress on the firewall, and the function of a network firewall is not to control these communications.

Enabling Support for Legacy Firewall Client/Winsock Proxy Clients

The ISA 2004 Firewall client uses a new and improved *Remote Winsock Proxy Protocol* that encrypts the communication channel between the Firewall client and the ISA 2004 firewall's Firewall service. This improves security because user credentials are transparently passed to the ISA 2004 firewall when the Firewall client makes an outbound connection request.

However, you have the option to allow non-encrypted Firewall client communications with the ISA 2004 firewall. This can provide you time to upgrade your existing Firewall client or Winsock Proxy 2.0 clients to the ISA 2004 Firewall client software.

Do the following to enable support for non-encrypted Firewall client connections from legacy Firewall/Winsock Proxy clients:

1. In the **Microsoft Internet Security and Acceleration Server 2004** management console, expand the server name, and then expand the **Configuration** node. Click on the **General** node.

2. On the **General** node, click the **Define Firewall Client Settings** link in the **Details** pane.

3. In the **Firewall Client Settings** dialog box, click the **Connection** node. Put a checkmark in the **Allow non-encrypted Firewall client connections** check box.

4. Click **Apply,** and then click **OK**.

5. Click **Apply** to save the changes and update the firewall policy.

6. Click **OK** in the **Apply New Configuration** dialog box.

If you have problems with Firewall client connections, make sure that the version of your Firewall client matches the encryption settings set on the ISA 2004 firewall. If you use legacy Firewall client software on your network, make sure that encryption is not enabled on the ISA 2004 firewall.

Client Side Firewall Client Settings

There are some configuration options available to users who have the Firewall client software installed. These options can be accessed by right-clicking on the Firewall client icon in the system tray and clicking the **Configure** command.

On the **General** tab (see Figure 5.13) of the **Microsoft Firewall Client for ISA Server 2004**, confirm that there is a checkmark in the **Enable Microsoft Firewall Client for ISA 2004** check box.

Figure 5.13 The Firewall Client Configuration Dialog box

The **Automatically detect ISA Server** option takes advantage of a WPAD entry in a DHCP or DNS server to automatically detect the location of the ISA 2004 firewall, and then automatically obtain Firewall client configuration information from the ISA 2004 firewall.

Figure 5.14 illustrates the effect of clicking **Detect Now** button.

Figure 5.14 The Detecting ISA Server Dialog Box

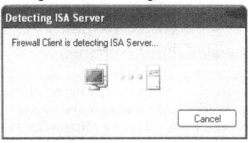

After the Firewall client finds the ISA 2004 firewall, you will see the dialog box shown in Figure 5.15.

Figure 5.15 The Detecting ISA Server Dialog Box

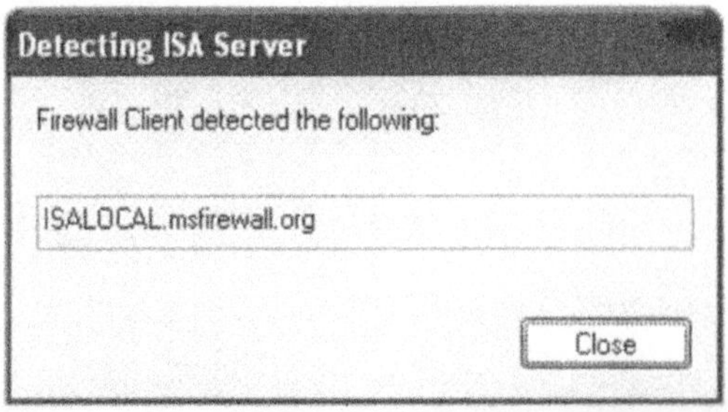

It's important to remember that autodetection will only work if you have configured a WPAD entry in a DHCP or DNS server. We will go through detailed procedures on how to configure the WPAD entries later in this chapter.

You also have the option to **Manually select ISA Server**. This option allows you to enter the IP address or DNS name of the ISA 2004 firewall and then click the **Test Server** button to find the firewall. When you enter an IP address, the client sends a request to TCP port 1745 and obtains the autoconfiguration information directly from the ISA 2004 firewall. Included in the autoconfiguration information is the name of the ISA 2004 firewall, which is listed in the **Detecting ISA Server** dialog box.

The Network Monitor trace shown in Figure 5.16 shows that a connection is made by the Firewall client and some of the information return to the Firewall client is shown in the Hex decode pane.

Figure 5.16 Firewall Client Packet Traces

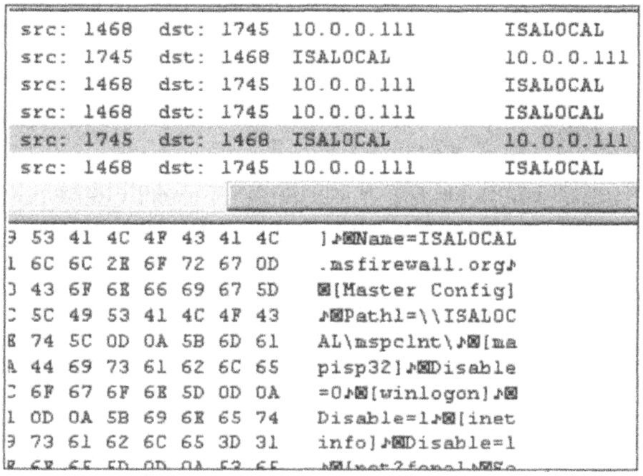

```
src: 1468  dst: 1745  10.0.0.111      ISALOCAL
src: 1745  dst: 1468  ISALOCAL        10.0.0.111
src: 1468  dst: 1745  10.0.0.111      ISALOCAL
src: 1468  dst: 1745  10.0.0.111      ISALOCAL
src: 1745  dst: 1468  ISALOCAL        10.0.0.111
src: 1468  dst: 1745  10.0.0.111      ISALOCAL


9 53 41 4C 4F 43 41 4C    ].@.Name=ISALOCAL
1 6C 6C 2E 6F 72 67 0D    .msfirewall.org.
3 43 6F 6E 66 69 67 5D    .@.[Master Config]
2 5C 49 53 41 4C 4F 43    .@.Path1=\\ISALOC
8 74 5C 0D 0A 5B 6D 61    AL\msplnt\.@.[ma
4 44 69 73 61 62 6C 65    pisp32].@.Disable
2 6F 67 6F 6E 5D 0D 0A    =0.@.[winlogon].@.
1 0D 0A 5B 69 6E 65 74    Disable=1.@.[inet
9 73 61 62 6C 65 3D 31    info].@.Disable=1
2 6E 6E 5D 0D 0A 52 6F    .@.[net2fone].@.o
```

Click on the **Web Browser** tab. Here you have the option to **Enable Web browser automatic configuration**. This option pulls information from the Web browser configuration you set earlier in the **Microsoft Internet Security and Acceleration Server 2004** management console. Users can click the **Configure Now** button, which makes it easy for users who inadvertently change the browser settings to get back to the ideal configuration with a click of a button. For this reason, you should not disable the Firewall client icon in the system tray.

TIP

You can disable the Firewall client icon in the system tray by putting a checkmark in the **Hide icon in notification area when connected to ISA Server** check box. You can automate this process by including an entry in the user's **management.ini** file, which is located in the **\Documents and Settings\user_name\Local Settings\Application Data\Microsoft\Firewall Client 2004** folder. You should include the entry as follows:

[TrayIcon]
TrayIconVisualState=1
You can use a log-on script to place this file in the user's directory. More information on Firewall client configuration file settings are included in the next section.

Firewall Client Configuration Files

The Firewall Client software adopts the centralized settings you configured by the ISA 2004 firewall. These settings determine things such as automatic Web Proxy client configuration, the ISA firewall's name, and ISA Server automatic detection and autoconfiguration. After the Firewall Client software is installed, ISA Server updates these client settings each time a client computer is restarted and every six hours after an initial refresh is made. The settings are also updated each time the user presses the **Test Server** button.

In addition to these settings, ISA firewall automatically updates the Firewall client with information about IP addresses that the client should consider local (the "Internal" network for that particular Firewall client).

For almost all Winsock applications, the default Firewall client configuration works without any further configuration. However, there may be times when you want to modify the default settings. The Firewall client can be configured for each user on the Firewall client computer. The configuration is done by making changes to .ini files, which are installed on the Firewall client computer.

You can change the default settings for all components after installation. The new configuration settings take effect only when the client configuration is refreshed.

Firewall Client Configuration .ini Files

The configuration information is stored in a set of files, which are installed on the Firewall client computer. When the Firewall client is installed, the following files (also seen in Figure 5.17) are created on the Firewall client computer:

- **common.ini**, which specifies the common configuration for all applications
- **management.ini**, which specifies Firewall client management configuration settings

Figure 5.17 Firewall Client Configuration Files

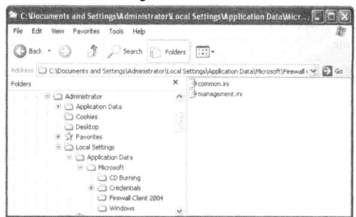

These files are created for all users who log onto the computer and may be created for each specific user on the computer. Per-user settings override the general configuration settings applying to all users of the same Firewall client computer. These files are created in different locations, depending on the operating system. Unfortunately, we only have information on where these files are located on a Windows XP computer. You can use the **Search** function for your version of Windows to determine the location of the configuration files.

On Windows XP computers the files are located at:

- **\Documents and Settings\All Users\\Local Settings\Application Data\Microsoft\Firewall Client** 2004 folder

- **\Documents and Settings***user_name***\Local Settings\Application Data\Microsoft\Firewall Client** 2004 folder

In addition to these files, the user may create another file called **Application.ini**, which specifies configuration information for specific applications.

There is an order of precedence regarding how the configuration .ini files are evaluated by the Firewall client. The order of evaluation is:

1. .ini files in the user's folder are evaluated first. Any configuration settings here are used by the Firewall client to determine how the Firewall client and applications that depend on the Firewall client will behave.

2. The Firewall client looks next in the **Documents and Settings\All Users** folder. Any *additional* configuration settings are applied. If a configuration setting specified contradicts the user-specific settings, it is ignored. The settings in the user's folder always take precedence.

3. The Firewall client detects the ISA Server computer to which it should connect and retrieves settings from the ISA 2004 firewall machine.

4. After retrieving the settings from the ISA 2004 firewall, the Firewall client examines the server-level settings. Any configuration settings specified on ISA Server are applied. If a configuration setting contradicts the user-specific or computer-specific settings, it is ignored.

Advanced Firewall Client Settings

The user on the Firewall client computer can create and modify the Firewall client configuration files and fine-tune the Firewall client behavior. The *common.ini* file, which is created when the Firewall client is installed, specifies the common configuration for all applications. The *application.ini* file controls configuration settings for applications on the client machine.

These files can be created for all users logged on to the computer and may be created for individual users on the computer. Individual user settings override settings that apply to all users of the computer. You can also use the **Microsoft Internet Security and Acceleration Server 2004** management console to modify the Firewall client configuration settings.

Table 5.6 lists entries you can include when configuring the Firewall client application settings. The first column lists the keys that can be included in the configuration files. The second column describes the values to which the keys can be set.

Be aware that some settings can be configured *only on the Firewall client* computer and not via the **Microsoft Internet Security and Acceleration Server 2004** management console.

Table 5.6 Firewall Client Configuration File Settings

Entry	Description
ServerName	Specifies the name of the ISA Server computer to which the Firewall client should connect.
Disable	Possible values: 0 or 1. When the value is set to 1, the Firewall client application is disabled for the specific client application.
DisableEx	Possible values: 0 or 1. When the value is set to 1, the Firewall client application is disabled for the specific client application. Applies only to the Firewall client for ISA 2004. When set, overrides the Disable setting.
Autodetection	(Can be set only on the Firewall client computer.) Possible values: 0 or 1. When the value is set to 1, the Firewall client application automatically finds the ISA Server computer to which it should connect.

Continued

Table 5.6 Firewall Client Configuration File Settings

Entry	Description
NameResolution	Possible values: L or R. By default, dotted decimal notation or Internet domain names are redirected to the ISA Server computer for name resolution and all other names are resolved on the local computer. When the value is set to R, all names are redirected to the ISA Server computer for resolution. When the value is set to L, all names are resolved on the local computer.
LocalBindTcpPorts	Specifies a Transmission Control Protocol (TCP) port, list, or range that is bound locally.
LocalBindUdpPorts	Specifies a User Datagram Protocol (UDP) port, list, or range that is bound locally.
RemoteBindTcpPorts	Specifies a TCP port, list, or range that is bound remotely.
RemoteBindUdpPorts	Specifies a UDP port, list, or range that is bound remotely.
ServerBindTcpPorts	Specifies a TCP port, list, or range for all ports that should accept more than one connection.
Persistent	Possible values: 0 or 1. When the value is set to 1, a specific server state can be maintained on the ISA Server computer if a service is stopped and restarted and if the server is not responding. The client sends a keep-alive message to the server periodically during an active session. If the server is not responding, the client tries to restore the state of the bound and listening sockets upon server restart.
ForceCredentials	(Can be set only on the Firewall Client computer.) Used when running a Windows service or server application as a Firewall Client application. When the value is set to 1, it forces the use of alternate user authentication credentials that are stored locally on the computer that is running the service. The user credentials are stored on the client computer using the Credtool.exe application that is provided with the Firewall Client software. User credentials must reference a user account that can be authenticated by ISA Server, either local to ISA Server or in a domain trusted by ISA Server. The user account is normally set not to expire. Otherwise, user credentials need to be renewed each time the account expires.

Continued

Table 5.6 Firewall Client Configuration File Settings

Entry	Description
NameResolutionForLocalHost	Possible values are L (default), P, or E. Used to specify how the local (client) computer name is resolved, when the gethostbyname API is called. The LocalHost computer name is resolved by calling the Winsock API function gethostbyname() using the LocalHost string, an empty string, or a NULL string pointer. Winsock applications call gethostbyname(LocalHost) to find their local IP address and send it to an Internet server. When this option is set to L, gethostbyname() returns the IP addresses of the local host computer. When this option is set to P, gethostbyname() returns the IP addresses of the ISA Server computer. When this option is set to E, gethostbyname() returns only the external IP addresses of the ISA Server computer—those IP addresses that are not in the local address table.
ControlChannel	Possible values: Wsp.udp or Wsp.tcp (default). Specifies the type of control channel used.
EnableRouteMode	Possible values are 0 and 1 (default). When EnableRouteMode is set to 1 and a route relationship is configured between the Firewall Client computer and the requested destination, then the IP address of the Firewall client is used as the source address. When the value is set to 0, the IP address of the ISA Server computer is used. This flag does not apply to older versions of Firewall client.

ISA 2004 Unsolved Mysteries

ISA 2004 and the official Microsoft stance on this issue is that Firewall client publishing is not supported. We will keep you up to date on any information we receive on this and publish workarounds when available.

You will also discover that the Firewall client settings you configure on the ISA 2004 firewall are not stored in the Firewall client configuration files located on the Firewall client machine. This is in contrast to how Firewall client configuration information was stored on ISA Server 2000 Firewall clients. The Firewall client configuration information is stored in memory and is not written to the hard disk. The reason for this, and why it is not documented, is an ISA 2004 Unsolved Mystery.

Firewall Client Configuration at the ISA 2004 Firewall

While the configuration files stored at the local Firewall client machine remain a bit of a mystery at the time we write this book, the centralized configuration of the Firewall client done at the **Microsoft Internet Security and Acceleration Server 2004** management console remains as useful as it was in ISA Server 2000. You can access the centralized Firewall client configuration interface by opening the **Microsoft Internet Security and Acceleration Server 2004** management console, then expanding the server name and the **Configuration** node. Click on the **General** node, and then click the **Define Firewall Client Settings** link.

Figure 5.18 The Define Firewall Client Settings link

Click the **Application Settings** tab. A list of the built-in Firewall client application settings is shown in Figure 5.19.

Figure 5.19 The Firewall Client Settings Dialog Box

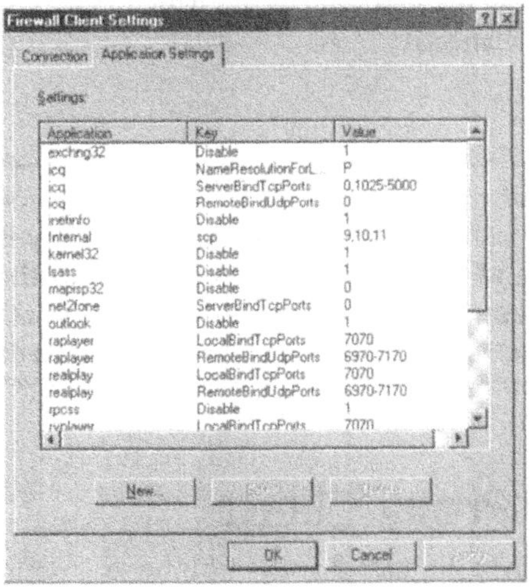

These settings are applied to all Firewall clients who obtain their settings from the ISA 2004 firewall. For example, you can see a setting **outlook Disable.** This setting tells the Firewall client software to bypass the Firewall client settings for the Microsoft Outlook application. This is an important setting, which allows the Outlook client to receive the proper new mail notification messages.

One especially of the Firewall client settings feature is to block applications. For example, you may want to block users from using the **kazaa.exe** application. You can use the **Disable** key to block the application. Do the following to block the **kazaa.exe** application:

1. In the **Firewall Client Settings** dialog box, on the **Application Settings** tab, click **New**.

2. In the **Application Entry Settings** dialog box, enter **Kazaa** (without the file extension) in the **Application** text box. Select **Disable** from the **Key** drop-down list. Select the value **1** from the **Value** list.

3. Click **OK**.

4. The new entry for **kazaa** appears in the **Settings** list. Click **Apply**, and then **OK**.

5. Click **Apply** (Figure 5.20) to save the changes and update the firewall policy.

Figure 5.20 Apply Changes to Firewall Configuration

6. Click **OK** in the **Apply New Configuration** dialog box

At this point, any user that has the Firewall client software installed will not be able to use the **kazaa.exe** application.

WARNING!

Users can get around this configuration by renaming the executable file. In order to completely block the **kazaa** application, you will need to configure the HTTP security filter and limit the users' access to only the HTTP protocol, or purchase a third-party application filter, such as the Akonix L7 for ISA Server product (www.akonix.com), that can detect peer-to-peer applications.

ISA 2004 Web Proxy Client

The Web Proxy client is any computer that has its browser configured to use the ISA 2004 firewall as its Web Proxy server. You do not need to add any new software to make a machine a Web Proxy client. The only requirement is that you configure the browser on the client machine to use the ISA 2004 firewall as its Web Proxy. The Web browser isn't the only application that can be configured as a Web Proxy client. Other applications, such as instant messengers and e-mail clients can also be configured as Web Proxy clients.

Advantages of the Web Proxy client configuration include:

- Improved performance for the Firewall and SecureNAT client configuration for Web access

- Ability to use the autoconfiguration script to bypass sites Direct Access

- Allows you to provide Web access (HTTP/HTTPS/FTP download) without enabling access to other protocols.

- Allows you to enforce user/group-based access controls over Web access.

- Supports RADIUS authentication for outbound Web Proxy client requests

- Allows you to limit the number of outbound Web Proxy client connections.

- Supports Web Proxy chaining, which can further speed up Internet access

Improved Performance for the Firewall Client and SecureNAT Client Configuration for Web Access

Web Proxy client machines communicate directly with the ISA 2004 firewall via the firewall's Web Proxy filter. The Web Proxy client connects directly to TCP port 8080 on the ISA 2004 firewall. TCP port 8080 is used by the ISA 2004 firewall's *Web Proxy listener*. The listener listens for outgoing Web requests and then exposes those communications to the firewall's Access Policies. Configuring the clients as Web Proxy clients improves performance because connections from Firewall and SecureNAT clients must be passed to the Web Proxy filter instead of being received directly by the filter. You will find during your own testing that Web Proxy client computers access Web content noticeably faster.

Ability to Use the Autoconfiguration Script to Bypass Sites (Direct Access)

One of the most useful features of the Web Proxy client configuration is the ability to use Direct Access to bypass the Web Proxy filter for selected Web sites. This requires that the Web Proxy client computer be configured to use the autoconfiguration script. There are two ways you can configure the Web Proxy client to use the autoconfiguration script:

- Manually configure the client to use the autoconfiguration script

- Configure WPAD entries in DNS and /or DHCP and configure the Web Proxy client to use autodetection to access configuration information

You can manually configure the Web Proxy client browser to use the autoconfiguration script. Any application that pulls its configuration from the Web browser settings can typically take advantage of the autoconfiguration script settings. Applications that do not pull their configuration from the Web browser are unlikely to be able to benefit from the autoconfiguration script settings.

A more efficient method of assigning the autoconfiguration script to the Web Proxy clients is to use WPAD entries in DNS and/or DHCP. The WPAD information will point the Web Proxy client to the IP address of the ISA 2004 firewall, from which the Web Proxy client will obtain autoconfiguration settings.

Support for the autoconfiguration script is critical for Web Proxy clients who want to access certain Java sites and also Hotmail e-mail. The autoconfiguration script provides a centralized list of Web sites that should be accessed via Direct Access. When these sites are configured for Direct Access, the Web Proxy client computer will bypass the Web Proxy filter and allow other methods, such as the machine's SecureNAT and/or Firewall client configuration, to connect to the Web site.

Allows You to Provide Web Access (HTTP/HTTPS/FTP Download) Without Enabling Users Access to Other Protocols

The Web Proxy client configuration allows you to provide Internet access to users who do not require the full range of Internet protocols. The Web Proxy client handles only the HTTP, HTTPS (SSL) and HTTP-tunnel FTP download. If a user's computer is configured as *only* a Web Proxy client, that user will have access to those protocols and no others. In fact, you can limit users to only a subset of those protocols.

Web Proxy clients use a tunneled connection when they send their Internet requests to the ISA 2004 firewall. For example, when a user sends a request to **www.microsoft.com**, the Web Proxy client wraps this request in another HTTP header with the destination address being the ISA 2004 firewall computer's internal interface and the destination port TCP 8080. When the ISA 2004 firewall receives the request, it removes the Web Proxy client's header and forwards the request to the Internet server at **www.microsoft.com**.

In the same way, when a Web Proxy client sends an FTP request to a site, such as **ftp://ftp.microsoft.com**, the Web Proxy client wraps the FTP request in the same HTTP header with the destination address of the Internal interface of the ISA 2004 firewall and the destination port TCP 8080. When the ISA 2004 firewall receives this request, it removes the HTTP header and forwards the request to the FTP server at **ftp.microsoft.com** as an actual FTP request, not an HTTP request. This is why we refer to the Web Proxy client's FTP support as HTTP-tunneled FTP.

NOTE

When using the Web Proxy client for FTP connections, the Web Proxy FTP client can perform only FTP *downloads*. In order to support FTP uploads the client machine will need to be configured as a SecureNAT or Firewall client. In adddition, the requests forwarded by the Web Proxy are sent as PORT (standard) mode connections

---

Allows You to Enforce User/ Group-based Access Controls Over Web Access

The Web Proxy client is able to send user credentials to the ISA 2004 firewall computer when required. In contrast to the Firewall client, which always sends user credentials to the ISA 2004 firewall, the Web Proxy client only sends credentials when asked to provide them. This improves performance, as authentication is only performed when required.

If the Web Proxy client has access to an Access Rule that allows access to the site and content in the request, and if the Access Rule allows for anonymous access (allows "All Users" access to the rule), then the Web Proxy client does not send credentials and the connection is allowed (assuming that the Access Rule is an "allow" rule)

This feature explains many of the anonymous entries you have in your Web Proxy log files. When the Web Proxy client sends a request to the ISA 2004 firewall, the first connection attempt does not include the Web Proxy client user credentials. This is logged as an anonymous request. If access to the site requires user credentials, then the ISA 2004 firewall will send an "access denied" message to the Web Proxy client machine and request the user to authenticate. Figure 5.21 illustrates that, at this point, the Web Proxy client has the option to authenticate using a number of different authentication protocols.

You can use the following authentication protocols for Web Proxy sessions:

- Windows-Integrated authentication
- Basic authentication
- Digest authentication
- Client Certificate authentication
- RADIUS authentication

WARNING

Web browsers can use Integrated, Basic, Digest, RADIUS, and Client Certificate authentication. It's important to note that Web browsers can only use Client Certificate authentication when connecting to published resources through a Web Publishing Rule. Web browser clients acting as Web Proxy clients cannot use Client Certificate authentication when accessing resources through the ISA 2004 firewall via an Access Rule. However, a downstream ISA 2004 firewall can use client certificate authentication to authenticate to an upstream ISA 2004 firewall in a WebProxy chaining scenario.

Figure 5.21 The Authentication Dialog Box

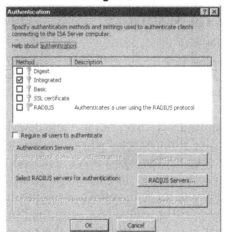

Credentials are passed to the ISA 2004 firewall transparently when Integrated authentication is enabled. However, both the ISA 2004 firewall and the Web Proxy client must be members of the same domain (or the ISA 2004 firewall must be a member of a domain that trusts the user account domain), or the ISA 2004 firewall must use RADIUS authentication to connect to the Active Directory or Windows NT 4.0 user account database. You can also get transparent authentication if you mirror user accounts in the local Security Account Manager (SAM) on the ISA 2004 firewall computer. However, for any but the smallest of organizations, the administrative overhead and the security risks of mirroring user accounts can be unacceptably high.

SSL certificate authentication is currently not available for browser to Web Proxy server connections. You can use SSL certificate authentication when configuring Web Proxy chaining. In this setup, a downstream Web Proxy server forwards Web requests to an upstream Web Proxy server. The downstream ISA 2004 Web Proxy server can authenticate with the upstream server by presenting a client certificate to the upstream ISA 2004 Web Proxy server. This provides a very secure Web Proxy chaining configuration that is not easily attainable with other Web Proxy solutions.

Users are prompted for user name and password when only **Basic** authentication is used. If the Web Proxy client and the ISA 2004 firewall are not members of the same domain, or if RADIUS authentication is not used, then Basic authentication is the best solution.

A new feature included with ISA 2004 is the ability to use RADIUS for Web Proxy authentication. When RADIUS is enabled as an authentication protocol for Web Proxy clients, the ISA 2004 firewall does not need to be a member of the user domain. This provides a slightly higher level of security because an attacker who may take control of the ISA 2004 firewall will not be able to leverage domain credentials to attack users on the protected network behind the ISA 2004 firewall. When a domain user tries to authenticate for a Web connection, the ISA 2004 firewall that is not a member of the user domain forwards the authentication request to a RADIUS server on the Internal network. The

RADIUS server forwards the request to an authentication server and then returns the response to the ISA 2004 firewall.

Note that when you configure the ISA 2004 firewall to support RADIUS authentication, the ISA 2004 firewall becomes a RADIUS client. You can use any RADIUS server, including Microsoft's RADIUS implementation, the Internet Authentication Server (IAS).

RADIUS authentication does require that you create a RADIUS server on the Internal network and configure the Web Proxy listener for the Web Proxy client's network to use the RADIUS server. In addition, there must be an Access Rule allowing the ISA 2004 firewall to communicate with the RADIUS server using the RADIUS protocol. There is a default firewall System Policy allowing RADIUS messages to the Internal network. If your RADIUS server is not located on the Internal network, you will need to configure the firewall System Policy allowing the RADIUS protocol to the RADIUS server at the alternate location.

We will go through the procedures required to create the RADIUS server and configure the RADIUS client later in this chapter. However, in order to support Web Proxy clients, you will need to perform the following:

■ Configure the Outgoing Web Requests listener to use RADIUS authentication

■ Configure the user account for Remote Access Permission or configure Remote Access Policy to enable access

■ Configure the Remote Access Policy to support PAP authentication

Do the following to configure the Web Proxy listener on the Web Proxy client's Network to use RADIUS:

1. In the **Microsoft Internet Security and Acceleration Server 2004** management console, expand the server name and then expand the **Configuration** node. Click on the **Networks** node and right-click on the **Internal** network (assuming that the Web Proxy clients are located on the Internal network, you would choose the appropriate network in your own configuration). Click **Properties**.

2. In the **Internal Properties** dialog box, click the **Web Proxy** tab.

3. On the **Web Proxy** tab, click the **Authentication** button.

4. In the **Authentication** dialog box, remove the checkmarks from the all the other check boxes. You will see dialog boxes informing you that there are no authentication methods available. Confirm that you have only the **RADIUS** option selected (see Figure 5.22) Do *not* select the **Require all users to authenticate** option. There have been many instances where this option causes repeated authentication boxes to appear..

Figure 5.22 The Authentication Dialog Box.

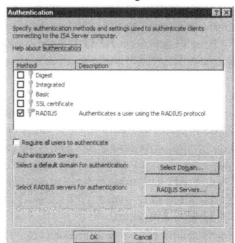

5. Click **RADIUS Servers**.

6. In the **Add RADIUS Server** dialog box, shown in Figure 5.23, enter a name or IP address for the RADIUS server in the **Server name** text box. If you enter a name, make sure that it's a fully-qualified domain name and that the ISA 2004 firewall can resolve that name to the correct IP address. Enter a description for the server in the **Server description** text box. Leave the **Port** and **Time-out (seconds)** values at their defaults unless you have a reason to change them. Confirm that there is a checkmark in the **Always use message authenticator** check box.

Figure 5.23 The Add RADIUS Server Dialog Box.

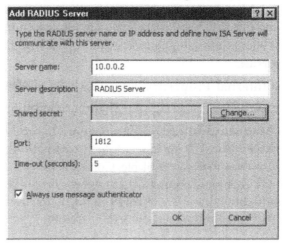

7. Click **Change**.

8. In the **Shared Secret** dialog box, enter and confirm a password in the **New secret** and **Confirm new secret** text boxes. This password is used to authenticate the RADIUS server and RADIUS client. Make sure that this is the same password you used when you configured the RADIUS client on the RADIUS server for the Internal network. Click **OK**. (NOTE: The RADIUS password should be long and complex; an ideal RADIUS password is one that is 24 characters and is created with a password generator application. The shared secret is used to generate an MD5 hash, which is used to authenticate the RADIUS client to the RADIUS server).

9. Click **OK** in the **Add RADIUS Server** dialog box.

10. The RADIUS server entry now appears on the list. Note that you can create multiple RADIUS servers and they will be queried in the order listed.

11. Click **OK** in the **Authentication** dialog box.

12. Click **Apply** and **OK** in the **Internal Properties** dialog box.

13. Click **Apply** to save the changes and update the firewall policy.

14. Click **OK** in the **Apply New Configuration** dialog box.

The next step is to configure the user account to enable dial-in access. Note that this procedure is *not* required if the domain is in Windows 2000 or Windows Server 2003 Native Mode. The reason for this is that you can control access policy via Remote Access Policy, and the default setting for user accounts controls access via Remote Access Policy when the domain is in Native Mode. For this reason, we highly recommend that you configure your Windows domains in Native Mode so that you do not need to enable each individual user account for dial-in access.

1. In the **Active Directory Users and Computers** console on a domain controller that contains the user accounts that you want to authenticate with Web Proxy RADIUS authentication, double-click on the account you want to allow to use RADIUS authentication.

2. In the user's **Properties** dialog box, click the **Dial-in** tab.

3. On the **Dial-in** tab, select the **Allow access** option.

4. Click **Apply**, and then click **OK**.

The user account is now able to use RADIUS for Web Proxy authentication.

The last step is to configure the Remote Access Policy so that PAP authentication is supported for Web Proxy client RADIUS authentication. It's important to note that PAP authentication is not secure, and you should use some method to protect the credentials as they as pass between the ISA 2004 firewall and the RADIUS server. Although the credentials are encyrpted using an MD5 hash, there should still be an additional layer of protection. The preferred method of protecting credentials is to use an IPSec transport mode connection.

Do the following to configure the Remote Access Policy:

1. At the IAS server on the Internal network, click **Start**, and point to **Administrative Tools**. Click **Internet Authentication Services**.

2. In the **Internet Authentication Services** console, click the **Remote Access Policies** node in the left pane of the console.

3. On the **Remote Access Policies** node, note that there are two Remote Access Policies in the right pane of the console. The first policy applies only to RAS connections from dial-up and VPN clients. The second policy, **Connections to other access servers** is the one used by the Web Proxy clients. Double-click **Connection to other access servers**.

4. In the **Connections to other access servers Properties** dialog box, click **Edit Profile**.

5. In the **Edit Dial-in Profile** dialog box, click the **Authentication** tab.

6. On the **Authentication** tab, put a checkmark in the **Unencrypted authentication (PAP, SPAP)** check box.

7. Click **Apply** and **OK**.

8. In the **Connections to other access servers Properties** dialog box (see Figure 5.24), confirm that the condition **Windows-Groups matches...** entry is included. This includes the groups of users who you want to have access to the Web Proxy service via RADIUS authentication. Use the **Add** button to add the group you want to have access. Also, confirm that the **Grant remote access permission** option is selected.

Figure 5.24 The Connections to other Access Servers Properties Dialog Box

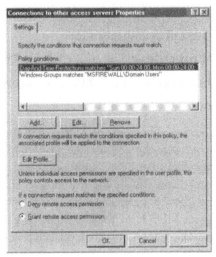

9. Click **Apply** and **OK** in the **Connections to other access server Properties** dialog box.

The policy will take effect immediately; you do not need to restart any equipment.

Allows you to Limit the Number of Outbound Web Proxy Client Connections

The number of Web Proxy client connections can be limited to a number that you specify. This can be helpful when you have limited bandwidth or you want to make sure that only a certain percentage of your users have access to the Internet at any single point in time.

You can access the configuration interface for the number of simultaneous Web Proxy client connections in the **Properties** dialog box of the network from which the Web Proxy clients access the Web. In the **Microsoft Internet Security and Acceleration Server 2004** management console, expand the server name, and then expand the **Configuration** node. Click the **Networks** node in the left pane of the console, and right-click the network in the **Details** pane. Click the **Properties** command.

In the network's **Properties** dialog box, click the **Web Proxy** tab. On the **Web Proxy** tab, click **Advanced**. In the **Advanced Settings** dialog box depicted in Figure 5.25, you can chose from the **Unlimited** and the **Maximum** options. When you select the **Maximum** option, you can enter a value for the maximum number of simultaneous connections. There is also a **Connection timeout (seconds)** value that you can customize. The default value is **120** seconds. You can shorten or extend this value depending on your requirements. If you find that idle connections are using up the number of allowed simultaneous connections, you can shorten the timeout value. If you find that users complain about Web sessions being disconnected prematurely, you can extend the timeout value.

Figure 5.25 Advanced Settings

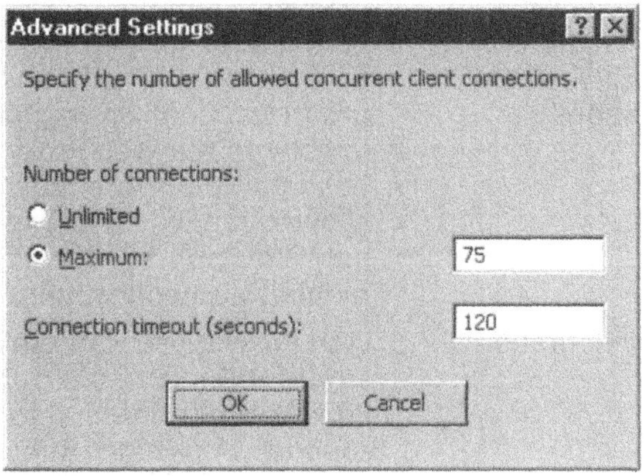

Supports Web Proxy Chaining, Which Can Further Speed Up Internet Access

Web Proxy chaining allows you to connect ISA 2004 and ISA Server 2000 firewall and Web Proxy servers to each other. The firewall Web Proxy servers represent a chain, where the ISA Web Proxy server farthest away from the central Internet access point represents the most "downstream" Web Proxy, and the ISA Web Proxy closest to the central Internet connection is the most "upstream" ISA Web Proxy.

There are a number of scenarios where ISA Web Proxy chaining can be configured. These scenarios include:

- Branch offices connecting to a main office ISA 2004 Web proxy firewall server

- Campus networks with multiple workgroup/departmental LANs connecting to upstream ISA 2004 firewall Web Proxies upstream on a campus backbone or services network

- Back-to-back ISA 2004 firewall configurations where the downstream ISA 2004 firewall uses Web Proxy chaining to forward corporate network Web Proxy requests to the front-end ISA 2004 firewall. This configuration adds to the already-strong security of the back-to-back ISA 2004 firewall configuration.

We will go into these scenarios in detail in Chapter 10 **Accelerating Web Performance with ISA 2004 Caching Capabilities**. Table 5.7 illustrates the advantages of the WebProxy client configuration.

Table 5.7 Advantages of the Web Proxy Client Configuration

Web Proxy Client Advantage	Implication
Improved performance over Firewall client only, SecureNAT client only, or Firewall/SecureNAT client only configurations	Machine configured as Web Proxy clients exhibit superior performance when connecting to the Internet using Web protocols. Connect requests are forwarded directly to the Web Proxy filter and connections that do not require authentication are allowed immediately. The Web Proxy will only request credentials when a connection requires authentication.
Ability to use autoconfiguration	Web Proxy clients can use Direct Access to script for Direct Access avoid using the Web Proxy when connecting to sites that do not support connections through Web Proxy servers. A Web Proxy client configured with the autoconfiguration script can be instructed to avoid the Web Proxy filter when connecting to Java sites or when connecting to Hotmail using Outlook Express. Without the autoconfiguration script and Direct Access, the user would have to

Continued

Table 5.7 Advantages of the Web Proxy Client Configuration

Web Proxy Client Advantage	Implication
	manually disable the Web Proxy configuration on the client to avoid the connecting via the Web Proxy.
Allows you to limit access to only "Web" protocols	Machines configured as only Web Proxy clients have access to the HTTP, HTTPS and FTP (download) protocols only.
Allows you to granular user/group based access controls for Web access	Web Proxy clients can send user credentials to the ISA firewall when required. This enables you to set fine-tuned granular access controls over what sites and content can be access on a per user/per group basis.
Supports RADIUS authentication for outbound Web Proxy requests	RADIUS authentication allows you to authenticate against any authentication server that supports RADIUS authentication. An Active Directory domain controller is one example of such an authentication server. RADIUS allows your Active Directory users to authenticate with the Web Proxy, even when the ISA firewall does not belong to the same Active Directory domain as the users.
Allows you to put Limits on the number of outbound connections	You can configure a limit on the number of Web Proxy client connections allowed to Web Proxy clients. Once that limit is reached, no more Web Proxy client connection are allowed through the ISA firewall. That provides a method of throttling Internet access without requiring strict bandwidth control.
Supports Web Proxy chaining	Web Proxy clients can directly benefit from Web Proxy chaining configurations where multiple ISA firewalls are configured in a Web Proxy chain. Authentication information from the Web Proxy client can be forwarded to upstream Web Proxy servers in the ISA firewall Web Proxy chain. The Web Proxy chaining configuration can provide significant improved performance for remote offices and machines located behind busy backbone network segments.

Table 5.8 Disadvantages of the Web Proxy Client Configuration

Web Proxy Client Disadvantage	Implication
None	There are no disadvantages to the Web Proxy client configuration. All machines should be configured as Web Proxy clients to improve performance and Internet access control.

ISA 2004 Multiple Client Type Configuration

A common point of confusion among ISA 2004 firewall administrators is whether or not a machine can be configured as multiple ISA 2004 client types. Many ISA firewall administrators are under the impression that a single machine cannot be configured as a Web Proxy, Firewall, and SecureNAT client.. This is a misconception. It is possible and sometimes preferred that a single computer be configured as all three types of ISA client.

The truth is that a single machine cannot be configured to *act* as both a Firewall client and a SecureNAT client. The reason for this is when a machine is configured as a Firewall client, all Winsock TCP and UDP communications are intercepted by the Firewall client software. Therefore, the SecureNAT client configuration does *not* have access to these communications. For non-Winsock TCP and UDP communications, and for all other non-TCP/UDP communications, the SecureNAT client handles the requests. For example, if the machine is configured as both a SecureNAT and Firewall client, the SecureNAT client configuration handles all ping, tracert and PPTP connections. Ping and tracert use ICMP, and PPTP uses GRE. Neither ICMP nor GRE uses TCP or UDP as a transport.

Table 5.9 describes the behavior of machines that are configured as multiple client types.

Table 5.9 Application Behavior on Multiple Client Configuration Machines

ISA 2004 Client Configuration	Application Behavior
SecureNAT and Firewall Client	Firewall client handles all TCP and UDP communications from Winsock applications. SecureNAT client handles all TCP/UDP communications from non-Winsock applications and all non-TCP/UDP communications
SecureNAT and Web Proxy Client	Web Proxy client handles HTTP/HTTPS/FTP download communications from the Web Proxy client application. From non-Web Proxy client applications, the SecureNAT client handles the HTTP/HTTP/FTP connections (both download and upload). If the Web Proxy

Continued

Table 5.9 Application Behavior on Multiple Client Configuration Machines

ISA 2004 Client Configuration	Application Behavior
	client-configured browser is not able to use the Web Proxy service to access FTP resources, the client will "fall back" on the SecureNAT client configuration. All other protocols are handled by the SecureNAT client configuration.
Firewall and Web Proxy Client	The Web Proxy client configuration handles HTTP/HTTPS/FTP download from Web Proxy client-configured applications. The Firewall client handles all other Winsock TCP and UDP communications, including HTTP/HTTPS/FTP download and upload from applications not configured as Web Proxy clients. FTP download from Web Proxy clients can fall back on Firewall client configuration. No access to non-TCP/UDP protocols and no access to TCP and UDP protocols for non-Winsock applications.
SecureNAT, Firewall, and Web Proxy Client	Access to HTTP/HTTPS/FTP download via Web Proxy client configuration for applications configured as Web Proxy clients. Fall back to Firewall client configuration for FTP download if Web Proxy client configuration does not support connection. All TCP/UDP communications from Winsock applications handled by Firewall client. All other communications handled by SecureNAT client configuration.

Deciding on an ISA 2004 Client Type

The ISA 2004 client type you decide on depends on the level of functionality and level of security you require. Table 5.10 rates the various ISA 2004 clients, based on functionality, security, ease of deployment and management, and operating system compatibility.

Table 5.10 Grading Security, Functionality, Ease and Compatibility of ISA 2004 Client Types, from Highest to Lowest

Functionality	Security	Ease of Deployment and Management	Operating System Compatibility
Firewall client	Firewall client	SecureNAT client	SecureNAT client
SecureNAT client	Web Proxy client	Web Proxy client	Web Proxy client
Web Proxy	SecureNAT client	Firewall Client	Firewall client

Table 5.11 describes a number of parameters you should consider when selecting the ISA 2004 client type to use in your environment.

Table 5.11 Choosing the Appropriate ISA 2004 Client Type

You require:	Suggested ISA 2004 Client type:
No software deployment to network clients.	The SecureNAT and Web Proxy client. The SecureNAT client does not require software installation and only requires that you set the appropriate default gateway address. The Web Proxy client does not require client software installation; you only need to configure the Web Proxy applications to use the firewall as their Web Proxy server.
Only Web protocols: HTTP, HTTPS and FTP download through a Web browser and other Web Proxy-aware applications and Web caching.	Web Proxy client or SecureNAT client. Both of these clients will be able to benefit from the Web Proxy cache on the ISA 2004 firewall. The advantage to using the Web Proxy client over the SecureNAT client in this scenario is that the Web Proxy client will send user information to the ISA 2004 firewall and allow you to enforce strong user/group-based access control over what sites and content users access via the Web.
Authentication before allowing access. User name included in logs.	Firewall or Web Proxy client. The Web Proxy client enables you to enforce user/group-based strong access control over HTTP/HTTPS/FTP download connections via Web Proxy client applications. The Firewall client allows strong user/group-based access controls over all Winsock applications using TCP and UDP protocols. Whenever a user authenticates with the ISA 2004 firewall, that user's name is included in the logs.

Continued

Table 5.11 Choosing the Appropriate ISA 2004 Client Type

You require:	Suggested ISA 2004 Client type:
Servers published to the The Internet using Web or Server Publishing Rules	The published server must be configured as a SecureNAT client if the original Internet client IP address is retained in the communication reaching the published server. This is the default configuration for Server Publishing Rules. For Web Publishing Rules, the default is to replace the original client IP address with the IP address of the ISA 2004 firewall's Internal interface (the interface that lies on the same Network as the published server). When the original source IP address is replaced with the ISA 2004 firewall's IP address, the published server only needs to know the route to the Internal IP address of the ISA 2004 firewall that forwarded the request. Note that for both Web and Server Publishing Rules you have the option to preserve the original client IP address.
Support for non-Windows operating systems	SecureNAT and Web Proxy clients. All operating systems support the SecureNAT client configuration because the SecureNAT client only requires the appropriate default gateway address configuration. All operating systems running applications supporting Web Proxy client configuration can connect to the ISA 2004 firewall via the Web Proxy client.
Support for Internet games	Firewall client. Most Internet games require multiple primary and secondary connections. Only the Firewall client supports complex protocols requiring secondary connections (unless there is an application filter installed on the ISA 2004 firewall to support that specific application).
Support for Voice/Video applications	Voice and video applications that do not require Session Initiation Protocol (SIP) generally require secondary connections (ISA 2004 does not support SIP signaling). Only the Firewall client supports secondary connections without the aid of an application filter.

Automating ISA 2004 Client Provisioning

There are several methods available for automating the Web Proxy and Firewall client installation and configuration. These include:

- Configuring DHCP Servers to Support Web Proxy and Firewall Client Autodiscovery

- Configuring DNS Servers to Support Web Proxy and Firewall Client Autodiscovery

- Automating Web Proxy Client Configuration with Group Policy

- Automating Web Proxy Client Configuration with Internet Explorer Administration Kit (IEAK)

The following sections discuss how to automate the configuration of Web Proxy and Firewall clients using the Web Proxy AutoDiscovery (WPAD) protocol and Active Directory Group Policy. We will not go into the details of how to use the Internet Explorer Administration Kit (IEAK) to automate Web proxy client configuration.

Note that there are two methods for supporting Autodiscovery for Web Proxy and Firewall clients: DNS and DHCP. Table 5.12 provides information that will help you decide which method best fits your needs.

NOTE

You can also automate the configuration of Web Proxy clients using Active Directory Group Policy. There are Group Policy elements that allow you to configure the behavior of all browsers that belong within the scope of the Group Policy Object. This feature is only available for Web browser configuration *is not* available for Firewall client configuration.

Table 5.12 DNS and DHCP Support for Web Proxy and Firewall Client Autodiscovery

DHCP	DNS
Client must be DHCP client	Client must be able to resolve DNS names on the Internal network
Internet Explorer 5.0 and above required	Internet Explorer 5.0 and above required
Must be able to send DHCPINFORM queries (Windows 2000, Windows XP, and Windows Server 2003 only)	Must be able to correctly qualify the unqualified name "WPAD" with a domain name to yield a FQDN that resolves to the ISA 2004 firewall's Internal IP address
User must be logged on as local administrator	Each domain must be configured with its own WPAD entry
ISA 2004 firewall can publish autodiscovery information on any available port on the ISA firewall	ISA 2004 firewall must publish autodiscovery information on TCP port 80

Continued

Table 5.12 DNS and DHCP Support for Web Proxy and Firewall Client Autodiscovery

DHCP	DNS
Each DHCP Server must be configured with a WPAD entry. If multiple DHCP servers are within the same broadcast range of the client, then all DHCP servers within that range must be configured with a wpad entry.	Each DNS server must be configured with a WPAD entry. Branch offices may require a custom configuration to prevent Branch office clients from using the WPAD entry pointing to ISA 2004 firewalls at the Main office.

NOTE

For more information about the WPAD protocol, please see the **ISA 2004** Help file at **www.microsoft.com/technet/treeview/default.asp?url=/ technet/prodtechnol/isa/proddocs/isadocs/CMT_AutoDetect.asp** For more information on how to configure IEAK to automate Web Proxy client configuration, please see Chapter 26 - **Using Automatic Configuration, Automatic Proxy, and Automatic Detection** at **www.microsoft.com/resources/documentation/ie/6/all/reskit/en-us/part6/c26ie6rk.mspx**

Configuring DHCP Servers to Support Web Proxy and Firewall Client Autodiscovery

DHCP clients can obtain autoconfiguration information from the ISA 2004 firewall computer by using DHCPINFORM messages. The Firewall client and Web browser software can issue DHCPINFORM messages to query a DHCP server for the address of a machine containing the autoconfiguration information. The DHCP server returns the address of the machine containing the autoconfiguration information, and the Firewall client or Web browser software requests autoconfiguration information from the address returned by the DHCP server.

The DHCP server uses a special DHCP option to provide this information. In this section on configuring Web Proxy and Firewall clients to use DHCP to obtain autoconfiguration information via WPAD, we will discuss the following steps:

- Installing the DHCP server
- Creating the DHCP scope
- Creating the DHCP 252 scope option
- Configuring the client as a DHCP client
- Configuring the client browser to use autodiscovery

- Configuring the ISA 2004 firewall to publish autodiscovery information
- Making the connection

Install the DHCP Server

The first step is to install the DHCP server. We went through the procedures for installing a DHCP server in Chapter 4.

Create the DHCP scope

A DHCP scope is a collection of IP addresses the DHCP server uses to assign to DHCP clients on the network. In addition, a DHCP scope can include additional TCP/IP settings to be assigned to clients, which are referred to as *DHCP options*. DHCP options can assign various TCP/IP settings such as a DNS server address, WINS server address, and primary domain name to DHCP clients.

Do the following on the DHCP server to enable the DHCP server and create the DHCP scope:

1. Click **Start**, and then select **Administrative Tools**. Click **DHCP**.

2. In the **DHCP** console, right click on your server name in the left pane of the console. Click on the **Authorize** command (see Figure 5.26).

Figure 5.26 Locating the Authorize Command

3. Click **Refresh** in the button bar of the console. You will notice that the icon to the left of the server name changes from a red, down-pointing arrow to a green, up-pointing arrow.

4. Right-click the server name in the left pane of the console again, and click the **New Scope** command.

5. Click **Next** on the **Welcome to the New Scope Wizard** page.

6. Enter a name for the scope on the **Scope Name** page. This name is descriptive only and does not affect the functionality of the scope. You can also enter a **Description** in the description box, if you wish. Click **Next**.

7. Enter a range of IP addresses that can be assigned to DHCP clients on the **IP Address Range** page. Enter the first address in the range into the **Start IP address** range text box and the last IP address in the range in the **End IP address** text box. Enter the subnet mask for your IP address range in the **Subnet mask** text box.

8. In the example in Figure 5.27, the Internal network is on network ID 10.0.2/24. We do not want to assign all the IP addresses on the network ID to the DHCP scope, just a selection of them. So in this example, we enter **10.0.2.100** as the **Start IP address** and **10.0.2.150** as the end IP address and use a **24**-bit subnet mask. Note that on production networks, it is often better to assign the entire network ID to the IP address range used in the scope. You can then create *exceptions* for hosts on the network that have statically-assigned IP addresses that are contained in the scope. This allows you to centrally manage IP address assignment and configuration using DHCP. Click **Next**.

Figure 5.27 Configuring the DHCP Scope IP Address Range

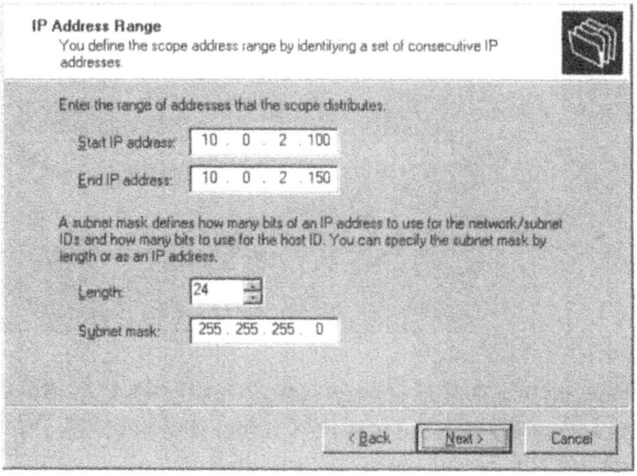

IP Address Range
You define the scope address range by identifying a set of consecutive IP addresses.

Enter the range of addresses that the scope distributes.

Start IP address: 10 . 0 . 2 . 100

End IP address: 10 . 0 . 2 . 150

A subnet mask defines how many bits of an IP address to use for the network/subnet IDs and how many bits to use for the host ID. You can specify the subnet mask by length or as an IP address.

Length: 24

Subnet mask: 255 . 255 . 255 . 0

< Back   Next >   Cancel

9. Do not enter any exclusions in the **Add Exclusions** dialog box. Click **Next**.

10. Accept the default settings on the **Lease Duration** page (8 days, 0 hours and 0 minutes), and click **Next**.

11. On the **Configure DHCP Options** page, select **Yes, I want to configure these options now,** and click **Next**.

12. Do not enter anything on the **Router (Default Gateway)** page. Note that if we were using SecureNAT clients on the network, we would enter the IP address of the Internal interface for the ISA 2004 firewall on this page.

However, with the current scenario, we want to test *only* the Web Proxy and Firewall client configurations. Click **Next**.

13. On the **Domain Name and DNS Servers** page, enter the **primary domain name** you want to assign to DHCP clients, and the **DNS server address** you want the DHCP clients to use.

14. The **primary domain name** is a critical setting for your Firewall and Web Proxy clients. In order for autodiscovery to work correctly for Firewall and Web Proxy clients, these clients must be able to correctly fully qualify the unqualified name WPAD. We will discuss this issue in more detail later. In this example, enter **msfirewall.org** in the **Parent domain** text box (see Figure 5.28). This will assign the DHCP clients the primary domain name msfirewall.org, which will be appended to unqualified names. Enter the IP address of the DNS server in the **IP address** text box. In this example, the IP address of the DNS server is **10.0.2.2**. Click **Add** after entering the IP address. Click **Next**.

Figure 5.28 Configuring the Default Domain Name for DHCP Clients

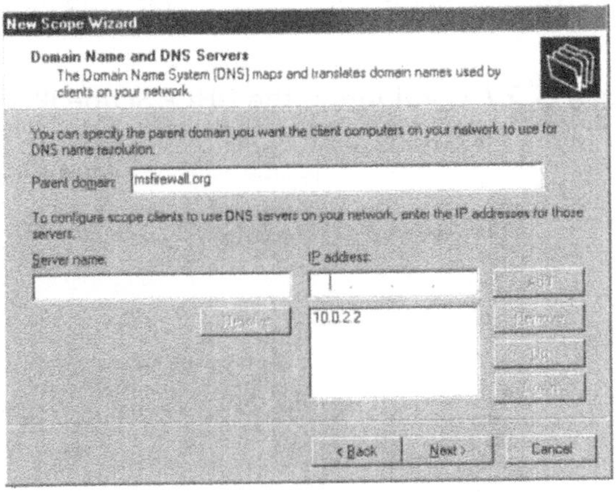

15. Do not enter a WINS server address on the **WINS Servers** page. In this example, we do not use a WINS server. However, WINS servers are very useful in VPN server environments if you wish your VPN clients to be able to browse the campus network using **My Network Places** or **Network Neighborhood** application. Click **Next**.

16. On the **Activate Scope** page, select **Yes, I want to activate this scope now**, and click **Next**.

17. Click **Finish** on the **Completing the New Scope Wizard** page.

18. In the right pane of the **DHCP** console, you see the two DHCP options you created in the Wizard, as seen in Figure 5.29.

Figure 5.29 Viewing the Scope Options

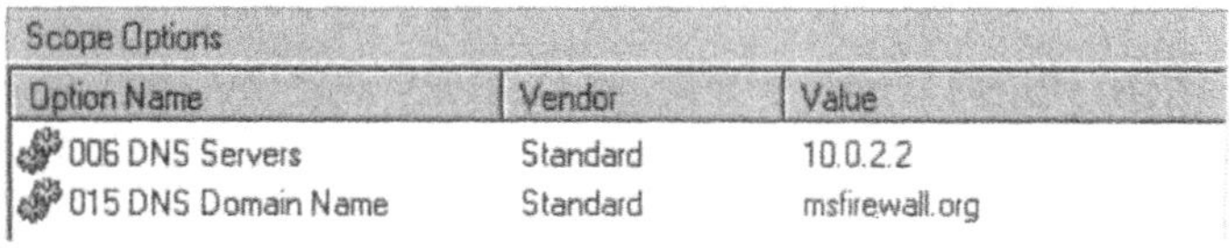

Scope Options		
Option Name	Vendor	Value
006 DNS Servers	Standard	10.0.2.2
015 DNS Domain Name	Standard	msfirewall.org

The next step is to create a custom DHCP option that will allow DHCP clients to autodiscover Web Proxy and Firewall client settings.

Create the DHCP 252 Scope Option and Add It to the Scope

The DHCP scope option number 252 is used to automatically configure Web Proxy and Firewall clients. The Web Proxy or Firewall client must be configured as a DHCP client, and the logged-on user must be a member of the local administrators group or Power users group (for Windows 2000). On Windows XP systems, the Network Configuration Operators group also has permission to issue DHCP queries (DHCPIN-FORM messages).

NOTE

For more information about the limitations related to using DHCP for autodiscovery with Internet Explorer 6.0, please see KB article **Automatic Proxy Discovery in Internet Explorer with DHCP Requires Specific Permissions** at http://support.microsoft.com/default.aspx?scid=kb;en-us;312864

Do the following at the DHCP server to create the custom DHCP option:

1. Open the **DHCP** console from the **Administrative Tools** menu and right-click your server name in the left pane of the console. Click the **Set Predefined Options** command, shown in Figure 5.30.

Figure 5.30 Selecting the Set Predefined Options Command

2. In the **Predefined Options and Values** dialog box (Figure 5.31), click **Add**.

Figure 5.31 The Predefined Options and ValuesDialog Box

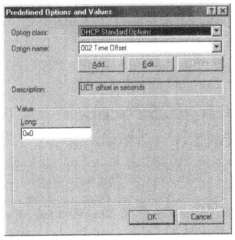

3. In the **Option Type** dialog box (Figure 5.32), enter the following information:

    Name: wpad

    Data type: String

    Code: 252

    Description: wpad entry

    Click **OK**.

Figure 5.32 The Option Type Dialog Box

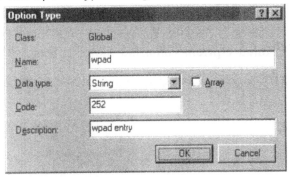

4. In the **Value** frame, enter the URL to the ISA 2004 firewall in the **String** text box. The format for this value is:

    http://ISAServername:Autodiscovery Port Number/wpad.dat

    The default autodiscovery port number is TCP 80. You can customize this value in the **ISA Management** console. If you do change the autodiscovery port number, then you will need to change the port number in the WPAD entry as well. We will cover this subject in more detail later.

As shown in Figure 5.33, enter the following into the **String** text box: http://isa2.msfirewall.org:80/wpad.dat

Make sure to enter wpad.dat in all *lower case* letters. For more information on this problem, please refer to KB article **"Automatically Detect Settings" Does Not Work if You Configure DHCP Option 252** at http://support.microsoft.com/default.aspx?scid=kb;en-us;307502

5. Click **OK**.

Figure 5.33 Predefined Options and Values Dialog Box

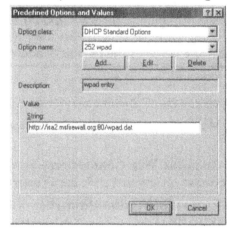

6. Right click the **Scope Options** node in the left pane of the console, and click the **Configure Options** command.

7. In the **Scope Options** dialog box (Figure 5.34), scroll through the list of **Available Options** and put a checkmark in the **252 wpad** check box. Click **Apply** and **OK**.

Figure 5.34 The Scope Options Dialog Box

8. The **252 wpad** entry now appears in the right pane of the console under the list of **Scope Options**.

9. Close the **DHCP** console.

The next step is to configure the client computer as a DHCP client.

Configure the Client as a DHCP Client

In order to use DHCP to obtain autodiscovery information for Web Proxy and Firewall clients, the client computer must be configured as a DHCP client.

> **NOTE**
>
> In this example, we configure a Windows 2000 machine as a DHCP client. The procedure varies a bit with each client operating system. All Windows TCP/IP operating systems use DHCP as the default IP address configuration.

Do the following on the client machine to configure it as a DHCP client:

1. Right click **My Network Places** on the desktop, and click the **Properties** command.

2. Right click the **Local Area Connection** entry in the **Network and Dial-up Connections** window and click the **Properties** command.

3. In the **Local Area Connection Properties** dialog box, click the **Internet Protocol (TCP/IP)** entry and click **Properties**.

4. In the **Internet Protocol (TCP/IP) Properties** dialog box, select **Obtain an IP address automatically** and **Obtain DNS server address automatically**. Click **OK**.

5. Click **OK** in the **Local Area Connection Properties** dialog box.

6. Close the **Network and Dial-up Connections** window.

Now you're ready to configure the browser to use autodiscovery for automatically discovering its Web Proxy client settings.

Configure the Client Browser to Use DCHP for Autodiscovery

The browser must be configured to use autodiscovery before it can use the DHCP server option 252 to automatically configure itself. This is the default setting for Internet Explorer 6.0, but the default setting may have been changed at some time during the life of the browser on a particular machine. In the following example, we manually configure the browser to use autodiscovery to autoconfigure itself. We will discuss methods you can use to automatically set this option later.

Do the following on the Web Proxy client computer:

1. Right click on the **Internet Explorer** icon on the desktop and click **Properties**.

2. In the **Internet Properties** dialog box, click the **Connections** tab. Click the **LAN Settings** button.

3. In the **Local Area Network (LAN) Settings** dialog box, put a checkmark in the **Automatically detect settings** check box. Click **OK**.

4. Click **OK** in the **Internet Properties** dialog box.

ISA 2004 firewall must be configured to publish autodiscovery information before the Web Proxy client can obtain configuration information. That's the next step.

Configure the ISA 2004 Firewall to Publish Autodiscovery Information

All the settings required for the Web browser to configure itself are contained on the ISA 2004 firewall computer. By default, this option is disabled. You can enable publishing of autodiscovery information on the ISA 2004 firewall computer so that the Web Proxy client can obtain autoconfiguration settings.

Do the following on the ISA 2004 firewall computer to enable it to provide auto-configuration information to Web Proxy and Firewall autodiscovery clients:

1. At the ISA 2004 firewall, open the **Microsoft Internet Security and Acceleration Server 2004** management console. Expand the server name in the left pane of the console, and then expand the **Configuration** node. Click the **Networks** node.

2. On the **Networks** node, click the **Networks** tab in the **Details** pane.

3. Right-click the **Internal** network on the **Networks** tab, and click **Properties** (see Figure 5.35).

Figure 5.35 Accessing the Internal Network Properties Dialog Box

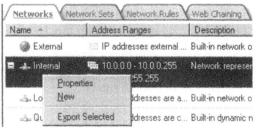

4. In the **Internal Properties** dialog box, put a checkmark in the **Publish automatic discovery information** check box. In the **Use this port for automatic discovery request** text box, leave the default **port 80** as it is.

5. Click **Apply** and **OK**.

6. Click **Apply** to save the changes and update the firewall policy.

7. Click **OK** in the **Apply New Configuration** dialog box.

Making the Connection

All the components are now in place for the Web browser to automatically connect to the ISA 2004 firewall's Web Proxy service using autodiscovery.

Do the following on the Web Proxy client computer:

1. Open **Internet Explorer** and enter the URL for the Microsoft ISA Server site at **www.microsoft.com/isaserver**

2. A Network Monitor trace shows the DHCPINFORM messages sent by the Web Proxy client. The Web Proxy client uses the DHCPINFORM messages, such as the one shown in Figure 5.36 to obtain the autodiscovery address contained in the DHCP option 252 entry.

Figure 5.36 Viewing the DHCPINFORM Request

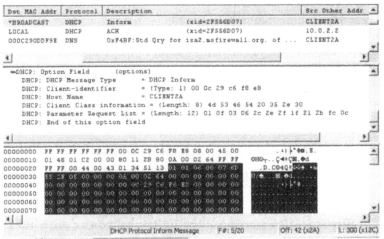

3. In Figure 5.37, you can see the ACK response to the Web Proxy client's DHCPINFORM message. In the bottom pane of the Network Monitor console, you can see that the DHCP server has returned the address you configured in the DHCP option 252 entry.

Figure 5.37 Viewing the contents of the DHCPINFORM request

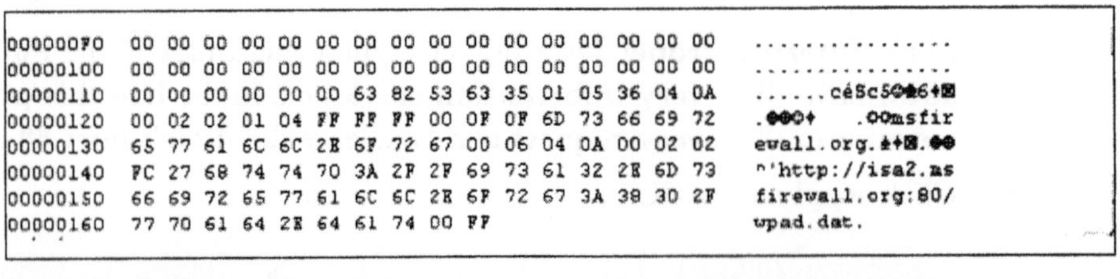

```
000000F0  00 00 00 00 00 00 00 00 00 00 00 00 00 00 00 00   ................
00000100  00 00 00 00 00 00 00 00 00 00 00 00 00 00 00 00   ................
00000110  00 00 00 00 00 00 63 82 53 63 35 01 05 36 04 0A   ......céSc5..6..
00000120  00 02 02 01 04 FF FF FF 00 0F 0F 6D 73 66 69 72   ...........msfir
00000130  65 77 61 6C 6C 2E 6F 72 67 00 06 04 0A 00 02 02   ewall.org.......
00000140  FC 27 68 74 74 70 3A 2F 2F 69 73 61 32 2E 6D 73   .'http://isa2.ms
00000150  66 69 72 65 77 61 6C 6C 2E 6F 72 67 3A 38 30 2F   firewall.org:80/
00000160  77 70 61 64 2E 64 61 74 00 FF                     wpad.dat.
```

4. After the Web Proxy client receives the address of the ISA 2004 firewall containing the autodiscovery settings, the next step is for it to resolve the name of the ISA 2004 firewall to its Internal IP address. Name resolution is critical for multiple aspects of ISA firewall 2004 function, and this is another example of this fact. You can see in the Network Monitor (Figure 5.38) that the Web Proxy client has issued a query for isa2.msfirewall.org, which was the URL contained in the DHCP 252 option.

Figure 5.38 Viewing the WPAD DNS Query

Dst MAC Addr	Protocol	Description		Src Other Addr
*BROADCAST	DHCP	Inform	(xid=2F556D07)	CLIENT2A
LOCAL	DHCP	ACK	(xid=2F556D07)	10.0.2.2
000C290DDF9E	DNS	0xF4BF:Std Qry for isa2.msfirewall.org. of ...	CLIENT2A

Configuring DNS Servers to Support Web Proxy and Firewall Client Autodiscovery

Another method you can use in deliver autodiscovery information to Web Proxy and Firewall clients is DNS. You can create a wpad alias entry in DNS and allow browser clients to use this information to automatically configure themselves. This is in contrast to the situation we saw with the DHCP method, where the logged-on user needed to be a member of a specific group in the Windows operating system.

Name resolution is a pivotal component in making this method of Web Proxy and Firewall client autodiscovery work . In this case, the client operating system must be able to correctly fully qualify the name *wpad*. The reason for this is that the Web Proxy and Firewall client only knows that it needs to resolve the name wpad; it does not know what specific domain name it should append to the query to resolve the name wpad. We will cover this issue in detail later.

NOTE

In contrast to the DHCP method of assigning autodiscovery information to Web Proxy and Firewall clients, you do not have the option to use a custom port number to publish autodiscovery information when using the DNS method. You must publish autodiscovery information on TCP 80 when using the DNS method.

We will detail the following steps to enable DNS to provide autodiscovery information to Web Proxy and Firewall clients:

- Creating the wpad entry in DNS
- Configuring the client to use the fully-qualified wpad alias

■ Configuring the client browser to use autodiscovery

■ Making the connection

Creating the wpad Entry in DNS

The first step is to create a wpad alias entry in DNS. This alias points to a Host (A) record for the ISA 2004 firewall, which resolves the name of the ISA 2004 firewall to the Internal IP address of the firewall. This Host (A) record must be created before you create the CNAME alias entry. If you enable automatic registration in DNS, the ISA 2004 firewall's entry will already be entered into DNS. If you have not enabled automatic registration, you will need to create the Host (A) record for the ISA 2004 firewall manually. In the following example, the ISA 2004 firewall has automatically registered itself with DNS.

WARNING

You should turn off DNS autoregistration on all network interfaces attached to the ISA 2004 fireall. This includes autoregistration for any demand-dial interfaces configured on the ISA 2004 firewall. If the ISA 2004 firewall has already autoregistered information in the DNS, you should remove all the autoregistered entries from the DNS after disabling autoregistration on each of the ISA 2004 firewall's adapters, and then re-enter the addresses. This will prevent problems with Internet connectivity when VPN clients connect to the ISA 2004 firewall's VPN server.

Do the following on the DNS server of the domain controller on the Internal network:

1. Click **Start** and select **Administrative Tools**. Click the **DNS** entry. In the **DNS** management console shown in Figure 5.39, right-click on the forward lookup zone for your domain, and click the **New Alias (CNAME)** command.

Figure 5.39 Selecting the New Alias (CNAME) Command

2. In the **New Resource Record** dialog box (Figure 5.40), enter **wpad** in the **Alias name** (uses parent domain if left blank) text box. Click the **Browse** button.

Figure 5.40 The New Resource Record Dialog Box

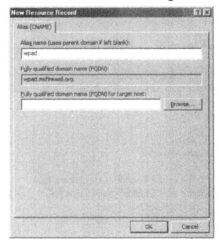

3. In the **Browse** dialog box, double-click on your server name in the **Records** list.

4. In the **Browse** dialog box, double-click on the **Forward Lookup Zone** entry in the **Records** frame.

5. In the **Browse** dialog box, double-click on the name of your forward lookup zone in the **Records** frame.

6. In the **Browse** dialog box, select the name of the ISA 2004 firewall in the **Records** frame. Click **OK**.

Figure 5.41 New Resource Dialog Box

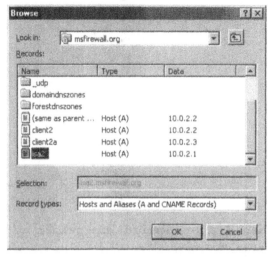

7. Click **OK** in the **New Resource Record** dialog box.

8. The **CNAME (alias)** entry appears in the right pane of the **DNS** management console.

Figure 5.42 Viewing the DNS WPAD Alias

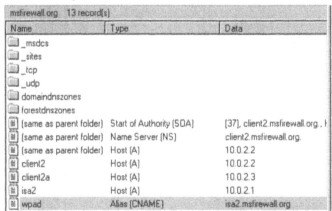

9. Close the **DNS Management** console.

Configure the Client to Use the Fully-Qualified wpad Alias

Web Proxy and Firewall clients need to be able to correctly resolve the name *wpad*. The Web Proxy and Firewall client configurations are *not aware of the domain containing the wpad alias*. The Web Proxy and Firewall client operating system must be able to provide this information to the Web Proxy and Firewall client software.

DNS queries must be *fully qualified* before the query is sent to the DNS server. A fully-qualified request contains a host name and a domain name. The Web Proxy and Firewall clients only know the *host name* portion, which in this case is *Wpad*. Web Proxy and Firewall client operating system must be able to provide the correct domain name, which it appends to the *wpad* host name, before it can send a DNS query to the DNS server.

There are a number of methods you can use to provide a domain name that is appended to the *wpad* name before the query is sent to the client's DNS server. Two popular methods for doing this are:

- Using DHCP to assign a primary domain name
- Configuring a primary domain name in the client operating system's network identification dialog box.

We will detail these two methods in the following steps:

1. Right-click **My Computer** on the desktop, and click the **Properties** command.
2. In the **System Properties** dialog box, click the **Network Identification** tab. Click the **Properties** button.
3. In the **Identification Changes** dialog box (see Figure 5.43), click **More**.

Figure 5.43 The Identification Changes Dialog Box

4. In the **DNS Suffix and NetBIOS Computer Name** dialog box shown in Figure 5.44, enter the domain name that contains your wpad entry in the **Primary DNS suffix of this computer** text box. This is the domain name that the operating system will append to the wpad name before sending the DNS query to the DNS server. By default, the primary domain name is the same as the domain name to which the machine belongs. If the machine is not a member of a domain, this text box will be empty. Note **Change primary DNS suffix when domain membership changes** is enabled by default. In the current example, the machine is not a member of a domain. Cancel out of each of the dialog boxes so that you do not configure a primary domain name at this time.

Figure 5.44 The DNS Suffix and NetBIOS Computer Name Dialog Box

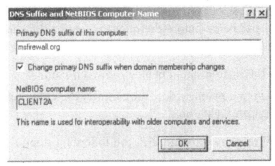

5. Another way to assign a machine a primary domain name is to use DHCP. A DHCP server can be configured to supply DHCP clients a primary domain name by configuring a DHCP scope option. We did this earlier when we created a scope on the DHCP server using the DHCP scope wizard. In the current example, the **DNS Domain Name** scope option was set to deliver the domain name *msfirewall.org* to DHCP clients. This option (shown in Figure 5.45) has the same effect as manually setting the primary domain name. DHCP clients will append this name to unqualified DNS queries (such as those for wpad) before sending the DNS query to a DNS server.

Figure 5.45 Viewing Scope Options

Scope Options		
Option Name	Vendor	Value
006 DNS Servers	Standard	10.0.2.2
015 DNS Domain Name	Standard	msfirewall.org

6. Go to the DHCP client system and open a command prompt. At the command prompt, enter **ipconfig /all** and press **ENTER**. Notice that the machine has been assigned a **Connection-specific DNS Suffix** of **msfirewall.org**.

DHCP is the most efficient way to assign a primary DNS suffix to clients on your network, as seen in Figure 5.46. This feature allows you to automatically configure a DNS suffix on DHCP clients that connect to your network, which are not members of your Active Directory domain. These clients can still correctly resolve the wpad name based on your current DNS infrastructure without requiring them to join the domain or manually configuring them.

Figure 5.46 DHCP client configuration

```
C:\>ipconfig /all

Windows 2000 IP Configuration

        Host Name . . . . . . . . . . . . : CLIENT2A
        Primary DNS Suffix  . . . . . . . :
        Node Type . . . . . . . . . . . . : Hybrid
        IP Routing Enabled. . . . . . . . : No
        WINS Proxy Enabled. . . . . . . . : No
        DNS Suffix Search List. . . . . . : msfirewall.org

Ethernet adapter Local Area Connection:

        Connection-specific DNS Suffix  . : msfirewall.org
        Description . . . . . . . . . . . : AMD PCNET Family PCI Ethernet Adap
r #2
        Physical Address. . . . . . . . . : 00-0C-29-C6-F8-E8
        DHCP Enabled. . . . . . . . . . . : Yes
        Autoconfiguration Enabled . . . . : Yes
        IP Address. . . . . . . . . . . . : 10.0.2.100
        Subnet Mask . . . . . . . . . . . : 255.255.255.0
        Default Gateway . . . . . . . . . :
        DHCP Server . . . . . . . . . . . : 10.0.2.2
        DNS Servers . . . . . . . . . . . : 10.0.2.2
        Lease Obtained. . . . . . . . . . : Sunday, January 11, 2004 4:17:20 I
        Lease Expires . . . . . . . . . . : Monday, January 19, 2004 4:17:20 I

C:\>
```

Note that if you have multiple domains and clients on your Internal network that belong to multiple domains, you will need to create wpad CNAME alias entries for each of the domains. In addition, DNS support for WPAD entries can be a bit problematic when you have a single Internal network domain that spans WAN links. You can only enter a single WPAD entry per domain, and all hosts that fully qualify the WPAD entry with that domain name will receive the same server address. This can lead to Branch office hosts attempting to access the Internet via an ISA 2004 located at the Main office. The best solution to this problem is to create subdomains in the DNS that support Branch office clients.

Configure the client browser to use autodiscovery

The next step is to configure the browser to use autodiscovery. If you have not already done so, configure the Web browser to use autodiscovery to automatically configure itself to use the ISA 2004 firewall's Web Proxy:

1. Right-click on the **Internet Explorer** icon on the desktop, and click **Properties**.

2. In the **Internet Properties** dialog box, click the **Connections** tab. Click the **LAN Settings** button.

3. In the **Local Area Network (LAN) Settings** dialog box, put a checkmark in the **Automatically detect settings** check box. Click **OK**.

4. Click **Apply**, and then click **OK** in the **Internet Properties** dialog box.

The next step is to configure the ISA 2004 firewall **Publish Autodiscovery Information** for autodiscovery Web Proxy and Firewall clients.

Special Considerations for VPN Clients

VPN clients can also be configured as Web Proxy clients of the network to which they connect via the VPN link. However, the Web Proxy client configuration is done on a per-connection basis. In order for the Web Proxy client to use the Web Proxy server on the destination network (the network the client is connected to via the VPN link), you must configure the VPN client to use the Web Proxy server for that specific VPN connection.

Perform the following steps to configure the VPN client to use a Web Proxy server on the remote network:

1. Right click on the **Internet Explorer** icon on the desktop and click **Properties**.

2. On the Connections tab, you'll see a list of your VPN connections in the Dial-up and Virtual Private Network Settings list. Select the **VPN connectoid** from the list and click Settings.

3. In the Settings dialog box for the VPN connectoid, select the appropriate Web Proxy settings. Depending on the Web Proxy support provided by the remote network, you can use the **Automatically detect settings, Use automatic configuration script** or **Use a proxy server for this connection option**.

4. Click **OK**, and then click **OK** again in the Internet Properties dialog box.

Allowing the VPN client to connect via the Web proxy allows the VPN client to be a Web Proxy client in addition to a SecureNAT client when connected to the ISA firewall/VPN server. This has the potential to significant enhance Web browsing performance and provides much better security than allowing split tunneling for the VPN client.

Configure the ISA 2004 Firewall to Publish Autodiscovery Information

Do the following on the ISA 2004 firewall to enable it to provide autoconfiguration information to Web Proxy and Firewall autodiscovery clients:

1. At the ISA 2004 firewall, open the **Microsoft Internet Security and Acceleration Server 2004** management console. Expand the server name in the left pane of the console, and then expand the **Configuration** node. Click the **Networks** node.

2. On the **Networks** node, click the **Networks** tab in the **Details** pane.

3. Right click the **Internal** network on the **Networks** tab, and click **Properties** (see Figure 5.47).

Figure 5.47 Accessing the Internal Network Properties Dialog Box

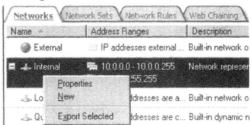

4. In the **Internal Properties** dialog box, put a checkmark in the **Publish automatic discovery information** check box. In the **Use this port for automatic discovery request** text box, leave the default port 80, as it is.

5. Click **Apply** and **OK**.

6. Click **Apply** to save the changes and update the firewall policy.

7. Click **OK** in the **Apply New Configuration** dialog box.

WARNING

Make sure that you do not install, or if already installed, disable, the IIS WWW service on the ISA 2004 firewall. If the IIS WWW service is running on the ISA firewall, it could prevent the ISA 2004 firewall from binding to TCP port 80. This type of *socket contention* is common when the ISA firewall has extraneous services running on it. For this reason, we recommend that you never run non-firewall services on the ISA firewall. This includes the IIS WWW service. An exception to this is when the WWW service is required for remote firewall management using third-party vendor management interfaces, such as the comprehensive Web interface provided by the **RoadBLOCK** firewall appliance (www.rimapp.com).

Making the Connection Using DNS for Autodiscovery

All the parts are now in place to allow the Web Proxy and Firewall client machine to use DNS to obtain autoconfiguration information. Perform the following steps on the Web Proxy client computer:

1. Open **Internet Explorer** and go to the **www.microsoft.com/isaserver/** home page.

2. A **Network Monitor** trace shows the Web Proxy client makes a DNS query for *wpad.msfirewall.org.* The DNS server responds to the query with the IP address (shown in Figure 5.48) of the ISA 2004 firewall computers.

Figure 5.48 Viewing DNS wpad Query Requests

Protocol	Description
DNS	0x406A:Std Qry for wpad.msfirewall.org. of type Host Addr on class INET addr.
DNS	0x406A:Std Qry Resp. for wpad.msfirewall.org. of type Host Addr on class INET
TCP	....S., len: 0, seq: 773548798-773548798, ack: 0, win:16384, src: .

3. After it obtains the IP address of the ISA 2004 firewall computer and the port from which it can obtain autoconfiguration information, the Web Proxy client sends a request (see Figure 5.49) for wpad autoconfiguration information. You can see this request in the bottom pane of the Network Monitor Window, **GET /wpad.dat HTTP/1.1**.

Figure 5.49 Viewing the Details of a DNS wpad Query Request

```
00000000  00 0C 29 30 5B 64 00 0C 29 C6 F8 E8 08 00 45 00   . +)0[d. +) ⊢"◆◘.E.
00000010  00 96 00 61 40 00 80 06 E1 FD 0A 00 02 03 0A 00   .û.a@.Ç±◘*◙.◆▼◙.
00000020  02 01 04 23 00 50 CE 1E 6A FF 16 CC EE 43 50 18   ◆✿◆#.P.←j -"≡CP↑
00000030  44 70 6C 3I 00 00 47 45 54 20 2F 77 70 61 64 2E   Dpl=..GET /wpad.
00000040  64 61 74 20 48 54 54 50 2F 31 2E 31 0D 0A 41 63   dat HTTP/1.1◙◙Ac
00000050  63 65 70 74 3A 20 2A 2F 2A 0D 0A 55 73 65 72 2D   cept: */*◙◙User-
00000060  41 67 65 6E 74 3A 20 4D 6F 7A 69 6C 6C 61 2F 34   Agent: Mozilla/4
00000070  2E 30 20 28 63 6F 6D 70 61 74 69 62 6C 65 3B 20   .0 (compatible;
```

Automating Installation of the Firewall Client

The Firewall client software can be installed on virtually any 32-bit version of Windows except Windows 95. There are a number of compelling reasons for installing the Firewall client software on all machines that supports its installation:

■   The Firewall client allows you to create user/group-based access controls for *all* TCP and UDP protocols. This is in contrast to the Web Proxy client configuration, which only supports HTTP, HTTPS and FTP.

■   The Firewall client has access to all TCP and UDP protocols, including those requiring secondary connections. In contrast, the SecureNAT client does not support application protocols that require secondary connections *unless* there is an application filter to support it.

■   The Firewall client provides much better performance than the SecureNAT client.

- The Firewall client sends application information to the ISA 2004 firewall service; this allows the Firewall service logs to collect application usage information and helps you determine which applications users are using to access Internet sites and services.

- The Firewall client sends user information to the Firewall service; this enables the ISA 2004 firewall to control access based on user account *and* record user information in the Firewall service's access logs. This information can be extracted and put into report form.

With these features, the Firewall client provides a level of functionality, security and access control that no other firewall in its class can match. For this reason, we always recommend that you install the Firewall client on any machine supporting the Firewall client software.

However, because the Firewall client configuration requires the Firewall client software to be installed, many firewall administrators are hesitant to avail themselves of the full feature set provided by the Firewall client. Many ISA 2004 firewall administrators don't have the time or the resources to "touch" (visit) each authorized computer on the corporate network in order to install the Firewall client software.

The solution to this problem is to automate the installation of the Firewall client. There are two methods that you can use. These methods require no additional software purchase and can greatly simplify the installation of the Firewall client software on large numbers of computers on the corporate network. These methods are:

- Group Policy-based software installation and management
- Silent installation script

In the following section, we will discuss these methods, as well as some key ISA Server client configuration settings you should make in the **ISA Management** console.

Configuring Firewall Client and Web Proxy Client Configuration in the ISA Management Console

There are a few configuration options you should set for the Firewall client *before* you configure a Group Policy or a silent installation script to install the Firewall client software. These settings, made at the **Microsoft Internet Security and Acceleration Server 2004** management console, determine issues such as Firewall client autodiscovery behavior and whether (and how) the Web browser is configured during installation of the Firewall client.

Perform the following steps on the ISA 2004 firewall to configure these settings:

1. In the **Microsoft Internet Security and Acceleration Server 2004 management console**, expand the server name, and then expand the **Configuration** node.

2. Click the **Networks** node, and then click **Networks** on the **Details** tab. Right-click the Internal network, and click **Properties**.

3. In the **Internal Properties** dialog box, click the **Firewall Client** tab.

4. On the **Firewall Client** tab, put a checkmark in the **Enable Firewall client support for this network** check box. In the **Firewall client configuration** frame, enter the name of the ISA 2004 firewall computer in the **ISA Server name or IP address** text box. The default setting is the computer name. However, you should replace the computer (NetBIOS) name with the fully-qualified domain name of the ISA 2004 firewall. When you replace the computer name with the FQDN, the Firewall client machines can use DNS to correctly resolve the name of the ISA 2004 firewall. This will avoid one of the most common troubleshooting issues with Firewall client connectivity. Make sure there is an entry for this name in your Internal network's DNS server.

The Web Proxy client configuration settings are available in the **Web browser configuration on the Firewall client computer** frame. These settings will automatically configure the Web browser as a Web Proxy client. Note that you can change the settings later, and the Web browsers will automatically update themselves with the new settings.

The **Automatically detect settings** option allows the Web browser to detect the Web Proxy and configure itself based on the settings you configure on the **Web Browser** tab of the **Internal Properties** dialog box, shown in Figure 5.50.

Figure 5.50 Internal Properties Dialog Box.

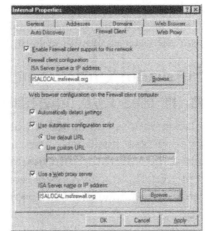

The **Use automatic configuration script** option allows you to assign a proxy autoconfiguration file (PAC) address to the Web browser. The Web browser will then query the location you specify or use the default location; the default location is on the ISA 2004 firewall. Note that when you use the default location, you obtain the same information you would receive if you had configured the Web browser to use the **Automatically detect settings** option. The **Use default URL** option automatically configures the browser to connect to the ISA 2004 firewall for autoconfiguration information. You can use the **Use custom URL** if you want to create your own PAC file that overrides the settings on the automatically-generated file at the ISA 2004 firewall. You can find more information on PAC files and proxy client autoconfiguration files in **Using Automatic Configuration and Automatic Proxy** at **www.microsoft.com/resources/documentation/ie/5/all/reskit/ en-us/part5/ch21auto.mspx**

The **Use a Web Proxy server** option allows you to configure the Web browser to use the ISA 2004 as its Web Proxy, but without the benefits of the autoconfiguration script information. This setting provides higher performance than the SecureNAT client configuration, but you do not benefit from the settings contained in the autoconfiguration script. The most important configuration settings in the autoconfiguration script include site names and addresses that should be used for *Direct Access*. For this reason, you should avoid this option unless you do not wish to use Direct Access to bypass the Web Proxy service to access selected Web sites.

NOTE

Web Proxy client Direct Access configuration allows you to bypass the Web Proxy service for selected Web sites. Some Web sites do not conform to Internet standards (Java sites are the most common offenders), and therefore do not work properly through Web Proxy servers. To configure these sites for Direct Access and the client machine, bypass the Web Proxy service and use an alternate means to connect to the destination Web site (such as via a SecureNAT or firewall client configuration). In order for the client to use an alternate connection method, the client machine must be configured as a Firewall and/or SecureNAT client.

5. Click the **Web Browser** tab, as shown in Figure 5.51. There are several settings in this dialog box that configure the Web Proxy clients via the autoconfiguration script. Note that in order for these options to take effect, you must configure the Web Proxy clients to use the autoconfiguration script either via autodiscovery and autoconfiguration or via a manual setting for the location of the autoconfiguration script.

The **Bypass proxy for Web server in this network** option allows the Web browser to use Direct Access to directly connect to servers that are accessible via a *single label name*. For example, if the user accesses a Web server on the Internal network using the URL **http://SERVER1**, the Web Proxy client browser will *not* send the request to the ISA 2004 firewall. Instead, the Web browser will directly connect to the SERVER1 machine. This reduces the load on the ISA 2004 firewall and prevents users from *looping back* through the ISA 2004 firewall to access Internal network resources. Note that the Bypass proxy for Web server in this network setting does not mean the browser will bypass the Web Proxy for accessing internal IP addresses. It will bypass the Web Proxy only when using a single label name when connecting to the resource.

The **Directly access computers specified in the Domains tab** option allows you to configure Direct Access to machines contained in the **Domains** tab. The **Domains** tab contains a collection of domain names that are used by the Firewall client to determine which hosts are part of the Internal network and bypass the ISA 2004 firewall when contacting hosts that are part of the same domain. The Web Proxy client can also use the domain on this list for Direct Access. We recommend that you always select this option as it will reduce the load on the ISA 2004 firewall by preventing Web Proxy clients from looping back through the firewall to access Internal network resources. In addition, this setting is a pivotal component of a split DNS infrastructure.

The **Directly access these servers or domains** list is a list of computer addresses or domain names that you can configure for Direct Access. Click the **Add** button.

Figure 5.51 Web Browser Tab on the Internal Properties Dialog Box

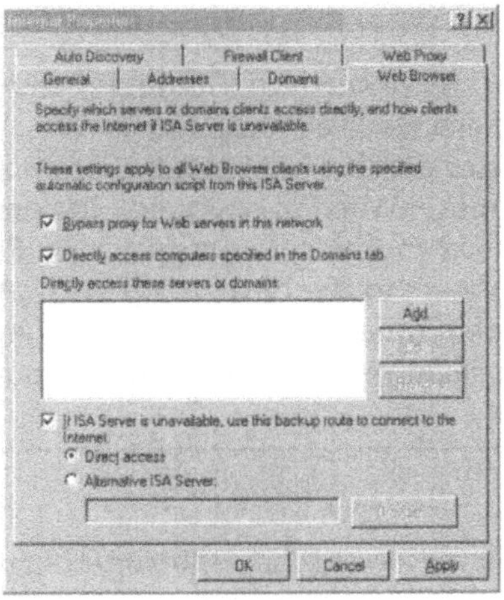

6. In the **Add Server** dialog box shown in Figure 5.52, you can select the **IP address within this range** option, and then enter an IP address or IP address range of machines that you want to Directly Access. You also have the option to select the **Domain or computer** option and enter the computer name or the FQDN of the machine that you want to access via Direct Access. A common domain name to enter for Direct Access is the **msn.com** domain, because this domain, along with the **passport.com** and the **hotmail.com**

domains must be configured for Direct Access to simplify Web Proxy client connections to the Microsoft Hotmail site.

Figure 5.52 The Add Server Dialog Box

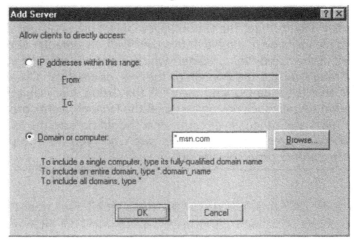

7. If the ISA firewall is unavailable, **use this backup route to connect to the Internet** option allows machines configured as Web Proxy clients to use other means to connect to the Internet. Typically, this means that the Web Proxy client will leverage its SecureNAT or Firewall client configuration to connect to the Internet. If the machine is not configured as a SecureNAT and/or Firewall client, then no access will be allowed if the Web Proxy service becomes unavailable.

8. Click **Apply**, and then click **OK**, after making the changes to the configuration in the **Internal Properties** dialog box.

9. Click **Apply** to save the changes and update the firewall policy.

At this point the Firewall and Web Proxy client configuration is ready, and you can install the Firewall client on machines behind the ISA 2004 firewall and have these settings automatically configured on them.

Group Policy Software Installation

You might not wish to install the Firewall client on all machines. For example, domain controllers and published servers should not be configured as Firewall clients. You can gain granular control over Group Policy-based software installation by creating an organizational unit for Firewall clients and then configuring an Organization Unit (OU) group policy object to install the Firewall client only on computers belonging to that OU.

NOTE

Placing machines in a Firewall client's OU is only one possible solution. If you have the requisite Active Directory (AD) expertise, you may wish to link the Group Policy Object to a higher level (domain or site) if you don't want to move the computer to another OU and create a Group Policy for each OU. However, you may need to filter the Group Policy Object using Groups or WMI filters, which incurs its own administrative overhead. By default, all computers are placed in the computer container (which is not an OU), and you must either link the Group Policy to the Domain or the Site, or create an OU and move the computer objects to the OU, and then link the Group Policy Object. Note that it's vital that not all machines be assigned the Firewall client software, as Domain Controllers and other server computers should not use the Firewall client unless it is absolutely required, such as the case when you want to publish servers that require complex protocol support.

Perform the following steps on the domain controller to create the OU, and then configure software installation and management to install the Firewall client on machines belonging to the OU:

1. Click **Start**, and select the **Administrative Tools** menu. Click **Active Directory Users and Computers**. Right-click on your domain name, and click **Organizational Unit**.

2. In the **New Object – Organizational Unit** dialog box, enter a name for the OU in the **Name** text box. In this example, we will call the OU **FWCLIENTS**. Click **OK**.

3. Click on the **Computers** node in the left pane of the console. Right-click your client computer, and click the **Move** command.

4. In the **Move** dialog box, click the **FWCLIENTS** OU, and click **OK**.

5. Click on the **FWCLIENTS** OU. You should see the computer you moved into this OU.

6. Right-click the **FWCLIENTS** OU, and click the **Properties** command.

7. Click the **Group Policy** tab in the **FWCLIENTS** dialog box. Click the **New** button to create a **New Group Policy Object**. Select the **New Group Policy Object** and click **Edit**.

8. Expand the **Computer Configuration** node, and then expand the **Software Settings** node. Right-click on **Software** installation, point to **New** and click **Package**.

9. In the **Open** text box, type the path to the Firewall client's Microsoft installer package (.msi file) in the **File name** text box. In this example, the path is:

   \\isa2\mspclnt\MS_FWC.MSI

Where **isa2** is the NetBIOS name of the ISA 2004 firewall computer or the name of the file server hosting the Firewall client installation files; **mspclnt** is the name of the share on the ISA 2004 firewall computer that contains the Firewall client installation files, and **MS_FWC.MSI** is the name of the Firewall client Microsoft installer package. Click **Open** after entering the path.

Figure 5.53 Entering the Installer Path

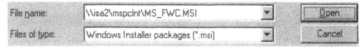

10. In the **Deploy Software** dialog box, select the **Assigned** option (see Figure 5.54) and click **OK**. Notice that you do not have the **Published** option when installing software using the **Computer Configuration** node. The software is installed before the user logs on. This is critical because only local administrators can install the Firewall client software. In contrast, you can assign software to machines and the software will install when no other user is logged onto the machine. Click **OK**.

Figure 5.54 Choosing the Assigned Option

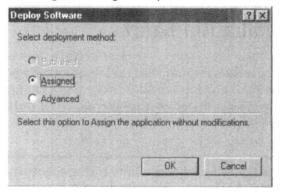

11. The new managed software package appears in the right pane of the console. All machines in the OU will have the Firewall client software installed when they are restarted. You can also manage the Firewall client software from here, as shown in Figure 5.55.

NOTE

For more details on how to take full advantage of Group Policy-based software installation and maintenance, please see the **Step-by-Step Guide to Software Installation and Maintenance** at www.microsoft.com/windows2000/tech-info/planning/management/swinstall.asp

Figure 5.55 Managed Software

Name △	Version	Deployment state	Source
Microsoft Firewall Client	3.0	Assigned	\\isa2\mspclnt\MS_FWC.MSI

12. Close the **Group Policy Object Editor** and the **Active Directory Users and Computers** console.

13. When you restart the machines in the **FWCLIENTS** OU, you will see the log-on dialog box (Figure 5.56) provide information about how managed software is being installed on the Windows client operating system.

Figure 5.56 Logging On

Silent Installation Script

Another useful method for installing the Firewall client software is to use a silent installation script. This method is useful when the logged-on user is a member of the local administrator's group. The silent installation script does not expose the user to any dialog boxes, and the user does not need to make decisions during the installation process.

TIP

In most situations, the Firewall client sends credentials of domain users to the ISA 2004 firewall. The ISA 2004 firewall must be a member of the user domain, or member of a domain that trusts the user domain, in order to authenticate users who authenticate with the Firewall client. Since users are already members of an Active Directory domain, a more efficient method of installing the Firewall client is to use Active Directory Group Policy. However, there are situations where there is no Active Directory domain, or you do not want to make the ISA 2004 firewall a member of the domain. In this case, you can mirror user accounts on the ISA 2004 firewall. The user accounts you configure on the ISA 2004 firewall will have the same user names and passwords that the users use to log on to their machines.

Open notepad; copy the following line into the new text document, and save the file as "fwcinstall.cmd": **msiexec /i \\ISA2\mspclnt\MS_FWC.msi /qn / l*v c:\mspclnt_i.log**

The **\\ISA2** entry is the computer name of the ISA 2004 firewall computer and will vary for each installation location. The rest of the line can be used exactly as listed above. Users can then go to a Web page, or click a link in an email message pointing them to this batch file. The process is very simple and only requires the user to click the link to run the script and from our experience with users and e-mail worms, we know they have no problems double clicking on exectuables. You could also place the .cmd file on a corporate Web site and send a message to users to visit the site and run the command. The installation is completely transparent, and the only thing the user will see is a momentary command prompt window and the Firewall client icon in the system tray when the procedure is completed.

WARNING

The user must be a member of the *local* Administrator's group to install the Firewall client software. If the user is not a member of the local Administrator's group, the software installation will fail. You can get around this problem by assigning the Firewall client software to machines. The software is installed before user log-on, so there are no issues with who the logged-on user is at the time of installation.

Systems Management Server (SMS)

Organizations using Systems Management Server (SMS) 2003 can use the software distribution feature of SMS to deploy the Firewall client software. The Software distribution routine in SMS 2003 provides the ability to deploy Windows Installer (.msi) files to any computer that is assigned to the SMS environment in a manner similar to the Active Directory Group Policy software management feature. Do the following to deploy the Firewall client using SMS 2003:

1. Create a collection that includes all the machines on which you want the Firewall client installed. An SMS collection is a group of network objects, such as computers or users, which are treated as an SMS management group. You can configure requirements such as IP address, hardware configuration, or add clients directly by name to group all computers that require the Firewall client software.

2. Create a package by importing the Firewall client Windows file (**MS_FWC.msi**). The Windows Installer file automatically includes a variety of attended and unattended installation options that can be used on a per-system or per-user basis. Programs are also created to uninstall the client. The per-system programs are configured to install the client with administrative

rights whether or not the user is logged on. The per-user programs install the client using the credentials of the logged-on user. This provides an advantage over the Group Policy method, which does not allow you to temporarily elevate privileges to install the Firewall client application.

3. Create an SMS advertisement, which specifies the target collection and program to install. In order to control deployment, you can schedule a time for the program to be advertised to collection members.

Summary

A server is of little use without clients, but the ISA firewall is unusual in that there are a number of different ways a computer can be configured to act as an ISA client. In fact, there are three distinct ISA client types: the SecureNAT client, the Firewall client and the Web Proxy client. Determining which is most appropriate in a given situation depends on a number of factors, including the client operating system, the protocols that need to be supported, and whether it is desirable or feasible to install client software on the client computers.

The SecureNAT client requires no software installation and no changes to the client computer's Web browser. By simply setting the client computer's TCP/IP settings so that the default gateway is that of the ISA firewall, any computer, running any popular operating system, can benefit from ISA Server 2004's firewall protections. This includes non-Microsoft operating systems such as Linux/UNIX and Macintosh, as well as older Microsoft operating systems, such as Windows 95, Windows 3.x and MS-DOS, which are not supported by the Firewall client software. All simple protocols are supported by SecureNAT, and even complex protocols can be supported by installing application filters on the ISA firewall. SecureNAT is the logical choice when you have a variety of different client operating systems that need ISA's protection, and the client systems need to access protocols other than HTTP/HTTPS or FTP.

The Web Proxy client will also work with all operating system platforms, so long as a compatible Web browser (one that can be configured to use a proxy server) is installed. However, the Web Proxy client is much more limited in the protocols it supports; only HTTP/HTTPS and HTTP-tunneled FTP (FTP download) are supported. In many cases, this will be all that is needed, and indeed, this limitation acts as an extra security measure by preventing access to other applications. One advantage of the Web Proxy client over SecureNAT is its ability to authenticate with the ISA firewall (if the firewall requests credentials). SecureNAT clients are able to authenticate only with client applications that support SOCKS 5 and only if a SOCKS 5 application filter is installed on the ISA firewall machine.

The Firewall client is the "client of choice" for modern Windows client machines— or at least, it should be. It can be installed on Windows 98 and all subsequent Windows operating systems, and it supports all Winsock applications that use TCP/UDP, including those that require complex protocols. No application filters are needed, reducing administrative overhead on the server side. Best of all, the Firewall client allows you to take advantage of strong user/group-based access controls, as credentials are sent to the ISA Server for authentication without any special configuration or action required on the part of the client. The Firewall client also gives administrators more control via logging of user and application information.

Client configuration problems are a common cause of access and security problems. However, configuring the Web Proxy client and installing the Firewall client don't have to be difficult or time-consuming. Both processes can be easily automated, and administrators have several automation methods from which to choose. DHCP servers can be configured to support Web Proxy and Firewall client autodiscovery, as can DNS servers.

Installation can be automated via Group Policy or a silent installation script, or you can use the Internet Explorer Administration Kit (IEAK) to configure the Web proxy client. If you have Systems Management Server (SMS) on your network, you can use it to deploy the Firewall client.

Selecting the correct client configuration and properly configuring the client computers is an essential ingredient in a successful deployment of ISA Server 2004, so it's important to understand the three client types and the step-by-step process for configuring each *before* you install your ISA Server.

Solutions Fast Track

Understanding the ISA 2004 SecureNAT Client

☑ The SecureNAT client does not require software installation. The only requirement is that the client operating system be configured with a default gateway address that can route Internet bound communications through the ISA 2004 firewall.

☑ The SecureNAT client supports all protocols not requiring secondary connections. Protocols requiring secondary connections (such as FTP) require an application filter on the ISA 2004 firewall.

☑ The SecureNAT client only supports protocols that are included in the Protocol list on the ISA 2004 firewall. If there is no protocol definition for the protocol, then the SecureNAT client will not be able to access the protocol, even if there is an Access Rule allowing the SecureNAT client machine access to all protocols.

☑ All operating systems can be configured as SecureNAT clients.

☑ The SecureNAT client is not a client/server relationship. There is no software on the SecureNAT client that directly communicates with the ISA 2004 firewall.

☑ The SecureNAT client does not send user or application information to the ISA 2004 firewall. The firewall records the source IP address of the connection and places only that information in the log files.

☑ The SecureNAT client is the only client that can access non-TCP/UDP protocols, such as ICMP (which is used by ping and tracert) and PPTP (which requires GRE, which does not use TCP or UDP as a transport).

☑ You cannot implement secure user/group-based authentication with non-TCP/UDP protocols because the SecureNAT client does not support sending user information to the ISA 2004 firewall.

☑ The SecureNAT client is designed for non-Microsoft operating systems. All Microsoft operating systems that support the Firewall client should have the

Firewall client installed. The exception to this is published servers and network infrastructure servers, such as domain controllers, DHCP servers, DNS servers, and IAS servers.

☑ In general, all published servers should be configured as SecureNAT clients. The exception to this is when the Web or Server Publishing Rule is configured to replace the original client IP address with the ISA 2004 firewall's IP address

☑ The SecureNAT client can take advantage of the ISA 2004 firewall's Web Proxy cache if the SecureNAT client accesses the Internet via a rule that has the Web Proxy filter enabled.

☑ The SecureNAT client is highly dependent on the current routing infrastructure; all routers along the path between the SecureNAT client and the Internet must be aware that all Internet-bound requests must leave via the Internal IP address of the ISA 2004 firewall.

Understanding the ISA 2004 Web Proxy Client

☑ All applications designed for Web Proxy support can be configured as Web Proxy clients.

☑ The Web Proxy client configuration does *not* require software installation; the only requirement is that the application that supports Web Proxy connections is configured to use the ISA 2004 firewall as its Web Proxy server.

☑ The Web Proxy client can send user credentials to the firewall; this enables strong user/group-based access control for Web Proxy clients.

☑ The Web Proxy client only supports HTTP, HTTPS (SSL/TLS), and FTP-tunneled download connections.

☑ You cannot perform FTP uploads via the Web Proxy client.

☑ The Web Proxy client automatically takes advantage of the Web Proxy cache on the ISA 2004 firewall.

☑ The Web Proxy client communicates directly with the ISA 2004 firewall, which makes it independent of the routing infrastructure. The only requirement is that the Web Proxy client machine knows the route to the Internal interface of the ISA 2004 firewall.

☑ The Web Proxy client can be automatically configured to connect to the Internet via the ISA 2004 firewall by using WPAD and the Web Proxy client autodiscovery. This allows all Web browsers on the network to automatically know what IP address to use for their Web Proxy client configuration without requiring the administrator to configure each client individually.

☑ The Web Proxy client may not be able to connect to some Web sites, such as those that use Java and embed private addresses in their communications or otherwise violate RFC Web Proxy behavior. You can configure Direct Access for sites that do not conform to RFC Web Proxy behavior.

☑ The Web Proxy client can be configured to use an autoconfiguration script; the autoconfiguration script provides the Web Proxy client information regarding the name of the ISA 2004 firewall and sites that the Web Proxy client should bypass via the Direct Access mechanism.

☑ Outbound Web Proxy client connections tunnel SSL through the firewall. Unlike Web Publishing scenarios where the published Web server is accessed via SSL-to-SSL bridging, the ISA 2004 firewall can not evaluate the content within an SSL tunnel made through the firewall.

Understanding the ISA 2004 Firewall Client

☑ The Firewall client can send user and application information to the ISA 2004 firewall and have this information stored in the log files.

☑ The Firewall client supports secondary connections without the aid of an application filter.

☑ The Firewall client does not require a protocol definition to access a protocol. If you configure an Access Rule that allows access to all protocols, the Firewall client will be able to access all TCP and UDP protocols, even if there is no Protocol Definition for a particular protocol.

☑ The Firewall client intercepts all TCP and UDP communications from Winsock applications and "remotes" them (sends them directly) to the ISA 2004 firewall. This makes the Firewall client relatively independent of the current routing infrastructure. The only requirement is that the Firewall client machine know the route to the Internal interface of the ISA 2004 firewall.

☑ The Firewall client can automatically find the ISA 2004 firewall through the use of WPAD entries in DHCP or DNS.

☑ The Firewall client can be deployed via Active Directory Group Policy, via SMS, or via a silent installation script.

☑ If you are not using SMS, the logged on user must be a member of the local administrators group to install the Firewall client software.

☑ You can automatically configure the Web browser as a Web Proxy client at the same time the Firewall client software is installed.

☑ The Firewall client requires software installation; the software is supported by all 32-bit Windows operating systems with the exception of Windows 95.

☑ The Firewall client is compatible with all ISA 2004 client types. However, a single machine cannot *act* as both a SecureNAT and Firewall client for Winsock applications that communicate using UDP or TCP.

Automating ISA 2004 Client Provisioning

- ☑ SecureNAT clients can be automatically configured using DHCP to assign the appropriate default gateway address.

- ☑ The Web Proxy client can be automatically configured to use the ISA 2004 firewall via WPAD entries in DNS and/or DHCP.

- ☑ The Web Proxy client can be automatically configured when the Firewall client is installed.

- ☑ The Web Proxy client does not require software installation; only applications that support Web Proxy connections can be configured as Web Proxy clients of the ISA 2004 firewall.

Automating Firewall Client Installation

- ☑ The Firewall client software can be installed using SMS, Active Directory Group Policy, or via a silent installation script.

- ☑ The Firewall client can automatically find the ISA 2004 firewall via WPAD entries in DNS and/or DHCP.

- ☑ The Firewall client can be manually configured to connect to a specific ISA 2004 firewall.

Frequently Asked Questions

The following Frequently Asked Questions, answered by the authors of this book, are designed to both measure your understanding of the concepts presented in this chapter and to assist you with real-life implementation of these concepts. To have your questions about this chapter answered by the author, browse to **www.syngress.com/solutions** and click on the **"Ask the Author"** form. You will also gain access to thousands of other FAQs at ITFAQnet.com.

Q: My computer is configured as a SecureNAT client and I cannot connect to an FTP site. What's the problem?

A: The ISA 2004 firewall includes an FTP application filter that allows connections to FTP sites without requiring the Firewall client. This means that you do *not* need the Firewall client software installed on the client machine to support the secondary connections the FTP protocol uses. You will need to investigate alternate reasons for your FTP connections failure, as installing the Firewall client software will not fix the problem.

Q: My computer is configured as a Firewall client. I am using Microsoft Outlook and I cannot connect to my POP3 server. Why can I connect to servers using other protocols but not POP3?

A: If you are using Outlook, the default Firewall client settings are configured to bypass the Firewall client. Therefore, there must be an alternate mechanism for the client to access the POP3 server. Make sure the client is also configured as a SecureNAT client, or configure the Firewall client settings so that Outlook uses the Firewall client. This can be done via the Firewall client settings in the Microsoft Internet Security and Acceleration Server 2004 management console.

Q: My computer is configured as a Web Proxy client. I am trying to connect to some chat and other Java sites but the Web Proxy client cannot connect. What can I do to make the connection?

A: There are several reasons why the connections to these sites are not working. The most common reason is that the Java code is not compliant with RFC Web Proxy servers. Since ISA 2004 is an RFC-compliant Web Proxy server, it will not always be able to present content from sites that are non-compliant. In addition, some chat and other online applications use additional protocols, in addition to HTTP. If this is the case, you will need to configure the client as a SecureNAT or Firewall client to support the additional protocols. For sites that are not compliant with RFC Web Proxy servers, you can configure those sites so that the Web Proxy clients use Direct Access via their SecureNAT and/or Firewall client configuration.

Q: I have configured the WPAD entry in my DHCP server, and some of my clients are able to automatically obtain the autoconfiguration information for the Web Proxy and Firewall client settings. However, most of my machines are not able to obtain the information from the DHCP server. What's going on here?

A: Keep in mind that when you use DHCP to assign autoconfiguration information via WPAD entries, only users logged on as local administrators can obtain the WPAD information. For users that do not log on as members of the local administrators group, you must configure a WPAD entry in DNS to support their connections.

Q: I need to access some Internet games and some voice applications over the Internet, like Yahoo games and Yahoo voice chat. My clients are configured as SecureNAT clients. My users are not able to make the connections. What can I do to enable these types of applications?

A: You will need to install the Firewall client to support applications that require secondary protocols. Most voice applications and many Internet games require secondary connections. While it is possible to use the SecureNAT client for these types of applications, you will need to create an application filter to support each Internet application requiring complex protocols. Another alternative is, if the client application supports SOCKS 4 proxies, you can configure the application to use SOCKS 4 to connect to the SOCKS 4 filter on the ISA 2004 firewall machine.

Q: I need to connect to an SSL Web site using TCP port 8081 but my Web Proxy client will not connect. What can I do to connect to the SSL Web site using an alternate port?

A: Check out Jim Harrison's **www.isatools.org** Web site. Jim has an excellent tool there that extends the SSL tunnel port range to any ports you desire. The name of the file, at the time of this writing, is **isa2k4_ssl_tpr.zip**.

Q: My SecureNAT clients can't get to the Internet. My Web Proxy clients and Firewall clients can get to the Internet without problems. The default gateway is set up correctly. Why can my Firewall and Web Proxy clients get to the Internet and not my SecureNAT clients?

A: The most likely reason is that your SecureNAT clients are not configured to use a DNS server that can resolve Internet host names. In contrast to Web Proxy and Firewall clients, which allow the ISA 2004 firewall to resolve names on their behalf, the SecureNAT client must resolve names on it own. Double-check the DNS settings on your SecureNAT client and configure them to use a DNS server that resolves Internet host names.

Chapter 6

Installing and Configuring the ISA Firewall Software

Topics in this Chapter:

Pre-installation Tasks and Considerations

There are several key pre-installation and tasks and considerations you need to address before installing the ISA firewall software. These include:

- System Requirements
- Configuring the Routing Table
- DNS Server Placement
- Configuring the ISA Firewall's Network Interfaces
- Unattended Installation
- Installation via a Terminal Services Administration Mode Session

System Requirements

The following are requirements for installing the ISA firewall software:

- Intel or AMD system with a 550 megahertz (MHz) or higher processor
- Windows 2000 or Windows Server 2003 operating system
- A minimum of 256 megabytes (MB) of memory; a practical minimum of 512 MB of memory for non–Web caching systems, and 1000 MB for Web-caching ISA firewalls
- At least one network adapter; two or more network adapters are required to obtain stateful filtering and stateful application-layer inspection firewall functionality
- An additional network adapter for each network connected to the ISA Server computer
- One local hard-disk partition that is formatted with the NTFS file system, and at least 150 MB of available hard disk space (this is exclusive of hard-disk space you want to use for caching)
- Additional disk space, which ideally is on a separate spindle, if you plan on using the ISA firewall's Web-caching feature

Special installation issues if you plan on installing the ISA firewall software on Windows 2000 include:

- Windows 2000 Service Pack 4 (SP4), or later, must be installed.
- Internet Explorer 6, or later, must be installed.
- If you are using the Windows 2000 SP4 slipstream, you must also install the hotfix specified in article 821887, "Events for Authorization Roles Are Not Logged in the Security Log When You Configure Auditing for Windows 2000 Authorization Manager Runtime," in the Microsoft Knowledge Base at http://support.microsoft.com/default.aspx?scid=kb;en-us;821887.

- You cannot configure the L2TP IPSec pre-shared key.

- VPN Quarantine is not supported when using RADIUS policy.

- All ISA Server services run using the local system account.

Another important consideration is capacity planning. While the above reflects minimal system requirements for installing and running the ISA firewall software, the ideal configuration is obtained when you size the hardware to optimize the ISA firewall software performance for your site. Table 6.1 provides basic guidelines regarding processor, memory, disk space and network adapter requirements based on Internet link speed.

Table 6.1 Basic Processor, Memory, Disk Space and Network Adapter Requirements Based on Link Speed

Internet	Up to 7.5 Mbps	Up to 25 Mbps	Up to 45 Mbps	Notes
Processors	1	1	2	
Processor type	Pentium III 550 MHz (or higher)	Pentium 4 2.0 - 3.0 GHz	Xeon 2.0 - 3.0 GHz	You can use other processors with comparable power that emulate the IA-32 instruction set. In deployments requiring only stateful filtering ("stateful packet inspection" — that is, when there is no need for higher security stateful application-layer inspection), the Pentium 4 and Xeon processor recommendations reach LAN wire speeds.
Memory	256 MB	512 MB	1 GB	With Web caching enabled, these requirements may be increased by approximately 256-512 MB.
Disk space	150 MB	2.5 GB	5 GB	This is exclusive of hard-disk space you need to use for caching and logging.
Network adapter	10/100 Mbps	10/100 Mbps	100/1000 Mbps	These are the requirements for the network adapters not connected to the Internet.

Continued

Table 6.1 Basic Processor, Memory, Disk Space and Network Adapter Requirements Based on Link Speed

Internet	Up to 7.5 Mbps	Up to 25 Mbps	Up to 45 Mbps	Notes
Concurrent Remote-access VPN connections	150	700	850	The Standard Edition of the ISA firewall supports a hard-coded maximum of 1000 concurrent VPN connections.

For an exceptionally thorough and comprehensive discussion on ISA firewall performance optimization and sizing, please refer to the Microsoft document **ISA Server 2004 Performance Best Practices** at www.microsoft.com/technet/prodtechnol/isa/2004/plan/bestpractices.mspx.

Configuring the Routing Table

The routing table on the ISA firewall machine should be configured before you install the ISA firewall software. The routing table should include routes to all networks that are not local to the ISA firewall's network interfaces. These routing table entries are required because the ISA firewall can have only a single default gateway. Normally, the default gateway is configured on the network interface that is used for the External Network. Therefore, if you have an internal or or other Network that contains multiple subnets, you should configure routing table entries that ensure the ISA firewall can communicate with the computers and other IP devices on the appropriate subnets. The network interface with the default gateway is the one used to connect to the Internet, either direction or via upstream routers.

The routing table entries are critical to support the ISA firewall's "network-within-a-Network" scenarios. A network within a Network is a network ID located behind a NIC on the ISA firewall that is a non-local network.

For example, Figure 6.1 is an example of a simple network-within-a-Network scenario.

Figure 6.1 Network within a Network

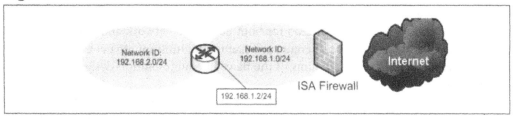

ISA Firewall

192.168.1.2/24

This small organization's IP addressing scheme uses two network IDs for the corporate network: 192.168.1.0/24 and 192.168.2.0/24. The network local to the ISA firewall's internal interface is 192.168.1.0/24. The network remote from the ISA firewall's internal interface is 192.168.2.0/24. A corporate network router separates the network and routes packets between these two network IDs.

The ISA firewall's networking model includes both of these networks as part of the same Network (Note: A capital "N" indicates an ISA firewall-defined network). You would naturally assume that the 192.168.1.0/24 would be an ISA-defined Network since it includes an entire network ID, but you might also assume that network ID 192.168.2.0/24 would be defined as a second ISA firewall-defined Network. That would be incorrect because the ISA firewall's Network model includes *all networks (all IP addresses)* reachable from a specific interface on the ISA firewall as being part of the same network.

The rationale behind this is that hosts on the same ISA-defined Network do not use the ISA firewall to mediate communications between themselves. It makes no sense for the ISA firewall to mediate communications between hosts on networks IDs 192.168.1.0/24 and 192.168.2.0/24, as this would require hosts to loop back through the firewall to reach hosts to which they should directly communicate.

In this example, there should be a routing table entry on the ISA firewall indicating that in order to reach network ID 192.168.2.0/24, the connection must be forwarded to IP address 192.168.2.1 on the corporate router. You can use either the RRAS console or the command line **ROUTE** and **netsh** commands to add the routing table entry.

The ISA firewall must know the route to *each* internal network ID. If you find that connections are not being correctly forwarded by the ISA firewall to hosts on the corporate network, confirm that there are routing table entries on the ISA firewall indicating the correct gateway for each of those network IDs.

TIP

You can greatly simplify your ISA firewall Network definitions and routing table entries by creating a well-designed IP addressing infrastructure with proper subnet design that allows for route summarization.

DNS Server Placement

DNS server and host name resolution issues represent the most common ISA firewall connectivity problems. Name resolution for both corporate network and Internet hosts must be performed correctly. If the company's name resolution infrastructure isn't properly configured, one of the first victims of the flawed name resolution design will be the ISA firewall.

The ISA firewall must be able to correctly resolve both corporate and Internet DNS names. The ISA firewall performs name resolution for both Web Proxy and Firewall clients. If the firewall cannot perform name resolution correctly, Internet connectivity for both Web Proxy and Firewall clients will fail.

Correct name resolution for corporate network resources is also critical because the ISA firewall must be able to correctly resolve names for corporate network resources published via Web Publishing rules. For example, when you create a secure-SSL Web Publishing Rule, the ISA firewall must be able to correctly forward incoming connection requests to the FQDN used for the common name on the Web site certificate bound to the published Web server on the corporate network.

The ideal name resolution infrastructure is the split DNS. The split-DNS infrastructure allows external hosts to resolve names to publicly-accessible addresses and corporate network hosts to resolve names to privately-accessible addresses. Figure 6.2 depicts how a split-DNS infrastructure works to enhance name resolution for hosts inside your corporate network, as well as those that roam between the corporate network and remote locations on the Internet.

Figure 6.2 The Miracle of the Split-DNS Infrastructure

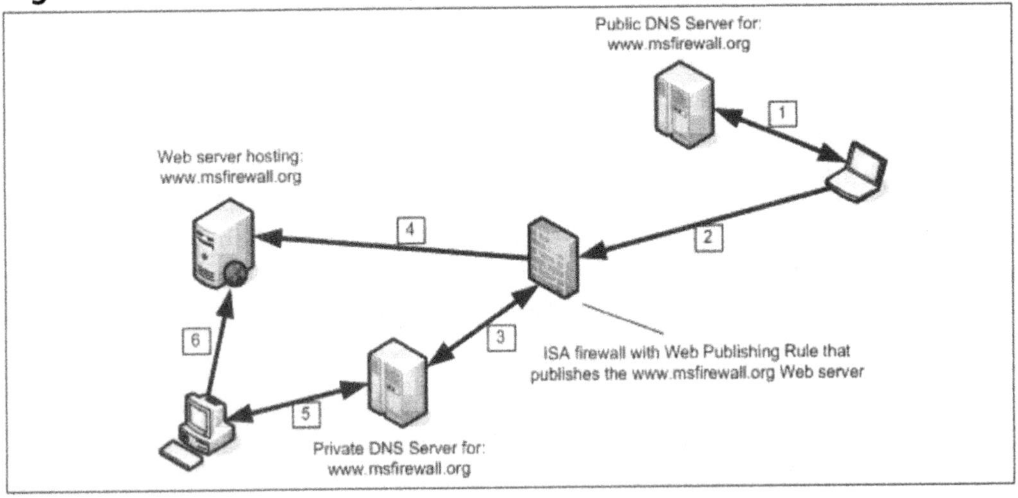

1. A user at a remote location needs to access resources on the corporate Web server, www.msfirewall.org. The www.msfirewall.org Web server is hosted on an ISA firewall-Protected Network and published using an ISA firewall Web Publishing Rule. The remote user sends a request to www.msfirewall.org, and

the name is resolved by the public DNS server authoritative for the msfire-wall.org domain. The name is resolved to an IP address on the external inter-face of the ISA firewall used by the Web listener designated in the Web Publishing Rule.

2. The remote Web client sends the request to the IP address on the external interface used by the Web Publishing Rules Web listener.

3. The ISA firewall resolves the name www.msfirewall.org to the actual IP address bound to the www.msfirewall.org Web site on the corporate network by querying the Internal network DNS server authoritative for the msfire-wall.org domain.

4. The ISA firewall forwards the connection to the actual IP address bound to the www.msfirewall.org Web site on the corporate network.

5. A host on the corporate network needs to access resources on the www.msfirewall.org Web site. The corporate user sends a request to the corpo-rate DNS server that is authoritative for the msfirewall.org domain. The corpo-rate DNS server resolves the name www.msfirewall.org to the actual IP address bound to the www.msfirewall.org Web site on the corporate network.

6. The Web client on the corporate network connects directly to the www.msfirewall.org Web server. The Web client doesn't loop back to reach the www.msfirewall.org Web site on the corporate network because Web Proxy clients are configured for direct access to resources on the msfirewall.org domain.

The split-DNS infrastructure provides transparent access to resources for users regardless of their location. Users can move between the corporate network and remote locations and use the same name to reach the same corporate resources. They don't need to reconfigure their mail clients, news clients, and other applications because *the same name* is used to access the resources regardless of location. Any organization needing to support users that roam between the corporate network and remote locations should implement a split DNS infrastructure.

Requirements for the split-DNS infrastructure include:

- A DNS server authoritative for the domain that resolves names for resources for that domain to the internal addresses used to access those resources

- A DNS server authoritative for the domain that resolves names for resources in that domain to the publicly-accessible addresses used to access those resources

- Remote users must be assigned DNS server addresses that forward requests for the domain to a public DNS server. This is easily accomplished using DHCP.

- Corporate users must be assigned DNS server addresses that forward requests for the domain to the private DNS server. This is easily accomplished using DHCP.

- The ISA firewall must be able to resolve names of published resources and all other resources hosted on a ISA firewall-Protected Network to the private address used to access that resource.

Most organizations that use the ISA firewall will have one or more internal DNS servers. At least one of those DNS servers should be configured to resolve both internal and Internet host names, and the ISA firewall should be configured to use that DNS server. If you have an internal network DNS server, you should never configure the ISA firewall's interfaces to use an external DNS server. This is a common mistake and can lead to slow or failed name resolution attempts.

TIP

Check out Jim Harrison's article **Designing An ISA Server Solution on a Complex Network** at http://isaserver.org/tutorials/Designing_An_ISA_ Server_Solution_on_a_Complex_Network.html for information on network designs supporting ISA firewalls.

Configuring the ISA Firewall's Network Interfaces

Perhaps one of the least understood ISA firewall configuration issues is how to correctly configure the IP addressing information on the ISA firewall's network interfaces. The reason for this is that name resolution issues have the potential for being complex, and fledging firewall administrators are often too busy to get lost in the details of DNS host name and NetBIOS name resolution.

There are two main networks interface configuration scenarios:

- An established name-resolution infrastructure on the corporate network protected by the ISA firewall
- *No* established name-resolution infrastructure on the corporate network protected by the ISA firewall

Tables 6.2 and 6.3 show the correct IP addressing information for both these scenarios in dual-homed ISA firewalls.

Table 6.2 Established Corporate Network Name-Resolution Infrastructure

Parameters	Internal Interface	External Interface
Client for Microsoft Networks	Enabled	Disabled
File and Print Sharing for Microsoft Networks	Enabled only if the ISA firewall hosts the Firewall client share	Disabled

Continued

Table 6.2 Established Corporate Network Name-Resolution Infrastructure

Parameters	Internal Interface	External Interface
Network Monitor Driver	Enabled when Network Monitor is installed on the ISA firewall (recommended)	Enabled when Network Monitor is installed on the ISA firewall (recommended)
Internet Protocol (TCP/IP)	Enabled	Enabled
IP address	Valid IP address on the network the internal interface is connected to	Valid IP address on the network the external interface is connected to. Public or private depending on your network infrastructure
Subnet mask	Valid subnet mask on the network the internal interface is connected to	Valid subnet mask on the network the external interface is connected to
Default gateway	NONE. Never configure a default gateway on any internal or DMZ interface on the ISA firewall.	IP address of upstream router (either corporate or ISP depending on next hop) allowing access to the Internet
Preferred DNS server	Internal DNS server that can resolve both internal and Internet host names	NONE. Do not enter a DNS server address on the external interface of the ISA firewall
Alternate DNS server	A second internal DNS server that can resolve both internal and Internet host names	NONE. Do not enter a DNS server address on the external interface of the ISA firewall.
Register this connection's addresses in DNS	Disabled. You should manually create entries on the Internal network DNS server to allow clients to resolve the name of the ISA firewall's internal interface.	Disabled
WINS	Enter an IP address for one more Internal network DNS server. Especially helpful for VPN clients who want to browse Internal network servers using NetBIOS name/browser service	NONE

Continued

Table 6.2 Established Corporate Network Name-Resolution Infrastructure

Parameters	Internal Interface	External Interface
WINS NetBIOS setting	Default	Disable NetBIOS over TCP/IP
Interface order	Top of interface list	Under internal interface

Table 6.3 *No* Established Corporate Network Name-Resolution Infrastructure

Parameters	Internal Interface	External Interface
Client for Microsoft Networks	Enabled	Disabled
File and Print Sharing for Microsoft Networks	Enabled only if the ISA firewall hosts the Firewall client share	Disabled
Network Monitor Driver	Enabled when Network Monitor is installed on the ISA firewall (recommended)	Enabled when Network Monitor is installed on the ISA firewall (recommended)
Internet Protocol (TCP/IP)	Enabled	Enabled
Default gateway	NONE. Never configure a gateway on any internal or DMZ interface on the ISA firewall.	IP address of upstream router (either corporate or ISP depending on next hop) allowing access to the Internet. May be assigned by ISP via DHCP
Preferred DNS server	External DNS server that can resolve Internet host names. Typically your ISP's DNS Server. **Note:** If the external interface uses DHCP to obtain IP addressing information, do not enter a DNS server on the ISA firewall's internal interface.	None, unless assigned by ISP via DHCP.

Continued

Table 6.3 *No* Established Corporate Network Name-Resolution Infrastructure

Parameters	Internal Interface	External Interface
Alternate DNS server	A second external DNS server that can resolve Internet host names **Note:** If the external interface uses DHCP to obtain IP addressing information from your ISP, do not enter a DNS server on the ISA firewall's internal interface.	NONE. Do not enter a DNS server address on the external interface of the ISA firewall unless assigned via DHCP by ISP.
Register this connection's addresses in DNS	Disabled	Disabled
WINS	NONE	NONE
WINS NetBIOS setting	Default	Disable NetBIOS over TCP/IP
Interface order	Top of interface list **Note:** If the external interface of the ISA firewall uses DHCP to obtain IP addressing information from your ISP, then do not move the internal interface to the top of the list.	Top of interface list if using ISP DHCP server to assign DNS server addresses

You should already be familiar with configuring IP addressing information for Windows Server interfaces. However, you may not be aware of how to change the interface order. The interface order is used to determine what name server addresses should be used preferentially.

TIP

You can track which interface is connected to what Network by renaming your network interfaces in the Network and dial-up connections user interface. Right-click on the network interface, and click **rename**. Enter the new name for the interface. For example, on a simple trihomed ISA firewall, we often name the interfaces LAN, WAN, and DMZ.

Perform the following steps to change the interface order:

1. Right-click **My Network Places** on the desktop, and click **Properties**.

2. In the **Network and Dial-up Connections** window, click the **Advanced** menu, then click **Advanced Settings**.

3. In the **Advanced Settings** dialog box (Figure 6.3), click the internal interface in the list of **Connections** on the **Adapters and Bindings** tab. After selecting the internal interface, click the up-arrow to move the internal interface to the top of the list of interfaces.

Figure 6.3 The Advanced Settings Dialog Box

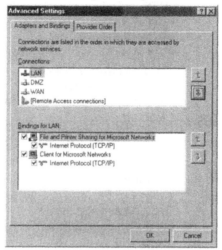

4. Click **OK** in the **Advanced Settings** dialog box.

Unattended Installation

You can perform an unattended installation of the ISA firewall to simplify provisioning multiple ISA firewalls using a common installation and configuration scheme. The unintended installation depends on the proper configuration of the **msiund.ini** file, which contains the configuration information used by ISA firewall setup in unattended mode.

TIP

Make a special note of the last entry in Table 6.4, which shows how you can include a pre-built ISA firewall policy in your unattended installation. This allows you to automate ISA firewall installation and configuration for thousands of ISA firewalls by running a simple command line entry.

The default **msisaund.ini** file is located on the ISA Server 2004 CD in the **\FPC** directory. Table 6.4 contains the salient entries and values that are configured in the **msisaund.ini** file.

Table 6.4 Entries and Values in the msisaund.ini File

Entry	Description
PIDKEY	Specifies the product key
INTERNALNETRANGES	Specifies the range of addresses in the Internal Network. **Msisaund.ini** must specify at least one Internet Protocol (IP) address. Otherwise, Setup fails. The syntax is: *N From1-To1,From2-To2,... FromN-ToN*, where *N* is the number of ranges, and *Froml* to *Tol* are the starting and ending addresses in each range.
InstallDir=*{install_directory}*	Specifies the installation directory for ISA Server. If not specified, it defaults to the first disk drive with enough space. The syntax is: *Drive:\Folder* The default folder is: %Program Files%\Microsoft ISA Server
COMPANYNAME=*Company_Name*	Specifies the name of the company installing the product
DONOTDELLOGS = {0|1}	If set to 1, log files on the computer are not deleted. The default is 0.
DONOTDELCACHE = {0|1}	If set to 1, cache files on the computer are not deleted. The default is 0.
ADDLOCAL= {**MSFirewall_Management**}, {**MSFirewall_Services**}, {**Message_Screener**}, {**Publish_Share_Directory**}, {**MSDE**}	Specifies a list of components (delimited by commas) that should be installed on the computer. To install all the components, set **ADDLOCAL=ALL.**
REMOVE={**MSFirewall_Management**}, {**MSFirewall_Services**}, {**Message_Screener**}, {**Publish_Share_Directory**}, {**MSDE**}	Specifies a list of components (delimited by commas) that should be removed from the computer. To remove all the components, set **REMOVE=ALL**.
IMPORT_CONFIG_FILE = Importfile.xml	Specifies a configuration file to import

Perform the following steps to effect the unattended installation of the ISA firewall:

1. Modify the **Msisaund.ini** file.

2. At a command prompt, enter

```
PathToISASetup\Setup.exe [/[X|R]] /V" /q[b|n]
FULLPATHANSWERFILE=\"PathToINIFile\MSISAUND.INI\""
```

PathToISASetup

The path to the ISA Server 2004 installation files. The path may be the root folder of the ISA Server CD-ROM or a shared folder on your network that contains the ISA Server files.

`/Q [b|n]`

Performs quiet unattended setup. If you specify **b**, a progress bar indicates the setup process. If you specify **n**, no dialog boxes are displayed.

`/R`

Performs unattended reinstallation

`/X`

Performs unattended uninstallation

`PathToINIFile`

The path to the folder containing the unattended installation information
Issues related to unattended installation of the ISA firewall include:

- You must be a member of the Administrators group to perform an unattended installation.

- You cannot perform an unattended installation on a computer with ISA Server 2000 installed.

- The INTERNALNETRANGES property in Msisaund.ini must specify at least one Internet Protocol (IP) address range that includes one of the IP addresses of your ISA Server computer. Otherwise, Setup fails.

- A sample answer file (Msisaund.ini) is provided on the CD, in the FPC folder.

- For example, **CD\FPC\setup.exe /v" /qn FULLPATHANSWER-FILE=\"C:\MSISAUND.INI\""** performs an unattended installation of ISA Server, using the Msisaund.ini file located in c:\.

- The MSDE component which is installed when you install the Advanced logging feature is not properly installed when you remotely install the ISA firewall using Terminal Services in application server mode. Use Terminal Services in administration mode to properly install MSDE.

Installation via a Terminal Services Administration Mode Session

You can install the ISA firewall via an Admin mode Terminal services connection. After installing is complete, a System Policy rule is configured to allow RDP connections only from the IP address of the machine that was connected during the ISA firewall software installation. This is in contrast to the default System Policy setting when installing the ISA firewall software at the console, where any host on the Internal Network can initiate an RDP connection to the ISA firewalls Internal interface.

Performing a Clean Installation on a Multihomed Machine

The following steps demonstrate how to install the ISA Server 2004 software on a dual-homed (two Ethernet cards) Windows Server 2003 machine. This is a "clean machine" that has only the Windows Server 2003 software installed and the IP addressing information configured on each of the machine's interfaces. The routing table has also been properly configured on this machine.

Perform the following steps to install the ISA firewall software on the multihomed machine:

1. Insert the ISA Server 2004 installation CD into the CD-ROM drive or connect to a network share point hosting the ISA Server 2004 installation files. If the installation routine does not start automatically, double-click the **isaautorun.exe** file in the root of the installation files folder tree.

2. On the **Microsoft Internet Security and Acceleration Server 2004** page, click the link for **Review Release Notes** and read the release notes. The release notes contain very important and topical information regarding changes in basic firewall software functionality. This information may not be included in the Help file or elsewhere, so we highly recommend that you read this information. After reviewing the release notes, click the **Read Setup and Feature Guide** link. You may want to read the guide now, just review the major topics covered in the guide, or print it out. Click the **Install ISA Server 2004** link.

3. Click **Next** on the **Welcome to the Installation Wizard for Microsoft ISA Server 2004** page.

4. Select **I accept the terms in the license agreement option on the License Agreement** page. Click **Next**.

5. On the **Customer Information** page, enter your name and the name of your organization in the **User Name** and **Organization** text boxes. Enter your serial number in the **Product Serial Number** text box. If you installed an evaluation copy of the ISA firewall software and now are installing a licensed version, then backup your configuration using the ISA firewall's integrated backup tool and uninstall the evaluation version. Restart the installation of the licensed version of the software. Click **Next**.

6. On the **Setup Type** page (Figure 6.4), select **Custom**. If you do not want to install the ISA Server 2004 software on the C: drive, click **Change** to change the location of the program files on the hard disk. The **Typical** option does not install the Firewall client share or the SMTP Message Screener. The **Complete** option installs the ISA firewall software, **Microsoft Internet Security and Acceleration Server 2004** management console, SMTP Message Screener, and the Firewall Client share. Click **Next**.

Figure 6.4 The Setup Type Page

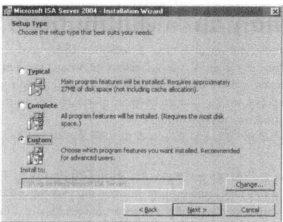

7. On the **Custom Setup** page (Figure 6.5), choose which components to install. By default, when you select **Custom**, the **Firewall Services**, **ISA Server Management**, and **Advanced Logging** features are installed. The **Advanced Logging** feature is MSDE logging, which provides superior log search and filtering features. The **Message Screener**, which is used to control spam and e-mail with certain file attachments from entering and leaving the network, is not installed by default. You must install the IIS 6.0 or IIS 5.0 SMTP service on the ISA firewall computer *before* you install the **Message Screener**. If you try to install the SMTP Message Screener on the ISA firewall before installing the IIS SMTP service, an error message is generated, and you will need to restart the installation of the ISA firewall. Use the default settings, and click **Next**.

Figure 6.5 The Custom Setup Page

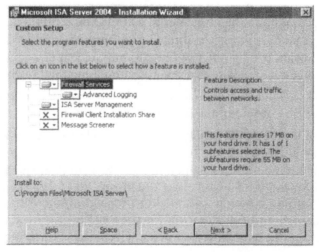

8. On the **Internal Network** page in Figure 6.6, click **Add**. The Internal
    Network is different from the internal network that was implied by the Local
    Address Table (LAT) was used by ISA Server 2000. In the case of ISA Server
    2004, the Internal Network contains trusted network services with which the
    ISA firewall must communicate. Examples of such services include Active
    Directory domain controllers, DNS servers, DHCP servers, terminal servers,
    and management workstations. The firewall System Policy uses the Internal
    Network for a number of System Policy rules. We will look at the System
    Policy later in this chapter.

9. Define the addresses included on the default Internal Network on the Internal
    Network setup page. You can manually enter the addresses to be included in
    the Internal Network by entering the first and last addresses in the Internal
    Network range in the **From** and **To** text boxes and then clicking the **Add**
    button. A better way to configure the default Internal Network is to use
    Select Network Adapter. This allows the ISA firewall setup routine to use
    the routing table to determine addresses used for the default Internal Network.
    This is one reason why it is important to make sure that you have correctly
    configured your routing table entries before installing ISA. Click **Select
    Network Adapter**. (See Figure 6.6.)

Figure 6.6 The Internal Network Address Page

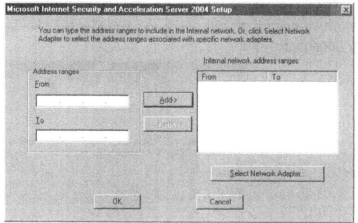

10. In the **Configure Internal Network** dialog box, remove the checkmark from
    the **Add the following private ranges**… checkbox. We prefer to uncheck
    this option because many organizations will use subnets of the private address
    network IDs throughout the organization on different ISA firewall-defined
    Networks. Leave the checkmark in the **Add address ranges based on the
    Windows Routing Table** checkbox, as shown in Figure 6.7. Put a checkmark
    in the box next to the Network Adapter representing the default Internal

Network. In this example, we have renamed the network interfaces so that the
interface name reflects its location. Click **OK**.

Figure 6.7 The Select Network Adapter Page

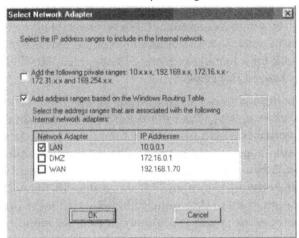

11.   Click **OK** in the dialog box (Figure 6.8, **Setup Message**) informing you that
      **The Internal network was defined, based on the Windows routing
      table.**

Figure 6.8 Warning Dialog Box Reminding You that the Routing Table must be
Properly Configured

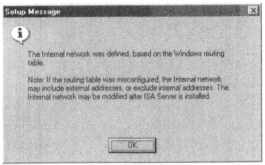

12.   Click **OK** on the **Internal network address ranges** dialog box, as shown in
      Figure 6.9.

Figure 6.9 Internal Network Address Ranges

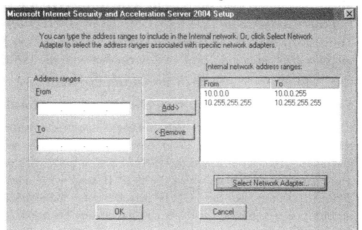

13.   Click **Next** on the **Internal Network** page.

14.   Put a checkmark by **Allow computers running earlier versions of Firewall Client software to connect** (Figure 6.10) if you want to support Firewall clients running previous versions of the Winsock Proxy (Proxy Server 2.0) or the ISA Server 2000 Firewall client software. This will allow you to continue using the ISA Server 2000 Firewall client software as you migrate to ISA Server 2004. When you migrate your Firewall clients to the ISA 2004 version of the Firewall client, the channel between the Firewall clients and the ISA firewall will be encrypted. The ISA 2004 Firewall client software encrypts the user credentials that are transparently sent from the Firewall client machine to the ISA firewall. Click **Next**.

Figure 6.10 The Firewall Client Connection Settings Page

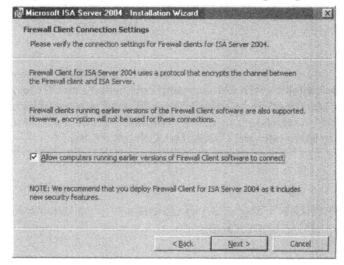

15. On the **Services** page, note that the **SNMP** and **IIS Admin Service** will be stopped during installation. If the **Internet Connection Firewall (ICF) / Internet Connection Sharing (ICF)**, and/or **IP Network Address Translation** (RRAS NAT service) services are installed on the ISA firewall machine, they will be disabled, as they conflict with the ISA firewall software.

16. Click **Install** on the **Ready to Install the Program** page.

17. On the **Installation Wizard Completed** page, click **Finish**.

18. Click **Yes** on the **Microsoft ISA Server** dialog box informing that you must restart the server (see Figure 6.11). Note that you will not need to restart the machine if you have installed the ISA firewall software on this machine before. The reason for the restart is that the TCP/IP stack is changed so that the dynamic port range of the TCP/IP driver is extended to 65535. If the installation routine recognizes that this range has already been extended, then the restart will not be required.

Figure 6.11 Warning Dialog Box regarding a Potential System Restart

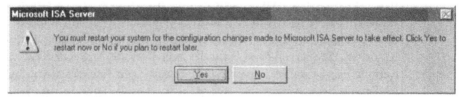

19. Log on as an **Administrator** after the machine restarts.

20. Click **Start**, and point to **All Programs**. Point to **Microsoft ISA Server**, and click **ISA Server Management**. The **Microsoft Internet Security and Acceleration Server 2004** management console opens and displays the **Welcome to Microsoft Internet Security and Acceleration Server 2004** page.

TIP

You can install the ISA Management console on any Windows XP or Windows Server 2003 machine. System Policy will need to be configured so that the machine on which you install the Remote Management MMC is added to the **Remote Management Computers** Computer Set.

Three setup logs are created on the ISA firewall machine. These are:

■ **ISAWRAP_*.log** Provides information about installation success and failure and MSDE log files setup

- **ISAMSDE_*.log** Provides detailed information about MSDE setup, if the Advanced Logging feature was selected
- **ISAFWSV_*.log** Provides detailed information about the entire ISA firewall installation process

If you choose to not install certain components, such as the Firewall client share or Advanced Logging (MSDE logging), you can use the Control Panel's **Add/Remove Programs** applet to re-run the installation routine and install these additional components at a later time.

WARNING

If the Microsoft Internet Authentication Service (IAS) was running on the machine during installation, you will need to restart the IAS service after installation completes. In addition, co-located IAS/ISA firewall installations are not supported on Windows 2000.

Default Post-installation ISA Firewall Configuration

The ISA firewall installation routine incorporates the settings you entered during the setup Wizard process. The install routine also sets up some default settings for User Permissions, Network Settings, Firewall Policy, and others. Table 6.5 lists the settings that you did not explicitly define during the installation process.

We can quickly summarize the default post-installation configuration with the following:

- System Policies allow selected traffic to and from the ISA firewall itself.
- No traffic is allowed through the ISA firewall because there is only a single Deny-access rule.
- A route relationship is set between the VPN/VPN-Q Networks to the Internal Network.
- A NAT relationship is set between the Internal Network and the default External Network.
- Only Administrators can alter ISA firewall policy.

Table 6.5 Post-Installation ISA Firewall Settings

Feature	Post-installation Settings
User permissions	Members of the Administrators group on the local computer can configure firewall policy. If the ISA firewall is a member of the domain, domain admins are automatically added to the local administrators group.
Network settings	The following Network Rules are created by the installation wizard: **Local Host Access** Local Host Access defines a Route relationship between the Local Host network and all networks. Allow communications from the ISA firewall to all other hosts is routed (does not use NAT; there would be no point to using NAT from Local Host to any Network). **Internet Access** Internet Access defines a Network Address Translation (NAT) relationship from the Internal network, Quarantined VPN Clients network, and the VPN Clients network to the External network. NAT is used from these three Networks for any communications sourcing from them to the External Network. Access is allowed only if you configure the appropriate access policy. **VPN Clients to Internal Network.** VPN Clients to Internal Network defines a Route relationship between the VPN Clients Network and the Internal Network. Access is allowed only if you enable virtual private network (VPN) client access.
Firewall policy	A default Access Rule (named **Default Rule**) denies traffic between all networks.
System policy	The ISA firewall is secure by default. Some system policy rules are enabled to allow necessary services. You should review the system policy configuration and customize it so that only services critical to your specific deployment are enabled.
Web chaining	A default rule (named **Default Rule**) specifies that all Web Proxy client requests are retrieved directly from the Internet. That is to say, there is no Web chaining configured by default. Web chaining rules were called Web routing rules in ISA Server 2000.
Caching	The cache size is set to 0. All caching is therefore disabled. You will need to define a cache drive to enable Web caching.
Alerts	Most alerts are enabled. You should review and configure alerts in accordance with your specific networking needs.

Continued

Table 6.5 Post-Installation ISA Firewall Settings

Feature	Post-installation Settings
Client configuration	Firewall and Web Proxy clients have automatic discovery enabled by default. Web browser applications on Firewall clients are configured when the Firewall client is installed.
Autodiscovery for Firewall and Web Proxy Clients	Publication of autodiscovery information is disabled by default. You will need to enable publication of autodiscovery information and confirm a port on which autodiscovery information is published.

The Post-installation System Policy

ISA Firewall Policy is a collection of Access Rules controlling access to and from the Local Host network. System Policy controls access to and from the *system*. You do **not** configure System Policy for network access between any other hosts. One of the most common errors made by new ISA firewall administrators is to use System Policy to control access from Protected Network hosts to non-Protected Network hosts.

Table 6.6 shows the list of System Policy rules and their status after installing the ISA firewall software. The **Order/Comments** column includes our advice regarding configuration of the specific System Policy Rule.

Table 6.6 Default Post-installation System Policy

Order/Comments	Name	Action	Protocols	From/Listener	To	Condition
1 Is the ISA firewall a member of the domain? If not, disable this rule.	Allow access to directory services for authentication purposes	Allow	LDAP LDAP (UDP) LDAP GC (global catalog) LDAPS LDAPS GC (Global Catalog)	Local Host	Internal	All Users
2 If no one is going to use the remote MMC to manage the ISA firewall, disable this rule.	Allow remote management from selected computers using MMC	Allow	Microsoft Firewall Control NetBIOS datagram NetBIOS Name Service NetBIOS Session RPC (all interfaces)	Remote Management Computers	Local Host	All Users
3 Confirm that the Remote Management Computers Computer Set has the addresses of the hosts that will manage the ISA firewall; if you don't want to allow RDP management of the ISA firewall, disable this rule.	Allow remote management from selected computers using Terminal Server	Allow	RDP (Terminal Services)	Remote Management Computers	Local Host	All Users

Continued

Table 6.6 Default Post-installation System Policy

Order/Comments	Name	Action	Protocols	From/Listener	To	Condition
4 (Disabled by default) Enable this rule if you want to log to	Allow remote logging to trusted servers using SQL servers.	Allow	NetBIOS Datagram NetBIOS Name Service NetBIOS Session	Local Host	Internal	All Users
5 Will you be using RADIUS authentication? If not, disable this rule.	Allow RADIUS authentication from ISA Server to trusted RADIUS servers	Allow	RADIUS RADIUS Accounting	Local Host	Internal	All Users
6 Will the ISA firewall be authenticating users? If not, disable this rule.	Allow Kerberos authentication from ISA Server to trusted servers	Allow	Kerberos-Sec (TCP) Kerberos-Sec (UDP)	Local Host	Internal	All Users
7 This rule must be enabled so that the ISA firewall can initiate DNS queries.	Allow DNS from ISA Server to selected servers	Allow	DNS	Local Host	All Net-works (and Local Host)	All Users
8 If the ISA firewall isn't going to act as a DHCP client, disable this rule.	Allow DHCP requests from ISA Server to all networks	Allow	DHCP (request)	Local Host	Anywhere	All Users

Continued

Table 6.6 Default Post-installation System Policy

Order/Comments	Name	Action	Protocols	From/Listener	To	Condition
9 If the ISA firewall isn't going to act as a DHCP client, disable this rule.	Allow DHCP replies from DHCP servers to ISA Server	Allow	DHCP (reply)	Internal	Local Host	All Users
10 Confirm that you have configured the proper IP addresses for the Remote Management Computers Computer Set.	Allow ICMP (PING) requests from selected computers to ISA Server	Allow	Ping	Remote Management Computers	Local Host	All Users
11 This rule must be enabled so that the ISA firewall can carry out network management tasks via ICMP.	Allow ICMP requests from ISA Server to selected servers	Allow	ICMP Information Request ICMP Timestamp	Local Host	All Networks (and Local Host Network)	All Users
12 **(disabled by default)** This rule is automatically enabled when you enable the ISA firewall's VPN server component.	All VPN client traffic to ISA Server	Allow	PPTP	External	Local Host	All Users
13 **(disabled by default)** This rule is automatically enabled when you enable a site-to-site VPN connection to this ISA firewall.	Allow VPN site-to-site traffic to ISA Server	Allow	NONE	External IPSec Remote Gateways	Local Host	All Users

Continued

Table 6.6 Default Post-installation System Policy

Order/Comments	Name	Action	Protocols	From/Listener	To	Condition
14 (disabled by default) This rule is automatically enabled when you enable a site-to-site VPN connection to this ISA firewall.	Allow VPN site-to-site traffic from ISA Server	Allow	NONE	Local Host	External IPSec Remote Gateways	All Users
15 Will you be trying to access file shares from the ISA firewall? If not, disable this rule	Allow Microsoft CIFS from ISA Server to trusted servers	Allow	Microsoft CIFS (TCP) Microsoft CIFS (UDP)	Local Host	Internal	All Users
16 (disabled by default) Enable this rule when you choose SQL logging.	Allow remote SQL logging from ISA Server to selected servers	Allow	Microsoft SQL (TCP) Microsoft SQL (UDP)	Local Host	Internal	All Users
17 Unless you want to allow the ISA firewall to contact the Windows Update site itself, disable this rule. I prefer to download updates to a management machine, scan them, and then copy them out of band to the ISA firewall and install them from that.	Allow HTTP/HTTPS requests from ISA Server to specified sites	Allow	HTTP HTTPS	Local Host	System Policy Allowed Sites	All Users

Continued

Table 6.6 Default Post-installation System Policy

Order/Comments	Name	Action	Protocols	From/Listener	To	Condition
18 (disabled by default) This rule is enabled when you create an HTTP/HTTPS connectivity verifier.	Allow HTTP/HTTPS requests from ISA Server to selected servers for connectivity verifiers	Allow	HTTP HTTPS	Local Host	All Networks (and Local Host Network)	All Users
19 (disabled by default) This rule is enabled if the Firewall client share is installed on the ISA firewall.	Allow access from trusted computers to the Firewall Client installation share on ISA Server	Allow	Microsoft CIFS (TCP) Microsoft CIFS (UDP) NetBIOS Datagram NetBIOS Name Service NetBIOS Session	Internal	Local Host	All Users
20 (disabled by default) Enable this rule if you want to perform remote performance monitoring of ISA firewall.	Allow remote performance monitoring of ISA iServer from trusted servers	Allow	NetBIOS Datagram NetBIOS Name Service NetBIOS Session	Remote Management Computers	Local Host	All Users
21 Unless you plan to access file shares from the ISA firewall, disable this rule.	Allow NetBIOS from ISA Server to trusted servers	Allow	NetBIOS Datagram NetBIOS Name Service NetBIOS Sessions	Local Host	Internal	All Users

Continued

Table 6.6 Default Post-installation System Policy

Order/Comments	Name	Action	Protocols	From/Listener	To	Condition
22 Unless you plan to use RPC to connect to other servers, disable this rule.	Allow RPC from ISA Server to trusted servers	Allow	RPC (all interfaces)	Local Host	Internal	All Users
23 This rule allows the ISA firewall to send error reports to Microsoft.	Allow HTTP/HTTPS from ISA Server to specified Microsoft error reporting sites	Allow	HTTP HTTPS	Local Host	Microsoft Error Reporting sites	All Users
24 (**disabled by default**) This rule should be enabled if SecurID authentication is enabled.	Allow SecurID authentication from ISA Server to trusted servers	Allow	SecurID	Local Host	Internal	All Users
25 (**disabled by default**) Enable this rule if you use MOM to monitor the ISA firewall.	Allow remote monitoring from ISA Server to trusted servers, using Microsoft Operations Manager (MOM) Agent	Allow	Microsoft Operations Manager Agent	Local Host	Internal	All Users
26 (**disabled by default**) Enable this rule if you want the ISA firewall to access CRL— required if the ISA terminates any SSL connections.	Allow all HTTP traffic from ISA Server to all networks (for CRL + downloads)	Allow	HTTP	Local Host	All Networks (and Local Host)	All Users

Continued

Table 6.6 Default Post-installation System Policy

Order/Comments	Name	Action	Protocols	From/Listener	To	Condition
27 You should change this rule by allowing contact with a trusted NTP server in your organization. The Internal entry allows it to contact all servers anywhere in the world.	Allow NTP from ISA Server to trusted NTP servers	Allow	NTP (UDP)	Local Host	Internal	All Users
28 If you don't plan on using SMTP to send alerts, you should disable this rule. If you do plan on sending SMTP alerts, you should replace the Internal Destination with a specific computer that will accept SMTP messages from the ISA firewall.	Allow SMTP from ISA Server to trusted servers	Allow	SMTP	Local Host	Internal	All Users
29 (disabled by default) This rule is automatically enabled when Content Download Jobs are enabled.	Allow HTTP from ISA Server to selected computers for Content Download Jobs	Allow	HTTP	Local Host	All Networks System and (and Local Network Service Host)	
30 Unless you plan on using the remote MMC, disable this rule	Allow Microsoft Firewall Control communication to selected computers	Allow	All Outbound traffic	Local Host	Remote Management Computers	All Users

The ISA firewall's System Policy Rules are evaluated before any user-defined Access Rules in the order listed in the **Firewall Policy** first column. View the ISA firewall's System Policy by clicking **Firewall Policy** in the left pane of the console and then clicking the **Tasks** tab. In the **Tasks** tab, click **Show System Policy Rules**. Click **Hide System Policy Rules** when you're finished viewing the firewall's system policy.

WARNING

You can make changes to only some components of the ISA firewall's default System Policy. You will find that there are several instances where you cannot make changes to the ISA firewall's System Policy with the System Policy Editor.

You can edit the ISA firewall's System Policy by clicking **Edit System Policy** on the **Tasks** tab. This opens the **System Policy Editor,** as shown in Figure 6.12. For each System Policy Rule there is a **General** tab and a **From** or **To** tab. The **General** tab for each **Configuration Group** contains an explanation of the rule(s), and the **From** or **To** tab allows you to control protocol access to or from the ISA firewall machine itself.

Figure 6.12 The ISA Firewall's System Policy Editor

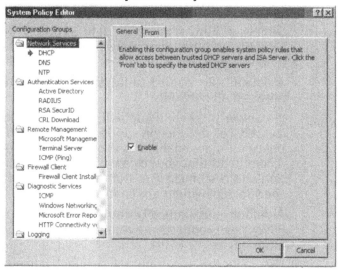

Table 6.7 Default Port-installation ISA Firewall System Configuration

Feature	Default setting
User permissions	Members of the Administrators group on the local computer can configure firewall policy. If the ISA firewall is a member of the domain, then the Domain Admins global group is automatically included in the local machine's Administrators group.
Definition of Internal network	The Internal network contains IP addresses you specified during setup of the ISA firewall software.
Network Rules	**Local Host Access** Defines a route relationship between the Local Host network and all networks. All connections between the Local Host network (that is, the ISA firewall machine itself) are routed instead of NATed. **Internet Access** Defines a NAT (Network Address Translation) relationship between the Internal Network, Quarantined VPN Clients Network, and the VPN Clients Network — to the External network. From each of these three Networks to the Internet, the connection is NATed. Access is allowed only if you configure the appropriate Access Rules. **VPN Clients to Internal Network** Defines a route relationship between the VPN Clients Network and the Internal Network. Access is allowed only if you enable virtual private network (VPN) client access.
Firewall policy	A default rule (named **Default Rule**) denies traffic between all networks.
System policy	ISA Server is secure by default, while allowing certain critical services to function. Upon installation, some system policy rules are enabled to allow necessary services. We recommend that you review the system policy configuration and customize it so that only services critical to your specific deployment are enabled.
Web chaining	A default rule (named **Default Rule**) specifies that all Web Proxy client requests are retrieved directly from the Internet.
Caching	The cache size is set to 0. All caching is, therefore, disabled.
Alerts	Most alerts are active. We recommend that you review and configure the alerts in accordance with your specific networking needs.
Client configuration	When installed or configured, Firewall and Web Proxy clients have automatic discovery enabled. Web browser applications on Firewall clients are configured when the Firewall client is installed.

Performing an Upgrade Installation

If you are currently running ISA Server 2000, you have the option to:

- Perform an in-place upgrade, or
- Migrate current ISA Server 2000 settings to a clean ISA 2004 installation.

Migrating and upgrading from ISA Server 2000 is a complex topic, and there are a number of issues that you must be aware of before upgrading or migrating. A number of complexities are introduced during the upgrade or migration process because:

- The ISA 2004 networking model is completely different from the ISA Server 2000 networking model,
- Bandwidth rules are not supported in the new ISA firewall,
- Active caching is not supported in the new ISA firewall,
- Permissions are not migrated to the new ISA firewall,
- Logging and reporting configuration is not migrated,
- Packet-filter configuration is not migrated because the new ISA firewall does not have, nor does it require, a packet-filter configuration,
- Application filters and Web filters for ISA Server 2000 are not compatible with the new ISA firewall, and
- The ISA firewall's Routing and Remote Access functionality and integration is quite different than that used by ISA Server 2000.

These and other issues can make the upgrade process somewhat complex. We hate to read computer books that refer you to the Help file for more information, but we're going to do that here. You will need to refer to the ISA Server 2004 Help file for information on the procedures and considerations related to an upgrade installation. The Help file contains information on how the ISA firewall interprets ISA Server 2000 policy and information that is retained and dropped.

However, if you want to do what we do, document your ISA Server 2000 configuration, and then replicate your policy once you understand how the new ISA firewall works and how it interprets your previous ISA Server 2000 firewall policy.

WARNING

You can only upgrade or migrate ISA Server 2000 Standard Edition to ISA 2004 Standard Edition. If you are using ISA Server 2000 Enterprise Edition, you will not be able to use the built-in upgrade and migration tools to move your current firewall policies to ISA 2004 Standard Edition.

Performing a Single NIC Installation (Unihomed ISA Firewall)

This ISA firewall software can be installed on a machine with a single network interface card. This is done to simulate the Proxy Server 2.0 configuration or the ISA Server 2000 caching-only mode. This 2004 ISA firewall does not have a caching-only mode, but you can strip away a significant level of firewall functionality from the ISA firewall when you install it in single-NIC mode.

When the ISA firewall is installed in single-NIC mode, you lose:

- Support for Firewall clients

- Support for full SecureNAT client security and functionality

- Server Publishing Rules

- All protocols except HTTP, HTTPS and HTTP-tunneled (Web proxied) FTP

- Remote Access VPN

- Site-to-Site VPN

- Multi-networking functionality (the entire IPv4 address space is the same network)

- Application-layer inspection except for HTTP

While this caponized version of the ISA firewall retains only a fraction of its ability to act as a network firewall protecting hosts on your corporate network, it does keep full firewall functionality when it comes to protecting itself. The ISA firewall will not be directly accessible to any host, external or internal, unless you enable system policy rules to allow access.

The NIC configuration on the unihomed ISA firewall should set the default gateway as the IP address of any current gateway on the network that allows the unihomed ISA firewall access to the Internet. All other non-local routes need to be configured in the unihomed ISA firewall's routing table.

If you only require a Web Proxy service to perform both forward and reverse proxy, then you can install the ISA firewall on a single NIC machine. The installation process differs a bit from what you find when the ISA firewall is installed on a multi-NIC machine.

Perform the following steps to install the ISA firewall software on a single-NIC machine:

1. Insert the ISA Server 2004 installation CD into the CD-ROM drive or connect to a network share point hosting the ISA Server 2004 installation files. If the installation routine does not start automatically, double-click the **isaautorun.exe** file in the root of the installation files folder tree.

2. On the **Microsoft Internet Security and Acceleration Server 2004** page, click **Review Release Notes**, and read the release notes. The release notes contain very important and topical information regarding changes in basic fire-

wall software functionality. This information may not be included in the Help file or elsewhere, so we highly recommend that you read it here. After reviewing the release notes, click **Read Setup and Feature Guide**. You may want to read the guide now, just review the major topics covered in the guide, or print it out. Click **Install ISA Server 2004**.

3. Click **Next** on the **Welcome to the Installation Wizard for Microsoft ISA Server 2004** page.

4. Select **I accept the terms in the license agreement option on the License Agreement** page. Click **Next**.

5. On the **Customer Information** page, enter your name and the name of your organization in the **User Name** and **Organization** text boxes. Enter your serial number in the **Product Serial Number** text box. If you installed an evaluation copy of the ISA firewall software and now are installing a licensed version, backup your configuration using the ISA firewall's integrated backup tool, and uninstall the evaluation version. Restart the installation of the licensed version of the ISA firewall software. Click **Next**.

6. On the **Setup Type** page, click the **Custom** option.

7. On the **Custom Setup** page you'll notice that the **Firewall Services**, **Advanced Logging**, and **ISA Server Management** options are selected by default. While you can install the **Firewall Client** share, keep in mind that the unihomed ISA firewall does not support Firewall or SecureNAT clients. The only client type supported is the Web Proxy client. However, if you have full service ISA firewalls on your network, you can install the Firewall client share on this machine and allow network clients to download the Firewall client software from the unihomed ISA firewall. There is no point to installing the SMTP message screener on the unihomed ISA firewall since this mode does not support Server Publishing Rules. Click **Next**.

8. On the **Internal Network** page click **Add**. On the **address ranges for internal network** page, click **Select Network Adapter**, as shown in Figure 6.13.

9. On the **Select Network Adapter** page, **Add the following private ranges** and **Add address ranges based on the Windows Routing Table** are selected. While you don't have to do anything is this checkbox, we recommend that you remove the checkmark from the **Add the following private ranges** option and put a checkmark in the box next to the single NIC installed on the unihomed ISA firewall. Click **OK**.

10. Click **OK** in the **Setup Message** dialog box informing you that the Internal Network was defined based on the routing table. This dialog box really doesn't apply to the unihomed ISA firewall, since all IP addresses in the IPv4 address range (except for the local host network ID) are included in the definition of

the Internal Network. The reason why the local host network ID is not included is that this address is included in the Local Host Network definition.

11. In the Internal network address range dialog box (Figure 6.13), you'll see that all IP addresses are included in the definition of the Internal network. Click **OK**.

Figure 6.13 The Internal Network Definition on the Unihomed ISA Firewall

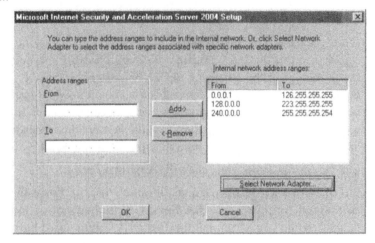

12. Click **Next** on the **Internal Network** page.

13. Click **Next** on the **Firewall Client Connection Settings** page. These settings don't mean anything because Firewall clients are not supported by the unihomed ISA firewall.

14. Click **Next** on the **Services** page.

15. Click **Install** on the **Ready to Install the Program** page.

16. Put a checkmark in the **Invoke ISA Server Management when the wizard closes** checkbox, and click **Finish**.

There are some significant limitations to the single NIC ISA firewall because there is no External network, there is lack of Firewall client support, and other factors. We discuss some of the implications of the unihomed ISA firewall and Access Policy related to this configuration in Chapter 7.

Quick Start Configuration for ISA Firewalls

Many of you will want to install and configure the ISA firewall as quickly as possible and then wait until later to get into the details of ISA firewall configuration. What you want to do is connect the ISA firewall to your network and your Internet connection, install the software, and create a rule that allows all hosts on your private network access to all protocols on the Internet as quickly as possible. Once you're up and running and connected to the Internet, you can then read the rest of this book at your leisure and get into the interesting and powerful configuration options available to you.

To help you, we have included a quick installationl and configuration section. In order to make this a quick installation and configuration guide, we're making the following basic assumptions about your network:

- You don't have any other Windows servers on your network. While you can have other Windows services running Windows network services, this guide will include instructions on how to install DNS and DHCP services on the ISA firewall. If you already have a DNS server on your network, you do not need to install a DNS server on the ISA firewall. If you already have a DHCP server on your network, you do not need to install a DHCP server on the ISA firewall.

- We assume that you are installing ISA Server 2004 on Windows Server 2003.

- We assume you have installed Windows Server 2003 on a computer using the default installation settings and have not added any software to the Windows Server 2003 machine.

- We assume your Windows Server 2003 computer already has two Ethernet cards. One NIC is connected to the Internal Network and the other is directly connected to the Internet via a network router, or there is a DSL or cable NAT "router" in front of it.

- We assume that machines on the Internal network are configured as DHCP clients and will use the ISA Server 2004 firewall machine as their DHCP server.

- We assume the Windows Server 2003 machine that you're installing the ISA Server 2004 firewall software on is not a member of a Windows domain. While we recommend that you make the ISA firewall a member of the domain later, the computer running the ISA firewall software does not need to be a domain member. We make this assumption in this quick installation and setup guide because we assume that you have no other Windows servers on your network (you may have Linux, Netware, or other vendors servers, though).

Figure 6.14 shows the ISA firewall and its relationship to the internal and external networks. The internal interface is connected to a hub or switch on the internal network, and the external interface is connected to a hub or switch that also connects to the router.

Figure 6.14 The Physical Relationships between the ISA Server 2004 Firewall and the Internal and External Networks.

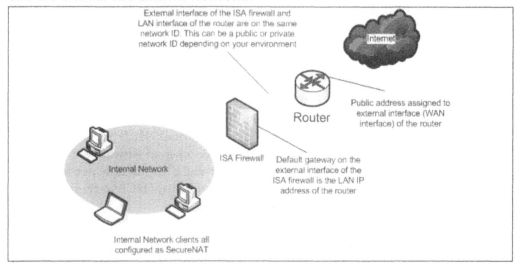

We will perform the following procedures to get the ISA firewall quickly set up and configured:

- Configure ISA firewall's network interfaces.
- Install and configure a DNS server on the ISA Server 2004 firewall computer.
- Install and configure a DHCP server on the ISA Server 2004 firewall computer.
- Install and configure the ISA Server 2004 software.
- Configure the internal network computers as DHCP clients.

Configuring the ISA Firewall's Network Interfaces

The ISA firewall must have at least one *internal* network interface and one *external* network interface. To correctly configure the network interfaces on the ISA firewall:

- Assign IP addresses to the internal and external network interfaces.
- Assign a DNS server address to the internal interface of the ISA firewall.
- Place the internal interface on top of the network interface order.

IP Address and DNS Server Assignment

First, we will assign static IP addresses to the internal and external interfaces of the ISA firewall. The ISA firewall also requires a DNS server address bound to its internal interface. We will not need to use DHCP on any of the ISA firewall's network interfaces because the internal interface should always have a static IP address, and the external interface doesn't need to support a dynamic address because it's behind a router.

If your Internet account uses DHCP to assign your public address, your DSL or cable router can handle the task of obtaining and renewing the public address. In addition, if you use PPPoE or VPN to connect to your ISP, your router can also handle these tasks. In this section, we discuss:

- Configuring the internal network interface, and
- Configuring the external network interface

Configuring the Internal Network Interface

The internal interface must have an IP address that is on the same network ID as other computers on the directly-attached network. This address must be in the private network address range, and the address must not already be in use on the network.

We will configure the ISA firewall to use its internal interface address as its DNS server address.

The ISA firewall must have a *static* IP address bound to its internal interface. Perform the following steps on the Windows Server 2003 machine that will become the ISA firewall:

1. Right-click **My Network Places** on the desktop, and click **Properties**.

2. In the **Network Connections** window, right-click the internal network interface, and click **Properties**.

3. In the network interface's **Properties** dialog box, click **Internet Protocol (TCP/IP)**, and then click **Properties**.

4. In the **Internet Protocol (TCP/IP) Properties** dialog box, select **Use the following IP address**. Enter the IP address for the internal interface in the **IP address** text box. Enter the subnet mask for the internal interface in the **Subnet mask** text box. Do *not* enter a default gateway for the internal interface.

5. Select **Use the following DNS server addresses**. Enter the IP address of the *internal* interface for the ISA firewall in the **Preferred DNS server** text box. This is the same number you entered in step 4 in the **IP address** text box. Click **OK** in the **Internet Protocol (TCP/IP) Properties** dialog box.

6. Click **OK** in the internal interface's **Properties** dialog box.

WARNING

If you already have a DNS server on your internal network, you should configure the ISA firewall's internal interface to use the Internal Network DNS server's IP address. You then configure the DNS server on the Internal Network to resolve Internet host names. The Microsoft DNS server will automatically resolve Internet host names as long as the Root Hints file is primed with Internet DNS Root Servers. The default Access Rule we will create at the end of this quick install and configuration section will allow the DNS server outbound access to Internet DNS servers for host name resolution.

WARNING

Never enter a default gateway address on the internal interface. An ISA firewall can have a single interface with a default gateway. Even if you have 17 NICs installed in the same ISA firewall, only one of those NICs can be configured with a default gateway. All other gateways must be configured in the Windows routing table.

Configuring the External Network Interface

Perform the following procedures to configure the IP addressing information on the external interface of the ISA firewall:

1. Right-click **My Network Places** on the desktop, and click **Properties**.

2. In the **Network Connections** window, right-click the external network interface, and click **Properties**.

3. In the network interface's **Properties** dialog box, click the **Internet Protocol (TCP/IP)** entry, and then click **Properties**.

4. In the **Internet Properties (TCP/IP) Properties** dialog box, select **Use the following IP address**. Enter the IP address for the external interface in the **IP address** text box. Enter the subnet mask for the external interface in the **Subnet mask** text box. Enter a **Default gateway** for the external interface in its text box. The default gateway is the LAN address of your router.

5. Click **OK** in the internal interface's **Properties** dialog box.

NOTE

You do not need to configure a DNS server address on the external interface. The DNS server address on the internal interface is the only DNS server address required.

Network Interface Order

The internal interface of the ISA Server 2004 computer is placed on top of the network interface list to ensure the best performance for name resolution. Perform the following steps to configure the network interface on the Windows Server 2003 machine:

1. Right-click **My Network Places** on the desktop, and click **Properties**.

2. In the **Network and Dial-up Connections** window, click the **Advanced** menu, then click **Advanced Settings**.

3. In the **Advanced Settings** dialog box (Figure 6.15), click the internal interface in the list of **Connections** on the **Adapters and Bindings** tab. After

selecting the internal interface, click the up-arrow to move it to the top of the list of interfaces.

Figure 6.15 The Advanced Settings Dialog Box

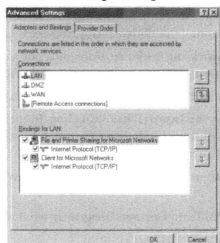

4. Click **OK** in the **Advanced Settings** dialog box.

Installing and Configuring a DNS Server on the ISA Server Firewall

We will install a caching-only DNS server on the ISA firewall. This will allow machines on the Internal Network and the ISA firewall to resolve Internet host names. Note that you *do not* need to perform this step if you already have a DNS server on your Internal network. Even if you already have a DNS server located on the Internal network, you might consider configuring the ISA firewall computer as a caching-only DNS server and then configure computers on the internal network to use the ISA Server 2004 machine as their DNS server or configure the Internal Network computers to use your Internal Network DNS server and configure the Internal Network DNS server to use the ISA firewall as a DNS forwarder.

Installing the DNS Service

The DNS Server service is not installed by default on Windows server operating systems. The first step is to install the DNS Server service on the Windows Server 2003 machine that will be the ISA firewall.

Installing the DNS Server Service on Windows Server 2003

Perform the following steps to install the DNS Server service on a Windows Server 2003 computer:

1. Click **Start**, point to **Control Panel**, and click **Add or Remove Programs**.

2. In the **Add or Remove Programs** window, click **Add/Remove Windows Components**.

3. In the **Windows Components Wizard** dialog box, select **Networking Services** from the list of **Components**. *Do not put a checkmark in the checkbox!* After highlighting the **Networking Services** entry, click the **Details** button.

4. In the **Networking Services** dialog box, put a checkmark in the **Domain Name System (DNS)** checkbox, and click **OK**.

5. Click **Next** in the **Windows Components** dialog box.

6. Click **OK** in the **Insert Disk** dialog box. In the **Files Needed** dialog box, provide a path to the i386 folder from the Windows Server 2003 installation CD in the **Copy files from** text box, then click **OK**.

7. Click **Finish** on the **Completing the Windows Components Wizard** page.

8. **Close** the **Add or Remove Programs** window.

Configuring the DNS Service on the ISA Firewall

The DNS Server on the ISA firewall machine performs DNS queries for Internet host names on behalf of computers on the internal network. The DNS Server on the ISA firewall is configured as a *caching-only* DNS server. A caching-only DNS Server does not contain information about your public or private DNS names and domains. The caching-only DNS Server resolves Internet host names and caches the results; it does not answer DNS queries for names on your private internal network DNS zone or your public DNS zone.

> **NOTE**
>
> DNS is an inherently complex topic. Do not be concerned if you do not completely understand the details of DNS operations. The DNS service will be correctly configured to resolve Internet host names when you complete the steps in this section.

If you have an internal network DNS server supporting an Active Directory domain, you can configure the caching-only DNS server located on the ISA firewall to refer client requests to your internal network domain to the DNS server on your internal network. The end result is that the caching-only DNS server on the ISA Server 2004 firewall computer will not interfere with your current DNS server setup.

Configuring the DNS Service in Windows Server 2003

Perform the following steps to configure the DNS service on the Windows Server 2003 computer:

1. Click **Start** and point to **Administrative Tools**. Click the **DNS** entry.

2. Right-click the server name in the left pane of the console, point to **View**, and click **Advanced**.

3. Expand all nodes in the left pane of the DNS console.

4. Right-click the server name in the left pane of the DNS console, and click the **Properties** option.

5. In the server's **Properties** dialog box, click **Interfaces**. Select **Only the following IP addresses**. Click any IP address that *is not* an IP address bound to the internal interface of the computer. After highlighting the non-internal IP address, click **Remove**. Click **Apply**.

6. Click the **Forwarders** tab, as shown in Figure 6.16. Enter the IP address of your ISP's DNS server in the **Selected domain's forwarder IP address list** text box, and then click **Add**. Put a checkmark in the **Do not use recursion for this domain** checkbox. This **Do not use recursion** option prevents the DNS server on the ISA firewall from trying to perform name resolution itself. The end result is if the forwarder is unable to resolve the name, the name resolution request stops. Click **Apply**.

TIP

If you find that name resolution performance isn't as good as you expect, disable the **Forwarders** entry. While a well-managed ISP DNS server can significantly improve name resolution performance, a poorly-managed ISP DNS server can slow down your ISA firewall's ability to resolve Internet host names. In most instances, you'll get better performance using your ISP's DNS server because it will have a larger cache of resolved host names than your ISA firewall's caching-only DNS server.

Figure 6.16 The Forwarders Tab

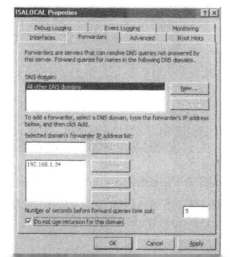

7. Click **OK** in the server's **Properties** dialog box.

8. Right-click the server name; point to **All Tasks,** and click **Restart.**

Perform the following steps *only if* you have an internal network DNS server that you are using to support an Active Directory domain. If you do not have an internal network DNS server and you do not need to resolve internal network DNS names, then bypass the following section on configuring a stub zone.

> **WARNING**
>
> *DO NOT* perform the following steps if you do not already have a DNS server on your internal network. These steps are only for those networks already using Windows 2000 Server or Windows Server 2003 Active Directory domains.

1. The first step is to create the reverse lookup zone for the Internal Network where the Internal DNS server ID is located. Right-click the **Reverse Lookup Zones** node in the left pane of the console, and click **New Zone.**

2. Click **Next** on the **Welcome to the New Zone Wizard** page.

3. On the **Zone Type** page, select **Stub zone,** and click **Next.**

4. Select **Network ID.** On the **Reverse Lookup Zone Name** page, enter into the **Network ID** text box the ID for the network where the internal network DNS server is located, as shown in Figure 6.17. Click **Next.**

Figure 6.17 The Reverse Lookup Zone Name Page

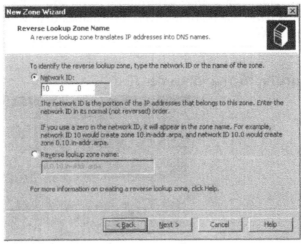

5. Accept the default file name on the **Zone File** page, and click **Next.**

6. On the **Master DNS Servers** page, enter the IP address of your internal network DNS server, and click **Add.** Click **Next.**

7. Click **Finish** on the **Completing the New Zone Wizard** page.

8. The next step is to create the forward lookup zone for the stub zone. Right-click the **Forward Lookup Zones** node in the left pane of the console, and click the **New Zone** command.

9. Click **Next** on the **Welcome to the New Zone Wizard** page.

10. On the **Zone Type** page, select **Stub zone**, and click **Next**.

11. On the **Zone name** page, type the name of your internal network domain in the **Zone name** text box. Click **Next**.

12. On the **Zone File** page (Figure 6.18), accept the default name for the zone file, and click **Next**.

Figure 6.18 The Zone File Page

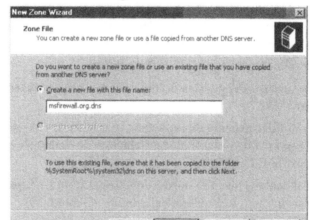

13. On the **Master DNS Servers** page, enter the IP address of your internal network's DNS server, and click **Add**. Click **Next**.

14. Click **Finish** on the **Completing the New Zone Wizard** page.

15. Right-click the server name in the left pane of the console; point to **All Tasks**, and click **Restart**.

Configuring the DNS Service on the Internal Network DNS Server

If your organization has an existing DNS infrastructure, you should configure your Internal network's DNS server to use the DNS server on the ISA Server 2004 firewall as its DNS forwarder. This provides a more secure DNS configuration because your Internal network DNS server never communicates directly with an untrusted DNS server on the Internet.

The Internal network DNS server forwards DNS queries to the DNS server on the ISA Server 2004 firewall, and the DNS server on the ISA Server 2004 resolves the name, places the result in its own DNS cache, and then returns the IP address to the DNS server on the Internal network.

WARNING

Perform the following steps only if you have an internal DNS server and you have configured the ISA firewall's internal interface to use the internal DNS server. If you do not have an internal network DNS server, do *not* perform the following steps.

Perform the following steps on the *Internal network DNS server* to configure it to use the DNS server on the ISA firewall as its forwarder:

1. Click **Start** and point to **Administrative** tools, then click **DNS**.

2. In the **DNS Management** console, right-click the server name in the left pane of the console, and click **Properties**.

3. In the server's **Properties** dialog box, click the **Forwarders** tab, as shown in Figure 6.19.

4. On the **Forwarders** tab, enter the IP address on the Internal interface of the ISA Server 2004 firewall in the **Selected domain's forwarder IP address list** text box. Click **Add**.

5. The IP address for the internal interface of the ISA Server 2004 firewall appears in the list of forwarder addresses (Figure 6.19).

Figure 6.19 The Forwarders Tab

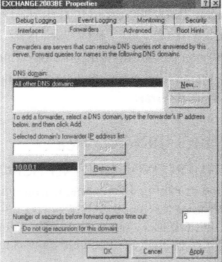

6. Put a checkmark in the **Do not use recursion for this domain** checkbox (Figure 6.20. This option prevents the Internal network DNS server from trying to resolve the name itself in the event that the forwarder on the ISA firewall is unable to resolve the name.

Figure 6.20 Disabling Recursion

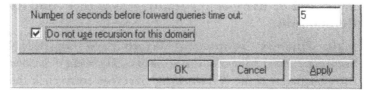

7. Click **Apply**, and then click **OK**.

Note that the DNS server on the Internal Network will not be able to resolve Internet host names yet. We still need to create an Access Rule allowing the DNS server access to the DNS server on the ISA firewall. We will create this Access Rule later in this section.

Installing and Configuring a DHCP Server on the ISA Server Firewall

Each of your computers needs an IP address and other information that allows them to communicate with each other and with computers on the Internet. The DHCP Server service can be installed on the ISA firewall and provide IP addressing information to Internal Network computers. We will assume that you need to use the ISA firewall as your DHCP server. If you already have a DHCP server on your network, you can bypass the following steps.

> **WARNING**
>
> You must not have any other DHCP servers on the network. If you have another machine on the network acting as a DHCP server, disable the DHCP service on that machine so that the ISA Server 2004 firewall acts as your only DHCP server on the network.

Installing the DHCP Service

The DHCP Server service can be installed on Windows 2000 Server and Windows Server 2003 computers. The procedure varies slightly between the two operating systems. In this section, we discuss procedures for installing the DHCP Server service on Windows 2000 Server and Windows Server 2003 computers.

*Installing the DHCP Server Service
on a Windows Server 2003 Computer*

Perform the following steps to install the DNS Server service on a Windows Server
2003 computer:

1. Click **Start**, point to **Control Panel**, and click **Add or Remove Programs**.

2. In the **Add or Remove Programs** window, click **Add/Remove Windows
   Components**.

3. In the **Windows Components Wizard** dialog box, select **Networking
   Services** from the list of **Components**. *Do not put a checkmark in the checkbox!*
   After highlighting the **Networking Services** entry, click the **Details** button.

4. In the **Networking Services** dialog box (Figure 6.21), put a checkmark in the
   Dynamic Host Configuration Protocol (DHCP) checkbox, and click **OK**.

Figure 6.21 The Networking Services Dialog Box

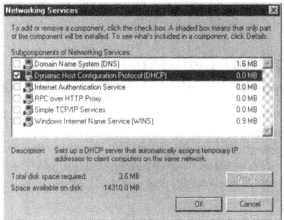

5. Click **Next** in the **Windows Components** dialog box.

6. Click **Finish** on the **Completing the Windows Components Wizard**
   page.

7. **Close** the **Add or Remove Programs** window.

Configuring the DHCP Service

The DHCP Server must be configured with a collection of IP addresses it can assign to
machines on your private network. The DHCP Server also provides information in
addition to an IP address, such as a DNS server address, default gateway, and primary
domain name.

The DNS server and default gateway addresses assigned to your computers will be
the IP address on the internal interface of the ISA firewall. The DHCP server uses a

DHCP scope to provide this information to the internal network clients. You must create a DHCP scope that provides the correct IP addressing information to your internal network clients.

NOTE

The DHCP server must not assign addresses that are already in use on your network. You must create *exclusions* for these IP addresses. Examples of excluded IP addresses might be static or reserved addresses assigned to print servers, file servers, mail servers, or Web servers; these are just a few examples of devices or servers that always have the same IP address assigned to them. These addresses are permanently assigned to these servers and network devices. If you don't create exclusions for these addresses, the DHCP server will perform a gratuitous ARP, and when it finds this address in use, will move it into a *bad address* group. In addition, a well designed network will group computers into contiguous blocks of IP addresses. For example, all computers that need static addresses would be placed into one contiguous block.

Perform the following steps to configure the Windows Server 2003 DHCP Server with a scope that will assign the proper IP addressing information to the internal network clients:

WARNING

If you already have a DHCP server on your corporate network, do not perform the following steps, and do not install the DHCP server on the ISA firewall. Only install the DHCP server on the ISA firewall if you do *not* have a DHCP server on your internal network.

---

1. Click **Start** and point to **Administrative Tools**. Click **DHCP**.

2. Expand all nodes in the left pane of the **DHCP** console. Right-click the server name in the left pane of the console, and click **New Scope**.

3. Click **Next** on the **Welcome to the New Scope Wizard** page.

4. Type **SecureNAT Client Scope** in the **Name** text box on the **Scope Name** page. Click **Next**.

5. On the **IP Address Range** page, enter the first IP address and the last IP address for the range in the **Start IP address** and **End IP address** text boxes. For example, if you are using the network ID 192.168.1.0 with a subnet mask of 255.255.255.0, then enter the start IP address as **192.168.1.1** and the end IP address as **192.168.1.254**. Click **Next**.

6. On the **Add Exclusions** page, enter the IP address of the internal interface for the ISA firewall in the **Start IP address** text box, and click **Add**. If you

have servers or workstations on the network that have statically-assigned IP addresses that you do not want to change, add those addresses to the exclusions list. Click **Next** after adding all addresses you want to exclude from the DHCP scope.

7. Accept the default value on the **Lease Duration** page, and click **Next**.

8. On the **Configuring DHCP Options** page, select **Yes, I want to configure these options now,** and click **Next**.

9. On the **Router** page, enter the IP address of the internal interface for the ISA firewall, and click **Add**. Click **Next**.

10. On the **Domain Name and DNS Servers** page, enter the IP address of the internal interface for the ISA firewall in the **IP address** text box, and click **Add**. *If you have an Active Directory domain on the Internal network*, enter the name of your Internal network domain in the **Parent domain** text box. Do *not* enter a domain name in the **Parent domain** text box *unless* you have an existing Active Directory domain on the internal network. Click **Next**.

11. Do not enter any information on the **WINS Servers** page unless you already have a WINS server on the internal network. If you already have a WINS server, enter that IP address in the **IP address** text box. Click **Next**.

12. Select **Yes, I want to activate this scope now** on the **Activate Scope** page, and click **Yes**.

13. Click **Finish** on the **Completing the New Scope Wizard** page.

Installing and Configuring the ISA Server 2004 Software

We're now ready to install the ISA firewall software.

The following steps demonstrate how to install the ISA firewall software on a dual-homed Windows Server 2003 machine:

1. Insert the ISA Server 2004 installation media into the CD-ROM drive or connect to a network share hosting the ISA Server 2004 installation files. If the installation routine does not start automatically, double-click the **isaautorun.exe** file in the root of the installation files tree.

2. On the **Microsoft Internet Security and Acceleration Server 2004** page, click **Review Release Notes** and read the notes. The release notes contain useful information about important issues and configuration options. After reading the release notes, click **Read Setup and Feature Guide**. You don't need to read the entire guide right now, but you may want to print it to read later. Click **Install ISA Server 2004**.

3. Click **Next** on the **Welcome to the Installation Wizard for Microsoft ISA Server 2004** page.

4. Select **I accept the terms in the license agreement** on the **License Agreement** page. Click **Next**.

5. On the **Customer Information** page, enter your name and the name of your organization in the **User Name** and **Organization** text boxes. Enter your serial number in the **Product Serial Number** text box. Click **Next**.

6. On the **Setup Type** page, select the **Custom** option. If you do not want to install the ISA firewall software on the C: drive, click the **Change** button to change the location of the program files on the hard disk. Click **Next**.

7. On the **Custom Setup** page, choose the components to install. By default, the **Firewall Services**, **ISA Server Management**, and **Firewall Client Installation Share** are installed. The **Message Screener**, which is used to control spam and file attachments from entering and leaving the network, is not installed by default. You must install the IIS 6.0 SMTP service on the ISA Server 2004 firewall computer *before* you install the **Message Screener**. We want to install the **Firewall Client Installation Share** so that we have the option later to install the Firewall client on Internal Network client machines. Click the "X" to the left of the **Firewall Client Installation Share** option and click **This feature, and all subfeatures, will be installed on the local hard drive**, as shown in Figure 6.22. The Firewall client adds a significant level of security to your network, and you should install the Firewall client on Internal network clients whenever possible. We discuss this issue in more detail in Chapter 5 on ISA Server client types. Click **Next**.

Figure 6.22 The Custom Setup Page

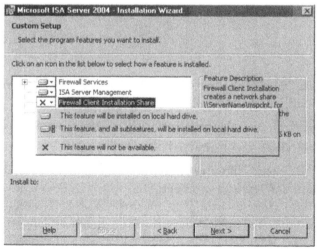

8. On the **Internal Network** page, click **Add**. The Internal network is different from the Local Address Table (LAT) used by ISA Server 2000. The Internal network contains trusted network services with which the ISA firewall must

communicate. Examples of such services include Active Directory domain controllers, DNS, DHCP, terminal services client management workstations, and others. The firewall System Policy uses the Internal network definition in many of its System Policy Rules.

9. On the **Internal Network** setup page, click the **Select Network Adapter** button.

10. In the **Configure Internal Network** dialog box, remove the checkmark from the **Add the following private ranges…** checkbox. Leave the checkmark in the **Add address ranges based on the Windows Routing Table** checkbox, as shown in Figure 6.23. Put a checkmark next to the adapter connected to the Internal network. In this example we have renamed the network interfaces so that the interface name reflects its location. Click **OK**.

Figure 6.23 The Select Network Adapter Page

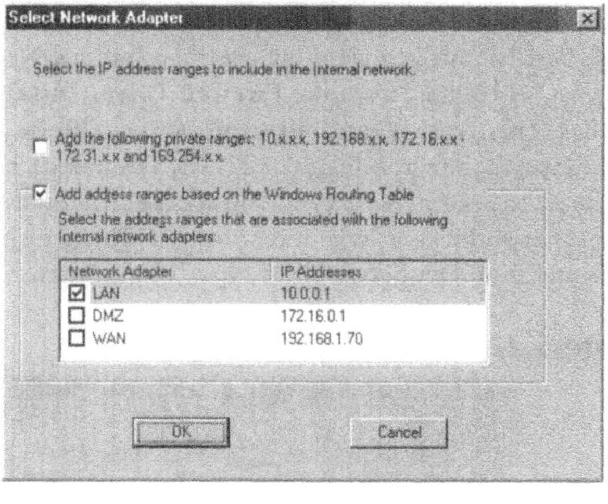

11. Click **OK** in the dialog box informing you that the Internal network was defined, based on the Windows routing table.

12. Click **OK** in the **Internal network address ranges** dialog box.

13. Click **Next** on the **Internal Network** page.

14. Do not check **Allow computers running earlier versions of Firewall Client software to connect**. This option requires that you use the new ISA firewall's Firewall client. Previous versions of the Firewall client (those included with Proxy 2.0 and ISA Server 2000) will not be supported. It also allows the Firewall client to send user credentials over an encrypted channel to the ISA firewall and allows the Firewall client to transparently authenticate with the ISA firewall. Click **Next**.

15. On the **Services** page, note that the **SNMP** and **IIS Admin Service** will be stopped during installation. If the **Internet Connection Firewall (ICF)** /

Internet Connection Sharing (ICF) and/or **IP Network Address Translation** services are installed on the ISA Server 2004 machine, they will be disabled, as they conflict with the ISA Server 2004 firewall software.

16. Click **Install** on the **Ready to Install the Program** page.

17. On the **Installation Wizard Completed** page, click **Finish**.

18. Click **Yes** on the **Microsoft ISA Server** dialog box informing that you must restart the server.

19. Log on as an **Administrator** after the machine restarts.

20. Click **Start** and point to **All Programs**. Point to **Microsoft ISA Server**, and click **ISA Server Management**. The **Microsoft Internet Security and Acceleration Server 2004** management console opens and displays the **Welcome to Microsoft Internet Security and Acceleration Server 2004** page.

Configuring the ISA Firewall

Now we're ready to configure Access Policy on the ISA firewall. We need to create the following five Access Rules:

- A rule that allows Internal Network clients access to the DHCP server on the ISA firewall

- A rule that allows the ISA firewall to send DHCP messages to the hosts on the Internal network

- A rule that allows the Internal Network DNS server to use the ISA firewall as its DNS server. Create this rule only if you have an Internal Network DNS server.

- A rule that allows Internal Network clients access to the caching-only DNS server on the ISA firewall. Use this rule if you do not have a DNS server on the Internal Network, or if you have a DNS server on the Internal Network and you want to use the ISA firewall as a caching-only DNS server with a stub zone pointing to your Internal Network domain.

- An "All Open" rule allowing Internal Network clients access to all protocols and sites on the Internet

Tables 6.8 through 6.12 show the details of each of these rules.

Table 6.8 DHCP Request to Server

Name	DHCP Request to Server
Action	Allow
Protocols	DHCP (request)
From	Anywhere
To	Local Host
Users	All Users
Schedule	Always
Content Types	All content types
Purpose	This rule allows DHCP clients to send DHCP requests to the DHCP server installed on the ISA firewall.

Table 6.9 DHCP Reply from Server

Name	DHCP Reply from Server
Action	Allow
Protocols	DHCP (reply)
From	Local Host
To	Internal
Users	All Users
Schedule	Always
Content Types	All content types
Purpose	This rule allows the DHCP server on the ISA firewall to reply to DHCP requests made by Internal network DHCP clients.

Table 6.10 Internal DNS Server to Forwarder

Name	Internal DNS Server to DNS forwarder
Action	Allow
Protocols	DNS
From	DNS Server*
To	Local Host
Users	All Users
Schedule	Always
Content Types	All content types
Purpose	This rule allows the Internal network DNS server to forward queries to the DNS forwarder on the ISA Server 2004 firewall machine. Create this rule only if you have an Internal Network DNS server.

* User defined

Table 6.11 Internal Network to DNS Server

Name	Internal Network to DNS Server
Action	Allow
Protocols	DNS
From	Internal
To	Local Host
Users	All Users
Schedule	Always
Content Types	All content types
Purpose	This rule allows Internal network clients access to the caching-only DNS server on the ISA firewall. Create this rule if you do not have an Internal Network DNS server, or if you have decided that you want to use the caching-only DNS server as your caching-only forwarder for all Internal Network clients, even when you have an Internal Network DNS server.

Table 6.12 All Open

Name	All Open
Action	Allow
Protocols	All Outbound Traffic
From	Internal
To	External
Users	All Users
Schedule	Always
Content Types	All content types
Purpose	This rule allows Internal network clients access to all protocols and sites on the Internet.

WARNING

This last rule, **All Open**, is used only to get you up and running. This All Open rule allows you to test the ISA firewall's basic Internet connection ability, but does not provide any outbound access control in a manner similar to most hardware packet-filter firewalls. The ISA firewall provides advanced inbound and outbound protection, so you want to be sure to disable the All Open rule and create per user/group, per protocol and per site rules after your basic Internet connections through the ISA firewall are successful.

In addition to these Access Rules, you should configure the firewall System Policy to allow DHCP replies from External network DHCP servers.

DHCP Request to Server Rule

Perform the following steps to create the **DHCP Request to Server** rule:

1. In the **Microsoft Internet Security and Acceleration Server 2004** management console, expand the server name, and click **Firewall Policy**.

2. In the **Firewall Policy** node, click the **Tasks** tab in the Task pane. On the Task pane, click **Create a New Access Rule**.

3. On the **Welcome to the New Access Rule Wizard** page, enter **DHCP Request to Server** in the **Access Rule name** text box. Click **Next**.

4. On the **Rule Action** page, select **Allow**, and click **Next**.

5. On the **Protocols** page, select the **Selected protocols** option from the **This rule applies to** list, and click **Add**.

6. In the **Add Protocols** dialog box (Figure 6.24), click the **Infrastructure** folder. Double-click the **DHCP (request)** entry, and click **Close**.

Figure 6.24 The Add Protocols Dialog Box

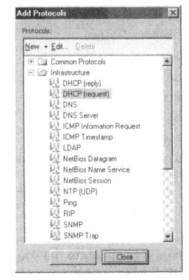

7. Click **Next** on the **Protocols** page.

8. On the **Access Rule Sources** page, click **Add**.

9. In the **Add Network Entities** dialog box, click the **Computer Sets** folder. Double-click the **Anywhere** entry, and click **Close**.

10. Click **Next** on the **Access Rule Sources** page.

11. On the **Access Rule Destinations** page, click **Add**.

12. In the **Add Network Entities** dialog box, click the **Networks** folder, and double-click **Local Host**. Click **Close**.

13. Click **Next** on the **Access Rule Destinations** page.

14. On the **User Sets** page, accept the default entry, **All Users**, and click **Next**.

15. On the **Completing the New Access Rule Wizard** page, review the settings, and click **Finish**.

DHCP Reply from Server Rule

Perform the following steps to create the **DHCP Reply from Server** rule:

1. In the **Microsoft Internet Security and Acceleration Server 2004** management console, expand the server name, and click **Firewall Policy**.

2. In the **Firewall Policy** node, click the **Tasks** tab in the Task pane. On the Task pane, click **Create a New Access Rule**.

3. On the **Welcome to the New Access Rule Wizard** page, enter **DHCP Reply from Server** in the **Access Rule name** text box. Click **Next**.

4. On the **Rule Action** page, select **Allow**, and click **Next**.

5. On the **Protocols** page, select the **Selected protocols** option from the **This rule applies to** list, and click **Add**.

6. In the **Add Protocols** dialog box, click the **Infrastructure** folder. Double-click **DHCP (reply)**, and click **Close**.

7. Click **Next** on the **Protocols** page.

Figure 6.25 The Protocols Page

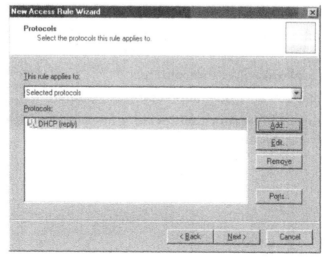

8. On the **Access Rule Sources** page, click **Add**.

9. In the **Add Network Entities** dialog box, click the **Networks** folder. Double-click the **Local Host** entry, and click **Close**.

10. Click **Next** on the **Access Rule Sources** page.

11. On the **Access Rule Destinations** page, click **Add**.

12. In the **Add Network Entities** dialog box, click the **Networks** folder, and then double-click the **Internal** entry. Click **Close**.

13. Click **Next** on the **Access Rule Destinations** page.

14. On the **User Sets** page, accept the default entry, **All Users**, and click **Next**.

15. On the **Completing the New Access Rule Wizard** page, review the settings, and click **Finish**.

Internal DNS Server to DNS Forwarder Rule

Perform the following steps to create the **Internal DNS Server to DNS Forwarder** rule:

1. In the **Microsoft Internet Security and Acceleration Server 2004** management console, expand the server name, and click **Firewall Policy**.

2. In the **Firewall Policy** node, click the **Tasks** tab in the Task pane. On the Task pane, click **Create a New Access Rule**.

3. On the **Welcome to the New Access Rule Wizard** page, enter **Internal DNS Server to DNS Forwarder** in the **Access Rule name** text box. Click **Next**.

4. On the **Rule Action** page, select **Allow**, and click **Next**.

5. On the **Protocols** page, select the **Selected protocols** option from the **This rule applies to** list, and click **Add**.

6. In the **Add Protocols** dialog box, click the **Infrastructure** folder. Double-click the **DNS** entry, and click **Close**.

7. Click **Next** on the **Protocols** page.

8. On the **Access Rule Sources** page, click **Add**.

9. In the **Add Network Entities** dialog box (Figure 6.26), click the **New** menu, then click **Computer**.

Figure 6.26 Selecting the Computer Command

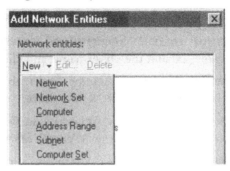

10. In the **New Computer Rule Element** dialog box, enter **Internal DNS Server** in the **Name** text box. Enter **10.0.0.2** in the **Computer IP Address** text box. Click **OK**.

11. In the **Add Network Entities** dialog box (Figure 6.27), click the **Computers** folder, and double-click **Internal DNS Server**. Click **Close**.

Figure 6.27 Selecting the New Computer Object

12. Click **Next** on the **Access Rule Sources** page.

13. On the **Access Rule Destinations** page, click **Add**.

14. In the **Add Network Entities** dialog box, click the **Networks** folder, and double-click **Local Host**. Click **Close**.

15. Click **Next** on the **Access Rule Destinations** page.

16. On the **User Sets** page, accept the default entry, **All Users**, and click **Next**.

17. On the **Completing the New Access Rule Wizard** page, review the settings, and click **Finish**.

Internal Network to DNS Server

Perform the following steps to create the **Internal Network to DNS Server** rule:

1. In the **Microsoft Internet Security and Acceleration Server 2004** management console, expand the server name, and click **Firewall Policy**.

2. In the **Firewall Policy** node, click the **Tasks** tab in the Task pane. On the Task pane, click **Create a New Access Rule**.

3. On the **Welcome to the New Access Rule Wizard** page, enter **Internal Network to DNS Server** in the **Access Rule name** text box. Click **Next**.

4. On the **Rule Action** page, select **Allow**, and click **Next**.

5. On the **Protocols** page, select the **Selected protocols** option from the **This rule applies to** list, and click **Add**.

6. In the **Add Protocols** dialog box, click the **Common Protocols** folder. Double-click the **DNS** entry, and click **Close**.

7. Click **Next** on the **Protocols** page.

8. On the **Access Rule Sources** page, click **Add**.

9. In the **Add Network Entities** dialog box, click the **Networks** folder. Double-click **Internal**, and click **Close**.

10. Click **Next** on the **Access Rule Sources** page.

11. On the **Access Rule Destinations** page, click **Add**.

12. In the **Add Network Entities** dialog box, click the **Networks** folder, and double-click **Local Host**. Click **Close**.

13. Click **Next** on the **Access Rule Destinations** page.

14. On the **User Sets** page, accept the default entry, **All Users**, and click **Next**.

15. On the **Completing the New Access Rule Wizard** page, review the settings, and click **Finish**.

The All Open Rule

Perform the following steps to create the **All Open** rule:

1. In the **Microsoft Internet Security and Acceleration Server 2004** management console, expand the server name, and click **Firewall Policy**.

2. In the **Firewall Policy** node, click the **Tasks** tab in the Task pane. On the Task pane, click **Create a New Access Rule**.

3. On the **Welcome to the New Access Rule Wizard** page, enter **All Open** in the **Access Rule name** text box. Click **Next**.

4. On the **Rule Action** page, select **Allow**, and click **Next**.

5. On the **Protocols** page, select **All outbound traffic** from the **This rule applies to** list, and click **Next**.

6. Click **Next** on the **Protocols** page.

7. On the **Access Rule Sources** page, click **Add**.

8. In the **Add Network Entities** dialog box, click the **Networks** folder. Double-click **Internal,** and click **Close**.

9. Click **Next** on the **Access Rule Sources** page.

10. On the **Access Rule Destinations** page, click **Add**.

11. In the **Add Network Entities** dialog box, click the **Networks** folder, and double-click **External**. Click **Close**.

12. Click **Next** on the **Access Rule Destinations** page.

13. On the **User Sets** page, accept the default entry, **All Users,** and click **Next**.

14. On the **Completing the New Access Rule Wizard** page, review the settings, and click **Finish**.

Your Access Rule should look like those in Figure 6.28. Note that in this example, you do not need to reorder the rules. When you start creating advanced Access Rules to control inbound and outbound access, you may need to reorder rules to obtain the desired results.

Figure 6.28 The Resulting Firewall Policy

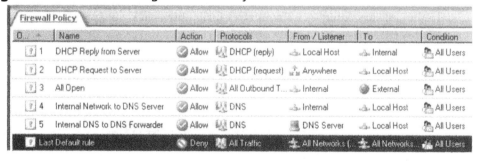

Configuring the Internal Network Computers

Internal Network computers are set up as ISA Server *SecureNAT* clients. A SecureNAT client is a machine with a default gateway address set to an IP address of a network device that routes Internet-bound requests to the internal IP address of the ISA Server 2004 firewall.

When Internal network computers are on the same network ID as the internal interface of the ISA firewall, the default gateway of the internal network computers is set as the internal IP address on the ISA firewall machine. This is how the DHCP scope on the DHCP server located on the ISA firewall is configured.

We will configure internal network computers that are on the same network ID as the internal interface of the ISA Server 2004 firewall and clients that may be located on network IDs that are not on the same network ID. This latter configuration is more common on larger networks that have more than one network ID on the internal network.

> **NOTE**
>
> The "network ID" is part of the IP address. Network IDs are part of advanced TCP/IP networking concepts. Typically, SOHO networks have only one Network ID and you do not need to be concerned about knowing your network ID. If you have a router anywhere *behind* the ISA firewall, you need to understand network IDs.

Configuring Internal Clients as DHCP Clients

DHCP clients request IP addressing information from a DHCP server. In this section, you will find out how to configure the Windows 2000 (Server or Professional) client as a DHCP client. The procedure is similar for all Windows-based clients. Perform the following steps to configure the internal network client and a DHCP client:

1. Right-click **My Network Places** on the desktop, and click **Properties**.

2. In the **Network Connections** window, right-click the external network interface, and click **Properties**.

3. In the network interface's **Properties** dialog box, click the **Internet Protocol (TCP/IP)** entry, and click **Properties**.

4. In the **Internet Protocol (TCP/IP) Properties** dialog box (Figure 6.29), select **Obtain an IP address automatically**.

Figure 6.29 The Internet Protocol (TCP/IP) Properties Dialog Box

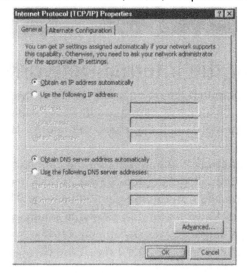

5. Select **Use the following DNS server addresses**. Enter the IP address of the internal interface in the **Preferred DNS server** text box. Click **OK** in the **Internet Protocol (TCP/IP) Properties** dialog box.

6. Click **OK** in the internal interface's **Properties** dialog box.

In figure 6.30, you can see a Network Monitor trace of a Windows XP client sending a request to the caching-only DNS server on the ISA firewall for an Internal Network domain for which we created a stub zone. The following eight frames are in the trace:

1. The client sends a reverse lookup query to the DNS server for the IP address of the DNS server itself. This allows the client to ascertain the name of the DNS server.

2. The caching-only DNS server on the ISA firewall responds to the Windows XP client with the answer to the query made in frame #1.

3. The Windows XP client sends a query to the caching-only DNS server on the ISA firewall for www.msfirewall.org. The msfireall.org domain is the name of the Internal Network domain.

4. An ARP broadcast is made by the ISA firewall to discover the IP address of the DNS server authoritative for the Internal Network domain.

5. The DNS server returns its IP address to the ISA firewall in an ARP broadcast.

6. The ISA firewall sends a query to the Internal DNS server to resolve the name of the Internal domain host.

7. The Internal DNS server returns the answer to the query to the ISA firewall.

8. The ISA firewall returns the response to the Windows XP client that made the original request.

Figure 6.30 DNS Queries in Network Monitor Trace

DNS	0x1:Std Qry for 1.0.0.10.in-addr.arpa. of type Dom. na...	10.0.0.5	10.0.0.1
DNS	0x1:Std Qry Resp. for 1.0.0.10.in-addr.arpa. of type D...	10.0.0.1	10.0.0.5
DNS	0x2:Std Qry for www.msfirewall.org. of type Host Addr ...	10.0.0.5	10.0.0.1
ARP_RARP	ARP: Request, Target IP: 10.0.0.2		
ARP_RARP	ARP: Reply, Target IP: 10.0.0.1 Target Hdwr Addr: 000C...		
DNS	0x30F8:Std Qry for www.msfirewall.org. of type Host Ad...	10.0.0.1	10.0.0.2
DNS	0x30F8:Std Qry Resp. Auth. NS is msfirewall.org. of ty...	10.0.0.2	10.0.0.1
DNS	0x2:Std Qry Resp. Auth. NS is msfirewall.org. of type ...	10.0.0.1	10.0.0.5

Figure 6.31 shows the domains cached on the caching-only DNS server located on the ISA firewall. You can enable the Advanced View in the DNS console and see the **Cached Lookups** node. After expanding the **.(root)** folder, you can see the domains for which the DNS server has cached DNS query information. If you double-click on any of the domains, you will see the actual resource records that the DNS server has cached.

Figure 6.31 DNS Domains Cached by the Caching-only DNS Server on the ISA Firewall

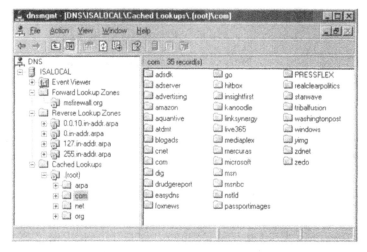

Hardening the Base ISA Firewall Configuration and Operating System

While the ISA firewall software does an exceptional job of protecting the firewall from attack, there are things you can do to further harden the ISA firewall configuration and the underlying operating system.

In this section, we'll discuss the following hardening and local security issues:

- **ISA firewall service dependencies** You need to know what services the ISA firewall depends on before disabling services on the firewall. In this section, we'll present the list of ISA firewall software dependencies.

- **Service requirements for common tasks performed on the ISA firewall** There are several maintenance tasks that you can run on the ISA firewall that depend on features provided by the underlying operating system. In this section, we'll examine some of these features and the services they depend upon.

- **Client roles for the ISA firewall client rules** This ISA firewall may need to act as a network client to a variety of network services. In this section, we'll review some of the network client roles and operating system services required for the ISA firewall to fulfill those roles.

- **ISA firewall administrative roles and permissions** Not all ISA firewall administrators are created equal. In this section, we'll discuss the ISA firewall administrative roles and how to provide users more granular control over the ISA firewall configuration and management.

- **ISA firewall lockdown mode** The ISA firewall needs to protect itself and the networks dependent on it in the event that an attack shuts down the ISA firewalls Firewall Service. In this section, we'll discuss the ISA firewall's Lockdown Mode.

ISA Firewall Service Dependencies

One of the more frustrating aspects of the ISA Server 2000 firewall was that there was never any definitive guidance regarding what services were required for full firewall functionality. Many ISA fans attempted to divine the service dependencies, but no hard and fast guidance was ever developed. To make life even more difficult for the ISA Server 2000 firewall administrator, the ISA Server 2000 System Hardening Templates invariably broke key features of the firewall and the underlying operating system.

These problems are corrected with the new ISA firewall. Now we know the exact services required by the ISA firewall software. Table 6.13 lists the core services that must be enabled for ISA Server and the ISA Server computer to function properly.

WARNING

Do not use any of the default security templates included with the version of Windows on which you've installed the ISA firewall software. You should create your own custom security policy on the ISA firewall and then create a template based on that policy.

Table 6.13 Services on which the ISA Firewall Software Depends

Service name	Rationale	Startup mode
COM+ Event System	Core operating system	Manual
Cryptographic Services	Core operating system (security)	Automatic
Event Log	Core operating system	Automatic
IPSec Services	Core operating system (security)	Automatic
Logical Disk Manager	Core operating system (disk management)	Automatic
Logical Disk Manager Administrative Service	Core operating system (disk management)	Manual
Microsoft Firewall	Required for normal functioning of ISA Server	Automatic
Microsoft ISA Server Control	Required for normal functioning of ISA Server	Automatic
Microsoft ISA Server Job Scheduler	Required for normal functioning of ISA Server	Automatic

Continued

Table 6.13 Services on which the ISA Firewall Software Depends

Service name	Rationale	Startup mode
Microsoft ISA Server Storage	Required for normal functioning of ISA Server	Automatic
MSSQL$MSFW	Required when MSDE logging is used for ISA Server	Automatic
Network Connections	Core operating system (network infrastructure)	Manual
NTLM Security Support Provider	Core operating system (security)	Manual
Plug and Play	Core operating system	Automatic
Protected Storage	Core operating system (security)	Automatic
Remote Access Connection Manager	Required for normal functioning of ISA Server	Manual
Remote Procedure Call (RPC)	Core operating system	Automatic
Secondary Logon	Core operating system (security)	Automatic
Security Accounts Manager	Core operating system	Automatic
Server*	Required for ISA Server Firewall Client Share (and others depending on your requirements)*	Automatic*
Smart Card	Core operating system (security)	Manual
SQLAgent$MSFW	Required when MSDE logging is used for ISA Server (not installed when Advanced Logging is not selected during installation)	Manual
System Event Notification	Core operating system	Automatic
Telephony	Required for normal functioning of ISA Server	Manual
Virtual Disk Service (VDS)	Core operating system (management)	Manual
Windows Management Instrumentation (WMI)	Core operating system (WMI)	Automatic
WMI Performance Adapter	Core operating system (WMI)	Manual

*The startup mode for the Server service should be set as **Automatic** in the following circumstances:

- You install Firewall client installation share on the ISA firewall

- You use Routing and Remote Access Management, rather than ISA Server Management, to configure a virtual private network (VPN). Required if you want to use EAP user certificate authentication for demand-dial VPN connections and troubleshooting of demand-dial VPN connections

- IF other tasks or roles table require the Server service

- The startup mode for the Routing and Remote Access service is Manual. ISA Server starts the service only if a VPN is enabled. Note that the Server service is required only if you need access to Routing and Remote Access console (rather than **Microsoft Internet Security and Acceleration Server 2004** management console) to configure a remote-access VPN or site-to-site.

Service Requirements for Common Tasks Performed on the ISA Firewall

Specific services must be enabled in order for the ISA firewall to perform necessary tasks. All services that are not used should be disabled. Table 6.14 lists a number of tasks the ISA firewall's underlying operating system may need to perform. Enable those services required to perform the tasks you want to perform on the ISA firewall and disable services responsible for tasks you will not be using.

Table 6.14 Services Required for Common Tasks Performed on the ISA Firewall

Task	Usage scenario	Services required	Startup mode
Application Installation locally using Windows Installer	Required to install, uninstall, or repair applications using the Microsoft Installer Service. Often required to install ISA firewall add-ins to enhance firewall functionality and protection	Windows Installer	Manual
Backup	Required if using NTBackup or other backup programs on the ISA firewall	Microsoft Software Shadow Copy Provider	Manual
Backup	Required if using NTBackup or other backup programs on the ISA firewall	Volume Shadow Copy	Manual
Backup	Required if using NTBackup or other backup program on the ISA firewall	Removable Storage Service	Manual

Continued

Table 6.14 Services Required for Common Tasks Performed on the ISA Firewall

Task	Usage scenario	Services required	Startup mode
Error Reporting	Required for error reporting, which helps improve Windows reliability by reporting critical faults to Microsoft for analysis	Error Reporting Service	Automatic
Help and Support	Allows collection of historical computer data for Microsoft Product Support Services incident escalation	Help and Support	Automatic
Host the Firewall client installation share	Required to allow computers SMB/CIFS connections to the ISA firewall to install the Firewall client software	Server	Automatic
MSDE logging	Required to allow logging using MSDE databases. If you do not enable the applicable service, you can log to SQL databases or to files. However, you will not be able to use the Log Viewer in off-line mode. Required only when ISA Advanced logging is installed	SQLAgent$MSFW	Manual
MSDE logging	Required to allow logging using MSDE databases. If you do not enable the applicable service, you can log to SQL databases or to files. However, you will not be able to use the Log Viewer in off-line mode. Required only when Advanced logging is installed	MSSQL$MSFW	Automatic
Performance Monitor—Background Collect	Allows background collecting of performance data on the ISA firewall	Performance Logs and Alerts	Automatic

Continued

Table 6.14 Services Required for Common Tasks Performed on the ISA Firewall

Task	Usage scenario	Services required	Startup mode
Print to a remote computer	Allows printing from the ISA Server computer (not recommended)	Print Spooler	Automatic
Print to a remote computer	Allows printing from the ISA Server computer (not recommended that you send print jobs from the ISA firewall)	TCP/IP NetBIOS Helper	Automatic
Print to a remote computer	Allows printing from the ISA Server computer (not recommended that you send print jobs from the ISA firewall)	Workstation	Automatic
Remote Windows administration	Allows remote management of the Windows server (not required for remote management of the ISA firewall software)	Server	Automatic
Remote Windows administration	Allows remote management of the Windows server (not required for remote management of the ISA firewall software)	Remote Registry	Automatic
Time Synchronization	Allows the ISA firewall to contact an NTP server to synchronize its clock. An accurate clock is important for event auditing and other security protocols.	Windows Time	Automatic
Remote Assistant	Allows the Remote Assistance feature to be used on this computer (not recommended that you run remote assistance sessions from the ISA firewall)	Help and Support	Automatic

Continued

Table 6.14 Services Required for Common Tasks Performed on the ISA Firewall

Task	Usage scenario	Services required	Startup mode
Remote Assistant	Allows the Remote Assistance feature to be used on this computer (not recommended that you run remote assistance sessions from the ISA firewall)	Remote Desktop Help Session Manager	Manual
Remote Assistant	Allows the Remote Assistance feature to be used on this computer	Terminal Services	Manual

Client Roles for the ISA Firewall

The ISA firewall may need to act in the role of client to network services located on protected and non-protected Networks. Network client services are required for the ISA firewall to act in its role of network client. Table 6.15 lists possible network client roles the ISA firewall may act as, describes when they may be required, and lists the services that should be enabled when you enable the role.

NOTE

You will also need to enable the automatic update services if you are using a WUS or SUS server on your network.

Table 6.15 Service Requirements Based on the ISA Firewall's Client Roles

Client role	Usage scenario	Services required	Startup mode
Automatic Update client	Select this role to allow automatic detection and update from Microsoft Windows Update.	Automatic Updates	Automatic
Automatic Update client	Select this role to allow automatic detection and update from Microsoft Windows Update.	Background Intelligent Transfer Service	Manual
DHCP client	Select this role if the ISA Server computer receives its IP address automatically from a DHCP server.	DHCP Client	Automatic

Continued

Table 6.15 Service Requirements Based on the ISA Firewall's Client Roles

Client role	Usage scenario	Services required	Startup mode
DNS client	Select this role if the ISA Server computer needs to receive name resolution information from other servers.	DNS Client	Automatic
Domain member	Select this role if the ISA Server computer belongs to a domain.	Network location awareness (NLA)	Manual
Domain member	Select this role if the ISA Server computer belongs to a domain.	Net logon	Automatic
Domain member	Select this role if the ISA Server computer belongs to a domain.	Windows Time	Automatic
Dynamic DNS registration	Select this role to allow the ISA Server computer to automatically register its name and address information with a DNS Server.	DHCP Client	Automatic
Microsoft Networking client	Select this role if the ISA Server computer has to connect to other Windows clients. If you do not select this role, the ISA Server computer will not be able to access shares on remote computers; for example, to publish reports.	TCP/IP NetBIOS Helper	Automatic
Microsoft Networking client	Select this role if the ISA Server computer has to connect to other Windows clients. If you do not select this role, the ISA Server computer will not be able to access shares on remote computers; for example, to publish reports.	Workstation	Automatic
WINS client	Select this role if the ISA Server computer uses WINS-based name resolution.	TCP/IP NetBIOS Helper	Automatic

After determining the appropriate service configuration for your ISA firewall, you can save the configuration in a Windows security template (.inf) file. Check www.isaserver.org for sample ISA security templates covering several common scenarios.

ISA Firewall Administrative Roles and Permissions

Not all firewall administrators should have the same level of control over the ISA firewall's configuration and management. The ISA firewall allows you to provide three levels of control over the firewall software based on the role assigned to the user.

The ISA firewall's Administrative Roles are:

- ISA Server Basic Monitoring
- ISA Server Extended Monitoring
- ISA Server Full Administrator

Table 6.16 describes the functions of each of these roles.

Table 6.16 ISA Firewall Administrative Roles

Role	Description
ISA Server Basic Monitoring	Users and groups assigned this role can monitor the ISA Server computer and network activity, but cannot configure specific monitoring functionality.
ISA Server Extended Monitoring	Users and groups assigned this role can perform all monitoring tasks, including log configuration, alert definition configuration, and all monitoring functions available to the ISA Server Basic Monitoring role.
ISA Server Full Administrator	Users and groups assigned this role can perform any ISA Server task, including rule configuration, applying of network templates, and monitoring.

Users assigned to these roles can be created in the ISA firewall's local SAM, or they can be domain users if the ISA firewall is a member of the Internal network Active Directory domain. Any users can be assigned to one of the ISA firewall's Administrative roles, and no special privileges or Windows permissions are required. The only exception to this is when a user needs to monitor the ISA Server performance counters using Perfmon or the ISA Server Dashboard; the user must be a member of the Windows Server 2003 Performance Monitors User group.

Each ISA Server role has a specific list of firewall administrator and configuration tasks associated with it. Table 6.17 lists some firewall tasks and the Administrative roles that are allowed to perform each task.

Table 6.17 ISA Firewall Tasks Assigned to ISA Firewall Administrative Roles

Activity	Basic Monitoring permissions	Extended Monitoring permissions	Full Administrator permissions
View Dashboard, alerts, connectivity, sessions, services	X	X	X
Acknowledge alerts	X	X	X
View log information		X	X
Create alert definitions		X	X
Create reports		X	X
Stop and start sessions and services		X	X
View firewall policy		X	X
Configure firewall policy			X
Configure cache			X
Configure VPN			X

WARNING

Users with ISA Server Extended Monitoring permissions can export and import all configuration information, including secret configuration information. This means that they can potentially decrypt secret information.

To assign administrative roles, perform the following steps:

1. Click **Start**, point to **All Programs**, point to **Microsoft ISA Server**, and click **ISA Server Management**.

2. Click the server name in the left pane of the **Microsoft Internet Security and Acceleration Server 2004** management console. Click **Define Administrative Roles** on the **Tasks** tab.

3. On the **Welcome to the ISA Server Administration Delegation Wizard** page, click **Next**.

4. On the **Delegate Control** page, click **Add**.

5. In **Group (recommended) or User** dialog box, enter the name of the group or user to which the specific administrative permissions will be assigned. Click the down arrow in the **Role** drop-down list and select the applicable administrative role. Click **OK**.

6. Click **Next** on the **Delegate Control** page.

7. Click **Finish** on the **Completing the Administration Delegation Wizard** page.

8. Click **Apply** to save the changes and update the firewall policy

9. Click **OK** in the **Apply New Configuration** dialog box.

Lockdown Mode

The ISA firewall sports a new feature that combines the need to isolate the firewall and all Protected Networks from harm in the event that the ISA firewall is attacked, to the extent that the Firewall services are shut down. The ISA firewall accomplishes a combination of protection and protective accessibility by entering *lockdown mode.*

Lockdown mode occurs when:

1. An attack or some other network or local host event causes the Firewall service to shut down. This can happen from a fault, or you can do it explicitly by configuring Alerts and then configuring an Alert Action that shuts down the Firewall service in response to the issue that triggered the Alert.

2. Lockdown mode occurs when the Firewall service is manually shut down. You can shut down the Firewall service if you become aware of an ongoing attack while configuring the ISA firewall and the network to effectively respond to the attack.

Lockdown Mode Functionality

When in lockdown mode, the following functionality applies:

1. The ISA Firewall's Packet Filter Engine (fweng) applies the lockdown firewall policy.

2. Firewall policy rules permits outgoing traffic from the Local Host network to all networks, if allowed. If an outgoing connection is established, that connection can be used to respond to incoming traffic. For example, a DNS query can receive a DNS response on the same connection. This does not imply that lockdown mode allows an extension of existing firewall policy for outbound access from the local host network. Only existing rules allowing outbound access from the local host network are allowed.

3. No new primary connections to the ISA firewall itself are allowed, unless a System Policy Rule that specifically allows the traffic is enabled. An exception is DHCP traffic, which is always allowed. DHCP requests (on UDP port 67) are allowed from the Local Host Network to all Networks, and DHCP replies (on UDP port 68) are allowed back in.

4. Remote-access VPN clients will not be able to connect to the ISA firewall. Site-to-site VPN connections will also be denied.

5. Any changes to the network configuration while in lockdown mode are applied only after the Firewall service restarts and the ISA firewall exits lockdown mode.

6. The ISA Server will not trigger any Alerts.

Connection Limits

The ISA firewall puts a limit on the number of connections made to or through it at any point in time. Connection limits allow the ISA firewall to block connections through the firewall for clients that may be infected with worms that attempt to establish large numbers of connections through the ISA firewall. Examples of such worms are mass mailing worms and the Blaster worm.

For Web Publishing Rules, you can customize a total number of connections limit by specifying a maximum number of concurrent connections in the Properties of the Web listener. Any new client requests will be denied when the maximum number of connections configured to the Web listener is reached.

You can limit the total number of UDP, ICMP, and other Raw IP sessions allowed by a Server Publishing Rule or Access Rule on a per-second basis. These limitations do not apply to TCP connections. When the specified number of connections is surpassed, new connections will not be created. Existing connections will not be disconnected.

You should begin by configuring low connection-limit thresholds. This enables the ISA firewall to limit malicious hosts from consuming resources on the ISA Server computer.

By default, connection limits for *non-TCP connections* are configured to 1000 connections *per second per rule* and to 160 connections *per client*.

Connection limits for TCP connections begin at 160 connections per client. You should not change these limits unless you notice that legitimate hosts are being blocked because the limiting is too low. You can determine if a host is being blocked because it has exceeded its connection limit by an associated Alert. The Alert will provide the IP address of the host exceeding its allowed number of connections.

Perform the following steps to configure connection limits:

1. Click **Start**, point to **All Programs**, point to **Microsoft ISA Server**, and click **ISA Server Management**.

2. Expand the server name in the left pane of the **Microsoft Internet Security and Acceleration Server 2004** management console, and expand the **Configuration** node. Click the **General** node.

3. Click **Define Connection Limits** in the details pane.

4. On the **Connection Limit** tab (Figure 6.32), check the **Limit the number of connections** checkbox. You can then configure the number of **Connections created per second, per rule (non-TCP)** and **Connection limit per client (TCP and non-TCP)**. Some machines may need access in excess of these numbers, such as busy published servers. In that case, you can

click **Add** and select a **Computer Set** to apply the **Customer connection limit** value.

Figure 6.32 The Connection Limits Dialog Box

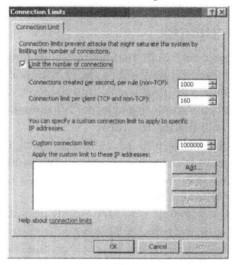

New connections will not be created after the specified number of connections is exceeded. However, existing connections will not be disconnected. Up to 1000 new connections are allowed per rule, per second by default. When this default limit is exceeded, an alert is triggered.

A log entry is recorded when the limit is exceeded:

- Action is Connection Denied
- Result code is FWX_E_RULE_QUOTA_EXCEEDED_DROPPED

You should limit the number of connections hosts can make to prevent flood attacks. Many requests are sent from spoofed source addresses when a UDP or IP flood attack occurs, and this can result in a denial of service.

Try the following when the limit is exceeded:

- If the malicious traffic appears to originate from an ISA firewall Protected Network, this may indicate a host on the Protected Network has a virus or worm infection. Immediately disconnect the computer from the network.

- Create a rule denying access to a computer set that includes the source IP addresses if the malicious traffic appears to originate from a small range of IP addresses on an external network.

- Evaluate the overall status of your network if the traffic appears to originate from a large range of IP addresses. Consider setting a smaller connection limit so that ISA Server can better protect your network.

If the limit has been exceeded due to a heavy load, consider setting a higher per-rule connection limit based on your analysis of your network's requirements.

In firewall chaining, and in some back-to-back ISA firewall scenarios, make sure to configure customized connection limits for the IP addresses of the chained server or back-end ISA firewall. Also, if your system publishes more than one UDP-based or raw IP-based service to the External network, you should configure smaller limits to help keep your network secure from flood attacks.

You can limit the total number of UDP, ICMP, and other Raw IP connections allowed per client. You can specify custom limits to apply to specific IP addresses. This is useful when you want to allow specific servers to establish more connections than allowed to other clients.

For TCP connections, no new connections are allowed after the connection limit is exceeded. Make sure you set connection limits high enough for TCP-based services, such as SMTP, so that SMTP servers can send outbound mail and receive inbound mail. For other connections (Raw IP and UDP), older connections are terminated when the connection limit is exceeded so that new connections can be created.

DHCP Spoof Attack Prevention

Some of you may want to use DHCP on the external interface of the ISA firewall so that it can obtain IP addressing information from your cable or DSL company's DHCP server. You might encounter problems with obtaining an IP address on the external interface when that interface is configured to use DHCP to obtain IP addressing information. A common reason for this problem is the DHCP Spoof Attack prevention mechanism.

It's important to understand the DHCP attack prevention mechanism to solve this problem. For each adapter on which DHCP is enabled, the ISA firewall maintains the list of allowed addresses. There is an entry in the registry for each DHCP enabled adapter:

The registry key name is

```
HKLM\SYSTEM\CurrentControlSet\Services\Fweng\Parameters\DhcpAdapters\<Adapter's MAC>/<Adapter's hardware type>
```

The values under the key are:

1. The adapter's name
2. The ISA network name of the adapter
3. The adapter's MAC address
4. ISA network addresses
5. The adapter's hardware type

Figure 6.33 shows an example of the registry key:

Figure 6.33 Registry Key for DHCP Attack Prevention

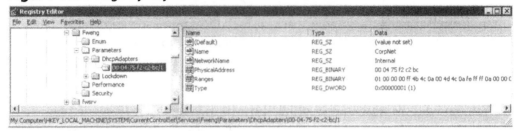

When the ISA firewall's driver sees a DHCP Offer message, it validates the offer using the following logic:

1. Using the DHCP "Client Ethernet Address" field and the "Hardware Type" field, the driver finds the corresponding registry key of the adapter.

2. If there is no registry key, the packet is allowed (this will be the case during initial setup of the ISA firewall software).

3. The driver verifies that "Your IP Address" field in the DHCP Offer contains an IP address within the addresses of the adapter's network element (as written in the registry).

4. If the verification fails, the packet is dropped, and an ISA alert is raised.

Figure 6.34 shows an example of a DHCP offer packet (the relevant fields are marked).

Figure 6.34 Network Monitor Capture of a DHCP Offer Packet

The invalid alert contains the following information (Figure 6.35):

Figure 6.35 An Invalid DHCP Offer Alert

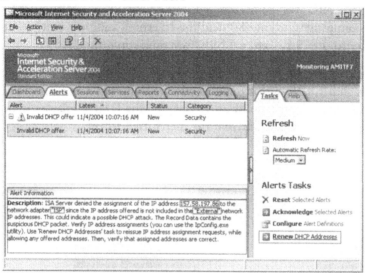

In case the network adapter should receive the offered address, the administrator should use the "Renew DHCP addresses" task that appears in the Task pane of the ISA firewall console. Figure 6.36 shows the warning dialog box you'll see when you click **Renew DHCP Addresses** in the Task pane .

Figure 6.36 The Renew DHCP Addresses Warning

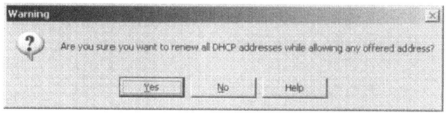

After clicking **Yes**, all registry keys related to DHCP attack prevention are deleted, and an "ipconfig /renew" is performed. This means that during this period, no offered address will be dropped by the driver (because there are no registry keys). Once the adapters receive their addresses, new registry keys are written with the new values, and the mechanism will be activated once again.

Dropped DHCP offers due to DHCP Attack Prevention may happen in the following scenarios:

1. If you have two DHCP adapters and you switched them. For example, the one that was connected to the internal network is now connected to the external network, and vice versa.

2. A DHCP adapter was moved to a different network. For example, ISA's external NIC was connected to a home network where another router made the connectivity to the ISP (and the Internet), and now you try replacing this router to use ISA's external NIC for connecting the ISP.

In such cases you need to use the **Renew DHCP Addresses** task, in order to allow the DHCP assignment. Note that once it's allowed, you will not need to allow it anymore. This procedure is needed only after changing the DHCP adapter in such a way that it becomes a member of a different ISA network element

Summary

In this chapter, we discussed many issues related to planning and installing an ISA firewall. We also discussed default System Policy and Firewall configuration after installation is complete. A quick start configuration was discussed and described which will allow you to get up and running quickly.

Solutions Fast Track

Pre-installation considerations

☑ The most important issues in server sizing for the ISA firewall is the link speed of the Internet connections.

☑ The routing table on the ISA firewall must be properly configured before installation of the ISA firewall.

☑ A split-DNS infrastructure will provide the best and most transparent name resolution solution for all organizations that require remote access to corporate resources.

☑ Correct DNS configuration on the ISA firewall's network interfaces is a critical factor to optimize speed and accuracy of Internet access.

☑ Consider whether you will use forward and reverse caching when planning the memory and disk requirements for your ISA firewall hardware.

☑ MSDE and file-based logging store information on the ISA firewall itself. Plan adequate disk space to support these logs.

Performing a clean installation

☑ You must install the IIS SMTP service on the server before installing the ISA firewall if you want to run the SMTP Message Screener on that machine,

☑ The Internal Network is defined as the network with the core network services used by the ISA firewall, such as Active Directory, DNS, DHCP, and Certificate services.

☑ If Firewall client encryption is enabled, only machines with the ISA 2004 version of the Firewall client are supported.

☑ You will not need to restart the ISA firewall after installation is complete if any version of ISA has been installed on the same machine previously.

Default Post-install System Policy and Firewall Configuration

- ☑ The Default Rule Access Rule blocks all traffic moving through the ISA firewall and is the only Access Rule enabled by the installation routine.

- ☑ The default Network Rule between the Internal Network and the Internet is set to NAT.

- ☑ Web caching is disabled by default after installation. It can be enabled by creating a cache drive.

- ☑ Autodiscovery information publishing is disabled by default.

Performing an upgrade installation

- ☑ Many features included with ISA Server 2000 are not included in ISA 2004, which may complicate upgrade and migration plans.

- ☑ You can upgrade ISA Server 2000 versions to like versions of ISA 2004.

Single NIC ISA Firewall installation

- ☑ Much of the ISA firewall's firewall functionality is lost in a single NIC configuration.

- ☑ The single NIC ISA firewall configuration is a holdover from the old Proxy Server 2.0 days.

- ☑ When installed in single NIC mode, the ISA firewall is able to protect itself effectively, but only secures HTTP, HTTPS, and FTP connections.

- ☑ Firewall and SecureNAT clients are not supported by the single NIC ISA firewall.

Quick-Start Configuration for ISA Firewalls

- ☑ The quick-start configuration in this chapter allows you to quickly install and configure a dual-NIC ISA firewall and get connected to the Internet as quickly as possible.

- ☑ The quick-start configuration is not meant to be a comprehensive guide to ISA firewall configuration, security, and optimization. Think of it as a baseline configuration that you can use until you have a better understanding of how the ISA firewall works.

Hardening the ISA Firewall's Configuration and Operating System

☑ You can enhance the security of the ISA firewall's base operating system by disabling services the ISA firewall's firewall services do not require.

☑ You will need to enable some services on the ISA firewall in order to provide

☑ ISA firewall Administrative roles can be assigned to users and groups to provide access to the firewall configuration and management components.

Frequently Asked Questions

The following Frequently Asked Questions, answered by the authors of this book, are designed to both measure your understanding of the concepts presented in this chapter and to assist you with real-life implementation of these concepts. To have your questions about this chapter answered by the author, browse to **www.syngress.com/solutions** and click on the **"Ask the Author"** form. You will also gain access to thousands of other FAQs at ITFAQnet.com.

Q: I tried to create an Access Rule allowing connections from Internal to External Networks on my unihomed ISA firewall, but the rule didn't work. What's up with that?

A: The unihomed ISA firewall does not have a default External Network. The reason for this is that all IP addresses in the IPv4 address range (except for those in the local host network ID) are considered part of the default Internal Network. If you want to create Access Rules from hosts on the corporate network to any other host, the rule should be from Internal Network to Internal Network. We highly recommend that you deploy the ISA firewall as a multi-homed firewall so that the ISA firewall can provide comprehensive network-based firewall protection.

Q: Do I have to install a DNS and DHCP server on the ISA firewall?

A: No. You do not need to install a DNS server or a DHCP server on the ISA firewall. In this chapter, we included a sample configuration where the ISA firewall acted as both a DNS and DHCP server. This configuration allowed the ISA firewall to simulate functionality provided by many simple packet filter-based small business firewalls. However, if you have a DNS server or DHCP server on your corporate network, you do not need to install the DNS or DHCP server on the ISA firewall.

Q: I tried to migrate my ISA Server 2000 configuration to ISA 2004, but the migration failed. Why?

A: There are a number of reasons for the migration process to fail. Failed migrations are most commonly seen when doing an in-place upgrade. We recommend that you document your current ISA Server 2000 settings and then replicate those settings on a fresh ISA firewall installation. However, if you wish to do an in-place upgrade, or if you want to migrate your ISA Server 2000 settings using the ISA migration tool, you should read the ISA Server 2004 Help file and learn the details of how the migration process works and what features are and are not supported when migrating from ISA Server 2000 to the new ISA firewall.

Q: What can network clients do when the firewall is in lockdown mode? Will intruders be able to attack the network or the firewall when it's in lockdown mode?

A: Intruders will not be able to attack your network when the ISA firewall is in lockdown mode. No new connections will be established through the ISA firewall during lockdown. Existing connections will not be disconnected, though. The ISA firewall enters lockdown mode when the firewall service fails. Lockdown mode is an example of how the ISA firewall "fails closed."

Q: Do I have to use a split-DNS infrastructure? I already have a domain with the dreaded .local top-level domain.

A: You never need to use a split-DNS infrastructure. However, a split-DNS infrastructure will greatly simplify life for your users who move between the corporate network and remote locations. While it would be easier to implement a split-DNS infrastructure when your internal domain name is also accessible from external locations, this is not a hard-coded requirement. For example, if your internal domain is domain.local, you can create a public domain named domain.com. Then you can create a forward lookup zone on your internal DNS servers for the domain.com domain. You then create a resource recorded in the domain.com domain that match the resources your remote users would use to access internal resources via Web and Server Publishing Rules on the ISA firewall. Both external and internal users would access resources using the same name, such as owa.domain.com, but the external DNS zone would resolve the name to the public address on the ISA firewall used to publish the site, while the internal zone would have resource records resolve owa.domain.com to the actual internal address of the OWA site on the corporate network.

Q: I have multiple network IDs on my corporate network. Do I have to create separate networks for all of them?

A: No. Remember that all IP addresses located behind a specific NIC are part of the same ISA firewall Network. For example, if you have five network IDs behind the same interface on the ISA firewall, the ISA firewall sees all those network IDs as part of the same Network (with a capital "N" indicating an ISA Network). You can create subnet objects or address set objects to group your network IDs if you need to exert access controls on the ISA firewall using those network IDs.

Chapter 7

Creating and Using ISA 2004 Firewall Access Policy

Solutions in this Chapter:

- **ISA Firewall Access Rule Elements**

- **Configuring Access Rules for Outbound Access through the ISA Firewall**

- **Using Scripts to Populate Domain Name Sets**

- **Creating and Configuring a Public Address Trihomed DMZ Network**

- **Allowing Intradomain Communications through the ISA Firewall**

Introduction

The ISA firewall's Access Policy (also known as firewall policy) includes Web Publishing Rules, Server Publishing Rules and Access Rules. Web Publishing Rules and Server Publishing Rules are used to allow inbound access and Access Rules are used to control outbound access.

The concepts of inbound and outbound access are somewhat more confusing with the new ISA firewall, when compared to their interpretations in ISA Server 2000. The reason for this is that ISA Server 2000 was Local Address Table (LAT) based. The definitions of inbound and outbound access were relative to the LAT. Inbound access was defined as incoming connections from non-LAT hosts to LAT hosts (external to internal). In contrast, the new ISA firewall does not have a LAT and there is not a comparable concept of an "internal" network in the same way that there was an internal network defined by the LAT in ISA Server 2000.

In general, you should use Web Publishing Rules and Server Publishing Rules when you want to allow connections from hosts that are not located on an ISA firewall Protected Network to a host on an ISA firewall Protected Network. Access Rules are used to control access between any two networks. The only limitation is that you cannot create Access Rules to control access between networks that have a Network Address Translation (NAT) relationship when the initiating host is on the non-NATed site of the relationship.

For example, suppose you have a NAT relationship between the default Internal Network and the Internet. You can create Access Rules that control connections between the Internal Network and the Internet because the initiating hosts are on the NATed side of the network relationship. However, you cannot create an Access Rule between a host on the Internet and the Internal Network because the Internet hosts are on the non-NATed side of the network relationship.

In contrast, you can create Access Rules in *both* directions when there is a route relationship between the source and destination Networks. For example, suppose you have a route relationship between a DMZ segment and the Internet. In this case, you can create Access Rules controlling traffic between the DMZ and the Internet and you can also create Access Rules that control traffic between the Internet and the DMZ segment.

The main job of the ISA firewall is to control traffic between source and destination networks. The ISA firewall's Access Policy permits clients on the source network to access hosts on a destination network and Access Rules also can be configured to block hosts on a source network from connecting to hosts on a destination network. Access Policy determines how hosts access hosts on other networks.

This is a key concept. The source and destination hosts must be on different networks. The ISA firewall should never mediate communications between hosts on the same ISA network. We refer to this type of configuration as "looping back through the ISA firewall". You should never loop back through the ISA firewall to access resources on the same network.

When the ISA firewall intercepts an outbound connection request, it checks both network rules and firewall policy rules to determine if access is allowed. Network Rules are checked first. If there is no Network Rule defining a NAT or Route relationship between the source and destination networks, then the connection attempt will fail. This is a common reason for failed connections and it is something you should check for when Access Policy does not behave the way you expect it to.

Access Rules can be configured to apply to specific source and/or destination hosts. Clients can be specified either by IP address (for example, by using Computer or Computer Set Network Objects) or by user name. The ISA firewall processes the requests differently depending on which type of client is requesting the object and how the Access Rules are configured.

When a connection request is received by the ISA firewall, the first thing the ISA firewall does is check to see if there is a Network Rule defining the route relationship between the source and destination networks. If there is no Network Rule, the ISA firewall assumes that the source and destination networks are *not connected*. If there is a Network Rule defining a route relationship between the source and destination network, then the ISA firewall processes the Access Policy rules.

After the ISA firewall has confirmed that the source and destination networks are connected, Access Policy is processed. The ISA firewall processes the Access Rules in the Access Policy from the top down (System Policy is processed before user-defined Access Policy).

If an Allow rule is associated with the outbound connection request, the ISA firewall will allow the request. In order for the Allow rule to be applied, the characteristics of the connection request must match the characteristics defined by the Access Rule. The Access Rule will match the connection request if the connection request matches the following Access Rule parameters:

- Protocol
- From (source location, which can include a source port number)
- Schedule
- To (destination location, which can include addresses, names, URLs and other Network Objects)
- Users
- Content groups

If the settings for each of these parameters match those in the connection request, then the Access Rule will be applied to the connection. If the connection request doesn't match the parameters in the Access Rule, then the ISA firewall moves to the next rule in the firewall's Access Policy.

WARNING

If there are no System Policy or user-defined Access Rules that apply to the connection request, then the **Last Default rule** is applied. This rule blocks all communications through the ISA firewall.

If the Access Rule matches the parameters in the connection request, then the next step is for the ISA firewall to check the Network Rules once again to determine if there is a NAT or Route relationship between the source and destination Networks. The ISA firewall also checks for any Web chaining rules (if a Web Proxy client requested the object) or for a possible firewall chaining configuration (if a SecureNAT or firewall client requested the object) to determine how the request will be serviced.

TIP

Web Chaining Rules and Firewall Chaining both represent methods of ISA firewall routing. Web Chaining Rules can be configured to forward requests from Web Proxy clients to specific locations, such as upstream Web Proxy servers. Firewall chaining allows requests from SecureNAT and Firewall clients to be forwarded to upstream ISA firewalls. Both Web Chaining and Firewall Chaining Rules allow the ISA firewall to bypass its default gateway configuration for specific connection requests from Web Proxy and Firewall clients.

For example, suppose you have an ISA firewall with two NICs: one NIC is connected to the Internet and the other connected to the Internal Network. You have created a single "All Open" rule which allows all users access to all protocol to connect to all sites on the Internet.

This "All Open" policy would include the following rules on the ISA firewall:

- A Network Rule defining the route relationship between the source network (the Internal Network) and the destination Network (the Internet).

- An Access Rule allowing all internal clients access to all sites at all times, using any protocol.

The default configuration is to NAT between the default Internal Network and the Internet. However, you can Route between the Internal network (and any other network) and the Internet if you like (as long as you have public addresses on the network).

ISA Firewall Access Rule Elements

You construct Access Rules using Policy Elements. One of the major improvements in the new ISA firewall over ISA Server 2000 is the ability to create all Policy Elements "on the fly". That is, you can create all Policy Elements from within the New Access Rule Wizard. This greatly improves on ISA Server 2000, where you have to plan out your Policy Elements in advance and then create Protocol Rules and Publishing Rules *after* you configure your Policy Elements.

The ISA firewall includes the following Policy Elements:

- Protocols
- User Sets
- Content Types

- Schedules
- Network Objects

Protocols

The ISA firewall includes a number of built-in protocols that you can use right out of the box to create Access Rules, Web Publishing Rules and Server Publishing Rules.

In addition to the built-in protocols, you can create your own protocols by using the ISA firewall's New Protocol Wizard. The pre-built protocols cannot be modified or deleted. However, you can edit or delete protocols you create yourself. There are some protocols that are installed with application filters that cannot be modified, but they can be deleted. You do have the option to unbind application filters from protocols. For example, if you don't want Web requests for SecureNAT and Firewall clients to be forwarded to the Web Proxy filter, you can unbind the Web Proxy filter from the HTTP protocol. We'll examine this issue in more detail later in this chapter.

When you create a new Protocol Definition, you'll need to specify the following information:

- **Protocol Type.** TCP, UDP, ICMP, or IP-level protocol. If you specify an ICMP protocol, then you'll need to include the ICMP type and code. Note that you cannot publish IP-level or ICMP protocols.

- **Direction.** For UDP, this includes Send, Receive, Send Receive, or Receive Send. For TCP, this includes Inbound and Outbound. For ICMP and IP-level, this includes Send and Receive.

- **Port range.** (for TCP and UDP protocols) This is a range of ports between 1 and 65535 that is used for the initial connection. IP-level and ICMP protocols do not use ports, as ports are part of the transport layer header.

- **Protocol number.** (for IP-level protocols). This is the protocol number. For example, GRE uses IP protocol number 47.

- **ICMP properties.** (for ICMP protocol). This is the ICMP code and type.

- (Optional) **Secondary connections.** This is the range of ports, protocol types, and direction used for additional connections or packets that follow the initial connection. You can configure one or more secondary connections. Secondary connections can be inbound, outbound or both inbound and outbound.

NOTE

You cannot define secondary connections for IP-level primary protocols.

User Sets

In order to enable outbound access control, you can create Access Rules and apply them to specific Internet Protocol (IP) addresses or to specific users or groups of users. When Access Rules are applied to a user or group, the users will have to authenticate using the appropriate authentication protocol. The Firewall client always uses integrated authentication and always sends the user credentials transparently. The Web Proxy client can use a number of different authentication methods.

The ISA firewall allows you to group users and user groups together in User Sets or what we like to call "firewall groups". User sets include one or more users or groups from any authentication scheme supported by the ISA firewall. For example, a user set might include a Windows user, a user from a RADIUS namespace, and another user from the SecurID namespace. The Windows, RADIUS and SecurID namespaces all use different authentication schemes, but users from each of these can be included in a single User Set.

The ISA firewall comes preconfigured with the following user sets:

- **All Authenticated Users.** This predefined user set represents all authenticated users, regardless of the method used to authenticate. An Access Rule using this set applies to authenticated users. When a rule applies to authenticated users, connections from SecureNAT clients will fail. An exception to this is when the SecureNAT client is also a VPN client. When a user creates a VPN connection to the ISA firewall, the VPN client automatically becomes a SecureNAT client. Although normally a SecureNAT client cannot send user credentials to the ISA firewall, when the SecureNAT client is also a VPN client, the VPN log on credentials can be used to authenticate the user.

- **All Users.** This predefined User Set represents all users. A rule defined using this set will apply to all users, both authenticated and unauthenticated, and no credentials are required to access a rule configured to use this User Set. However, the Firewall client will always send credentials to the ISA firewall, even when authentication is not required. You'll see this in effect in the **Microsoft Internet Security and Acceleration Server 2004** management console, in the **Sessions** tab when a user name has a question mark next to it.

- **System and Network Service.** This pre-built User Set represents the Local System service and the Network service on the ISA firewall machine itself. This User Set is used in some System Policy Rules.

Content Types

Content types specify Multipurpose Internet Mail Extensions (MIME) types and file extensions. When you create an access rule that applies to the HTTP protocol, you can limit what Content Types the Access Rule applies to. Content Type control allows you to be very granular when configuring Access Policy because you can control access not only on a protocol and destination basis, but also by specific content.

Content Type control only works with HTTP and tunneled FTP traffic. Content Type control will not work with FTP traffic that isn't handled by the ISA firewall's Web Proxy filter.

When an FTP request is made by a host on an ISA firewall Protected Network, the ISA firewall will check the file extension in the request. The ISA firewall then determines if the rule applies to a Content Type that includes the requested file extension and processes the rule accordingly. If the Content Type doesn't match, then the rule is ignored and the next rule in the Access Policy is checked.

When a host on an ISA firewall Protected Network makes an outbound HTTP request, the ISA firewall sends the request to the Web server via the Web Proxy filter (by default). When the Web server returns the requested Web object, the ISA firewall checks the object's MIME type (which is found in the HTTP header information) or its file extension (depending on the header information returned by the Web server.) The ISA firewall determines if the rule applies to the specified Content Type including the requested file extension, and processes the rule accordingly.

The ISA firewall comes with a pre-built list of Content Types that you can use right out of the box. You can also create your own Content Types. When you create your own Content Types, you should specify both MIME type and file extension.

For example, to include all Director files in a content type, select the following file name extensions and MIME types:

- .dir
- .dxr
- .dcr
- application/x-director

You can use an asterisk (*) as a wildcard character when configuring a MIME type. For example, to include all application types, enter **application/***.

> **TIP**
>
> The wildcard character can be used only with MIME types. You *cannot* use wildcards for file extensions. You can use the wildcard only once and that is at the end of the MIME type after the slash (/).

The ISA firewall comes with the following pre-built Content Types:

- Application
- Application data files
- Audio,
- Compressed files
- Documents
- HTML documents

- Images
- Macro documents
- Text
- Video
- VRML.

Controlling access via MIME type can be challenging because different MIME types are associated with different file name extensions. The reason for this is that the Web server controls the MIME type associated with the Web object returned to the user. While there is general agreement on how MIME types are defined, a Web site administrator has complete control over the MIME type associated with any content hosted by his Web server. Because of this, you will sometimes see that content that you had thought you had blocked using Content Types is not blocked. You can determine the MIME type used by the Web server returning the response by doing a Network Monitor trace. The HTTP header will show the MIME type returned by the Web server for the Web content requested by the requesting client.

The following table lists the Internet Information Services (IIS) default associations. You can use these for general reference.

Table 7.1 Default IIS MIME Types for common file extensions

File name extension	MIME type
.hta	application/hta
.isp	application/x-internet-signup
.crd	application/x-mscardfile
.pmc	application/x-perfmon
.spc	application/x-pkcs7-certificates
.sv4crc	application/x-sv4crc
.bin	application/octet-stream
.clp	application/x-msclip
.mny	application/x-msmoney
.p7r	application/x-pkcs7-certreqresp
.evy	application/envoy
.p7s	application/pkcs7-signature
.eps	application/postscript
.setreg	application/set-registration-initiation
.xlm	application/vnd.ms-excel
.cpio	application/x-cpio
.dvi	application/x-dvi
.p7b	application/x-pkcs7-certificates

Continued

Table 7.1 Default IIS MIME Types for common file extensions

File name extension	MIME type
.doc	application/msword
.dot	application/msword
.p7c	application/pkcs7-mime
.ps	application/postscript
.wps	application/vnd.ms-works
.csh	application/x-csh
.iii	application/x-iphone
.pmw	application/x-perfmon
.man	application/x-troff-man
.hdf	application/x-hdf
.mvb	application/x-msmediaview
.texi	application/x-texinfo
.setpay	application/set-payment-initiation
.stl	application/vndms-pkistl
.mdb	application/x-msaccess
.oda	application/oda
.hlp	application/winhlp
.nc	application/x-netcdf
.sh	application/x-sh
.shar	application/x-shar
.tcl	application/x-tcl
.ms	application/x-troff-ms
.ods	application/oleobject
.axs	application/olescript
.xla	application/vnd.ms-excel
.mpp	application/vnd.ms-project
.dir	application/x-director
.sit	application/x-stuffit
.*	application/octet-stream
.crl	application/pkix-crl
.ai	application/postscript
.xls	application/vnd.ms-excel
.wks	application/vnd.ms-works
.ins	application/x-internet-signup

Continued

Table 7.1 Default IIS MIME Types for common file extensions

File name extension	MIME type
.pub	application/x-mspublisher
.wri	application/x-mswrite
.spl	application/futuresplash
.hqx	application/mac-binhex40
.p10	application/pkcs10
.xlc	application/vnd.ms-excel
.xlt	application/vnd.ms-excel
.dxr	application/x-director
.js	application/x-javascript
.m13	application/x-msmediaview
.trm	application/x-msterminal
.pml	application/x-perfmon
.me	application/x-troff-me
.wcm	application/vnd.ms-works
.latex	application/x-latex
.m14	application/x-msmediaview
.wmf	application/x-msmetafile
.cer	application/x-x509-ca-cert
.zip	application/x-zip-compressed
.p12	application/x-pkcs12
.pfx	application/x-pkcs12
.der	application/x-x509-ca-cert
.pdf	application/pdf
.xlw	application/vnd.ms-excel
.texinfo	application/x-texinfo
.p7m	application/pkcs7-mime
.pps	application/vnd.ms-powerpoint
.dcr	application/x-director
.gtar	application/x-gtar
.sct	text/scriptlet
.fif	application/fractals
.exe	application/octet-stream
.ppt	application/vnd.ms-powerpoint
.sst	application/vndms-pkicertstore

Continued

Table 7.1 Default IIS MIME Types for common file extensions

File name extension	MIME type
.pko	application/vndms-pkipko
.scd	application/x-msschedule
.tar	application/x-tar
.roff	application/x-troff
.t	application/x-troff
.prf	application/pics-rules
.rtf	application/rtf
.pot	application/vnd.ms-powerpoint
.wdb	application/vnd.ms-works
.bcpio	application/x-bcpio
.dll	application/x-msdownload
.pma	application/x-perfmon
.pmr	application/x-perfmon
.tr	application/x-troff
.src	application/x-wais-source
.acx	application/internet-property-stream
.cat	application/vndms-pkiseccat
.cdf	application/x-cdf
.tgz	application/x-compressed
.sv4cpio	application/x-sv4cpio
.tex	application/x-tex
.ustar	application/x-ustar
.crt	application/x-x509-ca-cert
.ra	audio/x-pn-realaudio
.mid	audio/mid
.au	audio/basic
.snd	audio/basic
.wav	audio/wav
.aifc	audio/aiff
.m3u	audio/x-mpegurl
.ram	audio/x-pn-realaudio
.aiff	audio/aiff
.rmi	audio/mid
.aif	audio/x-aiff

Continued

Table 7.1 Default IIS MIME Types for common file extensions

File name extension	MIME type
.mp3	audio/mpeg
.gz	application/x-gzip
.z	application/x-compress
.tsv	text/tab-separated-values
.xml	text/xml
.323	text/h323
.htt	text/webviewhtml
.stm	text/html
.html	text/html
.xsl	text/xml
.htm	text/html
.cod	image/cis-cod
.ief	image/ief
.pbm	image/x-portable-bitmap
.tiff	image/tiff
.ppm	image/x-portable-pixmap
.rgb	image/x-rgb
.dib	image/bmp
.jpeg	image/jpeg
.cmx	image/x-cmx
.pnm	image/x-portable-anymap
.jpe	image/jpeg
.jfif	image/pjpeg
.tif	image/tiff
.jpg	image/jpeg
.xbm	image/x-xbitmap
.ras	image/x-cmu-raster
.gif	image/gif

Schedules

You can apply a Schedule to an Access Rule to control when the rule should be applied. There are three built-in schedules:

- **Work Hours** Permits access between 09:00 (9:00 A.M.) and 17:00 (5:00 P.M.) on Monday through Friday (to this rule)

- **Weekends** Permits access at all times on Saturday and Sunday (to this rule)
- **Always** Permits access at all times (to this rule)

Note that rules can be allow or deny rules. The Schedules apply to all Access Rules, not just allow rules.

WARNING

Schedules control only new connections that apply to an Access Rule. Connections that are already established are not affected by Schedules. For example, if you schedule access to a partner site during Work Hours, users will not be disconnected after 5PM. You will have to manually disconnect the users or script a restart of the firewall service.

Network Objects

Network Objects are used to control the source and destination of connections moving through the ISA firewall. We discussed the Network Objects Policy Elements in Chapter 4.

Configuring Access Rules for Outbound Access through the ISA Firewall

Access Rules always apply to outbound connections. Only protocols with a primary connection in either the outbound or send direction can be used in Access Rules. In contrast, Web Publishing Rules and Server Publishing Rules always use protocols with a primary connection with the inbound or receive direction. Access Rules control access from source to destination using outbound protocols.

In this section we'll go over in detail how to create an Access Rule and each of the options available to you when using the **New Access Rule Wizard,** along with additional options available to you in the **Properties** of the Access Rule.

To begin, open the **Microsoft Internet Security and Acceleration Server 2004** management console and expand the server name and click **Firewall Policy** node. Click the **Tasks** tab in the Task Pane and click the **Create New Access Rule** link. This brings up the **Welcome to the New Access Rule Wizard** page. Enter a name for the rule in the **Access Rule name** text box. In this example we'll create an "All Open" Access Rule that allows all traffic from all hosts outbound from the default Internal Network to the default External Network. Click **Next**.

The Rule Action Page

On the **Rule Action** page you have two options: **Allow** or **Deny**. In contrast to ISA Server 2000, the new ISA firewall has the **Deny** option set as the default. In this example, we'll select the **Allow** option and click **Next, as shown in Figure 7.1**.

Figure 7.1 the Rule Action page

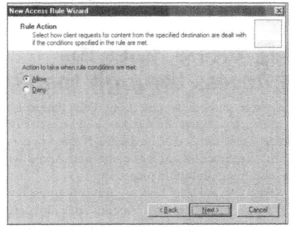

The Protocols Page

On the **Protocols** page, you decide what protocols should be allowed outbound from the source to destination location. You have three options in the **This rule applies to** list:

- **All outbound traffic** This option allows all protocols outbound. The effect of this option differs depending on the client type used to access this rule. For Firewall clients, this option allows all protocols outbound, including secondary protocols that are defined on the ISA firewall and some that are not defined. However, if a SecureNAT client attempts to connect via a rule that employs this option, outbound access will only be allowed for protocols that are included in the ISA firewall's **Protocols** list. If the SecureNAT client cannot connect to a resource when you use this protocol, try creating a new Protocol Definition on the ISA firewall to support the SecureNAT client's connection. However, if secondary connections are required, such as is the case with FTP, you must employ the Firewall client or create an application filter to support that protocol for SecureNAT clients.

■ **Selected protocols** This option allows you to select the specific protocols to which you want this rule to apply. You can select from the default list of protocols included with the ISA firewall right out of the box, or you can create a new Protocol Definition "on the fly". You can select one protocol or multiple protocols for a single rule.

■ **All outbound traffic except selected** This option allows you to enable all protocols outbound (dependent only the client type) *except* for specific protocols outbound. For example, you might want to allow Firewall clients outbound access to all protocols except those you explicitly want to deny because of corporate security policy, such as AOL Instant Messenger, MSN Messenger and IRC. See Figure 7.2.

Figure 7.2 The Protocols page

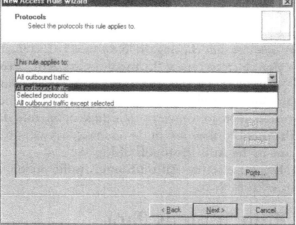

Highlight the **Selected Protocols** option and click the **Add** button. This brings up the **Add Protocols** dialog box. In the **Add Protocols** dialog box, you see a list of folders that group protocols based on their general use. For example, the **Common Protocols** folder contains protocols most commonly used when connecting to the Internet and the **Mail Protocols** folder is used to group protocols most commonly used when accessing mail services through the ISA firewall. The **User-Defined** folder contains all your custom protocols that you manually create on the ISA firewall. The **All Protocols** folder contains all protocols, both built-in and User-defined, configured on the ISA firewall.

Click the **All Protocols** folder and you'll see a list of all protocols configured on the ISA firewall. The ISA firewall comes with over 100 built-in Protocol Definitions you can use in your Access Rules, as shown in Figure 7.3.

Figure 7.3 the Add Protocols dialog box

If you need to use a protocol for which there isn't already a Protocol Definition, you can create a new one now but clicking the **New** menu. Clicking the **New** menu will allow you the option to create a new **Protocol** or new **RPC Protocol**. See the section earlier in this chapter on how to create new Protocol Definitions.

Once you identify the protocol you want to include in the rule, double click on it. Double click on any other protocol you want to include in the rule and then click **Close** in the **Add Protocols** dialog box. In this example, we want to allow access to all protocols, so click close in the **Add Protocols** dialog box.

On the **Protocols** page, select the **All outbound traffic** option from the **This rule applies to** list and click **Next**.

The Access Rule Sources Page

On the **Access Rule Sources** page, select the source location to which this Access Rule should apply. Click the **Add** button to add the source of the communication for which this rule will apply.

In the **Add Network Entities** dialog box you can choose the source location of the communication to which this Access Rule applies. If none of the source locations listed in the **Add Network Entities** dialog box works for you, you can create a new Network Object by clicking the **New** menu. Double click the location to which you want the rule to apply. Note that you can choose more than one source location by double clicking on multiple Network Objects.

In this example, click on the **Networks** folder to expand the folder and then double click on the **Internal** Network entry. Click **Close** to close the **Add Network Entities** dialog box as shown in Figure 7.4.

Figure 7.4 the Add Network Entities dialog box

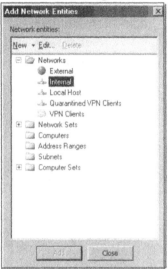

Click **Next** on the **Access Rule Sources** page.

The Access Rule Destinations Page

On the **Access Rule Destinations** page, select the destination for which you want this rule to apply. Click the **Add** button to add a destination location. The **Add Network Entities** dialog box appears and you can select a Network Object for the destination for which this Access Rule applies. As in the previous page of the Access Rule Wizard, you can create a new destination location by clicking the **New** menu and creating the new location.

In this example, we'll click on the **Networks** folder and then double click on the **External** entry. Click **Close** to close the **Add Network Entities** dialog box. Click **Next** on the **Access Rule Destinations** page.

The User Sets Page

On the **User Sets** page, you can set the users to which this Access Rule applies. The default setting is **All Users**. If you want to remove this User Set or any other one from the list of users to which this rule applies, select the User Set and click the **Remove** button. You can also edit a user set in the list by clicking the **Edit** button.

You can add a User Set to the list by clicking the **Add** button. In the **Add Users** dialog box, you can double click on a Firewall Group to which you want the rule to apply. You can also create new firewall groups by clicking the **New** menu and you can edit existing firewall groups by clicking the **Edit** menu.

In this example, we'll use the default setting, **All Users**. Click **Close** in the **Add Users** dialog box and click **Next** on the **User Sets** page as shown in Figure 7.5.

Figure 7.5 The User Sets page

The **Completing the New Access Rule Wizard** page appears next. Review your settings and click **Finish**.

> **NOTE**
>
> When you create a rule that allows outbound access for **All Users**, unauthenticated connections are allowed through the ISA firewall. A rule that applies to **All Users** can be used by SecureNAT clients. If an Access Rule requires authentication, SecureNAT client connections will fail because the SecureNAT client cannot authenticate.

Access Rule Properties

There are several options you can configure in an Access Rule that aren't exposed in the New Access Rule Wizard. You can select these options by going into the **Properties** dialog box of the Access Rule.

The **Properties** dialog box of an Access Rule contains the following tabs:

- The General tab
- The Action tab
- The Protocols tab
- The From tab

- The Users tab
- The Schedule tab
- The Content Types tab

Right click the Access Rule and click the **Properties** command.

The General Tab

The first tab you see is the **General** tab. You can change the name of the Access Rule by entering the new name in the **Name** text box. The rule can be enabled or disabled by placing or removing the checkmark in the **Enable** checkbox.

The Action Tab

The Action tab provides several options that were not exposed in the New Access Rule Wizard. The options available on the Action tab include:

- **Allow** Choose this option if you want connections matching the characteristics of this rule to be allowed through the ISA firewall

- **Deny** Choose this option if you want to connections matching the characteristics of this rule to be denied access through the ISA firewall

- **Redirect HTTP requests to this Web page** Choose this option if you want HTTP requests matching the characteristics of this rule to be redirected to another Web page. This option is only available if the rule is a Deny rule. When the user attempts to access a denied site, the request is automatically redirected to a Web page you configure in the text box below this option. Make sure that you enter the complete URL to which you want the user to be redirected, such as http://corp.domain.com/accesspolicy.htm.

- **Log requests matching this rule** Connection attempts matching the Access Rule are automatically logged after you create the rule. There may be times when you don't want to log all connections matching a particular rule. One example of when you would not want to log connections matching a rule is when you create a rule matching protocols you have little interest in investigating, such as NetBIOS broadcasts. Later in this chapter, we will describe a procedure you can use to reduce the size of your log files by creating an Access Rule that does not log connections matching NetBIOS broadcast protocols.

Figure 7.6 shows the contents of the Action tab.

Figure 7.6 The Action tab

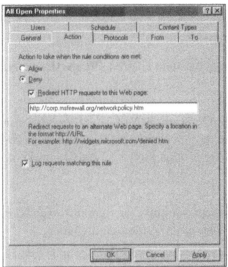

The Protocols Tab

The **Protocols** tab provides you many of the same options available in the New Access Rule Wizard. You have the same options in the **This rule applies to** list, which are: **Allow all outbound traffic**, **Selected protocols** and **All outbound traffic except selected**. You can use the **Add** button to add more protocols to the list. Use the **Remove** button to remove protocols that you select in the **Protocols** list and click the **Edit** button to edit protocols you select in the **Protocols** list.

> **NOTE**
>
> You can edit only user-defined protocols.

There are application filters that you can configure for any of the protocols you've included in the **Protocols** list on the **Protocols** tab. The filters available depend on the protocols you've included in the list. Click the **Filters** button to view the configurable filters for the list of protocols included in the Access Rule as shown in Figure 7.7.

Figure 7.7 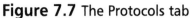The Protocols tab

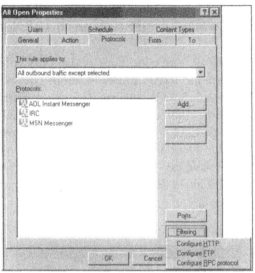

You also have control over the source ports allowed to access resources through the ISA firewall via each Access Rule. Click the **Ports** button and you'll see the **Source Ports** dialog box. The default setting is **Allow traffic from any allowed source port**. However, if you have applications for which you can control the source port, or those that use default source ports (such as SMTP), then you can limit the source ports allowed to access the rule by selecting the **Limit access to traffic from this range of source ports** option and enter the **From** and **To** source ports that represent the first and last ports in a range of source ports you want to allow. See Figure 7.8.

Figure 7.8 the Source Ports dialog box

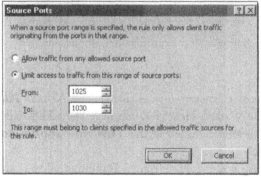

The From Tab

On the **From** tab you have options similar to those seen in the New Access Rule Wizard. However, an option not available in the Wizard is the ability to create an exception. If you want to add additional source locations for which this Access Rule should apply, click the **Add** button next to the **This rule applies to traffic from these sources** list. If you want to remove a source location, click the location and then click the **Remove** button. If you want to edit the characteristics of a location, click the **Edit** button.

You can apply this rule to all source locations in the **This rule applied to traffic from these sources** list *except* for certain source locations you specify in the **Exceptions** list. For example, suppose the Access Rule is configured to deny outbound access to the PPTP VPN protocol for all machines on the Internal Network. However, you want to allow machines that belong to the **Remote Management Computers** Computer Set access to this protocol. You can add the **Remote Management Computers** Computer Set to the list of **Exceptions** by clicking the **Add** button. Use the **Remove** and **Edit** button in the **Exceptions** list to remove and edit the locations in that list, as shown in Figure 7.9.

Figure 7.9 The From tab

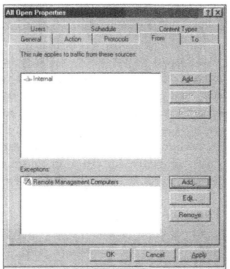

The To Tab

The **To** tab provides similar functionality as that on the **Access Rule Destination** page of the New Access Rule Wizard. However, you have the additional option to set an Exception to the destinations included in the **This rule applies to traffic sent to these destinations** list.

For example, suppose you create an Access Rule that allows outbound access to the HTTP protocol for all External sites. However, you do not want to allow users access to the Hotmail Web mail site. You can create a Domain Name Set for the domains required for Hotmail access and then use the **Add** button in the **Exceptions** section to add the Hotmail Domain Name Set. The rule will then will allow HTTP access to all sites *except* the Hotmail site. See Figure 7.10.

Figure 7.10 The To Tab

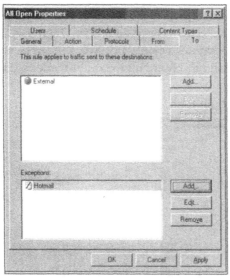

The Users Tab

The Users tab allows you to add firewall groups to which you want the Access Rule to apply , as shown in Figure 7.11. In addition, you have the option to add exceptions to the group to which the rule applies. For example, you could configure the rule to apply to **All Authenticated Users** but exclude other firewall groups, such as the built-in **System and Network Service** group.

Figure 7.11 The Users tab

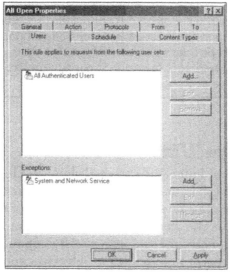

The Schedule Tab

On the **Schedule** tab, you set the times you want the rule to apply. The scheduling option isn't exposed in the New Access Rule Wizard interface. You can use one of the three default schedules: **Always**, **Weekends** or **Work hours,** or you can create a new custom schedule by clicking the **New** button, as illustrated by Figure 7.12.

Figure 7.12 The Schedule tab

The Content Types Tab

Another option not exposed in the New Access Rule Wizard is the ability to apply content type control over the connection. On the **Content Types** tab, you can specify what content types will apply to the rule. Content Type constraints are only applied to HTTP connections; all other protocols ignore the settings on the Content Types tab.

The default setting is to have the rule apply to **All content types.** You can limit the content types the rule applies to by selecting the **Selected content types (with this option selected, the rule is applicable only HTTP traffic)** option and putting a checkmark in the checkboxes next to the content types to which you want the rule to apply. See Figure 7.13.

If you unbind the Web Proxy filter from the HTTP protocol and then allow Firewall or SecureNAT client connections access to this rule, the connection attempt may fail because content inspection is dependent on the Web Proxy filter.

Figure 7.13 The Content Types tab

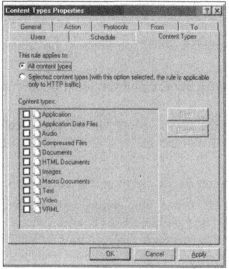

The name of the Access Rule appears in the title bar of that rule's **Properties** dialog box. This is true when you click from tab to tab in the Access Rule's **Properties** dialog box. However, if you click the **Content Types** tab and then click other tabs in the Access Rule's **Properties** dialog box, the name of the rule changes in the title bar to **Content Types Properties**. However, when you leave the dialog box, the name of the rule does not actually change. We would prefer to think of this as an Easter Egg, rather than a bug.

The Access Rule Context Menu Options

There are several options to choose from when you right click an Access Rule. These options include the following:

- **Properties** This option brings up the Access Rule's **Properties** dialog box.
- **Delete** This option deletes the Access Rule.
- **Copy** This option allows you to copy an Access Rule and then paste a copy of the rule to the Firewall policy.
- **Paste** This option allows you to paste an Access Rule that you've copied
- **Export Selected** This option allows you to export the Access Rule to an .xml file. You can then import this file to another ISA firewall to replicate the rule to another machine.
- **Import to Selected** This option allow you to import an Access Rule from an .xml file to the position selected in the Access Policy.
- **Move Up** This option allows you to move the rule up on the list of Access Rules.
- **Move Down** This option allows you to move the rule down on the list of Access Rules
- **Disable** This option allows you disable the Access Rule while keeping it on the list of Access Rules and allows you to re-enable it later if you require it again
- **Enable** This option allows you to enable an Access Rule that you've disabled.
- **Configure HTTP** This option appears when the Access Rule includes the HTTP protocol. The Configure HTTP option allows you to configure the HTTP Security Filter to exert access control over HTTP connections using the ISA firewall's advanced application layer inspection mechanisms
- **Configure FTP** This option appears when the Access Rule includes the FTP protocol. When it is selected, you are presented with a dialog box that allows you to enable or disable FTP uploads
- **Configure RPC Protocol** This option appears when the Access Rule includes an RPC protocol. When it is selected, you are presented with a dialog box that allows you to enable or disable strict RPC compliance (which has the effect of enabling or disabling DCOM connections).

TIP

The **Copy** option is very useful if you want to avoid using the New Access Rule Wizard to create new rules. Right click an existing rule and then click **Copy**. Right click the same rule and then click **Paste**. The pasted copy of the rule will have the same name as the original rule except that there will be a **(1)** appended to the name. You can then right click the rule and click **Properties** or you can double click the rule and then change the name and other characteristics of the rule. We find this useful when we're making small changes to Access Rules and do not want to lose the settings on the original rule. If the new rule doesn't work as expected, we can delete the new rule and return to the original rule. Try copying and paste rules a few times and see how this process works for you.

Configuring RPC Policy

When you create an Access Rule that allows outbound RPC, you have the option to configure RPC protocol policy. Access Rules that allow **All IP Traffic** also include RPC protocols. Right click the Access Rule and click **Configure RPC protocol** to configure RPC policy.

In the **Configure RPC protocol policy** dialog box, shown in Figure 7.14, you have a single option: **Enforce strict RPC compliance**. The default setting is enabled. When this setting is not enabled, the RPC filter will allow additional RPC type protocols, such as DCOM. If you find that some RPC-based protocols do not work correctly through the ISA firewall, consider disabling this option.

RPC policy is configured on a per-protocol basis. For example, you can enforce strict RPC compliance for one Access Rule and disable strict RPC compliance for another Access Rule in the ISA firewall's firewall policy.

Figure 7.14 The Configure RPC Protocol Policy Dialog Box

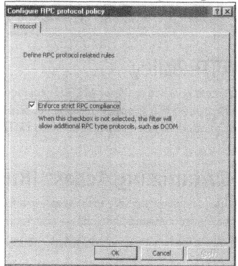

Configuring FTP Policy

When you created an Access Rule that allows the FTP protocol, you have the option to configure FTP policy. Right click the Access Rule and click the **Configure FTP** command. This brings up the **Configure FTP protocol policy** dialog box, shown in Figure 7.15. By default, the **Read Only** checkbox is enabled. When this checkbox is enabled, FTP uploads will be blocked. If you want to allow users to upload files using FTP, remove the checkmark from the checkbox.

FTP policy is configured on a per-rule basis.

Figure 7.15 The Configures FTP Protocol Policy Dialog Box

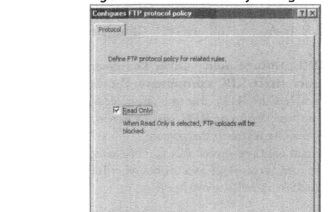

Configuring HTTP Policy

Whenever you create an Access Rule that allows HTTP connections, you have the option to configure HTTP policy. HTTP policy settings control the HTTP Security Filter. We discuss the configuration options available in the HTTP Security Filter in full detail in chapter 10.

Ordering and Organizing Access Rules

The ordering of Access Rules is important to ensure that your Access Policy works the way you expect it to work. We recommend the follow ordering of Access Rules:

- Put Web Publishing Rules and Server Publishing Rules on the top of the list
- Place anonymous Deny Access Rules under the Web Publishing Rules and Server Publishing Rules. These rules do not require user authentication and do not require the client to be from a specific location (such as part of a Computer Set)

- Place anonymous Allow Access Rules under the Anonymous Deny Access Rules. These rules do not require user authentication and do not require the client to be from a specific location (such as part of a Computer Set)

- Place Deny Access Rules requiring authentication below the anonymous Allow Access Rules

- Place Allow Access Rules requiring authentication below the Deny Access Rules requiring authentication.

It is important that anonymous rules that apply to the same protocol as an authenticated access rule be applied first if it is your intent to allow anonymous access for that protocol. If you do not put the anonymous access rule before the authenticated Access Rule, then the connection request will be denied to the anonymous user (typically a SecureNAT client) for that protocol.

For example, suppose you have two Access Rules: one rule allows all users access to the HTTP protocol and the second rule allows members of the EXECS firewall group access to the HTTP, HTTPS, FTP, IRC and MSN Messenger protocols. If you place the rule allowing the EXECS group access before the anonymous access rule, then all HTTP connections outbound will require authentication and the anonymous access rule located under the authentication required rule will be ignored. However, if you had an anonymous access rule for the NNTP protocol under the rule allowing the EXECS outbound access to the HTTP, HTTPS, FTP, IRC and MSN Messenger protocols, then the anonymous NNTP connection would be allowed because the NNTP protocol doesn't match the characteristics of the rule allowing the EXECS users outbound access.

We found this model a bit confusing at first. When we first starting working with the ISA firewall, we assumed that when a rule applies to a particular firewall group, a connection request from a user that does not supply credentials to the ISA firewall would be ignored and the firewall would then continue down the list of rules until an anonymous Access Rule matching the connection parameters was found. However, this is *not* the case. Anonymous users might be considered members of the "Anonymous Users" group and that group does not match any group for which you might require authentication. Since the "Anonymous Users" group never matches an actual group, any rule for which authentication is required matching the connection request will be denied.

How to Block Logging for Selected Protocols

You may want to prevent the ISA firewall from logging information about certain protocols that reach the firewall. Common examples are the NetBIOS broadcast protocols: NetBIOS Name Service and NetBIOS Datagram. Both of these protocols regularly broadcast to the local subnet broadcast address and can fill the ISA firewall's Firewall Service log with information that isn't very useful to the ISA firewall administrator.

You can create an Access Rule that includes these protocols and then configure the Access Rule to not log information about connections associated with the rule. For example, you can perform the following procedure to block logging of these NetBIOS protocols:

1. In the **Microsoft Internet Security and Acceleration Server 2004** management console, expand the server name and click the **Firewall Policy** node.

2. In the Task Pane, click the **Tasks** tab and click the **Create New Access Rule** link.

3. On the **Welcome to the New Access Rule Wizard** page, enter a name for the rule in the **Access Rule name** text box. In this example, we'll name the rule **Block NetBIOS logging**. Click **Next**.

4. Select the **Deny** option on the **Rule Action** page and click **Next**.

5. On the **Protocols** page, select the **Selected protocols** option from the **This rule applies to** list. Click the **Add** button.

6. In the **Add Protocols** dialog box, click the **Infrastructure** folder. Double click the **NetBIOS Datagram** and **NetBIOS Name Service** entries. Click **Close**.

7. Click **Next** on the **Protocols** page.

8. On the **Access Rule Sources** page, click the **Add** button.

9. In the **Add Network Entities** dialog box, click the **Computer Sets** folder and then double click the **Anywhere** entry. Click **Close**.

10. Click **Next** on the **Access Rule Sources** page.

11. On the **Access Rule Destinations** page, click the **Add** button.

12. In the **Add Network Entities** dialog box, click the **Computer Sets** folder. Double click the **Anywhere** entry and click **Close**.

13. Click **Next** on the **Access Rule Destinations** page.

14. Click **Next** on the **User Sets** page.

15. Click **Finish** on the **Completing the New Access Rule Wizard** page.

16. Right click the **Block NetBIOS Logging** rule and click **Properties**.

17. In the **Block NetBIOS Logging Properties** dialog box, remove the checkmark from the **Log requests matching this rule** checkbox.

18. Click **Apply** and then click **OK**.

19. Click **Apply** to save the changes and update the firewall policy.

20. Click **OK** in the **Apply New Configuration** dialog box.

The rule you created in this example not only prevents logging of NetBIOS broadcasts, but prevents these protocols to and from the ISA firewall. Thus, you get two benefits from one rule!

Disabling Automatic Web Proxy Connections for SecureNAT Clients

There may be times when you want Firewall and SecureNAT client to bypass the Web Proxy service. By default, HTTP connections from SecureNAT and Firewall clients are automatically forwarded to the Web Proxy filter. The advantage of this configuration is that both SecureNAT and Firewall clients are able to benefit from the ISA firewall's Web Proxy cache (when caching is enabled on the ISA firewall).

The problem is that some Web sites are poorly written and are not compliant with CERN compliant Web proxies. You can solve this problem by configuring these sites for Direct Access and then unbinding the Web Proxy filter from the HTTP protocol.

Perform the following steps to disable automatic Web Proxy connections for Firewall and SecureNAT clients:

1. In the **Microsoft Internet Security and Acceleration Server 2004** management console, expand the server name and click the **Firewall Policy** node in the left pane of the console.

2. In the Task Pane, click the **Toolbox** tab. On the **Toolbox** tab, click the **Command Protocols** folder and double click the **HTTP** protocol.

3. In the **HTTP Properties** dialog box, click the **Parameters** tab.

4. On the **Parameters** tab, remove the checkmark from the **Web Proxy Filter** checkbox. Click **Apply** and then click **OK**.

5. Click **Apply** to save the changes and update the firewall policy.

6. Click **OK** in the **Apply New Configuration** dialog box.

One side effect of bypassing the Web Proxy filter is that HTTP Policy is not applied to the SecureNAT and Firewall clients. However, HTTP Policy is applied to machines that are explicitly configured as Web Proxy clients, even when the Firewall, SecureNAT and Web Proxy clients access the site using the same Access Rule.

For example, suppose you create a rule named **HTTP Access**. The **HTTP Access** Access Rule allows all users on the Internal network access to all sites on the External Network using the HTTP protocol. Let's say you configure HTTP Policy for this rule to block connections to the www.spyware.com domain. When Web Proxy clients attempt to connect to www.spyware.com, the connection will be blocked by the **HTTP Access** Access Rule. However, when the SecureNAT and Firewall clients attempt to access www.spyware.com via the **HTTP Access** rule (when the Web Proxy Filter is unbound from the HTTP protocol), that Access Rule will allow the SecureNAT and Firewall clients through.

Another side effect of unbinding the Web Proxy Filter from the HTTP Protocol Definition is that the configuration interface (**Configure HTTP policy for rule** dialog box) for the HTTP filter is removed from the **Microsoft Internet Security and Acceleration Server 2004** management console. For all rules that have an HTTP policy already configured, that policy is still enforced on Web Proxy clients. However, to change HTTP Policy on existing rule, or to configure HTTP policy on new Access Rules, you will need to re-bind the HTTP Filter to the HTTP Protocol Definition. You can then unbind the Web Proxy Filter again after configuring the HTTP policy.

Of course, you could just configure all clients as Web Proxy clients (which is our recommendation) and avoid the administrative overhead.

WARNING

The HTTP Policy configuration interface is also removed from Web Proxy rules when the Web Proxy Filter is unbound from the HTTP Protocol Definition.

Using Scripts to Populate Domain Name Sets

One of the ISA firewall's strong suits is its exceptional stateful application layer inspection. In addition to performing the basic task of stateful filtering (which even a simple 'hardware' firewall can do), the ISA firewall's strong application layer inspection feature set allows the ISA firewall to actually understand the protocols passing though the firewall. In contrast to traditional second generation hardware firewalls, the ISA firewall represents a third-generation firewall that is not only network aware, but application protocol aware.

The ISA firewall's stateful application inspection mechanism allows you to control access not just to "ports", but to the actual protocols moving through those ports. While the conventional "hardware" firewall is adept at passing packets using simple stateful filtering mechanisms that have been available since the mid 1990's, the ISA firewall's stateful application layer inspection mechanisms bring the ISA firewall into the 21st century and actually control application layer protocol access. This allows strong inbound and outbound access control based on the firewall's application layer awareness, rather than through simple "opening and closing" of ports.

One powerful example is the ability to control what sites users can access through the ISA firewall. You can combine this ability to control the sites users can access by adding strong user/group based access control as well as protocol control.

For example, you might have a group of users called "Web Users," and you might want to block access to a list of 1500 URLs or domains for those users. You can create an Access Rule that blocks only those 1500 sites and allows access to all other sites when members of that group authenticate with the ISA firewall.

Another example might be this: you want to create a block list of 5000 domains that you want to prevent all users except for domain admins from reaching via any protocol. You can create a Domain Name Set and then apply this Domain Name Set to an Access Rule blocking these sites.

The trick is to find a way to get those thousands of domains or URLs into Domain Name Sets and URL Sets. You can, of course, enter these URLs and domains manually using the built-in tools included in the ISA Management console. The problem with this approach is that you'll need to get your clicking thumb ready for a long weekend as you click your way through the user interface to add all of these domains and URLs.

A better way is to import the sites you want to include in your URL Sets and Domain Name Sets from a text file. There are a number of places on the Internet where you can find such files (I won't mention any here because I don't want to create an implicit endorsement of any of them). Once you have a text file, you'll want use a script to import the entries in the text file into a URL Set or a Domain Name Set.

First, let's start with the scripts. The first script below is used to import the entries in a text file into a URL Set. Copy the information into a text file and then save it as **ImportURLs.vbs**.

```
< ------------------Start with the line below this one------->
Set Isa = CreateObject("FPC.Root")
Set CurArray = Isa.GetContainingArray
Set RuleElements = CurArray.RuleElements
Set URLSets = RuleElements.URLSets
Set URLSet = URLSets.Item("Urls")
Set FileSys = CreateObject("Scripting.FileSystemObject")
Set UrlsFile = FileSys.OpenTextFile("urls.txt", 1)
For i = 1 to URLSet.Count
  URLSet.Remove 1
Next
Do While UrlsFile.AtEndOfStream <> True
  URLSet.Add UrlsFile.ReadLine
Loop
WScript.Echo "Saving..."
CurArray.Save
WScript.Echo "Done"
< ------------------End with the line above this one--------->
```

The two entries in this file you need to change for your own setup are highlighted in yellow.

In the line:

```
Set URLSet = URLSets.Item("Urls")
```

Change the **Urls** entry to the name of the URL Set you want to create on the ISA firewall.

In the line:

```
Set UrlsFile = FileSys.OpenTextFile("urls.txt", 1)
```

Change the **urls.txt** entry to the name of the text file that contains the URLs you want to import into the ISA firewall's configuration.

The next script is used to import a collections of domains contained in a text file. Save the following information in a text file and name it **ImportDomains.vbs**.

```
< ------------------Start with the line below this one-------
Set Isa = CreateObject("FPC.Root")
Set CurArray = Isa.GetContainingArray
Set RuleElements = CurArray.RuleElements
Set DomainNameSets = RuleElements.DomainNameSets
Set DomainNameSet = DomainNameSets.Item("Domains")
Set FileSys = CreateObject("Scripting.FileSystemObject")
Set DomainsFile = FileSys.OpenTextFile("domains.txt", 1)
For i = 1 to DomainNameSet.Count
  DomainNameSet.Remove 1
Next
Do While DomainsFile.AtEndOfStream <> True
  DomainNameSet.Add DomainsFile.ReadLine
Loop
WScript.Echo "Saving..."
CurArray.Save
WScript.Echo "Done"
< ------------------End with the line above this one--------->
```

The two entries in this file you need to change for your own setup are shown below.

In the line:

```
Set DomainNameSet = DomainNameSets.Item("Domains")
```

Change the **Domains** entry to the name of the Domain Name Set you want to create on the ISA firewall.

In the line:

```
Set DomainsFile = FileSys.OpenTextFile("domains.txt", 1)
```

Change the **domains.txt** entry to the name of the text file that contains the domains you want to import into the ISA firewall's configuration.

Using the Import Scripts

Now let's see how the scripts work. The first thing you need to do is create the URL Set and the Domain Name Set in the **Microsoft Internet Security and Acceleration Server 2004** management console. This is easy and involves only a few steps.

First, we'll create a URL Set named **URLs**, since that's the default name in our script. Remember, you can change the URL Set name in the script if you like; just make sure you first create a URL Set in the **Microsoft Internet Security and Acceleration Server 2004** management console with the same name.

Perform the following steps to create a URL Set with the name **URLs**:

- In the **Microsoft Internet Security and Acceleration Server 2004** management console, expand the server name and then click on the **Firewall Policy** node.

- In the **Firewall Policy** node, click the **Toolbox** tab in the Task Pane. In the **Toolbox**, click the **Network Objects** tab.

- In the **Network Objects** tab, click the **New** menu and click **URL Set**.

- In the **New URL Set Rule Element** dialog box, shown in Figure 7.16, enter **URLs** in the **Name** text box. Click **OK**

Figure 7.16 The New URL Set Rule Element dialog box

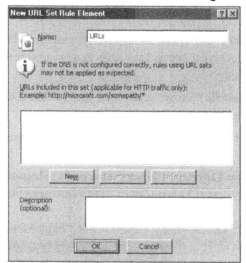

- The URL Set now appears in the list of URL Sets, shown in Figure 7.17.

Figure 7.17 The URL Sets list

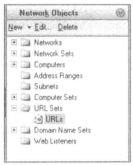

The next step is to create a Domain Name Set with the name **Domains**, which is the default name of the Set used in the ImportDomains script. Remember, you can use a different name for the Domain Name Set; just make sure the name is the same as the one you set in the script.

Perform the following steps to create the Domain Name Set with the name Domains:

1. In the **Microsoft Internet Security and Acceleration Server 2004** management console, expand the server name and then click on the **Firewall Policy** node.

2. In the **Firewall Policy** node, click the **Toolbox** tab in the Task Pane. In the **Toolbox**, click the **Network Objects** tab.

3. In the **Network Objects** tab, click the **New** menu and click **Domain Name Set**.

4. In the **New Domain Name Set Policy Element** dialog box, shown in Figure 7.18, enter **Domains** in the **Name** text box. Click **OK**.

Figure 7.18 The New Domain Set Policy Element dialog box

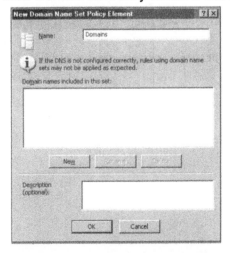

- The new entry appears in the list of **Domain Name Sets,** shown in Figure 7.19.

Figure 7.19 the Domain Name Sets list

- Click **Apply** to save the changes and update the firewall policy.
- Click **OK** in the **Apply New Configuration** dialog box.

Now we need to create two text files: **urls.txt** and **domains.txt.** Those are the default names used in the scripts. You can change the names of the files, but make sure they match the names you configure in the scripts.

The **domains.txt** file will contain the following entries:

stuff.com

blah.com

scumware.com

The **urls.txt** file will contain the following entries:

```
http://www.cisco.com
http://www.checkpoint.com
http://www.sonicwall.com
```

Next, copy the script files and the text files into the same directory. In this example, we'll copy the script files and text files into the root of the C: drive. Double click on the **ImportURLs.vbs** file. You'll first see a dialog box that says **Saving,** as shown in Figure 7.20. Click **OK**.

Figure 7.20 Saving the information

Depending on how many URLs you're importing, it will be a few moments or a few minutes until you see the next dialog box, shown in Figure 7.21, which informs you that the import was completed. Click **OK**.

Figure 7.21 Finishing the procedure

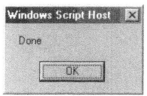

Now we'll import the Domains. Double click the **ImportDomains.vbs** file. You'll see the **Saving** dialog box again. Click **OK**. A few moments to a few minutes later, you'll see the **Done** dialog box. Click **OK**.

Close the **Microsoft Internet Security and Acceleration Server 2004** management console if it is open. Now open the **Microsoft Internet Security and Acceleration Server 2004** management console and go to the **Firewall Policy** node in the left pane of the console.

NOTE

You can avoid opening and closing the **Microsoft Internet Security and Acceleration Server 2004** management console by clicking the **Refresh** button in the **Microsoft Internet Security and Acceleration Server 2004** management console's button bar.

Click the **Toolbox** tab in the Task Pane and click the **Network Objects** bar. Click the **URL Sets** folder. Double click the **URLs** URL Set. You'll see that the URL Set was populated with the entries in your text file as shown in Figure 7.22. Cool!

Figure 7.22 URL Set entries

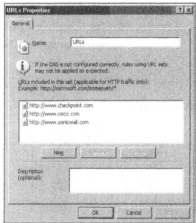

Click on the **Domain Name Sets** folder. Double click on the **Domains** entry. You'll see that the Domain Name Set is populated with domains you want to block, or allow, depending on your need. In this example we included a set of domains we'd like to block, shown in Figure 7.23.

Figure 7.23 Domain Name Set Properties

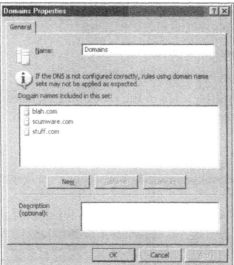

As you obtain more URLs, you can add them to the same text files and run the script again. The new entries will be added without creating duplicates of the domains or URLs that are already included in the Domain Name Set or URL Set.

Extending the SSL Tunnel Port Range for Web Access to Alternate SSL Ports

There will be times when your Web Proxy clients need to connect to SSL Web sites using an alternate port for the SSL link. For example, your users might try to access a banking Web site that requires an SSL connection on TCP port 4433 instead of the default port 443. This can also be problematic for SecureNAT and Firewall clients, since the default setting on the ISA firewall is to forward SecureNAT and Firewall client HTTP connections to the Web Proxy filter. Clients will see either a blank page or an error page indicating that the page cannot be displayed.

The problem here is that the Web Proxy filter only forwards SSL connections to TCP port 443. If clients try to connect to an SSL site over a port other than TCP 443, the connection attempt will fail. You can solve this problem by extending the SSL tunnel port range. However, to do so, you will need to download Jim Harrison's script at http://www.isatools.org, and enter the tunnel port range(s) you want the ISA firewall's Web Proxy component to use.

Perform the following steps to extend the ISA firewall's SSL tunnel port range:

- Go to www.isatools.org and download the isa_tpr.js file and copy that file to your ISA firewall. Do not use the browser on the firewall. Download the file to a management workstation, scan the file, and then copy the file to removable media and then take it to the ISA firewall. Remember, you should never use client applications, such as browsers, e-mail clients, etc. on the firewall itself.

- Double click the isa_tpr.js file. The first dialog box you see states This is your current Tunnel Port Range list. Click OK.

- The NNTP port is displayed. Click OK.

- The SSL port is displayed. Click OK.

- Now copy the isa_tpr.js file to the root of the C: drive. Open a command prompt and enter the following:

```
isa_tpr.js /?
```

- You will see the following dialog box, shown in Figure 7.24.

Figure 7.24 Help information for the isa_tpr.js script

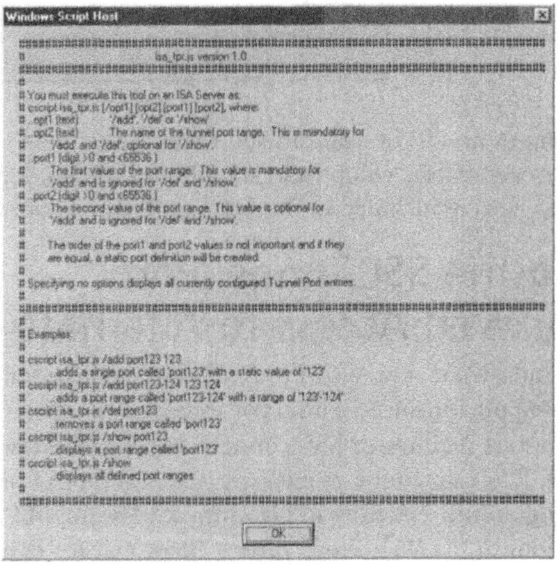

- To add a new tunnel port, such as **8848**, enter the following command and press ENTER:

```
Cscript isa_tpr.js /add Ext8848 8848
```

- You will see something like what appears in figure 7.25 after the command runs successfully.

Figure 7.25 Running the isa_tpr.js script to add a port to the SSL tunnel port range

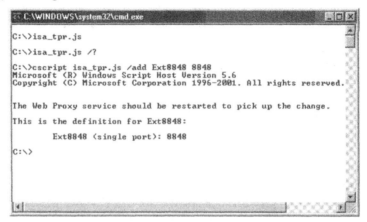

Alternatively, you can download the .NET application, **ISATpre.zip** file (written by Steven Soekrasno) from the www.isatools.org site and install the application on the ISA firewall. This application provides an easy to use graphical interface that allows you to extend the SSL tunnel port range. Figure 7.26 shows what the GUI for this application looks like.

Figure 7.26 Using Steven Soekrasno's .NET Tunnel Port Range extension application

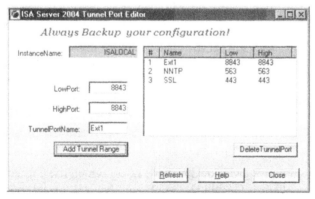

Avoiding Looping Back through the ISA Firewall for Internal Resources

A common error made by ISA firewall administrators involves allowing hosts on an ISA firewall Protected Network to loop back through the firewall to access resources on the same network where the client is located.

> **NOTE**
>
> Looping back through the ISA firewall can either reduce the overall performance of the ISA firewall, or prevent the communication from working at all.

For example, suppose you have a simple ISA firewall configuration with a single external interface and a single internal interface. On the Internal network located behind the internal interface, you have a SecureNAT client and a Web server. You have published the Web server to the Internet using a Web Publishing Rule. The Web server is accessible to internal clients using the URL http://web1 and to external clients using the URL http://www.msfirewall.org.

What happens when users on the Internal Network attempt to connect to the Web server using the URL www.msfirewall.org? If you don't have a split DNS in place, the clients on the Internal Network will resolve the name www.msfirewall.org to the IP address on the external interface of the ISA firewall that is listening for incoming connections to www.msfirewall.org. The host then will try to connect to the Internal resource by looping back through the ISA firewall via the Web Publishing Rule. If the client is a SecureNAT client, the connection attempt may fail (depending on how the ISA firewall is configured) or the overall performance of the ISA firewall is severely degraded because the firewall is handling connections for local resources.

You should always avoid looping back through the ISA firewall for resources located on the same network as the requesting host. The solution to this problem is to configure SecureNAT, Firewall and Web Proxy clients to use Direct Access for local resources (local resources are those contained on the same ISA firewall Network as the host requesting those resources). A Direct Access solution depends on the following components:

- Create a split DNS so that the clients can use the same domain name to reach the same resources both internally and externally. This requires two zones on two DNS servers. One zone is used by external clients and one zone is used by internal clients. The external client zone resolves names to the externally accessible address and the internal zone resolves names to internally accessible addresses. The key is that the zones are authoritative for the same domain name.

- Configure the properties of the network on which the Protected Network Web Proxy client is located to use Direct Access to reach both the IP addresses on the Internal network and the internal network domain names. This is done on the Web Proxy tab.

- Configure the properties of the network on which the Protected Network Firewall client is located to use Direct Access for internal domains

Details of this configuration are included in chapter 5 on ISA client installation and provisioning and in Chapter 4 on the ISA firewall's networking design.

Anonymous Requests Appear in Log File Even When Authentication is Enforced For Web (HTTP Connections)

A common question we encounter from ISA firewall admins relates to the appearance of anonymous connections from Web Proxy clients in the ISA firewall's Web proxy logs. These connections appear in spite of the fact that all rules are configured to require authentication. The short answer to this question is that this is normal and expected.

The long answer to this question involves how Web proxy clients normally communicate with authenticating Web proxy servers. For performance reasons, the initial request from the Web Proxy client is send *without* user credentials. If there is a rule that allows the connection anonymously, then the connection is allowed. If the client must authenticate first, then the Web proxy server sends back to the Web proxy client an access denied message (error 407) with a request for credentials. The Web proxy client then sends credentials to the ISA firewall and the user name appears in the log files.

Figure 7.27 shows the HTTP 407 response returned to the Web proxy client. On the right side of the figure, you'll see the ASCII decode of a frame taken from a Network Monitor trace. On the fifth line from the top, you'll see **HTTP/1.1 407 Proxy Authentication Required...** This is the 407 response the Web Proxy clients receive when an Access Rule requires authentication in order to connect to a Web site through the ISA firewall.

Figure 7.27 A 407 response is returned to the Web proxy client

```
00000000  00 0C 29 EE 9B C0 00 0C 29 5A 67 DB 08 00 45 00   ..)εc└..)Zg..E.
00000010  05 DC 9E D0 00 00 80 06 82 46 0A 00 00 01 0A 00   ...╨..ÇéF.....
00000020  00 05 1F 90 04 3A CF 99 3C 69 5A 18 D7 CE 50 10   ...É.:╧Ö<iZ.╫╬P.
00000030  F9 83 E8 2F 00 00 48 54 54 50 2F 31 2E 31 20 34   ·âΦ/..HTTP/1.1 4
00000040  30 37 20 50 72 6F 78 79 20 41 75 74 68 65 6E 74   07 Proxy Authent
00000050  69 63 61 74 69 6F 6E 20 52 65 71 75 69 72 65 64   ication Required
00000060  20 28 20 54 68 65 20 49 53 41 20 53 65 72 76 65    ( The ISA Serve
00000070  72 20 72 65 71 75 69 72 65 73 20 61 75 74 68 6F   r requires autho
00000080  72 69 7A 61 74 69 6F 6E 20 74 6F 20 66 75 6C 66   rization to fulf
00000090  69 6C 6C 20 74 68 65 20 72 65 71 75 65 73 74 2E   ill the request.
000000A0  20 41 63 63 65 73 73 20 74 6F 20 74 68 65 20 57    Access to the W
```

Blocking MSN Messenger using an Access Rule

Blocking dangerous applications is a common task for the ISA firewall. There are a number of methods you can use to block dangerous applications:

- Use the HTTP Security Filter to block the application if the application uses a Web (HTTP) connection to reach the site
- Use Domain Name Sets or URL Sets to block the sites the dangerous application needs to access to establish a connection
- Block the protocol, or do not allow access to the protocol, required by the dangerous application if the application uses a custom protocol

- If the application can use both a custom protocol and Web connection to access the Internet, then block the custom protocol and then use Domain Name Sets or URL Sets to block its ability to access the Internet using a Web connection

- Simplify your life by using the Principle of Least Privilege. When you use Least Privilege, you create rules to allow access. Anything not explicitly allowed is blocked. In this way, you'll almost never need to create a Deny rule of any kind

To demonstrate one method you can use to block dangerous applications, we'll create an Access Policy that blocks the MSN Messenger 6.2 application. The elements of the solution include the following:

- Create a Deny Rule that blocks the MSN Messenger Protocol

- Create an Access Rule that blocks the MSN Messenger HTTP header.

In this example, we will create an "all open" rule that allows all protocols outbound, but include a signature in the HTTP Security Filter that blocks the MSN Messenger. The second rule blocks the MSN Messenger protocol. Tables 7.2 and 7.3 show the properties of each Access Rule.

Table 7.2 All Open Rule with MSN Messenger 6.2 HTTP Security Filter signature

Setting	Value
Name	All Open -1
Action	Allow
Protocols	HTTP and HTTPS
From/Listener	Internal
To	External
Condition	All Users
Purpose	This rule allows all traffic through the ISA firewall to all users and all sites. An HTTP signature is created to block the MSN Messenger 6.2 HTTP header

Table 7.3 Access Rule that denies the MSN Messenger protocol

Setting	Value
Name	Deny Messenger Protocol
Action	Deny
Protocols	MSN Messenger
From/Listener	Internal
To	External
Condition	All Users
Purpose	Blocks the MSN Messenger Protocol TCP 1863

You can use the information given earlier in this chapter on how to create the Access Rules. The **Deny Messenger Protocol** Access Rule must be placed above the **All Open** rule. Deny rules should always be placed above allow rules. Your firewall policy should look something like that in figure 7.28.

Figure 7.28 Firewall Policy to block MSN Messenger

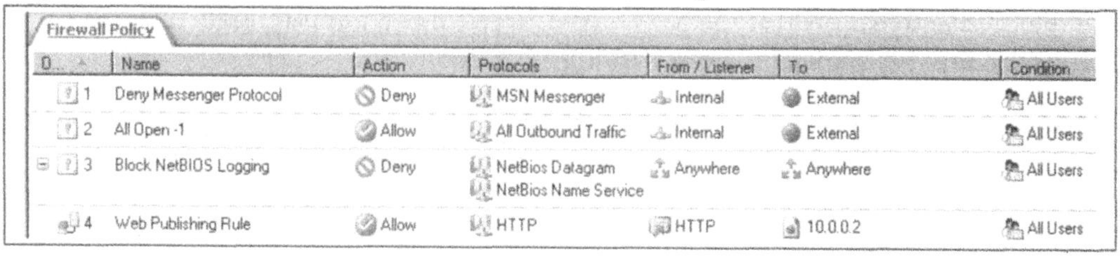

After creating the Access Rules, right click on the **All Open -1** Access Rule and click the **Configure HTTP** command. In the **Configure HTTP policy for rule** dialog box, click the **Add** button. In the **Signature** dialog box, shown in Figure 7.29, enter the following information:

> **Name:** Enter a name for the MSN Messenger blocking signature
>
> **Description (optional):** Enter a description for the rule
>
> **Search in:** Select the **Request headers** option from the drop down list
>
> **HTTP Header:** Enter **User-Agent:** in the text box
>
> **Signature:** enter **MSN Messenger** in the text box

Click **OK** to save the signature and click **OK** in the **Properties** dialog box. Click **Apply** to save the changes and update the firewall policy and Click **OK** in the **Apply New Configuration** dialog box.

Figure 7.29 The Signature dialog box

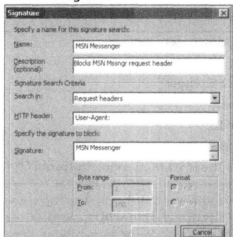

Figure 7.30 shows log file entries for the blocked connection from MSN Messenger. This first entry shows the connection using the MSN Messenger protocol being blocked and the third entry shows that the MSN Messenger connection was blocked by the HTTP Security Filter signature in the All Open rule.

Figure 7.30 Log file entries showing the HTTP Security Filter blocking the MSN Messenger connection

Destination Port	Protocol	HTTP Method	Action	URL	Rule	Filter Information
1863	MSN Messenger	-	Denied Connection	-	Deny Messenger Protocol	-
8080	http	GET	Allowed Connection	http://ISALOCAL/array.dll?Get.Routing.Script		
8080	http	POST	Denied Connection	http://gateway.messenger.hotmail.com/gatewa...	All Open -1	Blocked by the HTTP Security filter

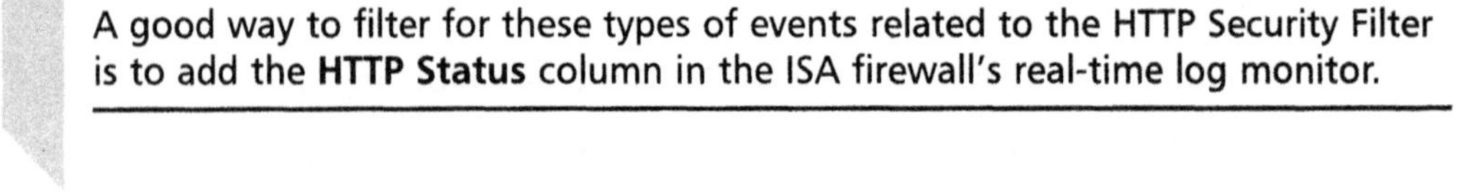

> **TIP**
>
> A good way to filter for these types of events related to the HTTP Security Filter is to add the **HTTP Status** column in the ISA firewall's real-time log monitor.

Allowing Outbound Access to MSN Messenger via Web Proxy

The MSN Messenger can access the Internet using its own protocol, or it can tunnel its communications in an HTTP header. However, you will run into problems if you want Web Proxy clients to access the MSN Messenger site because of an authentication issue that hounds both the MSN Messenger and Hotmail applications.

When the MSN Messenger sends credentials to the MSN Messenger site, those credentials are also sent to the ISA firewall. If the user name and password the user uses to access the MSN Messenger site aren't the same as the credentials the user uses on the corporate network, then the connection will fail. If you allow anonymous access to the MSN Messenger site, then you won't have problems because no credentials are sent to the ISA firewall because the firewall won't challenge the user for credentials.

You can get around this issue by enabling an anonymous access rule for Web Proxy clients so that they can use the HTTP and HTTPS protocols to reach the sites required by the MSN messenger. This limits your exposure because you're not allowing anonymous access to all sites, just MSN Messenger. However, you do lose out on user/group based access control. You can easily solve this problem by using the Firewall client on your hosts and enforcing authentication via the Firewall client and configuring the MSN sites for Direct Access.

You will need to allow anonymous access to the HTTP protocol to the following sites:

Config.messenger.msn.com

Gateway.messenger.hotmail.com

Loginnet.passport.net

Loginnet.passport.com

207.46.110.0/24 (this is a Subnet Network Object)

We obtained this information by viewing the log file entries in the ISA firewall console's real time log viewer. The subnet and domains may change over time, so if you find that the rule no longer works, you'll need to check your log files and see what sites are required by the Messenger.

Table 7.4 shows the settings in the Access Rule allowing Web Proxy clients access to the MSN Messenger site.

Table 7.4 Settings for a MSN Messenger Web Proxy Access rule

Setting	Value
Name	MSN Messenger Web Proxy Access
Action	Allow
Protocols	HTTP and HTTPS
From/Listener	Internal
To	Messenger Subnet Messenger Sites
Condition	All Users
Purpose	This rule allows Web Proxy clients access to the MSN Messenger Sites without requiring authentication. This rule must be above all other rules that require authentication for the HTTP and HTTPS protocols.

Changes to ISA Firewall Policy Only Affects New Connections

After a client initiates a request, the ISA firewall maintains an active state in the firewall state table for the session which permits the response to return to the client. The active state permits the client to send new requests. The ISA firewall removes the active state from the state table after the session is idle for an unspecified period of time (usually a minute or two).

For example, try the following:

■ Open a command prompt on a host on a Protected Network and ping a host through the ISA firewall using the "ping –n IP address" command. The –n allows the ping to continue unabated during your test. When you're finished with your test, you can use the CTRL+C command to stop the ping. Make sure there is a rule that allows the host to ping the host through the ISA firewall.

■ On the ISA firewall, apply a Deny rule for the Ping protocol and place it above any rule that currently allows the ping through the ISA firewall.

■ The ping continues unabated even after the rule is applied. This is because there is an active state table entry for the ping from that client and the destination address being pinged.

■ Open a second command prompt on the client that is pinging the remote host. Start a ping to a second host through the ISA firewall. The ping requests are denied because there is no state table entry for the ping protocol from that host to that destination host.

■ If you try to ping from a different client, the ping is denied.

Access Rules are applied immediately for *new* connections when you click **Apply** to save the changes and update firewall policy. To make changes apply to all existing connections, you can do either of the following:

■ Disconnect existing sessions in the **Sessions** tab of the **Monitoring** node. To disconnect a session, open the **Microsoft Internet Security and Acceleration Server 2004** management console, click the **Monitoring** node, click the **Sessions** tab in the middle pane, click the session that you want to disconnect, and then click **Disconnect Session** on the **Tasks** tab.

■ Another option is to restart the Microsoft Firewall service. In the **Microsoft Internet Security and Acceleration Server 2004** management console, click the **Monitoring** node, click the **Services** tab, click **Microsoft Firewall**, click **Stop Selected Service** on the **Tasks** tab, and then click **Start Selected Service** on the **Tasks** tab.

Creating and Configuring a Public Address Trihomed DMZ Network

One of the most significant improvements in the ISA Server 2004 firewall over the old ISA Server 2000 firewall is multinetworking. As discussed in Chapter 4, multinetworking refers to how the ISA Server 2004 firewall sees the world. Unlike the ISA Server 2000 firewall, which saw the world as "trusted versus untrusted (LAT versus non-LAT), the ISA Server 2004 firewall sees all networks as untrusted and applies firewall policy to all connections made through the ISA Server 2004 firewall. This includes hosts connecting through a VPN remote access client or VPN gateway connection.

ISA Server 2004 multinetworking allows you to connect multiple interfaces (or multiple virtual interfaces using VLAN tagging) and have complete control over the traffic that moves between networks connected by the ISA Server 2004 firewall. This is in stark contrast to the ISA Server 2000 networking model, where traffic moving between internal networks was not exposed to firewall policy and you had to create a "poor man's DMZ" using RRAS packet filters.

In this section, we'll examine how to publish hosts on a *public* address DMZ segment. You might remember that ISA Server 2000 required the use of public addresses on a DMZ segment. The ISA Server 2000 DMZ segment had to use public addresses; you didn't have the option to use private addresses because the ISA Server 2000 firewall routed (instead of NAT'd) connections to the trihomed DMZ segment using simple stateful packet filters (like a traditional packet filtering firewall). In contrast, the ISA Server 2004 firewall allows you to route between the Internet and a DMZ segment, or NAT between the Internet and DMZ segment. In fact, the ISA Server 2004 firewall allows you to decide how you want connections to be routed between any two networks: route or NAT.

Using public addresses is sometimes necessary if you have an established DMZ segment with multiple hosts using public addresses and you do not wish to change the addressing scheme because of overhead involved with making the appropriate public DNS changes. You still want to use the current IP addressing scheme on the servers so that Internet hosts reach the DMZ severs using the same IP addresses (actually, the same DNS mappings) used previously. You can do this with the ISA Server 2004 firewall by configuring a route relationship between the Internet and the DMZ segment containing the servers you want to "publish".

Note that we put *"publish"* in quotes. There's a reason for that. ISA firewall policy provides two methods you can use to control traffic moving through the firewall: Access Rules and Publishing Rules. Access Rules can participate in a route or NAT relationship. Publishing Rules always NAT the connection, even if you're using a public address segment and have a route relationship between the source and destination host.

If it sounds a bit confusing, it is. It's especially confusing if you're accustomed to the ISA Server 2000 way of doing things, where you always had to NAT between untrusted and trusted hosts. Before we get into the specifics of how to publish servers on a public address segment, let's take a look at some aspects of the new ISA firewall's networking model.

Figure 7.31 shows the sample network we'll use in the how-to portion of this section. The figure shows a route relationship between the Internet and the DMZ segment. When the PocketPC PDA client connects to the server on the DMZ segment, the name it uses to establish the connection resolves to the actual IP address of the DMZ host, which in this case is 172.16.0.2. The route relationship allows us to do this and preserve the existing DNS records mapping the DMZ host to its actual IP address. ISA Server 2004 Access Rules are used to make the DMZ host available to Internet clients.

Figure 7.31 The sample public address DMZ segment

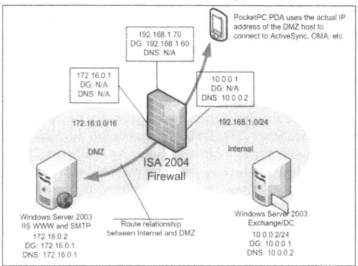

However, you can also use publishing rules to make the public address DMZ host available to Internet users. In this case, the PocketPC PDA host on the Internet uses an IP address on the *external interface* of the ISA firewall to access the DMZ host as shown in Figure 7.32. Note that the DMZ host still has a public address. Even though we are using public IP addresses, NAT is performed because we're using a publishing rule. This allows the Internet host to connect to the IP address on the external interface of the ISA firewall and effectively *hides* the IP address of the DMZ host. This *NAT hiding* is a common security measure for publicly available servers.

Figure 7.32 Public access network allows for NAT hiding

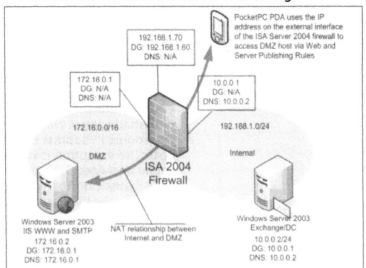

Note in the figures the IP address used by the DMZ host for the DNS server address. The address **172.16.0.1** is the IP address of the DMZ interface. The reason we use this IP address instead of the actual DNS server address is that we're publishing the DNS server on the Internal network. The DNS Server Publishing Rule listens on the IP address on the DMZ interface. You'll see the details of this configuration later in this section.

One of the major drawbacks of ISA Server 2000 Web publishing scenarios was that you always received the IP address of the ISA Server 2000 firewall in the published Web servers' log files. This was problematic for organizations that had already invested large sums of money in log analysis and reporting software that pulled information from the Web server's logs. ISA Server 2004 fixes this problem and allows you to choose to pass the original client IP address to a published Web server, or to use the ISA firewall's IP address. This is true for publishing rules on public and private address DMZs for all publishing rules: both Web and Server Publishing.

Table 7.5 describes the ISA firewall's behavior for allowing remote access to DMZ segments using public address and private addresses.

Table 7.5 Remote Access to DMZ Server using Private v. Public Addresses, NAT v. Route, Access Rules, and Publishing Rules

Addressing Scheme – Route Relationship – Rule Type	Result and Explanation
Public Address DMZ with Route Relationship using Access Rules	This configuration allows you connect to your DMZ hosts using their actual public addresses. The log files on the published servers will show the original source IP address of the remote host. The exception is when you create an Access Rule to connect to an HTTP server on the DMZ segment. In this case, the ISA Server 2004 firewall's IP address will appear as the source address. This can be corrected by disabling the Web Proxy filter on the rule.
Public Address DMZ with Route relationship using Publishing Rules*	This configuration requires that you connect to the published DMZ host via an IP address bound to the external interface of the ISA Server 2004 firewall. Connections are not made to the actual IP address of the DMZ host and your public DNS records may need to be changed to reflect this fact. Source IP address will be that of the ISA Server 2004 firewall, unless you configure the Server and Web Publishing Rules for forward the original source IP address (you have a choice of forwarding the original client's source IP address or the ISA Server 2004 firewall's IP address to the published server)
Public Address DMZ with NAT relationship using Access Rules	This configuration requires that you connect to the published DMZ host via an IP address bound to the external interface of the ISA Server 2004 firewall. Connections are not made to the actual IP address of the DMZ host and your public DNS records may need to be changed to reflect this fact. Source IP address will be that of the ISA Server 2004 firewall, unless you configure the Server and Web Publishing Rules for forward the original source IP address

Continued

Table 7.5 Remote Access to DMZ Server using Private v. Public Addresses, NAT v. Route, Access Rules, and Publishing Rules

Addressing Scheme – Route Relationship – Rule Type	Result and Explanation
	(you have a choice of forwarding the original client's source IP address or the ISA Server 2004 firewall's IP address to the published server). The result is that this setup is very similar to the last option
Public Address DMZ with NAT relationship using Publishing Rules*	This configuration requires that you connect to the published DMZ host via an IP address bound to the external interface of the ISA Server 2004 firewall. Connections are not made to the actual IP address of the DMZ host and your public DNS records may need to be changed to reflect this fact. Source IP address will be that of the ISA Server 2004 firewall, unless you configure the Server and Web Publishing Rules for forward the original source IP address (you have a choice of forwarding the original client's source IP address or the ISA Server 2004 firewall's IP address to the published server). Sound familiar?
Private Address DMZ with NAT relationship using Publishing Rules*	This configuration requires that you connect to the published DMZ host via an IP address bound to the external interface of the ISA Server 2004 firewall. Connections are not made to the actual IP address of the DMZ host and your public DNS records may need to be changed to reflect this fact. Source IP address will be that of the ISA Server 2004 firewall, unless you configure the Server and Web Publishing Rules for forward the original source IP address (you have a choice of forwarding the original client's source IP address or the ISA Server 2004 firewall's IP address to the published server). Yep, it's the same as the last two.

* Note that in all publishing rule configurations, the connection is NAT'ed. In no circumstance is a connection routed when you use a Web or Server Publishing Rule.

There are some interesting results based on whether the Web Proxy filter is enabled on an Access Rule. We'll explore this behavior later in this section.

Before finishing out this discussion, we should mention that you do lose some of the security for certain scenarios when you decide to use Access Rules instead of publishing rules to allow access to your DMZ hosts, to the extent that the ISA firewall provides little more security than a traditional packet filtering firewall. Reasons you might want to use publishing rules include:

- Web publishing rules allow you to prevent users from using IP addresses instead of FQDNs to access resources on the DMZ host. Many worms attack servers based on IP addresses, but rarely use a FQDN.

- Web publishing rules allow you to configure custom Web listeners, which provide features such as Exchange Forms-based authentication, delegation of basic authentication and RSA SecurID authentication.

- Web publishing rules allow you to perform SSL to SSL bridging. This prevents attackers from hiding exploits inside an SSL tunnel. When using SSL to SSL bridging, the ISA Server 2004 firewall "unwraps" the SSL tunnel, exposes the connection to the ISA Server 2004 firewall's deep stateful application layer inspection mechanisms, and drops connections containing exploits and suspicious characteristics. Connections deemed to be safe are then re-encrypted and sent to the published Web server via a second SSL link, which is created between the ISA Server 2004 firewall and the published Web server.

- Server publishing rules expose incoming connections to the application layer filters dedicated to protecting specific services. Examples include the SMTP filter that blocks buffer overflow attacks, the DNS filter that blocks a number of DNS exploits, and the POP3 filter that blocks POP3 buffer overflows. If you use Access Rules to publish the public address DMZ hosts, the application layer filters will not protect you against these exploits.

- If you publish a public address Web server on a DMZ segment using Access Rules, you are still protected by the HTTP security filter. The HTTP security filter provides very deep application layer inspection for all HTTP communications moving through the ISA Server 2004 firewall. The HTTP security filter allows you granular control and is configurable on a per-rule basis, so that you're not stuck with a single HTTP security policy for all the rules on the ISA Server 2004 firewall. This is a quantum leap over the URLScan method of filtering HTTP communications through the firewall that was used in ISA Server 2000 for HTTP stateful inspection.

The remainder of this section describes how to publish a public address DMZ host using Access Rules. This method allows you to continue to use the public addresses your servers have been using, but continue to leverage the full stateful application layer filtering power of the ISA Server 2004 firewall. Unlike traditional packet filter based firewalls, the ISA firewall performs stateful filtering and stateful application layer inspection on all communications moving through the firewall. This provides the highest level of protection and control of any firewall on the market.

To accomplish our goal, you'll need to perform the following steps:

- Configure the routing table on the upstream router
- Configure the network adaptors
- Install the ISA Server 2004 firewall software
- Install and configure the IIS WWW and SMTP services on the DMZ server
- Create the DMZ network
- Create the Network Rules Between the DMZ and External Network and for the DMZ and Internal Network
- Create an Server Publishing Rule allowing DNS from DMZ to Internal
- Create an Access Rule allowing DNS from Internal to External
- Create an Access Rule allow HTTP from External to DMZ
- Create an Access Rule allowing SMTP from External to DMZ
- Test the Access Rules from External to DMZ
- Change the Access Rule allowing External to DMZ by disabling the Web Proxy filter

Configure the Routing Table on the Upstream Router

The most common problem we've seen with ISA firewall admins who put together public address DMZ segments relates to the routing table entries on the upstream router. When you create a public address DMZ segment, you need to subnet your public block and assign one of the subnets to the DMZ segment. You can then bind the first valid address of a subnetted block to the DMZ interface and the first valid address of another subnetted block to the public interface.

That's where many ISA firewall admins stop and that's where they run into problems. You have to configure the upstream router with a route to the DMZ segment. You do this by configuring the router to use the IP address on the external interface of the ISA Server 2004 firewall as the gateway address for the DMZ segment's network ID. If this routing table entry is missing on the upstream router, no primary incoming connections and no responses to incoming connections, to and from the DMZ segment, will work.

In the lab network that we're using for the examples in this section, the external network host is on the same network ID as the external interface of the ISA firewall, which is 192.168.1.0/24. The external IP address on the ISA firewall is **192.168.1.70** and the external host will use an IP address assigned in the same network ID. The DMZ segment uses the network ID **172.16.0.0/16**. Therefore, on the Windows XP external network host we use in this section, we configured a routing table entry to tell it to use the external IP address of the ISA Server 2004 firewall to reach network ID **172.16.0.0/16**. Specially, here's what we did:

```
route add 172.16.0.0 MASK 255.255.0.0 192.168.1.70
```

Note that this example does not use a subnet of a public address block. In your production environment, you would subnet your public address block and create a routing table entry for your DMZ segment's subnetted block on your router upstream from the ISA Server 2004 firewall. This implies you have control over the upstream router, which makes public address DMZ segments a moot point for hobbyist ISP accounts. However, there's no reason why you can't create private address DMZs with a hobbyist ISP account.

Configure the Network Adaptors

Network adapter configuration was always a bone of contention for ISA Server 2000 admins and we anticipate that it will continue to be for ISA firewall admins. There are a number of reasons for this, with the primary issue being whether or not you host your own DNS services.

DNS is a critical issue for the ISA firewall because the firewall can perform proxy name resolution for Web Proxy and Firewall clients. The ISA firewall uses the DNS settings on its NICs to query the appropriate DNS server. If you have the incorrect DNS server configuration, you can experience either slow name resolution or no name resolution at all, which gives the end user the impression that "the ISA firewall doesn't work".

We can determine the correct DNS configuration on the ISA firewall by using the following guidelines:

- If you have a DNS server on your internal network, you should configure that DNS server to support Internet host name resolution

- If you choose to not allow your internal network DNS server to perform Internet host name resolution, you should consider putting a caching only DNS server on the ISA firewall, or on a DMZ segment

- If you choose to put a DNS sever on a DMZ segment which is authoritative for your publicly accessible domains, do **not** allow this DNS server to act as a DNS resolver. That is, your authoritative DNS server should only answer queries for the domains you host and return an error to users who try to resolve other names through that server

- If you do not wish to host your own DNS servers and do not use DNS on the internal network, you should configure the ISA firewall to use a public DNS server, such as your ISP's DNS server. Note that this configuration will cause problems with name resolution for internal network hosts, and may cause problems with Web Proxy and Firewall client connections. For this reason, you should choose another firewall for SOHO environments that do not have an established DNS infrastructure. However, if you have a SOHO environment and a DNS server, the ISA firewall is the ideal firewall to protect your company's assets

- Never, EVER put a public DNS server address on the same NIC that has your private DNS server address configured on it!

- The DNS server address should be configured on the *top listed* interface in the **Network and Dial-up Connections** window. For example, if you have a trihomed ISA firewall and a DMZ interface, an Internal interface and a public interface, the Internal NIC should be on the top of the list and the DNS server IP address should be configured on that interface. This is true whether you use an Internal DNS server, a DMZ DNS server or a public DNS server, such as your ISP's DNS server

If you don't understand these principles, consult someone who does. DNS settings are critical and if the DNS configuration on your ISA firewall is incorrect, you *will* experience connectivity problems that are difficult to troubleshoot and it will give you the false impression that the ISA firewall "does not work".

TIP

Get your DNS house in order before publishing your public address DMZ servers to the Internet.

Install the ISA Server 2004 Firewall Software

After the DNS situation is handled and the network interfaces on the ISA Server 2004 firewall are properly configured, you're ready to install the ISA Server 2004 firewall software. While we hate to tell people "please see blah blah blah" for instructions on how to do something (because you end up wasting a lot of time trying to figure out how the information at blah blah blah solves the specific problem at hand), in this case we are going to refer you to the Chapter 5 on how to install the ISA firewall.

Install and Configure the IIS WWW and SMTP Services on the DMZ Server

In this section, we will place a Windows Server 2003 machine in the public address DMZ. The machine will have the IIS 6.0 WWW service (W3SVC) installed and the IIS 6.0 SMTP service. We'll publish both of these services to the Internet using Access Rules. In your production network, you'll install and configure the services you require, which might include a front-end Exchange Serve publishing OWA, OMA, ActiveSync, RPC over HTTP and other services.

The host on the DMZ segment uses an IP address valid for your subnetted block used for the DMZ. The published DMZ host uses the IP address of the DMZ interface on the ISA Server 2004 firewall as its default gateway. The DMZ host does *not* use the Internal network IP address as its default gateway because it does not have access to addresses on the Internal network unless we give it access, and we're not going to do that.

The DNS server address on the DMZ host's NIC will be the IP address of the DMZ interface on the ISA firewall. We use this configuration because we will configure a NAT relationship between the DMZ segment and the Internal network and a Server Publishing Rule that publishes the DNS server on the DMZ interface's IP address.

The internal network DNS server is configured to resolve Internet host names. This is useful if you want to use the SMTP server on the DMZ segment as an outbound SMTP relay. The SMTP relay needs to be able to resolve the MX domain name for each outgoing mail message and it can use the DNS server on the Internal network to get this done.

Create the DMZ Network

With the DMZ server in place, we can now get in front of the ISA Server 2004 management console and create the rules to make it all happen. The first step is to create the DMZ Network. The ISA firewall needs to know the IP addresses used on the network and the route relationship it should use when connecting to any other network. In our current example, the DMZ network will be named **DMZ** and we will assign the entire IP address range for its network ID to the network. On your production network, you should include all the IP addresses in the subnetted block you created for the DMZ segment.

> **WARNING**
>
> You may have noticed that ISA comes with several Network Templates that purportedly simplify configuration of the trihomed DMZ network. However, we recommend against using these templates because they make assumptions about the route relationship between your networks and require you to configure firewall access policies that are not very well documented, nor are they very well understood by most ISA Server 2004 administrators. We have already seen a large number of network configuration and troubleshooting issues related to using the Network Templates. These problems would have been avoided by manually configuring the firewall. By avoiding the use of Network Templates, you will ensure that you have a secure configuration and that your firewall configuration and Access Policies are precisely what you intend them to be.

Perform the following steps to create the DMZ network:

- In the **Microsoft Internet Security and Acceleration Server 2004** management console, expand the server name and then expand the **Configuration** node. Click the **Networks** node.

- On the **Networks** node, click the **Networks** tab in the **Details** pane of the console. On the **Tasks** tab, click the **Create a New Network** link.

- On the **Welcome to the New Network Wizard** page, shown in Figure 7.33, enter a name for the rule in the **Network name** text box. In this example, we'll name the network **DMZ**. Click **Next**.

- On the **Network Type** page, select the **Perimeter Network** option. Click **Next**.

Figure 7.33 New Network Wizard

- On the Network Addresses page, click the Add Adapter button.

- In the Select Network Adapters dialog box, shown in Figure 7.34, select the DMZ network interface and then put a checkmark in the interface's checkbox. Note that you can put a checkmark in the checkbox without selecting the interface first. However, if you do not select the interface, you will not see the correct Network Interface Information in the frame at the bottom of the dialog box. Click OK.

Figure 7.34 The Select Network Adapters dialog box

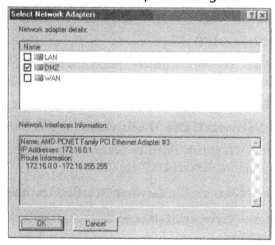

- Click **Next** on the **Network Addresses** page.

- Review your settings on the **Completing the New Network Wizard** page and click **Finish**.

Create the Network Rules Between the DMZ and External Network and for the DMZ and Internal Network

Now that the DMZ network is defined, the next step is to configure the route relationships between the DMZ network, the Internal network and the Internet (which is the External network, as the term applied to any network for which you haven't defined a network).

In our example, we want a route relationship between the DMZ network and the Internet, and a NAT relationship between the DMZ network and the Internal network. This allows us to use Access Rules to allow external hosts access to the DMZ segment and a server publishing rule to hide the IP address of the DNS server on the Internal network. Note that even if we used a route relationship between the DMZ and the Internal network, we could still create a Server Publishing Rule to allow the DMZ host access to the DNS server on the Internal network. It is important to use a Server Publishing Rule instead of an Access Rule so that the DNS filter can protect the DNS server on the Internal network.

Perform the following steps to create the Network Rule controlling the route relationship between the DMZ network and the Internet:

1. On the **Networks** node in the left pane of the console, click on the **Network Rules** tab in the Details pane. Click the **Create a New Network Rule** link on the **Tasks** tab in the Task Pane.

2. On the **Welcome to the New Network Rule Wizard** page, enter a name for the rule in the **Network rule name** text box. In this example, we'll name the **Network Rule DMZ<>External**. Click **Next**.

3. On the **Network Traffic Sources** page, click the **Add** button.

4. In the **Add Network Entities** dialog box, click the **Networks** folder and then double click on the **DMZ network**. Click **Close**.

5. Click **Next** on the **Network Traffic Sources** page.

6. On the **Network Traffic Destinations** page, click the **Add** button.

7. In the **Add Network Entities dialog** box, click the **Networks** folder and double click on **External. Click Close**.

   - Click **Next** on the **Network Traffic Destinations** page.

   - On the **Network Relationship** page, select the Route option and click Next.

- Review your settings on the **Completing the New Network Wizard** page and click **Finish**.

The next step is to create the route relationship between the DMZ Network and the Internal Network. In this case, we'll use the NAT route relationship between DMZ and Internal network.

Perform the following steps to create the NAT route relationship between DMZ and Internal networks:

1. On the **Networks** node in the left pane of the console, click on the **Network Rules** tab in the Details pane. Click the **Create a New Network Rule** link on the **Tasks** tab in the Task Pane.

2. On the **Welcome to the New Network Rule Wizard** page, enter a name for the rule in the **Network rule name** text box. In this example, we'll name the Network Rule **DMZ<>Internal**. Click **Next**.

3. On the **Network Traffic Sources** page, click the **Add** button.

4. In the **Add Network Entities** dialog box, click the **Networks** folder and then double click on the **Internal** network. Click **Close**.

5. Click **Next** on the **Network Traffic Sources** page.

6. On the **Network Traffic Destinations** page, click the **Add** button.

7. In the **Add Network Entities** dialog box, click the **Networks** folder and double click on **DMZ**. Click **Close**.

8. Click **Next** on the **Network Traffic Destinations** page.

9. On the **Network Relationship** page, select the **Route** option and click **Next**.

Review your settings on the **Completing the New Network Wizard** page and click **Finish**.

Create Server Publishing Rule Allowing DNS from DMZ to Internal

The DMZ host may need to resolve Internet host names. This is the case whenever the DMZ host needs to establish new outbound connections to servers on the Internet based on the destination host name. An example would be when you have an SMTP relay on the DMZ segment that's used to relay outbound mail for your organization.

We use a Server Publishing Rule in this example so that the DNS filter's protection is applied to connections from the DMZ host to the DNS server on the Internal network.

Perform the following steps to create the Server Publishing Rule:

1. In the **Microsoft Internet Security and Acceleration Server 2004** management console, click the **Firewall Policy** node. In the Task Pane, click the **Tasks** tab and then click the **Create a New Server Publishing Rule** link.

2. On the **Welcome to the New Server Publishing Rule Wizard** page, shown in Figure 7.35, enter a name for the rule in the **Server publishing rule name** text box. In this example, we'll name the rule **Publish Internal DNS Server**. Click **Next**.

3. On the **Select Server** page, enter the IP address of the DNS server on the Internal network. In this example, the IP address of the Internal Network DNS server is **10.0.0.2**, so we'll enter that into the text box. Click **Next**.

4. On the **Select Protocol** page, select the **DNS Server** protocol from the Selected protocol list. Click Next.

5. On the **IP Addresses** page, put a checkmark in the **DMZ** checkbox. This is the interface on which the Server Publishing Rule will listen for incoming connection requests to the Internal network DNS server. Click **Next**.

Figure 7.35 the New Server Publishing Rule Wizard

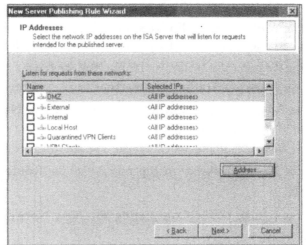

6. Review your settings on the **Completing the New Server Publishing Rule** page and click **Finish**.

Create an Access Rule Allowing DNS from Internal to External

1. In the **Microsoft Internet Security and Acceleration Server 2004** management console, click the **Firewall Policy** node. In the Task Pane, click the **Tasks** tab and then click the **Create a New Server Publishing Rule** link.

2. On the **Welcome to the New Server Publishing Rule Wizard** page, enter a name for the rule in the **Server publishing rule name** text box. In this example, we'll name the rule **Publish Internal DNS Server**. Click **Next**.

3. On the **Select Server** page, enter the IP address of the DNS server on the Internal network. In this example, the IP address of the Internal Network DNS server is **10.0.0.2**, so we'll enter that into the text box. Click **Next**.

4. On the **Select Protocol** page, select the **DNS Server** protocol from the **Selected protocol** list. Click **Next**.

5. On the **IP Addresses** page, put a checkmark in the **DMZ** checkbox. This is the interface on which the Server Publishing Rule will listen for incoming connection requests to the Internal network DNS server, as shown in Figure 7.36. Click **Next**.

Figure 7.36 Selecting IP addresses that will listen for requests

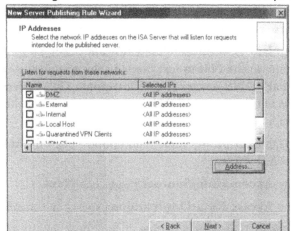

6. Review your settings on the **Completing the New Server Publishing Rule** page and click **Finish**.

Create an Access Rule Allowing DNS from Internal to External

The Internal network DNS server needs to be able to query an Internet DNS server to resolve Internet host names. We can create a DNS Access Rule that will allow the Internal network DNS server access to Internet DNS servers using the DNS protocol.

Perform the following steps to create the DNS Access Rule for the DNS server:

1. In the **Microsoft Internet Security and Acceleration Server 2004** management console, click the **Firewall Policy** node in the left pane of the console.

2. Click the **Tasks** tab in the Task Pane and then click the **Create New Access Rule** link.

3. On the **Welcome to the New Access Rule Wizard** page, enter a name for the rule in the **Access Rule name** text box. In this example, we'll call the rule **Outbound DNS Internal DNS Server**. Click **Next**.

4. On the **Rule Action** page, select the **Allow** option and click **Next**.

5. On the **Protocols** page, select the **Selected protocols** entry from the **This rule applies to** list. Click the **Add** button.

6. In the **Add Protocols** dialog box, click the **Common Protocols** folder and then double click the **DNS** entry. Click **Close**.

7. Click **Next** on the **Protocols** page.

8. On the **Access Rule Sources** page, click the **Add** button.

9. In the **Add Network Entities** dialog box, click the **New** button. Click the **Computer** entry.

10. In the **New Computer Rule Element** dialog box, enter a name for the computer in the **Name** text box. In this example, we'll enter the name **Internal DNS Server**. In the **Computer IP Address** text box, enter the IP address of the Internal DNS server. In this example, the IP address is **10.0.0.2**, so we'll enter that IP address. Click **OK**.

11. Click the **Computers** folder and double click the **Internal DNS Server** entry. Click **Close**.

12. On the **Access Rule Sources** page, click **Next**.

13. On the **Access Rule Destinations** page, click the **Add** button.

14. In the **Add Network Entities** dialog box, click the **Networks** folder. Double click the **External** entry and click **Close**.

15. Click **Next** on the **Access Rule Destinations** page.

16. On the **User Sets** page, accept the default entry **User Sets** and click **Next**.

17. Review the settings on the **Completing the New Access Rule Wizard** page and click **Finish**.

Create an Access Rule
Allow HTTP from External to DMZ

The next step is to create an Access Rule that allows HTTP from the External network to the DMZ host. While you do not benefit from the full firewall feature set provided by a Web publishing rule, this option allows you to expose the actual IP address of the Web server to the Internet and the security provided by the HTTP Security Filter still applies to the Access Rule. The basic configuration of the HTTP Security filter provides a good level of protection and you can customize the HTTP Security Filter to provide an enhanced level of security to your Access Rule published Web server.

Perform the following steps to publish your DMZ Web server using an Access Rule:

1. In the **Microsoft Internet Security and Acceleration Server 2004** management console, click on the **Firewall Policy** node in the left pane of the console and then click the **Create a New Access Rule** link in the **Tasks** tab of the Task Pane.

2. On the **Welcome to the New Access Rule Wizard** page, enter a name for the rule in the **Access Rule name** text box. In this example, we'll name the rule **Inbound to DMZ Web Server**. Click **Next**.

3. On the **Rule Action** page, select the **Allow** option and click **Next**.

4. On the **Protocols** page, click the select the **Selected protocols** option from the **This rule applies to** list and click **Add**.

5. In the **Add Protocols** dialog box, click the **Common Protocols** folder and double click the **HTTP** entry. Click **Close**.

6. Click **Next** on the **Protocols** page.

7. On the **Access Rule Sources** page, click the **Add** button.

8. In the **Add Network Entities** dialog box, click the **Networks** folder and double click the **External** entry. Click **Close**.

9. Click **Next** on the **Access Rule Sources** page.

10. On the **Access Rule Destinations** page, click the **Add** button.

11. In the **Add Network Entities** dialog box, click the **New** menu then click the **Computer** entry.

12. In the **New Computer Rule Element** dialog box, shown in Figure 7.37, enter a name for the DMZ Web server in the **Name** text box. In this example we'll use **DMZ Web Server**. Enter the IP address of the DMZ Web server in the **Computer IP Address** text box. In this example, the IP address of the DMZ Web server is **172.16.0.2**, so we'll enter that value into the text box. Click **OK**.

Figure 7.37 The New Computer Rule Element

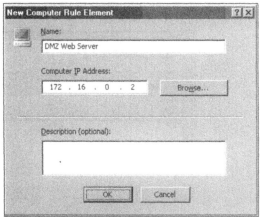

13. In the **Add Network Entities** dialog box, click the **Computers** folder. Double click the **DMZ Web Server** entry. Click **Close**.

14. Click **Next** on the **Access Rule Destinations** page.

15. On the **User Sets** page, accept the default entry **All Users** and click **Next**.

16. Review your settings on the **Completing the New Access Rule Wizard** page and click **Finish**.

Create an Access Rule Allowing SMTP from External to DMZ

Now that the Web server is published, we'll create another rule that allows inbound access to the SMTP server on the DMZ network. Again, we'll use an Access Rule. Note that when we use an Access Rule instead of a Server Publishing Rule, we will not benefit from the protection we get from SMTP filter.

Perform the following steps to create the Access Rule to allow inbound access to the SMTP server:

1. In the **Microsoft Internet Security and Acceleration Server 2004** management console, click on the **Firewall Policy** node in the left pane of the console and then click the **Create a New Access Rule** link in the **Tasks** tab of the Task Pane.

2. On the **Welcome to the New Access Rule Wizard** page, enter a name for the rule in the **Access Rule name** text box. In this example, we'll name the rule **Inbound to DMZ SMTP Server**. Click **Next**.

3. On the **Rule Action** page, select the **Allow** option and click **Next**.

4. On the **Protocols** page, click the select the **Selected protocols** option from the **This rule applies to** list as shown in Figure 7.38, and click **Add**.

5. In the **Add Protocols** dialog box, click the **Common Protocols** folder and double click the **HTTP** entry. Click **Close**.

Figure 7.38 The New Access Rule Wizard

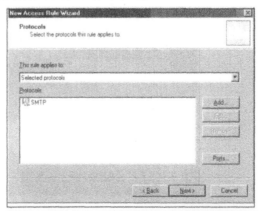

6. Click **Next** on the **Protocols** page.

7. On the **Access Rule Sources** page, click the **Add** button.

8. In the **Add Network Entities** dialog box, click the **Networks** folder and double click the **External** network. Click **Close**.

9. Click **Next** on the **Access Rule Sources** page.

10. On the **Access Rule Destinations** page, click the **Add** button.

11. In the **Add Network Entities** dialog box, click the **Computers** folder. Double click the **DMZ Web Server** entry. Click **Close**.

12. Click **Next** on the **Access Rule Destinations** page.

13. On the **User Sets** page, accept the default entry **All Users** and click **Next**.

14. Review your settings on the **Completing the New Access Rule Wizard** page and click **Finish**.

15. Click **Apply** to save the changes and update the firewall policy.

16. Click **OK** in the **Apply New Configuration** dialog box.

Figure 7.39 The Firewall Policy

Your Firewall Policy should look what what's seen in Figure 7.39 below.

Test the Access Rules from External to DMZ

Now you're ready to test the Access Rules. Perform the following steps to perform the tests:

1. Open the Web browser on the external host and enter the IP address of the DMZ Web server. In this case, the IP address of the DMZ Web server is **172.16.0.2**, so we'll enter **http://172.16.0.2** in the Address bar of the browser and press ENTER.

2. The default Web page of the IIS Web site appears. In this example, we haven't configured a special default Web page, so we'll see the **Under Construction** page. This demonstrates that the Access Rule allowing inbound access to the DMZ Web site worked correctly.

3. Now, let's look at the Web site's log file and see what shows up. Open the **Windows Explorer** and navigate to

C:\WINDOWS\system32\LogFiles\W3SVC1. Double click on the log file that has today's date on it. You'll see something like what appears below. Note the boldfaced entries. This indicates the source IP address as recorded in the Web server log. In this example, the source IP address is the IP address on the DMZ interface of the ISA Server 2004 firewall computer. This might not be what you expected. The reason for this is that the Web Proxy Filter is automatically associated with the HTTP protocol. We'll see how to disable the Web Proxy filter on the protocol later in this section.

```
#Software: Microsoft Internet Information Services 6.0
#Version: 1.0
#Date: 2004-06-18 05:47:14
2004-06-18 05:56:21 172.16.0.2 GET /iisstart.htm - 80 - 172.16.0.1
Mozilla/4.0+(compatible;+MSIE+6.0;+Windows+NT+5.1) 200 0 0
2004-06-18 05:56:25 172.16.0.2 GET /pagerror.gif - 80 - 172.16.0.1
Mozilla/4.0+(compatible;+MSIE+6.0;+Windows+NT+5.1) 200 0 0
```

1. Next, go to the Web Server on the DMZ segment and open the **Internet Information Services (IIS) Manager** console from the **Administrative Tools** menu in the **Start** menu.

2. In the **Internet Information Services (IIS) Manager** console, right click on the **Default Virtual SMTP Server** and click **Properties**. On the **General** tab, put a checkmark in the **Enable Logging** checkbox. Click **Apply** and then click **OK**.

3. At the external host computer, open a command prompt. In the command prompt window, enter **telnet 172.16.0.2 25** and press ENTER.

4. You'll see the SMTP service banner appear. Enter **help** and press ENTER. You'll see a list of the commands supported by the SMTP server as shown in Figure 7.40. Enter **quit** to disconnect from the SMTP server.

Figure 7.40 Commands supported by the SMTP server

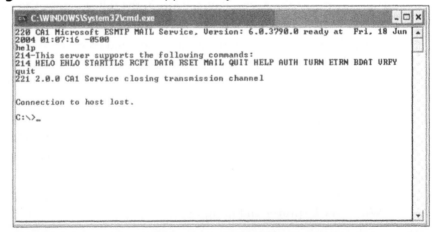

5. Navigate to the **C:\WINDOWS\system32\LogFiles\SMTPSVC1** on the DMZ host computer. Open the log file with today's date. You'll see something that looks like what you see below. Note the highlighted IP address. This is the address of the external host that made the inbound request to the DMZ Web server. In this case, the original client IP address is preserved because there is no application filter proxying the connection and replacing the source IP address with the ISA firewall's IP address.

```
#Software: Microsoft Internet Information Services 6.0

#Version: 1.0

#Date: 2004-06-18 06:07:22

#Fields: time c-ip cs-method cs-uri-stem sc-status

06:07:22 192.168.1.187 QUIT - 240
```

Test the DNS Rule from the DMZ to the Internal Network

We demonstrated that the Access Rules controlling inbound access from the Internet to the DMZ host work correctly using the procedures in the previous section. The next step is to confirm that the Server Publishing Rule allowing the DMZ host access to the DNS server on the Internal network works correctly.

Perform the following steps to test the DNS Server Publishing Rule:

1. At the DMZ host, open a command prompt. At the command prompt, enter **nslookup www.hotmail.com** and press ENTER.

2. You'll see the results of the nslookup that look like Figure 7.41. Note the first two entries triggered the **Publish Internal DNS Server** rule and the subsequent entries triggered the **Outbound DNS Internal DNS Server** rule. This shows that the DMZ host made a DNS query to the Internal network DNS server and the DNS server on the Internal network then queried Internet DNS servers to resolve the name.

Figure 7.41 Results of nslookup command

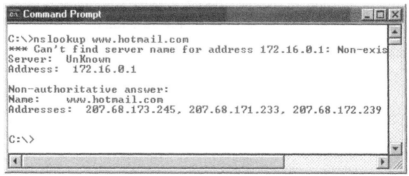

3. You should see entries like those in Figure 7.42 in the real time log monitor.

Figure 7.42 Log monitor entries

6/18/2004 2:23:32 AM	172.16.0.2	10.0.0.2	53	DNS Server	Initiated...	Publish Internal D...
6/18/2004 2:23:32 AM	172.16.0.2	10.0.0.2	53	DNS Server	Initiated...	Publish Internal D...
6/18/2004 2:23:32 AM	10.0.0.2	192.5.6.30	53	DNS	Initiated...	Outbound DNS Int...
6/18/2004 2:23:32 AM	10.0.0.2	206.16.0.71	53	DNS	Initiated...	Outbound DNS Int...
6/18/2004 2:23:32 AM	10.0.0.2	192.55.83.30	53	DNS	Initiated...	Outbound DNS Int...
6/18/2004 2:23:33 AM	10.0.0.2	216.239.126.10	53	DNS	Initiated...	Outbound DNS Int...

Change the Access Rule Allowing External to DMZ by Disabling the Web Proxy Filter

You may wish to see the original IP address of the external network host instead of the ISA Server 2004 firewall's IP address when you publish the Web server using a Access Rule. You can accomplish this goal by disabling the Web Proxy filter. This can be done within the properties of the HTTP Access Rule you created earlier.

Perform the following steps to disable the Web Proxy filter:

1. In the **Microsoft Internet Security and Acceleration Server 2004** management console, right click on the **Inbound to Web Server** rule and click **Properties**.

2. In the **Inbound to Web Server Properties** dialog box, click the **Protocols** tab.

3. On the **Protocols** tab, click the **HTTP** entry in the **Protocols** list and click the **Edit** button.

4. In the **HTTP Properties** dialog box, click the **Parameters** tab. On the **Parameters** tab, remove the checkmark from the **Web Proxy Filter** checkbox in the **Application Filters** frame. Click **Apply** and then click **OK**.

5. Click **OK** in the **Inbound to Web Server Properties** dialog box.

6. Click **Apply** to save the changes and update the firewall policy.

7. Click **OK** in the **Apply New Configuration** dialog box.

Now let's see what happens when we connect to the Web site again.

1. At the external client machine, open the Web browser and enter **http://172.16.0.2** in the Address bar and press ENTER.

2. The **Under Construction** page appears. Hold down the CTRL key on the keyboard and click the **Refresh** button in the browser's button bar.

3. Return to the DMZ Web server and open the Web server's WWW service's log file. You'll see something like what appears below. Note the highlighted IP addresses. The original IP address now appears in the log file.

```
#Software: Microsoft Internet Information Services 6.0
#Version: 1.0
#Date: 2004-06-18 07:42:37
#Fields: date time s-ip cs-method cs-uri-stem cs-uri-query s-port cs-
username c-ip cs(User-Agent) sc-status sc-substatus sc-win32-status
2004-06-18 07:42:37 172.16.0.2 GET /iisstart.htm - 80 - 192.168.1.187
Mozilla/4.0+(compatible;+MSIE+6.0;+Windows+NT+5.1) 200 0 0
2004-06-18 07:42:37 172.16.0.2 GET /pagerror.gif - 80 - 192.168.1.187
Mozilla/4.0+(compatible;+MSIE+6.0;+Windows+NT+5.1) 200 0 0
```

While disabling the Web Proxy filter on the HTTP protocol solves the problem of controlling the source IP address on the Access Rule published Web server, you do lose out on the Web Proxy filter for *all* Web communications that aren't made through the Web Proxy client configuration. This means that outbound connections from SecureNAT and Firewall clients will not be handled by the Web Proxy filter and they will not benefit from the Web Proxy cache and other features provided by the Web Proxy filter. In addition, there may be some unintended effects on Web Publishing rules. Note that we haven't yet completely tested the side-effects of disabling the Web Proxy filter on the HTTP protocol, so we cannot be sure what these unintended effects may be.

An alternative is to create your own Protocol Definition that is defined as TCP 80 Outbound. You can use this custom Protocol Definition to publish the DMZ HTTP server host using an Access Rule. The big problem with this approach is that you do not have the protection of HTTP Security filter or the Web Proxy filter. In this scenario, you really *do* have a traditional packet filtering firewall on your hands!

Allowing Intradomain Communications through the ISA Firewall

The new ISA firewall's enhanced support for directly attached DMZs has led to a lot of questions on how to allow intradomain communications through the ISA firewall from one network to another. You can now create multiple directly attached perimeter networks and allow controlled access to and from those perimeter networks. You can also safely put domain member machines on these DMZ segments to support a variety of new scenarios, such as dedicated network services segments that enforce domain segmentation.

For example, you might want to put an Internet facing Exchange Server or an inbound authenticating SMTP relay on a network services segment. In order to take advantage of the user database in the Active Directory, you need to join these machines to the Active Directory domain on the Internal network. Since the Internal network domain controllers are located on a network controlled by the ISA firewall, you need to configure the ISA firewall to allow the protocols required for intradomain communications.

TIP

Note that we don't "open ports" on the ISA firewall. The term "open ports" has its roots in simple packet filter based hardware firewalls. Since the ISA firewall is protocol aware, it can perform stateful filtering and stateful application layer inspection on all communications moving through the firewall. We highly recommend that you do *not* put your trust in only a simple packet filter hardware firewall to protect your critical corporate resources.

The basic network configuration used in this example is seen in Figure 7.43 below.

Figure 7.43 Basic network configuration for trihomed DMZ

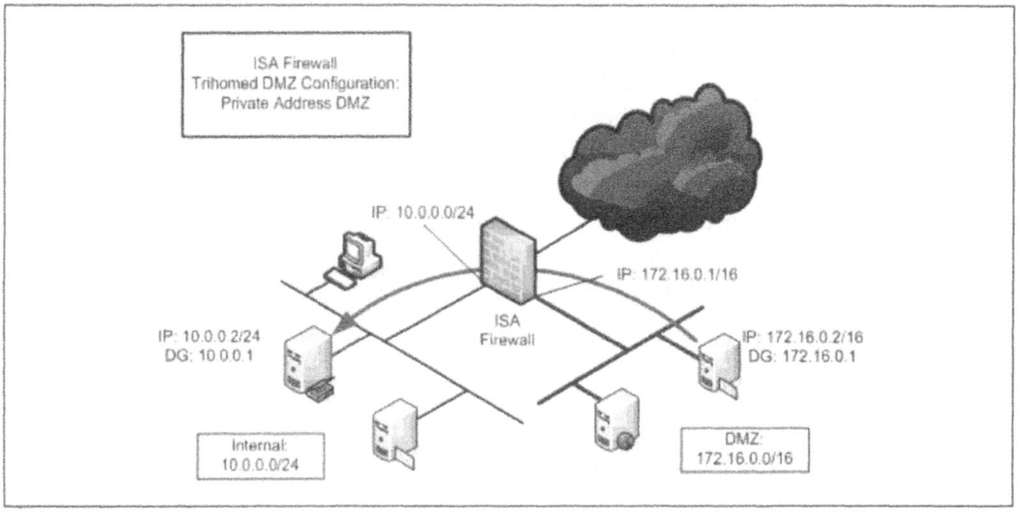

Table 7.6 shows the protocols required for intradomain communications, as well as other details included in an Access Rule we will create to support these communications.

Table 7.6 Protocols Required for Intradomain Communications

Name	Intradomain Communications
Action	Allow
Protocols	ADLogon/DirRep* Direct Host (TCP 445)** DNS Kerberos-Adm(UDP) Kerberos-Sec(TCP)

Continued

Table 7.6 Protocols Required for Intradomain Communications

Name	Intradomain Communications
	Kerberos-Sec(UDP)
	LDAP (TCP)
	LDAP (UDP)
	LDAP GC (Global Catalog)
	RPC Endpoint Mapper (TCP 135)∗∗∗
	NTP
	Ping
From	DMZ Member Server
	Internal Network DC
To	Internal Network DC
	DMZ Member Server
Users	All
Schedule	Always
Content Types	All content types

∗ADLogon/DirRep:Primary Connection: 50000 TCP Outbound (requires RPC key set on the back-end Exchange Server)

∗∗Direct Host:Primary Connection: 445 TCP Outbound (required to demonstrate an issue discussed in this section

∗∗∗RPC Endpoint Mapper: Primary Connection: 135 TCP Outbound (required to demonstrate an issue discussed in this section)

RPC services configure themselves in the Registry with a universally unique identifier (UUID), which is similar in function to a globally unique identifier (GUID). RPC UUIDs are well-known identifiers (at least to RPC services), and are unique for each service.

When an RPC service starts, it obtains an unused high or ephemeral port, and registers that port with the RPC service's UUID. Some services choose a random high port while others try to always use the same high port if that port is not already in use. The high port assignment is static for the lifetime of the service and changes only after the machine or service is restarted.

When a client communicates with an RPC service, it doesn't know in advance which high port the service is using. Instead, the RPC client application establishes a connection to the server's RPC portmapper (endpoint mapper) service (on TCP 135) and requests the service it wants by using the service's specific UUID. The RPC endpoint mapper returns the corresponding high port number to the client and closes the connection endpoint mapper connection.

Finally, the client makes a new connection to the server, using the high port number it received from the endpoint mapper.

Because it's impossible to know in advance which port an RPC service will use, the firewall needs to permit all high ports through.

We want to limit the ports required for RPC to a single port. This allows us to know in advance what port to use and configure on the firewall. Otherwise, we would need to allow all high ports from the DMZ to the Internal network. We can limit the ports to a single port by making a Registry change on each domain controller. The Registry Key is:

```
HKEY_LOCAL_MACHINE\SYSTEM\CurrentControlSet\Services\NTDS\Parameters\
```

NOTE

We actually do not need to do this, as the ISA firewall's RPC filter can dynamically control port access. The RPC filter listens to the RPC negotiations and then dynamically opens the required high port. However, we prefer to set the port manually as it makes it easier to analyze the logs and track the RPC communications moving between the DMZ segment and the Internal network. If the administrative overhead of setting a specific high port for RPC communications is too high, you can take advantage of the RPC filter and not worry about it. This is what we mean when we say the ISA firewall doesn't "open ports" – the ISA firewall actually understands the *protocols* required.

You need to add a DWORD value named **TCP/IP Port** and set the value to the port you want to use. You'll need to carry out this procedure on each of the domain controllers in your domain.

Perform the following steps on each of the domain controllers in your domain to limit the RPC replication port to **50000**:

1. Click **Start** and click **Run**. In the **Open** text box enter **Regedit** and click **OK**.

2. Go to the following Registry key: HKEY_LOCAL_MACHINE\SYSTEM\ CurrentControlSet\Services\NTDS\Parameters\

3. Click the **Edit** menu and point to **New**. Click **DWORD Value**.

4. Rename the entry from **New Value #1** to **TCP/IP Port**, then double click the entry.

5. In the **Edit DWORD Value** dialog box, select the **Decimal** option. Enter **50000** in the **Value data** text box. Click **OK**.

6. Restart the domain controller.

The ISA firewall allows you to control the route relationship between any two Networks. In this example, we will use a ROUTE relationship between the DMZ and the Internal network. Note that when you apply a Network Template to create a DMZ segment, the default route relationship is set as NAT. While there are some minimal advantages to using a NAT relationship, those advantages are outweighed by the limitations they impose in this scenario. If you used a Network Template, make sure to change the Network Rule that controls communications between the DMZ and Internal network to ROUTE as shown in Figure 7.44.

Figure 7.44 Configuring the Network Relationship

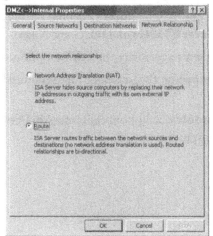

In the following example, we create a rule allowing intradomain communications between a single member server in the DMZ and a single domain controller on the Internal Network. We are using this scenario for simplicity's sake, but you are by no means limited to allowing communications between single servers.

For example, you might have several member server machines on the DMZ and multiple domain controllers on the Internal network. In this case, instead of creating computer objects representing single machines, you would create a Computer Set for the DMZ member servers and another Computer Set for the Internal Network domain controllers. You can then use the Computer Sets to control the Source and Destination locations for the intradomain communications rule.

NOTE

In the following exercise, you will create two Protocol Definitions that are *not required* since there are built in Protocol Definitions to support our requirements. However, we will create these Protocol Definitions to illustrate some important points that we discuss at the end of the section.

Perform the following steps to create the intradomain communications rule that will allow machines in the DMZ segment to communicate with domain controllers on the Internal network:

1. In the **Microsoft Internet Security and Acceleration Server 2004** management console, expand the server name and then click the **Firewall Policy** node.

2. In the **Firewall Policy** node, click the **Tasks** tab on the Task Pane. Click the **Create a New Access Rule** link.

3. On the **Welcome to the New Access Rule Wizard** page, enter a name for the rule in the **Access Rule name** text box. In this example, we will call the rule **Member Server®Internal DC**. Click **Next**.

4. On the **Rule Action** page, select the **Allow** option and click **Next**.

5. In the **This rule applies to** list, select the **Selected protocols** option. Click the **Add** button.

6. In the **Add Protocols** dialog box, click the **All Protocols** folder. Double click the following protocols:

```
DNS
Kerberos-Adm (UDP)
Kerberos-Sec (TCP)
Kerberos-Sec (UDP)
LDAP
LDAP (UDP)
LDAP GC (Global Catalog)
NTP (UDP)
Ping
```

7. Click the **New** menu and click **Protocol**.

8. On the **Welcome to the New Protocol Definition Wizard** page, enter **ADLogon/DirRep** in the **Protocol Definition name** text box. Click **Next**.

9. On the **Primary Connection Information** page, click **New**.

10. On the **New/Edit Protocol Connection** page, select **TCP** in the **Protocol type** list. Select **Outbound** in the **Direction** list. In the **Port Range** frame, enter **50000** in the **From** and **To** text boxes as shown in Figure 7.45. Click **OK**.

Figure 7.45 Creating a new Protocol Definitions

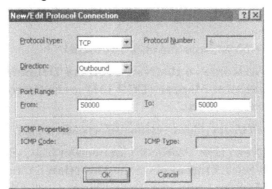

11. Click **Next** on the **Primary Connection Information** page.

12. Select the **No** option on the **Secondary Connections** page.

13. Click **Finish** on the **Completing the New Protocol Definition Wizard** page.

14. Click the **New** menu and click **Protocol**.

15. On the **Welcome to the New Protocol Definition Wizard** page, enter **Direct Host** in the **Protocol Definition** name text box. Click **Next**.

16. On the **Primary Connection Information** page, click **New**.

17. On the **New/Edit Protocol Connection page**, select **TCP** in the **Protocol type** list. Select **Outbound** in the **Direction** list. In the **Port Range** frame, enter **445** in the **From** and **To** text boxes. Click **OK**.

18. Click **Next** on the **Primary Connection Information** page as shown in Figure 7.46.

Figure 7.46 Configure the Primary Connection for the Protocol Definition

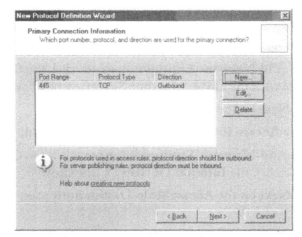

19. Select the **No** option on the **Secondary Connections** page.

20. Click **Finish** on the **Completing the New Protocol Definition Wizard** page.

21. Click the **New** menu and click **Protocol**.

22. On the **Welcome to the New Protocol Definition Wizard** page, enter **RPC Endpoint Mapper (TCP 135)** in the **Protocol Definition name** text box. Click **Next**.

23. On the **Primary Connection Information** page, click **New**.

24. On the **New/Edit Protocol Connection** page, select **TCP** in the **Protocol type** list. Select **Outbound** in the **Direction** list. In the **Port Range** frame, enter **135** in the **From** and **To** text boxes. Click **OK**.

25. Click **Next** on the **Primary Connection Information** page.

26. Select the **No** option on the **Secondary Connections** page.

27. Click **Finish** on the **Completing the New Protocol Definition Wizard** page.

28. In the **Add Protocols** dialog box, click the **User-Defined** folder. Double click the **ADLogon/DirRep, Direct Access** and **RPC Endpoint Mapper (TCP 135)** protocols. Click **Close**.

29. Click **Next** on the **Protocols** page.

30. On the **Access Rule Sources** page, click **Add**.

31. In the **Add Network Entities** dialog box, click the **New** menu. Click **Computer**.

32. In the **New Computer Rule Element** dialog box, enter **DMZ Member Server** in the **Name** text box. Enter **172.16.0.2** in the **Computer IP Address** text box. Click **OK**.

33. In the **Add Network Entities** dialog box, click the **New** menu. Click **Computer**.

34. In the **New Computer Rule Element** dialog box, enter **Internal DC** in the **Name** text box. Enter **10.0.0.2** in the **Computer IP Address** text box. Click **OK**.

35. In the **Add Network Entities** dialog box, click the **Computers** folder. Double click the **DMZ Member Server** entry. Click **Close**.

36. Click **Next** on the **Access Rule Sources** page.

37. On the **Access Rule Destinations** page, click **Add**.

38. In the **Add Network Entities** dialog box, click the **Computers** folder. Double click the **Internal DC** entry. Click **Close**.

39. Click **Next** on the **Access Rule Destinations** page.

40. On the **User Sets** page, accept the default entry, **All Users**, and click **Next**.

41. Review the settings on the **Completing the New Access Rule Wizard** page and click **Finish**.

42. Click **Apply** to save the changes and update the firewall policy.

43. Click **OK** in the **Apply New Configuration** dialog box, then you'll see what's shown in Figure 7.47 in the Firewall Policy tab.

Figure 7.47 Firewall Policy

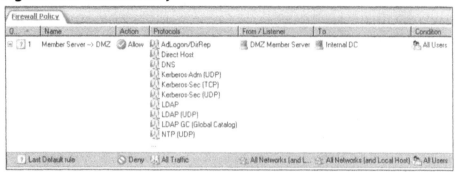

You can test the rule by joining a machine in the DMZ to the Active Directory domain on the Internal network and then logging into the domain after joining the domain. Note that this rule doesn't allow all protocols through from the member servers to the domain controllers. You will need to create other Access Rules for other protocols, and additional Access Rules for communications to other machines on other networks.

Figure 7.48 below shows some log file entries for communications between the member server and the domain controller on the Internal network. There are some entries in the log file that highlight some undocumented issues with the ISA firewall and its configuration.

Figure 7.48 Log file entries showing communications between member server and domain controller

Client IP	Destinat	Destination Port	Protocol	Action	Rule	Source Network	Destination Net
172.16.0.2	10.0.0.2	445	Microsoft CIFS (TCP)	Closed...	Member Server <--> DMZ	DMZ	Internal
172.16.0.2	10.0.0.2	389	LDAP	Closed...	Member Server <--> DMZ	DMZ	Internal
172.16.0.2	10.0.0.2	88	Kerberos-Sec (UDP)	Initiated...	Member Server <--> DMZ	DMZ	Internal
172.16.0.2	10.0.0.2	50000	AdLogon/DirRep	Initiated...	Member Server <--> DMZ	DMZ	Internal
172.16.0.2	10.0.0.2	135	RPC (all interfaces)	Initiated...	Member Server <--> DMZ	DMZ	Internal
172.16.0.2	10.0.0.2	88	Kerberos-Sec (UDP)	Initiated...	Member Server <--> DMZ	DMZ	Internal
172.16.0.2	10.0.0.2	88	Kerberos-Sec (UDP)	Initiated...	Member Server <--> DMZ	DMZ	Internal
172.16.0.2	10.0.0.2	389	LDAP	Initiated...	Member Server <--> DMZ	DMZ	Internal
172.16.0.2	10.0.0.2	88	Kerberos-Sec (UDP)	Initiated...	Member Server <--> DMZ	DMZ	Internal
172.16.0.2	10.0.0.2	88	Kerberos-Sec (UDP)	Initiated...	Member Server <--> DMZ	DMZ	Internal
172.16.0.2	10.0.0.2	88	Kerberos-Sec (UDP)	Initiated...	Member Server <--> DMZ	DMZ	Internal
172.16.0.2	10.0.0.2	445	Microsoft CIFS (TCP)	Initiated...	Member Server <--> DMZ	DMZ	Internal
172.16.0.2	10.0.0.2	389	LDAP (UDP)	Initiated...	Member Server <--> DMZ	DMZ	Internal
172.16.0.2	10.0.0.2	389	LDAP (UDP)	Initiated...	Member Server <--> DMZ	DMZ	Internal
172.16.0.2	10.0.0.2	389	LDAP (UDP)	Initiated...	Member Server <--> DMZ	DMZ	Internal
172.16.0.2	10.0.0.2	445	Microsoft CIFS (TCP)	Closed...	Member Server <--> DMZ	DMZ	Internal

Notice on the first line the connection to TCP port 445. In the protocol column, the name of the protocol is **Microsoft CIFS (TCP)** and not **Direct Host**, which is the name of the Protocol Definition we created for that protocol. The reason for this is that the built-in protocols will be used preferentially in the event that you create a Protocol Definition that has the same settings as a built-in Protocol Definition.

In the fifth line from the top, you'll see a connection made to TCP port 135. The **Protocol** column lists this as the **RCP (all interfaces)** protocol, instead of the **RCP Endpoint Mapper** protocol that we created. Again, the reason for this is that there is a built-in **RPC (all interfaces)** protocol and it is used preferentially over the one we created. In addition, this built-in Protocol Definition automatically binds the ISA firewall's RPC filter, which adds a significant amount of protection for the RPC communications.

We do see one of our custom Protocol Definitions being used in the fourth line from the top. The **ADLogon/DirRep** Protocol Definition is used to communicate on the custom RPC port we configured in the Registry of the domain controller.

Summary

In this chapter we discussed how the ISA firewall processes Access Policy and how to configure Access Rules to control outbound access through the ISA firewall. We also discussed a number of special topics in ISA firewall Access Policy that you can use to further lockdown your network.

You learned about the elements that make up the ISA firewall access rules, including protocols, user sets, content types, schedules and network objects. We discussed how you can create your own protocols or use those built into the ISA Server firewall. We also discussed the user sets (firewall groups) that come preconfigured in ISA Server: all authenticated users, all users, and system and network service. We talked about how content type control works with HTTP and tunneled FTP traffic, and you learned about the pre-built content types, as well as how to create your own content types. We also discussed how to apply schedules to access rules.

Next, we provided step by step details on how to create access rules and all the options that are available when creating or configuring a rule. You also learned how to bypass the Wizard and create new rules by copying and pasting, then making changes to an existing rule. We showed you how to configure RPC, FTP and HTTP policies, and how to order and organize your access rules.

We discussed using scripts to populate domain name sets, and provided a sample script that will allow you to import entries into a Domain Name set or URL set from a text file.

You learned about some specific examples of tasks you might want to perform, such as how to block MSN Messenger using an access rule and how to allow outbound access to MSN Messenger via Web Proxy.

In the next section, we discussed the details of creating and configuring a public address trihomed DMZ (perimeter) network. We discussed reasons for using access rules instead of publishing rules to allow access to DMZ hosts, and described how to publish a public address DMZ host using access rules and how to test the rules.

Finally, we covered how to allow intradomain communications through an ISA Server Firewall. We discussed protocols required for intradomain communications and showed you how to edit the registry on your domain controllers to limit ports required for RPC to a single port, in order to make it easier to analyze the logs.

Solutions Fast Track

Configuring Access Rules for Outbound Access through the ISA Firewall

☑ Only protocols with a primary connection in either the outbound or send direction can be used in Access Rules. In contrast, Web Publishing Rules and Server Publishing Rules always use protocols with a primary connection with the inbound or receive direction. Access Rules control access from source to destination using outbound protocols.

☑ On the **Rule Action** page you have two options: **Allow** or **Deny**. In contrast to ISA Server 2000, the new ISA firewall has the Deny option set as the default.

☑ The ISA firewall comes with over 100 built-in Protocol Definitions you can use in your Access Rules.

☑ There are several options you can configure in an Access Rule that aren't exposed in the New Access Rule Wizard. You can access these options by going into the Properties dialog box of the Access Rule.

☑ When you set a schedule for an Access Rule, the rule is applied only to new connections that match the characteristics of the rule. However, active connections to which this rule applies will not be disconnected.

☑ The Copy option is very useful if you want to avoid using the New Access Rule Wizard to create new rules. Right click an existing rule and then click Copy. Right click the same rule and then click Paste.

☑ A common error made by ISA firewall administrators involves allowing hosts on an ISA firewall Protected Network to loop back through the firewall to access resources on the same Network where the client is located. Looping back through the ISA firewall can either reduce the overall performance of the ISA firewall, or prevent the communication from working at all.

☑ You should always avoid looping back through the ISA firewall for resources located on the same Network as the requesting host. The solution to this problem is to configure SecureNAT, Firewall and Web Proxy clients to use Direct Access for local resources (local resources are those contained on the same ISA firewall Network as the host requesting those resources).

☑ Blocking dangerous applications is a common task for the ISA firewall. There are a number of methods you can use to block dangerous applications.

☑ When the MSN Messenger sends credentials to the MSN Messenger site, those credentials are also sent to the ISA firewall. If the user name and password the user uses to access the MSN Messenger site aren't the same as the credentials the user uses on the corporate network, then connection will fail.

☑ After a client initiates a request, the ISA firewall maintains an active state in the firewall state table for the session which permits the response to return to the client. The active state permits the client to send new requests. The ISA firewall removes the active state from the state table after the session is idle for an unspecified period of time (usually a minute or two).

Using Scripts to Populate Domain Name Sets

☑ In addition to performing the basic task of stateful filtering (which even a simple 'hardware' firewall can do), the ISA firewall's strong application layer inspection feature set allows the ISA firewall to actually understand the protocols passing though the firewall.

☑ The ISA firewall's stateful application inspection mechanism allows you to control access not just to "ports", but to the actual protocols moving through those ports.

☑ The first thing you need to do when using Import scripts is create the URL Set and the Domain Name Set in the **Microsoft Internet Security and Acceleration Server 2004** management console.

☑ As you obtain more URLs, you can add them to the same text files and run the script again. The new entries will be added without creating duplicates of the domains or URLs that are already included in the Domain Name Set or URL Set.

Creating and Configuring a Public Address Trihomed DMZ Network

☑ Unlike the ISA Server 2000 firewall, which saw the world as "trusted versus untrusted (LAT versus non-LAT), the ISA Server 2004 firewall sees all networks as untrusted and applies firewall policy to all connections made through the ISA Server 2004 firewall. This includes hosts connecting through a VPN remote access client or VPN gateway connection.

☑ ISA Server 2004 multinetworking allows you to connect multiple interfaces (or multiple virtual interfaces using VLAN tagging) and have complete control over the traffic that moves between networks connected by the ISA Server 2004 firewall.

☑ Using public addresses is sometimes necessary if you have an established DMZ segment with multiple hosts using public addresses and you do not wish to change the addressing scheme because of overhead involved with making the appropriate public DNS changes.

☑ ISA Server 2004 firewall policy provides two methods you can use to control traffic moving through the firewall: Access Rules and Publishing Rules. Access Rules can participate in a route or NAT relationship. Publishing Rules always NAT the connection, even if you're using a public address segment and have a route relationship between the source and destination host.

☑ One of the major drawbacks of ISA Server 2000 Web publishing scenarios was that you always received the IP address of the ISA Server 2000 firewall in the published Web servers' log files. ISA Server 2004 fixes this problem and allows you to choose to pass the original client IP address to published Web server, or to use the ISA Server 2004 firewall's IP address.

☑ When you create a public address DMZ segment, you need to subnet your public block and assign one of the subnets to the DMZ segment. You can then bind the first valid address of a subnetted block to the DMZ interface and the first valid address of another subnetted block to the public interface.

☑ You have to configure the upstream router with a route to the DMZ segment. You do this by configuring the router to use the IP address on the external interface of the ISA Server 2004 firewall as the gateway address for the DMZ segment's network ID. If this routing table entry is missing on the upstream router, then no primary incoming connections, and no responses to incoming connections, to and from the DMZ segment will work.

☑ DNS is a critical issue for the ISA Server 2004 firewall because the firewall can perform proxy name resolution for Web Proxy and Firewall clients. The ISA Server 2004 firewall uses DNS settings on its NICs to query the appropriate DNS server. If you have the incorrect DNS server configuration, you can experience either slow name resolution, or no name resolution at all.

☑ After the DMZ network is defined, the next step is to configure the route relationships between the DMZ network, the Internal network and the Internet (which is the External network, which is defined as any network for which you haven't defined a network).

☑ The DMZ host may need to resolve Internet host names. This is the case whenever the DMZ host needs to establish new outbound connections to servers on the Internet based on the destination host name.

☑ The Internal network DNS server needs to be able to query Internet DNS server to resolve Internet host names. We can create a DNS Access Rule that will allow the Internal network DNS server access to Internet DNS servers using the DNS protocol.

☑ You may wish to see the original IP address of the external network host instead of the ISA Server 2004 firewall's IP address when you publish the Web server using a Access Rule. You can accomplish this goal by disabling the Web Proxy filter.

Allowing Intradomain Communications through the ISA Firewall

☑ You can now create multiple directly attached perimeter networks and allow controlled access to and from those perimeter networks. You can now safely put domain member machines on these DMZ segments to support a variety of new scenarios, such as dedicated network services segments that enforce domain segmentation.

☑ You might want to put an Internet facing Exchange Server or an inbound authenticating SMTP relay on a network services segment. In order to take advantage of the user database in the Active Directory, you need to join these machines to the Active Directory domain on the Internal network.

☑ RPC services configure themselves in the Registry with a universally unique identifier (UUID), which is similar in function to a globally unique identifier (GUID). RPC UUIDs are well-known identifiers (at least to RPC services), and are unique for each service.

☑ ISA firewall's RPC filter can dynamically control port access. The RPC filter listens to the RPC negotiations and then dynamically opens the required high port.

☑ When you apply a Network Template to create a DMZ segment, the default route relationship is set as NAT.

Frequently Asked Questions

The following Frequently Asked Questions, answered by the authors of this book, are designed to both measure your understanding of the concepts presented in this chapter and to assist you with real-life implementation of these concepts. To have your questions about this chapter answered by the author, browse to **www.syngress.com/solutions** and click on the **"Ask the Author"** form. You will also gain access to thousands of other FAQs at ITFAQnet.com.

Q: I am using a dedicated FTP program to connect to my company's FTP server. I can authenticate and download information from the FTP site, but I can't upload. I have an Access Rule that allows the host access to the FTP protocol. Why can't I upload?

A: You need to right click on the Access Rule allowing the outbound FTP connection and click the **Configure FTP** command. Then configure the FTP Policy to allow FTP uploads.

Q: I want to authenticate all connections through the ISA firewall. Do I need the Firewall client?

A: Yes! The Firewall client significantly improves both the security and performance of the ISA firewall. Without the Firewall client, you will not be able to authenticate connections made using Winsock applications through the ISA firewall. While you can configure the clients as Web Proxy clients, you will only get user information for HTTP, HTTPS and HTTP tunneled FTP connections. We recommend that you install the Firewall client on all client operating systems and configure Access Rules to require authentication.

Q: I created an Access Rule on the ISA firewall that allows anonymous access using the FTP protocol to our company's FTP site. However, users are not able to establish FTP connections to the site. When I look at the ISA firewall service log, I see that a rule requiring authentication denied the request. Why was the request denied when I had an anonymous access rule allowing the request?

A: The problem is probably related to the ordering of your rules. If you have a rule that applies to the FTP protocol and also requires authentication and that rule is above the anonymous access rule, then the connection request will be denied because that rule was processed before the anonymous access rule. We recommend that you put anonymous Deny rules first, then anonymous Allow rules. Then put authenticated Deny rules after the anonymous Allow. Finally, put your authenticated allow rules at the end of your Access Rule list.

Q: I created a custom Protocol Definition for a custom application we use in-house. The Protocol Definition includes TCP port 4467 outbound and secondary connections for 5587-5600 inbound. I created an Access Rule allowing all users outbound access to this protocol but the connection is denied by the Default Access Rule. Our clients are configured as SecureNAT and Web Proxy clients. What can I do to get this Access Rule to work?

A: The problem you're having is that SecureNAT clients cannot negotiate secondary connections without the aid of application filter. You can get your developers to create an application filter to support your in-house customer protocol. However, a much better solution is to install the Firewall client on your client operating systems. The Firewall client can negotiate secondary connections because it communicates directly with the ISA firewall's Firewall Service.

Q: I have created an Access Rule to allow our SecureNAT clients outbound access to a Web server on our Internal Network that we've published using a Web Publishing Rule. External users have no problem accessing the published server via the Web Publishing Rule but our Internal Network SecureNAT clients cannot connect to the Web site. What can we do to make the Access Rule work correctly?

A: The problem isn't with your Access Rule per se, but rather with the fact that you're looping back through the ISA firewall to access Internal Network resources. We will assume that the published Web server and the SecureNAT clients are all on the same ISA Network. Hosts that are on the same ISA Network should always communicate directly with one another and not loop back through the ISA firewall. From your description, it appears that the SecureNAT clients are resolving the name of your published Web site to the IP address on the external interface of the ISA firewall. To solve this problem, you need to create a split DNS, so that external hosts resolve the name of the Web site to the IP address on the external interface of the ISA firewall that's used by the Web Publishing Rule, and Internal Network SecureNAT clients resolve the IP address of the published Web site to the actual IP address of the Web server (that it uses on the Internal Network).

Q: The clients on my Internal Network are configured as Web Proxy clients. I created an Access Rule allowing outbound access to authenticated users for the HTTP and HTTPS protocols. This rule works fine except for users who need to connect to MSN Messenger using HTTP. Each time the Web Proxy clients attempt to connect to MSN Messenger via the Web Proxy, the connection attempt fails. Why is this happening and how can I fix it?

A: The problem is that the MSN Messenger is sending the MSN user account credentials to the ISA firewall when the Web Proxy authentication request is returned to the MSN Messenger. Since it is unlikely that the user's MSN Messenger credentials are the same as the user's domain credentials, the authentication attempt fails. To solve this problem, you need to bypass the HTTP 407 response returned by the Web Proxy filter on the ISA firewall. The best solution to this problem is to configure the clients as Firewall clients, and then configure the MSN Messenger sites for Direct Access. You can configure Direct Access in the Properties dialog box for the Network(s) from which the client(s) connect to the MSN site. When Direct Access for the MSN Messenger sites is enabled, the Web Proxy client ignores connections for those sites and hands off the connection to the client's Firewall client or SecureNAT client configuration. If you want to require authentication for outbound access, you should install the Firewall client on all client operating systems. The Firewall client transparently sends user credentials to the ISA firewall's Firewall Service.

Chapter 8

Publishing Network Services with ISA 2004 Firewalls

Topics in this Chapter:

- **Overview of Web Publishing and Server Publishing**

- **Creating and Configuring Non-SSL Web Publishing Rules**

- **Creating and Configuring SSL Web Publishing Rules**

- **Creating Server Publishing Rules**

- **Creating Mail Server Publishing Rules**

☑ **Summary**

☑ **Solutions Fast Track**

☑ **Frequently Asked Questions**

Overview of Web Publishing and Server Publishing

Web Publishing and Server Publishing Rules allow you to make servers and services on ISA firewall Protected Networks available to users on both protected and non-protected networks. Web and Server Publishing Rules allow you to make popular services, such as SMTP, NNTP, POP3, IMAP4, Web, OWA, NNTP, Terminal Services, and many more available to users on remote networks or on other Internal or Perimeter Networks.

Web Publishing Rules and Server Publishing Rules provide very different feature sets and are used for very different purposes. In general, Web Publishing Rules should be used to publish Web servers and services, and Server Publishing Rules should be used to publish non-Web servers and services. There are exceptions to these rules, and we will discuss these exceptions in this chapter.

We will begin the chapter with a discussion of the features and capabilities of Web and Server Publishing Rules. After this general overview of Web and Server Publishing Rules, we will go into the details of how to create and configure Web and Server Publishing Rules. We will then complete this chapter with several scenarios that demonstrate how Web and Server Publishing Rules are used on production networks.

Web Publishing Rules

Web Publishing Rules are used to publish Web sites and services. Web Publishing is sometimes referred to as "reverse proxy." When you publish a Web site, the ISA firewall's Web Proxy filter always intercepts the request and then proxies the request to the Web site published by the Web Publishing Rule.

Web Publishing Rules sport the following features:

- Provide proxied access to Web sites protected by the ISA firewall
- Perform deep application-layer inspection of connections made to published Web sites
- Path redirection
- Pre-authentication of connections made to published Web sites (Forward Basic authentication credentials)
- Reverse Caching of published Web sites
- Ability to publish multiple Web sites with a single IP address
- Ability to re-write URLs returned by the published Web site using the ISA firewall's Link Translator
- Support for forwarding either the ISA firewall's IP address or the original client's IP address to the Web site
- Support for SecurID authentication
- Support for RADIUS authentication

- Ability to schedule when connections are allowed to Published Web sites
- Port and Protocol Redirection

Let's look at each of these features in more detail.

Provide Proxied Access to Web Sites Protected by the ISA firewall

Web Publishing Rules provide proxied access to Web sites located on an ISA firewall Protected Network. Any Network that is not part of the default External Network is considered an ISA firewall Protected Network. A proxied connection is more secure than a routed and NATed connection because the entire communication is deconstructed and reconstructed by the ISA firewall. This allows the ISA firewall to perform very deep application-layer inspection of Web requests made to published Web sites that have been published using Web Publishing Rules.

The ISA firewall's Web Proxy filter handles all incoming Web connections made through Web Publishing Rules. Even when you unbind the Web Proxy filter from the HTTP protocol definition, the Web Proxy filter is always enabled for Web Publishing Rules. This is a security decision made by the ISA firewall team. They determined that non-proxied incoming connections to Protected Network Web servers should always be proxied to allow for the highest degree of protection for published Web servers.

Perform Deep Application-Layer Inspection of Connections Made to Published Web Sites

One of the major advantages of using Web Publishing Rules to publish Web sites on protected networks is the ISA firewall's ability to perform very deep application-layer inspection on all connections made to published Web sites. This deep application-layer inspection prevents attackers from sending malicious commands or code to the published Web site. This allows the ISA firewall to stop attacks at the perimeter and prevents the attacker from ever reaching the published Web server itself.

Deep application-layer inspection for Web requests is the responsibility of the ISA firewall's **HTTP Filter**. The ISA firewall's HTTP filter allows you to control virtually any aspect of an HTTP communication and block or allow connections based on almost any component of an HTTP communication.

Examples of how you can control connections to published Web sites include:

- Setting the maximum payload length
- Blocking high-bit characters
- Verifying normalization
- Blocking responses containing Windows executable content
- Setting the exact HTTP methods that you want to allow to the published Web site and block all others

- Allowing only a specific list of file extensions

- Allowing only a specific list of Request or Response headers

- Creating fine-tuned signatures that can block connections based on Request URLs, Request headers, Request body, Response headers, or Response body

We will go into some of the details of the HTTP Security Filter (HTTP Filter) later in this chapter, and we will also go into the deep details of the HTTP Security Filter in Chapter 10 on the ISA firewall's application-layer filtering feature set.

Path Redirection

Web Publishing Rules allow you to redirect connections based on the path indicated by the external user. Path redirection allows you to redirect connections based on the user's indicated path to an alternate directory on the same Web server, or to another Web server entirely.

For example, a user sends a request to www.msfirewall.org/kits. You want the request to be forwarded to a server named **WEBSERVER1** and to a directory on the server named **/deployment_kits**. You can configure the Web Publishing Rule to direct the path in the request (which is **/kits**) to the path on the internal Web server, **/deployment_kits**.

You can also use path redirection to forward the request to another Web server entirely. For example, suppose users submit requests for the following sites:

- www.msfirewall.org/scripts

- www.msfirewall.org/deployment_kits

You can create two Web Publishing Rules, one for incoming requests to www.msfirewall.org/scripts and one for www.msfirewall.org/deployment_kits. The request for www.msfirewall.org/script can be redirected to a Web server named **WEB-SERVER1**, and the second can be redirected to **WEBSERVER2**. We can even redirect the request to alternate paths on each Web server.

We will go over some examples of path redirection in the scenarios section of this chapter.

Pre-authentication of Connections Made to Published Web Sites

Web Publishing Rules can be configured to forward basic authentication credentials (basic delegation). This means that you can pre-authenticate the user at the ISA firewall. This pre-authentication prevents unauthenticated connections from ever reaching the Web server. Pre-authentication blocks attackers and other malicious users from leveraging unauthenticated connections to exploit known and unknown weaknesses in Web servers and applications.

One popular use of pre-authentication is for OWA Web sites. Instead of allowing unauthenticated connections from reaching the OWA Web site, the ISA firewall's Web Publishing Rule for the OWA Web site can be configured to authenticate the user. If the user successfully authenticates with the ISA firewall, then the connection request is passed to the OWA site. If the user cannot authenticate successfully with the ISA firewall, then the connection attempt is dropped at the firewall and never reaches the published Web site.

Pre-authentication also allows you to control who can access Web sites. You can configure Web Publishing Rules to allow only certain user groups to access the published Web site. So even if users are able to authenticate successfully, they will only be able to access the published Web site if they have permission to do so. In this way, the ISA firewall's Web Publishing Rules allow authentication and authorization for access to published Web sites.

The ISA firewall's delegation of basic authentication option allows the ISA firewall to authenticate the user and then forward the user credentials to the published Web site when the Web site request credentials. This prevents the user from being subjected to double authentication prompts. Instead of the user answering the Web site's request for authentication, the ISA firewall answers the request after successfully authenticating the user.

Reverse Caching of Published Web Sites

The ISA firewall can cache responses from Web sites published via Web Publishing Rules. Once a user makes a request for content on the published Web site, that content can be cached (stored) on the ISA firewall. When subsequent users make requests for the same content on the published Web server, the content is served from the ISA firewall's Web cache instead of being fetched from the Web server itself.

Caching responses from published Web sites reduces the load on the published Web server and on any network segments between the ISA firewall and the published Web server. Since the content is served from the ISA firewall's Web cache, the published Web server isn't exposed to the processing overhead required to service those Web requests. And because the content is served from the ISA firewall's Web cache instead of the published Web site, network traffic between the ISA firewall and the published Web site is reduced, which increases overall network performance on the corporate network.

You can also control the reverse caching on content. You may want users to always receive the freshest versions of content in some locations on your published Web server, while allowing the ISA firewall to cache other content on the published Web servers for a pre-defined time period. You can create cache rules on the ISA firewall in order to have fine-tuned control over what content is cached and how long that content is cached.

Ability to Publish Multiple Web Sites with a Single IP Address

Web Publishing Rules allow you to publish multiple Web sites using a single IP address on the external interface of the ISA firewall. The ISA firewall can do this because of its ability to perform stateful application-layer inspection. Part of the ISA firewall's stateful application-layer inspection feature set is its ability to examine the host header on the incoming request and make decisions on how to handle the incoming request based on that host header information.

For example, suppose you have a single IP address on the external interface of the ISA firewall. You want to publish two Web servers on an ISA firewall Protected Network. Users will access the Web sites using the URLs www.msfirewall.org and www.tacteam.net. All you need to do is create two Web Publishing Rules. One of the Web Publishing Rules will listen for incoming connections for www.msfirewall.org and forward those requests to the msfirewall.org server on the ISA firewall Protected Network, and the other Web Publishing Rule will listen for requests to www.tacteam.net and forward those requests to the Web site on the ISA firewall Protected Network responsible for the tacteam.net Web site.

The key to making this work, as we'll discuss later in this chapter, is to make sure that the public DNS resolves the fully-qualified domain names to the IP address on the external interface of the ISA firewall. Once the DNS issue is addressed, publishing two or two hundred Web sites with a single IP address is very simple using the ISA firewall's Web Publishing Rules.

Ability to Rewrite URLs Returned by the Published Web Site using the ISA Firewall's Link Translator

The ISA firewall's link translator can rewrite the responses that published Web servers send to users making requests. The link translator is useful when publishing Web sites that include hard-coded URLs in their responses, and those URLs are not accessible from remote locations.

For example, suppose you publish a Web site that hard codes the URLs in its responses and the hard-coded URLs include the private names of servers on the Protected Network. Such URLs would have the form http://server1/documents or http://webserver2/users. Since these are not fully-qualified domain names that are accessible from the Internet, the connection requests fail. This is a common problem with some SharePoint Portal Server Web sites.

The link translator solves this problem by rewriting the responses returned to the user accessing the Web site. The links http://server1/documents and http://webserver2/users are rewritten http://www.msfirewall.org/documents and http://www.tacteam.net/users, both of which are accessible from the Internet.

Link translation is also useful in some SSL scenarios. For example, when you are not using SSL from the ISA firewall to the Web server, but you are using SSL between the Web client on the Internet and the ISA firewall, the link translator can change the HTTP response returned by the Web server to an SSL response in the links presented to the user. This prevents the users from encountering broken links on the published Web page.

We will discuss the usages and configuration options of the link translator in this chapter and in detail in Chapter 10 on application-layer filtering.

Support for Forwarding either the ISA Firewall's IP Address, or the Original Web Client's IP Address to the Web Site

One of the limitations with Web Publishing Rules in ISA Server 2000 was that logs on the published Web server always showed the IP address for the internal network adapter of the ISA Server. When you published Web servers using Web Publishing Rules, the source IP address of the client connecting to the published Web server was replaced with the internal IP address of the ISA Server. This was a major barrier to adoption for many potential ISA Server administrators because they already had sunk significant costs into log analysis software installed on the published Web servers. Their only option was to use Server Publishing Rules, which isn't a good option because Server Publishing Rules do not confer the same high level of security as Web Publishing Rules.

The good news is that the new ISA firewall gives you the choice between forwarding the ISA firewall's IP address to the published Web server or forwarding the actual remote Web client's IP address to the published Web server. If you don't need the actual client's IP address in the Web server's log files, then use the default option, which is to replace the client IP address with the ISA firewall's network interface address. If you need to preserve the remote Web client's IP address, then you can choose the option to preserve the IP address.

We'll discuss the advantages and disadvantages of each approach when we cover the details of creating and configuring Web Publishing Rules later in this chapter.

Support for SecurID Authentication

RSA's SecurID is a two-factor authentication mechanism that requires that the user have something (the SecurID token) and know something (their user credentials). The ISA firewall comes with built-in support for SecurID authentication for Web servers and services published via Web Publishing Rules.

Support for RADIUS Authentication

Some organizations will choose to put the ISA firewall in a location where making the firewall a member of the user domain is not the best option. For example, if you have a back-to-back firewall configuration where the front-end firewall is an ISA firewall, you should not make the front-end ISA firewall a member of the user domain. You can still take advantage of the domain user database for authentication and authorization by using RADIUS for Web Publishing Rule authentication.

The ISA firewall can be configured as a RADIUS client to a RADIUS server on the corporate network. The RADIUS server can then be configured to authenticate users against the Active Directory or any other RADIUS-compliant directory on the corporate network. RADIUS authentication can be used for both inbound and outbound connections through the ISA firewall's Web Proxy filter. Setting up Web Publishing Rules using RADIUS is very easy and allows the ISA firewall support back-to-back firewall scenarios where the ISA firewall is the front-end firewall.

Ability to Schedule when Connections are Allowed to Published Web Sites

ISA Firewall Web Publishing Rules allow you to control when users can access the published Web site. You may have some Web sites that you only want accessed during work hours, and other Web sites that have high bandwidth requirements that you only want accessed during off-hours. You can control when users access published Web sites by applying either built-in or custom schedules to your Web Publishing Rules.

Port and Protocol Redirection

Web Publishing Rules allow you to perform both protocol and port redirection. Port redirection allows the ISA firewall to accept a connection request on one port and then forward that request to an alternate port on the published Web server. For example, the ISA firewall can listen to incoming requests on its Web listener on TCP port 80 and then redirect that connection to TCP 8888 on the published Web server on the ISA firewall Protected Network.

You can also perform protocol redirection using Web Publishing Rules. In contrast to port redirection, where the only change is the destination port, the ISA firewall's support for protocol redirection allows you to publish FTP sites using Web Publishing Rules. The incoming HTTP GET request made to the Web Publishing Rule's Web listener is transformed to an FTP GET and forwarded to the published FTP site on a ISA firewall Protected Network. Web Publishing Rules support protocol redirection from HTTP to FTP.

Server Publishing Rules

Like Web Publishing Rules, you can use Server Publishing Rules to provide access to servers and services on ISA firewall Protected Networks. The following features and capabilities characterize Server Publishing Rules:

- Server Publishing Rules are a form of reverse NAT or "Port Mapping" and do not proxy the connection.

- Almost all IP level and TCP/UDP protocols can be published using Server Publishing Rules.

- Server Publishing Rules do not support authentication.

- Application-layer filtering can be applied to a defined subset of Server Published protocols.

- You can configure port overrides to customize the listening ports and the port redirection. You can also lock down the source ports the requesting clients use to connect to the published server.

- You can use IP address controls over who can access published resources.

- The external client source IP address can be preserved or can be replaced with the ISA firewall's IP address.

- You can apply schedules that limit when the published server can be accessed via the Server Publishing Rule.

- Support for "port redirection" (or PAT – Port address translation) where connections can be received on one port and redirected to another port, providing the same functionality as that seen in many "hardware" firewall solutions.

Let's look at each of these in a bit more detail.

Server Publishing Rules are a Form of Reverse NAT or "Port Mapping" and do not Proxy the Connection

Server Publishing Rules are a form of either reverse NAT or port mapping, depending on whether you have a NAT or route relationship between the published server and the host that is connecting to the published server via the Server Publishing Rule. The Server Publishing Rule configures the ISA firewall to listen on a specific port and then forwards those connections to the published server on an ISA firewall Protected Network.

In contrast, Web Publishing Rules proxy the requests to the published Web server. Server Publishing Rules just change the source port and IP address before forwarding the connection to the published server. Proxied connections are completely deconstructed and reconstructed by the ISA firewall, and thus, confer a much higher level of application-layer inspection than Server Publishing Rules.

Almost All IP Level and TCP/UDP Protocols Can be Published using Server Publishing Rules

Web Publishing Rules only accept HTTP and HTTPS connections and forward them as HTTP, HTTPS, or FTP connections. In contrast, Server Publishing Rules can be used to publish almost any IP Level, TCP, or UDP protocol. This provides a great deal of flexibility in what services can be made available to hosts via Server Publishing Rules.

Server Publishing Rules do not Support Authentication

One of the major drawbacks of Web Publishing Rules compared to Server Publishing Rules is that Server Publishing Rules do not support pre-authentication at the ISA firewall. Authentication must be done by the server published by the Server Publishing Rule.

Application-Layer Filtering can be Applied To a Defined Subset of Server Published Protocols

Deep stateful application-layer inspection for connections made through Web Publishing Rules is performed by the ISA firewall's HTTP filter. Server Publishing Rules also support application-layer inspection through the use of Application Filters. The ISA firewall comes out of the box with the following application filters:

- DNS (security filter)
- FTP Access Filter

- H.323 Filter
- MMS Filter
- PNM Filter
- POP Intrusion Detection Filter (security filter)
- PPTP Filter
- RPC Filter (security filter)
- RTSP Filter
- SMTP Filter (security filter)
- SOCKS v4 Filter
- Web Proxy Filter (security filter)

A number of these filters are used to mediate complex protocols in the same way that NAT editors allow the use of complex protocols through a NAT device. Examples of types of access filters are the H.323 Filter, the MMS Filter, and the RTSP filter. In contrast, there are several application filters whose main job is to secure connections made through the ISA firewall by performing compliance testing against the connection. Example of these security filters are the DNS filter, POP Intrusion Detection Filter, and the RPC Filter.

Some of the application-layer filters perform both duties. They mediate complex protocol management for SecureNAT clients, and they also secure the connections they mediate. Filters fitting into this category include the FTP Access Filter and the RPC Filter.

We will cover application-layer filters in detail in Chapter 10.

Configuring Port Overrides to Customize the Listening Ports and the Port Redirection

Within each Server Publishing Rule is the ability to control the listening port, the destination port, and the port that the requesting client can use as a source port to access the Server-Published server. This provides you very granular control over port redirection (port mapping) for any server you publish using Server Publishing Rules.

You can use IP Address Controls Over who can Access Published Resources

Although Server Publishing Rules do not allow you to pre-authenticate users at the ISA firewall, you can configure Server Publishing Rules to limit IP addresses that can connect to the published server via the Server Publishing Rule. This type of IP address-based access control is used for publishing servers that should have limited access. An example of such a server is a Terminal Server on the corporate network that only administrators located at pre-defined addresses can access.

External Client Source IP Address can be Preserved Or Replaced with the ISA Firewall's IP address

In ISA Server 2000, Server Publishing Rules always preserved the original client IP address when it forwarded the connections to the published server on the internal network. The new ISA firewall improves on this by allowing you to choose to either preserve the original client IP address or replace the original client IP address with the IP address of the ISA firewall itself.

Apply Schedules Limiting when the Published Server can be Accessed via the Server Publishing Rule

Like Web Publishing Rules, Server Publishing Rules can be put on a schedule so that connections can only be established to the published server during the times allowed by the schedule. You can use one of the built-in schedules or create your own custom schedules.

Support for Port Redirection or PAT (Port Address Translation)

Like Web Publishing Rules, Server Publishing Rules allow you to customize how connections are forwarded to the published server and what ports are used to accept and forward the connection requests. For example, you might want to accept incoming connections for your private SMTP server on TCP port 26 and forward them to TCP port 27 on a published SMTP server. You can do this using the ISA firewall's port redirection (PAT) feature.

Creating and Configuring Non-SSL Web Publishing Rules

You can create Web Publishing Rules by using the ISA firewall Web Publishing Rule Wizard. The Web Publishing Rule Wizard walks you through the steps of creating a Web Publishing rule that allows you to publish Web servers and services on any ISA firewall Protected Network. In this section, we will go through the Web Publishing Rule Wizard and discuss the options you're presented with and the implications of those options.

In this section, we'll focus on Web Publishing Rules that do not require SSL-secured connections. SSL security requires additional steps, and we'll cover those steps in the next section where we focus on secure SSL Web Publishing Rules.

To start the Web Server Publishing Rule Wizard, open the **Microsoft Internet Security and Acceleration Server 2004** management console, and expand the server name. Click the **Firewall policy** node, and click the **Tasks** tab. On the **Tasks** tab, click the **Publish a Web Server** link.

You'll first encounter the **Welcome to the New Web Publishing Rule Wizard** page. On this page, you'll enter a name for the rule in the **Web publishing rule name** text box. Click **Next**.

The Select Rule Action Page

On the **Select Rule Action** page, you have the option to **Allow** or **Deny** connections to the published Web server. Note that the default option on the **Select Rule Action** page is **Allow**. This is in contrast to the default action on the Access Rule Wizard, where the default action is **Deny**. Most Web Publishing Rules will allow access to Web sites and specific paths within those Web sites. However, you can create Web Publishing Rules that deny access to fine-tune Web Publishing Rules that allow access. Choose the **Allow** option and click **Next**. Figure 8.1 shows the default option on the Select Rule Action page.

Figure 8.1 The Select Rule Action Page

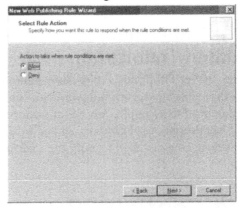

The Define Website to Publish Page

On the **Define Website to Publish** page, you provide information about the Web site on the ISA firewall Protected Network. As you'll see in Figure 8.2, you have the following options on this page:

- Computer name or IP address
- Forward the original host header instead of the actual one (specified above)
- Path
- Site

In the **Computer name or IP address** text box, enter either the IP address of the fully-qualified domain name of the Web server or the ISA firewall Protected Network. If you use a FQDN, make sure that the ISA firewall is able to resolve that name to the Web server's IP address on the corporate network and *not* the IP address on the external interface of the ISA firewall. This is a very common error among ISA firewall administrators.

You can ensure that the name is properly resolved to the private address of the Web server by creating a split DNS infrastructure or by using a HOSTS file entry on the ISA firewall.

One of the primary advantages of using a FQDN in the **Computer name or IP address** field is that the Web site name shows up in the URL field in the ISA firewall's Web Proxy log. If you use an IP address, only the IP address of the published server will appear in this field and make log analysis more difficult to perform efficiently.

We will discuss the virtues of the split DNS infrastructure and how to create one later in this chapter. Figure 8.2 shows the options on the Define Website to Publish page.

Figure 8.2 The Define Website to Publish Page

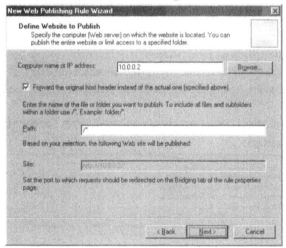

The **Forward the original host header instead of the actual one (specified above)** is an interesting option because its exact meaning is not entirely clear. What it's supposed to mean is that instead of the host header value in the **Computer name or IP address** text box being sent to the published server, the actual host header in the request sent by the external user is forwarded to the published Web server. This is an important issue if you are hosting multiple Web sites on a single Web server and differentiate the Web sites by using different host headers for each one.

You can see the effects of forwarding, or not forwarding, the original host headers in figures 8.3, 8.4, and 8.5. In Figure 8.3 you can see the host headers as seen on the external interface of the ISA firewall from a client connection request for **www.msfirewall.org**. The **HTTP: Host =www.msfirewall.org** host header appears in the network monitor trace.

Figure 8.3 HTTP Headers Seen on the External Interface of the ISA Firewall

```
HTTP: GET Request from Client
    HTTP: Request Method =GET
    HTTP: Uniform Resource Identifier =/
    HTTP: Protocol Version =HTTP/1.1
    HTTP: Accept = image/gif, image/x-xbitmap, image/jpeg, image/pjpeg, */*
    HTTP: Accept-Language =en-us
    HTTP: Accept-Encoding =gzip, deflate
    HTTP: User-Agent =Mozilla/4.0 (compatible; MSIE 6.0; Windows NT 5.1)
    HTTP: Host =www.msfirewall.org
    HTTP: Connection =Keep-Alive
```

When the Web Publishing Rule is configured to not forward the original Host header, and an IP address (or an alternate name) is used in the **Computer name or IP address** text box, you will see on the Network Monitor trace, in Figure 8.4, taken on the published Web server that the Host header entry is **HTTP: Host =10.0.0.2**, which isn't the Host header contained in the original client address. It's the entry we put in the **Computer name or IP address** text box. Figure 8.4 shows an example of HTTP headers seen on the Published Web Server when the original Host header is not forwarded.

Figure 8.4 HTTP Headers Seen on the Published Web Server when Original Host Header is not Forwarded

```
HTTP: GET Request from Client
    HTTP: Request Method =GET
    HTTP: Uniform Resource Identifier =/
    HTTP: Protocol Version =HTTP/1.1
    HTTP: Reverse-Via = ISALOCAL
    HTTP: Host =10.0.0.2
    HTTP: If-None-Match ="0325lecdac21:af2"
    HTTP: User-Agent =Mozilla/4.0 (compatible; MSIE 6.0; Windows NT 5.1)
    HTTP: If-Modified-Since =Sat, 22 Feb 2003 00:48:30 GMT
    HTTP: Accept = image/gif, image/x-xbitmap, image/jpeg, image/pjpeg, */*
    HTTP: Accept-Language =en-us
    HTTP: Connection =Keep-Alive
```

However, when we enable **Forward the original host header instead of the actual one (specified above)**, Figure 8.5 shows what appears on the published Web server. In this case, the Network Monitor trace shows that the host header seen on the Web server is **HTTP: Host =www.msfirewall.org**. See Figure 8.5 for headers seen on the published Web server when the original Host header is forwarded.

Figure 8.5 HTTP Headers Seen on the Published Web Server when Forwarding the Original Host Header

```
HTTP: GET Request from Client
    HTTP: Request Method =GET
    HTTP: Uniform Resource Identifier =/
    HTTP: Protocol Version =HTTP/1.1
    HTTP: Reverse-Via = ISALOCAL
    HTTP: Host =www.msfirewall.org
    HTTP: If-None-Match ="0325lecdac21:af2"
    HTTP: User-Agent =Mozilla/4.0 (compatible; MSIE 6.0; Windows NT 5.1)
    HTTP: If-Modified-Since =Sat, 22 Feb 2003 00:48:30 GMT
    HTTP: Accept = image/gif, image/x-xbitmap, image/jpeg, image/pjpeg, */*
    HTTP: Accept-Language =en-us
    HTTP: Connection =Keep-Alive
```

In the **Path** text box, you enter the paths you want accessible on the published Web server. You can enter a name of a specific file or folder, or you can allow access to all files and folders within a folder by using the /★ wildcard. This option allows you to restrict access to specified files and folders. Although this wizard page only allows you to enter a single path, we'll see later that we can enter the **Properties** dialog box of the Web Publishing Rule and create additional paths and even path redirections.

The **Site** box isn't a text box, so you can't enter anything in it. Instead, it shows you the URL that will be accessible on the published Web site..

In this example, we entered **10.0.0.2** for the **Computer name or IP address** and chose to forward the original host header. We entered a path of /★. Click **Next**.

The Public Name Details Page

On the **Public Name Details** page, you enter information about what FQDNs or IP addresses users will use to connect to the published Web site via this Web Publishing Rule. You have the following options on this page:

- Accept requests for
- Path (optional)
- Site

The **Accept requests for** drop-down list provides you with two choices: **Any domain name** and **This domain name (type below)**. If you choose **Any domain name**, any requests for a domain name or IP address are accepted by the Web listener for this rule. This is a *very poor selection* because it can potentially expose you to viruses or worm attacks, or attacks from malicious users.

For example, some prevalent worms will send requests to the TCP port 80 or to bogus domain names (such as www.worm.com) to the IP address used by the Web listener for this rule. If you select **Any domain name**, then the Web listener will accept these as valid requests and continue processing them. This is in spite of the fact that you are not hosting any resources for the bogus domain name the worm or the malicious user uses to access the IP address the Web listener is using on the external interface of the ISA firewall.

A better option, and the one we recommend that you always use for your Web Publishing Rules, is **This domain name (type below)**. When you choose this option, you enter the exact domain name that must be included in the users request to the Web listener. If you want to accept requests only for the www.msfirewall.org domain, then incoming requests for http://1.1.1.1 or http://www.worm.com will be dropped because they do not match the domain name you want this rule to apply to.

When you select **This domain name (type below)**, you must enter the domain name you want this rule to accept in the **Public name** text box. In this example, we entered the FQDN **www.msfirewall.org**. The **Public Name Details** Wizard page allows you to enter only a single domain name, but you can add more domain names after the wizard is completed. However, we highly recommend that you use a single domain name per Web publishing rule.

The **Path (optional)** text box allows you to restrict the path(s) that users can access via this Web Publishing Rules. You might want to allow users access to only specific directories on your Web site and not to the entire site. Although you can only enter a single path on the **Public Name Details** page (Figure 8.6), you can enter additional paths after the wizard is completed, in the **Properties** dialog box for this rule.

Figure 8.6 The Public Name Details Page

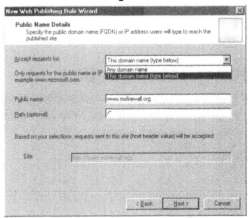

The Select Web Listener Page and Creating an HTTP Web Listener

You assign a Web listener to the Web Publishing Rule on the **Select Web Listener** page. A Web listener is a Network Object you use in Web Publishing Rules. The Web listener "listens" on an interface or IP address that you choose for incoming connections to the port you define. For example, if you create a Web publishing rule that allows HTTP public access to the www.msfirewall.org site, you would create a Web listener that listens on the external interface of the ISA firewall using the IP address that external users resolve www.msfirewall.org.

NOTE

We assume in the above example that the external interface of the ISA firewall has a public address bound to it. The situation is slightly different if you have a firewall in front of the ISA firewall and have a NAT relationship between the front-end firewall and the ISA firewall. In that case, external clients would resolve the name www.msfirewall.org to the public address on the front-end firewall that is mapped to the IP address used on the Web listener on the back-end ISA firewall.

You have two options on the **Select Web Listener** page if there are listeners already configured on the ISA firewall:

- Edit
- New

Edit allows you to configure existing Web listeners, and **New** allows you to create a new Web listener. In this example, there are no listeners yet created on the ISA firewall, so we click **New**.

On the **Welcome to the New Web Listener Wizard** page, enter a name for the Web listener in the **Web listener name** text box. In this example, we'll name the Web listener **HTTP Listener** (since we only have a single IP address bound to the external interface; if there were multiple addresses, we could add the number in the last octet to the listener definition to make it easier to identify). Click **Next**.

On the **IP Addresses** page, select the Networks and IP addresses on those Networks that you want the listener to listen on. Recall that each interface on the ISA firewall represents a Network, and all IP addresses reachable from that interface are considered part of that Network. The Web listener can listen on any Network defined on the ISA firewall.

In this example, we want to accept incoming connections from Internet users, so we'll select the **External** network by putting a checkmark in its checkbox. At this point, the Web listener will accept connection requests to all IP addresses bound to the external interface of the ISA firewall. We recommend that if you have multiple IP addresses bound to an interface that you configure the Web listener to use only one of those addresses. This provides you greater flexibility because you can customize the properties of each listener. If you allow the listener to listen on all IP addresses on the interface, then a single set of listener properties will be assigned to it.

Click **Addresses** on the **IP Addresses** page, as shown in Figure 8.7.

Figure 8.7 The IP Addresses Page

On the **Network Listener IP Selection** page (Figure 8.8) you have three options:

- All IP addresses on the ISA Server computer that are in the selected network
- The default IP address on the ISA Server computer in the selected network

■   Specified IP addresses on the ISA Server computer in the selected network

All IP addresses on the ISA Server computer that are in the selected network is the default and is the same as checking the checkbox on the previous page without making any customizations. This option allows the listener to listen on all addresses bound to the interface representing the Network(s) you select. When you select more than one Network, the Web listener will listen on IP addresses bound to each of the Networks you select.

The default IP address on the ISA Server computer in the selected network allows the listener to accept connections to the *primary* IP address bound to the Network interface. The primary address is the first address on the list of addresses bound to the Network interface. This is also the interface that is used for connections *leaving* that interface.

Specified IP addresses on the ISA Server computer in the selected network allows you to select the specific IP addresses you want the listener to use. The available IP addresses for the Network appear in the **Available IP addresses** section. You select the IP address you want the Web listener to use, and click **Add**; it then appears in the **Selected IP Addresses** section.

The example in Figure 8.8 demonstrates the Network centric nature of the ISA firewall. Before we selected an address, both **172.16.0.1** and **192.168.1.70** were in the **Available IP Addresses** list. These two addresses are actually bound to two *different* adapters. The **192.168.1.70** address is bound to the external interface (the one with the default gateway configured on it), and the **172.16.0.1** address is bound to a DMZ interface on the ISA firewall. The reason why both these addresses are included is that the default External Network includes *all IP addresses that are not defined as part of a Network*. Since we haven't defined the DMZ Network, the address bound to the DMZ interface is part of the default External network.

In Figure 8.8, we've selected the IP address bound to the external interface of the ISA firewall. Click **OK**. Then click **Next** on the **IP Addresses** page.

Figure 8.8 The External Network Listener IP Selection Dialog Box

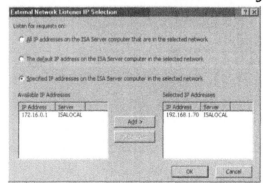

The **Port Specification** page in Figure 8.9 allows you to define the TCP port on which the Web listener accepts incoming connections. The default port is TCP port **80**.

You can change this port to any port you like, as long as it does not collide with a socket already in use on the ISA firewall.

You also have the option to enable an SSL listening port on the Web listener. We recommend that you configure your HTTP and SSL listeners separately. This is a new feature in the 2004 ISA firewall. We will cover the details of configuring SSL listeners in the next section of this chapter.

> **W**ARNING
>
> You cannot configure SSL on the listener unless you have a machine certificate stored in the ISA firewall's machine certificate store. We will discuss the details of this configuration in more detail later in this chapter.

In the example in Figure 8.9, we use the default port, and click **Next**.

Figure 8.9 The Port Specification Page

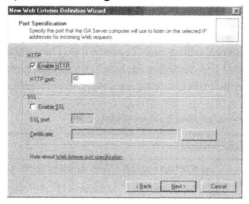

> **W**ARNING
>
> A socket is a combination of a transport protocol (TCP or UDP), an IP address, and a port number. Only one process can bind itself to a socket. If another process on the ISA firewall is using the same socket that you want to use for your Web listener, then you will need to disable the other process using the socket, or choose another port number for the Web listener to use. This is a common problem for ISA firewall administrators who attempt to publish Web resources located on the ISA firewall itself. As mentioned many other times in this book, you should *never* run services on the ISA firewall other than the ISA firewall services, services that the ISA firewall depends upon, and add-on services that enhance the ISA firewall's stateful application-layer inspection abilities.

Click **Finish** on **Completing the New Web Listener Wizard** page. The details of the Web listener appears on the **Listener properties** page. We can now click **Edit** to customize several aspects of the Web listener.

Click **Edit**, and then click the **Preferences** tab (Figure 8.10). Here you can configure the **Authentication** and **Advanced** properties for the listener.

Figure 8.10 The Preferences Tab

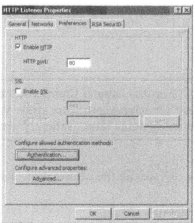

Click **Authentication**, and you'll see the authentication options available for the Web listener in the **Authentication** dialog box (Figure 8.11). The default authentication method is **Integrated**. Table 8.1 describes each of the authentication methods available for Web listeners and a short description of the important characteristics of each method.

Table 8.1 Web Listener Authentication Methods

Authentication Method	Details
Basic	Supported by all Web clients and servers
	User names and passwords are encoded (Base64), but not encrypted. Easy to obtain with any network analyzer
	Uses SSL to secure basic authentication
	Supports delegation of basic authentication
Digest	Credentials sent as one-way hash
	Web browser must support HTTP 1.1
	Requires domain controller to store password using reversible encryption
	WDigest encryption also supported (Windows Server 2003 only)
	User name and domain name case sensitive
	When both ISA firewall and DC are Windows Server 2003, WDigst is used by default
	Windows NT 4.0 user accounts do not support Digest authentication

Continued

Table 8.1 Web Listener Authentication Methods

Authentication Method	Details
Integrated	Uses NTLM, Kerberos and Negotiate authentication mechanisms
	User name and password hashed before sending
	Logged-on user credentials automatically sent to ISA firewall
	If logged-on user not authenticated, log-on dialog box appears
	Log-on dialog box continues to appear until valid credentials are entered or CANCEL is selected
RADIUS	RADIUS both authenticates and authorizes
	RADIUS users must enter credentials in DOMAIN\User format
	ISA firewall uses MD5 hash of the shared secret to authenticate with RADIUS server to encrypt user name, password, and characteristics of the connection
	Recommended to use IPSec to secure channel between ISA firewall and RADIUS server
	RADIUS servers configured on the ISA firewall are used for all rules and objects that use RADIUS authentication. You cannot configure separate lists of RADIUS servers for VPN and Web listener authentication. However, you can select separate RADIUS servers from the list for Web Publishing Rules and VPN authentication
	When using RADIUS for Web Publishing Rules, make sure you enable forwarding of basic authentication credentials in the Web Publishing Rule.
SecurID	Two-factor authentication
	Physical token and PIN (personal ID number) required
	SA ACE/Agent runs on ISA firewall
	RSA ACE/Agent passes credentials to RSA/ACE server
	Cookie placed on user's browser after successful authentication; cookie is held in memory and not written to disk. Cookie removed from memory when browser closed
	Use SSL to secure connection between Web browser and ISA firewall when using SecurID authentication
	Refer to ISA Server 2004 Help for details of configuration
	Cannot be used in combination with other authentication methods.

Continued

Table 8.1 Web Listener Authentication Methods

Authentication Method	Details
OWA Forms-based	Used to publish Outlook Web Access (OWA)
	ISA firewall generates log-on form
	Cookie sent to browser when authentication successful
	Credential information not cached on client browser
	Users must reauthenticate if browser is closed, leave the OWA Web site
	Can't set session time-out limits
	SSL connection between browser and ISA firewall recommended
	Can change password during session, but must reauthenticate after password change
	Can only be used with RADIUS authentication after a hotfix is applied. Check out http://support.microsoft.com/default.aspx?scid=kb;en-us;884560 for details on this configuration.
SSL Certificate	Users authenticate by presenting user certificates
	Most secure form of authentication

Authentication options are shown in Figure 8.11.

Figure 8.11 The Authentication Dialog Box

The authentication option you select applies only if you limit access to the Web Publishing Rule to a user or group. If you allow All Users access to the Web Publishing Rule, then the authentication option is ignored. These authentication options apply only to authentication performed by the ISA firewall itself, *not* to authentication that may be required by the published Web site.

All authentication methods except RADIUS require that the ISA firewall be a member of a domain. This is not a significant issue unless you have a back-to-back firewall configuration where the front-end firewall is an ISA firewall (the back-end firewall can be any kind of firewall you like, including ISA firewalls). If the ISA firewall is on the front-end and you want to authenticate users at the front-end server, we recommend that you use only RADIUS authentication. When the ISA firewall is on the back-end, we always recommend that you make the firewall a member of the Active Directory domain so that you can leverage the many security advantages inherent in domain membership. However, if there are political reasons why the back-end ISA firewall cannot be made a member of the domain, you can still leverage RADIUS authentication in the scenario, too.

Put a checkmark in the **Require all users to authenticate** checkbox if you require authentication for all Web Publishing Rules that will use this listener.

> ## WARNING
>
> While the **Require all users to authenticate** option should be used for Web listeners used for Web Publishing Rules, we *do not* recommend that you use this option for Web listeners used for outbound access through the ISA firewall for Web Proxy clients. We discuss this issue in more detail in Chapter 5.

Click **RADIUS Servers** to select or add a RADIUS server for RADIUS authentication.

Click **Select Domain** to set a default domain if you wish to choose Basic authentication.

Click **Configure,** to the right of **Configure OWA forms–based authentication**, to customize the cookie parameters for the OWA connection. We will discuss this issue in more detail later in this chapter.

Click **OK** to close the **Authentication** dialog box. Click **Advanced**, in the **HTTP Listener Properties** dialog box. This brings up the **Advanced Settings** dialog box, as shown in Figure 8.12. In the **Advanced Settings** dialog box, you can set the **Number of connections** you want to support on the listener and the idle connection timeout for the listener. Click **OK** to close the **Advanced Settings** dialog box.

> ## TIP
>
> Out of the box, you cannot use RADIUS authentication together with Forms-based authentication. There is a hotfix you can apply to the ISA firewall that will enable you to use Forms-based authentication together with RADIUS authentication. For more information on how to use FBA with RADIUS authentication, check out **You cannot use the RADIUS authentication protocol when you use the Outlook Web Access (OWA) Forms-Based Authentication on a Web publishing rule to publish an internal Web site such as OWA in ISA Server 2004** at http://support.microsoft.com/default.aspx?scid=kb;en-us;884560

Figure 8.12 Tthe Advanced Settings Dialog Box

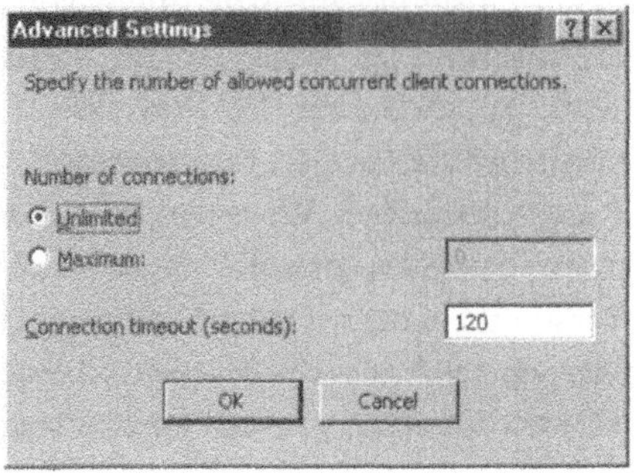

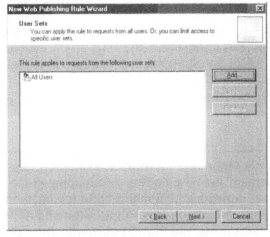

Click **OK** to close the **HTTP Listener Properties** dialog box and click **Next** on the **Select Web Listener** page.

The User Sets Page

On the **User Sets** page (Figure 8.13) you configure whether authentication is required to access the Web server published by this Web Publishing Rule. The default settings is **All Users**, which means that authentication is not required to access the Web server published by this Web Publishing Rule. Click the **Add** button if you want to require authentication. You will be presented with the **Add Users** dialog box where you can select the User Set representing the users you want the rule to apply to.

Note that the **All Users** option only means that authentication is not required when the Web listener is not configured to require authentication. To configure the Web Publishing Rule to allow the user of anonymous credentials, use the **All Users** user set.

Figure 8.13 The User Sets Page

We will discuss User Sets, how to create them and how to use them in Chapter 10. Click **Next** on the **User Sets** page and then click **Finish** on the **Completing the New Web Publishing Rule Wizard** page.

The Web Publishing Rule Properties Dialog Box

The new Web Publishing Rule appears in the **Firewall Policy** list. Right click the **Web Publishing Rule** and click **Properties**. The Web Publishing Rules **Properties** dialog box has twelve tabs:

- General
- Action
- From
- To
- Traffic
- Listener
- Public Name
- Paths
- Bridging
- Users
- Schedule
- Link Translation

Let's look at the options in each of these tabs. You'll find that there are many options on these tabs that were not exposed in the Web Publishing Rule Wizard.

The General Tab

On this tab you can change the name of the Web Publishing Rule by entering a name in the **Name** text box. You can also enter a description for the rule in the **Description (optional)** text box. You can enable or disable the Web Publishing Rule by enabling or disabling the **Enable** checkbox, as shown in Figure 8.14.

Figure 8.14 The General Tab.

Action

On the **Action** tab (Figure 8.15) you either Allow or Deny access to the site configured in the Web Publishing Rule. You also have the option to **Log requests matching this rule**. If you find that your log files are getting too large, and the site being accessed by the rule isn't of any particular interest to you, then you might consider not logging requests handled by this rule. However, we do not recommend that you disable logging for any publishing rules because most of these rules represent connections from untrusted Networks.

Click **Apply** to save the changes you make on this tab.

Figure 8.15 The Action Tab

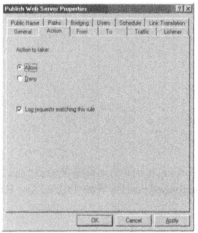

From

On the **From** tab, configure locations where you want the Web Publishing Rule to accept connections for the Published Site. The default location is **Anywhere**, which means that any host that can reach the IP address or addresses used for the Web listener can access this Web Publishing Rule.

You can limit access to this Web Publishing Rule by clicking **Anywhere** and then clicking **Remove**. After removing the **Anywhere** entry, click **Add**. In the **Add Network Entities** dialog box, click the folder that contains the Network Object you want to allow access to the Web Publishing Rule.

There is also the option to fine-tune access to the rule by setting exceptions in the **Exceptions** frame. For example, you might want to allow access to the Web Publishing Rule to all Networks *except* for hosts on the Network where the published server is located. This is generally a good idea because you do not want corporate network hosts looping back through the ISA firewall to connect to resources located on the corporate network.

Click **Apply** on the **From** page, Figure 8.16, after making your changes.

Figure 8.16 The From Tab

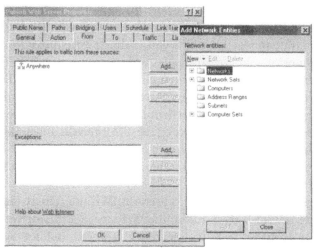

To

The **To** tab is one of the most important tabs in the **Properties** dialog box. The reason for this is that the entry you put in the **Server** text box defines the host name in the URL that Web Publishing Rule sends to the published Web site. The entry you put in the **Server** text box replaces the host header that was included in the original client request sent to the ISA firewall. If you don't want the ISA firewall to replace the entry in the host header with the entry in the **Server** text box, then put a checkmark in the **Forward the original host header instead of the actual one (specified above)** checkbox.

Another important option on the **To** tab is the ability to specify how the ISA firewall proxies the requests to the server listed in the **Server** text box. You have two options:

- Requests appear to come from the ISA Server computer
- Requests appear to come from the original client

Requests appear to come from the ISA Server computer is useful when you don't want to make the published Web server a SecureNAT client. One of the primary disadvantages of the SecureNAT client configuration is that the entire routing infrastructure must be aware that the ISA firewall should be the gateway to the Internet. Many organizations have an established routing infrastructure, and they don't want to make the ISA firewall the route of last resort for all hosts on the network. You can get around this problem by allowing the ISA firewall to replace the remote host's IP address with its own. When the published server returns its response, it only needs to know the route to the local interface on the ISA firewall. It doesn't need a route to the Internet and doesn't need to make the ISA firewall its default gateway.

Requests appear to come from the original client allows the ISA firewall to preserve the IP address of the remote host sending the request for published Web site resources. The advantage to this approach is that if you have log-reporting software on the Web server itself, you will be able to report on the actual IP addresses of the hosts connecting to the Web site. If you don't select this option, it will appear in the Web site's log files that all connections are coming from the ISA firewall's IP address.

One issue with this approach is that if you enable reverse proxy for the published Web site, you will notice a number of requests sourcing from the ISA firewall itself, and you might misinterpret this as the ISA firewall failing to preserve the IP address of the requesting host. This is not true, and there is no bug or problem with this ISA firewall software in this regard. The issue is that when performing reverse proxy, the ISA firewall serves the responses from its cache. However, the ISA firewall, in its role as reverse Proxy server, needs to check on the status of the objects on the Web site, and this status check generates requests from the ISA firewall's address to the published Web site, which subsequently appears in the Web site's logs.

For this reason and more, we prefer to perform Web site activity analysis on the ISA firewall's Web Proxy service logs instead of the Web site logs themselves. There are exceptions to this rule, but for sites that are public sites only and not accessed by internal users, the Web Proxy logs on the ISA firewall provide the most rich and most accurate information.

Options for the **To** tab are shown in Figure 8.17.

TIP

We recommend that you use a FQDN in the **Server** text box on the **To** tab. This will allow the Web Proxy log to include this name in the log file entries and make it easier for you to audit access to the published servers. In addition, the FQDN will appear in any reports you create.

Figure 8.17 The To Tab

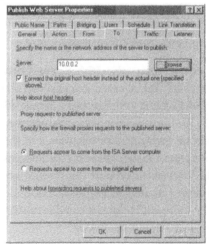

Traffic

On the **Traffic** tab, you'll see a list of protocols allowed by this Web Publishing Rule. The protocols are not configurable on this tab. Instead, the allowed protocols are determined by the protocol support set on the Web listener configured for this publishing rule.

Notify HTTP users to use HTTPS instead is disabled in this example because we are not using an SSL listener. When this option is available, it allows the ISA firewall to return an error page to the user accessing the Web site through the Web Publishing Rule showing that HTTPS, instead of HTTP, should be used. It's a common error for users to enter HTTP, instead of HTTPS, when accessing secure Web sites. Fortunately, it takes less than three seconds to resubmit the request by adding an "s" to the protocol in the request. Forcing users to enter the correct protocol also encourages users to use correct Internet hygiene.

Require 128-bit encryption for HTTPS traffic is also not available because this rule doesn't apply to SSL publishing. This option allows you to control the level of encryption security for SSL connections to the published Web site. All modern Windows clients support 128-bit encryption right out of the box, but there are outdated Windows clients and non-Windows clients that do not support 128-bit encryption, and you might want to block connections from these relatively unsecure clients.

Click **Apply** to save the changes you made on the traffic tab, as shown in Figure 8.18.

Figure 8.18 The Traffic Tab

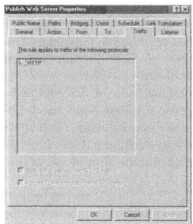

Listener

On the **Listener** tab, you can view the characteristics of the listener currently in use by the Web Publishing Rule, and you can change the properties of the listener here, as well, by clicking **Properties**. You can also create a new Web listener by clicking **New** and then applying the new listener to this Web Publishing Rule.

If you have already created multiple Web listeners on this ISA firewall, you can change the listener used by the Web Publishing Rule by clicking the down arrow on the **This rule applies to requests received on the following listener** drop-down box.

Click **Apply** after you make changes on the **Listener** tab (Figure 8.19).

Figure 8.19 The Listener Tab

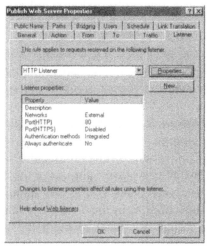

Public Name

The **Public Name** tab allows you to view and configure the names that can be used to access the Web server published via this Web Publishing Rule. In the Web Publishing Rule we created in this example, we chose the name **www.msfirewall.org** for the public name that can be used to access the Web server. If a request comes in on the Web listener used by this Web Publishing Rule for a FQDN that is different from this one, this rule will ignore the connection request. Note that if this Web listener is used by other Web Publishing Rules, the incoming request will be compared to the **Public Name** entries in those other Web Publishing Rules. If no Web Publishing Rule includes a **Public Name** that matches that in the Host header of the incoming Web request, the connection will be dropped.

Also, note that a single Web Publishing Rule can be used for multiple host names. The key to success is to make sure that each of these host names resolves to the IP address or addresses that the Web listener bound to this rule is listening on. For example, the Web listener for this rule might be listening on an IP address that resolves to both www.msfirewall.org and www.tacteam.net. If that is the case, then we could add www.tacteam.net to the **Public Name** list. However, this also means that the same Paths, Bridging, Users, Schedule, and other settings would be applied to the connections coming in to the www.tacteam.net Web site. This might not always be the case, and this is why we recommend that you create separate Web Publishing Rules for each site that you publish.

You can **Add** a new Public name to the list by clicking **Add**, and you can **Remove** or **Edit** a selected public name by clicking **Edit** and **Remove**.

Click **Apply** when you have made your desired changes to the **Public Name** tab, as shown in Figure 8.20.

Figure 8.20 The Public Name Tab

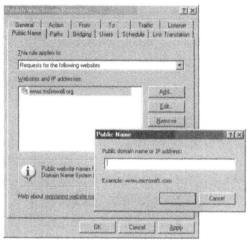

Paths

The **Paths** tab allows you to control how requests to different paths included in the requests are handled by the Web Publishing Rule. You'll notice in the path list that there are two columns: the **External Path** and the **Internal Path** column.

The **External Path** is the path in the request made by the user accessing the Web site through this Web Publishing Rule. For example, if a user enters the URL http://www.msfirewall.org/docs into the browser, then the external path is **/docs**. If a user enters the URL http://www.tacteam.net/graphics into the browser, then the external path is **/graphics**.

The **Internal** path is the path that the ISA firewall will forward the request to based on the entry for the **External** path. For example, suppose we set the **External Path** as **/docs** and the **Internal Path** as **/publicdocuments**. When the user enters the URL http://www.msfirewall.org/docs into the browser, and the ISA firewall's Web listener for this rule accepts the connection for the request, then the ISA firewall will forward the request to the site listed in the **To** tab to the path **/publicdocuments**. If the entry in the **To** tab is **10.0.0.2**, then the ISA firewall forwards the request to the published Web server as **http://10.0.0.2/publicdocuments**.

Path redirection provides you a lot of flexibility in your Web publishing rules and allows you to simplify the paths external users use to access published resources without requiring you to change directory names on the published Web server.

If you want access to all the folders and files under a particular directory, enter the path using the **/path/*** format. If you want to allow access to a single file in a path, enter the path in the **/path** format. For example, if you want to allow access to all the files in the **documents** directory on the Web server, enter for the **Internal** path **/doc-uments/***. If you want to allow access to only the **names.htm** file in the **documents** directory, then enter the path as **/documents/names.htm**. An example of the **Paths** tab is shown in Figure 8.21.

Figure 8.21 The Paths Tab

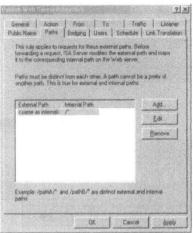

Click **Add** to add a new path. In the **Path mapping** dialog box, enter an *internal path* for **Specify the folder on the Web site that you want to publish. To publish the entire Web site, leave this field blank** text box. Next, select either the **Same as published folder** or **The following folder** option, as shown in Figure 8.22. If external users enter the same path, select the **Same as published folder**. If the users will enter a different path, select **The following folder** and enter the alternate path in the text box.

Figure 8.22 The Path Mapping Dialog Box

![Path mapping dialog box showing "Specify the folder on the Web site that you want to publish. To publish the entire Web site, leave this field blank." with a text field, "Examples: /mypath, /mypath/*", an External Path section with radio buttons "Same as published folder" (selected) and "The following folder", a text field, and OK/Cancel buttons.]

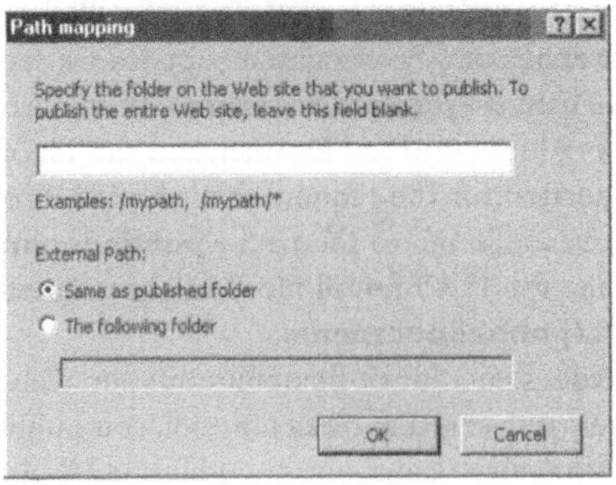

TIP

Many ISA firewall administrators wish to redirect to the root of the Web site based on the path entered by the user. For example, if the user enters the URL http://www.msfirewall.org/firewalldocs, then the request should be forwarded to the root of the internal Web server at **10.0.0.2**. You can do this by entering the external path as **/firewalldocs/*** and the internal path as **/** as seen in Figure 8.23. All connections made to the **firewalldocs** directory are now redirected to the root of the server listed in the **To** tab, which in this case is **10.0.0.2**.

Figure 8.23 Redirecting to the Web Root Using a Path

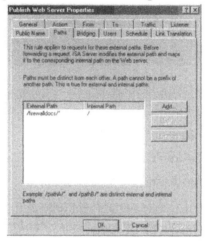

A common desire among ISA firewall administrators is to redirect connections to the root of a Web site to the /Exchange folder on Outlook Web Access (OWA) Web sites. This is easy to do by using a path redirection on the **Path** tab. In this case, the external path is /* and the internal path is **/Exchange**. Notice that you must use a backslash at the end of the path because there is already an entry for **/Exchange/** after running the Mail Server Publishing Wizard (we'll talk more about the Mail Server Publishing Wizard later in this chapter). The **Paths** tab with this type of OWA configuration would look like that seen in Figure 8.24.

The reason why this works is because the OWA Web site is kind enough to help hapless users who don't understand the difference between UNC and HTTP paths. The OWA Web site will accept the backslash as a valid request and convert it on the fly to a forward slash. This allows you to use the **Internal Path** statement /Exchange\ and /exchange/* in the **Path** tab, where it would, otherwise, not be possible to do this if you had to enter forward slashes for both entries because the ISA firewall will not allow you to enter multiple path mappings that use the same path prefix. The OWA configuration is shown in Figure 8.24.

Figure 8.24 Mapping the OWA Web Site Root to the Exchange Folder

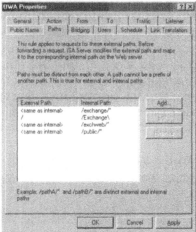

Another thing you can do with path statements is redirect to different servers. For example, take the following URLs:

■ www.msfirewall.org/scripts

■ www.msfirewall.org/articles

■ www.msfirewall.org/ids-ips

All three URLs point to the same FQDN and only differ in the path. You can create three Web Publishing Rules, each one using the same **Public Name** and each one including a different path configuration and a different server on the **To** tab. When a user makes a request using one of these three URLs, the request will be forwarded to the appropriate server based on the settings on the **Public Name**, **Paths**, and **To** tabs.

Bridging

The **Bridging** tab, as shown in Figure 8.25, allows you to configure port or protocol redirection for the Web Publishing Rule. You have the following options:

■ Web Server

■ Redirect requests to HTTP port

■ Redirect requests to SSL port

■ Use a certificate to authenticate to the SSL Web server

■ FTP server

■ Use this port when redirecting FTP requests

The **Web Server** option configures the Web Publishing Rule to forward HTTP or HTTPS requests. There is no protocol redirection with this option.

The **Redirect requests to HTTP port** option when checked allows you to redirect incoming HTTP requests for this Web Publishing Rule and Web listener to the published Web server using the port in the text box to the right of this option. The default port is TCP port **80**. You can choose any other port you like for the redirect. This allows you to use alternate port numbers on the published Web sites while still accepting requests on the default HTTP port used by the Web listener (although you do not need to use the default HTTP port on the Web listener if you have configured the Web listener to listen on an alternate port).

Redirect requests to SSL port allows you to redirect requests to the specified SSL port. Note that you can select both the HTTP and SSL checkboxes. When this is the case, incoming traffic is routed through its corresponding protocol and port. For example, if the incoming request is HTTP, then the request is forwarded to the HTTP port. If the incoming request is SSL, the request is forwarded to the SSL port. You can change the SSL port the request is forwarded to, which is helpful if you have SSL sites published on alternate ports.

One of the most misunderstood options in the ISA firewall's user interface is **Use a certificate to authenticate to the SSL Web server**. This option is *not* used by the ISA firewall to accept incoming SSL connections from users connecting to the published Web server. This option allows you to configure the ISA firewall to present a *user certificate* to the published Web site when the Web site requires user certificate authentication. The user certificate is bound to the Firewall service on the ISA firewall and enables the ISA firewall to present a user certificate for authentication to the Web site.

The **FTP server** option allows the Web Publishing Rule to perform protocol redirection. The incoming request can be either HTTP or HTTPS, and the connection is redirected as an FTP GET request to the published FTP site. Using SSL-to-FTP bridging is useful when providing remote access to FTP sites requiring authentication. Since FTP sites support only Basic authentication, you can protect user credentials by using an SSL link to the external interface of the ISA firewall. The **Bridging** tab is shown in Figure 8.25.

Figure 8.25 The Bridging Tab

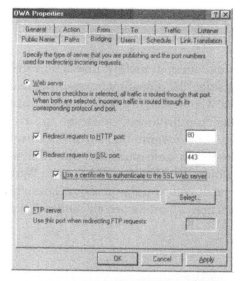

Users

The **Users** tab allows you to configure which users can access the published Web site via the Web Publishing Rule. Anyone can access the Web site through the ISA firewall when **All Users** are allowed access. However, this means that all users can get through the ISA firewall and have the unauthenticated requests forwarded to the published Web site. The Web site itself may require authentication. The user will still need to successfully authenticate with the Web site if the Web site requires authentication.

You can require authentication at the ISA firewall by removing the **All Users** group and adding any other user group via the **Add** button. The default groups included with the ISA firewall are **All Users**, **All Authenticated Users**, and **System and Network Service**. You can add your own firewall groups and fine-tune your authentication scheme. We'll talk more about firewall groups and how to use them in Chapter 7 on Creating and Configuring Firewall Policy for Outbound Access. See how to configure the **Users** tab in Figure 8.26.

Figure 8.26 The Users Tab

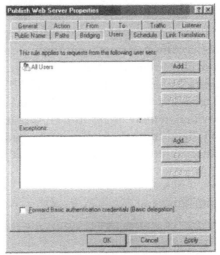

The ability to authenticate users at the ISA firewall provides a significant security advantage. Authenticating at the ISA firewall prevents unauthenticated connections from ever reaching the published Web server. Attackers and other malicious users and code can potentially leverage the unauthenticated connection to attack the published server. Authenticating at the firewall first removes the potential security risk.

Note that you can also require authentication at the Web site, so that users are required to authenticate at both the ISA firewall and at the Web site. In some circumstances, users will be presented with two log-on dialog boxes: the first authentication request is made by the ISA firewall, and the second authentication request is made by the published Web site.

You can avoid a dual authentication prompt by taking advantage of the single-sign feature provided by the ISA firewall's *delegation of Basic authentication*. This feature can be enabled when you select **Forward Basic authentication credentials (Basic delegation)** on the **Users** tab.

Delegation of Basic authentication allows users to authenticate with the ISA firewall using Basic authentication. The ISA firewall authenticates the user. If the authentication attempt is successful, the request is forwarded to the published Web site. If the published Web site requests credentials, then the ISA firewall forwards the credentials the user provided when it successfully authenticated with the firewall.

You will need to enable Basic authentication on the Web listener used by the Web Publishing Rule, and the Web site the user authenticates with will also need to use Basic authentication.

> **WARNING**
>
> You should always enable the **Forward Basic authentication credentials (Basic delegation)** when using RADIUS authentication for Web Publishing Rules. You will encounter inconsistent results and multiple log-on prompts with failed connections if you do not enable this option.

Schedule

On the **Schedule** tab (Figure 8.27) you can configure schedules that control when users can connect to the published Web site. There are three default schedules:

- **Always** The Web site is always available through the Web Publishing Rule.
- **Weekends** All day Saturday and Sunday
- **Work hours** Monday through Friday 9:00 A.M. to 5:00 P.M.

You can also create your own custom schedules. We cover this issue in Chapter 7 on outbound access policies.

Figure 8.27 The Schedule Tab

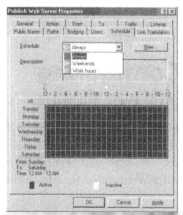

Link Translation

The ISA firewall's Link Translation feature allows you to rewrite the URLs returned by the published Web servers. URL rewriting is useful when you publish Web sites that hard code links in Web pages they return to users, and those links are not reachable from external locations.

For example, suppose we visit a Web site using the URL www.msfirewall.org. The www.msfirewall.org home page contains hard-coded links in the form of http://server1/users and http://server1/computers. When the Internet user clicks on one of these links, the connection fails because the Internet user isn't able to correctly resolve the name **server1** to the IP address on the external interface of the ISA firewall.

The ISA firewall's Link Translation feature allows you to rewrite the links containing **server1** to **www.msfirewall.org**. When the Web server returns the home page of the www.msfirewall.org site, the external user no longer sees the URLs with **server1** in them because the ISA firewall rewrote those URLs to include **www.msfirewall.org** instead of **server1**. The external user is now able to click on the links and access the content on the Web server. See Figure 8.28.

We go into more detail in about the ISA firewall's Link Translator in Chapter 10.

Figure 8.28 The Link Translation Tab

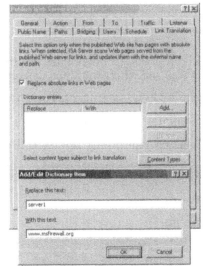

Creating and Configuring SSL Web Publishing Rules

You can publish secure Web servers using SSL Web Publishing Rules. Publishing Secure Web servers requires a bit more work up front because you need to obtain a Web site certificate for the published Web site, bind that certificate to the Web site on the published Web server and then bind a Web site certificate to the ISA firewall so that it can impersonate the Web server. This allows the ISA firewall to provide very high security for SSL Web sites published via Web Publishing Rules.

In this section we'll discuss the following:

- SSL Bridging
- Importing Web site certificates into the ISA Firewall's machine certificate store
- Requesting a Web site certificate for the ISA Firewall to present to SSL Web sites
- Creating an SSL Web Publishing Rules

SSL Bridging

SSL Bridging is a ISA firewall feature that allows the ISA firewall to perform stateful application layer inspection on SSL connections made to Web published Web servers on an ISA firewall Protected Network. This unique feature allows the ISA firewall to provide a level of stateful application layer inspection that no other firewall in its class can perform today.

SSL bridging prevents intruders from hiding exploits within an encrypted SSL tunnel. Conventional stateful filtering firewalls (such as most "hardware" firewalls on the market today) cannot perform stateful application layer inspection on SSL connections moving through them. These hardware stateful filtering firewalls see that an incoming SSL connection, check the firewall's Access Control List, and if there is an ACL instructing the stateful packet filter based firewall to forward the connection to a server on the corporate network, then the connection is forwarded to the published server without any inspection for potential application layer exploits.

The ISA firewall supports two methods of SSL bridging:

- SSL to SSL bridging
- SSL to HTTP bridging

SSL to SSL bridging provides a secure SSL connection from end to end. SSL to HTTP bridging ensures a secure connection between the Web client and the ISA firewall and then allows a clear text connection between the ISA firewall and the published Web server.

In order to appreciate how the ISA firewall works with SSL in protecting your Web server, let's look at the life cycle of a communication between the Web client on the Internet and the Web site on the ISA firewall protected network:

1. The OWA client on the Internet sends a request to the ISA firewall's external interface.

2. An SSL session is negotiated between the Web client on the Internet and the ISA firewall's external interface

3. *After* the SSL session is established, the Web client sends the username and password to the ISA firewall. The SSL tunnel that has already been established between the Web client and ISA firewall and protects these credentials.

4. The request is decrypted *before* the request is forwarded by the ISA firewall to the published Web server. The decrypted packets received from the Web client are examined by the ISA firewall and subjected stateful application layer inspection via the ISA firewall's HTTP security filter and any other application layer inspection filters you've installed on the ISA firewall. If the ISA firewall finds a problem with the request, it is dropped.

5. If the request is acceptable, the ISA Server firewall re-encrypts the communication and sends it over a *second* SSL connection established between the ISA firewall and the published Web site on the ISA firewall Protected Network.

6. The published Web server decrypts the packet and replies to the ISA firewall. The Web server encrypts its response and before sends it to the ISA firewall.

7. The ISA firewall decrypts the response received from the published Web server. It evaluates the response in the same way it did in step 4. If something is wrong with the response, the ISA firewall drops it. If the response passes stateful application layer inspection, the ISA firewall re-encrypts the communication and forwards the response to the Web client on the Internet via the SSL session the Internet Web client already established with the ISA firewall.

SSL "Tunneling" versus SSL "Bridging"

The ISA firewall actually participates in *two* different SSL sessions when SSL-to-SSL bridging is used:

- An SSL session between the Web client and the external interface of the ISA firewall

- A second SSL session between an internal interface of the ISA firewall and the published Web server

The typical stateful packet-filter firewall only performs forwards connections for published SSL sites. This is sometimes referred to as "SSL tunneling." The conventional stateful filtering firewall accepts SSL communications on its external interface and forwards them to the published SSL server. Application-layer information in the communication is completely hidden inside the SSL tunnel because the packet filter-based firewall has no mechanism to decrypt, inspect, and re-encrypt the data stream. Because traditional stateful filtering firewalls are unable to make allow and deny decisions based on knowledge of the contents of the encrypted tunnel, it passes viruses, worms, buffer overflows and other exploits from the Web client to the published Web site.

What About SSL-to-HTTP Bridging?

The ISA firewall can also perform SSL-to-HTTP bridging. In the SSL-to-HTTP bridging scenario, the connection between the Web client and the external interface of the ISA firewall is protected in the SSL tunnel. The connection between the ISA firewall's internal interface and the published Web server on the corporate network is sent "in the clear" and not encrypted. This helps performance because avoids the processor overhead incurred for the second SSL link.

However, you have to consider the implications of SSL-to-HTTP bridging. Steve Riley (http://www.microsoft.com/technet/treeview/default.asp?url=/ technet/columns/security/askus/auaswho.asp), a Program Manager on the ISA Server team at Microsoft, has mentioned that the external user connecting to the published Web site using SSL has an implicit agreement and expectation that the entire transaction is protected. We agree with this assessment. The external Web client enters into what can arguably be considered a "social contract" with the published Web server, and part of that contract is that communications are protected from "end to end."

SSL-to-SSL bridging protects the data with SSL and the ISA Server firewall services from end to end. SSL-to-HTTP bridging protects the data from the OWA client and while it's on the ISA Server firewall, but it is not safe once it's forwarded from the ISA Server firewall and the OWA site on the internal network.

Enterprise and Standalone Certificate Authorities

The topic of Certificate Authorities (CAs) and PKI (Public Key Infrastructure) is usually enough to drive many administrators away from even considering SSL. There are a number of reasons for this:

- The available documentation on certificate authorities and PKI, in general, is difficult to understand.

- The subject has the potential to be extremely complex.

- You need to learn an entirely new vocabulary to understand the CAs and PKI. Often the documentation on these subjects doesn't define the new words, or they use equally arcane terms to define the arcane term for which you're trying to get the definition.

- There doesn't seem to be any support for the network and firewall adminis-trator who just wants to get a CA setup and running so that he can use certifi-cates for SSL and L2TP/IPSec authentication and encryption.

We not going to do an entire course on PKI and the Microsoft CA, but we do want to help you understand some of the decisions you need to make when deciding what type of Certificate Authority to install and use.

The Microsoft Certificate Server can be installed in one of four roles:

- Enterprise Root CA
- Enterprise Subordinate CA
- Standalone Root CA
- Standalone Subordinate CA

Enterprise Root and Enterprise Subordinate CAs can only be installed on Active Directory member servers. If you want to install a CA on a non-domain member, then install a Standalone Root or Standalone Subordinate CA. If you install a single

Certificate Server, you'll install it as an Enterprise Root or Standalone Root. Subordinate CAs are used in organizations managing multiple CAs.

■ You can use the **Certificates MMC standalone snap-in** to obtain machine or user certificates – the snap-in is only available to domain member computers.

■ You can configure Group Policy to automatically issue machine and user certificates via *autoenrollment* – this feature is only available to domain member computers.

■ You can use the Web enrollment site to obtain certificates via a Web interface.

The **Certificates MMC standalone snap-in** or autoenrollment can't be used to obtain certificates from Standalone CAs. The only way to obtain a certificate from a standalone CA is to request one from the standalone CA's Web enrollment site. You must fill out a form and then submit the request. The certificate is not immediately issued, because the only thing the CA knows about the requestor is what's put in the form. Someone needs to "eyeball" the request and then manually approve the request. The requestor then needs to use the browser to return to the Web enrollment site and download the certificate.

The enterprise CA is less hassle because it has information about the requestor. Since the request is for a computer or user in the domain, someone has already qualified the domain user or computer and deemed that member worthy of a certificate. The enterprise CA assumes you have administrative control over all domain member users and computers and can evaluate the validity of the certificate requests against the information available to it in the Active Directory.

For these reasons, we recommend you use enterprise CAs. We will assume that you're using an enterprise CA for the remainder of this discussion.

For more information on Certificate Authorities and PKI, check out Microsoft's PKI page at www.microsoft.com/windowsserver2003/technologies/pki/default.mspx

SSL-to-SSL Bridging and Web Site Certificate Configuration

One of the most common reasons that ISA firewall admins give up on SSL, and SSL-to-SSL bridging is the problems they may experience in getting the SSL connections to work correctly. The most common reason for this is a configuration error that involves the relationship between the certificate configuration and the Web Publishing Rule used to publish the Web site.

Figure 8.29 and the list to follow provides details of the SSL-to-SSL bridged connection to a public Outlook Web Access Web site.

Figure 8.29 SSL-to-SSL bridging

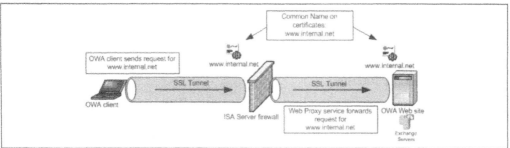

1. The Web client sends the request https://www.internal.net/exchange/ to the external interface of the ISA Server firewall publishing the OWA 2003 Web site

2. The ISA firewall checks its Web Publishing Rules to see if there is a Web Publishing Rule containing a Destination Set with the FQDN www.internal.net and the path **/exchange**. If there is a Web Publishing Rule matching this FQDN and path, the connection will be handled based on the forwarding instructions included in the Web Publishing Rule. However, *before* the ISA firewall can evaluate the URL, the SSL session must be established. The **common name** *on the certificate* the ISA firewall uses to impersonate the OWA Web site must be the *same* as the FQDN used by the Web client to connect to the site. In this example, the common name on the certificate the ISA firewall uses to impersonate the OWA Web site must be www.internal.net so that it matches the FQDN the external OWA client uses in its request.

3. The ISA firewall decrypts the packets, examines them, and then attempts to create a new SSL connection between itself and the internal OWA Web site. Just like when the external OWA client connects to the external interface of the ISA Server firewall, the ISA Server firewall's Web Proxy service acts as a client to the OWA 2003 Web site on the internal network. The request the Web Proxy service sends to the OWA 2003 site on the internal network must match the **common name** on the certificate on the OWA Web site. That is why we must configure the request to be forwarded to www.internal.net when we configure the Web Publishing Rule. I'll remind you of this important fact when we discuss the configuration of the Web Publishing Rule.

4. The packets are forwarded to the Web site after the SSL session is established between the ISA firewall and the Web server on the internal network.

NOTE

All machines participating in the SSL sessions (the Web client, the ISA firewall, and the Web site) must have the CA certificate of the root Certificate Authority in its **Trusted Root Certification Authorities** certificate store.

Things break when the common name on the server certificate doesn't match the name used by the client request. There are two places where things can break in the SSL-to-SSL bridging scenario:

- If the common name on the certificate used by the ISA Server firewall to impersonate the Web site doesn't match the name (FQDN) used by the Web client on the Internet.

- If the common name on the certificate on the Web site doesn't match the name (FQDN) used by the ISA firewall service to forward the request; the name in the ISA firewall's request to the published Web server is determined by the entry on the **To** tab in the Web Publishing Rule.

Keep these facts in mind as we work through our SSL-to-SSL bridging Web Publishing Rule later.

> **WARNING**
>
> You will encounter the dreaded **Internal Server Error 500** if there is a mismatch between the name in the request and the name on the certificate.

Importing Web Site Certificates into The ISA Firewall's Machine Certificate Store

The ISA firewall must be able to impersonate the published Web server so that it identifies itself to the remote Web client as the published Web server. The mechanism behind this impersonation is a common name on the Web site certificate. We must install the Web site certificate on the ISA firewall to accomplish this task.

The first step is to export the Web site certificate from the secure Web server's Web site. The IIS console has an easy-to-use Certificate Wizard where you can export the Web site certificate. When you export the Web site certificate, make sure that you include the private key. One of the most common reasons for failure in secure Web Publishing Rules is that the Web site certificate was not exported with its private key.

The Web site certificate is then imported into the ISA firewall's machine certificate store. Once the Web site certificate is imported into the ISA firewall's machine certificate store, it will be available to bind to a Web listener. You'll know that the certificate wasn't properly imported if you're unable to bind the certificate to a Web listener.

Perform the following steps to import the Web site certificate into the ISA firewall's machine certificate store:

1. Copy the Web site certificate to the ISA firewall machine.

2. Click **Start**, and then click the **Run** command. In the **Run** dialog box, enter **mmc** in the **Open** text box, and click **OK**.

3. In the console, click **File**, and then click **Add/Remove Snap-in**.

4. In the **Add/Remove Snap-in** dialog box, click **Add**.

5. In the **Add Standalone Snap-in** dialog box, click **Certificates** in the list of **Available Standalone Snap-ins**, and click **Add**.

6. On the **Certificates Snap-in** page, select the **Computer account** option and click **Next**.

7. On the **Select Computer** page, select **Local computer (the computer this console is running on)** and click **Finish**.

8. Click **Close** in the **Add Standalone Snap-in** dialog box.

9. Click **OK** in the **Add/Remove Snap-in** dialog box.

10. Expand the **Certificates (Local Computer)** node in the left pane of the console.

11. Expand the **Personal** node in the left pane of the console.

12. Right-click the **Certificates** node, point to **All Tasks** and click **Import**.

13. Click **Next** on the **Welcome to the Certificate Import Wizard** page.

14. On the **File to Import** page, use the **Browse** button to find the certificate you copied to the ISA firewall. Click **Next** after the certificate appears in the **File name** text box.

15. Enter the password you assigned to the Web site certificate in the **Password** text box on the **Password** page. Do *not* mark the certificate as exportable. Click **Next**.

16. Accept the default setting, **Place all certificates in the following store** on the **Certificate Store** page. Click **Next**.

17. Click **Finish** on the **Completing the Certificate Import Wizard** page.

18. Click **OK** on the **Certificate Import Wizard** dialog box.

19. The Web site certificate and the CA certificate appear in the right pane of the console. The CA certificate has the same name as the entry in the **Issued by** column.

20. Right-click the CA certificate and click **Cut**.

21. Expand the **Trusted Root Certification Authorities** node in the left pane of the console.

22. Right-click the **Certificates** node and click **Paste**. If the **Paste** command does not appear, repeat step 20, and then try again.

23. Return to the **Personal\Certificates** node in the left pane of the console and double-click the Web site certificate.

24. In the **Certificate** dialog box, click the **Certification Path** tab. The CA certificate should not have a red "x" on it. If there is a red "x" on the CA certificate, that indicates that the CA certificate was not successfully imported into the **Trusted Root Certification Authorities** node.

25. Close the **Certificate** dialog box.

26. Close the **mmc** console. Do not save the console.

Now that the Web site certificate is imported into the machine's certificate store, it'll be available to bind to the Web listener used in the SSL Web Publishing Rule.

Requesting a User Certificate for the ISA Firewall to Present to SSL Web Sites

The ISA firewall can be configured to present a user certificate to Web sites that require user certificates before connecting to the site. These user certificates are also referred to as *client certificates*. The published Web site can be configured to require that the client certificate be presented before a connection is allowed. Client certificates can be mapped to user accounts. This allows for user certificate authentication. However, you can require user certificates and then provide log on credentials via alternate authentication methods.

You can request a user certificate for the ISA Firewall's Firewall Service and then configure the Web Publishing Rule to present this certificate when Web sites request a client certificate. The first step is to request a certificate for the ISA firewall's Firewall Service account.

In the following example we will use the certificates MMC to import a certificate for the ISA Firewall's Firewall service account. We cannot use the Certificates MMC to request a certificate for the account, but we can import a user certificate using the Web enrollment site.

In order to request a certificate for the ISA firewall from the Web enrollment site, we must first create a user account for the ISA firewall. Create a user account name **isafirewall** in the Active Directory prior to performing the following procedures.

Perform the following steps to request a certificate for the Firewall service account:

1. At the ISA firewall machine, open the **Microsoft Internet Security and Acceleration Server 2004** management console, expand the server name, and click the **Firewall Policy** node.

2. Click the **Tasks** tab in the Task pane. On the **Tasks** tab, click the **Show System Policy Rules** link.

3. In the list of **System Policy Rules**, right-click Rule 2 **Allow all HTTP traffic from ISA Server to all networks (for CRL downloads)**, and click **Edit System Policy**.

4. On the **General** tab of the **System Policy Rule for CRL Download**, check the **Enable** checkbox. Click **OK**.

5. Click **Apply** to save the changes and update the firewall policy.

6. Click **OK** in the **Apply New Configuration** dialog box.

7. Open Internet Explorer on the ISA firewall and enter the URLhttp://<certificateserver>/certsrv, where **certificateserver** is the name or IP address of the enterprise CA on the corporate network.

8. In the **Connect to** dialog box, enter the credentials of the **isafirewall** account and click **OK**.

9. Click **Add** in the Internet Explorer dialog box, creating the blocking of the site.

10. Click **Add** in the **Trusted site** dialog box. Click **Close**.

11. On the **Welcome** page, click the **Request a certificate** link.

12. On the **Request a Certificate** page, click the **User Certificate** link.

13. On the **User Certificate – Identifying Information** page, click **Submit**.

14. Click **Yes** in the **Potential Scripting Violation** dialog box.

15. Click **Yes** in the dialog box informing you that you're sending information to the Web server.

16. On the **Install this certificate** page, click the **Install this certificate** link.

17. Click **Yes** in the **Potential Scripting Violation** dialog box.

18. Click the **Tools** menu in the browser, and click **Internet Options**.

19. In the **Internet Options** dialog box, click the **Content** tab.

20. On the **Content** tab, click **Certificates**.

21. In the **Certificates** dialog box, click **isafirewall** and click **Export**.

22. Click **Next** on the **Welcome to the Certificate Export Wizard** page.

23. On the **Export Private Key** page, select **Yes, export the private key**, and click **Next**.

24. On the **Export File Format** page, *remove* the checkmark from the **Enable strong protection** checkbox. Place a checkmark in the **Include all certificates in the certification path if possible** checkbox. Click **Next**.

25. On the **Password** page, enter a password and confirm the password for the certificate file. Click **Next**.

26. On the **File to Export** page, enter a path in the **File name** text box. In this example, we'll enter the file name **c:\isafirewallcert**. Click **Next**.

27. Click **Finish** on the **Completing the Certificate Export Wizard** page.

28. Click **OK** in the **Certificate Export Wizard** dialog box.

29. Click **Close** in the **Certificates** dialog box.

30. Click **OK** in the **Internet Options** dialog box.

Now we'll import the certificate into the Firewall service account:

1. Click **Start** and then click **Run**. In the **Run** dialog box, enter **mmc** in the **Open** text box, and click **OK**.

2. In the console, click **File**, and then click **Add/Remove Snap-in**.

3. In the **Add/Remove Snap-in** dialog box, click **Add**.

4. In the **Add Standalone Snap-in** dialog box, click **Certificates** in the list of **Available Standalone Snap-ins**, and click **Add**.

5. On the **Certificates snap-in** page, select the **Services account** option, and click **Next**.

6. On the **Select Computer** page, select **Local Computer (the computer this console is running on)**, and click **Next**.

7. On the **Select a service account to manage on the local computer** page, select **Microsoft Firewall** from the **Service account** list, and click **Finish**.

8. Click **Close** in the **Add Standalone Snap-in** dialog box.

9. Click **OK** in the **Add/Remove Snap-in** dialog box.

10. In the console, expand the **Certificates – Service** node and right-click **fwsrv\Personal**. Point to **All Tasks** and click on **Import**.

11. On the **Welcome to the Certificate Import Wizard** page, click **Next**.

12. On the **File to Import** page, click **Browse** to find the location of the user certificate file you exported from the browser. Click **Next**.

13. Enter the password you assigned the certificate in the **Password** text box. Do not put a checkmark in the **Mark this key as exportable** checkbox. You might also want to delete the certificate from the Web browser on the ISA firewall so that this certificate cannot be stolen by individuals who obtain physical access to the ISA firewall. Click **Next**.

14. On the **Certificate Store** page, use the default setting **Place all certificates in the following store**, and click **Next**.

15. Click **Finish** on the **Completing the Certificate Import Wizard** page.

16. Click **OK** in the **Certificate Import Wizard** dialog box.

The certificate is now associated with the Firewall service account. You might want to disable the System Policy Rule we created earlier so that you don't inadvertently use the browser on the ISA firewall. Remember, you should avoid using the browser, and all other client applications, on the firewall.

Creating an SSL Web Publishing Rule

Now that our certificates are in place, we can create the SSL secure Web Publishing Rule. In the **Microsoft Internet Security and Acceleration Server 2004** management console, expand the server name, and click the **Firewall Policy** node. On the **Firewall Policy** node, click the **Tasks** tab in the Task pane. In the Task pane, click **Publish a Secure Web Server**.

On the **Welcome to the SSL Web Publishing Rule Wizard** page, enter a name for the rule in the **SSL Web publishing rule name** text box. In this example, we'll name the rule **Secure Web Server**, and click **Next**.

The Publishing Mode Page

On the **Publishing Mode** page (Figure 8.30), you have two options:

- SSL Bridging
- SSL Tunneling

Figure 8.30 The Publishing Mode Page

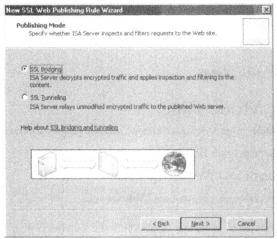

The **SSL Bridging** option is the more secure option. SSL bridging provides a secure end-to-end encrypted SSL connection while at the same time allowing the ISA firewall to perform both stateful filtering (like any conventional "hardware" firewall) and stateful application-layer inspection. This is the preferred option and the option we will use in this example.

The **SSL Tunneling** option is the less secure option. SSL tunneling bypasses the ISA firewall's stateful application-layer inspection functionality and reduces the overall level of security for the publishing rule that is provided by a conventional stateful filtering "hardware" firewall. Do not use the **SSL Tunneling** feature unless you encounter an unusual situation where you publish applications that are not compliant with HTTP 1.1 Web Proxies.

Select **SSL Bridging**, and click **Next**.

The Select Rule Action page

The **Select Rule** action page, as shown in Figure 8.31, has two options: **Allow** or **Deny**. **Allow** allows connections to the published server, and **Deny** denies connections to the published server. The default option is **Allow**. You can use **Deny** publishing rules to fine-tune existing Web Publishing Rules.

Figure 8.31 The Select Rule Action Page

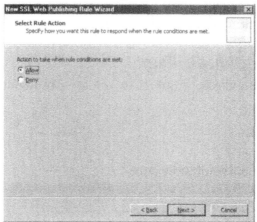

Select **Allow**, and click **Next**.

The Bridging Mode Page

On the **Bridging Mode** page you have three options (also shown in Figure 8.32):

- Secure connection to clients
- Secure connection to Web server
- Secure connection to clients and Web server

Each "secure connection" is in the context of the connection *from* the ISA firewall.

The **Secure connection to clients** option sets the connection up as SSL-to-HTTP bridging. This option secures the connection between the Web client and the ISA firewall, but allows the connection to travel in unsecured free text between the ISA firewall and the published Web server. We highly recommend against this practice, unless you use an alternate method of securing the connection between the ISA firewall and the published Web server (such as IPSec or a dedicated link between the ISA firewall and the Web server where the cable itself would need to be compromised in the fashion of a "vampire tap" such as cutting the cable and wiring each side of the twisted pairs to a listening device acting as a "man in the middle," or by picking up the signal using a Time Domain Reflectometer).

We do realize that there is always a trade-off between security and performance and the implicit contract you have with users who assume their connection is secure from end to end. If you believe that you have a strong, defensible reason for not using an end-to-end connection, then SSL-to-HTTP bridging is possible with the ISA firewall. Depending on the Web application you publish, you may need to use the ISA firewall's Link Translator feature to get things working properly. We'll talk more about the Link Translator in Chapter 10.

The **Secure connection to Web server** option allows you to perform HTTP-to-SSL bridging. The connection between the Web client is sent over HTTP, and the connection between the ISA firewall and the Web server is sent via SSL. This is a somewhat unusual scenario, where the client is on a more trusted network than the networks in the path between the ISA firewall and the published server. An example of this type of scenario is where a branch office has an ISA firewall connecting it to the main office using a dedicated WAN link. You can publish the main office Web server at the branch office ISA firewall and secure the connection over the WAN link to the main office and finally to the destination Web server.

Secure connection to clients and Web server (as shown in Figure 8.32) is the most secure and preferred option. This enables SSL-to-SSL bridging where the connection between the Web client and the ISA firewall is secured by SSL, and the connection between the ISA firewall and the published Web server is also secured by SSL. The ISA firewall is able to perform stateful application-layer inspection on the contents of the SSL connection when you use SSL bridging, while at the same time providing an end-to-end encrypted connection.

Figure 8.32 The Bridging Mode Page

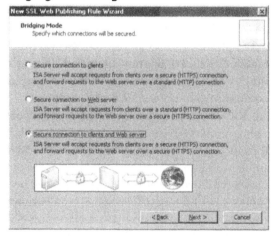

In this example, we will select **Secure connection to clients and Web server**, and click **Next**.

The Define Website to Publish Page

On the **Define Website to Publish** page, you have the following options:

- Computer name or IP address
- Forward the original host header instead of the actual one (specified above)
- Path
- Site

The **Computer name or IP address** text box includes the IP address or name for the published Web server. This is a critical entry for SSL publishing because the name in this text box *must match the common name on the Web site certificate on the Web server*. If the name you enter in the **Computer name or IP address** text box doesn't match the common name on the Web site certificate, the connection attempt will fail, and the user will see a **500 Internal Server** error.

For example, if the common name on the Web site certificate bound to the published Web site is **owa.msfirewall.org**, then you *must* enter **owa.msfirewall.org** in the **Computer name or IP address** text box. If you enter the IP address or NetBIOS name of the server, the connection will fail because the name doesn't match the common name on the Web site certificate.

' **Forward the original host header instead of the actual one (specified above)** works the same way as it does when you publish non-SSL sites. However, you must be careful with this option because if the remote user uses a FQDN that is different than the common name on the Web site certificate, the connection attempt will fail.

For example, if the remote user enters **http://www.msfirewall.org** to access the published Web site through the ISA firewall, then the ISA firewall will use **www.msfirewall.org** instead of **owa.msfirewall.org** when it proxies the connection to the published Web site, and the connection will fail with a 500 error. For this reason, we recommend that you use the same name from end to end for your Web Publishing Rules. However, this isn't required because if you do not enable the **Forward the original host header instead of the actual one (specified above)** option, and you use the same name from end to end, then the name the external user uses to access the Web site is the same as the common name on the Web site certificate.

The key to success is that the name in the **Computer name or IP address** text box matches the common name on the Web site certificate on the published Web site, and the ISA firewall resolves the name in the **Computer name or IP address** text box to the *internal* address, *not* the public address used by the Web listener, for that site. In this example, the name owa.msfirewall.org must resolve to the *internal* or non-public address. That is to say, the *actual* address bound to the Web site on the corporate networks.

The **Path** text box is used in the same way it's used for non-SSL connections. See the section in this chapter on publishing non-secure Web sites for details of this option.

The **Site** box lists the URL of the site that will be published on the Internal network.

The Define Website-to-Publish Rule Wizard is illustrated in Figure 8.33.

Figure 8.33 The Define Website to Publish Page

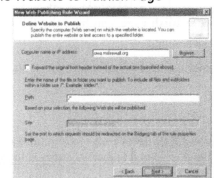

Click **Next** on the **Define Website to Publish** page.

The Public Name Details Page

On the **Public Name Details** (Figure 8.34) page, you define what names users can use to access the published Web site via this Web Publishing Rule. The **Public Name Details** page includes the following options:

- Accept requests for
- Public name
- Path
- Site

The **Accept requests for** drop-down list allows you to choose either **This domain name (type below)** or **Any domain name**. As we mentioned in our earlier discussion on non-SSL publishing, the **Any domain name** option is a low security option and should be avoided, if at all possible. This option allows the Web Publishing Rule to accept incoming requests using any IP address or FQDN that can reach the IP address that the Web listener for the Web Publishing Rule uses. The preferred option is **This domain name (type below)**. This option limits the name remote users can use when accessing the Web site published by this Web Publishing Rule.

You enter the name the remote user uses to access the published Web site in the **Public name** text box. This is a critical option. You must enter the name that the remote user uses to access the Web site, and the name *must match the common name on the Web site certificate bound to the Web listener* used by this rule.

We recommend that you export the Web site certificate bound to the published Web site and import that certificate into the ISA firewall's machine certificate store. When you do this, you can bind the original Web site certificate to the Web listener used by this Web Publishing Rule. You would then use the same name from end to end.

For example, if the Web site certificate used on the published Web site has the common name **owa.msfirewall.org**, and you export that Web site certificate and bind it to the Web listener used by this Web Publishing Rule, you should use the same name, **owa.msfirewall.org**, in the **Public name** text box. Remote users must be able to resolve this name to the address on the ISA firewall that the Web listener used by this rule accepts incoming secure connections.

The **Path** text box allows you to set what paths are accessible on the published Web site. For more details on how to use the **Path** option, review our discussion of this subject in the non-SSL Web publishing section of this chapter.

See an example of The Public Name Details page in Figure 8.34.

Figure 8.34 The Public Name Details Page

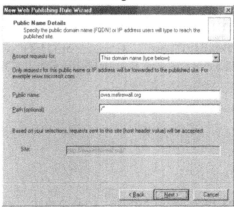

Click **Next** on the **Public Name Details** page.

The Select Web Listener Page

Select the Web listener you want to use for this Web Publishing Rule on the **Select Web Listener** page (Figure 8.35). If you have already created an SSL Web listener on this ISA firewall, you can select it from the **Web listener** list. If you do not have an SSL Web listener, you can create one by clicking **New**.

In this example, we will create a new SSL Web listener for this Web Publishing Rule. Click the **New** button as shown in Figure 8.35.

Figure 8.35 The Select Web Listener Page

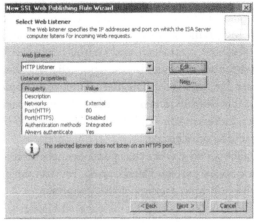

· On the **Welcome to the New Web Listener Wizard** page, enter a name for the Web listener in the **Web listener name** text box. In this example, we'll name the Web listener **SSL Listener**. Click **Next**.

On the **IP Address** page, select the Network you want the listener to listen on. In this example, we want the listener to listen for incoming requests to the published Web site on the **External** interface. Check the box next to the **Network** where you want the listener to listen for requests. However, we do not want the Web listener to listen on all IP addresses assigned to the External Network interface(s), so we'll click **Address** as shown in Figure 8.36.

Figure 8.36 The IP Addresses Page

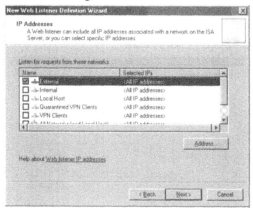

In the **External Network Listener IP Selection** dialog box, select **Specified IP addresses on the ISA Server computer in the selected network**. Select the address on the ISA firewall that resolves to the common name on the Web site certificate bound to the Web listener. In this case, the IP address that resolves to the name **owa.msfirewall.org** is **192.168.1.70**. Select the IP address in the **Available IP Addresses** list, and click **Add** to move it to the **Selected IP Addresses** list. Click **OK**. The External Network Listener IP Selection page is shown in Figure 8.37.

Figure 8.37 The External Network Listener IP Selection Page

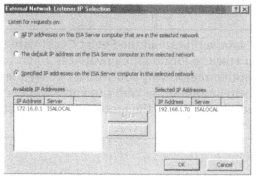

Click **Next** on the **IP Address Selection** page.

On the **Port Specification** page, set what TCP port(s) the Web listener will listen on. We recommend that you always create separate listeners for HTTP and SSL, since this provides you more flexibility in creating listeners and Web Publishing Rules. Since we are creating an SSL listener in this example, remove the checkmark from the **Enable HTTP** checkbox to prevent this Web listener from accepting incoming HTTP connections. Check the **Enable SSL** checkbox. The default listening port for the SSL listener is **443**. You can change this port if you like, but users will need to manually enter the alternate port if you do.

The SSL listener needs a Web site certificate bound to it so that it can impersonate the published Web site. Click the **Select** button to select the certificate, as shown in Figure 8.38.

Figure 8.38 The Port Specification Page

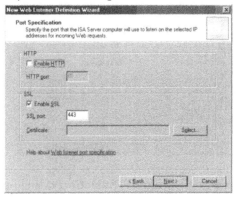

You'll see a list of Web site certificates in the **Select Certificate** dialog box. In our current example, we see two certificates: a machine certificate assigned to the ISA firewall that it uses for user certificate authentication with Web sites that require user certificates, and the Web site certificate for the Web site we're publishing. Select the Web site certificate (in this example, the Web site certificate is **owa.msfirewall.org**), and click **OK**. The Select Certification dialog box is illustrated in Figure 8.39.

> **WARNING**
>
> If you do not see your certificate in the **Select Certificate** list, the most likely reason is that you failed to include the private key when you exported the Web site certificate. Another reason why you would not see the Web site certificate in this list is that you imported the Web site into another certificate store. The certificate must be imported into the machine certificate store, not a user or service certificate store.

Figure 8.39 The Select Certificate Dialog Box

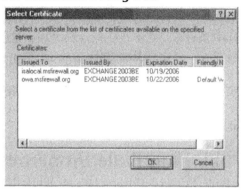

The certificate appears in the **Certificate** box on the **Port Specification** page as shown in Figure 8.40. Click **Next**.

Figure 8.40 The Certificate Appears on the Port Specification Page

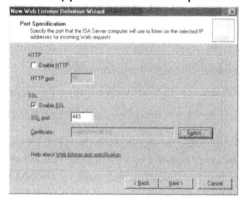

Click **Finish** on the **Completing the New Web Listener Wizard** page. The details of the SSL listener now appear on the **Select Web Listener** page (Figure 8.41). Click **Next**.

Figure 8.41 The Select Web Listener Page

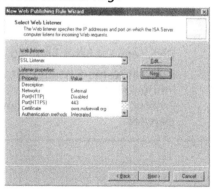

The User Sets Page

Configure the users you want to access the Web site on the **User Sets** page. The configuration options on the **User Sets** page are the same for both SSL and non-SSL publishing. Check out the discussion of the **User Sets** page in the non-SSL Web Publishing section of this chapter.

Click **Finish** on the **Completing the New Web Publishing Rule Wizard** page. Click **Apply** to save the changes and update the firewall policy. Click **OK** in the **Apply New Configuration** dialog box.

The SSL Web Publishing Rule Properties Dialog Box

The SSL Web Publishing Rule Properties dialog box is identical to that found in the non-SSL Web Publishing Rule Properties dialog box. Review the section on the Web Publishing Rule **Properties** dialog box in the non-SSL Web Publishing Rule section of this chapter.

Creating Server Publishing Rules

Creating Server Publishing Rules is simple compared to Web Publishing Rules. The only things you need to know when creating a Server Publishing Rule are:

- The protocol or protocols you want to publish
- The IP address where the ISA firewall accepts the incoming connections
- The IP address of the Protected Network server you want to publish

A Server Publishing Rule uses protocols with the primary connection set as **Inbound**, **Receive** or **Receive/Send**. For example, if you want to publish an SMTP server, the Protocol Definition for that protocol must be for SMTP, TCP port 25 Inbound. Outbound Protocol Definitions are used for Access Rules.

The ISA firewall comes with a number of built-in Server Publishing Protocol Definitions. Table 8.2 lists these built-in Protocol Definitions.

Table 8.2 Server Publishing Protocol Definitions

Protocol Definition	Usage
DNS Server	TCP 53 Inbound
	UDP 53 Receive/Send
	DNS Security Filter Enabled
	Domain Name System Protocol - Server. An inbound protocol used for server publishing. This Protocol Definition also allows for DNS zone transfer

Continued

Table 8.2 Server Publishing Protocol Definitions

Protocol Definition	Usage
Exchange RPC Server	TCP 135 Inbound
	RPC Security Filter enabled
	Only Exchange RPC interfaces are exposed (Exchange RPC UUIDs)
	Used for publishing Exchange server for RPC access from External network.
FTP Server	TCP 21 Inbound
	FTP Access Filter enabled
	File Transfer Protocol - Server. An inbound protocol used for server publishing. Both PASV and PORT modes are supported.
HTTPS Server	TCP 443 Inbound
	Secure HyperText Transfer Protocol - Server. An inbound protocol used for server publishing. Used for publishing SSL sites when Web Publishing Rules and enhanced security is not required.
IKE Server	UDP 500 Receive/Send
	Internet Key Exchange Protocol - Server. An inbound protocol used for server publishing. Used for IPSec passthrough.
IMAP4 Server	TCP 143 Inbound
	Protocol (IMAP) - Server. An inbound protocol used for server publishing.
IMAPS Server	TCP 993 Inbound
	Secure Interactive Mail Access Protocol (IMAP) - Server. An inbound protocol used for server publishing.
IPSec ESP Server	IP Protocol 50 Receive/Send
	IPSec ESP Protocol - Server. An inbound protocol used for server publishing. Used for IPSec passthrough.
IPSec NAT-T Server	UDP 4500 Receive/Send
	IPSec NAT-T Protocol - Server. An inbound protocol used for server publishing. Used for NAT Traversal for L2TP/IPSec and other RFC-compliant NAT traversal connections for IPSec.

Continued

Table 8.2 Server Publishing Protocol Definitions

Protocol Definition	Usage
L2TP Server	UDP 1701 Receive/Send
	Layer 2 Tunneling Protocol - Server. An inbound protocol used for server publishing. Used to publish the L2TP/IPSec control channel.
Microsoft SQL Server	TCP 1433 Inbound
	Microsoft SQL Server Protocol
MMS Server	TCP 1755 Inbound
	UDP 1755 Receive
	MMS Filter enabled
	Microsoft Media Server Protocol - Server. An inbound protocol used for server publishing.
NNTP Server	TCP 119 Inbound
	Network News Transfer Protocol - Server. An inbound protocol used for server publishing.
NNTPS Server	TCP 563 Inbound
	Secure Network News Transfer Protocol - Server. An inbound protocol used for server publishing.
PNM Server	TCP 7070 Inbound
	PNM Filter enabled
	Progressive Networks Streaming Media Protocol - Server. An inbound protocol used for server publishing.
POP3 Server	TCP 110 Inbound
	Post Office Protocol v.3 - Server. An inbound protocol used for server publishing.
POP3S Server	TCP 995 Inbound
	Secure Post Office Protocol v.3 - Server. An inbound protocol used for server publishing.
PPTP Server	TCP 1723 Inbound
	PPTP Filter enabled
	Point-to-Point Tunneling Protocol - Server. An inbound protocol used for server publishing.
RDP (Terminal Services) Server	TCP 3389 Inbound
	Remote Desktop Protocol (Terminal Services) - Server

Continued

Table 8.2 Server Publishing Protocol Definitions

Protocol Definition	Usage
RPC Server (all interfaces)	TCP 135 Inbound
	RPC Filter enabled
	Remote Procedure Call Protocol - Server. An inbound protocol used for server publishing (All RPC interfaces). Used primarily to intradomain communications through the ISA firewall.
RTSP Server	TCP 554 Inbound
	Real Time Streaming Protocol - Server. An inbound protocol used for server publishing. Used by Windows Media Server services Windows Server 2003
SMTP Server	TCP 25 Inbound
	SMTP Security Filter enabled
	Simple Mail Transfer Protocol - Server. An inbound protocol used for server publishing.
SMTPS Server	TCP 465 Inbound
	Secure Simple Mail Transfer Protocol - Server. An inbound protocol used for server publishing.
Telnet Server	TCP 23 Inbound
	Telnet Protocol - Server. An inbound protocol used for server publishing.

Any of the protocols in Table 8.2 can be used right out of the box for a Server Publishing Rule.

In the following example, we'll create a Server Publishing Rule for a RDP site on the default Internal Network. The RDP site could be a Terminal Server or a Windows XP machine running Remote Desktop:

1. In the **Microsoft Internet Security and Acceleration Server 2004** management console, expand the server name, and then click the **Firewall Policy** node. Click the **Tasks** tab in the **Task** pane, and click **Create a New Server Publishing Rule**.

2. On the **Welcome to the New Server Publishing Rule Wizard** page, enter a name for the rule in the **Server Publishing Rule name** text box. In the example, we'll name the rule **SPR – Terminal Server**. Click **Next**.

3. On the **Select Server** page, enter the IP address of the published server on the ISA firewall Protected Network in the **Server IP address** text box. In this example, we'll enter **10.0.0.2**. You can also click **Browse** to find the server, but the ISA firewall will need to be able to resolve the name of that server correctly. Click **Next**.

4. On the **Select Protocol** page (Figure 8.42), click the down-arrow for the **Selected protocol** list, and click the **RDP (Terminal Services) Server** protocol. You can see the details of the selected protocol in the **Properties** dialog box. You can also change the ports used to accept the incoming connections and the ports used to forward the connection to the published Web server. Click **Ports**.

Figure 8.42 The Select Protocol Page

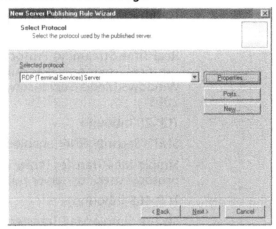

5. The following options are available to you in the **Ports** dialog box.

-   **Publish using the default port defined in the Protocol Definition** This option allows the ISA firewall to listen on the default port defined in the Protocol Definition for the selected protocol. In the current example, the RDP Protocol Definition listens on TCP port 3389. Using this option the ISA firewall listens on TCP port 3389 on the IP address you set for the listener for this Server Publishing Rule. This is the default setting.

-   **Publish on this port instead of the default port** You can change the port number used to listen for incoming requests. This allows you to override the port number in the Protocol Definition. For example, we might want the ISA firewall to listen for incoming RDP connections on TCP port 8989. We could select **Publish on this port instead of the default port**, and then enter the alternate port, **8989**, in the text box next to this option.

-   **Send requests to the default port on the published server** This option configures the ISA firewall to forward the connection using the same port the ISA firewall received the request on. In this example, the RDP Server Publishing Rule accepts incoming RDP connections on TCP port 3389. The connection is then forwarded to port 3389 on the published server. This is the default setting.

-   **Send requests to this port on the published server** This option allows you to perform port redirection. For example, if the ISA firewall accepts incoming requests for RDP connections on TCP port 3389, you can redirect the connection to an alternate port on the published RDP server, such as TCP port 89.

- **Allow traffic from any allowed source port** This allows the ISA firewall to accept incoming connections from clients that use any source port in their requests to the published server. This is the default setting, and most applications are designed to accept connections from any client source port.

- **Limit access to traffic from this range of source ports** You can limit the source port that the application connecting to the published server uses by selecting this option. If your application allows you to configure the source port, you can improve the security of your Server Publishing Rule by limiting connections from hosts using a specific source port and entering that port in the text box associated with this option. You can also list a range of allowed source ports if you want to allow multiple hosts to connect to the server.

    Click **OK** after making any changes. In this example, we will not change the listener or forwarded port number.

6. On the **IP Addresses** page, you can select the Network(s) where you want the ISA firewall to listen for incoming connections to the published Web site. The **IP Addresses** page for Server Publishing Rules works the same way as that used by Web Publishing Rules. For more information on how to use the options on this page, review the discussion about the **IP Address** page in the non-SSL Web Publishing Rules section of this chapter. In this example, we'll select **External** by putting a checkmark in the **External** checkbox. Click **Next**.

7. Click **Finish** on the **Completing the New Server Publishing Rule Wizard** page.

8. Click **Apply** to save the changes and update the firewall policy.

9. Click **OK** in the **Apply New Configuration** dialog box.

The Server Publishing Rule Properties Dialog Box

You can fine-tune the Server Publishing Rule by opening the Server Publishing Rules **Properties** dialog box. Double-click the Server Publishing Rule to open the **Properties** dialog box. The first tab you'll encounter is the **General** tab. Here you can change the name of the Server Publishing Rule and provide a description for the rule. You can also enable or disable the rule by changing the status of the **Enable** checkbox. The General tab is shown in Figure 8.43.

Figure 8.43 The General Tab

On the **Action** tab, set the rule for whether or not to log connections that apply to this rule. We recommend that you always log connections made via a Server Publishing Rule. However, if you have a reason why you do not want to log these connections (for example, privacy laws in your country do not allow logging this information), you can disable logging by removing the checkmark from the **Log requests matching this rule** checkbox shown in Figure 8.44.

Figure 8.44 The Action Tab

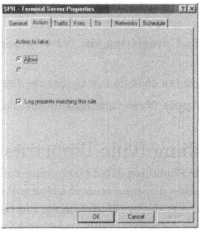

On the **Traffic** tab you can change the protocol used for the Server Publishing Rule by clicking the down arrow in the **Allow network traffic using the following protocol** drop-down list. You can create a new Protocol Definition for a Server Publishing Rule by clicking **New**, and you can view the details of the Protocol Definition used in the Server Publishing Rule by clicking **Properties**. You can also customize the source and destination ports allowed by the Server Publishing Rule using the **Ports** button. See options for the Traffic tab in Figure 8.45.

Figure 8.45 The Traffic Tab

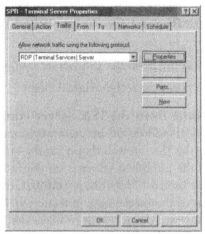

You can control what hosts can connect to the published server using settings on the **From** tab. The default location allows hosts from **Anywhere** to connect to the published server via this rule. However, connections will only be allowed from hosts that can connect via Networks configured on the **Networks** tab. So, while hosts from **Anywhere** can connect to the published server, connections are still limited to those hosts who can connect via the interface(s) responsible for the Networks listed on the **Networks** tab.

You can get more granular access control over who can connect to the published server by removing the **Anywhere** option and allowing a more limited group of machines access to the published server. Click **Anywhere**, and then click **Remove**. Then click **Add**, and select a Network Object defining the group of machines you want to allow access to the published server.

You can further fine-tune access control by setting exceptions to the list of allowed hosts and adding them to the **Exceptions** list. Click **Add** in the **Exceptions** section. See Figure 8.46 for options on the From tab.

Figure 8.46 The From Tab

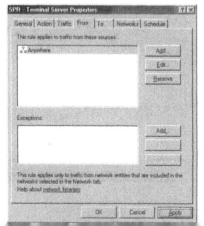

On the **To** tab, configure the IP address of the server published via this Server Publishing Rule. You can also control what client IP address is seen by the published server by your selection in the **Request for the published server** frame. You have two options:

- Requests appear to come from the ISA Server computer
- Requests appear to come from the original client

Requests appear to come from the ISA Server computer allows the published server to see the source IP address of the incoming connection to the IP address on the network interface on the ISA firewall that is on the same Network as the published server. For example, if the published server is on the Internal network, and the ISA firewall's interface on the Internal Network is **10.0.0.1**, then the published server will see the source IP address of the incoming connection as **10.0.0.1**.

This option is useful when you do not want to make the published server a SecureNAT client. The SecureNAT client is one where the machine is configured with a default gateway address that routes all Internet-bound connections through the ISA firewall. If you do not want to change the default gateway address on the published server, then use **Requests appear to come from the ISA Server computer**. The only requirement is, if the published server is on a different subnet from the ISA firewall, the published server needs to be able route to the IP address that the ISA firewall uses when it forwards the connection to the published server.

If you want the published server to see the actual client IP address, select **Requests appear to come from the original client**. This option requires that the published server be configured as a SecureNAT client. The reason why the machine must be configured as a SecureNAT client is that since the client IP address is from a non-local network, the published server must have a default gateway that routes Internet-bound communications through the ISA firewall. Figure 8.47 illustrates the options on the To tab.

Figure 8.47 The To Tab

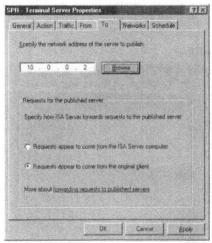

On the **Networks** tab, you can configure which Networks the ISA firewall can listen on to accept incoming connections to the published server. In this example, we set the Server Publishing Rule to accept incoming connections from hosts on the **External Network** (the default External Network includes all addresses that aren't defined in any other Network on the ISA firewall).

You can configure the ISA firewall to listen on any Network. For example, you can configure the Server Publishing Rule to listen for connections on the VPN Clients Network. VPN clients can then connect to the published server via this Server Publishing Rule. The Networks tab is shown in Figure 8.48.

Figure 8.48 The Networks Tab

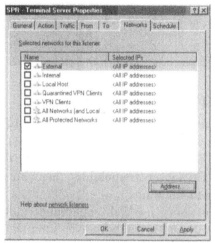

On the **Schedule** tab, you can set when connections can be made to the published server. There are three default schedules:

- **Always** Users can always connect to the published server.

- **Weekends** Users can connect to the published server from 12:00 A.M. to 12:00 A.M. Saturday and Sunday.

- **Work hours** Users can connect to the published server from 9:00 A.M. to 5:00 P.M. Monday through Friday.

You can also create your own schedule using the **New** button. We'll talk more about creating schedules in Chapter 10. Note that schedules control when users can connect to the published server, but they do not drop existing connections. The reason for this is that users who connected to the published server connected when connections are allowed, and they may have ongoing work that would be disturbed if the connection where arbitrarily halted by the schedule. You can script a disconnect by stopping the Microsoft Firewall service and restarting it if you must stop all connections. The Schedule tab is shown in Figure 8.49.

Figure 8.49 The Schedule Tab

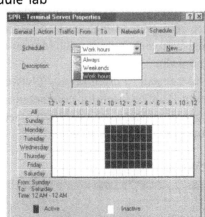

Server Publishing HTTP Sites

You might have noticed when going over the list of Protocol Definitions used for Server Publishing Rules that there wasn't a Protocol Definition for HTTP Server. There is a Protocol Definition for HTTPS servers but not for HTTP. If you want to create a Server Publishing Rule for HTTP server publishing then you will need to create your own HTTP server Protocol Definition.

We recommend that you always use Web Publishing Rules to publish Web sites, but there may be times when you want to publish a Web site that isn't compliant with Web Proxy servers. In this case you will need to use a Server Publishing Rule instead of a Web Publishing Rule.

Perform the following steps to create the Protocol Definition for HTTP Server publishing:

1. In the **Microsoft Internet Security and Acceleration Server 2004** management console, expand the server name and click the **Firewall Policy** node. Click the **Toolbox** tab in the **Task** Pane and click the **Protocols** header.

2. Click the **New** menu and click **Protocol**.

3. On the **Welcome to the New Protocol Definition Wizard** page, enter **HTTP Server** in the **Protocol Definition name** text box and click **Next**.

4. On the **Primary Connection Information** page, click the **New** button.

5. On the **New/Edit Protocol Connection** page, set the **Protocol type** to **TCP** and the **Direction** to **Inbound**. In the **Port range** frame, set the **From** and **To** values to **80**. Click **OK**.

Figure 8.50 The New/Edit Protocol Connection dialog box

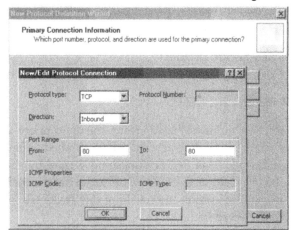

6. Click **Next** on the **Primary Connection Information** page.

7. On the **Secondary Connections** page, select the **No** option and click **Next**.

8. Click **Finish** on the **Completing the New Protocol Definition Wizard** page.

9. Click **Apply** to save the changes and update the firewall policy.

10. Click **OK** in the **Apply New Configuration** dialog box.

11. The new **HTTP Server** Protocol Definition appears in the list of **User-Defined** Protocol Definitions.

Figure 8.51 The new HTTP Server Protocol Definition

Creating Mail Server Publishing Rules

The ISA firewall includes a Mail Server Publishing Wizard right out of the box. You can use the Mail Server Publishing Wizard to publish the following mail-related services:

- Outlook Web Access

- Outlook Mobile Access

- Secure Exchange RPC

- IMAP4 and Secure IMAP4

- POP3 and Secure POP3

- SMTP and Secure SMTP

The Mail Server Publishing Wizard creates the appropriate Web or Server Publishing Rules required to allow access to the published mail server through the ISA firewall. You can access the Mail Server Publishing Wizard by clicking on the **Firewall Policy** node in the left pane of the **Microsoft Internet Security and Acceleration Server 2004** management console and clicking the **Tasks** tab in the **Task** pane. Click the **Publish a Mail Server** link.

On the **Welcome to the New Mail Server Publishing Rule Wizard** page, enter a name for the rule in the **Mail Server Publishing Rule name** text box. Give the rule a meaningful name so that you'll be able to identify the purpose of the rule. You may create several Web or Server Publishing Rules based on your selections, so keep this in mind when naming the rule. You can always rename the rules after the Wizard is completed. Click **Next**.

On the **Select Access Type** page (Figure 8.52), you have the following options:

- Web client access: Outlook Web Access (OWA), Outlook Mobile Access, Exchange Server ActiveSync

- Client access: RPC, IMAP, POP3, SMTP

- Server-to-server communication: SMTP, NNTP

Figure 8.52 The Select Access Type Page

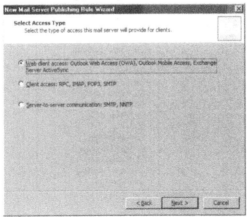

The **Web client access: Outlook Web Access (OWA), Outlook Mobile Access, Exchange Server ActiveSync** option publishes these services using Web

Publishing Rules. The Wizard configures the Web Publishing Rules for you. You can create SSL or non-SSL connections.

The **Client access: RPC, IMAP, POP3, SMTP** option publishes these protocols using Server Publishing Rules. You can publish one or more of these protocols when you select this option.

The **Server-to-server communication: SMTP, NNTP** option publishes these two protocols. You can select one or both.

Because the options available differ based on the selection you make on this page, we will cover each one separately in the following sections.

The Web Client Access: Outlook Web Access (OWA), Outlook Mobile Access, Exchange Server ActiveSync Option

Select this option and click **Next**. On the **Select Services** page, select the Exchange Web services you want to publish via a Web Publishing Rule. Your options are:

- Outlook Web Access
- Outlook Mobile Access
- Exchange ActiveSync

The Web Publishing Rule will contain the required paths to reach the Exchange Server services you select. The **Enable high bit characters used by non-English character sets** option allows users to view e-mail messages using extended characters. If you only want to support English characters, then remove the checkmark from this checkbox.

Figure 8.53 The Select Services Page

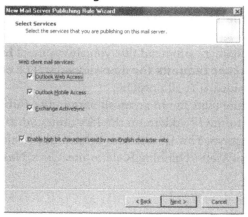

Click **Next**, as shown on the Select Services page in Figure 8.53.

On the **Bridging Mode** page, select how you want to publish the Web site. We highly recommend that you always use SSL-to-SSL bridging. This method is the most secure and minimizes compatibility issues. For more information on how to configure SSL bridging for Web Publishing Rules, see the Web Publishing section of this chapter.

On the **Specify the Web Mail Server** page, enter the name of the Web server on the ISA firewall Protected Network. We recommend that you use the FQDN of the machine and that this name be the same as the common name on the Web site certificate used on the Exchange OWA/OMA/ActiveSync Web site. The ISA firewall also needs to be able to resolve this name to the address that is actually bound to the Exchange Server on the corporate network and *not* the IP address on the ISA firewall's external interface. See the section on secure Web Publishing Rules in this chapter for more information on this subject. See Figure 8.54 for options on the Specify the Web Mail Server page.

Figure 8.54 The Specify the Web Mail Server page

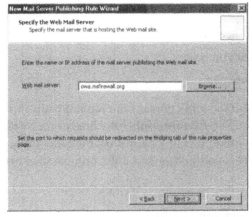

On the **Public Name Details** page, you can configure the name that the user who accesses the published server through the Web Publishing Rule must use when connecting to the site. We highly recommend that you always use **This domain name (type below)** in the **Accept requests for** drop-down list. The other option is not secure and should be avoided, if at all possible.

Enter the name remote users use to access the site in the **Public name** text box. This name must resolve to the IP address on the ISA firewall that listens for the incoming connection requests. This IP address is determined by the settings on the Web listener you configure this Web Publishing Rule to use. Click **Next**. See Figure 8.55.

Figure 8.55 The Public Name Details Page

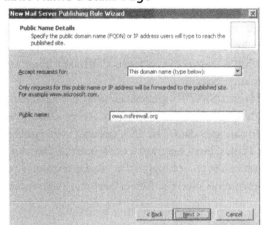

On the **Select Web Listener** page, select or create a Web listener for this rule. For details on creating and configuring Web listeners for Web Publishing Rules, please refer to the sections on creating HTTP and SSL Web Publishing Rules earlier in this chapter.

On the **User Sets** page, you can configure the rule to allow all users to connect to the published Web server, or you can have the ISA firewall pre-authenticate users before allowing them access to the published Web site. If you choose to have the ISA firewall to pre-authenticate users, you must make the ISA firewall a member of the user domain or a domain that trusts the user domain. An alternative is to configure the ISA firewall to use RADIUS authentication. We discuss how to configure the ISA firewall to use RADIUS authentication and configure RADIUS groups in Chapter 7 on outbound access through the ISA firewall. Click **Next**.

Click **Finish** on the **Completing the New Mail Server Publishing Rule Wizard** page. Click **Apply** to save the changes and update the firewall policy. Click **OK** in the **Apply New Configuration** dialog box.

The Client Access: RPC, IMAP, POP3, SMTP Option

Select this option and click **Next**. On the **Select Services** page you have the following options:

- Outlook (RPC)
- POP3: Standard ports and Secure ports
- IMAP4: Standard ports and Secure ports
- SMTP: Standard ports and Secure ports

The **Outlook (RPC)** option creates a Server Publishing Rule that allows inbound access for secure Exchange RPC connections. Secure Exchange RPC publishing allows Outlook 2000, 2002, and 2003 to "just work," regardless of where the user is located.

When combined with a well-designed split DNS infrastructure, users can roam between the corporate network and remote locations, open Outlook, and access their e-mail transparently without requiring reconfiguration of their e-mail application. Secure Exchange RPC is a very secure publishing protocol, and you can configure the Secure Exchange RPC Server Publishing Rule to force Outlook clients to encrypt their communications to the Exchange Server.

The **POP3**, **IMAP4**, and **SMTP** options allow you to publish both secure and non-secure versions of these protocols. Secure versions of these protocols use SSL to encrypt both user credentials and data. The ISA firewall will publish these protocols using Server Publishing Rules, but you must configure the Exchange Server with the appropriate Web site certificates to complete the configuration if you want to use the secure version of these protocols. See the Select Services page in Figure 8.56.

Figure 8.56 The Select Services Page

Notice the information box on this page. It says **For full SMTP filtering functionality the Message Screener must be installed**. When you create the SMTP Server Publishing Rule using this Wizard, the SMTP security filter is enabled. The SMTP security filter blocks buffer overflow attacks against the published SMTP server. You can enhance the stateful application-layer inspection for SMTP messages moving through the SMTP Server Publishing Rule by installing and configuring the SMTP Message screener on the ISA firewall, on a dedicated SMTP relay, or on the Exchange Server itself. We will discuss the SMTP Message Screener in detail in Chapter 10 on the ISA firewall application-layer filtering feature set. Click **Next** on the **Select Services** page.

On the **Select Server** page, enter the IP address of the published server on the corporate network in the **Select Server** text box. Click **Next**.

On the **IP Addresses** page, select the Network representing the Interface that should accept connection requests for the published server. You can limit the IP address used to accept the incoming connection if you have multiple addresses bound to any of these interfaces by clicking the **Address** button. For more information on how to configure the settings on the **IP Addresses** page, see the discussion on this subject in the Server Publishing Rules section of this chapter. Click **Next**.

Click **Finish** on the **Completing the New Mail Server Publishing Rule Wizard** page. Click **Apply** to save the changes and update the firewall policy. Click **OK** in the **Apply New Configuration** dialog box.

You'll see a number of new rules in the **Firewall Policy** for the ISA firewall (Figure 8.57). You can rename these rules to clean them up and have them be more consistent with your own rule-naming policy.

Figure 8.57 Firewall Policy after Running the Mail Server Publishing Wizard

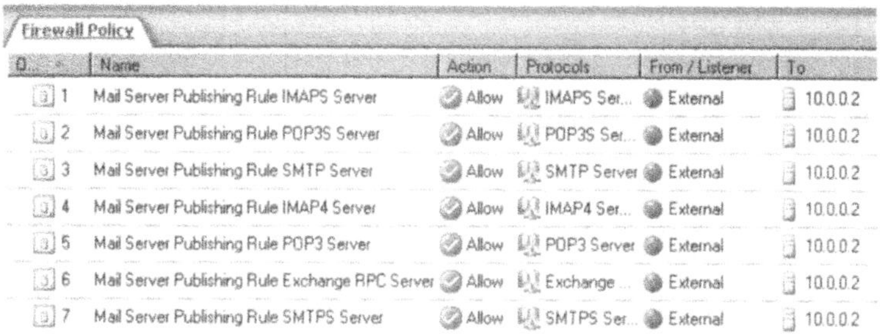

O...	Name	Action	Protocols	From / Listener	To
1	Mail Server Publishing Rule IMAPS Server	Allow	IMAPS Ser...	External	10.0.0.2
2	Mail Server Publishing Rule POP3S Server	Allow	POP3S Ser...	External	10.0.0.2
3	Mail Server Publishing Rule SMTP Server	Allow	SMTP Server	External	10.0.0.2
4	Mail Server Publishing Rule IMAP4 Server	Allow	IMAP4 Ser...	External	10.0.0.2
5	Mail Server Publishing Rule POP3 Server	Allow	POP3 Server	External	10.0.0.2
6	Mail Server Publishing Rule Exchange RPC Server	Allow	Exchange...	External	10.0.0.2
7	Mail Server Publishing Rule SMTPS Server	Allow	SMTPS Ser...	External	10.0.0.2

You can enhance the security for your secure Exchange RPC publishing rule by forcing the Outlook clients to use a secure connection. Right-click the **Exchange RPC Server** rule, and click **Configure Exchange RPC**. Put a checkmark in the **Enforce Encryption** checkbox, click **Apply** and then click **OK**. See Figure 8.58.

Figure 8.58 The Configure Exchange RPC Policy Dialog Box

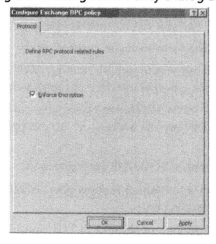

Summary

In this chapter we discussed methods you can use to provide secure access to servers and services protected by the ISA firewall. The two primary methods of providing secure remote access to corporate services are Web Publishing Rules and Server Publishing Rules. Web Publishing Rules can be used to publish HTTP, HTTPS, and FTP servers. Server Publishing Rules can publish almost any other protocol. We discussed the details of Web and Server Publishing and how to configure and create Web and Server Publishing Rules.

Solutions Fast Track

Overview of Web Publishing and Server Publishing

☑ Web Publishing Rules provide proxied access to published servers; this is more secure than reverse NAT'ing connections.

☑ Web and Server Publishing Rules expose connections to deep application-layer inspection depending on which protocols are published.

☑ The HTTP Security Filter exposes the HTTP and SSL connection to very deep inspection and allows you to control access based on virtually any aspect of the HTTP communications.

☑ Web Publishing allows you to perform path redirection.

☑ Web Publishing allows you to pre-authenticate users.

☑ Web Publishing allows you to cache content on the published Web sites.

☑ Web Publishing allows you to publish multiple Web sites with a single IP address bound to the external interface of the ISA firewall.

☑ For both Web and Server Publishing Rules, you can replace the client source address with the ISA firewall's address, or you can preserve the client IP address.

☑ Web publishing supports RADIUS authentication.

☑ Both Web and Server publishing support port redirection. Web Publishing supports protocol redirection.

☑ Server Publishing supports publishing all TCP and UDP protocols, including complex protocols.

☑ You can apply schedules that limit when published sites are available for both Web and Server Publishing Rules.

Creating and Configuring Non-SSL Web Publishing Rules

☑ You can create non-SSL Web Publishing Rules using the Web Publishing Rule Wizard.

☑ Use **Forward the original host header instead of the actual one (special above)** when you want the ISA firewall to forward the host name that the client on the Internet sent to the ISA firewall.

☑ Always use a specific public name for all Web Publishing Rules. Do not use the option to accept requests for **Any domain name**.

☑ Use the path option to control what paths on the published Web server remote users can access when connecting via the Web Publishing Rule.

☑ The authentication options configured on the Web listener determine what authentication protocols are supported when the ISA firewall pre-authenticates connections to the published Web site.

☑ Use delegation of basic authentication when publishing Web sites to prevent users from being exposed to multiple log-on dialog boxes.

☑ Configure Web listeners to listen on a specific IP address. Do not configure Web listeners to listen on all IP addresses unless you are using a dial-up connection to the Internet.

☑ Avoid socket contention and compromising the security of the ISA firewall by not installing any IIS service on the ISA firewall except for the IIS SMTP service.

☑ Enable **Require all users to authenticate** if all Web Publishing Rules using a particular Web listener will require pre-authentication by the ISA firewall.

☑ Configure separate Web listeners for HTTP and SSL connections, even when the listeners listen on the same IP address.

Creating and Configuring SSL Web Publishing Rules

☑ The ISA firewall supports both SSL bridging and SSL tunneling. SSL bridging is the more secure option.

☑ SSL-to-SSL bridging is the most secure method of SSL bridging and is the preferred SSL publishing method.

☑ The public name must be the same as the common name on the certificate bound to the Web listener.

☑ The name on the **To** tab on the Web Publishing Rule must be the same as the name bound to the Web site certificate on the published Web site.

☑ If there is a name mismatch, the user will see a 500 Internal Server Error.

☑ The most common reason for the Web site certificate not appearing in the list of certificates available to bind to the Web listener is that the private key was not included with the certificate.

Creating Server Publishing Rules

☑ Server Publishing Rules provide reverse NAT for published servers.

☑ Server Publishing Rules are exposed to stateful application-layer inspection depending on the protocol published.

☑ You can configure port redirection for any protocol used in a Server Publishing Rule.

☑ You can control the source ports allowed for any protocol Server Publishing Rule.

☑ You can configure Server Publishing Rules to retain the source IP address of the remote client or replace the source IP address with the IP address of the ISA firewall.

Creating Mail Server Publishing Rules

☑ The ISA firewall's Mail Server Publishing Wizard allows you to publish common mail server protocols.

☑ You can use the Mail Server Publishing Wizard to publish OWA, OMA and ActiveSync Web sites.

☑ The Mail Server Publishing Wizard can create SMTP, NNTP, POP3(S), and IMAP4(S) Server Publishing Rules.

☑ Additional configuration may be required on the published Web mail server to completely support the publishing configuration.

Frequently Asked Questions

The following Frequently Asked Questions, answered by the authors of this book, are designed to both measure your understanding of the concepts presented in this chapter and to assist you with real-life implementation of these concepts. To have your questions about this chapter answered by the author, browse to **www.syngress.com/solutions** and click on the **"Ask the Author"** form. You will also gain access to thousands of other FAQs at ITFAQnet.com.

Q: I can receive incoming mail from my SMTP Server Publishing Rule, but outbound mail isn't going out. How can I fix this?

A: The incoming mail from Internet SMTP servers to your corporate SMTP servers is controlled by the Server Publishing Rule allowing the mail through the ISA firewall to the SMTP server on your network. The external DNS also was configured to resolve your MX names to the IP address on the external interface of the ISA firewall. For outbound SMTP connections, you'll need to make sure the SMTP server is able to resolve the names for the SMTP servers responsible for mail in each Internet domain. You'll need to configure the ISA firewall with Access Rules allowing outbound SMTP from the SMTP server to the Internet. Also, you need to make sure that the SMTP server is configured with a DNS server that has access to a DNS Access Rule.

Q: I'm getting a 500 Internal Server Error when I try to access my OWA Web site. What's up with that?

A: The problem is that the common name on the Web site certificate bound to the published Web server is not the same as the name on the **To** tab in the Web Publishing Rule. Change the name or IP address you have listed in the **To** tab so that it's the same as the common name on the Web site certificate. Also, make sure that the ISA firewall is able to resolve that name to the actual IP address of the Web site (the exception being if the Web site is separated from the ISA firewall by a NAT device, in which case the name should resolve to the IP address of the interface on that device performing reverse NAT).

Q: My users are receiving multiple authentication prompts when connecting to my published Web site. How can I set the ISA firewall up so that users see a single prompt?

A: Configure the Web listener to use Basic authentication, and then configure the Web Publishing Rule to use delegation of Basic credentials. Then confirm that the published Web site supports Basic authentication. Users will no longer bet presented with multiple authentication prompts.

Q: I want to publish a mail server on an ISA Protected Network, but I do not want that machine to be a SecureNAT client. How can I configure the ISA firewall so that the machine doesn't need to be configured for SecureNAT?

A: You can configure the Server Publishing Rule so that the ISA firewall's IP address replaces the IP address of the source host. In this way, the only route the SMTP server needs to know is the route to the network ID on which the interface forwards the connection to the SMTP server.

Q: We want to allow VPN clients access only to our Microsoft Exchange Server via Secure Exchange RPC. Is this possible?

A: You can use the Mail Server Publishing Wizard to create a Secure Exchange RPC Server Publishing Rule with a listener on the VPN Clients Network. Then create a DNS Server Publishing Rule with a listener on the VPN Clients Network. Using the combination of these two Server Publishing Rules, you can publish your corporate network DNS and Exchange servers to members of the VPN Clients Network and allow them to connect to your Exchange Server using only secure Exchange RPC, and allow them access only to the Exchange and DNS servers and no other servers on the Network.

Q: SSL-to-HTTP bridging is configured for our published Web site, but it's not working. How can I fix the Web Publishing Rule so that SSL-to-HTTP bridging works correctly?

A: The of the problems with SSL-to-HTTP bridging is that Web servers often dynamically generate links based on the protocol used for the connection. Since the link between the ISA firewall and published Web server uses HTTP, the link generated by the Web server is an HTTP link, and this is returned to the Web client on the Internet. Since the connection between the Web client and the ISA firewall requires SSL, the connection fails. You may be able to solve this problem using the ISA firewall's Link Translation feature, but a better solution is to implement SSL-to-SSL bridging. Not only does SSL-to-SSL bridging solve the link problem, it also increases the overall level of security of your Web Publishing solution.

Q: We want to publish an HTTP Web server using a Server Publishing Rule because there's a Web app on the machine that doesn't support CERN-compliant Web proxies. How can we do this?

A: You can publish an HTTP Web server using a Server Publishing Rule instead of a Web Publishing Rule. You must make sure that no Web listener is using the socket you want to use for the Server Publishing Rule before using a Server Publishing Rule to publish the HTTP server. After confirming that no Web listener is using the socket (and the IIS WWW service is not installed on the ISA firewall), create a Protocol Definition for TCP port 80 Inbound. Then use this Protocol Definition to create the HTTP Server Publishing Rule.

Chapter 9

Creating Remote Access and Site-to-Site VPNs with ISA Firewalls

Topics in this Chapter:

Overview of ISA Firewall VPN Networking

Virtual private networking (VPN) has grown in popularity until it has become a standard for companies that have telecommuters, executives, and salespeople who need network access when on the road, and/or partners and customers who need access to resources on the corporate network. The purpose of VPN networking is to allow remote access to resources on the corporate network that would otherwise only be available if the user were directly connected to the corporate LAN. With a VPN connection, the user has a "virtual" point-to-point link between the remote VPN user and the corporate network. The user can work as if he/she were on site; applications and services running on the users' computers treat the VPN link as if it were a typical Ethernet connection. The Internet over which the client is connected to the corporate network is completely transparent to the users and applications.

One of the major advantages of using a VPN connection instead of a client/server Web application is that VPN users at remote locations can potentially access all of the protocols and servers on the corporate network. This means your users can access the full range of services on Microsoft Exchange Servers, Microsoft SharePoint Servers, Microsoft SQL Servers, and Microsoft Live Communication Servers just as they do when they are directly connected to the network at the corporate location. VPN client software is built into all modern Windows operating systems. A VPN user does not need any special software to connect to each of these services, and it's not necessary to create special proxy applications to allow your users to connect to these resources.

ISA Server 2000 was the first Microsoft firewall to provide tightly integrated VPN configuration and management. ISA Server 2000 included easy-to-use wizards that made it simple to create remote access and site-to-site (gateway-to-gateway) VPN connections to the ISA Server 2000 firewall/VPN server. However, there were still some improvements that could be made. The ISA Server 2000 VPN server still required the firewall administrator to spend a significant amount of time fine-tuning the VPN server configuration via the Routing and Remote Access console.

ISA 2004 significantly enhances the VPN components that are included with the Windows 2000 and Windows Server 2003 Routing and Remote Access Services (RRAS). Now an administrator can enable, configure, and manage the VPN server and gateway components directly from the ISA 2004 firewall management console, rather than having to go back and forth between the ISA MMC and the RRAS MMC. You will rarely need to use the Routing and Remote Access console to configure VPN components.

Other improvements to VPN functionality in ISA 2004 include:

- Firewall Policy Applied to VPN Client Connections
- Firewall Policy Applied to VPN Site-to-Site Connections
- VPN Quarantine
- User Mapping of VPN Clients
- SecureNAT Client Support for VPN Connections

- Site-to-Site VPN using Tunnel Mode IPSec
- Publishing PPTP VPN Servers
- Pre-shared Key Support for IPSec VPN Connections
- Advanced Name Server Assignment for VPN Clients
- Monitoring of VPN Client Connections

These new VPN server and gateway features make ISA 2004 one of the most powerful co-located VPN and firewall solutions on the market today. In the following subsections, we discuss these new features and how they work together to make the ISA 2004 VPN solution the VPN of choice for all organizations running Microsoft networks.

Firewall Policy Applied to VPN Client Connections

When a VPN remote-access client establishes a connection with the VPN server, the VPN client acts like a machine that is directly connected to the corporate network. This virtual link to the corporate network enables the remote VPN user access to almost every resource on the corporate network, limited only by the access controls configured on the servers and workstations. However, this power to access virtually any resource on the corporate network can be a security risk. Generally, you should not allow users to have a full range of access to corporate resources when they connect over a remote access VPN connection. That's because these users might be connecting from computers that aren't within your control and don't conform to corporate software and security policies, or they may be connecting from computers that are on untrusted networks, such as hotel broadband networks. You have no way of knowing whether these machines pose a threat to your network.

Your VPN policy should stipulate that only highly-trusted users who are connecting from known trusted machines on known trusted networks are allowed unfettered access to the corporate network over a remote-access VPN link. Examples of users who might be granted such access include your network, security, and firewall administrators, and perhaps some highly-placed executives. All other users should be restricted to accessing only the subset of network resources that they need to do their jobs when connected via the VPN link.

For example, many firewall administrators allow users to connect over VPN so that they can use the full Outlook 2000/2002/2003 MAPI client to access a Microsoft Exchange Server. Microsoft Exchange provides several different methods for remotely accessing Exchange Server resources. These include the SMTP, POP3, IMAP3, and Outlook Web Access (OWA) services. However, users like to keep the broad range of options available to them when using the full Outlook MAPI client.

There are basically three ways to satisfy users' needs in this situation:

- Publish the Exchange Server using the ISA Server secure RPC Server Publishing Rule

- Have your users use the Outlook 2003/Exchange 2003 RPC over HTTP protocol

- Grant your users VPN access to the corporate network

The ISA Server secure RPC Server Publishing mechanism enables remote Outlook MAPI clients to connect to the full range of Microsoft Exchange Server services from any remote location. The only problem is that, for security reasons, many firewalls and ISPs have blocked access to the RPC port mapper port (TCP 135). This port is required to make the initial secure connection to the Exchange Server using a secure Exchange RPC publishing rule, but the Blaster worm, which exploited this port, caused most administrators to shut it down. Consequently, RPC publishing has lost much of its former utility.

RPC over HTTP(S) can solve this problem by encapsulating the RPC connection inside an HTTP header. This allows the Outlook MAPI client to send requests to the Exchange Server using HTTP. HTTP is generally allowed by all corporate firewalls and ISPs, since it is used for Web communications. The problem with this solution is that not all organizations have upgraded to Outlook 2003 and Exchange Server 2003.

Granting users VPN access will circumvent the limitations of the other solutions, but providing such access can pose a security risk when all VPN clients can access the entire network. The ideal solution is to enforce Access Policy on VPN clients, based on user/group accounts. This way, users can access only the servers and protocols they require.

ISA 2004 is the only VPN server solution that gives administrators this level of access control. When VPN clients connect to the VPN server, those clients are placed on a built-in network entity called the *VPN Clients Network*. The ISA 2004 firewall treats this network like any other network, which means strong user- and group-based access controls can be placed on data that travels between the VPN Clients Network and the corporate network.

All you need to do is create the user accounts and create an access policy on the ISA 2004 firewall/VPN server that limits what machines and protocols the users/groups can access and use, and all those network devices are protected from the VPN remote-access users.

This feature virtually eliminates the need for SSL VPNs (except in those circumstances where remote users are behind extremely restrictive firewalls that block all but HTTP and SSL connections outbound) and other proprietary remote-access solutions aimed at providing per protocol, per server, per user/group access to corporate network resources. Most commercial broadband networks at hotels and conference centers allow outbound PPTP and L2TP/IPSec via NAT Traversal. This way, you can provide remote access for your VPN users without the security threat that typically accompanies VPN client connections.

Firewall Policy Applied to VPN Site-to-Site Connections

A site-to-site VPN connection connects two or more networks (instead of an individual client and a network) over the Internet. Using a VPN site-to-site link can create substantial cost savings in comparison to dedicated WAN links that use dedicated circuits (for example, linking two sites via T-1).

To use a VPN site-to-site link, each site requires a VPN gateway and a relatively inexpensive Internet connection. When the VPN gateways establish connections with one another, the site-to-site VPN link is established. Then the users on each end can communicate with other networks over the VPN site-to-site link just as they would with a routed connection on their own network. The VPN gateways act as routers and route the packets to the appropriate network.

VPN site-to-site connections use the same technologies as do client-to-server (remote access) VPN connections – and traditionally suffered from the same security problem. That is, all users had access to the entire network to which their own network was connected. The only thing that kept users out of network resources for which they had no permission to access was local access controls on the servers.

Site-to-site VPN connections are typically set up between branch office and main office networks. Providing branch office users with access to the entire main office network can pose a major security threat.

The ISA 2004 firewall/VPN server can solve this problem by controlling outbound data that travels through the site-to-site link. Users at the branch office can be limited to only the resources on the main office network required to do their jobs, and thus, prevented from accessing other computer resources on the main network. As with remote-access VPN clients, the users at the branch office should only be allowed to use the specific protocols they need on the servers they are allowed to access.

VPN site-to-site connections that take advantage of strong user- and group-based access controls can save money without sacrificing security.

VPN Quarantine

VPN Quarantine (VPN-Q) is a new feature that allows you to screen VPN client machines before allowing them access to the corporate network. The VPN Quarantine feature included with ISA 2004 is similar to the Network Quarantine feature found in Windows Server 2003 RRAS.

To use VPN-Q, you must create a CMAK (Connection Manager Administration Kit) package that includes a VPN-Q client and a VPN-Q client-side script. The client runs the script and reports the results to the VPN-Q server component on the ISA 2004 firewall/VPN server. The VPN client is moved from the "VPN Quarantine" network to the "VPN Clients" network if the script reports that the client meets the software requirements for connecting to the network. You can set different access policies for hosts on the VPN Quarantine network versus the VPN Clients network.

The ISA 2004 firewall extends the functionality of the Windows Server 2003 RRAS Quarantine controls because the Windows Server 2003 RRAS Quarantine feature does not let you set policy-based access controls. The RRAS Quarantine uses simple "port-based" access controls, but it this doesn't really provide any level of serious security. The ISA 2004 firewall applies strong firewall policy-based access controls over hosts on the VPN Quarantine network and exposes these connections to the ISA 2004 firewall's sophisticated application-layer filters.

TIP

Here is some good news for ISA 2004 firewall administrators who are planning to install the firewall on Windows 2000: When you install ISA 2004 on a Windows 2000 machine, the firewall will bring VPN-Q functionality with it. In other words, you don't have to have Windows Server 2003 to get the VPN-Q feature when ISA 2004 is installed on the Windows 2000 machine. (There is a limitation in that you have to use ISA 2004 VPN-Q policies rather than RADIUS policies, but the additional functionality ISA 2004 adds to the Windows 2000 RRAS VPN is significant).

User Mapping of VPN Clients

User mapping is a feature that allows you to map virtual private network (VPN) clients connecting to ISA Server using an authentication method that is not based on "Windows authentication" (such as RADIUS or EAP authentication) to the Windows namespace. With user mapping enabled and configured, firewall policy access rules specifying user sets for Windows users and groups are also applied to authenticated users that do not use Windows authentication. Default firewall policy access rules will not be applied to users from namespaces that are not based on Windows, unless you define user mapping for users.

The user mapping feature extends the strong user/group-based access controls you can apply to VPN clients that use an authentication method other than Windows.

This is important because Windows authentication of domain users is only available when the ISA 2004 firewall belongs to the domain that contains the users accounts, or to a domain that is trusted by the user accounts' domain. If the ISA 2004 firewall does not belong to a domain, then Windows authentication is used only for user accounts stored on the ISA 2004 firewall machine itself.

With user mapping, you can use RADIUS authentication of domain users, and you can apply user/group-based access control over VPN clients who authenticate via RADIUS. Without user mapping, you would not have access to strong user/group-based access control, and Access Policies from the VPN Clients Network to the Internal network would be limited to controlling protocol and server access to all users connecting to the VPN.

SecureNAT Client Support for VPN Connections

When a VPN client connects to the VPN server, the routing table on the VPN client changes so that the default gateway is the IP address of the VPN server. This causes a potential problem for VPN clients in that, while they are connected to the VPN, they cannot access resources on the Internet at the same time.

A problem with the ISA Server 2000 firewall/VPN servers was that, for VPN clients to access resources on the Internet, you had to choose from one of the three following options:

- Enabling split tunneling on the VPN client
- Installing the Firewall Client software on the VPN client machines
- Configuring the Dial-up and Virtual Private Network settings of the VPN connection with Proxy Server settings (this enables browsing with Internet Explorer only when the client is connected to the VPN)

Split tunneling refers to a configuration wherein the VPN client machine is *not* configured to use the default gateway on the remote network. The default setting for Microsoft VPN clients is to use the default gateway for the remote network. A VPN requires two connections: first, a connection is made to the Internet (with broadband or other always-on technology, this connection does not have to be manually established each time); second, the VPN connection is made *over* the Internet connection. When VPN clients are configured not to use the default gateway, they can access resources on the corporate network through the VPN connection, and they can also access resources on the Internet via the Internet connection that was established by the VPN client machine *before* the VPN connection took place.

There are some serious security threats that occur when the VPN client machine can access the Internet directly while at the same time being able to access the corporate network via the VPN link. This allows the VPN client computer to completely bypass all Internet access policies that were configured on the ISA Server 2000 firewall for the duration of the VPN connection. Split tunneling is like allowing users on the corporate network to have local modem connections along with their connections to the LAN. The modem connections would completely bypass the ISA Server 2000 firewall policy and allow the workstation access to the Internet that would not otherwise be allowed by the ISA Server 2000 firewall policies. This creates a potential for downloading worms, viruses, and other dangerous content. A malicious user on the Internet would even be able to route exploits from an outside computer through the machine that is performing split tunneling and into the corporate network.

Because of this risk, it was important to provide an alternate method of allowing VPN clients Internet access while connected to the ISA 2004 firewall/VPN server. The preferred alternative with ISA 2000 is to install the firewall client software on the VPN client machine. The Firewall Client will forward requests directly to the ISA Server firewall's internal IP address and does not require split tunneling to allow the client computer to connect to the Internet. In addition, the Firewall Client exposes the VPN client machine to the ISA Server 2000 firewall access policies.

ISA 2004 firewall/VPN servers solve the problem of split tunneling without requiring installation of the Firewall client by enabling Internet access for VPN SecureNAT clients. The VPN clients are SecureNAT clients of the ISA 2004 firewall by default, because they use the firewall as their default gateway. The ISA 2004 firewall/VPN server can use the log-on credentials of the VPN client to apply strong user- and group-based access controls in order to limit the sites, content, and protocols that the VPN client machines will be allowed to access on the Internet.

TIP

Even though the Firewall client software is not required on VPN client computers to allow them to access the Internet through the ISA 2004 firewall machine, you might still want to install the Firewall client on VPN client machines if you want to support complex protocols that require one or more secondary connections. SecureNAT clients can't use complex protocols that require secondary connections unless there is an application filter to support the secondary connections. Firewall client machines can access any TCP or UDP protocol, even those that require secondary connections, without the requirement of the Application Filter.

An alternative to using the Firewall client on the VPN client is to configure the Dial-up and Network settings of the VPN client connection object in Internet Explorer with Proxy Server settings. If you are using ISA Server 2000, you can configure the VPN connection object with the same Web Proxy settings that are used by internal clients. However, this approach allows VPN clients to use HTTP, HTTP(S) and FTP (download only) protocols for Internet access. This same feature is available when connecting to ISA 2004 firewall/VPN servers.

Site-to-Site VPN Using Tunnel Mode IPSec

With ISA Server 2000, VPN remote-access clients could use PPTP or L2TP/IPSec to connect to the ISA Server 2000 VPN server, and other VPN gateways could connect to the ISA Server 2000 VPN gateway and establish site-to-site VPN links between two geographically separate networks. However, most third-party VPN gateways (such as Cisco or other popular VPN gateway solutions) did not support PPTP or L2TP/IPSec for VPN gateway-to-gateway connections. Instead, they required IPSec tunnel mode VPN connections.

If you had ISA Server 2000 firewall/VPN servers on both sites, it was simple to create a highly secure L2TP/IPSec VPN connection between the two sites or a less secure PPTP VPN connection. However, if you had a third-party VPN gateway at the main office, and you wanted to install an ISA Server 2000 VPN gateway at a branch office, you couldn't establish a site-to-site VPN connection to the main office VPN gateway because the main office VPN gateway didn't support PPTP or L2TP/IPSec connections, and ISA Server 2000 didn't support IPSec tunnel mode connections for site-to-site links.

ISA 2004 firewalls solve this problem because you can now use IPSec tunnel mode for site-to-site links between an ISA 2004 VPN gateway and a third-party VPN gateway. You can still use PPTP or high security L2TP/IPSec to create site-to-site links between two ISA Server firewall/VPN gateways, but ISA 2004 enables you use a lower security IPSec tunnel mode connection to connect to third party VPN gateways.

> **NOTE**
>
> IPSec tunnel mode is supported only for site-to-site VPN connections. Client-to-server remote-access VPN connections still use only PPTP or L2TP/IPSec. When using IPSec tunnel mode, you should be aware that it is vulnerable to several well-known exploits, whereas L2TP/IPSec requires stronger authentication and is not as vulnerable to these attacks. Thus, when you have a choice, L2TP/IPSec is the preferred VPN protocol set for site-to-site VPN connections.

Publishing PPTP VPN Servers

In ISA Server 2000, Server Publishing Rules limited you to publishing servers that required only TCP or UDP protocols. In other words, you could not publish servers that required non–TCP or UDP protocols, such as ICMP or GRE. This meant you could not publish a PPTP server because it uses the GRE protocol, which is a non–TCP or UDP protocol. The only alternative with ISA Server 2000 was to put these servers on a perimeter network segment and use packet filters to allow the required protocols to and from the Internet.

ISA 2004 has solved this problem. You can now create Server Publishing Rules for any IP protocol using ISA 2004. This includes Server Publishing Rules for GRE. The ISA 2004 firewall's enhanced PPTP filter now allows inbound and outbound access. The new inbound access support means you can publish a PPTP VPN server located behind an ISA 2004 firewall.

This feature is sure to be very popular among former ISA Server 2000 firewall administrators who formerly had to create VPN pass-through connections in order to reach the Internal network.

Pre-shared Key Support for IPSec VPN Connections

A Public Key Infrastructure (PKI) is necessary in high-security environments so that computer and user certificates can be issued to the computers that participate in an IPSec-based VPN connection. Digital certificates are used for computer authentication for L2TP/IPSec remote access and gateway-to-gateway connections, and for IPSec tunnel mode connections. Certificates can also be used for user authentication for both PPTP and L2TP/IPSec connections.

Setting up a PKI is not a simple task, and many network administrators do not have the time or the expertise to implement one quickly. In that case, there is another way to benefit from the level of security provided by IPSec-protected VPN connections.

With ISA 2004, you can use pre-shared keys instead of certificates when you create remote access and gateway-to-gateway VPN connections. All VPN client machines running the updated L2TP/IPSec VPN client software can use a pre-shared key to create an L2TP/IPSec remote-access VPN client connection with the ISA 2004 firewall/VPN server. Windows 2000 and Windows Server 2003 VPN gateways can also be configured to use a pre-shared key to establish site-to-site links.

> **WARNING**
>
> Pre-shared keys for IPSec-based VPN connections should be used with caution. Certificates are still the preferred method.

Be aware that a single remote-access server can use only one pre-shared key for all L2TP/IPSec connections that require a pre-shared key for authentication. You must issue the same pre-shared key to all L2TP/IPSec VPN clients connecting to the remote-access server using a pre-shared key. Unless you distribute the pre-shared key within a Connection Manager profile (CMAK), each user will have to manually enter the pre-shared key into the VPN client software settings. This reduces the security of the L2TP/IPSec VPN deployment and increases the probability of user error and increased number of support calls related to L2TP/IPSec connection failures.

> **WARNING**
>
> If the pre-shared key on the ISA 2004 firewall/VPN server is changed, a client with a manually configured pre-shared key will not be able to connect using the L2TP/IPSec pre-shared key until the key on the client machine is also changed.

Despite its security drawbacks, the ability to easily use pre-shared keys to create secure L2TP/IPSec connections to the ISA 2004 firewall/VPN server is sure to be popular among firewall administrators. Pre-shared keys are an ideal "stop gap" measure that you can put into place immediately and use while in the process of putting together a certificate-based Public Key Infrastructure. When the PKI is complete, you can then migrate the clients from pre-shared keys to high-security computer and user certificate authentication.

Advanced Name Server Assignment for VPN Clients

The ISA Server 2000 VPN server/gateway was based on the VPN components included with the Windows 2000 and Windows Server 2003 Routing and Remote Access

Services. The RRAS VPN services allow you to assign name server addresses to VPN remote access clients. Proper name server assignment is very important to VPN clients because incorrect name server assignments can render the VPN client unable to connect to either Internal network resources or resources located on the Internet.

Alternatively, it is possible to configure the VPN client connectoid with the IP addresses of WINS and DNS server. You can automate this process by using the Connection Manager Administration Kit to distribute these settings. Client-side name server assignment requires that each connectoid object be manually configured or that you use CMAK to distribute these settings.

It is possible to distribute name resolution settings from the VPN server. However, if you wanted to distribute name server settings to a VPN client from the ISA Server 2000 VPN server, you had to use one of the following:

- Name server addresses that were bound to one of the network interfaces on the ISA Server 2000 firewall machine

- Name server addresses provided to the VPN client via DHCP options (this was available only if the DHCP Relay Agent was installed on the ISA Server 2000 firewall/VPN server)

You might sometimes want to assign VPN clients name server addresses that are not based on the network interface configuration on the firewall/VPN server, and you might not want to install the DHCP Relay Agent on the firewall. Unfortunately, if this was the case, you were out of luck with ISA Server 2000 because it did not support this scenario.

Good news: ISA 2004 firewall/VPN servers do not have this problem because they allow you to override the name server settings on the ISA 2004 firewall/VPN server and issue custom name server addresses to the VPN clients. This can be done within the ISA 2004 management console; you don't have to enter the RRAS console to create the custom configuration.

Monitoring of VPN Client Connections

The ISA Server 2000 VPN server was limited by the logging and monitoring capabilities of the Windows 2000 and Windows Server 2003 RRAS VPN. Determining who connected to the network via a VPN connection required that you sift through text files or database entries. And that's not all; because the firewall did not manage the VPN remote-access client connections, there was no central mechanism in place at the firewall to allow you to determine which resources were being accessed by VPN remote-access clients.

ISA 2004 solves this problem by applying firewall policy to *all* connections to the firewall, including VPN connections. You can use the real-time log viewer to look at ongoing VPN remote-access client connections and filter it to view only VPN client connections. If you log to an MSDE database, you can query the database to view an historical record of VPN connections. With ISA 2004 firewall/VPN servers, you not only get complete information about who connected to the ISA 2004 firewall/VPN, but you also get information about what resources those users connected to and what protocols they used to connect to those resources.

For example, you can filter VPN criteria in the log viewer if you are using live logging and are logging to a file. What you can't do with file-based logging is use the ISA firewall's log viewer to query the archived data. However, you can still filter and monitor real-time VPN connections in the log viewer. In addition, you can filter VPN connections in both the Sessions view and the Log view.

In the **Tasks** tab in the Task pane of the **Virtual Private Networks (VPN)** node in the **Microsoft Internet Security and Acceleration Server 2004** management console, you can click on a link that allows you to monitor the VPN client and gateway connections. If you choose this option, make sure you back up the default filter settings so that you can return to your baseline filtering configuration.

This ISA 2004 logging and monitoring feature is a big improvement over the logging and monitoring features included with ISA Server 2000 and is also much better than the standalone Windows 2000 and Windows Server 2003 Routing and Remote Access Service VPN.

Creating a Remote Access PPTP VPN Server

A remote access VPN server accepts VPN calls from VPN client machines. A remote access VPN server allows *single client machines and users* access to corporate network resources after the VPN connection is established. In contrast, a VPN gateway connects entire networks to each other and allows multiple hosts on each network to connect to other networks through a VPN site-to-site link.

You can use any VPN client software that supports PPTP or L2TP/IPSec to connect to a VPN server. The ideal VPN client software is the Microsoft VPN client, which is included with all versions of Windows. However, if you wish to use L2TP/IPSec with pre-shared keys and NAT traversal support, you should download and install the updated L2TP/IPSec client from the Microsoft download site. We'll go over the details on how to obtain this software later in the chapter.

In this section, we'll go over the procedures required to create a PPTP remote access VPN server on the ISA firewall. The specific steps we'll perform include:

- Enabling the ISA Firewall's VPN Server component
- Creating an Access Rule allowing VPN Clients access to the Internal network
- Enabling Dial-in Access for VPN User Accounts
- Testing a PPTP VPN Connection

Enable the VPN Server

You need to turn on the VPN server component, as it is disabled by default. The first step is to enable the VPN server feature and configure the VPN server components. You do this in the **Microsoft Internet Security and Acceleration Server 2004** management console and *not* in the RRAS console.

Most of the problems we've seen with the ISA firewall VPN configuration are related to fledgling ISA firewall administrators using the RRAS console to configure the VPN components. While there will be times when we want to use the RRAS console, the vast majority of the configuration for the ISA firewall's VPN server and VPN gateway is done in the **Microsoft Internet Security and Acceleration Server 2004** management console.

> ### WARNING
>
> You want to do most of your VPN server and gateway configuration in the **Microsoft Internet Security and Acceleration Server 2004** management console because the ISA firewall settings will overwrite most of the settings you create in the RRAS console. For more information on this issue, check out **Interoperability of Routing and Remote Access and Internet Security and Acceleration Server 2004** at
> http://support.microsoft.com/default.aspx?scid=kb;en-us;838374

Perform the following steps to enable and configure the ISA 2004 VPN Server:

1. Open the **Microsoft Internet Security and Acceleration Server 2004** management console and expand the server name. Click on the **Virtual Private Networks (VPN)** node.

2. Click on the **Tasks** tab in the Task pane. Click the **Enable VPN Client Access** link (Figure 9.1).

Figure 9.1 The Enable VPN Client Access link

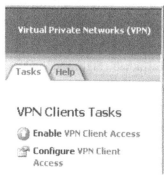

3. Click **Apply** to save the changes and update the firewall policy.
4. Click **OK** in the **Apply New Configuration** dialog box.
5. Click the **Configure VPN Client Access** link on the **Tasks** tab.

6. On the **General** tab in the **VPN Clients Properties** dialog box, change the value for the **Maximum number of VPN clients allowed** from **5** to **10**. The Standard Edition of the ISA firewall supports up to 1000 concurrent VPN connections. This is a hard-coded limit and it is locked-in regardless of the number of VPN connections supported by the Windows operating system on which the ISA firewall is installed. The exact number is unclear, but we do know that when the ISA firewall is installed on the Enterprise version of Windows Server 2003, you can create over 16,000 PPTP connections and over 30,000 L2TP/IPSec VPN connections to the ISA firewall. The General tab is shown in Figure 9.2.

Figure 9.2 The General Tab

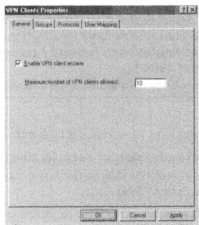

Make sure that you will have at least the number of IP addresses available to VPN clients as the number you list in the **Maximum number of VPN clients allowed** text box. Determine the number of VPN clients you want to connect to the ISA firewall, and then add one more for the ISA firewall itself. That's the number you want to enter into this text box.

1. Click on the **Groups** tab (Figure 9.3). On the **Groups** tab, click **Add**.

2. In the **Select Groups** dialog box, click the **Locations** button. In the **Locations** dialog box, click **msfirewall.org,** and click **OK**.

3. In the **Select Group** dialog box, enter **Domain Users** in the **Enter the object names to select** text box. Click **Check Names**. The group name will be underlined when it is found in the Active Directory. Click **OK**.

Figure 9.3 The Groups Tab

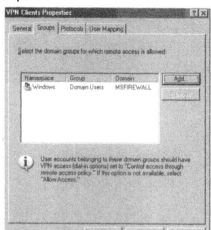

You can enter local groups that are configured on the ISA firewall machine itself, or you can use domain groups. The ISA firewall will use only domain Global Groups, it will not use Domain Local Groups. You configure domain Global Groups on the **Groups** tab *only* when the ISA firewall is a member of the domain. If the ISA firewall is not a member of the domain, then you can use RADIUS authentication to allow domain Global Groups access to the ISA firewall's VPN server. We will cover the details of configuring RADIUS authentication for VPN remote-access connections later in this chapter.

> **WARNING**
>
> The domain functionality must be set to Windows 2000 Native or higher in order to be able to **Control access through remote access policy**, or the users/group must be created on the ISA firewall's own SAM.

Another thing to keep in mind is that when you control access to the VPN server via a domain (or local) group, the users must have remote access permission. We'll discuss that issue later in this chapter.

1. Click the **Protocols** tab. On the **Protocols** tab, put a checkmark in the **Enable PPTP** check box only, as shown in Figure 9.4.

Figure 9.4 The Protocols Tab

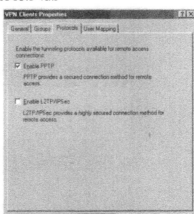

2 Click the **User Mapping** tab. Put a checkmark in the **Enable User Mapping** check box. Put a checkmark in the **When username does not contain a domain, use this domain** check box. Enter **msfirewall.org** in the **Domain Name** text box. Note that these settings will only apply when using RADIUS/EAP authentication. These settings are ignored when using Windows authentication (such as when the ISA 2004 firewall machine belongs to the domain and the user explicitly enters domain credentials). Click **Apply** and **OK.** You may see a **Microsoft Internet Security and Acceleration Server 2004** dialog box informing you that you need to restart the computer for the settings to take effect. If so, click **OK** in the dialog box. The User Mapping tab is shown in Figure 9.5.

Figure 9.5 The User Mapping tab

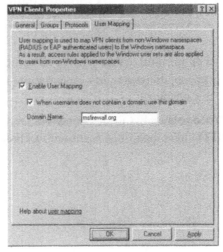

The User Mapping function is a bit obscure, and there isn't any good documentation on how the User Mapping functions with RADIUS (at this time). In fact, you can prevent all VPN connections to your ISA firewall if you enable user mapping and *do not* make the ISA firewall a member of the domain. From what we can tell, user mapping can be used when the ISA firewall is a member of your domain, and you use RADIUS authentication to support authentication for users that belong to multiple domains. In this case, you can enable user mapping to support creating user/group-based access control over users who log on via RADIUS and map those user accounts to accounts in the domain the ISA firewall belongs to, and then create Access Rules using those accounts by creating **User Sets** on the ISA firewall.

We have some information about **User Mapping** and how it works and doesn't work in an article, **Using RADIUS Authentication with the ISA Firewall's VPN Server**, at http://isaserver.org/articles/2004vpnradius.html. We will discuss this subject in more detail later in this chapter and also discuss how to use apply user/group-based access control over VPN clients that log on via RADIUS.

One area where User Mapping is well understood, and we have confirmed that it works correctly, is when you use EAP user certificate authentication. We will go over the details of how User Mapping works with EAP user certificate authentication later in the chapter.

3. On the **Tasks** tab, click **Select Access Networks**.

4. In the **Virtual Private Networks (VPN) Properties** dialog box, click **Access Networks**. Note that the **External** checkbox is selected. This indicates that the external interface is listening for incoming VPN client connections. If you want internal users to connect to the ISA firewall, select **Internal**. You also have the options to allow VPN connections from **All Networks (and Local Host) Network** and **All Protected Networks**. The Virtual Private Networks Properties dialog box is shown in Figure 9.6, **Select and Configure Access Networks Options**.

Figure 9.6 Select and Configure Access Networks Options

The ability to select VPN connections from multiple networks can be useful when you have unsecure networks located behind the ISA firewall. For example, suppose you have a trihomed ISA firewall that has an external interface, an Internal interface, and a WLAN interface. You use the WLAN for users who bring in laptops that are not managed by your organization. You also require users who have managed computers to use the WLAN segment as well when they bring laptops that are moved between the corporate network and untrusted networks.

You configure Access Rules on the ISA firewall to prevent connections from the WLAN segment. However, you configure Access Rules that allow VPN connections on the WLAN interface to connect to resources on the corporate Internal network. In this way, no users connected to the WLAN segment are able to access resources on the corporate Internal network segment except those corporate users who can VPN into the WLAN interface on the ISA firewall and present the proper credentials to complete a VPN link.

Another scenario where you might want to allow a VPN connection into the ISA firewall is when the ISA firewall is acting as a front-end firewall. In that case, you probably do not want to allow direct RDP or remote MMC connections to the ISA firewall. What you can do is allow RDP connections *only from VPN Clients* and then allow VPN clients RDP access to the Local Host Network. In this way, a user must establish a secure VPN connection to the front-end ISA firewall before an RDP connection can be established. Hosts connecting via any other means are denied access to the RDP protocols. Nice!

5. Click the **Address Assignment** tab (Figure 9.7). Select *Internal* from the **Use the following network to obtain DHCP, DNS and WINS services** drop down list box. This is a critical setting as it defines the network on which access to the DHCP is made.

Figure 9.7 The Address Assignment Tab

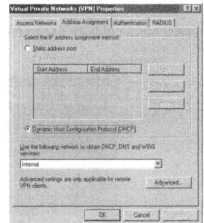

Note that this isn't your only option. You can select any of the adapters on the ISA firewall from **Use the following network to obtain DHCP, DNS and WINS**

services. The key issue is that you select the adapter that has the correct name server information on it, and the most likely candidate is the Internal interface of the ISA firewall.

You also have the option to use a **Static address pool** to assign addresses to the VPN clients. The problem with using a static address pool is, if you assign *on subnet* addresses (addresses in the same network ID as one of the interfaces on the ISA firewall), you will need to remove those addresses from the definition of the Network to which the ISA firewall is connected.

For example, suppose the ISA firewall has two network interfaces: an external and an internal interface. The internal interface is connected to your default Internal Network and the Internal Network ID is 192.168.1.0/24. If you want to assign VPN clients addresses in the Internal Network address range using a static address pool, such as 192.168.1.200/211 (total of 10 addresses), you will need to manually remove those addresses from the definition of the Internal Network before you can create a static address pool with these addresses. If you try to create a static address pool with these *on subnet* addresses, you'll see the following error (Figure 9.8).

Figure 9.8 A Network Warning Dialog Box.

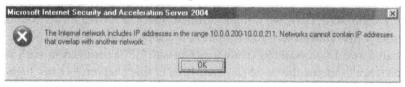

You can assign name server addresses to VPN clients that are independent of the name server configuration on any of the interfaces on the ISA firewall. Click the **Advanced** button, and you'll see the **Name Resolution** dialog box. The default settings are **Obtain DNS server addresses using DHCP configuration** and **Obtain WINS server addresses using DHCP configuration**. Of course, you cannot obtain DHCP options for VPN clients unless you install and configure a DHCP Relay Agent on the ISA firewall. The ISA firewall's RRAS service will only obtain blocks of IP addresses for the VPN clients, not DHCP options. We will discuss this issue in more detail later in this chapter.

If you want to avoid installing the DHCP Relay Agent, you can still deliver custom DNS and WINS server addresses to VPN clients by selecting **Use the following DNS server addresses** and **Use the following WINS server addresses**. See Figure 9.9.

Figure 9.9 The Name Resolution Dialog Box

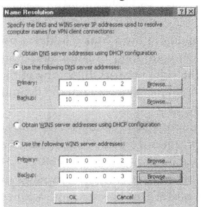

6. Click on the **Authentication** tab. Note that the default setting enables only
    Microsoft encrypted authentication version 2 (MS-CHAPv2). Note the
    Allow custom IPSec policy for L2TP connection checkbox. If you do
    not want to create a public key infrastructure (PKI), or, you are in the process
    of creating one but have not yet finished, you can enable this checkbox and
    enter a **pre-shared** key. You should also enable a custom IPSec policy pre-
    shared key if you want to create a site-to-site VPN connection with pre-shared
    keys. We'll discuss this issue in detail later in this chapter. For the highest level
    of authentication security, enable the **Extensible authentication protocol
    (EAP) with smart card or other certificate** option. We will discuss later in
    this chapter how to configure the ISA firewall and VPN clients to use User
    Certificates to authenticate to the ISA firewall. Figure 9.10 shows the
    Authentication tab options.

Figure 9.10 The Authentication Tab

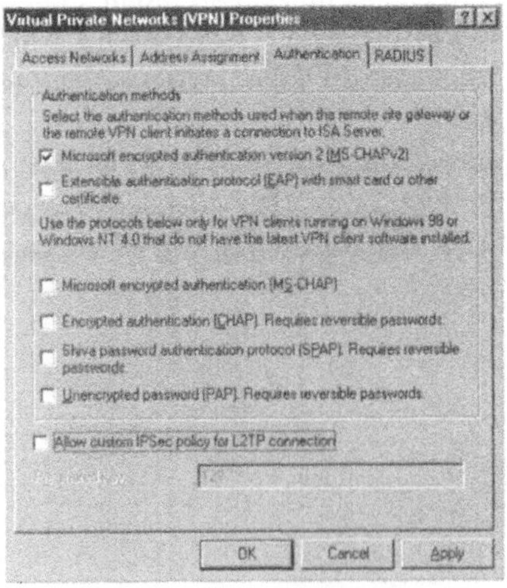

7. Click the **RADIUS** tab. Here you can configure the ISA 2004 firewall VPN server to use RADIUS to authenticate the VPN users. The advantage of RADIUS authentication is that you can leverage the Active Directory's (and other directories) user database to authenticate users without requiring the ISA firewall to be a member of a domain. See Figure 9.11. We'll go over the details of how to configure RADIUS support for VPN user authentication later in this chapter.

Figure 9.11 Virtual Private Networks Properties

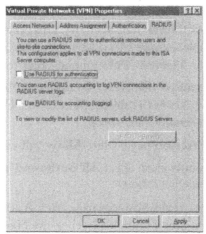

8. Click **Apply** in the **Virtual Private Networks (VPN) Properties** dialog box and then click **OK**.

9. Click **Apply** to save the changes and update the firewall policy.

10. Click **OK** in the **Apply New Configuration** dialog box.

11. Restart the ISA firewall machine.

The ISA firewall will obtain a block of IP addresses from the DHCP Server on the Internal network when it restarts. Note that on a production network where the DHCP server is located on a network segment remote from the ISA 2004 firewall, all interposed routers will need to have BOOTP or DHCP relay enabled so that DHCP requests from the firewall can reach the remote DHCP servers.

Create an Access Rule Allowing VPN Clients Access to Allowed Resources

The ISA firewall will be able to accept incoming VPN connections after the restart. However, VPN clients cannot access any resources because there are no Access Rules allowing the VPN clients to get to anything. You must create Access Rules allowing members of the VPN Clients network access to the resources you want them to access. This is a stark contrast to other combined firewall/VPN server solutions in that the ISA firewall VPN server applies stateful filtering and stateful application-layer inspection on all VPN client connections.

In the following example, you will create an Access Rule allowing all traffic to pass from the VPN Clients network to the Internal network. In a production environment, you would create more restrictive access rules so that users on the VPN Clients network have access only to resources they require. Later in this chapter, we will demonstrate how you can configure a more restrictive Access Policy using user/group-based access control on VPN clients.

Perform the following steps to create an unrestricted-access VPN clients Access Rule:

1. In the **Microsoft Internet Security and Acceleration Server 2004** management console, expand the server name and click the **Firewall Policy** node. Right-click the **Firewall Policy** node, point to **New** and click **Access Rule**.

2. In the **Welcome to the New Access Rule Wizard** page, enter a name for the rule in the **Access Rule name** text box. In this example, enter **VPN Client to Internal**. Click **Next**.

3. On the **Rule Action** page, select **Allow** and click **Next**.

4. On the **Protocols** page, select **All outbound protocols** in the **This rule applies to** list. Click **Next**.

5. On the **Access Rule Sources** page, click **Add**. In the **Add Network Entities** dialog box (Figure 9.12), click the **Networks** folder and double-click on **VPN Clients**. Click **Close**.

Figure 9.12 The Add Network Entities Dialog Box

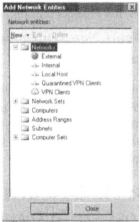

6. Click **Next** on the **Access Rule Sources** page.

7. On the **Access Rule Destinations** page, click **Add**. In the **Add Network Entities** dialog box, click the **Networks** folder, and double-click **Internal**. Click **Close**.

8. On the **User Sets** page, accept the default setting, **All Users**, and click **Next**.

9. Click **Finish** on the **Completing the New Access Rule Wizard** page.

10. Click **Apply** to save the changes and update the firewall policy.

11. Click **OK** in the **Apply New Configuration** dialog box. The VPN client policy is now the top-listed Access Rule in the Access Policy list as shown in Figure 9.13.

Figure 9.13 VPN Client Policy

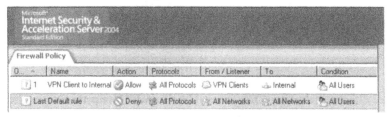

At this point VPN clients that successfully authenticate and have Dial-in permission will be able to access all resources, using any protocol, on the Internal network.

Enable Dial-in Access

In non-native mode Active Directory domains, all user accounts have dial-in access *disabled* by default. You must enable dial-in access on a *per account* basis for these non-native mode Active Directory domains. In contrast, native-mode Active Directory domains have dial-in access controlled by *Remote Access Policy* by default. Windows NT 4.0 domains always have dial-in access controlled on a per user account basis.

In the lab environment used in this book, Active Directory is in Windows Server 2003 mixed mode, so we will need to manually change the dial-in settings on each domain user account that requires access to the VPN server.

Perform the following steps on the domain controller to enable Dial-in access for the Administrator account:

1. Click **Start** and point to **Administrative Tools**. Click **Active Directory Users and Computers**.

2. In the **Active Directory Users and Computers** console, click on the **Users** node in the left pane. Double-click on the **Administrator** account in the right pane of the console.

3. Click on the **Dial-in** tab. In the **Remote Access Permission (Dial-in or VPN)** frame, select **Allow access** as shown in Figure 9.14. Click **Apply** and **OK**.

Figure 9.14 The account dial-in tab

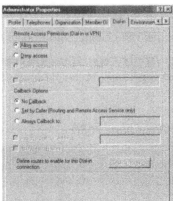

4.   Close the **Active Directory Users and Computers** console.

Another option is to create groups on the ISA firewall itself. You can create local users on the ISA firewall and then place those users into groups. This method allows you to use the default setting on the user accounts created on the ISA firewall, where the default dial-in setting is **control access via Remote Access Policy**.

While this option doesn't scale very well, it's a viable option for those organizations that have a limited number of VPN users and who don't want to use RADIUS or don't have a RADIUS server to use.

Perform the following steps to create a user group that has access to the ISA firewall's VPN server:

1.   On the ISA firewall, right-click **My Computer** on the desktop and click **Manage**.

2.   In the **Computer Management** console, expand **System Tools**, and expand the **Local Users and Groups** node. Right-click the **Groups** node, and click **New Group**.

3.   In the **New Group** dialog box, enter a name for the group in the **Group Name** text box. In this example, we'll name the group **VPN Users**. Click **Add**.

4.   In the **Select Users** dialog box, click **Advanced**.

5.   In the **Select Users** dialog box, select the users or groups you want to make part of the **VPN Users** group. In this example, we'll select **Authenticated Users**. Click **OK**.

6.   Click **OK** in the **Select Users** dialog box.

7.   Click **Create**, and then **Close**.

Now let's configure the ISA firewall's VPN server component to allow access to members of the **VPN Users** group:

1. In the **Microsoft Internet Security and Acceleration Server 2004** management console, expand the server name, and then click **Virtual Private Networking (VPN)**. Click **Configure VPN Client Access** on the **Tasks** tab in the Task pane.

2. In the **VPN Clients Properties** dialog box, click **Add**.

3. In the **Select Groups** dialog box, enter **VPN Users** in the **Enter the object name to select** text box, and click **Check Names**. The group name will be underlined when it's found. Click **OK**.

We enter the local **VPN Users** group in the **Groups** tab in this example because VPN access can be controlled via the **Control access through Remote Access Policy** setting on the user accounts of users in the local SAM of the ISA firewall. You can also enter domain users and groups (when the ISA firewall is a member of the user domain) when the domain supports Dial-in access via Remote Access Policy. We will talk more about domain users and groups and Remote Access Policy later in this chapter. See Figure 9.15 for controlling permission via Remote Access Policy.

Figure 9.15 Controlling permission via Remote Access Policy

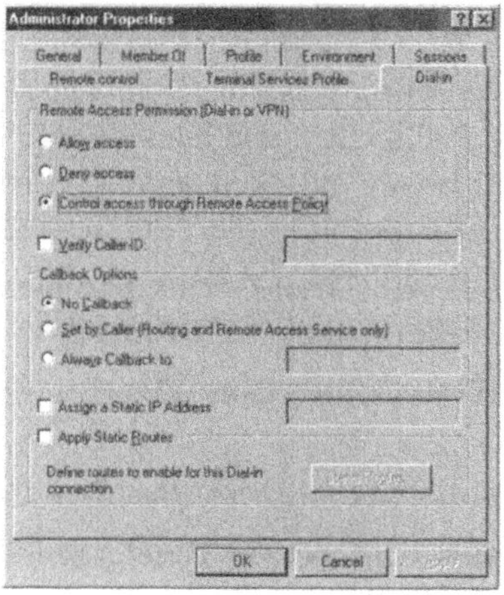

4. Click **Apply**, and then click **OK** in the **VPN Client Properties** dialog box (Figure 9.16).

Figure 9.16 The Groups Tab

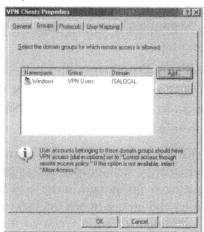

5. Click **Apply** to save the changes and update the firewall policy.

6. Click **OK** in the **Apply New Configuration** dialog box.

Test the PPTP VPN Connection

The ISA 2004 VPN server is now ready to accept VPN client connections. Set up the VPN connectoid on your VPN client, and then establish the VPN connection to the ISA firewall. In this book's test lab, we use a Windows XP client running Service Pack 1.

Perform the following steps to test the VPN Server:

1. On the Windows XP external client machine, right-click **My Network Places** on the desktop, and click **Properties**.

2. Double-click **New Connection Wizard** in the **Network Connections** window.

3. Click **Next** on the **Welcome to the New Connection Wizard** page.

4. On the **Network Connection Type** page, select **Connect to a private network at my workplace**, and click **Next**.

5. On the **Network Connection** page, select the **Virtual Private Network connection** page, and click **Next**.

6. On the **Connection Name** page, enter **VPN** in the **Company Name** text box, and click **Next**.

7. On the **VPN Server Selection** page, enter the IP address on the external interface of the ISA firewall (in this example, the external IP address is 192.168.1.70) in the **Host name or IP address** text box. Click **Next**.

8. Click **Finish** on the **Completing the New Connection Wizard** page.

9. In the **Connect VPN** dialog box, enter the user name **Administrator** and the password for the administrator user account. (**NOTE:** If the ISA firewall is

a member of a domain, enter the machine name or the domain name before the user name in the format NAME\username). Click **Connect**.

10. The VPN client establishes a connection with the ISA 2004 VPN server. Click **OK** in the **Connection Complete** dialog box informing that the connection is established.

11. Double-click the connection icon in the system tray, and click **Details**. You can see that **MPPE 128** encryption is used to protect the data and the IP address assigned to the VPN client (Figure 9.17). Click **Close**.

Figure 9.17 Details of PPTP connection

12. If you're using the lab setup for this book, click **Start** and **Run**. In the **Run** dialog box, enter **\\EXCHANGE2003BE** in the **Open** textbox, and click **OK**. The shares on the domain controller computer appear. Close the windows displaying the domain controller's contents. Note that we were able to use a single label name to connect to the domain controller because the ISA firewall assigned the VPN client a WINS server address. A single label name would also work via a DNS query if the VPN client machine were configured to fully qualify single label names with the correct domain name.

13. Right-click the connection icon in the system tray, and click **Disconnect**.

Creating a Remote Access L2TP/IPSec Server

In the last section, we discussed the procedures required to enable and configure the ISA firewall's VPN server component to allow remote access VPN client PPTP connections. In the following section, we'll build on the configuration we created in the last section and configure the ISA firewall to support a L2TP/IPSec remote access VPN client connection.

We'll perform the following procedures to allow L2TP/IPSec remote access VPN client connections to the ISA firewall:

- Issue certificates to the ISA 2004 firewall and VPN clients
- Test a L2TP/IPSec VPN connection
- Monitor VPN Client Connections

Issue Certificates to the ISA Firewall and VPN Clients

You can significantly improve the level of security on your VPN connections by using the L2TP/IPSec VPN protocol. The IPSec encryption protocol provides a number of security advantages over the Microsoft Point-to-Point Encryption (MPPE) protocol used to secure PPTP connections. While the ISA firewall supports using a pre-shared key to support the IPSec encryption process, this should be considered a low-security option and should be avoided if possible.

> **WARNING**
>
> While PPTP and MPPE are secure VPN protocols that can be used by organizations that do not want to use PKI and L2TP/IPSec, the level of security provided by PPTP/MPPE is directly related to the complexity of the user credentials and the PPP user authentication protocol. You should use only complex user passwords with MS-CHAPv2 or EAP user certificate authentication.

However, if you just aren't in the position to roll out a PKI, then a pre-shared key for L2TP/IPSec is still a viable option. Just be aware that it lowers the level of security for your L2TP/IPSec connections compared to those created using machine certificates. The secure IPSec solution is to use computer certificates on the VPN server and VPN clients. We'll discuss using pre-shared keys after going through the procedures for using certificate authentication for the L2TP/IPSec connection.

The first step is to issue a computer certificate to the ISA firewall. There are a number of methods you can use to request a computer certificate. In the following example, we will use the **Certificates** stand-alone MMC snap-in. Note that you can only use the Certificate MMC snap-in when the ISA firewall is a member of the same domain where an enterprise CA is installed. If the ISA firewall is not a member of a domain where there is an enterprise CA, then you can use the Web enrollment site to obtain a machine certificate.

In order for the stand-alone MMC snap-in to communicate with the certificate authority, we will need to enable an "all open" rule that allows all traffic from the Local Host network to the Internet network. We will disable this rule after the certificate request is complete.

Perform the following steps on the ISA 2004 firewall to request a certificate from the enterprise CA on the Internal network:

1. In the **Microsoft Internet Security and Acceleration Server 2004** management console, expand the server name in the left pane, and then click the **Firewall Policy** node. Click the **Tasks** tab in the Task pane, and then click **Create New Access Rule**.

2. On the **Welcome to the New Access Rule Wizard** page, enter a name for the rule in the **Access Rule name** text box. In this example, we will enter **All Open from Local Host to Internal**. Click **Next**.

3. On the **Rule Action** page, select **Allow**, and click **Next**.

4. On the **Protocols** page, accept the default selection, **All outbound traffic**, and click **Next**.

5. On the **Access Rule Sources** page, click **Add**. In the **Add Network Entities** dialog box, click the **Networks** folder. Double-click **Local Host**, and click **Close**.

6. On the **Access Rule Destinations** page, click **Add**. In the **Add Network Entities** dialog box, click the **Networks** folder. Double-click **Internal**, and click **Close**.

7. On the **User Sets** page, accept the default setting, **All Users**, and click **Next**.

8. Click **Finish** on the **Completing the New Access Rule Wizard** page.

9. Right-click the **All Open from Local Host to Internal** Access Rule, and click the **Configure RPC Protocol** command.

10. In the **Configure RPC protocol policy** dialog box, remove the checkmark from the **Enforce strict RPC compliance** checkbox. Click **Apply**, and then click **OK**.

11. In the **Microsoft Internet Security and Acceleration Server 2004** management console, expand the **Configuration** node, and click on the **Add-ins** node. Right-click on the **RPC Filter** entry in the Details pane, and click **Disable**.

12. In the **ISA Server Warning** dialog box, select **Save the changes and restart the services**. Click **OK**.

13. Click **Apply** to save the changes and update the firewall policy.

14. Click **OK** in the **Apply New Configuration** dialog box.

15. Click **Start** and the **Run** command. Enter **mmc** in the **Open** text box, and click **OK**.

16. In **Console1**, click the **File** menu and the **Add/Remove Snap-in** command.

17. In the **Add/Remove Snap-in** dialog box, click **Add**.

18. In the **Add Standalone Snap-in** dialog box, select the **Certificates** entry from the **Available Standalone Snap-ins** list. Click **Add**.

19. On the **Certificates snap-in** page, select **Computer account**.

20. On the **Select Computer** page, select **Local computer**.

21. Click **Close** in the **Add Standalone Snap-in** dialog box.

22. Click **OK** in the **Add/Remove Snap-in** dialog box.

23. In the left pane of the console, expand **Certificates (Local Computer)** and click on **Personal**. Right-click on the **Personal** node. Point to **All Tasks**, and click **Request New Certificate**.

24. Click **Next** on the **Welcome to the Certificate Request Wizard** page.

25. On the **Certificate Types** page, select the **Computer** entry in the **Certificate types** lists, and click **Next**.

26. On the **Certificate Friendly Name and Description** page, enter a name in the **Friendly name** text box. In this example, enter **Firewall Computer Certificate,**. Click **Next**.

27. Click **Finish** on the **Completing the Certificate Request Wizard** page.

28. Click **OK** in the dialog box informing you that the certificate request was successful.

29. Return to the **Microsoft Internet Security and Acceleration Server 2004** management console, and expand the computer name in the left pane. Click on the **Firewall Policy** node. Right-click on the **All Open from Local Host to Internal** Access Rule, and click **Disable**.

30. In the **Microsoft Internet Security and Acceleration Server 2004** management console, expand the **Configuration** node, and click on the **Add-ins** node. Right-click on the **RPC Filter** entry in the Details pane, and click **Enable**.

31. Click **Apply** to save the changes and update the firewall policy

32. In the **ISA Server Warning** dialog box, select **Save the changes and restart the services**. Click **OK**.

33. Click **OK** in the **Apply New Configuration** dialog box.

TIP

If you do not disable the RPC filter before attempting to request a certificate from the **Certificates** MMC, the certificate request will fail. If you then disable the RPC filter after requesting the certificate, the request will fail again. You will need to restart the ISA firewall in order to request the certificate. The moral of this story? Do *not* request the certificates from the **Certificates** MMC before you disable the RPC filter.

Note that you will not need to manually copy the enterprise CA certificate into the ISA firewall's **Trusted Root Certification Authorities** certificate store because CA certificate is automatically installed on domain members. If the firewall were not a member of the domain where an enterprise CA is installed, then you would need to manually place the CA certificate into the **Trusted Root Certification Authorities** certificate store.

TIP

Check out the ISA Server 2000 VPN Deployment Kit documentation for detailed information on how to obtain certificates using the Web enrollment site and how to import the CA certificate into the ISA firewall's Trusted Root Certification Authorities machine certificate store. Find the Kit at the ISAserver.org Web site at http://www.isaserver.org/articles/isa2000vpndeploymentkit.html

---

The next step is to issue a computer certificate to the VPN client computer. In this example, the VPN client machine is not a member of the domain. You need to request a computer certificate using the enterprise CA's Web enrollment site and manually place the enterprise CA certificate into the client's **Trusted Root Certification Authorities** machine certificate store. The easiest way to accomplish this is to have the VPN client machine request the certificate when connected via a PPTP link.

NOTE

In a production environment, untrusted client machines must not be issued computer certificates. Only managed computers should be allowed to install computer certificates. Domain members are managed clients and, therefore, under the organization's administrative control. We strongly encourage you to **not** allow users to install their own certificates on unmanaged machines. The computer certificate is a security principle and is not meant to provide free access to all users who wish to have one.

Perform the following steps to request and install the CA certificate:

1. Establish a PPTP VPN connection to the ISA firewall.

2. Open **Internet Explorer**. In the **Address** bar, enter **http://10.0.0.2/certsrv** (where 10.0.0.2 is the IP address of the CA on the Internal Network), and click **OK**.

3. In the **Enter Network Password** dialog box, enter **Administrator** in the **User Name** text box and enter the Administrator's password in the **Password** text box. Click **OK**.

4. Click **Request a Certificate** on the **Welcome** page.

5. On the **Request a Certificate** page, click **advanced certificate request**.

6. On the **Advanced Certificate Request** page, click **Create and submit a request to this CA**.

7. On the **Advanced Certificate Request** page, select the **Administrator** certificate from the **Certificate Template** list. Place a checkmark in the **Store certificate in the local computer certificate store** checkbox. Click **Submit**.

8. Click **Yes** in the **Potential Scripting Violation** dialog box.

9. On the **Certificate Issued** page, click **Install this certificate**.

10. Click **Yes** on the **Potential Scripting Violation** page.

11. Close the browser after viewing the **Certificate Installed** page.

12. Click **Start,** and then click **Run**. Enter **mmc** in the **Open** text box, and click **OK**.

13. In **Console1**, click the **File** menu, and click the **Add/Remove Snap-in** command.

14. Click **Add** in the **Add/Remove Snap-in** dialog box.

15. In the **Add Standalone Snap-in** dialog box, select the **Certificates** entry from the **Available Standalone Snap-ins** list. Click **Add**.

16. Select **Computer account** on the **Certificates snap-in** page.

17. Select **Local computer** on the **Select Computer** page.

18. Click **Close** in the **Add Standalone Snap-in** dialog box.

19. Click **OK** in the **Add/Remove Snap-in** dialog box.

20. In the left pane of the console, expand **Certificates (Local Computer) Personal**. Click on **\Personal\Certificates**. Double-click on **Administrator** certificate in the right pane of the console.

21. In the **Certificate** dialog box, click **Certification Path**. At the top of the certificate hierarchy seen in the **Certification path** frame is the root CA certificate. Click the **EXCHANGE2003BE** certificate at the top of the list. Click **View Certificate**.

22. In the CA certificate's **Certificate** dialog box, click the **Details** tab. Click **Copy to File**.

23. Click **Next** on the **Welcome to the Certificate Export Wizard** page.

24. On the **Export File Format** page, select **Cryptographic Message Syntax Standard – PKCS #7 Certificates (.P7B)**, and click **Next**.

25. On the **File to Export** page, enter **c:\cacert** in the **File name** text box. Click **Next**.

26. Click **Finish** on the **Completing the Certificate Export Wizard** page.

27. Click **OK** in the **Certificate Export Wizard** dialog box.

28. Click **OK** in the **Certificate** dialog box. Click **OK** again in the **Certificate** dialog box.

29. In the left pane of the console, expand the **Trusted Root Certification Authorities** node, and click **Certificates**. Right-click **Trusted Root Certification Authorities\Certificates**. Point to **All Tasks**, and click **Import**.

30. Click **Next** on the **Welcome to the Certificate Import Wizard** page.

31. On the **File to Import** page. Use the **Browse** button to locate the CA certificate you saved to the local hard disk, and click **Next**.

32. On the **Certificate Store** page, accept the default settings, and click **Next**.

33. On the **Completing the Certificate Import Wizard** page, click **Finish**.

34. In the **Certificate Import Wizard** dialog box informing you that the import was successful, click **OK**.

Disconnect from the VPN server. Right-click on the connection icon in the system tray, and click **Disconnect**.

Test the L2TP/IPSec VPN Connection

Now that both the ISA firewall and the VPN client machines have machine certificates, you can test a secure L2TP/IPSec remote-access client VPN connection to the firewall. The first step is to restart the Routing and Remote Access Service so that it registers the new certificate.

Perform the following steps to enable L2TP/IPSec support:

1. In the **Microsoft Internet Security and Acceleration Server 2004** management console, expand the server name, and click **Virtual Private Networking (VPN)**. Click **Configure VPN Client Access** on the **Tasks** tab in the Task pane. Click **Apply**, and then click **OK**.

2. Click **Apply** to save the changes and update the firewall policy.

3. Click **OK** in the **Apply New Configuration** dialog box.

4. Restart the ISA firewall machine.

The next step is to start the VPN client connection:

1. From the VPN client computer, open the VPN client connectoid. Click **Properties**. In the **VPN Properties** dialog box, click **Networking**. On the **Networking** tab, change the **Type of VPN** to **L2TP IPSec VPN**. Click **OK**.

2. Initiate the VPN connection to the ISA firewall.

3. Click **OK** in the **Connection Complete** dialog box informing you that the connection is established.

4. Double-click on the connection icon in the system tray.

5. In the **ISA VPN Status** dialog box (Figure 9.18), click the **Details** tab. You will see an entry for **IPSEC Encryption**, indicating that the L2TP/IPSec connection was successful.

Figure 9.18 L2TP/IPSec Connection Details

6. Click **Close** in the **ISA VPN Status** dialog box.

Monitor VPN Clients

The ISA firewall allows you to monitor the VPN client connections. Perform the following steps to see how you can view connections from VPN clients:

1. In the **Microsoft Internet Security and Acceleration Server 2004** management console, expand the server name, and click the **Virtual Private Networks (VPN)** node. Click the **Tasks** tab in the Task pane, and click **Monitor VPN Clients (Figure 9.19)**. Note that this option will change the nature of the Sessions filter. You might want to back up your current sessions filter so that you can get back to it after the VPN filter is created.

Figure 9.19 The Monitor VPN Clients Link

2. You are moved to the **Sessions** tab in the **Monitoring** node. Here you can see that the sessions have been filtered to show only the **VPN Client** connections.

3. Click on the **Dashboard** tab. Here you can see in the **Sessions** pane the **VPN Remote Client** connections (Figure 9.20).

Figure 9.20 The ISA Firewall Dashboard

4. You can also use the real-time logging feature to see VPN client connections. Click on the **Logging** tab, and then click the **Tasks** tab in the Task pane. Click **Start Query**. You can use the filter capabilities to focus on specific VPN clients or only the VPN Clients network. Figure 9.21 shows the log file entries.

Figure 9.21 Log File Entries for the VPN Client Connection

3/17/2004 9:14:57 AM	255.255.255.255	138	NetBios Datagram	Denied Connection	Default rule	10.0.0.108		VPN Clients	Local Host
3/17/2004 9:14:57 AM	10.0.0.2	137	NetBios Name Ser...	Initiated Connection	VPN Client to Internal	10.0.0.108		VPN Clients	Internal
3/17/2004 9:13:38 AM	10.0.0.2	53	DNS	Closed Connection	VPN Client to Internal	10.0.0.108	Administrator	VPN Clients	Internal
3/17/2004 9:15:48 AM	10.0.0.2	0	Ping	Initiated Connection	VPN Client to Internal	10.0.0.108	Administrator	VPN Clients	Internal

Using a Pre-shared Key for VPN Client Remote Access Connections

As mentioned earlier in this chapter, you can use pre-shared keys for IPSec authentication if you don't have a PKI setup. The ISA firewall can be configured to support both pre-shared keys and certificates for VPN remote access client connections. The VPN client must support pre-shared keys for IPSec authentication. You can download the updated Windows L2TP/IPSec VPN clients at http://www.microsoft.com/windows2000/server/evaluation/news/bulletins/l2tpclient.asp. This VPN client allows you to use pre-shared keys for Windows 9X, Windows NT 4.0, and Windows 2000 client operating systems.

The ISA firewall must be configured to support pre-shared keys. Perform the following steps to configure the ISA firewall to support pre-shared keys for IPSec authentication:

1. In the **Microsoft Internet Security and Acceleration Server 2004** management console, expand the server name, and click the **Virtual Private Networking (VPN)** node.

2. Click the **Select Authentication Methods** link on the **Tasks** tab in the Task pane.

3. In the **Virtual Private Networks (VPN) Properties** dialog box, put a checkmark in the **Allow customer IPSec policy for L2TP connection** checkbox. Enter a pre-shared key in the **Pre-shared key** text box. Make sure that the key is complex and contains letters, numbers, and symbols (see Figure 9.22). Make the key at least 17 characters in length.

Figure 9.22 The Authentication Tab

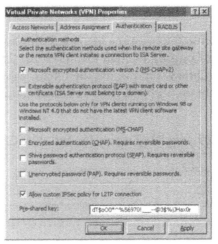

4. Click **Apply**, then click **OK** in the **ISA 2004** dialog box informing you that the Routing and Remote Access Service must be restarted. Click **OK** in the **Virtual Private Networking (VPN) Properties** dialog box.

5. Click **Apply** to save the changes and update the firewall policy.

6. Click **OK** in the **Apply New Configuration** dialog box.

You need to configure the VPN client to support a pre-shared key. The procedures will vary with the client you're using. The following describes how to configure the Windows XP VPN client to use a pre-shared key:

1. Open the VPN connectoid that you use to connect to the ISA firewall and click the **Properties** button.

2. In the connectoid's **Properties** dialog box, click the **Security** tab.

3. On the **Security** tab, click the **IPSec Settings** button.

4. In the **IPSec Settings** dialog box, put a checkmark in the **Use a pre-shared key for authentication** checkbox, and then enter the key in the **Key** text box as shown in Figure 9.23. Click **OK**.

Figure 9.23 Enter a pre-shared key on the L2TP/IPSec client

5. Click **OK** in the connectoid's **Properties** dialog box.

6. Connect to the ISA firewall. You can see that the pre-shared key is used for the IPSec connection by viewing the connection's characteristics in the **IPSec Security Monitor** MMC snap-in (Figure 9.24).

Figure 9.24 Viewing IPSec Information in the IPSec MMC

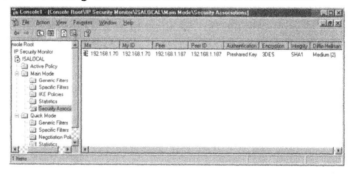

Creating a PPTP Site-to-Site VPN

Site-to-site VPNs allow you to connect entire networks to one another. This can lead to significant cost savings for organizations that are using dedicated frame relay links to connect branch offices to the main office, or branch offices to one another. The ISA firewall supports site-to-site VPN networking using the following VPN protocols:

■ PPTP (Point-to-Point Tunneling Protocol)

■ L2TP/IPSec (Layer Two Tunneling Protocol over IPSec)

■ IPSec Tunnel Mode

The most secure VPN protocol for site-to-site VPNs is the L2TP/IPSec VPN protocol. L2TP/IPSec allows you to require both machine and user authentication. The second most secure protocol for site-to-site VPNs is a matter of debate. If you have two ISA firewalls, or are connecting an ISA firewall to a Windows RRAS machine, then I recommend that you use PPTP and route certificate authentication. IPSec tunnel mode should only be used when you need to connect to downlevel VPN gateways. The major problem with IPSec tunnel mode is that most downlevel VPN gateway vendors require you to use a pre-shared key instead of certificate authentication, and there are a number of exploits that can take advantage of this situation.

Creating a site-to-site VPN can be a complex process because of the number of steps involved. However, once you understand the steps and why they're performed, you'll find that setting up a site-to-site VPN is a lot easier than you think. In this section we'll begin with creating a site-to-site VPN using the PPTP VPN protocol. After we establish the PPTP link, we'll use the link to connect to the Web enrollment site on the enterprise CA at the main office network and install a machine certificate on the branch office ISA firewall.

In the following exercise, the main office ISA firewall is named **ISALOCAL**, and the branch office ISA firewall is named **REMOTEISA**. We will be used the lab network setup described in Chapter 4, so if you don't recall the details of the lab setup, you should take a look at it now. Refreshing your knowledge of the lab setup will help you understand the site-to-site VPN procedures we'll be carrying out.

> **NOTE**
>
> In the following example, the ISA firewall at the branch office is not a member of the main office domain. However, it is possible to make the branch office ISA firewall a member of the domain and extend your domain to branch offices. Because of space limitations in this book, we cannot go into the procedures required to support this configuration. Make sure you subscribe to the RSS feed at www.isaserver.org so that you'll receive a notification when we post an article series on the ISAserver.org site on how to setup the branch office machines as domain members and how to extend your domain into branch offices.
>
> Another important consideration in the following walkthrough is that we are using DHCP to assign IP addresses to VPN clients and gateways. You can use either DHCP or a static address pool. However, if you choose to use a static address pool and you assign *on subnet* IP addresses to VPN clients and gateways, then you will need to remove those addresses from the definition of the Internal Network (or any other Network for which these might represent overlapping addresses).

You'll need to perform the following steps to get the PPTP site-to-site VPN working:

- **Create the Remote Network at the Main Office** A Remote Site Network is what the ISA firewall uses for site-to-site VPN connections. Whenever you connect the ISA firewall to another network using a site-to-site

VPN, you must first create the Remote Site Network. The Remote Site Network is then used in Access Rules to control access to and from that Network. The Remote Site Network we create at the main office will represent the IP addresses used at the branch office network.

- **Create the Network Rule at the Main Office** A Network Rule controls the route relationship between Networks. We will configure the site-to-site Network so that there is a Route relationship between the main office and the branch office. We prefer to use Route relationships because not all protocols work with NAT.

- **Create the Access Rules at the Main Office** The Access Rules at the main office will allow all traffic from the main office to reach the branch office and all the traffic from the branch office to reach the main office. On your production network, you will likely want to lock down your rules a bit so that branch office users can only access the information they require at the main office. For example, if branch office users only need to access the OWA sites at the main office, then create Access Rules that only allow users access to the HTTPS protocol to the OWA server.

- **Create the VPN Gateway Dial-in Account at the Main Office** We must create a user account that the branch office ISA firewall can use to authenticate with the main office ISA firewall. This account is created on the main office ISA firewall. When the branch office ISA firewall calls the main office ISA firewall, the branch office will use this user name and password to authenticate with the main office. The branch office ISA firewall's demand-dial interface is configured to use this account.

- **Create the Remote Network at the Branch Office** Once the site-to-site VPN configuration is done at the main office, we move our attention to the branch office's ISA firewall. At the branch office ISA firewall, we begin by creating the Remote Site Network that represents the IP addresses in use at the main office. We'll use this Network Object to control traffic moving to and from the main office from the branch office.

- **Create the Network Rule at the Branch Office** As we did at the main office, we need to create a Network Rule controlling the route relationship for communications between the branch office network and the main office network. We'll configure the Network Rule so that there is a Route relationship between the branch office and the main office.

- **Create the Access Rules at the Branch Office** We will create two Access Rules on the branch office ISA firewall. One allows all traffic to the branch office to reach the main office, and the second rule allows all traffic from the main office to reach the branch office. In a production environment you might wish to limit what traffic can leave the branch office to the main office. Note that you can set these access controls at either or both the branch office or the main office ISA firewall. We prefer to implement the access controls at both sites, but the access controls at the main office are more important because you often may not have change controls tightly regulated at the branch offices.

■ **Create the VPN Gateway Dial-in Account at the Branch Office** We need to create a user account on the branch office ISA firewall that the main office ISA firewall can use to authenticate when it calls the branch office ISA firewall. The demand-dial interface on the main office ISA firewall uses this account to authenticate with the branch office ISA firewall.

■ **Activate the Site-to-Site Links** We'll activate the site-to-site VPN connection by initiating a connection from a host on the branch office to a host on the main office network.

Create the Remote Site Network at the Main Office

We begin by configuring the ISA firewall at the main office. The first step is to configure the Remote Site Network in the **Microsoft Internet Security and Acceleration Server 2004** management console.

Perform the following steps to create the Remote Site Network at the main office ISA firewall:

1. Open the **Microsoft Internet Security and Acceleration Server 2004** management console and expand the server name. Click **Virtual Private Networks (VPN)**.

2. Click on the **Remote Sites** tab in the Details pane. Click on the **Tasks** tab in the Task pane. Click **Add Remote Site Network**.

3. On the **Welcome to the New Network Wizard** page, enter a name for the remote network in the **Network name** text box. In this example, we will name the remote network **Branch**. This name is very important because this will be the name of the demand-dial interface created on the ISA firewall at the main office, and it will be the name of the user account that the branch office ISA firewall will use to connect to the main office ISA firewall. Click **Next**.

4. On the **VPN Protocol** page, you have the choice of using **IP Security protocol (IPSec tunnel mode, Layer Two Tunneling Protocol (L2TP) over IPSec** and **Point-to-Point Tunneling Protocol.**

If you do not have certificates installed on the main and branch office machines and do not plan to deploy them in the future, you should choose the PPTP option. If you have certificates installed on the main and branch office firewalls, or if you plan to install them in the future, choose the L2TP/IPSec option (you can use the pre-shared key until you get the certificates installed). Do *not* use the IPSec option unless you are connecting to a third-party VPN gateway (because of the low security conferred by IPSec tunnel mode site-to-site links which typically depend on pre-shared keys). In this example, we will configure a site-to-site VPN using PPTP, so select the **Point-to-Point Tunneling Protocol (PPTP)** (as shown in Figure 9.25). Click **Next**.

Figure 9.25 Selecting the VPN Protocol

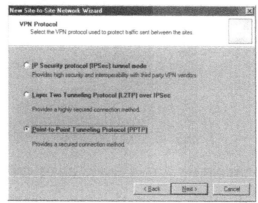

5. On the **Remote Site Gateway** page, enter the IP address on the external interface of the remote ISA firewall. In this example, the IP address is **192.168.1.71**, so we will enter this value into the text box.

Note that you can also use a fully-qualified domain name in this text box. This is helpful if the branch office uses a dynamic address on its external interface and you use a DDNS service like TZO (www.tzo.com). We have been using TZO for years and highly recommend their service. Click **Next**.

6. On the **Remote Authentication** page, put a checkmark in the **Local site can initiate connections to remote site using these credentials** checkbox. Enter the name of the account that you will create on the remote ISA firewall to allow the main office ISA firewall to authenticate to the branch office ISA firewall.

In this example, the user account will be named **Main** (the user account much match the name of the demand-dial interface created on the remote site; we haven't created that demand-dial interface yet, but we will when we configure the branch office ISA firewall). The **Domain** name is the computer name of the branch office ISA firewall, which in this example is **REMOTEISA** (if the remote ISA firewall were a domain controller, you would use the domain name instead of the computer name, since there are no local accounts stored on a domain controller). Enter a password for the account and confirm the password as shown in Figure 9.26. Make sure that you write down the password so you will remember it when you create the account later on the branch office ISA firewall. Click **Next**.

Figure 9.26 Setting Dial-in Credentials

7. Read the information on the **Local Authentication** page, and click **Next**.

The information on this page reminds you that you must create a user account on this ISA firewall that the branch office ISA firewall can use to authenticate when it initiates a site-to-site VPN connection. If you forget to create the user account, the authenticate attempt will fail and the site-to-site VPN link will not establish.

8. Click **Add** on the **Network Addresses** page. In the **IP Address Range Properties** dialog box, enter **10.0.1.0** in the **Starting address** text box. Enter **10.0.1.255** in the **Ending address** text box. Click **OK**.

This is a critical step in your site-to-site VPN configuration. You should include all addresses on the Remote Site Network. While you might create Access Rules that allow access only to a subset of addresses on that network, you should still include all addresses in use on that network. Also, keep in mind any network IDs that are reachable from the branch office ISA firewall. For example, there may be multiple networks reachable from the LAN interface (any of the internal or DMZ interfaces of the branch office ISA firewall). Include all those addresses in this dialog box. See Figure 9.27.

Figure 9.27 Configuring the IP Address Range for the Remote Site Network

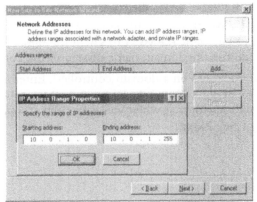

9. Click **Next** on the **Network Addresses** page.

10. Click **Finish** on the **Completing the New Network Wizard** page.

Create the Network Rule at the Main Office

The ISA firewall must know how to route packets to the branch office network. There are two options: **Route** and **NAT**. A Route relationship routes packets to the branch office and preserves the source IP address of the clients making a connection over the site-to-site link. A NAT relationship replaces the source IP address of the client making the connection. In general, the route relationship provides a higher level of protocol support, but the NAT relationship provides a higher level of security because it hides the original source IP address of the host on the NATed side.

One important reason for why you might want to use a Route relationship is if you plan to have domain members on the Remote Site Network. Kerberos authentication embeds the source IP address in the payload and has no NAT editor or application filter to make this work.

In this example, we will use a Route relationship between the main and branch office so that we have the option later to make machines on the branch office network members of the main office's Active Directory domain. Perform the following step to create a Network Rule to control the routing relationship between the main office and branch office networks:

1. Expand the **Configuration** node in the left pane of the console. Click **Networks**.

2. Click on the **Network Rules** tab in the Details pane. Click on the **Tasks** tab in the Task pane. Click **Create a New Network Rule**.

3. On the **Welcome to the New Network Rule Wizard** page, enter a name for the rule in the **Network rule name** text box. In this example, we will call the rule **Main to Branch**. Click **Next**.

4. On the **Network Traffic Sources** page, click **Add**.

5. In the **Add Network Entities** dialog box, click the **Networks** folder. Double-click on the **Internal** network. Click **Close**.

6. Click **Next** on the **Network Traffic Sources** page.

7. On the **Network Traffic Destinations** page, click **Add**.

8. In the **Add Network Entities** dialog box, double-click the **Branch** network. Click **Close**.

9. Click **Next** on the **Network Traffic Destinations** page.

10. On the **Network Relationship** page (Figure 9.28), select the **Route** relationship.

Figure 9.28 The Network Relationship Page

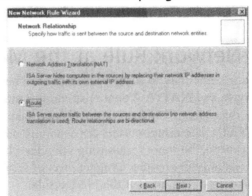

11. Click **Finish** on the **Completing the New Network Rule Wizard** page.

Create the Access Rules at the Main Office

We want hosts on both the main and branch office networks to have full access to all resources on each network. We must create Access Rules allowing traffic from the main office to the branch office and from the branch office to the main office.

> **NOTE**
>
> In a production environment, you would lock down access quite a bit and allow branch office users access only to the resources they require at the main office. In addition, you may not wish to allow main office users access to any resources at the branch office. Or perhaps you want to limit access from the main office to the branch office to only members of the Administrators group.

Perform the following steps to create Access Rules allowing traffic to move between the main and branch offices:

1. Click the **Firewall Policy** node in the **Microsoft Internet Security and Acceleration Server 2004** management console. Click the **Tasks** tab in the Task pane. Click **Create New Access Rule**.

2. On the **Welcome to the New Access Rule Wizard** page, enter a name for the rule in the **Access Rule name** text box. In this example, enter **Main to Branch**. Click **Next**.

3. On the **Rule Action** page, select **Allow**, and click **Next**.

4. On the **Protocols** page, select **All outbound traffic** in the **This rule applies to** list (Figure 9.29). Click **Next**.

Figure 9.29 The Protocols page

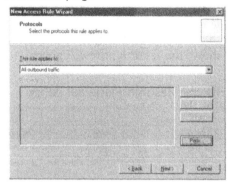

5. On the **Access Rule Sources** page, click **Add**.

6. In the **Add Network Entities** dialog box, click the **Networks** folder, and double-click the **Internal** network. Click **Close**.

7. Click **Next** on the **Access Rule Sources** page.

8. On the **Access Rule Destinations** page, click **Add**.

9. In the **Add Network Entities** dialog box, click on the **Networks** folder, and double-click on the **Branch** network. Click **Close**.

10. Click **Next** on the **Access Rule Destinations** page.

11. On the **User Sets** page, accept the default entry **All Users**, and click **Next**.

12. Click **Finish** on the **Completing the New Access Rule Wizard** page.

The second rule allows hosts on the branch office network access to the main office network:

1. Click the **Tasks** tab in the Task pane. Click **Create New Access Rule**.

2. On the **Welcome to the New Access Rule Wizard** page, enter a name for the rule in the **Access rule name** text box. In this example, enter **Branch to Main**. Click **Next**.

3. On the **Rule Action** page, select **Allow** and click **Next**.

4. On the **Protocols** page, select **All outbound protocols** in the **This rule applies to** list. Click **Next**.

5. On the **Access Rule Sources** page, click **Add**.

6. In the **Add Network Entities** dialog box, click the **Networks** folder, and double-click the **Branch** network. Click **Close**.

7. Click **Next** on the **Access Rule Sources** page.

8. On the **Access Rule Destinations** page, click **Add**.

9. In the **Add Network Entities** dialog box, click on the **Networks** folder, and double-click on the **Internal** network. Click **Close**.

10. Click **Next** on the **Access Rule Destinations** page.

11. On the **User Sets** page, accept the default entry **All Users**, and click **Next**.

12. Click **Finish** on the **Completing the New Access Rule Wizard** page. Figure 9.30 shows the resulting firewall policy.

Figure 9.30 The Resulting Firewall Policy

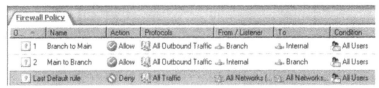

The last step is to enable access for VPN clients (although technically, the branch office VPN gateway isn't really a remote access VPN client):

1. Click on the **Virtual Private Network** node in the left pane of the console.

2. Click the **VPN Clients** tab in the Details pane. Click the **Tasks** tab in the Task pane. Click **Enable VPN Client Access**.

3. Click **OK** in the **ISA 2004** dialog box informing you that the **Routing and Remote Access** service must be restarted.

4. Click **Apply** to save the changes and update the firewall policy.

5. Click **OK** in the **Apply New Configuration** dialog box.

Create the VPN Gateway Dial-in Account at the Main Office

You must create a user account on the main office firewall that the branch office firewall can use to authenticate the site-to-site VPN link. This user account *must have the same name* as the demand-dial interface on the main office computer. You will later configure the branch office ISA 2004 to use this account when it dials the VPN site-to-site link.

User accounts and demand-dial interface naming conventions are a common source of confusion for ISA firewall administrators. The key here is that the calling VPN gateway must present credentials with a user name *that is the same as the name of the demand-dial interface answering the call*. In Figure 9.31, you can see how this works when the main office calls the branch office and when the branch office calls the main office.

The name of the demand dial interface at the main office is **Branch**. When the branch office calls the main office, the user account the branch office uses to authenticate with the main office ISA firewall is **Branch**. Because the name of the user account is the same as the name of the demand-dial interface, the main office ISA firewall knows that it's a remote VPN gateway making the call, and the ISA firewall does *not* treat this as a remote access VPN client connection.

When the main office calls the branch office, it presents the user credentials of a user named **Main**, which is the same name as the demand-dial interface on the branch office ISA firewall. Because the name of the user account presented during authentication is the same as the name of the demand-dial interface, the branch office ISA firewall knows that this is a VPN gateway connection (VPN router) and not a remote access client VPN connection. Figure 9.31 shows the demand dial interface configuration.

Figure 9.31 Demand Dial Interface Configuration on Local and Remote Sites

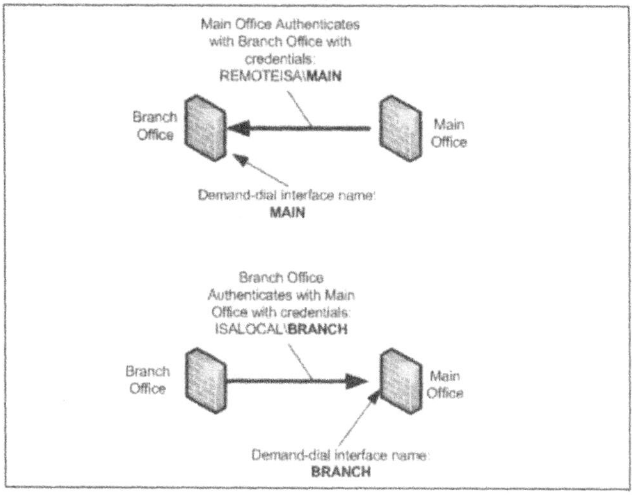

Perform the following steps to create the account the remote ISA 2004 firewall will use to connect to the main office VPN gateway:

1. Right-click **My Computer** on the desktop, and click **Manage**.

2. In the **Computer Management** console, expand the **Local Users and Groups** node. Right-click the **Users** node, and click **New User**.

3. In the **New User** dialog box, enter the name of the main office demand-dial interface. In our current example, the demand-dial interface is named **Branch**. Enter **Branch** into the text box. Enter a **Password** and confirm the **Password**. Write down this password because you'll need to use it when you configure the branch office ISA firewall. Remove the checkmark from the **User must change password at next logon** checkbox. Place checkmarks in the **User cannot change password** and **Password never expires** checkboxes. Click **Create**.

4. Click **Close** in the **New User** dialog box.

5. Double-click the **Branch** user in the right pane of the console.

6. In the **Branch Properties** dialog box, click the **Dial-in** tab. Select **Allow access**.

7. Click **Apply**, and then click **OK**.

8. Restart the ISA firewall computer.

Create the Remote Site Network at the Branch Office

We can now turn our attention to the branch office ISA firewall. We will repeat the same steps we performed on the main office ISA firewall, but this time we begin by creating a Remote Site Network on the branch office firewall that represents the IP addresses used on the main office network.

Perform the following steps to create the Remote Site Network at the branch office:

1. Open the **Microsoft Internet Security and Acceleration Server 2004** management console and expand the server name. Click the **Virtual Private Networks (VPN)** node.

2. Click **Remote Sites** in the Details pane. Click **Tasks** in the Task pane. Click **Add Remote Site Network**.

3. On the **Welcome to the New Network Wizard** page, enter a name for the remote network in the **Network name** text box. In this example, we will name the remote network **Main**. Click **Next**.

4. On the **VPN Protocol** page, select **Point-to-Point Tunneling Protocol (PPTP)**, and click **Next**.

5. On the **Remote Site Gateway** page, enter the IP address on the external interface of the main office ISA firewall. In this example, the IP address is **192.168.1.70**, so we will enter this value into the text box. Click **Next**.

6. On the **Remote Authentication** page, put a checkmark by **Local site can initiate connections to remote site using these credentials**. Enter the name of the account that you created on the main office ISA firewall to allow the branch office VPN gateway access.

In this example, the user account is named **Branch** (the user account much match the name of the demand-dial interface created at the main office). The Domain name is the name of the remote ISA 2004 firewall computer, which, in this example, is **ISA-LOCAL** (if the remote ISA firewall were a domain controller, you would use the *domain name* instead of the computer name). Enter the password for the account and confirm the password as shown in Figure 9.32. Click **Next**.

Figure 9.32 Configure Dial-in Credentials

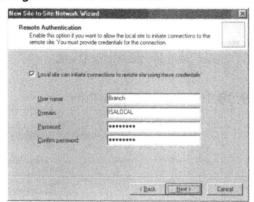

7. Read the information on the **Local Authentication** page, and click **Next**.

8. Click **Add** on the **Network Addresses** page. In the **IP Address Range Properties** dialog box, enter **10.0.0.0** in the **Starting address** text box. Enter **10.0.0.255** in the **Ending address** text box. Click **OK**.

9. Click **Next** on the **Network Addresses** page.

10. Click **Finish** on the **Completing the New Network Wizard** page.

Create the Network Rule at the Branch Office

As we did at the main office, we must create a Network Rule that controls the routing relationship between the branch and the main office networks. We will configure a route relationship so that we can get the highest level of protocol support.

Perform the following steps to create the Network Rule at the branch office:

1. Expand the **Configuration** node in the left pane of the console. Click on **Networks**.

2. Click on the **Network Rules** tab in the Details pane. Click on the **Tasks** tab in the Task pane. Click **Create a New Network Rule**.

3. On the **Welcome to the New Network Rule Wizard** page, enter a name for the rule in the **Network rule name** text box. In this example, we will call the rule **Branch to Main**. Click **Next**.

4. On the **Network Traffic Sources** page, click **Add**.

5. In the **Add Network Entities** dialog box, click the **Networks** folder. Double-click on the **Internal** network. Click **Close**.

6. Click **Next** on the **Network Traffic Sources** page.

7. On the **Network Traffic Destinations** page, click **Add**.

8. In the **Add Network Entities** dialog box, double-click on the **Main** network. Click **Close**.

9. Click **Next** on the **Network Traffic Destinations** page.

10. On the **Network Relationship** page, select **Route**.

11. Click **Finish** on the **Completing the New Network Rule Wizard** page. Figure 9.33 shows the new Network Rule.

Figure 9.33 The New Network Rule

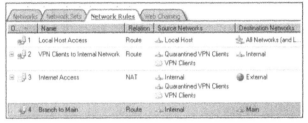

Create the Access Rules at the Branch Office

We will create two Access Rules, one allowing all traffic from the branch office to the main office, and a second allowing all traffic from the main office to the branch office.

Perform the following steps to create Access Rules allowing all traffic to move between the branch and main office networks:

1. Click **Firewall Policy** in the left pane of the console. Click the **Tasks** tab in the Task pane. Click **Create New Access Rule**.

2. On the **Welcome to the New Access Rule Wizard** page, enter a name for the rule in the **Access Rule name** text box. In this example, we will call it **Branch to Main**. Click **Next**.

3. On the **Rule Action** page, select **Allow**, and click **Next**.

4. On the **Protocols** page, select **All outbound traffic** in the **This rule applies to** list. Click **Next**.

5. On the **Access Rule Sources** page, click **Add**.

6. In the **Add Network Entities** dialog box, click the **Networks** folder and double-click the **Internal** network. Click **Close**.

7. Click **Next** on the **Access Rule Sources** page.

8. On the **Access Rule Destinations** page, click **Add**.

9. In the **Add Network Entities** dialog box, click on the **Networks** folder, and then double-click on the **Main** network. Click **Close**.

10. Click **Next** on the **Access Rule Destinations** page.

11. On the **User Sets** page, accept the default entry **All Users**, and click **Next**.

12. Click **Finish** on the **Completing the New Access Rule Wizard** page.

The second rule allows hosts on the main office network access to the branch office network:

1. Click the **Tasks** tab in the Task pane. Click **Create New Access Rule**.

2. On the **Welcome to the New Access Rule Wizard** page, enter a name for the rule in the **Access Rule name** text box. In this example, we will call it **Main to Branch**. Click **Next**.

3. On the **Rule Action** page, select **Allow**, and click **Next**.

4. On the **Protocols** page, select **All outbound traffic** in the **This rule applies to** list. Click **Next**.

5. On the **Access Rule Sources** page, click **Add**.

6. In the **Add Network Entities** dialog box, click the **Networks** folder and double-click the **Main** network. Click **Close**.

7. Click **Next** on the **Access Rule Sources** page.

8. On the **Access Rule Destinations** page, click **Add**.

9. In the **Add Network Entities** dialog box, click the **Networks** folder, and double-click the **Internal** network. Click **Close**.

10. Click **Next** on the **Access Rule Destinations** page.

11. On the **User Sets** page, accept the default entry **All Users** and click **Next**.

12. Click **Finish** on **Completing the New Access Rule Wizard** page. Figure 9.34 shows the resulting firewall policy.

Figure 9.34 The Resulting Firewall Policy

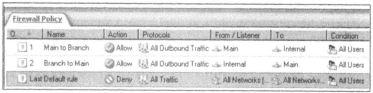

The next step is to enable access for VPN clients:

1. Click on the **Virtual Private Network** node in the left pane of the console.

2. Click the **VPN Clients** tab in the Details pane. Click the **Tasks** tab in the Task pane. Click **Enable VPN Client Access**.

3. Click **OK** in the **ISA 2004** dialog box informing you that the **Routing and Remote Access** service must be restarted as shown in Figure 9.35.

Figure 9.35 Restarting the Routing and Remote Access Service

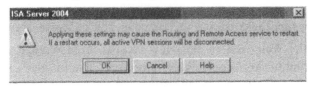

4. Click **Apply** to save the changes and update the firewall policy.

5. Click **OK** in the **Apply New Configuration** dialog box.

Create the VPN Gateway Dial-in Account at the Branch Office

We must create a user account the main office VPN gateway can use to authenticate when it initiates the VPN site-to-site connection to the branch office. The user account must have the same name as the demand-dial interface created on the branch office machine, which, in this example, is **Main**.

Perform the following steps to create the account the remote ISA 2004 firewall will use to connect to the main office VPN gateway:

1. Right-click **My Computer** on the desktop, and click **Manage**.

2. In the **Computer Management** console, expand the **Local Users and Groups** node. Right-click the **Users** node, and click **New User**.

3. In the **New User** dialog box, enter the name of the main office demand-dial interface. In our current example, the demand-dial interface is named **Main**. Enter **Main** into the text box. Enter a **Password** and confirm the **Password**. This is the same password you used when you created the Remote Site Network at the Main office. Remove the checkmark from the **User must change password at next logon** checkbox. Place checkmarks in the **User cannot change password** and **Password never expires** checkboxes. Click **Create**.

4. Click **Close** in the **New User** dialog box.

5. Double-click the **Main** user in the right pane of the console.

6. In the **Main Properties** dialog box, click the **Dial-in** tab (Figure 9.36). Select **Allow access**. Click **Apply**, and then click **OK**.

Figure 9.36 The Dial-in Tab

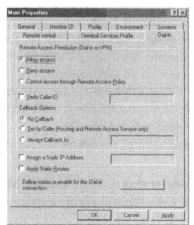

7. Restart the ISA firewall computer.

Activate the Site-to-Site Links

Now that both the main and branch office ISA firewalls are configured as VPN routers, you can test the site-to-site connection.

Perform the following steps to test the site-to-site link:

1. At the remote client computer behind the remote ISA 2004 firewall machine, click **Start**, and then click **Run**.

2. In the **Run** dialog box, enter **cmd** in the **Open** text box, and click **OK**.

3. In the command prompt window, enter **ping –t 10.0.0.2**, and press ENTER

4. You will see a few pings time out, and then the ping responses will be returned by the domain controller on the main office network.

5. Perform the same procedures at the domain controller at the main office network, but this time ping **10.0.1.2**.

TIP

If the site-to-site connection fails, check to make sure that you have defined valid IP address assignments to VPN clients and gateways. A common reason for failure of site-to-site VPN connections is that the ISA firewalls are not able to obtain an address from a DHCP server, and there are no addresses defined for a static address pool. When this happens, the ISA firewall assigns VPN clients and gateways IP addresses in the autonet range (169.254.0.0/16). When both gateways are assigned addresses in the autonet range, both machines' demand-dial interfaces are located on the same network ID and this causes the site-to-site link to fail.

Creating an L2TP/IPSec Site-to-Site VPN

We recommend that you use L2TP/IPSec as your VPN protocol for site-to-site VPN connections. L2TP/IPSec is more secure than PPTP and IPSec tunnel mode. However, to ensure that you have a secure site-to-site VPN connection using L2TP/IPSec, you must use machine certificates on all ISA firewall VPN gateways.

We can leverage the PPTP VPN site-to-site link we created in the previous section to allow the branch office ISA firewall access to the Web enrollment site of the enterprise CA located on the main office network.

We will perform the following procedures to enable the L2TP/IPSec site-to-site VPN link:

- **Enable the System Policy Rule on the Main office firewall to access the enterprise CA** We will enable a system policy rule that allows the ISA firewall to connect from the Local Host Network to all Networks. While, ostensibly, this rule is to allow for CRL checking, we can use it to allow the ISA firewall at the main office access to the Web enrollment site on the Internal network.

- **Request and install a Web site certificate for the Main office firewall** Once we connect to the Web enrollment site, we will request an Administrator certificate that we will install into the main office's local machine certificate store. We will also install the enterprise CA's certificate into the main office ISA firewall's Trusted Root Certification Authorities machine certificate store.

- **Configure the main office ISA firewall to use L2TP/IPSec for the site-to-site link** The Remote Site Network configuration that defines the branch office Network is set to use PPTP for the site-to-site link. We need to change this so that L2TP/IPSec is used instead of PPTP.

- **Enable the System Policy Rule on the Branch office firewall to access the enterprise CA** For the same reason we did so on the main office ISA firewall, we need to enable a System Policy rule that will allow the branch office's Local Host Network access to the Web enrollment site on the main office network.

- **Request and install a Web site certificate for the Branch office firewall** When the PPTP site-to-site link is established, the branch office ISA firewall will be able to connect to the Web enrollment site over that connection. We will install an Administrator certificate on the branch office firewall in its machine certificate store, and install the CA certificate for the main office enterprise CA in the branch office ISA firewall's Trusted Root Certification Authorities machine certificate store.

- **Configure the branch office ISA firewall to use L2TP/IPSec for the site-to-site link** The Remote Site Network representing the main office network must be configured to use L2TP/IPSec instead of PPTP for the site-to-site link.

- **Establish the IPSec Site-to-Site Connection** After we install the certificates and make the changes to the ISA firewall configurations, we'll trigger the site-to-site link and see the L2TP/IPSec connection in the ISA firewall's Monitoring node.

- **Configuring Pre-shared keys for Site-to-Site L2TP/IPSec VPN Links** This is an optional procedure. While we prefer that everyone use certificates for machine authentication, we realize that this is not always possible. We discuss the procedures you can use to support pre-shared key authentication for your L2TP/IPSec site-to-site VPN links.

Enable the System Policy Rule on the Main Office Firewall to Access the Enterprise CA

The ISA 2004 firewall is locked down by default and only a very limited set of protocols and sites are allowed outbound from the ISA firewall immediately after installation. As for any other communications moving through the ISA firewall, Access Rules are required to allow the firewall access to *any* network or network host. We will need to configure the ISA firewall at the main office with an Access Rule allowing it HTTP access to the Web enrollment site. We could create an Access Rule, or we could enable a System Policy rule. Creating an Access Rule allowing access from the Local Host Network to the enterprise CA using only the HTTP protocol would be more secure, but it's easier to enable the System Policy rule. In this example, we will enable a System Policy Rule that allows the firewall access to the Web enrollment site.

Perform the following steps to enable the System Policy rule on the Main Office firewall:

1. In the **Microsoft Internet Security and Acceleration Server 2004** management console, expand the server name, and click the **Firewall Policy** node.

2. Right-click **Firewall Policy**; point to **View**, and click **Show System Policy Rules**.

3. In the System Policy Rule list, double-click **Allow HTTP from ISA Server to all networks (for CRL downloads).** This is System Policy Rule #26.

4. In the **System Policy Editor** dialog box, check the **Enable** checkbox on the **General** tab as shown in Figure 9.37. Click **OK**.

Figure 9.37 Configuring System Policy

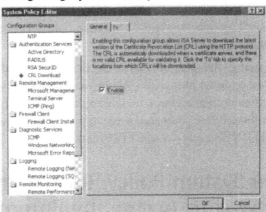

5. Click **Apply** to save the changes and update the firewall policy.

6. Click **OK** in the **Apply New Configuration** dialog box.

7. Click **Show/Hide System Policy Rules** (on the far right of the button bar in the MMC console) to hide System Policy.

Figure 9.38 The Show/Hide System Policy Rules Button

Request and install a Web Site Certificate for the Main Office Firewall

The next step is to request a certificate from the enterprise CA's Web enrollment site. After obtaining the certificate, we will copy the CA certificate into the ISA firewall's **Trusted Root Certification Authorities** certificate store.

Perform the following steps on the main office ISA firewall to request and install the certificates:

1. Open **Internet Explorer**. In the **Address** bar, enter **http://10.0.0.2/certsrv** (where 10.0.0.2 is the IP address of the enterprise CA), and click **OK**.

2. In the **Enter Network Password** dialog box, enter **Administrator** in the **User Name** text box, and enter the **Administrator's** password in the **Password** text box. Click **OK**.

3. In the **Internet Explorer** security dialog box, click **Add**. In the **Trusted Sites** dialog box, click **Add** and **Close**.

4. Click **Request a Certificate** on the **Welcome** page.

5. On the **Request a Certificate** page, click **advanced certificate request**.

6. On the **Advanced Certificate Request** page, click **Create and submit a request to this CA**.

7. On the **Advanced Certificate Request** page, select the **Administrator** certificate from the **Certificate Template** list as shown in Figure 9.39. Remove the checkmark from the **Mark keys as exportable** checkbox. Place a checkmark in the **Store certificate in the local computer certificate store** checkbox as shown in Figure 9.40. Click **Submit**.

Figure 9.39 The Advanced Certificate Request Page

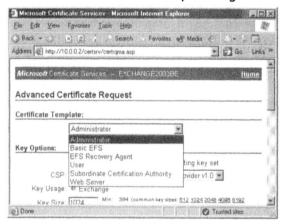

Figure 9.40 The Store Certificate in the Local Computer Certificate Store Option

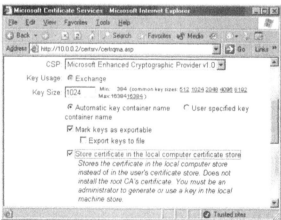

8. Click **Yes** in the **Potential Scripting Violation** dialog box.

9. On the **Certificate Issued** page, click **Install this certificate**.

10. Click **Yes** on the **Potential Scripting Violation** page.

11. Close the browser after viewing the **Certificate Installed** page.

12. Click **Start**, and then click **Run**. Enter **mmc** in the **Open** text box, and click **OK**.

13. In **Console1**, click the **File** menu, and then click **Add/Remove Snap-in**.

14. Click **Add** in the **Add/Remove Snap-in** dialog box.

15. Select the **Certificates** entry in the **Available Standalone Snap-ins** list in the **Add Standalone Snap-in** dialog box. Click **Add**.

16. Select **Computer account** on the **Certificates snap-in** page.

17. Select **Local computer** on the **Select Computer** page.

18. Click **Close** in the **Add Standalone Snap-in** dialog box.

19. Click **OK** in the **Add/Remove Snap-in** dialog box.

20. In the left pane of the console, expand **Certificates (Local Computer)**, and then expand **Personal**. Click on **\Personal\Certificates**. Double-click on the **Administrator** certificate in the right pane of the console.

21. In the **Certificate** dialog box, click the **Certification Path** tab. The root CA certificate is at the top of the certificate hierarchy seen in the Certification path frame. Click the **EXCHANGE2003BE** certificate (which is the CA that issued the Administrator certificate) at the top of the list. Click **View Certificate** (Figure 9.41).

Figure 9.41 The Certificate Path Tab

22. In the CA certificate's **Certificate** dialog box, click the **Details** tab. Click **Copy to File**.

23. Click **Next** in the **Welcome to the Certificate Export Wizard** page.

24. On the **Export File Format** page, select **Cryptographic Message Syntax Standard – PKCS #7 Certificates (.P7B)**, and click **Next**.

25. On the **File to Export** page, enter **c:\cacert** in the **File name** text box. Click **Next**.

26. Click **Finish** on the **Completing the Certificate Export Wizard** page.

27. Click **OK** in the **Certificate Export Wizard** dialog box.

28. Click **OK** in the **Certificate** dialog box. Click **OK** again in the **Certificate** dialog box.

29. In the left pane of the console, expand **Trusted Root Certification Authorities** and click the **Certificates** node. Right-click **Trusted Root Certification Authorities\Certificates**; point to **All Tasks**, and click **Import**.

30. Click **Next** on the **Welcome to the Certificate Import Wizard** page.

31. On the **File to Import** page, use **Browse** to locate the CA certificate you saved to the local hard disk, and click **Next**.

32. On the **Certificate Store** page, accept the default settings, and click **Next**.

33. Click **Finish** on the **Completing the Certificate Import Wizard** page.

34. Click **OK** in the **Certificate Import Wizard** dialog box informing you that the import was successful.

Configure the Main Office ISA Firewall to Use L2TP/IPSec for the Site-to-Site Link

The Remote Site Network on the main office ISA firewall representing the branch office network is configured to use PPTP for the site-to-site connection. We need to change this to L2TP/IPSec. Perform the following steps to make the change:

1. In the **Microsoft Internet Security and Acceleration Server 2004** management console, expand the server name, and then click the **Virtual Private Networks (VPN)** node in the left pane of the console.

2. On the **Virtual Private Networks (VPN)** node, click the **Remote Sites** tab in the Details pane. Double-click the **Branch** Remote Site Network entry.

3. In the **Branch Properties** dialog box, select the **L2TP/IPSec (provides a highly secure connection method)** option. Click **Apply** and then click **OK**.

4. Do *not* apply the new configuration to the Firewall Policy yet. This will break our PPTP site-to-site link, and we need this PPTP site-to-site link to stay up until we have installed a certificate on the branch office ISA firewall. After the branch office ISA firewall has been configured, then you can apply the changes to the Firewall Policy at the main office.

Enable the System Policy Rule on the Branch Office Firewall to Access the Enterprise CA

Now we'll switch our attention to the branch office ISA firewall. We need to enable the System Policy Rule allowing the branch office firewall to connect to the enterprise CA on the main office network.

Perform the following steps to enable the System Policy rule on the branch office firewall:

1. In the **Microsoft Internet Security and Acceleration Server 2004** management console, expand the server name, and click the **Firewall Policy** node.

2. Right-click **Firewall Policy**; point to **View**, and click **Show System Policy Rules**.

3. In the System Policy Rule list, double-click **Allow HTTP from ISA Server to all networks (for CRL downloads)**. This is System Policy Rule #26.

4. In the **System Policy Editor** dialog box (Figure 9.42), put a checkmark in the **Enable** checkbox on the **General** tab. Click **OK**.

Figure 9.42 Configuring System Policy

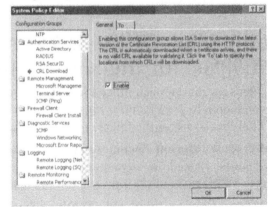

5. Click **Apply** to save the changes and update the firewall policy.

6. Click **OK** in the **Apply New Configuration** dialog box

Request and Install a Web Site Certificate for the Branch Office Firewall

Now we'll request a certificate for the branch office firewall. After we obtain the certificate, we will copy the CA certificate into the machine's **Trusted Root Certification Authorities** certificate store.

Perform the following steps on the branch office ISA firewall to request and install the certificates:

1. Open **Internet Explorer**. In the Address bar, enter **http://10.0.0.2/certsrv**, and click **OK**.

2. In the **Enter Network Password** dialog box, enter **Administrator** in the **User Name** text box, and enter the **Administrator's** password in the **Password** text box. Click **OK**.

3. In the **Internet Explorer** security dialog box, click **Add**. In the **Trusted Sites** dialog box, click **Add and Close**.

4. Click **Request a Certificate** on the **Welcome** page.

5. On the **Request a Certificate** page, click **advanced certificate request**.

6. On the **Advanced Certificate Request** page, click **Create and submit a request to this CA**.

7. On the **Advanced Certificate Request** page, select the **Administrator** certificate from the **Certificate Template** list. Remove the checkmark from the **Mark keys as exportable** checkbox. Place a checkmark in the **Store certificate in the local computer certificate store** checkbox. Click **Submit**.

8. Click **Yes** in the **Potential Scripting Violation** dialog box.

9. On the **Certificate Issued** page, click **Install this certificate**.

10. Click **Yes** on the **Potential Scripting Violation** page.

11. Close the browser after viewing the **Certificate Installed** page.

12. Click **Start** and **Run**. Enter **mmc** in the **Open** text box, and click **OK**.

13. In **Console1**, click the **File** menu, and then click **Add/Remove Snap-in**.

14. Click **Add** in the **Add/Remove Snap-in** dialog box.

15. Select the **Certificates** entry from the **Available Standalone Snap-ins** list in the **Add Standalone Snap-in** dialog box. Click **Add**.

16. Select **Computer account** on the **Certificates snap-in** page.

17. Select **Local computer** on the **Select Computer** page.

18. Click **Close** in the **Add Standalone Snap-in** dialog box.

19. Click **OK** in the **Add/Remove Snap-in** dialog box.

20. In the left pane of the console, expand **Certificates (Local Computer)**, then expand **Personal**. Click on **\Personal\Certificates**. Double-click on the **Administrator** certificate in the right pane of the console.

21. In the **Certificate** dialog box, click the **Certification Path** tab. The root CA certificate is at the top of the certificate hierarchy seen in the Certification path frame. Click the **EXCHANGE2003BE** certificate at the top of the list. Click **View Certificate**.

22. In the CA certificate's **Certificate** dialog box, click **Details**. Click **Copy to File**.

23. Click **Next** in the **Welcome to the Certificate Export Wizard** page.

24. On the **Export File Format** page, select **Cryptographic Message Syntax Standard – PKCS #7 Certificates (.P7B)**, and click **Next**.

25. On the **File to Export** page, enter **c:\cacert** in the **File name** text box. Click **Next**.

26. Click **Finish** on the **Completing the Certificate Export Wizard** page.

27. Click **OK** in the **Certificate Export Wizard** dialog box.

28. Click **OK** in the **Certificate** dialog box. Click **OK** again in the **Certificate** dialog box.

29. In the left pane of the console, expand the **Trusted Root Certification Authorities** node, and click **Certificates**. Right-click the **\Trusted Root Certification Authorities\Certificates** node; point to **All Tasks** and click **Import**.

30. Click **Next** on the **Welcome to the Certificate Import Wizard** page.

31. On the **File to Import** page, use **Browse** to locate the CA certificate you saved to the local hard disk, and click **Next**.

32. On the **Certificate Store** page, accept the default settings, and click **Next**.

33. Click **Finish** on the **Completing the Certificate Import Wizard** page.

34. Click **OK** on the **Certificate Import Wizard** dialog box informing you that the import was successful.

Configure the Main Office ISA Firewall to Use L2TP/IPSec for the Site-to-Site Link

The Remote Site Network at the branch office ISA firewall representing the main office network is configured to use PPTP for the site-to-site connection. We need to change this to L2TP/IPSec. Perform the following steps to make the change:

1. In the **Microsoft Internet Security and Acceleration Server 2004** management console, expand the server name, and then click the **Virtual Private Networks (VPN)** node in the left pane of the console.

2. On the **Virtual Private Networks (VPN)** node, click the **Remote Sites** tab in the Details pane. Double-click the **Main** Remote Site Network entry.

3. In the **Branch Properties** dialog box, select **L2TP/IPSec (provides a highly secure connection method)**. Click **Apply**, and then click **OK**.

4. Click **Apply** to save the changes and update the firewall policy.

5. Click **OK** in the **Apply New Configuration** dialog box.

6. Now you can save the changes to the Firewall Policy at the main office.

Activate the L2TP/IPSec Site-to-Site VPN Connection

Let's see if our L2TP/IPSec site-to-site VPN connection works:

1. First, you need to restart the **Routing and Remote Access Service** on both ISA firewalls so that the **Routing and Remote Access Service** recognizes the certificate.
2. In the **Microsoft Internet Security and Acceleration Server 2004** management console, expand the server name and click the **Monitoring** node.
3. On the **Monitoring** node, click the **Services** tab. Right-click the **Routing and Remote Access Service**, and click **Stop**.
4. When the service is stopped, right-click it again, and click **Start**.
5. From a host on the branch office network, ping the domain controller on the main office network.
6. When you receive ping responses, go to the branch office ISA firewall and open the **Microsoft Internet Security and Acceleration Server 2004** management console. Expand the server name, and then click the **Monitoring** node.
7. On the **Monitoring** node, click the **Sessions** tab. On the **Sessions** tab, right-click any of the column headers, and then click the **Application Name** entry (see Figure 9.43).

Figure 9.43 Adding the Application Name column

Activation
Source Network
10/10/2004 10:27:51 PM SecureN
10/10/2004 10:29:27 PM VPN Rer
10/10/2004 10:32:21 PM SecureN
Activation
Session Type
Client IP
Source Network
Client Username
Client Host Name
Application Name
Server Name
Add/Remove Columns...

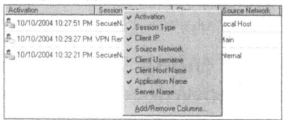

8. In the **Application Name** column you'll see that an L2TP/IPSec connection was established (see Figure 9.44).

Figure 9.44 Viewing the L2TP/IPSec

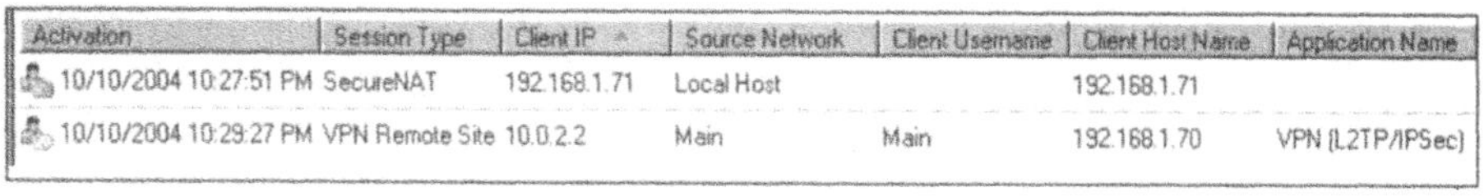

Activation
Session Type
Client IP
Source Network
Client Username
Client Host Name
Application Name
10/10/2004 10:27:51 PM SecureNAT 192.168.1.71 Local Host 192.168.1.71
10/10/2004 10:29:27 PM VPN Remote Site 10.0.2.2 Main Main 192.168.1.70 VPN (L2TP/IPSec)

Configuring Pre-shared Keys for Site-to-Site L2TP/IPSec VPN Links

In the previous example, we demonstrated the procedures required to create the site-to-site L2TP/IPSec connection using certificates for computer authentication. If you don't have a PKI in place yet, or if you do not plan on implementing a certificate infrastructure, you can use pre-shared keys for the computer authentication component of L2TP/IPSec connection establishment. This provides a more secure connection than you would see with IPSec tunnel mode and pre-shared keys, because you still have the user authentication requirement for the L2TP/IPSec connection.

Perform the following steps on both the main and branch office ISA firewalls to enable pre-shared keys for the site-to-site VPN connection:

1. In the **Microsoft Internet Security and Acceleration Server 2004** management console, expand the server name, and then click the **Virtual Private Networking (VPN)** node in the left pane of the console.

2. On the **Virtual Private Networking (VPN)** node, click the **VPN Clients** tab in the Details pane.

3. Click the **Tasks** tab in the Task pane. Click the **Select Authentication Methods** link.

4. In the **Virtual Private Networks (VPN) Properties** dialog box, put a checkmark in the **Allow custom IPSec policy for L2TP connection** checkbox.

5. Click **Apply** and then click **OK**.

6. Click **Apply** to save the changes and update the firewall policy.

7. Click **OK** in the **Apply New Configuration** dialog box.

IPSec Tunnel Mode Site-to-Site VPNs with Downlevel VPN Gateways

One of the major improvements that the new ISA firewall has over ISA Server 2000 is that it can be configured to use IPSec tunnel mode for site-to-site VPN connections. Most third-party VPN gateways require that you use IPSec tunnel mode for site-to-site VPN connections. It was very difficult to find a third-party VPN gateway that would work with ISA Server 2000. But with the new ISA firewall, you can establish a IPSec tunnel mode site-to-site link with just about any third-party VPN gateway.

Because of the number of third-party VPN gateways available on the market today, it's not possible for us to go into detail on how to configure the ISA firewall to connect to each of these devices. The good news is that Microsoft has published a comprehensive set of documents on how to connect the ISA firewall to a number of popular VPN gateways. At the time of this writing, there are documents on how to connect the ISA firewall to the following VPN gateways:

- Cisco PIX

- Astaro Linux

- SmoothWall Express

- Generic third-party gateways

You can find these documents and more on the Microsoft ISA 2004 VPN documentation site at http://www.microsoft.com/isaserver/techinfo/guidance/2004/vpn.asp

Using RADIUS for VPN Authentication and Remote Access Policy

We prefer to not join front-end ISA firewalls to the user domain. The reason for this is that the network segments between the front-end ISA firewall and back-end firewalls are unauthenticated DMZ segments, and we want to avoid passing domain information through those segments as much as possible.

When the ISA firewall is not a member of the user domain, we must use a mechanism other than Windows to authenticate and authorize domain users. The ISA firewall can authenticate VPN users with RADIUS (Remote Access Dial-In User Service). The RADIUS Protocol allows the ISA 2004 firewall to forward user credentials of a RADIUS server on the Internal network. The RADIUS server sends the authentication request to an authentication server, such as an Active Directory domain controller. The Microsoft implementation of RADIUS is the Internet Authentication Service (IAS).

In addition to authenticating users, the IAS server can be used to centralize Remote Access Policy. For example, if you have six ISA firewall/VPN servers under your administrative control, you can apply the same Remote Access Policy to all these machines by creating policy on an IAS server on your network.

The ISA firewall is not limited to working with just IAS, and it supports all types of RADIUS servers. However, the Microsoft IAS server is included with all Windows 2000 and Windows Server 2003 server family products, which makes it very convenient to use for any Microsoft shop.

In this section we will discuss procedures required to enable RADIUS authentication and RADIUS Remote Access Policy for VPN clients. We will carry out the following procedures:

- Configure the IAS Server

- Create a VPN Clients Remote Access Policy

- Enable the VPN Server on the ISA 2004 firewall and configure RADIUS Support

- Create a VPN Client Access Rule

- Make the connection from a PPTP VPN client

Configure the Internet Authentication Services (RADIUS) Server

If you have not installed the IAS server, you can install it now using the **Add/Remove Programs** Control Panel applet on your Windows 2000 or Windows Server 2003 machines on the Internal Network. You need to configure the IAS server to communicate with the Active Directory and then instruct the IAS server to work with the ISA 2004 firewall/VPN server machine. In our current example, the IAS server is installed on the domain controller on the Internal Network (EXCHANGE2003BE).

Perform the following steps to configure the IAS server:

1. Click **Start**; point to **Administrative Tools**, and click on **Internet Authentication Services**.

2. In the **Internet Authentication Services** console, right-click on the **Internet Authentication Service (Local)** node in the left pane of the console. Click the **Register Server in Active Directory** command.

3. This setting allows the IAS Server to authenticate users in the Active Directory domain. Click **OK** in the **Register Internet Authentication Server in Active Directory** dialog box.

4. Click **OK** in the **Server registered:** dialog box. This dialog box informs you that the IAS Server was registered in a specific domain and if you want this IAS Server to read users' dial-in properties from other domains, you'll need to enter this server into the **RAS/IAS Server Group** in that domain. This automatically places the machine in the RAS and IAS Server Group in the Active Directory. If you want to register the server in another domain, you must place it in the RAS and IAS Servers group in that domain or use the command **netsh ras add registeredserver** *Domain IASServer* command.

5. Right-click on the **RADIUS Clients** node in the left pane of the console, and click the **New RADIUS Client** command.

6. In the **New RADIUS Client** dialog box, type in a **Friendly name** for the ISA firewall. You can use any name you like. In this example we'll use the DNS host name of the ISA firewall, which is **ISALOCAL**. Enter either the FQDN or the IP address of the ISA 2004 firewall/VPN server in the **Client address (IP or DNS)** dialog box. Do not enter a FQDN if your ISA firewall has not registered its internal interface IP address with your internal DNS server. You can use the **Verify** button to test whether the IAS Server can resolve the FQDN. Click **Next**.

7. On the **Additional Information** page, leave the **RADIUS Standard** entry in the **Client-Vendor** drop-down list box. Your ISA firewall will use this setting. Enter a complex shared secret in the **Shared secret** text box, and confirm it in the **Confirm shared secret** text box. The shared secret

should be a complex string consisting of upper and lower case letters, numbers, and symbols. Put a checkmark in the **Request must contain the Message Authenticator attribute** checkbox. This option enhances the security of the RADIUS messages passed between the ISA firewall and IAS servers. Click **Finish**. See Figure 9.45.

> **WARNING**
>
> The shared secret should be very long and complex. We recommend that it be at least 20 characters and contain a mix of upper and lower case letters, numbers, and symbols.

Figure 9.45 Configuring the Shared Secret

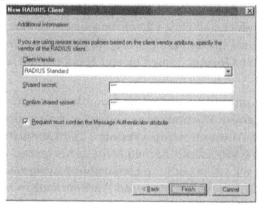

Create a VPN Clients Remote Access Policy

We're now ready to create a Remote Access Policy on the IAS Server. Remote Access Policies configured on the IAS Server are applied to VPN client connections made to the ISA firewall when the ISA firewall is configured to use RADIUS authentication and policy, and when the ISA firewall is configured as a RADIUS client. Fortunately for us, the Windows Server 2003 IAS server has a Remote Access Policy Wizard that makes it easy to create a secure VPN client Remote Access Policy.

Perform the following steps to create a VPN client Remote Access Policy on the IAS Server:

1. In the **Internet Authentication Service** console, right-click on the **Remote Access Policies** node, and click the **New Remote Access Policy** command.

2. Click **Next** on the **Welcome to the New Remote Access Policy Wizard** page.

3. On the **Policy Configuration Method** page, select **Use the wizard to set up a typical policy for a common scenario**. In the **Policy name** text box, type a name for the policy. In this example, we'll call it **VPN Access Policy**. Click **Next**.

4. Select the **VPN** option on the **Access Method** page. This policy is used for all VPN connections. You have the option to create separate policies for PPTP and L2TP/IPSec VPN links. However, to create separate policies for PPTP and L2TP/IPSec connections, you'll need to go back to the previous page in the Wizard and create two **custom** policies. In this example, we apply the same policy to all remote access VPN connections. Click **Next**.

5. You can grant access to the VPN server based on user or group. The best access control method is on a per-group basis because it entails less administrative overhead. You can create a group such as **VPN Users** and allow them access, or allow all your users access. In this example, we will select the **Group** option and click the **Add** button. This brings up the **Select Groups** dialog box. Enter the name of the group in for **Enter the object name to select**, and click **Check names** to confirm that you entered the name correctly. In this example, use the **Domain Users** group. Click **OK** in the **Select Groups** dialog box and **Next** in the **User or Group Access** dialog box.

6. Select user authentication methods you want to allow on the **Authentication Methods** page. You may wish to allow both **Microsoft Encrypted Authentication version 2** and **Extensible Authentication Protocol (EAP)**. Both EAP and MS-CHAP version 2 authentication are secure, so we'll select both the **Extensible Authentication Protocol (EAP)** and **Microsoft Encrypted Authentication version 2 (MS-CHAPv2)** checkboxes. Click the down arrow from the **Type (based on method of access and network configuration)** drop-down list and select the **Smart Card or other certificate** option, then click the **Configure** button (as shown in Figure 9.46). In the **Smart Card or other Certificate Properties** dialog box, select the certificate you want the server to use to identify itself to VPN clients. The self-signed certificate appears in the **Certificate issued to** drop-down list. This certificate is used to identify the server when VPN clients are configured to confirm the server's validity. Click **OK** in the **Smart Card or other Certificate Properties** dialog box (as shown in Figure 9.47), and then click **Next**.

Figure 9.46 The Authentication Method Page

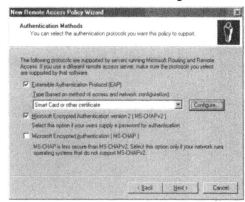

Figure 9.47 The Smart Card or other Certificate Properties Dialog Box

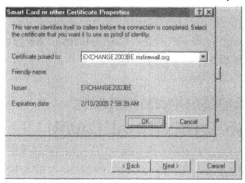

NOTE

If you do not see the certificate in the **Smart Card or other Certificate Properties** dialog box, then restart the RADIUS server and start over. The certificate will then appear in the dialog box after the restart. If you still do not see the certificate, this indicates that either the machine does not have a machine certificate installed on it, or that it has a machine certificate, but it does not trust the CA issuing the certificate. Double-check the machine certificate and the machine's Trusted Root Certification Authorities certificate stores to confirm that you have both these certificates installed.

7. Select the level(s) of encryption you want to enforce on VPN connections. All Microsoft clients support the strongest level of encryption. If you have clients that don't support 128 bit encryption, select lower levels, but realize that you lower the level of security provided by the encryption method used by the VPN protocol. In this example, we'll select all three options (see Figure 9.48). In a high-security environment, you should select on the strongest encryption

option. Just make sure all your VPN clients support this level of encryption. Click **Next**.

Figure 9.48 The Policy Encrypted Level

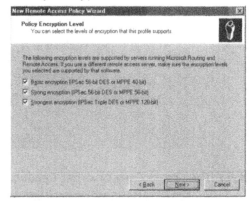

8. Review your settings on the **Completing the New Remote Access Policy Wizard** page and click **Finish**.

Remote Access Permissions and Domain Functional Level

The new Remote Access Policy requires the connection be a VPN connection. The VPN protocol can be either PPTP or L2TP/IPSec. The VPN client must use MS-CHAP v2 or EAP-TLS to authenticate, and the client must support the level of encryption set in the Remote Access Policy. The user must belong to the **Domain Users** group in the domain specified in the Remote Access Policy.

The next step is to configure Remote Access Permissions. Remote Access Permissions are different than Remote Access Policies.

When a VPN user calls the ISA firewall, the parameters of the connection are compared against Remote Access Policy (the remote access policy can be either on the ISA firewall itself or on a IAS server). Remote Access Policies are represented as a hierarchical list. The policy on top of the list is evaluated first, then the second-listed policy is evaluated, then the third, and so forth.

The VPN client's connection parameters are compared to the *conditions* in the policy. In the remote access policy we created above, there were two conditions:

■ The connection type is a virtual connection, and

■ The user is a member of the **Domain Users** group.

If the connection request matches both of those conditions, then Remote Access Permissions are determined. Remote access permissions are determined differently depending on the type of domain the user account belongs to.

Windows Server 2003 domains do not use the Mixed and Native Mode designations you might be familiar with in Windows 2000. Windows Server 2003 supports domains of varying *functional levels*. If all the domain controllers in your domain run Windows Server 2003, the default functional level is *Windows 2000 mixed*. All user accounts are denied VPN (Dial-up) access by default in Windows 2000 Mixed Mode functional level. In Windows 2000 Mixed Mode, *you must configure each user account* to have permission to log on to the VPN server. The reason is that user account permissions override Remote Access Policy permissions in Mixed Mode domains.

If you want to control Remote Access Permissions via Remote Access Policy, you must raise the domain functional level to Windows 2000 Native or Windows Server 2003. The default Remote Access Permission in Windows 2000 and Windows Server 2003 domains is **Control access through Remote Access Policy**. Once you are able to use Remote Access Policy to assign VPN access permission, you can take advantage of group membership to allow or deny VPN access to the VPN server.

When a VPN connection matches the *conditions* in the Remote Access Policy, and the user is granted access via either the user account Dial-in settings or Remote Access Policy, then the VPN connection parameters are compared to a number of settings defined by the *Remote Access Profile*. If the incoming connection does not comply with the settings in the Remote Access Profile, then the next Remote Access Policy is compared to the connection. If no policy matches the incoming connection's parameters, the VPN connection request to the ISA firewall is dropped.

The VPN Remote Access Policy you created earlier includes all the parameters required for a secure VPN connection. Your decision now centers on how you want to control Remote Access Permissions:

- **Enable Remote Access on a per group basis:** this requires that you run in Windows 2000 Native or Windows Server 2003 functional level.

- **Enable Remote Access on a per user basis:** supported by Windows 2000 Native, Windows 2000 Mixed and Windows Server 2003 functional levels.

- **Enable Remote Access on both a per user and per group basis:** this requires Windows 2000 Native or Windows Server 2003 functional level; granular user-based access control overriding group-based access control is done on a per user basis.

Procedures required to allow *per user* and *per group* access include:

- Change the **Dial-in** permissions on the user account in the Active Directory to control Remote Access Permission on a per user basis.

- Change the domain functional level to support Dial-in permissions based on Remote Access Policy.

- Change the Permissions settings on the Remote Access Policy.

Changing the User Account Dial-in Permissions

You enable dial-in permissions on a per account basis, or create Remote Access Policies that can be configured to enable dial-in permissions to entire groups.

Perform the following steps if you want to control access on a per user basis, or if you have no other choice because of your domain's functional level:

1. Click **Start**; point to **Administrative Tools**, and click on **Active Directory Users and Computers**.

2. In the **Active Directory Users and Computers** console, expand your domain name and click on the **User** node.

3. Double-click on the **Administrator** account in the right pane of the console. In the user account **Properties** dialog box, click on the **Dial-in** tab. The default setting on the account is **Deny access.** You can allow VPN access for the account by selecting the **Allow access** option. Per user account settings override permissions set on the Remote Access Policy. Notice the **Control access through Remote Access Policy** option is disabled. This option is available only when the domain is at the Windows 2000 or Windows Server 2003 functional level. Make no changes to the account setting at this time. See Figure 9.49.

Figure 9.49 Changing the Dial-in Permissions

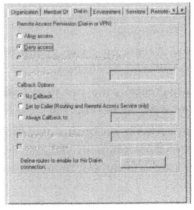

4. Click **Cancel** to escape this dialog box.

Changing the Domain Functional Level

If you want to control access on a per group basis, you will need to change the default domain functional level. Perform the following steps to change the domain functional level:

1. On a domain controller in your domain, open the **Active Directory Domains and Trusts** console. Click **Start**; point to **Administrative Tools** and click on **Active Directory Domains and Trusts**.

2. In the **Active Directory Domains and Trusts** console, right-click on your domain, and click on the **Raise Domain Functional Level** command.

3. In the **Raise Domain Functional Level** dialog box, click the down arrow in the **Select an available domain functional level** drop-down list and select either **Windows 2000 native** or **Windows Server 2003**, depending on the type of domain functional level your network can support. In this example, we will select the **Windows Server 2003** option. Click the **Raise** button after making your selection (as shown in Figure 9.50).

Figure 9.50 The Raise Domain Functional Level

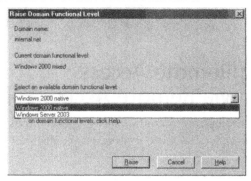

5. Click **OK** in the **Raise Domain Functional Level** dialog box. This dialog box explains that the change affects the entire domain and after the change is made, it cannot be reversed.

6. Click **OK** in the **Raise Domain Functional Level** dialog box informing you that the functional level was raised successfully. Note that you do not need to restart the computer for the changes to take effect. However, the default Remote Access Permission will not change for user accounts until Active Directory replication is completed. In this example, we will restart the computer. Restart the computer now and log in as Administrator.

7. Return to the **Active Directory Users and Computers** console and double-click on a user account. Click on the **Dial-in** tab in the user's **Properties** dialog box. Notice how the **Control access through Remote Access Policy** option is enabled and selected by default (Figure 9.51).

Figure 9.51 Controlling Access via Remote Access Policy

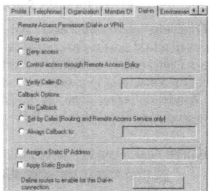

Controlling Remote Access Permission via Remote Access Policy

Now that we have the option to control access via Remote Access Policy (instead of a per user account basis), let's see how VPN access control via Remote Access Policy is performed:

1. Click **Start**; point to **Administrative Tools**, and click **Internet Authentication Service**.

2. Click **Remote Access Policies** in the left pane of the console. You will see the **VPN Access Policy** and two other built-in Remote Access Policies. You can delete the other policies if you require only VPN connections to your ISA firewall. Right-click on **Connections to other access servers**, and click **Delete**. Repeat with **Connections to Microsoft Routing and Remote Access server**.

3. Double-click on the **VPN Access Policy** in the right pane of the console. In the **VPN Access Policy Properties** dialog box there are two options that control access permissions based on Remote Access Policy:

    ■ Deny remote access permission

    ■ Grant remote access permission

Notice that this dialog box does inform you that the user account settings override the Remote Access Permission settings: **Unless individual access permissions are specified in the user profile, this policy controls access to the network**. Select the **Grant remote access permission** to allow members of the **Domain Users** group access to the VPN server (Figure 9.52).

Figure 9.52 Remote Access Policy Properties

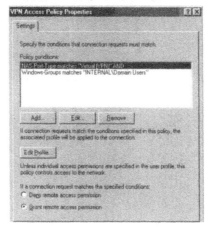

4. Click **Apply** and then click **OK** in the **VPN Access Policy Properties** dialog box to save the changes

Enable the VPN Server on the ISA Firewall and Configure RADIUS Support

After the RADIUS server is installed and configured and Remote Access Policies are in place, we can start configuring the ISA firewall. First, we will first enable the VPN server component and then configure the VPN server to support RADIUS authentication.

Perform the following steps to enable the VPN server and configure it for RADIUS support:

1. In the **Microsoft Internet Security and Acceleration Server 2004 management console**, expand the server name, and click on **Virtual Private Networks (VPN)**.

2. Click the **Tasks** tab in the Task pane. Click **Enable VPN Client Access**.

3. Click **Configure VPN Client Access**.

4. In the **VPN Clients Properties** dialog box, put a checkmark in the **Enable VPN client access** checkbox. Configure the number of VPN clients you want to allow in the **Maximum number of VPN allowed** text box.

5. Click the **Protocols** tab. Put checkmarks in the **Enable PPTP** and **Enable L2TP/IPSec** checkboxes. Click **Apply** and then click **OK** (Figure 9.53).

Figure 9.53 Enabling the VPN Protocols

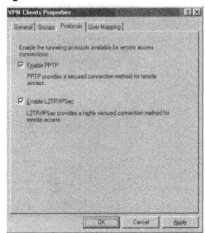

6. Click the **Specify RADIUS Configuration** link on the **Tasks** tab.

7. On the **RADIUS** tab in the **Virtual Private Networks (VPN) Properties** dialog box (Figure 9.54), put a checkmark in the **Use RADIUS for authentication** checkbox.

Figure 9.54 Configuring RADIUS Authentication

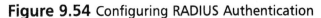
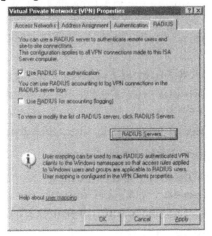

8. Click the **RADIUS Servers** button. In the **RADIUS** dialog box, click **Add**.

9. In the **Add RADIUS Server** dialog box, enter the name of the IAS server machine in the **Server name** text box. In this example, the name of the IAS server is **EXCHANGE2003BE.msfirewall.org**. Enter a description of the server in the **Server description** text box. In this example, enter the description **IAS Server**. Click the **Change** button (Figure 9.55).

Figure 9.55 The Add RADIUS Server Dialog Box

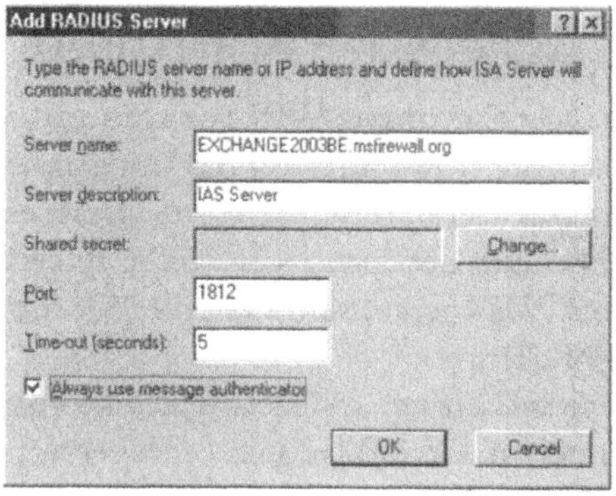

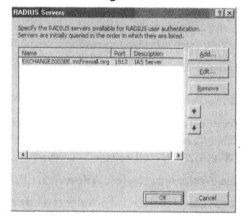

10. In the **Shared Secret** dialog box, enter a **New Secret** and then **Confirm new secret**. Make sure this is the *same secret* you entered in the RADIUS client configuration at the IAS server machine. Click **OK**.

11. Click **OK** in the **Add RADIUS Server** dialog box.

12. Click **OK** in the **RADIUS Servers** dialog box (Figure 9.56).

Figure 9.56 RADIUS Server Dialog Box

13. Click **Apply** in the **Virtual Private Networks (VPN) Properties** dialog box. Click **OK** in the **ISA 2004** dialog box informing you that the **Routing and Remote Access Service** may restart. Click **OK** in the **Virtual Private Networks (VPN) Properties** dialog box.

14. Click **Apply** to save the changes and update the firewall policy.

15. Click **OK** in the **Apply New Configuration** dialog box.

16. Restart the ISA firewall, and log on as **Administrator**.

Create an Access Rule Allowing
VPN Clients Access to Approved Resources

The ISA firewall can accept incoming VPN connections after the restart. However, the VPN clients cannot access any resources on the Internal network because there are no Access Rules enabling this access. You must create an Access Rule allowing machines belonging to the VPN clients network access to the Internal network. In contrast to other combined firewall VPN server solutions, the ISA firewall applies access controls for network access to VPN clients.

In this example, we will create an Access Rule allowing VPN clients access to the OWA server on the Internal network and no other servers. In addition, we'll limit the users to using only HTTP when making the connection.

This type of configuration would be attractive to organizations that want to allow secure remote access to their corporate OWA site, but that do not want to use SSL-to-SSL bridging because:

- There may be potential vulnerabilities in the SSL/TLS encryption implementations, and

- They want to allow non-encrypted communications through the corporate network to enable internal network IDS to evaluate the connections.

We will demonstrate other ways you can implement access control on VPN clients using user/group members later in this chapter.

Perform the following steps to create an unrestricted access VPN clients Access Rule:

1. In the **Microsoft Internet Security and Acceleration Server 2004** management console, expand the server name and click the **Firewall Policy** node. Right-click the **Firewall Policy** node, point to **New**, and click **Access Rule**.

2. In the **Welcome to the New Access Rule Wizard** page, enter a name for the rule in the **Access Rule name** text box. In this example, we will name the rule **OWA for VPN Clients**. Click **Next**.

3. On the **Rule Action** page, select **Allow**, and click **Next**.

4. On the **Protocols** page, select the **Selected protocols** option in the **This rule applies to** list. Click **Add**.

5. In the **Add Protocols** dialog box, click the **Common Protocols** folder, and double-click the **HTTP** and **HTTPS** Protocols. Click **Close**.

6. Click **Next** on the **Protocols** page.

7. On the **Access Rule Sources** page, click **Add**. In the **Add Network Entities** dialog box, click the **Networks** folder, and double-click **VPN Clients**. Click **Close**.

8. Click **Next** on the **Access Rule Sources** page.

9. On the **Access Rule Destinations** page, click **Add**. In the **Add Network Entities** dialog box, click the **New** menu, and click **Computer**.

10. In the **New Computer Rule Element** dialog box, enter the name of the OWA server in the **Name** text box. In this example, we'll name it **OWA Server**. Enter the IP address of the OWA server in the **Computer IP Address** text box. Click **OK**.

11. Click the **Computers** folder and double-click the **OWA Server** entry. Click **Close**.

12. Click **Next** on the **Access Rule Destinations** page.

13. On the **User Sets** page, accept the default setting, **All Users**, and click **Next**.

14. Click Finish on the **Completing the New Access Rule Wizard** page.

15. Click **Apply** to save the changes and update the firewall policy.

16. Click **OK** in the **Apply New Configuration** dialog box. The **OWA for VPN Clients** policy is now the top-listed Access Rule in the Access Policy list (Figure 9.57).

Figure 9.57 The resulting firewall policy

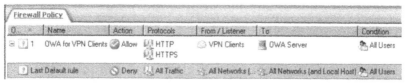

Make the Connection from a PPTP VPN Client

All the elements are in place to support RADIUS authentication for VPN clients. In the following exercise you will establish a PPTP VPN connection from an external network VPN client.

Perform the following steps to connect to the VPN server via RADIUS authentication:

1. In the **Dial-up and Network Connections** window on the external network client, create a new VPN connectoid. Configure the connectoid to use the IP address **192.168.1.70** as the address of the VPN server. Log on with the user name **Administrator**.

2. Click **OK** in the dialog box informing you that the VPN connection is established.

3. At the domain controller machine, click **Start** and point to **Administrative Tools**. Click **Event Viewer**.

4. In the **Event Viewer**, click on the **System** node in the left pane of the console. Double-click on the **Information** entry with the source as **IAS**. (See Figure 9.58).

Figure 9.58 Event Viewer Entry

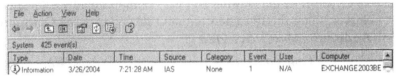

5. In the **Event Properties** dialog box, you will see a **Description** of the log-on request. The information indicates that the RADIUS server authenticated the request and includes the RADIUS-specific information sent to the domain controller. Review this information and close the **Event Properties** dialog box (Figure 9.59).

Figure 9.59 Log-On Request Details

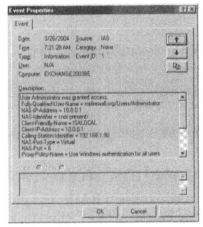

6. At the ISA firewall, you can see log file entries specific to this VPN request. Note the PPTP and the RADIUS connections (Figure 9.60).

Figure 9.60 Log File Entries for VPN RADIUS Authentication

192.168.1.90	192.168.1.70	1723	PPTP	Initiated Connection	Allow VPN client traffic to ISA Server	
192.168.1.90	192.168.1.70	0	PPTP	Initiated Connection	Allow VPN client traffic to ISA Server	
10.0.0.1	10.0.0.2	1812	RADIUS	Initiated Connection	Allow RADIUS authentication from ISA Server to trusted RADIUS servers	
10.0.0.108	10.0.0.109	0	WAN Miniport (PPTP)	Initiated VPN Connection		Administrator

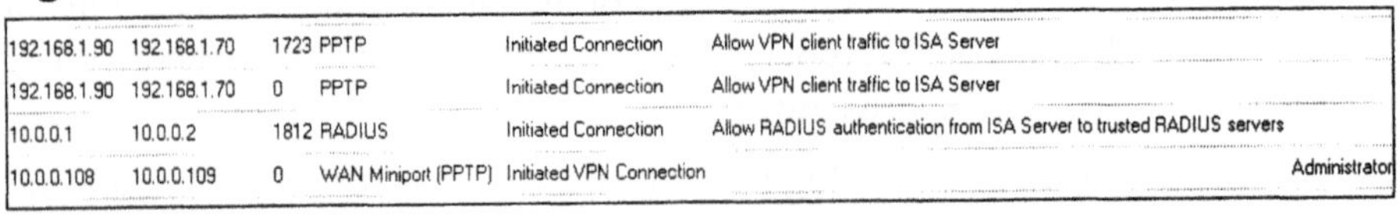

7. At the ISA firewall server, you can see the VPN client session in the **Sessions** tab in the **Monitoring** node of the **Microsoft Internet Security and Acceleration Server 2004** management console (Figure 9.61).

Figure 9.61 VPN Session Appears in Sessions Section

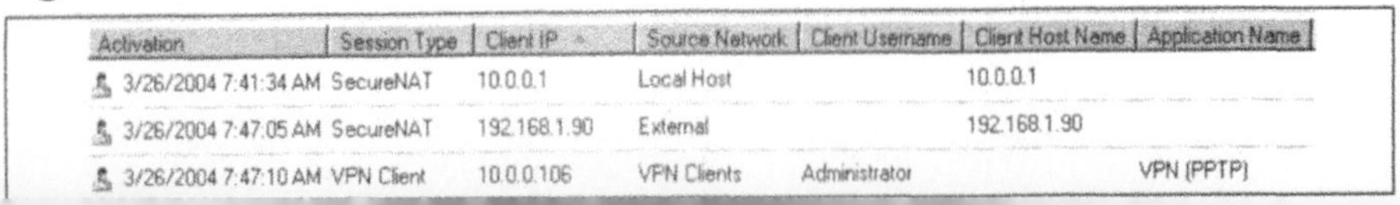

Activation	Session Type	Client IP ▲	Source Network	Client Username	Client Host Name	Application Name
🔒 3/26/2004 7:41:34 AM	SecureNAT	10.0.0.1	Local Host		10.0.0.1	
🔒 3/26/2004 7:47:05 AM	SecureNAT	192.168.1.90	External		192.168.1.90	
🔒 3/26/2004 7:47:10 AM	VPN Client	10.0.0.106	VPN Clients	Administrator		VPN (PPTP)

8. At the VPN client computer, disconnect the VPN connection.

9. If you run a **Network Monitor** session on the RADIUS server, you can see that a single RADIUS **Access Request** is sent from the ISA firewall to the RADIUS server and a single **Access Accept** message is sent to the ISA firewall from the RADIUS server (Figure 9.62).

Figure 9.62 RADIUS Messages in Network Monitor Trace

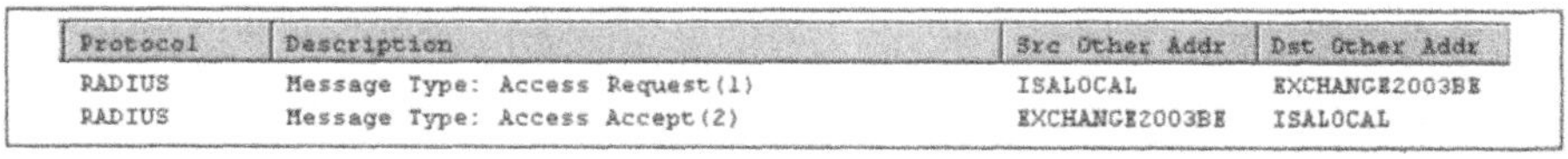

Protocol	Description	Src Other Addr	Dst Other Addr
RADIUS	Message Type: Access Request(1)	ISALOCAL	EXCHANGE2003BE
RADIUS	Message Type: Access Accept(2)	EXCHANGE2003BE	ISALOCAL

Using EAP User Certificate Authentication for Remote Access VPNs

You can significantly enhance the security of your ISA firewall's VPN remote access client connections by using EAP user certificate authentication. User certificate authentication requires that the user possess a user certificate issued by a trusted certificate authority.

Both the ISA firewall and the remote access VPN client must have the appropriate certificates assignment to them. You must assign the ISA firewall a machine certificate that the firewall can use to identify itself. Users must be assigned user certificates from a certificate authority that the ISA firewall trusts. When both the remote access client machine presenting the user certificate and the ISA firewall contain a common CA certificate in their Trusted Root Certification Authorities certificate stores, the client and server trust the same certificate hierarchy.

The steps required to support user certificate authentication for remote access client VPN connections to the ISA firewall include:

- Issuing a machine certificate to the ISA firewall
- Configuring the ISA firewall software to support EAP authentication
- Enabling User Mapping for EAP authenticated users
- Configuring the Routing and Remote Access Service to support EAP authentication
- Issuing a user certificate to the remote access VPN client machine

We have discussed the procedures for issuing a machine certificate to the ISA firewall in other chapters in this book and in the ISA Deployment Kits at www.isaserver.org, so we will not reiterate that procedure here. Instead, we'll start with configuring the ISA firewall software to support EAP authentication, and then discuss how to configure the RRAS service and the clients.

> **NOTE**
>
> The following exercises assume that you have already enabled and configured the ISA firewall's VPN server component before enabling EAP authentication support. Also note that this option is only available when the ISA firewall is a member of a domain. This provides another compelling reason for making the ISA firewall a domain member.

Configuring the ISA Firewall Software to Support EAP Authentication

Perform the following steps to configure the ISA firewall to support EAP authentication:

1. In the **Microsoft Internet Security and Acceleration Server 2004** management console, expand the server name, and click **Virtual Private Networks (VPN)** in the left pane of the console.

2. While in **Virtual Private Networks (VPN)**, click the **Tasks** tab in the Task pane. On the **Tasks** tab, click **Authentication Methods**.

3. In the **Virtual Private Networks (VPN) Properties** dialog box, put a checkmark in the **Extensible authentication protocol (EAP) with smart card or other certificate (ISA Server must belong to a domain)** checkbox (Figure 9.63).

Figure 9.63 Setting EAP Authentication

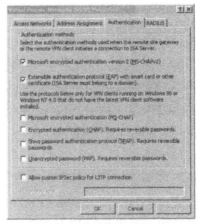

4. Read the information in the **Microsoft Internet Security and Acceleration Server 2004** dialog box. The dialog box reports that **EAP authenticated users belong to the RADIUS namespace and are not part of the Windows namespace. To apply user-based access rules to these users you can either define a RADIUS user set for them or you**

can use user mapping to map these users to the Windows namespace. If user mapping is enabled, access rules applied to the Windows users and group will be applicable to EAP authenticated users.

This is important information and describes the real utility of the User Mapping feature we discussed earlier in this chapter. Because EAP authentication doesn't use "Windows" authentication, you cannot by default apply user/group access policy on VPN clients authenticating with EAP user certificates. However, if we enable User Mapping for these users and map the user names of the EAP certificate authenticated users to domain users, then the same access rules that you apply to users who log on using Windows authentication will be applied to the EAP user certificate authenticated users. We'll go over the procedures of enabling and configuring User Mapping in the next procedures in this section.

Click **OK** (as shown in Figure 9.64) to acknowledge that you read and understand this information.

Figure 9.64 Warning about User Mapping and EAP

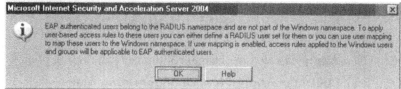

5. Click **Apply**, and then click **OK**.

Enabling User Mapping for EAP Authenticated Users

Perform the following steps to enable and configure User Mapping for EAP certificate authenticated users:

1. In the **Microsoft Internet Security and Acceleration Server 2004** management console, expand the server name, and click **Virtual Private Networks (VPN)** in the left pane of the console.

2. While in **Virtual Private Networks (VPN)**, click the **Tasks** tab in the Task pane. Click **Configure VPN Client Access** in the **Tasks** tab.

3. In the **VPN Clients Properties** dialog box, click the **User Mapping** tab.

4. On the **User Mapping** tab, put a checkmark in the **Enable User Mapping** checkbox. Put a checkmark in the **When username does not contain a domain, use this domain**. Since user certificates don't contain domain names, you should enable this option. In the **Domain Name** text box, enter a domain name for the domain that the ISA firewall belongs to. This allows the ISA firewall to map the user name of the EAP certificate-authenticated user to accounts in that domain, and then rules applying to those users will apply to

the EAP-authenticated users in the same way as they would if the users had authenticated using traditional "Windows" authentication.

5. Click **Apply** and then click **OK** (Figure 9.65).

Figure 9.65 Enabling User Mapping for EAP Authentication

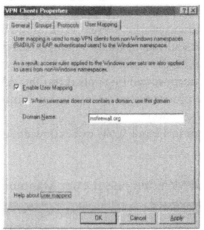

6 Click **Apply** to save the changes and update the firewall policy.

7. Click **OK** in the **Apply New Configuration** dialog box.

Issuing a User Certificate to the Remote Access VPN Client Machine

The VPN remote access client machines need to obtain user certificates and be configured to use the certificates to authenticate with the ISA firewall's remote access VPN server.

Perform the following steps to obtain a user certificate for the remote access VPN client:

1. Open **Internet Explorer**. In the **Address** bar, enter the URL for your certificate authority's Web enrollment site, and press **ENTER**.

2. Enter **Administrator** (or any name for which you want to obtain a user certificate) in the **User Name** text box. Enter the **Administrator's** password in the **Password** text box. Click **OK**.

3. On the **Welcome** page of the CA's Web enrollment site, click **Request a certificate**.

4. On the **Request a Certificate** page, click **User Certificate**.

5. Click **Submit** on the **User Certificate – Identifying Information** page.

6. Click **Yes** in the **Potential Scripting Violation** dialog box informing you that the Web site is requesting a new certificate on your behalf.

7. On the **Certificate Issued** page, click **Install this certificate**.

8. Click **Yes** in the **Potential Scripting Violation** dialog box informing you that the Web site is adding one or more certificates.

9. Close **Internet Explorer**.

We can configure the VPN connectoid to use user certificate authentication now that we have a user certificate installed on the remote access VPN client machine:

1. In the **Dial-up and Network Connections** window on the external network client, create a new VPN connectoid. Configure the connectoid to use the IP address **192.168.1.70** as the address of the VPN server.

2. When you complete the connection Wizard, you will see the **Connect** dialog box. Click **Properties**.

3. In the connectoid's **Properties** dialog box, click the **Security** tab. On the **Security** tab (Figure 9.66), select **Advanced (custom settings)**. Click **Settings**.

Figure 9.66 The Security Tab

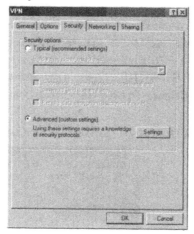

4. In the **Advanced Security Settings** dialog box (Figure 9.67), select **Use Extensible Authentication Protocol (EAP)**. Click **Properties**.

Figure 9.67 Enabling EAP Authentication

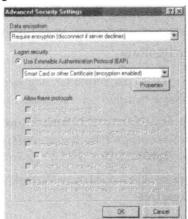

5. In the **Smart Card or other Certificate Properties** dialog box, select **Use a certificate on this computer**. Place a checkmark by **Validate server certificate**. Place a checkmark by **Connect only if server name ends with**, and enter the domain name of the authentication server. In this example, the domain name of our Active Directory domain is msfirewall.org, so enter that name in the text box. In the **Trusted root certificate authority** list, select the name of the CA that issued the certificates. In this example, the CA name is **EXCHANGE2003BE**, so select that option. Click **OK** in the **Smart Card or other Certificate Properties** dialog box (Figure 9.68).

Figure 9.68 The Smart Card or other Certificate Properties Dialog Box

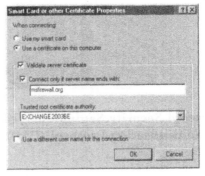

6. Click **OK** in the **Advanced Security Settings** dialog box.

7. Click **OK** in the connecoid's **Properties** dialog box.

8. A **Connect** dialog box appears which contains the name on the user certificate you obtained from the CA (Figure 9.69). Click **OK**.

Figure 9.69 Selecting the User Certificate for EAP User Authentication

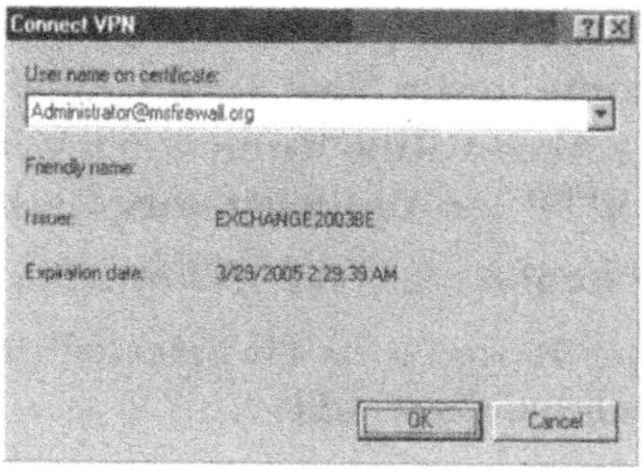

The VPN link will establish, and you'll be authenticated by the DC on the corporate network.

Supporting Outbound VPN Connections through the ISA Firewall

You can configure the ISA firewall to allow outbound access to VPN servers on the Internet. The ISA firewall supports all true VPN protocols, including PPTP, L2TP/IPSec, and IPSec NAT Traversal (NAT-T).

The ISA firewall can pass PPTP VPN connections from any Protected Network to the Internet with the help of its PPTP filter. The ISA firewall's PPTP filter intercepts the outbound PPTP connection from the Protected Network client and mediates the GRE (Generic Routing Encapsulation/IP Protocol 47) Protocol and the PPTP control channel (TCP 1723) communications. The only thing you need to do is create an Access Rule allowing outbound access to PPTP.

WARNING

In the following example, we configure outbound access to PPTP only from **Remote Management Computers**. We do this to emphasize that only highly-trusted hosts should be allowed outbound access to VPN servers. The VPN client connects to a network that you likely have no administrative control over. The VPN client acts as a potential security bridge between your network and the remote network. Therefore, you must be very strict on what machines are allowed outbound VPN access. This example also allows a connection to a specific VPN server. You should always pre-qualify VPN servers where your users connect to reduce the overall negative security impact outbound VPN connections can have on your corporate network.

Perform the following steps to allow outbound PPTP access through the ISA firewall:

1. In the **Microsoft Internet Security and Acceleration Server 2004** management console, expand the server name, and click **Firewall Policy**.

2. In the **Firewall Policy** node, click **Create a New Access Rule** on the **Tasks** tab in the Task pane.

3. On the **Welcome to the New Access Rule Wizard** page, enter a name for the rule in the **Access Rule name** text box. In this example, enter **Outbound PPTP for Administrators**. Click **Next**.

4. On the **Rule Action** page, select **Allow**, and click **Next**.

5. On the **Protocols** page, select the **Selected protocols** option from the **This rule applies to** list. Click **Add**.

6. In the **Add Network Entities** dialog box, click the **VPN and IPSec** folder and double-click the **PPTP** entry. Click **Close**.

7. Click **Next** on the **Protocols** page.

8. In the **Add Network Entities** dialog box, click the **Computer Sets** folder and double-click the **Remote Management Computers** entry. Click **Close**.

9. Click **Next** on the **Access Rule Sources** page.

10. On the **Access Rule Destinations** page, click **Add**.

11. In the **Add Network Entities** dialog box, click the **New** menu, and then click **Computer**.

12. In the **New Computer Rule Element** dialog box, enter a name for the external VPN server in the **Name** text box. Enter the IP address of the authorized VPN server in the **Computer IP Address** text box. In this example, enter **Authorized VPN Server**. Click **OK**.

13. Click the **Computers** folder and double-click the **Authorized VPN Server** entry. Click **Close**.

14. Click **Next** on the **Access Rule Destinations** page.

15. Click **Next** on the **User Sets** page.

16. Click **Finish** on the **Completing the New Access Rule Wizard** page.

TIP

Because the PPTP VPN protocol requires GRE (an IP level protocol that does not use TCP or UDP as a transport), machines configured as only Firewall and/or Web Proxy clients will not be able to connect to Internet VPN servers using PPTP. The machine must also be configured as a SecureNAT client to successfully complete the PPTP connection. The result is that you can not use strong user/group-based access controls to limit which users can use PPTP connections to Internet VPN servers. An alternative is to use Computer Objects or Computer Address Set Objects and achieve outbound access control for PPTP using the client's IP address. The same is true for IPSec NAT-T protocols (although for different reasons), as you'll see in the following discussion.

All modern IPSec-based VPN clients support some type of NAT traversal. The Microsoft L2TP/IPSec client supports the IETF Internet draft http://www.ietf.org/internet-drafts/draft-ietf-ipsec-nat-t-ike-08.txt for supporting IPSec through NAT devices. While historically a number of non-Microsoft VPN vendors fragmented the IPSec NAT-T market by implementing proprietary NAT-T solutions for their VPN clients, most of them are following Microsoft's lead and are implementing the IETF draft recommendations for their VPN clients and servers.

RFC-compliant NAT traversal requires that you allow outbound UDP 500 and UDP 1701 through the ISA firewall. UDP port 500 is for the Internet Key Exchange (IKE) negotiation and UDP 1701 is used for the L2TP control channel. For this reason, you might expect that using RFC-compliant IPSec NAT-T would allow you to control outbound VPN access on a user/group basis since most UDP and TCP protocols use Winsock. Unfortunately, this is not the case for the Microsoft L2TP/IPSec NAT-T and most other IPSec NAT-T protocols because the NAT-T client is implemented as a *shim* in the Windows TCP/IP protocol stack and allows it to bypass the Winsock interface.

WARNING

Not all IPSec NAT-T implementations are RFC-compliant and use proprietary UDP or TCP NAT-T headers. In order to support outbound access for these proprietary, non-RFC IPSec NAT-T VPN clients, you'll need to understand the protocols required by these clients and make sure that both client and server are configured to support the same IPSec NAT-T protocols. For a detailed discussion of this problem and possible solutions, please review Stefaan Pouseele's excellent article **How to Pass IPSec Traffic Through ISA Server** at http://isaserver.org/articles/IPSec_Passthrough.html

Perform the following steps to allow RFC-compliant IPSec NAT-T VPN connections (such as the Windows L2TP/IPSec client) through the ISA firewall:

1. In the **Microsoft Internet Security and Acceleration Server 2004** management console, expand the server name and click **Firewall Policy**.

2. In the **Firewall Policy** node, click **Create a New Access Rule** on the **Tasks** tab in the **Task** pane.

3. On the **Welcome to the New Access Rule Wizard** page, enter a name for the rule in the **Access Rule name** text box. In this example, we'll name it **Outbound L2TP/IPSec NAT-T for Administrators**. Click **Next**.

4. On the **Rule Action** page, select **Allow** and click **Next**.

5. On the **Protocols** page, select the **Selected protocols** option from the **This rule applies to list**. Click **Add**.

6. In the **Add Network Entities** dialog box, click the **VPN and IPSec** folder and double-click the **IKE Client** and **IPSec NAT-T Client** entries. Click **Close**.

7. Click **Next** on the **Protocols** page.

8. On the **Access Rule Sources** page, click **Add**.

9. In the **Add Network Entities** dialog box, click the **Computer Sets** folder and double-click the **Remote Management Computers** entry. Click **Close**.

10. Click **Next** on the **Access Rule Sources** page.

11. On the **Access Rule Destinations** page, click **Add**.

12. In the **Add Network Entities** dialog box, click **New** and **Computer**.

13. In the **New Computer Rule Element** dialog box, enter a name for the external VPN server in the **Name** text box. Enter the IP address of the authorized VPN server in the **Computer IP Address** text box. In this example, enter **Authorized VPN Server**. Click **OK**.

14. Click the **Computers** folder, and double-click **Authorized VPN Server**. Click **Close**.

15. Click **Next** on the **Access Rule Destinations** page.

16. Click **Next** on the **User Sets** page.

17. Click **Finish** on the **Completing the New Access Rule Wizard** page.

Installing and Configuring the DHCP Server and DHCP Relay Agent on the ISA Firewall

Many smaller organizations may wish to install a DHCP server on the ISA firewall itself. This allows smaller companies the ability to automatically assign IP addressing information to hosts on the corporate network without requiring them to install the DHCP server on a separate server on the corporate network. Many of these companies may have only one other Windows Server on their network, and that server is often a Windows domain controller. Because there are potential negative security implications of putting a DHCP server on a Windows domain controller, we consider placing the DHCP server on the ISA firewall a viable alternative.

The ISA firewall has a System Policy that enables the firewall itself to be a DHCP client. There are two System Policy Rules are listed in Table 9.1.

Table 9.1 System Policy Rules Enabling the ISA Firewall to be a DHCP Client

Rule #	Rule Name	Action	Protocols	From/Listener	To	Condition
8	Allow DHCP requests from ISA Server to all networks	Allow	DHCP (request)	Local Host	Anywhere	All Users
9	Allow DHCP replies from DHCP servers to ISA Server	Allow	DHCP (reply)	Internal	Local Host	All Users

The DHCP System Policy Rules allow DHCP requests from the ISA firewall, and DHCP replies from the Internal Network to the ISA firewall. These rules won't help us when we want to run the DHCP server on the ISA firewall itself because we want to allow DHCP requests *from the Internal Network* to the ISA firewall. We also want to allow DHCP Replies *from the ISA firewall* to the Internal Network. We'll need to create Access Rules to allow the required DHCP communications to and from the ISA firewall.

Perform the following steps to create the Access Rules allowing DHCP Requests to the ISA firewall and DHCP Replies from the ISA firewall:

1. In the **Microsoft Internet Security and Acceleration Server 2004** management console, expand the server name, and click the **Firewall Policy** node.

2. In the **Firewall Policy** node, click **Create a New Access Rule** on the **Tasks** tab in the Task pane.

3. On the **Welcome to the New Access Rule Wizard** page, enter a name for the rule in the **Access Rule name** text box. In this example, enter **DHCP Request**. Click **Next**.

4. On the **Rule Action** page, select **Allow** and **Next**.

5. On the **Protocols** page, select the **Selected protocols** option from the **This rule applies to** list. Click **Add**.

6. In the **Protocols** dialog box, click the **Infrastructure** folder and double-click the **DHCP (request)** entry. Click **Close**.

7. Click **Next** on the **Protocols** page.

8. On the **Access Rule Sources** page, click **Add**.

9. In the **Add Network Entities** dialog box, click the **Networks** folder and double-click the **Internal** entry. If you want clients from multiple Protected Networks to access the DHCP server on the ISA firewall, make sure to include those Networks, too. Click **Close**.

10. Click **Next** on the **Access Rule Sources** page.

11. On the **Access Rule Destinations** page, click **Add**.

12. In the **Add Network Entities** dialog box, click the **Networks** folder, and double-click the **Local Host** network.

13. Click **Next** on the **Access Rule Destinations** page.

14. Click **Next** on the **User Sets** page.

15. Click **Finish** on the **Completing the New Access Rule Wizard** page.

Next, we'll create the rule for the DHCP reply from the ISA firewall:

1. In the **Microsoft Internet Security and Acceleration Server 2004** management console, expand the server name, and click the **Firewall Policy** node.

2. In the **Firewall Policy** node, click **Create a New Access Rule** on the **Tasks** tab in the Task pane.

3. On the **Welcome to the New Access Rule Wizard** page, enter a name for the rule in the **Access Rule name** text box. In this example, we'll name it **DHCP Reply**. Click **Next**.

4. On the **Rule Action** page, select **Allow** and click **Next**.

5. On the **Protocols** page, select the **Selected protocols** option from the **This rule applies to** list. Click **Add**.

6. In the **Protocols** dialog box, click the **Infrastructure** folder and double-click the **DHCP (reply)** entry. Click **Close**.

7. Click **Next** on the **Protocols** page.

8. On the **Access Rule Sources** page, click **Add**.

9. In the **Add Network Entities** dialog box, click the **Networks** folder and double-click the **Local Host** entry. Click **Close**.

10. Click **Next** on the **Access Rule Sources** page.

11. On the **Access Rule Destinations** page, click **Add**.

12. In the **Add Network Entities** dialog box, click the **Networks** folder and double-click the **Internal** network. If you want the ISA firewall to respond to clients from multiple Protected Networks to access the DHCP server on the ISA firewall, make sure to include those Networks, too. Click **Close**.

13. Click **Next** on the **Access Rule Destinations** page.

14. Click **Next** on the **User Sets** page.

15. Click **Finish** on the **Completing the New Access Rule Wizard** page.

Creating a Site-to-Site VPN Between an ISA Server 2000 and ISA Firewall

Many ISA Server 2000 firewall administrators have an ISA Server 2000 firewall in place at their branch offices and are now replacing or supplementing packet filter-based "hardware" firewalls with ISA firewalls at main office. Because of this encouraging trend, we think it's important to cover the topic of joining an ISA Server 2000 firewall at a branch office to an ISA firewall at the main office.

The procedure isn't difficult, but if you haven't worked much with setting up site-to-site VPNs on both the 2000 and 2004 ISA firewalls, things can get a bit tricky, The good news is that when you've completed this article, you'll see how easy it is to get the site-to-site VPN link established between these two devices.

First, let's take a look at the lab network so we have a common point of reference. As usual, we highly recommend that you test the configuration using your lab network, or by using your favorite operating system virtualization software (be that Microsoft's Virtual Server/Virtual PC, or VMware's VMware Workstation or GSX Server (or even ESX Server)). Both VPC and VMware are good products for ISA firewall scenario testing.

Figure 9.70 depicts the lab network configuration:

Figure 9.70 Lab Network Configuration

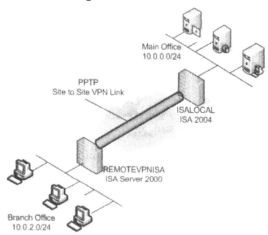

The virtual lab network is similar to that used for other exercises in this book, with some custom settings to support this scenario. IP addressing information for ISA firewalls is in Table 9.2.

Table 9.2 IP Addressing and Network Information for the ISA Firewall VPN Gateways

Parameter	ISALOCAL	REMOTEVPNISA
IP Address	External: 192.168.1.7024 Internal: 10.0.0.1/24	External: 192.168.1.71/24 Internal: 10.0.2.0/24
Default Gateway	External: None* Internal: None	External: None* Internal: None
DNS	External: None Internal: 10.0.0.2	External: None Internal: 10.0.2.2

Continued

Table 9.2 IP Addressing and Network Information for the ISA Firewall VPN Gateways

Parameter	ISALOCAL	REMOTEVPNISA
WINS	External: None Internal: 10.0.0.2	External: None Internal: 10.0.2.2
VPN Client IP Address Range	10.0.0.0 /24 (via DHCP)	10.0.3.0/24 (static address pool)
Server OS	Windows Server 2003	Windows Server 2003
ISA Firewall Version	ISA 2004	ISA Server 2000

* In your production environment, you use the LAN interface or your router as the gateway.

We will perform the following procedures to create a site-to-site PPTP VPN connection between the ISA Server 2000 firewall at the branch office and the ISA firewall at the main office:

- Run the **Local VPN Wizard** on ISA Server 2000.

- Change the **Password** for the **Remote VPN User Account** created by the **Local VPN Wizard**.

- Change the **Credentials** the ISA Server 2000 Firewall uses for the **Demand-dial Connection** to the main office.

- Change the **Idle Properties** of **the Demand-dial Interface** on the ISA Server 2000 VPN gateway.

- Create a **Static Address Pool** for VPN clients and Gateways.

- Run the **Remote Site Wizard** on Main Office the ISA firewall.

- Create a **Network Rule Defining the Route Relationship Between the Main and Branch Office**.

- Create **Access Rules Allowing Traffic from the Main Office to the Branch Office**.

- Create the user account for the remote VPN router.

- Test the connection.

In this section we'll focus on using PPTP, although you can use L2TP/IPSec since both ISA Server 2000 and the ISA firewall support L2TP/IPSec for site-to-site VPNs. We'll test the configuration using an "all open" Access Rule between the sites. On your production network, you'll want to limit what users at the branch office can access at the Main office.

Run the Local VPN Wizard on the ISA Server 2000 firewall

The first step is to run the Local VPN Wizard on the branch office ISA Server 2000 VPN gateway. The Local VPN Wizard does much of the heavy lifting for us, and we wish they still had it in the new ISA firewall.

Perform the following steps to run the Local VPN Wizard on the ISA Server 2000 VPN gateway at the branch office:

1. In the **ISA Management** console, expand the **Servers and Arrays** node, and then expand the **server** node. Click on the **Network Configuration** node.

2. Right-click the **Network Configuration** node, and click **Set Up Local ISA VPN Server**.

3. Click **Next** on the **Welcome to the Local ISA Server VPN Configuration** page.

4. Click **Yes** in the **ISA Virtual Private Network (VPN) Wizard** dialog box.

5. In the **ISA Virtual Private Network (VPN) Identification** page (Figure 9.71), enter **Branch** for **Type a short name to describe the local network**. Enter **Main** for **Type a short name to describe the remote network**. Click **Next**.

Figure 9.71 The ISA Virtual Private Network (VPN) Identification page

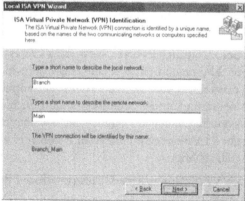

6. On the **ISA Virtual Private Network (VPN) Protocol** page, select **Use PPTP** and click **Next**.

7. On the **Two-way Communication** page, check **Both the local and remote ISA VPN computer can initiate the connection**. In the **Type the fully qualified domain name or IP address of the remote VPN computer** text box, enter the IP address of the main office ISA firewall. In this example, enter **192.168.1.70**. In the **Type the remote VPN computer name or the remote domain name** text box, enter the computer name of

the ISA firewall as the main office. In this example (Figure 9.72), the main office computer name is **ISALOCAL**. The only time you would enter a domain name is when the VPN gateway is a domain controller, and I know you would never make your ISA firewall a domain controller. Click **Next**.

Figure 9.72 The Two-way Communication Page

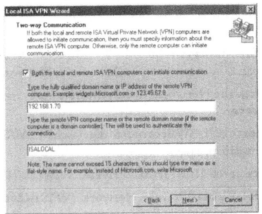

8. On the **Remote Virtual Private Network (VPN) Network** page, click **Add**. In the **ISA Virtual Private Network (VPN) Wizard** dialog box, enter the start and end IP addresses for the main office network. Since we are using the entire 10.0.0.0/24 network ID at the main office, we'll enter **10.0.0.0** in the **From** text box and **10.0.0.255** in the **To** text box. Click **OK**. Click **Next**.

9. On the **Local Virtual Private Network (VPN) Network** page, the IP addresses of the branch office are automatically added for you. You can click **Add** if you want to add more addresses representing the branch office network. However, since these addresses are automatically added from the Windows routing table, you might want to make sure the routing table on the branch office ISA Server 2000 firewall is correct before adding any more addresses. Click **Next**.

10. On the **ISA VPN Computer Configuration File** page, enter a file name in the **File name** text box. In this example, enter **C:\main**. Enter a password and confirm the password. Note that while we're going through the motions of creating this file, we will *not* be using it, since the ISA firewall does not support it. Click **Next**.

11. Click **Finish** on the **Completing the ISA VPN Setup Wizard** page.

> **NOTE**
>
> ISA Server 2000 does not perform stateful filtering or stateful application-layer inspection on its VPN remote access client or VPN demand-dial site-to-site interfaces. In contrast, the ISA firewall does perform both stateful filtering (stateful packet inspection) and stateful application-layer inspection on all VPN interfaces, including the demand-dial interface.

Change the Password for the Remote VPN User Account

Now we're ready to fix the user account created by the Local VPN Wizard. The Local VPN Wizard created a user account that the main office ISA firewall will use to authenticate with the branch office VPN gateway. However, we have no idea what password the Wizard assigned to this account. Therefore, we'll use the same account, but we'll reset the password.

Perform the following steps to reset the password on the VPN gateway user account:

1. Right-click **My Computer** on the desktop, and click **Manage**.

2. In the **Computer Management** console, expand the **System Tools** node and expand the **Local Users and Groups** node.

3. In the right pane, right-click the **Branch_Main** user account, and click **Set Password**. Click **Proceed** in the **Set Password for Branch_Main** dialog box.

4. Enter the new password and confirm the password on the **Set Password for Branch_Main** dialog box. Click **OK**.

5. Click **OK** in the dialog box informing you that the password has been set.

Remember that this is the user account you will configure the main office ISA firewall to use when it calls the branch office ISA Server 2000 VPN gateway.

Change the Credentials the ISA Server 2000 Firewall uses for the Demand-dial Connection to the Main Office

The Local VPN Wizard created a demand-dial interface to use to call the main office VPN gateway. It also made assumptions about the naming convention you would use for the demand-dial interface you'll create *at the main office*. We don't like the assumptions the Local VPN Wizard made, so we're going to change the credentials used by the ISA Server 2000 VPN gateway's demand-dial interface when it calls the main office ISA firewall.

Perform the following steps to change the credentials used by the ISA Server 2000 VPN gateway's demand-dial interface to call the main office ISA firewall:

1. Open the **Routing and Remote Access** console, and expand the server name. Click the **Network Interfaces** node.

2. Right-click the **Branch_Main** demand-dial interface that appears in the right pane of the console, and click **Set Credentials**.

3. In the **Interface Credentials** dialog box, change the **User name** to **Branch**. Enter a password and confirm the password. The demand-dial interface we create at the main office will be named **Branch**. We will also create a user account on the main office ISA firewall with the name **Branch**. Write this information down because we're going to need it when we create the **Branch** user account at the main office ISA firewall. Click **OK**.

4. Restart the **Routing and Remote Access Service**.

NOTE

The name **Branch** will be the name of the demand-dial interface we create on the main office ISA firewall. You'll see how this works later in this article.

Change the ISA Server 2000 VPN Gateway's Demand-dial Interface Idle Properties

The default setting on the demand dial interface on the branch office ISA Server 2000 VPN gateway is set to hang up after a five-minute idle time. We don't want the interface to ever hang up. We can fix this by going into the **Properties** of the demand-dial interface:

1. In the **Routing and Remote Access** console, expand the server name, and click the **Network Interfaces** node.

2. Right-click the **Branch_Main** demand-dial interface, and click **Properties**.

3. In the **Branch_Main Properties** dialog box, click the **Options** tab. On the **Options** tab, change the **Idle time before hanging up** to **never**.

4. Change the **Redial attempts** to **99** and set the interval at **10 seconds** (Figure 9.73). Click **OK**.

Figure 9.73 The Options tab on the Demand-dial Interface's Properties Dialog Box.

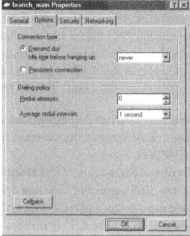

Create a Static Address Pool for VPN Clients and Gateways

In this example, we do not have a DHCP server at the branch office. We can create a static address pool on the branch office VPN gateway. This static address pool contains addresses the ISA Server 2000 VPN gateway can assign to calling VPN clients and VPN gateways. In this example, we'll create a static address pool that includes the entire 10.0.3.0/24 address range.

Perform the following steps to create the static address pool on the ISA Server 2000 VPN gateway at the branch office:

1. At the branch office ISA Server 2000 firewall machine, open the **Routing and Remote Access** console.

2. In the **Routing and Remote Access** console, right-click the server name, and click **Properties**.

3. In the **REMOTEVPNISA (local) Properties** dialog box, click the **IP** tab.

4. On the **IP** tab, select the **Static address pool** option. Click **Add**.

5. In the **New Address Range** dialog box, enter the **Start IP address** and the **End IP address**. In this example, the **Start IP address** is 10.0.3.1 and the **End IP address** is 10.0.3.254. Click **OK**.

6. Click **Apply**, and then click **OK** in the **REMOTEVPNISA (local) Properties** dialog box.

7. Restart the **Routing and Remote Access Service**.

Run the Remote Site Wizard on the Main Office ISA firewall

Now we'll focus our attention on the ISA firewall at the main office. The 2004 ISA firewall doesn't have a spiffy Local VPN Wizard like the ISA Server 2000 firewall. However, there is still a VPN wizard that will assist us in creating the Remote Site Network representing the addresses used at the branch office; it's just not as comprehensive.

Perform the following steps on the main office ISA firewall to create the remote network:

1. In the **Microsoft Internet Security and Acceleration Server 2004** management console, expand the server name, and click **Virtual Private Networks (VPN)**.

2. Click the **Remote Sites** tab in the **Details** pane of the console. Click the **Tasks** tab in the Task pane, and click **Add Remote Site Network**.

3. On the **Welcome to the New Network Wizard** page, enter **Branch** in the **Network name** text box. This is the name assigned to the demand-dial interface on the main office ISA firewall. Click **Next**.

4. On the **VPN Protocol** page, select **Point-to-Point Tunneling Protocol (PPTP)**, and click **Next**.

5. On the **Remote Site Gateway** page enter the IP address or the FQDN of the branch office ISA Server 2000 firewall's external interface. If you use a FQDN, make sure it resolves to the correct IP address. In this example, enter **192.168.1.71**. Click **Next**.

6. On the **Remote Authentication** page, check the **Local site can initiate connections to remote site using these credentials** checkbox. Enter the user name the main office ISA firewall will use to authenticate with the branch office ISA Server 2000 VPN gateway. This name is the same as the name used for the demand-dial interface created on the branch office ISA firewall. In this example, the name is **Branch_Main**. Enter the computer name of the branch office ISA Server 2000 VPN gateway in the **Domain** text box. In this example, enter **REMOTEVPNISA**. Enter the password and confirm the password of the **Branch_Main** user account created on the branch office ISA Server 2000 firewall. Click **Next** as shown in Figure 9.74.

Figure 9.74 The Remote Authentication Page

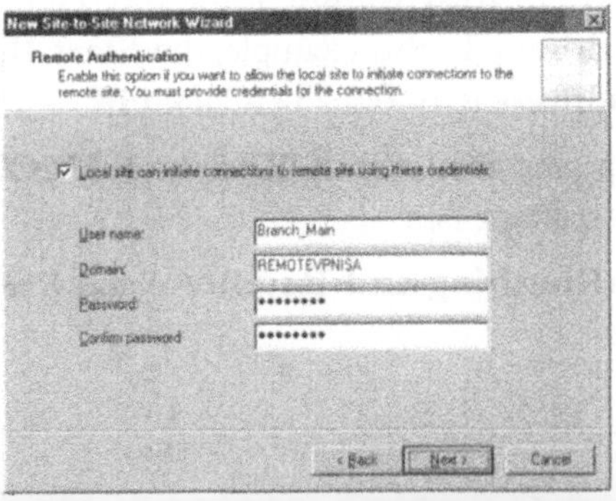

7. The **Local Authentication** page has information reminding you that a user account must be created on the main office ISA firewall that the branch office ISA Server 2000 VPN gateway can use to authenticate. We will create this user account later. The account must have the same name of the demand-dial interface created on the main office ISA firewall, which in this example is **Branch**. Click **Next**.

8. On the **Network Addresses** page, enter the IP addresses used on the branch office network. In this example, the branch office uses the entire network ID 10.0.2.0/24. Click **Add**. Enter **10.0.2.0** for the starting address and **10.0.2.255** as the ending address. Click **OK**. Click **Next**.

9. Click **Finish** on the **Completing the New Network Wizard** page.

Create a Network Rule that Defines the Route Relationship Between the Main and Branch Office

Like any stateful filtering (stateful packet inspection) firewall, the ISA firewall allows you to control the route relationship between the source and destination network. We prefer to use a route relationship between networks connected by a site-to-site VPN. However, you do have the option to use NAT. Just keep in mind that not all applications work through NAT.

> **WARNING**
>
> While you do have the option to choose NAT, we have not tested this configuration, so it may or may not work. Use NAT at your own risk. You can mitigate your risk by testing it in your lab first.

In this example, we'll create a route relationship between the main office and branch office. Perform the following steps to create the Network Rule that controls this routing relationship:

1. In the **Microsoft Internet Security and Acceleration Server 2004** management console, expand the server name and the **Configuration** node. Click **Networks**.

2. In the **Networks** node, click the **Network Rules** tab. Click the **Tasks** tab in the Task pane, and click **Create a New Network Rule**.

3. On the **Welcome to the New Network Rule Wizard** page, enter a name for the rule in the **Network rule name** text box. In this example, we'll name it **Main to Branch**. Click **Next**.

4. On the **Network Traffic Sources** page, click **Add**. In the **Add Network Entities** dialog box, click the **Networks** folder and double-click the **Internal** entry. Click **Close**.

5. Click **Next** on the **Network Traffic Sources** page.

6. On the **Network Traffic Destinations** page. Click **Add**. In the **Add Network Entities** dialog box, click the **Networks** folder, and double-click the **Branch** entry. Click **Close**.

7. Click **Next** on the **Network Traffic Destinations** page.

8. On the **Network Relationship** page (Figure 9.75), select **Route** and click **Next**.

Figure 9.75 The Network Relationship Page

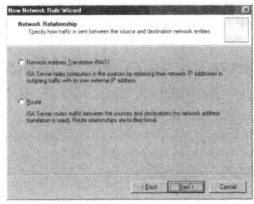

9. Click **Finish** on the **Completing the New Network Rule Wizard** page.

Create Access Rules Allowing Traffic from the Main Office to the Branch Office

While the branch office ISA Server 2000 VPN gateway doesn't perform stateful filtering or stateful application-layer inspection its VPN interfaces, the ISA firewall at the main office does. Therefore, we need to create Access Rules controlling traffic from the branch office to the main office and from the main office to the branch office.

Perform the following steps to create the Access Rules:

1. In the **Microsoft Internet Security and Acceleration Server 2004** management console, expand the server name, and click the **Firewall Policy** node.

2. Click the **Tasks** tab in the Task pane, and click the **Create New Access Rule** link.

3. In the **Welcome to the New Access Rule Wizard** page, enter the name of the rule in the **Access Rule name** text box. In this example, enter rule **All Open Main-Branch**. Click **Next**.

4. On the **Rule Action** page, select **Allow** and click **Next**.

5. On the **Protocols** page, accept the default entry in the **This rule applies to** list, and click **Next**.

6. On the **Access Rule Sources** page, click **Add**. In the **Add Network Entities** dialog box, click the **Networks** folder. Double-click **Internal**, and click **Close**. Click **Next** on the **Access Rule Sources** page.

7. On the **Access Rule Destinations** page, click **Add**. In the **Add Network Entities** dialog box, click the **Networks** folder. Double-click **Branch** and click **Close**. Click **Next** on the on the **Access Rule Destinations** page.

8. Click **Next** on the **User Sets** page.

9. Click **Finish** on the **Completing the New Access Rule Wizard** page.

10. Right-click the **All Open Main-Branch** rule, and click **Copy**.

11. Right-click the **All Open Main-Branch** rule, and click **Paste**.

12. Double-click the **All Open Main-Branch(1)** rule.

13. In the **All Open Main-Branch(1) Properties** dialog box, click the **General** tab. Change the name of the rule to **All Open Branch-Main**.

14. Click the **From** tab. Click the **Internal** entry and **Remove**. Click **Add**. In the **Add Network Entities** dialog box, click the **Networks** folder and double-click the **Branch** entry. Click **Close**.

15. Click the **To** tab. Click **Branch** and **Remove**. Click **Add**. Click the **Networks** folder and double-click **Internal**. Click **Close**.

16. Click **Apply** and then click **OK**.

17. Click **Apply** to save the changes and update the firewall policy.

18. Click **OK** in the **Apply New Configuration** dialog box.

19. Your Firewall Policy should look something like Figure 9.76 (you might have other rules, but put these rules above the other ones).

Figure 9.76 The Resulting Firewall Policy

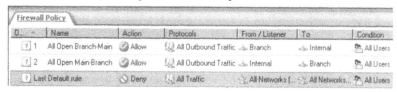

20. Restart the ISA firewall machine at the main office.

Create the User Account for the Remote VPN Router

The remote site Wizard doesn't create a user account for the ISA Server 2000 firewall at the branch office to authenticate to the main office ISA firewall. We'll have to create that user account ourselves

Perform the following steps to create the user account:

1. Right click **My Computer** on the desktop, and click **Manage**.

2. In the **Computer Management** console, expand the **System Tools** node, and expand the **Local Users and Groups** node.

3. Right-click on the **Users** node, and click **New User**.

4. In the **New User** dialog box, enter the name of the demand-dial interface on the ISA firewall at the main office. In the current example, the name of the demand-dial interface at the main office is **Branch**. Enter a password and confirm the password. Remove the checkmark from the **User must change password at next logon** checkbox. Place checkmarks in the **User cannot change password** and **Password never expires** checkboxes. Click **Create**, and then click **Close**.

5. Double-click on the **Branch** user account. In the **Branch Properties** dialog box, click the **Dial-in** tab. On the **Dial-in** tab, select **Allow access** in the **Remote Access Permission (Dial-in or VPN)** frame.

Test the connection

Now let's test the connection. From a host on the main office network, ping a host on the branch office network. You should see a successful ping reply after a couple of no responses as the demand-dial interface initializes. If you don't receive a reply after four pings, try again. Once the connection is established, try using Telnet to connect to an SMTP server on the remote site network

Figure 9.77 shows the log file entries from these two tests.

Figure 9.77 Log File Entries from Ping and SMTP Connections

Client IP	Destination IP	Destination Port	Protocol	Action	Rule	Source Network	Destination Net
10.0.0.2	10.0.2.3	0	Ping	Closed...	All Open Main-Branch	Internal	Branch
10.0.0.2	10.0.2.3	25	SMTP	Initiated...	All Open Main-Branch	Internal	Branch
10.0.0.2	10.0.2.3	25	SMTP	Closed...	All Open Main-Branch	Internal	Branch
10.0.0.2	10.0.2.3	25	SMTP	Initiated...	All Open Main-Branch	Internal	Branch
10.0.0.2	10.0.2.3	25	SMTP	Closed...	All Open Main-Branch	Internal	Branch
10.0.0.2	10.0.2.3	25	SMTP	Initiated...	All Open Main-Branch	Internal	Branch
10.0.0.2	10.0.2.3	25	SMTP	Closed...	All Open Main-Branch	Internal	Branch
10.0.0.2	10.0.2.3	0	Ping	Initiated...	All Open Main-Branch	Internal	Branch

A Note on VPN Quarantine

As mentioned in the introduction to this chapter, the ISA firewall has the ability to "prequalify" VPN clients before they are allowed to connect to the corporate network. This is the ISA firewall's *VPN Quarantine* feature. When properly implemented, the VPN quarantine feature can be used to place all VPN clients in a special VPN Quarantine Network and leave those VPN clients on the VPN Quarantine Network until the client passes a number of security tests. When the VPN client passes these security tests, the

VPN client is automatically removed from the VPN Quarantine Network to the VPN Clients Network.

The problem with the ISA firewall's implementation of VPN Quarantine is that it's of absolutely no use to the typical ISA firewall administrator unless he has advanced scripting or programming skills. Out of the box, the ISA firewall's VPN Quarantine provides only a *development platform* for a VPN Quarantine solution. In fact, without a development staff to assist you with rolling out a VPN-Q solution, you could completely lock out all VPN clients from reaching resources for which you have created Access Rules allowing them to reach.

The problem is that the ISA firewall's user interface can give the impression that enabling VPN Quarantine is a matter of putting a checkmark in a checkbox. To see what we mean, open the **Microsoft Internet Security and Acceleration Server 2004** management console, expand the server name, and then expand the **Configuration** node and click the **Networks** node.

While on the **Networks** node, right-click the **Quarantined VPN Clients** Network in the **Networks** tab in the details pane and click **Properties**.

In the **Quarantined VPN Clients Properties** dialog box, click on the **Quarantine** tab. Put a checkmark in the **Enable Quarantine Control** checkbox. You'll see the following dialog box (Figure 9.78).

Figure 9.78 Warning Regarding VPN Quarantine and VPN Client Access

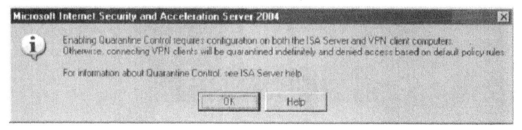

This dialog box states Enabling Quarantine Control requires configuration on both the ISA Server and VPN client computers. Otherwise, connecting VPN clients will be quarantined indefinitely and denied access based on default policy rules. This means that unless you have carried out the configuration and development procedures required to make VPN Quarantine work correctly, *all* VPN clients will remain assigned to the Quarantined VPN Clients Network and be able to access only resources available to members of the Quarantine VPN Clients Network. Of course, you could create Access Rules enabling members of the Quarantined VPN Clients Network to access any resource you want them to on the corporate network, but that defeats the purpose of using VPN-Q in the first place.

Once VPN-Q is enabled, you see that you have the following options:

- **Quarantine according to RADIUS server policies** This option is only available when the ISA firewall is installed on Windows Server 2003 machines. This allows you to implement RADIUS server VPN quarantine policy.

- **Quarantine according to ISA Server policies** This option can be used on Windows 2000 machines to enable VPN-Q.

- **Disconnect quarantined users after (seconds)** This option allows you to set the time-out on VPN clients placed in the Quarantined VPN Clients Network. If the VPN client can't perform the steps required to remove itself from quarantine in this period of time, then the VPN client is disconnected.

- **Exempt these users from Quarantine Control** You can prevent users or groups from ever being placed on the Quarantined VPN Clients Network by including those users in this list. See options for the Quarantine tab in Figure 9.79.

Figure 9.79 The Quarantine Tab on the Quarantined VPN Client Properties Page

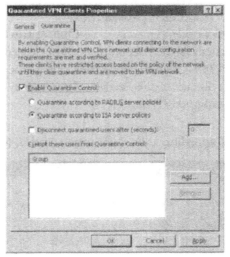

If you have development resources at your disposal, or if you have advanced scripting or programming skills, then check out Microsoft's documentation on VPN-Q at http://www.microsoft.com/isaserver/techinfo/guidance/2004/vpn.asp

However, there is some good news for those ISA firewall administrators who don't have access to advanced scripting or development resources. Frederic Esnouf, an ISA firewall MVP, has put together a full-featured, start-to-finish solution for VPN-Q called the Quarantine Security Suite (QSS). We highly recommend Frederic's solution, and you can find more information on it at http://fesnouf.online.fr/programs/QSS/QSS.htm.

Avanade also stepped in with some assistance to the VPN-Q puzzle. They have prototype software that will assist you in creating a functional VPN-Q solution at http://www.avanade.com/solutions/section.aspx?id=8&parentID=2.

TIP

If you consider yourself handy with Windows scripting, Microsoft has recently released some sample scripts that you can customize for your own environment. You can read about these scripts at the **VPN Quarantine Sample Scripts for Verifying Client Health Configurations** page (www.microsoft.com/downloads/details.aspx?FamilyID=a290f2ee-0b55-491e-bc4c-8161671b2462&display-lang=en)

Summary

In this chapter, we discussed the ISA firewall's VPN remote access server and VPN gateway features. The VPN remote access server supports both PPTP and L2TP/IPSec connection from remote access VPN clients. The ISA firewall's VPN gateway supports IPSec tunnel mode, PPTP and L2TP/IPSec connections from other VPN gateways. We also discussed other topics related to the ISA firewall's support for VPN clients and gateways, including EAP authentication and DHCP server configuration.

Solutions Fast Track

Overview of ISA Firewall VPN Networking

☑ Firewall policy with stateful filtering and stateful application-layer inspection is applied to the ISA firewall's VPN remote access client and VPN gateway interfaces.

☑ The ISA firewall includes a VPN Quarantine feature that allows you to pre-qualify VPN clients before they are allowed on the network. Pre-qualification includes confirming that the VPN client has the most recent security hotfixes, services, anti-virus definitions, and anti-spyware definitions installed.

☑ The ISA firewall's user mapping feature allows you to map users who authenticate via RADIUS or EAP to actual user accounts and use that information to perform strong user/group-based access control over remote access VPN and VPN gateway connections to the ISA firewall.

☑ SecureNAT client support now allows remote access VPN clients to access the Internet through the ISA firewall without requiring the Firewall client to be installed on the remote access VPN client machine

☑ IPSec tunnel mode support allows the ISA firewall to terminate site-to-site VPN connections with downlevel, third-party VPN devices, such as Cisco VPN concentrators.

☑ The new PPTP filter allows you to publish PPTP VPN servers.

☑ The ISA firewall supports both certificates and pre-shared keys for IPSec tunnel mode and L2TP/IPSec VPN connections. For L2TP/IPSec, this applies for both remote access client and VPN gateway connections.

☑ The new ISA firewall allows you to assign custom name servers to VPN clients so that you do not need to depend on the interface name server addresses for VPN client name server assignment.

☑ You can now monitor VPN client and VPN gateway connections moving through the ISA firewall. You can determine the user name, the application, the protocols, and the source and destination IP address, and much more by viewing this information in the ISA firewall's logging console.

Creating a Remote Access PPTP VPN Server

☑ You use the **Microsoft Internet Security and Acceleration Server 2004** management console to configure a remote access PPTP VPN server; do not use the RRAS console.

☑ If you use DHCP to assign addresses to VPN clients and gateways, make sure there are enough IP addresses in the scope to support the number of VPN client connections you want to support.

☑ ISA 2004 Standard Edition supports up to 1000 concurrent VPN connections, regardless of the operating system on which the firewall software is installed.

☑ You can enable remote access VPN permission via user account configuration or via Remote Access Policy.

☑ User Mapping is most useful when using EAP user certificate authentication. This allows you to perform user/group-based access control on users who authenticate via EAP user certificate authentication.

☑ Use DHCP to assign IP addresses to your VPN clients if you want to use *on-subnet* addresses for your VPN clients. If you use a static address pool, you will need to remove these address from the definition of the Network already defined on the ISA firewall using the addresses.

Creating a Remote Access L2TP/IPSec Server

☑ You can use either machine certificates or pre-shared keys for L2TP/IPSec remote access VPN client connections.

☑ You must temporarily disable the RPC filter to use the Certificates standalone snap-in to obtain a certificate for the ISA firewall from an online CA.

☑ The new L2TP/IPSec VPN client allows almost all versions of Windows to establish a remote access VPN connection to the ISA firewall using L2TP/IPSec. In addition, the new software enables pre-shared key support and NAT traversal.

☑ Pre-shared keys lack the scalability and security of certificate authentication, but are acceptable substitutes until you have implemented a public key infrastructure.

Creating a PPTP Site-to-Site VPN

☑ A site-to-site VPN connects entire networks to one another.

☑ The Remote Site Network wizard must be run on both sides of the site-to-site VPN connection.

☑ You must create a user account on each ISA firewall that the calling ISA firewall can use to authenticate with the answering ISA firewall.

☑ Access Rules must be created to allow traffic to and from each network connected via the site-to-site VPN link.

☑ A Network Rule that defines the route relationship between the local and remote Networks must be created on each ISA firewall participating in the site-to-site VPN link.

☑ You can use an IP address or FQDN when defining the address of the remote site gateway. This is helpful when the branch offices use dynamic addresses on their external interfaces.

☑ The demand-dial interface created by the Remote Site Network wizard defines the name of the user account that the calling ISA firewall must use to authenticate to that interface. If the calling VPN gateway does not use an account with the name of the interface that it's calling, then the connection is treated as a remote access VPN client connection and routing fails between the networks

Creating an L2TP/IPSec Site-to-Site VPN

☑ L2TP/IPSec is a more secure VPN Protocol than PPTP.

☑ Machine certificates are more secure than pre-shared key authentication for L2TP/IPSec site-to-site VPN connections.

☑ L2TP/IPSec uses UDP for its control channel, which may confer a greater degree of stability for site-to-site VPN connections using the L2TP/IPSec protocol.

Using RADIUS for VPN Authentication and Remote Access Policy

☑ In a front-end back-end ISA firewall configuration, you may not wish to make the ISA firewall a member of a domain. In that case, you can use RADIUS authentication for remote access VPN client connections.

☑ RADIUS can be used to centralize remote access policy throughout the organization. this obviates the need to replicate Remote Access Policy across multiple ISA firewall VPN remote access servers and gateways.

☑ RADIUS authentication for remote access VPN clients supports both Windows authentication and EAP user certificate authentication.

☑ Dial-in permissions can be configured on a per-account basis or controlled on a per-group basis using Remote Access Policy. Only local accounts on the ISA firewall's SAM or domain accounts in Native Mode or Windows Server 2003 Mode domains support Dial-in permissions via Remote Access Policy.

Using EAP User Certificate Authentication for Remote Access VPNs

☑ EAP user certificate authentication provides a higher level of security than that found with traditional username/password authentication.

☑ You can use the ISA firewall's User Mapping feature to support user/group-based access controls on users who authenticate via EAP. However, the ISA firewall must be a member of the domain.

Creating a Site-to-Site VPN between ISA Server 2000 and ISA Firewalls

☑ You can create site-to-site VPNs between ISA firewalls and ISA Server 2000. You use the Local VPN Wizard on the ISA Server 2000 machine and the Remote Site Network Wizard on the ISA firewall.

☑ The Local VPN Wizard on the ISA Server 2000 machine automatically creates an account for the calling VPN gateway to use. However, you must change the password of the user account because you do not know the password the Local VPN wizard assigned to the account.

A Note on VPN Quarantine

☑ VPN Quarantine allows you to pre-qualify VPN clients before allowing them access to the corporate network. The pre-qualification process can include checking that the VPN client has the latest security updates, hotfixes, anti-virus signatures, anti-spyware signatures, and more.

☑ The ISA firewall's VPN-Q implementation is more a platform for development than a feature that can be used by the average ISA firewall administrator "out of the box."

☑ Frederic Esnouf's Quarantine Security Suite is an effective solution to the VPN-Q problem.

☑ Avanade also provides a framework that you can use to create a functional VPN-Q solution using the ISA firewall.

Frequently Asked Questions

The following Frequently Asked Questions, answered by the authors of this book, are designed to both measure your understanding of the concepts presented in this chapter and to assist you with real-life implementation of these concepts. To have your questions about this chapter answered by the author, browse to **www.syngress.com/solutions** and click on the **"Ask the Author"** form. You will also gain access to thousands of other FAQs at ITFAQnet.com.

Q: I want to create a site-to-site VPN between my branch offices and main office networks. Do I need to change the IP address scheme on any of these networks?

A: It depends on your current IP addressing scheme. The ISA firewalls connecting the main office to the branch offices act as VPN routers. Routers route between different network IDs. So, if any of your branch offices use addresses on the same network ID as the main office, or over any of the other branch offices, then you will need to change the IP addressing scheme in that office so that all networks joined by the site-to-site VPN links are on different network IDs.

Q: I want to use a Voice over IP system (VoIP) for intraorganizational calls throughout our company's main and branch offices. I plan on using ISA firewall site-to-site VPNs to join the offices. Should I use a Route or NAT relationship between the networks connected via the site-to-site VPN links?

A: VoIP systems are legendary for not being NAT friendly because they often embed the client IP address on the application-layer data. If you plan on implementing VoIP, then definitely use Route Network Rules between all your networks joined by site-to-site links.

Q: I'm using EAP user certificate authentication with my ISA firewall remote access VPN server. However, whenever a user tries to connect to the VPN server, they immediately get disconnected. How can I fix this?

A: The most likely problem is that your ISA firewall is not a member of a domain. When using EAP user certificate authentication, the ISA firewall must be a member of the domain. Another situation where you might see this problem is when you use RADIUS authentication for VPN clients and enable User Mapping. If the ISA firewall is not a member of the domain, there is no Windows user database to map to, and so the VPN connection closes immediately after the connection request.

Q: My site-to-site VPN connections seem to disconnect frequently, and often, I need to reboot the server before they will reconnect. Is there anything I can do about this?

A: If you're using PPTP for your site-to-site VPN, you might consider using L2TP/IPSec. The L2TP/IPSec VPN connections have been reported to be more stable. Another option worth trying to is to make sure that only one side of the site-to-site VPN link is configured as the calling VPN gateway and one site is the answering VPN gateway. If both sides are configured as calling VPN gateways, there is the potential for a "collision" if they try to each other at the same time. If you're using a DSL connection, make sure there are no black hole routers in the path by testing and adjusting the MTU on the ISA firewall and clients. This is mostly a problem with PPPoE hobbyist accounts. It would be worth trying to get a business-class DSL connection to overcome the MTU issue.

Q: I installed a machine certificate on my ISA firewall so that I could use L2TP/IPSec for my remote access VPN client connections. However, the connections always fail. There are no problems when I try to connect using PPTP. What can I do to get L2TP/IPSec working?

A: One common reason for the L2TP/IPSec connection not working is that while the machine ISA firewall or the VPN clients have a computer certificate, the machine doesn't have the CA certificate of the root CA issuing the certificate in its Trusted Root Certification Authorities machine certificate store. Another reason why the L2TP/IPSec might fail is that the machines were assigned user certificates instead of machine certificates. Machine certificates are stored in the machine certificate store and user certificates are stored in the User certificate store.

Q: I want to create a site-to-site VPN between my main office and branch office using ISA firewalls. We currently have third-party firewalls/VPN gateways at both the main and branch office, and they are using IPSec tunnel more and pre-shared keys for the site-to-site link. Should I do the same thing when I replace these devices with ISA firewalls?

A: No. The highest level of security can be obtained by using L2TP/IPSec with EAP user certificate authentication for the PPP authentication sequence. We recommend that you only use IPSec tunnel mode for site-to-site VPN links when you want to support connections between the ISA firewall and downlevel VPN gateways.

Chapter 10

ISA 2004 Stateful Inspection and Application Layer Filtering

Solutions in this Chapter:

- Application Filters
- Web Filters

Introduction

The ISA firewall is able to perform both stateful filtering and stateful application layer inspection. The ISA firewall's stateful filtering feature set makes the ISA firewall a network layer stateful firewall in the same class as any hardware firewall that performs stateful filtering at the network and transport layers. Stateful filtering is often referred to as *stateful packet inspection*, which is a bit of a misnomer because packets are layer 3 entities and in order to assess connection state, layer 4 information must be assessed.

However, in contrast to traditional packet filter based stateful hardware firewalls, the ISA firewall is able to perform stateful application layer inspection. Stateful application layer inspection enables the ISA firewall to fully inspect the communication streams passed by the ISA firewall from one Network to another. In contrast to stateful filtering where only the network and transport layer information is filtered, true stateful inspection requires that the firewall be able to analyze and make decisions on all layers of the communication, including the most important layer, the application layer.

In this chapter we will discuss the following:

- Application Filter
- Web Filters

The Web filters perform stateful application layer inspection on communications handled by the ISA firewall's Web Proxy components. The Web Proxy handles connections for HTTP, HTTPS (SSL), and HTTP tunneled FTP connections. The Web filters take apart the HTTP communications and expose them to the ISA firewall's application layer inspection mechanisms, examples of which include the HTTP Security filter and the OWA forms-based authentication filter.

The Application filters are responsible for performing stateful application layer inspection on non-HTTP protocols, such as SMTP, POP3, and DNS. These application layer filters also take apart the communication and expose them to deep stateful inspection at the ISA firewall.

Web and Application filters can perform two duties:

- Protocol access
- Protocol security

Protocol access allows access to protocols that require secondary connections. Complex protocols may require more than one connection, either inbound or outbound through the ISA firewall. SecureNAT clients require these filters to use complex protocols because the SecureNAT client does not have the power of the Firewall client. In contrast to the Firewall client that can work together with the ISA firewall to negotiate complex protocols, the SecureNAT client is a simple NAT client of the ISA firewall and requires the aid of application filters to connect using these complex protocols (such as FTP or MMS).

Protocol security protects the connections moving through the ISA firewall. Protocol security filters such as the SMTP and DNS filters inspect the communications that apply to those filters and block connections that are deemed outside of secure parameters. Some of these filters block connections that may represent buffer overflows (such as the DNS and SMTP filters), and some of them perform much deeper inspection and block connections or content based on policy (such as the SMTP Message Screener).

Application Filters

The ISA firewall includes a number of Application filters. In this section, we discuss:

- SMTP filter and Message Screener
- DNS filter
- POP Intrusion Detection filter
- SOCKS V4 filter
- FTP Access filter
- H.323 filter
- MMS filter
- PNM filter
- PPTP filter
- RPC filter
- RTSP filter

The SMTP Filter and Message Screener

The SMTP filter and Message Screener are used to protect published SMTP servers. The SMTP filter protects published SMTP servers from buffer overflow attacks, and the SMTP Message Screener protects your company from unwanted e-mail messages.

The SMTP Message Screener can be placed in a number of locations:

- On the ISA firewall
- On a dedicated SMTP relay on a Protected Network Segment
- On the Exchange Server

We recommend that you put the SMTP Message Screener either on the ISA firewall or on a dedicated SMTP relay either on the corporate network or on a DMZ segment. The reason why we recommend that you do not place the SMTP Message Screener on the Exchange Server is that message screening consumes a great deal of processor cycles, which will have a negative impact on the Exchange Server's overall performance.

In this section, we focus on our preferred configuration, which is to put the SMTP Message Screener on a dedicated SMTP relay machine. This option is the most secure, provides the best performance, and introduces the SMTPcred tool, which is required when the SMTP Message Screener is used on a machine where the SMTP Message Screener is not installed on the ISA firewall itself.

Installing the SMTP Message Screener on a Dedicated SMTP Relay

Installing and configuring the SMTP Message Screener on a dedicated SMTP relay on a Protected Network Segment (corporate network or DMZ) is relatively easy. However, for the complete solution to work, you will need to perform other configurations and setup tasks:

- The Exchange Server will need to be able to resolve the MX domain names of mail it sends outbound, or the SMTP relay will need to be able to resolve MX domain names of outbound mail if the SMTP Message Screener machine will also act as an outbound SMTP relay.

- An Access Rule is required for the machine that performs the name solution for the Exchange Server. Ideally, this will be a DNS server on the corporate network that is capable of resolving Internet host names.

- You'll need to configure an Access Rule that allows outbound SMTP for any machine that needs to send outbound SMTP mail.

- You'll need to create a Server Publishing Rule to allow external SMTP servers to send mail to the SMTP relay running the SMTP Message Screener.

In this section, we discuss the installation and configuration of the SMTP Message Screener. Refer to the appropriate chapters in this book for details on the required Access Rules and Server Publishing Rules.

The SMTP Message Screener is an optional ISA Server 2004 component. This feature integrates with the IIS 6.0 SMTP service to examine and block SMTP mail based on parameters you configure in the Message Screener.

Install the SMTP Message Screener on the SMTP Relay

Perform the following steps to install the SMTP Message Screener on the ISA Server 2004 firewall computer:

1. Locate the ISA Server 2004 installation media and double-click the **isaautorun.exe** file.

2. In the Autorun menu, click the **Install ISA Server 2004** icon.

3. Click **Next** on the **Welcome to the Installation Wizard for Microsoft ISA Server 2004** page.

4. On the **Program Maintenance** page, select the **Modify** option and click **Next**.

5. On the **Custom Setup** page, click the **Message Screener** option, click **This feature**, and all subfeatures will be installed on local hard drive. Click **Next**. (See Figure 10.1.)

Figure 10.1 The Custom Setup Dialog Box

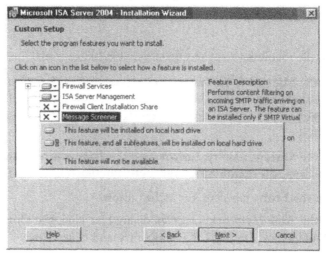

6. Click **Next** on the **Services** page that informs you that the **SNMP** and **IIS Admin Service** will be stopped during installation.

7. Click **Install** on the **Ready to Modify the Program** page.

8. Put a checkmark in the **Invoke ISA Server Management** when the wizard closes checkbox, and then click **Finish** on the **Installation Wizard Completed** page.

9. Close the Autorun menu.

The SMTP Message Screener must communicate with the ISA Server 2004 firewall to obtain settings information, including the keywords, domains, and attachments you want to block. You configure the SMTP Message Screener settings on the ISA Server 2004 firewall machine in the SMTP Filter interface, *not* on the SMTP relay machine on which the SMTP Message Screener is installed.

The smtpcred.exe tool is used to facilitate the transfer of information between the SMTP Message Screener machine and the ISA Server 2004 firewall. You will enter user, computer, and domain information in the smtpcred.exe tool to set up this connection.

> **WARNING**
>
> In ISA Server 2000, the communication between the Message Screener and the ISA Server 2000 machine used DCOM calls. The new ISA firewall removes this requirement and DCOM is not longer required. This improves the overall security for the connection between the SMTP Message Screener machine and the ISA firewall.

Perform the following steps to run the smtpcred.exe tool:

1. In the **Microsoft Internet Security and Acceleration Server 2004** management console, expand the computer name and then click the **Firewall Policy** node. Right-click the **Firewall Policy** node and click **Edit System Policy**.

2. In the **System Policy Editor**, find the **Remote Management** group and click the **Microsoft Management** subfolder. Click the **From** tab.

3. On the **From** tab, click the **Add** button.

4. In the **Add Network Entities** dialog box, click the **Computers** node. Double-click the **SMTP Relay** entry and click **Close**.

5. In the **System Policy Editor**, click **OK**. (See Figure 10.2.)

Figure 10.2 The System Policy Editor

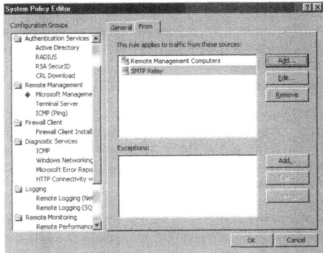

6. Click **Apply** to save the changes and update the Firewall policy.

7. Click **OK** in the **Apply New Configuration** dialog box.

8. At the **SMTPRELAY** computer, navigate to the **C:\Program Files\Microsoft ISA Server** folder and double-click the **smtpcred.exe** tool.

In the **Message Screener Credentials** dialog box, enter the name of the ISA Server 2004 firewall in the **ISA Server** text box. In the **Retrieve settings every … min** text box, enter a value for the number of minutes you want the SMTP Message Screener to wait between retrieving the configuration settings from the ISA Server 2004 firewall. In the **Authentication data** frame, enter the **Username**, **Domain**, and **Password** of a user who is an administrator on the ISA Server 2004 firewall. (See Figure 10.3.)

Figure 10.3 The Message Screener Credentials Dialog Box

9. Click the **Test** button. A **Warning** dialog box appears, informing you that some values have not been written to storage. Click **OK**.

10. An **SMTP Message Screener Configuration Test Completed** dialog box will appear, informing you that no errors were detected. Click **OK**.

11. Click **OK** in the **Message Screener Credentials** dialog box.

Configuring the SMTP Message Screener

We're now ready to configure the SMTP Message Screener, an application filter that examines all incoming messages that go through the ISA Server 2004 firewall via the SMTP Server Publishing Rule.

> **WARNING**
>
> You should be judicious about your configuration of the SMTP Message Screener. You need to be sure that your settings are not so restrictive that legitimate mail is blocked. As with all e-mail filtering applications, there is the potential for blocking mail required by your users.

Perform the following steps on the **Inbound SMTP Relay** Server Publishing Rule:

1. In the **Microsoft Internet Security and Acceleration Server 2004** management console, expand the server name and then expand the **Configuration** node. Click the **Add-ins** node.

2. In the **Add-ins** node, right-click the **SMTP Filter** in the **Details Pane** and click **Properties**. (See Figure 10.4.)

Figure 10.4 The SMTP Filter

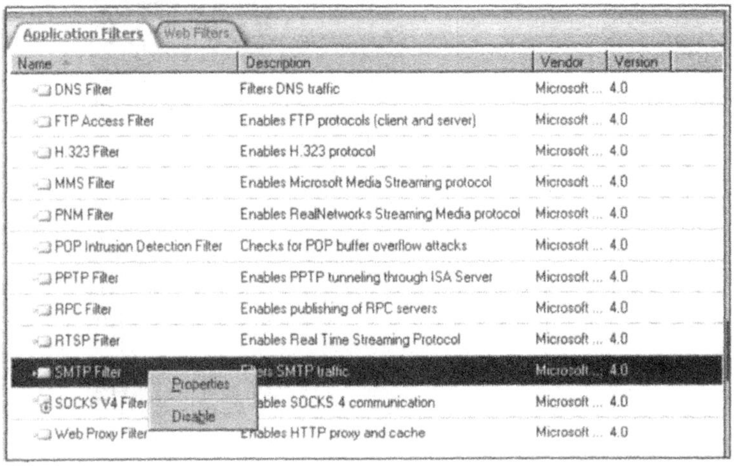

3. Click the **General** tab in the **SMTP Filter Properties** dialog box. Confirm that there is a checkmark in the **Enable this filter** checkbox.

4. Click the **Keywords** tab. Click the **Add** button. In the **Mail Keyword Rule** dialog box, enter **mail enhancement** in the **Keyword** text box. Select the **Message header or body** option. Select the **Hold message** option from the **Action** list. Click **OK**.

5. Click the **Keywords** tab. Confirm that there is a checkmark in the **Enable keyword rule** checkbox. You can select one of the following options in the **Apply action if keyword is found in** frame:

   ■ **Message header or body** If the keyword is found in *either* the message header or message body, the Action you configure for the rule will be applied.

   ■ **Message header** If the keyword is found in the header (subject line), the Action you configure for the rule will be applied.

   ■ **Message body** If the keyword is found in the body of the message, the Action you configure for the rule will be applied.

- Click the down arrow for the **Action** drop-down list box. You have the following options:

  - **Delete message** The SMTP message is deleted without being saved or notifying anyone that it has been deleted.

  - **Hold message** The SMTP message is held in the BADMAIL directory in the SMTP service's folder hierarchy. You can view components of the held message, but the message is not saved in a format that you can easily forward to the recipient.

  - **Forward message to** The SMTP message is forwarded to an e-mail address you configure in this rule. Each rule can have a different e-mail address to which the message is forwarded.

6. Click the **Add** button. In the **Mail Keyword Rule** dialog box, enter **mail enhancement** in the **Keyword** text box. Select the **Message header or body** option. Select the **Hold message** option from the **Action** list. Click **OK**. (See Figure 10.5.)

Figure 10.5 The SMTP Filter Properties Dialog Box

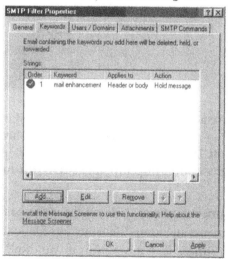

7. Click the **Users / Domains** tab. You can configure the SMTP Message Screener to block messages based on the sender's user account or e-mail domain on the **Users/Domains** tab. Enter a user e-mail account in the Sender's name text box and click **Add**. The sender's e-mail address appears in the Rejected Sender's list. Type in an e-mail domain in the **Domain name** text box and click **Add**. The e-mail domain appears in the Rejected Domains list.

E-mail messages processed by the SMTP Message Screener matching e-mail addresses or e-mail domains found in these lists are deleted. These messages are not stored anywhere on the server, nor are they forwarded to any user or administrator. If a message from a rejected sender or rejected domain also contains a keyword that matches a keyword rule, and that keyword rule is configured to hold the message, the message will not be held because it is rejected before the keyword search begins.

8. Click **Apply** and then click **OK**. (See Figure 10.6.)

Figure 10.6 The User / Domains Tab

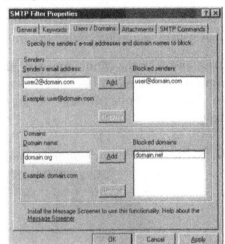

9. Click the **Attachments** tab and click the **Add** button. Confirm that there is a checkmark in the **Enable attachment rule** checkbox on the **Mail Attachment Rule** dialog box. You have three options in the **Apply action to messages containing attachments with one of these properties** frame:

- **Attachment name** Select this option and enter a name for the attachment, including filename and file extension, in the text box next to this option. Use this option if you don't want to block all attachments with a particular file extension, but you do want to block a specific filename. For example, you do not want to block all .zip files, but you do want to block a file named exploit.zip.

- **Attachment extension** It is more common to block all files with a specific file extension. For example, if you want to block all files with the exe file extension, select this option and then enter either **exe** or **.exe** in the text box to the right of this option.

■ **Attachment size limit (in bytes)** You can block attachments based on their size. Select this option and enter the minimum size of the file extensions you want to block.

10. Click the down arrow for the **Action** drop-down list box. You have the following options:

■ **Delete message** The SMTP message is deleted without being saved or notifying anyone that it has been deleted. Choose to delete the messages when you are sure that there will be no "false positives," meaning that no one would possibly want the deleted message.

■ **Hold message** The SMTP message is held in the **BADMAIL** directory in the SMTP service's folder hierarchy. You can view components of the held message, but the message is not saved in a format that you can easily forward to the recipient. Use the HOLD option when you think there is a possibility that someone may want the message. When the message is held, you will be able to retrieve it later if a user is concerned that mail was inadvertently deleted.

■ **Forward message to** The SMTP message is forwarded to an e-mail address you configure in this rule. Each rule can have a different e-mail address to which the message is forwarded. Use this option if you have an e-mail administrator dedicated to reviewing spam messages for potential false positives. You can also use this option to save spam messages that can be used to train other anti-spam applications using Bayesian filtering and other filter training mechanisms. (See Figure 10.7.)

Figure 10.7 The Mail Attachment Rule Dialog Box

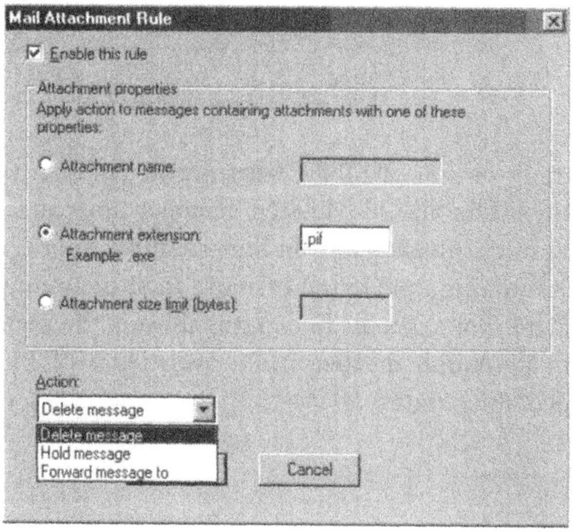

In this example, we'll select the **Forward message to** option so that you can see how to enter the forwarding address.

11. When you select the **Forward message to** option, a text box appears that allows you to enter an e-mail address to which the message will be forwarded. However, the server must be able to resolve the address of the mail domain of this user.

For example, in Figure 10.8, we entered the e-mail address **smtpsecurityadmin@ msfirewall.org**. The ISA Server firewall must be able to access an MX record for the internal.net domain. The ISA Server firewall forwards the message to the SMTP server responsible for the internal.net mail based on the information in the MX record.

In this example, the firewall is configured with a DNS server address of a DNS server on the internal network that can resolve both internal and external network names. The message is forwarded to the internal address of the Exchange server. You must configure a *split DNS infrastructure* if the internal.net domain is available to both internal and external users.

Figure 10.8 The Mail Attachment Rule Dialog Box

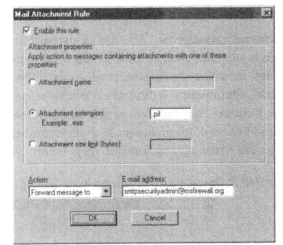

12. The settings on the **SMTP Commands** tab are mediated by the SMTP filter component. The SMTP Message Screener does not evaluate SMTP commands and does not protect against buffer overflow conditions. The commands in the list are limited to a predefined length. If an incoming SMTP connection sends a command that exceeds the length allowed, the connection is dropped. In addition, if a command that is sent over the SMTP channel is not on this list, it is dropped. (See Figure 10.9.)

Figure 10.9 The SMTP Commands Tab

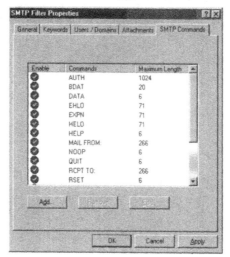

13. Click **Apply** and then click **OK** in the **Configure SMTP Protocol Policy** dialog box.

14. Click **Apply** to save the changes and update the Firewall policy.

15. Click **OK** in the **Apply New Configuration** dialog box.

Configuring SMTP Message Screener Logging

The ISA Server 2004 firewall keeps a separate log for messages that are processed by the SMTP Message Screener. This log provides valuable information regarding the messages that were blocked by the Message Screener and why they were blocked.

Perform the following steps to configure the SMTP Message Screener logging feature:

1. In the **Microsoft Internet Security and Acceleration Server 2004** management console, click the **Monitoring** node in the left pane of the console.

2. In the **Monitoring** node, click the **Logging** tab in the Details Pane.

3. Click the **Tasks** tab in the Task Pane. On the **Tasks** tab, click the **Configure SMTP Message Screener Logging** link.

4. In the **SMTP Message Screener Logging Properties** dialog box, click the **Log** tab. Note that the only logging method available is **File**. This option creates a text-based log file. Select the **ISA Server file format** option from the **Format** list. This allows the log to use local time in the log files. Confirm that there is a checkmark in the **Enable logging for this service** checkbox. (See Figure 10.10.)

Figure 10.10 The Log Tab

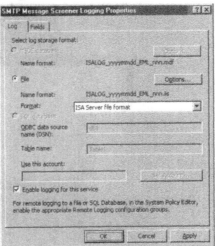

5. Click the **Options** button. The default location for the logs is in the **ISALogs folder** on the local hard disk. Make a note of the options in the **Log file storage limits** frame. Note that the text log files are compressed by default, using NTFS compression. Accept the defaults and click **Cancel**. (See Figure 10.11.)

Figure 10.11 The Options Dialog Box

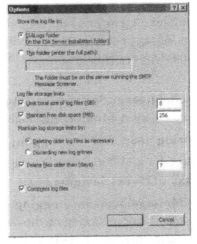

6. Click **Apply** and then click **OK** in the **SMTP Message Screener Logging Properties** dialog box.

Table 10.1 lists the SMTP service log fields and the nature of the information recorded in each. When a field is disabled in the SMTP Message Screener log, a dash "-"

will appear in that field when ISA Server log format is used. If W3C format is used, the field will not appear. The Field column indicates the position of that field when using the ISA Server log file format (the position is important to note because there is no "directive" or column header in the log indicating what that field is logging).

Table 10.1 SMTP Service Log Fields

Field	W3C	Description
1	date	The date that the logged event occurred.
2	time	The time that the logged event occurred. In W3C format, this is in Coordinated Universal Time (UTC).
3	cs-sender	The sender name, as specified in the "MAIL FROM:" SMTP header. Limited to 72 characters.
4	cs-recipient	The list of recipients, as specified in the "RCPT TO:" SMTP header. Limited to 72 characters.
5	cs-subject	The message subject. Limited to 72 characters.
6	cs-messageid	The ID of the message. The ID is either the unique message ID generated by the sender, or the ID automatically assigned by the Windows SMTP service, when it is received. Limited to 72 characters.
7	x-action	The action that ISA Server took. One of the following: **Delete** The message is deleted. **Hold** The message is stored in the BADMAIL queue. **Forward** The message is forwarded to a different recipient (not the recipient specified in the original message). **Pass** The message is sent to the specified recipients (in cs-recipient).
8	x-reason	The reasons why ISA Server executed the action (x-action) are listed following the table. Potential reasons why ISA Server executed the action are listed below: Some message properties could not be read. Taking default action. (The default action is Hold). Policy rule stamp could not be found in the message. Taking default action. (The default action is Hold). The policy rule stamp is an indication that ISA Server puts in the message to let the Message Screener know which rule should be applied to the message. This is generated if the message did not pass through the SMTP application filter before being passed to the SMTP Message Screener. Logger is not initialized yet. Taking default action.

Continued

Table 10.1 SMTP Service Log Fields

Field	W3C	Description
		(The default action is Hold).
		Policy rule could not be read. Taking default action.
		(The default action is Hold).
		Failed while trying to forward the message.
		The specific error code is also listed here.
		The SMTP Message Screener policy rule does not allow messages from sender.
		The SMTP Message Screener policy rule does not allow attachment.
		The SMTP Message Screener policy rule does not allow attachment extension.
		The SMTP Message Screener policy rule does not allow attachments of specified size.
		The SMTP Message Screener policy rule does not allow messages with specified subject.
		The SMTP Message Screener Policy rule does not allow messages with specified message body

The DNS Filter

The ISA firewall's DNS filter protects the DNS server published by the ISA firewall using Server Publishing Rules. You can access the configuration interface for the DNS filter's attack prevention configuration page in the **Intrusion Detection** dialog box. Expand the server name and then expand the **Configuration** node. Click the **General** node.

In the Details Pane, click the **Enable Intrusion Detection and DNS Attack Detection** link. In the **Intrusion Detection** dialog box, click the **DNS Attacks** tab. On the **DNS Attacks** tab, put a checkmark in the **Enable detection and filtering of DNS attacks** checkbox. (See Figure 10.12.)

Figure 10.12 The DNS Attacks Tab

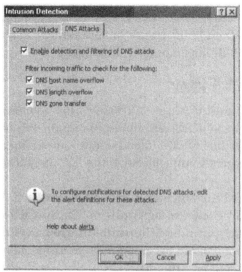

Once detection is enabled, you can then enable prevention. You can protect yourself from three attacks:

- DNS host name overflow
- DNS length overflow
- DNS zone transfer

The **DNS host name overflow** and **DNS length overflow** attacks are DNS denial-of-service (DoS) type attacks. The DNS DoS attack exploits the difference in size between a DNS query and a DNS response, in which all of the network's bandwidth is consumed by bogus DNS queries. The attacker uses the DNS servers as "amplifiers" to multiply the DNS traffic.

The attacker begins by sending small DNS queries to each DNS server that contain the spoofed IP address (see *IP Spoofing*) of the intended victim. The responses returned to the small queries are much larger, so if a large number of responses are returned at the same time, the link will become congested and denial of service will take place.

One solution to this problem is for administrators to configure DNS servers to respond with a "refused" response, which is much smaller than a name resolution response, when they receive DNS queries from suspicious or unexpected sources.

You can find detailed information for configuring DNS servers to prevent this problem in the U.S. Department of Energy's Computer Incident Advisory Capability information bulletin J-063, available at www.ciac.org/ciac/bulletins/j-063.shtml.

The POP Intrusion Detection Filter

The POP Intrusion Detection filter protects POP3 servers you publish via ISA firewall Server Publishing Rules from POP services buffer overflow attacks. There is no configuration interface for the POP Intrusion Detection filter.

The SOCKS V4 Filter

The SOCKS v4 filter is used to accept SOCKS version 4 connection requests from applications written to the SOCKS version 4 specification. Windows operating systems should never need to use the SOCKS filter because you can install the Firewall client on these machines to transparently authenticate to the ISA firewall and support complex protocol negotiation.

For hosts that cannot be configured as Firewall clients, such as Linux and Mac hosts, you can use the SOCKS v4 filter to support them. The SOCKS v4 filter is disabled by default. To enable the filter, open the **Microsoft Internet Security and Acceleration Server 2004** management console, expand the server name, and then expand the **Configuration** node. Click the **Add-ins** node. In the Details Pane, right-click the **SOCKS V4** filter and click **Enable**.

You will need to configure the SOCKS V4 filter to listen on the specific network(s) for which you want it to accept connections. Double-click the **SOCKS V4** filter. In the **SOCKS V4 Filter Properties** dialog box, click the **Networks** tab. On the **Networks** tab, you can configure the **Port** on which the SOCKS filter listens for SOCKS client connections. Next, put a checkmark in the checkbox next to the network for which you want the SOCKS filter to accept connections. Click **Apply** and then click **OK**. (See Figure 10.13.)

Figure 10.13 The SOCKS V4 Filter Properties Dialog Box

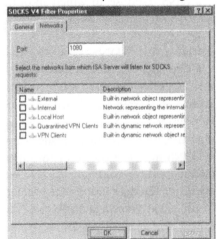

The SOCKS v4 filter supports SOCKS v4.3 client applications. The SOCKS filter is a generic sockets filter that supports all client applications that are designed to support the SOCKS v4.3 specification. The SOCKS filter performs duties similar to that performed by the Firewall client. However, there are some significant differences between how SOCKS and the Firewall client work:

- The Firewall client is a generic Winsock Proxy client application. All applications designed to the Windows Sockets specification will automatically use the Firewall client.

- The SOCKS filter supports applications written to the SOCKS v4.3 specification.

- When the Firewall client is installed on the client machine, all Winsock applications automatically use the Firewall client, and user credentials are automatically sent to the ISA firewall. In addition, the Firewall client will work with the ISA firewall service to manage complex protocols that require secondary connections (such as FTP, MMS, and many others).

- The SOCKS client must be configured on a per-application basis. Each application must be explicitly configured to use the ISA firewall as its SOCKS server. When the application is configured to use the ISA firewall as its SOCKS server, the SOCKS filter will manage complex protocols for the SOCKS client application.

- The SOCKS 4.3a filter included with the ISA firewall does not support authentication. SOCKS 5 introduced the capability to authenticate the client application that attempts to access content through the SOCKS proxy.

We always recommend that you use the Firewall client because of the impressive advantages it provides by allowing you the ability to authenticate all Winsock connections made through the ISA firewall. However, SOCKS is a good "second best" when you cannot install the Firewall client.

The FTP Access Filter

The FTP Access filter is used to mediate FTP connections between Protected Network clients and FTP servers on the Internet, and from external hosts and published FTP servers. The FTP Access filter supports both PASV and PORT (passive and standard) mode FTP connections.

The FTP Access filter is required for SecureNAT clients because FTP uses secondary connections for PORT-mode FTP connections. FTP is a complex protocol that requires outbound connections from the FTP PORT-mode client and new secondary inbound connections from the FTP server. While the Firewall client does not require application filter support for secondary connections, SecureNAT clients do require application layer filter support, which is why the ISA firewall dev team included the FTP Access application filter.

> **NOTE**
>
> If you plan to support PORT-mode FTP client connections, make sure that IP Routing is enabled on the ISA firewall (the default setting). When IP Routing is enabled, the secondary connections are handled in kernel mode rather than user mode. This kernel-mode handling of the secondary connections (which are data transfers from the FTP server to the FTP client) will significantly increase performance.

Stefaan Pouseele, an ISA Server MVP, has written an excellent article on the FTP protocol and how FTP challenges firewall security. Check out his article, *How the FTP Protocol Challenges Firewall Security* at http://isaserver.org/articles/How_the_FTP_protocol_Challenges_Firewall_Security.html.

This is no configuration interface for the FTP Access filter.

The H.323 Filter

The H.323 filter is used to support H.323 connections through the ISA firewall. To configure the H.323 filter, open the **Microsoft Internet Security and Acceleration Server 2004** management console and expand the server name. Next, expand the **Configuration** node and click the **Add-ins** node. Double-click the **H.323 Filter** entry in the Details Pane.

In the **H.323 Filter Properties** dialog box, click the **Call Control** tab (see Figure 10.14). You have the following options:

- Use this Gatekeeper
- Use DNS gateway lookup and LRQs for alias resolution
- Allow audio
- Allow video
- Allow T120 and application sharing

Figure 10.14 The Call Control Tab

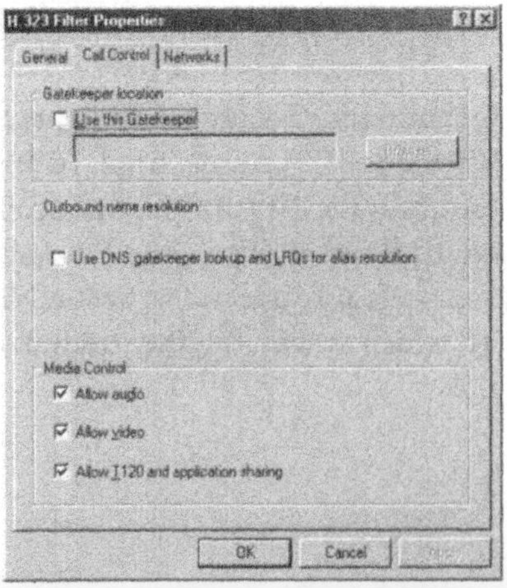

Click the **Networks** tab. On the **Networks** tab, put a checkmark in the checkbox to the left of the networks on which you want the H.323 filter to accept connections requests. (See Figure 10.15.)

Figure 10.15 The Networks Tab

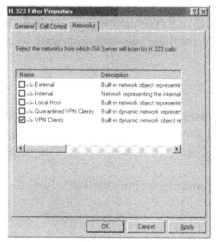

The MMS Filter

The MMS filter supports Microsoft Media Services connections through the ISA firewall for Access Rules and Server Publishing Rules. The MMS filter is an access filter that allows SecureNAT client access to the complex protocols and secondary connections required to connect to Microsoft Media Services hosted content. Firewall clients do not require the help of the MMS filter to connect to MMS servers. There is no configuration interface for the MMS filter.

The PNM Filter

The PNM filter supports connections for the Progressive Networks Media Protocol from Real Networks. The PNM filter is an access filter allowing SecureNAT client access to the complex protocols and secondary connection required to connect to Progressive Networks Media servers. There is no configuration interface for the PNM filter.

The PPTP Filter

The PPTP filter supports PPTP connections through the ISA firewall for outbound connections made through Access Rules and inbound connections made through Server Publishing Rules. The ISA firewall's PPTP filter differs from the ISA Server 2000 PPTP filter in that it supports both inbound and outbound PPTP connections. The ISA Server 2000 PPTP filter only supports outbound PPTP connections.

The PPTP filter is required by both SecureNAT and Firewall clients. In fact, a machine located on an ISA firewall protected network must be configured as a SecureNAT client to use the PPTP filter to connect to PPTP VPN servers through the ISA firewall. The reason for this is that the Firewall client does not mediate non-TCP/UDP protocols. The PPTP VPN protocol requires the use of the Generic Routing Encapsulation (GRE) protocol (IP Protocol 47) and TCP protocol 1723. The TCP session is used by PPTP for tunnel management.

When the outbound access to the PPTP protocol is enabled, the PPTP filter automatically intercepts the GRE and TCP connections made by the PPTP VPN client. You do not need to create an Access Rule allowing outbound access to TCP 1723 for VPN clients.

The RPC Filter

The RPC filter is used to mediate RPC connections to servers requiring Remote Procedure Calls (RPCs) for both outbound connections using Access Rules and inbound connections using Server Publishing Rules. This includes secure Exchange RPC publishing.

There is no configuration interface for the RPC filter.

The RTSP Filter

The RTSP filter supports Microsoft Real Time Streaming Protocol connections through the ISA firewall for Access Rules and Server Publishing Rules. The RTSP filter is an access filter that allows SecureNAT client access to the complex protocols and secondary connections required to connect to Microsoft Real Time Streaming Protocol hosted content (such as that on Windows Server 2003 Microsoft Media Servers). Firewall clients do not require the help of the MMS filter to connect to MMS servers.

There is no configuration interface for the RTSP filter.

Web Filters

ISA firewall Web filters are used to mediate HTTP, HTTPS, and FTP tunneled (Web proxied) connections through the ISA firewall. In this section, we discuss the following Web filters:

- HTTP Security filter
- ISA Server Link Translator
- Web Proxy filter
- SecurID filter
- OWA Forms-based Authentication filter

The HTTP Security Filter (HTTP Filter)

The ISA firewall's HTTP Security filter is one of the key application layer filtering and inspection mechanisms included with the ISA firewall. The HTTP Security filter allows the ISA firewall to perform application layer inspection on all HTTP communications moving through the ISA firewall and block connections that do not match your HTTP security requirements.

The HTTP Security filter is tightly tied to the Web Proxy filter. When the Web Proxy filter is bound to the HTTP protocol, all communications outbound through the ISA firewall with a destination port of TCP 80 are subjected to the HTTP Security filter's deep application layer inspection. We'll see later how to unbind the Web Proxy filter from the HTTP protocol if you do not want all communications to be scrubbed by the HTTP Security filter.

> **NOTE**
>
> While you can unbind the Web Proxy filter from outbound HTTP protocol con-
> nections, you cannot unbind the Web Proxy filter from Web Publishing Rules.
> Connections coming in through Web Publishing Rules will always be proxied.
> For more information on unbinding the HTTP filter from the HTTP protocol for
> Access Rules, refer to Chapter 6.

The HTTP Security filter is applied on a per-rule basis, and you can apply different HTTP filtering properties on each rule that allows outbound HTTP communications. This provides you very granular, fine-tuned control over what type of connections can move over the HTTP channel. In addition, you can bind the Web Proxy filter to other ports and enforce HTTP Security Filter policy over connections moving over alternate ports. This provides you another potent weapon against users and applications that try to subvert your network and Firewall Security policy by tunneling Web connections over alternate ports.

In this section, we discuss:

- Overview of HTTP Security Filter Settings

- HTTP Security Filter Logging

- Disabling the HTTP Security Filter for Web Requests

- Exporting and Importing HTTP Security Filter Settings

- Investigating HTTP Headers for Potentially Dangerous Applications

- Example HTTP Security Filter Policies

- Commonly Blocked Application Signatures

- The Dangers of SSL Tunneling

Overview of HTTP Security Filter Settings

The HTTP Security filter includes a number of tabs that allow you precise control over what HTTP communications are allowed through the ISA firewall on a per-rule basis. Configuration of the HTTP Security filter is done on the following tabs:

- General
- Methods
- Extensions
- Headers
- Signatures

The General Tab

On the **General** tab, you can configure the following options (see Figure 10.16):

- Maximum header length
- Payload length
- Maximum URL length
- Verify normalization
- Block high bit characters
- Block responses containing Windows executable content

Figure 10.16 The General Tab

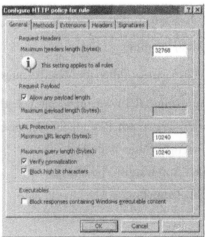

The **Maximum headers length (bytes)** option allows you to configure the maximum length of all headers included in a request HTTP communication. This setting applies to *all* rules that use the HTTP Security filter. This setting protects you from attacks that try to overflow Web site buffers by sending excessively long headers to the Web server. If you set the value too low, some applications on your site might not work correctly. If you set it too high, intruders may be able to construct a special HTTP request that could exploit known and unknown buffer overflow issues with your Web site or Web server. You might want to start with a value of 10,000 bytes and work upward from there. Your Web site administrator should be able to help you with the maximum header length required for sites your ISA firewall protects.

In the **Request Payload** frame, you have the option to **Allow any payload length** or to set a specific maximum payload length. The payload is the part of the HTTP communication that is not part of the HTTP header or command structure. For example, if you allow users to post content to your Web site (an ordering form or a discussion forum), you can set a limit on the length of their posts by unchecking the **Allow any payload length** checkbox and entering a custom value in the **Maximum payload length (bytes)** text box. Again, you may want to discuss your Web site's requirements with your Web site administrator or Web programmer to get specific details on maximum payload length requirements for your protected Web sites.

There are several options in the **URL Protection** frame. The **Maximum URL length (bytes)** option allows you to set the maximum URL that the user can send through the ISA firewall when making a request through the firewall for a Web site. Exploits can send excessively long URLs in an attempt to execute a buffer overflow or other attack against a Web server. The default value is **10240**, but you can increase or decrease this value based on your own site's custom requirements. The **Maximum query length (bytes)** value allows you to set the maximum length of the query portion of the URL. The query part of the URL appears after a question mark (?) in the request URL. The default value is **10240**, but you can make it longer or shorter, based on your requirements. Keep in mind that the **Maximum URL length** must be longer than the **Maximum query length** because the query is part of the URL.

The **Verify normalization** option is also included in the **URL Protection** frame. *Normalization* is the process of decoding so-called "escaped" characters. Web servers can receive requests that are encoded using escaped characters. One of the most common examples is when there is a space in the URL, as in the URL http://msfirewall.org/ Dir%20One/default%20file.htm. The %20 is an "escape" character representing a "space." The problem is that bad guys can also encode the "%" character and perform what is called "double encoded" requests. Double encoding can be used to attack Web servers. When the **Verify Normalization** option is selected, the HTTP Security filter will normalize or decode the request twice. If the request of the first and second decodings is not the same, the HTTP Security filter will drop the request. This prevents "double encoding" attacks. You should enable this feature, but keep in mind that poorly designed Web sites and Web applications are not always security aware, and may actually accept and require double encoded requests. If that is the case for sites you want to access on the Internet or for sites you publish through the ISA firewall, you will need to disable this option.

The **Block high bit characters** option allows you to block HTTP requests that include URLs with high bit characters in them. High bit characters are used by many languages that use extended character sets, so if you find that you can't access Web sites that use these extended character sets in their URLs, you will need to disable this option.

The **Block responses containing Windows executable content** option allows you to prevent users from downloading files that are Windows executable files (such as .exe files, but any file extension can be used on a Windows executable). The HTTP Security filter is able to determine if the file is a Windows executable because the response will begin with an **MZ**. This can be very helpful when you need to prevent your users from downloading executables through the ISA firewall.

TIP
_____

Remember that your HTTP policy is configured on a per-rule basis. Because you can configure HTTP policy on a per-rule basis, you can enable these settings for some rules, and disable them for other rules. This per-rule HTTP policy configuration option provides you a great deal of flexibility in what content is available from specific sites to specific users at specific times.

The Methods Tab

You can control what HTTP methods are used through an Access Rule or Web Publishing Rule using the settings on the **Methods** tab (see Figure 10.17). You have three options:

- Allow all methods
- Allow only specified methods
- Block specified methods (allow all others)

Figure 10.17 The Methods Tab

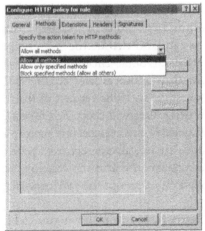

HTTP methods are HTTP commands that hosts can send to a Web server to perform specific actions; for example, GET, PUT, and POST. There are others that you, as a network and firewall administrator might not be familiar with, such as HEAD, SEARCH, and CHECKOUT. There are other methods that are proprietary and used by specific Web applications, such as Outlook Web Access. The **Allow all methods** option allows you to allow HTTP methods used in an HTTP communication through the ISA firewall.

NOTE

Other HTTP methods you'll encounter when allowing access to Microsoft applications include RPC_IN_DATA and RPC_OUT_DATA, which are used for securely publishing RPC over HTTP for Outlook 2003 clients. However, remember that the filter only *blocks* communications set in the HTTP policy filter, so be careful not to block methods you might require, even when you're not completely sure what the exact methods you might require will be. We recommend that you thoroughly test your filter settings and discuss with the Web application admins and developers what methods are required.

The **Allow only specified methods** option allows you to specify the exact methods you want to allow through the ISA firewall. If you can identify what methods are required by your Web site and Web application, then you can allow those only and block any other method. Other methods could be used to compromise your Web site, so if they're not needed, block them.

The **Block specified methods (allow all others)** option allows you to allow all methods except those specific methods you want to allow. This option provides you a bit more latitude in that even if you don't know all the methods your site might require, you might know some that are definitely not required. One example might be the POST method. If you don't allow users to post content to your Web site, then there's no reason to allow the POST method, and you can explicitly block it.

When you select either the **Allow only specified methods** or the **Block specified methods (allow all others)** option, you need to click the **Add** button to add the method you want to allow or block. The **Method** dialog box appears after clicking the **Add** button.

In the **Add** dialog box, you enter the method in the **Method** text box (Figure 10.18). You might also want to add a description of this method in the **Description** text box. This helps you remember what the method does and helps the next person who might need to manage your ISA firewall and isn't aware of the insides of the HTTP protocol command set.

Figure 10.18 The Methods Dialog Box

The Extensions Tab

On the **Extensions** tab, you have the following options (see Figure 10.19):

- Allow all extensions
- Allow only specified extensions
- Block specified extensions (allow all others)
- Block requests containing ambiguous extensions

Figure 10.19 The Extensions Tab

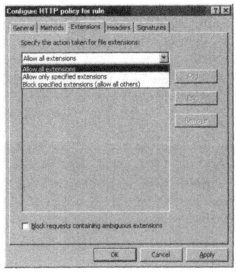

You can control what file extensions are allowed to be requested through the ISA firewall. This is extremely useful when you want to block users from requesting certain file types through the ISA firewall. For example, you can block users from accessing .exe, .com, .zip, and any other file extension through the ISA firewall.

The **Allow all extensions** option allows you to configure the Access Rule or Web Publishing Rule to allow users access to any type of file based on file extension through the ISA firewall. The **Allow only specified extensions** option allows you to specify the precise file extensions that users can access through the ISA firewall. The **Block specified extensions (allow all others)** option allows you to block specified file extensions that you deem dangerous.

If you select the **Allow only specified extensions** or **Block specified extensions (allow all others)** option, you need to click the **Add** button and add the extensions you want to allow or block.

The **Extension** dialog box appears after you click the **Add** button. Enter the name of the extension in the **Extension** text box. For example, if you want to block access to .exe files, enter **.exe** . Enter a description if you like in the **Description (optional)** text box. Click **OK** to save the new extension. (See Figure 10.20.)

Figure 10.20 The Extensions Dialog Box

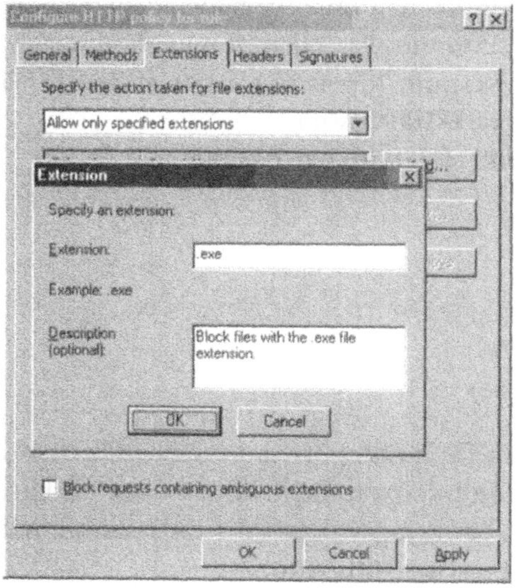

The Headers Tab

On the **Headers** tab, you have the following options (see Figure 10.21):

- Allow all headers except the following
- Server header
- Via header

Figure 10.21 The Headers Tab

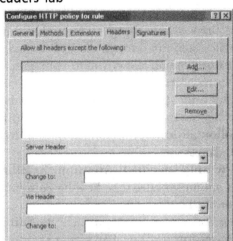

An HTTP header contains HTTP communication specific information that is included in HTTP requests made from a Web client (such as your Web browser) and HTTP responses sent back to the Web client from a Web server. These headers perform multiple functions that determine the status or state of the HTTP communications and other characteristics of the HTTP session.

Examples of common HTTP headers include:

- Content-length

- Pragma

- User-Agent

- Accept-Encoding

You can accept all HTTP headers or you can block certain specific HTTP headers. There are certain HTTP headers you might always want to block, such as the P2P-Agent header, which is used by many peer-to-peer applications. If you want to block a specific HTTP header, click the **Add** button.

In the **Header** dialog box, select either the **Request headers** or **Response headers** option from the **Search in** drop-down list. In the **HTTP header** text box, enter the HTTP header you want to block. Click **OK**. (See Figure 10.22.)

Figure 10.22 The Header Dialog Box

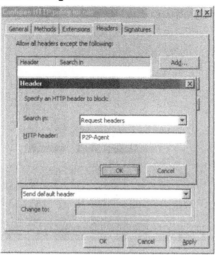

You can configure the Server Header returned in the HTTP responses by making a selection in the **Server Header** drop-down list. The Server Header is an HTTP header that the Web server sends back to the Web client informing the client of the type of Web server to which the client is connecting. Intruders can use this information to attack a Web server. You have the options to:

- Send original header
- Strip header from response
- Modify header in response

The **Send original header** option lets the header sent by the Web server go unchanged. The **Strip header from response** option allows the ISA firewall to remove the Server Header, and the **Modify header in response** allows you to change the header. You should change the header to confuse the attacker. Since this header isn't required by Web clients, you can change it to something like **Private** or **CompanyName** or anything else you like.

These options all help to prevent (or at least slow down) attackers. Attackers will have to expend more effort and use alternate methods to "fingerprint" your Web server. (See Figure 10.23.)

Figure 10.23 The Server Header Option

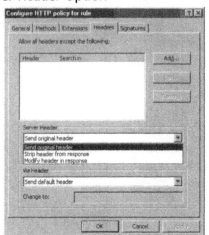

The **Via Header** option allows you to control the Via Header sent to the Web client. When Web Proxy servers are located between a client and Web server, the Web Proxy server will insert a Via Header in the HTTP communication informing the client that the request was handled by the Web Proxy server in transit. Each Web Proxy server in the request path can add its own Via Header, and each sender along the response path removes its own Via Header and forwards the response to the server specified in the next Via Header on the Via Header "stack." The **Via Header** settings allows you to change the name your ISA firewall includes in its own Via Header and enables you to hide the name of your ISA firewall. The default setting is for your ISA firewall to include its own Computer name in the Via Header.

You have two options:

- Send default header
- Modify header in request and response

The **Send default header** option leave the Via Header unchanged. The **Modify header in request and response** option allows you to change the name included in the Via Header inserted by your ISA firewall. We recommend that you change this to hide the actual name of your ISA firewall to prevent attackers from learning the actual name of your ISA firewall machine. (See Figure 10.24.)

Enter the alternate Via Header in the **Change To** text box.

Figure 10.24 The Via Header

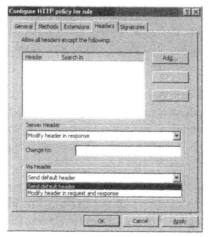

The Signatures Tab

The **Signatures** tab allows you to control access through the ISA firewall based on HTTP signatures you create. These signatures are based on strings contained in the following components of an HTTP communication:

- Request URL
- Request headers
- Request body
- Response headers
- Response body

You access the **Signature** dialog box by clicking the **Add** button. (See Figure 10.25.)

Figure 10.25 The Signatures Tab

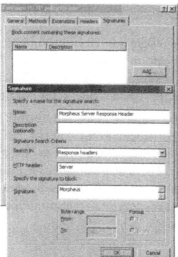

In the **Signature** dialog box, enter a name for the signature in the **Name** text box and a description of the signature in the **Description** text box. This is especially helpful so that you know the purpose and rationale for this signature.

In the **Search in** drop-down list, select where you want the ISA firewall to search for the specified string. You have the follow options:

- **Request URL** When you select this option, you can enter a string that when found in the Web client's request URL, the connection is blocked. For example, if you wanted to prevent all requests to sites that have the string **Kazaa** in the URL included in the Web client's request, you enter **Kazaa** in the **Signature** text box.

- **Request headers** When you select this option, you enter the specific HTTP header you want the ISA firewall to check in the **HTTP header** text box and then enter the string in the header you want the ISA firewall to block in the **Signature** text box. For example, if you want to block eDonkey P2P applications, you can select this option and then **User-Agent** in the **HTTP header** text box. In the **Signature** text box, you then enter **ed2k**. Note that this option gives you more granular control than you would have if you just blocked headers in the **Headers** tab. If you block a specific header in the **Headers** tab, you end up blocking all HTTP communications that use that specific header. By creating a signature that incorporates a specific header, you can allow that HTTP header for all communications that do not include the header value you enter for the signature.

- **Request body** You can block HTTP communications based on the body of the Web request outside of that contained in the HTTP commands and headers. While this is a very powerful feature, it has the potential to consume a great deal of resources on the ISA firewall computer. For this reason, you need to configure the byte range you want the ISA firewall to inspect in the **Byte range From** and **To** text boxes. We don't have any explicit recommendations on specific entries you might want to include in this section, but will provide updates on www.isaserver.org when we do.

- **Response headers** When you select this option, you enter the specific HTTP header you want to block based on the HTTP response returned by the Web server. You enter the specific HTTP header in the **HTTP header** text box and the HTTP header value in the **Signature** text box.

- **Response body** The response body option works the same as the **Request body** option, except it applies to the content returned to the Web client from the Web server. For example, if you want to block Web pages that contain specific strings that are identified as dangerous or inappropriate, you can create a signature to block those strings. Keep this in mind when reading about the latest Web-based attack and create a signature that blocks connections that employ such an attack.

Figure 10.26 shows some example signatures blocking some commonly encountered applications that might be considered a major security risk for corporate networks.

Figure 10.26 Example Signatures

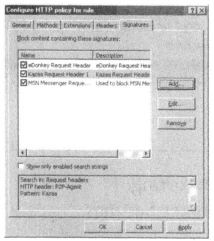

TIP

Another signature you might want to create is one that blocks the **<iframe src="?"/>** string in the response body. This string can potentially peg the processor on the victim machine and hang the operating system.

HTTP Security Filter Logging

How do you know if your security filters are working? One way to determine the effectiveness of the entries you've made in the HTTP Security filter is to use the ISA firewall's built-in log viewer. Perform the following steps to configure the ISA firewall's built-in log viewer to view HTTP Security Filter actions:

1. In the **Microsoft Internet Security and Acceleration Server 2004** management console, expand the server name and click the **Monitoring** node in the left pane of the console.

2. In the **Monitoring** node, click the **Logging** tab. In the **Tasks** tab of the Task Pane, click the **Start Query** link.

3. Right-click one of the column headers and click the **Add/Remove Columns** command.

4. In the **Add/Remove Columns** dialog box, click the **Filter Information** entry in the **Available Columns** list and click **Add**. The **Filter Information** entry now appears in the list of **Displayed columns**. Click **OK**.

5. Issue a request from a client behind the ISA firewall that would be blocked by your HTTP Security Filter settings. Figure 10.27 shows an example of a connection that was blocked because the URL contained a string that was disallowed by the HTTP Security filter.

Figure 10.27 Log File Entries Showing the HTTP Security Filter Blocking a Connection

Client IP	Destinatio...	Destination Port	Protocol	HTTP Method	URL	Filter Information
10.0.0.5	10.0.0.1	8080	http	GET	http://www.cisco.com/	Blocked by the HTTP Security filter: URL contains sequences which are disallowed
10.0.0.5	10.0.0.1	8080	Unidentifie...	·	·	·
10.0.0.1	10.0.0.2	53	DNS	·	·	·
192.168.1.70	192.168.1.34	53	DNS	·	·	·
10.0.0.5	10.0.0.1	8080	Unidentifie...	·	·	·
10.0.0.5	10.0.0.1	8080	http	GET	http://www.cisco.com/	Blocked by the HTTP Security filter: URL contains sequences which are disallowed

Exporting and Importing HTTP Security Filter Settings

An HTTP policy can be exported from or imported into an Access Rule that uses the HTTP protocol or a Web Publishing Rule. The **HttpFilterConfig.vbs** script located at **\sdk\samples\admin** can be used to export an existing HTTP policy that has already been configured in an Access Rule or Web Publishing Rule or an HTTP policy that has already been exported to a file can be imported into an existing Access Rule or Web Publishing Rule.

The **HttpFilterConfig.vbs** script greatly simplifies configuration of complex HTTP policies that include multiple entries for parameters such as signature, file extensions, and headers. We recommend that you export your HTTP policies after you create them in the **Microsoft Internet Security and Acceleration Server 2004** management console.

In this section, we discuss how you can export and import an HTTP policy from and to a Web Publishing Rule.

TIP

Jim Harrison, the Godfather of ISA firewall scripting, has several attack prevention tools and scripts on his site that automatically configure an HTTP policy as part of the attack prevention and mitigation configuration. Check out Jim's fantastic ISA firewall tools Web site at www.isatools.org.

Exporting an HTTP Policy from a Web Publishing Rule

HTTP policies can be exported from an Access Rule or Web Publishing Rule using the **HttpFilterConfig.vbs** file located on the ISA 2004 CD-ROM. Follow these steps to export the HTTP policy from an existing Web Publishing Rule:

1. Copy the **HttpFilterConfig.vbs** file from the ISA firewall CD-ROM to the root of the C: drive.

2. Open a command prompt and change the focus to the root of the C: drive. Enter the following command and press **Enter** (notice that if the rule name has a space in it you must enclose the name in quotes):

   ```
   C:\Httpfilterconfig.vbs import "Publish OWA Site" c:\webpol.xml
   ```

3. You will see a dialog box confirming that the information was successfully imported into the rule (see Figure 10.28).

Figure 10.28 Successful Import Dialog Box

Importing an HTTP Policy into a Web Publishing Rule

HTTP policies can be imported into Access Rules that include the HTTP protocol and Web Publishing Rules. We use the same script we used when exporting an HTTP policy, the **HttpFilterConfig.vbs** file. To import an HTTP policy saved to an .xml file into a Web Publishing Rule named **Publish OWA Site**:

1. Copy both the .xml file and the **HttpFilterConfig.vbs** file from the ISA firewall CD-ROM to the root of the C: drive. In this example, the .xml file is named **webpol.xml**.

2. Open a command prompt and change the focus to the root of the C: drive. Enter the following command and press **Enter** (notice that if the rule name has spaces in it, you must enclose the name in quotes):

   ```
   C:\Httpfilterconfig.vbs import "Publish OWA Site" c:\webpol.xml
   ```

3. You will see a dialog box confirming that the information was successfully imported into the rule (see Figure 10.29).

Figure 10.29 Successful Import Dialog Box

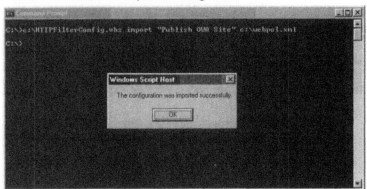

Investigating HTTP Headers for Potentially Dangerous Applications

One of your primary tasks as an ISA firewall administrator is to investigate characteristics of network traffic with the goal of blocking new and ever more dangerous network applications. These dangerous applications might be peer-to-peer applications, instant messaging applications, or other applications that hide by wrapping themselves in an HTTP header. Many vendors now wrap their applications in an HTTP header in an attempt to subvert your Firewall policy. Your goal as an ISA firewall administrator is to subvert the vendors' attempt to subvert your Network Usage policy.

As you can imagine, the vendors of these applications aren't very cooperative when it comes to getting information on how to prevent their applications from violating your firewall security. You'll often have to figure out this information for yourself, especially for new and obscure applications.

Your main tool in fighting the war against network scumware is a protocol analyzer. Two of the most popular protocol analyzers are Microsoft Network Monitor and the freeware tool Ethereal. Both are excellent, the only major downside of Ethereal being that you need to install a network driver to make it work correctly. Since the WinPcaP driver required by Ethereal hasn't been regression tested against the ISA firewall software, it's hard to know whether it may cause problems with firewall stability or performance. For this reason, we'll use the built-in version of Network Monitor included with Windows Server 2003 in the following examples.

Let's look at a couple of examples of how you can determine how to block some dangerous applications. One such application is eDonkey, a peer-to-peer file-sharing application. The first step is to start Network Monitor and run a network monitor trace while running the eDonkey application on a client that accesses the Internet through the ISA firewall. The best way to start is by configuring Network Monitor to listen on the Internal interface of the ISA firewall, or whatever interface eDonkey or other offending applications use to access the Internet through the ISA firewall.

Stop the trace after running the offending application for a while. Since we're only interested in Web connections moving through TCP port 80, we can filter out all other communications in the trace. We can do this with Display filters.

Click the **Display** menu and then click the **Filter** command. In the **Display Filter** dialog box, double-click the **Protocol == Any** entry. (See Figure 10.30.)

Figure 10.30 The Display Filter Dialog Box

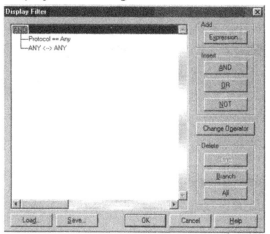

In the **Expression** dialog box, click the **Protocol** tab and then click the **Disable All** button. In the list of **Disabled Protocols**, click the **HTTP** protocol, click the **Enable** button, and then click **OK**. (See Figure 10.31.)

Figure 10.31 The Expression Dialog Box

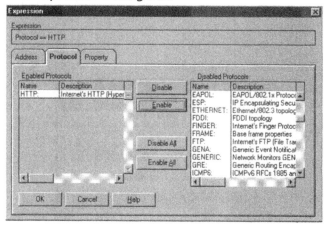

Click **OK** in the **Display Filter** dialog box. The top pane of the Network Monitor console now only displays HTTP connections. A good place to start is by looking at the **GET** requests, which appear as **GET Request from Client** in the **Description**

column. Double-click on the GET requests and expand the **HTTP: Get Request from Client** entry in the middle form. This displays a list of request headers.

In Figure 10.32, you can see that one of the request headers appears to be unusual (only if you have experience looking at Network Monitor traces; don't worry, it won't take long before you get good at this). The **HTTP: User-Agent =ed2k** seems like it might be specific for eDonkey2000. We can use this information to create an HTTP Security Filter entry to block the **User-Agent** Request Header value **ed2k**.

Figure 10.32 The Network Monitor Display Window

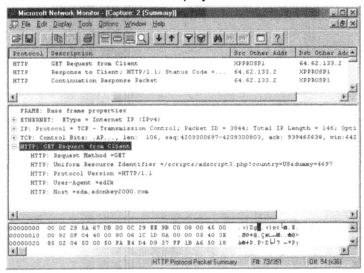

You can do this by creating an HTTP Security Filter signature using these values. Figure 10.33 shows what the HTTP Security Filter signature would look like to block the eDonkey application.

Figure 10.33 The Signature Dialog Box

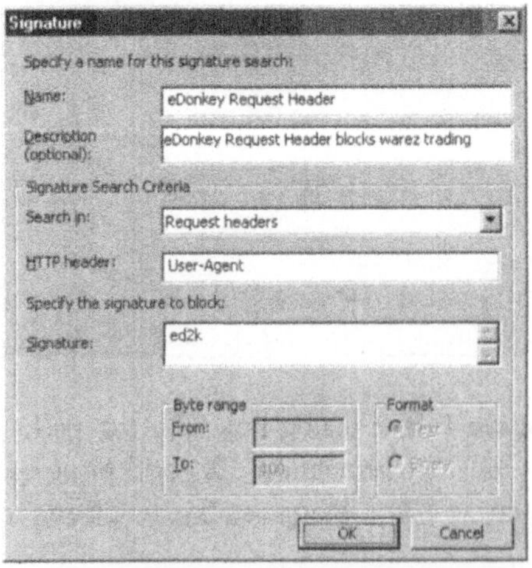

Another example of a dangerous application is Kazaa. Figure 10.34 shows a frame displaying the GET request the Kazaa client sends through the ISA firewall. In the list of HTTP headers, you can see one that can be used to help block the Kazaa client. The **P2P-Agent** HTTP request header can be blocked completely, or you can create a signature and block the **P2P-Agent** HTTP request header when it has the value **Kazaa**. You could also block the **Host** header in the HTTP request header when the value is set as **desktop.kazaa.com**.

Figure 10.34 Network Monitor Display Showing Kazaa Request Headers

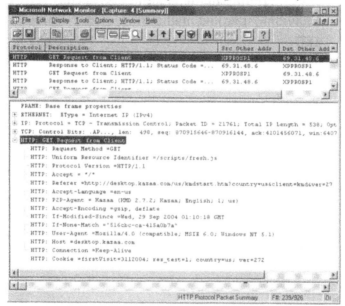

Example HTTP Security Filter Policies

Creating HTTP Security Filter policies can take some time. You need to run the required applications and then determine the required methods, extensions, headers, and other signatures that are specific for your application. While the effort is well spent, sometimes you need to get critical applications up and running quickly.

For this reason, we include a couple of example HTTP Security Filter policies you can use right away to protect IIS Web sites and Outlook Web Access sites.

Table 10.2 provides the defaults of a good default Web site HTTP Security Filter policy you can use. This policy allows the most common methods required for simple Web sites and restricts extensions that might allow an attacker to compromise your site. There are also several HTTP signatures included that block common strings that Internet criminals might use to compromise your Web site or server.

Table 10.2 Example HTTP Security Filter for Generic Web Sites

Tab	Parameter
General	Maximum header length is 32768.
	Allow any payload length is selected.
	Maximum URL length is 260.
	Maximum query length is 4096.
	Verify normalization is selected.
	Block high bit characters is not selected.
Methods	Allow only specified methods:
	GET
	HEAD
	POST
Extensions	Block specified extensions (allow all others):
	.exe
	.bat
	.cmd
	.com
	.htw
	.ida
	.idq
	.htr
	.idc
	.shtm
	.shtml
	.stm
	.printer
	.ini
	.log
	.pol
	.dat
Headers	No changes from the default.

Continued

Table 10.2 Example HTTP Security Filter for Generic Web Sites

Tab	Parameter
Signatures (Request URL)	Block content containing these signatures
	..
	./
	\
	:
	%
	&
Tab	Parameter

Table 10.3 provides settings you can use to configure an HTTP Security Filter policy for OWA publishing. Notice the methods required by OWA. You can see these in action by using the ISA firewall's built-in log filter and watching the HTTP Methods column.

TIP

You may not want to include the **&** character and **.exe** extension. You need to allow **.exe** for downloading of the S/MIME control. However, because HTTP Security Filter policy is applied on a per-rule basis, we suggest you create a separate rule allowing access for specific Outlook Web Access needs, and order it before the rule that blocks access based on Table 10.3. The allow rule would allow access only to the OWA directory containing those controls. If you do not allow the **&** character in requests, certain functions, like Calendaring, will not work correctly.

Table 10.3 HTTP Security Filter Settings for OWA Web Publishing Rules

Tab	Parameter
General	Maximum header length is 32768.
	Allow any payload length is selected.
	Maximum URL length is 260.
	Maximum query length is 4096.
	Verify normalization is selected.
	Block high bit characters is not selected.

Continued

Table 10.3 HTTP Security Filter Settings for OWA Web Publishing Rules

Tab	Parameter
Methods	Allow only specified methods:
	GET
	POST
	PROPFIND
	PROPPATCH
	BPROPPATCH
	MKCOL
	DELETE
	BDELETE
	BCOPY
	MOVE
	SUBSCRIBE
	BMOVE
	POLL
	SEARCH
Extensions	Block specified extensions (allow all others):
	.exe
	.bat
	.cmd
	.com
	.htw
	.ida
	.idq
	.htr
	.idc
	.shtm
	.shtml
	.stm
	.printer
	.ini
	.log
	.pol
	.dat
Headers	No changes from the default.

Continued

Table 10.3 HTTP Security Filter Settings for OWA Web Publishing Rules

Tab	Parameter
Signatures (Request URL)	Block content containing these signatures
	./
	\
	:
	%
	&

Table 10.4 shows entries for an HTTP Security Filter policy you can use for an RPC-over-HTTP Web Publishing Rule. Notice the unusual HTTP methods used by the Outlook 2003 RPC-over-HTTP protocol.

Table 10.4 HTTP Security Filter Policy Settings for RPC-over-HTTP Web Publishing Rule

Tab	Parameter
General	Maximum headers length is 32768.
	Maximum Payload Length: 2000000000.
	Maximum URL length is 16384.
	Maximum query length is 4096.
	Verify normalization is selected.
	Block high bit characters is not selected.
Methods	Allow only specified methods:
	RPC_IN_DATA
	RPC_OUT_DATA
Extensions	No changes from the default.
Headers	No changes from the default.
Signatures (Request URL)	No changes from the default.

Commonly Blocked Headers and Application Signatures

While we consider it an entertaining pastime spending long evenings with Network Monitor and discovering how to block dangerous applications, not all ISA firewall administrators share this predilection. For those of you who need to configure your ISA firewall to protect your network from dangerous applications as soon as possible, we provide the information in Tables 10.5 and 10.6.

Table 10.5 lists the information you need to include in signatures to block commonly encountered dangerous applications. You use the information in this table to create a signature entry in the HTTP Security filter.

Table 10.5 Sample Signatures for Blocking Commonly Encountered Dangerous Applications

Application	Location	HTTP Header	Signature
MSN Messenger	Request headers	User-Agent:	MSN Messenger
Windows Messenger	Request headers	User-Agent:	MSMSGS
Netscape 7	Request headers	User-Agent:	Netscape/7
Netscape 6	Request headers	User-Agent:	Netscape/6
AOL Messenger (and all Gecko browsers)	Request headers	User-Agent:	Gecko/
Yahoo Messenger	Request headers	Host	msg.yahoo.com
Kazaa	Request headers	P2P-Agent	Kazaa Kazaaclient:
Kazaa	Request headers	User-Agent:	KazaaClient
Kazaa	Request headers	X-Kazaa-Network:	KaZaA
Gnutella	Request headers	User-Agent:	Gnutella Gnucleus
eDonkey	Request headers	User-Agent:	e2dk
Internet Explorer 6.0	Request headers	User-Agent:	MSIE 6.0
Morpheus	Response header	Server	Morpheus
Bearshare	Response header	Server	Bearshare
BitTorrent	Request headers	User-Agent:	BitTorrent
SOAP over HTTP	Request headers Response headers	User-Agent:	SOAPAction

Table 10.6 contains some HTTP header values you can use to block dangerous applications. In contrast to signatures that require the HTTP header name and value, the entries in Table 10.6 can be configured in the **Headers** tab of the HTTP Security filter. These headers are specific for the listed dangerous applications and are not used for legitimate HTTP communications, so you do not need to specify a specific value for the HTTP headers blocked here.

Table 10.6 HTTP Headers Used to Bock Dangerous Applications

Application	Location	Type	Value
Kazaa	Headers	Request Header	X-Kazaa-Username: X-Kazaa-IP: X-Kazaa-SupernodeIP:
BitTorrent	Extensions	None	.torrent
Many peer-to-peer clients	Headers	Request Header	P2P-Agent

The Dangers of SSL Tunneling

As an ISA firewall administrator, your main concern is controlling what external users can access on your corporate network and what users on the corporate network can access on the Internet and other networks within the corporate network. You spend a lot of time configuring a Firewall policy so users have access only to the protocols you want them to use, connect only to the servers you want them to connect to, download only the content corporate Security policy approves, and access resources only at a specified time of day.

You must have the ability to allow or deny VPN connections, remote desktop connections, access to Web servers, and file transfer via Web or Instant Messenger connections. The truth is, you *need* to be able to explicitly allow or deny all communications moving through the ISA firewall.

Major problems occur when a firewall encounters encrypted communications. For example, what happens when users use an SSL encrypted connection to an OWA Web site? Conventional hardware firewalls (such as PIX or Sonicwall) see an incoming connection to TCP port 443. An access control list (ACL) on the hardware firewall tells it to allow the incoming connection and forward it to the OWA site on the corporate network.

The remote access OWA client negotiates an encrypted SSL connection with the OWA site. All communications moving through the hardware firewall are now encrypted and the hardware firewall has no clue about the contents of the encrypted SSL "tunnel." There is nothing the hardware firewall can do if an attacker or worm on the OWA client machine launches an attack against the OWA server through this SSL encrypted session. Simple stateful filtering hardware firewalls just say, "this is an SSL connection and I have an ACL to allow SSL connections to the OWA server, have a nice day."

This is a serious security problem, and one against which hardware firewalls are helpless to protect. The fact that attackers can leverage an encrypted channel *that you allow* through the firewall means you have lost access control, because the corporate Firewall policy *cannot* be enforced against the contents of the encrypted channel.

This situation gets even worse. Many application developers are getting into the HTTP tunneling act. They do this ostensibly to get around "restrictive firewalls" that allow only HTTP and/or HTTPS outbound or inbound. To get around these "restrictive firewalls," they "wrap" their application protocol in an HTTP header so that firewalls configured to allow HTTP/HTTPS communications allow their application through.

Examples of this type of HTTP tunneling of non–Web applications include RPC over HTTP(S), the GoToMyPC application, and a large number of HTTP tunneling applications explicitly designed to subvert a Firewall policy (http://www.google.com/search?hl=en&ie=UTF-8&q=HTTP+tunnel).

So-called "SSL VPNs" also belong to this group. SSL "VPNs" are used to bypass firewall security and tunnel an array of application protocols within an encrypted SSL link. All of these applications, whether designed to increase productivity (such as RPC over HTTP) or to explicitly violate Network Usage policy, have a common goal: hide the underlying application protocol inside an encrypted SSL tunnel.

NOTE

Most SSL "VPNs" are not VPN connections at all. Many vendors advertise an SSL "VPN" when in fact there is no IP-level VPN connection. Instead, these vendors provide application-specific gateways that tunnel their protocols in an SSL (HTTPS) header. The application gateway then forwards the connections to the server on the corporate network. Examples of so-called SSL "VPNs" are OWA and RPC over HTTP, although Microsoft does not advertise these services as SSL "VPN." In contrast, there are "network" SSL VPNs that tunnel PPP over SSL. There are problems inherent in these implementations because TCP is tunneled in TCP, but this is another topic for another time.

While hardware firewalls do not have the capability to inspect contents of an SSL tunnel and thus block access to application protocols hidden inside the tunnel, the ISA firewall is not hobbled by the limitations of hardware firewall architecture. The ISA firewall does much more than simple stateful filtering; it is able to break open the SSL encrypted tunnel, perform deep stateful application layer inspection of the contents, and then re-encrypt the communication and forward it to the site on the corporate network.

At this point, it should be clear that the ISA firewall provides a much higher level of security than a traditional stateful filtering hardware firewall. Today's attacks are at the application layer and are focused against servers and services on the corporate network that drive business.

This is not to say that the ISA firewall administrator's life is perfect. While the ISA firewall's "SSL bridging" feature allows it to provide a level of security orders of magnitude higher than what you see with hardware firewalls for *incoming* SSL connections, we still have to worry about SSL tunneled applications sourcing from the corporate network destined for Internet sites.

The ISA firewall performs inbound SSL bridging and stateful application layer inspection, but does not perform outbound SSL bridging. Outbound SSL bridging is what we need to prevent exploits contained in outbound SSL tunnels. Once outbound SSL bridging is available, you'll be able to block internal users from hiding HTTP tunneled applications in their encrypted SSL links.

Our advice is to be very wary of "SSL VPNs" and any other application that hides the real nature of its communications inside an SSL encrypted link. The ISA firewall can block or allow these applications when they must pass through a Web Publishing Rule, but not when they move through an Access Rule. It vital that you keep this in mind when creating Firewall policies.

Consider whether users really need outbound access to SSL sites. If so, you should strictly limit the sites to which they can establish SSL connection. Otherwise, users could leverage their permission to tunnel just about any protocol inside that SSL link, and you *do not* want that.

WARNING

Make sure that all users on your network and those who connect to resources through your ISA firewall are aware that you monitor communications moving through an encrypted tunnel (at the present time, only inbound connections using SSL bridging). Users must sign-off on this policy, and this policy should be reviewed and approved by corporate legal departments. Finally, you must do everything you can to prevent users from using SSL encrypted channels. You'll be surprised to find out that the overwhelming majority of SSL encrypted connections made through the ISA firewall are not for business purposes.

The ISA Server Link Translator

Link Translation solves a number of issues that may arise for external users connecting through the ISA firewall to an internal Web site.

The ISA firewall Link Translator is implemented as an ISA firewall Web filter. Because of the Link Translator's built-in functionality, and because it comes with a built-in default dictionary, you can use it right out of the box to solve many common problems encountered with proxy-based Web publishing scenarios.

For example, when pages on the internal Web site contain absolute URLs pointing to itself, the Link Translator will return the appropriate links to the external user, even when those URLs contain http:// prefixes and the external user connects to the Web site using https://.

The default Link Translator dictionary can also appropriately translate requests made to nonstandard ports. For example, if users connect to a Web site that is published on a nonstandard port, such as http://www.msfirewall.org:8181, link translation will include the port number in the URLs sent back to the external client.

When you enable link translation for a Web Publishing Rule, a Link Translation dictionary is automatically created. In most cases, you won't have to add to the default dictionary.

The default dictionary includes the following entries:

- Any occurrence on the Web site of the computer name specified on the **To** tab of the Web Publishing Rule Properties is replaced with the Web site name (or IP address).

   For example, if a rule redirects all requests for http://www.microsoft.com to an internal computer called SERVER1 (or 192.168.1.1), all occurrences of http://SERVER1 in the response page returned to the client are replaced with http://www.microsoft.com.

■ If a nondefault port is specified on the Web listener, that port is used when replacing links on the response page. If a default port is specified, the port is removed when replacing links on the response page. For example, if the Web listener is listening on TCP port 88, the responses returned to the Web client will include links to TCP port 88.

■ If the client specifies HTTPS in the request to the ISA firewall, the firewall will replace all occurrences of HTTP with HTTPS.

For example, suppose the ISA firewall publishes a site located on a machine with the internal name SERVER1. The ISA firewall publishes the site using the public name www.msfirewall.orgdocs. An external Web client then makes the following request:

```
GET /docs HTTP/1.1
Host: www.msfirewall.org
```

Note that the directory name in the request is not terminated by a slash (/). When the server running Internet Information Services (IIS) receives this request, it automatically returns a 302 response with the location header set to http://SERVER1/docs/, which is the internal name of the server followed by the directory name and terminated by a slash.

The ISA firewall's Link Translator then translates the response header value to http://www.msfirewall.org/docs/.

In this example, the following entries are automatically added to the Link Translation dictionary:

■ http://SERVER1 is mapped to http://www.msfirewall.org

■ http://SERVER1:80 is mapped to http://www.msfirewall.org

■ https://SERVER1 is mapped to https://www.msfirewall.org

■ https://SERVER1:443 is mapped to https://www.msfirewall.org

For security reasons, if an initial client request was sent via SSL, all links to the same Web server are translated to SSL. The following entries are automatically included in the Link Translation dictionary:

■ http://SERVER1 is mapped to https://www.msfirewall.org

■ http://SERVER1:80 is mapped to https://www.msfirewall.org

■ https://SERVER1 is mapped to https://www.msfirewall.org

■ https://SERVER1:443 is mapped to https://www.msfirewall.org

If the published Web site uses ports other than the default HTTP and SSL ports (for example, 88 for HTTP and 488 for SSL), links containing that port number will also be translated. For example:

- http://SERVER1:88 is mapped to http://www.msfirewall.org
- https://SERVER1:488 is mapped to https://www.msfirewall.org

In the same way, if the ISA firewall publishes the site using a Web listener on nondefault ports (for example, 85 for HTTP and 885 for SSL), links will be translated to the published ports:

- http://SERVER1 is mapped to http://www.msfirewall.org:85
- http://SERVER1:80 is mapped to http://www.msfirewall.org:85
- https://SERVER1 is mapped to https://www.msfirewall.org:885
- https://SERVER1:443 is mapped to https://www.msfirewall.org:885

NOTE

- Don't end the search string in the Link Translator dictionary with a terminating character. For example, use http://SERVER1, not http://SERVER1/.
- When adding an entry for a site name, also add an entry with the site name and port. For example, if you add the search string http://SERVER1 in the Link Translator dictionary, also add the search string http://SERVER1:80.
- Use both http:// and https://.
- Use caution when changing directory structures, as this will affect the settings in your Link Translation dictionary.
- Dictionaries with a large number of entries when applied to Web sites that have many links requiring translation could detrimentally impact ISA Server performance.

While the default dictionary is effective for most simple Web publishing scenario, things get a bit stickier when you publish more complex Web sites. For more complex Web publishing scenarios, or when complex ASP code is involved (for example, with SharePoint services), it's necessary to configure dictionary entries that map to names returned by the internal Web site.

The Link Translator checks the Content-type header of the response to determine whether link translation should be applied to the body of the message. The default settings allow for link translation only MIME types belonging to the HTML document's content group. The ISA firewall's Link Translator works by first looking for a Content-type header to determine if it needs to perform translation. If no Content-type header is present, the filter will look for a Content-location header to perform translation. If neither header is present, the filter will look at the file extension.

The Link Translator maps text strings according to the following rules:

- The Link Translator searches for the longest strings, then shorter strings, and finally the default strings.

- If the Link Translator finds a matching text string, it will then look at the next character to the right to see if it is a *terminating* character. The following are considered terminating characters:
  \t \r \n ;   ~ < !   "   & '   ) $)   *
  + ,   - /   > = ?   [\ ]   ^   { | }

- If the Link Translator finds a terminating character immediately to the right of the string, it will perform translation on that string.

For example, consider a scenario where the Link Translation dictionary is configured to replace "sps" with "extranet.external.net" and a response page returned by the Web server includes a hard-coded link to http://Sps/SpsDocs/. The Link Translator translates the string to http://extranet.external.net/SpsDocs/. However, if the response page includes a link to http://sps/sps-isa/, *both* instances of "sps" would be translated because they are both followed by a terminating character, resulting in http://extranet.external.net/extranet.external.net-isa/ being sent to the external client.

Because of these potential translation issues, it's critical that you understand the behavior of link translation mapping to prevent problems with your custom Link Translator dictionaries.

Determining Custom Dictionary Entries

You must test the behavior of the Link Translator to see if any custom dictionary entries are required. SharePoint Portal Services provides a fertile test bed for testing the Link Translator. Begin your test by connecting to a published SharePoint site using an external client and testing the functionality of the published site. You should look for links pointing to internal server names and links that use the wrong prefix (for example, http instead of https).

Be aware that some links will be included in client-side scripts returned to the browser for processing. You should therefore also view the HTML source code that is returned, not just the rendered HTML in the browser.

In the case of a published SharePoint site, it may be necessary to add custom dictionary entries. For example, even though the Link Translator is enabled, the search function on the SharePoint site may return results with both the wrong prefix (http instead of https) and internal server names.

In addition, after adding custom dictionary entries to fix these problems, the source code of the search results page contains JavaScript that includes references to the wrong prefix, causing errors to be returned to the browser when trying to perform an additional search from the search results page.

For example, after adding two dictionary entries to replace "http://" with "https://" and to replace "sps" with "extranet.external.net," the returned source code included the following strings in the client-side JavaScript code:

```
f.action='http:\/\/extranet.external.net\/Search.aspx', and
http:\\\/\\\/extranet.external.net\\\/Search.aspx
```

To fix this problem, it is necessary to explicitly map the shorter string "http:" to "https:". Importantly, it is necessary to include the colon (:) in the dictionary entry. Simply mapping "http" to "https" (without the colon) causes the entire site to be inaccessible.

It should be clear to you at this point that finding the correct custom dictionary entries can involve extensive and repetitive testing. Incorrect link translation mappings can break the Web site for external clients, so we highly recommend that you test configurations in your test lab before deploying link translation in a production environment.

Configuring Custom Link Translation Dictionary Entries

Custom Link Translation dictionaries are configured on a per-rule basis. Remember, link translation is only performed on links returned by Web servers published by Web Publishing Rules; you do not configure Link Translation for outgoing requests to Internet Web servers.

To configure Link Translation:

1. Right-click the Web Publishing Rule and click **Properties**.

2. In the Web Publishing Rule's **Properties** dialog box, click the **Link Translation** tab.

3. On the **Link Translation** tab, put a checkmark in the **Replace absolute links in Web pages** checkbox. Click the **Add** button.

4. In the **Add/Edit Dictionary Item** dialog box, enter the name of the string you want replaced in returned links in the **Replace this text** text box. Enter the value you want to replace the string in the **With this text** text box. Click **OK**. (See Figure 10.35.)

Figure 10.35 Add/Edit Dictionary Text Box

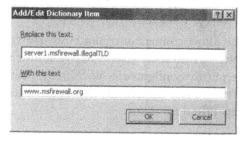

5. The dictionary entry appears in the list of dictionary entries. Click the **Content Types** button. (See Figure 10.36.)

Figure 10.36 Link Translation Tab in Web Publishing Rule Properties

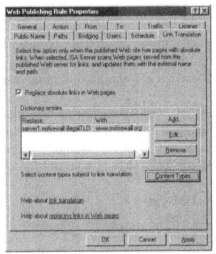

6. In the **Link Translation** dialog box, select the content types to which you want to apply Link Translation. By default, only the **HTML Documents** content type is selected. Your selection here is global and applies to all Web Publishing Rules. Even though you can create custom dictionaries for each Web Publishing Rule, the content types are the same for all dictionaries.

WARNING

The Web Publishing Rule must list an explicit fully qualified domain name (FQDN) or IP address in order to perform link translation. If you configure the Web Publishing Rule to redirect for all incoming connections to the listener, you will see an error dialog box informing you that you must use an explicit FQDN or IP address on the **Public** tab of the Web Publishing Rule's **Properties** dialog box.

The Web Proxy Filter

The Web Proxy filter allows connections from hosts not configured as Web Proxy clients to be forwarded to the ISA firewall's Cache and Web Proxy components. If you want only hosts that are explicitly configured as Web Proxy clients to use the ISA firewall's Web Proxy feature set, you can unbind the Web Proxy filter by removing the checkmark from the **Web Proxy Filter** checkbox.

Figure 10.37 The HTTP Properties Dialog Box

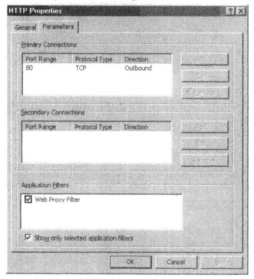

The SecurID Filter

The SecurID filter is used to mediate SecurID authentication with the ISA firewall. The SecurID filter configuration interface is accessed via the Authentication Properties dialog box for the Web listener. Figures 10.38 and 10.39 show the configuration interfaces.

Figure 10.38 The HTTP Properties Dialog Box and RSA SecurID Tab

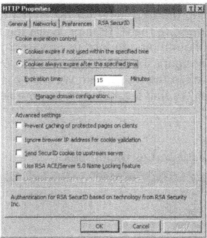

Figure 10.39 The Manage Domain Configuration Dialog Box

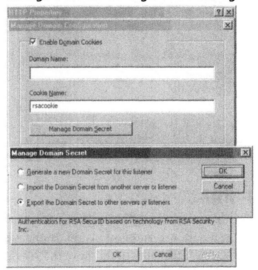

The OWA Forms-based Authentication Filter

The OWA Forms-Based Authentication filter is used to mediate Forms-based authentication to OWA Web sites that are made accessible via ISA firewall Web Publishing Rules. Figure 10.40 shows the configuration interface for the OWA Forms-Based Authentication filter, which is accessible from the Authentication dialog box for the Web listener.

For more information on the OWA Forms-Based Authentication filter, see Chapter 8, "Web and Server Publishing."

Figure 10.40 The OWA Forms-Based Authentication Dialog Box

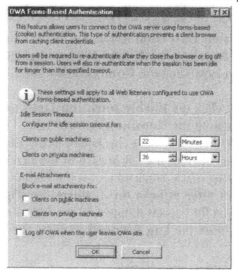

The RADIUS Authentication Filter

The RADIUS Authentication filter is used to mediate RADIUS authentication for Web Proxy clients and external hosts connecting to published Web sites via Web Publishing Rules.

The RADIUS filter is used by Web listeners when the listeners are configured to use RADIUS authentication. While the RADIUS filter provides you the ability to authenticate against any RADIUS-compliant directory (including the Active Directory), it does limit you to use only RADIUS authentication on the listener configured to use RADIUS. In contrast, when using other authentication methods, such as basic or integrated authentication, you can support multiple authentication protocols on a single Web listener.

For more information on using the RADIUS filter and configuring the RADIUS filter for forward and reverse Web Proxy scenarios, see Chapter 8 and Chapter 6, "Configuring Outbound Access through an ISA Firewall."

IP Filtering and Intrusion Detection/Intrusion Prevention

The ISA firewall performs intrusion detection and intrusion prevention. In this section, we discuss the following intrusion detection and intrusion prevention features:

- Common Attacks Detection and Prevention
- DNS Attacks Detection and Prevention
- IP Options and IP Fragment Filtering

Common Attacks Detection and Prevention

You can access the **Intrusion Detection** dialog box by opening the **Microsoft Internet Security and Acceleration Server 2004** management console, expanding the server name, and then expanding the **Configuration** node. Click the **General** node.

In the **General** node, click the **Enable Intrusion Detection and DNS Attack Detection** link. This brings up the **Common Attacks** tab.

On the **Common Attacks** tab, put a checkmark in the **Enable intrusion detection** checkbox. Put a checkmark to the left of each of the attacks you want to prevent. If you enable the **Port scan** attack, enter values for the **Detect after attacks … well-known ports** and **Detect after attacks on … ports**. (See Figure 10.41.)

You can disable logging for packets dropped by the Intrusion Detection filter by removing the checkmark from the **Log dropped packets** checkbox.

Figure 10.41 The Common Attacks Tab

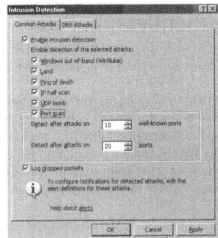

Denial-of-Service Attacks

Denial-of-service (DoS) attacks are one of the most popular choices of Internet hackers who want to disrupt a network's operations. Although they do not destroy or steal data as some other types of attacks do, the objective of the DoS attacker is to bring down the network, denying service to its legitimate users. DoS attacks are easy to initiate; software is readily available from hacker Web sites and warez newsgroups that will allow anyone to launch a DoS attack with little or no technical expertise.

NOTE

> *Warez* is a term used by hackers and crackers to describe bootlegged software that has been "cracked" to remove copy protections and made available by software pirates on the Internet, or in its broader definition, to describe any illegally distributed software.

In February 2000, massive DoS attacks brought down several of the biggest Web sites, including Yahoo.com and Buy.com.

The purpose of a DoS attack is to render a network inaccessible by generating a type or amount of network traffic that will crash the servers, overwhelm the routers, or otherwise prevent the network's devices from functioning properly. Denial of service can be accomplished by tying up the server's resources; for example, by overwhelming the CPU and memory resources. In other cases, a particular user/machine can be the target of DoS attacks that hang up the client machine and require it to be rebooted.

NOTE

> DoS attacks are sometimes referred to in the security community as "nuke attacks."

Distributed Denial-of-Service Attack

Distributed DoS attacks use intermediary computers, called *agents,* on which programs called *zombies* have previously been surreptitiously installed. The hacker activates these zombie programs remotely, causing the intermediary computers (which can number in the hundreds or even thousands) to simultaneously launch the actual attack. Because the attack comes from the computers running the zombie programs, which may be on networks anywhere in the world, the hacker is able to conceal the true origin of the attack.

Examples of DDoS tools used by hackers are TFN (Tribe FloodNet), TFN2K, Trinoo, and Stacheldraht (German for "barbed wire"). While early versions of DDoS tools targeted UNIX and Solaris systems, TFN2K can run on both UNIX and Windows systems.

Because DDoS attacks are so popular, many tools have been developed to help you detect, eliminate, and analyze DDoS software that may be installed on your network. The National Infrastructure Protection Center has recently announced one such tool to detect some types of DDoS programs on some systems. For more information, see www.fbi.gov/nipc/trinoo.htm.

NOTE

An excellent article that provides details on how TFN, TFN2K, Trinoo, and Stacheldraht work is available on the NetworkMagazine.com Web site, titled *Distributed Denial of Service Attacks,* at www.networkmagazine.com/ article/NMG20000512S0041.

It is important to note that DDoS attacks pose a two-layer threat. Your network could be the target of a DoS attack that crashes your servers and prevents incoming and outgoing traffic, and your computers could be used as the "innocent middlemen" to launch a DoS attack against another network or site.

SYN Attack/LAND Attack

SYN attacks exploit the TCP "three-way handshake," the process by which a communications session is established between two computers. Because TCP (unlike UDP) is connection-oriented, a *session*, or direct one-to-one communication link, must be created prior to sending data. The client computer initiates the communication with the server (the computer whose resources it wants to access).

The "handshake" includes the following steps:

1. The client machine sends a SYN (synchronization request) segment.

2. The server sends an ACK message and a SYN, which acknowledges the client machine's request that was sent in step 1, and sends the client a synchronization request of its own. The client and server machines must synchronize each other's sequence numbers.

3. The client sends an ACK back to the server, acknowledging the server's request for synchronization. When both machines have acknowledged each other's requests, the handshake has been successfully completed and a connection is established between the two computers.

Figure 10.42 illustrates how the process works.

Figure 10.42 TCP Uses a "Three-Way Handshake" to Establish a Connection between Client and Server

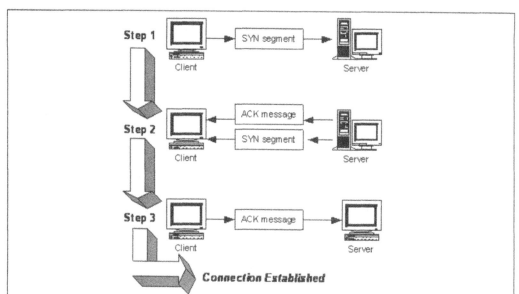

This is how the process normally works. A SYN attack uses this process to flood the system targeted as the victim of the attack with multiple SYN packets that have bad source IP addresses, which causes the system to respond with SYN/ACK messages. The problem comes in when the system, waiting for the ACK message from the client that normally comes in response to its SYN/ACK, puts the waiting SYN/ACK messages into a queue. This is a problem because the queue is limited in the number of messages it can handle. When it is full, all subsequent incoming SYN packets will be ignored. For a SYN/ACK to be removed from the queue, an ACK must be returned from the client, or the interval timer must run out and terminate the three-way handshake process.

Because the source IP addresses for the SYN packets sent by the attacker are no good, the ACKs that the server is waiting for never come. The queue stays full, and there is no room for valid SYN requests to be processed. Thus, service is denied to legitimate clients attempting to establish communications with the server.

The LAND attack is a variation on the SYN attack. In the LAND attack, instead of sending SYN packets with IP addresses that do not exist, the flood of SYN packets all have the same spoof IP address—that of the targeted computer.

The LAND attack can be prevented by filtering out incoming packets whose source IP addresses appear to be from computers on the internal network. ISA Server has preset intrusion detection functionality that allows you to detect attempted LAND attacks, and you can configure Alerts to notify you when such an attack is detected.

Ping of Death

Another type of DoS attack that ISA Server can be set to specifically detect is the so-called "Ping of Death" (also known as the "large packet ping"). The Ping of Death attack is launched by creating an IP packet larger than 65,536 bytes, which is the maximum allowed by the IP specification (this is sometimes referred to as a "killer packet"). This can cause the target system to crash, hang, or reboot.

ISA allows you to specifically enable detection of Ping of Death attacks.

Teardrop

The Teardrop attack works a little differently from the Ping of Death, but with similar results. The Teardrop program creates IP fragments, which are pieces of an IP packet into which an original packet can be divided as it travels through the Internet. The problem is that the offset fields on these fragments, which are supposed to indicate the portion (in bytes) of the original packet that is contained in the fragment, overlap.

For example, normally two fragments' offset fields might appear as:

```
Fragment 1:   (offset) 100 - 300
Fragment 2:   (offset) 301 - 600
```

This indicates that the first fragment contains bytes 100 through 300 of the original packet, and the second fragment contains bytes 301 through 600.

Overlapping offset fields would appear something like this:

```
Fragment 1: (offset) 100 - 300
Fragment 2: (offset) 200 - 400
```

When the destination computer tries to reassemble these packets, it is unable to do so and may crash, hang, or reboot.

Variations include:

- NewTear
- Teardrop2
- SynDrop
- Boink

All of these programs generate some sort of fragment overlap.

Ping Flood (ICMP Flood)

The ping flood or ICMP flood is a means of tying up a specific client machine. It is caused by an attacker sending a large number of ping packets (ICMP echo request packets) to the Winsock or dialer software. This prevents it from responding to server ping activity requests, which causes the server to eventually time out the connection. A symptom of a ping flood is a huge amount of modem activity, as indicated by the modem lights. This is also referred to as a *ping storm*.

The *fraggle attack* is related to the ping storm. Using a spoofed IP address (which is the address of the targeted victim), an attacker sends ping packets to a subnet, causing all computers on the subnet to respond to the spoofed address and flood it with echo reply messages.

> **NOTE**
>
> During the Kosovo crisis, the fraggle attack was frequently used by pro-Serbian hackers against U.S. and NATO sites to overload them and bring them down.

You can use programs such as NetXray or other IP tracing software to record and display a log of the flood packets. Firewalls can be configured to block ping packets, to prevent these attacks.

SMURF Attack

The Smurf attack is a form of "brute force" attack that uses the same method as the ping flood, but directs the flood of ICMP echo request packets at the network's router. The destination address of the ping packets is the broadcast address of the network, which causes the router to broadcast the packet to every computer on the network or segment. This can result in a very large amount of network traffic if there are many host computers, which can create congestion that causes a denial of service to legitimate users.

> **NOTE**
>
> The broadcast address is normally represented by all 1s in the host ID. This means, for example, that on class C network 192.168.1.0, the broadcast address would be 192.168.1.255 (255 in decimal represents 11111111 in binary), and in a class C network, the last or z octet represents the host ID. A message sent to the broadcast address is sent simultaneously to all hosts on the network.

In its most insidious form, the Smurf attacker spoofs the source IP address of ping packets. Then, both the network to which the packets are sent *and* the network of the spoofed source IP address will be overwhelmed with traffic. The network to which the spoofed source address belongs will be deluged with responses to the ping when all the hosts to which the ping was sent answer the echo request with an echo reply.

Smurf attacks can generally do more damage than some other forms of DoS, such as SYN floods. The SYN flood affects only the capability of other computers to establish a TCP connection to the flooded server, but a Smurf attack can bring an entire ISP down for minutes or hours. This is because a single attacker can easily send 40 to 50 ping packets per second, even using a slow modem connection. Because each is broadcast to every computer on the destination network, the number of responses per second is 40 to 50 times the number of computers on the network—which could be hundreds or thousands. This is enough data to congest even a T-1 link.

One way to prevent a Smurf attack from using your network as the broadcast target is to turn off the capability to transmit broadcast traffic on the router. Most routers allow you to do this. To prevent your network from being the victim of the spoofed IP address, you will need to configure your firewall to filter out incoming ping packets.

UDP Bomb or UDP Flood

An attacker can use the User Datagram Protocol (UDP) and one of several services that echo packets upon receipt to create service-denying network congestion by generating a flood of UDP packets between two target systems. For example, the UDP chargen service on the first computer, which is a testing tool that generates a series of characters for every packet that it receives, sends packets to another system's UDP echo service, which echoes every character it receives. By exploiting these testing tools, an endless flow of echoes goes back and forth between the two systems, congesting the network. This is sometimes called a *UDP packet storm*.

In addition to port 7, the echo port, an attacker can use port 17, the quote of the day service (quotd) or the daytime service on port 13. These services will also echo packets they receive. UDP chargen is on port 19.

Disabling unnecessary UDP services on each computer (especially those mentioned previously) or using a firewall to filter those ports/services will protect you from this type of attack.

UDP Snork Attack

The Snork attack is similar to the UDP bomb. It uses a UDP frame that has a source port of either 7 (echo) or 9 (chargen), with a destination port of 135 (Microsoft location service). The result is the same as the UDP bomb—a flood of unnecessary transmissions that can slow performance or crash the systems that are involved.

WinNuke (Windows Out-of-Band Attack)

The out-of-band (OOB) attack, sometimes called the *Windows OOB bug*, exploits a vulnerability in Microsoft networks,. The WinNuke program (and variations such as Sinnerz and Muerte) creates an out-of-band data transmission that crashes the machine to which it is sent. It works like this: A TCP/IP connection is established with the target IP address, using port 139 (the NetBIOS port). Then, the program sends data using a flag called MSG_OOB (or Urgent) in the packet header. This flag instructs the computer's Winsock to send data called out-of-band data. Upon receipt, the targeted Windows server expects a pointer to the position in the packet where the Urgent data ends, with normal data following. However, the OOB pointer in the packet created by WinNuke points to the end of the frame with no data following.

The Windows machine does not know how to handle this situation and will cease communicating on the network, and service will be denied to any users who subsequently attempt to communicate with it. A WinNuke attack usually requires a reboot of the affected system to reestablish network communications.

Windows 95 and NT 3.51 and 4.0 are vulnerable to the WinNuke exploit, unless the fixes provided by Microsoft have been installed. Windows 98/ME and Windows 2000/2003 are not vulnerable to WinNuke, but ISA Server allows you to enable detection of attempted OOB attacks.

Mail Bomb Attack

A mail bomb is a means of overwhelming a mail server, causing it to stop functioning and thus denying service to users. It is a relatively simple form of attack, accomplished by sending a massive quantity of e-mail to a specific user or system. There are programs available on hacking sites on the Internet that allow a user to easily launch a mail bomb attack, automatically sending floods of e-mail to a specified address while protecting the attacker's identity.

A variation on the mail bomb program automatically subscribes a targeted user to hundreds or thousands of high-volume Internet mailing lists, which will fill the user's mailbox and/or the mail server. Bombers call this *list linking*. Examples of these mail bomb programs include Unabomber, extreme Mail, Avalanche, and Kaboom.

The solution to repeated mail bomb attacks is to block traffic from the originating network using packet filters. Unfortunately, this does not work with list linking because the originator's address is obscured; the deluge of traffic comes from the mailing lists to which the victim has subscribed.

Scanning and Spoofing

The term *scanner,* in the context of network security, refers to a software program that is used by hackers to remotely determine what TCP/UDP ports are open on a given system, and thus vulnerable to attack. Scanners are also used by administrators to detect vulnerabilities in their own systems in order to correct them before an intruder finds them. Network diagnostic tools such as the famous Security Administrator's Tool for Analyzing Networks (SATAN), a UNIX utility, include sophisticated port scanning capabilities.

A good scanning program can locate a target computer on the Internet (one that is vulnerable to attack), determine what TCP/IP services are running on the machine, and probe those services for security weaknesses.

NOTE

A common saying among hackers is: "A good port scanner is worth a thousand passwords."

Many scanning programs are available as freeware on the Internet. An excellent resource for information about the history of scanning, how scanners work, and some popular scanning programs can be found at www.ladysharrow.ndirect.co.uk/ Maximum%20Security/scanners.htm.

Port Scan

Port scanning refers to a means of locating "listening" TCP or UDP ports on a computer or router, and obtaining as much information as possible about the device from the listening ports. TCP and UDP services and applications use a number of *well-known ports*, which are widely published. The hacker uses his knowledge of these commonly used ports to extrapolate information.

For example, Telnet normally uses port 23. If the hacker finds that port open and listening, he knows that Telnet is probably enabled on the machine. He can then try to infiltrate the system; for example, by guessing the appropriate password in a brute-force attack.

DNS Attacks Detection and Prevention

The ISA firewall's DNS filter protects DNS servers published by the ISA firewall using Server Publishing Rules. You can access the configuration interface for the DNS filter's attack prevention configuration page in the **Intrusion Detection** dialog box. Expand the server name and then expand the **Configuration** node. Click the **General** node.

In the Details Pane, click the **Enable Intrusion Detection and DNS Attack Detection** link. In the **Intrusion Detection** dialog box, click the **DNS Attacks** tab. On the **DNS Attacks** tab, put a checkmark in the **Enable detection and filtering of DNS attacks** checkbox. (See Figure 10.43.)

Once detection is enabled, you can enable prevention, and protect yourself from three attacks:

- DNS host name overflow
- DNS length overflow
- DNS zone transfer

Figure 10.43 The DNS Attacks Tab

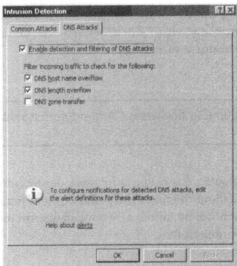

The *DNS host name overflow* and *DNS length overflow* attacks are DNS DoS type attacks. The DNS DoS attack exploits the difference in size between a DNS query and a DNS response, in which all of the network's bandwidth is tied up by bogus DNS queries. The attacker uses the DNS servers as "amplifiers" to multiply the DNS traffic.

The attacker begins by sending small DNS queries to each DNS server that contain the spoofed IP address (see *IP Spoofing*) of the intended victim. The responses returned to the small queries are much larger, so that if there are a large number of responses returned at the same time, the link will become congested and denial of service will take place.

One solution to this problem is for administrators to configure DNS servers to respond with a "refused" response, which is much smaller than a name resolution response, when they receive DNS queries from suspicious or unexpected sources.

Detailed information for configuring DNS servers to prevent this problem is contained in the U.S. Department of Energy's Computer Incident Advisory Capability information bulletin J-063, available at http://www.ciac.org/ciac/bulletins/j-063.shtml.

IP Options and IP Fragment Filtering

You can configure what IP Options are allowed through the ISA firewall and whether IP Fragments are allowed through. Figures 10.44 and 10.45 show the configuration interfaces for IP Options filtering and IP Fragment filtering. Figure 10.46 shows a dialog box warning that enabling Fragment filtering may interfere with L2TP/IPSec and streaming media services.

For more information on fragment filtering, see the discussion on common network layer attacks earlier in this chapter.

Figure 10.44 The IP Options Tab

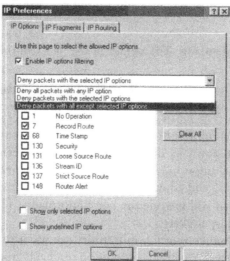

Figure 10.45 The IP Fragments Tab

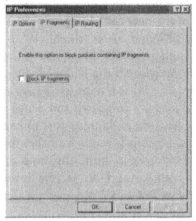

Figure 10.46 The IP Fragment Filter Warning Dialog Box

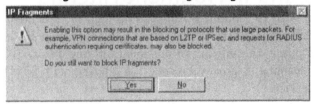

Source Routing Attack

TCP/IP supports *source routing*, which is a means to permit the sender of network data to route the packets through a specific point on the network. There are two types of source routing:

- **Strict source routing** The sender of the data can specify the exact route (rarely used).

- **Loose source record route (LSRR)** The sender can specify certain routers (hops) through which the packet must pass.

The source route is an option in the IP header that allows the sender to override routing decisions that are normally made by the routers between the source and destination machines. Source routing is used by network administrators to map the network, or for troubleshooting routing and communications problems. It can also be used to force traffic through a route that will provide the best performance. Unfortunately, source routing can be exploited by hackers.

If the system allows source routing, an intruder can use it to reach private internal addresses on the LAN that normally would not be reachable from the Internet, by routing the traffic through another machine that is reachable from both the Internet and the internal machine.

Source routing can be disabled on most routers to prevent this type of attack. The ISA firewall also blocks source routing by default.

Summary

In this chapter, we discussed the ISA firewall's application layer filtering feature set. We discussed the two main types of application filters employed by the ISA firewall: access filters and security filters. While we broke down the ISA firewall's filters into these two main categories, this is not to say that access filters are unsecure. Both the access filters and the security filters impose requirements that the connections meet specifications of legitimate communications using those protocols.

We finished the chapter with a discussion of the ISA firewall's intrusion detection and prevention mechanisms. You learned about common network layer attacks that can be launched against the ISA firewall and how the ISA firewall protects you against them.

Solutions Fast Track

Application Layer Filters

☑ Application layer filters perform stateful application layer inspection on non-Web protocols.

☑ There are application layers for the most common application layer protocols used to connect to the Internet.

Web Filters

☑ Web filters are used to filter HTTP, HTTPS, and FTP tunneled connections through the ISA firewall.

☑ You cannot disable the Web Proxy filter for Web Publishing Rules.

Intrusion Detection and Prevention

☑ The ISA firewall automatically protects you against common network layer attacks; this is the ISA firewall's intrusion protection feature.

☑ The ISA firewall can be configured to detect and report common attacks. This is the ISA firewall's intrusion detection feature.

☑ Even when the ISA firewall is not configured to detect an intrusion, it will protect you against it.

☑ The DNS filter protects published Web servers from common buffer overflow exploits, and prevents remote users from performing a zone transfer from your published DNS servers.

☑ You can configure the ISA firewall to allow specific IP Options when required for network diagnostics and then disable those options after the diagnostics are completed.

Frequently Asked Questions

The following Frequently Asked Questions, answered by the authors of this book, are designed to both measure your understanding of the concepts presented in this chapter and to assist you with real-life implementation of these concepts. To have your questions about this chapter answered by the author, browse to **www.syngress.com/solutions** and click on the **"Ask the Author"** form. You will also gain access to thousands of other FAQs at ITFAQnet.com.

Q: Can I use Forms-based Authentication for non-OWA sites?

A: Yes. You can use FBA for any site you publish using a Web Publishing Rule. However, some users have reported unexpected results, so you should test this feature thoroughly before using it for non-OWA sites in a production environment.

Q: Can I install the SMTP Message Screener on the ISA firewall machine?

A: Yes. The ISA firewall machine can be configured as an inbound and outbound SMTP relay for your company. In addition, you can install the SMTP Message Screener on the Exchange Server. However, we do not recommend that you install the SMTP Message Screener on the Exchange Server machine.

Q: Some of the URLs returned by my SharePoint site aren't reachable from remote clients via a Web Publishing Rule. I configured the Link Translator to changes the links, but it doesn't seem to work all the time. What's up with that?

A: While the Link Translator can reliably change the links returned to the Web client by the SharePoint site, some of the links are actually created on the client machine itself via a client-side script. Since the ISA firewall's Link Translator does not pre-process the client-side script during the translation, these links break. We expect either a feature pack or future versions of the ISA firewall to include enhanced support for SharePoint server publishing and solve this problem.

Q: Our security officer won't allow us to join the ISA firewall to the domain, although he can't come up with any cogent reason for not making the ISA firewall a domain member. However, we must go by his policy. We would like to use the ISA firewall's Forms-based Authentication feature for OWA publishing, but we will need to use RADIUS authentication. Is there any way we can do this?

A: Yes. However, at the time of writing, the fix is part of a hotfix. We expect the hotfix to be rolled up in the first ISA firewall feature pack. Check out *You cannot use the RADIUS authentication protocol when you use the Outlook Web Access (OWA)*

Forms-Based Authentication on a Web publishing rule to publish an internal Web site such as OWA in ISA Server 2004 at http://support.microsoft.com/default.aspx?scid=kb;en-us;884560 for more information.

Q: You didn't include much information about the SecurID filter and how to use SecurID in this chapter. Why is that, and how can I get more information on SecurID?

A: We wanted to put some detailed information on SecurID in this book, but unfortunately were not able to get anyone at RSA to answer our requests for information. If we are able to get someone at RSA to follow up with us, we'll include detailed SecurID authentication information at www.isaserver.org.

Q: Does the MMS filter work for both inbound and outbound connections? I tried to publish a Microsoft Media Server on a Windows Server 2003 machine using an MMS Server Publishing Rule but it didn't work. Is there a way to configure the filter to support MMS Server Publishing Rules?

A: .The MMS filter does work for both inbound and outbound connections. However, your site may be using RTSP instead of MMS. Try creating a Server Publishing Rule using the RTSP protocol and see if that solves your problem.

Chapter 11

Accelerating Web Performance with ISA 2004 Caching Capabilities

Topics in this Chapter:

- **Understanding Caching Concepts**

- **Understanding ISA Server 2004's Web Caching Capabilities**

- **Configuring ISA Server 2004 as a Caching Server**

- **Comparing ISA Server 2004 to Third-Party Caching Solutions**

With the growing emphasis on security and firewall capabilities, it's easy to forget that ISA Server 2004 provides a second important function: performance acceleration for your network's internal and external Web users. This is done via the caching feature, and it's a feature that most of ISA Server's top competitors in the firewall market don't include with their products.

The Web is a vital part of many of today's businesses. Members of your organization may access Web sites on the Internet every day, to gather information about particular subjects, conduct research on people and things, stay on top of the news affecting your industry, and so forth. At the same time, your own Web site(s) may be one of your best vehicles for advertising and promoting your business and providing information to partners and clients.

Within most Internet-connected organizations, the amount of Web traffic has been growing consistently. Users often visit the same Web sites on a regular basis, or multiple users within the organization visit the same sites and view the same pages. In addition, overall network and Internet traffic is steadily increasing, often to the point of near saturation of available Internet bandwidth. Caching can be the solution.

Understanding Caching Concepts

It can be costly to add additional Internet bandwidth. Some ISPs charge T-1 and T-3 users on a usage basis, so reducing bandwidth usage can result in real savings to the bottom line. Even if your organization buys bandwidth on an unlimited plan, reducing usage can increase performance for the network's users. There are two different types of caching—forward and reverse—that can benefit your organization, and we will discuss them in this section. Caching servers can also be deployed in groups, and these groups can be arranged in two different architectures, depending on your network's needs.

NOTE

Just in case you were anticipating that the two types of caching would be *active* and *passive*, please note that, as discussed in Chapter 2, ISA Server 2004 no longer supports active caching, although there is a setting for it in the interface.

In the following sections, we will look at the differences between the two types of Web caching, the architectures used to deploy multiple caching servers, and the protocols that are used by caching servers to communicate with one another.

Web Caching Types

As stated above, there are two basic types of Web caching:

- Forward caching
- Reverse caching

ISA Server 2004 performs both of these, so let's look at each a little more closely.

Forward Caching

One way to reduce Internet bandwidth consumption is to store frequently-accessed Web objects on the local network, where they can be retrieved by internal users without going out to a server on the Internet. This is called forward Web caching, and it has the added advantage of making access for internal users faster because they are retrieving the Web objects (such as pages, graphics, and sound files) over a fast LAN connection, typically 100Mbps or more, instead of a slower Internet connection at perhaps 1.5Mbps.

Forward caching is supported by all Web caching servers. Forward caching accelerates the response to outbound requests when users on the internal network request a Web object from a server on the Internet. Those objects that are requested frequently are stored on the caching server. This means they can be retrieved via the fast local network connection instead of over a slower Internet connection.

Forward caching takes place when a user on a network protected by the ISA Server 2004 firewall makes a request for Web content. The requested content is placed in the Web cache after the first user makes a request. The next (and subsequent) user who requests the same content from the Internet has the content delivered from the Web cache on the ISA Server 2004 machine instead of from the Internet Web server. This reduces the amount of traffic on the Internet connection and reduces overall network costs. In addition, the content is delivered to the user much more quickly from cache than it is from the actual Web server. This increases user satisfaction and productivity.

The primary "bottom line" benefit of ISA Server 2004's forward caching is cost savings realized by reduced bandwidth usage on the Internet connection.

Reverse Caching

Reverse caching, in contrast, reduces traffic on the internal network and speeds access for external users when the company hosts its own Web sites. Frequently-requested objects on the internal Web servers are cached at the network edge, on a proxy server, so that the load on the Web servers is reduced.

Reverse caching is appropriate when your organization hosts its own internal Web sites that are made available to external Internet or intranet users. The caching server stores those objects that are frequently requested from the internal Web servers and serves them to Internet users. This speeds access for the external users and it also lightens the load on the internal Web servers and reduces traffic on the internal network.

Reverse caching takes place when a user on the Internet makes a request for Web content that is located on a Web server published by an ISA Server 2004 Web Publishing Rule. The ISA Server 2004 firewall retrieves the content from the Web server on an internal network or another network protected by the firewall and returns that information to the Internet user who requested the content. The ISA Server 2004 machine caches the content it retrieves from the Web server on the internal network. When subsequent users request the same information, the content is served from the ISA Server 2004 cache instead of being retrieved from the originating Web site.

There are two principle benefits to the reverse caching scenario:

- Reverse caching reduces bandwidth usage on the internal network.

- Reverse caching allows Web content to be available when the Web server is offline.

How Reverse Caching Reduces Bandwidth Usage

Reverse caching reduces bandwidth usage on the internal network when cached content is served directly from the ISA Server 2004 machine. No bandwidth usage is required on the internal network; thus, this bandwidth becomes available to internal network users. Corporate networks that are already having issues with insufficient bandwidth will benefit from this configuration.

How Reverse Caching Increases Availability of Web Content

There is an even more compelling advantage to reverse caching: its ability to make Web site content available when the Web server is offline. This can be part of a high-availability plan for your Web services.

Web servers can go offline for several reasons. For example, the Web server will be down for a time when routine maintenance needs to be performed or after the server experiences a hardware or software crash. No matter why the server is offline, downtime can create a negative experience, ranging from a minor inconvenience to a serious problem, for Internet users when they try to access content on the site. The big advantage of the ISA Server 2004 reverse caching feature is that it makes it possible for you to take the Web server offline and still have Web site content available to Internet users because the content is served from the ISA Server 2004 cache.

Web Caching Architectures

Multiple Web-caching servers can be used together to provide for more efficient caching. There are two basic caching architectures that use multiple caching servers working together:

- Distributed Caching
- Hierarchical Caching

As the name implies, distributed caching distributes, or spreads, the cached Web objects across two or more caching servers. These servers are all on the same level on the network. Figure 11.1 illustrates how distributed caching works.

Figure 11.1 How Distributed Caching Works

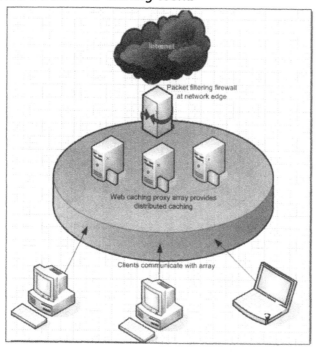

Hierarchical caching works a little differently. In this setup, caching servers are placed at different levels on the network. Upstream caching servers communicate with downstream proxies. For example, a caching server is placed at each branch office. These servers communicate with the caching array at the main office. Requests are serviced first from the local cache, then from a centralized cache before going out to the Internet server for the request.

Hierarchical caching is illustrated in Figure 11.2.

Figure 11.2 How Hierarchical Caching Works

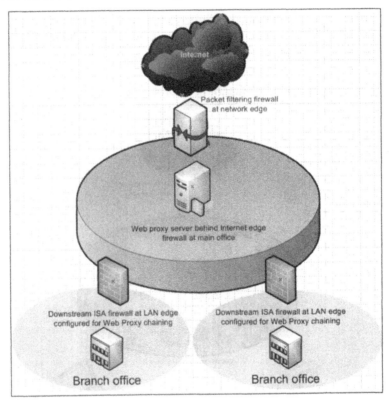

Finally, you can combine the two methods to create a hybrid caching architecture. The combination gives you the "best of both worlds," improving performance and efficiency. A hybrid caching architecture is shown in Figure 11.3.

Figure 11.3 A Hybrid Caching Architecture

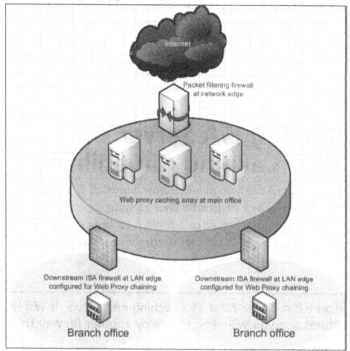

Web Caching Protocols

When multiple Web caching servers work together, they need a way to communicate with each other, so that if the Web object requested by the client isn't found in a server's cache, it can query other caching servers before the "last resort" of going out and retrieving the document from the Internet.

There are a number of different protocols that can be used for communications between Web caching servers. The most popular of these are the following:

- **Cache Array Routing Protocol (CARP),** a hash-based protocol that allows multiple caching proxies to be arrayed as a single logical cache and uses a hash function to ascertain to which cache a request should be sent. The hash function can also be used by the Web Proxy client to determine where the content is located in a distributed cache.

- **Internet Cache Protocol (ICP),** a message-based protocol defined in RFC 2186 that is based on UDP/IP and was originally used for hierarchical caching by the Harvest project, from which the Squid open-source caching software was derived.

- **HyperText Caching Protocol (HTCP),** which permits full request and response headers to be used in cache management.

- **Web Cache Coordination Protocol (WCCP),** a router-based protocol that removes distribution of requests from the caches and uses service groups to which caches belong. The router calculates hash functions.

- **Cache digests,** a hash-based protocol that is implemented in Squid, which uses an array of bits called a *Bloom filter* to code a summary of documents stored by each proxy.

Understanding ISA Server 2004's Web Caching Capabilities

ISA Server 2004 can act as a firewall, as a combined firewall and Web caching server (the best "bang for the buck"), or as a dedicated Web caching server. You can deploy ISA Server 2004 as a forward caching server or a reverse caching server. The Web proxy filter is the mechanism that ISA Server 2004 uses to implement caching functionality.

WARNING

If you configure ISA Server 2004 as a caching-only server, it will lose most of its firewall features and you will need to deploy another firewall to protect the network.

ISA Server 2004 supports both forward caching (for outgoing requests) and reverse caching (for incoming requests). The same ISA Server can perform both forward and reverse caching at the same time.

With forward caching the ISA Server sits between the internal clients and the Web servers on the Internet. When an internal client sends a request for a Web object (a Web page, graphics or other Web file), it must go through the ISA Server. Rather than forwarding the request out to the Internet Web server, the ISA Server checks its cache to determine whether a copy of the requested object already resides there (because someone on the internal network has previously requested it from the Internet Web server).

If the object is in cache, the ISA Server sends the object from cache, and there is no need to send traffic over the Internet. Retrieving the object from the ISA Server's cache on the local network is faster than downloading it from the Internet Web server, so internal users see an increase in performance.

If the object isn't in the ISA Server's cache, the ISA Server sends a request for it to the Internet Web server. When it is returned, the ISA Server stores the object in cache so that the next time it is requested, that request can be fulfilled from the cache.

With reverse caching, the ISA Server acts as an intermediary between external users and the company's Web servers. When a request for an object on the company Web server comes in from a user over the Internet, the ISA Server checks its cache for the object. If it's there, the ISA Server impersonates the internal Web server and fulfills the external user's request without ever "bothering" the Web server. This reduces traffic on the internal network.

In either case, the cache is an area on the ISA Server's hard disk that is used to store the requested Web objects. You can control the amount of disk space to be allocated to the cache (and thus, the maximum size of the cache). You can also control the maximum size of objects that can be cached, to ensure that a few very large objects can't "hog" the cache space.

Caching also uses system memory. Objects are cached to RAM as well as to disk. Objects can be retrieved from RAM more quickly than from the disk. ISA Server 2004 allows you to determine what percentage of random access memory can be used for caching (by default, ISA Server 2004 uses 10 percent of the RAM, and then caches the rest of the objects to disk only). You can set the percentage at anything from 1percent to 100 percent. The RAM allocation is set when the Firewall service starts. If you want to change the amount of RAM to be used, you have to stop and restart the Firewall service.

The ability to control the amount of RAM allocated for caching ensures that caching will not take over all of the ISA Server computer's resources.

NOTE

In keeping with the emphasis on security and firewall functionality, caching is *not* enabled by default when you install ISA Server 2004. You must enable it before you can use the caching capabilities.

Using the Caching Feature

Configuring a *cache drive* enables both forward and reverse caching on your ISA Server 2004 computer. We'll show you how to enable caching in the section titled *Configuring ISA Server 2004 as a Caching Server* later in this chapter.

There are a few requirements and recommendations for the drive that you use as the cache drive:

- The cache drive must be a local drive. You can't configure a network drive to hold the cache.

- The cache drive must be on an NTFS partition. You can't use FAT or FAT32 partitions for the cache drive.

- It is best (but not required) that you not use the same drive on which the operating system and/or ISA Server application are installed. Performance will be improved if the cache is on a separate drive. In fact, for best performance, not only should it be on a separate drive, but the drive should be on a separate I/O channel (that is, the cache drive should not be on a drive slaved with the drive that contains the page file, OS, or ISA program files). Furthermore, if performance of ISA Server is a consideration, MSDE logging consumes more disk resources than text logging. Therefore, if MSDE logging is used, the cache drive should also be on a separate spindle from the MSDE databases.

TIP

You can use the convert.exe utility to convert a FAT or FAT32 partition to NTFS, if necessary, without losing your data.

The file in which the cache objects are stored is named dir1.cdat. It is located in the urlcache folder on the drive that you have configured for caching. This file is referred to as the *cache content file*. If the file reaches its maximum size, older objects will be removed from the cache to make room for new objects.

A cache content file cannot be larger than 64GB (you can set a smaller maximum size, of course). If you want to use more than 64GB for cache, you must configure multiple drives for caching and spread the cache over more than one file.

WARNING

You should never try to edit or delete the cache content file.

Understanding Cache Rules

ISA Server 2004 uses cache rules to allow you to customize what types of content will be stored in the cache and exactly how that content will be handled when a request is made for objects stored in cache.

You can create rules to control the length of time that a cache object is considered to be valid (ensuring that objects in the cache don't get hopelessly out of date), and you can specify how cached objects are to be handled after they expire.

ISA Server 2004 gives you the flexibility to apply cache rules to all sites or just to specific sites. A rule can further be configured to apply to all types of content or just to specified types.

Using Cache Rules to Specify Content Types That Can Be Cached

A cache rule lets you specify which of the following types of content are to be cached:

- **Dynamic content** This is content that changes frequently, and thus, is marked as not cacheable. If you select to cache dynamic content, retrieved objects will be cached even though they are marked as not cacheable.

- **Content for offline browsing** In order for users to be able to browse while offline (disconnected from the Internet), all content needs to be stored in the cache. Thus, when you select this option, ISA Server 2004 will store all content, including "non-cacheable" content, in the cache.

- **Content requiring user authentication for retrieval** Some sites require that users be authenticated before they can access the content. If you select this option, ISA Server 2004 will cache content that requires user authentication.

You can also specify a **Maximum object size**. By using this option, you can set limits on the size of Web objects that will be cached under a particular cache rule.

Using Cache Rules to Specify How Objects are Retrieved and Served from Cache

In addition to controlling content type and object size, a cache rule can control how ISA Server will handle the retrieval and service of objects from the cache. This refers to the validity of the object. An object's validity is determined by whether its Time to Live (TTL) has expired. Expiration times are determined by the HTTP or FTP caching properties or the object's properties. Your options include:

- **Setting ISA Server 2004 to retrieve only valid objects from cache (those that have not expired).** If the object has expired, the ISA server will send the request on to the Web server where the object is stored and retrieve it from there.

- **Setting ISA Server 2004 to retrieve requested objects from the cache even if they aren't valid.** In other words, if the object exists in the cache, ISA Server will retrieve and serve it from there even if it has expired. If there is no version of the object in the cache, the ISA Server will send the request to the Web server and retrieve it from there.

- **Setting ISA Server to never route the request.** In this case, the ISA Server relies only upon the cache to retrieve the object. Objects will be returned from cache whether or not they are valid. If there is no version of the object in the cache, the ISA Server will return an error. It will *not* send the request to the Web server.

- **Setting ISA Server to never save the object to cache.** If you configure the rule this way, the requested object will never be saved to the cache.

NOTE

The default TTL for FTP objects is one day. TTL boundaries for cached HTTP objects (which are defined in the cache rule) consist of a percentage of the age of the content, based on when it was created or last changed.

You can also control whether HTTP and FTP content are to be cached for specific destinations, and you can set expiration policies for the HTTP and FTP objects. You can also control whether to enable caching of SSL content.

> **TIP**
>
> Because SSL content often consists of sensitive information (which is the reason it's being protected by SSL), you might consider *not* enabling caching of this type of content for better security.

If you have multiple cache rules, they will be processed in order from first to last, with the default rule processed after all the custom rules. The default rule is automatically created when you install ISA Server 2004. It is configured to retrieve only valid objects from cache, and to retrieve the object from the Internet if there is no valid object in the cache.

We show you how to configure cache rules in the section titled *Configuring ISA Server 2004 as a Caching Server.*

Understanding the Content Download Feature

The content download feature is used to schedule ISA Server 2004 to download new content from the Internet at pre-defined times so that when Web Proxy clients request those objects, updated versions will be in the cache. This enhances performance and ensures that clients will receive up-to-date content more quickly.

You can monitor Internet access and usage (see Chapter 13, *Using ISA Server 2004's Monitoring, Logging, and Reporting Tools*) to determine which sites users access most frequently and predict which content will be requested in the future. Then you can schedule content download jobs accordingly. A content download job can be configured to periodically download one page (URL), multiple pages, or the entire site. You can also specify how many links should be followed in downloading the site. You can configure ISA Server 2004 to cache even those objects that are indicated as not cacheable in the cache control headers. However, a scheduled content download job won't complete if the Web server on which the object is stored requires client authentication.

To take advantage of this feature, you must enable the system policy configuration group for Scheduled Content Download Jobs, and then configure a content download job. We'll show you how to do that in the section titled *Configuring ISA Server as a Caching Server.*

> **TIP**
>
> When you enable the **Schedule Content Download Jobs** system policy configuration group, this causes ISA Server to block unauthenticated HTTP traffic from the local host (the ISA server) – even if you have another policy rule configured that would allow such traffic. There is a workaround that will make it possible

to allow this traffic and still use content download jobs. This involves creating a rule to allow HTTP access to All Networks and being sure that another rule higher in the order is configured to allow HTTP access from the local host.

Tools and Traps

How Webmasters Control Caching via HTTP Headers

There are two different factors that affect how HTTP (Web) content is cached. The configuration of the caching server is one, but Webmasters can also place information within the content and headers to indicate how their sites and objects should be cached.

Meta tags are commands within the HTML code of a document that specify HTTP expiration or non-cacheable status, but they are only processed by browser caches, not by proxy caches. However, HTTP headers are processed by both proxy caches and browser caches. They aren't inserted into the HTML code; they are configured on the Web server and sent by the Web server before the HTML content is sent.

HTTP 1.1 supports a category of headers called cache control response headers. Using these headers, the Webmaster can control such things as:

- maximum age (the maximum amount of time the object is considered valid, based on the time of the request).
- cacheability
- revalidation requirements

ETags and Last-Modified headers are generated by the Web server and used to validate whether an object is fresh.

In Microsoft Internet Information Services, cache control response headers are configured in the HTTP Headers tab of the property pages of the Web site or Web page.

ISA Server 2004 does not cache responses to requests that contain certain HTTP headers. These include:

- cache-control: no-cache response header
- cache-control: private response header
- pragma: no-cache response header
- www-authenticate response header
- set-cookie response header
- cache-control: no-store request header

Continued

> ■ authorization request header (except if the Web server also sends a cache-control: public response header)
>
> For more information about how the Webmaster can control caching with HTTP headers, see www.mnot.net/cache_docs/#IMP-SERVER.

Configuring ISA Server 2004 as a Caching Server

Although caching is not enabled by default, it is easy to configure ISA Server 2004 to perform forward and/or reverse caching. In this section, we will show you the step-by-step procedures for the following:

- Enabling caching

- Configuring the cache size and memory allocation for caching

- Creating cache rules

- Configuring content download jobs

Enabling and Configuring Caching

In this section, we'll look at how to enable, disable, and configure general properties of caching. The first step in using ISA Server 2004 as a caching server is to enable caching.

How to Enable Caching in Standard Edition

From the **Configuration | Cache** node of the ISA management console:

1.   In the left pane of the ISA Server 2004 MMC, expand the server name, and then expand the **Configuration** node.

2.   Right-click the **Cache** node in the left pane and select **Define Cache Drives,** or click the **Cache Rules** tab in the middle pane, and select **Define Cache Drives (enable caching)** from the right **Tasks** pane.

3.   In the **Define Cache Drives** dialog box, select an NTFS drive and type the desired number into the **Maximum cache size** field, then click the **Set** button, as shown in Figure 11.4.

Figure 11.4 Setting Maximum Cache Size

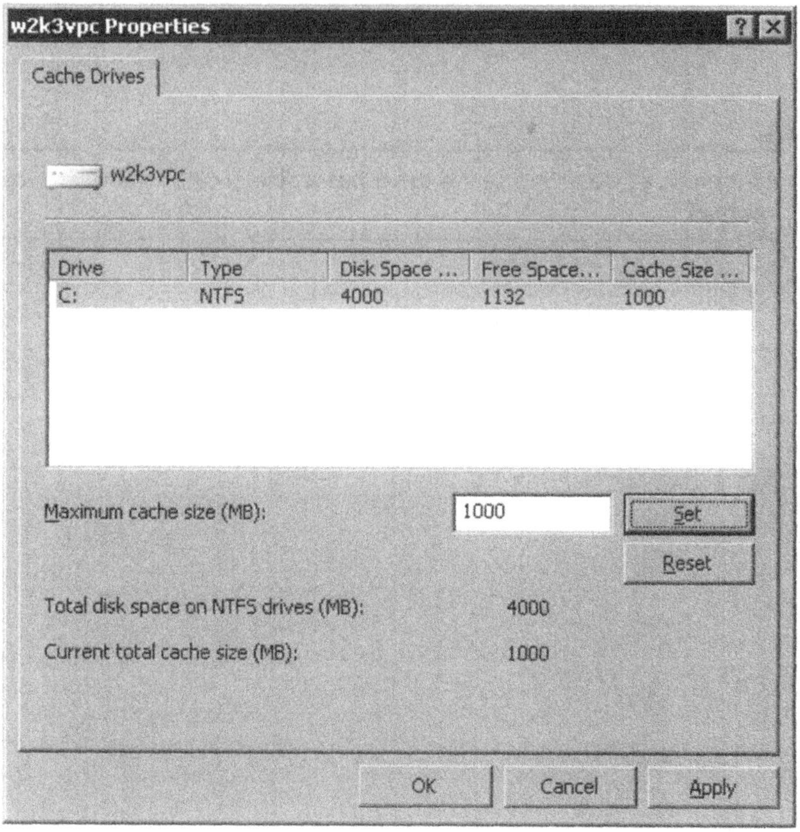

4.   Click **Apply** and then **OK.**

How to Disable Caching in Standard Edition

In ISA Server 2004 Standard Edition, you can disable caching by performing the following steps:

1. In the left pane of the ISA Server 2004 MMC, expand the server name, and then expand the **Configuration** node.

2. Right click the Cache node in the left pane and select **Disable Caching,** or click the **Cache Rules** tab in the middle pane and select **Disable Caching** in the right **Tasks** pane.

NOTE

Another way to set the drives to zero is by using the **Reset** button on the **Define Cache Drives** dialog box.

NOTE

As long as at least one cache drive has a size greater than zero, caching is enabled.

How to Configure Caching Properties

In this section, we look at how to configure general caching properties, including the following:

- Configuring which content to cache
- Configuring the maximum size of objects in the cache
- Configuring negative caching
- Configuring whether expired objects should be returned from cache
- Allocating a percentage of memory to caching

Let's address each of these, one at a time.

Configuring Which Content to Cache

To configure which content should be cached, follow these steps:

1. In the left pane of the ISA Server 2004 MMC, expand the server name.
2. Click the **Cache Rules** tab in the middle pane.
3. Click the **Tasks** tab in the right pane.
4. Click **Configure Cache Settings** in the **Related Tasks** section.
5. Click the **Advanced** tab in the **Cache Settings** dialog box.
6. Here you can select whether to cache objects that have an unspecified last modification time and objects that do not have an HTTP status code of 200 by checking or unchecking the appropriate checkbox, as shown in Figure 11.5. Both boxes are checked (thus, caching of these objects is enabled) by default.

Figure 11.5 Configuring Which Content to Cache

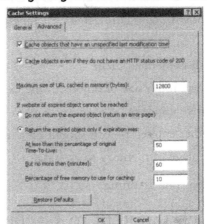

Configuring the Maximum Size of Objects in the Cache

This setting is made in the same **Cache Settings** dialog box as the previous setting.

1. In the left pane of the ISA Server 2004 MMC, expand the server name.
2. Click the **Cache Rules** tab in the middle pane.
3. Click the **Tasks** tab in the right pane.
4. Click **Configure Cache Settings** in the **Related Tasks** section.

5. Click the **Advanced** tab in the **Cache Settings** dialog box.

6. In the field labeled **Maximum size of URL cached in memory (bytes),** enter the desired number of bytes. This will limit the size of objects that can be cached and save space on your cache drive.

Configuring Whether Expired Objects Should be Returned from Cache

This setting, too, is made in the **Cache Settings** dialog box.

1. In the left pane of the ISA Server 2004 MMC, expand the server name.

2. Click the **Cache Rules** tab in the middle pane.

3, Click the **Tasks** tab in the right pane.

4. Click **Configure Cache Settings** in the **Related Tasks** section.

5. Click the **Advanced** tab in the **Cache Settings** dialog box.

6. If you prefer that an expired object not be returned if the Web site cannot be reached, select **Do not return the expired object.** An error page will be returned.

7. Alternatively, you can select to return the expired object if the expiration was less than a specified percentage of the original TTL, but no more than a specified number of minutes since the object expired. If you select this option, enter the desired numbers in the appropriate fields.

By default, ISA Server 2004 is configured to return the expired object only if the expiration was less than 50 percent of the original TTL and no more than 60 minutes.

Allocating a Percentage of Memory to Caching

This setting is also configured in the **Cache Settings** dialog box.

1. In the left pane of the ISA Server 2004 MMC, expand the server name.

2. Click the **Cache Rules** tab in the middle pane.

3. Click the **Tasks** tab in the right pane.

4. Click **Configure Cache Settings** in the **Related Tasks** section.

5. Click the **Advanced** tab in the **Cache Settings** dialog box.

6. In the field labeled **Percentage of free memory to use for caching,** enter the desired percentage.

The default amount of memory allocated for caching is 10 percent. When the percentage set here is exceeded, additional objects are cached only to disk (not to RAM).

Creating Cache Rules

In this section, we look at how to create and configure cache rules for various situations, how to modify an existing cache rule, and how to disable or delete a cache rule you have created, as well as how to change the order of rules. We also discuss how to copy, export, and import cache rules.

How to Create a Cache Rule

Creating a cache rule is made easy by the wizard that is built into ISA Server 2004. Just follow these steps:

1. In the left pane of the ISA Server 2004 MMC, expand the server name.

2. Click the **Cache Rules** tab in the middle pane.

3. Click the **Tasks** tab in the right pane.

4. In the **Cache Rule Tasks** section, click **Create a Cache Rule.** This will invoke the **New Cache Rule Wizard**, as shown in Figure 11.6.

Figure 11.6 Creating a New Cache Rule with the Wizard

5. Type in a name for your new cache rule, and then click **Next**.

6. On the next page, you'll be asked to select destination network entities. The rule will be applied to requests that are sent to these destinations. Click the **Add** button and select from the entities listed in the Add Network Entities dialog box, as shown in Figure 11.7.

Figure 11.7 Selecting Destinations to which the Cache Rule will Apply

7. Expand the top-level entities to see the specific entities beneath them. Highlight the entity you want to add, and then click **Add**. You can add multiple entities.

8. When you're finished adding entities, click **Close**.

9. Back on the **Cache Rule Destination** page of the wizard, click **Next**.

10. On the **Content Retrieval** page, you can control how cached objects will be retrieved when they are requested. Select from one of three choices for retrieving the object from cache:

   ■ Only if a valid version of the object exists in the cache (if no valid object exists, the request will be routed to the Web server where the original object is stored)

   ■ If any version of the object exists in the cache (if an invalid version exists in cache, it will be returned from cache. If no version exists in cache, the request will be routed to the Web server)

   ■ If any version of the object exists in cache (if no version exists in cache, the request will be dropped and the request will *not* be routed to the Web server)

   Make your selection and click **Next**.

11. On the **Cache Content** page, you can control whether particular types of content that are retrieved are to be cached. By default, an object is not stored in cache unless the source and destination headers instruct that it be cached. However, you can change that behavior here by making one of two selections: Never, (no objects will ever be cached); If source and request headers indicate

to cache (the default setting). If you select to cache objects, you can also control which of the following should be cached:

■   dynamic content

■   content for offline browsing

■   content requiring user authentication for retrieval.

By default, none of these is cached. You can select any number of these choices, as shown in Figure 11.8.

Figure 11.8 Configuring When to Store Content in Cache

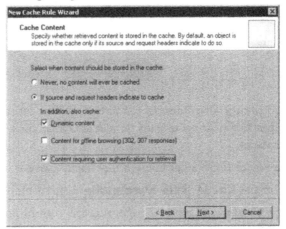

12.   After you have made your selections, click **Next**.

13.   On the **Cache Advanced Configuration** page, you can set a limit on the size of objects to be cached by checking the **Do not cache objects larger than:** checkbox and setting a size in kilobytes, megabytes or gigabytes, as shown in Figure 11.9.

Figure 11.9 Limiting the Size of Objects to be Cached and Caching SSL Responses

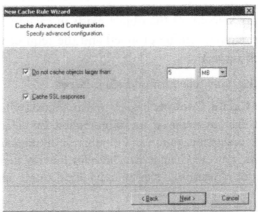

NOTE

By default, there is no limit set on the size of objects to be cached.

14. On this page, you can also select whether to cache SSL responses. By default, SSL responses are cached, but you might want to disable this for security purposes since SSL content may be sensitive, and you might not want copies of it sitting on the cache server.

15. After making your selections, click **Next**.

16. On the **HTTP Caching** page, you can enable or disable HTTP caching (it is enabled by default) and set the TTL of objects as a percentage of the content's age, based on when it was created or last modified. You can also set the TTL time boundaries, and select to apply the TTL boundaries to sources that specify expiration, as shown in Figure 11.10. By default, the TTL of objects is set at 20 percent of content age, and TTL time boundaries are set to no less than 15 minutes and no more than one day.

NOTE

The "created" and "last modified" dates are contained in the HTTP headers that are returned by the Web server.

Figure 11.10 Enabling HTTP Caching and Setting TTL Configuration

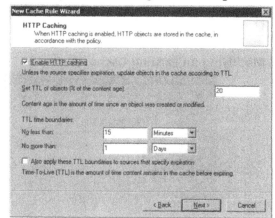

17. When you have made your selections, click **Next**.

18. On the **FTP Caching** page, you can enable or disable FTP caching (it is enabled by default). You can also set a TTL for FTP objects, as shown in Figure 11.11. The default TTL is one day.

Figure 11.11 Enabling FTP Caching and Setting the TTL Configuration

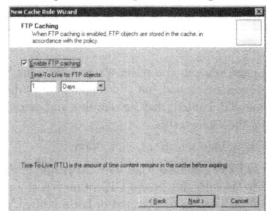

19   After making your selections, click **Next**.

20.   The last page of the wizard summarizes all the choices you have made. If you need to make changes, you can click the **Back** button to return to the appropriate page and modify your selections. Otherwise, click **Finish** to create the rule.

How to Modify an Existing Cache Rule

If you want to make changes to a cache rule that you've already created, highlight it in the **Cache Rules** tab in the middle pane of the ISA Server 2004 MMC, and click **Edit Selected Rule** in the right **Task** pane, or right-click the rule you want to modify and select **Properties**. Either method will open the **<Rule name> Properties** box, as shown in Figure 11.12.

Figure 11.12 Modifying an Existing Cache Rule

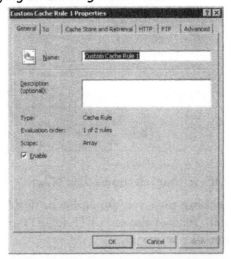

On the **General** tab, you can change the name of the cache rule or insert an optional description to describe the rule.

On the **To** tab, you can change, add, edit, or remove destination network entities. On this page, you can also configure exceptions, as shown in Figure 11.13. In our example, the cache rule will apply to all content requested from external entities, except those from shinder.net.

Figure 11.13 Configuring Exceptions to the Destination Network Entities

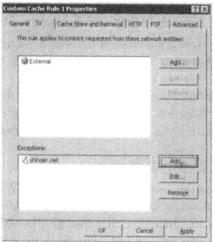

On the **Cache Store and Retrieval** tab, you can change the selections you made in the wizard regarding when to retrieve content from cache and when to store content in cache.

On the **HTTP** tab, you can enable or disable HTTP caching and modify your TTL configurations. You can also restore the defaults with the click of a button.

On the **FTP** tab, you can enable or disable FTP caching, change the TTL settings, or restore the defaults.

On the **Advanced** tab, you can set or change the size limit for objects to be cached and change your settings for caching SSL responses.

How to Disable or Delete a Cache Rule

If you want to disable a cache rule that you've created (but want to keep it because you might want to enable it again sometime in the future), you can do so by following these steps:

1. Highlight the rule you want to disable in the middle pane of the ISA Server 2004 MMC and click **Edit Selected Rule** in the right task pane, or right-click the rule and select **Properties.**

2. On the **General** tab, uncheck the checkbox labeled **Enable**.

3. Click the **Apply** button, and then click **OK**.

The rule will still show up in the **Cache Rules** list, but with a red down arrow icon to indicate that it is disabled. You can re-enable it by simply checking the box.

If you want to do away with a rule completely (you will not want to use it again), you can delete it. Simply highlight the rule you want to delete in the middle pane, and click **Delete Selected Rules** in the right **Tasks** pane. You can highlight multiple rules and delete them all at once. Alternatively, you can right-click the rule(s) you want to delete and select **Delete** from the context menu. You will be asked if you are sure you want to delete the rule(s). Click **Yes** to do so.

How to Change the Order of Cache Rules

Remember that the cache rules are processed in order from first to last (top to bottom in the list on the **Cache Rules** tab in the middle pane), with the Default rule always processed last.

You can change the order of the rules by highlighting a higher rule in the middle pane and selecting **Move Selected Rules Down** in the right **Tasks** pane, or by right-clicking the rule you want to move and selecting **Move Down** from the context menu.

How to Copy a Cache Rule

You can also copy and paste the cache rules you've created. Why would you want to do that? Well, if you've created a rule and now you want to create another rule with only one or two properties that are different, rather than go through the whole wizard process, you can take the easy way out and just right-click the first rule, and select **Copy** from the context menu.

Next, right-click on the rule again (*not* in an empty area of the Cache Rules list as you might intuitively expect), and select **Paste** from the context menu. Now you can open the copy's **Properties** box, change its name and make whatever other changes you want to make to it.

> **TIP**
>
> Note that copying and pasting are tasks that don't appear in the right Tasks pane. Unlike with most tasks, you will have to do these from the right context menu.

How to Export and Import Cache Rules

You can export your cache rules to an XML file, which can then be used to import the data to another ISA Server 2004 computer or back to the current machine. Here's how to export your cache rules:

1. In the left pane of the ISA Server 2004 MMC, expand the server name.
2. Click the **Cache Rules** tab in the middle pane.

3. Click the **Tasks** tab in the right pane.

4. In the **Related Tasks** section, click **Export Cache Rules.** This invokes the **Export** wizard. Click **Next** on the first page of the wizard.

5. On the **Export Preferences** page, you can choose to export optional confidential information (which includes user passwords, RADIUS shared secrets, and other confidential information), along with the rules themselves. By default, confidential data is not exported. If you choose to export it by checking the checkbox, you will be asked to enter and confirm a password. This password will be used to encrypt the confidential data. Click **Next.**

6. On the **Export File Location** page, type in or browse to the path of the file to which you want to save the exported data. The file must be an XML file. If you have not already created a file, you can do so by typing in the desired path and filename (for example, **c:\files\cacherules.xml**).

TIP

Although you can create a new file by typing in the path and file name on the Export File Location page, you must specify an existing path (that is, you cannot create a new folder in this way; if you try to do so, you will get an error message stating that the path does not exist).

---

7. The last page of the wizard summarizes the selections you have made. If you want to change anything, use the **Back** button to return to the appropriate page and make your changes. If not, click **Finish** to export the data to the specified file. A dialog box will inform you when the configuration has been successfully exported, as shown in Figure 11.14.

Figure 11.14 Successfully exporting cache rules to an XML file

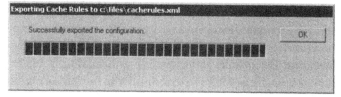

Now, to import cache rules that have been saved to XML files, simply follow these steps:

1. In the left pane of the ISA Server 2004 MMC, expand the server name.

2. Click the **Cache Rules** tab in the middle pane.

3. Click the **Tasks** tab in the right pane.

4. In the **Related Tasks** section, click **Import Cache Rules.** This invokes the Import wizard. Click **Next** on the first page of the wizard.

TIP

If you have made changes to the configuration that have not yet been applied, you will see a warning message advising you that if an error occurs during the import process, these changes might be discarded. You are asked if you want to import anyway. You can click **Yes** to proceed, or **No** to stop the import process so that you can go back and apply your changes. To apply your changes, click the **Apply** button at the top of the middle pane.

5. On the **Select Imported File** page, you will be asked to type in the path or browse for the XML file from which you want to import cache rules, as shown in Figure 11.15. Enter this information and click **Next**.

Figure 11.15 Selecting an Import File

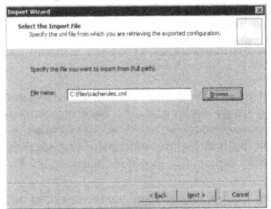

6. On the **Import Preferences** page, you can select to import server-specific information (such as cache drives and SSL certificates) by checking a checkbox. By default, server specific information is not imported. You should import server-specific information if you are importing information back to the same machine from which it was exported. If you import server-specific information to a different machine, you may find that the firewall service will not start because the machine does not have the same certificates.

7. The last page of the wizard summarizes the information you have entered. If you want to change anything, use the **Back** button and return to the appropriate page to make the changes. If not, click **Finish** to complete the import process. A dialog box will inform you when the cache rules have been successfully imported.

The process just described exports or imports all of your cache rules. You can also export or import just selected rules. To do so, highlight the rule you want to export or import and right-click it, then select **Export Selected** or **Import to Selected** from the right context menu.

Configuring Content Downloads

Content download jobs are handy tools for administrators as they allow you to automate the process of updating cached content. In this section, we'll show you how to do the following:

- Ensure a content download job can run
- Create and configure a scheduled content download job
- Make changes to an existing content download job
- Disable or delete a content download job
- Export or import content download job configurations
- Run a content download job immediately

Let's look at each of these in the following subsections.

How to Ensure a Content Download Job Can Run

Several requirements must be met before a content download job will run. Specifically:

- You must configure the Local Host network to listen for Web Proxy client requests.
- You must enable the system policy rules to allow content download.
- You must ensure that the Job Scheduler service is running.

There are two ways to meet these requirements. The first automates the process and is easiest. If you try to create a content download job before making the configuration changes, you will receive a message advising you that these changes must be made and asking if you want the settings configured, as shown in Figure 11.16.

Figure 11.16 Making Configuration Changes Automatically

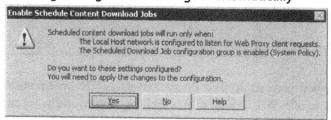

Click **Yes** to make the changes automatically (You will still need to click **Apply** at the top of the middle pane for the changes to take effect).

The second way is to make the configuration changes manually. In the following subsections, we show you how to make each of the changes.

Configuring the Local Host Network

To configure the Local Host Network to listen for Web Proxy client requests, perform the following steps:

1. In the left pane of the ISA Server 2004 MMC, expand the server name, then expand the **Configuration** node.

2. Click the **Networks** node.

3. In the middle pane, click the **Networks** tab.

4. Double click **Local Host** in the list of **Networks**, or right-click it and select **Properties.** This will open the **Local Host** properties dialog box.

5. Click the **Web Proxy** tab.

6. Check the box labeled **Enable Web Proxy clients** (it is unchecked by default), as shown in Figure 11.17.

Figure 11.17 Enabling Web Proxy Clients

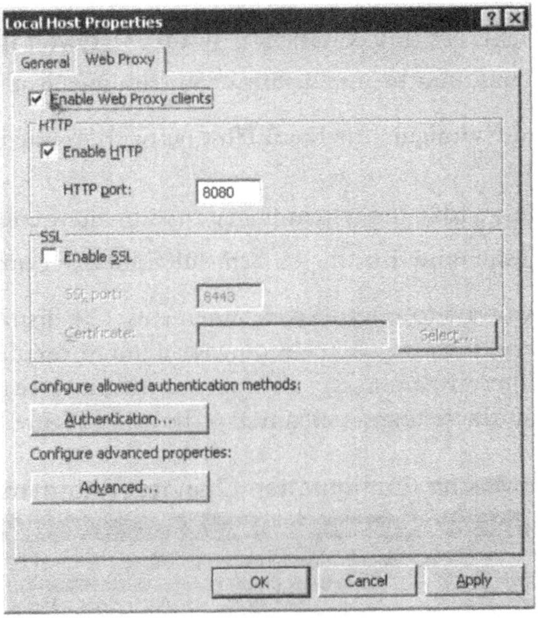

By default, when you enable Web Proxy clients, HTTP will be enabled, and SSL will not. You can enable SSL, if desired, by checking its box, and you can set different HTTP and SSL ports from the defaults (8080 and 8443), if needed.

If you enable SSL, you will need to select a server certificate by clicking the **Server Certificates** button, highlighting the server name and clicking **Select** to select from among the certificates installed on the server.

You can also configure authentication methods from among the following:

- Digest
- Integrated (the default)
- Basic
- SSL certificate
- RADIUS

To do so, click the **Authentication** button and check the box(es) of the authentication method(s) you want to use. You can also check a box here to require all users to authenticate.

You can select a default domain for authentication, select RADIUS servers, and configure OWA forms-based authentication.

NOTE

For more detailed information about configuring ISA Server to listen for Web Proxy clients and to configure authentication for Web Proxy clients, see Chapter 4, *Preparing the Network Infrastructure for ISA 2004*.

Enabling the System Policy Rules

To enable the system policy rule to allow content download, perform the following steps *after* you have configured the Local Host Network to listen for Web Proxy clients:

1. In the left pane of the ISA Server 2004 MMC, expand the server name.
2. Click the **Firewall Policy** node.
3. In the right Tasks pane, click **Show System Policy Rules.**
4. In the middle pane, scroll down to the rule **Allow HTTP from ISA Server computers for Content Download Jobs.** You will see a red down arrow on the icon that indicates that the rule is disabled.
5. To enable the rule, do the following: in the right **Tasks** pane, in the **System Policy Tasks** section, click **Edit System Policy,** or right-click the rule and select **Edit System Policy** from the context menu.
6. Under **Configuration Groups**, scroll down to the folder labeled **Various** and select **Scheduled Download.**
7. On the **General** tab, check the box labeled **Enable**, as shown in Figure 11.18.

Figure 11.18 Enabling the System Policy Configuration Group

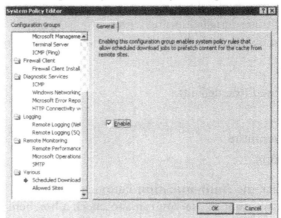

8. Click **OK**.

9. Click **Apply** at the top of the middle pane.

Running the Job Scheduler Service

To stop or start the Microsoft ISA Server Job Scheduler service from within the ISA 2004 MMC, perform the following steps:

1. In the left pane of the ISA Server 2004 MMC, expand the server name.

2. Click the **Monitoring** node.

3. In the middle pane, under the **Services** tab, if the **Job Scheduler** status is shown as **Stopped**, right-click it and select **Start** from the context menu, or highlight it and click **Start Selected Service** in the right **Tasks** pane under **Services Tasks**, as shown in Figure 11.19.

Figure 11.19 Starting or Stopping the Job Scheduler Service from the ISA Console

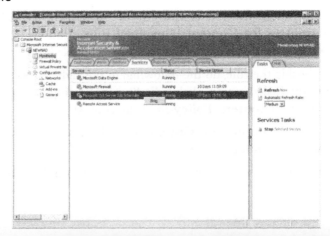

You can also start and stop the service from the **Services** node in the Windows 2000/Server 2003 Computer Management Console as you do with other Windows services. Click the **Start** menu and right-click **My Computer** (or right-click **My Computer** on the desktop) and click **Manage**, then expand the **Services and Applications** node in the left pane and click **Services**, as shown in Figure 11.20.

Figure 11.20 Starting or Stopping the Job Scheduler Service from the Computer Management Console

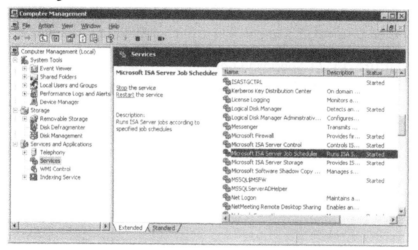

How to Create and Configure Scheduled Content Download Jobs

To create a scheduled content download job, perform the following steps:

1. In the left pane of the ISA Server 2004 MMC, expand the server name, then expand the **Configuration** node.

2. Click the **Cache** node.

3. In the middle pane, click the **Content Download Jobs** tab.

4. In the right **Tasks** pane, in the **Content Download Tasks** section, click **Schedule a Content Download Job.** This invokes the **New Content Download Job Wizard**.

5. On the first page of the wizard, give the content download job a name, and then click **Next**.

6. On the **Download Frequency** page, select how often to run the job. You can select from among the following choices: One time only, on completion of the wizard; one time only, scheduled; daily; weekly. Make your selection and click **Next**.

7. On the **Content Download** page, enter the URL of the page on the Internet server from which you want to download content. You can also set job limits, as shown in Figure 11.21. You can select not to follow links outside the URL's domain name, set a maximum depth of links per page, set a maximum number of objects to be retrieved, and set a maximum number of concurrent TCP connections to create for the job. By default, **Do not follow link outside the specified URL domain name** is disabled, so outside links will be followed. There is no maximum link depth set by default. The default limit on number of objects to be retrieved is 60,000, and the default maximum number of concurrent TCP connections is 4. After making your selections, click **Next**.

Figure 11.21 Specifying Content Download Details

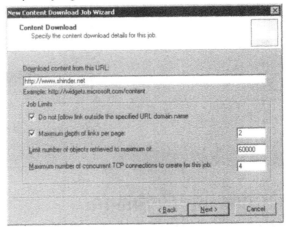

8. On the **Content Caching** page, you can control which content is to be cached and how long objects will stay in the cache before they expire (the TTL). First, select whether to cache all content, cache content if source and request headers indicate to cache *or* if content is dynamic, or cache if source and request headers indicate to cache (this is the default).

9. As shown in Figure 11.22, you can set the TTL according to one of three options: expire content according to the cache rule, set the TTL if it's not defined in the reponse, or override the object's TTL. By default, the content expires according to the cache rule. If you select to override the object's TTL, you can set a new TTL (in minutes) with which downloaded objects will be marked. The default is 60 minutes. After you have made your selections, click **Next**.

Figure 11.22 Configuring Content Caching

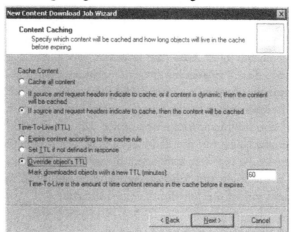

10. On the last page of the wizard, you'll see a summary of the selections you have made. If you want to make any changes, use the **Back** button to return to the appropriate page. Otherwise, click **Finish** to create the new content download job.

The new job you have created will now be listed in the middle pane on the **Content Download Jobs** tab of the **Cache** node, as shown in Figure 11.23.

Figure 11.23 The New Job Appears in the Content Download Jobs List

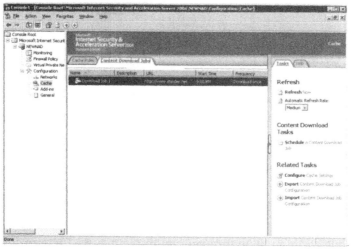

How to Make Changes to an Existing Content Download Job

If you want to modify a content download job that you previously created, highlight it in the middle pane, and click **Edit the selected job** in the right **Tasks** pane, or right-click the job, and select **Properties** from the context menu.

On the **General** tab, you can change the job's name and add an optional description.

On the **Schedule** tab, you can specify a date and time to start the download, and you can change the download frequency (once, daily, or weekly on a specified day of the week). You can also configure the daily frequency if you selected to run the job daily. As shown in Figure 11.24, you can have the job run once per day, or you can configure it to be repeated at specified intervals (either hours or minutes). You can also set a time after which a new run of the job should not be started.

Figure 11.24 Modifying the Job Schedule

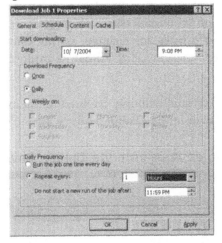

On the **Content** tab, you can change the URL from which the content is to be downloaded, and you can modify the job limits that you set when you created the job with the wizard.

On the **Cache** tab, you can change the options for which content to cache and the TTL options that you set when you created the job with the wizard.

How to Disable or Delete Content Download Jobs

If you do not want a job to run as scheduled but you will want to start running it on the same schedule again in the future, you can disable the job. To do so, highlight the job in the middle pane and click **Disable the Selected Jobs** in the right **Tasks** pane. You can highlight multiple jobs and disable them all at once. Alternatively, you can right-click the job and select **Disable** from the context menu.

If you want to do away with a job altogether because you will not be using it again in the future, you can delete it by highlighting it in the middle pane and clicking **Delete the Selected Jobs** in the right **Tasks** pane. You can highlight multiple jobs and delete them all at once. Alternatively, you can right-click the job and select **Delete** from the context menu.

How to Export and Import Content Download Job Configurations

You can export a content download job configuration by saving it to an XML file, just as you have exported other ISA Server 2004 configuration settings. To do so, highlight the job in the middle pane and click **Export Content Download Job Configuration** in the **Related Tasks** section of the right **Tasks** pane. Alternatively, you can right click the selected job and select **Export Selected** from the context menu. This invokes the **Export Wizard**.

Click **Next** on the first page of the wizard. On the **Export Preferences** page, specify whether to export confidential information. If you choose to do so, you need to enter and confirm a password with which the confidential information will be encrypted. Click **Next**.

Type in or browse to the path where you want to save the XML file. You can create a file by typing its path and name here, but you cannot create a folder.

On the last page of the wizard, your selections will be summarized. If you want to change anything, use the **Back** button to return to the appropriate page. Otherwise, click **Finish** to complete the Export process. A dialog box will inform you when the configuration has been successfully exported.

You can import a content download job that you saved from this or another ISA Server 2004 computer in much the same way. Click **Import Content Download Job Configuration** in the **Related Tasks** section of the right **Tasks** pane. This invokes the **Import Wizard**. Click **Next** on the first page.

Type in or browse to the path where the XML file you want to import is located, and click **Next**. Select whether to import server-specific information (such as cache drives and certificates). By default, server-specific information is not imported. You should import server-specific information if you are importing the configuration back to the same computer from which you exported it. If you are importing it to a different computer and select to import server-specific information, the firewall service might not start if the new computer does not have the same certificates installed. After you make your selection, click **Next**.

On the last page of the wizard, your selections will be summarized. If you want to change anything, use the **Back** button to return to the appropriate page. Otherwise, click **Finish** to complete the Import process. A dialog box will inform you when the configuration has been successfully imported.

How to Run a Content Download Job Immediately

In addition to running the content download jobs on the schedule you have configured, you can run any existing content download job manually at any time. To do so, highlight the job in the middle pane, and click **Start Selected Jobs Now** in the **Content Download Tasks** section of the right **Tasks** pane. You can highlight multiple jobs and run them all with a single click.

Alternatively, you can right-click the job you want to run, and select **Start** from the context menu.

Summary

Although Microsoft's marketing emphasis with ISA Server 2004 is on its firewall and VPN gateway functionality, it also provides companies with a viable Web caching solution that can save hundreds or thousands of dollars that would have to be spent for a separate caching product if you implemented competing firewall products that don't include caching functionality (and that's most of them).

ISA Server 2004's caching capabilities enhance your network's productivity by providing acceleration of access to external Web sites by your internal users, via the forward caching feature. It can also accelerate the access of external users who connect to your internal Web sites, via the reverse caching feature.

In larger, more complex network environments, multiple ISA Server 2004 computers can be used in distributed or hierarchical caching arrangements to provide for the best possible performance. Distributed caching distributes, or spreads, the cached Web objects across two or more caching servers. These servers are all on the same level on the network. In a hierarchical caching setup, caching servers are placed at different levels on the network. Upstream caching servers communicate with downstream proxies. For example, a caching server is placed at each branch office. These servers communicate with the caching array at the main office. Requests are serviced first from the local cache, then from a centralized cache before going out to the Internet server for the request.

ISA Server 2004 uses the Cache Array Routing Protocol (CARP), for communications between Web caching servers. CARP is a hash-based protocol that allows multiple caching proxies to be arrayed as a single logical cache and uses a hash function to ascertain to which cache a request should be sent. ISA Server 2004 uses cache rules to allow you to customize what types of content will be stored in the cache and exactly how that content will be handled when a request is made for objects stored in cache.

ISA Server 2004 can act as a combined firewall and Web-caching server, or as a dedicated Web-caching server, in addition to its default configuration (firewall only). In this chapter, you learned about the concepts of Web caching and how to configure an ISA Server 2004 computer to perform caching for your organization.

Fast Track

☑   There are two basic types of Web caching: forward and reverse. ISA Server 2004 performs both of these types of Web caching.

☑   Forward Web caching has the advantage of making access for internal users faster because they are retrieving the Web objects (pages, graphics, sound files, and so forth) over a fast LAN connection, typically 100Mbps or more, instead of a slower Internet connection at perhaps 1.5Mbps.

☑ The primary "bottom line" benefit of ISA Server 2004's forward caching is cost savings realized by reduced bandwidth usage on the Internet connection.

☑ Reverse caching reduces traffic on the internal network and speeds access for external users when the company hosts its own Web sites. Frequently requested objects on the internal Web servers are cached at the network edge on a proxy server so that the load on the Web servers is reduced.

☑ There are two principle benefits to the reverse-caching scenario: reverse caching reduces bandwidth usage on the internal network, and reverse caching allows Web content to be available when the Web server is offline.

☑ Multiple Web caching servers can be used together to provide for more efficient caching. There are two basic caching architectures that use multiple caching servers working together: distributed and hierarchical.

☑ You can combine the distributed and hierarchical methods to create a hybrid caching architecture. The combination gives you the "best of both worlds," improving performance and efficiency.

☑ There are a number of different protocols that can be used for communications between Web-caching servers. The most popular of these are CARP, ICP, HTCP, WCCP and Cache digests.

☑ ISA Server 2004 uses CARP for communications between distributed Web-caching servers.

☑ Web Proxy clients can also use CARP to locate the ISA Server that contains objects when distributed caching is enabled.

☑ The Web Proxy filter is the mechanism that ISA Server 2004 uses to implement caching functionality.

☑ The cache is an area on the ISA Server's hard disk that is used to store the requested Web objects. You can control the amount of disk space to be allocated to the cache (and thus, the maximum size of the cache). You can also control the maximum size of objects that can be cached to ensure that a few very large objects can't "hog" the cache space.

☑ Caching uses system memory. Objects are cached to RAM, as well as to disk. Objects can be retrieved from RAM more quickly than from the disk. ISA Server 2004 allows you to determine what percentage of random access memory can be used for caching (by default, ISA Server 2004 uses 10 percent of the RAM and then caches the rest of the objects to disk only).

☑ Enabling caching on your ISA Server 2004 computer is done by configuring a cache drive. When you configure a cache drive, this enables both forward and reverse caching.

☑ The file in which the cache objects are stored is named dir1.cdat. It is located in the urlcache folder on the drive that you have configured for caching. This file is referred to as the cache content file.

☑ ISA Server 2004 uses cache rules to allow you to customize what types of content will be stored in the cache and exactly how that content will be handled when a request is made for objects stored in cache.

☑ In addition to controlling content type and object size, a cache rule can control how ISA Server will handle the retrieval and service of objects from the cache. This refers to the validity of the object.

☑ If you have multiple cache rules, they will be processed in order from first to last, with the default rule processed after all the custom rules.

☑ The content download feature is used to schedule ISA Server 2004 to download new content from the Internet at pre-defined times so that when Web Proxy clients request those objects, updated versions will be in the cache.

Frequently Asked Questions

The following Frequently Asked Questions, answered by the authors of this book, are designed to both measure your understanding of the concepts presented in this chapter and to assist you with real-life implementation of these concepts. To have your questions about this chapter answered by the author, browse to **www.syngress.com/solutions** and click on the **"Ask the Author"** form. You will also gain access to thousands of other FAQs at ITFAQnet.com.

Q: What is negative caching?

A: Negative caching is a term that is used to describe ISA Server's ability to continue to serve Web pages and Web objects from the ISA Server cache even after those objects' Time To Live (TTL) has expired. Normally, items are cached for a specific period of time before they have to be updated from the Web server where they originated. Without negative caching, the cached object will no longer be available after the TTL expires (until it is once again refreshed by updating the object from the originating Web server). By using negative caching, ISA Server can continue serving the expired object after its expiration.

Q: Why does Microsoft use CARP for ISA Server 2004 communication between caching servers, instead of one of the other popular protocols?

A: In a word, efficiency. CARP allows caching servers and Web Proxy clients to locate cached objects based on a hash. This eliminates unnecessary traffic and duplication of cached objects among caching servers.

Q: What does the event log item 14193, "Cache was initialized with less memory cache than configured" mean?

A: You may see this event recorded when the ISA Server 2004 computer does not have enough free memory to allocate the percentage of free memory that you configured to be used for caching. If there is not enough free memory, a smaller amount of memory will be allocated for caching, but this event will be recorded in the event log.

Q: What happens when the cache fills up? Will this prevent new objects from being cached?

A: No. New objects will still be cached. If the cache is full, ISA Server 2004 will purge some objects from the cache to make room for new ones. URLs in the cache are removed according to a built-in logic so that the most recently used objects will be removed last.

Q: What does it mean if I see a message, when I start the ISA Server 2004 computer, that the cache did not initialize properly?

A: This message usually indicates that the ISA Server 2004 computer was not shut down properly. For example, if a power outage caused the ISA Server computer to turn off without going through the normal shutdown process, you might receive this message. Even if the computer did shut down normally, you could receive this message when an ISA Server service was stopped abruptly.

Q: I have a routing configuration specified in my content download job and a different routing configuration specified in Web chaining rules. Which one will be used?

A: The routing configuration that you have specified in the Web chaining rules will always take precedence over the one in the content download job. Thus, if you have a Web chaining rule that specifies that a request should be routed, it will be routed even though you specify in the content download job that it should not be routed. Web chaining rules let you route Web requests according to destination. With the Web chaining rule, you can choose to route a request from a Web

Proxy client to a specific upstream ISA server, redirect it to a specified Web site, or retrieve the requested object directly from a specified destination.

Q: Does ISA Server 2004 perform active caching? If not, why not?

A: Active caching was supported by ISA Server 2000. The purpose of active caching was to allow ISA Server to automatically go out and get updated versions of popular Web objects before they were requested by clients. ISA would monitor the TTL of the most frequently requested objects, and then, when they were close to expiring, refresh them from the Internet, preventing the objects from expiring. This "proactive" approach was intended to keep fresh copies of popular objects in the cache to reduce the time needed to refresh expired objects when a client requested them. However, Microsoft determined, after examining real world deployments of active caching, that it often did not benefit the overall network environment because of the extra bandwidth involved in automatically refreshing objects. Thus, the feature was discontinued in ISA Server 2004.

Q: How does ISA Server 2004's caching capability compare with that of other third-party competitors?

A: One of ISA Server 2004's primary advantages over most competitors is its combined firewall functionality and caching capability. Most popular firewalls offer caching only as an add-on module or through a separate product (at extra cost). The only major competitor that offers both is Blue Coat, with its SG appliances.

There are a number of third-party caching-only solutions. Some, such as Cisco's Content Engines (which are billed as "router-integrated content delivery systems that include caching), include other functions, and different models range in price all the way from under a thousand dollars to over $70,000. Others, such as the open-source Squid, are free of charge, but difficult to configure, requiring that you have Linux/UNIX expertise and use the command line interface and configuration files similar to the old Windows .ini files. Another popular caching solution is Novell's Volera Excelerator, which runs on Linux and Windows. It, too, is relatively expensive, ranging from $3,595 to $44,995, with a mid-range Enterprise license (1GB) costing $12,945 at the time of this writing.

Caching solutions also differ in features support and caching protocols used. For example, Blue Coat (formerly CacheFlow) appliances support forward, reverse, hierarchical, and distributed caching, as does ISA Server. It also supports active caching and streaming-media caching. Client browsers are configured via a Proxy Autoconfiguration (PAC) file, and reverse caching is done using a layer 4/7 switch or router that supports WCCP. Blue Coat supports ICP, HTCP and WCCP. Novell Excelerator can use ICP, proprietary HTTP, and WCCP, and supports hierarchical, distributed, forward, and reverse caching. Streaming-media caching is supported with the optional Media Excelerator (at extra cost). Squid runs on Linux/UNIX and supports a wide variety of protocols: ICP, HTCP, CARP, Cache digests, and WCCP. It supports forward, reverse, hierarchical,and distributed caching. It does not support active caching or streaming media caching. Squid does not include high availability/load balancing, as do ISA Server, Blue Coat, and Novell.

ISA Server holds its own against third-party caching solutions in terms of the feature/cost tradeoff.

Chapter 12

Using ISA Server 2004's Monitoring, Logging, and Reporting Tools

Topics in this Chapter:

- Exploring the ISA Server 2004 Dashboard

- Creating and Configuring ISA Server 2004 Alerts

- Monitoring ISA Server 2004 Sessions and Services

- Working with ISA Server 2004 Logs and Reports

- Using ISA Server 2004's Performance Monitor

Introduction

One of the biggest complaints we hear about firewall products from almost all vendors concerns the monitoring and reporting capabilities. It's not enough for a firewall to provide protection from Internet attacks and control what comes into and goes out of the local network; the name of the game in today's business world is documentation. Network administrators need to be able to track attempted intrusions and attacks from outside, as well as their own users' Internet use.

Logs and reports serve several important purposes:

- Awareness of failed or successful intrusions and attacks so you can take additional preventative measures

- Evidentiary documentation for forensics purposes when pursuing civil or criminal actions against intruders, attackers or insiders who misuse the network

- Tracking of bandwidth usage for planning expansion of the network

- Establishment of performance benchmarks for planning future capacity requirements

- Justification to management for budgetary considerations

- Paper trail for management and outside regulatory agencies to show compliance with policies and regulations

ISA Server 2004 includes an array of tools that can be used to monitor ISA Server activities, create and configure alerts to keep you apprised of changes, generate reports to summarize information in an easy-to-read form and provide a document trail, and monitor the ISA Server's performance. All of these tools are located in the Monitoring node, accessed via the console tree in the left pane of the ISA Server 2004 management console.

TIP

To access the Monitoring node in ISA Server 2004 Standard Edition, expand the ISA Server name in the left console tree and select Monitoring. In

---

In this chapter, we will examine each of these tools built into ISA Server 2004 and provide step-by-step instructions on how to use them. Specifically, we'll address the following:

- How to use the ISA Server 2004 Dashboard (section by section)
- How to create and configure notification alerts
- How to monitor sessions and services on the ISA Server
- How to configure logs and generate reports

■ How to use the ISA Server performance monitor (a specially-configured instance of the Windows Server System Monitor that is installed with ISA Server)

Exploring the ISA Server 2004 Dashboard

The Dashboard is a brand new feature in ISA Server 2004, and it's a handy way for the ISA Server administrator to tell, at a glance, what's going on in all the various monitoring subnodes. For more detailed information, you can click on the individual tabs for Alerts, Sessions, Services, Reports, Connectivity, and Logging, but if you want a "big picture" view, the Dashboard provides it in a single interface. The default Dashboard configuration on an ISA Server 2004 Standard Edition machine is shown in Figure 12.1.

Figure 12.1 The Dashboard on an ISA Server 2004 Standard Edition Computer

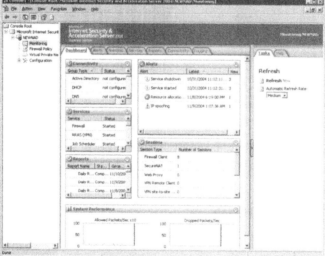

The Dashboard also provides you with system performance information. For example, you are able to see, in graph format, the number of packets allowed per second (times 10) and the number of packets dropped per second.

Each of the Dashboard sections contains an icon that indicates the status of that area:

■ **Checkmark inside a green circle:** indicates that all is okay

■ **Exclamation point inside a yellow triangle:** indicates a warning

■ **X inside a red circle:** indicates a problem or potential problem

You can think of the Dashboard as the starting point for identifying any problems or issues that the ISA Server might be having. You can also perform some tasks, such as resetting alert instances, directly from the Dashboard interface.

You can "roll up" various sections of the Dashboard if you don't want to view them. Just click the icon in the top right corner of the section you want to "roll up" (a circle with two small up-pointing arrows) and the section will "roll up," making more room for other sections. In Figure 12.2, the Connectivity, Reports and Alerts sections are "rolled up."

Figure 12.2 "Rolling up" Dashboard sections

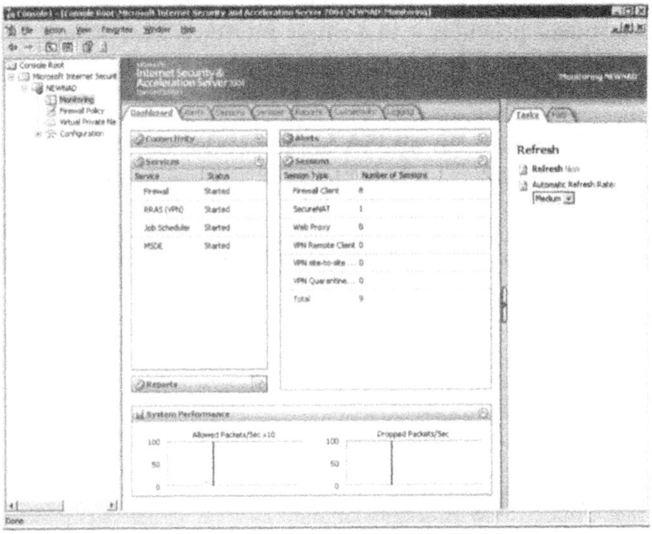

Dashboard Sections

The default Dashboard is divided into six sections:

- Connectivity
- Services
- Reports
- Alerts
- Sessions
- System Performance

Let's take a closer look at each of the Dashboard sections.

Dashboard Connectivity Section

The Connectivity section of the Dashboard allows you to monitor connections between the ISA server machine and other computers. You can monitor specific computers on the network, or even a connection to a particular Web server, by URL.

However, before you can monitor connections to specific computers, you will need to create a connectivity verifier and assign it to a group. Until you do this, the Dashboard Connectivity section will show all group types as "Not configured," as shown in Figure 12.3.

Figure 12.3 Default Connectivity Status Prior to Creating Connectivity Verifiers

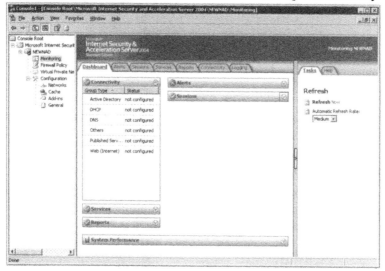

The groups to which computers can be assigned include the following:

- Active Directory
- DHCP
- DNS
- Published Servers
- Web (Internet)

After you've created one or more connectivity verifiers and assigned them to groups, the status will be shown for the configured group type, as shown in Figure 12.4.

Figure 12.4 Connectivity Status Shown After Creation of Connectivity Verifier

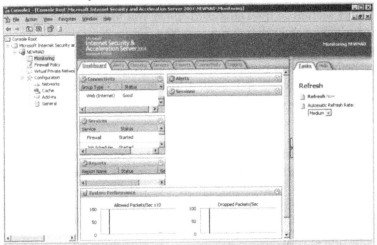

We discuss how to create connectivity verifiers in the section titled *Monitoring ISA Server 2004 Connectivity, Sessions and Services* later in this chapter.

Dashboard Services Section

The Services section of the Dashboard makes it easy for you to quickly check the status of the services that are running on the ISA Server computer. The following services are installed during the installation of the ISA Server 2004 software:

- The firewall service
- The ISA Server Control service
- The ISA Server Job Scheduler service
- The Microsoft Data Engine (MSDE)

We discuss each of these services in more detail in the section titled *Monitoring ISA Server Connectivity, Sessions and Services* later in this chapter.

From the Services section of the Dashboard (see Figure 12.5), you can view the status of each service (whether it is currently started or stopped).

Figure 12.5 The Services Section of the ISA Server 2004 Dashboard

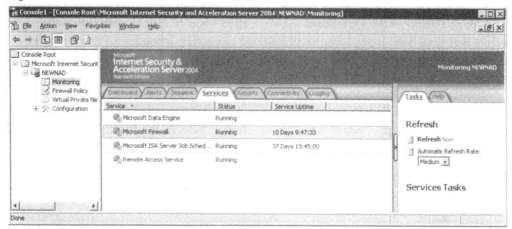

Dashboard Reports Section

The Reports section of the Dashboard tells you, at a glance, the names of reports that have been generated, their status (generating or completed), and the date of generation, as shown in Figure 12.6.

Figure 12.6 The Reports Section of the ISA Server 2004 Dashboard

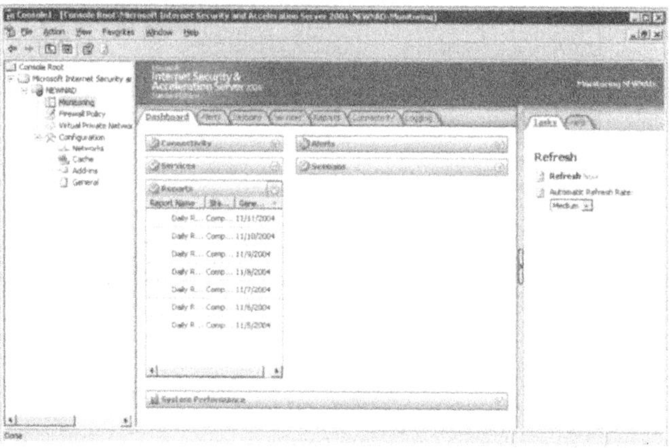

This section is handy for determining whether scheduled or manually generated reports have finished generating. You can open a listed report (if it has been completed) from the Dashboard interface by double-clicking its name in the Report Name column.

We discuss how to schedule automated report jobs, how to manually generate reports, and how to customize the content of reports in the section titled *Working with ISA Server 2004 Logs and Reports* later in this chapter.

Dashboard Alerts Section

The Alerts section of the Dashboard interface allows you to quickly determine the events that have been logged on the ISA Server computer, when each event occurred, the severity of the event (Information, Warning or Error), and the number of new instances when this event has occurred.

If you look in the Application log of the Windows Event Viewer (**Start | Administrative Tools | Event Viewer**), you'll see that the events displayed in the ISA Server 2004 Dashboard Alerts section are also shown there. In the Event Viewer, they will be shown with Microsoft Firewall as the source of the event, as shown in Figure 12.7.

Figure 12.7 Event Viewer Logs Show the Firewall Service Events Displayed on the Dashboard

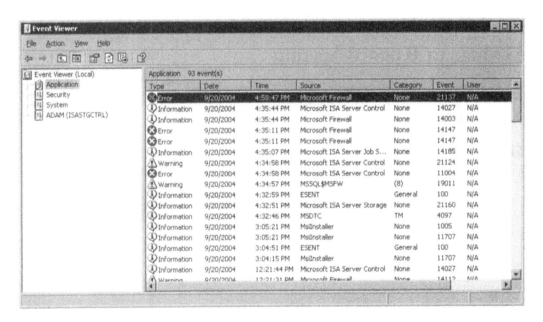

NOTE

The Event Viewer also shows events attributed to the Microsoft ISA Server Control service, Microsoft Server Job Scheduler, and other ISA Server services that are not displayed on the ISA Server 2004 MMC Dashboard or in the Alerts tab of the ISA Server management console. Thus, you should always check the Event Viewer for the most complete list of application-related events that have occurred on your ISA Server 2004 computer.

Dashboard Sessions Section

The Sessions section of the ISA Server 2004 Dashboard makes it easy to see, at a glance, the session types and number of sessions that are currently active through the ISA Server 2004 firewall that is being monitored. This includes the following session types:

- Firewall clients
- SecureNAT clients
- Web Proxy clients
- VPN Remote clients
- VPN site-to-site connections
- VPN quarantined clients

The total number of sessions is also shown, as you can see in Figure 12.8.

Figure 12.8 The Sessions section of the ISA Server 2004 Dashboard (Standard Edition)

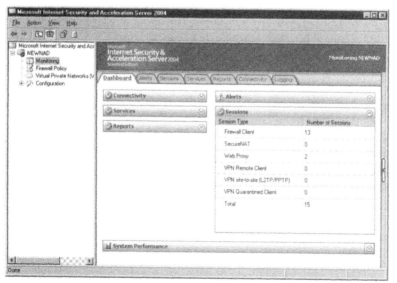

You can open the Sessions tab from the Dashboard interface to view details about each individual session by double-clicking the title bar of the Sessions section. We will discuss how to use the information on the Sessions tab in the section titled *Monitoring ISA Server 2004 Connectivity, Sessions and Services* later in this chapter.

Dashboard System Performance Section

The System Performance section of the ISA Server 2004 Dashboard interface provides a "quickie" view of the two most important performance counters for ISA Server:

- Allowed packets per second (times 10)
- Dropped packets per second

As shown in Figure 12.9, these counters are displayed in graph form on the Dashboard.

Figure 12.9 The System Performance Section of the ISA Server 2004 Dashboard

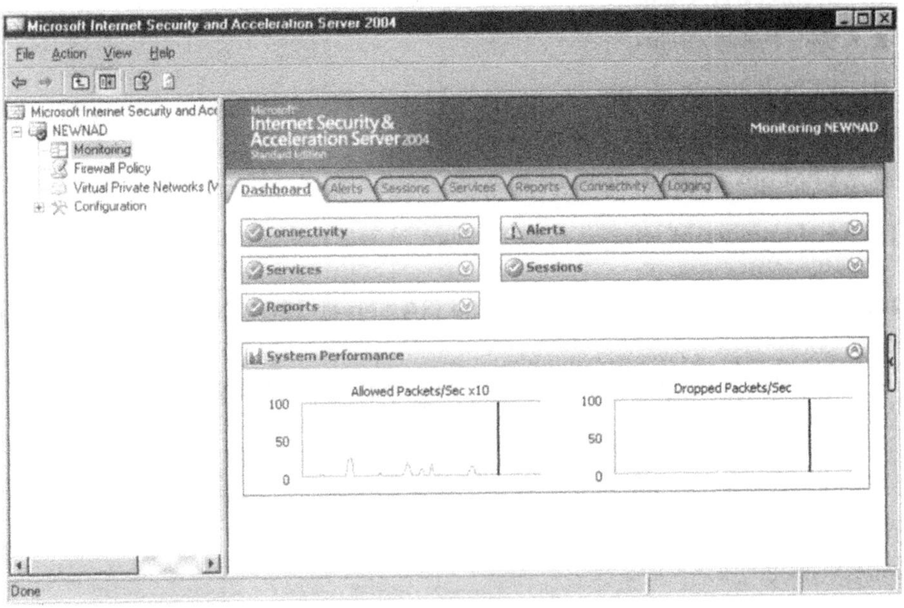

These same counters, along with a number of other counters specific to ISA Server 2004, are displayed by default in the ISA Server Performance Monitor console that is installed during the installation of the ISA Server 2004 software, as shown in Figure 12.10.

Figure 12.10 ISA Server Performance Monitor with Default Counters

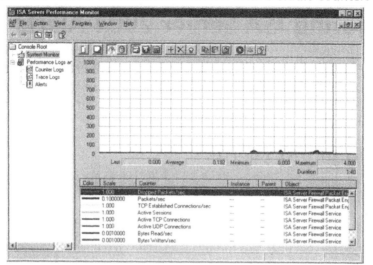

We will discuss how to use the ISA Server 2004 Performance Monitor in the section titled *Using ISA Server 2004's Performance Monitor* later in this chapter.

Configuring and Customizing the Dashboard

You can change the look of the Dashboard to suit your own preferences. As mentioned earlier, you can "roll up" or "unroll" any of the sections by clicking on the up or down pointing arrows in the upper right of the section.

You can also customize which columns are shown in each section by right-clicking one of the column headers (for example, Status) and selecting or deselecting column names.

To make more room for the Dashboard, you can close the console tree on the left by clicking its icon in the toolbar, and/or you can close the task pane on the right by clicking the right-pointing arrow between the Dashboard and task pane.

Once you have the Dashboard configured the way you want, you can use it as your "front page" overview of what's happening on your ISA server. Then you can drill down to the individual section tabs to get more detailed information. In the following sections, we show you how to use the tools you'll find on those tabs to create and configure all of ISA Server 2004's monitoring, logging, reporting and alerting functions.

Creating and Configuring ISA Server 2004 Alerts

ISA Server's alerting function means you can be notified of important ISA-related events as soon as they are detected. Rather than coming in to work to find that a hacker attempted to access or attack the system hours earlier, you can find out about it immediately. Or if one of ISA Server's services unexpectedly stops, you can be notified and take the appropriate action to minimize any loss of functionality.

Alert-triggering Events

Alerts can be configured to notify you of any of the following events (the official event name is in parentheses):

- An action associated with an alert fails (alert action failure)
- The cache container fails to initialize (cache container initialization error)
- A cache container is recovered (cache container recovery complete)
- An attempt to resize the cache file fails (cache file resize failure)
- Cache fails to initialize (cache initialization failure)
- Cache content is restored (cache restoration complete)
- There is an error in writing cache content (cache write error)
- A cached object is discarded (cached object discarded)
- An extension component fails to load (component load failure)
- There is an error during the reading of configuration data (configuration error)
- The connection limit is exceeded by a user or IP address (connection limit exceeded)
- The connection limit for a rule (the number of connections per second) is exceeded (connection limit for rule exceeded)
- The DHCP anti-poisoning intrusion detection feature is disabled (DHCP anti-poisoning intrusion detection disabled)
- A busy line or failure to answer causes a dial-on-demand connection to fail (dial on demand failure)
- There is a DNS zone transfer attack (DNS zone transfer intrusion)
- Information cannot be logged to the system event log (event log failure)
- The Firewall client and the ISA Server service fail to communicate (firewall communication failure)
- The FTP filter fails to parse the allowed FTP commands (FTP filter initialization warning)

- An attempted intrusion/attack from an outside user is detected (intrusion detected)

- A CRL is invalid, expired, or missing (invalid CRL found)

- DHCP offers an invalid IP address (invalid DHCP offer)

- ISA Server detects invalid dial-on-demand credentials (invalid dial-on-demand credentials)

- Credentials for the ODBC database are invalid (invalid ODBC log credentials)

- The source address on an IP packet is not valid (IP spoofing)

- Configuration changes have been made which require the ISA Server computer to be rebooted (ISA Server computer restart is required)

- A log fails (log failure)

- A log reaches its storage limits (log storage limits)

- The configuration of the network has been changed in a way that affects the ISA Server (network configuration changed)

- There are no ports available, resulting in a failure to establish a network socket (no available ports)

- The ISA Server is unable to connect to a requested server (no connectivity)

- One of the operating system components (NAT, ICS or Routing and Remote Access) presents a conflict with the ISA Server (OS component conflict)

- A UDP packet is greater than the maximum size specified in the registry, causing the ISA Server to drop it (oversized UDP packet)

- A buffer overflow exploiting the Post Office Protocol (POP) is detected (POP intrusion)

- A user is removed from the Quarantined VPN Clients network (Quarantined VPN Clients network changes)

- An error occurs while the report summary was being generated (report summary generation failure)

- A resource allocation failure, such as insufficient system memory, occurs (resource allocation failure)

- A routing (chaining) failure occurs (routing/chaining failure)

- A routing (chaining) recovery occurs (routing/chaining recovery)

- The RPC filter is unable to use the defined port, which is already being used (Bind failure)

- The RPC filter connectivity changes (RPC filter—connectivity changed)

- A server publishing rule is not configured correctly (server publishing failure)

- A server publishing rule cannot be applied (server publishing not applicable)

- A service cannot start (service initialization failure)

- A service stops unexpectedly (service not responding)

- A service stops properly (service shutdown)

- A service starts properly (service started)

- The ISA Server's connection to a requested server is slow (slow connectivity)

- An SMTP rule is violated (SMTP filter event)

- The SOCKS configuration fails because the port is being used by another protocol (SOCKS configuration failure)

- There is a SYN attack detected (SYN attack)

- An unregistered event occurs (unregistered event)

- Upstream chaining credentials are not correct (Upstream chaining credentials)

- A VPN client attempts to make a connection and fails (VPN connection failure)

The alert service determines when an event occurs and whether an alert is configured to provide notification or perform some other action. It then initiates the specified notification or other action.

Viewing the Predefined Alerts

You can see the predefined alert definitions by clicking the Alerts tab and opening the task pane if it is not already open. Click **Configure Alert Definitions** under **Alerts Tasks** on the task pane **Tasks** tab. This will open the Alerts Properties dialog box, as shown in Figure 12.11.

Figure 12.11 The Alerts Properties Dialog Box

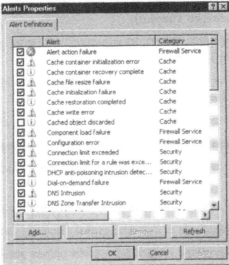

The Alerts Properties dialog box gives you a graphical representation of the severity of the alert, that is, whether it is an Error, Warning, or Information. You can modify the severity and other properties of the alert from this dialog box. You can also assign a level of severity to any new alert you create.

Creating a New Alert

To define a new alert, click the **Add** button. This will invoke the New Alert Configuration Wizard, as shown in Figure 12.12.

Figure 12.12 The New Alert Configuration Wizard

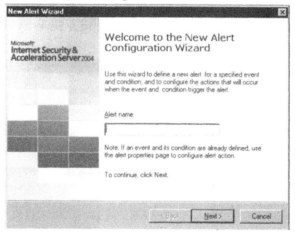

As you can see, you'll need to give the new alert a name. Then click **Next.**

On the next page of the wizard, you need to select an event and any additional conditions that will trigger the alert. The list of events from which you can select matches the list of events we described earlier in this section.

For example, as shown in Figure 12.13, you can select the Log Failure event and then select for the alert to be triggered by the log failure of any ISA Server service, the ISA Server Firewall service, or the ISA Server Web filter.

Figure 12.13 Selecting Events and Conditions to Trigger an Alert

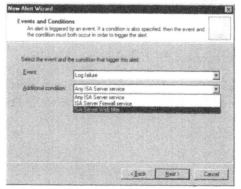

Next, you can assign a category for the alert from the following choices:

- Security
- Cache
- Routing
- Firewall Service
- Other

On the same page, as shown in Figure 12.14, you need to select a severity level (Error, Warning or Information).

Figure 12.14 Assigning a Category and Selecting a Severity Level for your New Alert

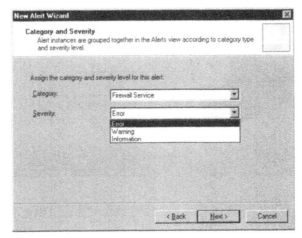

The next page allows you to define what action (if any) will be taken when the specified event and conditions occur. ISA Server can be configured to do any or all of the following when the conditions specified for an alert have been met: :

- Send an e-mail notification to yourself or another administrator(s)
- Run a program
- Log the event to the Windows event log (this option is enabled by default)
- Stop selected services on the ISA Server computer
- Start selected services on the ISA Server computer

You can select multiple actions. For example, you can select to send an e-mail message *and* report the event to the Windows event log, as we've done in Figure 12.15.

Figure 12.15 Defining Actions to be Performed when the Alert is Triggered

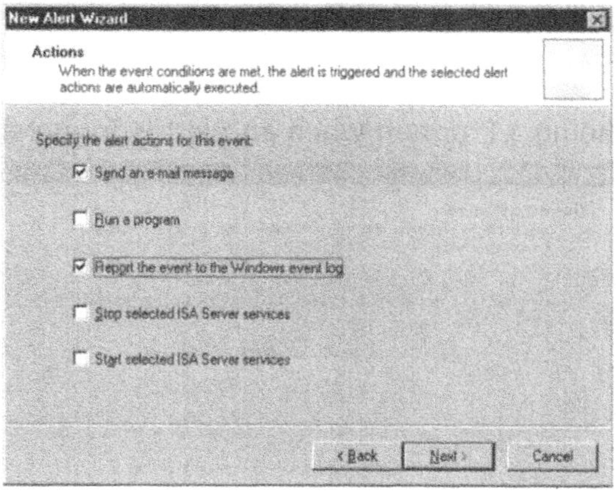

If you have selected to send an e-mail message, you will be asked to provide the name of the SMTP server to be used and enter "From" and "To" addresses for the message. You can send the message to multiple recipients using the CC: field, as shown in Figure 12.16.

TIP

You might be asked to enter the name and password of an account with permissions to access the SMTP server. In addition, you might need to create an access rule to allow the local host to access the External network using the SMTP protocol, if you configure the e-mail notification to use an external SMTP server. Furthermore, if SMTP messages to a server on the internal network fail, a possible cause is that the "Allow SMTP from ISA to Trusted Servers system policy" rule is not enabled. (Note that the Help file suggests you must enable a system policy rule to allow the Local Network to communicate with the Internal Network via SMTP. However, by default this rule is already enabled, so you won't need to worry about this unless you have disabled it).

Figure 12.16 Sending E-Mail Notification Messages

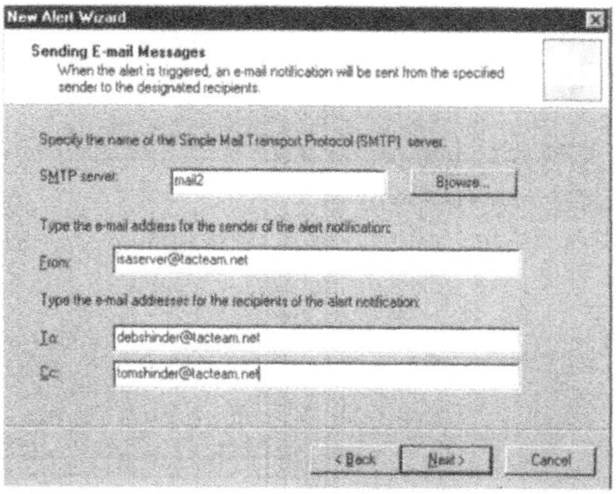

Similarly, if you select to run a program, you'll be asked to provide a path to the program's executable file and an account to use in running the program, as shown in Figure 12.17.

Figure 12.17 Running a Program when an Alert is Triggered

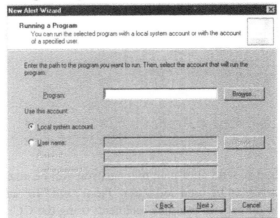

TIP

One of the more common uses of Running a Program is to invoke an executable that will send a pager message to an administrator. However, if the administrator's cell phone supports text messaging, it may be possible to use SMTP to deliver a message to the administrator's cell phone, eliminating the need to support paging mechanisms.

If you select to stop or start a service, you will be asked to choose the service(s) to stop or start, as shown in Figure 12.18.

Figure 12.18 Stopping or Starting a Service when an Alert is Triggered

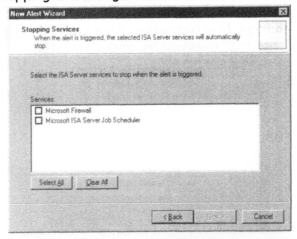

When you have configured all the properties for the new alert, the last page of the wizard summarizes the information you entered, as shown in Figure 12.19. Check it over and use the **Back** button to make any corrections, then click **Finish.**

Figure 12.19 Completing the New Alert Wizard

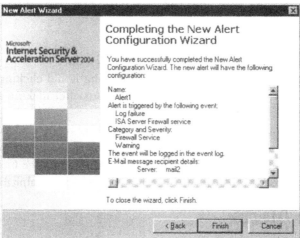

The new alert will now show up in the Alerts Properties dialog box, in the Alerts Definitions window, as shown in Figure 12.20.

Figure 12.20 New Alerts Show Up in the Alerts Definitions Window

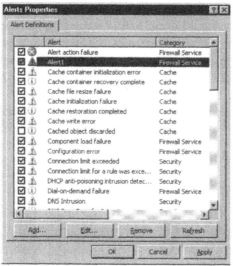

You can disable an alert here by unchecking its checkbox. You will notice that some alerts are predefined but disabled by default. These include:

- Cached object discarded

- Event log failure

- Network configuration changed

- Quarantined VPN Clients network changed

- Server publishing is not applicable

- SMTP filter event

The rest of the predefined alerts are enabled by default.

You can remove an alert completely by highlighting it and clicking the **Remove** button. You can refresh the view of the configured alerts after making a change by clicking the **Refresh** button.

You can rearrange the order of the alerts in the window by clicking the title of the column. For example, clicking the top of the Alerts column will rearrange the alerts in ascending or descending alphabetical order. Clicking the top of the Categories column will rearrange the alerts by category, in ascending or descending alphabetical order.

Modifying Alerts

You can modify the properties of your new alert, or those of any of the predefined alerts, by highlighting the alert you want to modify and clicking the **Edit** button. This will allow you to change the category and/or severity and disable or enable the alert from the General tab. On the Events tab, you can change the event and additional conditions.

When you modify an alert, you can specify the number of times that the event should occur before an alert is triggered, and/or you can specify the number of times per second that the event should occur before triggering the alert. You can also specify whether, when these time thresholds are met, the alert should be triggered immediately, only if the alert was manually reset, or only if a specified number of minutes have passed since the last execution of the alert. This is shown in Figure 12.21.

Figure 12.21 Modifying an Alert to Specify Time Thresholds

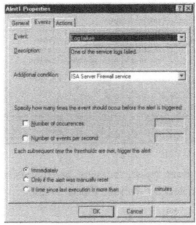

On the Actions tab, you can change, remove or add actions to be performed when the alert is triggered, just as you did when you originally created the alert.

Viewing Triggered Alerts

When you click the Alerts tab in the Monitoring node, the alerts that have been triggered are displayed in the middle pane, as shown in Figure 12.22.

Figure 12.22 Viewing Alerts that have been Triggered

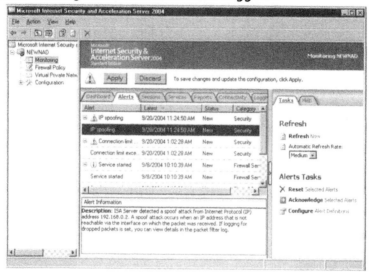

The display shows the alert name, the date and time it occurred, the status, and the category to which the alert has been assigned. Alerts are grouped together by alert type (such as "Service started"). Click the small square with a + sign to expand a group.

If you click on an individual alert, a detailed description will be displayed in the Alert Information window below the list of recent alerts. Again, this same information appears in the Event Viewer's application log, as shown in Figure 12.23.

Figure 12.23 Event Viewer Application Log Entry Showing Information
Displayed in Alerts Windows

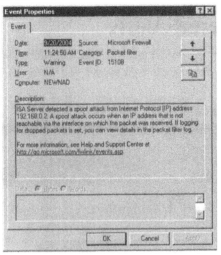

The alerts window is automatically refreshed by default at periodic intervals. You can set the refresh rate to one of the following:

- None
- Low
- Medium
- High

This is done in the right task pane. You can also force a manual refresh at any time by clicking the **Refresh Now** icon (refer back to Figure 12.23).

In addition to configuring alert definitions, you can perform the following Alerts Tasks:

- **Reset selected alerts:** You can reset alerts to remove them from the Alerts display. In the middle pane, highlight the alert that you want to reset, and click **Reset selected alerts** in the right task pane. You will be asked if you're sure you want to reset the alert. Click **Yes** to do so. The alert will then disappear from the middle pane. You can also reset a whole group of alerts by highlighting the group heading.

- **Acknowledge selected alerts:** You can acknowledge an alert to remove it from the Dashboard view. It will remain in the Alerts window on the Alerts tab, but its status will be shown as "Acknowledged." You can use this to indicate that you have seen the alert and are handling it. In the middle pane, highlight the alert(s) you want to acknowledge, and click **Acknowledge selected alerts** in the right task pane.

NOTE

When you reboot the ISA Server computer, all alerts will be reset.

Monitoring ISA Server 2004 Connectivity, Sessions, and Services

You can monitor connectivity between the ISA Server and other computers from the **Connectivity** tab. You can monitor current sessions for Firewall, Web Proxy, and SecureNAT clients from the **Sessions** tab. You can monitor the status of ISA Server services from the **Services** tab. In the following sections, we will look at each of these individually.

Configuring and Monitoring Connectivity

You can monitor the connections between the ISA Server and specific servers on any network (by server name or IP address) or between the ISA Server and a specific Web server (by URL). You can use one of three methods to verify the connectivity:

- **Ping:** The ISA server will send a ping (ICMP ECHO_REQUEST message) to the server. When the server sends back an ECHO_REPLY message, this confirms that it is reachable by the ISA server.

- **TCP Connect:** The ISA server will attempt to make a TCP connection to a specified port on the server. This can be used to ensure that a particular service is running on the server.

- **HTTP Request:** The ISA server will send an HTTP GET command to the specified Web server. A response indicates that the Web server is up and running and reachable by the ISA server.

To monitor connectivity to a server by any of these methods, you need to create a connectivity verifier and place it into one of the predefined groups. The groups include:

- Active Directory
- DHCP
- DNS
- Published servers
- Web (Internet)
- Others

The status of each group is shown in the Dashboard view. This will allow you to quickly determine if one of the servers in the group has a problem. Then you can click the **Connectivity** tab for details about which server(s) in the group has the connectivity problem.

In the following sections, we'll show you how to create connectivity verifiers, how to assign them to groups, and how to monitor connectivity with the verifiers you have created.

Creating Connectivity Verifiers

The first step in monitoring connections between the ISA server and other computers is to create a connectivity verifier. To do so, click the **Connectivity** tab in the Monitoring node, and then click **Create New Connectivity Verifier** in the right task pane. This invokes the New Connectivity Verifier Wizard. On the first page of the wizard, you need to give the verifier a name (for example, if you are going to monitor the connection to a Web site, you might give it the name of the site's URL).

Next, you'll be asked to provide connectivity verification details. First, enter a server name, IP address, or URL in the Connection details field (you can also browse to a location to monitor by clicking the **Browse** button).

Select the group type in the drop-down box, as shown in Figure 12.24.

Figure 12.24 Entering Connectivity Verification Details

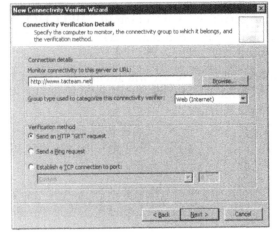

You can also select the verification method. If you are monitoring connectivity to a Web server (URL), you should select **Web (Internet)** as the group type and **Send HTTP "GET" request** as the verification method. If you want to verify that a specific program or service is running on the server connection you will be monitoring, select **Establish a TCP connection to port:** and select from the available applications in the drop-down box. The port number will be entered for you, or you can choose **Custom** and enter the port number.

Applications from which you can choose in the drop-down box include:

AOL Instant Messenger

Chargen (TCP)

Daytime (TCP)

Discard (TCP)

DNS

Echo (TCP)

Finger

FTP

Gopher

H.323 Protocol

HTTP

HTTPS

ICA

ICQ 2000

Ident

IMAP4

IMAP5

IRC

Kerberos-Adm (TCP)

Kerberos-Adm (TCP)

LDAP

LDAP GC (Global Catalog)

LDAPS

LDAPS GC (Global Catalog)

Microsoft CIFS (TCP)

Microsoft Operations Manager Agent

Microsoft SQL (TCP)

Microsoft Operations Manager Agent

Microsoft SQL (TCP)

MMS (Microsoft Media Server)

MS Firewall Control

MSN

MSN Messenger

Net2Phone Registration

NetBios Session

News

NNTP

NNTPS

PNM (Progressive Networks Media)

POP2

POP3

POP3S

PPTP

Quote (TCP)

RDP (Terminal Services)

Rlogin

RPC (all interfaces)

TRSP (Real Time Streaming Protocol

SMTPS

SSH

Telnet

Time

WhoIs

The last page of the wizard summarizes your choices. Use the **Back** button if you want to change anything. Otherwise, click **Finish.**

If you have selected to verify an HTTP connection, you will see a dialog box informing you that a rule allowing HTTP or HTTPS to the specified destination must be configured in order to do this, and asking if you want to enable the system policy rule to "allow HTTP/HTTPS requests from ISA Server to the selected servers for connectivity verifiers." This is shown in Figure 12.25. Click **Yes** to enable the rule.

Figure 12.25 Enabling a Rule to allow HTTP/HTTPS Requests

NOTE

If you delete or disable all of the verifiers that use the HTTP method, the system policy rule to allow HTTP/HTTPS requests for connectivity verifiers will be automatically disabled as a security measure. You'll have to enable it again if you later create or enable a verifier that is configured to use HTTP.

The new connectivity verifier will be shown in the middle pane when the **Connectivity** tab is selected, as shown in Figure 12.26.

Figure 12.26 The New Connectivity Verifier

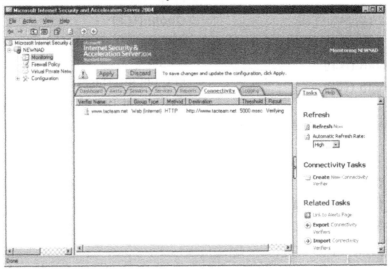

After you select to enable the rule, you must click **Apply** at the top of the console. This saves your changes and updates the configuration. You'll see a progress bar as the changes are applied, then the dialog box will advise that the changes to the configuration were successfully applied. Click **OK** to close the dialog box.

Now "Verifying" will disappear from the **Result** column and a result time (in milliseconds) will replace it.

You can delete or disable a verifier by right clicking it and selecting **Delete** or **Disable** from the context menu. You can also export or import verifiers from this menu. Another way to perform these tasks is to highlight the selected verifier and click the appropriate task in the right task pane (**Delete Selected Verifiers, Disable Selected Verifiers, Export Connectivity Verifiers** or **Import Connectivity Verifiers**).

If you want to change any of the properties of your connectivity verifier, right-click it and select **Properties** from the context menu, or highlight it and click **Edit Selected Verifier** in the right task pane.

On the **General** tab of the properties box, you can change the name, enable or disable the verifier, and type an optional description. On the **Properties** tab, you can change the URL, server name or IP address of the connection being monitored, change the group type, or change the verification method. You can also specify a timeout response threshold (by default, 5000 msec). Finally, you can select whether to trigger an alert if the server response is not within the specified timeout period (by default, an alert is triggered), as shown in Figure 12.27.

Figure 12.27 Modifying Properties of a Connectivity Verifier

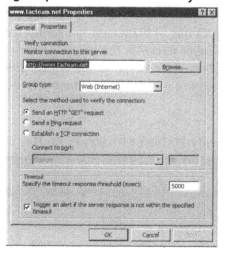

Monitoring Connectivity

Once you've configured your verifiers, you can tell at a glance whether there are any problems with the servers in a particular group by viewing the Connectivity section of the Dashboard. As you can see in Figure 12.28, the group types that have verifiers configured show a status of "Good" as long as the connections in that group type are verified.

Figure 12.28 Monitoring Connectivity from the Dashboard

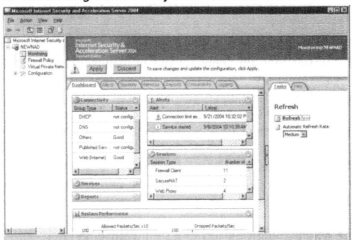

If there is a problem with one of the servers in a group, the group status will show the problem (even though other servers in the group may be connected without any problem). For example, if one of the servers in the Others group is experiencing a slow connection, this will be indicated in the **Status** column on the Dashboard, as shown in Figure 12.29.

Figure 12.29 Connectivity Problems Displayed on Dashboard

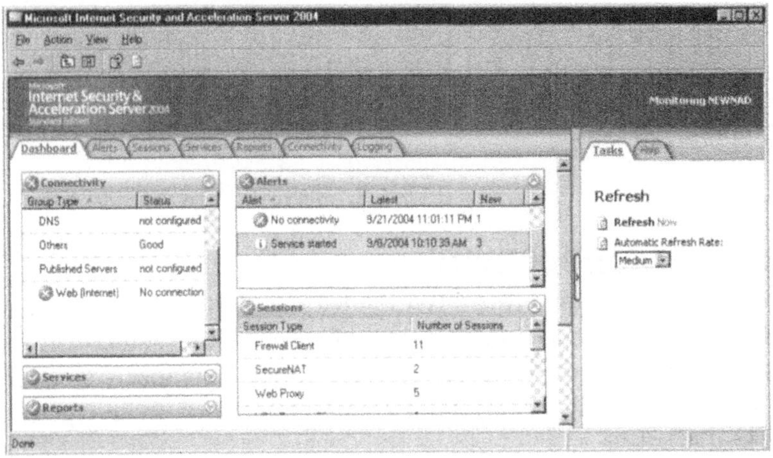

To determine which server has the problem, you'll need to go to the **Connectivity** tab. Then you'll be able to see exactly which verifier reports a problem, as shown in Figure 12.30.

Figure 12.30 The Connectivity Tab Shows Which Server Has a Problem

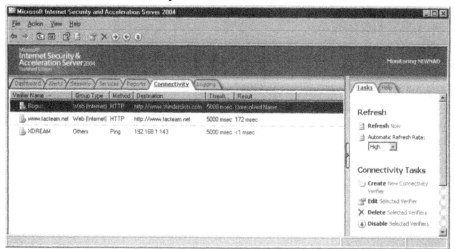

"Unresolved Name" is one of several status indicators that can occur for verifiers using the HTTP method. It occurs when the server's name cannot be resolved to an IP address. Other results, depending on the response from the Web server, include:

- **OK:** This result is reported when a 401 message (Web server authentication required) is returned from the server.

- **Error** (Windows Server 2003): This result is reported when a 407 message (proxy authentication required) is returned, because ISA Server could not verify connectivity to the actual Web server.

- **Authentication required** (Windows 2000 Server): This result is reported when a 407 message is returned if the server is running Windows 2000.

- **Error:** This result is reported if any 4xx message is returned (except 401 or 407) or if any 5xx message is returned.

- **Time-out:** This result is reported if the request times out before the server responds.

- **Unable to verify:** This result is reported if the ISA Server is down or the Firewall service is otherwise unavailable.

Tools and Traps...

Why Monitor Connectivity?

When should you create connectivity verifiers, and to which servers should you monitor connectivity? If you have mission critical servers on the network (for example, your Exchange e-mail server) that have been published to make them available to external clients, you might want to create a connectivity verifier so you can easily keep tabs on whether it's working properly.

You might also want to create connectivity verifiers to some popular external Web sites that are considered reliable in terms of up-time, so you can tell at a glance if the ISA Server has connectivity to those external sites.

Monitoring Sessions

A handy feature in ISA Server 2004 is the ability to monitor real-time *sessions,* that is, the activity of a particular client computer (IP address) by a particular user (account name). You can monitor sessions from all three types of clients: Firewall, Web Proxy, and SecureNAT.

NOTE

Because ISA Server sees a session as a unique combination of a user plus an IP address, you might show more current users in the Firewall service performance counters than the number of sessions shown in the Sessions window. That's because if a new connection is made from the same IP address and the same user, it is considered part of the same session. The System Monitor denotes every connection as a current user.

Viewing, Stopping and Pausing Monitoring of Sessions

To view current sessions being conducted through the ISA Server, click the **Sessions** tab and you will see a list of sessions as shown in Figure 12.31.

Figure 12.31 Viewing Current Sessions

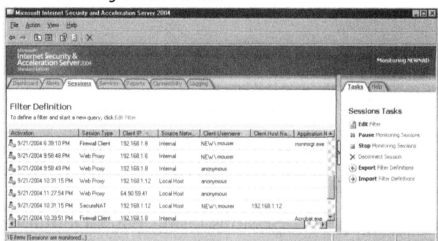

As you can see, the display shows you the following information about each session:

- Date and time the session was activated
- Session type (Firewall, Web Proxy, SecureNAT client, VPN client, or Remote VPN site)
- Client IP address
- Source network
- Client user name (if authentication is required)
- Client host name (for Firewall Client sessions)
- Application name (for Firewall Client sessions)
- Server name (name of the ISA Server)

The Server name and Application name columns are not displayed by default in Standard Edition. To display them, right-click on one of the column headers and check **Server name** or **Application name** in the context menu.

> **NOTE**
>
> Even if you have blocked anonymous connections, you may see anonymous sessions because, for performance reasons, the Web Proxy client sends the first message anonymously; the server then returns a 407 message requiring authentication, and subsequent communications include client credentials.

If you want to stop monitoring sessions, just select **Stop Monitoring Sessions** in the right task pane. All the sessions information will then disappear from the Sessions tab. To start monitoring again, click **Start Monitoring Sessions** (which only appears when you have stopped monitoring).

WARNING

If you stop monitoring sessions, all the information that ISA Server had collected about sessions up to that time will be lost.

You can also stop ISA Server from adding new sessions to the display by selecting **Pause Monitoring Sessions.** When you do so, that selection will be replaced by **Resume Monitoring Sessions.** When you are paused, the sessions that were already in the display will stay there.

Monitoring Specific Sessions Using Filter Definitions

If you have many sessions going through the ISA server, it can be difficult to find the ones in which you're interested. You can use ISA Server 2004's filtering mechanism to sort the sessions data and display only sessions that meet specified criteria. If you specify multiple criteria, only the sessions that meet *all* of your specifications will be displayed.

To define a filter, do the following:

1. In the right task pane, click **Edit Filter,** or right-click in the middle pane and select **Edit Filter** from the context menu.

2. In the **Edit Filter** dialog box, select filter criteria for the **Filter by** field from the drop-down box, as shown in Figure 12.32.

Figure 12.32 Setting Filter Criteria

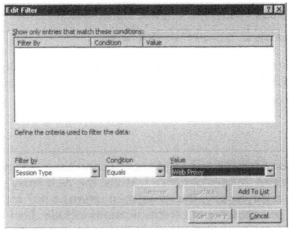

You can select to filter by any of the following:

■ Activation

■ Application name

- Client host name
- Client IP address
- Client user name
- Server name
- Session type
- Source network

3. Next, you'll need to select a condition (in this case, "equals" or "not equal").

4. In the Value field, your choices depend on which criteria you are filtering by. In our example, we chose to filter by session type, so our value choices are Firewall Client, SecureNAT, VPN Client, VPN Remote Site, or Web Proxy. We want to view all Web Proxy sessions.

5. Click **Add to list** to add your filter criteria to the list

If you want to further narrow the scope of sessions listed, you can add more criteria by going through the same process again. In our example, as shown in Figure 12.33, we want to view only the Web Proxy sessions for client IP address 192.168.1.121 (the local host).

Figure 12.33 Specifying Multiple Filtering Criteria

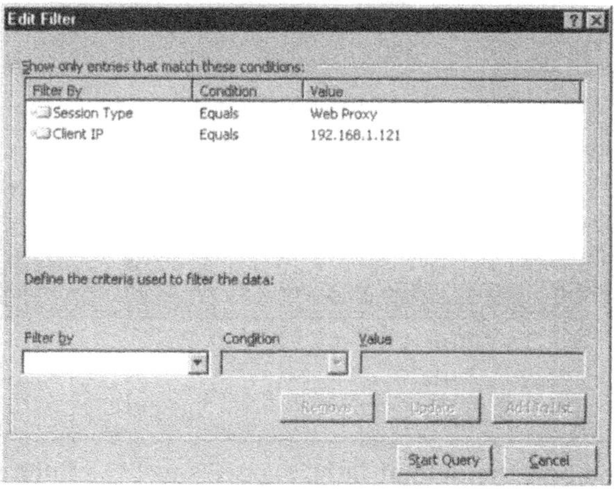

6. When you have added all the criteria that you want, click **Start Query** and the filtering process will begin. The session(s) that meet all of the specified criteria will be displayed as shown in Figure 12.34.

Figure 12.34 Result of Filtering

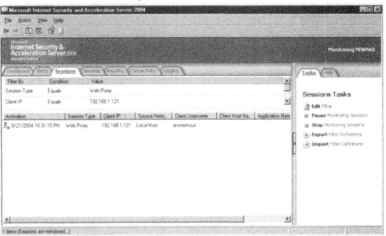

You can save a filter definition so you can use it again by exporting it to an .xml file. See *Exporting and Importing Filter Definitions* later in this section.

ISA Server Mysteries

The Missing Task Pane Functions

In the ISA Server 2004 Help files, you'll see instructions for saving filter definitions and "loading" filter definitions that tell you to select **Save Filter Definitions** or **Load Filter Definitions** on the **Tasks** tab. The problem is that no such selections exist (they did in some beta versions). In the final release of the product, you use the **Export** and **Import** functions for this purpose.

TIP

Before you edit the default filter, export (save) the filter definition. If you want to return to the default Sessions view, you can easily import the filter definition, and then stop and restart monitoring. ISA Server does not provide a reset button to return you to the default view (all sessions); this is a feature we would like to see in a future version of ISA Server.

Disconnecting Sessions

You can disconnect a session quickly and easily by right-clicking it in the Sessions window and selecting **Disconnect Session** in the context menu. You will be asked if you're sure you want to disconnect the session. Click **Yes** to do so. Alternatively, you can highlight the session, and then click **Disconnect Session** in the right task pane.

Exporting and Importing Filter Definitions

You can save filters by exporting them to .xml files, and then load them by importing them. If you do a lot of filtering, you will probably want to make a number of predefined filters so you can quickly view, for example, all Web Proxy sessions with one filter, all Firewall sessions with another filter, all sessions for a particular application with another, all sessions for a particular client user name with another, and so forth.

Once you have defined a filter you want to save and conducted a query with it, click **Export Filter Definitions** in the right task pane. Select a location in which to save it (we suggest creating a folder for all your filters) and give it a descriptive name (for example, FirewallSessionFilter). Click the **Save** button.

When you're ready to use that filter again, just click **Import Filter Definitions** in the right task pane, navigate to the location of the saved filter and select it, and click the **Load** button. You may need to click the **Refresh** button in the top toolbar to view the new filter results after loading the filter.

Monitoring Services

You can view the ISA Server services that are running on the firewall by using the **Services** tab in the Monitoring node. By default, the Services window in the middle pane will show the names of services, the status of each (running or stopped), and in some cases, the service uptime (how long the service has been running in days, hours, minutes, and seconds.

> **NOTE**
>
> The Service Uptime column does not update in real time. You will need to click the **Refresh** button on the toolbar or click **Refresh Now** in the right task pane to update the times.

You can stop and start services from this interface. Just right-click a running service and select **Stop,** or highlight a service and click **Stop Selected Service** in the right task pane. The service's status will change to "Stopped" as shown in Figure 12.35. You can then restart the service by right-clicking and selecting **Start,** or highlighting and selecting **Start Selected Service** in the task pane.

Figure 12.35 Stopping and Starting Services

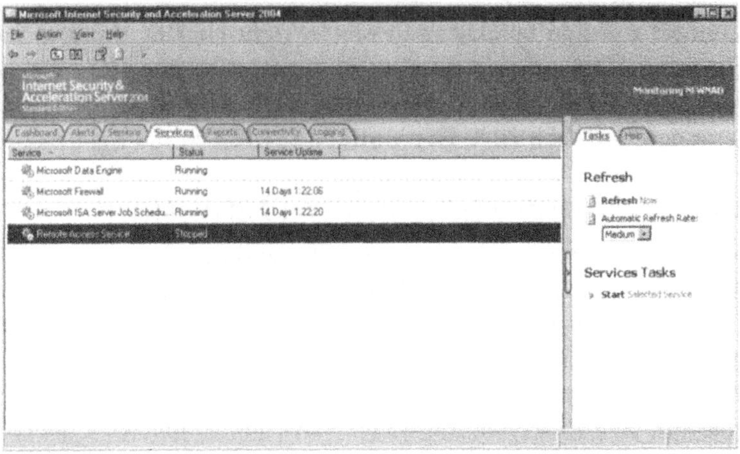

Working with ISA Server 2004 Logs and Reports

ISA Server 2004's logging and reporting features take monitoring a step further and provide you with permanent documentation of the activities related to your ISA server. In the following sections, we take a look at how ISA Server logs data, how to configure the logs, and how to generate reports based on the logged information.

Understanding ISA Server 2004 Logs

ISA Server 2004 logs all components by default. These logs include the following:

- Web Proxy
- Firewall Service
- SMTP Message Screener

Log Types

The default log type is a Microsoft Data Engine (MSDE) database. The MSDE service is installed along with ISA Server 2004. If you have a SQL server on the network, you can configure the logs to be saved to the SQL database, or you can save the information to a file (World Wide Web Consortium or W3C format, or ISA Server format). There are advantages and disadvantages to each.

NOTE

The SMTP Message Screener log cannot be saved to an MSDE or SQL database. It must be saved to a file.

Logging to an MSDE Database

You can use ISA Server 2004's log viewer to display information saved in an MSDE database. You can query the database to find specific information. This is one of the reasons we like the MSDE format. The logs themselves are limited to 2GB each, but the log viewer will display all the information in separate log files as if it came from the same file. If a log reaches the 2GB limit, ISA Server 2004 will automatically start a new one.

You can also export the information from the log viewer to a text file, which is handy if you use analysis tools that require text files.

By default, MSDE log information is saved to the ISALogs folder within the ISA Server installation folder.

Logging to a SQL Server

Logging to a SQL server allows you to use standard SQL tools to query the database. There is also some fault tolerance in having the logs located on a remote SQL server. However, if connectivity with the SQL server is lost, the Firewall service shuts down.

There are also a number of security issues involved in logging to a remote SQL server. If you choose to do so, Microsoft recommends using Windows authentication rather than SQL authentication, and you should also consider encrypting the log information and implementing IPSec for the data transmitted from the ISA Server to the SQL server. In order to log to a SQL database, you will need to ensure that the system policy rule to allow remote logging using NetBios transport to trusted servers is enabled on the ISA server.

Tip

The Microsoft Log Parser is a free command line tool that ships with Microsoft IIS and Windows Server 2003 Advanced Edition or can be downloaded from the Microsoft Web site. It can be used to mine information from ISA firewall logs. You can use it to search, analyze, cross-reference, and export log files. For more information about Log Parser and how to use it with ISA logs, see the *Microsoft Log Parser Toolkit*, by Gabriele Giuseppini and Mark Burnett (published by Syngress Publishing).

Logging to a File

If you select to use the W3C file format, the data is stored along with information about the version, log date, and logged fields. The W3C format creates a tab-delimited file.

If you select to use the ISA Server file format, only the data itself is saved, and all fields are logged, whether selected or not, but unselected fields are shown as empty (marked by a dash). This format creates a comma-delimited file.

Another difference between the two formats is that W3C files denote the date and time in Coordinated Universal Time (UTC), whereas the ISA Server format uses local time as configured on the computer.

The files are stored by default in the ISALogs folder. You can change this location if you want. If the partition on which the logs are stored is formatted in NTFS (which we recommend), you can compress the log files to save space, although this may cause a reduction in performance (access time).

W3C and ISA Server log files, like MSDE files, are limited to 2GB, but a new file is started automatically when the limit is reached. ISA Server monitors log file size at ten minute intervals.

NOTE

Regardless of the logging method you choose, logs should always be stored in a secure location. Access to logs should be tightly controlled to prevent accidental or deliberate modification.

How to Configure Logging

You can configure logging separately for each of the three services (Firewall, Web Proxy, and SMTP Message Screener). Click the **Logging** tab in the **Monitoring** node, and select **Configure Firewall Logging, Configure Web Proxy Logging**, or **Configure SMTP Message Screener Logging** in the right task pane, as shown in Figure 12.36.

Figure 12.36 Configuring Logging Separately

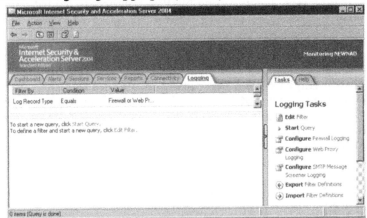

Configuration is basically the same for each service, with a few differences. In our example, we will configure logging for the Firewall service. The first step is to ensure that the **Enable logging for this service** box at the bottom of the **Log** tab is checked (it is enabled by default). Next, you need to configure the log storage format, as shown in Figure 12.37.

Figure 12.37 Configuring Log Storage Format

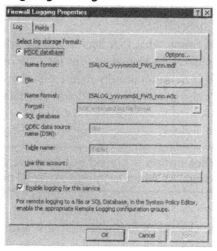

Configuring MSDE Database Logging

By default, the MSDE database format is selected. To configure it, click **Options**, which will display the **Options** dialog box shown in Figure 12.38.

Figure 12.38 Configuring MSDE Database Logging

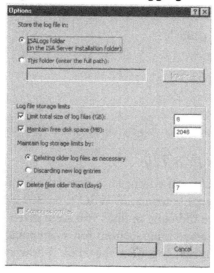

Here you can select whether to store the MSDE database files in the default location in the ISALogs folder, or in a different folder. To do the latter, type in the folder path or click the **Browse** button to browse to the folder where you want to store the logs.

Next, you can set a limit on the total size of all log files, in gigabytes. The default is 8 GB. You can also set an amount of free disk space that is to be maintained, in megabytes. The default is 2048MB (2 GB).

You can select also determine what ISA Server will do when the log limits are reached: either delete the oldest files to make room for new ones, or discard the new log entries. Finally, you can select to automatically delete files that are older than a specified number of days (by default, this option is selected and the default time period is 7 days).

> **NOTE**
>
> The **Compress log files** option is grayed out because you can't compress MSDE files. You can only compress when logging to a W3C or ISA Server format file.

On the **Fields** tab, you can check the fields that you want logged or uncheck those you don't want logged. If you want to log all fields, you can click the **Select All** button or you can clear all fields with the **Clear All** button. By default, all fields are logged except the following:

- Bidirectional
- Source proxy
- Destination proxy
- Client host name
- Destination host name
- Network Interface
- Raw IP Header
- Raw Payload

You can log only the default fields by clicking the **Restore Defaults** button.

Configuring Logging to a File

If you choose to log to a file, you will need to select the file format from the drop-down box: either ISA Server file format or W3C extended log file format. When you click **Options**, you will see the same options you were given for MSDE logging (location to store the log file, storage limits, actions for maintaining storage limits), but you will also see that the **Compress log files** checkbox is now available.

Configuring Logging to a SQL Database

If you choose to log to a SQL database, you will first need to set up a SQL server for ISA Server logging. This involves configuring the SQL server to accept the Open Database Connectivity (ODBC) connection from the ISA Server. You'll need to create a SQL server account if the SQL Server and the ISA Server aren't in the same Windows domain. If the two are in the same domain, you can use Windows authentication; if they are in different domains that do not have an appropriate trust relationship, you have to use SQL authentication.

Once you have the SQL server set up, on the **Log** tab of the **Firewall Logging Properties** dialog box, you'll need to enter the name of the ODBC data source and a table name. Then you may need to set a user account. To do so, click **Set Account**, and enter the user name and password (twice) in the **Set Account** dialog box. You can browse for a user by clicking the **Browse** button.

You'll need to enable the necessary Remote Logging configuration groups in the System Policy Editor.

> **NOTE**
>
> There are many complex issues related to configuring SQL server authentication and creating SQL databases that are beyond the scope of this chapter. Consult the SQL Server 2000 documentation or download the SQL Server 2000 Books Online (updated in 2004) from the Microsoft Web site at www.microsoft.com/sql/techinfo/productdoc/2000/books.asp.

To configure Web Proxy or SMTP Message Screener logging, the procedure is the same as for Firewall logging. The primary difference is in the available fields to be logged. In addition, you'll find that all log storage formats except **File** are grayed out in the SMTP Message Screener Logging properties dialog box.

How to Use the Log Viewer

The log viewer will show you entries being logged in real time as they happen. Each event is displayed in the log viewer as soon as it is logged. Click the **Logging** tab to use the log viewer. The default filter displays all log records for the Firewall or Web Proxy logs. To display these records, click **Start Query** in the task pane. Entries will continue to be added to the display in real time until you click **Stop Query.**

Because the log viewer contains many columns, you might want to close the console tree pane and/or the task pane to provide more room. Even if you do, you will probably still have to scroll to see all the default columns. The log viewer is shown in Figure 12.39.

Figure 12.39 The Log Viewer with Default Filter

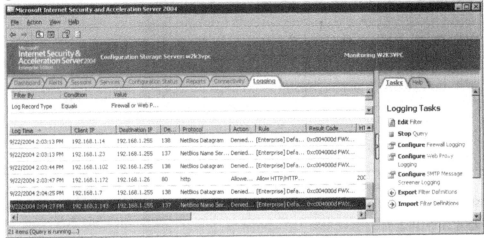

By default, the following columns are shown:

- Log time
- Destination IP
- Destination port
- Protocol
- Action
- Rule
- Client IP
- Client user name
- Source network
- Destination network
- HTTP method
- URL

You can add additional columns, such as MIME type, source or destination proxy, referring server, and many others. To do so, or just to view a list of available column headers, right-click any column header and select **Add/Remove Columns.**

How to Filter the Log Information

You can filter the information in log viewer similarly to the way you filtered the sessions information. As with the sessions filters, only those entries that meet all of your specified criteria will be displayed.

If you have logged to an MSDE database, you can also filter by log time. This allows you to display log data entered during a specific time period (rather than live data). You can only set the log time to something other than live for MSDE databases. This is referred to as offline viewing.

To configure a filter, click **Edit Filter** in the task pane. The **Edit Filter** dialog box is shown in Figure 12.40.

Figure 12.40 Editing a Log Filter

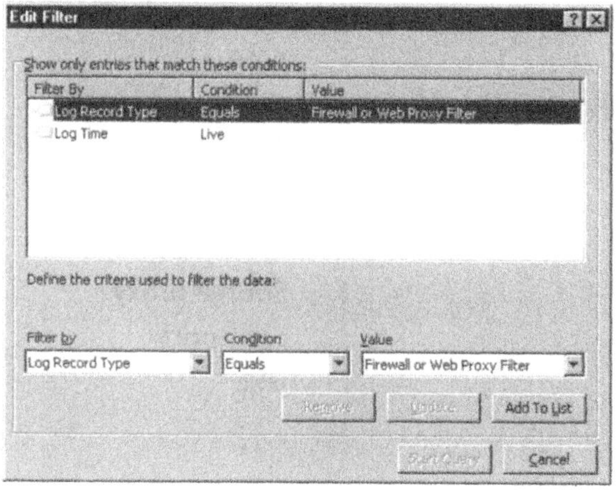

In the **Filter by** field, select the desired criteria.

ISA Server Mysteries

Can't Remove The Default Criteria

Note that you cannot remove the default entries. When you click either the Log Record Type or Log Time entry, the **Remove** button is grayed out. If you try to create a new entry for Log Record Type or Log time, when you click **Add to List**, you will get a message that only one Log Record Type (or Log Time) expression is allowed in a query.

Continued

> So how do you change these parameters? Here's the secret: Click the one you want to change to highlight it, make the change in the **Value** field, and then click **Update.**

You can choose from the following criteria by which to filter:

Action	Log time
Authenticated client	MIME type
Bidirectional	Network interface
Bytes received	Object source
Bytes sent	Original client IP
Cache information	Processing time
Client agent	Protocol
Client host name	Raw IP header
Client IP	Raw payload
Client user name	Referring server
Destination host name	Result code
Destination IP	Rule
Destination network	Server name
Destination port	Service
Destination proxy	Source network
Error information	Source port
Filter information	Source proxy
HTTP method	Transport
HTTP status code	URL
Log Record type	

Some of these criteria apply only to one or the other log type (Firewall or Web Proxy).

When you configure the log record type, you can select to display entries from the Firewall or Web Proxy filter, from the Firewall filter only, or from the Web Proxy filter only. Note that you cannot display entries from the SMTP Message Screener logs.

TIP

There will be no SMTP Message Screener log until you configure the Message Screener on the ISA Server computer.

When you configure the log time, in the **Condition** field the default is **Live** (and that is the only option if you are not logging to an MSDE database). If you're logging to MSDE, you can select any of the following:

- Last 24 hours
- Last 30 days
- Last 7 days
- Last hour
- Live
- On or after
- On or before

If you choose one of the last two, you'll need to select a date and time in the **Value** field.

After you have specified all the desired criteria for filtering, click **Start Query** to display the entries filtered by your criteria.

NOTE

If the Firewall service is stopped, either manually or automatically, the log viewer will stop updating information, and the ISA server will go into lockdown mode. The firewall service might shut down automatically because of an event trigger that is configured to stop the service if a particular event, such as an intrusion attempt, occurs. In lockdown mode, no incoming traffic other than DHCP traffic is allowed except for traffic specifically allowed by a system policy rule. To bring the ISA Server out of lockdown mode, restart the firewall service.

Saving Log Viewer Data to a File

You can save the data displayed in the log viewer to a file by copying all results, or only selected results, to the Windows clipboard. To copy selected results, highlight the entries you want to copy (you can select multiple entries by holding down the CTRL or SHIFT keys). Click **Copy Selected Results to the Clipboard.** To copy all results, click **Copy All Results to the Clipboard.**

Then you can paste the copied results into a text editor, such as Notepad, as shown in Figure 12.41.

Figure 12.41 Saving Log Viewer Data by Copying to the Clipboard

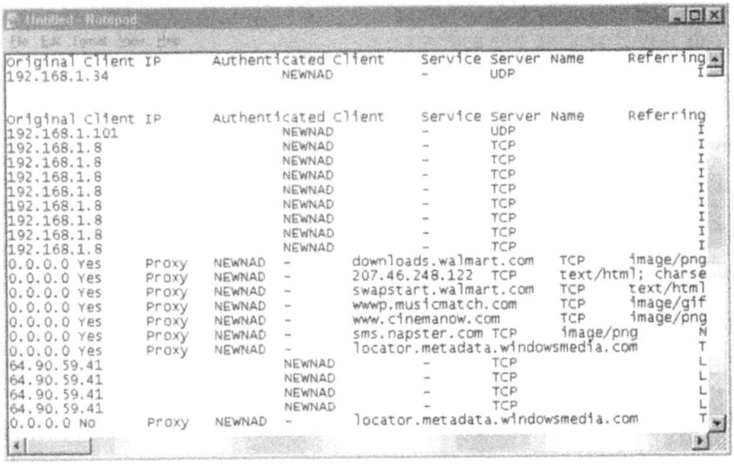

Once you have the data in a text editor, you can save it as a text file. However, note that you can only display up to ten thousand results in the log viewer, so even if you copy all results, you may not get all entries in the log.

Exporting and Importing Filter Definitions

You can save your filter definitions in the same way you did with sessions filters, by selecting **Export Filter Definitions** in the task pane and selecting a location and file name. The filters are saved as .xml files. You can then load them by selecting the **Import Filter Definitions** in the task pane.

Because there are so many different filtering criteria available for filtering log information, it is handy to be able to save a number of different filters and import them when they are needed.

Generating, Viewing, and Publishing Reports with ISA Server 2004

The reporting function is where it all comes together; this is where you create reports that summarize or detail the information in the log files in such a way that allows you to easily analyze the data and spot patterns, trends, and anomalies.

You can track usage for bandwidth allocation purposes, or you can track access for security purposes. With the reporting feature, you can generate reports manually or schedule report jobs to be run on a regular basis. The reporting component creates a database in the ISASummaries folder (by default) on the ISA Server computer. Reports are based on summaries of the Firewall and Web Proxy logs.

How to Generate a One-time Report

To create a report, click the **Reports** tab in the Monitoring node. This will show you a listing of all reports that have been generated, or are in the process of generating, as shown in Figure 12.42.

Figure 12.42 The Reports Display

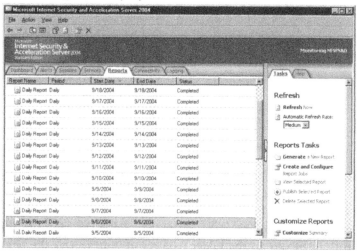

To create a new report, click **Generate a New Report** in the task pane. This will invoke the **New Report Wizard**. This wizard manually creates a single, one-time report as soon as you finish configuring the wizard. On the first page, you'll be asked to give your report a name.

On the next page of the wizard, you can select the type of content to include in this report. You can choose any of all of the following:

- Summary
- Web Usage
- Application Usage
- Traffic and Utilization
- Security

In our example, shown in Figure 12.43, we've selected to include only Web usage data.

Figure 12.43 Configuring Report Content

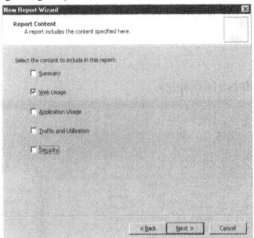

Click **Next,** and you'll be asked to specify a reporting period (start date and end date). Because the reports are based on daily log summaries, you cannot include the present date as the end date.

On the next page, you will have the option to publish the report to a directory. You can type in a path or browse to the folder where you want to save the report. If you click **Browse,** you can use the **Make New Folder** button to create a new folder in which to save the reports. It will be named New Folder by default, but you can right-click it and rename it from within the **Browse for Folder** dialog box.

You may need to enter an account name and password of an account that has permission to write to the specified directory. If so, check the **Publish using this account** checkbox, as shown in Figure 12.44, and click **Set Account** to enter the account name and credentials.

Figure 12.44 Configuring Report Publishing

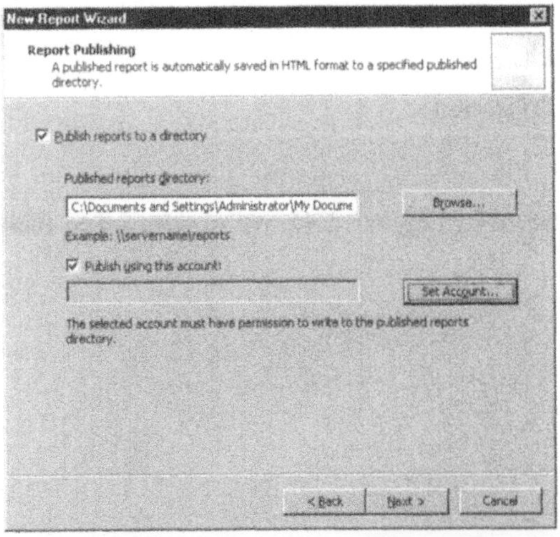

The report is automatically saved in HTML format.

On the next page, you can choose to have an e-mail notification sent when the report is completed. You'll need to enter the following information:

- SMTP server name or IP address
- Address from which the notification is to be sent
- Address to which the notification is to be sent
- CC: addresses of additional recipients, if any
- Message for the body of the e-mail.

You can also check a checkbox to include a link to the completed published report within the e-mail message.

The last page of the wizard summarizes your choices. Use the **Back** button to make any changes, then click **Finish** to begin generating the report. The report will immediately appear in the Reports list, with the status shown as "Generating," as shown in Figure 12.45.

Figure 12.45 Generating the Report Upon Completion of the Wizard

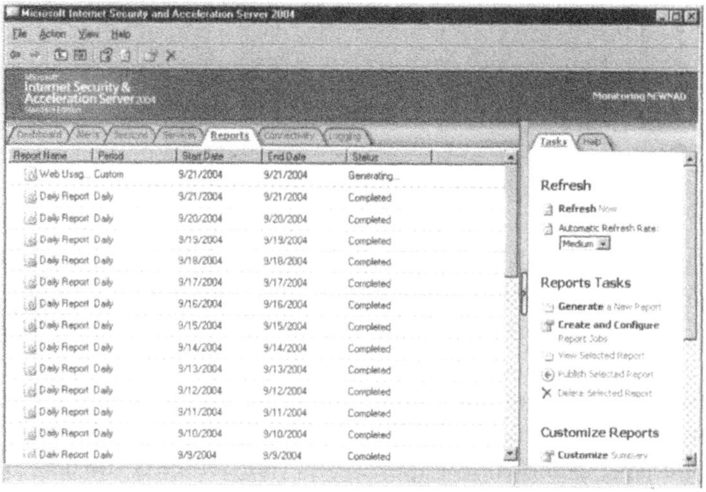

Because it is a one-time report, the **Period** column will indicate "Custom."

How to Configure an Automated Report Job

You can configure a report job to generate reports on a daily, weekly, monthly, or yearly basis. This is handy for comparative purposes. For example, you might want to create a daily summary report, or a weekly Web usage report.

> **NOTE**
>
> The ISA Server Job Scheduler Service must be running in order to generate reports from report jobs.

To create a report job, click **Create and Configure Report Jobs** in the right task pane. This will bring up the **Report Jobs Properties** dialog box, shown in Figure 12.46.

Figure 12.46 Creating Report Jobs

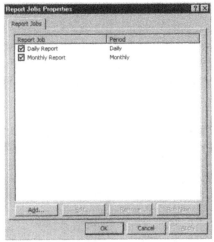

Here you will see a list of all scheduled report jobs. To add a new report job, click the **Add** button. This invokes the **New Report Job Wizard**. On the first page of the wizard, you'll be asked to give your report job a name (for example, Weekly Web Usage Report).

On the next page, you can configure the report content in the same way you did for a one-time report.

On the third page, as shown in Figure 12.47, you can select the time interval to run the report job: daily, weekly, or monthly.

Figure 12.47 Scheduling the Report Job

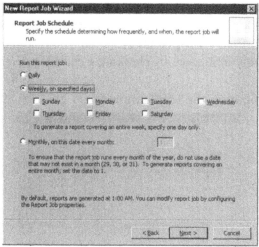

If you choose to run the job weekly, you can select on which day of the week to run the job. If you choose to run the job monthly, you will be asked to specify a day of the month on which to run the job. You should not use days that some months don't have (29, 30 or 31) if you want the job to run every month. If you want a report that covers the entire preceding month, you should set this value to 1.

On the next page, you can configure the job to publish the reports to a directory in the same way you did with the one-time report. The following page allows you to configure an e-mail message to be sent when the report completes, also in the same way as was done for the one-time report.

Finally, the last page of the wizard summarizes your choices. When you click **Finish,** the job will be scheduled to run on the day(s) you specified. By default, the report will start generating at 1:00 A.M. on the specified day. You can change this by selecting the report job in the **Report Job Properties** dialog box and clicking **Edit**. Click the **Schedule** tab, and you can change the generation hour, as shown in Figure 12.48.

Figure 12.48 Editing the Report Job Properties

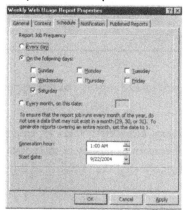

Other Report Tasks

There are a number of other report-related tasks you can perform from the task pane. You can configure the log summary by clicking **Configure Log Summary.** This brings up the **Log Summary Properties** dialog box, from which you can enable or disable daily and monthly summaries by checking a checkbox, as shown in Figure 12.49.

Figure 12.49 Configuring the Log Summary

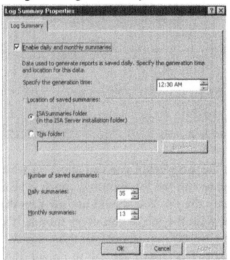

You can also change the default report generation time here, and specify where the summaries are to be saved (by default, they are saved in the ISASummaries folder). You can also configure the number of daily and monthly summaries to save (from a minimum of 35 to a maximum of 999 for daily summaries, and from a minimum of 13 to a maximum of 999 for monthly summaries).

NOTE

Remember, the log summaries are the basis for reports. If you disable the log summary database, ISA Server will create the missing summaries if you generate a report. However, if you delete summaries that were previously created, ISA Server will not re-create them.

You can also customize each of the report content types, using the following task pane selections:

- **Customize Summary Content:** You can specify the number of protocols to include, specify the number of top users to report on, specify the sort order for determining top usage, specify the number of top Web sites and the sort order for determining top sites, and specify the sort order for the cache hit ratio, either by requests or by bytes.

- **Customize Web Usage Content:** You can specify the number of top protocols to include and specify the sort order for determining top protocols (requests, users, bytes in, bytes out, or total bytes), specify the number of top Web sites and the sort order, specify the number of top users and the sort order, specify the number of object types and the sort order, specify the number of Web browsers and the sort order, and specify the number of operating systems and the sort order.

- **Customize Application Usage Content:** You can specify the number of top protocols and the sort order, number of top users and sort order, number of client applications and sort order, number of destinations and sort order, and number of operating systems and sort order.

- **Customize Traffic and Utilization Content:** You can specify the number of top protocols and the sort order for cache hit ratio.

- **Customize Security Content:** You can specify the number of clients who generate the most dropped packets and the number of users who cause the most authorization failures.

How to View Reports

Once a report has been generated, you can view it from the **Reports** tab in the **Monitoring** node of the **ISA Server Management** console. Double-click the report name, and it will open in your Web browser, as shown in Figure 12.50.

Figure 12.50 Viewing Reports

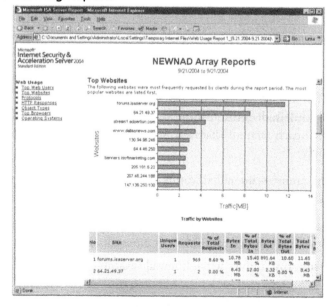

As you can see, the reports use graphs and tables to make the information easy to access and analyze. You can quickly move to different sections of the report by clicking the hyperlinks on the left side of the page.

Publishing Reports

If you didn't select to automatically publish the report to a directory when you configured the report job, you can publish it after it has been generated. Just highlight the report you want to publish and click **Publish Selected Report** in the task pane.

You will be asked to select a destination location for the report files folder. Click **OK**, and the report will be published to the folder. A new subfolder will be created within the selected folder (the folder name will be the report name plus the date). All the HTML and graphics files for the report will be stored there. To open the report itself from the folder, double-click the file named Report.htm.

Reports need to be published if you want to view them on computers other than the ISA Server computer.

Using ISA Server 2004's Performance Monitor

ISA Server 2004 installs the ISA Server Performance Monitor (a customized view of the Windows System Monitor that includes only ISA Server-related counters) when you install the ISA Server 2004 software.

The following counters are added to the Performance monitor for the ISA Server Firewall Packet Engine object:

- **Dropped packets** shows the total number of packets dropped.
- **Dropped packet/sec** shows the total number of packets dropped each second.
- **Packets** shows the total number of packets that the firewall packet engine driver has inspected.
- **Packets/sec** shows the total number of packets that the firewall packet engine driver inspects each second.
- **TCP established connections/sec** shows the number of TCP connections established each second (that is, a 3-way SYN handshake has been completed successfully).

The following counters are added to the Performance monitor for the ISA Server Firewall Service object:

- **Accepting TCP connections** shows the number of connections that are awaiting a TCP connection from the Firewall client.
- **Active sessions** shows active Firewall sessions.

- **Active TCP connections** shows the total number of TCP connections currently passing data.

- **Active UDP connections** shows the total number of UDP connections currently passing data.

- **Available UDP mappings** shows the number of mappings that are available for UDP connections.

- **Available worker threads** shows the number of Firewall Service worker threads that are waiting in completion port queue.

- **Bytes read/sec** shows the number of bytes that are read by the data pump in one second.

- **Bytes written/sec** shows the number of bytes that are written by the data pump in one second.

- **DNS cache entries** shows the number of DNS name entries cached by the Firewall service.

- **DNS cache flushes** shows the number of times the DNS domain name cache has been cleared.

- **DNS cache hits** shows the number of times a DNS domain name was found in the DNS cache.

- **DNS cache hits %** shows the percentage of DNS domain names retrieved by the Firewall service that are retrieved from cache.

- **DNS retrievals** show the number of DNS domain names retrieved by the Firewall service.

- **Failed DNS resolutions** shows calls to resolve host DNS domain names and IP addresses for Firewall service connections that failed.

- **Kernel mode data pumps** shows the number of kernel mode data pumps created by the Firewall service.

- **Listening TCP connections** shows the connection objects awaiting TCP connections from remote computers following a successful listen.

- **Pending DNS resolutions** shows calls to resolve DNS domain names and IP addresses for Firewall service connections that are pending.

- **Pending TCP connections** shows the number of TCP connections waiting for a connect call to finish.

- **SecureNAT mappings** show the number of mappings that were created by SecureNAT.

- **Successful DNS resolutions** shows calls to resolve host DNS domain names and IP addresses for Firewall service connections that were returned successfully.

- **TCP bytes transferred/sec** shows the number of TCP bytes transferred by the kernel mode data pump in one second.

- ■ **TCP Connections Awaiting Inbound Connect Call** shows connections from Firewall service to Firewall client after a connection from the Internet was accepted by the Firewall service on a listening socket.

- ■ **UDP bytes transferred/sec** shows the number of UDP bytes transferred by the kernel mode data pump in one second.

- ■ **Worker threads** shows Firewall service worker threads currently alive.

The following counters are added to the Performance Monitor for the ISA Server Web Proxy object:

Active Web sessions

Array bytes received/sec

Array bytes sent/sec

Array bytes total/sec

Average milliseconds/request

Cache hit ratio (%)

Cache hit ratio for last 10K requests

Client bytes received/sec

Client bytes sent/sec

Client bytes total/sec

Connect errors

Connect errors/total errors (%)

Current array fetches average milliseconds/request

Current cache fetches average milliseconds/request

Current direct fetches average milliseconds/request

DNS cache entries

DNDS cache flushes

DNS cache hits

DNS cache hits (%)

DNS retrievals

Failing requests/sec

Failing requests/total requests (%)

FTP requests

HTTP requests

HTTPS sessions

Incoming connections/sec

IO errors to array member

IO errors to array member/total (%)

IO errors to client

IO errors to client/total errors (%)

IO errors to server

IO errors to server/total errors (%)

Maximum users

Outgoing connections/sec

Requests from array member

Requests from array member/total errors (%)

Requests to array member

Requests to array member/total errors (%)

Requests with Keep Alive to array member

Requests with Keep Alive to array member/total errors (%)

Requests with Keep Alive to client

Requests with Keep Alive to client/total errors (%)

Requests with Keep Alive to server

Requests with Keep Alive to server/total errors (%)

Requests/sec

Reverse bytes received/sec

Reverse bytes sent/sec

Reverse bytes total/sec

Sites allowed

Sites denied

SNEWS sessions

SSL client bytes received/sec

SSL client bytes sent/sec

SSL client bytes total/sec

Thread pool active sessions

Thread pool failures

Thread pool size

Total array fetches

Total cache fetches

Total failing requests

Total pending connects

Total requests

Total reverse fetches

Total SSL sessions

Total successful requests

Total upstream fetches

Total users

Unknown SSL sessions

Upstream bytes received/sec

Upstream bytes sent/sec

Upstream bytes total/sec

You can add or remove counters by right-clicking any column header in the bottom pane of the **System Monitor** view, and selecting **Properties.** On the **Data** tab, select the counters you want to remove, and click **Remove.** To add a counter, click **Add** and select the computer (local or a computer in the drop-down list), performance object and counter(s) to add. You can add counters for any performance object, not just those related to ISA Server.

The ISA Server Performance Monitor is configured in the same way as the Windows Performance Monitor, and you can create counter logs, trace logs and alerts just as you do when monitoring other aspects of Windows computers.

Solutions Fast Track

Exploring the ISA Server 2004 Dashboard

☑ The Dashboard is a brand new feature in ISA Server 2004, and it's a handy way for the ISA Server administrator to tell, at a glance, what's going on in all the various monitoring subnodes.

☑ Each of the Dashboard sections contains an icon that indicates the status of that area.

☑ You can "roll up" various sections of the Dashboard if you don't want to view them.

☑ The Connectivity section of the Dashboard allows you to monitor connections between the ISA server machine and other computers. You can monitor specific computers on the network or even a connection to a particular Web server, by URL.

☑ The Services section of the Dashboard makes it easy for you to quickly check the status of the services that are running on the ISA Server computer.

☑ The Reports section of the Dashboard tells you, at a glance, the names of reports that have been generated, their status (generating or completed), and the date of generation.

☑ The Alerts section of the Dashboard interface allows you to quickly determine the events that have been logged on the ISA Server computer, when each event occurred, the severity of the event (Information, Warning or Error), and the number of new instances this event occurred.

☑ Sessions section of the ISA Server 2004 Dashboard makes it easy to see, at a glance, the session types and number of sessions that are currently active through the ISA Server 2004 firewall that is being monitored.

☑ The System Performance section of the ISA Server 2004 Dashboard interface provides a "quickie" view of the two most important performance counters for ISA Server.

☑ You can change the look of the Dashboard to suit your own preferences.

Creating and Configuring ISA Server 2004 Alerts

☑ ISA Server's alerting function means you can be notified of important ISA-related events as soon as they are detected.

☑ The alert service determines when an event occurs and whether an alert is configured to provide notification or perform some other action.

☑ To define a new alert, click the **Add** button. This will invoke the New Alert Configuration Wizard.

☑ You can assign a category for each alert and select a severity level.

☑ When the conditions specified for an alert have been met, ISA Server can be configured to perform an action.

☑ Some alerts are predefined, but disabled by default.

☑ You can modify the properties of your new alert, or those of any of the predefined alerts.

☑ When you click the Alerts tab in the Monitoring node, the alerts that have been triggered are displayed in the middle pane.

☑ The alerts window is automatically refreshed by default at periodic intervals.

Monitoring ISA Server 2004 Sessions and Services

☑ You can monitor connectivity between the ISA Server and other computers from the **Connectivity** tab.

☑ You can monitor current sessions for Firewall, Web Proxy, and SecureNAT clients from the **Sessions** tab.

☑ You can monitor the status of ISA Server services from the **Services** tab.

☑ You can use one of three methods to verify the connectivity: Ping, TCP Connect, or HTTP Request.

☑ To monitor connectivity to a server by any of these methods, you need to create a connectivity verifier and place it into one of the predefined groups.

☑ If you have selected to verify an HTTP connection, you will see a dialog box informing you that a rule allowing HTTP or HTTPS to the specified destination must be configured in order to do this.

☑ You can delete or disable a verifier by right-clicking it and selecting **Delete** or **Disable** from the context menu.

☑ Once you've configured your verifiers, you can tell at a glance whether there are any problems with the servers in a particular group by viewing the Connectivity section of the Dashboard.

☑ A handy feature in ISA Server 2004 is the ability to monitor real-time *sessions,* that is, the activity of a particular client computer (IP address) by a particular user (account name).

☑ You can monitor sessions from all three types of clients: Firewall, Web Proxy, and SecureNAT.

☑ To view current sessions being conducted through the ISA Server, click the **Sessions** tab and you will see a list of sessions.

☑ If you have many sessions going through the ISA server, it can be difficult to find the ones in which you're interested. You can use ISA Server 2004's filtering mechanism to sort the sessions data and display only sessions that meet specified criteria.

☑ You can save a filter definition so you can use it again by exporting it to an .xml file.

☑ You can disconnect a session quickly and easily by right-clicking it in the Sessions window and selecting **Disconnect Session** in the context menu.

☑ You can view the ISA Server services that are running on the firewall by using the **Services** tab in the Monitoring node.

☑ By default, the Services window in the middle pane will show the names of services, the status of each (running or stopped), and in some cases, the service uptime (how long the service has been running in days, hours, minutes and seconds).

Working with ISA Server 2004 Logs and Reports

☑ ISA Server 2004's logging and reporting features take monitoring a step further and provide you with permanent documentation of the activities related to your ISA server.

☑ ISA Server 2004 logs all components by default. These logs include the following: Web Proxy, Firewall Service, and SMTP Message Screener.

☑ You can use ISA Server 2004's log viewer to display information saved in an MSDE database.

☑ Logging to a SQL server allows you to use standard SQL tools to query the database. There is also some fault tolerance and improved security in having the logs located on a remote SQL server. However, if connectivity with the SQL server is lost, the Firewall service shuts down.

☑ The security of log files is an important consideration when implementing logging of any type.

☑ Configuring logging to a SQL database requires a good understanding of security issues specific to SQL Server.

☑ If you choose to log to a file, you will need to select the file format from the drop-down box: either ISA Server file format or W3C extended log file format.

☑ W3C and ISA Server log files, like MSDE files, are limited to 2GB, but a new file is started automatically when the limit is reached.

☑ You can configure logging separately for each of the three services (Firewall, Web Proxy, and SMTP Message Screener).

☑ If you choose to log to a SQL database, you will first need to set up a SQL server for ISA Server logging. This involves configuring the SQL server to accept the Open Database Connectivity (ODBC) connection from the ISA Server.

☑ The ISA Server installation CD contains the fwsrv.sql and w3proxy.sql scripts to automate the creation of the SQL tables.

☑ The log viewer will show you entries being logged in real time, as they happen.

☑ You can filter the information in log viewer similarly to the way you filtered the sessions information.

☑ When you configure the log record type, you can select to display entries from the Firewall or Web Proxy filter, from the Firewall filter only, or from the Web Proxy filter only. Note that you cannot display entries from the SMTP Message Screener logs.

☑ You can save the data displayed in the log viewer to a file by copying all results, or only selected results, to the Windows clipboard.

☑ You can save your filter definitions in the same way you did with the sessions filters, by selecting **Export Filter Definitions** in the task pane and selecting a location and file name.

☑ The reporting function is where it all comes together; this is where you create reports that summarize or detail the information in the log files in such a way that allows you to easily analyze the data and spot patterns, trends, and anomalies.

☑ To create a new report, click Generate a New Report in the task pane. This will invoke the **New Report Wizard**.

☑ You can configure a report job to generate reports on a daily, weekly, monthly or yearly basis. To create a report job, click **Create and Configure Report Jobs** in the right task pane.

☑ Once a report has been generated, you can view it from the **Reports** tab in the **Monitoring** node of the ISA Server Management console.

☑ If you didn't select to automatically publish the report to a directory when you configured the report job, you can publish it after it has been generated.

☑ Reports need to be published if you want to view them on computers other than the ISA Server computer.

Using ISA Server 2004's Performance Monitor

☑ ISA Server 2004 installs the ISA Server Performance Monitor (a customized view of the Windows System Monitor that includes only ISA Server-related counters) when you install the ISA Server 2004 software.

☑ A number of counters are added to the Performance Monitor for the ISA Server Firewall Packet Engine object, the ISA Server Firewall Service object and the ISA Server Web Proxy object.

☑ You can add or remove counters by right-clicking any column header in the bottom pane of the **System Monitor** view and selecting **Properties.**

☑ The ISA Server Performance Monitor is configured in the same way as the Windows Performance Monitor, and you can create counter logs, trace logs, and alerts just as you do when monitoring other aspects of Windows computers.

Frequently Asked Questions

The following Frequently Asked Questions, answered by the authors of this book, are designed to both measure your understanding of the concepts presented in this chapter and to assist you with real-life implementation of these concepts. To have your questions about this chapter answered by the author, browse to **www.syngress.com/solutions** and click on the **"Ask the Author"** form. You will also gain access to thousands of other FAQs at ITFAQnet.com.

Q: I have configured ISA Server to block anonymous users, but when I look at the logs, I see anonymous requests. What am I doing wrong?

A: Even though you require all users to authenticate, the initial request sent by a user is sent anonymously and logged as "anonymous." When authentication is required, the ISA Server sends back a 407 message in response to this anonymous request ("authentication required"). Then the user responds by sending the same request again with NTLM authentication credentials. ISA Server responds with another 407 message and sends an authentication challenge. The third time, the user responds with the same request and with an authentication response. Now the connection is logged with the user's account name. However, the first two communications will be logged as from anonymous users.

Q: I have configured an alert with an action to run a specific program when the alert conditions are triggered. The event is displayed in both the Alerts window of the ISA Server Monitoring node and in the Windows event viewer, but the program did not run as expected. What happened?

A: The most likely answer is that the user account that you specified to run the program did not have the correct permissions to do so. In order to perform an alert action, the account needs to have the **Logon as batch job** permission. If it doesn't, the action will fail. To solve the problem, either specify a different account to run the program (one that has the **Logon as batch job** permission) or assign the **Logon as batch job** permission to the user account.

Q: I configured an alert and chose to have an e-mail notification sent to my e-mail address when the alert is trigger. The event is displayed in the Alerts window of the ISA Server Monitoring node and in the Windows event viewer, but I did not receive the e-mail message? What happened?

A: You should check the configuration of the SMTP server that you specified to send the e-mail message. If it is an external SMTP server, the e-mail notifications cannot be sent unless you first define an access rule to allow the local host to access the external SMTP server. If it is an SMTP server on the Internal network, you will have to enable the system policy rule to allow the local host network to access the Internal network using the SMTP protocol.

Q: The Dashboard shows "No connectivity" for the entire Web (Internet) group, but when I check the Connectivity tab, only one of the five Web servers in the group shows a problem. Why did the Dashboard indicate that they were all disconnected?

A: The Dashboard gives you a "worst case" report so that you know there is a problem with one or more servers in a group, and you know what the problem is. If any server in a group has a problem, the group status will display that problem. Remember that the Dashboard is only intended to provide an "at a glance" overview of information. For details, you should always consult the appropriate tab (in this case, the Connectivity tab).

Q: I know I can set the refresh rates for the various tabs by selecting **None, Low, Medium**, or **High** in the right task pane. But what do those levels really mean? How often is the view refreshed at each selection?

A: If the refresh rate is set to None, the view never automatically refreshes (you can refresh it manually by clicking the Refresh button on the top toolbar or the Refresh Now icon in the right task pane). If the refresh rate is set to Low, the view is refreshed at 120 second intervals. If the refresh rate is set to Medium, the view is refreshed at 60 second intervals. If the refresh rate is set to High, the view is refreshed at 30 second intervals.

Q: I configured an alert to trigger when a DNS intrusion attempt occurs five times, by setting the **Number of occurrences** value to 5 on the **Events** tab of the DNS intrusion properties dialog box. However, I can see in the log that a DNS intrusion event did occur exactly five times, but the alert did not trigger. Why not?

A: When you set a value in the **Number of occurrences** field, the alert will be triggered on the next attempt *after* the number you specified. Thus, if you set the value to 5, the alert will not be triggered until the 6th occurrence of the event.

Q: I have set up a monthly Web Usage report to run on the last day of every month (the 31st) so I can get the data for the entire month. However, last month (September), the report did not run. Do I have to manually run a report every month in order to get the entire previous month? If I had specified the 28th (since all months have at least 28 days), I wouldn't get data for the last days on those months that have more days.

A: When the day of the month you have specified doesn't exist (e.g., September has only 30 days), the report won't run on those months that don't have that day. The solution is simple: run the report on the 1st day of every month. Since reports are created from log summaries, the data for the 1st will not yet be available on the 1st when you run the report. Thus, you will get all of the data for the previous month, regardless of how many days it has.

Index

Printed and bound by CPI Group (UK) Ltd, Croydon, CR0 4YY

03/10/2024

01040341-0008